GUIDE TO
HONEYMOON DESTINATIONS

by Risa Weinreb

1988–89 Edition

Copyright © 1988
by Risa Weinreb

Published by Prentice Hall Press
A Division of Simon & Schuster, Inc.
Gulf + Western Building
One Gulf + Western Plaza
New York, NY 10023

ISBN 0–13–331745-5

Manufactured in the United States of America

*Although every effort was made to ensure the accuracy
of price information appearing in this book,
it should be kept in mind that prices
can and do fluctuate in the course of time.*

CONTENTS

| Introduction | **FROMMER'S GUIDE TO HONEYMOON DESTINATIONS** | **1** |

Chapter I   **PLANNING YOUR HONEYMOON**   **4**
1. Honeymoon Checklist   **4**
2. Choosing Your Destination   **5**
3. All About Travel Agents   **8**
4. A Glossary of Travel Terms   **8**

Chapter II   **PREPARING TO GO AWAY**   **10**
1. Choosing Your Accommodations   **10**
2. Getting There   **11**
3. The Practicalities   **14**
4. Some Special Tips for Honeymooners   **18**

PART ONE   **THE UNITED STATES**

Chapter III   **NEW ENGLAND INNS**   **24**
1. Practical Facts   **24**
2. Connecticut's River Towns   **28**
3. North of the Litchfield Hills   **32**
4. The Berkshires of Massachusetts   **34**
5. Cape Cod   **38**
6. Manchester and the Mountains   **42**
7. The Heart of Vermont   **45**

Chapter IV   **CALIFORNIA**   **48**
1. Practical Facts   **50**

	2. San Francisco	53
	3. Monterey, Carmel, and the Monterey Peninsula	69
	4. Big Sur	82
	5. San Simeon	85
	6. Santa Barbara	86
	7. Los Angeles and Environs	91
Chapter V	**FLORIDA**	108
	1. Practical Facts	110
	2. Sanibel and Captiva Islands	113
	3. Marco Island	118
	4. Central Florida, Disney World, and EPCOT	122
	5. Boca Raton	132
	6. Palm Beach	135
	7. Fort Lauderdale	139
	8. Miami/Miami Beach	145
	9. Key West	156
Chapter VI	**GEORGIA**	163
	1. Practical Facts	165
	2. Savannah	167
	3. The Golden Isles	168
	4. Atlanta	171
	5. The Mountains	174
Chapter VII	**HAWAII**	177
	1. Practical Facts	179
	2. Oahu	183
	3. Maui	192
	4. Kauai	199
	5. The Big Island	207
Chapter VIII	**MISSOURI: LAKE OF THE OZARKS**	216
	1. Practical Facts	218
	2. Romantic Interludes	219
	3. Honeymoon Hotels and Hideaways	220
	4. Romantic Restaurants	222

Chapter IX	NEVADA: LAS VEGAS	225
	1. Practical Facts	225
	2. Romantic Interludes	228
	3. Honeymoon Hotels and Hideaways	229
	4. Romantic Restaurants	231
Chapter X	NEW YORK	233
	1. New York City	233
	2. Niagara Falls	252
Chapter XI	PENNSYLVANIA: THE POCONOS	260
	1. Practical Facts	262
	2. Romantic Interludes	265
	3. Honeymoon Hotels and Hideaways	266
Chapter XII	SOUTH CAROLINA	274
	1. Practical Facts	275
	2. Myrtle Beach	277
	3. Pawleys Island to Georgetown	280
	4. Charleston	282
	5. The Island Resorts	285
Chapter XIII	TEXAS: SAN ANTONIO	290
	1. Practical Facts	291
	2. Romantic Interludes	294
	3. Honeymoon Hotels and Hideaways	296
	4. Romantic Restaurants	301
	5. Nightlife	304
PART TWO	CANADA	
Chapter XIV	INTRODUCING CANADA	308
	1. Practical Facts	308
Chapter XV	TORONTO	310
	1. Practical Facts	312
	2. Romantic Interludes	314
	3. Honeymoon Hotels and Hideaways	315

		4. Romantic Restaurants	317
Chapter XVI	MONTREAL		320
		1. Practical Facts	321
		2. Romantic Interludes	323
		3. Honeymoon Hotels and Hideaways	326
		4. Romantic Restaurants	328
Chapter XVII	NOVA SCOTIA		330
		1. Practical Facts	332
		2. Halifax/Dartmouth	335
		3. Nova Scotia's Trails	341
		4. More Suggestions in Nova Scotia	352
PART THREE	MEXICO		
Chapter XVIII	INTRODUCING MEXICO		356
		1. Practical Facts	357
Chapter XIX	ACAPULCO		366
		1. Romantic Interludes	367
		2. Honeymoon Hotels and Hideaways	368
		3. Romantic Restaurants	371
Chapter XX	PUERTO VALLARTA		373
		1. Romantic Interludes	374
		2. Honeymoon Hotels and Hideaways	374
		3. Romantic Restaurants and Night Spots	377
Chapter XXI	MORE MEXICAN BEACH RESORTS		378
		1. Manzanillo	378
		2. Ixtapa/Zihuatanejo	380
		3. Cancún	382
		4. Cozumel	386

PART FOUR   **THE CARIBBEAN, THE BAHAMAS, AND BERMUDA**

Chapter XXII   **ARUBA**   **390**
1. Practical Facts   392
2. Romantic Interludes   394
3. Honeymoon Hotels and Hideaways   395
4. Romantic Restaurants and Night Spots   397

Chapter XXIII   **THE BAHAMAS**   **399**
1. Practical Facts   400
2. Nassau/Cable Beach/ Paradise Island   404
3. Freeport/Lucaya   409
4. The Family Islands: The Abacos, Eleuthera, The Exumas   412
5. More Suggestions in the Bahamas   418

Chapter XXIV   **BARBADOS**   **419**
1. Practical Facts   420
2. Romantic Interludes   424
3. Honeymoon Hotels and Hideaways   426
4. Romantic Restaurants   429

Chapter XXV   **BERMUDA**   **431**
1. Practical Facts   434
2. Romantic Interludes   440
3. Honeymoon Hotels and Hideaways   441
4. Romantic Restaurants in Hamilton   455
5. Nightlife in Hamilton   457
6. Romantic Restaurants Elsewhere in Bermuda   458

7. Nightlife Elsewhere in
   Bermuda   **459**

Chapter XXVI **BONAIRE** **460**
1. Practical Facts **461**
2. Romantic Interludes **464**
3. Honeymoon Hotels and
   Hideaways **465**
4. Romantic Restaurants **466**
5. Nightlife **467**

Chapter XXVII **BRITISH VIRGIN ISLANDS** **468**
1. Practical Facts **469**
2. Tortola **473**
3. Virgin Gorda **477**
4. Jost Van Dyke **481**
5. Peter Island **482**
6. More Suggestions in the B.V.I. **483**

Chapter XXVIII **THE CAYMAN ISLANDS** **485**
1. Practical Facts **486**
2. Grand Cayman **490**
3. Cayman Brac **495**
4. Little Cayman **497**

Chapter XXIX **CURAÇAO** **499**
1. Practical Facts **500**
2. Romantic Interludes **502**
3. Honeymoon Hotels and
   Hideaways **503**
4. Romantic Restaurants and
   Night Spots **504**

Chapter XXX **GUADELOUPE** **506**
1. Practical Facts **507**
2. Romantic Interludes **510**
3. Honeymoon Hotels and
   Hideaways **511**
4. Romantic Restaurants and
   Night Spots **513**

Chapter XXXI   **JAMAICA**   **516**
1. Practical Facts   **518**
2. Montego Bay   **526**
3. Negril   **535**
4. Mandeville   **538**
5. Ocho Rios   **539**
6. Port Antonio   **548**

Chapter XXXII   **MARTINIQUE**   **553**
1. Practical Facts   **554**
2. Romantic Interludes   **557**
3. Honeymoon Hotels and
   Hideaways   **558**
4. Romantic Restaurants and
   Night Spots   **561**

Chapter XXXIII   **PUERTO RICO**   **564**
1. Practical Facts   **565**
2. Romantic Interludes   **568**
3. Honeymoon Hotels and
   Hideaways   **570**
4. Romantic Restaurants   **573**
5. Nightlife   **574**

Chapter XXXIV   **ST. MAARTEN/ST. MARTIN**   **575**
1. Practical Facts   **577**
2. Romantic Interludes   **582**
3. Honeymoon Hotels and
   Hideaways   **584**
4. Romantic Restaurants   **588**

Chapter XXXV   **UNITED STATES VIRGIN ISLANDS**   **591**
1. Practical Facts   **593**
2. St. Thomas   **599**
3. St. Croix   **609**
4. St. John   **617**

Appendix I   **SUGGESTED READING**   **623**
Appendix II   **THE $35-A-DAY TRAVEL CLUB**   **625**

MAPS

Connecticut and Rhode Island 29
The Central Berkshires 35
Massachusetts 39
Vermont and New Hampshire 43
California 49
Downtown San Francisco 56–57
The Monterey Peninsula 70
The Big Sur Coast 83
Los Angeles and Environs 92–93
Florida Orientation 109
Orlando and Vicinity 123
Miami and Vicinity 147
Georgia 164
The Hawaiian Islands 178
Oahu 185
Kauai 200
Hawaii—The Big Island 208
Lake of the Ozarks 217
Las Vegas and Environs 226
Getting In and Out of New York City 234
Greenwich Village 240
Central Park 242–243
Midtown Manhattan 246
SoHo, Little Italy, and Chinatown Area 250–251
Niagara Falls 255

The Poconos 261
South Carolina 276
Downtown San Antonio 292
Downtown Toronto 311
Vieux Montreal 324
Montreal: Centre-Ville 327
Nova Scotia, Prince Edward Island, and
   Cape Breton Island 331
Mexico 358–359
The Caribbean Islands 391
The Bahamas and Turks and Caicos 401
Barbados 421
Bermuda 433
Netherlands Antilles 462
British Virgin Islands 470
Guadeloupe 508
Jamaica 517
Martinique 553
Puerto Rico 566
Saint Martin / Sint Maarten 576
The Virgin Islands 592

IN APPRECIATION

I am deeply grateful to all the talented, dedicated people who worked hard and long to make this book informative, accurate, and fun to use.

First and foremost, a great big "thank you" goes to the various contributing editors, who scouted the Western Hemisphere for the best honeymoon hideaways and romantic restaurants. All of them are experienced travel writers, and I think you'll find it interesting to get to know a bit about them.

Naomi Black (New England Country Inns, St. Martin) is the coauthor of the *East Coast Bed and Breakfast Guide* (Simon & Schuster / Prentice Hall Press, 1986).

Yvette Cardoza and Bill Hirsch (Cayman Islands) are a husband-and-wife writing and photography team who explored the Caymans from the top of the Brac to 800 feet underwater on the Cayman Wall.

Rachel Jackson Christmas (The Bahamas, Guadeloupe, Martinique) has written for *Travel & Leisure, Woman's Day, Ms, Diversion, Essence,* and *Modern Bride.*

Laura Del Rosso (Mexico, San Francisco hotels) works as San Francisco Bureau Chief for *Travel Weekly,* a national travel industry news magazine.

Richard Gehr (New York City, Niagara Falls) writes frequently for such diverse publications as the *Village Voice, New York Post, Film Comment, Music & Sound Output,* and *Video.*

Robin D. Hill (Florida) is author of the Florida Department of Tourism's *Florida Vacation Guide,* and works as a copywriter for a major Florida advertising agency.

Barbara A. Koeth (Aruba, Bonaire, Curaçao) is a freelance writer and photographer who specializes in writing about off-the-beaten-track adventures.

Melanie Menagh (Georgia, South Carolina) has written several travel guides, as well as articles for *Mademoiselle, Savvy, Signature, USA Weekend, Modern Bride,* and *Vanity Fair.*

Robert F. Miller (Puerto Rico) is a freelance writer who frequently covers that island.

George Pandi (Montreal) has spent two decades in the city he writes about and has also lived in and written about cities all over the world—Vienna, London, Budapest, New York, and San Francisco.

Elizabeth Tener (Barbados) has written travel articles for *Modern Bride, Family Circle, Cosmopolitan,* and *Mid-Atlantic Country,* as well as a regular career column for *Self* magazine.

Mary Shank (Lake of the Ozarks) has written travel articles for various publications, including *Missouri Getaway Magazine, Travelhost Magazine,* and *Vacation's Guide.*

Douglas Watt (Toronto) has contributed to the *Toronto Star, Montréal Gazette, Hamilton Spectator, London (Ontario) Free Press,* and *The News and Travel International Magazine,* London, England.

Marty Wentzel (Hawaii) is the former editor of *Spotlight Hawaii* and the *Hawaii Hotel Network.*

Joyce Wiswell (Las Vegas) is a New York City–based writer and editor who has written for a number of publications, including *Modern Bride.*

Melanie Young (San Antonio) is a freelance writer and is also Travel Editor of *San Antonio Monthly* magazine.

None of this book would have been possible without the devoted efforts of Carol A. Knapp, who worked many long hours in preparing this manuscript. Her diligence and attention to detail are much appreciated.

A salute also goes to Alan David for his technical help and computer wizardry. And many, many thanks (plus *mille grâces* and *muchas gracías*) to all the people at the various tourist boards and visitors bureaus for the help they have extended. On a personal note, I could not have accomplished any of this without the support of my editor, Marilyn Wood, and the rest of the Travel Team at Simon & Schuster / Prentice Hall, most notably Gloria McDarrah.

Finally, I owe special recognition to my family and friends for the patience, understanding, and support they tendered during my work on this book, which caused me to be late for (and beg out of) many dinner dates and special events. (Stand up and take a bow, guys!) And, most of all, I'd like to thank my best friend, Steen Hansen, for sharing the spirit of romance and adventure.

DEDICATION
To Cele Goldsmith Lalli, Editor in Chief, and
George E. Morrissey, Publisher, of Modern Bride
magazine, for caring so much about all the brides
and grooms—and all their editors.

FROMMER'S GUIDE TO HONEYMOON DESTINATIONS

EVER SINCE ADAM AND EVE, lovers have tried to return to the Garden of Eden. For most couples, the closest they'll ever come is their honeymoon.

Honeymoons rank among the oldest of human rituals. The word "honeymoon" itself is derived from a custom of the early Anglo-Saxons, who celebrated weddings by drinking mead (fermented honey) for the period of time between full moons—about 30 days.

Although the word is an ancient one, honeymoons themselves are a fairly recent invention. At first only the rich and famous could afford them. In one of the first honeymoons to gain widespread attention, Napoleon's younger brother, Jerome, came to America and took his bride, Betsy Patterson, to Niagara Falls in the early 1800s. The modern honeymoon was born.

Not so long ago, marriages were arranged, and honeymoons were important getting acquainted periods. Today, even after the "sexual revolution," 98% of all newlyweds take honeymoons to symbolize a deeper commitment to each other for a variety of reasons.

In this book, we've taken the point of view of unabashed romantics. We've focused on places and activities that most stir the heartbeats of honeymooners. It's not meant to be the most complete guidebook on the market. It doesn't list every historic old fort or musty museum. But what the book does have is detailed information about the most popular honeymoon destinations in the United States, Canada, Mexico, and the Caribbean. For each destination area, we'll discuss:

ROMANTIC INTERLUDES: What are the most sensuous—and fun—pastimes for couples in love? We'll give you the inside scoop on secluded beaches prime for picnics-for-two, sunset perches, idyllic day-cruises . . . as well as rollicking amusement parks, active volcanoes, free concerts, and hot-air balloon rides. You'll notice that throughout this book, we use "vacation" as a synonym for "honeymoon"—we believe this trip should be fun!

HONEYMOON HOTELS AND HIDEAWAYS: Your choice of accommodations matters more on your honeymoon than on any other trip you'll ever take. You will want to spend every moment in memorable, romantic surroundings. In recognition of the fact that every couple harbors different boudoir fantasies, we've included a wide range of where-to-stay options. Sexy little love nests and high-rise pleasure palaces. Thatch-roofed hales in the tropics and columned plantations down south. And, because the most romantic room of all is one you can afford, we've also sought out the most attractive budget properties.

ROMANTIC RESTAURANTS: Because there comes a time when you can't live on love alone, we'll point out some of the most delectable dining possibilities. Once again, our selections are skewed toward the eclectic. You'll find high-toned meccas of classic cuisine as well as Formica lunch counters that serve the best slice of Neapolitan pizza in town. Whatever you crave, you'll surely find something to satisfy your appetite.

PRACTICAL FACTS: In addition, since even starry-eyed lovers need to know what plane to catch and what travel documents they need, there's a full section covering everything from telephone area codes to the rainy seasons.

Some Important Topics

Prices: Every effort has been made to assure that all price information was accurate at the time the book went to press. Unfortunately, it is a fact of life that rates constantly change—almost always in an upward direction. Consult your travel agent or the establishment for the most up-to-date information.

Hotel Rates: Whenever possible, we have listed the Honeymoon Package rate. However, many hotels also have other packages (tennis, diving, sailing), as well as longer or shorter stays that couples might find attractive. In addition, hotels frequently change the components of their honeymoon packages. Ask your travel agent for details.

Restaurants: Write-ups either list typical prices of menu items, or else give an approximate cost for a complete dinner for two people. In the latter case, prices are based on a couple ordering a moderately priced appetizer, entrée, dessert, and coffee. Cost of drinks is not included.

Honeymoon Hotline: This is the first edition ever of *Frommer's Guide to Honeymoons,* and we'd like to get feedback from our readers. Your comments and suggestions about this book will be invaluable in planning future volumes. Also, we'd appreciate receiving your own personal reviews of the hotels and restaurants we've covered—as well as letting us know about any new romantic hideaways you've found. Future honeymooners will thank you for sharing your joy. Send your responses to: Risa Weinreb, c/o Frommer Books, Prentice Hall Press, One Gulf + Western Plaza, New York, NY 10023.

A popular wedding toast goes: "May you enjoy your work as much as your vacations; and may you love each other always with loyalty, trust, and joy." It is our hope that you begin fulfilling all the promise of your futures together on your honeymoon.

Chapter I

PLANNING YOUR HONEYMOON

1. Honeymoon Checklist
2. Choosing Your Destination
3. All About Travel Agents
4. A Glossary of Travel Terms

MAKING A SCHEDULE. Setting the date. Choosing the wedding dress. Deciding where to have the reception. These count among your most important wedding arrangements. Now another series of crucial decisions await—planning your honeymoon. Just as you have a schedule for mailing your invitations and finalizing the seating plan, you need a calendar for making your honeymoon arrangements.

1. Honeymoon Checklist

By planning your trip ahead, you can make sure you'll select the honeymoon destination that's right for you; get the most convenient airline reservations at the cheapest price; and reserve the most romantic room at your favorite resort. Here's a checklist:

6 to 12 Months Beforehand
- Start discussing what sort of honeymoon destination you want—a beach, the country, the ski slopes? What kind of ambience—elegant, casual?
- Ask family and friends about their recommendations, not only for destinations, but also about travel agents.
- Get travel brochures from tourist boards, hotels, and your travel agent.

4 to 6 Months Beforehand
- Make your airline, hotel, and car rental reservations. (Note: Do this even further in advance if you will be traveling during peak season, such as the Christmas holidays in the Caribbean.) Send any deposits necessary.
- Get passports and/or visas, if needed.

2 to 4 Months Beforehand
- Have you received all your confirmations?
- Consider your luggage requirements and purchase any new pieces needed.
- Analyze your wardrobe. Shop for clothes for your honeymoon.
- Check that the camera you intend to take is in good working order.

1 Month Beforehand

- Reconfirm all your arrangements through your travel agent.
- If you will be driving your own car to your destination, take it in to the service station for a complete mechanical check-up.

1 to 2 Weeks Beforehand

- Reconfirm all your arrangements through your travel agent.
- Pack everything except the clothes and toiletries you will need for the coming week. Is everything clean, ironed, and repaired?
- Purchase traveler's checks.
- Arrange to stop the mail delivery, newspaper, etc. while you are away.

1 to 2 Days Beforehand

- Reconfirm all your arrangements through your travel agent.
- Pack your remaining items.
- Be sure you have your passports, airline tickets, traveler's checks, hotel confirmation, rental car confirmation, credit cards.
- Bon voyage!

2. Choosing Your Destination

"Where should we go on our honeymoon?" That's probably the question that's uppermost in your mind (and, incidentally, it's the question couples most frequently ask me when they find out that I'm a travel writer). The answer is, "That depends."

And what it depends on is what you both like to do. What do you want from your honeymoon? Relaxation? Adventure? New scenery? Every newlywed couple has a unique honeymoon style. The knack of creating a perfect honeymoon (or a perfect vacation in the years to come) comes from planning a trip around your interests. Start by discussing what each of you wants from the trip. Here are some main areas to consider:

SETTING: What kind of setting do you want? Shall it be a cosmopolitan whirl of theater, museums, and shopping in a big city—or a beachy retreat to a tropical isle with only the coconut palms for company? A secluded cabin by a mountain lake or a self-contained resort with tennis courts, a golf course, gourmet restaurants, and discos right on the property? Talk about all your interests and desires. If you have different hobbies, don't despair. Some locations can satisfy both your inclinations. There are big cities within an hour's drive of the ski slopes and Caribbean islands with both duty-free shopping and world-class scuba diving, places that offer both game-fishing and gambling, and country villages where quaint stores sell museum-quality furniture from around the world. With a little research, you can uncover the locale that's right for you both.

WHEN TO GO: When are you going? If you're heading to a beach resort, you want sunshine. At the ski slopes, you need snow. What places offer peak conditions during the time you'll be on your honeymoon? Some resort areas have "seasons," meaning that the weather varies at different times of the year. Sometimes the seasonality is obvious: Vermont in the summer is quite different from Vermont in the winter. Other times, variations are subtle: California weather along the coast tends to be sunniest in autumn; diving conditions in the Caribbean are usually clearest from April to June. Seasonality might have nothing to do with the weather, but rather with special events and cultural activities. New York's music, dance, and theater scene is liveliest in winter; Barbados hosts its celebrated "Crop Over" festival in August. In the introduction to all the areas covered by this book, we've given an accurate assessment of the annual weather, so read carefully before you go.

Don't write off a place just because it's the so-called "off" season. Some destinations—particularly in the U.S. Sunbelt, Hawaii, Mexico, and the Caribbean—have virtually the same weather all year. In the Caribbean, for example, many islands have only a 5° temperature difference between the winter and the summer. By going during the low season, you can save up to 50% on airline and hotel prices over the high season. Another advantage: In the low season, you'll find fewer crowds on beaches, in stores, and in restaurants.

THE TIME FACTOR: How much time do you have? Your schedule strongly influences your honeymoon choice. If you only have a week, you should not spend a full day traveling each way, or head to a far-away destination where you'll experience a lot of jet lag. The time factor also can determine how you travel; for example, if your honeymoon locale can be reached easily either by car or plane. Flying will usually save you time; driving will save you money. Which works best for you?

THE COST: How much can you afford? Enter Reality. Exactly how much money do you want to spend on your honeymoon? This is a very personal decision—no two couples earning, let's say, $40,000 a year are going to spend their money the same way. Some will go all out on a honeymoon splurge. Others, saving to buy a house, a car, or furniture will opt for a more modest expenditure. It's up to you, as a couple, to set priorities. It might be interesting for you to know, however, how much a "typical" honeymoon might cost. According to the latest figures from *Modern Bride* magazine, the average couple spent $1,264 on a honeymoon within the continental United States; $2,694 on a trip outside (which would also include Hawaii and the U.S. Virgin Islands).

Obviously, how much you're willing to allocate will determine which honeymoon destinations you can realistically consider. What is not so obvious is that on vacation there are different ways to spend money. Some couples will devote a large chunk of their budget to flying to an exotic location, then stay in cheap digs once they get there. Others want to stay in the best hotel in town—even if the "town" in question is only a 60-mile drive from where they grew up. What do you two want to do?

Often, honeymoon budgeting is the first time a couple has to sit down and discuss their financial facts of life. This can cause some strains and tensions in your relationship. To help avoid the rough spots, see the section on "Coping with Honeymoon Stress."

Making a Budget

Let's get down to the nitty-gritty here. You've scribbled out all the dollar figures on paper and have a good idea how much you can spend on your trip. Can you afford that dream honeymoon? Use the chart below to calculate approximate expenses.

Want to make your money go even further? Here are some tried-and-true tips for cutting costs.

1. Travel during the off-season, if possible. Airfares and hotel rates can be up to 50% cheaper. See the individual destination chapters in this book for details about when each area offers its lowest rates.

2. Book your airline tickets in advance. Advance purchase fares (APEX) can save you over 80% on many routes. Many airlines only make 10% to 15% of their seats available at the lowest fare; by booking early, you have a better chance of getting these low rates.

3. To save some money on meals, have some picnic lunches with wine and cheese. Who ever said economizing can't be romantic?

EXPENSES

Transportation
Main transportation
(air, ship, car): $_____

Airport transfers: $_____

Gas/tolls/parking: $_____

Rental car: $_____

Taxis: $_____

TOTAL TRANSPORTATION: $_____

Accommodations
Room rate: $_____

Tips: $_____

Misc. (laundry, taxes, etc.): $_____

TOTAL ACCOMMODATIONS: $_____

Food (per couple)
Breakfast
$_____ per day × _____ days $_____

Lunch
$_____ per day × _____ days $_____

Dinner
$_____ per day × _____ days $_____

TOTAL FOOD: $_____

Amusements and Entertainment
Sports equipment/fees $_____

Movies/theater/concerts $_____

Admission fees $_____

Nightclubs/discos $_____

TOTAL ENTERTAINMENT: $_____

Shopping and Gifts

TOTAL SHOPPING: $_____

Miscellaneous

TOTAL MISCELLANEOUS: $_____

TOTAL EXPENSES: $_____

3. All About Travel Agents

Whether you know exactly where you want to go—or if you're still casting about for helpful suggestions—a travel agent can help you plan and arrange all the honeymoon details. Important to know: In most cases, using a travel agent is free. Agents earn money through commissions on airline tickets, car rentals, and hotel reservations. All you might have to pay for would be special services, such as long-distance telephone calls. Ask the travel agent in advance.

A good travel agent will be up-to-date on the latest vacation information: air fares, hotels, special packages. In addition, because most of them have computer hook-ups with airlines, hotels, and rental car agencies, they can make reservations quickly and easily. Travel agents can not only book flights and hotels; they can also reserve theater tickets, sightseeing tours, and advise you about the climate and customs of a country. In brief, they are your personal travel advisers.

Remember to stay open to suggestions. An agent often can recommend a destination you had not thought of but which might be just right for your honeymoon.

How can you find a good travel agent? Your best bet is to ask family and friends for recommendations. Also, look for someone who is a member of ASTA (American Society of Travel Agents) or is a CTC (Certified Travel Counselor). In particular, the CTC designation helps assure expertise. To qualify, an agent must have been in the business for at least five years, and must have passed an eighteen-month course.

4. A Glossary of Travel Terms

"Super APEX" is not Clark Kent's alter ego, and a MAP is not something you buy from Rand McNally. Like any other business, travel uses trade lingo, slang, and abbreviations. Here's a rundown of some of the most common terms you'll encounter when talking with your travel agent or reading through brochures. Many are also used in this book. If you have any specific questions, ask your travel agent or contact the program operator directly.

Airlines

Nonstop flight: The plane flies from one place to another with "no stops."

Direct flight: The plane will stop en route to pick up additional passengers, but you do not need to change planes to reach your final destination.

Connecting flight: You will need to change planes in order to get where you want to go.

Hotels

Concierge desk: A special-service desk at many fine hotels, staffed by an employee who can help make airline and restaurant reservations, arrange sightseeing excursions, and perform other personal services.

Double-occupancy rate: Price per person, based on two people sharing a room.

Double-room rate: Price per room, based on two people sharing the room.

Guaranteed late arrival: In most cases, a hotel will only hold a room until 6 p.m. To assure your room will be waiting no matter what time you arrive, you can arrange a guaranteed late arrival. It requires that you give a credit card number. If you fail to arrive that night, the room cost will still be charged to your credit card.

Honeymoon Packages: Plans that offer accommodations—plus such goodies as air transportation, car rental, or sightseeing jaunts—in one neat "package." Often, the programs offer extremely good value, giving you all the honeymoon features you want at a comparatively inexpensive price. As with any present, however, you want to make sure this package gives you something of real value—not mere gift wrapping.

When you glance through this book, you'll see that honeymoon packages vary widely. In general, you'll get one of the best rooms in the house (with king-size bed and a great view) and a welcoming gift (such as a fruit basket or bottle of champagne). Other features run the full gamut: from sunset cocktail cruises to scuba-diving lessons. Usually, the room rate offers you significant savings over the ''rack'' rate (the standard price for the accommodations). When evaluating different honeymoon packages, try to put a dollar value on all those bonus items you're getting. How much do those flowers cost? The tennis court fee? Even more important—will you take advantage of all the opportunities?

Oceanfront: Means that the room directly overlooks the water.

Oceanview: While you will have some view of the water, the room won't completely front it.

Service charges: In some locales, a fixed percentage (usually 10% to 15%) is added to hotel and/or meal bills. This eliminates the need for tipping.

Taxes: Federal and local taxes can also be levied against hotel and restaurant bills.

Meals

EP (European Plan): No meals are included in your room rate.

CP (Continental Plan): Room rate includes a continental breakfast, generally bread or croissants, jam, and coffee or tea.

BP (Bermuda Plan): Named for the country where it was first popularized, this option includes a full breakfast: juice, eggs, bread, coffee, tea, etc.

MAP (Modified American Plan): Includes breakfast and either lunch or dinner. Also known as half-board or half-pension.

AP (American Plan): Includes breakfast, lunch, and dinner daily. Also known as full-board or full pension.

Chapter II

PREPARING TO GO AWAY

1. Choosing Your Accommodations
2. Getting There
3. The Practicalities
4. Some Special Tips for Honeymooners

WHERE YOU STAY is more important on your honeymoon than on any other trip. After all, many of you have been planning this vacation since you were five years old—all you needed was the right roommate. Now that you've found him or her, you want to share each moment together in the most romantic surroundings possible.

1. Choosing Your Accommodations

The perfect honeymoon hideaway—where can it be found? Here once again we get into personal preferences—the "right" hotel is the one that suits both of you. Before making your room reservations, you should consider what kind of accommodations you would prefer. High-rise hotel? Cozy little love nest? Here are some of your options.

HOTELS: Skyscrapers with mirrored windows, plant-filled atriums, and clear-glass elevators that ascend, like bubbles, to distant penthouses. Gargoyled grand hotels where red carpets cascade down the entrance stairs. Hotels certainly come in all shapes and sizes. What they usually have in common is a deluxe atmosphere emphasizing personal service in all its manifestations: porters, a concierge, bellhops, room service. In addition, you'll generally find many amenities right in-house: boutiques, car rental offices, beauty salons, laundry services. Usually, they are located in cities.

SELF-CONTAINED RESORTS: Often these are also hotels, but they can also be low-rise villas, condos, or cottages. What differentiates them from just plain hotels? The fact that everything necessary for human survival—and even a honeymoon's survival—is located right on the property. A multiplicity of tennis courts, golf courses, swimming pools with waterfalls and swim-up bars, discos, enough restaurants that you need never dine in the same one twice even if you stay there for a week—that's what you'll find at these resorts, which are actually complete worlds unto themselves.

MOTELS: At motels or motor lodges, you can drive up and park your car right outside your door. Convenience and economy are the usual bywords here.

CONDOMINIUMS AND VILLAS: Enjoy all the comforts of a home—while away on your honeymoon. Condos and villas have became an increasingly popular option for couples because they combine the privacy and spaciousness of a residence (bedroom, bathroom, kitchen, living and dining areas) with all the services of a hotel—front desk, porters, daily maid service, and sports facilities such as tennis courts and swimming pools. In particular, the kitchen facilities come in handy.

INNS: These can range from historic old lodgings where George Washington slept to modern structures that bear a striking physical (if not semantic) resemblance to a hotel. For the purposes of this book, we'll consider an inn a small hotel that also has a dining room that serves meals to the public.

BED-AND-BREAKFASTS: Usually, "B&Bs" are private residences that take in paying guests, offering both a bedroom and breakfast (either full or continental). Settings can range from gingerbread-trimmed Victorian mansions to an extra bedroom in a city apartment. Be aware that not all B&B accommodations offer a private bath—sometimes you'll have to share the one down the hall.

ACCOMMODATIONS CHECKLIST: No matter what type of accommodations you prefer, keep the following points in mind when deciding where to stay.

    1. Location: What is it near—sightseeing, shopping, the beach? Although centrally located properties are convenient, they usually charge higher rates.

    2. Ground transportation: How do you get from the airport to the hotel? How much will it cost you? Does the hotel offer guests free transfers? How long will the journey take?

    3. Amenities: Does the property have the facilities you want (as tennis courts, swimming pools, restaurants, a health spa)? How good are the facilities? Are the tennis courts lit for night play? What brand of exercise equipment is in the gym? How much will it cost you to use the facilities?

    4. Rooms: What kind of view does the room have? Make sure you reserve a room with a double, queen-, or king-size bed.

    5. Meals: Does the room rate include any meals? Which ones? Hotel meal plans generally will save you money, but you miss out on the fun of trying out new places.

    6. Confirmation: Make sure you get a written confirmation for your room, specifying all the details: honeymoon package, dates, view, even the king-size bed.

    7. Guaranteed late arrival: As mentioned earlier, most hotels will only hold rooms until 6 p.m. It's a good idea to guarantee late arrival using your credit card, especially if you encounter unforeseen travel delays, you want that room ready!

2. Getting There

BY AIR: Here's a guide to help you plan your travel by air.

Making Reservations

    The easiest way to make airline reservations is through a travel agent. Most agents have on-line computer hook-ups to the airlines, and so have instant access to information about fares and seat availability. Travel agents are also up-to-date on rate information, and can fully explain any restrictions, requirements, or cancellation penalties. Once again, using a travel agent is generally free.

    If you want to do it yourself, you can get flight information from the Official

Airline Guide (OAG), a book available at many libraries. The OAG lists all domestic and international flights with their airport departure and arrival times. Many airlines in the United States have toll-free "800" numbers you can call for reservations and information. To get the number, call 800/555-1212. In order to find out which airlines fly to which cities or countries, you can call the area tourist board.

Fares

First the good news: It probably costs less to reach your preferred destination than ever before. Now the bad news: Air fares and airline routes change at such a dizzying rate, even travel agents and airline reservations agents have trouble keeping up with the latest events. Your best bet for assuring that you get the low-down on low fares: Skim the daily newspapers for advertisements about new promotions and ask your travel agent for details about requirements and restrictions.

In general, rates will vary depending on whether you fly first class or economy/coach, and how far in advance you purchase your tickets. APEX (Advance Purchase Excursion) fares are usually the cheapest. As the name implies, you must buy your tickets a specified number of days in advance. Other restrictions often apply, such as staying a minimum number of days, staying over a weekend, etc. In addition, you might be liable for a penalty if you change or cancel your plans.

Air fares are usually most expensive during high ("peak") season, especially during holiday periods. Low ("off") season rates can often be up to 50% lower. In "shoulder" seasons (airline parlance for those periods in between high and low seasons), air fares will be somewhat in the middle. When you travel during the week also affects air fares. It usually costs less to fly to a resort destination Monday through Thursday than on weekends. (It's often the opposite for flying to major cities that are popular business destinations: It's cheaper on the weekends.) In addition, evening or overnight ("red-eye") flights are generally the cheapest of all.

Airline Check-in

Plan to arrive at the airport at least an hour in advance of departure time for domestic flights, two hours in advance for international flights. This gives you plenty of time to check in your luggage and make seat selections. A time-saving tip: Get your boarding passes in advance if possible. You can get them through your travel agent for flights on most of the major airlines. This is a big advantage, because if a flight is overbooked, passengers without boarding passes get bumped first.

Baggage

According to current airline regulations, each person is usually permitted to check in two pieces of luggage weighing a total of 44 pounds. If your baggage weighs more, you may have to pay a penalty. Tag each bag you check with your name and home phone number. (Many police officers advise against including your home address, which could tip off burglars. You can put your complete address inside the suitcase.) For an added safety precaution, lock each bag. When you hand over your baggage, make sure the ticket on each piece corresponds with your flight number and final destination. Also verify that you have a claim ticket for each bag.

The smartest travel tip we can give you: Always, always take essentials with you in a carry-on bag. (For honeymooners, essentials mean not only toiletries, medications, and eyeglasses, but also bathing suits and contraceptives.) Carry-on baggage must fit securely underneath the seat or in the overhead compartment. Each airline has different size requirements, so check with your travel agent in advance. Often you can carry on hanging garment bags, which can either be hung in airplane closets or placed in the overhead compartments.

Best of all, follow the advice of frequent fliers. Don't check in any baggage at all—just take a carry-on bag and hanging garment bag. If you pack the right clothes, you should be able to travel for a month—or more. See the "How to Pack" section for details.

TRAVEL BY CAR: Obviously, driving is not an option if you live in Des Moines and will be honeymooning in the Cayman Islands. But it's something to consider if your destination is within 1,000 miles of home. When you drive, getting there is half the fun. On the way to your final destination, you can explore charming old towns, make detours to historic houses, and stop for picnics by secluded waterfalls.

Your Own Car Versus a Rental Car

If you're not going too far, and if your own vehicle is in good shape, you'll probably want to save money and use your own car. Important: Take your car in for a complete mechanical check-up about a month before the wedding. The last, last-minute worry you want is a balky transmission or other mishap. If you'll be driving long distances consider renting a car. Not only does this save wear-and-tear on your own vehicle, but you can have a bit of fun and splurge on a luxury or sports model, such as a convertible.

If you'll be flying to your honeymoon destination, ask your travel agent whether or not you should rent a car. It's a virtual necessity in many vacation areas. Many airlines and hotels often have special fly/drive or fly/stay rates that give you extremely low rates for a rental vehicle. Even if you plan on spending most of your honeymoon at your resort hotel, you might want to rent a car for a day. It's the best way to get acquainted with a new area.

Most car rental companies will ask for a major credit card. Renting a car without one demands considerable advance planning. You'll have to undergo a credit check and furnish bank references, proof of employment, and other financial disclosures. You'll also have to pay the full rental amount in advance, plus an additional deposit that will be refunded when you return the car.

Important: Most car rental companies require you to be at least 21 years of age to rent a car—and even 25, under certain circumstances. You must have a valid driver's license. Call the rental car company's toll-free 800 number if you have any questions.

Here's a rundown of factors that influence rental car rates.

Make, size, model: The bigger the car and the more loaded with features, the more it will cost. You'll usually find the cheapest rate on a subcompact.

Equipment: Features such as air conditioning and automatic transmission cost extra in some destinations. If you want either of these options, make sure your request is noted on your reservation.

Locale: It simply costs more to rent a car in some places.

Drop-off charge: If you rent a car in one state or city, and return it in another, you may have to pay a fee. This can be as much as $75.

Length of rental: Because of special deals, it sometimes costs less to rent a car for a week than for five days; weekday rentals can run less than weekends. Ask your travel agent for details.

Peak seasons: Just as with airline seats, it costs more to rent a car during the high season.

Unlimited mileage versus mileage charge: With unlimited mileage, you can drive as far as you like without paying a per-mile fee. Mileage charges generally run anywhere from 10 to 30 cents per mile, which really adds up if you intend to drive far.

Collision damage waiver: You'll hear varying viewpoints about its necessity. The cost is usually minimal—less than ten dollars per day. We'd recommend it if you'll be traveling long distances in the United States; it is essential when driving in foreign countries such as Mexico.

Corporate discounts: Many large companies receive corporate discounts from car rental companies. Often, employees can benefit from these discounts even if they are using the car for vacation travel. Ask your company travel representative for details.

3. The Practicalities

HOW TO GET A PASSPORT: You must apply in person at one of the 12 passport agencies in the United States (see addresses which follow), the county clerk's office, or a major post office. Bring with you:

1. The application, available at major post offices.
2. Two photos taken within the past six months.
3. An official birth certificate with a raised seal, which you can obtain from the Department of Health in the area you were born. Allow plenty of time; it often takes four to six weeks to obtain the birth certificate.

The passport application fee is $42. It generally takes three weeks to process, but can sometimes take longer.

Passport Renewals

Save time by renewing your passport by mail. You can do so if your current passport was issued within the last eight years, and it was issued after your eighteenth birthday. You can obtain the proper forms at one of the passport offices or a major post office; you will also need two new photos. Renewal fee is $35; it takes about three weeks to receive the new passport.

A good service to know about is **Passport Plus,** located at 677 Fifth Avenue, New York, NY 10022 (tel. 212/759-5540, or toll free 800/367-1818). They operate nationwide and can help you obtain all travel documents, from passports to visas. Fees vary: A passport renewal runs from $35 (plus the $35 renewal fee) for one-week service, to $150 for same-day delivery. Call them for complete details.

A Word to the Bride

If you already have a passport under your maiden name, it will remain valid for your honeymoon. If your airline tickets are in your married name, bring a copy of your marriage certificate with you. (Immigration officials check whether the name on the passport and on the airline ticket are the same.) If you will be using your husband's last name after marriage, you can have your passport amended by mail. This service is free.

Passport Offices

The following are the locations and phone numbers for passport agencies in the United States. Outside of these areas, main post offices will be able to process applications.

Boston: John F. Kennedy Building, Room E-123, Government Center, Boston, MA 02203 (tel. 617/565-3930).

Chicago: 230 S. Dearborn St., Chicago, IL 60604 (tel. 312/353-7155).

Honolulu: Room C-106, New Federal Building, 300 Ala Moana Blvd., P.O Box 50185, Honolulu, HI 96850 (tel. 808/541-1919).

Houston: 500 Dallas St., Houston, TX 77002 (tel. 713/229-3608).

Los Angeles: 11000 Wilshire Blvd., Room 13100, Los Angeles, CA 90024 (tel 213/209-7070).

Miami: 51 S.W. First Ave., Miami, FL 33130 (tel. 305/536-5395).

New Orleans: 701 Loyola Ave., Room T12005, New Orleans, LA 70113 (tel 504/589-6161).

New York: 630 Fifth Ave., Room 270, New York, NY 10111 (tel 212/541-7700).

Philadelphia: 600 Arch St., Philadelphia, PA 19106 (tel. 215/597-7482).

San Francisco: 525 Market St., Suite 200, San Francisco, CA 94105 (tel. 415/974-7972).

Seattle: 915 Second Ave., Seattle, WA 98174 (tel. 206/442-7941).

Stamford: One Landmark Square, Broad and Atlantic Streets, Stamford, CT 06901 (tel. 203/325-4401).

Washington, DC (main office): 1425 K Street NW, Washington, DC 20524 (tel. 202/783-8200).

TIPS ABOUT TIPPING: *Le pour-boire. La propina.* Although the amount and the

nature of the acknowledgment may vary in different countries, it is customary to reward excellent service. Here are some guidelines for how much and who to tip in the United States. Customs vary in different countries; see the "Practical Facts" section for each area.

Transportation

Taxi: 15% to 20% of the fare; plus 50 cents to $1 per suitcase.

Hotel limousine driver: 10% to 15% of the fare. If the service is complimentary, 50 cents to $1 per bag.

Private limousine: 10% to 15% of the fare.

Train: Sleeping-car attendants, $1 per day; dining-car waiter, 15% of the bill.

Hotels

Bellhops: 50 cents to $1 per bag.

Doorman: 50 cents to $1 for getting a cab.

Parking attendant: 50 cents to $1.

Maid: $1 per day.

Restaurants

Waiter: 15% to 20% of bill.

Wine steward: 5% of wine cost.

Maître d': $1 to $10, depending on service rendered.

Miscellaneous

Beach or pool attendant: $1 per couple per day.

Sightseeing guide (group tour): $2 per couple.

In several foreign countries and in some U.S. hotels, resorts, and restaurants, a service charge of 10% to 15% is automatically added to bills. Additional tipping is not necessary. If you have any queries, ask in advance.

HANDLING FOREIGN CURRENCY: Whether you'll be looking after pounds or

pesos, the following pointers will help smooth the way when dealing with foreign currencies:

● Exchange rates for the U.S. dollar can fluctuate daily. You'll usually get the best rate of exchange at a national bank; rates tend to be less favorable at hotels, restaurants, and shops.

● Never change money on the street. Fast-talking con artists with nimble fingers often give unwary tourists the wrong change—or even wrap a single bill of foreign currency around a wad of cardboard.

● Try to change money only as you need it. You lose money every time you convert currency.

● Very useful: a small pocket calculator or currency converter. It's the fast, accurate way to keep track of how much something costs in dollars.

MAKING PHONE CALLS FROM ABROAD: Americans enjoy some of the lowest

telephone rates in the world. As a consequence, it often costs far more than you would expect to call home from a foreign country. In addition to the higher phone rates, many hotels outside the United States add a substantial surcharge to the cost of the call—sometimes as much as 100% to 300%. To avoid excessive telephone charges:

1. Always ask the hotel about telephone surcharges before you place a call.

2. If dialing from your hotel, call your party and ask them to call you back. The call costs less if placed from the United States. You can reimburse the person for the cost when you return home.

3. If you can, place your call from a pay phone at a telephone or post office. These offices do not levy surcharges.

4. Charging your call to an international calling card can also save you money. You can get these cards free from your local telephone company.

5. Find out if your hotel participates in American Telephone and Telegraph's TELEPLAN. Under this program, participating hotel chains, such as Hilton International and Marriott, agree to add only a reasonable surcharge for calls. To find out if your hotel is a member of TELEPLAN, call toll free 800/874-4000.

SHOPPING TIPS: A word hovering on many honeymooners' lips is "bargains." The Caribbean islands are especially well known for offering savings on many luxury items. Depending on which island you visit, you might encounter one of the following shopping opportunities. "Duty-free" shopping means that the country does not tax imported goods (or taxes them at a very low rate). "In-bond" shopping is similar in principle, in that no duties are levied on imports. It operates slightly differently, though, since it treats the imported goods as if they never entered the country. Usually, the in-bond merchandise you buy will be delivered to your airplane or cruise ship when you depart; you will not be able to take it with you directly from the store. Meanwhile, some countries will not tax imports from their mother countries, although they will levy duties on merchandise from other nations. This means that you can usually find good values on English goods in British islands, French goods on islands such as Martinique and Guadeloupe, etc. You might want to consult *A Shopper's Guide to the Caribbean* for further details and tips (published by Prentice Hall Press, New York).

You'll find good shopping values not only in the duty-free ports of the Caribbean, but also in diamond merchants' stalls along 47th Street in Manhattan, the factory outlets of the Poconos, even on the racks of swank Beverly Hills boutiques during clearance sales. Another potential source of bargains: airport duty-free stores. Wherever you shop, here are some pointers for assuring that what you buy is a really good value.

1. **Have shopping priorities.** Be firm with yourselves. Plan in advance exactly what items you most want—and concentrate your search on them.

2. **Comparison shop in advance.** This is a corollary of no. 1 above. Before your honeymoon journey, check the price range of items you want in stores back home. That way, when you get to the alleged bargain center of the universe, you'll know exactly how much of a good value you're actually getting.

3. **Research specific items.** If you're looking to fill in your china or crystal pattern, know that not all stores carrying famous lines (such as Wedgwood and Waterford) carry all patterns. To find out which store carries the pattern you want, contact the local tourist board.

4. **Beware of fakes.** Counterfeits have become big business worldwide. Check merchandise carefully. Be on the lookout for shoddy workmanship. Items like cameras or watches should carry serial numbers.

5. **Shop around.** Be aware that just because one store offers the best price on jewelry, it isn't necessarily the bargain leader on liquor.

6. **Haggle.** In many places, prices are negotiable.

7. **Ask about warranties and service.** You can't always get them at duty-free or discount outlets—something to consider.

8. Always buy it because you like it, not because it's a bargain. That way, it will continue to give you pleasure in years to come.

CLEARING U.S. CUSTOMS: If you honeymoon abroad, you will have to clear U.S. Customs when you return. By knowing the basic rules and regulations, you'll be able to pass through smoothly.

1. All returning Americans must fill out a Customs form that you'll receive on your return flight or cruise ship. For convenience, you can also get the declaration form from your travel agent before you leave and fill it in as you make purchases.

2. From most countries, you are permitted to return with $400 worth of goods per person duty free. You can make a simple oral declaration to the Customs inspector; you do not need to enumerate your purchases. Your $400 allowance is based on the retail value of the articles; the goods must be for your personal use. Exceptions: From the U.S. Virgin Islands, your duty-free allowance is $800 per person. From Puerto Rico, you can bring back an unlimited amount of goods, except for alcohol, for which you must prove that taxes have been paid.

3. Liquor and cigarettes: If you are 21 or older, your exemption includes one liter of alcohol and one carton of cigarettes. If you are returning from the U.S. Virgin Islands, your exemption includes one gallon of alcohol and 1,000 cigarettes.

4. If you buy more, you will have to pay Customs duty. You'll be charged a flat rate of 10% (5% if you are returning from the U.S. Virgin Islands) on the first $1,000 worth of purchases over the exemption. You will need to make a written declaration—a complete list of everything you've bought and how much you paid.

5. Keep all your sales receipts handy to support your statements. Since Customs officials can ask to inspect your bags, pack all your new purchases together in one suitcase.

6. Customs officers are usually kind to people who exceed the $400 limit, and will try to include the items subject to the highest duty in the exemption.

7. Fruits, flowers, and plants are either prohibited or strictly regulated. Narcotics are forbidden.

8. Over and above your duty-free allowance, you can also send gifts to family and friends—up to $100 per person per day, duty free. You cannot mail perfume, liquor, or tobacco.

9. For complete details about U.S. Customs regulations, send for the free booklet *Know Before You Go*, available from the U.S. Customs Service, 1301 Constitution Avenue NW, Washington, DC 20229.

EATING RIGHT: Any change in your familiar routine—from the excitement of the wedding to traveling halfway around the globe—can cause stomach jitters.

The best way to stay healthy is by eating right. Here are some tips:

1. The general rule is: If you can't peel it, boil it, or cook it, don't eat it.

2. In areas where the water is a problem, only drink purified water. Use the purified water for brushing your teeth; avoid drinks with ice cubes (beer is a good substitute).

3. Do not eat raw vegetables. Peel all fruits. Avoid raw or rare meat (even if you take it that way back home).

4. Avoid dairy products such as milk or cheese.

5. Stay away from buffets, where foods are prepared in advance and are exposed to the air for a long time.

ABOUT DRUGS: In a word—don't. Marijuana, hallucinogens, and other drugs are illegal in every country covered in this book. You can be dealt with very severely for possession of even a small quantity, and being an American citizen won't prevent you from being jailed: You are subject to the laws of the country you are visiting. Forget it.

4. Some Special Tips for Honeymooners

IF YOU'RE REMARRYING . . . : Whether or not either of you has been married previously, much of the advice that appears on the previous pages applies to you. Nonetheless, couples who are remarrying have some special needs.

One factor to consider is the wedding itself. Whatever their previous marital history, couples today are free to plan a wedding that suits their lifestyle and social circle. Often, people who eloped the first time or had a very simple ceremony will choose an all-out party to celebrate their new happiness. Someone who has already been through a splashy reception might prefer a more quiet, intimate event. One idea previously married individuals might want to consider is getting married at their honeymoon locale. The paradisiacal setting—a tropical beach, hidden waterfall, or bounteous garden—seems fitting for the new life that's beginning. Psychologically, it also frees couples from any family pressures or unstated objections regarding the marriage. One bride we talked with who had been married previously told us, "The first time I was married, I went along with a lot of the ideas my parents had about the wedding. This time, the marriage ceremony is what *we* want." For more information about combining your wedding with your honeymoon, see the next section, "Getting Married There."

It should go without saying, but we'll mention it anyway. Do not honeymoon where either of you has been with an ex-spouse. Dr. Maryellyn Duane, a New York City psychologist who specializes in family and marital practice, stresses, "Don't do it the way you did it the first time. Try to do something different and something that speaks to the uniqueness of your own relationship, and get away as much as you can from the memories of 'what was.' " People who have been married before should be prepared for feeling a twinge of sadness even as they plan for their new happiness. It's a natural emotion, and yet a complicated one, that might cause some insecurities if you share it with your new spouse. Instead, therapists recommend talking it out with a close friend, your parents, or a professional.

Someone who is marrying for the first time who is marrying a divorced person will experience some different anxieties. Cele Goldsmith Lalli, editor-in-chief of *Modern Bride* magazine, says, "It's only natural that the one who hasn't been would be concerned about living up to previous expectations. You just have to put all of that out of your mind. This is a new life, this is a different relationship, and there is no basis for comparison. You have nothing to be concerned about if you just concentrate on being yourself."

If either of you has children by a previous marriage, the question of taking them along on your trip may already have come up. The response of the experts varies from "no—never" to a qualified "perhaps." The general feeling is that the partners need some time to be together as a couple. But each situation is different, and each couple should decide what works best for their family. Mrs. Lalli adds, "In general, it is better to go away together and get some distance and objectivity—and relaxation—and not have to deal with these responsibilities that are going to be such a demanding part of your everyday lives together. And there will be plenty of time in the future for family vacations."

GETTING MARRIED THERE: If planning to get married at your honeymoon locale, pay particular attention to:

1. **Time frames:** Some places require that you be in the area for a certain number of days before a license can be issued or a wedding performed.
2. **Fees:** This can range from about $5 to several hundred.
3. **Identification:** Do you have to produce either proof of identity or proof of

age? What documents are acceptable? Driver's license? Certified birth certificate? Passport?

4. Local rules: These can be quite different from what you're accustomed to back home. In Bermuda, for example, a marriage notice must be published in the newspapers two weeks before a license can be issued.

5. Other documentation: If either one of you is divorced or widowed, you usually have to furnish the official certificate. If you will be marrying in a non-English-speaking country, you probably will need a translated, notarized copy of the papers.

Arranging a wedding long distance can be simplified if you contact a local specialist. In many areas, you can consult a wedding service. Often, your best bet will be telephoning the social activities director of the hotel where you will be staying and discussing your plans. The hotel can frequently handle all the details, from arranging for the officiant to ordering flowers—even finding someone to videotape the ceremony.

Wherever you choose to marry, try to incorporate local customs into your wedding. In the U.S. Virgin Islands, this might mean hiring a steel band for the music. In Hawaii, you can wear the traditional maile leis that symbolize long life, health, and prosperity. You'll add special meaning to this most special event.

COPING WITH HONEYMOON STRESS: You're madly in love. The air fare you have just paid to reach your honeymoon destination outstrips the annual budget of several small nations, and your suite outglitters anything on *Lifestyles of the Rich and Famous*. Yet you have just burst into tears because your partner announces that s/he is heading down to the beach to play volleyball with the gang instead of going antiques shopping with you. Is it all over?

Relax—you're dealing with honeymoon stress.

Honeymoon stress is just the flip side of taking The Trip of a Lifetime. For most couples, the honeymoon is the most significant vacation they'll ever have. And, as with anything important—and that also costs a lot of money—you want it to be perfect. Worse, you're constantly worrying whether everything measures up. (Please note that ''everything'' also often includes your new mate.) This feeling of tension can manifest itself several different ways: Anything from arguing over inconsequential matters to sudden, inexplicable attacks of sheer dumbness—like forgetting to take your airline tickets when you head for the airport. The factors contributing to honeymoon stress are varied:

● **The wedding.** When most couples start planning their honeymoons, they little anticipate how downright exhausted they'll be by the time the wedding night rolls around. Between the nervous tension about details that go awry—plus the sheer joy when the ceremony and reception turn out as gloriously as planned—you'll be emotionally frazzled by the day after the wedding. This fatigue makes you susceptible; petty annoyances that would not usually upset you instead get under your skin.

● **The commitment of marriage.** Even for couples who have lived together before marriage, the honeymoon marks the official start of a transition from single to married life. Stuart R. Johnson, a marital and family therapist in New Haven, Connecticut, points out that even today, ''Marriage is a lot more than a piece of paper, psychologically speaking.'' Marriage represents a major commitment, and each party feels—and fears—that he or she is surrendering some of their independence. ''There are two fundamental human issues that make marriages work or not work,'' Mr. Johnson continues. ''They come down to how do people deal with intimacy—not just sex, but anything they do together: love, companionship, problem solving, playing. Autonomy is the other issue—the sense of being a separate person and doing autonomous activities . . . careers and work, but also separate hobbies.'' On their honeymoon, couples are first beginning to grapple with this issue of "we" versus "I," the fact that it is impossible to meld two separate individuals into one entity. Until a workable balance is established, there will be strains in the relationship.

● **Getting to know each other.** During courtship, couples are often distracted from their relationship by career pressures and other responsibilities. The honeymoon gives people a chance to really concentrate on each other. Also during courtship, most men and women stay on their best behavior and try to please each other. They worry that if certain of their traits or quirks are uncovered—an inability to calculate a waiter's tip, crankiness in the morning—their mate won't love them any more. Likewise, each partner will learn new things about the person they married.

● **Defining new roles.** As mentioned at the beginning of this introduction, honeymoon planning is often the first time a couple discusses nitty-gritty finances with each other. One partner may tend to be an epicurean spendthrift, the other wants to save for a rainy day. Naturally, they'll run into conflicts. In addition, while traveling together, each partner will start to assume new responsibilities. One person might become the car driver, the other the map reader. Someone will be the budget planner, the other the tour guide. Until these roles are clearly defined, couples will encounter some rough spots.

● **Exaggerated expectations.** So much time and energy has gone into planning this trip that couples tend to expect too much from it: perfect weather, complete compatibility, a string of magic moments. Mr. Johnson points out, "The image of the honeymoon is wall-to-wall intimacy. It captures all the romantic mythology about intimacy: 'We become as if we are one.' Well, that's nonsense. Two human beings are not one." The problem is compounded by movies and television soap operas, which present an unrealistic image of love and romance. American culture is so imbued with these myths that even people who wouldn't be caught dead watching these programs accept the myths of unmitigated sweetness and light that Hollywood presents. Of course, life and love just don't work like that, and often the honeymoon is the first glimpse of that reality.

● **"Great sexpectations."** Perhaps the biggest myth surrounding honeymoons concerns the sexual relationship; couples expect not only the hearts and flowers of intimacy, but also the rockets and fireworks of passion as well. And although couples put tremendous pressure on themselves for peak sexual performance, conditions for a loving relationship are far from optimal. The wedding planning, ceremony, and reception sap a lot of energy out of people—they're absolutely zonked by their wedding night.

● **Travel is stressful.** People who don't travel much often believe that trips unfold in complete pleasure. Not true. Travelers constantly worry about catching that flight, paying with foreign currencies, finding that left-hand turn to the hotel. When you add in the anxieties associated with the wedding, you'll often find that extremely well-organized, experienced travelers will suddenly pull real bloopers, and forget to take their wallets, hotel reservations, passports, or other necessities.

It's important for honeymooners to realize that feeling stress is not necessarily bad—it's part of the growing pains involved in forming a deeper relationship. Dr. Duane comments, "When stress is actually due to change, it can be very, very productive. It means that you are having deep, emotional feelings. It's a process of growth and change. So how can a honeymoon not be a time of stress?" Although some anxiety is natural, there are ways to help assure that stress won't interfere with a happy honeymoon.

● **Consider delaying your honeymoon departure.** In all likelihood, you'll be pooped the day after the wedding. By postponing your departure by at least a day, you can catch up with your sleep and spend time with wedding guests visiting from out of town. In many cases, delaying your honeymoon for several weeks or months may be the smartest way to give yourselves the honeymoon you always dreamed of, especially if both of you also face substantial career pressures. It just may be too difficult to take the time away from work for the wedding planning and for the honeymoon too. Cele Lalli recommends, "If it is too complicated to take your honeymoon right after the wedding, you should postpone such an important trip to a little later time when you can do it without conflict."

- **Do your honeymoon your way.** Plan your trip around what you would like to do, instead of what you think you ought to do or what is romantic to do. One couple, for example, spent their honeymoon cross-country skiing with friends. It was comfortable, natural—and, most important, it felt right for them.

- **Make a list of items you must bring with you.** Do this several weeks before your departure so that last-minute anxiety attacks won't numb you into forgetfulness.

- **Consider choosing a resort area that's especially popular with honeymooners.** Most newlyweds discover that they enjoy being with other just-marrieds, because they all have so much in common. From her conversations with couples from around the country, Mrs. Lalli finds that newlyweds "really will enjoy being with others who are on their honeymoon, because you can share the interesting wedding experiences that all of you have had—it can make everything more fun." Many of the most popular resorts for honeymooners offer a wide range of social activities—from party boats to volleyball games. With so much to do, you'll have plenty of new events to talk about.

- **Plan a realistic budget.** Be practical about what you can afford, but also allow some money for splurges. When we've asked married couples what they would have done differently on their honeymoon, the most common response was, "Gee, I wish we'd paid extra to get an oceanfront room." "I wish we'd taken that helicopter tour." "I love the poster that we took home—but we should have bought the original watercolor painting of the beach we always went to." Don't shortchange your honeymoon memories.

- **Relax.** Enjoy every moment of the honeymoon trip for what it is. Don't let inflated expectations or overambitious planning interfere with the real fun you're having. You don't have to schedule activities for every moment. A honeymoon is a time to get away and unwind. Also, don't put pressure on yourselves to have the greatest sex of your lives. Dr. Duane reminds newlyweds, "Any sexual relationship is something a couple has to work on. Defocus the sex, and instead find other activities you enjoy doing in common. You'll find that sex will come more naturally then."

- **Communicate.** Since the honeymoon marks the transition into married life, there's no better time to start good habits—like talking things over. If you feel uncomfortable when your spouse automatically assumes all responsibility for travel finances, or rejected if he or she doesn't share your enthusiasm for pre-Mayan artifacts, talk about it. Communication forms a stronger basis for a relationship than sulking.

- **Each of you should have some time alone.** Realize that you don't have to spend every moment together. You have different interests—indulge them. While one of you goes to the baseball game, the other can scope out the shopping mall. Private time doesn't even mean that you have to be apart. You can have that same feeling of space while sitting on the beach together, each reading a book.

- **Keep your sense of humor.** If things go wrong on your journey, remember that the mishaps will probably turn into the funniest stories you'll tell in years to come. And that's good advice for both traveling . . . and marriage.

Part One

THE UNITED STATES

Chapter III

NEW ENGLAND INNS

1. Practical Facts
2. Connecticut's River Towns
3. North of the Litchfield Hills
4. The Berkshires of Massachusetts
5. Cape Cod
6. Manchester and the Mountains
7. The Heart of Vermont

NEW ENGLAND'S HEART AND SOUL lie along its back roads, where general stores still sell sodas in long slender bottles and pretzel rods for a penny. Time hasn't stood still; it's just accommodated itself to Yankee stubbornness. Whether you're in the dramatic Green Mountains of Vermont or the coast off Cape Cod, you'll begin to understand why New England has managed to keep its rural ways despite the sprawl of its big cities. The people are tied to the land—to the cranberry bogs, to the birch trees, to the sunken meadows. A visit to the inns and bed and breakfasts of these northern states means spending time just observing the passing of the seasons, even subtle changes from day to day.

Whole books have been written about the wide range of charming inns this region offers. Since we cannot possibly cover them all in this volume, we have instead focused on what we consider to be the most romantic honeymoon locales in Connecticut, Massachusetts, and Vermont.

1. Practical Facts

GETTING THERE: Although airline, bus, and train service are all available to take you into New England, most of the small towns are accessible by car only.

By Air

To southern Connecticut: The closest major airport, Bradley International, is located in Windsor Locks just north of Hartford and about 40 miles from East Haddam. Over a dozen airlines fly into Bradley. The **Delta Connection,** one of Delta's commuter airlines (tel. toll free 800/221-1212), offers flights called "The Business Express" into Tweed Airport in New Haven (about 40 miles from the East Haddam / Chester area) and into the Groton / New London Airport (approximately 25 miles away).

To northwestern Connecticut and the Berkshires: Bradley International Airport in Windsor Locks is a little over 50 miles from the Salisbury area; the Albany, N.Y., airport, about 75 miles.

To Cape Cod: Airports in Hyannis and Provincetown provide regularly scheduled service to the Cape. The most popular airlines are **Gull Air** (tel. toll free 800/832-9700), and **PBA** (Provincetown-Boston Airline), which is now owned by Texas Air (tel. toll free 800/722-3597).

To Vermont: Although Burlington is the nearest large airport that welcomes major carriers, you can fly into Rutland via **Precision Airlines.** Driving time from Rutland to Ludlow or Manchester is less than 30 minutes.

By Bus

Greyhound and **Bonanza** bus lines, in conjunction with smaller, regional bus companies, have a fairly extensive network that runs throughout New England. Contact Bonanza (tel. toll free 800/556-3815), an independent working out of Providence, RI, for information to Lee, Lenox, and Hyannis, Mass., and Canaan, Conn. Greyhound goes to Lee, Lenox, and Stockbridge, Mass, and New Haven, Conn.; in addition, they also have schedule and fare information for **Vermont Transit** (tel. toll free 800/451-3292), a part of Greyhound that runs up to Manchester and Ludlow.

By Train

To southern Connecticut: The closest stop is in Old Saybrook, although you can take Amtrak (tel. toll free 800/872-7245) into New London or New Haven.

To northwestern Connecticut and the Berkshires: From Boston, you can get off the Lake Shore Limited in Pittsfield, which is just a hop away from Lenox and Lee. From New York, the only train to the area stops in Albany.

To Cape Cod: The Cape Cod & Hyannis Railroad chugs along between Boston and Hyannis. The slow and scenic trip is a treat for romantic rail riders.

To Vermont: Amtrak's Montrealer runs through Vermont, stopping in Bellows Falls and White River Junction. But because it's a night train, it is not a viable option unless you can arrange to be picked up at the station by someone who knows their way around.

GETTING AROUND: Public transportation is almost nonexistent in most small towns. A **car** is the only way to take advantage of New England. Be advised that most gas stations in small towns close down by 7 p.m., and even along main highways, many service stations close by 10 p.m. Keep an eye on your gas gauge.

By Taxi

Taxis can be prohibitively expensive for touring, but drivers can be arranged through most tourist offices; the charge for two hours usually hovers around $25 or $30.

By Rental Car

The major rental car companies have offices scattered throughout New England, including facilities at the main airports. Call **Hertz** (tel. toll free 800/654-3131), **Avis** (tel. toll free 800/331-1212) or **National Rental Car** (tel. toll free 800/328-4567) for more specific information.

WEATHER: New England's temperate weather means mild springs, warm but not blistery summers, and crisp, cool autumns. If you're by the shore, winter temperatures log in around 25° to 30°. Head to Vermont, though, and the nights can be bitter cold, plummeting below zero. In Vermont, there's an extra season that usually falls in April: mud season. As the thaw sets in, rivers rise and the unpaved roads turn to unpassable mud. Venture to the north country only if you have a four-wheel-drive vehicle at your disposal.

CLOTHING: Although dress is casual in the countryside, there's a general trend for clothing to become more fashionable the closer you get to New York City. Jeans and comfortable shirts are acceptable for traveling, but bring along dinner clothes for evenings at gourmet restaurants. Most innkeepers dress casually and expect that their guests will do the same.

TIME: All the New England states are on Eastern Standard Time in winter and go on Daylight Savings Time in the summer.

TELEPHONES: The area code for Connecticut is 203; for Vermont, 802. In Massachusetts, the area code for the Berkshires is 403; for Cape Cod, 617. Most inns and bed and breakfasts have a house phone that guests can use. In many cases, however, the phone is also used for reservations, so keep your calls brief. It is easiest to use a credit card.

SHOPPING: New England offers a cornucopia of crafts and antiques at stores that are as quaint and charming as the towns in which they stand. On the other extreme, however, are the fabulous outlet stores—in Manchester Center, Vermont, and Hyannis, Cape Cod—that offer no-nonsense bargains on clothing, tableware, and the like.

Take a special side trip to a local event: a harvest fair, fruit celebration, or school fund-raiser. (Schedules are available from the tourism offices.) The shopping's sure to include homemade crafts and baked goods—and you just might find that white elephant that endears you to the area forever.

ABOUT ACCOMMODATIONS: Inns. Bed-and-breakfasts. Bed-and-breakfast inns. They all sound alike, and in many cases, they are alike. Much to the dismay of travelers, there are no standardized definitions that outline the facilities and amenities of these unique accommodations.

As a general rule, most **inns** have a dining room that offers meals to the outside public. Professionally run **bed-and-breakfast inns** usually don't serve afternoon or evening meals, and if they do, it's to guests only. The owners also tend to keep their living quarters separate from that of their guests'. **Bed-and-breakfasts** that are mom-and-pop operations, in most cases, tend to have community rooms that are shared, and only open up guest rooms on an irregular schedule. They don't offer as much privacy and comfort as the bed-and-breakfast inns.

In many cases, the terms "bed-and-breakfast" and "inn" will be used interchangeably once it is established that a place offers dinner. All of the accommodations listed in this book provide good mattresses, private baths, and a special, unique touch that you can't get anywhere else.

Deposit and cancellation policies: Most inns and bed-and-breakfasts follow strict rules concerning deposits and necessary cancellations. A deposit equal to 50% of the cost of your stay is not unusual. If you must cancel at the last minute, you will probably be required to pay a small service charge (approximately $10) in addition to the full sum. Notify innkeepers as soon as you know of a change in your plans, because most hosts will refund your money if they can rent the room.

Peak season: Definitions differ from one inn to the next. In Massachusetts and Connecticut, peak seasons are usually summer and autumn; in Vermont, autumn and winter.

Minimum stays: Partly as a reminder that guests tend to relax only after they've stayed more than one night and partly as good business practice, many inns have instituted a minimum stay policy. Many innkeepers require a two-night stay for peak season weekends and three-day holidays. Don't be put off by the rules. Hopping from inn to inn is not necessarily as pleasant as it may sound. Stay an extra day, and you'll enjoy your honeymoon so much more.

What to Expect: Good bedding and a private bath to start. No room phones, no television, and no children. Beyond that the amenities vary dramatically from inn to inn. Air conditioning, often not provided, is not really very important when you're out in the country. Most of the houses have wonderful cross breezes. If you're fussy about heat in the cool seasons, ask in advance if the room has individual temperature controls. Most inns lack this luxury, but then again, most innkeepers are happy to raise or lower the heat if you ask. Breakfasts are included in the room rate; taxes and gratuities are not.

Breakfasts: In general, the breakfasts served are above average. Hosts bring out the finished products based on the secret recipes of who knows how many generations back. To clarify the terms used here, **continental** means the basics: coffee or tea, muffins or breads or croissants, and juice. An **expanded continental** breakfast is an enlargement on the theme; in addition to what you get in a continental breakfast, you usually can choose from cold cereals, granola, cheeses, and fruit. **Full** breakfast denotes a hot meal, usually some sort of egg dish, pancakes, or French toast, or the like, plus everything on the continental breakfast. Sometimes it even includes an appetizer such as a baked pear or fruit compote.

Rates and Payments: Room rates may change with the seasons. Also, prices may vary for different rooms at the same inn or B&B, depending on views, size, and amenities. Few places have honeymoon packages; however, if you let your hosts know in advance that you are newlyweds, they will often have a chilled bottle of champagne waiting in your room when you arrive.

Regarding payment, be aware that not all inns and B&Bs accept credit cards. Some will honor "plastic" for the room deposit, but not the complete payment. Ask in advance.

DINING OUT: When you make your room reservation, don't be surprised if innkeepers ask you where you will want to dine, even if it's months in advance. Some of the finest restaurants outside of New York, Chicago, and San Francisco are in New England's tiny inn towns. Make your reservations as soon as possible and confirm them once you arrive at your destination.

New England's gourmet restaurants generally change their menus seasonally, adding more fresh fish in the summer and game in the winter. Let the maitre d' know you're on your honeymoon. He or she may know of a special dessert or appetizer that's not on the menu but that can be whipped up just for you.

HOW TO GET MARRIED IN NEW ENGLAND: Bed-and-breakfasts and inns thrive on romance, and the majority of innkeepers are willing and eager to help with wedding plans. Newlyweds-to-be should take advantage of innkeepers' knowledge if they wish to be married or have their reception at the inn. The locals know the best florists, caterers, bakers, etc.

In Connecticut: Couples must obtain a certificate from the Registrar of Vital Statistics in the town in which the marriage is to be celebrated. The certificate will be issued four days after filing with proof of identity and marital status and with physician's statement (a rubella test for brides-to-be under 50 and capable of pregnancy is the only necessary test). The marriage must be solemnized within 65 days.

In Massachusetts: You must file your notice of intention to marry at least three days before the marriage ceremony. You both have to go in person to the clerk or registrar of any town in the state. Both members of the couple must submit to a medical exam no more than 30 days before filing. The license will be issued 3 or more (but not more than 60) days after filing. If you plan to ask a nonresident clergyman to perform the ceremony, you may need special permission. Ask the clerk or registrar in advance if this will be a problem.

In Vermont: You must file for a marriage certificate from the town clerk of the groom's hometown, or if he is not a resident, from the bride's hometown. Nonresidents must file in the town where the ceremony will be performed and must provide an affidavit that the proposed marriage is not contrary to the laws of their home states. Both members of the couple must have a premarital medical examination within 30 days before application. After the marriage certificate is obtained, three days must elapse before the ceremony can take place.

In all three states, waivers from the various requirements may be obtained from the probate judge for the area in which the marriage will be solemnized.

FOR FURTHER INFORMATION: Contact the **New England Vacation Center,** 630 Fifth Avenue, New York, NY 10020 (tel. 212/307-5780).

For Connecticut: Contact **The Connecticut Tourism Office,** 210 Washington Street, Hartford, CT 06106 (tel. 203/566-2496, or toll free Maine to Virginia 800/243-1685). **Connecticut Valley Tidewater Commission,** 70 College St., Middletown, CT 06457 (tel. 203/347-6924). **Litchfield Hills Visitors Commission,** P.O. Box 1776, Marbledale, CT 06777 (tel. 203/868-2214).

For Massachusetts: Contact **The Spirit of Massachusetts,** Division of Tourism, 100 Cambridge St., 13th floor, Boston, MA 02202 (tel. 617/727-3201). **Berkshire Visitors Bureau,** Berkshire Common Plaza Level, Dept. MA, Pittsfield, MA 01201 (tel. 413/443-9186). **Cape Cod Chamber of Commerce,** Dept. MA, Hyannis, MA 02601 (tel. 617/362-3225).

For Vermont: Contact the **Vermont Travel Division,** 134 State St., Montpelier, VT 05602 (tel. 802/828-3236). **Ludlow Area Chamber of Commerce,** P.O. Box 174, Ludlow, VT 05149 (tel. 802/228-5318). **Manchester and the Mountains Chamber of Commerce,** Manchester Center, VT 05255 (tel. 802/362-2100).

CONNECTICUT

2. Connecticut's River Towns

Often overlooked by tourists, the villages of East Haddam, Chester, Deep River, and Ivoryton offer a taste of past eras. Situated in Middlesex County on the Connecticut River, which bisects the state, all are within a five- to ten-minute drive north of the beautiful and beach-studded Long Island Sound. The location encouraged shipbuilding and ivory trade, which helped shape the character of the towns. Many of the residents here are relearning the history that surrounds them. Attractions include the **Goodspeed Opera House,** known for its musical revivals, and its neighbor, the **Goodspeed-at-Chester,** which stages new musical productions.

East Haddam, spurred to growth by the theater, is the busiest of the four towns; Chester, with its restored buildings and mill river is the quaintest; and Ivoryton, the grandest. But for a real glimpse of the area before tourism, stroll through Deep River.

Bordered by New Haven, New London, and Hartford counties, this little cutout of Connecticut retains its small-town feel even though it is only a short drive away from the state's biggest cities. **Sports** enthusiasts can take advantage of good bicycling roads, canoeing on the Connecticut, and swimming at the lakes or in the Sound.

SHOPPING: Best bets in southeastern Connecticut include Barbara Barlow's antique store down the road from Riverwind (tel. 526-2014 for exact location), the gift and clothing shops along Chester's main street, and if you don't mind driving into a more crowded and touristy area, **Olde Mistick Village** in Mystic—no more than half an hour away off exit 90 on I-95. More than 60 stores in an 18th-century setting comprise the village, among them **Franklin's General Store** featuring handmade items, **Bestemors Scandinavian Gifts, Mystick Pewter Shop, Ye Olde 1776 Shoppe** for

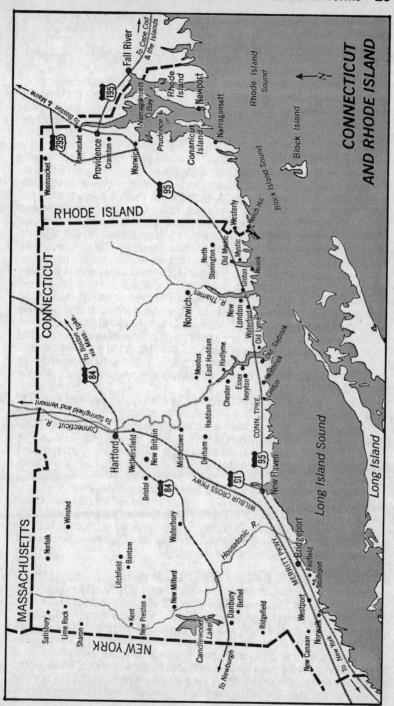

scrimshaw, and the **Rocking Horse Shop** with—what else?—rocking horses (and other gifts).

ROMANTIC INTERLUDES: This deceptively quiet river valley offers romantic adventure aloft, afloat, and aground.

Rise above the Connecticut River Valley in a **seaplane.** From the small three-seater you can see Selden's Creek, Gillette Castle, and Long Island Sound. Plan to take off in the morning so you can land in the river before the pleasure boats come out (May to November). Or opt for a land plane and go any time you desire. Contact **Eagle Aviation** for information about the $30 per person ride, which leaves from the Goodspeed Airport at Goodspeed Landing (tel. 873-8568).

All aboard! The **Valley Railroad** (tel. 767-0103) takes you back in time to circa 1910 as you chug along from Essex to Chester in restored vintage steam-train cars. Experience first-class travel in the Pullman parlor car *Wallingford* with its revolving plush seats, carpets, leaded-glass partitions, and music. The train connects with a riverboat at Deep River for an hour-long ride past Gillette Castle and by the Goodspeed Opera House. The schedule varies seasonally. Allow two hours and ten minutes for the train and cruise, which costs $11.90 ($1.95 less if you opt for the more simple bench-seating cars). Arrive 45 minutes ahead of time for the best seats. The train runs during the spring, summer, and fall, and around the Christmas holidays, weather permitting.

Built of native stone and southern white oak, **Gillette Castle** stands atop a rocky ridge that overlooks the Connecticut River. The building resembles a child's turreted sand castle but much larger and grander. Walking trails snake through the 122-acre property, which includes a picnic area and a very romantic arched stone bridge. Stop at **The Wheatmarket** (tel. 526-9347) in Chester before you go and pick up their Lover's Picnic, a hefty lunch of brie cheese, country pâté, celeriac salad, marinated mushrooms, French bread, and sparkling cider ($20 for two people). If you haven't already discovered it, take the **Chester-Hadlyme** ferry (50¢ for car with two passengers or two bicyclists) back across the river. A wonderfully picturesque road leads from the ferry toward Rte. 9A.

Imagine paddling up to a silent, wooded cove that's all your own for the day. The placid **Connecticut River** is dotted with islands and private inlets perfect for newly-weds equipped with a bottle of champagne and a treat-laden picnic basket. For $25 to $30 for the two of you, **Down River Canoes** (tel. 346-3308 or 345-8355) will provide the boat and arrange to pick you up at the end of the day. If you don't mind company, ask about their overnight canoe trip that highlights a candlelit waterfront steak or shad-and-clam bake.

For a tamer trip on the Connecticut, reserve a dinner cruise aboard the luxury yacht **The Camelot** (tel. 345-4507). The chef, who also advises American Cruise Lines, prepares a delectable array of seasonal foods for an all-you-can-eat buffet. The lunch trip leaves Haddam at noon for a 2½-hour trip to the tunes of Dixieland jazz ($22 per person plus tax and tip). The three-hour evening cruise features a live band and dinner dancing ($32 per person plus tax and tip).

IDYLLIC INNS AND BED-AND-BREAKFASTS: The romantic settings of southern Connecticut fall as backdrops to the wonderful array of homey places to stay.

Riverwind, 209 Main Street, Deep River, CT 06417 (tel. 203/526-2014). Situated by the village green, this 1850s clapboard house embodies warmth and whimsy. Innkeeper Barbara Barlow, who hails from Smithfield, Virginia, has captured the magic that comes from combining Yankee ingenuity with Southern graciousness. The eight guest rooms, all with impeccable private baths, ooze charm and coziness; decorated with country American crafts and beautiful antiques, each room offers something special—for instance, a canopied bed or a maple four-poster that rises 2 ½ feet above the polished pine floors. Candlelit buffet breakfasts with delicious baked goods such as blueberry pound cake or an incredibly good coffee cake are the norm, and when there's a chill outside, the fire in the dining room is kept roaring. As one visitor wrote in the guest diary: "Every detail is perfect." Let Barbara know you're newlyweds; she's sure to sneak a bottle of champagne into your room. Rates: $60 to $70 with full breakfast.

Stonecroft Inn, 17 Main St., East Haddam, CT 06423 (tel. 203/873-1754). This gracious, Federal-style inn sits on a low rise just down the street from the Goodspeed Opera House. An atmosphere of refined relaxation predominates. Guests take their cues from retired banker Paul Higgins, who furnished the house with many of his family's exquisite antiques. The appointments subtly complement the subdued colors of the Federal era with silk and bargello chairs, a chintz-covered canopy bed, and crystal candelabras on the mantel. Request one of the rooms with a working fireplace, although only one of the five rooms is unsuitable for honeymooners (it has twin beds). Paul usually serves cheese in the afternoon and has been known to surprise newlyweds with a complimentary bottle of champagne. Rates: $75 to $85 with full breakfast.

A stately addition to the area's bed-and-breakfasts, **Selden House,** 20 Read St., Deep River, CT 06417 (tel. 203/526-9195), emphasizes a simple, almost spare, elegance. The details of the house are splendid—lovely moldings, pocket doors in the living room, original hardware. An inviting living room highlights an autumn-colored oriental rug, a Chinese silk Empire sofa, and chairs carved by the man who designed Mount Rushmore. The eight rooms, which are more plainly furnished, still reflect the house's gracefulness, especially the spacious room number one, which has a nice size working fireplace. Outside, on the land's four acres, a beautiful weeping cherry tree stands within sight of terraced stone steps, and you'll find many perfect places for a wedding ceremony or an evening drink before dinner. Rates: $55 to $90 with continental breakfast.

Copper Beech Inn, Main Street, Ivoryton, CT 06426 (tel. 203/767-0330). Guests now have a choice of accommodations at this fine inn, once the residence of an ivory magnate. In 1986, the owners, Paul and Louise Ebeltoft, rebuilt the carriage house to include nine capacious rooms characterized by crisp, reproduction colonial furniture, king-size beds, televisions, and whirlpool tubs. First-time inn visitors may feel more comfortable in the carriage house, while old hands will prefer the four rooms in the main house. The uniquely furnished older rooms each convey a different mood, influenced by the wonderful beds: Take your choice among brass, white wicker, Hitchcock, or a four-poster. If you want to be on your own, you won't miss having a common living room. The inn's celebrated dining rooms stand where the parlors and billiard rooms originally were. Rates: $70 to $125 with continental breakfast.

ROMANTIC RESTAURANTS:

Some of the finest restaurants in Connecticut are clustered here by the Connecticut River. Most couples dress for dinner, although no code dictates such formality.

Fine Bouche, 79 Main St., Centerbrook (tel. 767-1277). Chef-owner Steven Wilkinson takes his job seriously, and it's reflected in the consistent quality and character of the extraordinarily good French menu he's prepared. Specialties include a succulent quail stuffed with a chicken and truffle mousse, salmon filet with a cream and chervil sauce, and crisp but moist sautéed duck breast with black currants and cassis. Wilkinson's desserts are equally enticing, as is his wine list, which offers an array that begins under $10 and includes an excellent selection of rare wines as well. Lunch features sandwiches on croissants or sourdough rye bread, hearty soups, salads, and reasonably priced hot entrées. The food is so good you may not even notice the simple but romantic surroundings, complete with fireplace. Prix-fixe, five-course dinner, $34.50; à la carte appetizers from $5.50 to $9.50, entrées from $16.50 to $19.50; lunch options from $2.50 to $8.95; plus wine. Make reservations several weeks in advance if possible.

Restaurant du Village, 59 Main St., Chester (tel. 526-5301). Tucked into a row of winsome buildings on Chester's main street, this small, formal restaurant epitomizes French country charm. White linens, Laura Ashley service plates, and a diminutive bouquet share the glow from small votive candles. In warm weather the French doors open out onto the red brick path that leads to the entrance. The doors open at 5:30 p.m. to serve the pretheater crowd. Try the mussels in curry cream sauce to start. This is French country cooking at its best. Dinner with drinks comes to about $70 for two.

Fiddlers Seafood Restaurant, 4 Water St., Chester (tel. 526-3210). A treasure trove for seafood lovers! Each day's specials can be mesquite grilled, poached, or pan sautéed on request. In addition there are 13 standard fish and shellfish entrees, ranging from whole lobster to a well-sauced pan-fried filet of sole. A rare treat is the broth-based Rhode Island clam chowder. Desserts change daily, but the chocolate terrine appears often and shouldn't be passed up. The setting is cheery and sweet: candlelight, a nosegay of fresh flowers, and blue scallop shells hand-stenciled on the walls. Dinner for two with appetizer and dessert: about $40. Lunch, about $12 for two.

Copper Beech Inn, Ivoryton (tel. 767-0330), voted Most Romantic in the county by readers of *Connecticut* magazine. Fine French food, good wine list, and scrumptious desserts. Chef Paul Gaffney is a Culinary Institute of America graduate. Entrées priced from $19.95. For continental food while overlooking the Connecticut River try **Gelston House,** East Haddam (tel. 873-1411), right next to the Goodspeed Opera House. Sunday brunch includes a fresh fruit and homemade pastry buffet. Brunch starts at $6.50; lunch, from $4.50; dinner, from $10.95. Monday is steak night ($11.95 to $14.95).

Grab lunch at **Robbie's** in Chester (tel. 526-3679)—sandwiches and Robbie's famous crab soup. Lots of ice cream too. You won't spend more than $6 per person with all the extras.

3. North of the Litchfield Hills

Litchfield, judged by some to be the prettiest example of an 18th-century New England village, has been "discovered" in the past decade; but travel north to the old resort towns of Lakeville, Salisbury, and Norfolk and you'll find yourself in countryside that's punctuated with cascading streams, village greens surrounded by stately mansions, and a quietness that lends itself to romance.

Tucked into the top northwest corner of Connecticut near the Housatonic River, these small towns share a border with New York to the west and Massachusetts to the north, a location that led people to dub the area the "Connecticut Berkshires." In fact, the Indian name for the river means "Place Beyond the Mountains." And although the peaks may not be as lofty as they are across the state line, their beauty is just as compelling.

While warm weather brings musicians and tourists to Music Mountain in Falls Village and the summer home of the Yale School of Music in Norfolk, Lime Rock Park in Lime Rock attracts serious car racing fans, especially during the major summer holidays. For those travelers who want to take a more active part in their time, the sporting activities here include skiing, canoeing on the Housatonic, and horseback riding in addition to the year-round hiking.

SHOPPING: If you're looking for auto art, you can't beat northwestern Connecticut, which has the largest collection of contemporary automotive artwork in the world at **Auto Art** in West Cornwall (tel. 672-6055). Other notables include the **Cornwall Bridge Pottery Store** near the covered bridge in West Cornwall (tel. 672-6545), open Thursday through Sunday; **Undermountain Weavers** (tel. 435-2321), with its fine selection of hand-loomed articles of cashmere and Shetland wool; and **Friendship Artisans,** a craft gallery in Salisbury that features traditional floor cloths, jewelry, leather, and other unique goods from New England craftspeople. The **Designing Woman,** also at Salisbury Square, has custom-designed needlepoint canvases and yarn.

ROMANTIC INTERLUDES: Spend some time traveling the unmarked roads to really appreciate this corner of Connecticut. You'll fall in love all over again.

Connecticut's two **covered bridges** still open to automobile traffic are easily reached from Salisbury. West Cornwall along Rte. 128 boasts one of native oak that was built in 1837; the other, **Bull's Bridge,** in Kent on Rte. 7, dates back to the Revolution. Although you can see both by car, you may want to stop in at the **Village Store** in Salisbury (tel. 435-9459) to rent a bike ($10 for the day) or call **Clarke Outdoors** in West Cornwall (tel. 672-6365) for a canoe. For $34 Clarke will take you up to Falls Village and let you wend your way down through calm and easy white water on the Housatonic (class I and II), past the red-hued covered bridge in West Cornwall and down to their pick-up point. Remember to pack a picnic!

Day Dreamer I and **II,** festive multicolored **charter balloons,** leave the Johnnycake Airport in Plymouth for a 1-to-1½-hour float over rolling hills, serene countryside, and picture perfect, white-steepled New England towns. Owner Steve Jalbert uncorks a champagne-and-cheese brunch after landing. Contact Adventure Rides (tel. 283-8736) for more information about the $150 per person flights, which run all year, weather permitting.

A dark burgundy and gold pinstripe reproduction of a French **vis-à-vis** drawn by a **draft horse** will take you around the back roads of Norfolk for $30 for two. **Horse & Carriage Livery** (tel. 542-6085) will make arrangements to provide a picnic basket and a bottle of wine or champagne on request, or you can bring your own for the hourlong ride. Proprietor Beth Denis also gathers folks for hay rides and sleigh rides according to the season.

Capture the sunset from the pavilion atop **Dennis Hill** (two miles south of Norfolk on Rte. 272), a 1,627-foot elevation that affords a sweeping view of the countryside. Haystack Mountain, one mile north of Norfolk on Rte. 272, commands an equally impressive vista from its 34-foot-high stone tower. Visit the latter on a clear evening and you can see Long Island Sound.

INNS AND BED-AND-BREAKFASTS: Wake up to the sound of wind in the trees or to the smell of breakfast and you'll never want to stay in a hotel again.

Blackberry River Inn, P.O. Box 326, Rte. 44, Norfolk, CT 06058 (tel. 203/ 542-5100). Dick and Joy Pygman are slowly turning this unusual exposed-shingle house into a premier inn. Listed in the National Register of Historic Places, the colonial building was built in 1763. The rooms, however, combine the best of modern comforts with beautiful antiques. Sunrise and Sunset, ultraspacious sister rooms across the hall from one another, both sport sun porches (heated in winter) with views on three sides. A fireplace makes Sunrise even more special. Lace curtains, white chenille bedspreads, and muted colors barely begin to capture the amorous essence that's infused in these rooms. A tennis court and cross-country ski trails enhance the 27 scenic acres. If Dick knows you're newlyweds, he'll have champagne waiting for you on arrival. And you can request breakfast in bed! Good restaurant. Rates: $70 to $125 with continental breakfast.

Mountain View Inn, Rte. 272, Norfolk, CT 06058 (203/542-5595). The marriage of Victoriana and Americana succeeds in this country manse within walking distance of the timeless Norfolk green. The living room tempts guests to stay up and linger until the wee hours of the morning. Lit predominantly by the fireplace, the textured, red wallpaper reflects a warmth that is carried through in the tapestry fabrics of the loveseat and parlor chairs. The low light picks up the glow of the wood in the Eastlake rocker as well. The reigning mood is casual, though, as guests chat or read. Upstairs, the third-floor rooms are coziest with slanted ceilings and country antiques.

You can request white eyelet linens for an extra touch of romance. Breakfast is served in a wraparound multiwindowed enclosed porch. Dining room. Rates: $55 to $90 with expanded continental breakfast.

For a more rustic environment, try the **Ragamont Inn,** Rte. 44, Salisbury, CT 06068 (tel. 203/435-2372). Suite no. 11 has a simple charm, with a private parlor that overlooks the main street. Strong colonial reds and browns predominate, so don't opt for this if you want soft pastels. Yet the wallpaper and curtains match the sofa, loveseat, and chair for an overall restful effect. The bedroom of this suite is down a short, private hall away from what little traffic noise there is. The restaurant, renowned for its German and Swiss food, is nicely set off from the guests' common rooms. No credit cards accepted. Rates: $50 to $70 with breakfast.

ROMANTIC RESTAURANTS: Casual is the keynote in this corner of the state, where many celebrities come to relax.

Ragamont Inn, Rte. 44, Salisbury (tel. 435-2372). Nestled between two white-columned facades, the awning-covered patio dining area refreshes visitors after a full day's exploration. The decor inside, a lush splash of verdant leaves, continues the warm weather theme. You're given no menus here, only the specials that are written up each day on blackboards. The Swiss and German cuisine draws an interesting crowd. Owner Rolf Schenkel dishes up some very good veal entrées as well as raclette, Sauerbraten, and hasenpfeffer. The menu is varied to suit less adventurous palates. Lunch offerings range between $5.50 and $11; a complete dinner for two is about $35.

Freshfields, Rte. 128 West Cornwall (tel. 672-6601), is the area's answer to nouvelle cuisine. Chef Steve Mangan is another Culinary Institute of America graduate who has come up with excellent, unpretentious fare. The service is congenial, and the airy surroundings are quite pleasant, with butcher-block tables, stoneware bud vases, and lace curtains. But the food. Ah, the food. Our dinner began with a complimentary spinach–pine nut quiche. The mâche, duck, and wild mushroom salad surpassed our expectations, as did the rack of lamb and tender mesquite-grilled chicken. Care was taken even to choose an unusual house wine: Rutherford Hills Merlot. Even so, the desserts stole the show. Lunch is about $12 for two; complete dinner with wine, about $40; brunch, about $25.

Holley Place, Pocketknife Square at Holley Street, Lakeville (tel. 435-2727). Sophisticated and friendly, this factory-turned-restaurant makes a bold, utterly romantic design statement with its buff-colored granite walls. Tracklights and a skylight give depth to the stone's texture, while pastel peach linens and floral Villeroy & Boch china soften the effect. The tavern room is less intimate and attracts a more informal crowd. It's great for lunch. Another Culinary Institute of America grad works the kitchen here, turning out good, solid continental fare. Grilled dishes and desserts are his specialties. Lunch, from $11 per couple; dinner, from $36 per couple plus drinks.

Pleasant outdoor dining at **Chez Riette,** Rte. 44, Lakeville (tel. 435-2889) includes French fare for dinner and salads and pasta for lunch. Prices are reasonable, hovering around $6 per person in the afternoon, $15 for entrées only at night.

The classic club sandwich and chili and chips make **Lakeville Cafe,** Main Street, Lakeville (tel. 435-2083) a popular lunch spot for townies and tourists alike. Lunch selections priced from $4.75 to $6.75; dinner, from $5.95 to $14.75; plus appetizers, dessert, and wine.

MASSACHUSETTS
4. The Berkshires of Massachusetts

Midway up the western border of Massachusetts, right where the turnpike cuts through, is a series of rolling hills and valleys renowned for their beauty, culture, and history.

Sophisticated and cosmopolitan, Lenox and Stockbridge have welcomed elegant

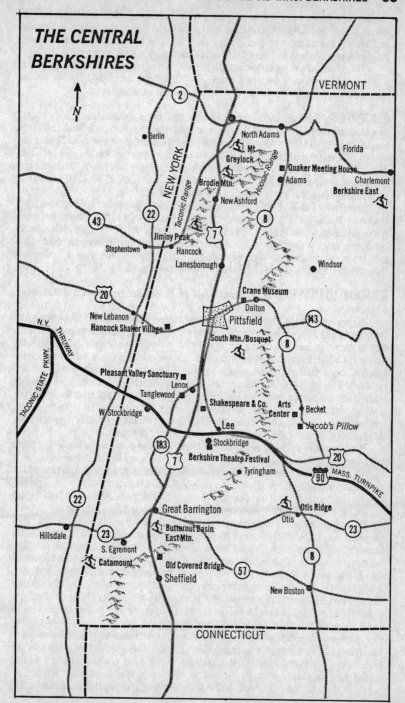

THE CENTRAL BERKSHIRES

visitors for over a century. The unusually well-maintained towns are beautifully restored, with many summer "cottages" still standing as private residences. In contrast, neighboring Lee is more of a working class town. It is also the home of the **Jacob's Pillow Dance Festival** and the 15,710-acre October Mountain State Forest.

The whole area comes alive in the summer, so much so that traffic slows down to a halt sometimes along the main streets. You'll escape the cities here but not the charged energy that marks these towns as preeminent vacation spots.

SHOPPING: The Berkshires are a veritable gold mine for antiques of every kind. Stopping in to browse is part of the fun. Also look in on the **Hancock Shaker Village** outside of Pittsfield (tel. 443-0188) for teas, stencils, and reproductions of Shaker furniture. At the **Norman Rockwell Museum** on Main Street in Stockbridge (tel. 298-3822) you'll find prints and reproductions for sale in the gift shop. If you don't buy something at **Great Barrington Pottery** in Housatonic (tel. 274-6259), you can at least tour the Japanese gardens and ceremonial tea house.

Don't miss **L&R Wise Goldsmiths** in Lenox, who do custom goldwork and gem sculpture (tel. 637-1589). For handmade kites, windsocks, and banners, go to **Lenox Kites** on Main Street (tel. 637-2115). **Design Works** (tel. 232-4235) also features handmade items in their store in West Stockbridge—a full line of American contemporary crafts. And to top the shopping day off, **Catherine's Chocolates** in Lenox and Stockbridge (tel. 528-2510) should satisfy most sweet tooths!

ROMANTIC INTERLUDES: Romance in the Berkshires begins with al fresco cultural events.

Experience a picnic beyond your wildest dreams. Choose from a five-course formal menu ($32.50), a three-course informal meal ($16.25), and a more practical Sunday brunch that includes either the Sunday *New York Times* or the *Boston Sunday Globe* ($12.50). Everything's taken care of: The service provides a white lawn cloth, napkins, cups, plates, utensils, even a bouquet of flowers and two white helium-filled balloons. This is no ordinary food either. A sample meal might include fusilli noodles with Szechuan peanut sauce; mesquite-broiled swordfish en brochette; duck with endive, mushrooms, and raspberry vinaigrette; coeur à la crème with raspberry purée; and something sinfully chocolate. Call **The Elegant Picnic** in Stockbridge (tel. 298-4010) or in Lenox (tel. 637-1621) for the full range of possibilities.

Shakespeare at the Mount (637-1197). Bring your picnic to the house that Edith Wharton built. A magnificent but aging beauty, this mansion in Lenox stands as a backdrop for outdoor professionally staged Shakespeare during the summer. Make your reservations as far in advance as possible. As darkness descends the night becomes magical, and you'll feel that you've entered another era. Admission is $3.50 per person for a tour of the premises, from $8 to $16 per person for tickets to the shows.

World renowned as the summer home of the Boston Symphony Orchestra, **Tanglewood** (tel. 637-1940) pampers its listeners with much more. The estate includes beautiful vistas of the Stockbridge Bowl, a formal labyrinth of hedges, and, most important, an expanse of perfectly tended lawn where lovers can stretch out and dream as they listen to music under the stars. Arrive early to avoid the heaviest traffic, and bring a warm wrap, because the night air can get chilly. You can now order your tickets through Ticket Master (call information if you're in the NYC area or Boston; otherwise call 800/682-8080). Tickets for the lawn, where you can bring a picnic, range from $6 to $8.50, while tickets in the shed cost from $10 to $50.

Matthew Arnold described the view from **Chesterwood** as "beautiful and soul-satisfying." The turn-of-the-century Georgian Revival–style house overlooks the Housatonic River and Monument Mountain. But it's the wooded nature trail that makes the estate extraordinary. Daniel Chester French, sculptor of the "Seated Lincoln" in the Lincoln Memorial, laid out the walking path with stone benches and pieces of his sculpture. The cool woods contrast with the brilliant garden adjacent to the house and artist's studio. The National Trust for Historic Preservation maintains the property, which is open May through October (tel. 298-3579). A small admission fee is charged.

If you're hardy, take the right-hand trail from the parking lot to the top of Great Barrington's **Monument Mountain,** just 2½ miles south of Stockbridge. You won't need anything but each other to appreciate the stunning views in all directions.

INNS AND BED AND BREAKFASTS: Even though inns line the street in downtown Lenox, you'll have to make your reservations far in advance of your arrival date if it's in the summer or during fall foliage. You'll be glad you did.

The Inn at Stockbridge, Rte. 7, Stockbridge, MA 01262 (tel. 413/298-3337). Don and Lee Weitz have turned this dignified, white-columned Georgian home into a delightful, classic bed-and-breakfast inn. Formal Williamsburg-style appointments in the dining room give way to an airy parlor with chintz-covered couches and a piano. Guests often curl up in front of the fire in the second living room. Upstairs, the house is just as lovely. Decor varies from a Laura Ashley–type dusty blue room with white wicker furnishings to an ecru and turquoise Chinese-inspired room. Lee pays scrupulous attention to all details; her extraordinarily good breakfast, for example, is served on Spode, Wedgwood, or other bone china. Don and Lee *love* weddings and newlyweds, and if you're staying a while, will help to make your honeymoon memorable. Rates: $60 to $160 including full breakfast.

Haus Andreas, R.R. 1, Box 605-B, Stockbridge Road, Lee, MA 01238 (tel. 413/243-3298). Hosts Lilliane and Gerhard Schmid split their time between the formal bed and breakfast here at the Haus and The Gateways, their larger, more imposing inn and restaurant in Lenox, so you may not see much of them. Their absence is filled with amenities not found in most inns: a swimming pool, volleyball, tennis, croquet, and badminton on the property; a nine-hole golf course across the street; and a tandem bicycle, yours for the asking. Built by a Revolutionary War soldier, the house stands as an eloquent reminder of the beauty of the summer cottages of the area. Many of the rooms have views of the orchard and mountains, and two have fireplaces. Rates: $60 to $150, including continental breakfast.

Wheatleigh, P.O. Box 824, Lenox, MA 01240 (tel. 413/637-0610) is most definitely not a charming inn. This luxurious, imposing estate was fashioned after a 16th-century Italian palazzo as a wedding present from father to daughter. Although it doesn't quite follow the rules for inclusion, Wheatleigh stands as an exception in every sense of the word. For a truly patrician experience, stay in one of the terraced rooms—with fireplace—that overlooks the Stockbridge Bowl. Grand proportions may intimidate the fainthearted, but for the cavalier romantic, this place is heaven. Dining room. Rates: $90 to $325 with continental breakfast.

ROMANTIC RESTAURANTS: From a renovated barn to an Italian palazzo, Berkshire restaurants cultivate romance in a variety of settings. Although there are no requirements, you'll probably feel more at ease if you dress for dinner.

Candlelight Inn, 53 Walker St., Lenox (tel. 637-1555). *Gourmet* magazine called chef Marsha Heller a "culinary genius" for good reason. In addition to the crisp, surprisingly good complimentary antipasto, you'll be treated to a refreshing lemon sherbet after the appetizer. The house special on many nights is a shrimp scampi that begs comparison with the very best restaurants in New York. There is a decent, abbreviated wine list that includes French, American, and sparkling wines. As the name hints, dinner is by candlelight with a complimentary nosegay of fresh flowers. Ask to be seated near the window on the enclosed porch, where you can see the semicircular drive and the goings-on of the street beyond. Appetizers start at $6.50; entrées, from $12.95.

Federal House, Rte. 102, South Lee (tel. 243-1824). Some of the best food in the Berkshires can be found in the three intimate dining rooms of this tidy, white-pillared, red brick house. The chef, Ken Algren, began his career as a pastry chef and has since worked at Stonehenge in Connecticut and Windows on the World in New York. His oysters in beer batter are an elegant rendering of an American classic and demonstrate the magic he can let loose from the kitchen. The setting is subdued and tasteful and terribly romantic. Bouquets of fresh flowers adorn all the tables and the mantels of the restaurant's two fireplaces. Good wine list. Complete dinner from about $50 per couple plus drinks.

There's no mistaking **Embree's,** Main Street, Housatonic (tel. 274-3476). It's the only lit facade in the whole town. From the outside, as you peer in through the floor-to-ceiling plate-glass windows, Embree's looks enticingly warm and inviting. And it is. Unique specials such as curried tempeh, mushrooms, and snow peas; roast duck pie; and curried ground lamb with custard and chutney have made this a local favorite. For traditionalists, there's a superb pot roast and grilled chicken. Entrees are priced from $8.75 to $18.75.

Dine in ultimate luxury amid Italian-inspired splendor at **Wheatleigh,** Hawthorne Road, in Lenox (tel. 637-0610). The cuisine is "new classic French." Prix fixe dinner costs $49 per person. **Truc Orient Express,** behind Main Street in W. Stockbridge (tel. 232-4204) serves up great, authentic Vietnamese food with dinners for two priced about $20 plus drinks. Exposed beams and collections of old tools set the scene at the **Old Mill,** Rte. 23 in South Egremont (tel. 528-1421). The menu changes but always includes fresh fish, veal, chilcken, and beef. A bargain. A complete dinner for two from $25 plus drinks. **Sebastian's,** just down the road from the Old Mill on Rt. 23 (tel. 528-3469), satisfies cravings with good, homemade pasta. Appetizers from $3.95, pastas and entrées from $7.95.

Head for the **Shaker Mill Tavern,** Rte. 102 in West Stockbridge (tel. 232-8565) for burgers ($4.50 to $5.50) and a look at the "scene." The Tavern plays host to area performers on Thursdays, Latin rhythms on Fridays, professional comedians on Saturdays, and piano sing-alongs on Sundays.

5. Cape Cod

Separated from the mainland by the Bourne and Sagamore bridges, within commuting distance from Boston, the Cape has been described as a flexed arm with Route 6A running the length of the inner arm and Provincetown at the end of the curled fingers. The more placid waters of the bay lap against the towns of Sandwich, Barnstable, Dennis, and Brewster. Falmouth and Chatham, with Hyannis in between, carve out the area from shoulder to elbow on the outer arm; Nantucket Sound crashes onto the shore there. But it's at the stretch from Chatham to Truro, the outer arm from elbow up, that promises the most dramatic surf.

The Cape attracts a crowd of summer visitors every year. Yet the bay side retains a peaceful, unpretentious atmosphere, especially along the Old Kings Highway, Rte. 6A, which parallels the busier Rte. 6. Only those going to or from the slumbering towns from Sandwich to Orleans pass by. The roadway—lined with cranberry bogs, salt ponds, and tidy weather-worn shingled houses, also boasts unobtrusive crafts shops, old bookstores, galleries, and antique stores.

Glorious white-sand beaches complement intriguing estuarine marshes, so visitors can either swim, hike, or both. Golf, tennis, bicycling, boat charters, and the like fill out Cape life.

SHOPPING: Cape Cod has its own recent history of craftspeople. One of the more interesting shops is **Scargo Pottery** in Dennis (tel. 385-3894), run by the Holl family. Birdfeeders fashioned to look like Italian castles, paintings, and sculpture sit side by side with dishes and flameware pottery. You can get decoys in Mashpee at **Decoys of**

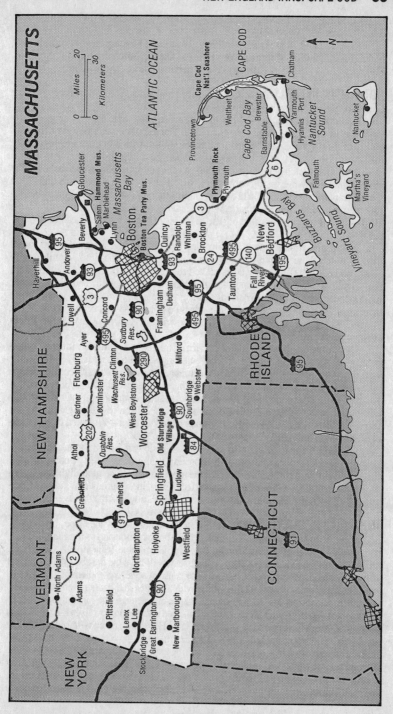

Cape Cod (tel. 477-9368) and braided rugs at the **Cape Cod Braided Rug Co.** in South Dennis (tel. 398-0089).

Rtes. 132 and 28 in Hyannis and Rte. 28 in East Falmouth have a lion's share of outlet stores: **Quoddy Moccasin, Van Heusen, Dansk, Kitchen Etc.** (with Noritake, Pfaltzgraff, and Oneida at 10% to 60% off) to name a few.

ROMANTIC INTERLUDES: Great beaches and quiet, wooded landscapes make Cape Cod a honeymooner's haven.

In mid-April through early May, the herring run upriver to the spawning pools by **the old grist mill** in Brewster. It's fascinating! The rest of the year, however, the tranquility of the two pools soothes the soul. Stone walkways and fragrant greenery make this an ideal spot for an early morning walk when the mist is just beginning to rise.

A 40-mile stretch of protected seashore awaits you at the **National Seashore.** The most impressive white-sand beaches are Race Point near Provincetown and Coast Guard near Orleans. When you tire of the unremitting sun, take the surprisingly beautiful swamp hike along the Atlantic White Cedar Swamp Trail or the Nauset Marsh Trail. Visitor centers are located off Rte. 6 in Eastham and by the dunes in Provincetown.

For **whale watching** the Dolphin Fleet offers morning, afternoon, and sunset trips to watch these magnificent, awesome creatures (tel. 255-3857, or toll free in Mass. 800/826-9300). Right whales, called thus because whalers thought they were the "right" whale to kill, humpbacks, and finbacks appear often. The lesser known, more slender minkes show up periodically, and once in a great while sei whales grace the waters. The *Ranger V* has a similar schedule (tel. 487-3322, or toll free in Mass. 800/992-9333). Both operate out of Provincetown from April through October. Prices are competitive, about $15 per person.

Quaint and untouched by many modern distractions, **Martha's Vineyard** happily survives without stoplights, fast-food enterprises, and billboards. The Vineyard's well-deserved reputation stems from its natural beauty as well as its celebrities. Rent a bike or reserve a rental car for exploration; there are numerous purveyors of both. If you plan to stay the night in the summertime, make reservations for the room well in advance. The same caveat applies for car rentals, or, if you're bringing a car, for the ferry. For ferry reservations, call the **Woods Hole, Martha's Vineyard & Nantucket Steamship Authority** (tel. 540-2022).

Cross the Cape to Hyannis to pick up the classic gaff-rigged ketch, the *Spray,* a beautiful 56-foot replica of the boat that Joshua Slocum sailed when he completed the first successful solo circumnavigation of the globe in 1895. The **moonlight sail** leaves the docks on Fridays and Saturdays at about 8:30 p.m. in the summer. Windsong Charters (tel. 775-1630) schedules other two-hour sails throughout the day.

INNS AND BED-AND-BREAKFASTS: The quiet side of the Cape, on the bay, specializes in lovers' retreats hidden away from heavy traffic and touring families.

With **Charles Hinckley House,** Box 723, Barnstable Village, MA 02630 (tel. 617/362-9924), Miya and Les Patrick may very well have the best bed-and-breakfast in New England. Miya has used her unerring sense of style to complement Les's restoration of the circa 1809 colonial building with antiques and handcrafted accessories. Romance, relaxation, and a homespun elegance characterize the inn. Miya attends to the smallest details, from toiletries and thick-piled cotton bath towels in the bathrooms to her trademark flower on the breakfast plate. Her vision extends into the stunning front-yard wildflower garden, which provides many of the blooms in the house. But that doesn't satisfy Miya; she orders in striking exotic blossoms and adds them to the bouquets. Care and thoughtfulness are apparent at every level. Although all four guest rooms are well heated and have working fireplaces, when the cold weather sets in, Miya still changes the linens from the pressed all-cotton sheets and handcrafted quilts to flannel bed dressings and down comforters. Honeymooners are treated to a bottle of champagne, and if they wish, breakfast in bed. Rates: $85 to $115 with a full breakfast.

Beechwood, 2839 Main St., Rte. 6A, Barnstable, MA 02630 (tel. 617/362-6618). Just a few miles up from the Charles Hinckley House, this 1853 Queen Anne-style Cape "cottage" has been restored to Victorian splendor. Owners Myles and Sandra Corey delight in the romance of the Victorian age. They serve afternoon tea each day in the elegant, fire-lit parlor, and will provide tea at bedside at newlyweds' request. You may be tempted not to leave your room. The Rose and Marble rooms each have a fireplace to banish the evening's chill. A huge lace-canopied four-poster dominates the former, while a substantial brass bed and red-velvet rocking chair lend romance to the latter. But each is furnished as a silent tribute to passion. Hanging out and relaxing are the big pastimes. The wraparound veranda, says Myles, "is one of the biggest sports here." Except maybe eating the hearty breakfasts. Rates: $75 to $105 with full breakfast.

Captain Dexter House, 100 Main St., P.O. Box 2457, Vineyard Haven, MA 02568 (tel. 617/693-6564). If you decide on an extended jaunt to Martha's Vineyard, stay at this restored sea captain's house around the corner from the ferry landing. The Captain Harding Room is a favorite with honeymooners. A lace canopy adorns the reproduction rice-carved four-poster bed, and a very comfortable loveseat is positioned next to the fireplace. The bay window on the opposite side of the room overlooks the town's main street and the harbor beyond. Throughout the house, there's an ample scattering of unusual antiques, including two portraits painted in 1843, the same year the house was built. Beyer Parker, the owner, jests that these stern-faced overseers are Captain Dexter and his wife. Rates: $50 to $110 with continental breakfast.

ROMANTIC RESTAURANTS: Zany to formally romantic, Cape Cod's restaurants love honeymooners.

The Cranberry Moose, Rte. 6A, Yarmouth Port (tel. 362-8153 or 362-3501), will capture your imagination from the very first glance at the Edward Gorey illustration on the menu's cover. The atmosphere—elegant with a touch of big-city funk—is genial and fun. Flowers "à la La Grenouille" (of New York City) assume center stage. As for the food, specialties include a rack of lamb persillé, roast duck, lots of fresh fish and shellfish, and if it's in season, cranberry mousse. A short but good wine list. Full dinner for two, about $65.

The Regatta, 217 Clinton St., Falmouth (tel. 548-5400), is blissfully romantic. The views of moonlight and the ocean set the scene as much as the soft pinks and mauve of the decor. Creative American food is the hallmark, with fresh fish featured nightly.' Try the roast lobster stuffed with crabmeat soufflé and served with sauce buerre blanc for a memorable meal. A "dessert trilogy" allows you to sample three of the most popular sweets. All in all, a gem. Appetizers from $6.25; entrées, $16.50 to $24, plus desserts and wine. No hard liquor or beer.

Chillingsworth, Rte. 6A, Brewster (tel. 896-3640). Reserve your table weeks—if not months—in advance of your visit and request one of the smaller, more intimate dining rooms. If you're lucky, you'll get the table for two in front of the fireplace. This is an old sea captain's house—approximately 250 years old—and some of the original wallpaper has even been left intact. People ooh and aah over the Limoges china, but it's the nouvelle cuisine that keeps them returning. The menu, which changes often, is in French, but the waiters and waitresses have their recitation, which explains what may be unfamiliar to you. The five-course dinners are prix-fixe, ranging from $35 to $45 depending on your entrée.

If you're in Hyannis for the Melody Tent summer theatre, plan to eat at **The Paddock** at the West Main rotary (tel. 775-7677) next door. They'll reserve a special table or do something out of the ordinary for you if you let them know you're newlyweds. Entrées, from $11.50 to $17.95, are a traditional continental-American mix. For an informal lunch after walking on the beach, stop in at **The Marshside,** on Bridge Street off of Rte. 6A in East Dennis (tel. 385-4010). Sandwiches, snacks, and seafood salads are their specialty: from $3.95. Generous gourmet deli sandwiches, terrific take-out fare, and a great selection of imported beers are for the asking at the **Dennis Village Mercantile,** Rte. 6A in Dennis (tel. 385-3877). And if **Kate's** drive-in on 6A in Brewster is open, stop for homemade ice cream and the best lobster roll on the Cape.

VERMONT

6. Manchester and the Mountains

Just before southern Vermont classifies as mid-Vermont, about half an hour northeast of Albany, New York, Manchester and the mountains greet you with picture postcard perfection.

Manchester Village is a tidy town of white clapboard houses with black shutters, a requisite white-steepled church, and a gracious resort that fronts the wide main street of the town. Equinox Mountain, rising to 3,816 feet provides a dramatic backdrop. The effect is simple elegance; the atmosphere, dignified yet casual. Townspeople take their afternoon constitutionals, stopping at the rare-books store or the stencil shop by the Equinox hotel.

Depending on the season, visitors usually take off early in the morning for the ski slopes, the hiking trails, or the back roads. The lingerers tend to golf, fish on the world famous Battenkill, or stroll along main street with the old-timers.

SHOPPING: Vermont, too, is known for its factory outlets. In Manchester, you can get **Ralph Lauren, Anne Klein, Dexter** shoes, and more. You can also satisfy your antiques cravings at **Carriage Trade Antiques Center, Danby Antiques Center,** or any one of a score of others. Ask your hosts for their favorite shops. Woodcarver Bill Herrick often works out of the **Jelly Mill** in Manchester (tel. 362-3629). For antique clocks, try the **Clock Emporium** (tel. 362-3328); for miniatures and dolls, the **Enchanted Doll House** (tel. 362-1327); and for baskets, **Basketville** (tel. 362-1609). Fly fishermen will appreciate the **Orvis** store (tel. 362-1300) with its range of fishing tackle and hunting accessories.

ROMANTIC INTERLUDES: Sports enthusiasts as well as antique hunters call this place paradise.

It doesn't take long before you're **cross-country skiing** along groomed and mapped trails enjoying the winter sunshine. One of the prettiest alpine centers is at **Hildene,** Robert Todd Lincoln's estate (tel. 362-1788) right in Manchester; trail fees vary from $5 to $6; equipment rental is $10 daily. At **Wild Wings** (tel. 824-6793) you can stop in for complimentary hot bouillon after you've explored their 12 miles of groomed and primitive trails. Trail fees range from $5 to $7; equipment rental, which includes use of the grounds, from $10 to $15. **Viking,** one of the largest centers, has extensive trails in Londonderry (tel. 824-3933).

From mid-May through October, the lovely, 412-acre estate that belonged to Robert Todd Lincoln—Abraham Lincoln's son—is open to the public for **tours and picnics** on the grounds (admission to the grounds is free; $5 for house tour). With sweeping views of the mountains and about three miles of hiking and nature trails, **Hildene** (tel. 362-1788) is much more than a historic home. The formal garden, gazebo, and observatory shouldn't be missed. Brides often choose the terrace for their receptions. It's located in Manchester.

What more need be said? In the light of day or under the glow of a full moon, **horsedrawn rides** give lovers a chance to snuggle together. **Village Carriage Company** (tel. 362-1998)—situated in front of the Equinox hotel in Manchester Village— has coachmen who come attired in top hat and tails to take you to your chosen restau-

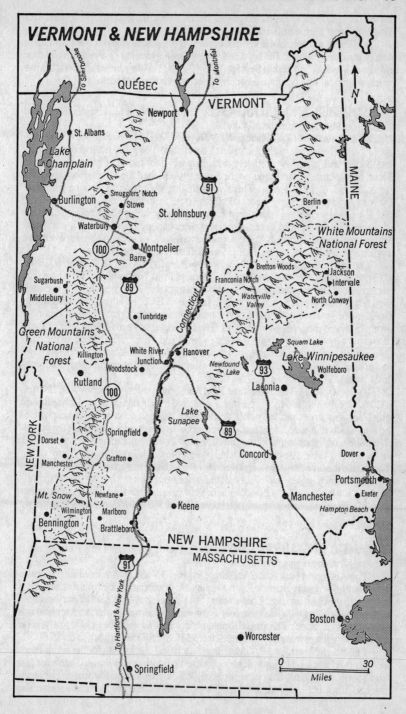

rant or for a ride ($30 per carriage per hour). For a more countrified jaunt, call **Windhill Farm Stable and Tack Shop** (tel. 362-2604).

You'll feel a shiver of excitement when you see something you want held up in front of a mass of people. Bid on it and you've got a memento of a very special time and place. **Wessner's Auction Service** (tel. 362-3482) in Manchester Center takes in a variety of goods. Call beforehand or check area newspapers for details.

INNS AND BED-AND-BREAKFASTS: The area around Manchester blossomed with bed-and-breakfasts in the past decade.

1811 House, Rte. 7A, Manchester Village, VT 05254 (tel. 802/362-1811). Anglophiles take heart. Mary and Jack Hirst have created a superbly put together, sophisticated bed and breakfast complete with English pub and after-hunt atmosphere. Guests help themselves to drinks on the honor system, then head to the basement for a game of pool or table tennis. There's a stunning collection of antique furniture, dishware, and prints, many pieces of which come from the Hirsts' families. All the double-bedded rooms are appropriate for honeymooners, but the fireplace suites are exceptionally lovely, with queen-size four-poster canopy beds. Expect a traditional British breakfast dish such as kippers, grilled tomatoes, or sautéed chicken livers as a supplement to eggs and bacon. Rates: $80 to $120 with full breakfast.

The Inn at Sunderland, R.R. 2, Box 2440, Arlington, VT 05250 (tel. 802/362-4213). Peggy and Tom Wall migrated to Vermont from Washington, DC, where they met, married, and decided they wanted to work together. This cheerful, tidy bed-and-breakfast is the result. They added five new rooms in 1986, including one accessible to handicapped guests. Both old and new rooms contain a comfortable mix of Victorian-era antiques and modern accoutrements. The house and hosts make lounging around a pleasure. Peggy puts out a boursin cheese spread and offers refreshments in the early evening; it's a nice way to share stories about the day's adventures. If Peggy knows you're honeymooners, she prepares a silver tray with a split of champagne and crystal flutes. Rates: $75 to $95 with full breakfast.

It's hard to miss **The Reluctant Panther,** Manchester Village, VT 05254 (tel. 802/362-2568); it's the only purple house with gold trim in this domain of white houses with black shutters. Singular, novel, and atypical begin to describe the atmosphere of the inn, which strives to "enhance your romance" by making you aware of the unusual. Unlike most other country inns, this one provides a complimentary bottle of wine for everyone, cable television, and in some rooms, whirlpool baths. Many of the rooms have modern fireplaces, and the Mary Porter Suite has an additional fireplace in the bath. Purples, golds, and pinks predominate throughout the inn, so state your preference if you want a more subdued milieu. Plan time to sit around the hearth in the bar area. It's the most romantic spot in the house. Rates: $69 to $160 including continental breakfast.

ROMANTIC RESTAURANTS: Vermont's varied restaurants make eating out a pleasure for many nights running.

The Arlington Inn, Rte. 7A, Arlington (tel. 375-6532). A refined air permeates this beautifully restored Greek Revival mansion, Victorian embellishments adding a richness to the crisp interior. Chef-owner Paul Kruzel shows off his Culinary Institute of America training with such specials as lobster-and-corn chowder, and venison in a maple-chestnut sauce. The printed menu offers less adventurous but equally good entrées. Appetizers from $4.50; entrées from $13.50; Sunday brunch from $5.50.

The Black Swan, Rte. 7A, Manchester (tel. 362-3807). Ask for the dining room with exposed brick walls and country wreaths tied with pretty bows. The decor and food together bespeak years of experience, which chef-owner Richard Whisenhunt has: Le Cirque in New York and Le Club in San Francisco are his alma maters. The sweetbreads of veal and the lobster and truffle pasta hint at the inventiveness here. If you crave a soufflé or baked Alaska with dinner, you can request these treats when you make your reservation; tell them it's your honeymoon. Lunch includes salads, pasta, fish, and burgers; prices range from $2.50 for soup to $7.75 for sautéed calf's liver with bacon. Dinner appetizers run from $2.75 to $6; entrées from $14 to $17.

Reluctant Panther, West Road and Rte. 7A, Manchester Village (tel. 362-2568). For a meal of many tastes, head for the purple house with gold shutters. Their "lite dining" special allows you to choose up to five items—from appetizers, soups, and salads—for $18. The standard prix-fixe dinner highlights their specialties: brace of quail and loin of lamb. Enjoy a drink in the fire-lit bar room for an especially romantic experience. Five-course, prix-fixe dinner from $42 to $50 per couple plus drinks.

The Equinox, Rte. 7A in Manchester Village (tel. 362-4700, or toll free 800/362-4747) stands as the central focus of the town. Go for lunch; they have interesting sandwiches. Prices range from $6.25 to $9.50. After shopping, try **Gourmet Deli,** Rte. 7A in Manchester Center (tel. 362-1254) for a casual lunch. Sandwiches for two will come to about $10. **Mother Myrick's Confectionery and Ice Cream Parlor,** Rte. 7 in Manchester Center (tel. 362-1560) is *the* place to go to satisfy your sweet tooth. If you get addicted, you can order their goodies through the mail.

7. The Heart of Vermont

The rural roads that lead from Ludlow to Belmont and Weston describe Vermont: sugar maples and white birches that rise and fall as the land does, hidden cabins that give themselves away by the single plumes of smoke from their chimneys, country stores advertising Maple Syrup Made Here. It's a countryside rich with impressions.

This trio of towns falls on the southern boundary of the middle region of the state. Forming a triangle just south and east of Rutland, they are connected by routes 155, 103, and 100—an area that passes by Terrible Mountain (2,844 feet) and rings the ski center at Okemo Mountain (3,343 feet).

Visitors come to be outside. The Long and Appalachian trails run through the 295,007-acre **Green Mountain National Forest** here, where store owners hop out for a quick hour of cross-country skiing at lunch and natives share news and packages from the capital. The seasons fall heartily; pungent, wet springs give way to sun-drenched summers and flaming autumns. Then the snow falls and high season arrives. Winter becomes a joyful challenge.

SHOPPING: The Ludlow area boasts the **Society of Vermont Craftsmen Center** open daily in July and August (tel. 362-1609). The **Weston Village Store** (tel. 824-5477) has everything from fiddlehead ferns in season to flannel nightgowns to hardware. **Mountain Stitchery** (tel. 824-6431), also in Weston, offers natural fiber yarns, stencil supplies, calico fabrics, and more. Stop in at **Meadowsweet Herb Farm** (tel. 492-3566), a bit down the road in North Shrewsbury, for herb wreaths, potpourri, and seasonings.

ROMANTIC INTERLUDES: The natural beauty of this area creates a romantic backdrop spring, summer, fall, and winter.

Try sampling Vermont specialties.

All within a few miles of each other in Ludlow, the **Crowley Cheese Factory** (tel. 259-2340), the **Green Mountain Sugar House** (tel. 228-7151), and the **Vermont Country Store** (tel. 463-3855) invite visitors to come and see their operations. In the spring the Sugar House offers sweet pick-your-own strawberries; in the fall, a cider mill operation. Year-round the crisp, crumbly Vermont Common Crackers are available for the tasting at the Country Store.

No matter what religion you call your own, the **Weston Priory,** a monk's retreat nestled amid the Green Mountains near Ludlow, is worth a trip. Call (tel. 824-5409) for the hours of service. The brothers, who can usually be found outside wearing jeans and working the land, are world renowned for their singing. Bring a picnic. The roads leading to and from the priory are some of the most photographed in Vermont.

Pick a perfect summer weekend day to call **Kinhaven Music School** (tel. 824-9592) in Weston for their schedule of free concerts. You'll feel a part of a small community as you listen to works of classical music played by very able, polished students. The drive and the grounds are beautiful, so bring a snack and a blanket if not a full picnic.

INNS AND BED-AND-BREAKFASTS: Skiing is the number one attraction in this corner of the state, so for relative quiet head to the mountains in the summer.

Located away from tourist traffic—any traffic for that matter—the **Parmenter House,** P.O. Box 106, Belmont, VT 05730 (tel. 802/259-2009), has found the perfect balance between Victorian beauty and down-home comfort and congeniality. Both Cynthia and Lester Firschein gave up anthropology to open up this dream bed-and-breakfast. Their intelligence and gentle respect for humanity make this a pearl among inns. Cynthia serves a breakfast buffet on the imposing dining table her mother carved. If the weather's nice, though, you may be happiest on the deck in back. Sit back and enjoy afternoon tea amid the antiques and oils painted by innkeeper Cynthia's grandfather. The parlor highlights a room set of hand-pulled Bradbury and Bradbury wallpaper based on an original William Morris design. Flowers and champagne are gratis if you announce you're on your honeymoon. You can also rent trail bikes for the day for $25 per person, including a box lunch. Rates: $50 to $70 including expanded continental breakfast.

Black River Inn, 100 Main St., Ludlow, VT 05149 (tel. 802/228-5585). "We don't sell rooms. We sell romance," commented innkeeper Tom Nunan. The 1835 house has a cozy lived-in feel. Guests gather around the fireplace in the tasteful, comfy living room, or wander down to the Black River out back. Each guest room commands a distinct personality. The imposing first-floor Lincoln Room gets its name from the four-poster bed our former president once slept in. For added privacy, choose the quiet, floral-motif Romance Room, with brass bed, spool chest, and sloped-ceiling bathroom. A sitting area in every room serves as your breakfast nook in the morning. In the Maple Room, the table stands in front of the window looking down on the stream. The real warmth of this understated inn, however, comes from its hosts Nancy and Tom. Their openness and friendliness make this a very special place. Rates: $110 for two, including breakfast and dinner. Ask about weekend packages.

ROMANTIC RESTAURANTS: Some of the finest romantic atmospheres in all of New England are here.

The Inn at Weston, Rte. 100, Weston (tel. 824-5804). The scenic drive from Belmont or Ludlow to Weston is an appropriate predinner treat. Take a few minutes to explore the town before you go in to dine. The atmosphere is relaxed and casual in this 1848 restored farmhouse. Choose from Vermont veal, scampi with sun-dried tomatoes, and a gingered duckling among other entrées. For dessert you'll have to share bites of the apple crisp and white-chocolate mousse. Dinner for two, approximately $45.

Nikki's, Pond Street at the foot of Okeno, Ludlow (tel. 228-7797). The locals tend to go here for a casual but elegant dinner. Stained-glass artwork and wide pine floorboards set the ambience as much as the glass-globed "candles." Owner Robert Gilmore heartily recommends the mixed grill—a tasty combination of breast of chicken, jumbo shrimp, and sweet Italian sausage cooked with herb butter. Nikki's has earned an award-winning reputation from its use of compound butters, fresh seafood (delivered three times a week), and black Angus beef. For a special treat, sample a number of wines by the glass; Nikki's offers an extensive wine list as well as eight vintage wines from its Cruvinet. Appetizers priced between $3.50 and $5.95, entrées from $10.95 to $16.95.

For an intimate meal with more than a modicum of friendliness, reserve a table at the **Black River Inn,** 100 Main St. in Ludlow (tel. 228-5585). The 7 p.m. seating features a set menu, so let them know in advance if you have any food allergies. Call early for reservations at the **Governor's Inn,** 86 Main St. in Ludlow (tel. 228-8830). A six-course creative American meal awaits you at $60 per couple; after-dinner cordial is included. If you're on the road, stop in at **The Village Green Deli** on the green in Chester (tel. 875-3898). Antiques, charm, and a community jigsaw puzzle make this little spot an especially nice way station. Lunch for two about $12.

Chapter IV

CALIFORNIA

1. Practical Facts
2. San Francisco
3. Monterey, Carmel, and the Monterey Peninsula
4. Big Sur
5. San Simeon
6. Santa Barbara
7. Los Angeles and Environs

OVER 300 YEARS before Horace Greeley wrote, "Go West, young man, go West," long before James Marshall culled some sparkling nuggets out of the American River, and before dream-weavers such as Samuel Goldwyn, Cecil B. deMille, and Louis M. Mayer began spinning celluloid fantasies, 16th-century writers had dreamed of a land of gold. "Know then, that west of the Indies, but to the East of Eden, lies California . . . [this] island, the most rugged in the world, abounds in gold," novelist Garci Ordóñez de Montalvo had penned.

So from the very beginning, California has beckoned as the place of the dream, the land of the myth. Over the years, its romantic magnetism has continuously lured newcomers. The same promise of riches and fame that brought grizzled old prospectors westward still draws hopeful young starlets from Duluth, or Coral Gables, or Albany, who stalk the beach at Malibu waiting to be discovered. The vocabulary remains the same: strike it rich; getting that one big break; finding a pot of gold. Even its nickname recognizes that glittering image: California is known as "The Golden State." This mother lode of promise, this newness, and the spirit of good things to come is what makes California such a treasure-trove for honeymooners.

California's cities and towns offer honeymooners a wide array of experiences. You can gawk at the stars while dining at an "in" West Hollywood bistro—or watch the whales spy hop and breach while you cruise the Pacific. Go to San Francisco's Chinatown for dim sum, nibble pastries at a thatch-roofed Danish bakery (complete with a stork nesting in the chimney) in Solvang, or munch an enchilada along Olvera Street in Los Angeles at a fiesta to celebrate the Cinco de Mayo. Head for a big-city swirl of theater, concerts, and art galleries; spend some time with Mickey, Minnie, and friends at Disneyland, or retreat to a mountain spa and soak your cares away at the mineral springs. Whatever you do, spend a lot of time staring off at the Pacific Ocean. As you contemplate the surging waters from the edge of a rocky, wave-tossed promontory, at Point Reyes, for example, or the Monterey peninsula, you'll surely find something awe-inspiring in the knowledge that you are

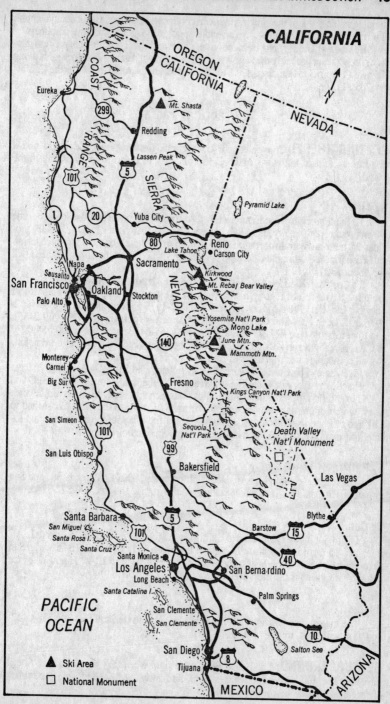

CALIFORNIA

Eureka

OREGON

CALIFORNIA

NEVADA

N

COAST RANGE

299

▲ Mt. Shasta

Redding

Lassen Peak

5

101

SIERRA

Pyramid Lake

20

Yuba City

1

80

Lake Tahoe

Reno

● Carson City

Sacramento

Napa

Kirkwood

▲ Mt. Rebal Bear Valley

Sausalito

San Francisco

Oakland

Stockton

NEVADA

Palo Alto

Yosemite Nat'l Park

Mono Lake

140

▲ June Mtn.

▲ Mammoth Mtn.

Monterey

Carmel

Big Sur

Fresno

Kings Canyon Nat'l Park

San Simeon

Sequoia Nat'l Park

Death Valley Nat'l Monument

101

99

San Luis Obispo

Bakersfield

Las Vegas

Santa Barbara

Blythe

San Miguel

Santa Rosa I.

5

Barstow

15

Santa Cruz

101

Santa Monica

40

Los Angeles

San Bernardino

Long Beach

Santa Catalina I.

Palm Springs

PACIFIC
OCEAN

San Clemente

San Clemente I.

10

Salton Sea

San Diego

8

ARIZONA

▲ Ski Area

Tijuana

□ National Monument

MEXICO

standing at the brink of the North American continent, upon the last substantial chunk of terra firma for 8,000 miles . . . an endless, golden vista for two honeymooners.

Because of California's tremendous expanse and diversity, this chapter concentrates on what are probably the state's most popular travel destinations: the sights along Highway 1 from San Francisco south to Laguna Beach, the route known as the California Coast Drive.

1. Practical Facts

GETTING THERE: Convenient air connections from all over the world and a first-rate system of highways make California easy to reach from anywhere in the world.

By Air

To San Francisco: **San Francisco International Airport (SFO)** is located some 14 miles south of the city, near San Mateo. The SFO Airporter (tel. 673-2433) provides 24-hour-a-day transportation from SFO to major hotels or the downtown terminal. Fare for the 30-minute ride is $6 per person. A taxi from the airport to SFO will run about $30.

To Los Angeles: **Los Angeles International Airport (LAX)** is located south of the city. If you're not renting a car, you can get ground transportation via Airport Service, Inc. (tel. 778-3141; or toll free 800/962-1975 nationwide; toll free 800/962-1976 in CA); B.T.C. Shuttles (tel. 389-8104); Eden Airport Express (tel. 459-0465); and SuperShuttle (tel. 777-8000; or toll free 800/554-6458 nationwide; 800/554-0279 in CA). Fares will run about $25 per couple, but vary according to your destination. Not all companies serve all areas of L.A., so ask in advance.

Elsewhere: There are local airports in Monterey and Santa Barbara.

Practically every major airline—and a bevy of the smaller ones—serve SFO and LAX. In addition, passengers to these cities often benefit greatly from the airline price wars, which often make it cheaper to fly from New York to the West Coast than to Chicago or Phoenix. Check the daily newspapers and ask your travel agent for up-to-date information about the latest air fares and purchase requirements.

By Rail

Amtrak serves both Los Angeles (Union Station, 800 N. Alameda St.) and San Francisco (in Oakland, 16th Street Station). Call Amtrak: toll free 800/872-7245.

By Car

The major highways leading to California are Interstate 10 from Phoenix to L.A., Interstate 15 from Las Vegas to L.A., and Interstate 80 from Salt Lake City into San Francisco. Route 5 is the fastest route from San Francisco to L.A.; Highway 1 (see details that follow) is the most scenic.

By Bus

The major lines serving California are **Greyhound** (tel. toll free 800/528-0447) and **Trailways** (tel. toll free 800/527-1566).

GETTING AROUND: The Beach Boys were right when they harmonized, "She'll have fun, fun, fun 'til her daddy takes her T-bird away." Most California good times are predicated on having your own wheels.

By Air

The main intra-California airlines are **AirCal** and **PSA.**

By Car

Definitely the modus operandi for getting around California. The state is the largest rental car market in the United States, and good deals on hired wheels are common. **Avis Rent-A-Car,** for example, charges $87 per week for a subcompact car, with no mileage charge for the first 1,000 miles (14-day advance reservation required). If you'll be doing the California Coast Drive between Los Angeles and San Francisco (or vice versa) you'll have to pay a $75 drop-off charge if you leave the car in L.A.; $50 if you leave the car in San Francisco.

If you're any kind of driving enthusiasts, spend the bucks to rent a good sports car. Avis rents Camaros and Firebirds for $147 per week (14-day advance reservation required). Or, for the ultimate romance (and to impress the local movie kingpins) you can rent a Corvette, Porsche, or Rolls-Royce. A 'Vette convertible goes for about $890 per week, plus 55¢ a mile; the Porsche Carrera convertible for around $925 per week, plus 55¢. Call **Autoexotica** at 415/673-4653 in San Francisco; 213/271-4879 in Los Angeles.

If you don't want to drive, but do want to see the California coast, consider the **California Parlour Car Tours** (tel. 415/474-7500). Their three-day San Francisco/ Los Angeles tour, including the Monterey Peninsula, San Simeon, Solvang, and Santa Barbara, costs about $400 per person, which covers hotel accommodations and all meals on tour. Highly recommended.

San Francisco is the only city covered in this chapter with a well-developed **public transportation network.** Most beloved of all, of course, are the cable cars, with their tinkling bells and hairpin turns (see the details under San Francisco "Romantic Interludes"). The San Francisco Municipal Railway (MUNI) operates both the trolleys (fare: $1.50) and buses (fare: 75¢), exact change required. Route information is published in the Yellow Pages telephone directory, or call tel. 673-MUNI. The Bay Area Rapid Transit system (BART) is one of the most modern train systems in the world. It connects San Francisco with the East Bay area, including Oakland (tel. 788-BART). San Francisco also has a large fleet of taxi cabs, which you can usually hail right on the street. You can also call for a pickup. Yellow Cab is the largest fleet in the city (tel. 415/626-2345).

About the California Coast Drive: Welcome to one of the most famous roadways in the world—California's Highway 1, officially known as the Cabrillo Highway. This switchbacked, two-lane highway skims the California coast from just south of Los Angeles to a bit north of Mendocino, a slender gray ribbon perched, just barely, between steep mountain flanks and a sheer plummet to the Pacific Ocean.

For maximum pleasure, count on spending at least three to four days on the drive, meaning you'll spend two to three overnights en route. Approximate driving distances between main places of interest are:

San Francisco to Monterey	185 miles (highway / good road)
Monterey to Big Sur	30 miles (very winding)
Big Sur to San Simeon	63 miles (very winding)
San Simeon to Santa Barbara	156 miles (good road)
Santa Barbara to Los Angeles	92 miles (highway)

On the winding stretches, figure that you will average no more than 35 mph, al lowing for curves and stops at the scenic overlooks.

WEATHER: Since the state is so large, you might reasonably expect that differer areas have different climates. True—but California is also known for its multiple microclimates, which produce such phenomena as the dense fog in San Francisco proper —and brilliant sunshine in Sausalito, just a few miles away. Here's an overview of weather patterns.

Northern California (San Francisco and the Monterey Peninsula)

You basically have a wet, cool season (December through February), and a dry, warm season (April through October), with fairly even temperature distribution throughout the year. The average daily high in San Francisco is 55° in January, 72° in July. What messes up any generalities, however, is the famous fog, which often envelops San Francisco and much of the northern coast in a damp, white blanket during the summer. This gives rise to such famous remarks as Mark Twain's: "The coldest winter I ever spent was a summer in San Francisco." Often the nicest months of all are September and October, which tend to have the sunniest weather along the coast.

Southern California (Santa Barbara and Los Angeles)

Once again, count on experiencing a variety of microclimates, based on the interaction between the cool Pacific Ocean, warm land mass, and mountains. The wet season tends to be November through March, while the driest months are June through September. The average daily high runs about 65° in January, 84° in August. You can enjoy beach weather all year (many Californians spend Christmas Day at the beach); but the swimming season (for all but the wet-suit-clad surfer boys) runs from April to October. North of Santa Barbara, most people consider the ocean too cold for swimming.

CLOTHING: Casual clothing is the rule here. At night, even the fanciest restaurants will usually require only a jacket for men, no tie. California lives up to its reputation for liberalism and tolerance in manners of dress: In San Francisco, it is not uncommon to see three-piece-suited financiers frequenting the same establishments as sandal-wearing members of the counterculture.

Given the whimsical vagaries of California climate, the best advice is to dress in layers. During Northern California winters, you will need a warm coat and wool clothing; in Southern California, tropical-weight wools and a light overcoat are the most you'll require. From November through March, an umbrella is a good idea for all of California.

TIME: California is in the Pacific Time zone, and observes Daylight Savings Time in the summer. When it is noon in Los Angeles, it is 3 p.m. in New York.

TELEPHONES: The area codes for the places covered in this chapter are: San Francisco, 415; Carmel/Monterey, 408; Santa Barbara, 805; Greater Los Angeles area, 213 and 818.

SHOPPING: You name it, you can find it in California—everything from Alcatraz key chains to a Georgian dining table that seats 20. See the shopping section of each destination for details.

ABOUT ACCOMMODATIONS: Sleek, big-city hotels where you might run into a famous rock star in the elevator. Tiny bed-and-breakfast inns, with crocheted antimacassars on the sofas and real Tiffany lamps. Very plush mountainside villas, where the floor-to-ceiling plate-glass windows overlook the blue Pacific. These are just a few of the honeymoon choices you'll find in California. Be sure to make your reservations as far in advance as possible, especially if you'll be honeymooning from May through October, the most popular tourist months along the coast.

If you're interested in B&Bs, you can get a free directory, *The California Bed and Breakfast Inns Directory,* published by the California Lodging Industry Association, in cooperation with the California Office of Tourism. The guide lists more than 200 different inns. To order a copy, send a self-addressed, stamped (39¢) legal-size envelope to: **California Office of Tourism,** Dept. BBC, 1121 L St., Suite 103, Sacramento, CA 95814.

DINING OUT: The freshest natural ingredients, perfectly prepared—that summarizes the appeal of California cookery, which has practically reinvented the concept of American cuisine. Dedicated chefs use an international repertoire of cooking techniques to prepare foods—from stir-frying to mesquite-grilling. Because California is an important agricultural state, you'll be able to choose from a bounty of just-harvested produce: tender young green-leaf lettuce, baby carrots, vine-ripened tomatoes. You'll find that menus at the best restaurants change almost daily, to take advantage of fresh seasonal fruits, vegetables, fish, and game. To accompany your meal, choose a bottle of California wine, which is now internationally recognized to rank with the finest French Bordeaux and burgundies.

HOW TO GET MARRIED IN CALIFORNIA: A garden gazebo overlooking the crashing waves of the Pacific . . . a red-roofed mission church . . . a gilded ballroom with crystal chandeliers . . . even a hot-air balloon. These are just a few of the places you can say, "I do" in California. In order to be married in California, you both must have proof of age and identification, as well as a health certificate issued within the last 30 days. If either of you is divorced, you must furnish proof of the final judgment. You both must appear in person at the County Clerk's office for the license to be issued; fee is $35 (out-of-state checks are not accepted). The marriage license is valid for 90 days, and the marriage can be performed anywhere in the state of California. For complete details, contact the County Clerk in the area in which you wish to get married. In addition, the guest relations director at many hotels and inns can help you make complete wedding arrangements.

FOR FURTHER INFORMATION: Contact the following tourist offices: **California Office of Tourism,** 1121 L St., Suite 103, Sacramento, CA 95814 (tel. 916/322-2881); **Carmel Business Association,** Vandervort Court, San Carlos and 7th, P.O. Box 4444, Carmel-by-the-Sea, CA 93921 (tel. 408/624-2522); **Greater Los Angeles Visitors and Convention Bureau,** Manulife Plaza, 11th Floor, 515 South Figueroa St., Los Angeles, CA 90071 (tel. 213/624-7300); **Monterey Peninsula Visitors and Convention Bureau,** 380 Alvarado St., P.O. Box 1770, Monterey, CA 93942 (tel. 408/649-1779); **San Francisco Convention and Visitors Bureau,** 201 Third St., Suite 900, San Francisco, CA 94103 (tel. 415/974-6900); **Santa Barbara Conference and Visitors Bureau,** 1330 State St., Suite 200, P.O. Box 299, Santa Barbara, CA 93102 (tel. 805/965-3023).

2. San Francisco

The screech of the gulls and the mournful wail of foghorns. A sprightly cling-clang of the cable-car bells. The warm aroma of baking sourdough bread, briny steam rising from the boiling crab pots, foamy spurt of espresso into the china cup. Cadences of foreign tongues spoken on city streets—Chinese on Grant Avenue, Italian on the bocce courts in North Beach, Spanish at the bodegas in the Mission District. Yes, even if you were blindfolded, you would immediately know that you have arrived in San Francisco.

If the sounds and smells alone don't win you over, the sights of San Francisco certainly will. Pastel-painted Victorian mansions snuggle together, side by side. The burnished towers of the Golden Gate Bridge soar above the pale-white fog. Impossibly crooked streets, such as Lombard, zigzag down the hillside, and steep sidewalks clamber to the top of Nob Hill. ("When you get tired of walking around San Francisco, you can always lean against it," goes one local joke.) No wonder San Francisco has been voted the city that Americans would most like to visit, and "I Left My Heart in San Francisco" is viewed less as a theme song than a statement of fact.

San Francisco sits at the top of a 32-mile-long peninsula located between the Pacific Ocean and San Francisco Bay. Its steep contours derive from the fact that it is built on over 40 hills (7 principal ones). Although the city proper has about 700,000 residents, about 5.8 million reside in the greater San Francisco Bay Area, making it the fourth largest metropolis in the country. Make your way to the top of Coit Tower, or other of San Francisco's vantage points, and you'll get a sense of what makes the city tick. In contrast to the quaint, gingerbread-trimmed Victorian houses, you'll see the sleek skyscrapers of the financial district. You'll quickly realize how important nautical activity is to San Francisco. At the piers of the Embarcadero at the northeastern part of the city, huge container ships from all over the globe tie up, helping maintain the city's reputation as a "window on the world." Along Fisherman's Wharf, trawlers and crab-fishing boats tug gently at their lines. Glancing over toward the Marina, you'll see much smaller vessels—sailboats, their shrouds pinging against the masts, seemingly eager to go zipping off across the sparkling blue bay.

Today, San Francisco reigns as the premier business nexus of the western United States. (Perhaps prophetically, much of the financial district was constructed on landfill made up of scuttled vessels that had brought prospectors west for the Gold Rush.) In addition, the city is a major center for the arts, known for its M. H. de Young Memorial Museum, Asian Art Museum, San Francisco Symphony, San Francisco Ballet, and War Memorial Opera House. As you walk its streets (San Francisco is a city for strollers), you'll feel tempted to agree with Will Rogers, who remarked, "Cities are like gentlemen. They are born, not made. I bet San Francisco was a city from the very first time it had a dozen settlers."

One final pointer: Never, ever refer to it as 'Frisco, the sure mark of an insensitive out-of-towner. San Francisco is always called "The City," because to the many people who love it, there can be no other.

SHOPPING: Whether you're looking for souvenirs or future family heirlooms, you'll enjoy prowling the streets of San Francisco. Conveniently, many stores cluster together on certain streets or in distinct shopping areas, making it fun to browse. Some of the areas you will want to investigate:

San Francisco cherishes its past, and old buildings find new uses as up-to-date boutiques and restaurants. The brick complex of **Ghirardelli Square** (Beach Street between Polk and Larkin) was originally constructed as a woolen mill during the Civil War; it was later converted into a chocolate factory. Today, it has been beautifully refurbished and houses over 80 shops and restaurants. Check out Bears to Go for stuffed teddies, L'Armoire for lacy lingerie and slips, and Tutwilers Brass for everything from andirons to door knockers. Kabutoya Galleries carries very reasonably priced original prints and lithographs; By Design features snappy items for you and your home—desk sets to high-tech toothbrushes; Plumage offers one-of-a-kind ceramic necklaces depicting clowns, macaws, and morning glories.

The Cannery (Beach Street at Leavenworth) is another renovated building; this time, Del Monte's circa 1894 produce cannery. Stand-out shops here include Bazaar Cada Dia, which gathers treasures from all over the world: baskets and carvings from Africa, brightly painted papier-mâché parrots from Mexico, woven-cotton handbags from India. Kites and Delights displays a collection of highfliers so pretty, you might prefer to hang them from a wall, rather than launch them overhead. Compositions in Art and Wood is a gallery exhibiting items from some of the finest American and European craftspeople, priced from $20 to $10,000. Hint: From the Cannery's many outdoor terraces and walkways, you'll have superb views of the bay and the Golden Gate Bridge.

More mass than class, **Pier 39** (at Pier 39 on the waterfront) is definitely the place to go for souvenirs. There are a few shops of note. The NFL Shop features jackets, sweats, caps, and banners all emblazoned with the logos of all the NFL teams. Get Framed gives you a large selection of designer sunglasses, including Calvin Klein and Vuarnet. For butter-soft leatherwear (jackets, skirts, bikinis, and pants for both him and her) in a rainbow of scrumptious colors, top choice is North Beach Leather.

Bargain-hunters, get ready to feel that surge of adrenalin! **Cost Plus** (Bay and Taylor Streets, near Fisherman's Wharf) has been a San Francisco tradition for years. The store carries over 100,000 items from 48 different countries: brass jugs from India, perfumed soaps from China, bright piñatas from Mexico. There's a lot of junk —but a lot of good buys too.

San Francisco's answer to New York's Fifth Avenue or Beverly Hills' Rodeo Drive, the **Union Square** area is where you'll find the toniest meccas for shopping nirvana. It's bounded by Powell, Stockton, and Post Streets, and Geary Avenue. Right on the square, you'll find outposts of Macy's, Neiman-Marcus, I. Magnin, Saks, and Bullock & Jones. On neighboring streets, cruise past boutiques for Louis Vuitton, Ellesse, Dunhill, Brooks Brothers, Cartier, and Gucci.

North Beach is definitely the up-and-coming neighborhood for shopping trends, it's located just north of Chinatown and south of Fisherman's Wharf. Best street for browsing: Grant Avenue. Try Spellbound for antique clothing, and East/West Leather for big, squishy bags, and soft, soft leather jackets in eye-popping shades such as shocking pink and fire-engine red. If your tastes encompass the absurd, don't miss The Shlock Shop at 1418 Grant, which carries a rummage-worthy hodgepodge of old Salvation Army hats, rare beer cans, British bobby hats. "Neat junk," says the owner, a bohemian painter. They also have a superb selection of Panama hats.

Union Street (between Van Ness and Steiner) is one of San Francisco's nicest and trendiest areas. Many of the smart shops are housed in restored Victorian buildings. Various boutiques sell fashionable clothing, art, antiques, and accent pieces for your home.

ROMANTIC INTERLUDES:
There are two ways to view San Francisco—as unabashed tourist and as intimate friend. Here are some recommendations that should allow honeymooners to appreciate both sides of this memorable city.

The cable cars are the nation's only mobile national monuments, with a design virtually unchanged since Andrew Hallidie invented them in 1873. Three routes still operate, including the Powell-Mason line, which terminates near Fisherman's Wharf; and the California Street line, which climbs through Chinatown to Van Ness. But, as the long waiting lines will demonstrate, the best ride of all is on the Powell-Hyde line. You board at the corner of Powell and Market Streets, then hang on as the cable car chugs resolutely up and over Nob Hill and Russian Hill, making several gasp-producing hairpin turns. Finally, the car gets up to about 9 ½ mph as it hurtles down to Aquatic Park, bells clanging joyfully, affording its human companions a magnificent view of San Francisco Bay. You can buy tickets at the automatic vending machines at the most popular stops; fare is $1.50 per person (have exact change).

Well before dawn, the fishing fleet casts off from **Fisherman's Wharf** every day.

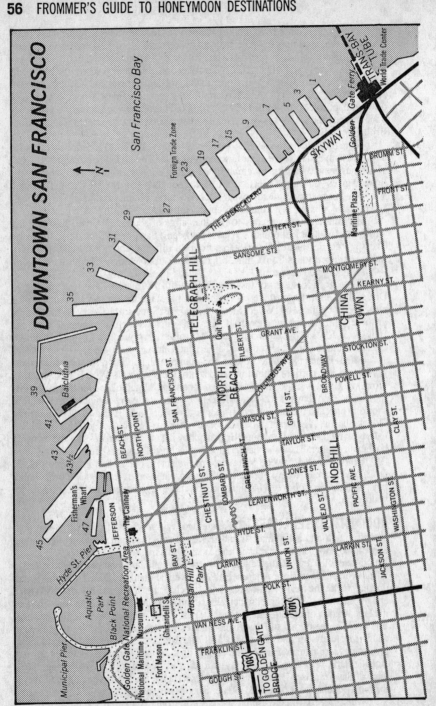

DOWNTOWN SAN FRANCISCO

San Francisco Bay

Foreign Trade Zone

THE EMBARCADERO

SKYWAY

Golden Gate Ferry

TRANS-BAY TUBE

World Trade Center

DRUMM ST.

FRONT ST.

Maritime Plaza

BATTERY ST.

SANSOME ST.

MONTGOMERY ST.

KEARNY ST.

TELEGRAPH HILL

Coit Tower

FILBERT ST.

GRANT AVE.

CHINA TOWN

STOCKTON ST.

NORTH BEACH

COLUMBUS AVE.

BROADWAY

POWELL ST.

GREEN ST.

MASON ST.

TAYLOR ST.

JONES ST.

NOB HILL

PACIFIC AVE.

CLAY ST.

LEAVENWORTH ST.

VALLEJO ST.

WASHINGTON ST.

HYDE ST.

LARKIN ST.

JACKSON ST.

SAN FRANCISCO ST.

BEACH ST.

NORTH POINT

CHESTNUT ST.

LOMBARD ST.

GREENWICH ST.

UNION ST.

POLK ST.

Russian Hill Park

LARKIN

BAY ST.

JEFFERSON

The Cannery

Hyde St. Pier

Fisherman's Wharf

Aquatic Park

Black Point

Municipal Pier

Golden Gate National Recreation Area

National Maritime Museum

Ghirardelli Sq.

Fort Mason

VAN NESS AVE.

FRANKLIN ST.

GOUGH ST.

101

TO GOLDEN GATE BRIDGE

101

Balclutha

39

41

43

43½

45

47

29

31

33

35

27

23

19

17

15

9

7

5

3

1

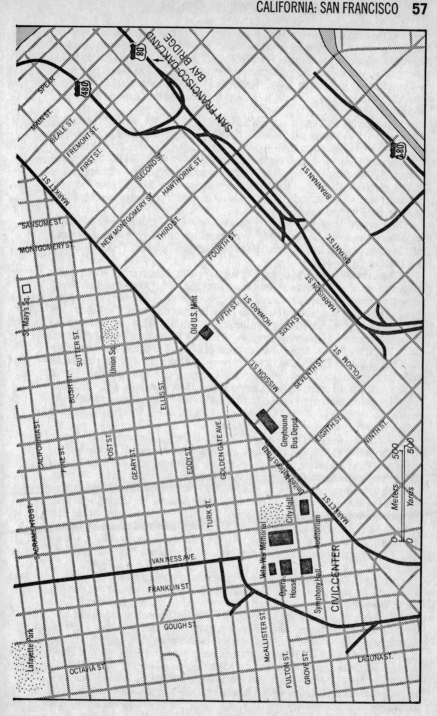

Much of the fresh catch with which the ships return—petrale sole, rockfish—appears on the menus of the famous restaurants that line the wharf, including Alioto's, Tarantino's, Sabellas, and others. The whole wharf pulsates with activity: crabs boil in giant cauldrons, caricaturists will sketch your portrait for $2.50, and street performers—from mimes to string quartets—will entertain. Across the street, feel like a kid again with visits to the Ripley's Believe It Or Not! Museum and the Guinness Museum of World Records.

Romantic it's not—but it sure is a heck of a lot of fun. Known as "The Rock," **Alcatraz** (tel. 546-2896 or toll free 800/445-8880 in California) served as a maximum security federal penitentiary from 1934 to 1963; today it is operated by the National Park Service. Over the years, it housed such notorious criminals as the "Bird Man of Alcatraz," "Machine-Gun" Kelly, and Al Capone. Join up with one of the hour-long park ranger tours. The rangers will regale you with legends of the lockhouse, clang the cell doors open and shut, and even lock you up in solitary confinement—only for 30 seconds, but it feels like an eternity.

To reach Alcatraz, take the ferry operated by the Red & White Fleet. It leaves from Pier 41 and costs $4 per person. In summer, you must buy your tickets several days in advance. You can also purchase tickets through Ticketron, P.O. Box 26430, San Francisco, CA 94126.

Chinatown is one of the largest Chinese communities outside of the Orient. For maximum visual impact, enter by the Chinatown Gate, Grant Avenue at Bush Street. Most of the tourist shops and restaurants line Grant Avenue, but to get a glimpse of the "real" Chinatown, head over to Stockton. Here, fresh produce such as bok choy, long beans, and winter melon spill over from the sidewalk stalls, and live carp swim in tanks in the fish markets. Back on Grant, browse through the various stores, which sell everything from T-shirts to fine antiques. Arts of China (843 Grant) features decorative Chinese fans ($20) as well as splendid ivory necklaces ($150). Shanghai Bazaar (645 Grant) carries cotton kimonos (very comfortable for lounging), as well as china tea sets, and paper lantern shades. Canton Bazaar (616 Grant) has it all—fashions, rugs, antiques, cloisonné, porcelain, furniture, and screens. When you get hungry, try Brandy Ho's Hunan Food (217 Columbus at Pacific), or Pot Sticker (150 Waverly Place), which is known for its fried dumplings.

Take a break in a real urban oasis; **Golden Gate Park** is three miles long, ½-mile wide, and lush with stands of redwoods and eucalyptus, dells of rhododenrons, and exotic trees from around the world. Drop in at the Morrison Planetarium for the laser show, the Conservatory of Flowers Botanical Gardens, or explore the bicycle paths, bridle paths, and jogging trails that tread their way across this 1,000 acres of green expanse. For hand-in-hand strolls, your best bet is the Japanese Tea Garden, with wishing pools, carp ponds, a bronze Buddha, and a small tea house (fortune cookies were invented here). Or rent a small rowboat at Stow Lake, then head over to Strawberry Hill Island, in the middle, for a picnic. And children of all ages will delight in the 1912-vintage Hershel-Spillman Carousel, sparkling like new after six years of restoration.

San Francisco has a fine selection of **museums,** most notably:

M. H. de Young Memorial Museum, Golden Gate Park (tel. 221-4811 or 750-3659). The oldest and largest museum in the west, the de Young is well known for its permanent collection, including works by El Greco, Rembrandt, and Gainsborough. The museum also has hosted many of the major traveling exhibitions, such as the Impressionists and King Tut. Open Wednesday through Sunday, 10 a.m. to 5 p.m.; admission $3 per person (also permits entry into the Asian Art and Legion of Honor museums on the same day). Call to verify holiday hours.

Asian Art Museum—The Avery Brundage Collection, Golden Gate Park, next to the de Young (tel. 668-8922). Rotates exhibits from its extensive collections, such as exquisite jade miniatures from China, 18-inch-tall vases carved from a solid piece of rock crystal, earthenware horses from Japan, bronze gods and goddesses from Nepal, Thailand, and Cambodia. Open Tuesday to Sunday, 10 a.m. to 5 p.m.; admission $3 per person.

California Palace of the Legion of Honor, Lincoln Park (tel. 221-4811 or 750-3659). A bronze cast of Rodin's "The Thinker" stands at the entrance to this museum that features an all-French collection: decorative arts, as well as fine paintings by Corot, Degas, Fragonard, Manet, Monet, and Renoir. Open Wednesday to Sunday, 10 a.m. to 5 p.m.; admission $3 per person.

If you enjoy the **performing arts,** the city provides plenty of choices.

War Memorial Opera House, Van Ness Avenue and Grove Street (tel. 431-1210). Regular season at this 3,535-seat hall runs from September to December, attracting world-class stars. They also host a summer opera festival. Be advised—tickets are very hard to get.

San Francisco Ballet, Opera House, Van Ness Avenue and Grove Street (tel. 762-BASS). The oldest permanent company in the United States, the San Francisco Ballet performs in the Opera House. The season runs late January to May; artistic director is Helgi Tomasson.

San Francisco Symphony, Davies Symphony Hall, Van Ness Avenue and Grove Street (tel. 431-5400). Under music director Herbert Blomstedt, the orchestra just celebrated its 75th anniversary. The season runs from October through May, and features special attractions, such as a Mostly Mozart and an All Beethoven festival.

Theater offerings range from major productions straight from Broadway *(Cats, La Cage aux Folles)* to experimental productions by new playwrights. One of the most interesting companies is the **American Conservatory Theatre (ACT),** recognized as one of America's finest resident theater companies. To get an idea of what's playing where, pick up a copy of the Sunday *San Francisco Chronicle*.

Some ticket outlets you should know about: BASS has several convenient ticket centers in the city; for information or to charge by phone, tel. 762-2277. **Ticketron** also has multiple outlets; for information or to charge by phone, tel. 392-SHOW. STBS (San Francisco Ticket Box Office Service) sells half-price day-of-performance tickets for selected music, dance, and theater events. They're located on the Stockton Street side of Union Square. Cash only, no reservations or telephone sales accepted. Open Tuesday to Saturday, noon to 7:30 p.m. For recorded information, tel. 433-STBS.

If you want to get the best scenic vistas of San Francisco, here are some options.

Fort Point National Historic Site was completed in 1861 to defend San Francisco harbor (presumably against attacks by Confederate privateers), though not one of its 149 original cannon was ever fired in anger. Here you get right under the Golden Gate Bridge, giving you one of the best vantage points to admire the graceful, mile-long span that symbolizes the city.

Vista Point is a scenic overlook just across the Golden Gate Bridge in Marin County. This is the best location for getting photos of the two of you with San Francisco shimmering in the background (for the best light, go in the afternoon).

Mrs. Lillie Hitchcock Coit, an honorary member of Knickerbocker Number Five Fire Company, donated $100,000 to build **Coit Tower** (top of Lombard Street on Telegraph Hill) to honor the city's firefighters. From the top of the 210-foot observation platform, the 360° views take in downtown San Francisco, the Bay Bridge, the Embarcadero, Angel Island, and the Golden Gate Bridge. Admission is $1.50. Downstairs, there's also an excellent gift shop with beautiful posters and classy T-shirts.

Photography buffs will want to get one of the classic shots of San Francisco: a row of pastel-painted Victorian houses, eaves covered with curlicued trim, contrasting with the futuristic San Francisco skyline, highlighted by the Transamerica and Bank of America towers. The place to go is **Alamo Square,** looking towards Steiner Street.

Get above it all with a **helicopter** flight above the city. Commodore Helicopters will take you aloft for four minutes for a gull's-eye perspective of the bay and Golden Gate Bridge. It costs $16.50 per person (tel. 981-4832). Longer airborne jaunts are available, including a day-trip to Napa Valley, where a limousine will squire you around to the wineries in style. About $300 per person (tel. 332-4482).

Slightly raffish, distinctly prosperous with an artsy undercurrent, **Sausalito** often draws comparisons to the hilltop villages along the Riviera. It's located just across the bay from San Francisco in Marin County. Sausalito was originally a summer community for wealthy San Franciscans, who would moor their houseboats here. Today, the houseboats remain down at the waterfront, but are now joined by pricey wood-and-glass houses cantilevered out over the hillsides. Along the bayside promenade called Bridgeway, you'll find trendy boutiques—a wonderful place to browse for arts and crafts and unusual clothing. Stop for lunch or dinner at one of the waterside restaurants, such as Scoma's or Ondine's.

Getting here is half the fun: Drive your car across the Golden Gate Bridge (the passenger gets to appreciate the spectacular city views), or take the Golden Gate Ferries from the Ferry Building at the foot of Market Street (tel. 332-6600) or the Red & White Fleet from Pier 41 at Fisherman's Wharf (tel. 546-2896). Fare is about $3.50 per person.

Located some 44 miles north of San Francisco (about an hour's drive), **Napa Valley** is probably the best-known wine growing region in America. Flanked by the Mayacamas and Howell mountains, the peaceful, green valley is dotted with wood-frame houses, stone wineries, and acre after acre (about 24,000 in all) of well-ordered vineyards. Thanks to Napa's consistent, sunny weather and rich volcanic soil, the area produces wines that equal or surpass the great vintages of France. Highway 29 cuts north right through the heart of the valley through towns such as Yountville, Oakville, Rutherford, and St. Helena. Many of the best-known wineries sprawl on the broad plains on either side of the roadway, and most of the larger vineyards are open for regular tours and tastings. These include the Robert Mondavi Winery in Oakville (tel. 707/963-9611), Inglenook in Rutherford (tel. 707/963-9411), Beaulieu Vineyards in Rutherford (tel. 707/963-2411), and Domaine Chandon in Yountville (tel. 707/944-2280). Hours vary seasonally, but if you arrive between 11 a.m. and 4 p.m., you're usually in good shape. Smaller wineries can be visited by appointment.

For the thrill of a lifetime, view wine country aboard a hot-air balloon flight, lifting off about an hour after sunrise to take advantage of the best weather conditions. The spectacle is beautiful—on a weekend morning, nearly 20 different balloons may go aloft, all with bright rainbow colors and zippy stripe, herringbone, and zigzag patterns. Climb into the gondola (balloon basket), and you're off—soaring above the green, rolling contours of the valley. The experience is guaranteed to make a "balloon dog" out of you in no time. Price for the hour-long flight, followed by a champagne toast, is about $155 per person. Contact Balloon Aviation of Napa Valley (tel. 707/252-7067). And, if you're looking for something different for your wedding, owner Chuck Foster can marry you aloft.

To fully appreciate all there is to do and see in Napa, consider staying over for a night or two. Top hostelries include the Silverado County Club and Resort (tel. 707/257-0200), with its superb golf and tennis facilities; and the Auberge du Soleil (tel. 707/963-1211), where rooms have fireplaces and decks overlooking the valley.

It seems fitting that Napa, the region of great wines, has also become celebrated for fine cuisine. Miramonte in St. Helena (tel. 707/963-3970) is one of the valley's premier restaurants. Chef Udo Nechutnys, a protegé of Paul Bocuse, creates memorable dishes, such as a scallop mousse flecked with finely grated orange peel and served with a white-wine-and-spinach sauce; or breast of muscovy duck, served rare with a red-currant-and-raspberry sauce, and accompanied by black mushrooms. Five-course, prix-fixe dinner, $46 per person plus wine. Domaine Chandon (tel. 707/944-

2892) has a beautiful terrace restaurant, overlooking rolling green lawns and neat rows of vines. Because of the pastoral views, it's especially nice for lunch. Start off with a warm chèvre salad or a seafood terrine, then try a maigret of duck in cabernet sauce with a purée of yams and garlic; or a bowl of steamed seafood, served in its own juices and accented with light cream and snipped chives. Lunch runs about $75 for two people, including champagne.

Part of the fun of a vacation in San Francisco is getting out of the city, and exploring some of the beautiful natural settings that surround it.

A day in the country is no farther than a ferry-ride away on **Angel Island State Park,** a green dot in the bay just off Tiburon in Marin County. The entire 750-acre island is uninhabited except for some 200 deer and a few resident park rangers. It offers excellent hiking—follow North Ridge Trail to the top for panoramic views of the bay. Most fun of all—rent bikes in San Francisco and take them along to pedal the route that circles the island. Bring a picnic lunch with some sourdough bread and Napa Valley cabernet—no food is sold on the island.

The Red & White Fleet ferries to Angel Island run from Pier 43½ and Tiburon; tel. 546-2896 for schedules. The round-trip fare is $6.75 per person.

Stinson Beach. If the sun's out and you want to feel the sand scrunch under your toes, Stinson offers nearly a mile of beach, perfect for surfcasting, picnics, or a game of Frisbee (only the relentlessly hardy will swim here). Located north of San Francisco in Marin County off Highway 1 (tel. 415/383-1644).

See the oldest living things on earth—the famous sequoias that stand up to 200 feet tall, measure some 16 feet in diameter . . . and are about 1,200 years old. In the 500-acre **Muir Woods** preserve (tel. 388-2595), marked trails wind their way past ferns, groves of oaks, and madronas. About 15 miles north of San Francisco off Highway 1, the park is open daily from 8 a.m. until sunset.

Mount Tamalpais (tel. 388-2070). Located just beyond Muir Woods, Mount Tam, as it is known familiarly hereabouts, soars 2,600 feet up. Drive to the summit, or follow one of the well-marked hiking trails. On a clear day, you can see over 100 miles.

Point Reyes National Seashore (tel. 663-1092). Follow Highway 1 about 40 miles north of San Francisco to this stunning peninsula thrust out into the Pacific, a place of windswept, foggy beauty. The 73,000-acre recreational area encompasses secluded beaches, rocky cliffs, grassy bluffs, all reachable by 150 miles of hiking trails. First stop by the Bear Valley Visitor Center for a map, and then set off. In particular, walk down the 312 steps to the historic lighthouse, with a seaside deck that provides an excellent vantage point for viewing the gray whales that migrate past here from December through April.

HONEYMOON HOTELS AND HIDEAWAYS: Thankfully for visitors, San Francisco is a compact 46.6 square miles, so no matter the hotel you choose, it's close to a cable-car line, other public transportation, or a short cab ride to restaurants, attractions, and nightlife. Some areas are both convenient and especially romantic, Union Square, Nob Hill, and Pacific Heights, among them. (The hotels listed below are located in those three areas.)

You'll find hotels in San Francisco less expensive than New York, but more costly than many other U.S. cities. Boosting the price is the city's 11% hotel tax, a fact to consider in figuring your honeymoon cost.

It's advised that you reserve well in advance during peak convention months of October and November, especially at the major, chain hotels which cater to this business. However, reservations are recommended at any time of the year.

For the *San Francisco Convention & Visitors Bureau Lodging Guide,* covering 330 motels and hotels in all categories, pensions and inns, send $1 for postage and handling to SFCVB, P.O. Box 6977, San Francisco, CA 94101.

Expensive

For three years, guests have been oohing and aahhing at the magnificence of **The Sherman House,** 2160 Green St., San Francisco, CA 94123 (tel. 415/563-3600), a stunning white mansion considered the most luxurious small hotel in San Francisco. It is the result of the dream of Manouchehr Mobedshahi, an Iranian-born businessman who purchased the Pacific Heights landmark in 1980 and spent four years meticulously restoring it, the carriage house, and the formal gardens. The mansard-roofed house was originally built by Leland Sherman, founder of the Sherman Clay Music Company and a lover of the arts. Sherman's guests included stars of opera and stage—Enrico Caruso among them—who performed to high society in the home's three-story recital hall. The 15 rooms and suites are individually furnished in Biedermeier, English Jacobean, or French Second Empire antiques. Each room contains a marble, wood-burning fireplace, and beds canopied in rich tapestry fabrics and covered with feather-down comforters. Bathrooms are lovely, with black marble whirlpool baths and a mini-TV set above the vanity. In the middle of the formal gardens, the Carriage House contains three suites, all in romantic pastel colors. The spacious Garden Suite opens onto its own private flower garden and gazebo. Like most rooms, it has views of the Golden Gate Bridge and the bay. At mealtime, you'll want to try out the fine restaurant. Rates (EP): $170 to $300 per couple per night; $300 to $475 for junior suites; $500 to $600, executive suites.

The Fairmont Hotel, atop Nob Hill, 950 Mason St. at California Street, San Francisco, CA 94108 (tel. 415/772-5000; reservations: toll free 800/527-4727 nationwide; 800/492-6622 in Texas). The Fairmont's regal facade is familiar to millions as the site of the St. Gregory in the TV series *Hotel.* The grande dame of Nob Hill hotels has retained its grand character, with musicians' balconies and boxes along one side of the lobby, still splendid with its marble columns, gold-leaf trim and velvety red carpeting. The hotel contains seven restaurants and San Francisco's best-known supper club, the Venetian Room, which attracts big-name entertainers. Rooms contain such added touches as terry bathrobes, bath accoutrements, chocolates on the pillows, and in-room movies. The main building's guest rooms are slightly larger than those in the modern tower addition, but many tower rooms have better views. For honeymooners with infinite budgets, there's always the Fairmont's historic, eight-room penthouse suite, which boasts the biggest price tag of any hotel accommodation in San Francisco —$4,000 per night. For those of more modest means, there's a honeymoon package (EP): $177 per couple per night in the main building or $213 per night in the tower, including a deluxe room, champagne on arrival, fruit basket, personalized stationery, and a brunch for two. Rates are $160 per night thereafter and upgrades to suites are offered, if available. Regular rates: $170 to $210 for a double standard room.

Campton Place, 340 Stockton St., San Francisco, CA 94108 (tel. 415/781-5555; reservations: toll free 800/647-4007 nationwide; 800/235-4300 in California), has combined the luxury of large, top-of-the-line hotels with the friendly, personal service of small inns. A deteriorating Union Square hotel just a few years ago, it is now favored by visiting celebrities and dignitaries. Impeccably groomed and courteous doormen set the mood at the entrance to the marble-floored lobby, which is decorated with Oriental art and a large crystal chandelier. Guest rooms are as elegant, resembling rooms in a private home furnished by a top interior designer. There are king-size beds with beige down bedspreads, armoires hiding TV sets, remote-control lighting, and limited-edition artwork. Baths are in Roman Travertine marble with brass fixtures whose shine proves they are polished daily. The hotel provides such services as a valet to assist with packing and unpacking, immediate pressing, prompt shoe shining and turn-down service. The restaurant at Campton Place is consistently ranked in the city's top ten, and the cozy little bar serves cocktails mixed and hand-shaken in the traditional manner. The location a few steps from Union Square can't be beat. Honeymoon packages: None. Rates (EP): $170 to $230 per couple per night. Two-room suites are from $475.

The Mandarin Oriental, 222 Sansome St., San Francisco, CA 94102 (tel. 415/885-0999; reservations: toll free 800/622-0404 in the U.S.; 800/663-0787 in Canada). One of the world's most acclaimed hotel companies opened its first U.S. hotel in San Francisco in mid-1987 and it quickly garnered accolades as one of the city's most sumptuous properties. Although in the bustling financial district, the Mandarin's twin towers rise so high you'll feel you are floating in the clouds above it all. The hotel's 160 rooms actually occupy the 38th through 48th floors of the third-highest building in San Francisco. (The lobby and restaurant are on the ground and second floors.) Italian marble in several shades, Oriental furnishings with a European touch, brass and chandeliers set the scene in the lobby and guest rooms. The high standards for which the Mandarin is known are evident in the beautifully decorated rooms. The bathrooms, lined with marble, have some of the best views in San Francisco: floor-to-ceiling windows overlooking the city line one side of each bathtub. Just so your feet won't get cold stepping on all this marble, the maid each evening sets out silk slippers from Thailand on an Irish linen mat at the side of the bed. Honeymoon package: Three days/two nights (EP): $545 per couple. Includes a Mandarin room with king-size beds, chilled champagne, room service breakfast one morning, and personalized stationery. Available add-ons are a dinner at Silks with a special menu, a tour of San Francisco with a Rolls-Royce and a romantic picnic, a bay sailing trip on a private yacht or a helicopter ride over the bay. Regular rates: $195 to $210 per couple per night for superior and deluxe rooms; $260 for Mandarin rooms; $285, $750, and $900 for suites.

Moderate

Casa Madrona Hotel, 801 Bridgeway, Sausalito, CA 94965 (tel. 415/332-0502). Casa Madrona's baby-blue, Cape Cod–style cottages and flower-covered latticed arbors climb a steep hill above the picturesque town of Sausalito. A sailboat marina, the bay, and the city of San Francisco are the views from its hideaway-like rooms. The three parts of the hotel are connected by red-brick pathways and steps: an 1885 Victorian-style Italianate mansion with 13 cozy rooms furnished with antiques, floral-printed wallpaper, white wicker, and claw-foot bath tubs; the cottages, the three most romantic hideaways in Sausalito; and new Casa Madrona, 17 suite-like rooms individually decorated in such wide-ranging styles as Art Nouveau, country French, rustic mountain cabin, Southwest, a Parisian artist's loft, elegant Oriental, and frilly Victorian. Of the cottages, La Tonnelle is the most romantic, with wood-burning stove, a tile tub for two, and a garden deck. In the new Casa Madrona, several suites are recommended for honeymooners, but, with their fireplaces and sweeping views from private balconies or decks, all are suitable. Some examples are Chateau Charmant, with melon and peach tones, canopied bed, elevated bathtub, and fireplace. Kathmandu transports you to an exotic mountain hideaway with secret alcoves, mirrors, a tub for two, and huge cushions for whiling away the hours. The hotel also has a hot tub under a vine-covered arbor that can be reserved for a private party of two. Also sumptuous is the Casa Madrona restaurant, with sweeping views, peach-and-white motif, and a roll-back glass roof for an al fresco feeling. The hotel is in the heart of Sausalito's waterfront. Ferries to San Francisco depart just a few hundred yards from its doorstep. Honeymoon package: None. Rates (EP): $65 to $125 per couple per night in the Victorian House; $140 to $160 for the cottages; $125 to $175 for new Casa Madrona suites.

"Not your ordinary hotel," proclaims **The Mansion,** 2220 Sacramento St., San Francisco, CA 94115 (tel. 415/929-9444), in its brochure, and that becomes delightfully clear at every turn in this Victorian fantasyland. Once in the grand foyer of the 1887 Queen Anne building, guests can see the ecletic collection of furnishings, murals, and fanciful artifacts, all from the creative—some say offbeat—mind of owner Bob Pritikin. His pig paintings and "porkabilia"—the largest such collection in the world—are on display everywhere. The usually packed weekend magic/music concerts in the Music Room feature Pritikin himself, billed as America's Foremost Concert Saw Player. This is in addition to the nightly appearance of the Mansion's ghost, Claudia, who, seated in her Victorian wheelchair, is pushed to the keyboard of a grand piano to play classical selections. For more romance and fun, there's the flower gardens, the billiard room with a live macaw looking on, a nickelodeon with drums and tambourines, and valuable Turner and Reynolds paintings to feast your eyes upon. The hotel's candlelit dining room is supervised by master chef David Coyle, formerly personal chef to the duke and duchess of Bedford. Rooms run the gamut size-wise, from the tiny Tom Thumb room, just barely big enough for two people standing, to the large, opulent Josephine room, a favorite of such celebrities as Barbra Streisand and Robin Williams. Some rooms have marble fireplaces, private terraces, and even ceilings that slant to the floor. Freshly picked flowers and colorful murals dominate many of them. The hotel is in a residential area four blocks from a cable-car line. Rates (BP) range from $89 per couple per night for the Tom Thumb room to $200 per couple for the Josephine Room. Full breakfast and the music/magic shows are included.

The Inn at Union Square, 440 Post St., San Francisco, CA 94102 (tel. 415/397-3510), may be the narrowest hotel in San Francisco; wink as you walk past it and you'll miss its elegant entrance. But, once you've seen the sumptuously decorated rooms and experienced the quiet graciousness of the staff, you won't want to pass it up. The Inn at Union Square is one of San Francisco's many refurbished downtown hotels, transformed in the last five years to an intimate hostelry that captures the style of a European inn. Its rooms have been decorated individually by the owner's wife, San Francisco interior designer Nan Rosenblatt. Some are in warm neutral tones, others burst with color and prints. Most rooms contain king-size, four-poster beds with goose-down pillows, Georgian furniture, and comfortable sitting areas. The sixth-floor suite has its own fireplace, bar, whirlpool bath, and sauna. The hotel doesn't have a lobby per se, but each floor has its own cozy lounge with fireplaces, where guests are served flaky croissants, fresh juice, fruit, and coffee each morning as well as cucumber sandwiches, cakes, and tea in the afternoon—all included in the room price. The hotel is ½ block west of Union Square and the Powell Street cable cars. Honeymoon package: None. Rates (CP) begin at $95 per couple per night for the smallest rooms with king-size beds; $130 to $170 for larger rooms and suites with king-size beds and sitting areas. It's $300 for the lavish penthouse suite.

The Union Street Inn, 2229 Union St., San Francisco, CA 94123 (tel. 415/346-0424), a tranquil six-room bed-and-breakfast, has all the charm of a 19th-century Edwardian home, yet it's smack in the midst of San Francisco's most fashionable residential area and trendiest shopping district. Owner Helen Stewart bought the 85-year-old house in 1978 and lovingly decorated the living room and each of the six guest rooms with antiques, oriental carpeting, and bric-a-bracs. In the main house, the most sumptuously romantic room is the New Yorker, with a canopied queen-size bed, elegant English armoire, and a sexy, salmon-colored chaise longue. But the inn's pièce de resistance is the Carriage House, actually a suite with a plant-shrouded Jacuzzi bathtub that can be entered from the bedroom or bathroom. A skylight opens above the tub for viewing the stars or sky. Difficult to believe that just beyond the brick path and through the quiet garden are some of San Francisco's best restaurants and nightlife. Honeymoon package: None. Rates (CP): $115 to $125 per couple per night for the Carriage House; other rooms, with shared bath, are $75 to $85. Rates include a continental breakfast of French pastries and muffins.

Petite Auberge, 863 Bush St., San Francisco, CA 94108 (tel. 415/928-6000). **White Swan Inn,** 845 Bush St., San Francisco, CA 94108 (tel. 415/775-1755). These two French and English "sisters," practically side by side on the lower slopes of Nob Hill, are romantic reminders of England and France, transported here by businessman-turned-hotel-owner Roger Tost. When you enter the Petite Auberge you'll feel transported to the French countryside by the calico-printed wallpaper, antiques, a carousel horse, and fresh-cut flowers everywhere. The inn's 26 rooms are individually decorated with quaint print wallpaper, curtains, and down comforters, French-style antiques, a collection of novels by the beds, and wood-burning fireplaces (in all but eight rooms). You'll have company—cuddly teddy bears, which share the queen-size beds in each room. The 27-room English-style White Swan offers the added warmth of a flower garden, curved bay windows, and handsome English antiques. The library, living room, and dining room are decorated in rich, warm woods. Rooms all have fireplaces. In both hotels, guests are served bountiful breakfasts of egg dishes, fresh fruit, homemade breads and pastries, and freshly squeezed juices. Afternoon tea is provided in both inns' sitting rooms: A fire is usually crackling in the fireplace at both hotels to ward off the chills of foggy afternoons. The hotels are within easy walking distance of Union Square, Nob Hill, and the cable-car lines. Honeymoon packages: None, but honeymooners receive fresh flowers and champagne in their rooms. Rates (BP) at the Petite Auberge are $95 to $145 per couple per night. The suite with a private deck and Jacuzzi-bathtub is $185. At the White Swan Inn, rates (BP) are $115 to $145 per couple per night; $225 for the Ashleigh Suite with large separate sitting room, wet bar, and two baths.

The 144-room **Hotel Bedford,** 761 Post St., San Francisco, CA 94109 (tel. 415/673-6040; reservations: toll free 800/227-5642 nationwide; 800/652-1889 in California; 800/327-5642 in Canada), was the first of five old San Francisco buildings to be renovated into stylish accommodations at reasonable prices. The Bedford's lobby is warm and inviting, its walls and upholstered furniture in peach, with small seating groups separated by glass-panel screens and wooden plantation shutters gracing tall bay windows. Rooms have been recently redecorated in soft pastel tones of lavender, salmon, and sky blue with modern white furniture. They have king-size beds, attractive new baths, small refrigerators, color TVs, VCRs, and views of San Francisco. The hotel's restaurant, the Café Bedford, is known for serving excellent California-style cuisine in a handsome pink, black, and gray dining room. The hotel is three blocks from Union Square and two blocks from the theater district. Honeymoon package (BP): $95 per couple per night for a deluxe room with views, $145 for two-room suite, including bottle of champagne, full American breakfast, two tickets for the cable cars, and a package for a Pier 39 visit. Regular rates: $85 per couple per night.

Inexpensive

Hotel Beresford Arms, 701 Post St., San Francisco, CA 94109 (tel. 415/673-2600; reservations: toll free 800/227-4048 nationwide; 800/652-1244 in California). A grand old lobby with carved, molded ceilings and red-velvet upholstered Victorian love seats greets guests at this reasonably priced 90-room hotel. Standard rooms have queen-size beds with white cotton bedspreads, attractive dark-wood furniture, modern bathrooms with sliding glass doors opening onto the tubs, small refrigerators, and color TVs. Suites have whirlpool baths, bidets, and full kitchens. Every morning, complimentary coffee and pastries are served in the lobby. The location is excellent, two blocks from Union Square and from the theater district. Honeymoon packages: None. Rates (EP): $60 per couple per night for standard rooms; $75 to $95 for suites. If this hotel is full, you might try its sister hotel, the Beresford, a block away on Sutter. Rates are the same.

The King George Hotel, 334 Mason St., San Francisco, CA 94102 (tel. 415/781-5050; reservations: toll free 800/227-4240 nationwide; 800/556-4545 within California; and 800/345-4240 in Canada), is a 144-room charmer. Refurbished several years ago in a English country motif, it has retained its inn-style character even though a renovation in mid-1987 gave it a more sophisticated look. The lobby has floor-to-ceiling drapes and Corinthian columns. Rooms are now bright, airy, and elegant, with cream-colored walls, cherry-wood furniture, and floral print bedspreads. The rooms are on the small side, but quite adequate and comfortable. A great place to relax after a day of sightseeing or shopping at Union Square (a block away) is at the hotel's Bread and Honey Tearoom above the lobby, serving traditional afternoon high tea (pastries) to the accompaniment of live, classical piano music. Honeymoon package: Inquire—it is sometimes available. Rates (EP): $69 per couple per night.

The Bed and Breakfast Inn, Four Charlton Court, San Francisco, CA 94123 (tel. 415/921-9784). This plant-covered turn-of-the-century building with creaky floors was opened as a bed-and-breakfast inn by Robert and Marily Kavanaugh in 1975. Although it's in the popular shopping and restaurant district of Union Street, the inn is just off Union on a tiny alleyway that will take you back to the narrow mews of old London. The inn has only nine rooms, four of which share bathrooms. The five with private baths are quite appropriate for anyone's romantic dreams, especially The Mayfair, a private flat with living room, kitchen, latticed balcony, and spiral staircase to the bedroom loft. One of the most charming rooms, often recommended for honeymooners, has a large Jacuzzi bathtub lined by a mirror. The queen-size bed is in a cozy alcove, decorated in dainty Laura Ashley prints. Guests can enjoy the garden, brew a cup of tea in the library, and share the continental breakfast in the English country–style dining room. Honeymoon package: None. Rates (CP): $68 to $85 per couple per night for "pension" rooms with shared baths; $108 to $129 for rooms with private baths, telephones, and TV; and $184 for the flat with spiral staircase.

The Cartwright, 524 Sutter St., San Francisco, CA 94102 (tel. 415/421-2865; reservations: toll free 800/227-3844 nationwide; 800/652-1858 in California; 800/654-1858 from Canada), has many loyal guests who cite its friendly, almost familial service, moderate rates, and excellent location a block from Union Square and on the cable-car line as reasons for their repeat visits. In 1986, they added another reason: the completion of a five-year renovation that has significantly upgraded the hotel, turning the lobby into an elegant showpiece and adding romantic brass and wood-carved beds, floral-print bedspreads, and newly tiled baths to each of its 114 rooms. The new decor is the work of Aroline Adams, who owns the hotel with her husband, Jerome (their children and son-in-law are also involved in the family-owned hotel). Rooms have small refrigerators, fresh flowers, large bathtubs and showers, color TV, and telephones. Complimentary tea is served in the lobby from 4 to 6 p.m. The hotel's Town and Country Tea Room serves breakfast and lunch in a country setting with blue-and-white floral print tablecloths, white rattan chairs, and hardwood floors. Honeymoon package: None. Rates (EP): $72 to $78 per couple per night.

Very Inexpensive

Grant Plaza, 465 Grant Ave., San Francisco, CA 94108 (tel. 415/434-3883; reservations: toll free 800/472-6899 nationwide; 800/472-6805 in California). This small gem at the entrance of Chinatown inevitably gets listed in most budget guides to San Francisco. But, besides being a bargain, the Grant Plaza is pretty, spotlessly clean, and attractively decorated. Its lobby of chandeliers, elegant burgundy carpeting, and potted plants belies the budget price. The rooms are a bit small, but all were redecorated in 1985 with furnishings that you'd find in a hotel whose rates are three times these. All rooms have color TVs, private baths, and direct-dial telephones. Unfortunately, the corner rooms (with the best views) have twin beds, but queen-size beds are available in others. Don't miss the cozy sitting area on the top floor, under the domed stained-glass skylight. The hotel does not have a bar or restaurant, but it is a five-minute walk from the Union Square shopping area, the theater district, and a ten-minute stroll from the nightlife and restaurants of North Beach. Cable cars are a block away. Honeymoon package: None. Rates (EP): $32 to $42 per couple per night.

ROMANTIC RESTAURANTS: San Francisco is one of the world's great dining cities, a place where there's one restaurant for every 164 residents—many of whom seem to live to eat, rather than eat to live. San Francisco's renowned chefs take pride in using only the freshest ingredients (many work with farmers who grow produce exclusively for their restaurants). Often, the lettuce in your dinner salad had the fresh dew on it only that morning; a petrale sole was just off-loaded a few hours earlier at Fisherman's Wharf.

Expensive

Located in one of San Francisco's most fashionable new hotels, **Campton Place Restaurant,** 340 Stockton (tel. 781-5155), offers a plush setting in the Grand European manner. When you enter, you'll feel as if you're sinking ankle-deep into the thick carpeting. Mirrors strategically placed hither and yon catch reflections. You can dine by the windows, in straight-backed chairs, or against the wall, ensconced in a cushy banquette. A spotlight draws attention to the huge floral display in a celadon vase; Wedgwood china gleams on the table. If the decor is classic, the food is innovative American, featuring regional specialties in season: poached lobster served with blue-corn cakes; or a grilled quail served with matchstick-thin sweet potato sticks. All perfectly prepared and impeccably served. Dinner for two with wine could easily run $150. Open for breakfast, lunch, and dinner; reservations recommended.

Moderate

Square One, 190 Pacific at Front (tel. 788-1110). The decor is Italian modern—terra cotta tiles, blonde wood furniture, soft, soothing shades of beige, taupe, and pastels all around. But what really gets your libido racing here is the food. Run by Joyce Goldstein, who used to manage the Chez Panisse Café in Berkeley, Square One has rapidly zoomed to the top rank of San Francisco's restaurant galaxy. The menu changes daily to take advantage of seasonal specialties, and Goldstein delights in adapting spices and techniques from different countries—perhaps a Brazilian churrasco, or an Algerian chick-pea soup, lushly seasoned with saffron. The Italian dishes equal those served in the finest restaurants in Tuscany: pollo all'arrabbiata, a grilled baby chicken in a marinade of garlic, hot peppers, tomatoes, and olive oil; or farfalle (bow-shaped pasta) served with prosciutto, artichokes, mushrooms, peas, and onions. Every day Square One features a different, home-baked Italian bread, such as a crusty panmarino, lustily spiced with rosemary. The staff is congenial and knowledgeable about the extensive (and reasonably priced) wine list. Don't miss the outstanding desserts, such as a frozen peach sorbet, with the flavor of fresh-harvested fruit. Dinner appetizers run from $4.50 to $9; entrées from $13.50 to $20. Open for lunch and dinner; reservations recommended.

Chez Panisse Café, 1517 Shattuck Ave., Berkeley (tel. 548-5049). In a sense, it all began here—the revolution launched by owner Alice Waters, who first popularized the idea of using just-harvested produce and regional menus to create a uniquely American cuisine. Today, serious food lovers continue to call at this small, cedar-fronted building in Berkeley, and sample the imaginative specialties. There are now two Chez Panisses: the downstairs restaurant, and the upstairs café. We strongly prefer the upstairs café, where you can enjoy equally fine cuisine—at about ⅓ the price. The café ranks as one of the liveliest, most animated spots in the Bay area. It's reminiscent of a French bistro, complete with small, black-marble tables and oak floor. The best tables for lovers occupy either the front or rear rooms—the main bar area gets a tad noisy with high spirits. As for the food—heavenly. You'll probably want to order one of everything on the menu—the baked Sonoma goat cheese with fresh garden lettuce ($7); or chicken saltimbocca, made with tender free-range chicken, sage, prosciutto, and marsala ($15.50). For dessert, see if you can negotiate with your waiter to reserve one of the light-as-air lemon-curd tarts ($4.75)—they usually get gobbled up fast. The café is open for lunch (reservations accepted) and dinner (first come, first seated—no reservations).

Greens, Building A at Fort Mason (tel. 771-6222), is certainly one of the most intriguing restaurants in San Francisco—and one of the most beautiful. Set in a former army fort warehouse, the room retains a high-tech approach with gray, industrial-type carpeting and the original high ceiling. Colorful abstract art brightens the walls, and natural wood tables soften the hard-edge feel. But the pièce de résistance is the view through the floor-to-ceiling windows—a postcard-perfect outlook over the marina to the Golden Gate Bridge. The restaurant is run by a Zen Buddhist group (only in San Francisco would you find Buddhists operating a first-class restaurant in what once was an army supply depot). You'll know the ingredients are fresh—many of the vegetables are grown on the group's own farm near Muir Woods. The cuisine can best be described as haute vegetarian, with dishes so richly satisfying and zestily flavorful, you'll never notice the lack of meat. At lunch, you might be able to start off with mesquite-grilled polenta, served with warm gorgonzola cheese and walnuts on a bed of lettuce ($4), or a picked-from-the-garden salad. Greens' pastas are excellent, such as linguine gently tossed with lentils, ricotta cheese, sweet peppers, garlic, and herbs. For dessert, try a blackberry tart, or chocolate-nut torte. At night, Greens turns the lights down to highlight the bay views. Selections might include mesquite-grilled brochettes with mushrooms, cherry tomatoes, peppers, and potatoes ($9.25) or pizza with zucchini, tomatoes, red onions, fontina, and pesto ($9.50). Several times a week, they also offer a five-course, fixed-menu dinner for $27.50 per person. Open for lunch and dinner; reservations necessary.

Guaymas, 5 Main, Tiburon (tel. 435-6300). If it weren't for the panoramic view of San Francisco out the windows, you'd probably swear you were dining in the Mexican town on the Sea of Cortès that lends the restaurant its name. Guaymas serves authentic Mexican regional cooking: tacos sudados ("sweating tacos"), filled with chicken or beef and steamed in a banana leaf; and pechuga ranchera con chile, a poached chicken breast served with a pungent, deep-red sauce made from ground guajillo chiles. Each of you should order something different so you can try several dishes. In addition to having magnificent views of San Francisco, the restaurant itself is beautiful, done with a sophisticated Mexican decor, with brightly painted tiles, a stuccoed fireplace, and flower boxes lining the outdoor decks. Dinner for two—including margaritas and beer—shouldn't cost you more than $45. Note: even if you don't have a car, Tiburon is easy to reach via a 15-minute ferry ride from the Ferry Building or Fisherman's Wharf. For schedules, call the restaurant or Red & White Ferries (tel. 546-2896). Guaymas is located right at Tiburon's ferry dock.

Fog City Diner, 1300 Battery St. at the Embarcadero (tel. 982-2000) is the place that originated the concept of "grazing"—downing a bevy of tasty, appetizer-size portions rather just one entrée. Go light with crabcakes ($5), or hunker down seriously with a grilled skirt steak ($8). And you've never seen such a glamorous diner. **Cliff House,** 1090 Point Lobos at Ocean Beach (tel. 386-3330), has been a favorite place to watch the sunset, as well as the surfers and seals. While the sunsets are spectacular, the food is just O.K., so drop by for cocktails only.

Very Inexpensive

Who says you have to spend a lot of money to dine well—and romantically? The best two meals in town are, if not free, about $6 per person. All along Fisherman's Wharf, sidewalk stands such as the **Lighthouse, Borruso's,** and **Guardino's** sell "walk-away" cocktails of shrimp or the famous Dungeness crab (about $2.50) and clam chowder ($2.25). When accompanied with some sourdough bread, it makes for a satisfying meal. For dessert, point your toes toward the **Ghirardelli Chocolate Manufactory,** where you can down an ice-cream soda, sundae, or the definitive chocolate malted, topped with a dollop of whipped cream. Good to the last slurp.

Or enjoy a lunch of dim sum (appetizers) in Chinatown at a restaurant such as **Tung Fong** (808 Pacific off Stockton; tel. 362-7115). Waiters push a trolley laden with tasty choices: spring rolls, barbecue chicken tidbits, steamed dumplings, and bow (puffy buns stuffed with ingredients such as black mushrooms and peppers)—just point to make your selections. The waiters are extremely helpful and will identify any items you don't recognize. Each dish costs about $1.65; figure on three per person. Then saunter up Grant Avenue toward the nearby Italian quarter in North Beach and polish off a cappuccino and gelato (ice cream) in a sidewalk café.

3. Monterey, Carmel, and the Monterey Peninsula

For residents as well as vacationers, the Monterey Peninsula and the towns along its shores represent the best of California's coast drive. Here, all the images that embody California seem to swirl together in one massive montage of splendid scenery. Two-hundred-year-old, red-roofed adobe structures line Monterey's broad streets. The indomitable Lone Cypress clings tenaciously to its rocky promontory off the 17-mile drive. Along the coast where the Pacific Ocean whips furiously into the cliffs, the pencil-thin outline of Highway 1 spirals its way along the shore. Although this is one of California's most historic regions, large stretches of terrain remain untouched. Yet in seaside towns such as Carmel and Monterey, civilization—in the form of gourmet restaurants, art galleries, and Bach festivals—reaches a chic refinement comparable to European communities along the Riviera.

Located about 120 miles south of San Francisco and 330 miles north of Los Angeles, the Monterey Peninsula forms the southernmost nub of Monterey Bay. Roughly rectangularly shaped, the peninsula embraces four distinct communities. Moving counterclockwise around the peninsula, they are Monterey, Pacific Grove, Pebble Beach, and Carmel-by-the-Sea. Although each retains a distinct personality, you'll find it easy to travel from one to another. Only three miles separate Carmel from Monterey, so have no hesitations about flitting from one to another—perhaps visiting the Monterey Bay Aquarium in the morning, lunching and shopping in Carmel, then spending the night at a B&B in Pacific Grove.

ABOUT ACCOMMODATIONS: Although accommodations on the Monterey Peninsula embody romance, the amorous ambience does not come cheap. Count on spending between $80 and $100 a night at a charming bed-and-breakfast inn, about $150 to $200 at one of the renowned resort hotels.

If you will be staying on the Monterey Peninsula during the weekend, be aware that many of the bed-and-breakfasts require a minimum stay of two nights. Also, since the region ranks as a popular weekend getaway for folks from San Francisco and Los Angeles, the choicest properties book up fast for Fridays, Saturdays, and Sundays. Reserve your room several months in advance, especially if you will be honeymooning during the summer.

Honeymoon packages are the exception, rather than the rule, on the Monterey Peninsula. Unless otherwise noted, prices quoted are per couple, per night. When making room reservations, let the hotel know that you are on your honeymoon—often, you'll receive a complimentary bottle of champagne.

ROMANTIC DINING: Superb—that describes dining on the peninsula known for just-caught seafood, just-picked fruits and vegetables, and just simply marvelous

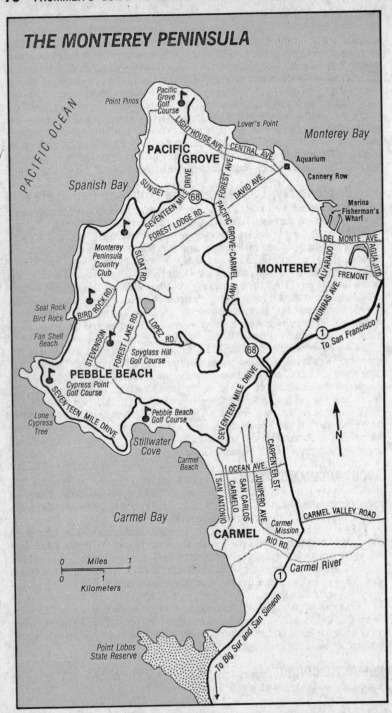

THE MONTEREY PENINSULA

PACIFIC OCEAN

Point Pinos

Pacific Grove Golf Course

Lover's Point

Monterey Bay

PACIFIC GROVE

Spanish Bay

LIGHTHOUSE AVE.

CENTRAL AVE.

Aquarium

Cannery Row

SUNSET

FOREST AVE.

DAVID AVE.

Marina

Fisherman's Wharf

SEVENTEEN MILE DRIVE

FOREST LODGE RD.

68

PACIFIC GROVE-CARMEL HWY.

DEL MONTE AVE.

AGUAJITO

SLOAT RD.

Monterey Peninsula Country Club

MONTEREY

MUNRAS AVE.

ALVARADO

FREMONT

BIRD ROCK RD.

Seal Rock
Bird Rock

FOREST LAKE RD.

LOPEZ RD.

1

To San Francisco

Fan Shell Beach

STEVENSON

Spyglass Hill Golf Course

68

PEBBLE BEACH

Cypress Point Golf Course

SEVENTEEN MILE DRIVE

SEVEN-TEEN MILE DRIVE

Pebble Beach Golf Course

Lone Cypress Tree

Stillwater Cove

Carmel Beach

CARPENTER ST.

OCEAN AVE.

SAN ANTONIO

SAN CARLOS

CARMELO

JUNIPERO AVE.

CARMEL VALLEY ROAD

Carmel Bay

Carmel Mission

CARMEL

RIO RD.

N

0	Miles	1
0		1

Kilometers

1

Carmel River

Point Lobos State Reserve

To Big Sur and San Simeon

views of the ocean. Some Monterey specialties to know about: petrale sole and Monterey Bay shrimp. Do not hesitate if either appear on the menu.

Picnicking

For lovers such as you, the most romantic meal will undoubtedly be a picnic on one of the secluded beaches that line the coast from Carmel to Big Sur. Picnic etiquette is simple. All beaches have public access; be cautious that incoming tides don't strand you on some tenuous sandy promontory; and take all your garbage with you for disposal back at your hotel. Many stores and delis in Carmel and Monterey specialize in picnic provisioning.

WINE-TASTING ROMANTIC INTERLUDES: Although Monterey County is one of the finest up-and-coming wine-growing regions in California, viniculture in the region has a long tradition. Over 200 years ago, Franciscan friars planted the first **vineyards** in California near Monterey. Thanks to the rich soil and sun-kissed climate, about 35,000 acres of vineyards flourish in the county. Among the properties open to visitors: **Almadén** in San Jose (tel. 448-9225); **Jekel Vineyards** in Greenfield (tel. 674-5522); **J. Lohr Winery** in San Jose (tel. 288-5057); and **Château Julian** in Carmel Valley (tel. 624-2600). Call for hours and appointments.

MONTEREY: In 1602, Spanish explorer Sebastían Vizcaíno discovered this broad, curving harbor. Because of its excellent anchorages and fine weather, Monterey served as the capital of Alta California—first for the Spanish, then for the Mexicans. It was not replaced as the number one city until a little shanty town up north—then named Yerba Buena, now called San Francisco—struck it rich during the Gold Rush. Reflecting the region's dependence on the sea, the town first served as port for trading schooners unloading their wares after a perilous journey around Cape Horn. Between the wars, Monterey ruled as the sardine-packing capital of the world, an era immortalized in John Steinbeck's novel, *Cannery Row*. Today Monterey continues to be a zesty blend of the old and the new.

Shopping

Monterey's Cannery Row also has an excellent selection of shops. **Trade Winds** (700 Cannery Row) is known for its "treasures from the sea," such as shell jewelry and vases, bowls and plates inlaid with abalone, and framed posters and prints of peninsula scenes. **The Monterey Bay Company** (711 Cannery Row) displays arts and crafts from all over the world, and **Winborne Kites** (585 Cannery Row) carries over 600 rainbow-hued kites and wind socks.

Romantic Interludes

Get a feel for Monterey's Spanish colonial past along the **Path of History,** a three-mile, self-guided walking tour. The marked route takes you past 45 beautifully preserved, 18th- and 19th-century white-washed adobe structures with red tile roofs and graceful black wrought-iron balconies. The historic houses that are open to the public include Larkin House (510 Calle Principal), built in the 1830s and considered one of the finest examples of Monterey colonial-style architecture; the Custom House (near Fisherman's Wharf), which was constructed in 1827 and now contains a museum of early California history; and Colton Hall and the Old Jail (Pacific between Madison and Jefferson), where California's first constitution was written in 1849. Also stop by Stevenson House (530 Houston St.), a former hotel where Robert Louis Stevenson lived. Most are open daily from 10 a.m. to 4 p.m.

From the 1920s to about 1946, Monterey was the sardine capital of the Western Hemisphere, with 16 canneries packing over 240,000 tons of sardines annually. The period is vividly recorded in John Steinbeck's novel *Cannery Row,* which depicts the raucous lives of the factory workers, fishermen, and hustlers. For reasons that are not completely understood, the sardines disappeared from area waters in 1948, and the old canneries went bankrupt. Today, the Row has been reborn—this time, as a fashionable stretch of restaurants and boutiques, where art galleries have replaced brothels, and pastel-painted bookstores occupy former bars where sailors once brawled. It's a fun spot for strolling and browsing, still filled with plenty of salty atmosphere.

Built, appropriately enough, around the old Hovden sardine cannery at the end of the row, the $40-million **Monterey Bay Aquarium** is the newest star on the peninsula and the largest aquarium in the United States. Most of all, it's a heck of a lot of fun, and the next best thing to being 20,000 leagues under the sea. Get eye-to-eye with bizarre denizens of the deep, such as wolf eels, giant sea stars, and the chambered nautilus, and meet strangely named creatures, such as the rubberlip sunperch and a striped "convictfish." The most impressive exhibit is unquestionably the three-story-tall kelp forest aquarium, where leopard sharks and schools of silvery sardines cruise. Then, find out what's more fun than a barrel of monkeys—which is a tank-full of playful sea otters. These aquatic clowns float on their backs and use small stones to whack open clams, which they hold on their tummies. Try to visit them at feeding time, 11 a.m., 2 p.m., and 4:30 p.m. daily.

The Monterey Bay Aquarium (tel. 375-3333) is open daily (except for Christmas Day) from 10 a.m. to 6 p.m.; admission is $7 per person. Tickets for weekends or holidays must be bought in advance through Ticketron; they are not available at the door. Advance purchases are also strongly recommended during the summer months. On weekends and holidays, parking is just as hard to come by as aquarium tickets, and the lots near Cannery Row fill up fast. Avoid the hassle by taking the free shuttle bus that runs between Monterey's Custom House parking garage (at the corner of Tyler and Del Monte), to the Aquarium. It also stops at Fisherman's Wharf and Cannery Row.

Monterey's **Fisherman's Wharf** area still throbs with nautical sound effects. Sea lions bark and beg for tidbits, halyards ping against sailboat masts, foghorns blast across the bay, gulls squeal and cry. The wharf itself has a good-times, carnival atmosphere, complete with an organ grinder and his monkey and souvenir shops where you can buy T-shirts or a starfish. From here, you can leave on a deep-sea fishing expedition, or go on a whale-watching cruise. Most fun of all—invest 50¢ and feed the sea lions that hang around the pilings. Each crafty old beggar has his own technique. Some emit a series of short, ear-piercing barks; others sound off in one long, mournful bellow.

Honeymoon Hotels and Hideaways

The Mariposa Inn, 1386 Munras Ave., Monterey, CA 93940 (tel. 408/649-1414), is a real charmer—modern, sophisticated, sensuous—a whole new, deluxe breed of motor inn. And the reasonable prices make it one of the best deals on the peninsula. The 51-unit lodge is built Spanish-style, surrounding a tranquil garden courtyard—where daisies, primroses, and dahlias bloom in abundance. The central location, high up on Carmel Hill, places the Mariposa conveniently near shopping, restaurants, and attractions. Someone who really cares about your comfort put this place together. Period pieces such as English-style highboys counterpoint the mostly modern furnishings. The color palette soothes—soft beiges, restful blues, and warm mauves. Most rooms have fireplaces. In the garden, there's a heated pool open April through December, and a hot tub open all year. Rates: deluxe queen-bedded rooms with fireplaces are $84 per couple; executive suites, with mirrored wet-bar, minifridge, sitting area, and fireplace: $100 per couple; honeymoon suites, complete with an ardently proportioned whirlpool spa surrounded by mirrors, a king-size bed, a double shower, a fireplace, and more: $143 per couple.

Casa Munras, 700 Munras Ave., Monterey, CA 93940 (tel. 408/375-2411 or toll free 800/222-2558). A large, heated swimming pool in the garden courtyard, brass beds topped off with comforters, and history dating back over 150 years—place Casa Munras at the head of the class for personable motels. The Casa occupies the original site of the hacienda belonging to Don Estebán Munras, last Spanish diplomat to California. Two-story adobe buildings with shingle roofs surround a colorful garden with fragrant roses and giant-size calla lilies. Accommodations reflect cheerful, contemporary good taste, and the rooms with king-size beds and fireplaces offer honeymooners exceptionally good value. The Casa is located near the "Path of History" and an easy five blocks' walk from Fisherman's Wharf. The Casa Cafe serves breakfast, lunch, and dinner daily, and locals congregate at the Happy Hour Oyster Bar for drinks and shellfish cocktails. Rates: poolside suites with living room, king-size brass beds, a corner fireplace, color TV, and large bathroom, $149 per couple; regular room with king-size brass bed, fireplace, and color TV, $120 per couple. (December through April, the Casa sometimes offers these at a special $99 rate. Ask!)

A sign in the lobby announces that the **Colton Inn,** 707 Pacific St., Monterey, CA 93940 (tel. 408/649-6500 or toll free 800/255-3050), is "the friendliest inn in town," and general manager Pamela Pinnix and her helpful staff work hard to live up to that reputation. This cozy motor lodge is located in downtown Monterey, right near the famous "Path of History," and the low adobe structure blends right in with the buildings where California history was made. The rooms are impeccably clean and comfortable, many with king-size beds and fireplaces. Rates: $60 per couple weekdays, $80 per couple weekends. But the real find is room no. 313, with a fireplace, king-size bed—and a private enclosed patio with a hot tub overlooking lush greenery and a rushing stream. It's the only one at the inn—and it goes for $137 a night.

Romantic Restaurants

Stained-glass windows, weathered cedar-board walls, fresh flowers, and mirrors weave a romantic mood at the **Whaling Station Inn,** 763 Wave St., Monterey (tel. 373-3778), right near Cannery Row. The staff is extremely congenial—the couple just ahead of us were greeted so royally, we thought they were regulars, but it turned out that this was the first time they had visited. The chef / owner, born in Monterey but of Sicilian descent, has a way with both the local veggies and the homemade pastas. Appetizers include linguine tossed with morels, grilled calamari, and fresh artichoke. You'll have a wide choice of entrée—veal piccata or marsala, sautéed prawns, even venison in season. Dinner for two, about $60 per couple plus drinks.

Set in an 1840s adobe house right on Monterey's Path of History, the **Old House,** 500 Hartnell St., Monterey (tel. 373-3737), is one of the peninsula's most beautiful restaurants, with the warm, elegant feel of a French country inn. You'll be served on fine Villeroy et Boch china, and drink California wine from crystal goblets. The menu highlights French recipes, prepared with fresh ingredients from Salinas and Carmel Valley, considered the "breadbasket" of California. Sample entrées include California abalone, Idaho trout, beef Wellington, and other specialties. Dinner for two, about $70 plus wine.

For seafood-by-the-bay, choose one of Monterey's Fisherman's Wharf establishments. **Domenico's** (tel. 372-3655) has been newly refurbished and has big glass windows overlooking the harbor. Fresh fish entrées range from $11 to $20. The two-level **Wharfside Restaurant and Lounge** (tel. 375-3956) also has terrific views. They specialize in pasta and seafood specialties such as bouillabaisse ($15.50) or homemade shrimp ravioli ($13.25), plus landlubber treats such as New York–cut steak ($16.50).

PACIFIC GROVE: This town is one of the best-kept secrets on the Monterey Peninsula. Many visitors come to the area frequently—sometimes even for years—without following Lighthouse Avenue beyond the hustle and bustle of Cannery Row to this peaceful community at the northernmost point of the peninsula.

The area is probably best known as "Butterfly Town, U.S.A." because of the millions of monarch butterflies that winter here each year—some from places as distant as Alaska and Mexico. Since butterflies are rather finicky creatures who only like certain trees, many of them congregate in the cypress and eucalyptus branches in George Washington Park. You can look, but don't touch—the butterflies are strictly protected by law.

At the turn of the century, Pacific Grove prospered as a Methodist summer community. Because of the strong religious beliefs that governed the town, many strict laws stayed on the books for a long time. Until the 1930s, everybody—including married couples—was required to sleep with the window shades up. Liquor could only be bought with a prescription, until a referendum ended Pacific Grove's dubious distinction of being California's last dry town in 1969. Today, Pacific Grove has attracted many young adults, drawn by the friendly, hometown feeling and reasonably priced real estate.

What remains from Pacific Grove's past are many fine Victorian buildings, graced by gables, turrets, and leaded-glass windows. Several houses have been restored as bed-and-breakfast inns, enabling honeymooners to dwell in the charm of another era.

Honeymoon Hotels and Hideaways

A good choice for honeymooners who crave seclusion and privacy, Pacific Grove also gives easy access to the main tourist sights.

Seven Gables Inn, 555 Ocean View Blvd., Pacific Grove, CA 93950 (tel. 408/372-4341). This is it—our vote for the most romantic bed-and-breakfast inn on the Monterey Peninsula. The house, a multigabled 1886 showplace, commands unobstructed views of Monterey Bay and Lover's Point. Inside, you'll see a world of frothy Victorian fantasy—Oriental carpets, lace doilies, stained glass, fringed lampshades, crystal chandeliers, canopy beds, armoires, bombé chests, knickknacks, needlepoint pillows, gilded wall sconces—all assembled with love by the Flatley family, innkeepers on the peninsula since 1958. Many of the pieces are museum quality, including a real Tiffany window. There are 14 rooms, each one unique. The Cypress Room, for example, has a sitting area in the bay window, from which you enjoy a 180° view of Monterey Bay. The Lover's Point Room, overlooking the promontory, features a canopied bed and marble-topped sink. All rooms offer ocean views and spiffy, modern, private bathrooms; fabrics, towels, and wallcoverings are plushly new. No smoking.

At breakfast time, no one goes away hungry from the ample continental spread of fresh-squeezed orange juice, fresh fruit, and hot-from-the-oven croissants and muffins. At 4:00 p.m., high tea is served, and Mrs. Flatley tempts all young lovers with her homemade fudge, cookies, and cakes. Rates: Prices range from $121 to $138 per night, depending on the size of the room. Since each room is so different, you should call the Flatleys to discuss the various layouts, and choose the one that best fulfills your honeymoon daydreams.

The Green Gables Inn, 104 Fifth St., Pacific Grove, CA 93950 (tel. 408/375-2095; toll free 800/841-5252). As you walk in the door, you'll hear strains of classical music and smell the warm, sweet aroma of baking bread. Teddy bears cavort in armchairs, a fire blazes in the hearth, and sunlight streams through the stained-glass window. Immediately, you'll fall under the spell of this half-timbered, step-gabled, 100-year-old house set on the edge of the Pacific. The guest accommodations include five rooms and a suite in the main house, and five bedrooms in the adjacent carriage house. The rooms in the main house offer the most atmosphere, with period details such as mirrored commodes, claw-foot bath tubs, wrought-iron bedsteads, and four-poster beds. However, not all of them have fireplaces, and most share a bathroom. The Carriage House rooms offer more privacy. Each has a fireplace, a color TV, and a private bath; although they too are furnished with traditional English-style pieces, the feeling is more modern. In the morning, breakfast is served in the dining room overlooking Monterey Bay; in the afternoon, guests gather in the parlor for afternoon tea, sherry, and wine, accompanied by hors d'oeuvres and music from the player piano. Rates: Main house rooms range from $121 for the Gable Room with queen-size bed, ocean view, and shared bath to $154 for the Lacey Suite with queen-size bed, sitting room with fireplace, and private bath with antique tub. Carriage House rooms are all $138.

"So romantic—you're going to love it." "A real winner." These are just some of the rave reviews recorded in the **Gosby House Inn,** 643 Lighthouse Ave., Pacific Grove, CA 93950 (tel. 408/375-1287; toll free 800/342-4888), guest book. Located in the heart of downtown Pacific Grove, this Victorian structure was built in 1887 and has been operating as a hotel since 1894. It has been placed on the National Historic Register, and is operated by the same group that runs Green Gables Inn.

In the front parlor, English- and French-style period furnishings surround the fireplace. A glass cabinet displays a fine collection of antique dolls. More contemporary Teddy bears pose here and there—on mantelpieces, Queen Anne armchairs, bannisters. Rooms reflect the intimacy of European country inns: polished natural woods, wrought-iron headboards, fluffy comforters, mirrored armoires, and delicate floral wallpapers. Fine details abound—even the tissue caddy is edged in lace. Each room is different: some share baths, some have fireplaces. The room price includes a hearty breakfast buffet (with granola, muffins, eggs or quiche, fresh fruits and juices), plus afternoon tea. Rates: For a room with a queen-size bed, from $105 to $127, depending on view, availability of a private bath, and fireplace.

When the **Centrella,** 612 Central Ave., P.O. Box 51157, Pacific Grove, CA 93950 (tel. 408/372-3372), opened in 1889, the local newspaper hailed it as the "largest, most commodious, and pleasantly located private boarding house in 'The Grove.'" That description remains true today. Completely restored, the Centrella enthralls honeymooners with its hand-rubbed oak and maple furnishings, beveled glass windows, and wainscotted hallways. It is listed on the National Register of Historic Places. The inn is very centrally located—just one block from town, only two blocks from the beach. Period decor sets the mood in the bedrooms—wrought-iron headboards, wicker sofas and chairs, floral chintz bedspreads with ruffled pillows, lace curtains. The rooms are a bit small, but there's a good reason—after the recent million-dollar renovation, practically everyone has a private bath. Several rooms have king-size beds—reserve these in advance. Also request a room facing the garden, with giant ferns, creamy white calla lilies, colorful impatiens, and a huge monkey tree holding court in garden center. Which brings us to the garden cottages, each entered by its own wooden gate. The two-room cottages provide a veritable home away from home, with overstuffed sofas, wicker tables, a fireplace, and a TV in the sitting room, and a wrought-iron bed and antique furnishings in the bedroom. Rates: Double rooms with private bath, $107 per couple. Cottages for two, $165. Prices include breakfast and evening social hour with wine and hors d'oeuvres.

A Romantic Restaurant

Old Bath House, 620 Ocean View Blvd., Pacific Grove (tel. 375-5195). Appropriately enough for honeymooners, this shingled building with a tall turret is located near Lover's Point in Pacific Grove. The interior is warm, cozy, and inviting, with rich wood paneling, etched glass, and an antique Victorian bar where you'll certainly want to sip a cocktail before dinner. For an appetizer, start with some pasta—perhaps linguine in a zesty red clam sauce ($7.15) or pasta primavera with fresh vegetables and cream ($6.60). As your entrée, choose from a medley of veal dishes, such as saltimbocca à la Romana, topped with prosciutto and mozzarella ($19.80) or roast rack of lamb ($20.90).

PEBBLE BEACH: In this private community that skirts the western edge of the peninsula, blue-blood cars (Jaguars, Porsches, and every conceivable model of Mercedes-Benz) crowd the parking lot at the local post office, and million-dollar price tags are not uncommon on the mansions that stand behind formidable wrought-iron gates. The area, which is also known as the Del Monte Forest, encompasses over 5,300 acres, including that spectacular stretch of scenery known as the 17-mile drive.

Romantic Interludes

Schedule several hours for this leisurely ride, and bring along your camera to record some truly memorable scenic images.

Called "the slowest way between Carmel and Monterey," the two-lane **17-Mile Drive** meanders its way along the western coast of Monterey Peninsula. It is part of the privately owned Pebble Beach / Del Monte Forest property. The route follows the former trails along which horsedrawn carriages brought vacationers to the original Del Monte Hotel in Monterey. Watch the antics of gulls and cormorants, seals and sea lions off Seal and Bird rocks (the beach area has tables and benches perfect for a picnic lunch). From the Cypress Point Lookout, you can often see over 20 miles down the California coast, all the way to the Point Sur Lighthouse. Finally, there's the Lone Cypress, the symbol of the Monterey Peninsula, which stands grandly on nearly barren rock facing the sea. Along the route, the road winds past the emerald-green Pebble Beach Golf Links and palatial mansions surrounded by cypress, oaks, and sycamores.

There are four entrances to 17-Mile Drive: at Highway 1, Carmel, Pacific Grove, and the country club. The road is privately owned; a $5 entrance fee per car helps maintain the route as well as the open spaces.

Honeymoon Hotels and Hideaways

Honeymooners who love the sporting life should choose exclusive Pebble Beach, where world-class golf, tennis, and equestrian facilities lie right outside your doorstep.

After nearly 70 years, **The Lodge at Pebble Beach,** 17-Mile Drive, Pebble Beach, CA 93953 (tel. 408/624-3811), still reigns as the grand resort of the Monterey Peninsula. The Lodge occupies a choice site on the brink of the Pacific Ocean within the private 5,328-acre Del Monte Forest, overlooking the Pebble Beach Golf Links, Carmel Bay, and the Santa Lucia Mountains.

From the moment a liveried attendant swings open the heavy wooden door in the columned entryway, you'll enter a world of Old World gentility and graciousness. Old World spaciousness, too, for the Lodge dates from a time when ample proportions were the rule, rather than the exception. Six-foot-tall hearths, full-grown ficus trees, and overstuffed sofas grace the Terrace Lounge—all practically dwarfed by the 20-foot-high ceilings. Guest accommodations occupy low, two-story buildings, all nicely spread out (there are only 161 rooms, 140 of which have working fireplaces). Each room is different—most have balconies, some also have ocean views. Even the decor varies. King-size bedded accommodations in the Portola Building have contemporary panache: track lighting, a mirrored wall to reflect the views of the 18th green and fairway, a huge bathroom with a marble sink, and splashes of brilliant color—turquoise and salmon. In the Vizcaino building, the furnishings are updated French country style, accented by such luxuries as a marble bathroom. Also, ask about the new luxury Inn at Spanish Bay resort, set in the sand dunes and pines at the northern edge of Pebble Beach. It's slated to open in late 1987.

Sports lovers will be in jock heaven. Golfers can tee off on their choice of three Pebble Beach courses, where they enjoy reduced greens fees. During their stay, guests have membership privileges at the Beach and Tennis Club, with its 14 courts and heated swimming pool. At the Pebble Beach Stables, horseback riders can mount up and explore the 34 miles of bridle paths that wind through every corner of the Del Monte Forest. Pebble Beach is also known for its full calendar of special events. One favorite: the August Concours d'Elegance vintage car show. The active life helps work up an appetite, and the Lodge has four fine restaurants to choose from, including the elegant Cypress Room for breakfast, lunch, and dinner (see description that follows). Rates: king-bedded rooms, from $192.50 to $330 per couple per night, depending on view and amenities, such as fireplaces.

A Romantic Restaurant

The Cypress Room, The Lodge at Pebble Beach, 17-Mile Drive (tel. 624-3811). Overlooking the 18th green, Carmel Bay, and the silhouette of Point Lobos in the distance, this elegant restaurant provides the perfect setting for the exquisite beauty of the Monterey Peninsula at breakfast, lunch, and dinner. A pianist plays softly on the baby grand piano, tall potted palms add an aura of Old World grandeur, and a color scheme culled from Nature's palette—sea-foam greens and sunset mauves—enhance the landscape views. The inventive menu highlights the best of American regional cuisine: a rare breast of pheasant, or homemade ravioli stuffed with crab meat. In season, dinner appetizers might include Pacific oysters on the half shell ($7.70) or a cream of artichoke soup ($3.60). As an entrée, try the seafood brochette with garlic butter ($12.10) or the New York steak with Zinfandel sauce ($13.20)—all excellent.

CARMEL-BY-THE-SEA: Why is this seaside town, less than a square mile in size, known throughout the world? When actor Clint Eastwood was elected Carmel's mayor in 1986, it didn't increase the town's celebrity, but seemed more like a logical consequence of it.

Perhaps Carmel is best explained by enumerating what it doesn't have. No buildings more than two stories tall. No neon signs. No courthouse or jail. Few sidewalks and even fewer street lamps. Instead of street numbers, houses are identified by location (such as "on Monte Verde, between Seventh and Eighth), or evocative names, such as "The Grey Whale" or "Sea Spirit." Residences range from tiny dollhouse-like cottages covered with climbing roses to ultramodern, wood-and-glass showplaces on the oceanfront Scenic Road. Trees are protected by a special 1916 ordinance that created an extensive urban forest that now requires the ministrations of a city forester and several full-time employees. (A local cartoon depicts a burning house, and the frantic owner screaming, "Never mind the house—save the trees!")

The word "Carmel" means "at rest," and true to its name, the village offers enchanted ways to do nothing at all. Linger on Carmel Beach, a long, pure-white crescent of sand that draws you to lounge, stroll, or sunbathe. The surf is always high; sandpipers on spindly legs always play a mad game of tag with the breaking waves. Sunsets are crimson wonders, with vistas stretching from Point Lobos to Pebble Beach.

Shopping

Despite the popularity of tennis, golf, horseback riding and the like, Carmel's number one sport is, unquestionably, shopping. (A local poster jokes: "Carmel. Population, 4,102. Gift shops, 17,210.") While not really in the thousands, the actual count of shops, galleries, and boutiques numbers about 100. The most amazing thing about this mercantile abundance is that none of the shops carries schlock—all the goods are absolutely first-rate. Most of the shops are clustered along Ocean Avenue and the neighboring cross streets from San Carlos to Casa Nova. Here are some establishments you might want to check out.

Carmel Bay Company (Ocean at Lincoln) offers great stuff for your new home: blue glass dishes from Mexico (plates are $8 each), ceramic pitchers for $13.75, heavy green wine glasses from Spain ($8), as well as posters, tote bags, and garden supplies. **Laub's Country Store** or the **Varsity Shop** (both on Ocean at San Carlos) are the places to pick up classy Carmel T-shirts. **Amourette** (Dolores, off Ocean) carries some of the nicest naughty lingerie you can imagine. **Handworks** (Dolores, off Ocean) carries exquisite crafts items: handwoven scarfs for $45; ceramic clocks decorated with bunnies or teddy bears, $50; turquoise or mother-of-pearl letter knives, $25; and original prints from $125. **Ladyfingers** (Dolores, off Ocean), offers one-of-a-kind jewelry, with many pieces designed by local artists, including some stunning rings using gold and semiprecious stones. Also beautiful sparkly earrings, with "moon and the stars" and other motifs, from $50 to $450. **Great Things Antiques** features top-of-the-line heirlooms, from major pieces such as English sideboards or a dining room table big enough to seat 18, to candlesticks, sherry decanters, and biscuit tins (the latter items in the $65 to $100 price range). They have two locations: on Lincoln, off Ocean; and on Ocean and Monte Verde. **The Village Straw Shop** (Lincoln, off Ocean) displays straw goods from as far away as Botswana and Sri Lanka, priced from $5 to $50.

Romantic Interludes

Here are two special places, one evokes the spirit of old California and the other the natural beauty of its spectacular shoreline.

Step back in time at the **Basilica of Mission San Carlos Borromeo del Rio Carmelo**—best known simply as the Carmel Mission. Footsteps echo down the Mexican tile aisles, water splashes in the garden fountain—sounds unchanged for over 200 years. The mission is closely associated with Padre Junipero Serra, the Franciscan friar who nurtured the establishment of 21 different California missions. From the time of its founding on June 3, 1770, Carmel served as Father Serra's headquarters. He is buried at the foot of the church altar. The Carmel Mission is one of only two basilicas in the entire western United States; it is possible that the church will soon elect Father Serra to sainthood.

Despite its celebrity, Carmel Mission is a simple place. Hand-lettered signs identify the various exhibits that trace the mission's history. Stop by the gift shop to see if they have any of the folk art from La Palma, El Salvador, in stock. The town craftspeople create brightly painted wooden ornaments that would look just right on your Christmas tree. Carmel Mission is open weekdays from 9:30 a.m. until 4:30 p.m.; Sundays from 10:30 a.m. until 4:30 p.m. Suggested donation is $1.

Just south of Carmel Bay is the spot that Robert Louis Stevenson praised as "the most beautiful meeting of land and sea on earth"—**Point Lobos.** In this 1,276-acre preserve, you can hike past stands of cypress twisted by the ocean winds, stand atop jagged cliffs, stroll along hidden coves and lagoons. Just offshore, sea lions and spotted harbor seals bark a noisy welcome from their rocky perches. From mid-December through mid-April, you can often watch gray whales migrating to their spawning waters off Baja California. The reserve makes a wonderful place for a picnic, especially in the white sand beaches at Whaler's Cove and Weston Beach. Open daily from 9 a.m. to 5 p.m. There's an entrance fee of $2 if you come by car; no admission if you walk or bike in. At the entrance, you can pick up a map of the reserve.

Honeymoon Hotels and Hideaways

Highlands Inn, P.O. Box 1700, Highway 1 South, Carmel, CA 93921 (tel. 408/624-3801; reservations: toll free 800/538-9525 nationwide; 800/682-4811 in California), is that very rare entity—the perfect hotel in the perfect place. Carmel Highlands, just a stone's throw from Carmel proper, is one of the most beautiful spots on earth, a place where wind-bowed Monterey cypress, rocky cliffs, and Pacific surf come together in a boisterous celebration of land and sea. Highlands Inn's two-storied, cedar-shingled villas harmonize with this setting, conveying the feel of an ultrasophisticated mountain lodge. Done up in tones of teal blue, mauve, and beige, the rooms are accented with light, natural oak trim and beams that bring a little bit of the outdoors inside. Furnishings are high-tech, without being hard-edged. Two cushions are positioned invitingly by the fireplace, a comfortable, well-lit couch makes you want to curl up for a good read . . . or a good backrub. Two thick terry-cloth bathrobes hang in the closet—typical of the thoughtful amenities you'll find here. In the morning, you'll wake up to the sound of the surf, with sunshine streaming through the pine trees. Perhaps order breakfast from room service, served on your own private balcony.

The Inn's lobby and lounge areas occupy the golden granite building that was the original lodge, which has been lightened by natural woods and brightened with skylights and picture windows to take advantage of the panoramic views. What remains from the original, however, are the ample proportions and the two massive stone fireplaces at each end of the lounge. No wonder Highlands Inn attracts so many honeymooners—the most famous newlywed guests being Sean Penn and Madonna. Many couples also choose to be married at the Inn's rose-covered gazebo, overlooking cypress trees, pines, and the endless Pacific Ocean. Superb bar and restaurant—see details which follow. Rates: Rooms are from $132 per couple per night. One-bedroom spa suites with whirlpools are $250 to $275 per couple. From December through April, Highlands Inn offers midweek "Hideaway Days," with spa suites reduced to just $130 per night, Sundays through Thursdays. Call for details.

Tickle Pink, 155 Highlands Dr., Carmel Highlands, CA 93923 (tel. 408/624-1244). Take a superb location on a bluff overlooking Point Lobos. Add oceanview decks for sunbathing, spacious accommodations for lounging, and flowers blooming from window boxes and planters. Color it all pink—and you've got this sweetheart of a retreat for honeymooners. Located at the start of the Coast Highway drive to Big Sur, just four miles from Carmel-by-the-Sea, and right next door to Highlands Inn, Tickle Pink is the most captivating motor lodge you can imagine. Because the inn is family-owned, service is very personal and personable. There's a high-powered telescope set up in the office, for example, so guests can do some whale watching. All rooms boast large picture windows and private balconies facing the ocean. Furnishings are modern and comfortable and most will be newly refurbished by 1988. Fabrics employ soft pastel colors, patterned into shell or floral motifs. The black-and-white-tiled bathrooms have an Art Deco look, and the room rates offer you the most view for the money on the peninsula. Rates: king-size bed, $124 per couple; fireplace rooms, $153 per couple; one-bedroom suites, $211 per couple. All rooms have minirefrigerators and color TVs; rates include complimentary continental breakfast and the morning newspaper.

La Playa Hotel, Camino Real at 8th, Carmel-by-the-Sea, CA 93921 (tel. 408/624-6476), is the only full-service resort hotel in the center of Carmel. Set in a quiet residential area just two blocks from the beach and four blocks from the downtown shops and galleries, this dazzling, Mediterranean-style resort would look right at home on the French Riviera or Italy's Amalfi coast. The villa blossomed from a mansion built in 1904 by a Carmel artist. In 1984, it was completely restored and refurbished, from brick patio to red-tiled roof. The lobby creates a regal first impression, with Mexican tile floors, antiques, hand-loomed area rugs, and white marble fireplace flanked by two statues (which come from Hearst Castle). Built into the gentle hillside, landscaped terraces descend, palazzo-style, to the heated pool in the center of the garden courtyard.

In keeping with the architecture, the 75 rooms contain Mediterranean-style furnishings (curlicued chairs, low chests, marble-topped side tables), with many wood pieces specially hand-carved with La Playa's mermaid logo. Bathrooms compensate for their smallish proportions with pampering amenities—soaps, shampoos, and lotion from Neutrogena, and a hair dryer. You have your choice of outlooks—ocean, gardens, patio, or the neighboring private houses—there isn't really a bad view. All rooms have color TVs and minirefrigerators. If you want to splurge, consider La Playa's two suites. The Executive Suite stars a huge black marble fireplace in the living room, a 100-of-your-most-intimate-friends-size patio with views stretching all the way to Pebble Beach, and a whirlpool tub (the apartment was designed as a private apartment for the former owners). The Penthouse boasts even more expansive ocean views and opulent features such as a marble bathroom and gilt mirrors. La Playa is known for friendly, personalized service, and the concierge in the lobby can help you with golf, tennis, or dining arrangements. La Playa's own Spyglass restaurant is also excellent. Rates: double rooms, $99 to $154 per couple, depending on view; suites, $198 to $203 per couple.

The Stonehouse Inn, 8th below Monte Verde, P.O. Box 2517, Carmel-by-the-Sea, CA 93921 (tel. 408/624-4569). Step into another era, when young bohemian writers such as Sinclair Lewis and Jack London would gather at this unique country house built from stones hand-shaped by local Indians. Josephine "Nana" Foster, the original owner, often invited notable artists living in the San Francisco Bay Area to stay in her Carmel residence. Today, the house has been exquisitely restored to turn-of-the-century elegance, with antiques, comfy quilts, and silk flowers. The six bedrooms, each different, are named after some of Nana Foster's most celebrated guests. The Jack London room, all done up in moss greens and dusty roses, features gabled ceilings and a splendid ocean view, for $110 per couple. (We wonder a bit about what the author of *The Call of the Wild* and *The Sea Wolf* would think about the lodger who recorded in the guestbook, "The Jack London room is cool!") The tranquil Lola Montez room offers a four-poster bed, gabled ceiling, and garden view, for $88 per couple. All rooms share baths. Breakfast is a hearty affair, with hot entrées such as quiche or soufflés, homemade bread, fresh-ground coffee, and seasonal fruits served up in the sunny, greenhouse-like breakfast room. In the afternoon, guests gather around the large stone hearth for wine, sherry, and hors d'oeuvres. (Ask the manager to show you the secret safe built into the fireplace.) The sun porch entices you to curl up with a good book, or you can wander through the charming garden with stone pathways and a white minigazebo. Just two blocks from the center of Carmel. Rates: $88 to $116 per couple. No smoking is permitted.

The Green Lantern, 7th and Casanova, P.O. Box 1114, Carmel-by-the-Sea, CA 93921 (tel. 408/624-4392). White-painted cottages with peaked roofs, dormer windows, and zigzagging stairways. Stone patios among the flower beds. Splashing fountains and antique furnishings. Such is the stuff honeymoon dreams are made of—and made to come true, at the captivating Green Lantern Inn. Set in a quiet residential neighborhood just a block from town, the bed-and-breakfast inn has welcomed guests since 1915. Although each of the 19 rooms is unique, all have private bath and color cable TV, and are decked out with fresh flowers. In keeping with the bosky atmosphere, each of the rooms is named after a tree. Spruce, for example, is done up in Dresden blue, with a white eyelet canopy over the bed, English-style furnishings, and an ocean view through the trees. Redwood has a cozy fireplace and a big brass bed in the loft bedroom. Breakfast consists of croissants, muffins, and fresh fruits, and in the afternoon guests can sip a glass of sherry in front of the fireplace in the wood-paneled common room. Rates: $71 to $137 per couple, depending on size, view, and availability of fireplace.

Located in the heart of Carmel just a few steps from Ocean Avenue, the **Sundial Lodge,** Monte Verde at Seventh Street, P.O. Box J, Carmel-by-the-Sea, CA 93921 (tel. 408/624-8578), has a charming brick courtyard bright with petunias, cyclamen, daisies, and primroses. Rooms are all different. From some, you can glimpse the Pacific glimmering through the treetops. Several units feature full kitchens. Decor might be country French or English drawing room, you might find brass bedsteads or wicker headboards. Plump quilts, ruffled pillows, and floral-patterned wallpapers add to the ambience. All accommodations have color TVs and private bathrooms (some have showers but no tubs). The continental breakfast includes homemade rolls, and afternoon tea or sherry warms the spirit. Rates: $77 to $99 per couple.

Although the **Sandpiper Inn,** 2408 Bayview at Martin Way, Carmel-by-the-Sea, CA 93923 (tel. 408/624-6433), sits a scant 50 yards from Carmel Beach, you'll feel more like you're a guest in a country house in the Scottish Highlands, because the owner-hosts are Scottish-born Graeme and Irene Mackenzie. The greeting "ceud mile failte"—"a hundred thousand welcomes"—hangs over the parlor door, and that accurately describes the warm atmosphere. Decor is homey, not high fashion, but that's exactly what charms the guests, many of whom are repeat visitors. Quilted floral bedspreads and authentic antiques grace the 13 rooms in the main house and the two private cottages. The inn is quiet and secluded, and there are no room telephones or television—on purpose. At night, you can fall asleep to the sound of the surf crashing against Carmel Point. Rates: oceanview or fireplace rooms, from $94. Corner rooms with king-size beds, from $116. Includes continental breakfast and afternoon sherry.

As its name implies, the **Colonial Terrace Inn,** San Antonio Avenue between 12th and 13th Avenues, P.O. Box 1375, Carmel-by-the-Sea, CA 93921 (tel. 408/624-2741), is a little bit of New England transplanted to the Pacific. White clapboard cottages with green shutters and shingled roofs front a secluded street lined with towering cypress trees. It's just a few steps from Carmel Beach. You'll want to kick off your shoes and relax in front of the big fireplace in the lounge, an inviting room with brick walls, English-style sideboard, needlepoint pillows, and resident cat lolling in an armchair. (The complimentary continental breakfast is served here in the morning.) Outside, brick walkways through the flower-filled gardens lead to the cottages. Each room has its own warm personality, accented by colonial-style furniture, white quilted bedspreads, and wooden headboards. Some have kitchens, fireplaces, or views of the Pacific sparkling through the trees. Rates: Room with queen-size bed, from $61 per couple; suites, from $105.

Romantic Restaurants

You are indeed at the very edge of the Pacific, at **Pacific's Edge,** Highland Inn, Carmel Highlands (tel. 624-3801), with the ocean dramatically framed by towering Monterey cypress that are spotlit at night. Through the floor-to-ceiling glass windows, you see it all—the gnarled trees, tempestuous surf, gyring gulls. And, thanks to the two-tiered seating levels, every table enjoys a panoramic view. The excellent food matches the splendid setting. Under the direction of food and beverage manager David Fink, the menu takes advantage of the seasonal bounty of the Monterey Peninsula: tender young lettuce from Watsonville, Castroville artichoke, Monterey salmon, local pheasant, duckling, and free-range chicken. Dishes are innovative, such as the basil-cured salmon with Maui onion marmalade, or veal chop with roasted shallots and fresh berries. The attentive waiters are knowledgeable about the wine list, which features the finest labels from Napa and Sonoma, as well as showcasing a different local Monterey County vintage each week. Dinner for two, about $80 plus drinks.

At happy hour time, mosey on over to **The Hog's Breath Inn** (Carmel, on San Carlos between Fifth and Sixth; tel. 625-1044)—owner Clint Eastwood sometimes drops by.

Picnic Suppliers

California Market at Highlands Inn (tel. 624-3801) sells upscale goodies such as prosciutto, pâté, brie, and chocolate mousse cake. They also turn out a mean roast beef sandwich. Or stop by Monterey's Fisherman's Wharf. Various stands and vendors sell Dungeness crab for $3.25 per pound, shrimp or crab walkaway cocktails for $1.75, or smoked salmon filets for $10 per pound.

Pick up dessert at one of the superb bakeries that line Carmel's Ocean Avenue. **Carmel Bakery** carries scones, breads shaped like crocodiles, and marzipan goodies.

L'Amandine appeals to chocoholics with éclairs and chocolate truffles. **Monterey Baking Company** features individual chocolate walnut tarts, almond-flavored jam drops with raspberry or apricot preserves, and wonderful breads baked fresh daily.

4. Big Sur

"Hill curves—next 74 miles" reads the yellow, diamond-shaped road sign as you drive south on Highway 1 past the Carmel River. Well, you can't say they didn't warn you. You are about to embark on the most incredibly scenic portion of the California coast drive—the stretch from Carmel to San Simeon, including the sinuous curves through Big Sur.

The area called Big Sur lies about 26 miles from Carmel—roughly a 45-minute drive. Here, Highway 1 sidewinds the coastal cliffs, looking exactly like it does in all those movies and car commercials; a two-lane ribbon of asphalt. Silver, spindly bridges that look like they were spun by drunken spiders. Nothing between you and yonder blue Pacific but a sheer, 1,000-foot drop. Yes, the drive is breathtakingly beautiful. It also can be undertaken by any good driver. And there are plenty of scenic overlooks so you can pull over to the side and admire the views. Often you can park your car at one of these turnoffs and hike down to the rocky beaches at water's edge.

Big Sur itself isn't only a place—it's a state of mind, a style of life, a tribute to the artistic spirit and imagination. Over the years, it has attracted writers, painters, and actors with impeccable avant-garde credentials, people such as Orson Welles, Henry Miller, Jack Kerouac, as well as miscellaneous blue-jean-clad hippies looking for a live-and-let-live environment where they could pursue an alternate lifestyle and groove on the sunsets. Civilization never has taken firm root here. The name of this vast region comes from the Spanish, who referred to the entire unmapped, unexplored region south of their settlement in Monterey as El Sur Grande. Electricity only arrived here in the early 1950s; power still does not reach into some mountainous recesses. You won't find anything that remotely resembles a town: the area's 1,200 or so residents drive up to the Monterey Peninsula when they need a new oil filter for the pickup, or some pâté for their pantry. The region offers contrasts: rocky coastline broken by smooth, white beaches . . . dense redwood forests and sun-baked ridges covered by bristly chaparral . . . hot springs and tide pools.

ROMANTIC INTERLUDES: In Big Sur, activity—like swimsuits in the hot tubs— is purely optional. Snooze all day on the sun deck or go off on a hike—it's up to you. However, if you do decide you want to actively explore, rather than just mellowing out and letting the experience come to you, you have several appealing options.

Vast areas of Big Sur have been set aside for public use. One of the best ways to appreciate the Ventana Wilderness Area and the Los Padres National Forest is along the hundreds of miles of hiking trails. You might encounter deer, raccoons, and opossum, as well as spot red-tail hawks, golden eagles, owls, and kingfishers soaring overhead. You must get a permit and should buy a trail map; both are available at the U.S. Forest Service Station about two miles north of Ventana Inn. A favorite both of locals and visitors, Pfeiffer Beach has jagged rock formations, tall sand dunes, and a lagoon. Although the water is too rough for swimming, this is a terrific beach for hanging out and strolling. Nearby, Pfeiffer Big Sur State Park has many easy hiking trails leading through the redwoods, as well as a river where you can swim. Garrapata Beach, another local favorite, has beautiful trails leading to the surf and hidden caves. Located at the mouth of the Big Sur River, Andrew Molera State Park has another fine stretch of beach (you have to wade across the river to get there). Partington Cove, about seven miles south of Big Sur, is the quintessential smuggler's cove, complete with a 200-foot tunnel that was officially used to ship tanbark—and unofficially used for. . . . ? Esalen Institute, the center of the human potential movement, is a private facility, but its natural hot springs are open to the public from 1 a.m. to 5 a.m. You can also make

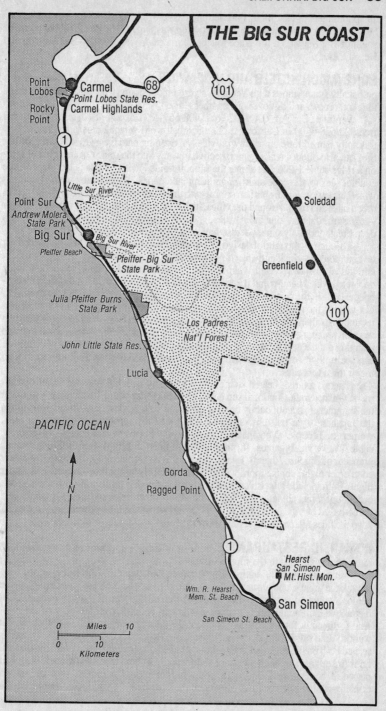

THE BIG SUR COAST

Point Lobos
Carmel
Point Lobos State Res.
Rocky Point
Carmel Highlands
68
101
Soledad
Little Sur River
Point Sur
Andrew Molera State Park
Big Sur
Big Sur River
Pfeiffer Beach
Pfeiffer-Big Sur State Park
Greenfield
Julia Pfeiffer Burns State Park
Los Padres Nat'l Forest
John Little State Res.
101
Lucia
PACIFIC OCEAN
N
Gorda
Ragged Point
1
Hearst San Simeon Mt. Hist. Mon.
Wm. R. Hearst Mem. St. Beach
San Simeon
San Simeon St. Beach
0   Miles   10
0   10
Kilometers

an appointment to visit for an outstanding massage (tel. 667-2335 for arrangements). Search for pieces of California jade that often wash up at Jade Beach, about 35 miles south of Big Sur (it's a fun place to stop if you're driving down to San Simeon and Hearst Castle).

HONEYMOON HOTELS AND HIDEAWAYS: The spectacular Big Sur region is practically synonymous with Ventana, a very unique country inn where couples come to relax, renew, and discover one another.

Ventana, Big Sur, CA 93920 (tel. 408/667-2331 or 624-4812; reservations: toll free 800/628-6500 in California). The Spanish word ventana means a window, and this aptly named retreat not only provides an opening onto the awesome vistas of Big Sur, but also offers a peaceful perspective inward, into the soul. Located on 240 acres on a ridge some 1,200 feet above the sapphire-blue Pacific, Ventana is a place where couples seek total escape amid magnificent landscapes. The two-story cedar buildings with their latticework fronts harmonize with the golden foothills dotted with thickets of green oaks and bays. Around the villas, lush flower beds add brilliant splashes of color —alyssum, daisies, zinnias, pansies, and row upon row of regal calla lilies. Take a deep breath: not only pine, but also bay laurel, sage, and wild basil perfume the air.

Through its thoughtful design, Ventana proves that rustic and luxurious need not be contradictory. Inside, the accommodations carry out the look of an elegant mountain lodge. One of the walls is built from rough-hewn cedar planks. Headboards are decorated with a hand-painted Pennsylvania Dutch–style motif; a handmade quilt covers the bed. In the corner, the wood-burning stove stands with logs already arranged, just waiting the touch of a match. Every room is different; some face the Santa Lucia mountains, others the Pacific. Each has a cozily secluded terrace or balcony where two wooden rocking chairs await, highly conducive to hand holding, sunset watching, and planning out the next 50 years of your life together. When you sit out here at night, you can see millions of stars glittering against the black velvet sky, because there's no major town for miles.

There's a large, heated swimming pool set up with lap lanes for serious swimmers. On the clothes-optional sun deck, you can bronze yourselves while overlooking the shimmering ocean, balmy breezes caressing your bodies. And, finally, unwind in the Japanese-style hot tubs or saunas, both tactfully separated into areas for men, women, and couples. Ventana has no (and never will have) tennis courts, golf courses, cable TV, or video games. It offers instead a quiet, reflective oasis set in the scenic grandeur of Big Sur. Rates (CP): standard room (no fireplace): $137.50 to $159.50 per couple per night; deluxe room with fireplace and private hot tub: $295 per couple per night. Both include a lavish continental breakfast with a medley of fresh fruits (kiwi, cantaloupes, pineapple, watermelon), bowls of strawberries and cream, granola, and home-baked banana bread and strudel, served warm and honey-sweet from the oven. Also includes afternoon wine and cheese.

ROMANTIC RESTAURANTS: Both of Big Sur's memorable restaurants take maximum advantage of the superb views.

Ventana, one mile south of Big Sur State Park (tel. 667-2331). If ever one were to rank the great scenic vistas of the world, the view from Ventana's restaurant would belong, without question, in the top ten. Poised on the edge of a summit about 1,000 feet above the Pacific, the restaurant panoramas embrace over 50 miles of seacoast. And fortunately for serious gastronomes, the cuisine soars as well. At lunch, you'll want to dine on the broad, wooden deck, looking south down the coast. Dinner is served both on the deck and in the high-ceilinged, skylit dining room with the unusual floor (made from six-inch blocks of solid wood). At both lunch and dinner, the menu pays full homage to California's bountiful harvests. For dinner, start off with a crunchy garden salad or fresh oysters on the half shell. As your main course, try the roast leg of lamb or grilled duck breast, accompanied by kiwi fruit, broccoli, cauliflower, Mexican corn, and a wild-rice pancake. Every day, the chef offers different fish specialties. For dessert, chocoholics will want to sample the chocolate mousse pie with pralines and just a hint of orange. Lunch, from $30 per couple; dinner, about $60 per couple plus drinks.

Nepenthe, three miles south of Big Sur State Park (tel. 667-2345). There's no place else on earth quite like it. Yuppies from San Francisco and L.A. sit next to hippies who dropped out during the 1960s—and decided never to come back. Red BMW's sporting "Life is a cabernet" license-plate holders park next to rusting VW beetles. Somehow, all the juxtapositions work, and Nepenthe ranks as one of the most popular ports of call on the California coast drive.

Nepenthe has always been unusual. The house was designed by Rowan Maiden, a student of Frank Lloyd Wright, using native materials—adobe and redwood. Lolly and Bill Fassett, the original owners, wanted the house to be an island of no care, and so chose the name Nepenthe, from the Greek word meaning "no sorrow." During the 1940s, Orson Welles and Rita Hayworth lived on the property for a time. During the 1950s, novelist Henry Miller dwelled on nearby Partington Ridge.

Both of Nepenthe's restaurants offer unsurpassed views of the Big Sur coastline and pine-covered mountains. Since the food is fine, but definitely secondary to the mood and the view, both are best recommended for brunch or lunch. The self-service Cafe Amphora, downstairs, has a huge sun deck where you can improve your pallor while munching bagel sandwiches with lox or turkey melt (from $7.65 to $8.70), or whole-grain sandwiches such as a turkey and avocado twosome for $7.65. They also concoct excellent fruit smoothies (with banana or strawberry) for $3.50. Nepenthe restaurant upstairs offers table service. It has both an outdoor deck and a small, enclosed dining area perfect for cooler weather. Lunch choices include soups, salads, burgers, and quiche (about $7 to $8).

When you can pry yourselves off the sun deck, check out Nepenthe's Phoenix boutique, a treasure trove of gifts and handicrafts.

5. San Simeon

At the southernmost reaches of the vast Big Sur region, on the top of a ridge named La Cuesta Encantata (the enchanted hill), stands a real-life castle that surpasses in richness all the citadels of our dreams—Hearst Castle.

Hearst Castle, east of Highway 1, San Simeon, CA 93452 (tel. 927-4621 for information only; see details about reservations at the end of this section). "Pleasure is worth what you can afford to pay for it," declared publishing magnate William Randolph Hearst. And at a time when a loaf of bread cost 4¢, and Hearst was earning some $50,000 a day, he spent $3 million to build what is truly a palace, combining Italian, Spanish, Moorish, and French architectural styles. The castle contains over 115 rooms, and could sleep over 80 people, both in the main house and mansion-like guest "cottages." Hearst heirs donated the castle to the state of California in 1958, and the Department of Parks and Recreation runs four different tours covering various parts of the property. For first-time visitors, the best tour is no. one, which includes a guest house, the esplanade and gardens, the ground floor of the castle (Casa Grande), the assembly room, the dining room, the theater, and the Roman-style pool. You'll be truly flabbergasted by what you see.

At one time, the Hearst family owned 40 miles of prime California seacoast, which they used as a cattle ranch. (About 90,000 acres still belong to the family.) The sprawling dimensions led houseguest W. C. Fields to remark, "You know, you could send your kids out to play, and they'd be grown up when they came back." Hearst started constructing the castle in 1919, and he devoted the better part of 30 years to building the estate and adding to its rich furnishings, spending about one million depression-era dollars a year on collecting art treasures from around the world. The effect is dazzling: the Neptune pool with its white and black marble design, and statuary carved from Carrera marble; the assembly room paneled with 500-year-old Italian choir stalls; intricate tapestries designed by Rubens; a 1710 wine bucket made from over 30 pounds of pure silver. In this opulent setting, at the height of his power, Hearst entertained luminaries from the worlds of politics (Jimmy Walker, Winston Churchill, and Calvin Coolidge); royalty (the duke and duchess of Windsor); and Hollywood (Carole Lombard, Cary Grant, Jean Harlow, and Charlie Chaplin).

Because of the tremendous popularity of Hearst Castle, it is absolutely essential that you purchase tickets in advance. Each of the four tours costs $8 per person. You can make telephone reservations seven days a week, from 9 a.m. to 6 p.m., by calling 452-1950 nationwide; toll free 800/446-PARK in California only. Reservations can be made up to eight weeks in advance; Visa and MasterCard are accepted.

HOTELS AND RESTAURANTS: The castle itself is a don't-miss sight, but the immediate area is not all that interesting. Unless you're a scion of the Hearst family and can stay at the castle, try to plan your route so that you will sleep elsewhere. In San Simeon itself, the only accommodations are roadside motels and small hotels; the new Holiday Inn is definitely the pick of the bunch. You will probably have to stop for a bite in the area. There is a completely dependable snack bar near the admission gates, as well as some equally predictable coffee shops in San Simeon. Better yet—pack your own picnic.

6. Santa Barbara

"God gave us the land, but the people made the city." Carved in Spanish over the entranceway to the courthouse, these words crystallize all that is special about Santa Barbara. The setting—a long, crescent-shaped indentation in the coastline, cupped in the embrace of the Santa Ynez mountains—equals that of any village on the Amalfi coast or the Côte d'Azur. The city of Santa Barbara, happily, is in keeping with its spectacular setting, a town of white adobe houses with red-tile roofs, all of which rise and fall over the curves of the foothills.

Located 335 miles south of San Francisco and 90 miles north of Los Angeles, Santa Barbara lies at the heart of Southern California. With its red-tile roofs, terrazzo walkways, and long, beachside boulevard lined with palm trees, Santa Barbara looks like a sleepy Spanish mission town. But in its own conservative way, it resembles Los Angeles, New York, and London. This is a major power center: The area has always appealed to captains of industry such as the Armours and the Firestones, as well as to weekend escapists from the Hollywood movie mills, such as John Travolta, Robert Mitchum, Michael Douglas, and Bo Derek. But recently, when a local boy named Ronald Reagan made good, Santa Barbara became the site of the White House West, and Cabinet officials, reporters, and Secret Service people became ubiquitous sights in the city's restaurants and shops. An interesting contrast: Although Santa Barbara shares Southern California's outdoor lifestyle—sailing, fishing, surfing, horseback riding—it has always nurtured the mind. The University of California has a campus here. The year-round roster of cultural attractions includes the Santa Barbara Ballet, live theater, rows and rows of art galleries, lectures and special events at the university, the Symphony Orchestra, and the Brooks Institute photography exhibits, to name just a few. Every sunny Sunday (and most of them are), there's the Santa Barbara Arts and Crafts Show, held under the fronds of Palm Park. Throughout the year, various events and festivals are scheduled: polo matches, the Summer Solstice Parade, whale-watching trips, film festivals, chili cook-offs, the Semana Nautica land and sea sporting event. . . . The list just goes on.

The city was named by the Spanish explorer Sebastian Viscaino, who sailed into the broad harbor on December 4, 1603—the feast of Santa Barbara. By 1786, it had become a major Spanish stronghold, with soldiers stationed at El Presidio; the gracious

Mission Santa Barbara overlooked everything from its hillside perch. Much of the city remains beautifully preserved, including several fine old adobes, made from the local clay. To best appreciate Santa Barbara's fine architecture, follow the marked, 90-minute "Red Tile Tour" that leads past some of the most historic sites: the "Historic Adobe" was the headquarters of Colonel John C. Fremont after he captured the city from the Mexicans in 1846; and La Caneda Adobe and El Cuartel, part of the original Spanish fortifications at El Presidio. To get the best view of Santa Barbara and its yacht harbor, head out to the end of Stearns Wharf, the oldest operating wharf on the west coast.

As you stroll through Santa Barbara or loll on its 30 miles of unspoiled beaches, you might notice an interesting phenomenon. Somehow, the sunshine always seems, well, sunnier here than elsewhere along the California coast. A friend finally explained why. Santa Barbara has the only beach that faces due south, allowing full frontal sunbathing all day. I still prefer my original explanation. Sheer magic.

SHOPPING: Santa Barbara is a place for people who appreciate the finer things of life, such as great art, sleek polo ponies, and clothes that you won't see on every other man and woman in the street. For the best and most atmospheric browsing, head over to **El Paseo,** Spanish for "the street" (808 to 810 State St.), a picturesque shopping arcade built in and around the 1827 adobe home that belonged to the De la Guerra family. Here, Neville and Hon displays Southeast Asian and primitive art; Astra Gallery sells original art priced from $150; A. & P. Williams Gallery exhibits watercolors and signed posters by owners Andrew and Pamela Williams; and Nature's Own carries shells, minerals, and gems. Save lots of time for what is indeed rubber-stamp paradise, Stampa Barbara (tel. 962-4077). Here, owner Gary Dorothy has a selection of over 30,000 rubber stamps, with designs that will please cat and dog fanciers, car fiends, airplane mavens, computer buffs, you name it. Prices for the stamps range from $3.50 to $17.50.

Other excellent areas for shopping include **upper State Street** (the 800 to 1300 numbers), where you'll find shops such as Tienda Ho (1017 State St.) for reasonably priced imports from Bali, Green and Yellow Basket (911 State St.) for gifts, and Elizabeth Fortner Gallery (1114 State St.) for fine crafts and wearable art. La Cumbre Plaza is Santa Barbara's largest shopping mall, with department stores such as Robinson's and Sears, and outlets of the Pottery Barn, Benetton, and Victoria's Secret (lingerie) nearby. Perhaps the most elegant shops are found in the Montecito enclave. If you're looking for something different in jewelry, head for Silverhorn (1155 Coast Village Rd.), where Michael and Carol Ridding create very beautiful, very modern designs using quartz glass and rough-cut gemstones. Bird in Paradise (1165 Coast Village Rd.) carries bold fashions for women, including Laise Adzer's lines. At Memaw's (1253 Coast Village Rd.) owner Carol Goodell stocks anything that strikes her fancy, from $1.50 pens to $1,000 stuffed tigers. Definitely worth a go-see.

ROMANTIC INTERLUDES: A city this beautiful holds infinite possibilities for honeymooners.

Called "The Queen of the Missions," the old **Mission Santa Barbara** is characterized by its two matching towers, which pose a serene picture against a backdrop of the eucalyptus-clad foothills. Founded on December 4, 1786, the Santa Barbara Mission is the tenth of the Spanish missions. Today, it houses a fine museum, which you can visit on a self-guided tour that makes California's Spanish colonial history come alive. One of the most fascinating artifacts on exhibit is a sketch of Santa Barbara in 1793, drawn by John Sykes, who accompanied Captain George Vancouver on his exploratory voyage up the Pacific coast. You'll want to linger in the central courtyard, with its fountain surrounded by towering palms, and lush gardens, where small, hand-lettered signs identify the various flowers and herbs.

To best appreciate Santa Barbara, choose other ways of locomotion than a car.

The county has several well-planned, scenic **bike paths** that take you through Santa Barbara, Goleta, Montecito, Summerland, and Carpinteria. Perhaps the most popular route of all is the 9.6-mile Goleta Valley Bikeway, which connects with the Atascadero Recreational Trail that branches off to the beach. You can rent ten-speed bikes for about $7 per hour, or $20 for a half-day. Contact Beach Rentals (tel. 963-2524) or Bike 'n' Hike Sports (tel. 969-0719).

Among the favorite area **hikes** are the Cold Springs Trail, a moderate-to-steep climb that passes waterfalls and swimming holes; Rattlesnake Trail (named for its twists rather than the critters), which leads to a grassy meadow edged by pine trees; and the five miles of trails in the Santa Barbara Botanic Garden (tel. 682-4726). The Sierra Club sponsors free public group hikes every Saturday and Sunday; call 965-8709 for starting times and details.

2 Much Fun (tel. 805/963-9021) runs guided mountain, beach, and moonlight **horseback rides,** from $20 per hour per person. San Ysidro Stables (tel. 969-5046) offers guided tours of scenic mountain trails, from $20 per hour per person. Call for schedules and reservations.

The **Channel Islands**—Anacapa, Santa Cruz, Santa Rosa, and San Miguel—are one of America's newest national parks, established in 1980. They are places of stark and primeval beauty. Thousands of elephant seals gather on the shores, and the islands have peaceful tide pools, reefs, caves, coves, and unique plant and wildlife. Island Packers offers several different day trips. The most popular is the excursion to Anacapa, giving you three hours to explore the island itself ($30 per person). Or take a gourmet cruise aboard the 81-foot schooner *Shearwater,* which also generally moors off Anacapa. The chef prepares specialties such as chicken tetrazzini, fresh steamed veggies, and hors d'oeuvres platters keep circulating throughout the day ($66 per person). Call for schedules and reservations (tel. 642-1393). Other outfits offering Channel Islands tours include Channel Charters (tel. 964-1656); Sea Landing Aquatics Center (tel. 963-3564), and Navigators Channel Island Cruise (tel. 969-2393).

HONEYMOON HOTELS AND HIDEAWAYS: Santa Barbara's accommodations capture the ambience of this old mission town.

A splendid hacienda by the sea, **Marriott's Santa Barbara Biltmore,** 1260 Channel Dr., Santa Barbara, CA 93108 (tel. 805/969-2261; reservations: toll free 800/228-9290), reigns as the queen of Santa Barbara. Opened in 1927 as part of the original Biltmore chain, the hotel captures the spirit of the Roaring '20s—but in keeping with the Southern California setting. Built Spanish-style with tranquil green courtyards, the two-story, white stucco buildings sprawl across from Butterfly Beach, the red-tile roofs, open archways, and wrought-iron grillwork harmonizing with the hazy blue Santa Ynez Mountains in the distance. Towering palm trees and fragrant eucalyptus dot the 24 acres of the property. The lobby has a gracious Spanish feel, with its high, exposed-beam ceilings, Mediterranean furnishings, archways, and iron-grillwork door. There are 229 guest rooms offering views of the ocean, pool, gardens, or mountains. Many rooms have balconies or private patios, vaulted ceilings, and ceiling fans; some have fireplaces. Floral prints in either sunny California colors or soft earth tones brighten the decor, which has a substantial, if a bit stolid, feel.

Biltmore guests have full privileges at the Coral Casino Beach and Cabana Club just across the street, which has an Olympic-size pool, private beach, cocktail lounge, and dancing. The Coral Casino is also slated to add health spa facilities in 1988. On the property are three lighted tennis courts, a swimming pool, and a putting green; golf can be arranged. Honeymoon package: None. Rates (EP): gardenview room: $187 per couple per night; poolview room with fireplace: $209 per couple per night; oceanview room, $231 per couple per night. If you let the Biltmore know in advance that you are honeymooners, they will have a bottle of champagne ready for your arrival.

El Encanto Hotel and Garden Villas, 1900 Lasuen Rd., Santa Barbara, CA 93103 (tel. 805/687-5000). The name, meaning "the enchanted one," says it all. El Encanto is situated on ten gardened acres on a hilltop in Santa Barbara's very exclusive Riviera district.

The most romantic accommodations are the cottages, which make you think that you're sleeping in an English garden. Springtime flowers seem to be everywhere—on the wallpaper and matching bedspread—unfurling petals of blue, pink, peach, and coral. Touches of brass add glamour, on the headboard, desk lamps, and drawer-pulls on the English-style furnishings. Baskets of silk flowers create a pleasing trompe l'oeil effect against the floral wallpaper. Windows are all around, covered with louvres so you can let in daylight and the garden views when you wish. Unusual for a hotel room, the lighting is well designed, with a combination of strategically placed lamps and track lighting allowing you to control the scheme for romance. Standard rooms offer similar nice touches, though on a smaller proportioned scale.

The pride of El Encanto must be the magnificent gardens, centered around a brick-columned pergola overhung with vines and surrounded by regal blue-and-gold bird of paradise plants. There's a tennis court and a solar-heated swimming pool on site, and the resort can arrange golf privileges nearby. Honeymoon package: None. Rates (EP): $110 to $330 per couple per night, depending on size, views, and lavishness of furnishings.

Hideaway is the word that comes to mind when describing the **San Ysidro Ranch,** 900 San Ysidro Lane, Montecito, CA 93108 (tel. 805/969-5046), in the foothills of the Santa Ynez Mountains and the very exclusive Montecito residential area. After all, if you can't find seclusion at a resort that has only 40 rooms—and 550 acres of prime real estate—where else could you? Among your escapist predecessors were Winston Churchill (who wrote one of his books here), Laurence Olivier and Vivien Leigh (who married here), and John and Jacqueline Kennedy (who honeymooned here). The ranch has a colorful history, having begun life in 1893 as a way station for Franciscan monks, who sold their homemade wine here. In the late 1920s, the spread was purchased by actor Ronald Colman.

The current owners, Jim and Susie Lavenson, preside over a luxurious getaway, a member of the prestigious Relais et Château group. Susie has charge of the decorating, which mingles Lavenson family leftovers, spot-buys from the Salvation Army, and priceless antiques. There is no "typical" room—each has a unique personality. The cottages have different names and fascinating pasts: Somerset Maugham penned several of his short stories in "Geranium," Sinclair Lewis wrote in the closet at "Oak" (he found the beautiful views too distracting). One of our favorites was "Lilac-One," with a pink quilt on the seductive, curtained bed and a Jacuzzi bubbling nicely on the outdoor deck surrounded by latticework ($417 per couple per night). Whichever cottage you choose, a sign will be hanging on the door, with your surname carved in wood. San Ysidro is that kind of place.

Cozy as these nests might be, you should take advantage of your awesome surroundings. Ride off into the hills on a sleek quarter horse from the stables ($22 per hour). See if you can keep your eye on the ball on the tennis courts (you'll find yourself gazing off at the Pacific or the mountains instead). Mix yourself a drink at the honor bar in the hacienda lounge and swim a few laps in the heated pool (preferably not in that order). Home on the range has never been so sweet. Honeymoon package: None. Rates (EP): $154 for rooms to about $500 for a private cottage with Jacuzzi. If your ménage includes the family horse, equine guests are boarded for $22 per night (AP). Includes gourmet hay.

Occupying 24 prime oceanfront acres between Stearns Wharf and the Santa Barbara Zoological Gardens, **Fess Parker's Red Lion Resort,** 633 East Cabrillo Blvd., Santa Barbara, CA 93103 (tel. 805/564-4333; Reservations: toll free 800/547-8010), is the city's first new luxury hotel in over 50 years; its grand opening was in

January 1987. Built in classic Spanish-colonial style, with a red-tile roof and white stucco walls, the resort is partially owned by actor Fess Parker, who was television's Daniel Boone. The western-based Red Lion chain is rapidly earning a stellar reputation, and a 1986 *Consumer Reports* survey ranked it among the top-three moderately priced chains nationwide. The new Santa Barbara addition lives up to this tradition. Rooms are oversized and feature all the amenities found in luxury hotels: air conditioning, mini-bar, remote-control color TV, and a private balcony overlooking the ocean, garden, or mountains. The blue-and-beige color scheme picks up on the tones of the Pacific and surrounding hills. Take advantage of the complete resort facilities: swimming pool, Jacuzzi, exercise room, sauna, and three lighted tennis courts. Honeymoon package: None. Rates (EP): $149 to $193 per couple per night, depending on view.

ROMANTIC RESTAURANTS: Santa Barbarans claim their city has the most restaurants per capita in the United States. And, we may add, some of the best and most reasonably priced. Because of its proximity to the great fishing waters, the seafood particularly merits a "10." Try fresh albacore tuna, swordfish, rockfish, white bass, or Pacific lobster. But when it appears on the menu, head straight for the Santa Barbara shrimp, generally served with their roe—definitely a foretaste of heaven.

Expensive

Michael's Waterside Inn, 50 Los Patos Way, Montecito (tel. 969-0307). The decor is unmistakably French, with floral print portières framing the windows, and crisp white linens on the table. And the cuisine features classic French techniques enlivened with innovative California twists, such as serving cultured abalone with a limpid buerre blanc sauce tinged with fresh dill, squab with a wine sauce based on a local cabernet, or roast duck combined with Santa Barbara olives. There's no innovation just for innovation's sake—these recipes are well thought out and the textures and flavors marry beautifully. The three-course, prix-fixe dinner, from $35 per person, includes appetizer, entrée, and dessert (such as the ambrosial crêpe soufflé with raspberries).

Moderate

The Palace Café, 8 East Cota St. (off State), Santa Barbara (tel. 966-3133). For a little bit of Dixieland gone west, head on over to the happening Palace Café. The decor sets a trendy New Orleans mood, with posters and paintings celebrating jazz, catfish festivals, Mardi Gras, and a bright neon sign heralding Louisiana's own Dixie beer. Best of all, the food delivers that real New Orleans flavor, with good ol' Southern delicacies such as crawfish, soft-shell crabs, and redfish airlifted in daily. Try not to stuff yourselves too much on the homemade breads they serve you for starters—banana muffins and jalapeño/cheddar sticks that will set your eyeballs jumping. Appetizers spotlight such yummies as black-bean soup with andouille sausage ($3.85) or crab claws dipped in a spicy batter, deep-fried, and served with a smooth remoulade sauce. For entrées, recommendations include the real thing jambalaya, packed with prawns, chicken breast, crawfish, andouille sausage, and served on a bed of "dirty" rice ($13), and the crawfish étouffée, thickened with a dark roux ($17.50). Pace yourselves so you can last till dessert, most notably, the Key lime pie ($3.85). The place is always packed, so be prepared to wait.

Paradise Café, 812 Anacapa St., Santa Barbara (tel. 966-2428). The building looks like it stepped straight out of a movie, with its original 1940s wall murals and neon signs. Take advantage of the balmy Santa Barbara climate, and eat on their large patio or veranda. The specialty here is oak-grilled steaks and fresh fish, priced from $8.50 for red snapper to $14.50 for a 22-ounce T-bone steak. Dinner entrées come complete with garlic bread, soup or salad, vegetables, rice, or shoestring potatoes.

Locals in the know ask for the huevos Valenzuela: scrambled eggs, black beans, avocado, and cheese packed into a huge tortilla. A steal at $5.25.

The Harbor Restaurant, Stearns Wharf, Santa Barbara (tel. 963-3311), is the place if you want to dine on the water—located right on Stearns Wharf. Try to time your arrival so you can enjoy some steamed mussels and cocktails on deck while you watch the sunset, gulls swirling over the harbor. Fresh fish is the specialty here, including a bouillabaisse ($20) or coconut-fried shrimp served with a variety of Indian accompaniments—chutney, Indian rice, and vegetables ($18.50). Choices also include steak, pasta, and chicken dishes, and entrées are served with a choice of New England–style clam chowder or salad. After dinner, head upstairs to the bar, which features live entertainment.

7. Los Angeles and Environs

Freeways. Surfers. Movie stars. U.C.L.A. Dodger Stadium. Valley Girls. Palm trees. Swimming pools. A sign that spells out H-O-L-L-Y-W-O-O-D. It seems only fitting that Los Angeles presents itself in montage images. Not only is L.A. linked, twin-like, with the movie industry, but also the city itself isn't so much a place as it is places, 140 different cities and communities loosely stitched together, like a patchwork quilt: Beverly Hills, Westwood, and Bel Air; Burbank, Hollywood, and Century City; Santa Monica, Venice, and Marina del Rey, and all the other cityscapes and townlets.

With a population of about 13 million, Greater Los Angeles is the second largest metropolitan area in the country. Los Angeles County itself is huge, encompassing over 4,083 square miles, surrounded on one side by the San Gabriel Mountains, on the other by the Pacific Ocean. Its lowest point lies some nine feet below sea level; its tallest, Mt. Baldy, towers some 10,080 feet above it. The experiences it offers are as wide as all humanity. There's the surfing, of course, at the beaches that gave the Beach Boys their name: Surfrider in Malibu, as well as Manhattan Beach, Hermosa Beach, and Redondo Beach. Yet just a two-hour's drive away, Big Bear Lake offers top-notch downhill skiing. You can give yourselves over shamelessly to celebrity gawking, driving past the homes of the stars on Beverly Drive, getting the best of *Jaws* on the Universal Studios tour, and poking each other in the ribs in excitement when you see "you know, what's his name?" sit down at an adjoining table at Primi, 72 Market, or whatever new spot the rich and famous have chosen to frequent this month. And despite such put-downs as Gertrude Stein's, "There is no there, there," Los Angeles actually has a downtown, a rather spectacular one, a futuristic core of silver skyscrapes that glitter like a mirage when you approach the city from the San Diego Freeway. If you're coming to L.A. for the first time, you will probably increase the number of Roll-Royces, Jaguars, and Porsches you have seen in your life at least tenfold—and that's just in the parking lot of the Hotel Bel-Air. But L.A. is also one of the most "happening" art scenes in the country, and perhaps the world, with the opening of the stunning new Museum of Contemporary Art (MOCA) downtown and the rapidly growing collection at the Getty Museum in Malibu, where practically every *objet* seems to be sporting a just-typed "recent acquisition" tag.

On your visit, make it a point to get to know L.A.'s various neighborhoods, to develop a sense for what makes swank Bel-Air different from posh Beverly Hills (Bel-Air is where the really, really rich live). Spend each day poking around a different area. Perhaps start off in downtown L.A., strolling through the state historic park along Olvera Street, the oldest thoroughfare in town. Stop in at the Avila Adobe, home of one of the pueblo's early mayors. Sample L.A.'s ethnic neighborhoods, with visits to Chinatown, Little Tokyo, Koreatown, and the corazón of the Mexican neighborhood, the Grand Central Market. Pack your beach towels and drive off to Malibu, Zuma, or the string of shores that stretch all along the county's coast. Celebrate L.A.'s romance with the road by driving—follow winding, two-lane Mulholland Drive, which climbs 1,400 feet into the Hollywood Hills, or Coldwater Canyon Drive, deep into the hills.

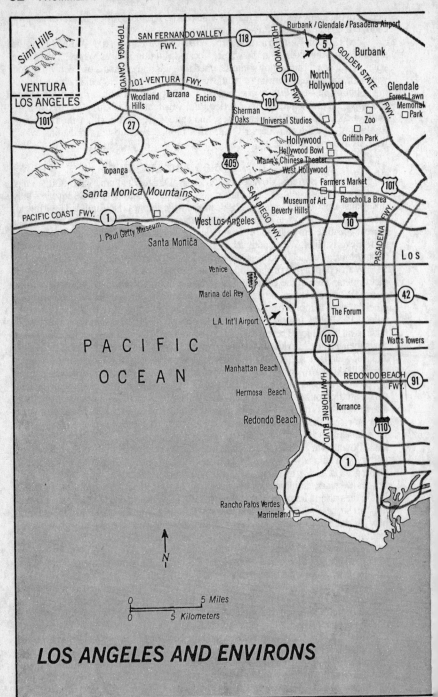

LOS ANGELES AND ENVIRONS

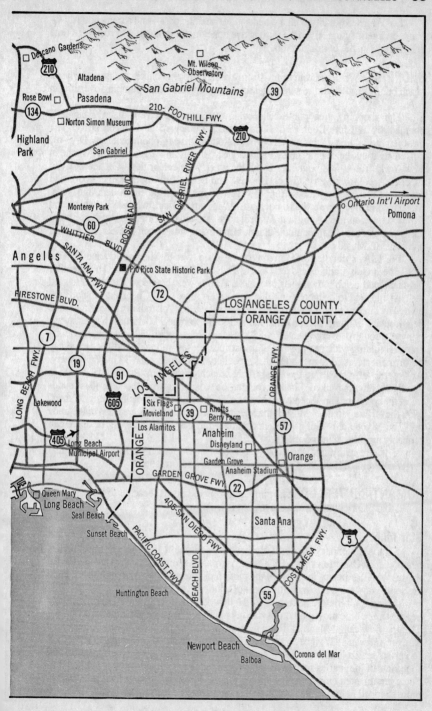

Los Angeles is a city with a wonderfully romantic past—and a tremendously vibrant, energetic future. Even the most active honeymooners are sure to run out of time before they run out of things to do.

SHOPPING: Whatever your taste—from classic European haute couture to the latest beach bunny craze—you're sure to get that shopping adrenaline pumping overtime in L.A.

The shopping area par excellence is the aptly named "Golden Triangle," bounded by Wilshire Boulevard, Santa Monica Boulevard, and Cañon Drive. The most famous address in this gilded district is Rodeo Drive (pronounce it Row-DAY-o), ranked right up there with rue du Faubourg St. Honoré in Paris and Fifth Avenue in New York. You'll find boutiques by all the worldwide celebrities—Cartier and Van Cleef & Arpel for jewelry; Gucci, Hermès, and Louis Vuitton for leather goods and handbags; plus beauty salons from Georgette Klinger, Elizabeth Arden, and Vidal Sassoon. Finally, there's that uniquely L.A. nirvana, Bijan, where $700 shirts and $13,000 fur coats are sold by appointment only. Around the corner on Wilshire Boulevard, you can browse through the classic department stores such as Saks, I. Magnin, and Neiman-Marcus.

For L.A.'s trendiest accoutrements, head on over to Melrose Avenue in West L.A., the stretch running between Doheny Drive and Highland Avenue. This friendly, old-fashioned neighborhood has become L.A.'s newest hot spot. The stores toward the east end tend to be more punk, the west end is more chic. Check out Koala Blue, owned by singer Olivia Newton-John, which showcases Australian designs; and Fred Segal, which contains several different men's and women's boutiques. Not far away, browse through Beverly Center at 8500 Beverly Boulevard. The gigantic reddish-colored building with the pink-and-purple stripes houses Bullock's and The Broadway department stores, designer boutiques, specialty food stores, and 14 movie theaters. At street level, you'll find the West Coast branch of the Hard Rock Café, which is practically always packed. Finally, you may be wondering what that blue-glass building at the corner of San Vicente and Melrose is. The answer: the Pacific Design Center, a/k/a the "Blue Whale." Most of the interior design showrooms are open to the trade only, but if you are working with a decorator to furnish your new home, he or she can probably arrange an introduction.

If you're really into shopping, check out *The Serious Shopper's Guide to Los Angeles* (Prentice Hall Press, New York) for further information.

ROMANTIC INTERLUDES: From star gazing to fine art, beaches to horse racing, you'll find plenty of thrills and excitement in L.A.

Star Tours

Scrape the phoney tinsel off Hollywood, and you'll find the real tinsel underneath, pianist Oscar Levant said. To most visitors, Los Angeles means a chance to visit the scene of the dream, the heart of the motion picture and television industries. Here are some ways for you to make the most of your time in Tinsel Town.

Mann's Chinese Theatre, 6925 Hollywood Blvd. (tel. 464-8111). For many years, some of the most glamorous movie openings took place at Grauman's Chinese Theatre (now called Mann's). From the time of the first premiere (Cecil B. deMille's *King of Kings* in 1927) it became the tradition for Hollywood celebrities to leave their footprints sealed in concrete in the courtyard. Here you can gaze at the signatures and footprints of luminaries such as Marilyn Monroe, Judy Garland—169 at latest count. Some left an even more personal impression: Al Jolson left knee prints, John Barrymore stamped in his profile, and Betty Grable registered her famous legs.

Walk of Fame, Hollywood Boulevard between Sycamore and Gower, and Vine between Sunset and Yucca. Right near Mann's Chinese Theatre, stroll along the sidewalks inlaid with more than 1,500 stars representing celebrities from the world of film, radio, television, or music.

Set in the Hollywood Hills on the slopes of Mount Lee, the **Hollywood sign** is looking good these days, after a recent refurbishment.

Universal Studios, Box 8620, Universal City, CA 91608 (tel. 818/777-3794), is located on the Hollywood Freeway at Lankershim or Cahuenga. Get behind the scenes at this working movie studio, where classic films have been made since 1915. The 5½-hour tour includes a tram ride through the famous back lot and a visit to the Entertainment Center, where you'll be treated to five action-packed live shows. In the back lot, you'll see the sets for movies such as *Back to the Future, The Sting,* and *Earthquake.* For the biggest highlights, you'll enter the amazing world of special effects, featuring a shark attack by the great white of *Jaws,* and a confrontation with King Kong, who will shake the Brooklyn Bridge, derail an elevated train, and cause a spectacular helicopter crash. Open summer and holidays, 9 a.m. to 5 p.m.; winters, from 10 a.m. to 3:30 p.m. on weekdays, and 9:30 a.m. to 3:30 p.m. on weekends. Admission is $14.95 per person.

NBC Television Studio Tour, 3000 West Alameda Ave., Burbank, CA 91523 (tel. 818/840-3537). Originally designed to show visiting VIPs how TV programs were made, the network now opens the studios to the public on a 75-minute walking tour. This is truly a backstage visit: What you see depends on what exactly is in production that day. You'll view set construction, wardrobe, dressing rooms, the KNBC News Studio, and the set of the *Tonight* show. New for visitors—a special-effects set, where you might be chosen to fly like Superman over the L.A. skyline. Tours depart at regular intervals all day. Weekdays: 9 a.m. to 4 p.m. Saturdays: 10 a.m. to 4 p.m. Sundays: 10 a.m. to 2 p.m. Closed Easter, Thanksgiving, Christmas Day, New Year's Day. Admission is $5.50.

Live NBC Show Tapings, c/o TICKETS, NBC Television Network, 3000 West Alameda Ave., Burbank, CA 91523 (tel. 818/840-3537). If you'd like to watch a live taping of a network TV show, you can pick up free tickets daily at the studio complex. You can also get tickets by mail by writing to the above address. Include the name of the show, number of tickets, date desired, and be sure to enclose a stamped, self-addressed envelope.

Movie Stars Homes. At various L.A. bookstores and from miscellaneous entrepreneurs hawking their wares from the back of 1967 stationwagons, you can pick up a $5 map of where different movie stars live or once lived. Although you probably won't run into Ann Margret mowing the front lawn, it's a fun way to drive through some of the posh neighborhoods, such as Beverly Hills, Bel Air, and Brentwood. Some of the best routes for eyeballing the palatial real estate: Beverly Drive through Beverly Hills (this is the road with all the palm trees that you see in movies such as *Beverly Hills Cop*), Stone Canyon Road in Bel Air, and Mulholland through Hollywood.

Hollywood on Location, 8644 Wilshire Blvd., Beverly Hills, CA (tel. 659-9165). Lights, action, camera! If you really want to see the stars, this may be your best bet in town. Every weekday morning at 9 a.m., Hollywood on Location releases a list telling you where movie and TV crews are filming that day—and night. For $19, you get a list of locations and a very detailed map pinpointing each location. The location list contains the name of each TV series and movie filming that day, the stars in it, gives the exact address and location, and also describes the scheduled type of filming, stunts, and special effects you might see. On most days, you'll have a roster of more than 20 different locations, practically always within ten miles of the Hollywood on Location office in Beverly Hills. You make up your own schedule based on the productions you most want to watch.

Go to the Beach

You'll have fun, fun, fun if you spend the day frolicking on one of the fine Southern California **beaches.**

Once known as the Gold Coast, **Santa Monica** was the first, great L.A. beach. The area has undergone a sizable renaissance recently and is once again a fashionable residential and resort area. In addition to playing some beach blanket bingo down on the sand, stroll down the landmark Santa Monica pier, originally built in 1909. Its most beloved attraction is the colorful carousel, originally built in 1922, with its brightly painted horses and glittery mirrors. Exhibits trace the history of the pier, and there are also some marvelous pre–video-era amusement games for 25¢, such as the Iron Claw, Estrella's Prophesies, and a Personality Tester. When you get the munchies, you can buy walkaway shrimp or crab cocktails on the pier, about $2.50 each. To our mind, much of the appeal of Santa Monica comes from the broad, palm-lined park that runs along the cliff above the beach, a green promenade that recalls the boulevards that line the waterfront in Cannes and Nice. A perfect spot for strolling, roller skating, picnicking, and sunset watching.

Malibu isn't just one beach, but rather is a 27-mile-long stretch of sands edging the Pacific north of Santa Monica. It is best known as Hollywood-by-the-sea, a popular residential area for celebrities such as Barbra Streisand, Johnny Carson, Sissy Spacek, Warren Beatty, and Goldie Hawn. Although the rich and famous generally keep to their own hot tubs behind the gates, the beach (and bathing-suit-clad bodies) make the trip well worthwhile. Check out the section known as Surfrider Beach, just north of Malibu Pier, said to be the original Beach Boys' hangout. The waves attract some of the best surfers.

Well, you just know **Venice** has to be a bit off the wall, since its original developer, Abbot Kinney, originally envisioned turning this area of marshy tidal flats into a second Venice, Italy, complete with singing gondoliers. The canal-cum-lagoon idea never quite took hold—but then, with Venice, you'll never know. It still might. Venice has long been a refuge for Southern California bohemia—from Alan Ginsberg and Jack Kerouac in the 1950s, to Janis Joplin in the early 1970s. Among its major contributions to humankind have been the Frisbee, the skateboard, and the resurrection of roller skates. Today, Main Street, U.S.A., it decidedly ain't. Part bazaar, part bizarre, the waterfront sidewalk is lined with hawkers and gawkers, cruising bodybuilders in full flex, musicians, sword swallowers, fortune-tellers, and broken-bottle jumpers. You can buy a watch for $1.99, or sunglasses for $3.99. To blend in with the crowd, you can rent roller skates ($3 per hour) or bikes ($3.30 per hour) from one of the shacks at the beach. You might see a swami on roller skates, or a beachboy on a skateboard, being towed by his mastiff. Oh yes, by the way, there's also a beach. Note: Although somewhat outlandish, Venice is safe by day. At night, things get a bit raunchy, so shove off before sunset.

The most popular strand for Valley Girls and their sun-bleached-blond surfer boyfriends is **Zuma Beach,** north of Santa Monica. **Manhattan Beach** is young and sporty, attracting surfers, joggers, bicycle riders, and volleyball players. **Hermosa Beach,** just south, is fairly similar, with a tad more locals (it's hard to find a parking spot). **Redondo Beach,** south of Hermosa, is where California surfing first made its debut in 1907, and is known as the best winter-surfing spot.

The Museums

Perhaps the biggest happening on the cultural front has been the emergence of L.A. as a formidable power in the art world, with several area **museums** making major acquisitions and undertaking expansions.

The **J. Paul Getty Museum,** 17985 Pacific Coast Hwy., Malibu (tel. 458-2003), occupies ten acres of the 65-acre Getty estate in fashionable Malibu. It is generally considered to be the richest museum in the world, with an endowment of over $2.3

billion. The setting is grand enough. Getty designed his museum after a second-century Roman palazzo, complete with colonnaded walkways, pools, and fountains. The first floor of the museum houses an extraordinary collection of Greek and Roman art. On the second floor, you'll find works by Rembrandt, Cézanne, Van Dyck, Goya, and others. Since the museum must spend $100 million a year, you can count on finding new treasures sporting the "recent acquisition" tag by the time you visit. The museum is open Tuesday through Sunday, 10 a.m. to 5 p.m. Admission and parking are free. However, the quirky feature is that you must call in advance to reserve a parking space; absolutely no "drive-ins" are permitted.

The **Museum of Contemporary Art (MOCA),** 250 South Grand Ave. at California Plaza, Downtown L.A. (tel. 621-2766). The splendidly designed building by Japanese architect Arata Isozaki only opened in December 1986, and it has become one of the most talked about museums in the world. Outside, the museum is breathtaking, faced with rough-cut sandstone and composed of carefully arranged geometric shapes, with arches and pyramids. Inside, the wide-open, white-painted galleries with their light-wood floors provide the perfect setting for works by Robert Rauschenberg, Claes Oldenburg, Louise Nevelson, and Eric Fischl. Open Tuesday to Sunday, 11 a.m. to 6 p.m. (until 8 p.m. on Thursday and Friday). Closed Thanksgiving, Christmas, and New Year's Day. Admission is $4 per person.

The **Temporary Contemporary,** 152 North Central Ave., Los Angeles (tel. 621-2766). This cavernous police warehouse in Little Japan served as the temporary home for MOCA until it moved into its permanent home in late 1986; the locale proved so popular that the Temporary Contemporary will continue to be a museum in its own right, spotlighting the latest innovations in postmodern art. Open Tuesday to Sunday, 11 a.m. to 6 p.m. (until 8 p.m. on Thursday and Friday). Closed Thanksgiving, Christmas, and New Year's Day. Admission is $4 per person.

Other Attractions

Disneyland, 1313 South Harbor Blvd., Anaheim (tel. 714/999-4000). Mickey, Minnie, and all your favorite Disney characters are waiting to greet you at this magical land filled with fantasy and adventure. The newest attraction is Captain EO, a three-dimensional, 70mm film directed by Francis Coppola, produced by George Lucas, and starring Michael Jackson as a heroic intergalactic warrior. The special effects of space ships and creatures seem so real, you'll be ducking in your seats. At Space Mountain in Tomorrowland, climb aboard a thrilling roller-coaster ride that seems to hurl you through outer space. See if the spirits move you in the Haunted Mansion. And even if you'd sooner buckle than swash, you'll be yo-ho-hoing with the best of the buccaneers at Pirates of the Caribbean. Disneyland is open Wednesday through Sunday, mid-September until mid-March; daily from mid-March through mid-September. Admission is $15 per person. Anaheim is about a 45-minute drive south of L.A.

The Hollywood Bowl, a shell in the Hollywood Hills, is the summer home of the Los Angeles Philharmonic, and also hosts a summer concert series. For a schedule of concert dates, call 856-5400.

Whatever your favorite **sport,** you can probably find top-flight events in Los Angeles. Baseball fans should check out the schedule at Dodger Stadium (tel. 244-1500). The gigantic Forum sports arena in Inglewood is home to the Los Angeles Lakers basketball team and L.A. Kings hockey team (tel. 673-1300 for ticket information). The Coliseum, which hosted the track and field events for the 1984 Olympics, is where the Los Angeles Raiders football team plays (tel. 322-5901). And you can see the sport of kings at its finest at Santa Anita Park (racing late December through mid-April; tel. 818/574-RACE), or Hollywood Park (racing late April to mid-July, mid-November to late December; tel. 419-1574).

HONEYMOON HOTELS AND HIDEAWAYS: It is only fitting that the movie capital of the world would dream up some of the most captivating accommodations imaginable. But, like everything else in L.A., romance has its price. Do not expect anything smacking of seductive ambience for under $70 per couple per night. Since L.A. is so spread out, your biggest decision in choosing a hotel should be location: Where do you envision spending most of your time? Beverly Hills and West Hollywood are centrally located both to downtown and Burbank—and provide the most recognizable L.A. addresses, the places where Rolls-Royces purr curbside, hopefuls have themselves paged by the pool, and moguls cut deals in penthouse suites. Westwood attracts L.A.'s young garde of actors and rock stars, as well as an arty and literary crowd that gathers around U.C.L.A. (it also has great movie theaters, a neighborhood feeling, and real sidewalks where you can stroll). Probably because it's right at the beach, Santa Monica has a more relaxed, laid-back feeling. You might be able to watch the sunset from your window, then stroll along the main street where many of L.A.'s hottest new restaurants are located.

One other eccentricity of L.A. lodging nomenclature should be noted: the "bungalow." This resembles nothing you might have inhabited at summer camp. Just like Marie Antoinette enjoyed playing a shepherdess at the Trianon in Versailles, Hollywood's royalty has a fondness for retreating into pastoral splendor in these elegant minimanses and villas found at several of Beverly Hills' swankiest hotels. If you want to splurge, you've come to the right place.

Unless indicated, none of the following hotels have honeymoon packages. Rates quoted are per couple per night.

For honeymooners on a tight budget, your best bet is one of the clean and dependable inns and motels in downtown L.A., especially the very good Best Western properties: **The Best Western Dragon Gate Inn,** 818 N. Hill Street, Los Angeles, CA 90012 (tel. 213/617-3077), **Best Western Inntowne Hotel,** 925 S. Figueroa Street, Los Angeles, CA 90015 (tel. 213/628-2222), and **Best Western Kent Inn Motel,** 920 S. Figueroa Street, Los Angeles, CA 90015 (tel. 213/626-8701), or toll free 800/528-1234. Rates run about $50 per couple per night.

Very Expensive

Hotel Bel-Air, 701 Stone Canyon Rd., Los Angeles, CA 90077 (tel. 213/472-1211). The setting is enchanted. Swans glide and preen in the lagoon, backdropped by the blush-pink, Spanish-mission–style buildings with the red-tile roofs. Long corridors lined with archways wind through gardens where the dominant color is pink: primroses, hibiscus, azaleas, magnolias, roses, impatiens. The lemon trees sprout absolutely massive fruits. In the distance, rugged mountains seem to cup the palm trees, the fountains, the porticos, the pools, setting you off from the rest of the world. Incredibly, this secluded Shangri-la is only one mile from Rodeo Drive in Bel-Air, probably the most exclusive residential enclave in Los Angeles.

After a $6-million refurbishment under the knowledgeable eye of Caroline Hunt Schoellkopf, whose Rosewood Hotels bought the property for $23 million in 1983, the Bel-Air radiates the savoir faire of a truly great hotel. Rosewood kept the best of the old Bel-Air—the personalized service and attention to detail—and completely renovated the hotel rooms and bungalows. Each of the 92 rooms is different. Many are done in ice-cream pastels: pistachio, strawberry, lemon, peach. Appointments might include marble sinks, gold-tone faucets, Mexican-tile floors, dhurrie rugs. Even the least expensive room has its own private terrace, screened from view by cascades of flowers. You'll enjoy complete seclusion: The property meanders over 11 park-like acres with splashing fountains, a gazebo, and a luxurious green backdrop of ferns, palms, California sycamores, and live oaks. The restaurant has also been redone in country French style, in shades of pink and beige, and the California-style cuisine is excellent. In nice weather, tables are set up on the terrace overlooking Swan Lake. The hotel's oval swimming pool is heated year-round, and the concierge can arrange for tennis, golf, and other sports activities. Rates (EP): rooms, $236 to $346 per couple per night; suites, $440 to $1,430 per couple per night.

The Beverly Wilshire, 9500 Wilshire Blvd., Beverly Hills, CA 90212 (tel. 213/275-4282; reservations: toll free 800/421-4354 nationwide; 800/282-4804 in California). Warren Beatty lived here for a while. Paul Newman and Joanne Woodward like the honeymoon suite. When you check into this hotel, you aren't just getting a place to stay—you're living a legend. Originally built in 1927, the hotel has been impeccably renovated and looks in tip-top shape, from the grand entrance lobby with the gilt ceiling and the tall marble pillars, to the newer Beverly Wing, built in 1971. Part of the prestigious Regent Hotel chain, the Beverly Wilshire would merit star billing just for its location, right at the intersection of Wilshire Boulevard and Rodeo Drive. "Mi casa es su casa" (my house is your house) is the motto of the hotel, and you'll find that standard upheld by all members of the staff.

In the newer Beverly Wing, each floor is decorated in a different style, retracing the history of California: Spanish, Mexican, early California, Italian, French, and Contemporary. There's also a floor of champagne suites, accented by *objets* donated by the great French champagne houses. Be sure to amble over for a peek at the Grand Ballroom, with its mirrored arches of white Carrara marble, hand-wrought iron balconies, and hand-carved marble balustrades designed in the style of Versailles. Rooms in the original building, the Wilshire Wing, are all different, including some absolutely dream-come-true suites. Suite 9A2 is traditionally elegant, in tones of pearly gray and rose, highlighted by gilt mirrors, and graced with two different balconies ($390 per couple per night). Our personal favorite is no. 798, which used to be a private apartment. The bedroom is nice enough, done up with traditional pieces and peach and lavender fabrics. But what you'll surely remember is the opulent bathroom, lined in pink and green Carrara marble in a Moorish design. ($308 per couple per night). The Honeymoon Suite is an oriental fantasy, with paisley fabrics, brass lamps, low sofa piled with pillows, and the subtle perfume of incense ($390 per couple per night). Although not as endowed with the sheer extravagance of the suites, the standard rooms make you feel very grand. You might find a Moorish-style headboard and black-and-white Art Deco–style bath, with tiles forming a checkerboard design. Two other hotel features should be mentioned: the palazzo-type Don Quixote pool, where hand-painted Mexican tiles recount the tale of Cervantes' knight-errant; and the masseur, recently rated no. one in the nation. Honeymoon package: None. However, the weekend packages can suit two lovers nicely. Three days/two nights, suites (CP): $495 per couple. Standard rooms (CP): $192.50 per couple per night, for Friday, Saturday, or Sunday arrival. Includes a bottle of champagne, complimentary use of sauna and swimming pool, and free valet parking.

When celebrities want to get away—in the best of circles—they head over to the landmark **Beverly Hills Hotel,** 9641 Sunset Blvd., Beverly Hills, CA 90210 (tel. 213/278-1487 or 213/276-2251; reservations: toll free 800/R-WARNER), built in 1912, affectionately known as the "Pink Palace." Set on a 16-acre enclave right in the heart of Beverly Hills, the hotel has the secluded feel of a country resort. Thanks to the park-like setting, you'll enjoy many sports right on the property. And the Beverly Hills pool is famous as an outdoor conference room, a place where agents and producers often must wipe suntan oil off their palms before shaking hands on a deal.

The guest register includes Clark Gable and Carole Lombard, F. Scott Fitzgerald, Marilyn Monroe—and, more recently, Eddie Murphy, Debra Winger, Lee Iacocca, and Mike Wallace. The hotel's current owners are primping, painting, and renovating, to embellish the ample proportions and gracious details of this 75-year-old hotel. Many accommodations have fireplaces, private patios, terraces, and kitchens; all now have fully stocked bars. The most attention is being lavished on the private "bungalows," more like private homes.

The restoration and refurbishment not withstanding, the Beverly Hills traditions are being preserved: the corridors in the main hotel will still be lined with the flamboyant palm-frond wallpaper, and a welcoming fire always blazes in the lobby hearth.

Honeymoon package: Standard room (EP): $148.50 to $176 per couple per night. One-bedroom bungalow suite (EP): $418 to $550 per couple per night.

Expensive

If the Beverly Hills Hotel is the bastion of Los Angeles' old guard, the **Westwood Marquis,** 930 Hilgard Ave., Los Angeles, CA 90024 (tel. 213/208-8765; reservations: toll free 800/421-2317 nationwide; 800/352-7454 in California), is the gathering place par excellence for the new crew of celebrities: superstars such as the rock group Duran Duran, Prince, Debra Winger, and the Rolling Stones. As the name implies, the 15-story hotel is located in the highly fashionable Westwood area, a stone's throw from Beverly Hills, Bel-Air, and Century City. This is an all-suite hotel in the grand European tradition, intimately scaled and opulently decorated with fine marble, Oriental rugs, tapestries, oil paintings, huge vases filled with spectacular floral displays, and an eclectic assemblage of objets d'art. If you arrive during afternoon high tea, you'll be greeted with the relaxing sounds of a harpsichord tinkling softly.

Individually decorated, each of the 256 suites is sophisticated and plush, with different accent pieces and colors: peach, sky blue, raspberry, forest green. Often, you'll find chinoiserie: bamboo-backed chairs, Chinese vase lamps, lacquer cabinets and chests. If you're preparing for a big night on the town, the bathroom has plenty of mirrors, as well as a separate makeup vanity. We counted three phones in our suite (including one in the bathroom), handy for accepting calls from agents and producers. Each suite has a separate dining area, so a room service breakfast can be enjoyed in leisurely comfort.

A special pride of the hotel is the beautiful garden leading to the pool area. The hotel has full health spa facilities, with separate men's and women's saunas, steam rooms, and treatment centers with hydrotherapy, massages, and facials. Both the Dynasty Room and Garden Terrace restaurants are excellent. And, the ultimate luxury: The hotel offers complimentary limousine service to surrounding areas, including Rodeo Drive. Honeymoon package: none. The Westwood Marquis has attractive weekend packages, for Friday or Saturday arrival for one or two nights. Parlor and one-bedroom suite (BP): $143 per couple per night. Includes full American breakfast, bottle of California champagne, special rate on valet parking, and late checkout. Regular rates for a suite are $176 to $242 per couple per night.

L'Ermitage Hotels (reservations: toll free 800/424-4443). Luxurious . . . innovative . . . comfortable . . . . It's hard to decide how to begin any description of these five elegant Los Angeles hotels founded by the Ashkenazy brothers, Arnold and Severyn. Instead of feeling like you're lodging in a hotel, you'll feel much more as if you're staying in a posh apartment lent you by friends—that is, if your friends have the taste and the megabucks to buy superb original art by the likes of Renoir, Utrillo, Chagall, and Van Gogh. The hotels are situated in all the best neighborhoods, such as Beverly Hills and West Hollywood. L'Ermitage, Bel Age, and Mondrian are the most luxurious "Hotels de grande classe," while Le Dufy and Le Parc are "Hotels de luxe." Although none has a honeymoon package, the weekend packages offer exceptionally good values. Each property also offers guests free limousine service in the immediate neighborhood. Here's a rundown on the collection:

L'Ermitage Hotel, 9291 Burton Way, Beverly Hills, CA 90210 (tel. 213/278-3344), well merits its "Hotel de grande classe" designation. You'll find every conceivable pampering amenity: 24-hour room service; gilt-framed original oil paintings from the English, French, Dutch, and Russian schools; a private bar where complimentary caviar and pâté are served each evening; and even someone to help you pack or unpack, upon request. You'll have fresh flowers in your room, and chocolates and cordials by your pillow each night. The hotel is situated in a tranquil, residential section of Beverly Hills; rooms face either tree-lined Burton Way or the Hollywood Hills. The lobby resembles an elegant French country inn, a motif that is carried out in the furnishings of the various suites, each of which has a fireplace. One of the hotel's biggest attractions is the multileveled rooftop garden, with swimming pool, mineral-water whirlpool, and huge trees in planters. At night the entire deck is illuminated with hundreds of tiny white lights. There's also the very elegant Café Russe, reserved exclusively for hotel guests. Weekend package: Three days / two nights (some meals): $715 per couple. Includes limousine transfers to and from L.A. airport if necessary, valet parking, all taxes and gratuities. Plus—a sumptuous, five-course candlelight dinner served in the privacy of your suite, including champagne, wine, cordial, espresso, *and* a musical serenade during your dinner. Regular rates: From $225 per couple per night for an executive suite.

Nestled between West Hollywood and Beverly Hills, the **Bel Age Hotel,** 1020 N. San Vicente Blvd., West Hollywood, CA 90069 (tel. 213/854-1111), pays homage to la Belle Époque—the splendid early years of the 20th century. The lobby is graciously French, with tall potted palms, Oriental carpets, and light-wood paneling. Each suite features hand-carved furniture, gilt-framed paintings, a private terrace with views of the Hollywood Hills, Los Angeles, or Beverly Hills, and a kitchenette. There's a lovely roof garden with swimming pool and whirlpool spas, and the Bel Age restaurant serves fine Russian cuisine. Because of its intimacy and luxury, the hotel attracts many visiting celebrities. A friend of ours remained calm when encountering Michael J. Fox in the restaurant, but did admit to a twinge of excitement while sharing an elevator ride with a hand-holding Sean Penn and Madonna. Weekend packages: Two days / one night (some meals): $325 per couple. Three days / two nights (some meals): $462 per couple. Both packages include a welcome basket of fresh fruit, mineral water, and wine; Sunday champagne brunch, all taxes and gratuities. Plus—a Saturday evening five-course, prix-fixe dinner at the Bel Age Restaurant, including Russian vodkas, oysters Muscovite, chicken Kiev, and a charlotte russe, among other gourmet tidbits. Regular rates: From $209 per couple per night.

Mondrian Hotel, 8440 Sunset Blvd., West Hollywood, CA 90069 (tel. 213/ 650-8999). Imagine a colorful Mondrian design splashed over the exterior of a white concrete hotel, and you'll get the picture of the very modern, ultra-elegant Mondrian Hotel. Artist Yaacov Agam has worked the hotel facade with 54 different colors to create what is, in effect, an abstract painting with a high-rise hotel for a canvas. You can't beat the Sunset Boulevard location, right at the heart of L.A.'s trendy Sunset Plaza district, near the Pacific Design Center, "restaurant row" on La Cienega Boulevard, and the boutiques of Melrose Avenue. Many celebrities—especially rock musicians—stay here. The 188 rooms use the bright, primary colors that Dutch painter Piet Mondrian was known for: the eye-catching combination of black couches, red lacquer tables, gray carpeting, and original artwork has won the hotel many design awards. Every suite has a kitchenette and a wet bar, and some have extra-deep whirlpool tubs. The health spa facilities are excellent, with a heated, ground-level swimming pool, exercise machines, men's and women's sauna and steam rooms, and massage rooms. Weekend package: Two days / one night (CP): $215 per couple. Three days / two nights (CP): $358 per couple. Both packages include a welcome basket of fresh fruits, mineral water, and wine; a 45-minute workout in the health club with a private trainer; valet parking; evening turn-down service; all taxes and gratuities. Regular rates: rooms, from $154 per couple; suites, from $187 per couple.

Le Dufy, 1000 Westmount Dr., West Hollywood, CA 90069 (tel. 213/657-7400). Soft, Impressionist-painter tones of gray, rose, salmon, and blue; hand-screened bedspreads that could have been designed by Jackson Pollock; a corner fireplace; these are just a few of the ingratiating touches you'll savor at Le Dufy. The lobby is small, but a true knockout, with a lavish use of pink marble, blond-wood furniture, a massive cocktail table incorporating a concrete slab, and brass railings and fixtures to add the right sparkle. The all-suite hotel is a big favorite with movie and record company executives, because of its proximity to the major studios, as well as the fashionable restaurants on La Cienega and shops on Melrose. The junior suites are compact, but beautifully appointed with pastel fabrics, light foods, and original art in soft, rainbow colors. Almost all the junior suites have mirrored ceilings in the bedroom. In addition, guests enjoy complimentary wine, beer, and liquor. On the landscaped roof garden, you can swim in the heated pool, soak in the whirlpool spa, or perfect your tan on the sun deck. Weekend package (CP): Friday or Saturday arrival, $98 per couple per night. Includes continental breakfast, parking, and evening turndown service. Regular rates: $135 per couple per night.

Le Parc, 733 North West Knoll, West Hollywood, CA 90069 (tel. 213/855-8888), is an especially fitting choice for sports-minded couples. On the rooftop overlooking L.A. and the Hollywood Hills, there's a lighted tennis court surrounded by the flags of the world. Use is free to guests—just sign up. At the rooftop pool area, you might find movie executives taking calls or making deals in the cozy, low-key setting brightened with flowers and citrus trees. There's also a health spa, sauna, and exercise equipment. Each of the 154 spacious suites has a fireplace, wet bar, separate dressing area, private balcony, and a VCR; you can choose your evening's entertainment from their library of over 80 tapes. Set on a very quiet residential street in West Hollywood, Le Parc is just one block from La Cienega restaurants and one block from the boutiques and galleries on Melrose Avenue. You'll very much feel at home, not only because of the contemporary, comfortable surroundings, but also thanks to the friendly staff, many of whom have worked at Le Parc for years. Weekend package: Three days / two nights (some meals): $242 per couple. Four days / three nights (Friday arrival): $347 per couple. Both packages include a fruit basket upon arrival, continental breakfast on Saturday, champagne brunch on Sunday, valet parking, all taxes and gratuities. Regular rates: $160 to $193 per couple per night.

Located right at the end of Wilshire Boulevard on the beach in Santa Monica, the **Miramar Sheraton Hotel,** 101 Wilshire Blvd., Santa Monica, CA (tel. 213/394-3731; reservations: toll free 800/325-3535), has been a longtime favorite of people who want to be right on the water in Santa Monica. The ten-story property is getting a lobby-to-penthouse renovation; the new decor features sophisticated tones of smoky rose, mauve, and beige, and contemporary furnishings. Rooms face either the ocean or the Santa Monica Mountains. Our favorite accommodations are the secluded lanai rooms, which surround the gardens and pool area—Greta Garbo, Humphrey Bogart, and Howard Hughes were among the guests here. On the property, you'll find all the amenities you'd expect of this fine hotel chain, including a large outdoor swimming pool you can really swim laps in, shops, a beauty salon, and rental car and airline desks. The best amenity of all is Adrienne Miley, the chief concierge. She literally knows L.A. like the back of her hand and can recommend fun, romantic escapades such as renting bikes and heading for the string of beaches south of Santa Monica. Honeymoon package: None. Room rates (EP): from $132 to $170 per couple per night, depending on view and availability of a terrace. Lanai rooms are $154 per couple per night.

The **Beverly Hills Comstock Hotel,** 10300 Wilshire Blvd., Los Angeles, CA 90024 (tel. 213/275-5575; reservations: toll free 800/343-2184), is one of Los Angeles' best-kept secrets, an all-suite hotel that is friendly and casual, yet superbly nestled between Beverly Hills, Westwood, and Century City, right across from the Los Angeles Country Club. Because the hotel was previously an apartment building, the suites are amply proportioned and come with all the amenities of a private residence, such as a fully equipped kitchen and a dining area. The Comstock is built around a lushly gardened pool courtyard; you reach your room via open walkways lined with flower boxes. Furnishings tend toward the eclectic: French provincial settees, a Chippendale-style dining set, and modern crystal chandeliers. Our favorite quarters are in the new wing, which is more private. The rooms are modern, and surround a luxuriant garden crammed with giant ferns, reeds, umbrella plants, and a little waterfall that flows into a goldfish pond. In the midst of this jungle splendor, a whirlpool percolates invitingly. Honeymoon package: None. Rates (EP): one-bedroom suite, $138 to $165 per couple per night; penthouse suite: $154 to $248 per couple per night.

Moderate

Westwood Plaza Hotel, Holiday Inn, 10740 Wilshire Blvd., Los Angeles, CA 90024 (tel. 213/475-8711; reservations: toll free 800/HOLIDAY or 800/472-8556 nationwide; 800/235-7973 in California). From the moment you pull into the driveway, you'll know that this is no ordinary Holiday Inn: The doorman wears a morning suit, and other staff members are nattily attired in dinner jackets. The lobby has a British accent, with Queen Anne–style wing chairs and Oriental carpets. Located in Westwood, the 19-story hotel is conveniently near Beverly Hills and Century City. Rooms are tastefully decorated in shades of blue and beige with English-style furnishings; standard and superior rooms are practically identical (the superior rooms have a mini-bar). On the sun deck, you can relax in the pool and whirlpool. For your convenience, the hotel runs a free shuttle to Beverly Hills' Rodeo Drive and to the Century City complex. There's also free parking. Honeymoon package: None. Weekend package (Friday and Saturday night): $110 per couple per night for a suite, including a bottle of champagne. Regular rates: $120 per couple per night for a standard; $143 per couple per night for a superior room.

Good value at a great location—that's what you'll find at the **Del Capri Hotel,** 10587 Wilshire Blvd., Los Angeles, CA 90024 (tel. 213/474-3511), located right on choice Wilshire Boulevard in Westwood. The two-story hotel surrounds a central courtyard with a heated, free-form pool. Although the rooms are simply decorated with Mediterranean-style furnishings, they offer pleasurable features. After a recent refurbishing, many bathrooms now feature a combination whirlpool / bathtub, and the dressing mirror comes with Hollywood-style bulbs around the perimeter. Beds are adjustable, so you can sit up and read. The number of king-size beds is limited, so make sure you state your preferences in advance. Honeymoon package: None, but if you advise the friendly staff that you are newlyweds, they'll usually proffer a bottle of champagne. Rates (CP): $96 per night for a room; $123 per night for a suite.

Moderately Inexpensive

Hotel Shangri-La, 1301 Ocean Ave., Santa Monica, CA 90401 (tel. 213/394-2791), is a true Art Deco gem, facing out over Palisades Park, the beach, and the ocean in lively Santa Monica. Built in 1939 as an apartment house, the hotel retains its Art Deco features. Every room has a beautiful view of the Southern California coastline. If you want something really special, choose the Penthouse ($300 per couple per night), which has an unbelievably long terrace that wraps around the building and views that stretch all the way to Malibu. Inside, mirrored walls reflect the panorama of sky and ocean. Colors come in wonderful seaside shades of pink and aqua. The suite has a fully equipped kitchen, marble master bathroom, and a mirrored headboard in the bedroom. Every room is different—some have balconies, some face directly over the ocean—but all have Deco touches, such as the custom-made furniture done all in curves and angles, etched mirrors, shell-design lamps. Even the studio rooms have plenty of panache. The hotel has just added a new garden courtyard, with imported Italian tile, charming gazebo, and refreshing fountain. Owned and managed by the Adaya family, the Shangri-La has become a favorite hideaway for stars who want a low-key yet elegant atmosphere. Cyndi Lauper, Lauren Hutton, Diane Keaton, Gene Hackman, and Brooke Shields have all stayed here. Rates (CP): studio, $88 per couple per day; one-bedroom suite, from $110 to $176 per day, depending on view and availability of terrace. Includes continental breakfast and afternoon tea. If you let the Adayas know that you're honeymooners, they will generally offer you T-shirts and special amenities.

BayView Plaza Holiday Inn, 530 West Pico Blvd., Santa Monica, CA 90405 (tel. 213/399-9344; reservations: toll free 800/HOLIDAY), is quite a wonderful place —extremely modern, designed somewhat like a step pyramid, and just a five-minute walk from the Santa Monica beach. Thanks to all those sharp angles, every room overlooks the mountains or the Pacific Ocean (you can see all the way to Catalina on clear days). To get in the California groove, choose one of the minisuites, four of which have a Jacuzzi-with-a-view on the terrace. Some of the suites are English-style; others have light rattan furnishings. Standard rooms are cheerful and breezy, with contemporary light-wood furnishings and seashore colors, such as beige, blue, dusty mauve, and sea-foam green. The hotel has two swimming pools and an art gallery selling watercolors and posters by local artists. All in all, it adds up to a well-thought-out hotel and the only L.A. hotel that offers bargain-price romance. Honeymoon package: None. Rates (EP): $72 per couple per night for an economy room; $127 per couple per night for a superior room; $275 per couple per night for the Jacuzzi suite. And—at certain times of the year, the BayView Plaza drops its weekend rates by 50% as part of Holiday Inn's "Great Rates Plus" program. This means that you can get an oceanview room for as little as $63.50 per couple per night. A limited number of rooms is available at this price. Ask your travel agent for details.

In Laguna Beach: Located about 60 miles south of Los Angeles, Laguna Beach is a popular weekend retreat for Angelenos, thanks to the five-mile-long strip of beach. The frontage is well utilized by all ilk of beach-goers—joggers, surfers, volleyball players, dog walkers, bikinied beach-party lasses, all seemingly blessed with sunbleached hair, even tans, and toothpaste-commercial-caliber teeth.

For over 150 years, Laguna Beach has been known as an artists colony, hosting several festivals annually. The most unusual event—not only in Laguna Beach, but perhaps in the world—must be the Pageant of the Masters held in July and August, when a cast of thousands (literally) poise themselves in tableaux and re-create various Old Master paintings. All year-round, you can enjoy the perfect Southern California weather (85° in the summer, 70° in the winter), and browse through the art galleries and shops in town.

The Ritz-Carlton, 33533 Shoreline Dr., Laguna Niguel, CA 92677 (tel. 714/240-2000; reservations: toll free 800/241-3333 nationwide; 800/821-3101 in California). Putting on the Ritz, Southern California–style, means checking into the Ritz Carlton Hotel, spectacularly perched on a 150-foot-high bluff over the ocean. With its red-roofed, Mediterranean-style architecture, and marble terraces that spread out over the hillside, the hotel would look suitably at home in either St. Tropez or Positano. Reminiscent of the grand hotels of Europe, the columned lobby area has leather armchairs and a giant-size lounge gallery with a high, vaulted ceiling, marble floors, and an Oriental carpet that seems to run for the length of a football field. Throughout the hotel, a $2-million collection of 18th- and 19th-century American and European art and antiques is on display (the works even have their own curator and information pamphlet). In spite of all this Old World splendor, the hotel is a virtual youngster, having first opened its doors in 1984.

Pamper yourselves by staying in accommodations on the top Club Floor, where a concierge ministers to your every need—from mixing a cocktail to setting up an appointment with the masseur. In the morning, you can help yourself to a lavish continental breakfast; in the afternoon, enjoy tea and crumpets while looking out over the Pacific. On the Club Floor, rooms are very large and very luxurious, with a king-size, four-poster bed and country French furnishings, elegantly done in cream, Wedgwood blue, and green. On your balcony, you can sit and watch the sunset over the Pacific. For sheer, unmitigated glamour, you can't outdo the opulent bathroom, where shiny chrome fixtures and crystal chandeliers enhance the gray-and-white marble floors and walls. Although the standard rooms are not quite as expansive, they too have marble bathroom and country French decor. The staff-to-guest ratio is about 1:1, including a full-time member of the housekeeping staff whose main responsibility is to fluff pillows and stamp the distinctive Ritz Carlton lion's-head logo in the ash urns.

Follow the winding paths down through the gardens to the beach (you can also hop the free jitney). The hotel is located on a stretch called Salt Creek Beach, popular with area surfers who bob out beyond the breakers, waiting for the perfect wave. The Ritz Carlton has an excellent fitness center, with exercise equipment and frequent aerobics classes; there are also tennis courts, two outdoor swimming pools, and two Jacuzzis. When you work up an appetite, the three restaurants are excellent. On a typically balmy California day, you can't ask for anything nicer than lunch on the Café Terrace, shaded by a pergola and overlooking the main pool. Honeymoon package: None. Rates: From $231 to $341 per couple per night for a room; $259 to $407 per couple per night on the concierge floor; rate depends on view.

ROMANTIC RESTAURANTS: The trend in L.A., as elsewhere in the state, is toward what has become known as California cuisine: ultrafresh ingredients, cooked to enhance the natural flavors. In addition, L.A. restaurants tend to mix some of the dramatic flair of show business into their recipes: dining out in L.A. is part food, part theater. People do not so much eat to live, as eat to look at who else is eating there. The ''hot'' new restaurant changes just about as rapidly as the ''hot'' new star. For our restaurant recommendations, we've concentrated on places that are romantic, serve good food, are ''in''—and have earned their fashionable reputations over a bit of time. Reservations are practically always necessary.

The crowd starts pouring into **Nicky Blair's,** 8730 Sunset Blvd., Los Angeles (tel. 659-0929), in earnest, about 9 to 9:30 p.m. at this very fashionable restaurant owned by the well-known character actor. Definitely a place to see and be seen, Nicky Blair's also has first-rate Italian food and stunning modern decor. The menu tends toward light, summery fare such as you might enjoy on a terrace overlooking the Italian Riviera. Appetizers include a mixed seafood salad ($9.40), fried baby calamari ($8.25), and stuffed mushrooms ($6.10). Perhaps split a pasta dish, such as the agnolotti, filled with spinach and ricotta, or the pasta al pesto. Entrées include excellent chicken and veal dishes, priced from $17.25 to $25, and many fish selections, such as grilled salmon with tarragon sauce ($20.50) and white fish with capers, lemon, and white wine ($20.50). Ask about specials: They have fresh Santa Barbara shrimp in season, and they are superb.

Ivy at the Shore, 1541 Ocean Ave., Santa Monica (tel. 393-3113). Believe it or not, sunny Los Angeles has never had many sidewalk cafés. Ivy at the Shore fills that gap in style with a bistro right in the center of all the Santa Monica action. Seated on a white wicker chair on the terrace, you'll be able to gaze at the passing parade as well as the palm-lined promenade, beach, and Pacific Ocean. Indoors, the seating is equally charming, with rattan furnishings, 1930s pink, floral-print fabric on the rattan chairs, and ceiling fans. The food is truly excellent, with many mesquite-grilled dishes, as well as pastas and pizzas. Every day, fresh fish is flown in from New Orleans: gulf shrimp, lump crabmeat, and redfish. And you probably never have tasted anything as delicious as their tropical drinks made from scratch: If you order a piña colada, the barman slices up a pineapple, adds fresh coconut and rum, and whips it up in the blender. Lunch, $30 to $40 per couple; dinner, $50 to $60 per couple.

A lively atmosphere and very, very good food—that's what you'll find at **Hamlet Gardens,** 1139 Glendon Ave., Westwood (tel. 824-1818), located right in the heart of Westwood. The restaurant has light, Mexican tile floors, big ficus trees in planters, exposed brick walls; the wooden banquettes are brightly hand-painted with flowers. Background piano music sets the mood. The excellent cuisine culls recipes and seasonings from all over the world. Start with gravlax, marinated with dill and aquavit ($8.70), roasted oysters baked with green chile pesto ($9.40), or prosciutto with marinated goat cheese and sliced tomatoes ($9.40). Pastas are absolutely splendid, such as the piselli carbonara with cream, peas, pancetta, and radicchio ($13.75). Entrées include grilled quail on fried polenta ($18.15), grilled strip steak with French fries ($22), or a grilled tuna niçoise served rare ($19.80). Menus change frequently to take advantage of seasonal specialties. Do not miss the desserts, such as chocolate pecan pie or fresh raspberries.

If only the tables could talk. . . . **The Polo Lounge,** the Beverly Hills Hotel on Sunset Boulevard, Beverly Hills (tel. 276-2251), has acted as Hollywood's unofficial club-cum-conference room ever since Will Rogers, Darryl Zanuck, and Spencer Tracy used to pile in here after playing a few chukkers in an adjacent polo field. It was here that the concept of the "power breakfast" and the "power lunch" originated, here that W. C. Fields reserved a table for two and arrived accompanied by a carnivorous plant. This famous rendezvous has three different seating areas. The Green Room, right in front of the entrance, is where the superstars and the main power brokers sit—when they want to be seen. If they don't want to be seen, they'll opt for the pink-and-white Patio, surrounded by flowers. For seclusion, patrons choose the Loggia, separated from the main area by a glass partition. For us mere mortals, the nice thing about the Polo Lounge (and the whole Beverly Hills Hotel, for that matter) is the fact that it's a friendly place. If you come here, you won't get the best table in the house, but at least you'll be treated with respect and courtesy. It's a nice way to step into a favored milieu of the rich and famous. The food is good enough, but remember that you've come here for the atmosphere. Breakfast, about $35 per couple. Lunch, sandwiches, from $11.50; salads, from $13.75; hot entrées, $17 and up.

The drive down to **Gladstone's 4 Fish,** 17300 West Pacific Coast Hwy., Pacific Palisades (tel. 454-3474), is beautiful, leading you to the westernmost tip of Sunset Boulevard. Gladstone's is an "in" spot, noisy, wildly animated—and its outdoor deck overlooks the Pacific. As the name implies, the specialties of the house are the denizens of the deep. Start with fried calamari or a rich, creamy chowder, then check out what the fisherman has brought back that day—it might be salmon, trout, or yellowtail grilled over mesquite charcoal. For shellfish lovers, there's Maine lobster fresh from the tank. For the finale, sip espresso and share a hot-fudge sundae, chocolate chip cheesecake, or strawberry shortcake. Dinner for two, about $50 to $60 plus drinks.

The Hollywood Diner, 945 North Fairfax, West Hollywood (tel. 655-7051) is one of L.A.'s new, trendy spots, owned by Patrick Terrail, the moving spirit behind Ma Maison, which reigned as the Numero Uno on the Hollywood circuit for years. The menu highlights simple American and Californian fare, such as hamburgers, fresh fish, salads, and oysters, with entrées priced from $11 to $19 each. Wine and beer only are served—no hard liquor. **72 Market Street,** at (you've guessed it) 72 Market Street in Venice (tel. 392-8720), also attracts the in crowd. The restaurant serves home-style American cooking. How home-style? Well, the specialty of the house is meatloaf, but the rendition here elevates this humble favorite into the realm of the classic, accompanied by garlicky spinach and savory mashed potatoes. There's also an oyster bar, salad platters, and grilled items. Entrées priced from $13.50 to $28.50. **Nipper's,** 421 North Rodeo Dr., Beverly Hills (tel. 859-8747) is for ultimate sybarites: They serve sevruga caviar ($38 a serving), pâté with truffles ($22), and brie ($22), which you can nibble while sipping from their cellar of fine imported French champagne. The bottle of Dom Perignon at $200 might set you back a bit, but they do offer Laurent-Perrier Brut and Mirassou Blanc des Noirs for about $11 a glass. If you get more basic urges, such as a hankering for pizza and a movie, head over to **Mario's,** 1001 Broxton in Westwood (tel. 208-7077). In addition to classic pies with pepperoni and mushrooms, they offer some California-type toppings, such as eggplant, pesto, and fresh basil. Small pies, $7.50; medium, $9.50; and large, $11.50. Also in Westwood, **Yester-**

day's at 1056A Westwood Blvd. (tel. 208-8000), attracts an exuberant crowd from U.C.L.A. They are best known for their potent drinks and live music nightly. **Primi,** 10543 West Pico Blvd., West L.A. (tel. 475-9235), is one of the hottest addresses in town, serving appetizer-size portions of over 60 different Italian dishes daily. The menu rotates, but might include such tempting delicacies as baby salmon with pasta, tortelli stuffed with chicken, homemade ravioli cupped around duck and sage, or grilled Santa Barbara shrimp. The restaurant is an offshoot of the exquisite Valentino owned by Piero Selvaggio. Count on about two to three different items for each of you, for about $40 per couple. **Saint Estephe,** 2640 North Sepulveda in Manhattan Beach (tel. 545-1334), wins kudos for its innovative Mexican cuisine, which is not only delicious to eat, but also beautiful to behold. Favorite dishes include the salmon "Painted Desert," aswirl in three different colored sauces ($25); marinated veal chop with sopapilla ($27.50), and the enchilado shrimp, lined up and served with blue-corn tortillas. For dessert, head for the chocolate chile relleño, chocolate molded in the shape of a pepper, and served with lime-caramel sauce. **The Ivy,** 113 North Robertson, Beverly Hills (tel. 274-8303), will enthrall you with its authentic 18th- and 19th-century antiques, roses picked from the gardens of the owners, and superb food—many of the herbs are grown in their own gardens. No wonder specialties such as the mesquite-grilled chicken, steak, and Pacific shrimp seem to get extra zing from their "secret" marinades. Fabulous desserts. About $80 per couple, plus drinks.

Chapter V

FLORIDA

1. Practical Facts
2. Sanibel and Captiva Islands
3. Marco Island
4. Central Florida, Disney World, and EPCOT
5. Boca Raton
6. Palm Beach
7. Fort Lauderdale
8. Miami / Miami Beach
9. Key West

FLORIDA IS EXACTLY as you'd expect . . . and *nothing* like it. There are miles of sugar-white shoreline and swaying palms, but also underground caves, moss-draped cypress, and the Everglades, a last haven for near-extinct animals and birds. Spend a day lazing on the gulf doing nothing, or try everything from billfishing to spelunking to wagering on a jai alai match. Float into cloudless skies with your love in the gondola of a hot-air balloon or dive below the depths for an underwater spectacle of reefs, colorful tropical fish, and sunken wrecks.

Located in the southeastern United States, Florida is the southernmost state; subtropical with plenty of warmth and winter sunshine. Its proximity to the rest of the South makes it a great place to find cotton plantations, Civil War battlegrounds, and down-home cooking such as southern-fried chicken and grits. It is a peninsula surrounded by the Atlantic on the east coast and the Gulf of Mexico on the west; no other state can boast as many miles of shoreline and sunny beaches.

Florida is not one destination, it is many destinations, each with its own ambience and charm.

Driving around Florida is as diverse and scenic as a trip across the entire United States—Pensacola is separated from Key West by 900 miles. The road between Miami and Key West and any route from Orlando south will find you surrounded by Everglades saw grass, acres of fragrant orange groves or tall cypress eerily draped in Spanish moss. Coastal roads feature water views, resort towns, and high-rise condominimums, but inland, discover Indian reservations, natural springs, waterfalls, and underground caverns. One of the best ways to see Florida is to *not* plan too much and stop along the road when you see something interesting. The destinations in this chapter are just starting points for finding *your* place in the sun.

Take a bumpy airboat ride through wild marshland in the morning, visit a Southern plantation in the afternoon or climb to the top of a century-old lighthouse for incredible vistas, have dinner in an old castle while cheering on your favorite knight in a

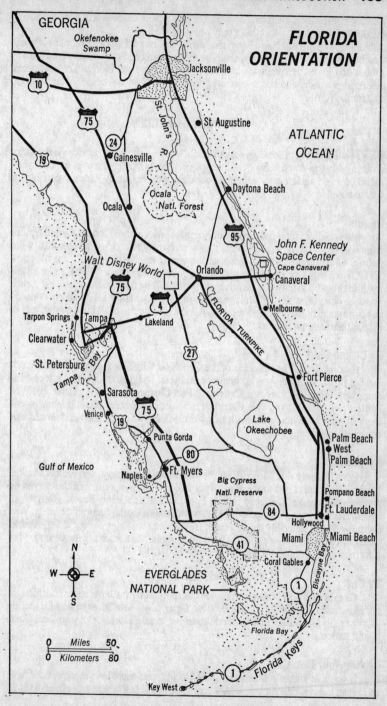

FLORIDA ORIENTATION

jousting competition, then kick up your heels as a New Orleans jazz band cranks out 1920s Dixieland tunes. And that's only one day!

Florida has all you plan a honeymoon for—and more. Hundreds of miles of warm beaches and the hush of history; shady woodlands and endless water sports; Mickey Mouse and Ernest Hemingway; baseball spring training and Florida Cracker homes; and enough sunshine to last an eternity. Welcome to Florida—come for the beaches, stay for the fun!

1. Practical Facts

GETTING THERE: Florida is easy to reach, thanks to frequent service via the major airlines and a top-notch network of interstate highways. Keep your eyes open for year-round deals on air fare and car rental packages, they're usually the most economical way to travel.

By Air

Many airlines offer packages to one or more cities within Florida. Remember that rates will probably be higher during the winter months and holiday periods, when throngs of northerners crowd hotels and resorts to escape the cold. Disney World / EPCOT packages are especially popular, so be sure to check for specials and availability of flights well in advance. Nearly every major airline flies to *somewhere* in Florida. To reach cities other than Miami, Orlando, or Tampa you may need to hop a connecting commuter flight once you're here. Almost all commuter airlines operate out of Miami International Airport.

By Cruise Ship

A cruise from The Bahamas or the Caribbean with a final destination in Florida can be a truly romantic way to begin or end your honeymoon. Ports are located in Tampa/St. Petersburg, at Cape Canaveral (Port Canaveral, servicing Orlando), West Palm Beach, Miami, and Port Everglades in Fort Lauderdale. If you'd like to spend more of your honeymoon on land, many cruise lines offer day trips and dinner sails departing from many cities.

By Train

For a leisurely ride, **Amtrak** serves the Midwest, northeast, and southern United States with connections to the West. Pull into one of over a dozen cities served by Amtrak: Clearwater, Deerfield Beach, Fort Lauderdale, Delray Beach, Hollywood, Miami, Jacksonville, Kissimmee, Lakeland, Orlando, Ocala, Sanford, Sebring, West Palm Beach, St. Petersburg, and Tampa. If you want to bring your car along, Amtrak offers an auto-ferry service out of Lorton, Virginia, to Sanford, near Orlando. For information, call Amtrak's toll-free number: 800/424-1111.

By Bus

Greyhound and **Trailways** provide transportation from other states and throughout Florida. Many smaller companies (i.e., **Gray Line**) have buses strictly for touring purposes. To find out about bus schedules to and around Florida, call your local Greyhound station.

Driving Your Own Car

If you live within 300 miles or so of Florida, you could save money on air fares and rental cars by driving yourself. Access to Florida is a breeze from Interstates 10 and 65 from the west; I-75 or I-95 from the north. Welcome Centers at all major entrance points offer maps, information, and brochures on sights, attractions, restaurants, and hotels as well as a free glass of Florida citrus juice. Plan where you're going to stop if you're driving to south Florida from anywhere—it's a 900-mile trek from Pensacola in the Panhandle to Key West on Florida's southernmost tip!

GETTING AROUND: When you make your hotel reservation, ask about complimentary transportation to major shopping malls and attractions. Many hotels have them, especially in the Orlando area. Often hotels (not just in large cities) have shuttles to and from the airport. If you really want to do some serious sightseeing, a rental car is almost a must. It's usually inexpensive and, let's face it, it's fun!

By Taxi

Taxis may be your best bet for areas where parking is a problem. If you're hailing a cab in Orlando, Miami, Tampa, or other major tourist centers, be aware that "special events fares" for Broadways plays, gallery openings, and symphony concerts may add up to $3 to the cost of the ride.

By Rental Car

The deals are sweet almost year-round for weekly rentals in Florida. Some of the larger companies give you two free days when you pay for five, unlimited mileage, and many other driver benefits. If you plan on visiting more than one destination in Florida, this may be the best way to get around. Here's a rundown on the kind of deals you might be able to find; they change frequently, so ask your travel agent for the latest scoop. **Alamo Rent A Car** (tel. toll free 800/327-9633) has mid-size cars for $25 a day; you can rent in your home state and drive to Florida without paying for mileage. **Avis** (tel. toll free 800/331-1212) has a "free two days when you rent for five" deal with 100 free miles per day. **National Car Rental** (tel. toll free 800/CAR-RENT) lets you rent for three days for the regular price and pay $20 a day thereafter. **Hertz** (tel. toll free 800/654-3131) has a great deal in Florida: Use your Eastern Airlines boarding pass to rent a car in Orlando or Miami for a week for just $59.

WEATHER: From Pensacola in the north to Key West in the south, temperatures can vary as much as 20° on any given day. In the summertime, temperatures range from warm to hot, so your bikinis and shorts should be sufficient wherever you travel in the state (average is 76° in the north; 81° in the south). In the winter, however, it is always best to prepare for the occasional cold snap that occurs as far south as Miami. Winters average 55° in the north, 68° in the south. In south Florida, rain is common in June and July, a factor you may consider when planning picnics or other outdoor activities. Tropical storm season is June through November.

CLOTHING: Lightweight clothing, swimsuits, and sandals are good choices for your Florida honeymoon. You'll also want to pack a good pair of walking shoes. A lightweight jacket or sweater and a pair of long pants will come in handy during the winter months or for restaurants where air conditioning may be chilly. For most restaurants, attractions, and hotels, casual attire is accepted and expected. However, many restaurants in the more upscale hotels require jackets for gentlemen, sometimes even ties are requested, so it's best to be prepared.

TIME: Florida spans two time zones—Central and Eastern, with most of the state being in the Eastern time zone. If you're entering Florida on I-10 from the west, you'll be on Central time for about two hours into the state.

TELEPHONES: Calling Florida will be easier if you know which area code belongs to which part of the state. All of northwest Florida over to Daytona Beach on the east coast uses 904. Tampa–St. Pete and all down the west coast is 813; the central east coast and south to Miami and the Keys is in the 305 area.

SHOPPING: If you're looking for T-shirts, ashtrays, or painted sand-dollar clocks, you'll find such souvenirs at drug stores, in malls, and in assorted shops on assorted beaches. Some real finds might be a bushel basket of real Florida citrus (many places will ship to your home so you don't have to carry it with you), or some rare shells you've collected yourself. Since Florida is dotted with shipping ports, shopping almost anywhere has an international flair. **Coconut Grove** in Miami is a mecca for goods from all over the world, as is **Park Avenue** in Winter Park near Orlando and the Vacation Kingdom's **EPCOT Center,** featuring authentic art objects, dolls, toys, and souvenirs from 10 different countries around the world.

Worth Avenue in Palm Beach has been called *the* most exclusive shopping district in the country, if not the world. The rental on most Worth Avenue shops for one year is more than what most of us earn in three. Don't feel intimidated by the clientele or the prices, though; Palm Beach has recently made a big push for vacationers using Garfield as a spokescat, trying to minimize the old "wealthy only" label. You'll find shops and restaurants very affordable, and you will certainly find treasures sold nowhere else. Gucci, Saks, and Godiva chocolates are here, as well as wonderfully pricey small boutiques. Check out the fancy new part of the strip called The Esplanade for even more mouth-watering delights. If you can't find it on Worth Avenue, you probably don't need it.

ABOUT ACCOMMODATIONS: Although not all Florida hotels have honeymoon packages, the wide range of vacation packages more than compensates. Summer rates can offer especially attractive deals in some resort areas; prices can drop by 30% to 50%. Where applicable, we've listed both low and high season rates in this chapter. A 15% tax will be added to your room rate.

DINING OUT: Nearly all of Florida is "come as you are," restaurants included, even the more expensive establishments. The occasional restaurant may require a jacket for men, sometimes even a tie, but if you're planning to pay $100 or more for a night out, you'll both probably want to dress up anyway.

Florida is part of the South, so along with the best international cuisine you'll find traditional favorites like corn bread, biscuits, and red-eye gravy. Of course, you must try any number of seafood delicacies cooked hundreds of different ways: Grouper, flounder, snapper, Gulf shrimp, pompano, and oysters are standard fare in many restaurants.

HOW TO GET MARRIED IN FLORIDA: To obtain a marriage license, you both need a blood test in Florida and proof of U.S. citizenship, such as a birth certificate. After the license is issued, you must wait three days before the actual ceremony can take place. Contact the city hall in the particular area in which you wish to marry.

How about a wedding at sea? If you'll be traveling to or from Florida aboard a cruise ship, many captains are licensed to officiate at weddings. If your perfect wedding involves a ship of smaller dimensions, some paddle wheelers or yachts can be chartered for the wedding and the reception. Outdoor gazebos at hotels and parks are favorite settings for weddings for many couples, but probably the number one choice in Florida is the beach. Sunset makes an especially nice setting. At many hotels, the social director can assist you in making all the arrangements.

FOR FURTHER INFORMATION: There are more than 200 chambers of commerce throughout the state that can provide you with maps, restaurant and hotel guides, brochures, and any other pertinent information you need on the areas you'll be visiting. For general information, write to the **Florida Chamber of Commerce,** P.O. Box 5497, Tallahassee, FL 32301 (tel. 904/222-2831). Chambers of commerce for the areas listed in this chapter follow:

Greater Boca Raton Chamber of Commerce, P.O. Box 1390, Boca Raton, FL 33432 (tel. 305/395-4433).

Coconut Grove Chamber of Commerce, 3437 Main Hwy., Coconut Grove, FL 33133 (tel. 305/444-7270).

Fort Lauderdale / Broward County Chamber of Commerce, P.O. Box 14516, Fort Lauderdale, FL 33302 (tel. 305/462-6000).

Key Biscayne Chamber of Commerce, 95 W. McIntyre St., Key Biscayne, FL 33149 (tel. 305/361-5207).

Greater Key West Chamber of Commerce, 402 Wall St., Key West, FL 33040 (tel. 305/294-2587).

Marco Island Chamber of Commerce, P.O. Box 913, Marco Island, FL 33937 (tel. 813/394-7549).

Miami-Dade Chamber of Commerce, 6255 Northwest Seventh Ave., Miami, FL 33150 (tel. 305/751-8648).

Miami Beach Chamber of Commerce, 1920 Meridian Ave., Miami Beach, FL 33139 (tel. 305/672-1270).

Orlando Area Chamber of Commerce, P.O. Box 1234, Orlando, FL 32802 (tel. 305/425-1234).

Palm Beach Chamber of Commerce, 45 Coconut Row, Palm Beach, FL 33480 (tel. 305/655-3282).

Sanibel / Captiva Island Chamber of Commerce, Causeway Road, Sanibel Island, FL 33957 (tel. 813/472-1080).

2. Sanibel and Captiva Islands

Exotic, unhurried, meticulously preserved and teeming with wildlife, the barrier islands of Sanibel and Captiva are truly a tropical paradise—a wonderfully diverse destination to "get away from it all." Residents fought hard to keep their islands isolated from the rest of Florida, but since the causeway linking the islands to the mainland opened in 1963, thousands can now visit these two pearls of the Gulf of Mexico.

The two islands are located north of Fort Myers and south of Tampa. Sanibel is the larger of the two (12 miles long and 3 miles wide), extending in an east-west direction into the Gulf of Mexico; Captiva is only six miles long and two miles wide. They are connected to the mainland by a $3 toll bridge; you'll save money by buying a $10, 20-trip pass if you plan to make frequent trips to and from.

You won't find a lot of glitz and glitter here; the islands' real appeal lies in their solitude and amazing variety of wildlife. Resorts offer a return to civilization but honeymooners with a real love of outdoor life will find Sanibel and Captiva most appealing. In order to protect its fragile natural splendor, Sanibel seceded from Lee County and set up its own government, which immediately put a stop to high-rise development. Sanibel Island is also home to the J. N. "Ding" Darling National Wildlife Refuge, the wonders of which will be discussed later, and is the best place for shelling in the western hemisphere.

ROMANTIC INTERLUDES: Just walking hand in hand along the shoreline with the surf washing over your bare feet conjures up a picture of romance in anyone's book, but keep your eyes open for the beautiful and strange birds and other wildlife all around you.

For a day of shelling, the islands are a conchologist's (shell collector's) delight; there are almost more shells than sand on Sanibel. Bring a bucket and wire scoop and dig in for lion's paws, tulips, cowries, jingles, sand dollars, and calico scallops. The tides wash them ashore by the thousands. Pick up a shelling guide at any one of the local shops to identify your finds. You'll probably be in good company; hundreds of bent-over diggers can be seen engaging in the popular posture called the "Sanibel stoop."

You'll spot brown pelicans, gulls, Louisiana herons, and other tropical birds all over the islands, but nowhere is the bird and wildlife watching better than in the 5,000-acre **J. N. "Ding" Darling Wildlife Refuge** on Sanibel Island, named for political cartoonist and naturalist J. N. "Ding" Darling. Bring along a camera, a pair of binoculars, and a bird book to identify such local inhabitants as the roseate spoonbill snapping up a meal of fish with its spatula-shaped beak, and "snake" birds who can swim underwater but must air-dry their wings before flying. There's also a five-mile drive through a mangrove swamp. Rent a canoe at **'Tween Waters Inn** on Captiva Island (tel. 472-5161) or the **Tarpon Bay Marina** (tel. 472-3196) and see the refuge from a different angle. Canoe trails twist and turn and the current can be swift at times, so this journey may be better left to experienced boaters.

A variety of cruises are available to the outlying keys of Boca Grande and Cabbage Key, leaving from the **'Tween Waters Marina** on Captiva Island (tel. 472-5463). It's possible to reach Boca Grande by car, but you have to travel for miles, so take the water route; it's more direct and infinitely more scenic. The main attractions on both islands are the lovely mansions set among the lush greenery. Fifty or so years ago, those with money and power opted to build their own island refuges where "commoners" could not reach; fortunately all of us can now view at least the *outside* of these lovely gabled and turreted homes. Hop on the **Cabbage Key Luncheon Cruise** aboard the *Island Queen II* from 10 a.m. to 3 p.m. daily for $15 per person; or the **Dinner Cruise** from 5:30 to 10:30 p.m. for $20 per person (they'll even throw in the sunset). The **Boca Grande Cruise** leaves at 10:30 a.m. daily and returns at 5:15 p.m. Price is $25. You'll cruise Pine Island Sound to see Cabbage Key and Useppa Island, then enter the Tarpon Triangle to Boca Grande. Dine at your choice of restaurants on the Boca Grande cruise and see the sights of "Old Florida" on Gasparilla Island, named for famed pirate and plunderer Jose Gaspar. Your captain will provide lighthearted and informative narrative along the way. A shorter sightseeing cruise is available from 3:30 to 5:30 p.m. daily for $10. It's a good idea to make reservations as far in advance as possible.

HONEYMOON HOTELS AND HIDEWAYS: From luxury hotels to furnished condominiums to private villas, the islands of Sanibel and Captiva welcome you to their tropical hideaways. Where applicable, prices shown reflect the spread between low- and high-season rates.

On Sanibel

Tucked cozily among royal palms and surrounded by shimmering crystal waters and an endless blue sky, the **Casa Ybel Resort**, 2255 West Gulf Dr., Sanibel Island, FL 33957 (tel. 813/472-3145; reservations: toll free 800/237-8906 nationwide; in Florida 800/282-8906), blends perfectly with these romantic islands in southwest Florida. As you step onto the footbridge leading to the resort's entrance, the reflection of the picturesque Thistle Lodge in the serene pond below welcomes you to "a little slice of paradise." Your warmly furnished one-bedroom villa will make you feel instantly at home; but once you walk out onto your private balcony to a view of a sun-washed white beach, palm trees, and emerald water dotted with pleasure craft, you'll know you've landed in a truly enchanted place. All villas are furnished with fully equipped kitchens and beachfront screened-in balconies. Rent sailboats, catamarans, bicycles, and beach cabanas for a whole honeymoon worth of outdoor activity. Or there's a refreshing swim in the pool, an invigorating set of tennis, or a leisurely round of golf to be enjoyed. Honeymoon package: Four days / three nights (EP): $484 per couple. Includes a one-bedroom villa, champagne, flowers, and a fruit basket on arrival, and a Casa Venture coupon book for free items and discounts. Seven-night package also available for $830 per couple (EP).

Sundial Beach & Tennis Resort, 1246 Middle Gulf Dr., Sanibel Island, FL 33957 (tel. 813/472-4151; reservations: toll free 800/237-4184 nationwide; 800/282-3405 in Florida). The waters of the Gulf of Mexico lap gently to the beach just steps away from your very own island hideaway. Four-story, white buildings sprawl out along the shore, just steps away from the shell-strewn sands. This resort is so complete, you'll never have to leave. You play golf or tennis, take a dip in one of the Sundial's five pools, dine to the music of the surf with the gulf as a backdrop, or sip drinks poolside. The Sanibel trolley can transport you on shopping or sightseeing excursions several times a day. Three restaurants, one lounge and a poolside bar are all on the grounds. "Island Honeymoon" package: Four days / three nights (EP): $575 per couple. Includes garden suite accommodations, chilled champagne and souvenir glasses, a trolley tour of the island or bicycle rentals, a souvenir beach towel, and a coupon for a free night at Sundial on your first anniversary. Seven night package available for $1225 (EP).

Song of the Sea, 863 East Gulf Dr., Sanibel Island, FL 33957 (tel. 813/472-2220). You may feel more like you're somewhere in the Mediterranean rather than Florida at this Old World inn with whitewashed walls, red tile roofs, and sculptures scattered throughout the grounds. Swim in the heated pool while playful stone cherubs and delicately carved seashores look on. Relax with a good book from the lending library or treat yourselves to a luxurious soak in the Jacuzzi. After a stroll around the grounds or a few hours of beachcombing in search of shells, cook some juicy steaks or fresh gulf seafood on one of the gas barbecue grills. Rent a boat and catch a breeze for a moonlight sail around Sanibel's Lighthouse Point. Tennis and golf are two privileges you may enjoy as a guest of Song of the Sea, and rented bicycles offer a different perspective of the island. Efficiencies and apartments are modestly but beautifully furnished in soft colors; some offer separate living rooms, fully equipped kitchens, and gulf-front screened balconies. Honeymoon package: None. Room rates: $132 to $155 (EP) per couple per night.

Sonesta Sanibel Harbour Resort, 15610 McGregor Blvd., Fort Myers, FL (tel. 813/466-4000; reservations: toll free 800/343-7170 nationwide). Sitting on 80 acres at the mouth of San Carlos Bay and the gateway to Sanibel and Captiva islands, the resort offers the best of both worlds, with easy access to both the islands and the mainland. Tennis is the big sport here, with Jimmy Connors as the touring professional. There's also a 5,500-seat tennis stadium, 12 lighted courts, a pro shop, clinics, and private lessons. But even if you don't play tennis, there's plenty to keep you busy. A fitness center provides a 40,000-square-foot spa, aerobic and strength-training equipment, an indoor pool, racquetball courts, Swiss showers, whirlpools, saunas, and steam rooms. Spend a day being pampered by the trained staff with massages, facials, herb wraps, and loofah scrubs. Just in case that isn't enough, spend prime tanning time on the private beach, improve your swing at the nearby championship golf course, charter a boat on Sanibel Island, or do some shelling in one of the finest spots on earth. Two

12-story towers offer one- and two-bedroom vacation apartments with two baths, a fully equipped luxury kitchen, living and dining rooms, and a screened balcony with views of San Carlos Bay and those great Sanibel sunsets. Suites offer views on two sides of the towers. Honeymoon package: None. Vacation apartment (one bedroom) rates (EP): $108.90 to $152.90 per couple per night in summer; $165 to $231 per couple per night in winter, depending on views.

Sanibel Arms West Condominium, 827 East Gulf Dr., Sanibel Island, FL 33957 (tel. 813/472-1138; reservations: toll free 800/237-8093 nationwide; in Florida call collect). These spacious condominium suites are bordered by a large private beach on the Gulf of Mexico. On the grounds find a large clubhouse, screened-in pool, sundeck, and two tennis courts. Cast a fishing line into the surf right from the beach. Take a bicycle tour of the island or seek out the many restaurants and shops nearby. Your two-bedroom condominium has two baths, a living and dining area, private balcony, screened porch, and fully equipped kitchen. Bright white kitchen appliances and cabinets, white wicker furniture throughout, checked wallpaper, and tropical print upholstery make you feel that you're far from winter's chill or the bustle of the city you left behind. Honeymoon package: None. Room rates are weekly only (EP): $650 to $850 per couple for gulf front; $550 to $725 per couple for gulf side. At Christmas time and in early spring (February to April 10), a two-week minimum stay is required.

On Captiva

Travel and Leisure magazine describes **South Seas Plantation Resort,** Yacht Harbour, P.O. Box 194, Captiva Island, FL 33924 (tel. 813/472-5111; reservations: toll free 800/237-6000 nationwide), as "Florida's Tahiti," spread over 330 acres on the northern tip of the island. Accommodations range from hotel rooms to one-bedroom villas to four-room houses right on the beach. The new Harbourside Village deluxe hotel rooms are especially honeymoon-right, overlooking the yacht harbor and Pine Island Sound. The feeling is tropical and islandy, with wicker headboards, rattan chairs, shell-motif pastel fabrics, and a green carpet that matches the palm trees outside. All the rooms have balconies facing the gulf or marina. For a ringside view of the famous gulf sunset, choose a one-bedroom beach villa. Each is uniquely decorated, and you can walk right out to the beach. Go shelling on the resort's 2 ½ miles of private beach, swimming in one of 17 pools scattered around the property, or hiking around the miles of resort trails. Play tennis on one of 22 courts or tee off on the resort's own nine-hole golf course. Try a new challenge by spending the day on a deep-sea fishing charter. Learn to sail, windsurf, or jet ski. Or spend a day on the *Silver Lady* boat excursion to legendary Useppa Island and Boca Grande. "Tropical Honeymoon" package: Seven days / six nights (EP): $1,010 per couple for the Harbourside Village hotel room; $1,373 per couple for the Beach Villa suite. It includes champagne and fruit delivered to your suite, use of bicycles for one day, complimentary beach towels, one day's use of beach cabanas, welcome cocktails, and a romantic cruise to nearby Historic Island. A huge range of packages is available; call for details.

Started in 1926 with one cottage, **'Tween Waters Inn,** Captiva Road, Captiva Island, FL 33924 (tel. 813/472-5161; reservations: toll free 800/223-5865 nationwide; 800/282-7560 in Florida), has changed hands and expanded, but has kept the original flavor and charm of 1920s Florida. The Inn is situated on a narrow strip of land between the gulf and Pine Island Sound; hence its name. Lushly landscaped with native trees and flowers, the popular inn has undergone extensive renovation to offer honeymooners the expected and unexpected amenities of modern resort hotels. The bayside marina provides rental of boats, canoes, and bicycles, and to see this island in all its splendor, try all the boats, bikes and footpaths you can find. 'Tween Waters Inn caters to those who crave the outdoors *and* those who prefer the civilized bounty of finely prepared cuisine in a dining room built early in the century. "Florida Fantasy Honeymoon" package: Four days / three nights (EP): $215 per couple. Includes a deluxe waterview unit with compact kitchen, a discount coupon book for food, drinks, and gifts, champagne, and a full day's use of canoes or bicycles. Seven-night package available for $500 (EP).

ROMANTIC RESTAURANTS AND NIGHTSPOTS: Take a break from your busy vacation schedule to enjoy dinner and cocktails in a quaint, romantic setting on these tropical isles.

Expensive

Outside, **La Vendée,** Andy Rosse Lane, Captiva Island (tel. 472-6866), gives the impression of a tropical summer home with an awning entranceway on one side, a cupola crowning the other side, and the entire structure surrounded by tall palms. Inside, it is a most elegant French restaurant with a tropical theme. Polished wooden tables mingle with rattan furnishings, indoor palms, luxurious place settings, and French touches (pictures, china, curtains). The menu is in French with English translations, so you can order in either language. Begin with a cold cream of leek soup with domestic caviar ($4.25), or try an appetizer of sautéed shrimp, tomatoes, and cilantro dressing ($7.50). Of course the specialty is seafood, prepared with French herbs in the native manner—roasted lotte, sliced, served with fresh pasta, saffron bouillon, and sauce rouille ($18) or braised halibut on top of warm cucumber with lobster butter sauce ($17). Baked duck, marinated lamb chops, filet mignon, and other meat and poultry dishes are offered ranging in price from $13.50 to $19. Cordials and coffee specialties round out a fine meal. Expect to pay $70 to $80 per couple for a full dinner. Open daily 5 to 10 p.m. Reservations accepted.

Moderate to Inexpensive

The Thistle Lodge Restaurant and Lounge at Casa Ybel Resort (tel. 472-3145). Over a century ago, the Reverend George Barnes built the Victorian gingerbread Thistle Lodge as a wedding gift for his daughter. With its turrets and balconies, fine-trimmed lawn and lush foliage, there could be few places on earth better suited for an evening tête-à-tête. The Chef takes foods indigenous to this area—Sanibel shrimp, shark, yellowtail, pecans, and oranges, and created menus to capture "the taste of Florida." Many specialties such as the Cajun beef Wellington and the creole onion soup rely heavily on the blackening techniques and roux sauces of New Orleans. Menus change monthly to reflect the freshest ingredients. Luncheon is served Monday through Saturday from 11 a.m. until 2 p.m. Sandwiches, soups, and specialty menu items are priced in the $3 to $10 range. Dinner is served 6 p.m. to 10 p.m., with entrées priced between $16 and $26. Brunch on Sunday is an event in itself, featuring seafood crêpes Punta Rassa, Belgian waffles, and café Orleans with praline liqueur and Kahlúa. Brunch is served from 10 a.m. until 2 p.m. and prix fixed at $12.95. And, if you'd like to be married here, the Lodge staff would be more than happy to assist you with everything from flowers to limousines.

J. Todd's next to the Ramada Inn, Sanibel Island (tel. 472-4123) is currently open for breakfast at 7 a.m. and carries on into the wee hours with live entertainment and dancing (dinner is served until 9 p.m.; 10 p.m. on weekends); it has been newly expanded and refurbished—an all-out attempt to become the liveliest night spot on the island. The dining room has undergone a facelift to offer diners an upbeat but casual atmosphere in rattan and warm gold with unusual shell chandeliers, a fitting ambience for J. Todd's new gourmet delights. The entire menu has been revamped to offer top-quality dishes like chateaubriand for two and slow-roasted prime rib at moderate prices. Dinner specials include your choice of shrimp cooked ten different ways, or the veal, beef, or chicken feature of the day plus the salad bar for $7.95 between 5:00 and 6:30 p.m. Friday night is prime rib night—all you can eat for $12.95. Save Saturday night for J. Todd's "Buffet of the Islands" from 5 to 10 p.m. There you'll find specialties such as oysters Rockefeller, crabmeat-stuffed artichokes, and seafood newburg for $13.51 a person. Visit the beachside raw bar for sandwiches, frozen drinks, oysters, and shrimp in a "come as you are" atmosphere.

The Mucky Duck, Andy Rosse Lane, Captiva Island (tel. 472-3434). This English-style pub at the gulf's edge opened in 1976 and quickly gained a reputation for excellence in dining. The warm, cozy feel of the Mucky Duck fits in beautifully with those spectacular water views; it's a local hangout, so don't be surprised if other diners or staff members walk up to your table and start a conversation. The lunch menu ranges from something on the light side (shrimp salad, fruit plate) to real rib-stickers like Scottish-style meat pie or Sam's Samwich with ham, turkey, and Swiss on rye, about $3.25 to $6.95. Dinner gets dressed up when the chef pulls out all the stops to create roast duckling à l'orange, steak and sausage pie, and Polynesian chicken; prices range from $9.50 to $14.95. The Mucky Duck's famous New England clam chowder is not to be missed. Lunch hours are 11:30 a.m. until 2:30 p.m.; dinner is from 5:30 to 9:30 p.m. Choose a delicate wine with your meal or a hearty mug of imported beer. No reservations are ever needed and The Mucky Duck takes cash or traveler's checks only.

'Tween Waters Restaurant at 'Tween Waters Inn, Captiva Island (tel. 472-5161). Relax in the cozy 1920s Florida Victorian dining room; it's the kind of place where the staff will go out of the way to make a fuss over visiting honeymooners. The food is good and prices are moderate. Sketches made by "Ding" Darling adorn the walls, and frilly curtains remind you of mom's kitchen. You may want to plan ahead for the feast that begins here about 5:30 p.m. and continues until 10 p.m. Each day features a different menu—Monday there is an Italian buffet, prime rib on Tuesday, a seafood buffet on Friday, and a special Captiva brunch on Sunday from 9 a.m. until 1 p.m. Most dinners are $9.95 to $14.95, and reservations should be made for dinner and Sunday brunch. Not flashy or fancy, but a nice taste of old Florida.

The Old Captiva House at 'Tween Waters Inn, Captiva Island (tel. 472-5161). Rustic and quaint inside and out, the Old Captiva House is set in one of the original parts of the hotel. It's clean and pleasant, but if the decor doesn't bowl you over, the food certainly will. Dinners like Florida flounder Véronique (baked in a white wine sauce and topped with white grapes) or medallions Rossini (center-cut filet mignon sautéed in white wine and topped with tomato and mozzarella cheese sauce) include a salad, fresh breads, vegetables, and potato or linguine. All you add is your beverage and dessert. Prices range from $9.95 to $16.95. The Old Captiva House opens at 7 a.m. for breakfast and closes at midnight.

Chadwick's at South Seas Plantation, Captiva Island (tel. 472-5111). "Tropical" is the key word at this recently redone restaurant. Huge paintings of parrots, toucans, and hibiscus flowers decorate the walls, bright greens and pinks spike interest in the furnishings. Seafood is the specialty here, especially at the all-you-can-eat seafood buffet on Friday nights ($21.50 per person). Help yourself from heaping platters of grouper, shrimp, oysters, and red snapper. Every Tuesday, there's a Hawaiian-style luau ($17 per person) and a champagne brunch on Sundays ($14.85) per person. A live band plays on Friday and Saturday nights.

3. Marco Island

Still one of Florida's last frontiers, Marco Island is beautifully remote from the more populated tourist centers that dot the west coast of Florida. The Calusa Indians called this serene island home for 2,000 years and archaeologists are still uncovering artifacts dating back to 500 B.C. Modern man has left his mark on the island, as the high-rise hotels and condominiums attest. But it certainly hasn't dissuaded the locals from moving right in and making themselves at home—bald eagles are sighted occasionally and some have even returned to the island to rear their young, attracted by artificial nests developers have put under the eaves of condominiums.

Take Florida 41 south of Fort Myers for a nice taste of rural Florida. There's only one road that will take you to the island, so keep an eye out for it (Florida 953). Marco Island is only about four miles long from stem to stern and so narrow the Jolly Green Giant could straddle it (about ½ mile across). Once you cross the bridge, it seems you're far from the mainland—gleaming sugar-white beaches contrast with sparkling emerald and turquoise gulf waters, and lush scrub brush and tall trees seem to grow out of the snowy-white sands.

This is the place where the Ten Thousand Islands begin, a conglomerate of mangrove trees that, because of their enormous root system, pick up pieces of shell, driftwood, and other debris and eventually form their own islands. The islands are great fun to explore by boat, but bring along a guide, as the maze of trees can be confusing.

ROMANTIC INTERLUDES: Far from the big city crowds, Marco Island offers you a chance to get back to nature and enjoy a quiet respite without going too far from civilization.

For a taste of the Everglades wilderness without actually venturing in, **Collier-Seminole State Park** (tel. 657-3771) has 6,500 acres of marshland for canoeing (a favorite spot is the 13-mile loop trail at the Blackwater River) and hiking. A catwalk winds its way through the mangrove swamps. Camping facilities are available and the fishing is fabulous! No admission fee. Follow U.S. 41 (the Tamiami Trail) 16 miles east to find the park.

Ready for a real adventure? Welcome to the wildest part of Florida—**The Everglades.** Spend a day or two exploring this magnificent subtropical wilderness. Everglades National Park takes up most of Florida's southern tip; at 1.4 million acres, that's more area than the entire state of Delaware. Once you venture by boat into the vast sea of marshland and sawgrass, watch carefully for the incredible variety and sheer numbers of plant, bird, and reptile species you are about to encounter. In an environment hostile to man, alligators, bald eagles, and snowy egrets live harmoniously. It's your chance to see what Florida would be like had man never intervened.

Boat tours are available so you can spend more time watching and picture taking and less time navigating. Everglades tours can be found at Everglades National Park from the National Park Service in Everglades City (tel. 695-2591 or toll free 800/233-1821 nationwide; 800/455-7724 in Florida), or from Eden of the Everglades, where you can talk to Ervin Stokes in Everglades City (tel. 695-2800). Air boat rides are offered through M. Douglas House, Everglades City (tel. 642-5777 or toll free 800/282-9194.

The pretty little **Marco Island Trolley** (tel. 394-2120) will delight you with a 1½-hour tour of this largest of the Ten Thousand Islands. Trolleys leave from all major hotels and shopping areas 11 times a day (every 45 minutes), but don't fret if it's not exactly on schedule; you're running on island time now. One of your stops will be the Calusa Indian burial mounds where 6,000-year-old artifacts have been uncovered. Relax and enjoy the ride while spotting pelicans, spoonbills, and perhaps even a dolphin or two (bring binoculars!). The trolley costs $4.50 per person and runs Monday through Saturday.

HONEYMOON HOTELS AND HIDEAWAYS: It's the best of two worlds; the open wilderness beyond Marco Island and the bustling civilization of cottages and towering hotels that line the beach. Where applicable, prices shown reflect the difference between low- and high-season rates.

Expensive

There's never a dull moment at Marriott's **Marco Island Resort,** 400 South Collier Blvd., Marco Island, FL 33937 (tel. 813/394-2511; reservations: toll free 800/228-9290; nationwide: 800/GET-HERE in Florida), with activities like sailing, fishing, waterskiing, windsurfing, mini-golf, or tennis on one of 16 courts. Stroll or swim along the 3½ miles of private beach or swim in one of three pools. Volleyball games are organized regularly if you care to join in the fun. If you go out for a day of bird watching or deep-sea fishing, chances are you'll be ready for a romantic dinner for two when you get back—you have five restaurants to dine at, from elegant to casual. Just for fun, ask for extra everything on your sundae at the Ice Cream Parlor next to the health club (is that a hint?). Many of the rooms overlook the Gulf of Mexico, others the pool or garden area. Each room is tastefully appointed in soft, pleasant, pastel hues and light woods. All have separate dressing rooms with vanity, cable TV and in-room movies, radio, refrigerator, mini-bar, and coffee maker. And every room has a private balcony. In addition to the tower rooms, there are Hawaiian-style lanais with direct access to the beach. Honeymoon package: Four days / three nights (EP): $588 per couple. Five-night package (EP) also available for $830 per couple.

At the **Marco Beach Hilton,** 560 South Collier Blvd., Marco Island, FL 33937 (tel. 305/394-5000; U.S. reservations: toll free 800-HILTONS), you'll have ringside seats for some of the most spectacular sunsets on the gulf. Imagine waking to fresh tropical breezes blowing into your room off your private gulf-front balcony. Your honeymoon suite has its own TV with Home Box Office—even a phone in the bathroom. Spend your days sunning, shelling, shopping, surfing, swimming, or enjoying any number of activities the Hilton can help you set up. Honeymoon package: Four days / three nights (EP): $470 (standard) to $635 (deluxe) per couple. Two- and seven-night packages also available. Includes chilled champagne, fresh flowers, and a catered breakfast in bed the first morning.

Moderate

The Olde Marco Inn, 100 Palm St., Marco Island, FL 33937 (tel. 813/394-3131), provides the comfort and fine dining one would expect at an elegant resort, but preserves the hospitality and charm of the 19th century wayside inn it once was. The inn is currently owned by Marion Blomeier, a former German concert singer, who has made restoring the Inn a life's work. She has included such museum pieces as a 2,000-prism cranberry-colored glass chandelier, original Audubon prints, and wildlife prints by Ray Harin, a former guest at the Inn. If you arrive by boat, you dock at the pier, where you can fish or enjoy the great sunsets. A new addition to the Inn is the Boat House (tel. 813/642-7700) adjacent to the Inn just off the Marco River at the entrance to Collier Bay. The lovely guest house, built in keeping with the historic white facade of the Inn, features 20 guest rooms with custom-designed interiors. Built-in sitting nooks, overstuffed pillows, and queen- and king-size beds with percale sheets create a cozy tropical ambience. French windows and doors with wooden shutters bring in maximum light and air, while paddle fans, rattan furnishings, and plenty of olive plants provide guests with the warm, friendly atmosphere of a bygone era. More modern conveniences like the cable TV, computer module capability, and direct-dial phones with an automatic wake-up feature remind you that you're not so far away from civilization. Honeymoon package: None. Standard rate (EP) is $99 to $121 per couple per night, including continental breakfast.

ROMANTIC RESTAURANTS AND NIGHTSPOTS: From quiet and intimate, to upbeat and stirring, Marco Island is filled with great eateries and nightclubs, all with those intoxicating gulf views surrounding them.

Moderate

Dress up for this evening's romantic dinner for two. **Sandcastles Restaurant** at the Marco Beach Hilton (tel. 394-5000), is elegant and intimate with lovely pool views. Low lighting and the white linen and burgundy color scheme offer a romantic setting. Choose the upper balcony for truly intimate dining. Fresh seafood is the specialty here, with exotic treats like swordfish, coconut fried shrimp, or the catch of the day served one of six different ways. Veal, filet mignon, juicy New York sirloin, and breast of chicken round out the menu, painstakingly prepared, elegantly presented, and overwhelmingly enjoyed. Take your time to savor the scenery both inside and out, and linger over after-dinner drinks. Dinners, which will cost a bit over $20 per person before appetizers and dessert, are served between 5:30 and 10 p.m. Sunday through Thursday; one hour later on the weekends. Reservations and jackets are requested.

When you hear strains of "In the Mood" and other classics, you may find it hard to keep your seat, but there's plenty of time to do everything on the island, and dinner at the **Marco Dining Room** at Marriott's Marco Island Resort (tel. 394-2511) should be savored slowly. The cool gray-green color scheme and softly lit chandeliers provide just the proper backdrop for the tuxedoed waiters who come complete with white gloves. Many of the restaurant's specialty dishes are prepared tableside so you may dine, listen to some great dance music, and watch the chef's floor show all at once! You'll spend about $50 per couple on your dinner, not including dessert and cocktails. Try a glass or bottle of excellent wine from the Marco Dining Room's considerable list. Dinner is served from 6:30 until 11 p.m., with reservations required until 9:30.

Olde Marco Inn, 100 Palm St. (tel. 813/394-3131). This lovely, restored, 1883 inn gets more beautiful every week. All of the six dining rooms are decorated in Victorian-era furnishings, curtains, and table settings, from the summerhouse setting of the veranda to the formal wood-paneled Audubon room with its original prints and crystal wall sconces. The continental menu compliments the period ambience. Start your meal with an appetizer of stone-crab claws, marinated Icelandic herring, or Jerry's extra, a specialty of the house that changes daily. Fresh fish might include snapper, grouper, shrimp, scallops, stone-crab claws, or whatever comes off the boat that day. Then there are favorites such as southern-fried chicken, wienerschnitzel, or veal Madagascar. Ask about Marion's preference; that's another name for the specialty entrées of the evening. Dinner, including appetizer, soup, and entrée, will run close to $50 per couple. Open for dinner only from 5:30 to 10 p.m. Monday through Saturday; 5 to 10 p.m. Sunday. Entertainment is provided nightly in both the piano lounge and the Crystal Room for dance music. Reservations for dinner requested.

Inexpensive

The **Paradise Cafe** at the Marco Beach Hilton (tel. 394-5000), is completely glass enclosed, decked out in soft turquoise and rose with wrought-iron chairs and plants. On the far end, old-time beach chairs overlook the Hilton's pool. Start each island morning off with a continental breakfast or select from heartier fare. Eggs sandcastle is a thinly sliced filet mignon and an English muffin topped with poached eggs and béarnaise sauce. You'll spend between $4.95 and $7.95 for your main breakfast course. Appease your luncheon hunger with a meal of French onion soup and a fiesta salad (beef, beans, cheese, guacamole, and all the trimmings in a tortilla shell), or seafood salad (shrimp, scallops, crabmeat, and whitefish), or bite into a grouper sandwich or order the catch of the day grilled or blackened in Cajun spices. Lunch entrées range from $5.25 to $10.95. The Paradise Cafe is open from 7 a.m. to 10 p.m. daily.

Beer steins, diagonally paneled windows, plate art, and Lederhosen accent the authentic German menu at **The Bavarian Inn,** opposite the Marco Beach Hilton (tel. 394-7233). Fill up a stein of foamy brew and toast great dishes like sauerbraten, Yaeger schnitzel, kasseler Rippschen, and roast kalbsharxe; waiters will happily help with pronunciations! Serving 4:30 to 10 p.m.; the midnight menu is in effect from 10 p.m. until 1 a.m. Complete dinners are all in the $10 per person range, sans beer.

4. Central Florida, Disney World, and EPCOT

Up until the 1970s, visitors escaped to Central Florida for the cool serenity of moss-draped cypress, clear natural springs, and sprawling horse farms. Then a man with a vision bought 27,400 acres of swamp land—twice the size of Manhattan—and transformed it into the largest tourist attraction in the world: Walt Disney World and EPCOT Center, jointly known as the Vacation Kingdom. Now Florida cracker homes and thoroughbred farms coexist with technological wonders of the 21st century. Add to that Central Florida's multitude of spectacles—Sea World, Cypress Gardens, and throngs of other razzle-dazzle attractions—and you just may have the most action-packed and delightfully diverse honeymoon vacation this side of the Milky Way.

Nothing in Disney's world has been left out or left to chance. Each attraction, hotel, restaurant, shop—even landscaping and maintenance—has been planned down to the last detail for visitors from all over the world, honeymooners being no exception. Certainly Disney must have had romance in mind when he designed lazy boat rides through mysterious Louisiana bayous, grottos, and lagoons, cascading waterfalls, even waterside dining with a simulated night sky overhead, complete with the reflected twinkle from Disney-manufactured fireflies.

Orlando is to Central Florida what Mickey Mouse is to the Magic Kingdom—the very center of things and the star attraction. The area is bordered by shady, sleepy southern towns with friendly-sounding names: Fellowship, Lake Placid, Winter Haven, and Kissimee (pronounce it Kuh-SIM-ee unless you *really* want to get friendly). It is about 90 miles from Florida's east and west coasts, which is why it has become such a popular place to live. And for vacations, well, need I say more? There are sure to be all the right ingredients in Central Florida for a memorable honeymoon. It's a place everyone can afford and an experience no one should miss.

ROMANTIC INTERLUDES: If you don't see another thing on your Central Florida honeymoon, take in **The Walt Disney World Vacation Kingdom** (Walt Disney World and EPCOT Center), P.O. Box 40, Lake Buena Vista, FL 32830 (tel. 824-4321). Perhaps the eighth wonder of the world, it can be the centerpiece for an entire vacation. There is so much to see and do, a week would not be too long to spend here. Couples will find romantic boat cruises, dining in several different "countries" with authentic cuisine, goods from around the world, fascinating and informative exhibits, and of course, the fun and child-like innocence of Disney character parades, haunted houses, and roller coasters. You're almost guaranteed a perfect honeymoon!

The best time to visit is any time school is in session—early spring or late fall. Crowds thin out a bit at these times, making your stay more enjoyable and lines shorter. A one-day World Pass, which entitles you to visit either Walt Disney World *or* EPCOT, is $18 per person. Three-day passports good for admission to both attractions are $45 per person; five-day passes are $65 per person. If you plan to stay at one of the hotels owned by Walt Disney World, you may get a few dollars off the price of your ticket.

Whole guidebooks have been written about Walt Disney World and EPCOT. What we've done here is focus in on the attractions that most appeal to fun, action-loving honeymooners like yourselves.

By no means for kids only, **Walt Disney World** is a thrill-a-minute entertainment showcase that provides rides, live entertainment, restaurants, and shopping every day of the year. Begin at Main Street, U.S.A., a look at turn-of-the-century America.

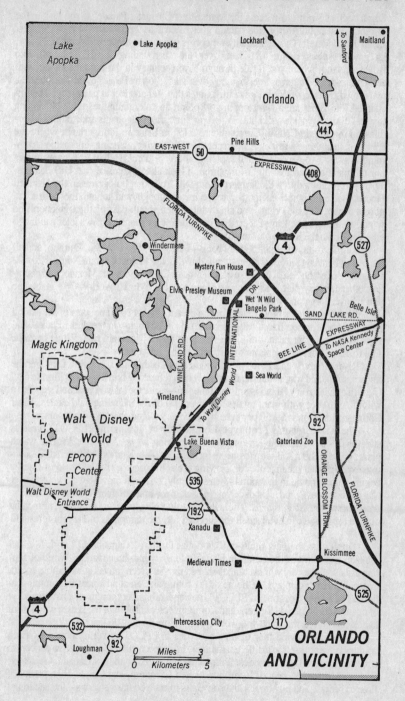

Lake Apopka
Lake Apopka
Lockhart
To Sanford
Maitland
Orlando
44
EAST-WEST 50 Pine Hills
EXPRESSWAY 408
FLORIDA TURNPIKE
4
527
Windermere
Mystery Fun House
Elvis Presley Museum
Wet 'N Wild
Tangelo Park
Belle Isle
SAND LAKE RD.
BEE LINE EXPRESSWAY
To NASA Kennedy
Space Center
Magic Kingdom
Sea World
Vineland
Walt Disney
World
EPCOT
Center
Lake Buena Vista
Gatorland Zoo
Walt Disney World
Entrance
535
92
192
Xanadu
Medieval Times
Kissimmee
4
525
N
Intercession City
17
532
ORLANDO
AND VICINITY
Loughman 92
0 Miles 3
0 Kilometers 5
INTERNATIONAL DR.
VINELAND RD.
To Walt Disney World
ORANGE BLOSSOM TRAIL
FLORIDA TURNPIKE

Come back at 3 p.m. to witness the Main Street Character Parade. If you visit in the summer or at holiday time, the parade goes electric at 9 p.m. and 11 p.m. Straight ahead the Cinderella Castle officially welcomes you to the wonderful world of Disney, its golden spires rising 181 feet over the surrounding moat. Take off into Adventureland, where you'll ride through bayou country in flat-bottomed boats with eerie moss-draped cypress trees hanging overhead. Stop by Pirates of the Caribbean, a real crowd pleaser, with rum-guzzling pirates that jeer and leer at passersby. The Enchanted Tiki Birds are a fun stopping-off point, an entertaining respite with singing tropical birds set inside a tiki hut. Watch out for curious elephants and smiling crocodiles on the Jungle Cruise. Climb aboard a log raft ride in Frontierland, where the sound of steamboat whistles is interspersed with singing, dancing, and banjo strumming in a salute to America's first settlers. Liberty Square's Hall of Presidents relives our turbulent but fascinating history through look-alike figures of past U.S. leaders. Then you're invited to a dinner party with 999 frolicking holograms in the Haunted House. Hang on tight to each other as you travel through, and get into the "spirit" as ghosts dance, play the organ, and sing while flying about, passing through doors and windows. Before you leave Liberty Square, there's a vintage stern-wheeler waiting to take you down the Rivers of America.

Your favorites of childhood are back—Peter Pan, Snow White, Dumbo, and all the rest in Fantasyland, plus an in-depth, down-under look at Captain Nemo's 20,000 Leagues Under the Sea. Then take a slow boat to China, Holland, Mexico, and countless other faraway places as you sing along to "It's a Small World." We guarantee you'll never forget the words!

Tomorrowland is more than simply a dream of what *could* be, part of the exhibit has been transformed into a roller-coaster ride at 65 mph—in the dark! Planets and stars whirl past your head within the elaborate Space Mountain ride. While here, be sure to check out the video tour of America in the 360° theater.

River Country and Discovery Island charge additional admission fees, but the flumes, rafts, and water slides can certainly be a refreshing break on a hot Florida day! Getting to Discovery Island is only half the fun—cross the lake by boat and step into a wildlife preserve with giant turtles and over 500 birds, including bald eagles. River Country admission is $9.50 per person; Discovery Island charges $4 per person.

The **Experimental Prototype Community of Tomorrow** (EPCOT) presents state-of-the-art technology in unusual and exciting ways. At Future World, watch plants grow without soil—up to twelve inches a day!—in Kraft's The Land, an innovative experimental greenhouse for growing crops in space. Exxon's World of Energy begins with a movie in the round, then suddenly, one wall moves away, your theater seat starts to move, and all at once you're back in the times of giant *Tyrannosaurus rex*, *pterodactyl*, and *Stegosaurus*. There they are, looming huge and ominous, munching on tree tops. You can even smell the dirt and feel the dampness of the rain forest climate.

Don't miss the new multi-million-dollar thriller, "Captain EO" with Michael Jackson and a cast of thousands in Kodak's Journey into Imagination. World of Motion puts you in a car, while a tunnel-shaped movie screen moves at incredible speed; Spaceship Earth displays the home of the future and great advances in communications; The Living Sea, one of EPCOT's newer exhibits, lets you in on a fish-eye view of ocean floor life; and Horizons and Communicore will delight the senses with lots of hands-on exhibits that keep you wondering, "How do they do that?"

Take a whirlwind tour of nine countries in EPCOT's World Showcase. Each country presents itself in a different manner, from spectacular films to native dancers to street vendors to lazy boat rides. Take in the sights and sounds of Canada, Germany, France, Mexico, Morocco, Japan, the United Kingdom, and China. Take plenty of time to browse and buy goods and souvenirs in each country's shops—the section of art objects and handcrafted dolls is as complete and authentic as if you'd actually visited each country. Lastly, our story, an "American Adventure," is told in part by Ben Franklin and Mark Twain. Once you see them walk, gesture, and talk, you'll find it hard to believe they aren't the genuine article.

Look for three new Walt Disney attractions opening in the next two years. Pleasure Island is a nighttime entertainment complex on Buena Vista Lagoon. Designed around a mythical 19th-century tale of shipbuilder Merriweather Adam Pleasure, Pleasure Island will feature six themed nightclubs to suit all musical tastes and a variety of shops and restaurants to complete the six-acre complex. Visitors will be able to take a Disney-MGM Studio Tour right on the grounds in 1989. Also scheduled at EPCOT's World Showcase is the Norway Pavilion, Gateway to Scandinavia. You'll be able to take a fantastic voyage aboard a 10th-century Viking ship. A screen tour of modern Norway will also be featured.

Right here in the same town, check out **Sea World,** 7007 Sea World Dr. (look for the I-4 Sea World exit), Orlando, FL 32821 (tel. 351-0021), the largest marine-life theme park in the world. The shows are the big attraction here, with skillful waterskiing exhibitions, talented seals, choreographed dolphins, and Shamu, the killer whale, trained to perform tricky maneuvers and high jumps with his human entourage. There's more entertainment in store with the "New Friends" whale and dolphin show, 60s-themed waterski show, feeding demonstrations, Japanese pearl-diving exhibitions, and the Shark Encounter, where you can view the creatures from moving sidewalks that glide past the huge shark tanks. But most fun of all is undoubtedly the brand-new, $13-million Penguin Encounter, which showcases about 300 of the dapper black-and-white birds, whose "formal attire" would rival the best-dressed wedding party. Six thousand pounds of manufactured "snow" falls on the exhibit daily. Don't miss it! Open 8:30 a.m. to 7:30 p.m., later in summer and on holidays. Admission: $13.95 per person. Parking is free.

Cypress Gardens, P.O. Box 1, west of U.S. 27 on Rte. 540 at Cypress Gardens Boulevard in Winter Haven, FL 33880 (tel. 324-2111) is a bit off the beaten path, Cypress Gardens was created over 50 years ago from a cypress swamp. Exotic flowers, clear reflecting pools, in a maze of nature trails, make up the gardens. The waterski shows are some of the best in the state. You'll want to spend the better part of a day here drinking it all in. Open 8 a.m. to 6 p.m., 365 days a year. Shows are 10 a.m., 2 p.m., and 4 p.m. Admission is $12.95 per person and parking is free.

There's a cozy little town just north of the crowds and feverish pace of Orlando where you may want to spend a whole day. In fact, some folks who visit **Winter Park** go back home, pack the rest of their belongings, and return to stay. Streets are quiet and shady with turn-of-the-century homes adorned with graceful lattice-work gables and porches. Man-made canals weave finger-like through the city. For a leisurely tour of the "Venice of America," hop aboard an excursion boat on one of three lakes. Call the **Winter Park Chamber of Commerce** (tel. 644-8281) for a list of boat excursions, times, and prices.

Because of its proximity to Orlando, the town can no longer be called rural—**Park Avenue** is now an exclusive shopping district. After shopping walk over to Rollins College to view the well-known Walk of Fame, 800 stones inscribed with the names of famous people, brought from their homes and birthplaces. There's also Mead Botanical Gardens, a quiet place to walk and picnic while viewing native Florida flora.

A good day trip by car (about two hours from Orlando), the lure of **Busch Gardens** (The Dark Continent), I-275 to the Busch Boulevard exit, 3000 Busch Blvd., Tampa, FL 33612 (tel. 971-8282), is not its free beer (although that may cause you to linger a bit), it is the wild giraffes, wildebeests, antelopes, elephants, and zebras that roam the *veldt* just as they would in Africa. Be sure to bring a camera for some great close-ups in this park, where animals roam free separated from the public by a large moat. Boat rides offer another perspective of these jungle-like habitats. Open 9:30 a.m. to dusk. Admission, $18.95 per person; parking is $1.

From the folks who brought you Sea World and Cypress Gardens, **Boardwalk and Baseball**, P.O. Box 800, Orlando, FL (tel. 422-0643 or 424-2424) offers a different type of theme park. Reminiscent of Coney Island or Atlantic City, every ride, show, and attraction in the park is connected by a wooden boardwalk. The other half of the name comes in with daily exhibition baseball games in February, March, and April, when Boardwalk and Baseball hosts the Kansas City Royals during spring training. For hard-core baseball fans, there are also batting cages, pitching machines, baseball memorabilia exhibits, and baseball films. For everybody else, Boardwalk and Baseball offers 30 thrill rides, including roller coasters, log flumes, and ferris wheels. Live shows are featured several times daily. Colorado Riders has a western theme complete with horses, wagons, cowboys, and can-can girls. Illusions combines magic with high-tech mechanics in this unusual offering. Admission is $16.95 per person, which is all-inclusive with the exception of the games on the midway. Parking is free.

HONEYMOON HOTELS AND HIDEAWAYS: Go all the way or sleep cheap, Central Florida has the largest variety of accommodations in all of Florida; your opportunity to find that one perfect place for romance in a land of magic and fun. Stay right on the Disney grounds in one of several "official" Walt Disney World hotels, or stay for less (usually) in the surrounding towns of St. Cloud, Kissimmee, or Winter Park.

Expensive

A gleaming 841-room, 27-story resort along the lakefront, **Buena Vista Palace** inside Walt Disney World Village, Lake Buena Vista, FL 32830 (tel. 305/827-3333; reservations: toll free 800/327-2990 nationwide; 800/432-2920 in Florida) towers over the Central Florida skyline, overlooking all of the Vacation Kingdom. This palace "designed for the 21st century" features four interconnected towers faced with reflective glass. The entire "World" is at your doorstep or a quick ride via the complimentary transportation system. All rooms have private balconies; many open onto either a central atrium or a courtyard. You're also sure to like the ceiling fans, remote-control color TV, and Mickey Mouse phones (there's even a bathroom extension). "Palace Promise" honeymoon package: Five days / four nights (EP): $980 per couple. Includes a candlelight dinner at Arthur's 27 (see restaurant section), deluxe accommodations with queen- or king-size bed, three-day World Passports for unlimited admission to the Magic Kingdom and EPCOT Center, one breakfast in bed, $100 in savings on dining and entertainment in the Official Bonus Cheque Pack, and a bottle of champagne and a fruit basket.

As an official Walt Disney World resort, the **Hotel Royal Plaza,** Lake Buena Vista, FL 32830 (tel. 305/828-2828; reservations: toll free 800/327-2990 nationwide; 800/432-2920 in Florida), rolls out the red carpet for honeymooners. For sheer extravagance, it's possible to rent the Michael Jackson or Bob Hope suites. They are both frequent guests of the hotel and received the honor of designing their own suites. Michael Jackson's suite offers one bedroom and a parlor for a mere $407 (EP) per night; $814 (EP) a night for the full four-bedroom suite. Bob Hope's suite goes for $572 (EP) a night for living and dining rooms, kitchen, and one bedroom; or $775.50 (EP) for two bedrooms. The Plaza's other rooms are beautifully appointed and come at a more affordable rate. Take your choice from English Tudor, old Key West, and garden motifs. Each guest room has a private balcony or patio with solid oak furnishings and separate vanity and dressing rooms. In addition to its easy access to Disney's worlds and other attractions, shops, and restaurants, delight in the hotel's many extras—a heated pool, lighted tennis courts, a health spa, game room, even a shuffleboard court! "Royal Honeymoon" package six days / five nights (EP): $1,023 per couple. Includes deluxe accommodations with champagne, fruit, a complimentary cocktail; a candle-light dinner for two at El Cid Steak & Seafood House (see restaurant section); and an Official Bonus Cheque Pack for savings up to $100 on dining and entertainment.

Moonlight on the waves, sipping cool drinks while gentle ocean breezes tempt you to fall in love all over again—cruises just seem to appeal to people in love. **Premier Cruise Lines,** the official cruise line of Walt Disney World, 101 George King Blvd., Cape Canaveral, FL 32920 (tel. 305/783-5061), can make fairy-tale honeymoons come true with their combination cruise and Walt Disney package. For the price of a four-night cruise ($1,088 per couple—EP), couples can take a full seven-day vacation. Four nights of your honeymoon will be spent on a luxury liner cruising to The Bahamas with dancing, live entertainment, a casino, fabulous cuisine, sports, movies, and more. When you return, you're treated to a three-night stay at a fine hotel in the Walt Disney World Vacation Kingdom—free! (The hotel varies.) A rental car and a three-day pass to the Magic Kingdom and EPCOT Center are also included—free! You just pay for the cruise. It works like magic. Honeymooners are greeted on board the cruise ship with champagne in their cabin, a honeymoon certificate, and an invitation to a honeymooner's party hosted by the ship's captain. Double- and queen-bedded cabins and suites are available at an additional cost. You can even get married on board!

With 1,503 guest rooms and an incredible sweeping panoramic view, Marriott's **Orlando World Center,** World Center Drive, Orlando, FL 32830 (tel. 305/239-4200), rates as the largest and certainly one of the most diverse resort hotels in all of Florida. Each room has a private balcony. Furnishings are contemporary, done up in soothing tones of peach and gray, with a separate sitting area. There are 10 restaurants, an 18-hole golf course on the grounds, 12 lighted tennis courts, palms, waterfalls, a lagoon, 4 pools, whirlpools, and more amenities to discover for yourselves as guests of this palatial honeymoon retreat. The views are spectacular. The free-form pool contains a half-million gallons of water, and the World Center would, of course, have to have its own shops that are as unique and diverse and extravagant as those at the Walt Disney World Shopping Village. Honeymoon package: Two days / one night (EP): $249 per couple. Includes a deluxe room with private balcony, welcome champagne and chocolates, and a dinner for two in the Regent Court restaurant or with room service. Disney packages for up to seven nights are also available and range in price from $394 (EP) for two nights to $1,379 (EP) for seven nights.

Walt Disney World Travel Company, Inc., P.O. Box 22094, Lake Buena Vista, FL 32830 (tel. 305/828-3237). Brought to you by the people who practically invented fun—a honeymoon package with villa accommodations at the Walt Disney World Resort. There are several different villa developments; honeymooners might prefer the woodsy Club Lake Villas. These secluded lagoon-side villas are far enough away from the Magic Kingdom crowds for you to feel like you're off on your own private island, but close enough to be convenient. Inside the villa, admire the skylights, vaulted ceiling, stocked refrigerator, and wet bar. "Honeymoon Magic" package: six days / five nights (EP): $1,124 per couple with limo service; $1,202.30 with rental car; $137.50 per couple each additional night. Includes round-trip limo transfers from the airport to your private villa or a National Car Rental, transportation to the Magic Kingdom or EPCOT Center, three-day passes to either Disney attraction, one dinner at your choice of selected restaurants inside the resort, champagne and souvenir glasses, a souvenir photo of the two of you, T-shirts, Mickey Mouse travel bags, and many more extras.

For an upbeat but romantic atmosphere; for fancy accommodations and fanciful nights; for sheer unexcelled delights on a grand scale, spend a night or two or seven at the **Stouffer Orlando Resort,** 6677 Sea Harbor Dr., Orlando, FL 32821 (tel. 305/

351-5555; reservations: toll free 800/822-4200). The lobby of this world-class honeymoon haven is breathtaking. Ten stories of rooms with private balconies flank a 65,000-square-foot atrium capped by giant skylights. Take a ride up one of the seven glass elevators to really appreciate the view. Look down upon diners in the café-like L'Orangerie. Exotic birds, fish, and plants add to the tropical setting amidst pools and waterfalls. You might guess that all the rooms and suites here provide the ultimate in comfort and luxury. Honeymoon package: Four days / three nights (EP): $697.40. One- and seven-night packages also available for $206.25 (EP) and $1,012.60 (EP), respectively. Includes superior accommodations with private balcony, champagne, breakfast in bed the first morning, access to health club facilities, transportation to area attractions, tickets to Sea World for one day, and three-day passports to Walt Disney World or EPCOT. The seven-night package also includes tickets to Cypress Gardens, Boardwalk and Baseball, and unlimited tennis.

The **Howard Johnson Fountain Park Hotel,** 5150 West Space Coast Parkway, Kissimmee, FL 32741 (tel. 305/396-1111; reservations: toll free 800/327-9179 nationwide; 800/432-0763 in Florida), treats newlyweds like family, and has surprisingly luxurious rooms and one terrific honeymoon package. Many rooms have a nice view of the pool or courtyard and although they're not fancy, you can expect a bright and cheery room decorated in Florida floral, with a color TV and a separate sitting area. Night games can be played on lighted tennis courts, and paddleboats are available. The challenge exercise course, saunas, heated pool, Jacuzzi, nine-hole putting green, and game room place the Fountain Park way up on the list of hotels with amenities. Fountain Suite honeymoon package: Four days / three nights (EP): $591.80. Includes welcome champagne, a deluxe pool-view suite with king-size bed, full breakfast each morning, and a three-day passport to the Vacation Kingdom, including round-trip transportation.

Moderate

Along with the Buena Vista Plaza and Hotel Royal Plaza, the **Hilton** at Walt Disney World Village, 1751 Hotel Plaza Blvd., Lake Buena Vista, FL 32830 (tel. 305/827-4000; reservations: toll free 800-HILTONS), is an "official" Walt Disney World hotel, meaning there is a quality of service and satisfaction that must be maintained, so the only surprises will be good ones. Adjacent to the Walt Disney World Shopping Village, the ten-story hotel is as luxurious as it is convenient. Complimentary transportation to the Magic Kingdom and EPCOT Center is available for all guests. Built on 23 acres, the Hilton's design complements its lush surroundings, encircling a picturesque waterfall and fountain. Enter through the palm-lined drive past a tropical background and two ponds. Rooms feature soothing colors and plush furnishings plus state-of-the-art telephones that control everything from the TV to the room temperature. Two swimming pools, tennis courts, a health club, six restaurants, and lounges and golf are available to you during your stay. There's horseback riding and sailing nearby that the Hilton will be happy to set up for you. Honeymoon package: Five days / four nights (EP): $567 per couple. Includes deluxe room with private balcony, bottle of champagne, and a breakfast buffet each morning, or call room service for an intimate breakfast on your very own veranda. Suites cost an extra $40 per night.

Las Palmas Inn, 6233 International Dr., Orlando, FL 32819 (tel. 305/351-3900; reservations: toll free 800/327-2114 nationwide; 800/432-1175 in Florida), is located in the "heart of the entertainment district," within walking distance of 150 shops and restaurants, and is also conveniently close to Disney World, EPCOT, and all the rest. Refreshingly tranquil, the newly decorated hotel has a breezy Mediterranean feel to it, with its white stucco walls and red-tile roof. Soak up those warm Florida rays at the courtyard pool or have a drink in the poolside cabana. The staff here is anxious to arrange every detail beforehand to assure you of a memorable honeymoon. Guests are treated to transportation to nearby attractions, and if you'd like to play a round of golf or a fast set of tennis, Las Palmas can get you there, too. "Beautiful Beginnings" honeymoon package: Four days / three nights (EP): $395 per couple. Includes deluxe accommodations with a king-size bed, chilled champagne and two keepsake toasting glasses, a full breakfast each day, one-day tickets to the Magic Kingdom or EPCOT, and one-day tickets to Sea World and Wet 'n' Wild theme parks.

Inexpensive

It's nice to know there are still some attractive, very affordable places in Florida —like the **Gateway Inn,** 7050 Kirkman Rd., Orlando, FL 32819 (tel. 305/351-2000; reservations: toll free 800/327-3808 nationwide; 800/432-1179 in Florida), which is close to all the attractions (transportation is complimentary of course). Start off your morning with a refreshing swim before planning your exciting day shopping and sightseeing. The Gateway can arrange admissions to any of the attractions for you and can even rent you a car. For your leisure hours at the hotel, try the mini-golf course, the video game room, or meet other vacationing couples for a drink poolside. Rooms are basic, modern, clean, and comfortable. Honeymoon package: Four days / three nights (EP): $201 per couple. Includes a chilled bottle of wine in your room, a free three-minute call home for the bride, and a "Florida Fun Book" with discount coupons. Seven-night package also available for $456.50 per couple (EP).

Just one mile from the Vacation Kingdom, the easy and relaxed atmosphere of the **Ramada Resort Maingate,** 2950 Reedy Creek Blvd., Kissimmee, FL 32741 (tel. 305/396-4466; reservations: toll free 800/327-9127 nationwide; 800/432-9195 in Florida), might be the perfect spot for a break from your frenetic daytime pace. It's a two-story motel; rooms are a bit small, but furnished with all the basics. Ask for a poolside room for shady tranquility, or wake up to a garden view. Buses leave from Ramada to the front door of all of Central Florida's main attractions. Honeymoon package: None. The Ramada offers many regular packages in two-, three-, or five-night versions from $124 (EP) to $283 (EP) based on double-room accommodations. A poolside room is $10 extra; a king-size bed $5 extra. Includes deluxe breakfast buffet or à la carte breakfast daily; one-day admission to Walt Disney World or EPCOT Center; one-day admission to Sea World, and unlimited free tennis on two lighted courts.

ROMANTIC RESTAURANTS AND NIGHT SPOTS: We'll concentrate on the
best spots in the greater Orlando area, including everything from New Orleans jazz to Shakespeare-flavored fare. Remember, this is only a very small sampling. From wherever you're staying in the area, you more than likely have access to at least 50 different places to eat and drink.

Expensive

Inside Walt Disney World Village at Buena Vista Palace Hotel, **Arthur's 27** (tel. 827-2727) has established itself as one of America's finest restaurants since it opened in 1983. The seasonal menu is nouvelle continental, and the impeccable service is matched only by the 27th-floor views overlooking EPCOT, the Magic Kingdom, and Walt Disney World Village. Expect to be well taken care of, with several waiters catering to your every desire. If that weren't enough, this ultimately romantic restaurant serenades you with strolling musicians and a live pianist. *Felicimo!* Among Arthur's specialties is the warm duck salad with grilled peppers and walnut vinaigrette; crayfish bisque in puff pastry; baked Florida snapper with sautéed pecans, oranges and key lime butter; medallions of lobster and fresh fennel, shallots, and cream; sautéed veal rib eye with chiva-calvados sauce and wild mushrooms; and medallions of veal, lamb, and beef prepared with three different peppercorns. The six-course prix-fixe dinner includes choice of appetizer, soup, entrée, salad, cheeses, dessert, coffee, and petits fours for $55 per person. Be sure you make reservations; jackets required for gentlemen.

Plus, pricey but nice, the **Royal Orleans** at 8445 International Dr. in Mercado Festival Center (tel. 352-8200) offers superb Louisiana-heritage cuisine (entrées $14 to $15), fine wines, and impeccable service for a special night out. The menu changes monthly to maintain the finest and freshest products at the peak of their season. The terraced courtyard serves hot chocolate New Orleans-style, chicory coffee, and *beignets* (French doughnuts with powdered sugar).

Moderate

"Let the good times roll" as you cavort through the **Church Street Station,** 129 West Church St., Orlando (tel. 422-2434), dining and entertainment complex. Located in historic downtown Orlando, Church Street Station is one stop you must make while in Orlando. Any night of the week, any day of the year, you're guaranteed some great Dixieland jazz, high-stepping dancing girls, and terrific dining. From Apple Annie's Courtyard serving crispy salads and deli sandwiches (meals are around $10 per person and folk and bluegrass music is provided in the evening) to Lili Marlene's Aviator Pub and Restaurant for a hearty drink or a light snack to a full meal (you'll spend about $30 per person for dinner here), to the rip-roarin', foot-stompin' Rosie O'Grady's saloon complete with Red Hot Mamas, Rosie O'Grady's Good Time Jazz Band, and can-can, bar-top dancers, there's food, drinks, dancing, and entertainment nearly every moment of the day. Eat 'em raw in Cracker's Oyster Bar (oysters, shrimp, crab, and cocktails; average entrée about $7); belly up to the bar in the Cheyenne Saloon and Opera House, Church Street's most recent addition; or be swept up in the light and video extravaganza at Phineas Phogg's Balloon Works for 80s' style discoing. Book a champagne balloon flight from Phineas Phogg's for $100 a person—this could be the most intimate, exciting, romantic part of your honeymoon. Church Street Station is open from 11 a.m. until 2 a.m., and there's an entertainment cover charge of $5.95 per person.

Just down the street from Church Street Station is another full evening of eating, drinking, and merrymaking. **Shakespeare's,** 15 West Church St., Orlando (tel. 841-4144), is a chapter out of Merry Olde England. You'll need to book yourselves in well ahead of time, as this popular night spot is filled virtually every night of the year. The Renaissance flavor is carried through from the huge, picnic-type tables to utensils such as pewter plates and cups to authentic cuisine like "Poultrye strewn well from ye salt kit. Basted well with brewet syder." Watch acts from William Shakespeare's best-loved plays interspersed with sword fights, jesters, jugglers, magicians, and lots of singing and dancing. Don't expect a quiet, intimate dinner—the house cast of players will encourage you to participate in their antics. The banquet begins promptly at 7:30 p.m. and your evening's fun will cost $24.95 a person.

If you're staying in the Kissimmee area (that's closest to Disney World), and even if you're not, you may still opt for a drive to **Medieval Times,** 4510 Vine St., Kissimmee (tel. 396-1518), a castle-looking structure where a night's (knight's?) fare may include roasted chicken flambé, spare ribs, pastries, and a hearty mug of ale. Seating is by reservation only (those coming early get the best seats) in an arena-type hall where jousting exhibitions, javelin throwing, and sword fighting make up your dinnertime entertainment. The $19 per person price includes your dinner, beverages, show, and tax. The castle opens at 6 p.m. with the two-hour show beginning at 6:45 p.m.

El Cid Steak and Seafood House, inside Walt Disney World Village at the Hotel Royal Plaza (tel. 828-2828), is formal but relaxed, so you needn't wear your finery here. Tables are draped in white linen with soft lighting overhead, fresh flowers adorn sideboards and tables, and warm gold walls are decked with Spanish-flavored paintings. The new mesquite grill (perhaps they call it "Texas-style" because of its mammoth size!) enhances the flavor of beef and seafood with a genuine wood-smoked, char-broiled taste. Many specialties are prepared for two tableside and flambéed (all part of the spectacle) including their shrimp Diane, shrimp scampi, and steak au poivre. With your entrée, you'll receive a salad, freshly baked bread, and steamed or grilled vegetables. Dinner will cost between $18 and $38 per person. Open 5 p.m. to 11 p.m. with reservations requested.

Selected by *Florida Trend* magazine as one of Florida's top 100 restaurants, **American Vineyards** inside Walt Disney World Village at the Hilton Hotel (tel. 827-4000, ext. 3092), is a place to save for a special night out. California wine-country memorabilia grace the walls, including wine posters, labels, and antique wine-making tools. The peach, burgundy, and gray color scheme is warm and intimate; alcove booths make for a pleasant evening of fine dining just for two. Regional American cuisine might include New England lobster and medallions of veal California. All wines are American vintage. Soft piano music accompanies your meal, which will run about $60 per couple. American Vineyards is open from 6 to 10:30 p.m. for dinner and serves Sunday brunch from 10 a.m. to 2 p.m. Reservations are suggested.

At **King Henry's Feast,** 8984 International Dr., Orlando (tel. 351-5151), another full evening's fun awaits you in an English manor house with its own tower and moat. The king's six wives are portrayed in paintings on the walls of the entrance hall. The theme is King Henry's surprise birthday feast as he seeks out a seventh bride—one that won't, um, lose her head. Wenches serve up jugs of free beer and wine, and refer to red-bibbed diners as "m'Lord" and "m'Lady." The evening begins with a welcome mead (wine and honey) reception, moves on to a five-course banquet consisting of the Lord Mayor's soup, Suffolk salad, mix'd Normandy berries, main roasts, and young wife's pudding, then the real entertainment begins. Sing-alongs, magic shows, dancing, singing, and balancing acts are the main attractions, with all performers clad in period costumes. The singing and carrying-on get louder and generally wilder as the evening wears on. Showtime begins promptly at 7:30 p.m. and lasts up to three hours. Admission price is $20.95 per person.

"Bienvenu!" "Welcome!" At **Mardi Gras,** at Mercado Festival Center, 8445 International Dr., Orlando (tel. 351-5151; reservations: toll free 800/641-5151 nationwide; 800/521-5152 in Florida), you will enjoy an evening of southern hospitality, carnival excitement, and the delicacies of an authentic New Orleans–style dinner all rolled into one. The evening starts off with a traditional mint julep or famous hurricane cocktail, followed by a four-course, lightly seasoned creole dinner including cream of broccoli soup, fruit ambrosia, seafood casserole or baked chicken breast, a corn-and-tomato vegetable casserole, and a great praline parfait dessert prepared by New Orleans chef James "Beany" Macgregor. A New Orleans jazz band performs during dinner, then a one-hour cabaret show features a 22-member cast with elaborate costumes and sterling choreography. The show combines a medley of Caribbean, Latin American, and West Indian Mardi Gras numbers. Showtime is 8 p.m. and reservations are essential. Admission is $22.95 per person.

Another in a series of themed restaurants owned by "Orlando Entertains," this newest undertaking, the **Fort Liberty Wild West Dinner Show and Trading Post,** Scott Boulevard, U.S. 192 East, Kissimmee (tel. 351-5151; reservations: toll free 800/641-5151 nationwide; 800/521-5152 in Florida), cost $3.5 million to build and seats 500 in a realistic 11-acre western complex with a stockade and western memorabilia. Fort Liberty features the essence of American pioneer days, complete with western music and food, and a medicine man and his traveling entertainment show. The evening starts off with a five-course western banquet with unlimited beer and soft drinks served by cowpokes and rustlers in authentic costume. After dinner comes the hootin', hollerin' 12-performer show. Be prepared to participate and sing along with songs everybody knows. Showtimes vary according to season and last about two hours. Open daily; reservations are requested. Admission price is $22.95 per person.

5. Boca Raton

The entire 47-mile strip of beachfront from Palm Beach to Fort Lauderdale is known as the Gold Coast, a fitting name for this area of sprawling mansions, impeccable gardens, and conspicuously wealthy residents. Nestled somewhere in the middle is lovely Boca Raton, dubbed "mouth of the rat" by Spanish conquistadors because of the jagged rocks lining the shore. A hazard to sailing vessels of the time, it seemed a fine spot to hide pirate treasure; no man would dare venture close enough to the rocks to come ashore.

But come ashore they did, and in droves. First the pineapple farmers and traders arrived, then the railroad brought ailing northerners who had heard of Boca Raton's year-round beauty and sought the southern sun's recuperative powers. It was for this reason that Addison Mizner, a wealthy eccentric and self-professed architect came to Boca Raton in 1918. Thinking he would pass his last months on earth here, he began planning the Everglades Club with Paris Singer (of sewing machine fame) who had also come south for his health. Using Mizner's architectural skills and Singer's financial backing, the swank club, still in use today, was eventually built in Palm Beach.

Mizner's dream still lay in Boca Raton. He set out with his brother to build "the greatest resort in the world—a little Greco-Roman glory and grandeur thrown in." The Cloister Inn opened in 1926 at a cost of $1.25 million—the most expensive 100-room hotel ever built. It attracted the famous, the wealthy, the social upper crust. (Today, it's part of the Boca Raton Hotel and Club.)

The seed was planted by Mizner decades ago for this oceanfront town to be one of unlimited riches. Fashionable shops and restaurants epitomize class and good taste; you'll have fun looking for fancy treasures to take home. Boca Raton can be a special environment for honeymooners seeking all the best in their Florida vacation.

ROMANTIC INTERLUDES: Because of its proximity to both Palm Beach and Fort Lauderdale, honeymooners have easy access to all the attractions and happenings along the Gold Coast. And remember the fun of snorkeling, windsurfing, scuba diving, deep-sea fishing, waterskiing, and canoeing in a city with year-round summer.

Witness the ancient sport of kings at Royal Palm Polo Sports Club, 6300 Clint Moore Rd., Boca Raton (tel. 994-1876), as played by the country's finest team. Set up a tailgate picnic if you'd like and watch the United States go head-to-head and mallet-to-mallet with teams from many nations. The "gentleman's sport" is rich in history, color, and gallantry, and will make a delightful afternoon outing. Matches are played December through April, Sundays and Wednesdays at 1 and 3 p.m. General admission: $4 per person; $8 per person for reserved box seats; reserved tailgate parking also available.

Pack a picnic and meander along winding trails to the beach at **Spanish River Park,** 3001 North State Rd. A1A, Boca Raton (no phone). With the oceans on one side and serene Lake Rogers on the other, there are more than enough quiet lakefront and oceanside picnic spots for you and your love to enjoy. Parking fee: $4 daily; $6 on weekends.

HONEYMOON HOTELS AND HIDEAWAYS: For your honeymoon in Boca Raton, nothing but the best. Where applicable, prices reflect the difference between low- and high-season rates.

Expensive

Located about halfway between Palm Beach and Fort Lauderdale on Florida's fabulous Gold Coast, the **Boca Raton Hotel and Club,** 501 E. Camino Real, Boca Raton, FL (tel. 305/395-3000; reservations: toll free 800/327-0101), embodies the good life that Boca's residents relish. The guest roster at this architectural masterpiece in stucco and cypress has included movie stars, royalty, Wall Street wealthy, and the international social set. You'll have access to the 18-hole golf course, 4 swimming pools, fitness facilities, 22 tennis courts, a marina with facilities for boating and fishing, and a ½-mile of beachfront with equipment for every water sport you can think of. There are acres of landscaped grounds to explore, or perhaps you'd like to attend a lecture on native sea life or learn the culinary secrets of international chefs.

Take your pick of accommodations, which consist of The Cloister, with antique furnishings, tiled walkways, resplendent gardens, and the famed Mizner fountain, now restored to its original grandeur; the majestic 27-story Tower overlooking Lake Boca Raton, contemporary with every luxury imaginable; or the Golf Villas, suites with kitchens located on the golf course. But the seven-story Beach Club is the spot reserved for honeymooners. It is the hotel's newest offering, with a long list of niceties attached. You're immediately served a glass of Florida orange juice or a champagne cocktail when you walk in the door. Your room faces either a private beach or a lush courtyard where exotic flowers bloom year-round. Step through the oak door to your 1980s, pastel-colored room. Wicker furniture gives the feeling of a beach house, but you'll know it's much more than that with extras such as a stocked refrigerator, chocolates on your pillow, and nightly turndown service, his-and-hers terry robes, and Gucci soap. Honeymoon package: Four days / three nights (MAP): $825 to $1,282 per couple. Includes an oceanfront room at the Boca Beach Club, breakfast and dinner daily, welcome gifts in your room, a honeymoon portrait, and lots more. Seven-night package also available for $2,755 (EP).

Moderate

With every room a suite, honeymooners will find plenty of room to stretch out and relax at the **Park Place Suite Hotel,** 661 Northwest 53rd St., Boca Raton, FL 33431 (tel. 305/994-8200; reservations: toll free 800/228-5250 nationwide; 800/325-2884 in Florida). Elegant yet understated, your Park Place suite will feel like home but include the fancy touches that make you feel like you're very special guests. A morning newspaper on your doorstep, valet parking, AM / FM clock radios, bath accessories, and complimentary safety deposit boxes are all part of Park Place's regular service. Deep rust and burgundy blend with neutral tones to create a pleasant living environment. Spacious rooms are wall-to-wall carpeted and floor-to-ceiling modern, with molded furniture mixed with soft velour couches and chairs, and with huge crystal chandeliers in sitting areas that have vaulted ceilings. Turndown service and bedtime mints are a nice touch, and Park Place has its own fitness center with sauna, Jacuzzi, and a heated swimming pool. You'll also love being this close to Worth Avenue shops. Honeymoon package: Two days / one night (CP): $183.90 per couple. Includes a deluxe suite with private balcony, champagne, continental breakfast, cocktails, and late check out. Package not available December through March.

Inexpensive

The mammoth, 11-story **Bridge Hotel,** 999 E. Camino Real, Boca Raton, FL 33432 (tel. 305/368-9500; reservations: toll free 800/327-0130), structure offers views of both the Atlantic Ocean and the Intracoastal Waterway from private balconies off every room. A lovely circular pool is built out over the waterway, as is the Café and Patio Bar. Rooms are modern, decorated in tones of deep amber, bright gold, beige, and soft brown. Parlor suites have separate living and dining area. Honeymoon package: None. Standard rates (EP): Double: $77 to $121 per couple per night; bedroom / parlor suite: $132 to $187 per couple per night.

ROMANTIC RESTAURANTS AND NIGHTSPOTS: Discover some great eating in and around shopping areas, but some of your finest meals may be closer to home, right in your hotel.

Expensive

The Boca Raton Hotel and Club handily provides eight restaurants and lounges to please every taste from wildly exotic to comfortable casual, and **The Top of the Tower,** 501 East Camino Real (tel. 395-3000), there is at the top of the price list for dining out. The exquisite crystal, linens, fresh flowers on your table, and window walls offering splendid views are well worth the cost. Your dinner promises to be a gourmet's delight, with dishes such as Maine lobster and Dover sole, lamb loins wrapped with spinach and prosciutto, salads of hot spinach and breast of duckling with raspberry vinegar. Main courses are priced from $24 to $35, with hors d'oeuvres and salads from about $9 to $15. Not only is the menu tempting, the view from 27 stories up is breathtaking. Open for dinner from 7 to 10 p.m.; closed Tuesdays. Jacket and tie required for men.

La Vieille Maison, "The Old House," 770 East Palmetto Park Rd. (tel. 391-6701), is a restored Addison Mizner two-story. Wrought-iron gates lead you past tropical gardens, gas lights, cascading fountains, and a fish pond to a series of dining rooms both upstairs and downstairs. Antique French furniture, tiled fireplace mantels, wood-beam ceilings, and finely crafted porcelain chandeliers create a cozy atmosphere even in larger rooms. If you get here early, ask to be seated on the balcony nestled right into an enormous tree! Begin your meal with fresh Florida lobster in a hot terrine with butter sauce, or the salade Floridienne with pink grapefruit, lump crabmeat, and sour-cream dressing. Choose a main course of jumbo shrimp, sautéed with onions, green peppers, tomatoes, garlic, and Pernod; or the delicate noisette of lamb with a béarnaise sauce. The combination of venison and venison liver terrine is perfectly blended with pistachios and spices to create a unique taste experience. As part of your five-course, prix-fixe dinner for $40 per person (there are fewer course versions for $34 and $23), you'll receive an appetizer, entrée with vegetables, salad, a selection of cheeses and fruits, and dessert.

Moderate to Inexpensive

Located near the Boca Raton Hotel and Club on the Intracoastal Waterway, the **Wildflower,** 551 East Palmetto Park Rd., (tel. 391-0000), is a nice stopping-off point from a day of shopping at Town Center Mall. Stained-glass windows enhance the comfortable atmosphere without disrupting the magnificent view of the water. For lunch, dinner, happy hour, or late-night dancing, you'll find Wildflower a place to let your hair down in Boca Raton. Sandwiches and meal-size salads are in the $5 to $7 range, while teriyaki New York strip steak, shrimp scampi, Cajun veal, and other hearty dinners are priced between $10 and $16. Open Monday through Saturday 11:30 a.m. until 2 a.m.; Sunday 1 p.m. to 1 a.m. with Sunday brunch from 1 to 4 p.m.

Tucked into Park Place's seven-story atrium, the **Cafe in the Park** at the Park Place Suite Hotel, 661 Northwest 53rd St. (tel. 994-8200), is surrounded by tropical greenery and shimmery reflecting pools. It serves light, California-style meals for breakfast, lunch, and dinner. The soup and salad bar is extensive, or if you prefer, try a mesquite-cooked meal from the grill. Soup and salad bar is $5.25; light lunch under $10; dinners are in the $11 to $16 range. Open 6 a.m. until 10 p.m. After dinner, try out Champ's, Park Place's nightclub with their "Extended Ecstatic Hour"—special drink prices and complimentary buffet served Monday through Friday.

6. Palm Beach

With a Rolls seemingly in every drive, stone lions and iron gates leading to 30-plus room homes, and lawns that could win *House and Garden* landscape awards, Palm Beach may be only a nice place to visit for most of us. This is not a place where the upwardly mobile live; these people have already *made* it and want their community and its inhabitants to reflect the wealth and good taste for which Palm Beach is known. The upper-crust resort area is actually an island, linked to the mainland (West Palm Beach) by bridges. Ever since Henry Morrison Flagler made his fortune in oil and built an incredible mansion (now a museum), "the Taj Mahal of North America," for his third wife, Palm Beach has been a haven for the polo set. People who take up residence here abide by their own strict set of laws: In Palm Beach, it is illegal to own a kangaroo or hang a clothesline.

ROMANTIC INTERLUDES: Some days will be just you and the sea, but for a bit more excitement, try some of the local attractions and spectator sports. Day or night, Palm Beach can fill your honeymoon vacation with pizzazz.

Put the **Henry Morrison Flagler Museum,** on Whitehall Way off Coconut Row (tel. 655-2833), at the top of your list for its centuries of antiques, objets d'art, and almost sinful opulence. The 1901 mansion-turned-museum was originally a gift from Flagler to his socialite third wife, Mary. Now the museum pays tribute to Flagler, the great railroad tycoon and developer who created Palm Beach as a playground for his wealthy friends. Open Tuesday through Saturday, 10 a.m. to 5 p.m.; Sunday noon to 5 p.m., Admission is $3 per person.

Try a day at the **polo matches.** This ancient game, once only enjoyed by the very rich, is now as popular as car racing in Florida. Polo players from England, Spain, Australia, Pakistan, Mexico, Argentina, and the United States are represented on the playing field. If you have never experienced the fast-paced thrill of mounted warfare, superb horsemanship, and the beauty, grace, and pageantry of the sport, then spend an afternoon at one of the three polo clubs in the area. General admission tickets are $4, with box seats going for $8 per person. Parking is free. Matches are on Wednesdays and Sundays, with the season running from December through April. Take in the action at the **Royal Palm Polo Club,** Boca Raton (tel. 994-1876); the **Gulfstream Polo Field** on Lake Worth Road off the Sunshine Skyway in Palm Beach (tel. 965-2057); or at the Palm Beach Polo & Country Club, 13198 Forest Hills Blvd. in Palm Beach (tel. 793-1113).

Heeerre commmes Swifty! That's the name of one of several mechanized rabbits used in the sport of **greyhound racing.** The dogs are in top form, sleek, and silent as they race for the gold. Wager to win the daily double, quinielas, trifectas, or the Pic Six jackpot with payoffs of up to $145,000! The **Palm Beach Kennel Club** has races daily at 12:30 p.m. and 8 p.m. Admission is just 50¢ per person. It's located north of Palm Beach International Airport, and is easily accessible from I-95 and the Turnpike on Belvedere Road and Collins Avenue in West Palm Beach (tel. 683-2222).

Spend a day at sea aboard the *Viking Princess* and you'll feel like you've been on holiday for a week. The cruise ship features shipboard games, casino gambling, an evening floorshow, plus live music and dancing. Then there's the swimming pool, theater, and even skeet shooting to keep you busy! You're sure to meet many fellow shipmates to dine with in the Crown or Tiara Dining rooms—no one can be a stranger for long there. The one-day ocean cruise leaves from the Port of Palm Beach at 10 a.m. and returns at 10 p.m.; price is $79 per person (tel. 845-SHIP).

Treat yourself to an exciting evening of **Jai-alai,** which utilizes a small ball thrown at high speed to an opponent who catches it in a netted cup-shaped contraption and hurls it back at lightning speed—rather like racquetball without the side walls. The fun part is wagering on one of the players—you just may take home more money than you came with! The **Palm Beach Jai-Alai Fronton** is located at 1415 West 45th St. (tel. 844-2444). Open November through April, Wednesdays and weekends (Friday and Saturday). Admission tickets range from $1 to $5.

HONEYMOON HOTELS AND HIDEAWAYS: There are many fine hotels in and around Palm Beach, but for the sheer take-your-breath-away luxury and attention to every detail, The Palm Beach Hilton and The Breakers win top prizes. Even if you choose to stay in one of the other hotels, pay a visit just to see how the other half vacations. Where applicable, prices reflect the difference between low- and high-season rates.

Expensive

Known the world over, the turn-of-the-century landmark, **The Breakers,** One S. County Rd. Palm Beach, FL 33480 (tel. 305/655-6611; reservations: toll free 800/833-3141), is reminiscent of richly adorned Italian villas. Twin Belvedere towers, graceful arches, and a Florentine fountain embellish the sun-washed pastel exterior. Frescos and decorated vaulted ceilings overlook courtyards and loggias with fountains and flowers leading to the grand ballroom, where American and European society mingle in bejeweled splendor. Stroll around 140 acres of lush gardens beside the Atlantic Ocean. *Lifestyles of the Rich and Famous* has recognized The Breakers as one of the world's top ten resorts. Huge rooms are deep-wood paneled with matching furniture and many have ocean-view private balconies. Sink into the thick carpet and marvel at the size of both bathrooms and closets. Honeymoon package: Four days/three nights (BP): $755. Includes a deluxe room with breakfast each morning, one dinner, bicycling, sailing, use of the health club, a champagne welcome basket in your room, an evening Rolls-Royce tour of Palm Beach, and complimentary use of his and her terry bathrobes. Five-night package also available for $1,246 (EP) (price includes service charge and tax).

If you're going to visit Palm Beach, you might as well join the elite and indulge yourselves to the hilt at the **Palm Beach Hilton,** 2842 S. Ocean Blvd., Palm Beach, FL 33480 (tel. 305/586-6542; reservations: toll free 800/HILTONS). Throw yourselves into the lap of luxury with decorator-furnished guest rooms or suites with thick carpets and cherry white-wicker accents, in-room stocked bar and refrigerator, and a spacious bath with telephone, TV, and hairdryer. Palm Beach awaits you at the touch of the telephone: Boating, deep-sea fishing, swimming, volleyball, bike rentals, golf, tennis, jogging, and exercise classes can all be set up from your hotel room. Or rent a jeep and tour around yourself. Honeymoon package: Three days/two nights (EP): $350. Includes a standard or deluxe room, welcome chilled champagne and flowers in your room, breakfast in bed your first morning, cocktails for two, and souvenir sun visors. Seven-night package also available for $1,528 (EP).

Moderate

Perhaps your honeymoon fantasy is staying at a private place, away from crowds, at a spacious, elegantly decorated residence on a secluded country club estate. At the **Palm Beach Polo and Country Club,** 13198 Forest Hill Blvd., West Palm Beach, FL 33414 (tel. 305/798-7000), guest lodging is clustered around one of many sports facilities—golf, polo, or tennis on the 2½-square-mile grounds. Each residence, fully furnished with a comfortable tropical ambience, includes expansive views of manicured grounds, waterways, or sporting complexes. Guests have access to sports facilities as well as three private dining areas. Play croquet (two lawns lit for night play), golf on one of two 18-hole courses, tennis on one of 17 courts, or take advantage of 11 polo fields and a show-barn complex. One-, two-, and three-bedroom suites have fully equipped kitchens, washer and dryer, color TV, direct-dial phones, and individual air conditioning controls. Spacious rooms are tastefully furnished, emphasizing light and space. All have a terrace or balcony. Most studio bedrooms feature kitchenettes and a balcony or terrace. All suites and rooms are custom designed so no two are alike, but typically, rooms may offer fireplaces, over-size beds, live plants, and window transoms. Honeymoon package: None. Room rates (EP): studio: $104.50 to $181.50 per night. One-bedroom suite (EP): $170.50 to $269.50 per night.

PGA Sheraton Resort, 400 Avenue of the Champions, Palm Beach Gardens, FL 33418 (tel. 305/627-2000; reservations: toll free 800/325-3535). Set around a lush lakefront golf course, this 2,340-acre country club community is a complete, self-contained resort. The famous PGA National Golf Club is just part of the complex, which also gives sports enthusiasts an alternative—a championship-level racquet club with 19 courts, 7 lighted for night play. And of course, the resort is also equipped with a wonderful lakeside sandy beach and a large freshwater pond. Add to that a fitness center, a fleet of sailboats, paddleboats and canoes, miles of jogging and bicycle paths, and a 240-acre wilderness preserve and you've got the most activities this side of Palm Beach. Three restaurants, two lounges, and a poolside bar give you endless dining possibilities. At the end of your active day, the Sheraton's impressive guest rooms are great to come home to. Large rooms are softly decorated in shades of pale coral and blue. Step out on your private balcony for breakfast or warm breezes and moonlight. Honeymoon package: None. Standard rates (EP): Standard $82.50 to $176 per night; superior $93.50 to $203.50; deluxe $104.50 to $214.50; club cottage $110 to $247.50; junior suite $110 to $236.50; suite $302.50 to $687.50. Many packages are also available that include use of golf and tennis facilities and instruction by resident pros.

The main drawing card at the **Palm Beach Lakes Inn,** 1800 Palm Beach Lakes Blvd., West Palm Beach, FL 33401 (tel. 305/683-8810); reservations: toll free 800/331-9569 nationwide; 800/843-5108 in Florida), is location. Situated right on the golf course and across the street from the trendy Palm Beach Mall, you're sure to be kept busy. The West Palm Beach Auditorium and Municipal Stadium, where you can see the Atlanta Braves and Montreal Expos in exhibition play during spring training, is only five minutes away. Many fine restaurants are within walking distance. The two-story, 200-room hotel is built around a meticulously landscaped courtyard with a heated pool and shuffleboard courts. The inn serves all guests a complimentary continental breakfast daily from 7 a.m. to 11 p.m. Rooms overlook the pool area, golf course, or landscaped grounds and all have music and color TV. Honeymoon package: None. Room rates: Standard double (EP): $72.60 to $79.20 per night. Suites slightly higher.

Inexpensive

Holiday Inn—Turnpike, 6255 Okeechobee Blvd., West Palm Beach, FL 33409 (tel. 305/686-6000; reservations: toll free 800-HOLIDAY). Many Holiday Inns across the country have recently updated and upscaled their rooms and restaurants—including this lovely property in America's winter playground. Although rooms are modest, there's enough room for two double beds with bright pink, purple, and blue floral designs, mauve or soft-colored carpet, and walnut-colored wood furnishings. This hotel now offers king leisure rooms with king-size beds and more space. There's an outdoor pool, free parking, valet cleaning service, and golf, tennis, and water sports aren't far away. Honeymoon package: None. Room rates (EP): Standard $48 to $54; king leisure room $54 to $58 per night.

ROMANTIC RESTAURANTS AND NIGHTSPOTS: Your honeymoon happens just once in a lifetime. So go ahead . . .

Expensive

No matter where you stay in Palm Beach area, your honeymoon *must* include the **Florentine Dining Room,** inside the Breakers Hotel (tel. 655-6611). Every president from Warren Harding on down has sampled the magnificent cuisine and superb wines served here. The Breakers even maintains its own wine cellar, where up to 200,000 bottles can be stored. The richly ornate dining room is filled with carvings, curved archways, thick red draperies, and tapestries. Expect your table to be set with only the finest linens, china, crystal, and silver money can buy. Get a good look at the hand-painted, beamed ceiling lit by a massive Venetian chandelier that hangs from a glorious circular skylight. Dinner is served from 6 to 10 p.m., and there is a different menu for each day of the week. Entrées might include Long Island duckling, fresh poached salmon or pompano, and a daily chef's specialty. Complete seven-course dinners run $36 per person and a 17% service charge will be added for tax and food and beverage service. A live orchestra accompanies a fine meal, and when you finish dining, feel free to get up and dance.

Moderate

Oh, if your friends could see you now! Just the two of you at a cozy corner table, sipping cocktails over a meal of veal piccata or lobster tails, gazing lovingly into each other's eyes while the Atlantic surf reflects the moonlight outside your window. **Sandcastles,** inside the Palm Beach Hilton (tel. 586-6542), and its adjoining lounge could very well create a perfect evening out for the two of you. It's intimate, with lovely pool views, terribly elegant and *very* Palm Beach. There's a small balcony seating about 25 people if you'd like to be up and away from the main dining room. The whole restaurant is colored a cool gray-green with white tableclothes and burgundy napkins. Start with steaming fettucine, Alfredo ($3.95) or oysters florentine ($6.50) unless you just *can't* pass up Florida's most popular delicacy, stone-crab claws. From beyond the Atlantic beaches, sample stuffed flounder ($15.50), sea scallops ($14.25), or swordfish steak ($14.50). From the land, bite into New York sirloin, so tender you can cut it with a fork ($15.95) or a mini rack of lamb ($22.95). It will be a night to remember. Open 6:30 a.m. until 10 p.m. Reservations requested.

Since 1921, **Testa's,** 221 Royal Poinciana Way (tel. 832-0992), has been a favorite of the locals for great food in a casual, friendly atmosphere. Choose your seating from the large indoor dining room (the original restaurant) with buff-colored paneling, tile floors, and original ceiling fans; the sidewalk cafe in front of the restaurant protected from the sun by large awnings and Plexiglas curtains that roll down in case of inclement weather; or the tropical garden with a retractable roof for dining beneath the stars. Oak tables and rattan chairs and bar stools are found throughout; there's also a huge multicolored awning over the entire bar area. Now—what folks come here for is the great kosher-style, Italian, and seafood dishes. Try yummy corned beef and cabbage, a Tuesday and Thursday special; swordfish, kingfish, and haddock, or spaghetti Testa with diced chicken, green peppers, and mushrooms au gratin ($8.25). The menu choices also include ham, veal, stone-crab claws, and terrific sandwiches. There's also a full breakfast menu which begins at 7 a.m. A full breakfast will only cost about $10 per couple; lunch will be about $16 per couple and $40 for dinner. Open until 1 a.m. The owners vacation in Maine for the summer months, so Testa's is closed from May to mid-December.

Chuck and Harold's, 207 Royal Poinciana Way, Palm Beach (tel. 659-1440). Two owners—two ideas of how to run a restaurant. But vive la différence! They must have agreed on a few things because the place is always full. Hand-painted cypress beams adorn the ceiling, while handmade Mexican tiles are inlaid into the walls. So how come they serve Italian? It's because Chuck and Harold *like* the way the place looks, but want to serve food they know best. The poppy-seed pizza crust has become a favorite. The menu is trendy and imaginative, with dishes such as seafood pasta Pagliari (cape scallops, salmon, shrimp, and mussels in a garlic/herb sauce), $14.75; salmon Doria, broiled and topped with yogurt, cucumber, and fresh dill, $18.50; and Harold's traditional grilled calves' liver and onions, $13. Dinner with wine will run about $25 a person. Open daily for dinner from 4:30 to 11 p.m.

Inexpensive

Stop in to the casual **Golf Club,** inside The Breakers (tel. 655-6611), after an early morning of shopping or a round of golf. (If you're interested in golfing at The Breakers, green fees are $24 for guests; $26 for carts, and equipment rental is available.) From your table watch others try the challenges of the Ocean Course while you enjoy a luncheon cocktail and perhaps a taco salad ($7.25) or a Philly cheesesteak ($8.25). Green touches inside as well as outside blend elegantly with the rich wooden furnishings. Open daily for lunch only, from 11:30 a.m. to 3 p.m.

7. Fort Lauderdale

It's a sunny, scenic, and usually serene continuation of Florida's Gold Coast for most of the year (it's south of Palm Beach and north of Miami along A1A), but come spring break time, Fort Lauderdale turns into a scene right out of *American Graffiti*. Lines of cars cruise the strip along A1A with radios blaring, while oceanfront nightspots pack college students elbow to elbow. But it has always been that way and residents start gearing up for it early.

So what has made Fort Lauderdale a haven for higher education? There is an incredible 6½-mile stretch of beachfront here that will actually hold all of those spring breakers at once and still leave room for regular vacationers. But putting the college scene aside, Fort Lauderdale has some unusual features that make it one of America's most unique oceanfront cities.

This town, like Winter Park, has been called "the Venice of America" with its over 250 miles of natural and man-made canals dotted now with picturesque homes and landscaped gardens. Boat tours will give you a good look at "the other side" of Fort Lauderdale. Then there's the downtown area. Scrubbed and ready for visitors, there is quite a collection of shops, including many antique stores. Arts and culture have also found a permanent place in the city, with its many museums and galleries, playhouses and theaters, and opera guild and a symphony. But the real lure to vacationers is the dark and wide New River, where canals dotted with yachts divide the city into islands connected by graceful bridges, plus that almost endless stretch of beach on the Atlantic.

ROMANTIC INTERLUDES: Rich in cultural activities, Fort Lauderdale is also a water wonderland. Its proximity to other vacation centers (Palm Beach to the north, Miami to the south, and Orlando to the east), assures honeymooners that they'll never run out of things to do.

You may have seen it on the old TV show *Gentle Ben*—the boat with a huge propeller in back, zipping over the swampy Everglades marshland. **Everglades Holiday Park,** 30 minutes west of Fort Lauderdale at 21940 Griffin Rd. (tel. 434-8111) will give you one of these thrilling, bumpy air boat rides through seas of sawgrass for $7 per person. If it's wildlife you're looking for, rent a quieter type of transport such as a canoe at the park. Airboat rides are given every 30 minutes daily between 9 a.m. and 5 p.m.

Stranahan House, 333 S. Federal Hwy. (tel. 544-4736), is located at Fort Lauderdale's oldest meeting place, a site where Seminole Indians traded furs for ammunition and cooking supplies. This small two-story home was Fort Lauderdale's first mansion, built out of Dade County pine by Frank Stranahan for his new bride, Ivy Julia Cromartie. With its restoration complete, the pine walls, the huge brick fireplace, and the lovely view from open, airy porches make the Stranahan House an idyllic spot for weddings. Picture yourself descending the steps to join your husband-to-be at the gazebo in the Virginia English garden. Exchange your vows on the intricate coral patio with its profusion of fragrant, tropical flowers and shady trees; it is large enough to accommodate up to 400 guests! If you're interested in just touring the house, it's open to the public on Wednesday, Friday, and Saturday from 10 a.m. to 4 p.m.; Sunday from 1 p.m. to 4 p.m. Admission price, which includes a guided tour, is $3 per person. To reserve a wedding date, call the Stranahan House; a member of the Fort Lauderdale Historical Society will be glad to help you.

Located in the Himmarshee Village area on the New River, the 1907 two-story pine **King-Cromartie House,** 229 S. W. 2nd Ave. (tel. 764-1665), was relocated by barge up the river to its present location downtown. The house is now a museum, filled with antiques and period furnishings right down to authentic clothes hung in the closet. Tour guides in period costume lead you through the house on weekends in the winter; Tuesday through Sunday in summer. Hours are Tuesday to Friday 2 to 5 p.m. and Sunday 1 to 5 p.m. Donation is $2 per person.

Fort Lauderdale is the winter home of the **New York Yankees** as well as the **Texas Rangers.** Get in on some Yankees exhibition baseball action in February and March at Fort Lauderdale Stadium, 5301 N.W. 12th Ave. (tel. 776-1921). The Rangers play at the Pompano Beach Municipal Stadium at 1700 N.E. 8th St., Pompano Beach (tel. 943-4873). Tickets to the games are $3.50 to $7 per person.

A European sport foreign to most of us in the U.S., jai-alai is exciting and fast paced. You can see the game at the **Dania Jai-Alai Fronton,** 301 East Dania Beach Blvd., Dania (tel. 945-4345 or 426-4330) from late June through mid-April. Jai-alai is a parimutuel sport, meaning you can plunk some money down on a *pelotari*—a player of the sport—and do a little wagering. Stadium opens at 7:30 p.m., 7 p.m. on Saturday. Admission is just $1.

What more refreshing and delightful way to spend an afternoon or evening on your honeymoon than aboard one of these restored antique floating showplaces—a **paddle-wheel boat?** As you travel along the Intracoastal Waterway, you'll view some of Fort Lauderdale's finest real estate.

A tradition for 40 years, these daily cruises on the *Jungle Queen,* Bahia Mar Yacht Basin, 801 Seabreeze Blvd., Rte. A1A (tel. 462-5596), are a must for all visitors to Fort Lauderdale. Cruises at 10 a.m. and 2 p.m. feature the captain's delightful commentary along the way, a stop at the Indian village Island, which includes a zoo, alligator show, snack stand, and a scenic cruise back up New River. Day cruise price is $6.25 per person; tickets should be reserved the morning of the cruise. At 7 p.m., the 550-passenger, 2-deck *Jungle Queen* pulls out for its barbecue-and-shrimp dinner cruise. Watch for lights in the homes of the stately mansions flicker on and off signaling a welcome to passengers on board the boat. The *Jungle Queen* docks on its own island, and passengers are directed toward the dining room, where a delicious dinner of ribs, chicken, and shrimp plus all the trimmings await. Alcoholic beverages are available at extra cost. The highlight of the evening is the hilarious *Vaudeville Revue,* followed by the return trip with everyone joining in a sing-along. Dinner cruise is $37.70 per couple, reservations must be made one week in advance for this popular attraction.

This plush 400-passenger sternwheeler replica of the *Paddlewheel Queen,* 2950 N.E. 32nd Ave. (tel. 564-7659), made its cruise debut in 1965. The first two decks are glass-enclosed and climate-controlled for summer or winter travel. The third level is an open observation deck. Tables and comfortable upholstered chairs offer nice river views all around. The *Paddlewheel Queen*'s "Sunlight" cruise welcomes you aboard from the docks one block west of A1A, at 12:30 p.m. The cruise is from 2 p.m. to 4:30

p.m. daily, offering taped commentary and music for just $9.90 per couple. Luncheon and cocktails are available on board. Weddings can be performed on board by the captain before the ship sets sail. Make arrangements for booking by calling the reservation number. Evening "Starlight" cruises board at 6:30 p.m., when you are escorted to your reserved nautical table. Order a cocktail and settle back to enjoy the *Paddlewheel Queen*'s band. Then the gangplank is hoisted and promptly at 7:30 p.m., the boat pulls onto the tropical starlit Intracoastal Waterway. A candlelight dinner is served at 8—a sumptuous U.S. choice grade charcoal steak with salad and appetizer. Enjoy dancing to the band or star gazing on the top deck on this most romantic of honeymoon excursions. The captain requests dresses or dressy pantsuits for ladies; sports jackets or dressy shirts for gentlemen. Tickets are $45 per couple and reservations must be made in advance.

HONEYMOON HOTELS AND HIDEAWAYS: Take your choice of the more than 60 hotels and motels in the Greater Fort Lauderdale area including Deerfield Beach, Pompano Beach, Lauderdale-by-the-Sea, Fort Lauderdale, Dania, Hollywood, and Hallandale. There are numerous villas, condominiums, and apartments also rented by the night, the week, or the month. Where applicable, prices reflect the difference between low- and high-season rates.

One of the area's newest and most unique resorts, the **Marina Bay Resort and Hotel,** 2175 State Road 84, Fort Lauderdale, FL 33312 (tel. 305/791-7600; reservations: toll free 800/321-2619 nationwide; in Florida 800/824-4434), features 125 floating guest suites opening onto the bay and a private dock. The accommodations resemble giant two-story houseboats with balconies. Jogging and hiking trails wind through Marina Bay's 37 acres of tropical landscaping. Make a splash in the heated Olympic-size pool or soak in the whirlpool. The marina adjacent to the resort's yacht slips offers boat rentals and dive boats. Challenge each other to a tennis match on one of 13 clay and Laykold courts. Add to that two award-winning restaurants, two lounges with live entertainment, a pro shop, golfing privileges, and easy access to Port Everglades and beach attractions. Spacious two-bedroom suites and efficiency apartments feature king-size beds with curved wicker headboards, French doors opening onto private balconies, deep wood paneling in suites or bright wallpaper in efficiencies, steam baths, closed-circuit movies, and much more. Honeymoon package: Three days/two nights, Friday through Sunday (EP): $218.90 per couple. Includes deluxe floating suite, chilled champagne, and long-stemmed rose on arrival, two complimentary cocktails, dinner for two from one of the restaurants or from room service, breakfast each morning from either the restaurant or room service, complimentary airport transportation, and private club privileges.

A world-class resort recently renovated and refurnished at a cost of $56 million, the 388-room **Pier 66 Hotel and Marina,** 2301 S.E. 17th St., Fort Lauderdale, FL 33316 (tel. 305/525-6666; reservations: toll free 800/327-3796 nationwide; 800/432-1956 in Florida), rises above the Intracoastal Waterway like a shimmering beacon. It is located ten minutes from the Fort Lauderdale airport and across the waterway from Port Everglades, one of Florida's busiest cruise-ship ports. Guest rooms feature private balconies with panoramic views of both the inland waterway canals and the Atlantic Ocean. Newly completed are 132-story lanai accommodations with their own tropical sunning area, 2 swimming pools, 2 tennis courts, and a 40-person Jacuzzi. A 142-slip yacht marina is adjacent to the hotel. Guests who want to sail the waterways or open sea may charter a yacht from the hotel's own fleet (one vessel comes with its own chef!) Arrangements can also be made through Pier 66 for deep-sea fishing and scuba diving. Two restaurants and a lounge offer great day and night water views as well as American and continental specialties. At night, guests can dance to live music at the Pier Top Lounge, while the entire floor slowly revolves 360° every 66 minutes! A complimentary shuttle is available four times daily to Fort Lauderdale's seven miles of beachfront and the exclusive Galleria Shopping Mall. Rooms give you more space than you've probably ever had in a hotel before. Lanai rooms have a two-story living area surrounded by windows. Wicker, glass, subdued upholstery, and lots of big pillows everywhere combine into an unmatched vacation retreat. Honeymoon package: Two days/one night (EP): $82.50 to $143 per couple; extra nights $55 to $115.50 per couple (EP). Includes deluxe accommodations with view of the ocean, waterway, or the pool area; valet parking, champagne in your room, breakfast in bed and 5 p.m. check-out.

Right smack in the middle of the strip between the Atlantic Ocean and the Intracoastal Waterway sits **The Breakers** of Fort Lauderdale, 909 Breakers Ave., Fort Lauderdale, FL 33304 (tel. 305/566-8800; reservations: toll free 800/525-2535 nationwide; 800/325-9702 in Florida), majestically soaring 15 stories above the city. You're only 200 yards from the ever-popular beachfront, and water views are great all around. The Breakers is an all-suite hotel for folks who want all the comforts of home. Relax in the heated pool, saunas, or bubbling Jacuzzi, or treat yourself to a massage, manicure, pedicure, or facial. Perfect your Florida tan on the sun deck, where you hardly need to miss a minute of sunshine to get a cool drink from the Patio Bar. Don't be surprised if you catch a glimpse of a couple of frisky spider monkeys playing among the trees; they're from the neighboring Bartlett Estate. Right across the street find bicycle paths, nature trails, picnic areas, and great fishing at the 80-acre Birch State Park. When you finish sunning and seeing the sights, come home to your luxurious one-bedroom suite with fully equipped kitchen. A nice way to start the day is to enjoy breakfast on your private balcony. Rooms are decorated in shades of pink, light blue, mauve, lavender, sea green, and ivory with molded ivory furniture and ginger jar lamps. Honeymoon package: Four days/three nights (EP): $434.50 to $643.50 per couple. Includes deluxe one-bedroom suite (ask for the 18th-floor honeymoon suite with ocean view, separate kitchen, living room, and patio), fresh flowers in your suite, a welcome basket with champagne, chocolates, and bubble bath, welcome cocktails, a dinner in Chatters restaurant with a carafe of wine, half-day bicycle rental, complimentary chaise longues and towels, the manager's wine and cheese party (Monday evenings only), use of the pool, Jacuzzi, sauna, and nearby tennis courts. Penthouse floor accommodations: $25 more in winter; $15 more in summer. One- and seven-night packages also available.

Within the city's 165 miles of waterways is an island retreat set out into the water, surrounded by palm trees and luxury yachts. **Bahia Mar Resort and Yachting Center,** 801 Seabreeze Blvd., Fort Lauderdale, FL 33316 (tel. 305/764-2233; reservations: toll free 800/327-8154), is just five miles from the Fort Lauderdale Airport, minutes from dog racing, jai-alai matches, and major league baseball, or shopping on Las Olas Boulevard or in the Galleria Mall. Nearby are dozens of challenging golf courses and tennis courts. Right outside your window, you'll see the 350-slip marina where charter boats depart for fishing and sailing. This is also where the *Jungle Queen* sternwheeler docks. Two restaurants, a snack bar, and a lounge with live entertainment give guests all they'll ever need under one roof. The 300 guest rooms are completely soundproof, and have color TVs, oversize beds, and flowery modern decor mixing pastels with deep greens and navy. Honeymoon package: Three days/two nights (EP): $324.50 per couple; extra nights $110 per couple. Includes deluxe accommodations, champagne in room on arrival, and breakfast each morning.

Marriott's Harbor Beach Resort, 3030 Holiday Dr., Fort Lauderdale, FL 33316 (tel. 305/525-4000; reservations: toll free 800/228-9290), starts like the big city—a massive white-stepped skyscraper towering over Fort Lauderdale. It turns into a country club with small villas, a magnificent golf course at Bonaventure Country Club, a large pool, a place where your whims are satisfied. Then it becomes a tropical paradise. This is Marriott's Harbor Beach, a 16-acre spectacle offering luxury and privacy all in one. Jog on 1,100 feet of private beachfront, work out in the health club, relax in the whirlpool, swim in the 8,000-square-foot pool. Five tennis courts await you along with windsurfer and sailboat rentals. Sport fishing and ocean sailing are available to you, too. The Harbor Beach Resort's 645 guest rooms are modern and convenient, with 24-hour room service, HBO, individual climate controls, and soft, comfortable furnishings in beach pastels and neutrals. Rooms are contemporary, chic, spacious, and many offer ocean views. Honeymoon package: Four days/three nights (BP): $493.90 to $867.90 per couple. Includes a welcome bottle of champagne with fresh fruit and hand-made chocolates; an oceanfront room; breakfast for two each morning (or Sunday brunch); one dinner for two in Sheffield's, the resort's gourmet restaurant; a one-hour boat rental; a private cabana for one day; one lunch for two at the poolside Cascades restaurant, and a photo album and gift when you depart.

ROMANTIC RESTAURANTS AND NIGHTSPOTS: Earthly delights and sensual pleasures abound in the area, with somewhere in the neighborhood of 3,500 restaurants, nightclubs, and eateries. A few places that are tops on our list are included here, but for more good bets ask your concierge or some of the locals.

Expensive

How about a taste of France in an old Fort Lauderdale building with a hint of New Orleans thrown in? That's **The French Quarter,** Las Olas and Eighth Avenue, Fort Lauderdale (tel. 463-8000). Several intimate dining areas offer honeymooners a wide range of dining environments. There's a comfortable pub-type room with a wood-beamed ceiling and cane chairs, or the outdoor café-like area with curved brick archways, wicker furniture, and tiled floors. The atrium room offers a garden setting with lush greenery all around. The French Quarter also offers a lounge and a dance floor with music every evening in the Upstairs Room. Now try a bit of French cooking with crêpes fourrées princesse stuffed with asparagus and chicken and topped with a delicate mornay sauce; soufflés made with Grand Marnier; or shrimp Fru-Fru (jumbo shrimp, mushrooms, white grapes, and pineapples in a light curry cream sauce). You'll also find your old standard here disguised under gourmet French names: mariage creole (filet mignon and lobster tail); steak au poivre vert or poivre noir (steak in butter with a cognac and green peppercorn sauce); and bouillabaisse Louisiane (snapper, grouper, clams, mussels, and lobster in a saffron bouillon). Say "oui" to dessert here; there are many tempting offerings like the crêpes Suzette or fresh strawberries au Sabayon. Average luncheon price will be around $36 per couple; close to $80 per couple for dinner. Open Monday to Friday for lunch noon to 3 p.m.; Monday through Saturday 6 to 11 p.m. for dinner. Closed Sundays.

Casa Vecchia, 209 North Birch Rd., Fort Lauderdale (tel. 463-7575) a former private estate (thus the name "Casa Vecchia") on the Intracoastal Waterway, has been given an old-world facelift for exciting dining pleasure. (If you're planning a small wedding, there is a small "wine room" for intimate parties of 12 or less). Museum-calibre pieces furnish the rooms and adorn the walls, creating a gracious atmosphere. Casa Vecchia serves Northern and Riviera Italian cuisine. Sauces are very light and mixed just minutes before serving. Pasta is usually homemade and again very light—a nice appetizer that won't fill you up. Start with carpaccio, thinly sliced raw beef served with an herb mayonnaise ($6.20). Or try one of those delicate pasta dishes as an appetizer or an entrée (double the price for the entrée), such as the capellini or linguine al pesto (angel hair pasta tossed with fresh basil, garlic, pine nuts, parmesan, and olive oil, $5.80). Of 35 entrées, from grouper Fiorentina (with spinach and mozzarella on a bed of tomato sauce, $16.80) to scaloppine di vitello (veal scallops layered with pancetta ham, sage, basil, provolone, and mozzarella, $19) to the breast of chicken (stuffed with chopped veal, spinach, pistachios, and spices, $15), everything you order will be a real treat. Fresh herbs are grown on the grounds and picked as needed; pastas, ice creams, and sorbets are made fresh daily in the kitchen, and the 14-page wine list will provide you well. The final tab will be about $70 to $80 per couple if you opt for one of the lower priced wines. Reservations are essential. Open for dinner daily 6 to 9:30 p.m. during the week; 6 to 10:30 p.m. on weekends.

Moderate

The Historic Bryan Homes Restaurant, 301 North New River Drive W., Fort Lauderdale (tel. 523-0177). Philomen Bryan and two of his sons came south in 1895 to help build Henry Flagler's East Coast Railroad and decided to stay. Bryan built his sons' neighboring homes on the north bank of the New River in 1904. Owner/host Anthony Gillette has turned these Fort Lauderdale treasures into one of the city's most popular restaurants. The Bryan Homes reflect the charm and grace of the turn-of-the-century lifestyle. Inside are ten separate dining areas complete with period furniture and decor. One of the homes has a wrapped veranda on three sides; it's a particularly nice place to sit under the shade of massive oaks. For an after-dinner cordial, you may elect to sit out on the front porch of one of the homes; comfortable wicker furniture makes room for plenty of guests to enjoy the warm night breezes. The cuisine is "New Florida," using many local ingredients. Start with a conch chowder ($2.50) or chilled strawberry soup ($2.25). Favorite hot and cold appetizers include a jumbo shrimp cocktail ($7.95) and the seafood pie with lobster, crabmeat, and shrimp ($4.50). Dive into one of the unusual seafood entrées like swordfish Captiva, southern-fried shark or snapper in a bag (the Caribbean way to cook seafood). There are also many excellent meat and poultry dishes—veal, steak, lamb, and duckling—to choose from. Dinner for two will cost about $50 before drinks and dessert. Dress is informal, and do linger. Open Tuesday through Thursday and Sunday, 5:30 to 10 p.m.; Friday and Saturday 5:30 to 11 p.m.

At **Mai-Kai,** 3599 North Federal Hwy., Fort Lauderdale (tel. 563-3272), take a side trip to the South Seas with authentic surroundings, native dancers, a Cantonese menu, and a magical aura of romance and friendliness. In business for 30 years, the owners are obviously doing something right and unrelenting attention to detail may be one reason the Mai-Kai is so popular. A Polynesian paradise has been created bit by bit right here in river city. Tiki huts, exotic jungle plants and flowers, and South Seas artifacts get the ball rolling when you walk in the door. Just for tonight, break away from the routine and order one of those frothy drinks that comes in a totem-pole glass with fresh fruit. You will be seated in one of several dining rooms, but the main one is where you'll see the show ($11.90 per couple) at 7:30 p.m., 10:30 p.m., or midnight. Entrées will be in the $10 to $20 range; drinks between $3 and $5. Order from Cantonese delicacies like Shanghai chicken, crab Rangoon, and scallops Singapore, or more traditional fare—steaks, chops, and ribs prepared to perfection over the Mai-Kai's oak-log fires. Pretty Tahitian dancers with dark eyes and hip-length black hair wear fancy grass skirts and headpieces in the Polynesian Revue. Not to worry, they wear something on their upper half, too! A trendy place for tourists, but kind of a nice change of pace.

Now here's a place that looks and *sounds* fun. **Shirttail Charlie's Native Fish & Honest Bar,** at Riverfront Marina, 400 S.W. 3rd Ave., Fort Lauderdale (tel. 463-FISH), loves to poke fun at itself, but that's part of the charm. The menu is a souvenir newsletter giving directions to the restaurant by car, by canoe, or barefoot. Directly on the water, Charlie's can offer "still strugglin'" seafood and a free after-dinner cruise up the New River on their own boat. Here you're gonna find some unusual fish dishes like topneck clams, cracked alligator tail, shark bites (!), blackened tuna (*not* out of a can!), coconut-fried shrimp, and sautéed alligator. If your tastes don't run to seafood, try Charlie's steaks, poultry, or pasta as a main course. Lunches range between $10 and $24 per couple; dinner $30 to $50. If you're hankering to go on the cruise, you need to make reservations to eat *upstairs*. Otherwise, you go on a "space available" ticket for $2 per person. Cruises last 30 minutes and leave at 7:30 p.m., 8:15 p.m., and 9 p.m. The Downstairs Docks and Turtle Bar features nightly live entertainment and a raw-bar kitchen. Come early for a table by the window for great riverside dining. Open for lunch Monday to Friday 11:30 a.m. to 2 p.m. Open for dinner daily from 5:30 p.m. to 10 p.m. Dress requirements: Men need a collared and sleeved shirt; no sandals.

Waterfront dining is everywhere in Fort Lauderdale, with a wide selection of unusual decors, prices, and menus; for seafood, though, the locals think first of the **15th Street Fisheries**, 1900 S.E. 15th St., Fort Lauderdale (tel. 763-2777). It's not just for the great views of the busy Intracoastal Waterway: Step into an eclectic nautical theme with huge nets hanging from suspended wood beams, antique lobster traps, metal pails, buoys, anchors, and other nautical memorabilia set up on shelves above the heads of diners. The area's favorite catches are immortalized in picture frames. The candlelight and small low-hung overhead lamps create a rosy glow in the evening without obstructing your night view of yachts, cruise ships, and marina lights. The Fisheries has a famous bouillabaisse that gets rave reviews, and a summer-only lobster dinner for $9.95. Other seafood entrées are available as well as porterhouse steaks. Dinners run about $40 per couple, including appetizer, salad, bread, vegetable, and a frosty fresh fruit ice. Opens at 11:30 a.m.; dinner served Monday, Thursday, and Sunday 5 to 10 p.m.; Friday and Saturday 5 to 11 p.m.

The old brick and natural woods decor accented by lots of tropical plants and huge windows has been copied over and over, but was a novel idea when **The Down Under**, 3000 East Oakland Park Blvd., Fort Lauderdale (tel. 563-4123) opened in 1968. A seven-foot wooden Beefeater guard greets you at the entrance. Move on into the dining area to find fresh flower arrangements, a working fireplace, valuable antique furnishings and accessories, expensive china, and delicate stemware. The 40 entrées are basically French, with a little New York, New Orleans, and California thrown in for flavor. And this lovely waterfront restaurant also emphasizes the best of Florida seafood. The recent addition of the waterfront greenhouse room provides great food and scenic views of the Intracoastal Waterway. Dinner with wine per couple will cost around $40 to $50, and with 700 wines to choose from, you ought to find one you love. Open weekdays for lunch from 11:30 a.m. to 2 p.m.; dinner daily from 6 to 10:30 p.m.

Inexpensive

Who-Song & Larry's Restaurant & Cantina, 3100 North Federal Hwy., Fort Lauderdale (tel. 566-9771). Feel a part of Old Mexico and old Fort Lauderdale (the restaurant's been here for 32 years) with a strolling mariachi band and the best Mexican chow this side of Tijuana. Sit in the Cantina for fine margaritas served in frosty glasses, then make your move past Mexican memorabilia, cacti, and scurrying waiters and waitresses to your table for some famous fajitas or hot, homemade tortillas, both made in their own exhibition kitchen. Who-Song & Larry's squeezes its own orange and grapefruit juice daily, so if you order mixed drinks, the juice will be fresh from the tree (almost). Lunches are about $10 per couple; dinners from $10 to $20 per couple. Open Monday through Thursday 11:30 a.m. to 11 p.m.; Friday and Saturday 11 a.m. to midnight; Sunday from 10:30 a.m. to 11 p.m.

8. Miami / Miami Beach

Miami is as different from Miami Beach as a Jeep is from a BMW: Both can be very exciting, but in very different ways.

The two are next-door neighbors. If you're driving south along the coast, you can follow Interstate 95 or U.S. 1 from Fort Lauderdale south into Miami, or take A1A south for the island route: Sunny Isles, Bal Harbour, and on into beautiful Miami Beach. It is only about ten miles long but those are about the most visitor-oriented, fun-filled, nightlife- and attraction-packed ten miles you'll ever see. Miami Beach is linked to Miami by several causeways, giving you easy access from four different points.

Key Biscayne is an island south of the beach, with Virginia Key and Fisher Island in between. It can only be reached by the Rickenbacker Causeway through Virginia Key from U.S. 1 in south Miami. The Key is only a couple of miles long, but offers water views all around and *seclusion* in this busy tourist town. The famous Tamiami Trail (U.S. 41) connects Florida's east and west coasts, is a direct route from Miami to Coral Gables southeast of Miami. Here and in most of Miami, you'll want to brush up on your Spanish—it's the second language here and may make it easier for you when dealing with taxi drivers, airport porters, and waiters. South of Coral Gables on Biscayne Bay is glitzy, wealthy Coconut Grove.

GUIDE TO THE NUMBERED POINTS OF INTEREST ON THE MIAMI AND VICINITY MAP: 1.—Seminole Okalee Indian Village; 2.—Dania Jai Alai Fronton; 3.—Gulfstream Park Racetrack; 4.—Calder Race Course; 5.—Monastery of St. Bernard; 6.—Biscayne College; 7.—Biscayne Kennel Club; 8.—Barry College; 9.—Hialeah Park Racetrack; 10.—Miami Jai Alai Fronton; 11.—Miami Stadium; 12.—Watson Park; 13.—Miami Municipal Auditorium; 14.—Orange Bowl Stadium; 15.—Dade County Auditorium; 16.—Flagler Kennel Club; 17.—Miami Merchandise Mart; 18.—Tamiami Trail; 19.—Miamarina—Bayfront Park; 20.—Miami Beach Convention Center; 21.—Ocean Front Auditorium; 22.—Marine Stadium; 23.—Planet Ocean; 24.—Seaquarium; 25.—Vizcaya Art Museum; 26.—Museum of Science & Planetarium; 27.—Historical Museum of So. Florida; 28.—"Miracle Mile"; 29.—Little Havana; 30.—Coconut Grove artist district; 31.—City Hall & Marina Dinner Key; 32.—University of Miami; 33.—Bill Baggs State Park—Cape Florida Lighthouse; 34.—Fairchild Tropical Garden; 35.—Parrot Jungle; 36.—Serpentarium; 37.—Monkey Jungle; 38.—Miami Seaquarium; 39.—Miami Wax Museum; 40.—Coral Castle; 41.—Orchid Jungle

---

If you've never considered Miami and its most famous beach as a honeymoon destination, think again. The upbeat, thriving feel of a resort city on the move is back, offering tourists sunshine, accommodations, and nightlife.

ROMANTIC INTERLUDES: There is an enormous amount of sightseeing to be done in and around Miami.

Built as a winter refuge for Evanston, Illinois, native John Deering, the incredible **Vizcaya Museum and Gardens**, 3251 South Miami Ave. (tel. 579-2813), a mansion-turned-museum, took two years (1914–1916) and 1,000 people to build. Deering, not to be confused with John Deere of tractor fame, earned his great wealth as cofounder and vice president of International Harvester Company. Because the mansion overlooks Biscayne Bay, he named the property "Vizcaya," a Basque word meaning elevated place. Deering used the palatial home as a showcase for his European and Oriental art pieces. As you take the guided tour through the home you will learn, among many other things, of the 150 types of marble used in the floors, shipped here from all over the world.

The entire estate, once 180 acres, has shrunk to only 30, but the entrance roads are still jungle-like vegetation, in contrast to the neatly landscaped gardens. It is possible to have your wedding in the gardens of Vizcaya with advance permission of the

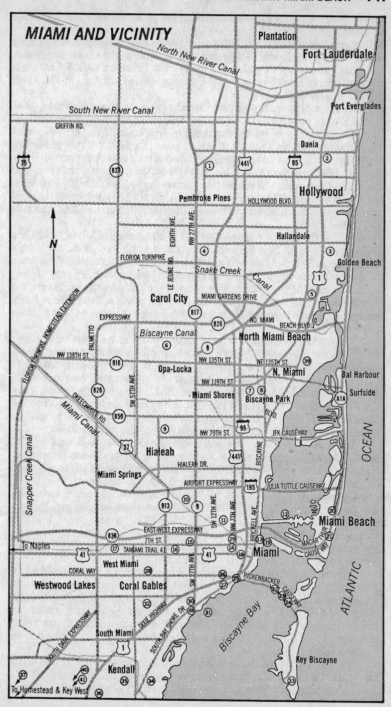

MIAMI AND VICINITY

museum and some planning to accommodate the museum's many restrictions. The house-and-garden tour is $5 per person; $3.50 per person for the garden alone. Open daily except December 25 from 9:30 a.m. to 5 p.m. Gardens close at 5:30 p.m. From January to May, the Florida Shakespeare Festival stages its plays in a setting plucked from the Renaissance—the gardens of Villa Vizcaya. Tickets are $10 to $16 and can be obtained from the South Florida Theater Company, 444 Brickell Ave., M-124, Miami 33131 (tel. 372-0305).

For a taste of Miami's wilder side, spend a day at the **Miami Metrozoo,** 12400 S.W. 152nd St. (tel. 251-0400). Over 100 species of animals, birds, and reptiles roam cageless, separated from the viewing public by large moats. Many exhibits are still under construction, but when it's all said and done, the Metrozoo may be Florida's finest. Open 10 a.m. to 5:30 p.m. daily. Admission price is $4.50 per person.

The **Bill Baggs State Park** in Key Biscayne is a shady, peaceful place away from the bustle of downtown Miami (take the causeway from Miami). The big draw here is the view of land, sea, and sky from the top of a restored 1830s lighthouse (122 steps up!). Other than that, it's quiet with lots of shade trees and flowers. And it's open to the public at no charge.

Just past the Latin side of town, the middle-class suburb of Miami called **Coral Gables** gets its name from the hard coral rock on which most of the city is built. George Merrick, turn-of-the-century entrepreneur, began this community as a peaceful diversion from city life. The combination of Mediterranean, French, Chinese, South African, and Dutch-influenced architecture you'll find here is more like art, with its whimsical gingerbread and palatial facades. It might help to identify the styles and get around if you pick up a map at City Hall, 405 Biltmore Way (tel. 442-6441), before you begin your tour.

The Venetian Pool at Almeria Avenue and Toledo Street must be at the top of your sightseeing list. Designed by Merrick and now open for public use, this lovely pool is surrounded by waterfalls, caves, lagoons, and grottos. For hours, days, and fees for the pool, contact the **Coral Gables Chamber of Commerce,** 50 Aragon Ave. (tel. 446-1657). Merrick's own gabled house of coral is close by, appropriately called Coral Gables House, at 907 Coral Way (tel. 442-6566). Admission is $1 per person. Open Wednesdays 1 to 4 p.m. The main entrance to the city, "La Puerta del Sol," and the newly renovated Biltmore Hotel (see hotel listings) also merit your time.

You'll need to rent a car for **Coral Castle,** 28655 U.S. 1, Homestead (tel. 248-6344), but you will never again see anything like it, and the drive to Homestead is scenic with lots to do and see along the way. Take the beach road (U.S. 1) or the Florida Turnpike to Homestead, about 35 miles south of Miami. The "castle" was built by one 97-pound Latvian immigrant for his "Sweet Sixteen" woman who remains a mystery, but supposedly had jilted Edward Leedskalnin on their wedding day. This massive structure took him 15 years to build (1925–1940) and is made entirely from coral rock. How he completed it remains a mystery. Leedskalnin used no heavy machinery and worked entirely solo, moving pieces of coral weighing several tons each. Open 9 a.m. to 9 p.m. daily. Admission is $6 per person.

Slip into the Florida of 50 years ago in Miami Beach's **Art Deco District** filled with blocks of oceanfront buildings splashed in shades of pink, light blue, ocean green, coral, and yellow. Now on the National Register of Historic Places, the district is bordered by Ocean Drive on the south, 9th Street north to Washington Avenue, and east to 13th Street. Here, tuxedos and designer jeans can co-exist in the same elegant restaurant, where a feeling of vitality and rebirth breathes life into an area that was once cast aside.

The best way to get a feel for the excitement and glamour of this era is to stop by the **Miami Design Preservation League** at 1236 Ocean Dr., Room 11 (tel. 672-1836). Each Saturday at 10:30 a.m., the MDPL conducts 90-minute walking tours of the district for $5 a person. If you don't happen to be in the area on a Saturday, stop by their office for self-guided tour maps. A tip for camera buffs: Try experimenting to create some dramatic effects. Look for port holes, curved balconies, glass-block windows, and lots of neon—all typically used in this district where construction began after the hurricane of 1926 and ended during World War II.

HONEYMOON HOTELS AND HIDEAWAYS: In town or on the beach, you're never very far from a wealth of shops, restaurants, and those great views of the ocean and the bay. If you're considering staying in one of the Art Deco hotels, you'll find them cozy and pretty, much as they must have been in the 1920s and 1930s; don't expect to see marble Jacuzzis and suite-size accommodations. The best part: The Art Deco hotels are right across from the ocean and are for the most part inexpensive. Where applicable, prices shown reflect the spread between low- and high-season rates.

In Miami

The **Hotel Intercontinental Miami,** 100 Chopin Plaza, Miami, FL 33131 (tel. 305/577-1000), seizes the opportunity to lure lovers of a fast-paced lifestyle by offering panoramic views from every floor. Its strategic location close to downtown and a quick taxi ride to almost anywhere allows honeymooners to take full advantage of attractions in town and on the beach. The centerpiece of the huge lobby is Sir Henry Moore's marble sculpture *The Spindle*, soaring 18 feet into the domed atrium. Elsewhere, look for marble from Italy, granite from Brazil and Africa, black mahogany from Central America, English oak, and Asian teak, all used as backdrop for eighteenth-century Belgian tapestries and a collection of rare English prints. Rooms are spacious with a Far Eastern feel—red sculpted chairs, black armoires painted with oriental designs, and deep floral prints on bedspread and curtains. Fully stocked refrigerators and the Lancôme soap, shampoo, and conditioner amenities give the place tip-to-toe class. There's no beach, but the good-size pool helps compensate. Honeymoon package (EP): $215 per couple per night; $110 (EP) each additional night. Includes a luxury parlor suite with a bottle of fine dry champagne, all VIP amenities, all sports and recreation facilities, breakfast in bed one morning (order from room service), or take a $30 credit in the Royal Palm Court restaurant. With its floor-to-ceiling glass windows, it offers unequalled views of Miami.

Built on what is almost its own private island on the bay, you can pick the **Biscayne Bay Marriott,** 1633 North Bayshore Dr., Miami, FL 33132 (tel. 305/374-3900; U.S. reservations: toll free 800/228-9290), out of Miami's dynamic skyline, rising 31 stories over the city. Choose a room with a balcony for sharing that skyline over a romantic nightcap, with water views on every side. Furnishings reflect classic good taste, with dark wood pieces and beds with carved headboard. In-room movies are standard in all rooms. Pool only, no beach. Honeymoon package (EP): $132 per couple per night; $93 each additional night. Includes a deluxe room (choice of queen- or king-size bed), welcome champagne, and your choice of breakfast in bed the first morning or lunch in the Bayview Restaurant. For a bit more money you can have a lot more room with a minisuite (EP): $186 per night and $148.50 each additional night.

On Miami Beach

The **Fontainebleau Hilton,** 4441 Collins Ave., Miami Beach, FL 33140 (tel. 305/538-2000; U.S. reservation: toll free 800/HILTONS). When this massive Miami Beach landmark was first constructed in the 1950s, no sign announced its name at the driveway entrance: If you didn't *know* this was the famed Fontainebleau, no one was going to tell you. After the recent $25-million facelift, there's finally an identifying marker. Now under the management of Hilton, the Fontainebleau still sets the standards for quality service and luxury on the Beach. The ornate lobby is somewhat over-whelming with its huge fountains, full-size trees, and tiny shimmering lights. Every-thing the Fontainebleau does is a spectacle, though, which has kept it a favorite for so many years. The rooms have all been redone recently, and they positively exude ele-gance, with reproduction antiques, plush carpeting, and rich pastel fabrics.

The hotel has recently opened its own health club and spa. The hotel is one of the few on the Beach with tennis courts: seven of them, all lit for night play. The grotto swimming pool is made as intimate as a 140-foot pool can be by the tropical foliage, giant rocks, and cascading waterfalls. In its restaurants, the hotel maintains a staff of the finest chefs in the state. The Steak House and Poodle Lounge are very much in the art deco style with black everything and bald-headed female mannequins floating on pedestals. The Dining Galleries is also an art gallery—the hotel has purchased price-less paintings, furniture, and sculpture to enhance its posh decor. "Honeymoon Cele-bration" package: Three days/two nights (EP): $359 per couple; $159.50 per couple (EP) each additional night. Includes deluxe oceanview accommodations, a bottle of iced champagne in your room on arrival, breakfast in bed your first morning, a Christine Valmy Evening Glamour Treatment for the bride (facial, cosmetic makeover, manicure, and pedicure); Fontainebleau Hilton his-and-her robes, and a Fontainebleau Hilton Passport, entitling you to special values on dining and entertain-ment.

The beach's resurgence of visitors in the past few years has prompted hotels to renovate, expand, and provide their guests with every possible convenience during their stay. The **Doral-on-the-Ocean**, 4833 Collins Ave., Miami Beach, FL 33140 (tel. 305/532-3600; U.S. reservations: toll free 800/327-6334), has recently opened its two presidential suites on their own floor for $2,500 each—per night! You may find the Doral's other accommodations a bit more affordable. All are decorated in soft pastels with cozy furnishings and include minirefrigerators, hair dryers, makeup mirrors, remote-control color TVs, and two phones per room. You'll have access to tennis, the aqua sports club, and the health and fitness center. Honeymoon package: None. Junior suites are recommended for honeymooners, though. These oversize rooms have king-size beds. Junior suite rates: $176 to $193.50 per couple per night.

The **Art Deco Hotels**, 13th and Ocean Drive, Miami Beach, FL 33139 (tel. 305/534-2135; reservations: toll free 800/327-6306). (Note: These are the central reserva-tions numbers for all the hotels.) Several art deco classics have been restored to their 1920s and 1930s splendor.

Quaint and charming, these hotels could become one of your Miami honey-moon's brightest memories. All are picturesque and unique. Aside from the bright pastel colors on the outside, architecture and decor are all quite different from one an-other. Waldorf Towers at 860 Ocean Dr.; the Hotel Leslie and The Carlyle next door to each other at 13th and Ocean, and the Cardozo, Victor, and Cavalier, newly opened and located within a block of the Carlyle each offers its own cozy ambience, authenti-cally decorated in the Art Deco style.

The Waldorf Towers has a small, intimate lobby with rattan furniture and lots of indoor palms; one side serves as a café for the daily continental breakfast. Rooms are European style; that means smaller than you might expect and modestly furnished in bright colors. Some rooms have *twin* beds—be sure to specify a double or a queen-size. And since a jazz club occupies the lower floor of the hotel, ask for a room above the first floor if you're looking for peace and quiet!

The Carlyle has transformed its lobby into the famous Carlyle Grill (see restau-rant section), so there is really no lobby to speak of. The hotel is a little fancier than the Waldorf Towers, but is also a very popular gathering place, meaning that the restaurant and adjoining bar are full most of the day and night. All hotels have an oceanfront terrace for lunch or drinks, or just to catch some of that warm Miami sun. Honeymoon package: None. Standard rates (EP): $66 per couple per night for a standard room; $137.50 per couple per night for a superdeluxe suite with many offerings in between.

In Coconut Grove

The **Grand Bay Hotel**, 2669 S. Bayshore Dr., Miami, FL 33133 (tel. 305/858-9600; U.S. reservations: toll free 800/327-2788), rates among the top 15 hotels in the world according to a 1987 list compiled by *Lifestyles of the Rich and Famous*. The lobby decor features the finest marble, inlaid woods, highly polished brass, shimmering chandeliers, and elegant clusters of cozy seating. Custom-designed rooms each have different furnishings in a variety of color schemes so on a return visit you'll again be surprised. Even though guests pass through constantly, it's still a wonderfully serene spot for reading or afternoon tea. Pool, no beach. "La Romantica" honeymoon package: Four days / three nights (EP): $438-per couple. Includes deluxe bayview accommodations with a private balcony, a glass of freshly squeezed Florida orange juice, a bottle of chilled French champagne, breakfast on your balcony or in the Grand Cafe, health club privileges, sauna, and Jacuzzi. A Grand Bay Shopping Card entitles you to 20% off your purchases at Mayfair Mall, home of some of the most fashionable shops in Miami (complimentary limo service will whisk you there and back!). The private, internationally known nightclub Regine's atop the Grand Bay gives you a membership for one year as part of the package. Seven-night package available for $1,216 (EP). The seven-night package also includes dinner for two in the Grand Café PLUS use of a Mustang convertible or Dodge 600—yours with unlimited mileage for *seven days!*

Each room of **Mayfair House**, 3000 Florida Ave., Miami, FL 33133 (tel. 305/441-0000; U.S. reservations: toll free 800/433-4555 nationwide; 800/341-0809 in Florida), is a work of art, from the salmon-and-black marble foyer to the French and oriental period pieces gracing the Mayfair Grill and Bar. Strawberries are served in your suite every afternoon. Caviar and pâté are complimentary when you order cocktails. And the white-glove service is free. Rooms are suite-size with expensive antiques, oriental rugs, and original oil paintings. Headboards are beautifully carved, and separate sitting areas provide a cozy place for relaxing or reading. The rooftop garden bar and pool overlook Biscayne Bay. Honeymoon package: Two days / one night (EP): $192.50 per couple. Includes a welcome glass of champagne and a fruit basket in your suite with private terrace and Japanese hot tub, guest membership to the private Ensign Bitters club, a souvenir T-shirt, a bottle of champagne, souvenir Mayfair kimonos for both of you, complimentary limousine service, valet parking, and a Mayfair Preferred Shopping Card with discounts at most Mayfair shops.

In Key Biscayne

Practically an island all to itself, the **Sonesta Beach Hotel**, 350 Ocean Dr., Key Biscayne, FL 33149 (tel. 305/361-2021; U.S. reservations: toll free 800/343-7170), lords over ten acres of Atlantic beachfront. Originally built to resemble a Mayan temple, the inside has been redone, so the similarities end there. Find cool fountains, soft pastels, 9 restaurants, and 300 rooms. The hotel makes a fine choice for tennis lovers, with ten Laykold courts, three lit for night play. Honeymoon package: None. However, many regular packages are available that should suit honeymooners and include choice of rooms with private balconies, villas, or resort homes. Newlyweds will be warmly welcomed with an oceanfront room and a complimentary bottle of champagne. "Florida Fantasy" package: Seven days / six nights: $792 to $974 per couple. Includes four days and three nights at the Sonesta Beach, three nights at the Sonesta in Orlando, and a rental car for six days with unlimited mileage. The "Sonesta Spree" package: Four days / three nights: $478 to $658 per couple. Includes luxury accommodations with private balcony (honeymooners automatically get an oceanfront room), unlimited tennis, use of the new fitness center, a welcome fruit basket, one dinner with a carafe of wine in any of the restaurants, and transportation for shopping trips.

In Coral Gables

Towering, majestic . . . the magnificent old **Biltmore Hotel**, 1200 Anastasia Ave., Coral Gables, FL 33134 (tel. 305/445-1926), once the tallest building in the south, has come to life after a long silence with a major multi-million-dollar renovation. George Merrick's dream hotel, erected in Coral Gables in 1926, still boasts the largest hotel pool in the country (there's no beach however). A pool, incidentally, where Johnny Weismuller taught and Ginger Rogers, Bing Crosby, and Judy Garland swam. The Spanish-style loggias, facade, and courtyard walkways are now proudly gleaming in tones of sienna and aqua. Doormen still greet guests as griffins playfully watch from atop stairwells. The original flavor of opulence and luxury has been carried throughout the hotel, from bellhops to room service. Spacious rooms have been preserved as much as possible—wood beams or painted ceilings have been kept, and tapestries, oriental rugs, and antiques brought in to capture the old hotel flavor. Every room is different, but elegant, in a classical, traditional style. Plumbing and vanity areas have been updated for modern travelers. Honeymoon package (EP): $125 per couple per night (includes tax and gratuities). Includes an upgrade to the best available room (the best in the house), fruit, and champagne, a continental breakfast served in your room, complimentary poolside cocktails, and limousine transport to the airport.

ROMANTIC RESTAURANTS AND NIGHT SPOTS: Whether you prefer an ambience that is wonderfully romantic or playfully whimsical, choose your place for a special night out with crystal and linens or a good-time atmosphere for a less expensive meal. Many of the finest restaurants are located in Miami-area hotels.

On Miami Beach

Expensive: The beautifully restored 1941 art deco hotel has turned its lobby into a showplace called the **Carlyle Grill** (inside the Carlyle Hotel), 1250 Ocean Dr., Miami Beach (tel. 534-2135). Pastel walls feature original sconces on either side of the fireplace, a huge black curved bar (formerly the reception desk), and curved bronze mirrors. Sit by the window for an ocean view or enjoy your lunch under umbrellas on the veranda. For starters, try a hearts-of-palm salad or escargot. Quiche Lorraine, chicken crêpes, or London broil are main course features. With Miami Beach's large Jewish population, you'll find kosher-style deli favorites everywhere—roast beef or corned beef on rye are two popular items. Luncheon entrées are priced between $4 and $10. Dinner at the Carlyle is a fancier affair with frogs' legs, lobster tails, cornish hen, or duckling to choose from, priced from $60 to $100 per couple for a full seven-course meal, depending on what you order. Open for breakfast at 7 a.m.; lunch is served noon to 3 p.m.; dinner from 6 p.m. on.

For the one night of your honeymoon stay you want to feel catered to, your every whim satisfied, reserve your table at **Dominque's Famous French Restaurant** (inside the Alexander Hotel) 5225 Collins Ave., Miami Beach (tel. 865-6500). Tables have individual lighting controls to suit your preferences and are set with the finest china, silver, crystal, and linens. Try for a table near the bay windows overlooking a fountain cascading over coral grottoes into two lagoon pools. Past that—the white sands of Miami Beach. Start with exotic appetizers such as buffalo sausages, diamondback rattlesnake salad, and alligator tail. Of course, there's also plenty of regular fare. A sampling of entrées include grilled salmon with watercress and dill sauce; Maine lobster; prime New York sirloin steak stuffed with escargots and garlic butter; and the house specialty—marinated rack of lamb. For dessert, house sorbet, glacés, rich pastries, or the special pistachio soufflé created for *Miami Vice* star Don Johnson. Dinners will cost around $100 per couple, more with drinks. Open 7:30 a.m. to 2:30 p.m. for breakfast and lunch; 6 to 11 p.m. for dinner. Reservations are requested. Dress up.

Moderate: The Tropics inside the Edison Hotel, 960 Ocean Dr., Miami Beach (tel. 531-5335). Delightfully colorful and fun, this avant-garde art deco–flavored restaurant is a gathering place for artists and socialites from early morning right into the wee hours. The huge floor-to-ceiling windows flood the place with the warm Miami sunshine, especially lovely at sunrise or sunset. The chefs have found a fun way to serve food, too: Your lox, bagels, and cream cheese may be served on a platter with carrot and carved green-pepper palm trees. Breakfast items are $2.25 to $6 each; luncheon $3.95 to $9. Dinner is a little of everything—chicken flambé with cognac, paella, blackened lamb, or fettuccine with onions, pepper, cured ham, and cream. The service is first-class. Dinners are priced from $24 to $50 per couple. Breakfast is served from 7 a.m. to noon; lunch noon to 3 p.m.; and dinner from 7 p.m. to midnight daily. On weekends, appetizers are served until 3 a.m. Enjoy live entertainment from 10 p.m. until 2 a.m. nightly and a weekend brunch Saturday and Sunday from 10 a.m. until 4 p.m.

"The First Eating House on Miami Beach," **Joe's Stone Crab Restaurant,** 227 Biscayne St., Miami Beach (tel. 673-0365), has upheld a tradition for great food in elegant surroundings since 1913. A huge stone fireplace and fancy chandeliers are focal points of the spacious dining room. French doors on two sides offer lovely garden views of a fountain and blooming hibiscus. Have whatever you want here as long as it's stone crab, the hearty little crabs now on the endangered list; fishermen are only allowed to break off the claws and then must throw the crabs back to grow another. Actually, Joe's offers other seafood delights and meat and poultry items, but if you've never sampled the delicate flavor of cold claws drenched in drawn butter, it would be almost criminal not to at least try them while you're here. Something to remember before you walk in to Joe's—they require long pants or skirts, and tank tops are a no no, too. If you do slip up, Joe's will lend you sweat pants and/or long-sleeve shirts to wear during your meal, which will cost about $32 per couple (the meal, not the clothes). Open for lunch from 11:30 a.m. until 2 p.m. Tuesday through Saturday; 5 to 10 p.m. daily for dinner (closed mid-May to October). Make reservations (lunch included) or get in line early for this popular Miami Beach stop.

The Twenties inside the Sheraton Bal Harbour, 9701 Collins Ave., Bal Harbour (tel. 865-7511) is set in an award-winning art deco room, and you'll get a floor show before you see the floor show. Waiters and waitresses sing, dance, and cavort while serving you delicious continental entrées like dry-aged steaks and fresh seafood. Dinners at The Twenties will run from $18.95 (pasta) to $20.95 for twin rock-lobster tails for two. Menu selections have Prohibition-era names like Bonnie and Clyde (surf and turf), Flapper Snapper, and the Great Gatsby (chateaubriand for two). Open for dinner from 5:30 to 10:30 p.m.

The Sheraton also has one of the finest nightly floor shows in the area. The Las Vegas–style revue "It's Hot" at the Bal Masque Supper Club sparkles and shimmers with glitzy dance routines, magic shows, and hilarious juggling acts that will bring you to your feet! Shows are at 9 p.m. Tuesday through Saturday with an extra 11 p.m. show on the weekends. Two shows Sunday at 2:30 p.m. and 8 p.m. You can also dine at the Bal Masque for about $60 per couple. It's $15 for the show only, which includes one drink. Reservations are required.

The Dining Galleries inside the Fontainebleau Hilton Resort, 4441 Collins Ave., Miami Beach (tel. 538-2000) is like dining in a museum. There are European statues, original oils, and an 1882 grand piano from Hamburg that was once owned by the late Liberace. Many of the dishes are named after works in the gallery. Try "The Three Graces," three petite medallions of veal tenderloin enhanced with three different sauces (sorrel, villeroy, and tomato fondue) for $22.50. Or the "Chicken Rosa di Maggio"—a sautéed breast of chicken with fresh poached oysters and roasted sweet peppers in a delicate sauce choron ($16.95). Entrées are priced from $16.95 to $25.50, which includes vegetable; other courses are à la carte. Make reservations for dinner from 6 p.m. until midnight or join them for luncheon on Sunday between 10 a.m. and 3 p.m.

Adjoining The Dining Galleries, **The Poodle Lounge and Steak House** inside the Fontainebleau Hilton (tel. 538-2000) has been "deco-ized." In true 1930s fashion, almost everything is black, including the walls, carpet, tables, and chairs. The stark white napkins really stand out. On each table, a single flower floats in a glass vase lit by an overhead light. Dinner is hearty and delicious; there are a few gourmet specialties, but meat and potato people will also find lots to like. The blackened pompano has to be their finest offering and comes heartily recommended ($18.95). Duckling, pork steak, veal, prime rib, New York strip, and lamb chops are all good eating; dinner may land in the $60 to $80 per couple range. Don't miss the baba au rhum cake. If you've never tried it, you're in for a treat! Open for dinner from 6 p.m. to midnight; the lounge stays open until 3 a.m.

The Starlight Roof Supper Club at the Doral-on-the-Ocean (tel. 532-3600). Grand views of the Atlantic Ocean, Miami Beach, and Biscayne Bay surround you at this 18th-floor club. Tiny lights twinkle on the ceiling that can even be seen from street level. It's a romantic place to dine (dinners are around $50 per couple) and see the glitzy song-and-dance routines Tuesday through Sunday. Dinner begins at 7 p.m. with the show at 9 p.m.; on Saturday the show starts at 10 p.m. and Sunday's show at 8:30 p.m. with dinner at 6 p.m. For Friday and Saturday performances the price is slightly higher ($64 per couple); show-only tickets are $24 per couple; $36 per couple for Friday and Saturday evenings.

The Bayview inside the Biscayne Bay Marriott (tel. 374-3900) has a lovely one —from the second floor overlooking the marina. It's casual and comfortable all day and all night, serving breakfast, a lunch buffet Monday through Friday, Sunday brunch, and a daily Early Bird Dinner Buffet. Continental specialties, deli sandwiches, and homemade desserts are served. Prices are comfortable, too: Complete dinners range from $34 to $68 per couple. Open for breakfast 7 to 10 a.m.; lunch 11:30 a.m. to 2 p.m.; dinner 7 to 10 p.m., and champagne brunch on Sunday served 11 a.m. to 2:30 p.m.

Club Ovo, 1450 Collins Ave. (tel. 531-9500). Newly refurbished with huge door handles that spell "OVO," this exclusive nightclub was one of the great jazz clubs on Miami Beach in the 1930s, when it was the Warsaw Ballroom. Come for an evening of dancing to popular hits from the last two decades or be entertained by a jazz trio for lunch (11:30 a.m. to 5 p.m.) or dinner (5 to 10 p.m.).

Inexpensive: At **Wolfie's 21,** Collins Avenue and 21st Street (tel. 538-6626) the walls are decked with photos of Clark Gable, Frank Sinatra, and Judy Garland. Whether they were here or not doesn't really matter. The atmosphere is early deli, the waitresses look like they have worked here since the turn of the century, and the food is good and cheap—you can get out of here with a full meal for about $6 per person. Late nights are when Wolfie's comes alive—theatergoers and other social-scene types stop in for kosher-style favorites while an accordion player serenades from 11 p.m. until 1 a.m. on weekends. Joseph Nevel, owner of Wolfie's, can be seen strolling around the place, making sure his guests are enjoying themselves. Open 24 hours every day.

In Miami and Vicinity

Expensive: A favorite spot for a special night out, **The Pavilion Grill**, at Hotel

Intercontinental Miami, 100 Chopin Plaza, Miami (tel. 577-1000). Look around at the rich French and Italian interior, with its rosewood and green marble, leather booths, and upholstery. The menu offers regional dishes from all 50 states: cactus leaves from Texas, king crab from Alaska, wild rabbit from Wyoming. And you didn't think anything from your own turf could taste so heavenly! How about fresh Florida lobster rolled up in a chicken breast and mesquite grilled ($20) or Key West tuna steamed in ginger, sake, and chili peppers ($19)? A full dinner with wine will run about $120 per couple on the average.

Moderate: Le Grand Cafe at the Grand Bay Hotel, 2669 South Bayshore Dr., Coconut Grove (tel. 858-9600) is an intimate, charming spot. Rattan tables and chairs are umbrella-covered and, along with lush plants and Impressionist-inspired prints, give an outdoor garden ambience. Try one of the unusual dishes here, such as black linguini with calamari ($7.95); terrine of fresh foie gras ($8.95) as an appetizer; or one of the other Mediterranean menu items. A dinner for two will be about $45. The Sunday brunch is a lavish spectacle, served from 11:30 a.m. to 3 p.m. Breakfast is served Monday through Saturday, 7 to 11 a.m.; lunch 11:30 a.m. to 3 p.m.; and dinner daily from 6 to 11 p.m.

The **Cafe at the Biltmore** inside the Biltmore Hotel, Coral Gables (tel. 445-1926), serves up very good, moderately priced meals, with enough variety that you wouldn't get tired of the food or the ambience of the place even if you ate here every day. Try huevos rancheros ($7) or Belgian waffles ($6) for breakfast, with breads and croissants made in the Biltmore bakery daily. Lunch can be plain—Biltmore hamburger with bacon and cheese ($7.25), or fancy—sautéed Norwegian salmon, Noilly Prat Italian parsley sauce ($10.50), all served with added finesse. For your honeymoon dinner here, don't be surprised if the maitre d' sends over a bottle of wine or serves the champagne himself, toasting your good health and a happy life together. Appetizers are priced from $3.50 to $9, with entrées in the $6.50 to $18.50 range. Top it all off with a steaming cup of cappuccino for a relaxing end to a fine meal. Breakfast served 6:30 to 11 a.m.; lunch from 11 a.m. to 2:30 p.m.; late lunch 2:30 to 6 p.m.; and dinner 6 p.m. to 11 p.m.

A favorite of both visitors and locals for casual fun, entertainment, great food and views of tropical Biscayne Bay, **Monty Trainer's Bayshore Restaurant, Lounge, Raw Bar, and Marina,** 2560 South Bayshore Dr., Coconut Grove (tel. 858-1431), is the gateway to the Grove, by land or by sea. The indoor restaurant has a nautical setting with dark-pine paneling and shipboard memorabilia. The 30-plus entrées are mostly seafood specialties, but MT's ribs, prime rib, and sirloin are the finest corn-fed midwestern beef available, aged three to four weeks. Delectable entrées such as island mahi mahi Coconut Grove–style or amadine, paella, or conch will run about $15; meat and poultry are a little less than that. A full meal will run about $50 to $60 per couple. After dinner, visit the lovely MT's Lounge and Indoor Garden Patio, then stroll over to the Bay Front Bar at Monty Trainer's Outdoor Raw Bar and Marina, where you can enjoy a drink under a grass tiki hut or dance under the stars. There's live entertainment every night of the week. Open daily Monday to Friday 11 a.m. to 1 a.m.; Saturday and Sunday 8 a.m. to 3 a.m.

Inexpensive: The Royal Palm Court, Hotel Intercontinental Miami, 100 Chopin Plaza, Miami (tel. 577-1000), is located in the grand lobby and is a terrific spot for a cozy brunch. Try the tempting Bayfront, snow crab and diced bell peppers topped with Swiss cheese ($7.25). For lunch or dinner, there are club sandwiches and burgers along with specialties such as salmon coulibiac for $9.95 and Hungarian-style stuffed cabbage for $9.50. There is also a nice selection of American and French wines and domestic and imported beer. Open daily 6 a.m. to 11 p.m.

9. Key West

"It's not the end of the earth, but you can see it from here," is a good description of Key West. The little island at the end of the road is 100 miles from Miami, 90 miles from Cuba, and as far as you can get from just about anywhere in the United States. The drive from Miami to Key West is delightful, and there's a time-saving shortcut if you're so inclined. As you approach Miami from the north, look for exit 4 to Homestead and Key West. This is the West Dade Tollway (821) that connects with U.S. 1 at Florida City leading to Key Largo. You may want to take the Card Sound Bridge Road at Florida City; it's a little longer but more scenic. Take your time and stop a lot on your way to the islands that make up the rest of the Florida Keys. You'll see the underwater John Pennecamp Coral Reef State Park in Key Largo (the snorkeling is terrific), and tiny Key deer on Big Pine Key, where the vegetation and wildlife differ dramatically from the rest of the Keys.

To become a "conch" (pronounced konk), a Key West native, you first must pack away your watch, slip off your shoes, and give up any hopes of following a set itinerary. Relish this most amazing place frequented by the likes of Audubon, Hemingway, Tennessee Williams, and Jimmy Buffett. Soon after you arrive, you'll be operating on "island time" where the locals follow only the position of the sun to know when to open their shops or return from a day of conch fishing. Or, as Tennessee Williams once wrote, "Time past has a lovely habit of remaining time present in Key West."

ROMANTIC INTERLUDES: Time past and time present have a lovely way of blending with the scenery here; take your time and enjoy the sights, sounds, and sensations of Key West.

See the sights of old and new Key West while listening to a charming narration of the island's bizarre and unscrupulous history on a **Conch Tour Train.** Hear tales of pirates, buried treasure, and wreckers, those who made a fortune plundering vessels loaded with jewels and money. The 1½-hour tour takes you through Old Town, the heart of Key West; the Old Lighthouse; and past the homes of John James Audubon, Ernest Hemingway, and Harry Truman. Tours board at 501 Front St., Mallory Square, and 3850 North Roosevelt Blvd. The trains run seven days a week between 9 a.m. and 4 p.m. Price is $6 per person (tel. 294-5161).

An intimate and old Key West way to sightsee is a **horse-drawn carriage** just for two. The tour lasts 45 minutes, costs $10 per couple, and can be boarded at Front and Whitehead Streets from 9 a.m. until dark.

If you're not a snorkeler, the Fireball **glass-bottomed boat** is the next best thing to being there. View a living coral reef teeming with exotic plant and aquatic life from the safety of your vessel. The sunset cruise is spectacular, but times vary according to sunsets, so check beforehand. Price is $8.50 per person for a two-hour cruise leaving the gulf end of Duval Street (tel. 296-6923). Daytime trips depart at about 9:30 a.m., noon, and 2:30 p.m., varying a bit at different times of the year.

Yes, the famed novelist gave us *For Whom the Bell Tolls, A Farewell to Arms,* and *The Snows of Kilimanjaro* from the second-floor study of the pool house, but few remnants of his actual presence remain. Hemingway purchased this Spanish colonial home in 1931, but took all of his personal effects with him when he moved to Cuba ten years later. Still, the rooms are furnished in "Hemingwayesque" style—bare floors, limited and modest furnishings, and, of course, *lots* of books and Hemingway photos. You'll hear about the legendary six-toed cats that roamed about the house and of which Hemingway became enamoured. Descendants still pad through the shady yard looking for handouts from the visitors. The **Ernest Hemingway Museum** is located at 907 Whitehead St. (tel. 294-1575); admission is $3 per person. Open daily 9 a.m. to 5 p.m.

Just down the road from the Hemingway house at 205 Whitehead St. (tel. 294-2116) is the famed residence where artist and naturalist John James Audubon spent a few weeks sketching local birds. The 1830 home has been completely renovated and reopened as a museum with period furnishings, many of which were recouped from shipwrecks. Open 9 a.m. to 5 p.m. every day. Admission price is $2 per person.

At sunset, it has become a Key West tradition to see what type of characters **Mallory pier** has stirred up on any given day. Long-haired, unshaven guitar players, dapperly dressed tap dancers, prophets, psychics, vegetarians, conch-shell peddlers, even folks like us can be found there. The performers are merely a prelude of the main attraction—a hint of pink streaks through the deep blue, fanning out into lavender before bursting into reds, golds, and oranges. A particularly memorable sunset will elicit a standing ovation from the crowd. And best of all . . . it's free.

Key West may be the end of the road, but it's by no means the end of Florida. Sixty-eight miles west of Key West is the massive, hexagonally shaped **Fort Jefferson on Garden Key in the Dry Tortugas.** The citadel saw little fighting; instead it served as a prison after the Civil War. Among its most famous inmates was Dr. Samuel Mudd, who had set the broken leg of John Wilkes Booth. He was not aware that Booth had just assassinated President Abraham Lincoln, but that's what makes the story even more moving. There is a large plaque on the wall of the fort honoring his tireless care of prisoners ill with malaria. The fort is just one highlight of the four-hour seaplane trip that leaves at 8:30 a.m. and 12:30 p.m. You can also enjoy some excellent snorkeling (gear is provided), bird watching, or swimming. Enroute the planes fly at low altitude so you are able to take pictures of marine life—sharks, stingrays, porpoises, and the giant sea turtles after which Ponce de Leon named the island ("Las Tortugas"). Cost for the half-day trip is $95 per person, but longer trips—all day or overnight camping—are available for $190 per person. Contact the Key West Seaplane Service (tel. 294-6978) for reservations.

Some of us sit around and tell stories of sunken wrecks and a king's ransom in buried treasure; Mel Fisher and his crew have sought the wrecks out and gone after the alleged treasure. And treasure they found—aboard ships like the *Nuestra Señora del Antocha* and the *Santa Margarita,* which sank in the Straits of Florida during a violent hurricane in 1622. The treasure is beyond compare: Heavy, ornate, gold chains, solid gold bars, a gold "poison cup," a 23-piece gold belt studded with rubies and diamonds, a stupendous emerald crucifix—adding up to more wealth than you'll probably see in a lifetime. The greatest treasure find of all time is on exhibit at **Treasure Salvors, Inc.,** 206 Greene St., Key West (tel. 296-9936). Open 10 a.m. to 6 p.m. daily. Admission is $5 per person.

HONEYMOON HOTELS AND HIDEAWAYS:
Capture the charm of Old Key West in Old Town or one of the newer resorts. No matter where you stay, nothing is far away. Where applicable, rates quoted reflect the spread between low- and high-season rates.

Moderate to Expensive

Key West's newest beachfront resort, **The Reach,** Simonton Street at the Ocean, Key West, FL 33040 (tel. 305/296-5000; U.S. reservations: toll free 800/874-4118 nationwide; 800/423-9953 in Florida), touts itself as "outrageously romantic." Victorian gingerbread Key West architecture washed in subtle peach and white looks stunning against the deep blue of the ocean. She's a beauty outside, and indoors, you'll find all the nice extras that take a resort hotel from pleasant to perfect: sunny terraces for an intimate breakfast for two; wicker and pine furniture for a spacious and airy feel; white walls, neutral shades of upholstery, and white lamps; Mexican tile floors and Indian dhurrie rugs; an alarm that wakes you to a fresh pot of coffee. The attentive European-style service and light, breezy feel of the place can only be described as a 24-hour celebration. Choose works by your favorite authors while your "librarian" dispenses tea and sherries in the lending library. Honeymoon package: Four days / three nights (EP): Deluxe oceanview room, $577 per couple; minisuite, $930 per couple. Includes breakfast in bed, champagne on arrival, and all taxes.

If you want more room than a hotel and more privacy than a guest house, **Ocean Key House,** Zero Duval St., Key West, FL 33040 (tel. 305/296-7701; U.S. reservations: toll free 800/328-9815 nationwide; 800/231-9864 in Florida), offers space and intimacy in their brand new all-suite accommodations. Right on the Gulf of Mexico, just steps from the charm of historic Key West, the Ocean Key House is pure luxury without being stuffy. The open-air lobby sets the mood of the place with a long inlaid wood reception desk with a huge arched window behind it and lots of plants all around. Rooms are downright luscious, with nothing left out. Decorated in soft peaches, pinks, and neutrals, the white furniture and live plants carry the island theme. Private balconies overlook the waterfront; a rather spectacular view to wake up to because it's where the Atlantic Ocean and the gulf meet. Sip champagne in your private Jacuzzi, cook up a feast in your own gourmet kitchen, or swim in the sparkling pool with the gulf as a backdrop. For avid boating enthusiasts, sightseeing and fishing boats are available at the Ocean Key House Marina. "The Suite Start" honeymoon package: Three days / two nights (EP): $361.90 per couple. Includes a deluxe gulf-view one-bedroom suite, champagne, a breakfast basket, a sunset harbor cruise on the *Miss Key West,* and a Key West "Island Bonus Check" book for discounts on shopping, dining, and entertainment. A five day / four night package is also available for $647.90 per couple (EP).

Marriott's Casa Marina Resort, Reynolds Street on the Ocean, Key West, FL 33040 (tel. 305/296-3535; U.S. reservations: toll free 800/228-9290 nationwide; 800/235-4837 in Florida). The original 1921 Spanish Renaissance La Casa Marina was created by Henry Morrison Flagler to give the tourists who rode the Overseas Railroad a place to stop and visit at the end of the line. The railroad, destroyed by a 1935 hurricane, has been replaced by a highway, but visitors still flock to this elegant resort, which has been a haven for politicians, movie stars, artists, and socialites. Many additions have been made as the resort grew up, and modern amenities added to keep pace with today's traveler. Breakfast on a patio by the ocean or wander around the estate grounds. Sun on the beach or sail away from the private pier. Your room combines the lovely posh surroundings of the old resort with the amenities of the new one. Thick carpets and pastel wallpaper complement the natural wicker furniture. Think of the rich, the powerful, and the influential who must have gazed in the heavy mirrored vanity before you. Many of the nice old touches have been left alone—paddle fans, tall columns, high-beamed ceilings. Honeymoon package: Four days / three nights (EP): $462 per couple. Includes welcome cocktails in the lounge and chilled champagne in your room; deluxe accommodations; transportation to and from the airport; one morning's breakfast for two; one dinner for two at Henry's, a Gatsby-era restaurant; a tour on the Conch Train or the Old Town Trolley; admission to the Hemingway House; full use of the resort facilities; and use of a Sunfish, snorkeling equipment, or bicycles. Price slightly higher for a lanai room with a balcony.

Holiday Inn La Concha Resort Hotel, 430 Duval St., Key West, FL (tel. 305/296-2991; U.S. reservations: toll free 800/HOLIDAY). The grande dame of Old Key West, this 1925 hotel marks the place where Tennessee Williams put his final touches on *A Streetcar Named Desire*. In the heart of the historic district, La Concha has spared no expense making every detail in renovation historically accurate. Pinks, violets, whites, and beiges blend with deep-green awnings and marble stairways to create the elegantly casual ambience. Sunset colors accent The Top's lounge and rooftop garden where guests may watch Atlantic sunrises and gulf sunsets from the island's tallest building. Rooms are adorned with 1920s resort furnishings, lots of wicker and rattan, and white-lace curtains billowing with fresh sea air. "The Romance of the 1920s" honeymoon package: Four days / three nights (EP): $368 midweek; $400 on weekends. Includes chilled champagne and a fruit basket in your room, one breakfast in bed, a trip aboard the Conch Tour Train, and a cruise on a glass-bottomed boat.

Inexpensive

The Colony, 714 Olivia St., Key West, FL 33040 (tel. 305/994-6691). Yet another neat alternative to flashy hotels, these seven cottages and efficiencies tucked away in the heart of Key West's residential district can't be seen from the street, so you're ensured the utmost in privacy. The cottages are set sporadically around a ceramic swimming pool, fish ponds, and fountains. All the cottages are decorated differently, but what they all have in common are French doors, a private patio, cathedral ceilings, TV with remote control, full kitchens with cookware, dishes, and utensils, and a safe in each closet for your valuables. There are no phones in the cottages, but the office may allow you to make calls from their phone. The Colony asks for a $200 deposit to reserve a cottage. Honeymoon package: None. Weekly rate (EP): $385 to $577.50 per couple. $385 off season.

Guest Houses

If you'd like to experience living in one of these grand old Key West homes for a day or a week, they are filled with lots of charm and old south graciousness. Most are very affordable, but remember sometimes you must share a bath. It's a great way to go if you don't have a great amount of money to spend, and many of the homes offer breakfast as part of the deal. In addition, the managers will truly bend over backwards for honeymoon couples.

Heron House, 512 Simonton St., Key West, FL 33040 (tel. 305/294-9227), is actually three restored homes, the oldest of which was built in 1856. Renovation has included making rooms larger to offer two-room suites and three-room luxury apartments with a light and airy spaciousness that gently blends old and new. Stroll around the shady grounds; there's a park right across the street, and the beach is only three blocks away. Heron House is located in a residential area so it's far from the noise and crowds in the busier tourist areas. Room with shared bath down the hall, $41.80 to $60.50 per couple per night. Room with private bath $55 to $71.50 per couple per night.

Pat Hoffman has just taken over the **Merlinn Guest House,** 811 Simonton St., Key West, FL (tel. 305/296-3336), which was formerly owned by an interior designer. Each room is individually decorated to perfection with wood-beam ceilings, Bahama fans, and polished wood floors. Every room has a private bath. Breakfast is served daily on the deck overlooking the guest house's small pool. Vegetable quiche, fresh biscuits, juice, and coffee are just a few of the menu items you might find waiting when you awaken. Complimentary cocktails and hors d'oeuvres welcome you to this quiet and pleasant place. Honeymoon package: None. Standard rates (EP): $75.90 per couple per night. Larger rooms are $97.90 (EP) per couple per night. Two rooms of note here are the patio house with a kitchen and sitting area and a king-size bed under a large skylight ($97.90 EP per night) and "The Treehouse" honeymoon suite on the second floor jutting out from the rest of the house so it is actually set into the trees. It has a queen-size bed with a mosquito net canopy and a private sundeck for $97.90 (EP) per night.

ROMANTIC RESTAURANTS AND NIGHTSPOTS: Historic hangouts abound

if you want to follow the footsteps of the greats, but there's also plenty of history in resort restaurants. The ocean or gulf views can also pick you up at several local nightspots.

Moderate

Four plant filled, candlelit dining rooms plus the enclosed Buttery Garden Room at **The Buttery**, 1208 Simonton St. (tel. 294-0717), offer diners as much variety in seating as eating. Managers Toni and Paul have revamped this beautiful old building from scratch. The garden room is glass-enclosed to keep diners comfortable, and French doors, high ceilings, and skylights added to keep that open outdoor-like atmosphere. The Audubon Room is very formally decorated with a crystal chandelier and Queen Anne chairs upholstered in silk brocade. The Fountain Room is a misnomer; the fountain fell into disrepair and has been removed, but the room now has a tropical feel to it, with parroted upholstery, lots of palms, and rattan chairs and tables. The Cape Cod and Buttery rooms are earthy with deep-wood paneling and captain's chairs, and the new room (it hasn't grown a name yet) has lace curtains and antiques. An intimate table in the corner of this room is a favorite spot for wedding proposals! Try gamberetti de mare with Key West shrimp, Buttery steak Richardo, or the catch of the day prepared any of six different ways. Entrées priced from $15 to $22. Open at 7 p.m.

Henry's at Casa Marina Resort (tel. 296-3535) prepares sumptuous cuisine. Your butter is served on chilled lemon leaves and salads are presented with chilled forks on cloth napkins. Entrées such as yellowtail snapper, drunken lobster, and steak Diane are favorites, but save room for conch chowder and Key lime pie. Entrées are priced from $14.95 to $27.95. Sultry piano music plays in the natural rattan and burgundy dining area while you eat, the moon glistens on the ocean waves, paddle fans whirr, and there you are with your favorite person in the world. Enjoy! After dinner, trip the lights fantastic with live entertainment in the Calabash Lounge from 9 p.m. until 2 a.m. A truly "honeymoonish" night out.

La Terraza De Marti, 1125 Duval St. (tel. 294-8435). Called "La-Te-Da" for short, this European-style hotel in the historic district is better known for its superb cuisine than its modest accommodations. Breeze through an entranceway adorned with bougainvillea and passion flowers to the dining area with a double-decker porch overlooking a truly gem-like pool. If you prefer, dine outdoors at one of several intimate poolside tables. Get a delicious start on your day with croissants with brie and tropical fruit ($9.50) or eggs served nine incredible ways from Benedict with oyster (Key West style), to five layers of omelets and fillings baked in cream custard. You might guess that luncheon and dinner menus are equally as tempting and exotic. Try dolphin rouge in a roasted red bell pepper purée, tortellini Martinique—tender dumplings dressed with Florida lobster and broccoli in a Pernod cream sauce, stone-crab claws with dijonaise sauce, or roulades de poisson—turbans of yellowtail, snapper, and salmon filets. Among 18 dinner entrées are—lobster boreale, a trio of quail, poulet roti champagne (roast chicken with forcemeat stuffing of chicken and pork in champagne-and-celery cream sauce), lamb Montmorencey (grilled and sliced, dressed with a port-and-garlic sauce with fresh cherries). Breakfast entrées $5.50 to $19; luncheon $6.50 to $14.75; dinner $8.25 to $19.50. Open seven days.

Built in 1909, **Louie's Backyard**, 700 Waddell Ave. (tel. 294-1061) is listed on the National Register of Historic Places. Patrons may dine seaside in the shade of flowering sea-grape trees outdoors under the stars or in one of Louie's elegant dining rooms, where period furnishings mingle with 1980s' wicker and plants. Louie's four-star rating from the *Miami Herald* is well deserved. Begin your meal with chilled avocado soup with gazpacho sorbet or fricassee of rabbit with corn cakes and root vegetables. Five salads are offered combining ingredients like black beans and spinach with corn, bell pepper, red onion, and cumin vinaigrette. The best part is still to come: citrus soy marinated grouper, Asian vegetables, ginger garlic vinaigrette, grilled beef tenderloin, and Missouri pecan butter. Desserts are very special, too: chocolate cake and chantilly cream with chocolate peanut sauce, Louie's lime tart with raspberry sauce. Louie's serves lunch from 11:30 a.m. to 3 p.m. and the entrées average about $6.50 per person. Dinner is served from 7 to 11 p.m. in the summer; 6 to 10:30 p.m. in the winter. Entrées average about $18.50. The Afterdeck Bar sits a transom's height above the water, and upstairs, lively jazz can be enjoyed nightly in the Billy Webb Bar, open noon to 2 a.m.

A Mallory Pier sunset will put you in the mood for the **A & B Lobster House,** 700 Front St., Key West, (tel. 294-2536). Ride the elevator to the main dining room or walk around the building to the raw bar directly on the water. The upstairs room offers a wonderful view of the harbor; the interior features polished terrazo floors and a carpeted gazebo in the center. From the restaurant, you can buy a ride on a sailing schooner, take a sunset cruise or visit a coral reef. All boats are privately owned and dock at the A & B Marina.

Did we mention food? In addition to all the sights and sails, there's a tremendous selection of exotic specialty drinks (there's even a separate menu just for them) and good, good food at moderate prices. Shrimp scampi, lobster tail, London broil, stuffed flounder, grouper, yellowtail, chicken, prime rib, conch, scallops, stone-crab claws, and filet mignon give everyone a choice of their favorites. Entrées start at $8.95 and range all the way up to $23.95 for a whole lobster tail with New York strip steak. Dinners come with everything but the kitchen sink and the dessert—can you possibly leave without a slice of THE Key lime pie? The main dining room serves Monday through Saturday 5 to 10 p.m. The raw bar serves daily from 10:30 a.m. to 10 p.m.

People watching is a popular pastime for diners at **Claire,** Gingerbread Square, 900–904 Duval St., Key West (tel. 296-5558). All seating areas are great for views: either indoors, in the garden, on the porch, or on the deck. Tables are covered with white paper and customers are issued crayons to doodle. Try one of Claire's regular favorites, such as fettuccine "Marco Polo"—stir-fried broccoli, snow peas, red peppers, fresh ginger, soy, and parmesan alone or with your choice of tofu, breast of chicken, or Key West shrimp ($9.95 to $15.50). Daily specials might include cream of zucchini soup with romano basil butter ($3.50), yellowtail, grouper, Florida spiny lobster, dolphin, or snapper ($12 to $17). Complete dinners should run around $50 per couple. Dinner menu in effect 5:30 p.m. to 2 a.m.; late-night menu from midnight to 1:30 a.m.

Inexpensive

Dine directly on south beach on the ocean side of Key West in **The Eatery,** 1405 Duval St. (tel. 294-2727), a delightful home-style buffet restaurant. The brick floor, whitewashed walls with natural cedar frames and latticework, combine with paddle fans and greenery to create an authentic Key West feel. Huge windows on the front and side of The Eatery look out onto the ocean. Haitian and palm-weave artwork by local talent is proudly displayed on the walls. This is an "all-you-can-eat" buffet restaurant so come hungry. Breakfast might include baked apples, home fries, or chipped beef in gravy ($5.75 per person). Dinner selections include local fresh fish, baby back ribs, conch chowder, or fritters, and a selection of five vegetables for about $12 per person. Open daily from 6 a.m. to 9 p.m.

When it was known as the Midget Bar, **Sloppy Joe's** at the corner of Greene and Duval (tel. 294-5717) was a place where Hemingway spent many hours downing a few cold beers or picking a fish fight. The new Sloppy Joe's, with its loud top-40 music and carnival atmosphere, is now a trendy hangout for college students on vacation, but a plaque in the bar blatantly announces that Hemingway *was here*. Meanwhile, **Captain Tony's Saloon** looks more like a Sloppy Joe's—in fact, it was the original at 428 Greene St. (tel. 294-1838). Business cards and newspaper clippings adorn the walls.

This place has got atmosphere by the ladleful and a trip to Key West isn't complete until you've at least walked through Captain Tony's and read one newspaper clipping dating back to the early 1930s.

Chapter VI

GEORGIA

1. Practical Facts
2. Savannah
3. The Golden Isles
4. Atlanta
5. The Mountains

JUST BEING IN THE LAND OF LUSCIOUS PEACHES, imperious debutantes, Ted Turner, florid politicoes, R.E.M., and Coca-Cola creates infinite possibilities for partying your honeymoon away. As you cross the northern Georgia border, you'll come upon Savannah. Set a little ways up the Savannah River from the coast, the city does double duty as a busy modern port and a stunning antebellum town. Here youthfulness and energy cohabit easily with the old ways of Savannah's venerable aristocracy. Savannah is fast becoming a hot item on the list of relatively undiscovered, wonderful cities in America. A huge influx of innkeepers and restaurateurs catering to an upscale clientele provides a pretty good indication of the continued gentrification—or rather regentrification—of Savannah.

The Golden Isles spill down the Georgia coast from South Carolina to Florida. Some of the South's poshest accommodations are to be found here; conversely, some of the South's most unspoiled campgrounds are also scattered throughout the island's forests. Whether you choose a resort jammed with amenities, or pitch your tent on a pristine island devoid of "improvements," the Golden Isles are the place to go for getaway honeymoons.

Atlanta, in contrast, lays all the possibilities of a chic, fast-paced metropolis at your feet. Indulge your palate at any of a number of fine restaurants. Wreak fiscal havoc with your credit cards at Saks Fifth Avenue, Neiman-Marcus, and Rich's. Pamper yourselves in a suite at one of Atlanta's world-class hotels. Atlanta is just the kind of magical city that serves as a mecca for beautiful people and beautiful things, just the place for honeymooners in the market for the best in culture, cuisine, and creature comforts.

The mountains of northeast Georgia are one of America's fastest-growing honeymoon destinations. Much of the land has yet to be developed; what is being done is proceeding gracefully, gradually, keeping in mind a new generation of honeymooner who demands exquisite serenity and escape on one hand, haute cuisine, riding, and tennis on the other. Georgia's northern mountains are festooned with forests and coursed by cascading rivers that tumble into glassy lakes. Just going for a hike or a drive can be the most wonderful way to pass the day.

Whether your passion is for a quiet mountain retreat, a quaint cobbled street, an empty beach, or a city packed with diversions, Georgia has plenty of treats to tickle your fancy.

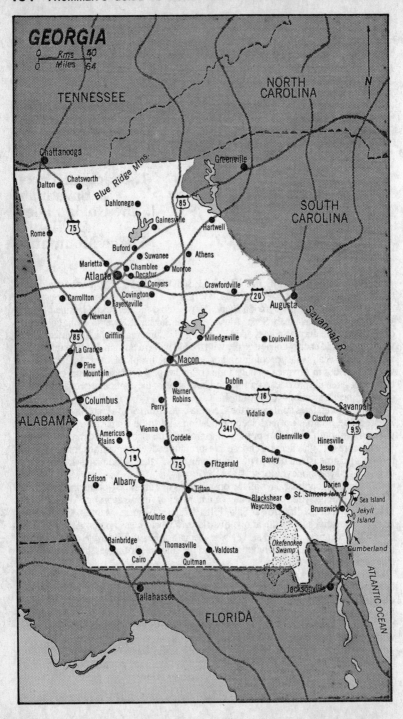

1. Practical Facts

GETTING THERE: Because Atlanta is virtually the hub of the southeast, Georgia is serviced by many airlines and interstates.

By Air

The Savannah airport, servicing the northern Georgia coast, has daily connecting service to most major east coast destinations on **Eastern Airlines.**

The Atlanta airport, one of the nation's busiest, has nonstop service from all major U.S. cities on **Delta, Eastern, Piedmont, Continental, Pan Am,** and **TWA.** This airport serves, of course, the Atlanta area, and the northeast mountains region as well.

The airport in Jacksonville, Florida, is closest to the southernmost of the Golden Isles—Cumberland and Jekyll. **Continental, Eastern, TWA,** and **Piedmont** connect this airport with the Northeast and Midwest.

By Car

Interstate 95 connects Georgia to Florida to the south, and to the entire Northeast up to Maine to the north.

Atlanta spins off interstates like spokes on a wheel: **Interstates 75** and **85** run north-south; **Interstate 20** goes east-west.

The Northeast Mountains are crisscrossed by some beautiful but tricky back roads. By all means come armed with a good map and detailed directions. You can reach the region by driving north from Atlanta on **Route 85** and **985** or on **Route 19.**

GETTING AROUND: For the Golden Isles and the Northeast Mountains, a car is a must. Savannah can be seen on foot, but should you want to do any exurban exploring, a car is necessary. In Atlanta, there is a newly expanded **subway** system, MARTA. Service is reliable and the ride is relatively safe during the day. **Taxis** are also available. Distances are great in Atlanta: The city is quite spread out. Renting a car is probably a good idea.

All airports and many of the better Atlanta hotels can supply you with a **rental car.** Unfortunately, unlike Florida there are no car-rental price wars, so rates in Georgia tend to be steep. A midsize car cost about $150 per week.

WEATHER: Since we are concerned with three very different areas, the weather for each must be considered separately.

Savannah and the Golden Isles

The best time to visit the Georgia coast is March through May or September through November. The weather is warm during the day, up to 80°, and sweater-necessary cool at night, with temperatures of 50° to 60°. Summer can be very hot and muggy. Winter, while rarely very cold, can be stormy.

Atlanta

This city is best in the springtime starting in March, when the dogwood blooms, on through azalea season and then magnolia season in May. Summer is hot and muggy. Winters are often icy and rainy.

The Northeast Mountains

Because of the elevations, the region's weather tends to be a bit behind the coast and Atlanta. Spring comes later, April instead of March; autumn finishes early, October instead of November. Summers can be hot, but generally stay breezy.

CLOTHING: Atlanta is a very sophisticated city. Better restaurants require tie and/or jacket for the gentlemen in the evening.

Savannah's tonier restaurants have similar dress-code requirements, but the city is generally more relaxed than Atlanta, sartorially speaking.

If you're headed for Sea Island, dressing up for dinner and dancing is a requisite part of the fun. The other Golden Isles mentioned are very low-key, and comfortable, casual clothing is the norm.

TIME: The entire state is in the Eastern Time zone, and observes Daylight Savings Time.

TELEPHONES: The Golden Isles and Savannah use the 912 area code. Atlanta and the mountains have 404 prefixes. Toll-free reservations and information numbers will be included in this chapter when available.

SHOPPING: Shopping in Savannah centers on the stores along the cobbled street of **Riverfront Plaza,** continuing to the Hyatt. Other havens for browsers and treasure hunters are the sidewalks of **Bull Street** and the cross-streets radiating therefrom. Some of the best spots in town are the shops at **The Savannah College of Art and Design,** which face each other across Bull Street on Madison Square. **The Gallery** is basically an artists/artisans' co-op run by the school, featuring weavings, pottery, and jewelry made by students, graduates, and local artists of note. **Design Works** is the school's book store stocked with art supplies and art books; sandwiches and ice cream are also available in this former apothecary shop.

In Atlanta, chic **malls** will supply you with everything you need. Two of the nicest (and consequently priciest) malls, set catty-corner across Peachtree at the intersection of Lenox Road, are **Lenox Square** and **Phipps Plaza,** featuring names like Saks Fifth Avenue, Neiman-Marcus, and Tiffany and Company.

The North Georgia Mountains are terrific places to find mountain crafts such as patchwork quilts, homemade preserves and handwoven baskets. One of the best places to seek the work of local craftspeople is the **Mark of the Potter,** set right beside Soque River in an old mill on Rte. 197 in Clarkesville.

ABOUT ACCOMMODATIONS: The hotels and resorts along the coast and in the mountains offer considerable discounts to those honeymooning in the off-season, which tends to be between November and March, give or take a week or two. Often the same room during these months will be 50% less than during the high season.

Most of the fine hotels in Atlanta offer special getaway weekend packages that typically include upgraded accommodations, breakfast in bed one day, champagne, flowers, free parking, and use of health club facilities.

DINING OUT: Both Savannah and Atlanta abound in fine restaurants. Along the coast and in the mountains, up-to-the-minute cuisine is less of a highlight than in the cities; however, local cuisine uses fresh traditional ingredients.

The sea provides fresh shrimp, scallops, and oysters for most of the year. Sweet bass and trout are pulled from mountain streams. Traditional Georgia cooking pleases the healthy appetite with rib-sticking classics like fried chicken and biscuits, cornbread, fritters, and such. The big breakfast including eggs; ham and grits are the norm.

HOW TO GET MARRIED IN GEORGIA: You must be at least 18 years of age to get married without parental consent. A blood test is required and women are tested for sickle-cell anemia. You must apply at the county office in the locale where you plan to marry in person or by phone/mail at least 24 hours in advance. Marriage license fee is $13 in cash.

FOR FURTHER INFORMATION: Contact: **Georgia Department of Industry and Trade,** 230 Peachtree St. NW, P.O. Box 1776, Atlanta 30301 (tel. 404/656-3545); **Savannah Area Convention & Visitors Bureau,** 301 West Broad St., Savannah, GA 31499 (tel. 912/233-6651). **Brunswick-Golden Isles Welcome Center,** Glynn Avenue, Brunswick, GA 31520 (tel. 912/264-5337). **Atlanta Convention and Visitors Bureau,** 233 Peachtree St., NE, Suite 200, Atlanta, GA 33043 (tel. 404/521-6600).

2. Savannah

Savannah is the first port of call you'll hit crossing the border of South Carolina into Georgia. From the outset, the city was not settled in a haphazard manner, but rather was planned for the ease and comfort of her citizenry. Founder James Oglethorpe had the town laid out on paper even before he left England for the New World in 1733. Today, Savannah remains a lovely place, with parks and squares, serene beside the Savannah river. A wise, contemplative town, yet one that offers a wide array of entertainment.

ROMANTIC INTERLUDES: As you wander along the oak-arched streets and down the tiny alleys, you will discover how bewitching Savannah is.

For a twist on the same old tour, try sightseeing from the plush seats of an antique **carriage** drawn by a matched set of horses. An evening's champagne outing just for the two of you is the most romantic way imaginable to explore the gas-lit streets of Old Savannah. The carriage picks you up right at your lodging, takes you for a spin around the town and deposits you—a bit better for the bubbly—at the door of whatever restaurant or hotel you choose. The price begins at $50 per couple for a half-hour tour with champagne. Contact **Carriage Tours of Savannah** (tel. 236-6756).

You can take a two-hour **daylight cruise** aboard a paddle-wheeler to get a good look at everything, or you can opt for an evening's odyssey on a **moonlight dinner cruise.** There's nothing quite like steaming upstream under the stars, the scent of magnolias wafting from the shore, to put a body in mind of the sweet days of Old Georgia. Itineraries and prices vary, so call Captain Sam at 234-7248. Day cruises, $13 per couple; dinner cruises, $50 per couple.

HONEYMOON HOTELS AND HIDEAWAYS: If you sat up nights for months fantasizing about the most heavenly honeymoon spot, you couldn't even begin to dream up what Hugh and Roberta Lineberger have in store for you in their 13 rooms and suites at **The Gastonian,** 220 East Gaston St., Savannah, GA 30401 (tel. 912/232-2869). The Caracalla Suite, named for a Roman emperor is decadent enough for Nero, featuring an immense canopy bed, 19th-century English antiques, fireplaces, a wet bar, and an eight-foot Jacuzzi. Honeymoon package: None. Rates for standard double rooms vary from $95 to $200 per couple per night (the $200 is for the Caracalla). Includes a full (delicious) breakfast with the newspaper of your choice, wine and fruit basket, an outdoor hot tub, and full concierge service.

The Foley House Inn, 14 West Hull St., Savannah, GA 31401 (tel. 912/232-6622), is conveniently located on Cheppewa Square in a beautiful townhouse built in 1796. The rooms all have a cold bottle of white zinfandel to greet you and a gas fireplace that ignites with a flip of a switch. Many of the rooms have oversized Jacuzzis or whirlpools, or you can enjoy the hot tub outdoors on the deck. Honeymoon package:

None. Tariffs range from $95 to $175 per couple per night, including afternoon tea or sherry, breakfast, and nightly turndown.

Magnolia Place, 117 West Perry St., Savannah, GA 31401 (tel. 912/234-4088), calls itself "the Grand Inn of Savannah" and grand it is indeed, situated across from beautiful Forsyth Park. The 1871 house has 13 rooms furnished with Georgian antiques; 6 also have a Jacuzzi. Should you require in-room entertainment, an extensive VCR library is available. Innkeepers Dirk Brown and Ron Stahan attend to all the little details to make sure your stay is perfect. Honeymoon package: $150 per couple per night. Includes continental breakfast, a champagne carriage tour, and a Jacuzzi-equipped room. Standard room rates range from $75 to $135 per couple per night.

ROMANTIC RESTAURANTS: Dining could and should be the highlight of your day every day in Savannah.

Moderate

People tend to agree **Elizabeth on 37th,** (named for chef/owner Elizabeth Terry), 105 East 37th St. (tel. 236-5547), is the choicest spot in town. Set in a tiny turn-of-the-century house, it features local specialties such as chicken and fresh seafood with Elizabeth's special twists—unusual fresh vegetables or quirky seasonings. One caveat: They do not take reservations and the wait tends to be quite long during peak hours. Dinner for two with wine, about $70.

Restaurant La Toque, 420 East Broughton St. (tel. 238-0138), is a recent and welcome addition to the Savannah culinary scene. It's large and airy, with a formal feel: white linen tablecloths, luxuriously upholstered chairs, fine crystal, and equally fine Swiss cuisine. Dinner is served Monday through Saturday from 6:30 p.m., with an earlier seating for lighter dining from 5 p.m. to 7 p.m. Dinner for two with wine, about $60.

Rivers End, Tasseys Pier, 3122 River Dr. (tel. 354-2973), is a bit out of the way, but certainly worth the drive. Tell them you're honeymooning and they'll be sure to give you a window seat whence you can watch the shrimp boats passing by. You know the seafood is fresh—some of it comes right off the boats you see gliding by. The desserts are supplied by Mrs. Bowdi, a Savannah matron, who started in the sweets business years ago in her own kitchen. Accompany one of her lip-smacking selections with Rivers End Special Coffee—an intoxicating amalgam of six different liqueurs. Dinner for two with all the trimmings goes for about $60.

Inexpensive

There's no sign, but you can't miss **Mrs. Wilkes' Boarding House,** 107 West Jones St. (tel. 232-5997), which usually has a long line out front. Some of the best grub around can be had here in this noisy, congenial restaurant. For a mighty low price you can grab a place at the table and fatten yourself silly on fried chicken, biscuits, grits, succotash served family style. Breakfast, $3.50 per person; lunch, $5.50 per person. (Dinner is not served.)

3. The Golden Isles

Ahh, and it's golden they certainly are. The name conjures up both the extravagant elegance of Sea Island and the luxurious simplicity of Cumberland Island. For quite some time the well-heeled have chosen this stretch of coastline as a retreat. Names like Rockefeller, Carnegie, Vanderbilt once graced the mailboxes (and in some cases, still do).

These islands, about a dozen in all, are strewn along the coast between Savannah in the north and Jacksonville, Florida, in the south. Some are tiny, privately owned dots of land in the ocean. Others, like Cumberland, are close to 20 miles long.

ROMANTIC INTERLUDES: Don't think it strange that we suggest a trip through a swamp. Canoeing through the **Okeefenokee** allows you to be about as far away from it all as the law allows. Bring a good map with you or take a tour by reservations. The cost is $9.36 per day for a two-person canoe (without guide). Contact: **Sewanee Canal Recreation Area,** Rte. 2, Box 336, Folkston, GA 31537 (tel. 496-7156).

If you prefer the element, air, **Head in the Clouds Kite Shop,** 128 Mallery St. (tel. 638-5483), has all that your boreal heart could desire. What could be more exhilarating than feeling the tug of your kite sailing far overhead above the beach? Head in the Clouds' flying aces give kiting exhibitions of their wares Sundays at noon near the beach at the King and Prince Hotel on St. Simons Island. Spend a wonderful afternoon flying a kite and take it back as a souvenir. Kite prices begin at $5 and rise above $50 for some high-tech, space-age models.

HONEYMOON HOTELS AND HIDEAWAYS: Most of the individual Golden Isles are synonymous with the resorts that occupy them. Prices at each resort tend to be all-inclusive, depending upon the package you choose, so you can enjoy three meals, golf, tennis, fishing, riding, swimming, and have a good idea of what it will all cost you *before* your honeymoon begins. Prices quoted reflect the difference between low- and high-season rates, if appropriate.

Sea Island

The **Cloister,** Sea Island, GA 21561 (tel. 912/638-3611 or toll free 800/SEA-ISLE), on Sea Island is unrivaled along the coast as the first and last word in well-equipped honeymoon destinations, the alpha and omega of fine-tuned, understated service. Sea Island has catered to discerning visitors, and especially to newlyweds, since 1928. That they've been at it so long does not, however, mean the service is formulaic, but, rather, that it is effortless, old school. The Cloister's philosophy is, how else *would* it be?

The whitewashed, tile-roofed buildings look a bit like a Mediterranean cloister with Gothic archways and filigree. Rooms are decorated in pretty florals with Sea Island's signature rich green predominating. In your accommodations, you'll find all you need, from sweet-scented soaps to stationery to hair dryers.

For your diversion there is golf, tennis, picnicking on the beach, skeet shooting, fishing, sailing, dancing, ocean and pool swimming—even a cooking school.

Honeymoon package: Prices vary widely according to which accommodations you choose. Sample package rates: An ocean front room ranges from $188 to $284 per couple per night. Includes all meals, nightly dancing, champagne welcome, breakfast in bed, lawn sports, and special honeymooner activities.

Little St. Simons Island

Little St. Simons Island, P.O. Box 1078, St. Simons Island, GA 31522 (tel. 912/638-7472). Good morning! The boat to Little St. Simons Island picks you up in the morning from St. Simon just to the south, and buzzes you through the marsh creeks. At the island you are ushered into a 1917 hunting lodge—trophies on the wood-paneled walls, ample chairs inviting lollygagging in the corner.

Once you arrive on the 10,000-acre island, a staff of naturalists, chefs, and managers display endless imagination when it comes to thinking up fun things for the 20 or so overnight guests to see and do. Served at lodge tables set up in the dining room, dinner frequently consists of the contributions of guests who've been out catching sea bass or blues in the surf, or unloading the claw-clacking blue crabs from the traps, or foraging for wild mushrooms with the help of naturalists. After dinner you might like to be initiated into the mystical world of fish printing, a project under the special supervision of the naturalists.

On the long, long beach, there often is nobody, but *nobody* but the two of you within a mile and a half in either direction. Have the kitchen pack a picnic for you or arrange a crab roast. Walk barefoot. Swim naked. Go crazy. Little St. Simons is the perfect place for it.

Ask for the honeymoon cottage, slightly secluded and simply decorated with rough-hewn camp furniture. It has a sitting room with a fireplace, two bedrooms, and an outdoor tub for lounging or soaking under the sky. Honeymoon package (Full AP): $225 per couple per night (two-night minimum). Includes accommodations, all meals, canoeing, boating, fishing, tours with the naturalists, jeep rides, horseback riding, crabbing.

Jekyll Island

Jekyll Island Club, P.O. Box 3124, Jekyll Island, GA 31520 (tel. 912/635-2600; reservations: toll free 800/822-1886) used to be the private enclave of a handful of millionaires. You can still tour through some of their palatial "cottages," which are outfitted with period furniture and open to the public.

When the number of guests outgrew the number of rooms in the various cottages, the Jekyll Island Association erected a clubhouse to lodge the overflow. After the millionaires left the area, the clubhouse was sold to the state of Georgia and eventually fell into disuse and disrepair. Now completely restored by the Radisson Corporation, the Clubhouse opened again to visitors at Christmas 1986. Renovations have retained the intricate latticework, original Tiffany glass, and ornate fireplaces (which grace all the guest rooms). One-bedroom suites are also available with Jacuzzis. The club offers (some with a moderate surcharge) deep-sea fishing tennis, swimming, bocce, and golf at any one of Jekyll's four excellent courses. Honeymoon package: None. Rates (BP) for double rooms range from $60 to $95 per couple.

Cumberland Island

Cumberland Island National Seashore, P.O. Box 806, St. Marys, GA 31558 (tel. 912/882-4335). The early morning boat to Cumberland Island leaves the pier at St. Marys River in the mist at 9 a.m. The vapor rises off the water enveloping the shrimp boats, the sleepy fishing village and the boats bobbing at the dock.

An island the size of Manhattan, Cumberland is mostly national park, but with never more than 300 souls—rather than 10 million—around. The demand for space on the ferry is keen, so boat and campsite reservations are best made as far in advance as possible.

If you're camping on Cumberland (there are 120 permanent or backcountry sites available), you have to bring all the food, water, and gear you'll need, because nothing is available to buy once you're on the island. The campsite at Sea Camp Dock is as quiet as a cathedral, except for the wind tossing about the treetops. The beach lies beyond several barriers of high dunes, between which feed wild ponies and deer. The beach itself is wide, made of sable-soft, pearly sand.

Greyfield Inn, P.O. Drawer B, Fernandina Beach, FL 32034 (tel. 904/261-6408), is run by some of the more recent descendants of the Carnegies, who owned the isle early this century. Greyfield, built in 1901, offers 9 rooms to a maximum of 18 guests. A pair of porch swings, generously supplied with cushions, sway in the breeze at either end of the veranda. There is a fire crackling in the sitting room, a well-stocked library, and an equally well-stocked honor bar with Stolly in the fridge.

The honeymoon suite contains a massive bed of Honduras mahogany, a row of windows looking out into the treetops, and an old-style clawfoot tub in the bathroom. Many of the furnishings and books are Carnegie heirlooms. Meals are served in the dining room, or if you choose, you can have breakfast in bed or a picnic lunch at the beach. Whenever possible, the inn's cooking staff utilizes whatever is grown in the garden or pulled in fresh from the Atlantic. Honeymoon package: None. Standard rates (Full AP): $170 to $190 per couple per night. Includes three meals daily, hiking with Greyfield's naturalist, use of bicycles, and of course unlimited swimming and fishing.

ROMANTIC RESTAURANTS: Most Golden Isle accommodations include all your meals. There is, however, one worthwhile epicurean detour to consider.

Alfonzo's Plantation Supper Club (tel. 638-9883), is tucked down an obscure road in an obscure part of St. Simon Island. Inside the restaurant, the Elks might be having a boisterous party in the back room, and the couches surrounding the fireplace are decorated with life-size, stuffed (as in with sawdust) mannequins, dressed up as good ole boys in their overalls and Amway caps. Don't ask how or why, but somehow they look just right there in a state of blissful collapse.

Alfonzo himself is a man of generous girth and disposition. He'll be strolling from table to table, checking up on this and that. The cuisine is country coastal, fish cooked all ways, fresh veggies, plump steaks. Just about anything you order is great. Alfonzo, however, is a little vain, so all the best dishes are named for him, such as Oysters Alfonzo or Alfonzo's Special, a spirited after-dinner beverage. Dinner for two with *all* the trimmings, $40.

4. Atlanta

Hot 'Lanta reigns unchallenged as the big-city mecca of the Southeast. Nowhere else within hundreds of miles can you be privy to a world-class art museum like the High, or a roster of music, theater, first-run and foreign films, clubs, and those niceties you'd expect from a cosmopolitan center that takes its culture to heart.

Atlanta epitomizes the new southern city, extending its condos, glass-and-steel skyscrapers, and shopping malls into the surrounding (former) farmland. If one side of town seems miles away from the other side, that's because it is. Atlanta is also a sports-lover's city. You can catch Ted Turner's Braves or Hawks, the Falcons, or Georgia Tech football. And of course, the coveted green jacket of champions is handed out yearly at the Masters Golf Tournament in nearby Augusta.

ROMANTIC INTERLUDES: While you're in town, be sure to take advantage of some of the cosmopolitan choices unavailable in the backcountry. In Atlanta, that certainly means **nightlife.** Catch greats from rock to jazz and back at the **Fox Theatre,** 660 Peachtree St. NE (tel. 881-1977). The interior looks like the Sultan's pleasure palace. It's not just another huge, cavernous arena, but a beautiful auditorium with good acoustics.

For a more intimate setting, try **Blind Willie's** or **Walter Mitty's,** practically next door to each other in Virginia Highlands, a neighborhood known for its funky and frivolous atmosphere. Blind Willie's, 828 North Highland Avenue NE (tel. 873-2583), serves up "booze, blues and cajun food," according to the T-shirts, and favors Mississippi and Chicago blues men with underchin stubble and gravelly voices—the best kind.

Walter Mitty's, 816 North Highland Avenue NE (tel. 876-7115), has cool jazz nightly, but is best when Bernadine Mitchell holds court with the Mose Davis Trio. Ms. Mitchell is a warm and exuberant presence with a knockout voice and an impeccable ability to choose numbers from Josephine Baker to Stevie Wonder. Both places serve food, but neither serves great food, so eat elsewhere and arrive in time for the sets.

About 70 miles southwest of the city is **Callaway Gardens,** an all-inclusive resort set in the mountains. Its sylvan serenity perfectly complements Atlanta's urban sophistication. The list of things to do at Callaway is as long as your shooting or golf or tennis arm. There is fishing, sailing, and windsurfing on one of several lakes, hiking and biking on a network of trails, many featuring themes such as "Rhododendrons," "Roses," or "Wildflowers." On the must-see list is the Sibley Horticultural Center, an immense greenhouse of seasonal blooms, sibilant waterfalls, and paths to lose yourselves along. Any time you visit there is bound to be a special event or two to amuse: an azalea festival, waterskiing tournament, marathon race, and the Columbus Steeplechase Riding event, to name a few.

Atlantans drive down for the day to revel in the verdure. You can also spend the night there. The Callaway Gardens Hotel, Mountain Creek Villas, and Country Cottages have accommodations with full kitchens, fireplaces, and porches overlooking the mountains, woods, and streams. Villa prices start at $115 per couple per night; cottages at $100 per couple per night. Rooms at the inn are small, but pleasant, grouped around waterfall-freshened courtyards. Inn room prices start at $60. Rates include accommodations and entrance to the gardens. Contact **Callaway Gardens at Pine Mountain,** U.S. Hwy. 27, Pine Mountain, GA 31822 (tel. toll free 800/282-8181).

What strikes you when you pull up to **Stone Mountain Park,** a half hour's drive from downtown Atlanta, is not so much the size of the famous carving of Jefferson Davis, Robert E. Lee, and Andrew Jackson. Sure it's big, the size of a football field, but what is truly astonishing is how even its formidable dimensions are dwarfed by the immensity of the granite mountain in which it is carved. At the visitors center, you can hear a stirring account of the Civil War and the part that each of these three heroes played.

The park offers lots of activities. Take the gondola up to the top of that huge slab of rock to get a view of the environs and to plan your strategy for seeing the rest of the attractions. The Plantation is a group of buildings transported intact from all over the state and clustered to recreate antebellum days. The buildings are furnished with antiques and guides wearing hoop skirts.

If you have a touch of the wanderlust you can step back in time by taking a leisurely chug around the lake on an old paddle wheeler—great place for a picnic. You can also puff around a track in a model reconstruction of a steam train that girdles the base of the mountain and toot-toots through the woods. Admission prices: $4 per car; the attractions are an additional $2.50 per person per attraction. Contact **Stone Mountain Park,** P.O. Box 778, Stone Mountain, GA 30086 (tel. 498-5600).

HONEYMOON HOTELS AND HIDEAWAYS: Atlanta's hotels offer the finest in American new-style convenience and older European panache and hospitality. Check out the special weekend packages, which generally include big-value extras such as upgraded accommodations, champagne, and breakfast in bed.

Expensive

The Ritz-Carlton Buckhead, 3434 Peachtree Rd. NE, Atlanta, GA 30326 (tel. 404/237-2700; reservations: toll free 800/241-3333), is the flagship of the Ritz hotels, and needless to say, the corporation has pinched no pennies to assure that everything is *just so.* From high tea in the Lobby Lounge to the use of fluffy robes for your bath, to twice-daily maid service, a smiling, capable staff member will sweep in and attend to whatever's necessary. Rooms are decorated with canopy-draped beds, Queen Anne and Ming Dynasty reproduction furnishings. The color TV is discreetly ensconced in a mahogany armoire.

Guests can start or spend the day at the indoor swimming pool and its sun deck; slim down at the fitness center with weight machines, sauna, and steam room; or freshen up with nonstop valet, concierge, and room service.

One very special treat: dinner in the Dining Room. The name sounds generic, but the experience is anything but run-of-the-mill. Unquestionably some of Atlanta's most thoughtful, delicate cooking awaits your choice.

Special weekends start at $195 for two, including deluxe accommodations for two nights and use of all fitness facilities.

Moderate

The lobby of the **Marriott Marquis,** 265 Peachtree Center Ave., Atlanta, GA 30303 (tel. 404/521-0000; reservations: toll free 800/228-9250), is breathtaking even in these days of increasing atrium jadedness. A stabile sculpture tumbles down from the roof, a stabile you can view from all angles as you zoom skyward in a glass elevator. The hotel's restaurants are arranged like satellites orbiting the core of the lobby. At any one restaurant you might find Mexican or Indian, continental, or Cajun cuisine.

If you're in the mood to splurge, try one of the suites on the Concierge Level. You'll be pampered with check-in facilities, afternoon tea, morning coffee, and the nation's newspapers. Honeymoon package: None. Weekend packages start at $69 per couple per night and rise to $170 for concierge-level suites. Includes champagne on arrival, free parking, breakfast in bed, and accommodations in a luxury hospitality suite.

ROMANTIC RESTAURANTS: Atlantans all have their favorite haunts, from a dark little dive that serves the world's best ribs, to a soigné cut-glass-and-champagne dining room. Here are just a few favorites.

Moderate

Dante's Down the Hatch, 3380 Peachtree Rd. NE (tel. 266-1600), would be worth looking in on, even if it didn't serve the freshest, richest fondues in town. The place is a rough-and-ready re-creation of an old-time port town, complete with a full-size ship's stern, live turtles and crocodiles swimming around the hull, and cozy nooks for noshing clapped with names like The Poop Deck, The Bishop's Den, and The Bordello.

The food is not fussy but delicious, featuring fondues such as beef, Mandarin (with a Chinese kick), and cheese. Drinks are generously poured and skimpily priced. To top it off, there is live jazz nightly except Mondays on the lower deck with the Paul Mitchell trio. Dinner for two: $50 including drinks.

Cafe Society, 571 Peachtree St. NE (tel. 872-9000). Thanks to the clean-line deco decor, you'll feel you should be wrapped in a beaded silk frock, puffing on a cigarette in a long ebony holder. The menu tends toward the continental, with a healthy helping of local favorites plus the chef's whimsical variations thrown in for good measure. The crowd tends to be (or at least look) artsy and literary. Try a bowl of the creamy, melt-in-your-mouth tomato soup for starters, continue with a deft preparation of veal or game hen, and for dessert relish rich chocolate silk pie. The service is quiet and expert, the food, superb, and the ambience—from the floral fantasies to the vintage posters—magnifique. Dinner for two will cost about $80 including drinks.

Inexpensive

The lush, plush eateries aside, if we had to pick an Atlanta favorite, it would have to be **The Varsity,** corner of Spring Street and North Avenue (tel. 881-1706), an Atlanta tradition. The red, black, gray, and cream interior is vast, deafening, and packed with people ordering, chatting, chomping, or catching their favorite soap opera on a TV screen in one of the many "dining rooms." Even ordering is an adventure here. Step up to the counter: "Waddayahave? Waddayahave? Waddayahave?" You can have a P.C. (pure chocolate milk over ice), a naked dog (plain frank), or a "hot" dog (with chili), and whatever you do *don't* miss those inimitable Varsity onion rings. If you're in a rush just order all that "walking"—to go. Lunch or dinner for two is a steal at about $3 apiece!

5. The Mountains

The eyes of the nation's honeymooners are set square upon the mountains of East Georgia: the quiet, sinuous roads climbing through oak and rhododendron forests, the spectacular storms, the crisp air, the hawk's-eye view from the summit of Brasstown Bald (Georgia's highest peak). This is for the most part unadulterated country—the radio plays Waylon and Willie, the local folks rattle around in their pickups. It's the province of the time-trusted tales and traditions of the series of *Foxfire* books.

Recently, the region has been gearing up as a new and relatively untrammeled honeymoon destination. Seventy percent of the land is owned by the forest service, so should remain unspoiled. With the exception of Helen (Georgia's answer to Bavaria) during Oktoberfest, when seven million people cram into that town, the area is largely sparse of tourists. All of this translates into plenty of privacy and reasonable prices for honeymooners with the taste and discernment to head for the Blue Ridge Mountains, nestled at the confluence of Georgia, South Carolina, North Carolina, and Tennessee.

ROMANTIC INTERLUDES: Take a heavenly drive through the mountains' nooks and crannies. Trek along the forest-scented trails. Just being here will make you feel like new and start your new life together beautifully.

While you're near Forge Mill, if it's springtime, take a trek over to **Mercier Orchards** on Hwy. 5 in Blue Ridge (tel. 632-2364). During the season, you can pick your own berries—raspberries or strawberries. Spend the afternoon gathering and tasting and turning your tongue and the tips of your fingers scarlet. During apple season you can select a bagful from bins loaded with any of the 25 varieties of apples the Merciers grow and ship all over the country. If you don't feel like lugging your apples home with you, they'll giftpack and ship them UPS anywhere in the country.

What could be better on a hot summer day than gliding down the **Chattahoochie River** with the one you love? In Helen you can rent inner tubes, tie a six-pack and a waterproof picnic around the nub, and spend the afternoon rolling on the river. You'll be joined by people in canoes, kids at the swimming holes, fishermen on the shore, and perhaps a deer coming down to wet his whistle. You can drop anchor and enjoy your lunch or dine as you drift. And if you work up a sweat from all this "exertion," you have only to flip over into the flowing stream to cool off. Different outlets rent tubes each season, but prices tend to be the same everywhere. Your best bet is to inquire at Riverhaus Pizza; they know everything that's going on in town. Price for a whole day's good, clean fun? About $5 per innertube.

Another great way to scope out the countryside is from the saddle, riding **horseback,** through the mountains. In Dillard there are scheduled trail rides with a guide to show you the way and to point out the indigenous flora and fauna. The bridle paths wind up around the hills to country so remote, you'll wonder if anyone's ever made it there on their own two legs. Experienced riders who have demonstrated competence can ride off by themselves. Pack some wine and fruit and make a day of it. Trail rides run daily during the summer, weekends off-season. Contact Lynn Dillard for information and reservations; tel. 746-5348.

HONEYMOON HOTELS AND HIDEAWAYS: Stovall House, Rte. 1, Box 103-A, Sautee, GA 30571 (tel. 404/878-3355). The Sautee environs offer hiking in the mountains, trout fishing in the creeks and rivers, shopping at local stores full of mountain crafts. Stovall House sits high on a bluff amid a country of rolling hills and pastures. The house, now on the National Register, was built in 1837, and stands on 28 acres of farmland, including an impressive garden (whence come many of the fresh veggies that grace your dinner table—see "Romantic Restaurants").

Current owners Ham and Kathy Schwartz have made improvements where necessary, but mostly have left well enough alone. They have a nice, homey place, comfortable, laid-back. You can enjoy the porch swing on the 270° veranda, or the tree swing out back overlooking the meadow and the corn fields.

Rooms are stenciled and furnished with simple, sturdy antiques; some have fireplaces, all have private bath. Honeymoon package: None. Rooms are $65 per couple per night, including breakfast.

In the backcountry high in the mountains is Rabun Gap—a post office more than a town—host to **Moon Valley,** Rte. 1, Box 680, Rabun Gap, GA 30568 (tel. 404/746-2466). Down at the end of a gravel road, set around a lake reflecting a bowl of mountains, you'll find the cabins and lodge that comprise this away-from-it-all resort.

The fishing is tip-top, and the trails are marked out so you won't get lost—unless you plan to. The biggest bonus has to be the wonderful food, the cooked to perfection steaks and chops, or the shrimp in a delicate froth of cream and wine. All is served on the patio in summer, before a roaring fire in winter. Buck Moon does all the cooking and insists his only training was "just getting in and doing it," and his only inspiration, his imagination. Meals are complemented by a good selection of wines, very reasonably priced—your champagne will arrive in the biggest bucket you'll ever see.

The rustic but fun cabins include a front porch and kitchenette. They start at $64.50 per couple. The lodge accommodations, $74.50 per couple per night, are more modern, including TV and a Jacuzzi, with loft beds under a skylight, so you can watch the stars spill around the sky all night. Rates include all meals.

Chalet Village, P.O. Box 329, Dillard, GA 30537 (tel. 404/746-5321). You'll be enchanted by this out-of-the-way, place where the air is clear and so is the living—clear, wholesome, and simple.

John Dillard's Chalet Village is a cluster of villas set back in the woods on the side of a hill overlooking the mountains. Four of the most luxurious units include a full kitchen and Jacuzzi opening out onto the back deck. Villas are decorated with four-poster, cherry-wood beds and have high cathedral ceilings. Tennis, an outdoor pool, and horseback riding are available.

The A-frame cabins are somewhat less sumptuous, but offer, as John observes, "a great view at a great price." The cabins are $50 to $55 per night. The chalets are $89 per night, or $275 for a three-night honeymoon package, including champagne, dinner at one of several area restaurants, horseback riding, and golf.

ROMANTIC RESTAURANTS: Should you not have the good fortune to secure accommodations at **Stovall House,** Rte. 1, Sautee (tel. 878-3355), you can console yourself with a fabulous feed instead. Since Kathy Schwartz plans her meals for her guests, it is wise and courteous to make reservations. The food is country cooking—with a dash of nouvelle to keep things interesting. Lunch features soups, salads, sandwiches. Dinner offers a variety of meats, fish—whatever is fresh at the market. You can eat on the glassed-in porch surveying the fields, or in the warmly lit dining room, by the fire. Service is attentive, but discerning enough to recognize when the two of you want to be alone. Dinner for two, $60 including drinks.

Situated in a turn-of-the-century house, **Rudolphs,** 700 Green St., Gainesville (tel. 534-2226), is one good reason to take a drive down Green Street (the lacy Victorian houses lining the avenue are another). You'll be treated to fish caught in local waters, veal and game when available. The decor is reminiscent of a small-scale English manor house with medieval overtones. Do save some room for their generous desserts—the fried ice cream is particularly good. Dinner for two, expensive but delicious, $80 including drinks.

Come to **The Forge Mill Crossing Restaurant,** off Rte. 76, Morganton (tel.

374-5771), for good food at great prices. The room is simple—country-style wood carvings on the walls, fresh daisies and honey bears on the tables. Light lunches and dinners are accompanied by steaming loaves of raisin bread and fresh apple butter. Apples are a prevalent theme, and hostess Kay Kendau has concocted all manner of tempting apple desserts. Stop in for a Sunday country brunch—all you can eat for $4.80 per person.

Chapter VII

HAWAII

1. Practical Facts
2. Oahu
3. Maui
4. Kauai
5. The Big Island

YOU DECIDE: Your honeymoon in Hawaii can be an action-packed adventure or a calm, beachside reverie.

Located in the Pacific Ocean 2,397 miles southwest of San Francisco, Hawaii is a sparkling string of four major tourist islands, four smaller islands, and some tiny volcanic outcroppings. Oahu is the most visited, but Maui, Kauai, and the big island of Hawaii—collectively known as the "Neighbor Islands"—also hold countless honeymoon possibilities. All four islands lie within just 236 miles of each other, yet each one is quite different from the next.

On Oahu's south coast, Waikiki shimmers with all the hustle and bustle of a cosmopolitan city, while the island's north shore boasts miles and miles of pristine beaches and backcountry towns. On Maui, resplendent resort areas such as Kaanapali, Kapalua, and Wailea rise in dramatic contrast to the gently rolling pasturelands of heavenly Hana. On the large island of Hawaii (generally referred to as the Big Island, to distinguish it from the name of the entire state), you can shiver at the summit of a 10,000-foot-high volcano or bask on world famous black-sand beaches. On Kauai, a hike through the wilderness of the Na Pali (cliffs) coast is set off by lazy days on golden beaches. The options are many, the choice is all yours.

The ethnic mix—Japanese, Filipino, Samoan, Caucasian, Thai, and Chinese contributes an array of international flavors so that Hawaii combines the exotica of a foreign country with the easy familiarity of the United States. Everything and everyone are extremely accommodating in the 50th state. Rainbow-hued tropical fish are so friendly they'll eat right out of your hand, and the air and water temperatures always seem to be exactly perfect. All year long, heady flowers bloom, waterfalls rush down the sides of volcanic cliffs, and the colors of earth, sea, and sky are vibrant. Activities and lodgings abound on the isles, and tours and transportation are generally quite easy to arrange.

Most of all, Hawaii's gracious people make it the epitome of heaven on earth. The natural warmth and friendliness of the islanders—will embrace you with what is known as the "aloha spirit." From the lei of flowers that you receive upon arrival to the helpful tips from a passerby, the aloha spirit springs freely from this rich land and its one million residents making Hawaii a harbor of love.

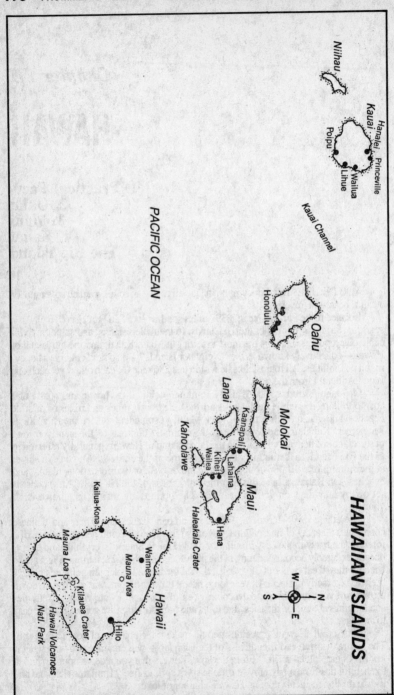

HAWAIIAN ISLANDS

1. Practical Facts

Although Hawaii is some 2,400 miles from the North American mainland, it is the 50th of the United States. Absolutely no border formalities are required for Americans—it's as easy as going from New York to New Jersey. Since farming is a major Hawaiian industry, an agricultural inspection takes place at the airport to prevent certain fruits and flowers from entering or leaving Hawaii. For details, contact the **Department of Agriculture,** 1428 South King St., Honolulu, HI 96814 (tel. 808/548-2211).

GETTING THERE: The most convenient transportation to Hawaii is by air, although cruise ships do dock as well.

By Air

From New York it takes about ten hours to fly to Hawaii, from Los Angeles, about five hours. **United, American, Delta, Continental,** and **TWA** provide service into Honolulu, and a local airline, **Hawaiian Air,** now offers flights from the West Coast to Hawaii.

You can also take a direct flight to the Neighbor Islands from the mainland. The principal island airports are in Kahului on Maui, Lihue on Kauai, and both Kona and Hilo on the Big Island. United offers nonstop service to Maui from Chicago, Seattle, and San Francisco, as well as one-stop service to Kauai from Los Angeles. United also flies to the Big Island: from Los Angeles to Hilo, and from both Los Angeles and San Francisco to Kona.

Or you can copy the Oahu "natives" and hop on an interisland flight from Honolulu. Major interisland carriers are Hawaiian Air, **Mid Pacific Air,** and **Aloha Air.** Flights from Honolulu to Maui take 30 minutes, to Kauai 20 minutes, and to the Big Island 40 minutes. These flights depart from the interisland terminal directly adjacent to the main terminal. Interisland flights from Honolulu are particularly convenient if you want to fly to the Kapalua / West Maui Airport (near Kaanapali on Maui) or Princeville Airport (on Kauai's north shore).

By Sea

American Hawaii Cruises, 550 Kearny St., San Francisco, CA 94108 (tel. toll free 800/227-3666), offers seven-day interisland excursions on glittering "love boats" that depart Honolulu on Saturdays. Prices range from $2,400 to $6,000 per couple for this all-inclusive cruise, which features stops on the Big Island, Kauai, and Maui.

GETTING AROUND OAHU: On Hawaii's most populated island, Oahu, for $10 an **airport shuttle bus** will take both of you plus your luggage the nine miles into Waikiki.

Taxis are used less frequently in Honolulu than in other major U.S. cities, but they'll take you where you need to go if you phone ahead. Two such companies are **Charleys** (tel. 955-2211) or **Aloha State** (tel. 847-3566). Rates are $1.20 for each mile, and the fare runs about $12 from the airport to Waikiki.

For 60¢ in exact change, you can go just about anywhere on Oahu's efficient public transportation system, dubbed **"TheBus"** (tel. 531-1611).

With so many sights in so many places, Oahu begs to be seen by car. **Renting a car** is not necessary in order to get around, but it's certainly nice to have one available for that early morning spin to the beach or an impulsive moonlight drive.

To rent a car you must be 18 years old and have a valid driver's license and a major credit card. A wide variety of major rental-car companies stand ready to help you, and the competition has kept prices fairly low, between $25 and $35 a day. Automatic shift usually costs a few dollars more than manual shift. Rentals generally offer insurance on your car, and several have money saving "fly / drive" deals tied in with

U.S. mainland carriers as well as the interisland airlines. Ask your travel agent for complete details.

For $35 to $60 an hour you can hire a fancy chauffeured limousine to see Oahu in style. Write ahead to **Silver Cloud Limousine Service,** P.O. Box 15773, Honolulu, HI 96830 (tel. 808/524-7999).

Be sure to buckle up, because Hawaii's seat-belt law is strictly enforced.

GETTING AROUND THE NEIGHBOR ISLANDS: Although there are other alternatives, a rental car is the preferred mode of transportation for visitors to Maui, Kauai, and the Big Island.

Airport Transportation

On Maui, a reservations-only shuttle from Kahului Airport to the Kaanapali Beach resort area costs $16 a couple (tel. 808/877-5507). So does the shuttle to Wailea-area hotels.

On Kauai, a free shuttle runs from Princeville Airport to Princeville Resort. No regular shuttles run from Lihue, which is the main airport.

On the Big Island, a shuttle from Keahole Airport to Kona costs $15 for two. No shuttles run from Hilo Airport.

By Taxi: On Maui, a cab ride from Kahului Airport to Kaanapali runs about $20 for two. On Kauai, to get from Lihue Airport to Princeville costs about $40, from Lihue to Poipu beach, about $25. On the Big Island, it's $20 from Keahole Airport to the Kona resorts, and $6 from the Hilo airport to your Hilo hotel.

Island Buses

Hilo's **Hele-On** bus makes a morning and afternoon trip around the town (tel. 935-8241). Buses also operate between the major attractions of the Big Island, every day but Sunday. It costs the two of you anywhere from $1.50 to $10, and a schedule is available at the State Visitor Information booth at the airport. No public buses run on Maui or Kauai.

Rental Cars

A rental car offers you maximum mobility to explore the far reaches of the neighbor islands.

On Maui, Kauai, and the Big Island, the major car-rental companies have offices that are either immediately adjacent to the airport or within a free van ride away. Fly/drive deals offered through interisland airlines include cars for as little as $16.95 a day. If you plan to really explore the island, sign up with a rental agency that offers a flat rate and unlimited free mileage.

LANGUAGE: In Hawaii, the English language is enlivened with many Hawaiian words that are used in everyday conversation. Instead of compass directions, say *mauka* (toward the mountains) or *makai* (seaward). *Mahalo* means thanks, and *pau* means finished. For the most romantic, get a hotel room with a *lanai* (balcony). Call your new mate *ipo* (sweetheart). If you forget all of that, just say *aloha,* which means everything from hello and goodbye to ''I love you.''

MONEY: Most of Hawaii's banks are open Monday to Friday from 8:30 or 9 a.m. until 3 p.m. (6 p.m. on Friday). Major credit cards and traveler's checks are widely accepted. Personal checks from out of town require at least two pieces of identification.

WEATHER: The Hawaiian weather report sounds like a broken record: sunny skies, light showers over the mountains, high in the mid-to-upper-80s. There are just two seasons. Summer runs from May to October, and while temperatures climb into the 90s during the warmest months of August and September, constant trade winds keep the climate comfortable. Winter (November through April) brings cooler weather, ranging from 65° at night to 85° during the day, along with 20- to 30-foot waves that often pound the north shores of all the islands. It rains more frequently during winter, but the sun returns quickly, and you can count on nice beach weather just about every day of the year.

CLOTHING: The word for Hawaiian fashion is casual. Dress tends to reflect the comfortable lifestyle of this easygoing place. Bring bathing suits, sports clothes, informal shirts and shorts, and sandals or informal shoes, and you'll be covered for almost every occasion. Don't forget your sunglasses, which are imperative in this bright climate. For an evening out, women should bring a summery dress or a skirt and blouse, and men should bring slacks, a light jacket, a tuck-in shirt, and dress shoes. A handful of the finer restaurants require men to wear jackets and ties, and casual eateries generally insist that all diners wear shirts and shoes. Be sure to leave room in your suitcase so you can buy some traditional aloha fashions. These colorful Hawaiian fabrics are turned into casual dress shirts for men, long and short muumuus (loose-fitting dresses) for women, and action-wear for everyone.

TIME: Hawaii's days are long and luxurious, so there is no need here for Daylight Savings Time. In winter, Hawaii is five hours behind the U.S. east coast: When it is noon in New York, it is 7 a.m. in Hawaii. In summer, when the mainland goes on Daylight Savings Time, there is a six-hour time difference: When it is noon in New York, it is 6 a.m. in Hawaii.

TELEPHONES: The area code for the entire state is 808. A call to any number within each island is considered a local call and costs 25¢ from a pay phone. Higher rates apply to interisland calls. For directory assistance dial, 1-411. In an emergency dial, 911.

SHOPPING: A variety of international goodies is available in this Pacific melting pot, and souvenir prices range from $1.50 for a strand of shiny black nuts from the kukui tree to $3,000 for an elegant oriental rug. Hawaii's pride and joy, however, are goods created in the islands. These local products reflect the spirit of the islands and offer cherished mementos of your Hawaiian honeymoon.

Koa and rosewood are prized island woods that make beautiful souvenirs such as bowls, furniture, and sculptures. Tapa, or bark cloth, is stenciled with handsome designs and used as a wall hanging or decorative covering. Other natural materials are used to create fascinating woven goods, such as baskets of coconut fronds and hats of *lauhala* (pandanus). Feather bands are worn to add color to the brim of a hat, and leis made of seeds, shells, and nuts last a lifetime. The most precious keepsakes are the leis and necklaces made from the tiny, delicately colored shells gathered on Niihau, the island that is *kapu* (off-limits) to people not of Hawaiian blood. The necklaces are very expensive—about $300 for a simple choker, and up into the thousands for a shell lei. All of these items are available at arts and crafts stores in the major cities and towns, as well as at outdoor fairs held frequently on the weekends.

Delectable local edibles make great souvenirs because they literally capture the flavor of the isles. Macadamia nuts are grown and packaged on the Big Island, as is

Kona coffee, a gourmet brew, but you can buy these products in any grocery store on any island. (You'll often find the cheapest prices at the local Woolworth's outlet.) Several distributors make it easy to ship home a carton or two of juicy Hawaiian pineapples and papayas. Often you can find a coupon or bargain on this service by looking in the free publications distributed in Waikiki street stands and at Neighbor Island airports.

If you want to send home some Hawaiian-bred flowers such as orchids, anthuriums, and proteas, the major flower shops can handle that for you. A dozen of each costs about $30 including shipping. It's fun to watch the lei-stringers in the flower shops, and even more fun to buy and bring home one of these traditional garlands of love, priced anywhere from $5 to $30. If you want to surround yourselves with the heady scents of Hawaii's blooms on a more permanent basis when you return home, you can choose from one of the several lines of locally produced tropical perfumes and colognes sold in hotel gift shops.

For the widest selection of resort wear, visit the major department stores. A smaller, more select, and usually more expensive variety is available in hotel fashion boutiques. For specific store recommendations, refer to the information about the appropriate islands.

ABOUT ACCOMMODATIONS: Each island features a diversity of accommodations. They range from the clean yet simple hotels off the beach with the basic amenities (air conditioning, television, telephone, comfortable beds, bathroom with shower, wall-to-wall carpeting, room service, and a small pool) to the luxurious beachfront apartment-hotels that pull out all the stops (ocean views off the *lanai*, a kitchenette, refrigerator, bar, stereo, king-size beds, sitting area, whirlpool, cable television and movies, turndown service, and so on).

Condominiums are becoming increasingly popular among honeymooners who are looking for all the comforts of home. In Hawaii, quite often the condo is more than just an apartment. Not only does it offer spacious accommodations and a fully equipped kitchen, complete with an oven, large refrigerator, and all your cooking needs, but it also features the amenities of a fine hotel, such as maid service, bell and front desks, sports facilities, and fine restaurants. It's a luxurious way to set up housekeeping on your honeymoon, and costs about the same as comparable hotel accommodations.

DINING OUT: Hawaii has every type of cuisine imaginable, from seaside snacks to continental feasts. The influence of many different cultures makes each meal an international treat, be it shave ice for two (a snow cone laced with exotic Hawaiian fruit syrups) or Japanese sashimi (bite-size slices of tender, raw fish enhanced with rice, vegetables, and tangy mustard).

For starters, there are American, Hawaiian, Korean, Chinese, Japanese, Thai, Italian, Vietnamese, Indian, and Filipino eateries spread across the islands. Go ahead, dig in! Begin your meal with a hearty round of *pupus* (appetizers), which can be anything from crispy *gau gee* (meat-filled dumplings) to spicy Portuguese sausage with fresh pineapple. Your entrée can come laced with a fiery teriyaki sauce or graced with a garnish of rich macadamia nuts. Traditional dishes become culinary works of art when prepared with one of Hawaii's homegrown foods, like the sweet Maui onion, so mild you can eat it all by itself. And fresh coconut ice cream and Kona coffee make the most decadent of desserts.

Ah, and the fresh fruit! Juicy pineapples and papayas, lovely green kiwi and star fruits, generous guavas and passion fruit, sweet bananas and quenching mountain apples tempt you both. Honeymoon when the mangoes are ripe and you'll insist on eating one with every meal.

Then, of course, there's Hawaiian food, best sampled at one of the many fine commercial luaus. The featured attraction is kalua pig, succulent and smoky after having been cooked for hours in an *imu* (underground oven). Try a little of everything, from the zesty lomilomi salmon, marinated with onions and tomatoes, to a thick taro pudding called poi, which Hawaiians love to eat with their fingers.

Sample as much of the fresh fish as possible, because it's bound to be a prize catch. One of the most delectable dishes from Hawaiian seas is *opakapaka*, a pink snapper which is tender and tempting whether it's broiled, fried, or served as sashimi. Equally magnificent is *mahimahi*, a white dolphin fish that often appears as the catch of the day. *Uku* and *onaga* are other types of snapper, and *ahi* and *aku* are two popular types of tuna. *Ulua* is a highly prized jack fish that is often the key ingredient to the tantalizing local chowder, and Hawaii's lobster, shrimp, and prawns taste as delicate as any.

Most restaurants take reservations, and many of the finest are found in hotels. If you order wine with your meal, be advised that the drinking age in Hawaii is 21.

HOW TO GET MARRIED IN HAWAII: Nearly one-quarter of the couples who marry in Hawaii are visitors, testimony to the alluring magic of the islands. Your Hawaiian wedding is all the more special when you incorporate traditional local touches. The bride wears the *holoku,* or formal Hawaiian gown with a long train, and the man dons a long-sleeved white shirt and white pants with a colored sash around his waist. The favorite wedding lei is *maile,* an aromatic green leaf often interwoven with delicate white pikake blossoms. And no wedding in paradise is complete without the beloved strains of "The Hawaiian Wedding Song."

A permit for getting married in Hawaii costs $8 and is valid for 30 days. You must be at least 20 years old, and the bride-to-be must show proof of rubella immunization. If you plan to get married on Oahu, apply in person to the **Hawaii Department of Health,** 1250 Punchbowl St., in Honolulu. The office is open from 8 a.m. until 4 p.m., Monday through Friday, except holidays. There are approximately 50 agents statewide who can be contacted for marriage permits on all the neighbor islands. For a complete information package, write to the **State Department of Health,** P.O. Box 3378, Honolulu, HI 96801 (tel. 808/548-5862).

Most couples choose to marry in one of the splendid beach or garden settings of their hotel. In that case, the marriage license is issued right at the hotel, and the hotel staff takes care of all the details, including paperwork, officiant, music, cake, flowers, photography, and the reception.

FOR FURTHER INFORMATION: The **Hawaii Visitors Bureau** is a goldmine of information about every activity under the sun. Contact them on Oahu: 2270 Kalakaua Ave., Honolulu, HI 96815 (tel. 808/923-1811). Mainland offices include New York, 441 Lexington Ave., Rm. 1407, New York, NY 10017 (tel. 212/986-9203); Chicago, 180 N. Michigan Ave., Suite 1031, Chicago, IL 60601 (tel. 312/236-0632); San Francisco, 50 California St., Suite 450, San Francisco, CA 94111 (tel. 415/392-8173).

In Canada: 4915 Cedar Crescent, Delta, B.C., Canada, V4M 1J9 (tel. 604/943-8555).

2. Oahu

If you tend to equate Oahu with Waikiki, guess again! It's true that Waikiki is a stimulating amalgam of sights and delights, but its famous beach area is only a tiny portion of the island Hawaiians call "The Gathering Place."

Third largest in the Hawaiian chain, Oahu is more than just a cosmopolitan sprawl. Stretched along the island's southeastern shore, the state's capital city of Honolulu is where about 80% of Hawaii's people live and work. It takes 15 minutes to drive from the Honolulu Airport to downtown Honolulu, and another 10 minutes to Waikiki, which is part of Honolulu.

Honolulu presents a charming mix of the old and new, from the modest homes of the first missionaries and America's only royal palace, to dazzling skyscrapers and fashionable shopping malls. Luxurious ocean liners still dock at historic Aloha Tower, while salty fishermen show off today's big catch at bustling Fisherman's Wharf.

Rising above it all are the magnificent Koolau Mountains, rugged reminders of the island's volcanic beginnings and the setting for much Hawaiian history and legend. In the hillsides of the Nuuanu Pali, King Kamehameha and his army fought off Oahu warriors in the famous Battle of Nuuanu (1795), conquering the enemy and unifying the islands under his rule. At the Nuuanu Pali Lookout, stop for magnificent panoramas of the island and ocean.

On the other side of the mountains, Oahu's north shore abounds with ancient fish ponds and haunting *heiaus* (sacred places). Ivory sands and shady beach parks invite lovers to picnic, swim, and linger in the serenity of the north shore, the "flip side" of Honolulu. World famous surfing havens like Sunset Beach and the Banzai Pipeline attract championship riders to perpetuate a sport once reserved for Hawaii's royalty. And to the west are the Waianae Mountains, steadfast guardians of the pristine sugarcane and pineapple fields that have played a dominant role in Hawaii's economy.

After your day tours of Oahu, you'll most likely be drawn back to Waikiki, an effervescent hub flanked by what's called "life's greatest beach" and an unmistakable volcano called Diamond Head. Today nearly all of Oahu's visitors stay in here, and with good reason. The best restaurants on the island are in Waikiki, as are the top draws in Hawaii's entertainment field. Despite its large number of day- and nighttime attractions, Waikiki is compact, and getting around by foot is easy. In fact, the beach is never more than a few blocks away from all the hotels. TheBus runs regularly up and down its streets, and pedicabs (Hawaiian-style rickshaws) offer a leisurely pace for getting from one end of Waikiki to the other.

Waikiki is conveniently adjacent to the Honolulu Zoo, the Waikiki Aquarium, and tree-lined Kapiolani Park, a favorite spot for jogging, kite flying, and picnics for two. This is the home of the free Kodak Hula Show, which traces the history of the hula, as well as the Kapiolani Bandstand, site of numerous free community concerts. Also in Kapiolani Park is the Waikiki Shell, an outdoor amphitheater where, for a moderate admission, you can enjoy entertainment by a variety of artists, from the Honolulu Symphony to international stars such as Al Jarreau, Bill Cosby, the Beach Boys, and Julian Lennon. Its sloping green lawns are perfect for relaxing under the stars, sipping some wine, and gazing at the silhouette of Diamond Head as music fills the air. Check the newspapers for concert dates.

Waikiki is there for your pleasure; indulge yourselves!

SHOPPING: The **Royal Hawaiian Shopping Center** in Waikiki on Kalakaua Avenue boasts more than 280,000 square feet of excellent shops, the most appealing of which is the **China Friendship Store**, with gifts and clothing from the People's Republic of China. For a crowded yet colorful assortment of products, try the **International Market Place** between Kalakaua and Kuhio Avenues, a riot of souvenir stands, T-shirt shops, and upbeat eateries. Colorful Hawaiian-wear awaits at the Watumull's hotel outlets in Waikiki: Hilton Hawaiian Village, Moana Hotel, Ilikai Hotel, and Royal Hawaiian Hotel. There's also a fine **Liberty House** department store on the Kalakaua strip, with quality Polynesian fashions for men and women.

A ten-minute drive west from Waikiki takes you to **Ala Moana Shopping Center,** an indoor / outdoor mall with 155 shops selling everything from delightful Japanese products at **Shirokiya** to Hawaiian-style footwear at the **Slipper House.**

Five minutes farther west, **Ward Centre** and **Ward Warehouse** offer elegant

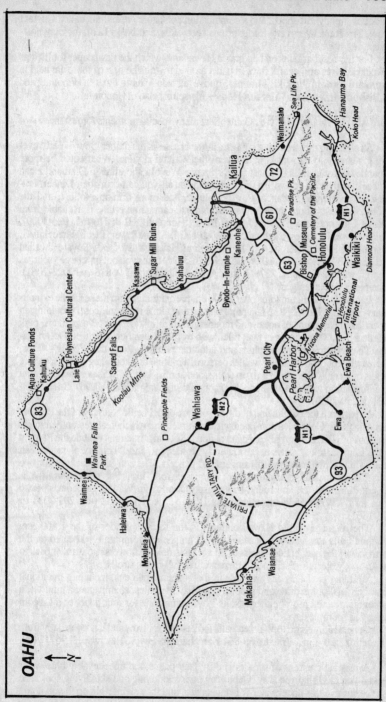

boutiques, trendy gift shops, and a combination bookstore / restaurant called **Upstart Crow.** Try **Rare Discovery** for luxurious keepsakes, and **Neon Leon** for zany postcards.

For the best bargains on handmade Hawaiiana, watch the newspaper for listings of weekend **arts and crafts fairs** in parks around town. The best of these are held in **Kapiolani Park** in Waikiki; **Thomas Square** and **Ala Moana Park** in Honolulu; and the **Bishop Museum** and **Mission Houses Museum,** also in Honolulu.

ROMANTIC INTERLUDES: Oahu offers many special moments for just the two of you.

Stroll along the deck on a **sunset dinner cruise** as the amber glow of early evening gives way to the sparkling lights of the Waikiki skyline. What could be more romantic? Most cruises sail past the distinctive Waikiki shoreline to Diamond Head and back, and lavish you with a lei greeting and an all-you-can-drink bar. Dinner, Polynesian entertainment, dancing to live music, and more drinking follow, and the whole affair lasts about three hours. An intimate catamaran cruise is available from **Aikane Catamarans,** 677 Ala Moana Blvd., Honolulu, HI 96813 (tel. 926-3009), while the world's largest catamaran is the **Ali'i Kai,** Aloha Tower, Pier 8, Street Level, Honolulu, HI 96813 (tel. 524-1800). **Diamond Head Cruises,** 305 Royal Hawaiian Ave., Suite 308, Honolulu, HI 96815 (tel. 926-3696) takes you out on a large yacht, as does **Hawaiian Cruises,** 2379 Kuhio Ave., Honolulu, HI 96815 (tel. 923-2061). Price per couple averages $50.

Fat Fred the Penguin joins over 2,000 unique creatures from the sea at the extraordinary **Sea Life Park.** The Makapuu Point setting alone is magnificent, providing an unparalleled panorama of ocean and mountains. Highlights of this 62-acre theme park include a 300,000-gallon reef tank filled with tropical Hawaiian creatures, Ocean Science Theater showcasing dolphins and adorable penguins, and the Whaler's Cove, where two 1,600-pound killer whales perform a routine of astounding stunts. Sea Life Park is open daily from 9:30 a.m. to 5 p.m. and admission is $15.50 per couple. Write for information to: Sea Life Park, Makapuu Point, Waimanalo, HI 96795 (tel. 923-1531 or 259-7933).

Experience the culture and traditions of the South Pacific courtesy of the **Polynesian Cultural Center,** a top-rated visitor attraction, which features authentic recreations of villages from seven island nations. Special attractions include the Pageant of the Long Canoes, meals at the Gateway Restaurant, and "This is Polynesia," an exhilarating show featuring 150 singers and dancers. The complete package for two costs $78 and includes entry to the park, admission to "This is Polynesia," an all-you-can-eat dinner buffet, and round-trip transportation from Waikiki, an hour's scenic drive away. Write 55370 Kamehameha Hwy., Laie, HI 96762 (tel. 293-3333 or 923-1861).

The romance of old Hawaii endures in the forest splendor of the 1,800-acre **Waimea Falls Park** valley, once the site of an ancient community. Located on the north shore, the park entices lovers of all ages to smell the flowers and wander back to the 45-foot waterfall. Each month there are free full-moon strolls.

Wedding packages are available in the botanical gardens, including traditional Hawaiian leis for the bride and groom, Hawaiian melodies, champagne, a minister, a photographer, and use of either a Rolls-Royce limousine for four hours or a Lincoln Town Car for three days.

General admission to Waimea Falls Park is $15 for two, and it is open daily from 10 a.m. to 5:30 p.m. Write to: 59-864 Kamehameha Hwy., Haleiwa, HI 96712 (tel. 638-8511).

A pristine crescent of sand ringed by lacy palms and unbelievably blue water beckon you to **Hanauma Bay,** Oahu's premier snorkeling and skindiving spot. The fish are tame in this underwater volcanic crater, and they swim right up to you if you offer them frozen peas. Hanauma Bay, which also offers bathroom and snack bar facilities, is a 20-minute drive from Waikiki. If you don't want to drive, Steve's Diving Adventures takes you there and back and provides equipment, beach mats, and fish food for $12 per couple. Contact them at 1860 Ala Moana Blvd., Honolulu, HI 96815 (tel. 947-8900).

Built in 1882, **Iolani Palace** has been restored to the initial splendor envisioned by its first occupant, King David Kalakaua, the "Merry Monarch" whose penchant for opulence helped dub his reign the "Champagne Dynasty." Guided tours are scheduled every 15 minutes from 9 a.m. to 2:15 p.m., Wednesdays through Saturdays, and the cost for two is $8. Your tour guide will provide you with slippers to protect the highly polished floors. The bandstand on the grounds adds a charming touch to this regal attraction, and every Friday at 12:15 p.m. the Royal Hawaiian Band performs there for your picnicking pleasure. Write to: P.O. Box 2259, Honolulu, HI 96804 (tel. 523-0141).

There's no view more precious than from atop **Diamond Head,** the famous extinct volcano rising 760 feet above town. From Waikiki you can drive through a tunnel into the crater. It's an easy half-hour hike up the inside trail, which culminates in 99 steps and a diversion through some wartime bunkers. Go when the gates open at 6 a.m. and the early morning lights make the whole ocean glimmer. Later in the day, the panoramic mountains reflect the rosy hues of the sunset. For details write **Hawaii State Parks and Recreation,** P.O. Box 621, Honolulu, HI 96809 (tel. 548-7455).

HONEYMOON HOTELS AND HIDEAWAYS: Be it a modest beach bungalow or the island's most luxurious suite, Oahu's variety of lodgings fits the bill for a honeymoon of any size and shape.

Expensive

Originally a private beachfront estate, **Halekulani,** 2199 Kalia Rd., Honolulu, HI (tel. 808/923-2311; reservations: toll free 800/367-2343), has been accommodating discriminating travelers to Waikiki Beach since 1917. The carefully restored main building, dating back to 1931, remains the focal point of the new Halekulani today. Steeped in nostalgia, this 456-room oasis links the elegance of the past with that of the present, and its five interconnecting buildings surround tranquil gardens and a century-old kiawe tree. White doves strut over gracious lawns lined with coconut palms, the beautiful pool is lined with an intricate mosaic depicting an orchid blossom, and the freshly swept beach offers a deck-chair view of the ocean and Diamond Head. Each room is tastefully furnished in accents of white, beige, blue, and gray, and has central air conditioning, separate sitting areas with lounge chairs, a tiled lanai, a love seat, a coffee table, three telephones, a refrigerator, a wet bar, and a color cable TV. Honeymoon package: none. However, Halekulani congratulates honeymoon couples with a split of champagne. Standard seven day / six night rate (EP): $1,280 per couple. Includes guaranteed ocean view, continental breakfast each day, welcome gift of Halekulani chocolates, jogging and aerobics classes, maid service, personalized check-in, and food and beverage gratuity.

The world's rich and famous have often chosen the **Kahala Hilton,** 5000 Kahala Ave., Honolulu, HI 96816 (tel. 808/734-2211; reservations: toll free 800/367-2525), as their Hawaiian host, for its peaceful beachside location in the prestigious Kahala area and its private, protected environment. It's still only ten minutes to Waikiki via the shuttle bus. Dolphins, penguins, and sea turtles cavort in the glistening lagoon, and tiny songbirds serenade you as you dine on the Hala Terrace, where you just might rub elbows with the likes of Henry Kissinger, Queen Elizabeth, Sylvester Stallone, and Linda Evans. *Magnum P.I.* usually films a part of each episode by the oceanside terrace. Most of its 370 rooms have lanais offering fine views of Kahala Bay or the Koolau mountains. Spacious living quarters are designed in bright island colors and feature his-and-her dressing areas, refrigerators and well-stocked mini-bars, cable TV, clock radios, house slippers, and his-and-her robes. Honeymoon package: Four days / three nights: $629 per couple (mountain view, no balcony), $751 per couple (mountain view with balcony), and $940 per couple (ocean view) per couple. Includes full American breakfast on the first morning, a convertible car for three days, and a greeting of flowers, fruit, and champagne.

Moderate to Inexpensive

The centerpiece of the **Hyatt Regency Waikiki,** 2424 Kalakaua Ave., Honolulu, HI 96815 (tel. 808/922-9292; reservations: toll free 800/228-9000), is its open-air Great Hall Atrium, with three cascading waterfalls, gardens of tropical foliage, and a custom-designed 45,000-pound chandelier suspended from a height of six floors. Oriental art prints decorate the walls of each 425-square-foot guest room, which is designed in warm earth tones and features air conditioning, wall-to-wall carpeting, private balcony, color TV, enclosed bathroom, twin mirrors, and a combination desk / game table with chairs. You can get almost anything you need from the many shops and boutiques in the hotel, and you can keep busy with the elaborate Hawaiian activities program. Its central location makes Waikiki sightseeing a snap. There's an award-winning restaurant, hot jazz in the first-floor lounge, and dancing in one of Honolulu's hottest discos, Spats. Honeymoon package: Five days / four nights (EP): $756.80 per couple. Includes champagne greeting, a tradewinds sail on the Mauna Kai catamaran along Waikiki Beach, and dinner at the elegant Bagwells 2424 restaurant. Upgrade available to include amenities such as a limousine, continental breakfast, and use of the Regency Club.

Spread over 20 acres, the **Hilton Hawaiian Village,** 2005 Kalia Rd., Honolulu, HI 96815 (tel. 808/949-4321; reservations: toll free 800/445-8667), commands the largest hotel beachfront in Waikiki. Catamaran sails are offered daily from the Hilton's private dock, and outrigger canoes, Hobie cats, surfboards, and snorkeling gear make this an outdoor-lover's nirvana. An entire city-within-the-city has been created here, to the extent that you may never need to venture beyond its 100 shops and services, 9 restaurants, 13 lounges, and 4 swimming pools. The open-air lobby is surrounded by feathery palms, blossoming trees, cascading waterfalls, an outdoor stage, a multilevel swimming pool, pristine lagoons, colorful fish, and exotic birds. Now nearly all the 2,522 rooms have some sort of ocean view, although the best views are from the Rainbow or Ocean Towers. Rooms are done in delicious shades of raspberry or aqua, with beige rugs and furniture designed in rattan and bamboo. For a feeling of true exclusivity, ask to stay in the pricey yet plush corner or penthouse suites of the Ocean Tower, which pamper you with a state-of-the-art exercise room, private sun deck, swimming pool, and bar. Honeymoon package: Three days / two nights (EP): $341 per couple. Includes the Don Ho cocktail show and a champagne breakfast catamaran sail.

Smack dab on Waikiki Beach, the **Outrigger Waikiki Hotel,** 2335 Kalakaua Ave., Honolulu, HI 96815 (tel. 808/923-0711; reservations: toll free 800/367-5170), is one of the most popular and convenient destinations for honeymooners. It's right on Kalakaua Avenue, the sparkling main drag of Waikiki, yet it also opens up to a glorious strip of sand and sea. Every room is decorated in a crisp, clean, Polynesian motif and offers such amenities as a lanai with views of the beach and ocean, air conditioning, color TV, and telephone. Kitchenette units are available for a higher price. The main showroom hosts top entertainment stars, led by the dynamic Society of Seven, a popular local septet in a sizzling Las Vegas–style revue. Honeymoon package: Four days / three nights: $452 per couple. Includes luxury accommodations in the exclusive Kuhio Club, a special level of rooms high atop the hotel, plus welcoming champagne and fruit, a dinner show, memento stationery, and a convertible car for one day. Same package is also available at the Outrigger Prince Kuhio Hotel, just a few blocks away.

Affectionately dubbed the "Pink Palace," the legendary **Royal Hawaiian**

Hotel, 2259 Kalakaua Ave., Honolulu, HI 96815 (tel. 808/923-7311; reservations: toll free 800/325-3535), is a pastel fairyland set right on the beach. Inaugurated in 1927, it is the second oldest of Waikiki's hotels, and it has been beautifully maintained in the stucco style of the original hotel. In the original building, gardenview rooms open up to groves of flowers and coconut palms, oceanview rooms offer a spacious old-world charm, and deluxe oceanview rooms are the largest and most luxurious, complete with a sitting room. Built in 1969, the Royal Tower offers private lanais and oceanfront views. All rooms have double doors, air conditioning, color TV with first-run movies, refrigerators, and electronic safes. A wide range of dining is available, including the elegant Monarch Room, a celebrated dinner showroom. For the ultimate trip into Hawaii's romantic past, go tea dancing each Monday. Choose from 579 rooms and suites. Honeymoon package: None. Standard rates (EP): $126.50 to $192.50 per couple per night for rooms; suites from $209 per couple per night.

Meet "the first lady of Waikiki," the **Sheraton Moana Hotel,** 2365 Kalakaua Ave., Honolulu, HI 96815 (tel. 808/922-3111; reservations: toll free 800/325-3535), a superb hostelry that opened in 1901. Fronting the ivory sands of Waikiki Beach, the white colonial-style hotel is somewhat dwarfed by the surrounding high rises, but it remains equally convenient to the exciting shopping, dining, and sightseeing attractions of the area. Renovations have preserved the original charm of this classic South Seas retreat, and the rooms are larger than their modern counterparts. The decor is decidedly Victorian, with brass beds, marble-top end tables, glass lamps, and cherry-wood writing desks. Some of the 390 rooms have private lanais and tropical ceiling fans, and all feature air conditioning, tub / shower combinations, and color TV. The H-shape of the design creates a center courtyard dominated by a century-old banyan tree, once the favorite writing spot of Robert Louis Stevenson and now the site of a thrilling Polynesian revue. Fine dining, private sunbathing, barber shop, beauty salon, and specialty shops. Honeymoon package: None. Standard rates (EP): $66 to $143 per couple per night.

Located in the "country" on the west coast of the island, a 30-minute drive from the airport and an hour from Waikiki, the **Sheraton Makaha Resort and Country Club,** P.O. Box 896, Makaha, HI 96792 (tel. 808/695-9511; reservations: toll free 800/325-3535) combines easy access to Honolulu attractions with the serenity of a summer estate. Just minutes away via Sheraton's free shuttle service awaits the world-famous Makaha Beach, home of annual surfing championships. The weather is usually pleasant here, with comfortable tradewinds ideal for golf, tennis, water sports, biking, jogging, and horseback riding. Gardens surround the 200 guest rooms and suites, which feature views of either the Makaha Coast or the rugged Waianae Mountains. The architecture is Polynesian, with low-rise cottages, open-air pavilions, and an elegant use of natural woods that blend into the country setting. Your room features a private lanai, individually controlled air conditioning, a telephone, a refrigerator, and a color TV, and the hotel includes two restaurants and a lounge, a fountain-fed swimming pool, gift shops, and Waikiki shuttle service. Honeymoon package: None. Standard rates (EP): $88 to $137.50 per couple per night (rooms), suites from $192.50 per couple per night.

Located on an 808-acre oceanfront resort on Oahu's scenic north shore, **Turtle Bay Hilton and Country Club,** Kahuku, HI 96731 (tel. 808/293-8811; reservations: toll free 800/445-8667), offers a Neighbor Island atmosphere while remaining accessible to Honolulu, just a scenic hour's drive away. There are three wings of 486 rooms and suites, and from your private lanai you get a magnificent view of the bay. The simple yet gracious room furnishings are done in wicker, brass, pastels, and light-colored woods, with prints of tropical flowers on the walls and plenty of living space. Five restaurants and three cocktail lounges offer superb ocean views, as do the two swimming pools, the adjacent private cottages, the 18-hole golf course, and the tennis courts. Honeymoon package (EP): $130.90 per couple per night. Includes deluxe oceanfront accommodations, champagne upon arrival, and full American champagne breakfast in bed.

ROMANTIC RESTAURANTS: Whatever you hunger for, you're sure to satisfy your appetite at one of Oahu's long list of fine restaurants and night spots. Unless otherwise noted, all these restaurants are in the Waikiki area.

Expensive

Treat yourselves like royalty at the oceanside **Michel's at the Colony Surf,** 2895 Kalakaua Ave. (tel. 923-6552), set right on the beach for panoramic views of the ocean. Sterling silver, beveled glass, white linen, and fresh orchids on each table are naturally illuminated by Hawaiian sunshine by day and Waikiki moonlight by night. This is one of the very few places on Oahu where men must wear dinner jackets. Lunch includes outstanding salads, sandwiches, soufflés, and hot entrées. Dinner's highlights include a fine lobster bisque laced with cognac, opakapaka Veronique, veal Oscar, and duckling flambé. Breakfast for two costs about $22, lunch $30, dinner $100, plus drinks.

Maile Restaurant, 5000 Kahala Ave. (tel. 734-2211). Dine and dance amidst tropical flowers, plants, and fountains as the waves gently lap on the nearby shore at the Kahala Hilton's signature restaurant, located about 15 minutes from Waikiki. The restaurant is noted for its formal elegance, extensive wine list, and unquestionably superb continental cuisine spiced with touches of Hawaii and the orient. For $72 per couple, the four-course table d'hôte dinner regales you with the best of the best, from escargots to steamed uhu, prime rib, and delectable pastries. À la carte dinners add up to about $100 for two plus drinks. Live entertainment is featured in the Maile Lounge, and jackets are requested of the men.

Moderate

Ranked among the world's top Italian restaurants, the **Trattoria,** 2165 Kalia Rd. (tel. 923-8415), a Waikiki landmark, serves an extensive menu of traditional and exotic fare in a setting as sumptuous as the food. High ceilings and chandeliers add a distinctly European flair to the atmosphere, and a handsome Italian troubadour strolls from table to table. Your intimate candlelit meal might include fresh island mahimahi Veronica, a sautéed island fish served with lemon sauce and seedless grapes. Trattoria also offers a unique presentation of manicotti glazed in a rich cream and tomato sauce. Dinner runs about $40 for two, plus drinks.

At **Hy's Steak House,** 2440 Kuhio Ave. (tel. 922-5555) Tuxedoed waiters cater to your every need. Specializing in charbroiled steaks of distinction, Hy's is also famed for its broiled lobster tail, the kiawe-broiled rack of lamb, fresh opakapaka, and a superb steak tartare. After dinner, slip into the softly lit rosewood lounge for an after-dinner drink by the piano bar. Dinner costs about $54 for two plus drinks.

Designed with plush red carpeting and jet-black leather, **Nick's Fishmarket,** 2070 Kalakaua Ave. (tel. 955-6333) is a favorite haunt for Honolulu's elite as well as out-of-town celebrities. Mood lighting, comfy booths, and impeccable table settings of the finest china put stars in the eyes of lovers. The menu promises such gifts of the sea as broiled fresh ulua amandine, cherrystone clams, swordfish, and ono. The aptly named Special Salad costs $5.50, and it's big enough to share. Get decadent over bananas flambé, the best in town. Nick's lounge is an upbeat forum for local talent, and you might even catch a star or two in the audience. Dinner is $50 for two plus drinks.

Canlis, 2100 Kalakaua Ave. (tel. 923-2324), a 1954 landmark at the entrance of Waikiki, has been the constant winner of dining awards. Lava-stone walls, tropical plants, and kimono-clad waitresses add a touch of the exotic to this calm oasis. Steak lovers meet their match in the filet mignon, pepper steak, and New York sirloin. The seafood is superb as well, particularly the broiled northwest salmon and fresh mahimahi. The blueberry cheesecake is a Canlis favorite. Dinner runs about $60 for two plus drinks.

The place to try the latest chic cuisine is **Keo's Thai Cuisine,** 625 Kapahulu Ave. (tel. 737-8240). The bamboo and brass decor, accented by striking arrangements of purple orchids is soothing, but the food's the real story here. Start with spring rolls wrapped in lettuce and fresh mint, garnished by cucumber and a piquant sauce. Keo's Evil Jungle Prince is a classic entrée, seasoned with just the right degree of intensity of hot peppers, fresh basil, and coconut milk. Spicy green papaya salad, crispy fried beef, and ginger shrimp are just a few of the consistently delicious offerings of this crowning achievement. Dinner for two is $30 plus drinks.

A favorite with the locals, **Tahitian Lanai,** 1811 Ala Moana Blvd. (tel. 946-6541), a casual tropical restaurant next to the Hilton Lagoon offers informal dining amid fresh ocean breezes. Breakfast, lunch, and dinner are all fun here. Morning fare features a great eggs Benedict and very special banana muffins. Lunch and dinner offerings of note are a robust French onion soup, Tahitian-style chicken, Hawaiian dinner plate, and London broil. For a sweet taste of the islands, top it off with the superb macadamia nut ice cream. For two, breakfast ranges from $6 to $15; lunch from $7.50 to $18.50; dinner from $18 to $48. Behind the restaurant is the Papeete piano bar.

Designed to resemble the dining room of a splendid ocean liner, **Captain's Table,** 2570 Kalakaua Ave. (tel. 922-2511) in the Holiday Inn Waikiki takes you on an excursion through Hawaii's unique seas, offering fresh ono sautéed with capers and lemon butter, broiled salmon with dill sauce, and other fine seafood. Try the stuffed grape leaves as an appetizer, and the herbed cream cheese that is served with lavosh crackers. Veal marsala, Malaysian-style lamb chops, and Australian lobster tail broaden this cosmopolitan menu for a meal you want to linger over for a good, long time. The Captain's Table lounge offers live entertainment. Dinner for two costs about $40 plus drinks.

Get a taste of Hawaiian paniolo (cowboy) traditions at **Hawaiian Hoe-Down,** Olomana Ranch, Waimanalo (tel. 259-9300): high-kicking saloon girls, cowboy hula, singers, and callers. Dance the two-step and the cotton eye Joe. The dinner spread includes an all-you-can-eat barbecue buffet with ribs, teriyaki chicken, corn on the cob, mai tais, beer, and lots more. It costs $74 per couple, including hotel pickup and round-trip transportation.

Set on a private estate a half-hour's drive from Waikiki, **Germaine's Luau,** south shore (tel. 949-6626), offers traditional Hawaiian fun. Hosting as many as 800 people per night, this outdoor affair is far from intimate, but it does offer a healthy dose of the aloha spirit and an entertaining introduction to the luau. An all-you-can-drink bar warms things up as you watch the procession of the royal court and the ceremonial lifting of the pig from its imu. You sit at long, rectangular tables where the food just keeps on coming: kalua pig, fried chicken, lomilomi salmon, mahimahi, macaroni and tossed salads, fresh pineapple spears, banana bread, and *haupia* (coconut) pudding. As the stars twinkle over the Pacific, a spellbinding Polynesian revue wraps up the evening with island songs and dances plus zany comedy. The luau costs $71 for two, including transportation from Waikiki, and it's held nightly except Fridays.

Restaurant Suntory, Royal Hawaiian Shopping Center (tel. 922-5511), is the place to try Japanese cuisine at its best. Choose from the Sushi Bar, the Teppanyaki Room (seafood, beef, or lobster cooked in a hearty stew), or the Shabushabu Room (specializing in tempura, which is fish and vegetables deep-fried in a light batter). Teppanyaki dinners cost from $40 to $60 per couple plus drinks. Rise above it all at one of Honolulu's elevated eateries, such as **Windows of Hawaii,** 1441 Kapiolani Blvd. (tel. 941-9138), a revolving restaurant high above Ala Moana Shopping Center. Dinner for two costs $64 plus drinks.

Inexpensive

How about dinner on the beach at **Shore Bird Beach Broiler,** 2169 Kalia Rd. (tel. 922-2887)? This broil-your-own eatery sits right on Waikiki Beach, a great spot for a fun night out. You're the chefs, and you stand around big open fires cooking your meal while gazing at the panorama of sand and sea, just a stone's throw away. Ribs, kebobs, chicken, and fish are the featured attractions, and all dinners come with an exceptionally generous salad bar. Dinners run from $12 to $25 for two plus drinks. Afterward, boogie down in Waikiki's only beachfront disco, complete with two dance floors and a ten-foot video screen.

Eggs 'n' Things, 463 Ena Rd. (tel. 949-0820). Most visitors don't know about it, and most locals love it. This cramped, tiny breakfast nook serves up phenomenal breakfasts at cheap prices, including a $1.75 early riser special of three pancakes and two eggs. Fancy crêpes and omelets cost about $10 for two, plus coffee. It's open at odd hours for a late breakfast or a midnight snack (from 11 p.m. to 2 p.m. the next day).

If your tastes run to Chinese food, go to **Maple Garden,** Isenberg Street (tel. 941-6641), a bright dining room with comfy booths and smiling waitresses who regale you with smoky Szechuan duck, sautéed scallops with snow peas, and an eggplant with garlic sauce to write home about. Dinner for two costs $25 plus drinks. Or try **Pizzeria Uno,** 2256 Kuhio Ave. (tel. 926-0646), whose second-story balcony juts out over the busy Kuhio Avenue scene, making for fun people-watching while you munch tasty pizza. Pizzas range from $3.95 to $16.95.

3. Maui

Ever since Maui, the legendary demigod, snared the sun and demanded longer days, his island namesake has been the sunniest link in the Hawaiian chain. In fact, it feels as if he may have cast a spell over the whole island, for Maui is filled with a magic that begs you to extend the honeymoon just a little bit longer.

The most visited of the Neighbor Islands is actually formed by two volcanoes connected by an isthmus. Maui is the second largest Hawaiian island, with an area of 729 square miles. Just to the west lie the islands of Molokai, Lanai, and Kahoolawe, which are considered part of Maui country.

Maui's east and west sections are as different in attractions as the people who visit them. Some head west toward seaside Lahaina, once the capital of all of Hawaii and a bustling whaling village, and now a popular forum for sightseeing, shopping, and dining. North of Lahaina lie the sun-drenched shores of Kaanapali, where a once-thriving old Hawaiian community has given way to glistening condos and hotels of Maui's most popular vacation area. Backed by the towering West Maui Mountains, the resort invites the active to swing golf clubs and tennis racquets while the serene sip refreshing mai tais by a stretch of sand and sea once prized by Hawaiian *alii* (royalty). Whether you go in for shopping or windsurfing by day, dining or disco dancing by night, it all adds up to Kaanapali, the most cosmopolitan pocket on the Valley Isle.

Beyond Kaanapali, the public beaches of Honokowai, Kahana, and Napili offer more secluded spots for swimming, snorkeling, picnicking, collecting shells, and napping to the sound of gentle waves. Farther north awaits Kapalua, which means "arms embracing the sea," a peaceful, ultra-elegant resort area hosting a classy hotel, fancy condominiums, and a tasteful array of European-style shops.

Compared to the west, eastern Maui is larger and more diverse, with its fields of sugar and pineapple flanking the "big cities" of Kahului and Wailuku. You'll most likely fly into the airport in Kahului, home of several busy shopping centers, Maui Community College, botanical gardens, and a zoo. Wailuku's pride and joy is Iao Valley State Park, where King Kamehameha defeated enemy forces in the bloody battle of 1790. Jutting high above the park is Iao Needle, an impressive 2,250-foot cinder cone, accompanied by an even higher peak called Puu Kukui, at 5,788 feet.

Heading south along Maui's west coast, you encounter Kihei, whose remote beaches were created with only the two of you in mind, and whose golf courses offer panoramic views of the nearby islands of Lanai, Kahoolawe, and Molokini. Nearby is Wailea, where desert cactus and barren landscapes of the early 1900s have been transformed into an exclusive resort area brimming with hotels, condominiums, shopping, land and water sports, and swinging night life.

At the easternmost corner of Maui awaits Hana, country home of just a few small accommodations and all the peace and quiet you may seek. Winding roads take you past homes and churches built in the 1800s, and families still farm and fish these reaches in the manner of their ancestors. Hiking and horseback trails beckon you to explore Hawaii's past in this region so aptly dubbed "heavenly Hana."

Inland stretch Maui's soothing, green highlands, where rough 'n' tumble *paniolos* (cowboys) ride the upcountry ranges and white-face Hereford cattle graze in seemingly endless pasturelands. Above it all reigns 10,000-foot Haleakala, the dormant volcano whose crater embraces a vast lunar landscape. As he gazed upon the warm reds, greens, and purples of the sunrise across the lava and cinder cones, Mark Twain called Haleakala "the sublimest spectacle I ever witnessed, and I think the memory of it will remain with me always."

Just like that cunning demigod Maui, you will wish you could command the sun to shine forever during your honeymoon on the Valley Isle.

SHOPPING: On Maui, the place to get your matching "Just Mauied" T-shirts is **David's of Hawaii** in Lahaina. As the former whaling capital of the isles, this quaint port features many shops with nautical overtones, including **The Whaler, Ocean Magic,** and **Waterfront Gifts Gallery.** You'll find some of the most beautiful island treasures at the **Sea and Shell Gallery** on Front Street, including gracefully curved nautilus shells plucked from Pacific Seas and a superb selection of shell jewelry. At **Alexia,** also on Front Street, women can find cotton and raw silk fashions by Georgiou —very island-right in their cool, casual elegance.

The maritime theme continues in nearby Kaanapali at **Whaler's Village,** an elegant mini-mall boasting the most elaborate selection of scrimshaw (**The Scrimshaw Factory**). You can also add to your antique map collection with a selection from **Lahaina Printsellers,** or go for a pair of glass whales for $4 at the **Narwhal Shop.**

Many of the fancy resorts have their own shopping arcades, the most glamorous of which is found in the Hyatt Regency Maui. **The Shops** at Kapalua are also appealing, though pricey; its most distinctive boutique is **Distant Drums.**

You get the most for your money at one of the island's large shopping centers, such as Kahului's **Kaahumanu Shopping Center** on Kaahumanu Street. Its 50-plus stores including **Nani Pacifica,** a terrific place to buy calendars and posters by local artists. For Hawaiian wear at wholesale prices go to **Island Muumuu Works** in the nearby **Maui Mall** also on Kaahumanu. In Kihei try the **Rainbow Connection** for elegant keepsakes; it's in a shopping center called **Azeka's Place** on Route 35.

Some of the most inventive island arts and crafts can be found in the local shops of Paia, including the **Maui Crafts Guild** and the **Tropical Emporium,** both on Hana Highway. And a must for Hana honeymooners is **Hasagawa General Store** on Highway 36, a legendary landmark where you can get just about anything you need (and plenty of things you've never heard of before).

ROMANTIC INTERLUDES. Go ahead! Bicycle down a volcano, then luxuriate in a seaside resort. On Maui, the emphasis is on variety.

On the west coast, the picturesque seaside town of **Lahaina** recalls the golden years of whaling in Hawaii. Just 15 minutes from Kaanapali, this beautifully restored historic burg brings to life the 1850s, when as many as 100 ships anchored in the original Hawaiian capital. It also reflects the efforts of the prim and proper missionaries who lived in Lahaina in the 1830s. The Baldwin House, the old prison, and several other simple homes and churches are preserved by the Lahaina Restoration Foundation. Now a National Historic Landmark, the city brims with narrow streets and old homes alongside colorful boutiques and delightful open-air restaurants and nightclubs, which are particularly lively in the evenings.

There's lots to do and see in Lahaina, day or night. Visit the **Pioneer Inn, a** whimsical 1901 homestead full of nautical memorabilia, and the **Carthaginian,** a restored 19th-century whaling vessel turned into a floating museum. If you're there between early November and late May, join a cruise to watch for the **whales,** which migrate annually through Lahaina's warm seas. Then hold hands in the shade of the world's largest-known **banyan tree,** measuring a quarter-mile in circumference and covering four city blocks.

For $15 per couple, a restored sugarcane train takes you from Kaanapali Resort to Lahaina, with a singing conductor as your guide. Contact **Lahaina-Kaanapali & Pacific Railroad,** Box 816, Lahaina, HI 96761 (tel. 661-0089).

Molokini Island, a tiny crescent just a short boat ride off Maui's southern shore, is actually the top of a dormant volcano and the home of exotic Hawaiian fish by the hundreds. Hop on a half-day snorkel cruise out of Maalaea Harbor, Kihei, or Lahaina and treat yourselves to an underwater adventure straight out of Jacques Cousteau. Butterfly fish frolic along with ulua, palani, taape, and other pretty swimmers. Most Molokini tours include equipment, lessons, breakfast, and lunch. **Dive Maui,** Lahainaluna Marketplace, Lahainaluna Road, Lahaina, HI 96761 (tel. 667-2080), charges about $100 per couple for snorkelers, $150 for scuba-divers.

Get up *real* early, fill a thermos with coffee, borrow blankets from your hotel, and prepare yourselves for an unrivalled sunrise from the top of a 10,023-foot-high dormant volcano. Translated "House of the Sun," **Haleakala** boasts a crater that is 20 miles in circumference, 19 square miles in area, and 3,000-feet deep. That's big enough to hold all of Manhattan island! Allow yourselves at least 2½ hours to drive from Kaanapali to the observatory (two hours from Wailea).

After sunrise, you can hike along more than 30 miles of trails through the 28,665-acre national park, which includes three cabins in the crater (available by advance lottery). Or take a guided horseback trip past the indigenous silversword, an eerie plant related to the sunflower. **Pony Express Tours,** P.O. Box 507, Makawao, HI 96768 (tel. 667-2202), offers full-day horseback tours of the crater for $240 a couple, and half-day tours for $160. Yet another option for "doing" Haleakala is to join a bicycle tour from the summit to the beach with **Cruiser Bob's Haleakala Downhill,** 505 Front St., Lahaina, HI 96761 (tel. 667-7717), or **Maui Downhill,** 440A Alamaha St., Kahului, HI 96732 (tel. 871-2155). It costs about $160 per couple.

A taste of Hawaii-gone-by lingers on in "Heavenly **Hana.**" To get there follow the road east from Kahului, take off your wristwatches, and set aside a whole day to drive the 50 miles past lush pasturelands, glorious rain forests, lacy waterfalls, sparkling bays, and breathtaking sea cliffs. All along the way you feel compelled to park the car, snap giddy pictures, smell the flowers, dunk in bracing mountain pools, and forget the rest of the world. If the surf's up, stop to watch daredevil windsurfers tackle the huge waves near Paia.

Once in Hana, plan to spend the night. A few small condominiums and a gracious hotel have been designed and landscaped to blend into Hana's simple beauty. This is truly the "old country" of Maui, where life is unhurried and people take pride in their heritage. You can visit the simple, touching burial site of Hana resident Charles Lindbergh and swoon over the views from the top of Mt. Lyons. Just beyond the town you can visit the frothy cascades of Wailua Falls as well as Seven Sacred Pools, a series of ponds dancing down to the sea—remote swimming spot indeed.

Where else but Hawaii could you find such ambrosia as pineapple wine? On the cool, upper slopes of Haleakala is the **Tedeschi Winery,** P.O. Box 953, Ulupalakua, HI 96790 (tel. 878-6058). Acres of pineapples and grapes are cultivated and transformed into a well-respected line of **fine wines.** Drive on Hwy. 37, the mountain road beyond Kula, to the Ulupalakua Ranch, whose owner joined forces with vintner Emil Tedeschi about ten years ago. The result of their union must be sampled firsthand, and at free daily wine tastings you can do just that. Toast each other in the tasting room, a former jail built in 1856, and be sure to try Tedeschi's pink champagne. Cheers!

HONEYMOON HOTELS AND HIDEAWAYS: Maui's major resort areas offer wonderful options for a honeymoon supreme.

Expensive

Kapalua Bay Hotel and Villas, One Bay Dr., Kapalua, HI 96761 (tel. 808/669-5656); reservations: toll free 800/367-8000). The ultimate in seclusion and luxury, Kapalua offers 23,000 acres by the sea, where palm and pine trees preside over two championship golf courses, tennis courts, glittering beaches, and a wealth of gourmet restaurants and elite boutiques. A grand vaulted lobby overlooks verdant lawns that roll down to the water's edge, and throughout the hotel you find native plants and flowers of all shapes and sizes. Your room is decorated in soothing shades of blue or rust warmed by natural woods, including mahogany paddle fans, wicker chairs, and rattan headboards. The 194 rooms afford breathtaking views of Kapalua Bay as well as the neighboring isles of Molokai and Lanai. Within each room you'll find such South Seas touches as high ceilings and shutters leading to your roomy lanai. If you opt for one of the condominium villas, your hosts pull out all the stops: sunken tiled baths, complete kitchens, and daily maid service, for starters. Honeymoon package: Four days/three nights (EP): $770 per couple. Includes oceanview hotel room, basket of fruit, champagne, midsize rental car, dinner for two, and a pair of designer kimonos.

In a word, the **Hyatt Regency Maui,** 200 Nohea Kai Dr., Lahaina, HI 96761 (tel. 808/667-7474; reservations: toll free 800/228-9000), is spectacular. A tropical fantasyland by the sea in Kaanapali, it encompasses 18 exotic acres graced with flamingos, swans, peacocks, penguins, and parrots, who strut amid Japanese gardens, underground grottoes, and graceful waterfalls. A rope bridge crosses a stream linking the gardens to the hotel, and the half-acre swimming pool features a grand, 130-foot waterslide and a secretive sunken bar. Subtle tones of beige, rust, and blue create a quiet elegance in each of the 815 rooms, which offer lounging areas, private phones, full bathrooms, air conditioning, color television, and local artworks as well as views of the mountains or ocean. Honeymoon package: Five days/four nights (EP): $1,078 per couple. Includes champagne, a cocktail sail, and dinner in the award-winning Spats. Upgraded package with concierge service, health club membership, and continental breakfast daily: $1,309 per couple.

Although a bit more low-key than the neighboring Hyatt Regency, the **Maui Marriott Resort,** 100 Nohea Kai Dr., Lahaina, HI 96761 (tel. 808/667-1200; reservations: toll free 800/831-9290), is equally luxurious. Spread across 15 oceanfront acres along Kaanapali Beach, it is surrounded by extensive landscapes laced with waterfalls, pools, and coconut groves. The hotel meets the sea in an open grouping of low-rise wings along its own stretch of golden sand. The beach is the focal point here, and the Marriott offers free sailing, surfing, and windsurfing demonstrations for fun in the sun. Designed to complement the softly colorful lithographs of Hawaiian artist Pegge Hopper, the decor of the 720 rooms features soft green carpets, subdued floral bedspreads in peach, beige, coral, and green, and rattan easy chairs. Each room has its own private lanai and ocean view, mirrored closet doors, a king-size bed, sitting area, refrigerator/bar, and color television. Come evening time, sip exotic drinks in the Makai Bar. Honeymoon package: Four days/three nights (EP): $693 per couple. Includes car rental, champagne and logo glasses upon arrival, and free breakfast buffet.

Kaanapali Beach Hotel, 2525 Kaanapali Pkwy., Lahaina, HI 96761 (tel. 808/661-0011; reservations: toll free 800/227-4700), is a casual beachside resort ideally situated between the ocean and two superb golf courses, just four miles from Lahaina and adjacent to Whalers Village Shopping Center. Its 431 rooms and four wings embrace a courtyard with a whale-shaped swimming pool. Each room has a private lanai from which you can see pristine neighbor islands on an azure sea or glorious panoramas of the West Maui mountains. Rooms feature air conditioning, color television, refrigerator, ironing board, daily maid service, telephone message alert, special shampoos and hand lotions, and full tub with shower. In the evenings the courtyard fills with friendly folks for open-air dining and dancing under the stars. Honeymoon package: Four days/three nights: $645 per couple. Includes deluxe accommodations, cocktail cruise, champagne, fruit basket, dinner show, helicopter flight over West Maui, and *Maui on My Mind* gift book. Eight days/seven nights: $910 per couple. Also includes a full-day snorkel and swim cruise to the island of Molokini.

If you both love the sun, you'll find plenty of it at **Maui Prince Hotel,** 5400 Makena Alanui Dr., Kihei, HI 96753 (tel. 808/874-1111; reservations: toll free 800/321-6284) at Makena Beach Maui's south shore. The 1,000 well-landscaped acres make for a sports-lover's paradise, with endless opportunities for oceanside golf and tennis, swimming and sailing in calm waters, and sunning on a white sand beach. You may find yourselves lingering in the stunning 30,000-square-foot courtyard, whose cascading waterfalls, fish ponds, rock gardens, foot bridges, and Hawaiian ferns, orchids, and anthuriums create a Garden of Eden in your own backyard. Three fine restaurants specialize in American cuisine, but when you both feel impetuous, you can call on the 24-hour room service and order a treat from the particularly diverse menu. Each of the 300 cheery rooms and suites has an ocean view, air conditioning, television, phone, and plenty of room for relaxing after an active day outside. Honeymoon package: Four days/three nights (EP): $690 per couple. Includes fruit basket and champagne upon arrival, a complimentary souvenir, and a midsize rental car.

The advantages of **Kaanapali Alii,** 50 Nohea Kai Dr., Lahaina, HI 96761 (tel. 808/667-1400; reservations: toll free 800/642-6284) are many. It's "your place" on the beach, a large one- or two-bedroom condominium apartment with fully equipped kitchen, washer/dryer, and fine furnishings. Daily maid and bell services are provided, and freshwater pools, saunas, and an exercise room enhance this oceanside experience. Plenty of privacy on your own balcony, perfect for that breezy breakfast or a drink at sunset. Honeymoon package: Eight days/seven nights: $1,373 (garden view) to $1,618 (ocean view) per couple. Includes a one-bedroom condominium, compact deluxe car, flowers, and champagne upon arrival. Upgrade to the ultimate honeymoon suite: Eight days/seven nights: $2,600 per couple. Includes ocean view apartment, midsize sedan, full bar, large tropical flower arrangement, Maui morning grocery package delivered every third day, two daily newspapers (*Wall Street Journal* and a local paper), assorted Hawaiian magazines, use of a VHS video recorder, luxury bath amenities, twice-daily housekeeping, and concierge service.

Built around its own tropical gardens on 15 sloping acres, **Stouffer's Wailea Beach Resort,** 3550 Wailea Alanui Dr., Wailea, HI 96753 (tel. 808/879-4900; reservations: toll free 800/468-3571) 347-room beachfront resort urges you to celebrate the senses. Come alive with a splash in the south Maui surf, and gaze in awe at the majestic stillness of Haleakala. Run your hands over the smooth furnishings of your room, which is designed in koa, a rich Hawaiian hardwood, and spoil yourselves with such complimentary amenities as your custom-designed refreshment center, digital clock, air conditioning, plush carpeting, in-room refrigerator, and color television with a daily selection of movies. For an unforgettable treat, ask to be served the gourmet candlelight dinner for two on your private lanai. Honeymoon package: Four days/three nights: $797 per couple. Summer discounts may be available. Includes oceanview room, air-conditioned compact car, dinner for two, champagne, a mai tai welcome, and a tropical fruit plate upon arrival.

Getting you to unwind and enjoy life Hawaiian-style is what the **Hotel Hana Maui,** Hana, HI 96713 (tel. 808/248-8211; reservations: toll free 800/321-4262), does best. In a remote region beneath Haleakala's east face, the Hotel Hana Maui consists of many one-story bungalows scattered over 20 acres of broad green lawn. Everywhere there are vistas of the volcano, with its deep-cut valleys and rain forests of koa and bamboo. Below, beaches of black and gold sand curve among lava cliffs glistening with spray. The hotel's spacious 82 rooms and suites, many with open lanais, are inspired by plantation life and decorated with discretely elegant rattan and cool tropical prints. The management really emphasizes hospitality by inviting guests to the plantation house for cocktails with the general manager and his wife. No television except in the lounge, but there's a library with comfy couches and chairs, jigsaw puzzles, and other simple pleasures. A windowed wall in the dining room looks out to Hana Bay, and the Paniolo Bar's fourth side opens to a view of mountain pastures. Sign up for one of the resort's guided trail rides through the misty mountains and down to the beach. Honeymoon package: Five days/four nights: $995 per couple. Includes Hana Airport transfers, leis upon arrival and departure, champagne, Tuesday night barbecue cookout at Lehoula Beach, fresh fruit bowl, hula and ukulele lessons, a one-hour horseback ride, and a Friday night luau at Hamoa Beach.

Moderate

What could be better for two people in love than a private bungalow on the beach at **Papakea Beach Resort,** 3543 Honoapiilani Hwy., Lahaina, HI 96761 (tel. 808/ 669-4848; reservations: toll free 800/367-5637). These one-bedroom, oceanview condominiums in Kaanapali are ideal if you're looking for an informal home away from home, framed by coconut palms and adjacent to waters so clear you can count your toes. It's so nice to have all the comforts of home at your fingertips, such as a blender to whip up something tropical, and a complimentary assortment of basics such as coffee, tea, salt, pepper, sugar, and a juicy Maui pineapple to get you started. Cook in your own private kitchen or do a little outdoor barbecuing by one of the swimming pools. Three night-lit tennis courts, putting greens, two whirlpool spas, and two saunas will keep you amply entertained. Honeymoon package: Four days/three nights (EP): $464.20 per couple. Includes a car, champagne, and fruit basket upon arrival.

At **Royal Lahaina Resort,** 2780 Kekaa Dr., Lahaina, HI 96761 (tel. 808/661-3611; reservations: toll free 800/227-4700), each of the 350 guest rooms is designed in pastels with rattan, wicker, plants, and ceiling fans that set a tropical island scene. Intimate garden and oceanfront cottages are perfect for a private honeymoon, and you'll find it all amid 30 landscaped acres right on Kaanapali Beach. The hotel has earned a five-star ranking as a tennis resort. Honeymoon package: Four days/three nights (EP): $510 per couple. Includes a deluxe oceanview room in the Lahaina Kai Tower, in-room champagne breakfast, admission to the Royal Lahaina Luau, champagne sunset sail, and *Maui on My Mind* gift book.

Maui Inter-Continental Wailea, P.O. Box 779, Wailea, HI 96753 (tel. 808/ 879-1922; reservations: toll free 800/327-0200), a deluxe 18-acre vacation resort, sprawls across both lush, green hills and a magnificent crescent of south shore beach, from which you can see the neighboring islands of Lanai and Kahoolawe. The outdoors is the key here. The open-air lobby is lush with ferns, palms, lava-rock walls, and island woods, and each of the 600 rooms uses earthy colors of green, orange, yellow, and brown intermingled with rattan and bamboo furnishings. The rooms are quite comfortable, and feature private balconies, color televisions, air conditioning, radios, room service, laundry, and valet. If you love tennis, this is the place for you; it is called "Wimbledon West" because of its superior 14-court tennis facility (including three grass courts). Honeymoon package: Four days/three nights: $520 per couple.

Includes oceanview room, compact car, daily breakfast, champagne, fruit basket, sun visors, beach bag and towels, and fresh orchids on the pillow every evening.

ROMANTIC RESTAURANTS: Whether you dine by candlelight or sup by the sea, Maui offers whatever your hearts desire.

Expensive

Named after the French explorer who discovered La Perouse Bay in 1786, **La Perouse,** Maui Inter-Continental Wailea, Wailea (tel. 879-1922), has been designed with the eclectic decor of oriental silk tapestries, unusual seashells, a horned candelabra from Africa, and a ceramic fountain bowl. Equally varied is the fine bill of fare that might include a special callaloo crabmeat soup made with taro leaves, coconut milk, and chunks of crab. Try hukilau and tiger prawns en papillote, the day's catch and prawns steamed with spinach, herbs, and brandy. Be sure to sample the wilted salad made with Maui's own Kula spinach, and Caesar salad prepared at your tableside—for two, of course. Fine wines. A concert pianist plays pretty background music. Dinners for two range from $63.50 to $140 plus drinks.

Moderate

A quaint country inn setting complements the fine French food at **La Bretagne,** 562-C Front St., Lahaina (tel. 661-8966). Pretty checkered tablecloths, tidy tile floors, and fresh cut flowers set the tone as you discover the joys of the Maui onion, prepared here in a tart and served as an appetizer. We recommend the breaded veal in mustard seed sauce, along with the superb duck with blueberry sauce. The French desserts are marvelous, especially when topped off by a rich café Français. Dinner costs $40 for two plus drinks.

Mama's Fish House, 799 Kiaholo Pl., Paia (tel. 579-9672). The drive to this sleepy town is well worth it when this beachfront restaurant is your goal. The spic-and-span dining room done in a Hawaiian-Tahitian motif offers ocean views and fresh island fish in creative preparations. It's hard to beat the Pacific abalone, flown in from Baja, California, and made to perfection by the same chef for 15 years. Chilled papaya coconut soup is an island delicacy, and the catch of the day is usually outstanding. Desserts roll by on a cart filled with such treats as lemon cheesecake and banana crisp. Dinner for two runs about $45 per couple plus drinks.

By all means, don't miss **Longhi's,** 888 Front St., Lahaina (tel. 667-2288) a popular café fashioned in a fantastic two-tiered, black-and-white design. Set across from the ocean, Longhi's presents smashing views of Lahaina harbor and the glorious Pacific, particularly as the day gives way to a vermilion sunset. Instead of handing out printed menus, waiters recite the dishes with dramatic flair, regaling you with such possibilities as fresh opakapaka, prawns amaretto, pasta with pesto, and gorgonzola cheese bread. Come here for brunch and feast on a medley of continental delights such as Italian sausage frittata and homemade sweet rolls. Dinner for two costs $60 plus drinks.

Swan Court, Hyatt Regency Maui, Kaanapali (tel. 667-7474). Yes, swans really do swim by you in this dreamy al fresco dining room by a peaceful pond. Come here to linger, and linger some more, under the hypnotic spell of Japanese gardens, trickling waterfalls, and muted stained glass. This is one of the most romantic dining experiences you'll discover on Maui. Swoon over such joys as shrimp bisque with cognac, roast duck glazed with honey and macadamia nuts, fresh fish with ginger butter, and veal with morel mushrooms. Dinner costs about $64 per couple plus drinks. The daily breakfast buffet covers several tables with tantalizing international fare, from fresh island fruit to tailor-made omelets created according to your whims. It's a beautiful way to start your day in paradise, and costs $21 per couple.

A country party, island-style! That's **Maui's Tropical Plantation Barbecue,**

Waikapu Valley (tel. 244-7643). Recalling Hawaii's plantation days, this sunset shindig starts out with an old-fashioned horse-drawn hayride through fields of pineapple, sugarcane, macadamia nuts, bananas, and tropical flowers. An all-you-can-drink selection of beer, wine, and mai tais loosens you up for the square dancing and socializing, followed by a big paniolo feast: Portuguese bean soup, chili con carne, steaks from the grill, a salad bar, and your choice of apple cobbler, macadamia nut cream pie, or pineapple cake. It's a one-of-a-kind celebration of island food and hospitality on a 120-acre plantation. Held every Monday and Wednesday, it costs $76 per couple, plus $10 for transportation from Kaanapali, Lahaina, Kihei, Wailea, and Kahului.

Work off that big dinner with some dancing in **Spats II,** Hyatt Regency Maui, Kaanapali (tel. 667-7474). It's a new disco with Roaring '20s speakeasy decor. Also in the Hyatt is **Drums of the Pacific,** a big Polynesian revue offered for cocktails ($40 per couple) or as a dinner show ($68 per couple). An open-garden setting beckons you to **Dillon's Hideaway,** 89 Hana Hwy., Paia (tel. 579-9113). Fresh-fish dinner is about $30 per couple, and happy hour features special drink prices. **The Old Lahaina Luau,** 505 Front St., Lahaina (tel. 667-1998), takes place on the beach and comes complete with Hawaiian dancers, Polynesian food, crafts demonstrations, and plenty of aloha spirit. It costs $66 per couple.

Inexpensive

Gaspare's Place, Island Surf Building, Kihei (tel. 879-8881), a pizza palace, is full of old Italian favorites, perfect for that casual meal on your sightseeing docket. Watch the chef toss the pizza dough until it's just right, then taste the results in a prize pizza known as Gaspare's Special, which costs $13.95. Submarine sandwiches, fettuccine, and spaghetti with meatballs are all quite tasty, not to mention affordable. Dinner, which includes salad and garlic bread, costs about $15 a couple plus drinks.

4. Kauai

Remember the "special island" that beckoned in *South Pacific?* The movie could have been filmed only on Kauai, a legendary "Bali Hai" that beckons every day, every night, whispering love songs from the mountains to the sea.

Kauai is the northernmost of Hawaii's major islands, and the fourth largest. It is also the oldest of the populated islands, and some eight million years of nature's handiwork have sculpted the jagged pinnacles and furrowed the emerald cliffs that characterize Kauai's stunning beauty. The island is dominated by 5,240-foot Mt. Waialeale, which rises from the great Alakai Swamp, source of Kauai's seven main rivers and home to rare plants and birds.

The island is steeped in ancient folklore, particularly tales of the *menehunes.* According to legend, the menehunes were an industrious race of little people, like leprechauns, who performed prodigious feats of construction. They supposedly labored in the secrecy of night, accepting in payment for their efforts only one shrimp per worker. The Menehune Fishpond in Nawiliwili and Menehune Ditch in Waimea are said to be two of their construction projects.

You can see both these sites while touring Kauai. Because of the island's compact proportions (about 33 miles long and 25 miles wide), sightseeing by car is easy. One main road runs around Kauai, ending on each side of the breathtaking 13-mile Na Pali coast in sheer-faced cliffs that rise 3,000 feet out of the sea. The lush, moist, northern areas from Lihue up to Haena are steeped in the past, from the spiritual dry and wet caves of the gods near Ke'e Beach, to the banks of the Wailua River where the first Polynesians made their homes. Lining the northern coastline are quiet coves of sea and sand, including Lumahai Beach ("Nurses Beach" in *South Pacific*) and dreamy Hanalei Beach Park, offering overpowering views of the Na Pali Coast.

Southern Kauai is almost always sunny and is well loved for its generous gifts of sand and sea. From windsurfing to boogie-boarding, water sports abound at Poipu

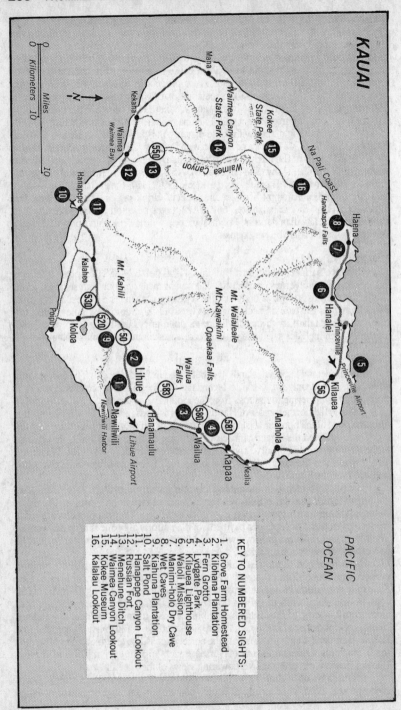

KAUAI

PACIFIC OCEAN

KEY TO NUMBERED SIGHTS:

1. Grove Farm Homestead
2. Kilohana Plantation
3. Fern Grotto
4. Lydgate Park
5. Kilauea Lighthouse
6. Waioli Mission
7. Maniniholo Dry Cave
8. Wet Caves
9. Kiahuna Plantation
10. Salt Pond
11. Hanapepe Canyon Lookout
12. Russian Fort
13. Menehune Ditch
14. Waimea Canyon Lookout
15. Kokee Museum
16. Kalalau Lookout

Beach, the number one resort area of the south shore. Poipu boasts a string of gleaming hotels and condominiums that are interspersed with eateries and miles of ivory beaches.

Just inland from Poipu awaits Koloa, the island's oldest sugar plantation and a quaint little town with renovated historic buildings. Open-air restaurants, tiny boutiques with colorful resort wear, a tempting family-owned bakery and ice creamery, and a mom-and-pop general store called Sueoka's are some of the irresistible attractions of Koloa, whose name, appropriately enough, means "long cane."

Heading west you find Hanapepe's fascinating salt ponds, the only ones of their kind in all Hawaii. Here saltmakers evaporate seawater to create salt just as their ancestors have for over 200 years. The old Hawaiian towns of Hanapepe, Lawai, Kalaheo, and Eleele stretch along the southern shoreline and offer plenty of local color in their casual shops and tidy residential communities. Farther west is Waimea, which was a favorite vacation spot for Hawaii's ancient alii as well as site of Captain James Cook's first landing in Hawaii in 1778. Yes, there are more excellent beaches to the west, where the isolated reaches of Barking Sands and Polihale invite you to stroll together down endless sands. Meanwhile, in the "high country" above Waimea, unusually cool forests invite outdoor lovers to camp, fish, and hike on the brink of a gaping chasm called Waimea Canyon.

Whatever your pleasure, each adventure is a delight on Kauai, your special island, where "some enchanted evening" happens every night.

SHOPPING: The compact capital of Lihue offers a fairly large range of shopping alternatives thanks to its large **Kukui Grove Center.** Here you'll find good prices on prints by local artists (**Stone's Gallery**) and budget aloha wear (**Hawaiian Wear Factory to You**). Its **Woolworth's** and **Long's Drugs** can handle your sundries needs, and **See You in China** presents a fine selection of gifts and crafts, including tie-dyed dresses and handmade muumuus starting at $50.

Wailua is home of the **Market Place at Coconut Plantation,** another enormous shopping emporium where you can find everything from elegant Niihau shell jewelry (the **Necklace Gallery**) to Hawaiian-style wind chimes (**Pottery Tree**). Farther north in Hanalei, find more fine island crafts at **Pua & Kawika's Place** and **Shanora of Kauai,** both in the **Ching Young Village Shopping Center.** While in Hanalei, check out the **Native Hawaiian Cultural Center,** where arts and crafts are sold by native Hawaiians.

When you're feeling playful, go buy and fly a kite from the **Hawaiian Kite Company,** one of the sweet little stores in Koloa town. The products in these restored boutiques are hard to resist, particularly the Old Koloa Town shirts at the **Logo Shop.** Although they're a bit expensive, the stores in Poipu's **Kiahuna Shopping Village** are worth a glance, particularly the elegant resort wear shop, **Pomare Fashions.**

ROMANTIC INTERLUDES: By land, sea, or air, Kauai is fun to explore. Try a little of each activity on the Garden Isle, a truly appropriate nickname for this South Pacific haven.

Whirlybirds give you a tremendous look at places that would otherwise be inaccessible on Kauai. Within an hour you can see all the highlights, from hidden valleys of Waimea Canyon to the cascades of Mt. Waialeale. Zoom over the Poipu coastline and ancient salt ponds of the south, or marvel from above at Lumahai Beach, where South Pacific was filmed. A one-hour tour costs about $100 per couple, and features narration, appropriate background music, and personal microphones for communication with the pilot. Reliable operations include **Blue Sky Aviation,** P.O. Box 724, Kilauea, HI (tel. 828-1334), **Na Pali Helicopters,** P.O. Box 3101, Lihue, HI 96766 (tel. 245-6959), and **Menehune Helicopter Tours,** 3222 Kuhio Hwy., Lihue HI 96766 (tel. 245-7705).

Kauai's only navigable river is the Wailua, and its banks are rich with blossoming ginger and burgeoning palms. Today you can chug up this idyllic waterway on a charming riverboat. Your destination is **Fern Grotto**, a series of yawning lava tubes curtained with giant tropical plants. This natural amphitheater provides a truly inspirational setting for couples in love, who can listen to "The Hawaiian Wedding Song" echoing through the ferns. Jolly entertainers strum ukuleles and croon happy Hawaiian melodies as you cruise up to the grotto and back. Cost is $16 per couple. Contact **Smith's Motor Boat Service**, P.O. Box 141, Kapaa, HI 96746 (tel. 822-7405). The Smith's twilight torchlight trip creates an especially romantic vision of this hallowed Hawaiian treasure, and various wedding packages are also available.

The **trail to Hanakapiai Beach** winds through groves of guavas and bananas, wanders past babbling brooks, and offers some of the island's most precious scenery. The two-mile trek makes the perfect day hike, beginning at Ke'e Beach on the north shore and ending at a prized beach flanked by razor-edged cliffs. The first mile of this ancient Hawaiian trail takes you up, up, up, but the climb is worth it, for from the edge of windswept cliffs you get a thrilling look at the Na Pali Coast. Then you head a mile down into Hanakapiai Valley, site of crystal ocean waters, perfect sands, enormous shade trees, and a bracing mountain stream. If you're looking for more adventure, follow the side trail from the beach into the lush hanging valley with its cascading waterfalls. Wild orchids, pungent guavas, sweet mangoes, and mountain apples surround you.

Another way to explore the inaccessible reaches of the Na Pali coast is on board a **Zodiac**, an inflatable rubber raft with a lot of power. Sit on the sides of the boat and let your able captain take you on a thrilling adventure, maneuvering into sea caves, across exotic reefs, and, if you're lucky, past schools of dolphins, flying fish, and sea turtles. Wear a swimsuit, bring your camera, and get ready for a rollicking ride! **Na Pali Zodiac Expeditions**, P.O. Box 456, Hanalei, HI 96714 (tel. 826-9722), offers half-day trips with snorkeling for $100 per couple. All-day trips with snorkeling plus a stop for lunch on a secluded beach go for $170 per couple.

"The Grand Canyon of the Pacific." That's what Mark Twain called **Waimea Canyon**, ten miles long, one mile wide, and 2,800-feet deep. Every lookout along Waimea Canyon Road inspires a slightly different reaction to this wonder of the world, and the layers of earth and vegetation seem to change colors throughout the day as the sunlight plays games with its ridges and ledges. Waimea Canyon Road ends at an equally awesome perch: the Kalalau Lookout, 4,120 feet above sea level. Dramatic cliffs, dense rain forests, shining waterfalls, and the never-ending sea spread out before you. On the way back down the hill, stop at delightful Kokee Lodge for a cozy drink by the roaring fireplace (tel. 335-6061).

Where do you go to really get away from it all? At the end of the main road (Highway 50) heading west there's a small marker pointing you left. Follow the signs along a bumpy cane-haul road, and sure enough, you'll find it: **Polihale Beach,** a remote state park flanked by mammoth cliffs and crashing surf. It's almost always sunny at this big beach, so bring along your visor for a beach experience par excellence. Buy your picnic provisions in Waimea, a half-hour's drive away, because Polihale is untouched by commercial enterprise. And if you're looking for the ultimate camping destination, pick up a free permit from the **State Park Office**, Box 1671, Lihue, HI 96766 (tel. 254-4444), and head west to this beach on the brink of the wilderness.

HONEYMOON HOTELS AND HIDEAWAYS: The oldest inhabited Hawaiian island offers some of the newest and most delightful accommodations this side of the Pacific, and they are grouped in three areas. The first-class resorts in sunny Poipu are ideally situated on a stretch of sandy beaches with gentle surf. Heading north takes you to the Wailua-Kapaa hub, a series of small country towns and fine oceanside accommodations near the Wailua River and Fern Grotto. The third destination is the

Princeville and Hanalei area, where toney resorts overlook Hanalei Bay and the spires of the Na Pali coast.

Expensive

The Waiohai Resort, R.R. 1, Box 174, Koloa, HI 96756 (tel. 808/945-6121; reservations: toll free 800/227-4700). This handsome seaside resort in Poipu is one of Hawaii's best hotels, hands down. Silk, bronze, teak, mahogany, and etched glass accent the interiors which include flowering courtyards and garden-like restaurants. The resort is uniquely shaped like a "W" to maximize the number of oceanview rooms, and your room is fashioned in the bold colors of the isles along with warm rattan and wood. Each of the 434 suites and rooms features a wet bar, refrigerator, sitting area, and big, private balcony. Bathrooms are spacious, with large closets and, most memorable of all, brass sinks. This place is dreamy; curl up with a couple of good books in the browsing library, then sip a love potion at the sunken island bar. Honeymoon package: Four days/three nights: $565 per couple. Includes welcome leis, continental breakfast in bed on the first morning, two logo beach towels, and a deluxe picnic basket for two.

Kauai Hilton and Beach Villas, 4331 Kauai Beach Dr., Lihue, HI 96766 (tel. 808/245-1955; reservations: toll free 800/445-8667). The swimming pools themselves are worth seeing, a veritable fantasyland of waterfalls and fountains that play around volcanic rock formations at this resort located midway between Wailua and Lihue. Set on 25 oceanside acres filled with lush gardens, exotic birds, and gentle palms, the 350-room hotel built in a dramatic horseshoe shape, has one main building of five floors and three adjacent buildings of two, three, and four floors. Reflecting the plantation-style architecture of the past, the main lobby is airy, with soaring floor-to-ceiling windows framing views of the gardens, pools, and the blue Pacific. Hotel rooms are fashioned in muted tones of mulberry ice, deep raspberry, and sea foam against an off-white background, and offer private lanais, sitting rooms, air conditioning, telephones, refrigerators, and color TV. In addition, the 150 one- and two-bedroom villas offer large living areas, fully equipped kitchens, and laundry facilities. Honeymoon package: Two days/one night (EP): rooms $169.40 per couple; villas $195.80 per couple. Includes king-size bed, champagne, orchid turndown, breakfast in bed, and a personal welcome from the manager.

Draped down a cliff by Hanalei Bay, the gargantuan **Sheraton Princeville Hotel,** P.O. Box 3069, Princeville, HI 96722 (tel. 808/826-9644; reservations: toll free 800/325-3535) on Kauai's north shore is terraced in order to give maximum exposure to the spectacular views of the bay and mountain peak known as Bali Hai in the distance. Special touches reflect the personalized hospitality of an old Hawaiian plantation home, including complimentary early morning coffee, a library, game tables, and afternoon tea service. Each room has a Hawaiian quilt on the bed, and the once-essential pie safe of 19th-century cooks (used for storing baked goods) has been adapted to house the latest in television design. Delicate pastels decorate the rooms, which feature private lanais, telephones, radio, full-length mirrors, and sitting areas. Three outstanding restaurants include the open-air Café Hanalei overlooking the bay, the country-style Hale Kapa and the supremely elegant signature restaurant called Nobles. If golf's your game, play a round together on the famous 27-hole Princeville Course, where every tee sports magnificent panoramas of the mountains and ocean. A couple of miles up the road awaits Princeville Center and its small assortment of shopping and dining experiences. Honeymoon package: None. Rates (EP): $132 to $192.50 per couple per night.

Moderate

Kiahuna Plantation, R.R. 1, Box 73, Koloa, HI 96756 (tel. 808/742-6411; reservations: toll free 800/367-7052). Looking for a beach house for two? Look no further than this penultimate Poipu condominium resort. The 200 shoreside acres are dotted with 333 lovely one- and two-bedroom cottages, and the best of these are perched right by the water. Warm greens and yellows brighten your cottage, and bamboo furniture adds a naturally tropical touch. Kiahuna spares no expense to make you comfortable, from the all-electric, fully equipped kitchens to the daily maid service. Don't look for a TV here; instead, Kiahuna encourages you to get outside and experience the glories of Poipu. Its famed 18-hole championship golf course was designed by Robert Trent Jones, Jr., and ten tennis courts make this the perfect place for the active set. Brennecke Beach is nearby for swimming, snorkeling, and scuba diving, and the resident surfing coach stands by to offer advice. Honeymoon package: None. Standard four day/three night package: $325 per couple. Includes one-bedroom condo, lei greeting, breakfast basket, and champagne.

Location is the big draw for **Poipu Beach Hotel,** R.R. 1, Box 174, Koloa, HI 96756 (tel. 808/724-1681; reservations: toll free 800/227-4700) a casual little getaway, whose three buildings, with a total of 142 guest rooms, are tucked away under a grove of palms right on Poipu Beach. Whether you face the pool, the ocean, or the mountains, all the rooms offer the same amenities, including open-air balconies, large dressing rooms, and small refrigerators. Best of all, your room features a well-equipped kitchenette, so you can fix a snack and get back outside quickly. If you prefer, breakfast, lunch, and dinner are offered in the restaurant, and a steak fry/buffet and Polynesian show heat things up every Tuesday. Wrap up your nights by dancing cheek-to-cheek in the Mahina Lounge as the waves crash right outside the windows. Honeymoon package: Four days/three nights: $290 per couple. Includes superior room, complimentary champagne, and welcoming leis. Upgrade to seven days/six nights: $557 per couple.

Coco Palms Resort Hotel, P.O. Box 631, Lihue, HI 96766 (tel. 808/822-4921; reservations: toll free 800/542-2626), a 45-acre resort, is nestled in a secluded coconut grove where Hollywood movie moguls have made several fantasy films. In fact, hundreds of couples get married and renew their vows at the Chapel in the Palms, originally built on the grounds for the movie *Sadie Thompson*. Set across from a one-mile stretch of white sand beach where the Wailua River meets Wailua Bay, Coco Palms offers 390 guest rooms, junior suites, suites, and thatched-roof cottages, interspersed with crystal lagoons and lava-rock waterfalls. An evening torch-lighting ceremony outside recalls the days when ancient alii strolled these hallowed grounds. Guest rooms have been newly refurbished in a cool, white-on-pastel motif with island rattan furnishings, and include exotic touches such as giant clam-shell basins in the bathrooms, plus air conditioning, color TV, and refrigerators. Some cottages offer tropical lanais and private garden hot tubs. Honeymoon package: Four days/three nights: $339 per couple January through March (peak season); $324 other times. Includes deluxe accommodations, champagne on arrival, fresh fruit basket, a remembrance gift from the staff, and the manager's cocktail party with special viewing area for torch-lighting ceremony. Upgrade to $695 per couple January through March; $680 other times. Includes King's Cottage accommodations, champagne, fruit basket, wine on the second day, luxury car, and manager's party.

With its unspoiled beauty and quiet serenity, **Hanalei Bay Resort,** P.O. Box 220, Hanalei, HI 96714 (tel. 808/826-6522; reservations: toll free 800/367-7052), is the perfect setting for pure relaxation. This sloping complex on Kauai's north shore features one-, two-, and three-bedroom low-rises that wind their way down to Hanalei Beach encompassing 20 acres. Explore the glorious gardens laced with gurgling streams. The resort itself boasts condominium apartments at their very best, including electric kitchens, large baths and living areas, rattan furniture, and island art on the walls. Princeville's lauded tennis and golf facilities are within walking distance, and if you're feeling even more active, horseback riding, snorkeling, and boogie-boarding are easily arranged. Ready to take it easy? Then grab your towels and loll around one of the swimming pools, or sip mai tais on the Bali Hai cocktail terrace on the top level. Honeymoon package: Four days/three nights (EP): $246.40 to $391.60 per couple. Includes lei greeting, continental breakfast on the first morning and champagne.

ROMANTIC RESTAURANTS: Kauai has scores of good restaurants, from mom-and-pop shops to fancy-dress establishments.

Expensive

Tamarind, Waiohai Resort, Poipu (tel. 742-9511). Deluxe dining in a world-class hotel means jackets for the men, but that's part of the attraction of this plush restaurant. A blend of mirrors and chrome works perfectly in tandem with earth colors of rusts and browns to create an atmosphere of tropical decadence. Settle back in your cushy bentwood chairs and enjoy the formal presentation, from fine cut-glass and gold-rimmed dishes to fresh flowers on every table. Order a different paté each night: It's always superb. Impeccable service accompanies such entrées as lamb marinated in mustard and garlic. Duckling, veal, lobster, and jumbo shrimp are all a real treat here. Be sure to save room for a temptation from the dessert and espresso carts. À la carte dinners range from $73 to $90 per couple plus drinks. Your dinner concludes with a complimentary liqueur served in a tiny chocolate cup. On Sundays, folks flock to the breezy Waiohai Terrace for a lavish champagne brunch featuring hundreds of items—from pineapples and papayas to omelets and fresh island seafood. All you can eat for $18.50 per person.

At **Nobels,** Sheraton Princeville Hotel, Princeville (tel. 826-9644), French doors lead you into a dining room of handpainted tile, fine chandeliers, leaded bevel glass, and archways touched with walnut. In this marvelous setting you dine on a masterful meal, be it saddle of venison with cognac cream sauce and a poached pear, or breast of duckling with black bing cherries. Everything is artistically presented, right down to the rosettes of butter on your bread plate. For appetizers, go for the goose-liver brandy soufflé with brioche—out of this world! A dessert tray tops it all off in style. The fixed dinner price per couple is $78 plus drinks.

Moderate

One look at **Bull Shed,** 796 Kuhio Hwy., Waipouli (tel. 822-3791) and you'll understand why it's an island tradition. The rustic A-frame restaurant is cradled by the curving shoreline and offers dreamy views of the sparkling Pacific. Inside, an airy design of exposed wood gives the place a relaxed, homey feeling, and it's easy to find a large table where the two of you can quaff some cocktails and gaze at the waves. Specializing in steak and seafood, Bull Shed offers such fine entrées as fresh fish, tenderloin fillet, steak and lobster combination, prime rib, and New Zealand rack of lamb. The salad bar is big and impressive. Hot rolls and rice come with the dinners, which cost about $24 for two.

Come as you are to **Brennecke's Beach Broiler,** Poipu (tel. 742-7588), right across from Poipu beach. Settled in on the second floor, you get wonderful aerial views of water while you dive into scrumptious seafood. Colorful petunias and geraniums decorate the pretty flower boxes by the window, beyond which lies that resplendent Poipu shoreline. You can actually see the cooks kiawe-broiling your yummy meals, which range from fresh fish to beach burgers, plus buckets of fresh clams, luscious island fruit, and great exotic drinks. Save room for the desserts—creamy homemade gelati (ice cream) and delicious island sherbets in flavors like guava and mango. Light lunches cost $16 per couple. Dinner costs about $28 per couple plus drinks.

Step back to the days when sugar was king in **JJ's Broiler,** 2971 Haleko Rd., Lihue (tel. 245-3841), a grand, century-old plantation home. Kauai's original (and many say, best) steak house, it lures many residents back time and time again. Perhaps the appeal is the softly lit atmosphere of the stylish courtyard, filled with European-style statues and soft green ferns. Even more alluring is JJ's unforgettably delicious Slavonic steak, the only one of its kind on the island. At $21 per couple, it comes with garlic bread and as many trips to the soup-and-salad bar as you can handle. Mainland chilled beef, lobster, scallops, prime rib, beef kabobs, crab legs, and mahimahi are all quite good. You can order the soup-and-salad bar only for $14 per couple.

Since 1948 **Green Garden,** Hanapepe (tel. 335-5422), located in a family home has served a menu of local favorites with a spirit of aloha. And what a garden it is! There are orchids on every table and an assortment of lush, tropical plants raised by the owner herself. You can order just about anything here: home-style soups, salad, vegetables, rolls, sandwiches, steaks, Chinese food, and more. Kiawe-broiled selections run from $11 to $28 for two, served with soup, salad, coffee, or tea. Other dinners are $8 to $12 per couple. Best of all is the *lilikoi* (passion fruit) chiffon pie, a legend in these parts. A perfect stop on your way to Waimea Canyon.

Once a plantation home and now a botanical wonderland, **Plantation Gardens,** Kiahuna Plantation, Poipui (tel. 742-1695), welcomes honeymooners into its tropical setting and offers wonderful open-air views of the surrounding gardens, ponds, and palm trees. The fresh catch of the day is the best choice here, be it onaga, opakapaka, ulua, ono, or mahimahi. Caesar salad is a super way to start, and the chicken teriyaki with vegetables and rice is tasty. Entrées cost between $28 and $34 per couple, and dinner comes with salad, soup, veggies, and bread. Plantation Gardens is well known for its Naughty Hula pie, a sinfully sweet dessert with macadamia nuts. Settle into the Poi Pounder Room after dinner for a drink amid Polynesian artifacts, or outside in the garden bar.

Flames of Fantasy Luau, Kauai Hilton, near Lihue (tel. 245-1955), an open-air feast for the senses, is definitely Kauai's best luau. A shell-lei greeting, contemporary Hawaiian music, and mai tai reception kick things off, followed by the spectacular torch-lighting ceremony and unearthing of the imu. A casual Hawaiian fashion show entertains you as you dig into the lavish buffet of lomilomi salmon, sautéed ono, kalua pig, poi, fresh fruits and greens, pineapple cake, and more. After dinner the seaside sky lights up with a musical trip through Hawaiian history starring some of the island's freshest young singers and dancers. The whole affair costs $36 for two.

Inexpensive

A rustic inn, **Kokee Lodge,** Kokee State Park (tel. 335-6061) offers hearty breakfasts and lunches daily, enough to fuel you for those invigorating walks through the surrounding high country. Situated midway between Waimea Canyon and Kalalau Lookout, the lodge is set in a grove of pine trees with a dozen furnished cabins nearby for those who decide to stay. Dinner, which is available on the weekends for about $18 a couple, includes steak, ribs, Cornish game hens stuffed with mushrooms and rice, mahimahi, and vegetarian fettuccine. Mud pie is high on the dessert list, and cocktails are best around the fireplace in the lounge. For two, breakfast costs $8 and lunch is $9.

For good fun and great food in a casual setting, try **Koloa Broiler,** Koloa (tel. 742-9122), with the big open windows. You cook your own entrée, be it barbecued chicken, mahimahi, steak, beef kebobs, or hamburgers, all of which come with a salad bar and baked beans. A couple of burgers at lunch adds up to $7, while dinner prices range from $12 to $16 for two. Relax in the roomy, rustic bar before and after your meal, and they'll whip up the best mai tai you've ever tasted.

Banana Joe's, Kilauea (tel. 828-1092) is a tropical fruit farm with such sightseeing refreshers as fruit frosties, which are $3 for two, and cut pineapple for $1 a pound. While you're visiting this roadside stand, take a tour of Joe's glorious groves. **Tropical Taco,** Kapaa Shopping Center (tel. 822-3622) makes inexpensive Mexican food with a creative Hawaiian touch. Dig into all your favorites: enchiladas, tostadas, tacos, and burritos. For dessert, try a tortilla with apple pie filling and cheese. Dinner for two costs $16 plus drinks. And believe it or not, you can round up some of the best Mexican food in the United States at **Keoki's Paradise,** Kiahuna Shopping Village in Poipu (tel. 742-7534). Start off at the taco bar in the lounge, where appetizers run $3 to $10, then move on to the restaurant for fresh fish and fine steaks ($7 to $19 for entrées; the huge prime rib at $16.95 is a steal).

NIGHTLIFE: When you're ready to boogie, try **Park Place,** Harbor Village Shopping Center, Nawiliwili (tel. 245-5775), with the largest dance floor on Kauai. Top-40 tunes and a video system enliven the triangular bar, where happy hour lasts all the way to midnight.

Another longtime Kauai favorite is **Club Jetty** in Nawiliwili (tel. 245-4970), which features live entertainment Wednesday through Saturday. In Hanalei, you can experience Old Hawaii at **Tahiti Nui** (tel. 826-6277). Friday and Saturday nights, there's live entertainment, ranging from Hawaiian tunes strummed on the ukulele to rock bands from Honolulu. Shell necklaces and primitive paintings of hula dancers hang on the wall, and "Auntie Louise," a Tahitian, helps make sure everyone has fun.

5. The Big Island

Located in the south of the Hawaiian archipelago, this isle is roughly twice as large as all the other islands combined. Although the island's official name is Hawaii, it is referred to as the Big Island, to differentiate it from the state. Because it is also the youngest of the Hawaiian chain, the Big Island bubbles and breathes through its active volcanoes, which occasionally send rivers of molten lava down to the sea. This is a vital, vivid landscape filled with rushing waterfalls, teeming rain forests, fields ripe with fruits and flowers, and pastures full of horses and cattle. You can bet that such a diverse island holds an equally wide variety of activities and accommodations for your honeymooning pleasure.

The Big Island was created by five volcanoes: Mauna Kea, Kohala, Hualalai, Mauna Loa, and Kilauea, the latter two of which are still active today. Mauna Loa ("long mountain") stands at 13,677 feet, and its extinct neighbor Mauna Kea ("white mountain") is the world's tallest seamount, peaking at 13,796 feet. These two monoliths rise from the center of the island, and around them circle six very distinctive districts. Allow plenty of time for your explorations: Because the Big Island is about 93 miles by 73 miles, it takes most of a day to drive around it.

When you explore the Big Island, you're discovering Hawaii's sacred past. You can see it in the petroglyphs carved into rocks along the Kona Coast. You can feel it at a 13th-century leeward landmark called Mookini, which was the birthplace of King Kamehameha the Great, unifier of the islands, and at Pu'u Kohola heiau, built by the king himself. You can sense it at the Kau beaches where Polynesian explorers landed their canoes as early as A.D. 550. You can hear it in the legends of the volcanoes, and see it in the dances through which island residents honor the gods.

How do you explore such a vast and varied island?

Perhaps you'll want to begin with a tour of the county seat of **Hilo,** a charming combination of the old and the new. Get up with the fishermen and catch the multiethnic action at the Suisan Market fish auction. Poke around botanical gardens full of exotic plants and flowers. Find out nutty secrets about growing macadamias at the **Mauna Loa** orchards, and pick up some free samples of those tasty little gems. Browse through the shops of downtown Hilo, then learn about the island's steadfast missionaries at the **Lyman House Museum.**

Another day you'll want to take a drive up the Hilo Coast to jungles thick with monster-size heliconia, bamboo, ginger, bird of paradise, and the star of the show, a 420-foot cascade called **Akaka Falls.** Farther north is **Waipio Valley,** a broad, deep, rain forest surrounded by 2,000-foot-high cliffs. Its twin **waterfalls of Hiilawe** tumble 1,300 feet down to a river, which in olden times was so well stocked that men caught fish with their bare hands. Hop on a four-wheel drive and explore the black sand beach

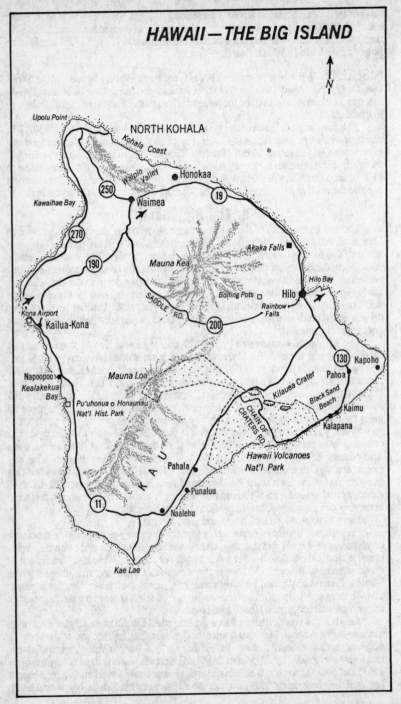

and inner reaches of this lush paradise, once a thriving Hawaiian community before *tsunamis* (tidal waves) robbed the valley of its civilization.

It's a totally different world on the expansive Kohala-Kona coast, where world-class resorts rise up amid fields of ancient lava flows. Play golf and tennis on championship courses by the sea. Visit **Hulihee Palace** in Kailua Village, where King David Kalakaua used to vacation. Stop by **Kealakekua Bay,** where Captain James Cook died in 1779. Nearby, observe the workings of the **Royal Kona Coffee Mill and Museum,** and share a cup of that exceptional brew. Catch the marlin of your dreams in the fabled waters of Kona, site of an annual international deep-sea fishing contest. Doze on beaches of green and ivory, and be back in time for sunset from your oceanview suite. More Big Island adventuring takes you to the summit of steaming **Kilauea Volcano,** where you can walk and drive around primitive lava landscapes.

If you're looking for a "horse of a different color," you'll want to mosey around the pasturelands of **Waimea,** with its rolling hills and soft pine trees. Learn about the life of the paniolo, eat a hearty country meal, and watch a rip-snortin' rodeo, Hawaiian-style. It's all waiting for you on the Big Island, where super-big thrills enliven your vacation for two.

SHOPPING: Sally Mermel calls her establishment **The Most Irresistible Shop in Hilo,** and souvenir lovers will agree after perusing her various goods: ceramics, postcards, hand-screened T-shirts for $20, koa wood products, books, local jams, and so on. The quaint old downtown section of Hilo also features the **Potter's Gallery,** where handmade wares go on display and sale. The newer section of Hilo offers **Kaikoo Hilo Mall,** where the **Book Gallery** presents an extensive Hawaiiana collection, as well as **Prince Kuhio Plaza,** a shopping center with reliable department stores like **Liberty House.**

Posters, books, slides, postcards, and other memorabilia relating to Kilauea are assembled at the **Hawaii Volcanoes National Park Visitor Center.** Next door is the **Volcano Arts Center,** absolutely the best place in Hawaii for paintings, sculptures, jewelry, and trinkets by top island craftspeople.

Looking for some paniolo duds? In Waimea, the **Paddock Shop** has belt buckles, cowboy hats, and Parker Ranch T-shirts. Their unusual feather hatbands cost $30 and up. Two well-known Hawaiian fashion boutiques also have outlets in Waimea: **Reyn's** and **Alfred Shaheen.**

When in Kona don't miss the **Kona Arts & Crafts Gallery** and the **Akona Kai Gallery,** offering one-of-a-kind artworks small and large. Also in Kona is the **Shellery,** presenting a dazzling selection of gifts from the sea, as well as **Original Maui Divers,** home of colored coral jewelry. Both these stores are located in the **Kona Inn Shopping Village.** The shopping arcade in the Hotel King Kamehameha is a fun place to scout out souvenirs, including **Gifts for All Seasons,** where Mrs. DeAguiar boasts a unique combination of goods from Hawaii and the Philippines. Across the street is the **Seaside Mall,** where the **Muumuu Factory to You** tempts you with its low prices, and **Butterfly Boutique** has sun-and-fun wear for those bright Kohala Coast days.

ROMANTIC INTERLUDES: This island of life is erupting with romantic escapades to fill your days and nights.

Kilauea, the world's largest active volcano, is surrounded by legends and lore that enhance an already dramatic landscape. The fiery goddess Pele is said to live in the seething abyss, and her moods regulate the changes in climate and geography. As you stroll along some of the 130 miles of paths around this national park, it's easy to get caught up in the stories attached to the area. The **Kilauea Visitor Center,** Volcano, HI 96718 (tel. 965-8936), fills you in on the history of the volcano, and an observatory displays the seismographic equipment used in detecting the tremors. If your timing is right, you'll get a chance to see Pele do her thing during one of the frequent eruptions. Park rangers will direct you to the safest spot for viewing her pyrotechnics. There's even a volcano hotline (tel. 967-7977). Wear warm clothes when you visit the volcano. It tends to get very chilly at 4,000 feet! Also, be sure not to take rocks from the park; it's considered to be very bad luck to do so. In fact, in the visitor center you can peruse a whole display of letters written by people who brought lava rocks home and suffered the consequences.

The best way to watch the volcano in action, and to tour the Big Island in general is by **Whirlybirds** that will spirit you away to such far reaches as Puu Oo vent, a real hot spot which is miles off the beaten track. Flightseeing also offers rare aerial views of the 442-foot Akaka Falls, sea cliffs, ancient Hawaiian ruins, and panoramic ranchlands. The cost ranges from $200 to $500 per couple, including in-flight narration by a knowledgeable pilot and background music to sweeten the views. Try **Kenai Helicopters,** P.O. Box 4118, Kailua-Kona, HI 96745 (tel. 885-7361), and **Big Island Air,** P.O. Box 1476, Kailua-Kona, HI 96740 (tel. 329-4868).

Set at the base of Mt. Hualalai, an 8,721-foot dormant volcano, the sunny port of **Kona** is full of sightseeing goodies. King David Kalakaua fell in love with the area and summered at **Hulihee Palace,** a beautifully restored building now open as a museum. Hawaii's missionaries also cherished Kona, where they built their first church, **Mokuaikaua.** You can still visit this prim little New England–style house of worship, which dates back to 1827. Then take a turn through **Puuhonua o Honaunau** (the Place of Refuge), where ancient lawbreakers retreated for protection from their crimes. This highly spiritual site has been restored and preserved as a national historical park, and offers demonstrations of traditional Hawaiian arts, crafts, and games.

Head up the hill to the **Royal Kona Coffee Mill and Museum,** where that wonderfully rich bean is grown and harvested. Go down to the sea for a visit to **Kealakekua Bay,** where Capt. James Cook was killed in 1779. Then stroll through **Kona Gardens,** a botanical park full of tropical plants, sacred sites, crafts demonstrations, and assorted displays of Hawaiiana. Contact **Kona Coast Activities,** P.O. Box 5397, Kailua-Kona, HI 96740 (tel. 367-5105).

From the first Spanish immigrants, called *espagnol,* came the first Hawaiian cowboys, called paniolos, that rare breed of cowpokes who work the tropical ranges. In the shadow of Mauna Kea in little Waimea town you'll find the **Parker Ranch,** whose 224,000 acres make it one of the largest privately owned spreads in America. Here the paniolos sing Hawaiian songs, wear aloha shirts, and sport flowers in their hatbands, while leading the rough-and-tumble life of six generations. The 15-minute presentation at the Parker Ranch Visitor Center fills you in on the days when John Palmer Parker jumped a whaling ship and spearheaded this 140-year-old legacy. Down the road is the **Kamuela Museum,** offering more down-home memorabilia, plus the Parker Ranch Broiler, home of a super-duper paniolo burger. Contact **Parker Ranch,** P.O. Box 458, Kamuela, HI 96743 (tel. 885-7655).

Each day at about 8 a.m., scores of fisherfolk leave Kailua-Kona pier in search of buried treasure: **fish,** that is, and lots of 'em! The waters off the Kona coast are world famous for their abundance of *opakapaka* (pink snapper), *ulua* (jack crevalle), *ono* (wahoo), *ahi* (tuna), *mahimahi* (dolphin fish), and the grand prize, the Pacific blue marlin, tipping the scales as high as 1,000 pounds. Charter a boat to share with others or for your very own. While you're at sea, take time to catch a few rays, snap some photos, eat your picnic lunch, and drink some beer. And don't forget to work on those great "fish stories" you'll tell the folks back home. Contact the **Kona Activities Center,** P.O. Box 1035, Kailua-Kona, HI 96740 (tel. 329-3171) or the **Kona Charters Skippers Association,** 75-5663 Palani Rd., Kailua-Kona, HI 96740 (tel. 367-8047). They'll set up the two of you for a full day for about $500 exclusive, and $125 shared, including tackle and bait.

Green sand? No kidding! Deposits of olivine crystals add a definite emerald hue to **Green Sand Beach,** a southeastern destination near South Point Park. Summer makes the best time to swim here, as the winter seas can be rough, but all year long you can sunbathe in privacy on green sand. All it takes is a two-mile hike from the boat ramp.

Gorgeous **black sand beaches** line the east coast from South Point up to Kalapana, including Punaluu Beach Park, Harry K. Brown Beach Park, Isaac Hale Beach Park, and Kaimu Beach Park. On the west coast, two miles of black sand grace Kiholo Bay, and Honomalino offers good swimming and snorkeling. Richardson's black sand beach is the finest of its kind on Hilo Bay.

HONEYMOON HOTELS AND HIDEAWAYS: Everything's big on the Big Island, including the selection of places to stay. By far the most unusual destination is the Volcano House, the sole hotel by Kilauea caldera and a perfect base of operations as you explore the national park.

The Kona and Kohala coast is the resort center of the island.

Enjoying more sunny days than anywhere else in Hawaii, the breezy Kohala coast makes a predictably perfect locale for your honeymoon. Its stunning beaches and gentle waves are ideal for water sports of all kinds, such as swimming, snorkeling, sailing, and surfing, while the cool countryside of Waimea is just 12 miles away for hiking, horseback riding, hunting, and exploring. Nearby sports buffs are lured to Kona's waters in particular for deep-sea fishing, which is the best in the whole state.

Expensive

Kona Village Resort, P.O. Box 1299, Kaupulehu-Kona, HI 96745 (tel. 808/ 325-5555; reservations: toll free 800/367-5290). Very few maps show Kaupulehu. Like all the best places, it's hidden, and its charm lies in what it does NOT have: big shopping arcades, tour groups, and crowds. Instead, this hypnotic haven drips with old-fashioned charm, as it creates an historic Polynesian village around a picturesque bay. One hundred plush, thatched cottages (called *hales*) surround peaceful lagoons and Kaupulehu's natural sandy beach. No room phone, no radio, no TV, but instead, a wide range of amenities in secluded surroundings. Recreational facilities include sailboats, outrigger canoes, snorkeling gear, tennis, and excursions on the resort's 27-foot glass-bottom boat. At day's end, torches are lit along the beach and flames flicker on the bay: Beautiful! Honeymoon package: Five days/four nights: $1,625 per couple. Includes round-trip transportation from Keahole-Kona Airport, lei greeting, welcoming rum punch, champagne upon arrival, breakfast, lunch, and dinner daily, three-hour snorkeling sail to a secluded beach or two one-hour massages, unlimited use of tennis courts, glass-bottom boat trips, and an 11-by-14-inch art reproduction of your "Honeymoon Hale."

Since its opening in 1965, the **Mauna Kea Beach Hotel,** P.O. Box 218, Kohala Coast, HI 96743 (tel. 808/882-7222; reservations: toll free 800/228-3000), has maintained an international reputation for excellence that has attracted a steady flow of discriminating guests such as Robert Wagner, Meryl Streep, Steven Spielberg, George Lucas, and Danny Kaye. Best-selling author Danielle Steele, a recent visitor, enjoyed the Mauna Kea so much that she used it as a honeymoon setting in her new novel. The award-winning design of this ultimate retreat capitalizes on a hillside location, with terracing to make the most of panoramic views of Kaunaoa Bay. Interior walkways and courtyards open to refreshing trade winds, and throughout the buildings and grounds you see over 1,000 ancient and contemporary works of art from Asia and the Pacific, including a majestic 7th-century Indian Buddha and 30 stunning handmade Hawaiian quilts. Your room is brightened by rainbow-inspired decor and large, floral lithographs by Hawaii's Lloyd Sexton, and as you stand arm-in-arm on your private lanai you get views of the Kohala coastline, the Kohala Mountains, or Mauna Kea. An 18-hole golf course covers an ancient lava flow and offers panoramas of the Pacific from every green. Honeymoon package: Five days/four nights (EP): $1,566.40 to $1,654.40 per couple. Includes full breakfast and dinner, champagne, floral bouquet, orchid turndown, sunset cruise, manager's reception, and a special take-home gift.

Commanding a three-mile shoreline of bays and beaches, the **Mauna Lani Bay Hotel,** P.O. Box 4000, Kohala Coast, HI 96743 (tel. 808/885-6622; reservations: toll free 800/992-7987), is far away from other hotels. Pick your own secluded cove and make the rest of the world go away! Done in a bold, contemporary design, this arrow-shaped, six-story hotel points to the crystal-clear waters of Makaiwa Bay, where swimming, diving, and boating are all excellent. Shady coconut and milo trees, springwater pools, lush green golf courses, and a sea of brilliant bougainvillea turn the chocolate-covered lava landscape into a rich oasis of luxury. Your room is fashioned with soft beige carpeting, teak and rattan furnishings, mahogany shutters, colors of off-white, gray, and rose, and accents of burgundy or blue, all beneath a 9½-foot-high ceiling. Comfort is the word here, with soft chairs, a couch, a marble coffee table, an oversize color TV, a dry bar and refrigerator, a clock radio, a guest-room safe, a spacious closet, a private lanai, and air conditioning. Honeymoon package: Six days/five nights (EP): $1,320 per couple. Includes oceanview room with private balcony, limousine transfer to and from the airport, champagne upon arrival, fruit basket, and a remembrance from the staff.

Moderate

One of Hawaii's most spectacular resorts, the **Kona Surf Resort,** 78-128 Ehukai St., Kailua-Kona, HI 96740 (tel. 808/322-3411; reservations: toll free 800/367-8011), covers 15 acres of natural and man-made delights at the edge of Keauhou Bay near Kona. Rivers of ancient lava laid the foundation for this seaside resort, a modern white design enlivened by emerald shade trees and thousands of flowering plants. An open-air design invites paradise inside as well, as waterfalls dance down lava rocks and unhindered breezes rustle giant ferns. The hotel goes out of its way to make your honeymoon fun, with a fabulous pool-slide, fitness programs, water sports, jogging and hiking trails, Hawaiian arts and crafts, golf at the 27-hole Keauhou championship course, three Laykold tennis courts, and volleyball. After a sauna and massage, slip into your private sunken bathtub and talk about tomorrow's plans. Each of the 537 rooms features a private lanai, color TV, radio, courtesy coffee-maker, and all-day room service. Honeymoon package: none. Room rates: $90 to $140 per couple per night.

Named after the great king who lived and died on the Big Island, the **Hotel King Kamehameha,** 75-5660 Palani Rd., Kailua-Kona, HI 96740 (tel. 808/329-2911; reservations: toll free 800/227-4700), in the heart of Kailua-Kona, is rich in Hawaiiana, and it houses an extensive collection of artifacts, including a restored *heiau* (shrine). Two six-story towers flank an air-conditioned shopping arcade. To the east, Mt. Hualalai rises up more than 8,000 feet, while at its foot the sandy coves of Kamakahonu Bay offer the best swimming, scuba, snorkeling, and sunbathing in town. Your room offers a private balcony, air conditioning, refrigerator, TV, and sitting area. Die-hard tennis fans rave about the hotel's video machine for stroke analysis, and the 18-hole Keauhou-Kona Golf Course is a short drive away. Honeymoon package: Four days/three nights: $650 per couple. Includes deluxe room, chilled champagne, tropical fruit basket, unlimited free tennis, plus dinner for two at Moby Dick's or a dinner and show at the hotel's bayside luau.

Kona Hilton Beach and Tennis Resort, P.O. Box 1179, Kailua-Kona, HI 96745 (tel. 808/329-3111; reservations: toll free 800/445-8667). The rugged lava-rock rim of Kailua Bay sets the scene for this hotel's unique architecture, with sweeping balconies following the contour of the mountains. Lush landscapes of exotic plants and fish-filled ponds await outside, while inside the 452 guest rooms and suites offer contemporary Polynesian decor of dark woods and tropical colors. From your private lanai you can see the gardens, Kailua Bay, or Kailua-Kona Village, and your room comes with air conditioning, refrigerator, color TV with a movie channel, coffeemaker, and his-and-her dressing areas. Dine and dance by the sea in one of the four restaurants and lounges. Honeymoon package (EP): $108 per couple per night. Includes deluxe room, champagne, honeymoon certificate, welcome letter, free cocktails for two in the Windjammer Lounge, orchid turndown, American breakfast with room service, and a newspaper in the morning.

Inexpensive

Volcano House, Hawaii Volcanoes National Park, Volcano, HI 96718 (tel. 808/967-7321; reservations: toll free 800/334-8484). Overlooking the very rim of creation, this one-of-a-kind hotel perches on the edge of active Kilauea crater, and is just a few steps away from the visitor center. It offers a large lounge furnished with deep-leather couches and chairs, with a floor-to-ceiling lava-rock fireplace that welcomes guests and warms the chill of the air at 4,200 feet above sea level. Of the 37 rooms, all the deluxe and most of the superior front the crater, while the lower-priced rooms are located in a separate building. The rooms are smallish, and their country-inn decor is simple and attractive, with wall-to-wall carpeting but no TV, radio, or (needless to say) air conditioning. A steam-vent sauna helps you unwind in natural style. Honeymoon package: None. Rates (EP): $40.70 to $52.80 per couple per night.

ROMANTIC RESTAURANTS: From fresh-grown fruits and vegetables to filet mignon for two, the Big Island boasts a bonanza of fine foods served in restaurants both casual and cosmopolitan. Bon appetit!

Expensive

Dining Pavilion, Mauna Kea Beach Hotel, Kohala Coast (tel. 882-7222). This freestanding, wood-frame structure seats 300 guests throughout three levels, and the open-air design offers you glorious views of Kaunaoa Bay. There's a fascinating blend of the foreign and familiar here. For instance, Thai china table settings reflect the restaurant's international scope, while rose-colored linens remind you that nearby Waimea is the rose capital of Hawaii. The daily menu reflects the market's best offerings, and every evening you can choose from such continental masterpieces as a hearty wienerschnitzel and tender veal medallions with butter noodles. You'll love the imaginative preparations of island foods, such as leg of lamb with Maui onions, banana and papaya soup, and sautéed mahimahi with capers and limes. Dinner costs about $80 for two, plus drinks. Folks flock in from miles around to eat their fill at the big luncheon buffet by the sea, which costs $31 (hotel guests) or $33 (nonguests) per couple.

Tiare Restaurant, Sheraton Royal Waikoloa, Kohala Coast (tel. 885-6789). Make your grand entrance through an etched-glass hallway as the heavenly strains of a harpist signal your arrival. You've come to one of the island's best restaurants, where fine French service is combined with an intimate atmosphere of crystal candelabras and plush gold-and-aqua decor. Appetizers of caviar, escargots, and lobster are all delicious beyond words. For $26 the chateaubriand printanier is specially prepared for two and served with fresh vegetables, potatoes, and béarnaise sauce. Other excellent entrées are the succulent roast duckling Waialae and the flamed steak Madagascar. Sip a selection from the extensive wine list and, after dinner, try a liqueur served in a chocolate cup, plucked from an ornamental brass tree especially for your pleasure. The shimmering Tiare Lounge offers live music before and after your meal. Dinner for two costs $90 plus drinks.

Moderate

The Pottery, 75-5995 Kuakini Hwy., Kona (tel. 329-2277). The owners of this candlelit inn want you to remember them in years to come, so they give you the pot in which your dinner was prepared! As the name implies, this homespun restaurant is a pottery as well, and on the wood-paneled walls are displays of handmade bowls, teapots, platters, and other ceramic delights that you can purchase at meal's end. Try something out of the steak kiln, or order the Cornish game hen, presented to you in a clay pot. All entrées come with salad, rice or potato, bread, and fresh vegetables. Look at your coffee mug, because it just may be a collector's item. Dinner for two in this creative hideaway costs from $24 to $35 plus drinks.

Huggo's, 75-5828 Kaha Kai Dr., Kona (tel. 329-1493). Dine by the water's edge and savor the expansive views of the waves washing up on the black lava rocks. Some say there's no better place to watch the sunset over Kailua Bay. One thing's certain: Huggo's offers the perfect forum for scrumptious seafood like oysters on the half shell, or such fresh catches of the day as opakapaka and mahimahi. Another favorite is barbecued shrimp as well as steaks, prime rib, and lobster. The super salad bar has a great variety of accompaniments, and the dressings are especially unique. Weekends you'll find live musical entertainment in the lounge. Dinner ranges from $16 to $40 for two plus drinks.

Kona Hilton Luau, Kailua-Kona (tel. 329-3111). A treasured Hawaiian tradition comes alive on the majestic Kona coastline. This open-air affair begins with an aloha shell-lei greeting and a good-hearted hour of *okole maluna!* (bottom's up!) in a romantic coconut grove. The featured entrée—roast kalua pig—is raised from the ground during the imu ceremony, and then you dine on the celebrated Hawaiian and oriental delicacies of the luau feast, from "three-finger" poi to yummy haupia pudding. Flames of torchlight flicker against the night sky as the Polynesian revue captivates you with South Pacific songs and dances. For two, it costs $62.

The SS James Makee, Kona Surf Resort, Kona (tel. 322-3411) invites you to gaze at the glorious sunset while sipping cocktails from the terrace. Dinner in the restaurant is notable for its fresh catch of the day, and costs about $40 per couple plus drinks. **Parker Ranch Broiler,** Waimea (tel. 885-7366) takes you to the world of the paniolo with "90/10" hamburgers ($8 for two) plus steak sandwiches, "Very Portuguese" bean soup, and missionary seafood chowder. Dinner runs about $25 per couple, and you can dine by views of lush green pastures. For dining and dancing, try **Mitchells,** Keauhou Shopping Village, Kona (tel. 322-9966). They feature live music nightly, and dinner is about $30 per couple plus drinks.

Inexpensive

KK Tei, 1550 Kamehameha Hwy., Hilo (tel. 961-3791). A taste of the Orient comes to the Big Island capital. Choose from several surroundings, including a serene Japanese garden where you sit on the floor, and a more traditional dining room. American food is available, but we recommend going the Japanese route at this superb teahouse. Tempura and teriyaki entrées are good here, and all dinners come with such side dishes as miso soup, delectable sushi, and steaming rice. Indulge yourselves in a glass of hot sake (rice wine) and warm up your special honeymoon dinner. Price for two is about $16 plus drinks.

Old Kailua Cantina, 75-5669 Alii Dr., Kona (tel. 329-8226). Kailua Bay is your view at this al fresco restaurant, where meals are memorable. Kick up your heels with a pitcher of margaritas to start things off in south-of-the-border style. Ever tried a margarita with fresh bananas? Or pineapple? How about papaya? At $9.95 a pitcher, this is the place to experiment. Chips and salsa are complimentary, and there's a wide choice of Mexican beers. Try the shrimp quesadilla appetizer, a tasty combination of seafood and spice. The Mauna Loa burrito is made with spicy pork, rice, beans, and cheese in a flour tortilla, and fresh island fish, meat, and chicken dishes are all available. Dinner costs about $15 per couple plus drinks.

Teshima Restaurant, Kealakekua-Kona (tel. 322-9140). For comfy decor and local-style dining, try this little gem on Hwy. 11, open since 1943. As soon as you walk in, you're treated like family, as Mrs. Teshima escorts you to your table and welcomes you with free sake. Relax in your booth over such Japanese dishes as shrimp tempura and teishoku with miso soup. They stuff a giant omelet full of spicy Portuguese sausage and fried rice, a popular combination with regular guests. Sashimi is particularly good here, but you can order just about anything and be guaranteed of the Teshima touch. Dinner for two costs $17 per couple, plus drinks.

Chapter VIII

MISSOURI: LAKE OF THE OZARKS

1. Practical Facts
2. Romantic Interludes
3. Honeymoon Hotels and Hideaways
4. Romantic Restaurants

IF YOUR IDEA OF A PERFECT HONEYMOON includes outstanding recreation and the great outdoors, Lake of the Ozarks will fit the bill. Set in the very heart of Missouri, the area lures visitors to its untouched forested hills and dramatic bluffs at water's edge. From any point along its shoreline, the lake seems moderately sized and relatively secluded, but it is in fact 129 miles long and boasts 1,300 miles of weaving, wooded shoreline—longer than either Lake Michigan or the California shorelines.

Lake of the Ozarks traces its beginnings back to 1929 when the Union Electric Company dammed the Osage River to tap its hydroelectric power potential. In the early years, the region was known for its fishing camps and shoreside cabins. In the 1940s and 1950s, small resorts with a few cottages began dotting the shoreline and it wasn't long before the large developers moved in.

Numerous communities have sprung up around the lake in the past 50 years. Lake Ozark, the site of Bagnell Dam, has grown from a campsite for construction workers to a bustling tourist town with historic buildings, restaurants, arcades, and excursion boat and plane rides. Just down U.S. Highway 54 on the east side of the lake is Osage Beach, a progressive young community experiencing tremendous expansion.

Camdenton, on the southern end of the lake, is the Camden County Seat and is another thriving young community. On the west side of the lake are the communities of Sunrise Beach, Laurie, and Gravois Mills, all offering a variety of interesting shopping, good dining, and beautiful views.

The Lake of the Ozarks draws over 2.5 million visitors every year and has developed into one of the premier honeymoon destinations in middle America. Yet despite its booming growth, the region still offers seclusion. Take directly to the lake for waterskiing, parasailing, boating, fishing, sailing, and jet skiing (marinas and resorts offering boat rentals are ample), or, you may prefer a scenic cruise aboard an excursion boat or a bird's-eye view of the lake from a helicopter or seaplane ride.

There is plenty to do on land as well. Lake of the Ozarks has earned a reputation for fine dining, golfing, shopping, entertainment, attractions, and Missouri's

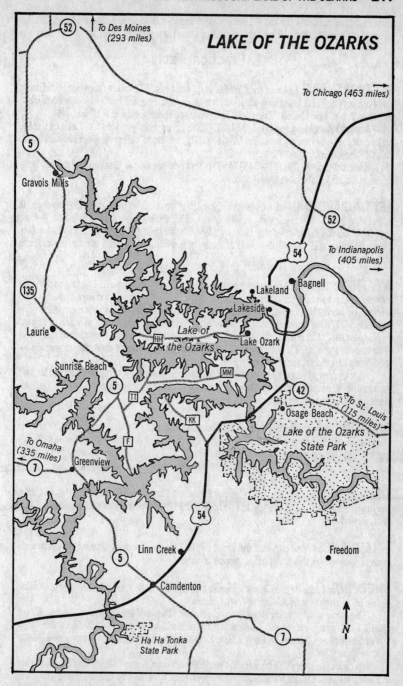

LAKE OF THE OZARKS

most outstanding state parks. Whatever your honeymoon speed, Lake of the Ozarks offers the diversity that allows you to realize your honeymoon dreams.

1. Practical Facts

GETTING THERE: Lake of the Ozarks is located just 175 miles from both St. Louis and Kansas City and is an easy day's **drive** from Chicago, Indianapolis, Des Moines, Omaha, Tulsa, and Dallas. The main interstates to the region are I-70 and I-44.

Trans-World Express (tel. 314/423-2888) currently services the Lake of the Ozarks daily. Flights originate in St. Louis and fly into Lee C. Fine Airport located in the Lake of the Ozarks State Park.

Kincaid Coach (tel. 314/348-3457) offers **bus** service to Osage Beach from both Springfield and Columbia, Missouri.

GETTING AROUND: Most visitors drive their own car to the Ozarks. However, if you arrive by air, rental cars are available at Lee C. Fine Airport. **Dollar Rent-A-Car** (tel. 314/365-2366) offers daily rates of $39 with unlimited mileage. **Circle Lake Delivery Service** (tel. 314/365-4743) also shuttles visitors from the airport to lodging properties.

WEATHER: The weather varies greatly depending on the season. During the winter months, plan to snuggle up beside the cozy fireplaces offered in many cottages and resorts, because the average daytime temperature is 49° and evening temperatures dip to around 27°. As spring weather warms, the dogwoods bloom a vibrant pink and white over the rolling hills, showcasing the Ozarks at their finest. Average spring daytime temperature is 72°, evening is 48°. Summer brings average daytime temperatures at 89° and around 64° in the evening.

As summer gives way to cool fall breezes, the autumn foliage is spectacular and the weather is most conducive for a long walk or boat ride to admire the colors, with an average daytime temperature of 78°, evening at about 50°.

CLOTHING: Comfortable, casual, and relaxed describes the dress code at Lake of the Ozarks. During summer months bathing suits, shorts, or a cover-up are the norm during the day. Evening activities are casual as well. Jackets are acceptable but not required for men.

TIME: Lake of the Ozarks is on Central Standard Time from the last Sunday in October until the first Sunday of April. The rest of the year, Central Daylight Savings Time is observed.

TELEPHONES: You can call the Lake of the Ozarks direct by dialing 314 (the area code) followed by the seven-digit phone number.

SHOPPING: Lake of the Ozark shopping ranges from the quaint to the cosmopolitan —but all with an Ozark flair and friendliness.

The area offers several shopping centers: Two enclosed malls—**Stone Crest Mall,** in Osage Beach; and **Laurie Terrace Mall,** in Laurie—as well as the **High Point Shopping Center,** in Osage Beach, feature everything from the practical to the extraordinary.

Two unique shopping centers in Osage Beach are **Osage Village** and **Main Street** at Poverty Flats. Osage Village, a picturesque mall accented by lavish landscaping and attractive lighting, is a factory merchants' outlet center. About 50 different stores offer name-brand products at reduced prices. Main Street at Poverty Flats Village has taken on the appearance of a Victorian village with wooden sidewalks and the familiar water-wheel and wishing well. Everything from clothing to crafts to musical instruments can be found here.

Plan to spend a casual afternoon strolling Bagnell Boulevard in Lake Ozark. There you will find historic buildings, restaurants, snack bars, crafts, and souvenir shops.

Set aside plenty of time to explore the many smaller, unique specialty stores. **Wilhelmi's Something Special** on Bagnell Boulevard, and **The Saltbox** in Osage Beach specialize in a large array of handmade country crafts.

If boutique shopping appeals to you, many of the larger resorts feature specialty shops on the premises. The downtown communities of Eldon, Camdenton, and Versailles are also a shopper's oasis.

HOW TO GET MARRIED AT LAKE OF THE OZARKS: You must apply for a

license three days before you can be married. Licenses can be obtained from the county recorder at either the Camden County Court House, Camdenton, MO 65020 (tel. 314/346-4440) or the Miller County Court House, Tuscumbia, MO 65082 (tel. 314/369-2911). Blood tests and identification are not necessary. After obtaining a license (fee is $15), an officiant of your choice or a qualified representative from the county registrar's office can perform the ceremony.

If you are interested in the unusual, check out Bridal Cave. As legend has it, the cave was the site of an Indian wedding centuries ago. Since it was opened to the public in 1948, Bridal Cave has been the site of over 1,000 weddings. Weddings are performed here April through October. The fee of $125 includes the use of the chapel, minister, music, photographer, and flowers (tel. 314/346-2676).

FOR FURTHER INFORMATION: Contact the **Greater Lake of the Ozarks Con-**

vention and Visitors Bureau, P.O. Box 98, Lake Ozark, MO 65049 (tel. toll free 800/325-0213 nationwide; or 800/392-0882 in Missouri).

2. Romantic Interludes

Pack a picnic, grab your camera and head to Missouri's newest state park, **Ha Ha Tonka**, located on Hwy. D off of Hwy. 54 West, near Camdenton on the Niangua Arm of Lake of the Ozarks. Here you'll find a rich mixture of natural beauty, geological oddities, and romantic history. Among the most prominent attractions at the park are the ruins of Ha Ha Tonka castle, a spectacular 3½-story structure destroyed by fire in 1942. The impressive castle ruins are reason enough for a visit to Ha Ha Tonka, but the natural surroundings are equally interesting. Now open to the public, the park is characterized by sinkholes, caves, underground streams, springs, and natural bridges. A number of hiking trails are available, and the park is lovely any season of the year. There is no admission charge. For hours of operation call 346-2986.

The Lake of the Ozarks is fast becoming a **golfer's** paradise and you may want to spend time on any of the lake's nine lush golf courses. Courses are geared for every level of golfer, from novice to amateur to champion. Golfing conditions are excellent from the first of March through the end of November.

For more information on golf packages contact: Dogwood Hills Golf Course, Rte. 1, Box 1300, Osage Beach, MO 65065 (tel. 348-1735); Indian Rock Golf Course, P.O. Box 1129, Laurie, MO 63038 (tel. 372-3023); Lake Valley Golf and Country Club, P.O. Box 304, Camdenton, MO 65020 (tel. 346-7218); Marriott's Tan-Tar-A Resort and Golf Club, P.O. Box 188, Osage Beach, MO 65065 (tel. 348-3131); Lodge of the Four Seasons, P.O. Box 408, Lake Ozark, MO (tel. 365-3001); Eldon

Golf Course, Rte. 1, Eldon, MO 65026 (tel. 392-4172); Rolling Hills Country Club, Rte. 5, Versailles, MO 65084 (tel. 378-5108).

A visit to the Lake would not be complete without spending at least one evening enjoying some of the best music shows in the Midwest. For a truly world-class show, visit the **Denny Hilton Showplace,** Rte. 2, Box 3350, Osage Beach, MO 65065 (tel. 348-1767) featuring a state-of-the-art light-and-sound show, comedy, and country and contemporary music nightly except Sunday at 7:30 p.m. April through October. (Cost is $9.25 per person).

You'll also find an enjoyable combination of country, bluegrass, and gospel music at **Jerry Prunty's Country Jubilee Show,** Rte. 2, Box 3635, Osage Beach, MO (tel. 348-2901) nightly except Monday at 7:30 p.m. April through October. (Cost is $8 per person).

Also well worth your time is the **Lake of the Ozarks Water Show,** P.O. Box 327, Lake Ozark, MO (tel. 348-3100). Ranked among the top four such shows in the country, this two-hour performance combines ski, stage, and high diving to present a daily extravaganza similar to the famed Cypress Gardens. Showtimes are 1:30 p.m. (cost $7 per person) and 8:30 p.m. (cost $8 per person), June through September.

Since much of the region's beauty can be seen best from water, it is advisable to rent a boat and explore the lake for yourself. The Missouri Department of Natural Resources has marked a nine-mile aquatic trail between **Public Beach No. 1** and the **Grand Glaize Beach** in the Lake of the Ozarks State Park. Along this trail, which should take about two hours to travel, you can see the site of an old logging chute, a small cave, a glade, a natural window, overhanging rock formations that have been used as Indian shelters, and much more.

Ski boats and runabouts can be rented for about $25 to $35 per hour, plus gas. Pontoons are a fun way to spend a leisurely afternoon cruising the lake and are available for $35 plus gas for the first hour, $25 per hour plus gas for each of the next three hours. Fishing boats can be rented for $12 per hour or $50 per day plus gas. Contact **Bridgeport Boat Rental** in the State Park (tel. 348-2280) or **Link's Landing** nearby (tel. 348-2741).

For a firsthand look at the lake with a captain in control, take a **scenic cruise** aboard the **Captain Larry Don.** One-hour and two-hour cruises depart hourly every day during season. (Cost is $5 and $6 per person respectively.) Enjoy the breakfast buffet cruise from 9 a.m. to 11 a.m. (cost is $9.50 per person), or the two-hour dinner cruise featuring an Ozark-style barbecue, 5 to 7 p.m. or 7 to 9 p.m. (cost is $16.75 per person). After dark, the *Captain Larry Don* turns into a floating dance floor featuring live bands nightly (cost is $8.50 per person). Contact: Casino Pier, P.O. Box 85, Lake Ozark, MO 65049 (tel. 365-2020).

3. Honeymoon Hotels and Hideaways

Lake of the Ozarks has earned a reputation for offering accommodations well within the reach of most budgets, and that is still the case. For complete information on resort, condominium, and camping rates contact the Greater Lake of the Ozarks Convention and Visitors Bureau at the address given above.

Summer is considered the high season (approximately June through September); rates quoted reflect the spread between low- and high-season prices.

Quietly nestled on the beautifully lush Horseshoe Bend peninsula overlooking the Lake of the Ozarks, the **Lodge of the Four Seasons,** P.O. Box 408, Lake Ozark, MO 65049 (tel. 314/365-3001 or toll free 800/THE-LAKE), possesses great natural beauty and an endless array of year-round activities. The unique use of natural stone, exotic Japanese gardens, and cascading waterfalls creates the ambience of rustic luxury. The accommodations vary from an elegantly furnished lakeside room to a suite or a secluded villa, but every facility you could possibly want is within easy walking distance of your room or villa. During your stay you can: Challenge the 18-hole Robert Trent Jones championship golf course; swim in one of the five indoor or outdoor swimming pools; revive in the health spa; hike or ride horse through woodland trails; fish; play tennis and racquetball; trapshoot; jog; shop; take in a movie; in winter go cross-country skiing or ice skating. And you can dine in one of the five award-winning restaurants. The honeymoon package: Three days/two nights (EP): $250 to $263 per couple. Includes: minisuite with private balcony and a tub-for-two, breakfast in bed daily, one dinner, fruit and cheese basket, a bottle of champagne and souvenir glasses, plus free use of the spa, sauna, whirlpool, and activity tickets for a lake cruise, bowling, trail rides, and the cinema.

Marriott's Tan-Tar-A Resort and Golf Club, P.O. Box 188, Osage Beach, MO 65065 (tel. 314/348-3131), situated on 400 beautiful acres of quiet woods and a mile of private shoreline just off State Road KK, offers almost every amenity imaginable. The guest rooms are lavishly furnished and appointed in earth tones. They offer a variety of floor plans and settings that range from hotel suites in the eight-story complex, to low-rise villa-style homes. Complementing the accommodations are more than 27 different recreational opportunities including 27 holes of championship golf, tennis, racquetball, bowling, ice skating, trap shooting, a full-service marina, health spa, indoor and outdoor pools, heated fishing dock, and a series of indoor shops. The honeymoon package: Three days/two nights (MAP): $360 to $399 per couple plus tax. Includes one-bedroom suite, breakfast and dinner daily, free recreation, champagne, a souvenir gift, and a one-hour moped rental per person. For those honeymooners staying through Monday, the package will also include a champagne cruise and a culinary class.

Located two miles south of Bagnell Dam on Business Highway 54, **Holiday Inn,** Rte. 72, Box 45, Lake Ozark, MO 65049 (tel. 314/365-2334) is an out-of-the-ordinary Holiday Inn. Amenities include indoor and outdoor swimming pools, a complete health club, 18-hole miniature golf course, restaurant, lounge, and live entertainment. It is conveniently located right on the lake just minutes from many attractions, restaurants, and shops. Honeymoon package: Two nights/three days (BP): $150 to $185 per couple plus tax. Includes luxury room with king-size bed, champagne with souvenir glasses, a newspaper and breakfast each morning, mini-golf, certificate for the gift shop, and use of all pools and health club facilities.

Set on a peninsula surrounded by water, **Millstone Lodge,** Box 515, Gravois Mills, MO 65037 (tel. 314/372-5111), has long been a landmark at Lake of the Ozarks. The guest rooms have been recently remodeled in vibrant autumn colors, adding new luxury. Millstone offers a swimming pool, a restaurant with a panoramic view of the lake, tennis courts, horseback riding, and a golf course nearby. A popular spot for boaters and guests alike is the lakefront patio, which has live entertainment. Honeymoon package: Two nights/three days. (MAP): $210 to $225 per couple. Includes lakeside room, champagne, dinner and breakfast daily, one-hour boat rental, unlimited tennis, and a Millstone souvenir.

Located near the Grand Glaize Bridge, **The Inn at Grand Glaize,** P.O. Box 964, Osage Beach, MO 65065 (tel. 314/348-4731) is one of the newest resorts at the lake. Just minutes away from area attractions, restaurants, and shops, The Inn is built at water's edge, has complete marina services, a restaurant, tennis courts, heated swimming pool, and a warm atmosphere from the minute you set foot in the lobby. The rooms, decorated in contemporary colors of green and mauve, are brand new and sparkle with freshness. Honeymoon package: Three days/two nights (EP): $89 to $145 per couple. Also available are one-bedroom condominiums with living room, kitchen, and fireplace. Condo rates: $60 to $100 per couple per day.

Located off State Road KK near golf courses, shopping, and area attractions, **The Knolls Resort Condominiums,** Rte. 1, Box 190-43, Osage Beach, MO 65065 (tel.

314/348-2236), has a waterfront, a full-service marina with boat rentals, indoor and outdoor pools, indoor and outdoor tennis, sauna, whirlpool, and a steam room. Each unit is luxuriously furnished and has a fireplace, private balcony, and cable television. Honeymoon package: Three days/two nights (EP): $210 to $250 per couple. Includes one bedroom condominium with hot tub, fruit and cheese basket, and bottle of champagne.

Houseboating on Lake of the Ozarks is becoming increasingly popular. Houseboats vary somewhat in size and amenities, but all include most of the following features: air conditioning, full bath, on-deck barbecue grill, stove, microwave, refrigerator, dishes, flatware, linens, bedding, full patio, penthouse sleeper, water slide, wet bar, and more. Houseboats can be rented for as low as $239 to $319 per couple per week. Contact the following companies for specific rates and information on houseboat amenities: Three Buoys Houseboat Vacations, Rte. 71, Box 1870, Camdenton, MO 65020 (tel. toll free 800/423-1021 nationwide, or toll free 800/334-5676 in MO); Link's Landing, Osage Beach, MO 65065 (tel. 314/348-2741); Fantasy Cruz, Lake Ozark, MO 65049 (tel. toll free 800/882-4006 nationwide, or 800/882-4005 in Missouri); Bridgeport Marina, P.O. Box 186, Osage Beach, MO 65065 (tel. 314/348-2280); Professional Management Group, Rte. 72, Box 76, Lake Ozark, MO 65049 (tel. toll free 800/238-3434 nationwide, or 800/237-3434 in MO).

4. Romantic Restaurants

The quality, variety, and unique settings for dining at the lake equal the area's famed recreational amenities. Reservations are not required at most restaurants. Moderately priced restaurants run around $40 for a dinner for two; inexpensive ones are under $20.

MODERATE: Ask locals where to go to for the best view of the lake and chances are they will send you to the **Blue Heron,** State Hwy. HH, Horseshoe Bend (tel. 365-4646), situated atop a large bluff with a panoramic view of the lake from both directions. Sip a glass of wine around a beautiful outdoor pool before you sit down to an elegant dinner inside amid a Dutch decor. The international menu is as highly acclaimed as the spectacular view. Specialty is the batter-fried lobster; impressive wine list. Dinner entrées are $14.95 to $24.95. Open March through November.

Arrowhead Lodge, Business 54, Lake Ozark (tel. 365-2345), draws a breakfast, lunch, and dinner crowd 365 days of the year. The restaurant has been a favorite of locals and visitors for years and for good reason. Their famous Arrowhead breakfast ($3 to $4 per person) and prime rib, catfish, fried chicken, and steaks, plus the rustic decor and unique log furniture keep the crowds coming back. Dinner prices vary from $7.95 to $22.95 per person.

Located by water on the seven-mile marker, **The Barge,** Bittersweet Road off Horseshoe Bend (tel. 365-5788) is an honest to goodness floating restaurant and lounge serving breakfast, lunch, and dinner. Specialties are the barbecue ribs, steaks, and catfish. Breakfast menu items run around $3, lunch items $3 to $6, and dinner entrées are $5 to $15. Open April through October.

For a cozy Olde English atmosphere head for **Bentley's,** Business 54, Lake Ozark (tel. 365-5301). Succulent prime rib and superb steaks are the specialties. Dinner for two, about $30, plus drinks. Open March through December.

The Cliff Room, Marriott's Tan-Tar-A Resort, Osage Beach (tel. 348-3131), well known for its prime rib and scrumptious Sunday brunch, serves American cuisine in rustic elegance and a classic hunt-club atmosphere. Ornately decorated tables with overstuffed chairs and a fire blazing in the fireplace in the winter, set the mood for a romantic dinner. Dinner for two is about $40, plus drinks; brunch is $12.50 per person. Open all year.

Happy Fisherman, Highway 54 and Lake Road 29, Osage Beach (tel. 348-3311). As the name implies this is a nautical-style restaurant complete with oversize clam shells that greet you at the entrance. All-you-can-eat shrimp and catfish make the Happy Fisherman popular. Lunch and dinner for two are about $12.50 and $30 respectively. Drinks, of course, are extra. Open March through November.

J. Bruner's, Lake Road 54-40, Osage Beach (tel. 348-2966). J. Bruner's American menu is fast earning a reputation for excellent steaks, seafood, and outstanding appetizers. The cozy, country decor make this a great spot for honeymooners. Dinner for two, about $40, plus drinks. Open all year.

Fresh fish, steaks, and barbecue ribs are served in contemporary elegance at **J.D. Waddles,** Inn at Grand Glaize, Osage Beach (tel. 348-4731). Lots of brass and glass accented by pleasing shades of green make this a dining experience to remember. Easily accessible by water or land, the restaurant serves lunch (about $5 per person), and dinner (around $13 per person). Open all year.

The open-air rooftop at **Mike Fink's Rooftop and Water Restaurant,** Bagnell Dam Boulevard, Lake Ozark (tel. 365-6771), makes for a spectacular view and an out of the ordinary afternoon or evening. Steak sandwiches are the rage. Lunch is $2.50 to $5, dinner, $5 to $15 per person. Open May through September.

Millstone Restaurant, Route O, Laurie (tel. 372-5111), is located at the six-mile marker and boasts a panoramic view of the lake from the dining room. Offering a complete American menu, the seafood buffet ($14.50 per person) is a Millstone favorite. Breakfast is $2 to $5 per person, lunch is $4 to $6 per person and dinner is $7 to $25. Open April through October.

Go south of the border one evening at **Vista Grande Mexican Restaurant,** Highway 54 across from Osage Village (tel. 348-1231). You will easily recognize the distinctive adobe facade and inside you will find authentic Mexican artifacts. The fajitas and chimichangas are fantastic, but the restaurant has earned its claim to fame by serving what satisfied customers say are the best margaritas in the United States. Lunch and dinner for two are about $8 and $20 respectively. Drinks are extra. Open all year.

The **Windrose,** Marriott's Tan-Tar-A Resort, Osage Beach (tel. 348-3131), provides a truly romantic lakeside dining experience. The wickered elegance of this restaurant complements the all-seafood menu. Scallops Windrose and shrimp Diavolo are favorites. Dinner for two, about $40, plus drinks. Open April through October.

INEXPENSIVE: Great family food and fun is the specialty at the famous **Clown,** near Grand Glaize Bridge, Osage Beach (tel. 348-2259) floating restaurant. Waitresses in swim suits serve up some of the best burgers and shrimp in town. Breakfasts run about $3, lunches and dinners vary from about $3 to $6. Great libations and a lounge with dance floor can be found at The Poop Deck and The Topsider, located just above The Clown. Open May through September.

Live lobster, crab legs, and a touch of Cajun can be savored at the **Fish Market,** Lodge of the Four Seasons, Lake Ozark (tel. 365-3001), along with a host of other fresh fish that is flown in daily. As a bonus, the Fish Market offers candlelight dining, a nautical decor, and a fantastic view overlooking the lake. Dinners start as low as $7.95 up to $17.50. Open March through November.

At **Just Like Home,** Highway 54 at Lake Road 56, Osage Beach (tel. 348-1135), the name says it all; the casual country atmosphere lends itself well to the all-you-can-eat family-style meals and menu. Home cooking is served at breakfast ($3 to $5); lunch ($3 to $5); and dinner ($7.95). Open March through November.

For the best homemade soups, breads, quiches, and desserts, pull up a chair at **Peace 'N' Plenty Country Cafe,** off Highway 54, Poverty Flats Village (tel. 348-1462). The quaint Americana decor highlights the fresh and interesting menu items.

Breakfasts are about $2 to $5, lunches are $4 to $7, and dinners are $5 to $12. Open all year.

To really get the flavor of the Ozarks, you must visit **Ozark Barbecue,** Route TT off of Hwy. 5, Sunrise Beach (tel. 374-7769). Located near the 11-mile marker by water, it's a popular spot for boaters. Nothing fancy here, just great barbecued beef, pork, ribs, and out-of-this-world desserts. Open for lunch and dinner, approximately $5 per plate. Open April through September.

Chapter IX

NEVADA: LAS VEGAS

1. Practical Facts
2. Romantic Interludes
3. Honeymoon Hotels and Hideaways
4. Romantic Restaurants

WHEN YOU DRIVE down the famed "strip" in Las Vegas, everything looks as you always pictured it would. Each hotel/casino is bigger and brassier than the one before, with undulating neon facades flickering and glowing in blinding fashion. Gaily lit marquees confirm that everyone who's anyone in the world of show business is playing in town: Rodney Dangerfield, Frank Sinatra, Bill Cosby, Joan Rivers. Glamour and excitement lies around every corner; the promise of instant riches beckons around every bend.

Much of the action in town centers along Las Vegas Boulevard, better known as the "strip." Here's where most of the giant casino/hotels are located, and each strives to outdo the others in flash and tack. Or head for the downtown area, a bit homier and more laid back than the strip. The casinos here are generally smaller, so you'll find it easier to walk from one to the other. And prices in the downtown area are generally cheaper than along the strip, though it should be noted that the entire city is one big bargain, whatever your budget.

Las Vegas is located in southwest Nevada, just 30 miles from the California border and 280 miles from Los Angeles. Although casino gambling was first voted in by the Nevada state legislature in 1931, the area didn't really start booming until after World War II. But since then it's been incredible growth here in this desert oasis—a one-of-a-kind glittering mecca that attracts 10 million visitors a year.

1. Practical Facts

GETTING THERE: Because of the city's popularity, it is easy to reach Vegas from anywhere in the United States.

By Air

Fly into Las Vegas's McCarran International Airport, which is just one mile from the strip, five miles from downtown. Most of the major airlines, as well as 30 charter companies, service McCarran, so you'll be able to shop around for bargain fares.

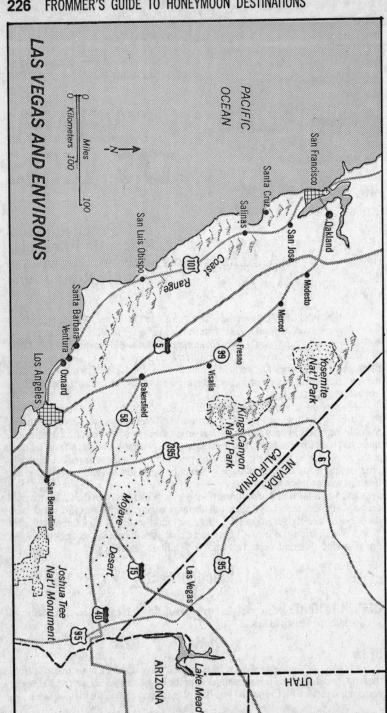

By Car

Hop on Interstate 15 in Los Angeles, which leads directly into Las Vegas some 280 miles later. Be advised that it's a boring drive with little in the way of scenery—just flat desert.

GETTING AROUND: There are more than 400 taxis cruising the city, and you'll have no problem flagging one down at your hotel or along the strip and downtown. It's about an $8 fare from the airport to the strip; about $12 from the airport to downtown. If you plan on doing lots of exploring, and casino hopping, you're probably better off renting a car. There's a multitude of car companies (you can hire anything from a bargain "wreck" to a brand-new Mercedes), and rates are quite competitive. For example, **Dollar Rent-A-Car** offers compact cars for about $32 a day; the first 100 miles are free, then there's a 15¢ per mile charge. This is a pretty standard fee in Las Vegas.

WEATHER: Las Vegas is in the middle of the desert, which means hot, dry days and cool nights most of the year. Only about four inches of rain falls annually, and perhaps the surest odds in town ride on the sunshine—a healthy 85% of the days are sunny. Winter temperatures generally hover in the 50s; spring and fall days average in the 70s, and summer daytime temperatures often top 100°.

CLOTHING: Casual clothes are fine just about everywhere, even in the casinos, though you'll need to dress up a bit for the finer restaurants (jackets required for men). April through October you'll be comfortable in shorts and sun dresses by day, with lightweight evening wraps for evening. You'll need heavier clothes and a warm coat for the nippy nights November through March.

TIME: Las Vegas is on Pacific Standard Time—the same as Los Angeles.

TELEPHONES: The area code for Las Vegas is 702.

SHOPPING: There are lots of upscale boutiques for splurging with your winnings. Virtually every major hotel has extremely fine (and expensive) clothing and jewelry arcades. **The Fashion Show Mall,** located in the heart of the strip, has more than 140 specialty shops and such tony department stores as Neiman-Marcus and Saks. Or try the **Meadows Mall,** just off the Las Vegas Expressway at Meadows Lane. This spacious shopping venue has 140 shops spread out among greenery, fountains, and works of art.

HOW TO GET MARRIED IN LAS VEGAS: Nothing could be easier than arranging a wedding in Las Vegas, even if the urge strikes you at 2 a.m.! No wonder it's the place where 55,000 couples say "I do" each year. The city is known for its wonderfully tacky wedding "chapels"; there are 18 in all, and most are open 24 hours. There's no blood test or waiting period required—just pick up a marriage license at the Clark County Clerk's office on South Third Street (tel. 702/455-3156 weekdays, 702/455-4415 weekends). The license is $25, and the ceremony will range from $25 to $30, though you'll pay extra for such frills as video taping.

You can pick up a list of the wedding chapels at the County Clerk's office.

FOR FURTHER INFORMATION: Contact: **The Las Vegas Convention and Visitors Authority,** 3150 Paradise Rd., Las Vegas, NV 89109 (tel. 702/733-2323).

2. Romantic Interludes

There's so much to see here in the land of glitter and glitz, you'll be kept busy morning till night. And you'll be amazed at the vast, gorgeous, unspoiled scenery just outside city limits.

You name it, Las Vegas will **dance** to it in one of the many extravagant shows staged throughout town. Nearly every casino has some type of flash dance, and they're a grand mix of magic, comedy, and outlandish, bare-breasted dancing. It seems nothing is sacred—one show (at **Bally's**) even jazzily reenacts the sinking of the Titanic!

Reservations are recommended especially for headliner shows; make your plans as soon as you arrive in town to avoid disappointment. Call the **Visitors Authority** (tel. 733-2323) for a list of upcoming shows. But you usually can't make reservations until a week or two in advance—a rather strange and inconvenient practice here.

Shows generally run about $16, which includes two drinks. When available, dinner shows are about $23 to $25 per person. If you want an especially good seat, it is essential that you tip the maître d'. Arriving early will do you no good, so be ready to shell out at least a $10 tip. (This is not to say that you won't get a decent seat otherwise, but if you're yearning to be ringside, plan on at least $20.)

Headliner shows vary widely in price, but generally fall in the $18 to $30 per person range for the show only. A hot star like Bill Cosby, though, can fetch as much as $45 a ticket.

The scenic **Colorado River** is less than an hour's drive from Las Vegas. The best way to experience the River is via a day-long rafting trip. The ride is rather mellow, and you'll be awestruck by the unique geological formations of the rocks on either side as you lazily float by. Try the package offered by **Black Canyon Tours** (tel. 293-3776). From Hoover Dam, you'll float 11 miles down the river to the resort of **Willow Beach** in Arizona. There you'll partake in a scrumptious buffet, then later be bused back to Las Vegas. Buses leave the Gold Strike Casino at 10 a.m. daily, 11 a.m. on Sundays. Cost is $49.95 per person from the Gold Strike (a 45-minute drive from Las Vegas to Hoover Dam); if you need to be picked up at your hotel in Vegas, add an additional $10 each.

Visit **Hoover Dam,** less than an hour's drive from downtown. One of the world's seven man-made wonders, the dam is the equivalent of a 70-story building! Guided tours are offered throughout the year for $1 per person (tel. 293-1081). You'll pass through the town of Boulder City on your drive; a pleasant bedroom community that is the only city in Nevada with absolutely no gambling—not even a slot machine.

One of the most popular additions to Las Vegas in recent years is the **Wet 'n' Wild** theme park, on the strip next to the Sahara. Here you can careen down enclosed tube slides, ride through churning rapids, or just lazily float along crystal blue waters in an innertube. Open mid-April through late September, 10 a.m. to 5 p.m. weekdays, 10 a.m. to 6 p.m. on weekends. The admission fee is $11 per person (tel. 737-3819).

A lake in the middle of the desert? That's what you'll find at **Lake Mead,** the largest man-made body of water in the country. And the people who created it (in 1931, during the construction of Hoover Dam) knew what they were doing—this lake is breathtaking, with 550 miles of craggy shoreline offering lots of secluded coves and romantic stretches of beach. You can rent a boat, waterski, even scuba dive in the crystal clear waters. For a really romantic day "at sea," rent a houseboat! Try **Willow Lake Marina,** about an hour from Las Vegas (tel. 767-3311). Open year-round, they even rent houseboats for $160 to $225 per day. For general information, call **Lake Mead Recreation Area** (tel. 293-4040).

Mount a horse at **Spring Mountain Ranch State Park** (tel. 363-1921) and you'll be cantering through some extraordinary desert scenery. Magnificent sandstone formations, desert blooms, even bighorn sheep combine to paint a dreamy western landscape. **Bonnie Springs Old Nevada** (tel. 875-4191) rents horses for $13 per person per hour. It's about a 30-minute drive from downtown Las Vegas; take Charleston Boulevard West.

Take advantage of Las Vegas' proximity to the **Grand Canyon** by hopping aboard a helicopter or small plane that offers an incredible, unparalled bird's-eye view of this world wonder. Not recommended for the faint of heart, these flights can be rather bumpy, but worth every minute! Flight time to the canyon is about 40 minutes; prices start at about $100 per person. Operators include **Scenic Airlines** (tel. 739-1900) and **Adventure Airlines** (tel. 736-7511).

3. Honeymoon Hotels and Hideaways

There are more than 60,000 hotel rooms in Las Vegas. Your only problem in finding a room to fit your budget is choosing one. While none of the hotels offer honeymoon packages per se, most do run seasonal specials, usually midweek two-night, three-day packages that include at least one meal (usually buffet) and a show. Be sure to ask exactly what your package includes, since they vary so widely from one hotel to the next.

All the hotels in Las Vegas are modern. None is older than 30 years old, and most are less than; they are all constantly refurbished. The contemporary furnishings are all quite similar. Each room has modern decor, color cable TV, air conditioning, full bath with shower and tub. What makes the hotels different are their facades (incredible sums of money go into the "image" of each hotel) and their casinos.

All room rates quoted here are double occupancy per night. Rates vary by day and season. You'll find the best bargains on rooms in February, March, July, and August, and midweek throughout the year.

MODERATE TO EXPENSIVE: The only major hotel in Las Vegas without a casino, **Alexis Park Resort,** 375 East Harmon Ave., Las Vegas, NV 89109 (tel. 702/796-3300; reservations: toll free 800/223-0888), provides peaceful respite from the hustle bustle of the strip. Though it's just four blocks from the strip (four *long* blocks, so the hotel provides complimentary limousine service), it's really another world here, with impeccable landscaping (waterfalls, streams, three lovely swimming pools) and elegant, luxury suites. A fitness center, two lighted tennis courts, and a nine-hole putting green complete the scene. Honeymoon package: None. Room rate: $85 to $140 per couple per night for standard suite; $115 to $170 per couple per night for king suite with whirlpool and fireplace.

One of the biggest and best-loved properties in town, **Caesars Palace,** 3570 Las Vegas Blvd. South, Las Vegas, NV 89109 (tel. 702/731-7222; reservations: toll free 800/634-6661), is a royal wonderland of glitz. It's arguably the nicest hotel in Las Vegas, and you'll immediately pick it out of the strip by its rows of arcing fountains, Roman statues, and giant "people-movers" (moving sidewalks). It's also right in the heart of the strip, within easy walking distance of many other casinos. Especially nice is the huge pool area (appropriately dubbed "the garden of the gods") with two pools and a giant Jacuzzi. The hotel has three casinos, a giant "sports book" (where you bet on sports events and televised horse races), and nine restaurants and lounges. The only drawback is that in some ways, Caesars is almost too big, and even the hotel's coffee shop is quite expensive. Try Cleopatra's Barge for romantic cocktails upon a giant "gondola." Honeymoon package: None. Room rate: $95 to $105 per couple per night; $145 per couple per night for petite suite. (Request the Olympic Tower—the rooms have mirrored ceilings, round beds, and sunken tubs.)

Desert Inn, 3145 Las Vegas Blvd. South, Las Vegas, NV 89109 (tel. 702/733-4444; reservations: toll free 800/634-6906), is a gorgeous, sprawling resort right in the middle of the action. From the front, the Desert Inn looks like any other hotel on the strip, but hiding behind the facade is a veritable country club, with 200 acres of golf,

10 tennis courts, and lots of hot whirlpools dotted about. There's also the wonderfully pampering spa, where (for an extra charge) you can take exercise classes or simply lie back and enjoy a facial, massage, or loofa scrub. Back inside, the small casino is among Las Vegas' more subdued and quiet. Honeymoon package: None. Room rate: $85 to $105 standard; $150 for minisuites; $175 to $265 for deluxe one-bedroom suite.

Located in Las Vegas' downtown section (a few miles from the strip), the **Golden Nugget,** 129 East Fremont, Las Vegas, NV 89101 (tel. 702/385-7111; reservations: toll free 800/634-3454), is lovely and elegant. The downtown location means less crowds and traffic, though there's still plenty of action. The Nugget is just a few years old and is so beautiful—lots of white marble, glass walls, and a festive yellow-and-white pool area. There are six restaurants (including what most locals consider to be the best buffet in town), a showroom, and an outstanding spa and beauty salon where you'll feel pampered. Just across the street is the Horseshoe Casino, one of the oldest and most popular in town and always packed with friendly, enthusiastic gamblers. Honeymoon package: None. Room rate: $54 to $90 per couple per night; $210 to $300 per couple per night for a suite.

Holiday Casino / Holiday Inn, 3475 Las Vegas Blvd. South, Las Vegas, NV 89109 (tel. 702/369-5000; reservations: toll free 800/634-6765). Its flashy showboat facade stands out gaily on the strip, and this hotel won't disappoint you once inside. Action in the casino is fast and furious, and there's even a bingo parlor! Rooms are both gracious and spacious, and the Olympic-size pool is perfect for soaking up Las Vegas' sunny climate. Honeymoon package: None. Room rate: $66 to $78 per couple per night.

Las Vegas Hilton, 3000 Paradise Rd., Las Vegas, NV 89109 (tel. 702/732-5111; reservations: toll free 800/732-7117), is the largest hotel in the world (3,174 rooms) and it is practically a city unto itself. It has one of the most beautiful casinos in town, with shimmering glass chandeliers and pulsating lights spotlighting the action. Even the women's bathroom is a work of art—incredibly elegant! There's an upscale shopping arcade with gleaming brass and marble accents, as well as 14 restaurants and lounges and a huge recreation area that includes a heated pool, picturesque lagoons, six lighted tennis courts, and an 18-hole putting green. And all this is actually situated on one ten-acre deck! Honeymoon package: None. Room rate: $60 to $120 per couple per night for a standard; $300 and up for one-bedroom suite.

Billed as the "island of Las Vegas," the **Tropicana,** 3801 Las Vegas Blvd. South, Las Vegas, NV 89109 (tel. 702/739-2222; reservations: toll free 800/634-4000), really does live up to its slogan. The hotel is situated right at the start of the strip, so it's a bit removed from the action farther down the road. But the facilities are all first-rate, and the casino is just stunning with its "cathedral" ceiling of orange stained-glass. Try the Atrium Bar for finger-snapping entertainment nightly, or check out the free bird shows that run continuously through the day. What really makes the Trop special, though, is its outlandish pool area, which goes on and on with waterfalls, ponds, lagoons, hot spas, water slides, and cascades of flowers. There's also 18 holes of golf across the street, 4 tennis courts, a spiffy health club and, of course, swim-up blackjack! Honeymoon package: None. Room rate: $65 to $95 per couple per night; $250 per couple per night for a suite.

INEXPENSIVE: An attraction in itself, the **Circus Circus,** 2880 Las Vegas Blvd. South, Las Vegas, NV 89109 (tel. 702/734-0410; reservations: toll free 800/634-3450), is aptly named—circus acts appear a full 13 hours each day on the mezzanine under the Big Top—and it's free! From flying trapeze artists to spine-tingling tightrope antics, it's all here. The festive carnival atmosphere also includes a nostalgic "midway" with the kind of games you used to play on the Jersey boardwalk—toss the hoop, skee ball, ring toss. For 25¢ to $1, these games are a better bet than the casino. Circus Circus also has two casinos and its own wedding chapel. Rooms are modern but rather basic. Honeymoon package: None. Room rate: $18 to $38 per couple per night for a standard.

A few minutes from the strip, the **Palace Station,** 2411 West Sahara Ave., Las Vegas, NV 89102 (tel. 702/367-2411; reservations: toll free 800/634-3101), incorporates a nostalgic turn-of-the-century theme throughout, highlighted by the impressive facade, a replica of an old-time railroad station. The railroad theme is carried out throughout the entire hotel and casino, with railcar lights, old maps, and lounge names such as the "Trackside Station." There's a bustling casino and sports book on-site, as well as several restaurants and, for late-night entertainment, the Loading Dock Lounge. Soak up the sun at the two swimming pools and bubbling spas, or hop the complimentary shuttle to the strip. Honeymoon package: None. Room rate: $40 to $50 per couple per night.

As their slogan attests, **Sam's Town,** 5111 Boulder Hwy., Las Vegas, NV 89122 (tel. 702/456-7777; reservations: toll free 800/634-6371), is a true original—a sort of Wild West "town" on the outskirts of Las Vegas (about seven miles from the strip). The bustling casino is among the locals' favorites, and it's easy to see why—there's a real down-home, comfortable feeling here. Try Roxy's Saloon for live entertainment, or don your cowboy boots for square dancing at the Western Dance Hall. There's also 56 lanes of bowling and great homemade ice cream at Calamity Jane's Ice Cream Parlour, where you can inspect vintage Coca-Cola memorabilia. Honeymoon package: None. Room rate: $43 per couple per night.

4. Romantic Restaurants

Most restaurants are located in the major hotels, and like room rates, the food prices are extremely competitive. Las Vegas is especially known for its lavish buffets, where you can find breakfast for as little as 99¢ per person, lunch for about $1.49, dinner for $2.49! Be prepared to wait on long lines for the buffets, but you sure can't beat the price. Especially recommended for gourmet fare in an elegant atmosphere is the dinner buffet at the Golden Nugget ($7.95). Jacket and tie required for men.

EXPENSIVE: Bacchanal, Caesars Palace (tel. 731-7110). An opulent Roman feast awaits the two of you in a forum that truly borders on the decadent. First, you enter a "Roman garden" of ornate statues, columns, flaming torches, and a lighted pool. Overhead a grape arbor loops among the ceiling beams. You'll be met by "wine goddesses" dressed in exotic costumes who'll see to your every whim. Next comes a beautifully orchestrated seven-course meal of hors d'oeuvres, soup, seafood, entrée, salad, vegetables and—to top it off—flaming desserts. (You choose the entrée, the rest of the menu is set.) After dinner, your wine goddess will even rub your neck and shoulders! The fixed price is $50 per person, which includes all the white wine, red wine, and champagne you can drink. Reservations are a must, as is proper attire.

The place for executives and high rollers in Las Vegas, **Michael's,** Barbary Coast Hotel (tel. 737-7111), is a small, elegant restaurant where you can just feel the power. Perhaps it's the huge red-velvet chairs and stained-glass dome overhead that adds to the heady ambience. Steaks, veal, and seafood dominate the menu; the Dover sole is among Michael's specialties. Appetizers start at $8.50; entrées from $21 to $38. Proper attire required.

MODERATE: Dome of the Sea, Dunes Hotel (tel. 737-4110). This dark and quiet restaurant oozes sensuality with its hushed, secret ambience that conjures up the sea at its most mysterious. A small lagoon running throughout offers a floating harpist, whose lilting melodies blend with the background trickle of water. Known for outstanding seafood, specialties of the house include frogs' legs and fisherman's stew. This intimate place is a must! Appetizers from $7, entrées from $19 to $30.

Benihana Village, Las Vegas Hilton (tel. 732-5801). Actually, this place is three restaurants in all, situated around a dreamy Japanese landscape of lush gardens, running streams, stone lanterns, and pine and willow trees. Try tempura for deep-fried seafood and lightly seasoned vegetables. (Appetizers from $4.50, entrées $10 to $24.) Hibachi cooking right at your table is the specialty at Teppanyaki, where complete dinners are priced from $11 to $30. Or try Robata, a Japanese barbecue where the preparation of your meal is a show in itself. (Appetizers from $2, entrées from $11 to $33.) All three feature the continuously running "Jambirdee," an animated show of birds, flowers, and a talking tree to boot. Jacket and tie is optional for men.

Fishermans Broiler, Palace Station Hotel (tel. 367-2408). This seafood eatery is a favorite with locals, and with good reason: The fresh seafood—proudly on display —is the greatest! Choose from mahimahi, catfish, and shark among the more unusual delights of the sea. The $4.95 soup-and-seafood salad bar for lunch is an especially good deal; don't miss the fresh seafood salad. The decor is simple and inviting—large brass ship's lanterns and vintage seascapes combine for the feel of an old New England boat house. Appetizers from $2.95, entrées $6.95 to $14.95. Dress casual.

Liberace's Tivoli Gardens, E. Tropicana Avenue (tel. 798-8546). Founded by Liberace himself, Tivoli Gardens is pretty much what you expect from the late king of sequins—lots of glitter and flash. Based on Copenhagen's Tivoli Gardens (but with a wickedly Liberace twist), the restaurant serves up specialties from a number of countries. The extensive menu includes tantalizing pasta appetizers, rack of lamb, tender veals and fresh seafood. Appetizers start at $6.95; dinners range from $17.50 to $32.50. A six-course fixed-price dinner, highly recommended, is $32.50 per person. There's piano lounge entertainment nightly except Mondays. Dress up.

Willy & Jose's Cantina, Sam's Town Hotel (tel. 456-7777). "Gringo" giant antique slot machines stand guard over this upbeat, offbeat Mexican eatery, a favorite among locals. Resembling an adobe hut, with beamed ceilings and lots of earthen pottery, Willy & Jose's has one of the silliest (and longest) menus around. But it's seriously good food here. Of course, you must start off with a margarita, then it's off to appetizers like taquitos and nachos, entrées like tostadas, fajitas, and burritos. Wash it all down with shots of tequila and really get into the atmosphere! Appetizers start at $3.50; entrées from $5.25 to $10.95. Dress casual.

Chapter X

NEW YORK

1. New York City
2. Niagara Falls

FOR FOREIGNERS, New York State embodies the spirit of America, home of such instantly identifiable national symbols as the Statue of Liberty and the Empire State Building. For Americans, it represents the pinnacle of success, the touchstone by which achievements in all walks of life—from theater to sports and finance—are measured. If you make it in New York, the song goes, you can make it anywhere.

Although New York is only the second-largest state in terms of population, and ranks as an also-ran number 30 in total area, it remains one of the Top Ten honeymoon destinations, according to a recent research survey by *Modern Bride* magazine. In this chapter, we will concentrate on the state's two most popular attractions: New York City and Niagara Falls.

1. New York City

Paris may well be the loveliest of cities, Rome the most eternal, but New York is certainly the sexiest and most energetic. Something about its dense vitality demands that it be shared with another, preferably beloved, person.

When people refer to New York City, they usually mean just the borough of Manhattan, and so will we in this chapter. Actually, New York City is comprised of five boroughs, of which Manhattan is but one (the others are Queens, Staten Island, the Bronx, and Brooklyn). Manhattan is the most densely populated part of New York City, with eight million inhabitants residing on an island 12 miles long and 3 miles wide.

So beautiful from so many angles, New York's charms defy simple description. Something resembling perspective, however, may be attained from the Observation Deck of the Empire State Building. Look toward the south and you'll see old New York: Greenwich Village, Chelsea, the Lower East Side, SoHo, Little Italy, and Chinatown. Farther on, the concrete and glass canyons of the financial district confront you along with the World Trade Center's twin towers. Past Battery Park at Manhattan's southern tip you'll spy the Statue of Liberty in all her proud, newly restored glory. Ellis Island, the entry point into the United States for more than ten million immigrants, lies beside it.

To the east, Brooklyn and Queens; to the west, the state of New Jersey. As you look north past the metallic forest of steel spires known as midtown, the lush, green rectangle of Central Park asserts itself, an 840-acre pastoral oasis amid the concrete-towered isle. To the right of Central Park, you can view the Fifth Avenue and Park Avenue apartments of the Upper East Side's well-heeled residents. To the park's left, the Upper West Side bustles with the vigor of a newly settled frontier as an ever-increasing army of yuppies settles in, bringing with them dozens of chic restaurants

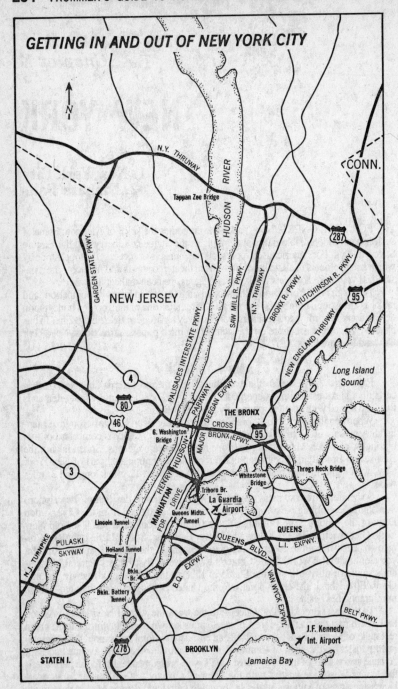

GETTING IN AND OUT OF NEW YORK CITY

and fashion-conscious boutiques. On the northwest corner of Central Park, Columbia University and St. John's Cathedral mark the lower boundary of Harlem. Gazing even farther north, you may be able to see Fort Tryon Park, home of the Cloisters, and across the Harlem River, the Bronx (also known as "DA BRONX!").

You could plan your entire honeymoon around just a single aspect of New York's many possibilities. A couple could spend a week exploring just a few of its 120 museums (not to mention its 400 art galleries), for example. Or attending Broadway, off-Broadway, and off-off-Broadway shows staged at more than 350 theaters. Or listening to jazz in intimate Greenwich Village clubs, or tasting their way through Chinatown, or shopping fashionable Fifth Avenue—the options are unlimited.

Most honeymooners, however, will probably want to mix and match, combining the town's more popular tourist spots—such as the Empire State Building, the Statue of Liberty, the Staten Island Ferry—with such relaxing delights as an afternoon in the Cloisters, coffee in an outdoor café in Central Park, or a quiet drink in a secret former speakeasy (ask for Chumley's Bar on Bedford Street in the West Village). It's amazing how romantic even the most public of settings can be in New York. Please don't feel like you should skip the city's best-known attractions simply because you've heard about them your entire life; each and every one is famous for good reason.

At night New York City becomes a mecca of culture and pleasure. Between the aesthetic options offered by its hundreds of stages, theaters, and concert halls, as well as its enormous gastronomic possibilities and nightclubs that don't warm up until well after midnight (such as Tunnel or the Palladium), honeymooners will quickly realize why New York is called "the city that never sleeps."

PRACTICAL FACTS: In this section you'll find out some basic New York City information—

Getting There

New York is a major transportation nexus. You'll have no trouble reaching it from anywhere in the world.

By Air: The three large airports that serve New York City, in order of their proximity to midtown Manhattan, are La Guardia Airport in northern Queens, John F. Kennedy (J.F.K.) International Airport in southeastern Queens, and Newark International Airport in New Jersey. Such major airlines as **United, TWA, Continental,** and **Pan Am** frequently offer low-cost fares from all parts of the country.

From J.F.K. to Manhattan, you can either take the JFK Express ("Train to the Plane"), a bus / subway combination ($6.50 per person) that leaves every 20 minutes and stops at many points from southern to northern Manhattan (tel. toll free 800/AIR-RIDE); the Carey Transportation motorcoach ($8 per person; tel. 718/632-0500), which leaves at least every 30 minutes and stops at both the Port Authority Bus Terminal's AirTransCenter, 42nd Street and Ninth Avenue, and Grand Central Station, 42nd Street and Park Avenue; or a taxi (between $17 and $23 for the cab ride).

From LaGuardia to Manhattan, you should take either the Carey motorcoach ($6 per person; tel. 718/632-0500), which goes to the Port Authority Terminal and Grand Central Station at least every 30 minutes, or catch a taxi at one of the two stands outside the main LaGuardia terminal ($8 to $13 for the cab ride).

From Newark, the Express Motorcoach Service leaves about every 15 minutes for the Port Authority Bus Terminal ($4 per person; tel. toll free 800/772-2222); the Olympia Trails Coach leaves about every 25 minutes for the World Trade Center in lower Manhattan and Grand Central Station ($5 per person). Taxi fare is about $25 to $30.

Information on transportation to all three New York City–area airports is available from the Port Authority of New York and New Jersey (tel. toll free 800/AIR-RIDE).

By Train: Trains entering Manhattan from cities all over the country terminate either at Grand Central Terminal (42nd Street and Park Avenue) or at Pennsylvania Station (Seventh and Eighth avenues between West 31st and 33rd streets).

By Bus: Greyhound and **Trailways** buses serve Manhattan from cities all around the country. The hectic Port Authority building on Eighth Avenue at West 45th Street receives thousands of commuter and long-distance bus passengers every day.

By Car: If you are considering driving to Manhattan, you should know in advance that there is *no* daytime street parking in midtown, and parking garages are very expensive (about $7 to $17 per day); see details in "Getting Around." Due to parking difficulties and the generally overcrowded streets, driving in New York is something you will probably want to avoid. Since Manhattan is an island, you will enter by one of its bridges or tunnels. The most scenic arrivals are via the George Washington Bridge on Manhattan's Upper West Side, the Triboro Bridge on the Upper East Side, or on the approach to the Lincoln Tunnel, all offering extraordinary views of the Manhattan skyline. When driving in town watch out for pedestrians, bicycle messengers, and taxis.

Getting Around

Once you get the hang of it, getting around New York City is easy.

By Taxi: The nearly 12,000 licensed "medallion" taxis are painted bright yellow. Taxis are metered and charge fixed rates: $1.15 for the first ⅛ mile and 15¢ for each subsequent ⅛ mile and / or for 60 seconds of standing time. One fare covers up to four passengers (five in the roomier "Checker" cabs). Most taxis cruise the city for passengers; you can hail them on the street. Fleet cabs (identifiable by stickers on the door or by illuminated advertisements on top of the car) charge an extra 50¢ from 8 p.m. to 6 a.m.

By Subway: At $1 per ride, the New York subway system is still one of the fastest and most reliable transportation bargains around. The system carries 3.4 million passengers daily, and runs 24 hours a day every day of the week. Purchase tokens at change booths in subway stations and insert them in turnstiles to enter the subway. You'll find the subway most useful for north-south trips (the 1, 2, and 3 "Broadway" lines serve the west side; the 4, 5, and 6 "Lexington Avenue" lines serve the east); crosstown trains are also available between Times Square and Grand Central Station and along 14th Street. Get a free subway map before you leave home by sending a large (at least six-by-eight inch) stamped, self-addressed envelope to Customer Services, Room 875, New York City Transit Authority, 370 Jay St., Brooklyn, NY 11201. Route information is available 24 hours a day from the New York Transit Information office (tel. 718/330-1234).

By Bus: Buses are equally reliable, a little safer, and much slower than subways. The $1 bus fare is payable only by exact change in coins or by subway token. Buses run both north-south along most of the main avenues, and crosstown (east-west) on such major streets as 14th, 34th, 42nd, 57th, and through Central Park on 68th, 79th, and 86th streets. Most midtown bus stops have route maps, and complete route maps may be found in most subway stations and in several of the easily obtainable New York pocket atlases.

By Car: Public transportation is a much more efficient, relaxing, and colorful way to enjoy the city. But if you want to bring a car into Manhattan, the parking lots on the west side and Upper East Side (above 66th Street) are much less expensive than midtown and hotel lots. Parking in the theater district can cost anywhere from $8 to $17 for a couple of hours, not necessarily including the city's 14% parking tax. If you park on the street, carefully read the red-and-white signs that explain parking restrictions. An illegally parked car will be heavily fined, and if towed will cost you at least $125.

If you need to rent a car, you can do so either at the airport or midtown. Sample rental car rates for a compact car run about $200 a week with no mileage charge for the first 700 miles; about $53 per day with no mileage fee for the first 100 miles. Various specials and discounts may also be available, so check with your travel agent. On weekends during the summer months, rental cars in Manhattan are usually reserved at least a week in advance, so make sure you plan ahead.

Weather

What kind of weather do you want? New York has it all, ranging from temperatures in the 20s and 30s (often accompanied by wind, rain, and snow) during the winter months (December through February) to the 80s and 90s during the humid summer (mid-June through September). Spring and autumn provide the most acclimate weather for appreciating the city.

Clothing

Dress corresponds to where you go and what time of year you go there. Bring your shorts and swimsuits for the summer, but in the winter you'll want to bundle up in overcoats, scarves, gloves, and a hat. Otherwise, wear whatever makes you feel comfortable, but remember that certain tonier dining spots may require gentlemen to wear a jacket and tie.

Time

New York is on Eastern Standard Time, and observes Daylight Savings Time during the summer months.

Telephones

The area code for Manhattan and the Bronx is 212; in the other boroughs it's 718. Local calls on pay phones cost 25¢. For directory information in Manhattan and the Bronx, dial 411; for the outer boroughs, dial 718/555-1212. The emergency number for police, fire, or ambulance assistance is 911.

Shopping

New York sells at least one of just about everything under the sun.

Macy's in midtown West 34th Street and Broadway (tel. 971-6000), the world's largest department store, is a good place to start a shopping expedition, with a dozen floors of reasonably priced clothing and housewares for a wide range of tastes. **Bloomingdale's,** East 60th Street and Lexington Avenue (tel. 705-2000), has an upscale selection of (mostly) women's clothing, plus men's clothes, housewares, and home furnishings, with prices competitive with Macy's. **Saks,** 49th Street and Fifth Avenue, (tel. 753-4000), is another fashion institution. The best department store sales take place around the major holidays.

New York's garment district, along Seventh Avenue in the 30s, offers excellent fashion bargains. Other popular shopping streets for fashion (and more) include **Fifth Avenue** in the 50s, with **Tiffany's, Cartier,** and other famous names; and **Madison Avenue** between 61st and 86th streets, known for upscale boutiques such as **Pierre Balmain, Yves Saint Laurent,** and **Kenzo.** Chic one-of-a-kind fashions will be found in the many small boutiques in **SoHo** (the area south of Houston Avenue). **Chinatown** contains dozens of small shops that offer a large range of inexpensive gifts and souvenirs. On the **Upper West Side,** the streets of the major avenues (Broadway, Amsterdam, and Columbus) are lined with boutiques, bookstores, gift shops, and toy stores.

Music fans shouldn't pass up **Tower Records,** 692 Broadway at West 4th Street (tel. 505-1500) and 66th Street and Broadway (tel. 799-2500), which lay claim to being the largest record stores in the world. Likewise, the **Strand,** just up the street at 829 Broadway at East 12th Street (tel. 473-1452), is one of the world's biggest book stores, with eight miles of used books and half-priced reviewers' copies.

Many electronics and clothing stores offer name-brand goods at a substantial discount. For jewelry, shop 47th Street between Fifth Avenue and Avenue of the Americas (Sixth Avenue). Electronic goods such as cameras, stereos, TVs, and videocassette recorders are sold substantially below list price at **Uncle Steve's,** 343 Canal (tel. 226-4010), **47th Street Photo,** 67 West 47th St. (tel. 260-4410), and by **The Wiz** and **Crazy Eddie** chains. (Note: Be advised, discounted electronics items are sometimes sold without manufacturers' warranties.)

Discount women's clothing is available at the **S & W Designers Apparel Discount Center,** 287 Seventh Ave. (tel. 924-6656), **The New Store,** 289 Seventh Ave. (741-1077), and in the many **Bolton's** outlets.

The **Odd Lot Trading Co., Third Avenue Bazaar,** and **Duane Reade** drugstores all offer large selections of miscellaneous discounted, discontinued, and / or slightly damaged goods.

Theater

Amid New York's hundreds of theaters, something is bound to appeal to any taste. Ticket prices run from about $50 for the best Broadway seats on a weekend, down to $10 or less for off-off-Broadway productions. The TKTS booths in Times Square and the World Trade Center, however, are one of New York's best bargains, since they sell half-price tickets for a wide selection of its older productions and previews on the day of the show. The booths open at noon for matinee performances (Wednesdays at 2 p.m. and Sundays at 3 p.m.), and at 3 p.m. for evening performances. Most theaters are dark on Monday.

How to Get Married in New York

You can get married 24 hours after obtaining a marriage license for $10 from the Marriage License Bureau in the Municipal Building downtown, 1 Center St. at Chambers Street (tel. 269-2900). No blood test or physical is necessary, but you should have original identification, such as a valid driver's license, passport, or birth certificate. If either of you is between the ages of 18 and 23, original proof of age is required. If you are 16 or 17 years old, your parents need to be present to sign a consent form. The bureau is open Monday through Friday from 9 a.m. to 4 p.m. You must wait a full 24 hours before the marriage ceremony. Marriages can be performed for $5 in the City Clerk's office, 1 Center St., Monday through Friday from 9:30 a.m. to noon, and from 1 p.m. to 4 p.m.

For Further Information

Contact: **New York Convention & Visitors Bureau,** Two Columbus Circle, New York, NY 10019 (tel. 212/397-8200). An information center located near Times Square, 158–160 West 42nd St., is open Monday through Friday from 9 a.m. to 6 p.m., and Saturday and Sunday from 10 a.m. to 6 p.m.

ROMANTIC INTERLUDES: The only problem honeymooners may have in New

York is deciding what romantic activities might have to be postponed for their next visit—there's too much to do in a short period of time.

Cruising New York

Take one of the **Circle Line's** Manhattan circumnavigations and get the big picture on the Big Apple. The double-decked boats depart every 45 minutes from Pier 83 at 42nd Street and Twelfth Avenue for the leisurely 2¾-hour trip ($12 per person), complete with well-informed guides. There's a snack counter and bar on board.

On Wednesday and Thursday evenings from June through August, Circle Line's Twilight Cruises offer even more romantic two-hour trips. Enjoy hot and cold hors d'oeuvres, dance to live music, sip cocktails served by one of several cash bars, and gaze at the Brooklyn Bridge and Manhattan's illuminated skyline. $70 per couple, jacket required for men, reservations necessary. Contact: **Circle Line Sightseeing Yachts, Inc.,** Pier 83, West 43rd Street and Twelfth Avenue, New York, NY 10036 (tel. 563-3200).

A Medieval Museum

Almost no New York vista is more romantic than the sight of the sun setting over New Jersey as seen from the **Cloisters** (tel. 923-3700), a branch of the Metropolitan Museum located close to the northern tip of Manhattan, in Fort Tryon Park, overlooking the Hudson River. Constructed in medieval style, the Cloisters was pieced together in 1938 from parts of a 12th-century chapter house, parts of cloisters from five medieval monasteries, a Romanesque chapel, and a 12th-century Spanish apse. Medieval festivals and concerts are held intermittently during the nonwinter months. Admission is a donation. Open Tuesday through Sunday, 9:30 a.m. to 4:45 p.m. (November through February) or until 5:15 p.m. (March through October). To get to the Cloisters by subway, take the IND Eighth Avenue A train to 190th Street–Overlook Terrace, exit by elevator, then either take the number 4 bus or walk through Fort Tryon Park to the museum. For those who wish to avoid the subways, the Madison Avenue bus no. 4, "Fort Tryon Park–The Cloisters," goes right to the door of the museum.

A Little Night Music

Spend a romantic musical evening in Greenwich Village, the world's jazz capital. Begin at the **Village Vanguard,** Seventh Avenue just below West 11th Street (tel. 255-4073), $12 cover and $6 minimum, a classic basement mecca where the cream of the straight-ahead jazz crop still checks in regularly. Then mosey down the street to **Sweet Basil Jazz Restaurant,** Seventh Avenue and Bleecker Street (tel. 242-1785), $12 cover and two-drink minimum, a comfortable, sophisticated room that takes the genre's new sounds seriously. **The Blue Note,** Sixth Avenue and West 3rd Street (tel. 475-8592), $15 cover and $7.50 minimum, **Bradley's,** University Place between West 10th and West 11th streets (tel. 228-6440), $5 cover and $5 minimum, and the **Village Gate,** Bleecker and Thompson streets (tel. 475-5120), variable cover, should also be on your jazz agenda. Slightly further south, **S.O.B.**'s, which stands for Sounds of Brazil, Varick and King streets (tel. 243-4940), $15 cover and two-drink minimum, specializes in music from the Caribbean, Africa, and—of course—Brazil.

Uptown, the Algonquin Hotel's **Oak Room,** West 44th Street between Fifth and Sixth Avenues (tel. 840-6800), about $25 cover and $15 minimum, a warm, masculine bastion of tradition; and the **Carlyle Cafe** in the Carlyle Hotel, Madison Avenue and East 76th Street (tel. 744-1600), $15 minimum, provide unequaled opportunities to enjoy romantic music in beautiful settings. No matter who is appearing during your stay—the great Bobby Short, George Shearing, and Michael Feinstein are all regulars in one or the other of these rooms—you'll hear the standards of such great composers

GREENWICH VILLAGE

as Cole Porter, Noel Coward, Irving Berlin, and the Gershwins sung and played at their sentimental best.

Views from on High

New York City's most popular tourist attraction is still **The Empire State Building,** Fifth Avenue at 34th Street (tel. 736-3100), $3 admission. Open daily from 9:30 a.m. to midnight, it offers an unmatchable view of the city and surrounding environs. It's especially romantic on a clear evening, when Manhattan turns into an unbelievable light show. There's a great souvenir shop on the 86th floor.

Downtown, the twin towers of the **World Trade Center** offer amazing views of Manhattan and its environs. In the southern tower, 2, the 107th floor observation deck is open from 9:30 a.m. to 9:30 p.m. (tel. 466-7377; $2.95 per person admission). In Tower 1, you can either dine (at considerable expense) in the famous 107th-floor Windows on the World (tel. 938-1111) or enjoy grilled entrées, snack on hors d'oeuvres, or just have a romantic late-night dessert or drink in the equally fabulously positioned Hors d'Oeuverie (tel. 938-1111), which features numerous appetizers such as crab fritters, chicken yakitori, and Thai spring rolls (all in the $4 to $5 range) as well as one or two entrées such as Korean short ribs (kalbi) or grilled Mexican chorizo with refried beans and tostadas. Hours are Monday through Saturday, from 3 p.m. to 6 p.m. and from 7:30 p.m. to 10:30 p.m., Sundays from noon to 9 p.m. During lunch, the Hors d'Oeuverie is a private club, but nonmembers are admitted for a $7.50 surcharge. The adjoining City Lights Bar is open Monday through Friday from 3 p.m. to 1 a.m., Saturday from noon to 1 a.m., and Sunday from noon to 9 p.m.

A Walk in the Park

On a warm spring or summer day, **Central Park** becomes a magnet for young New Yorkers. However, the **Conservatory Gardens** on Fifth Avenue at 104th Street is a well-kept New York horticultural secret and perfect for a romantic stroll. Open from 8 a.m. to a half-hour before dusk, this unpopulated piece of paradise is surrounded by rose bushes and features a large floral centerpiece whose beds are changed seasonally. The spring tulips are a floral marvel. A visit to the Conservatory Gardens is like being in another world.

Central Park proper is a green 2½-mile sanctuary amid the concrete jungle of Manhattan. Designed in 1856, its pedestrian and bike paths, tunnels and bridle paths form maze-like patterns in which many remarkable treasures are hidden. The **Central Park Zoo,** for example, is open daily from 10 a.m. to 5 p.m. Or pack a picnic and just wander around and visit such attractive spots as the elliptical **Conservatory Pond** with its fairy-tale motif, **Central Park Lake** (where you can rent paddleboats during the day), the **Great Lawn,** the **Reservoir,** the **Victorian Carousel** (10:30 to 6 p.m.), and the newly renovated **Wollman ice skating rink** (open during the winter only; tel. 517-4800 for skate rental information).

Or pick up a bottle of champagne, a couple of glasses, and take a leisurely **moonlight carriage ride** through the park—or any other time of day, for that matter. Carriages park along 59th Street, and the legally set rates are $17 for the first half hour, $5 for each additional 15 minutes.

Romance on a Budget

Although the best things in life may not be free, they needn't cost a fortune either. New York offers many inexpensive or free staples of civilized life that are at least as enjoyable as its pricier attractions. For a mere 25¢, the **Staten Island Ferry** departs from the South Ferry Terminal adjacent to Battery Park every half hour for a 30-minute round-trip to Staten Island and back, passing Governors Island, the Statue of Liberty, and Ellis Island, as well as giving a unique view of lower Manhattan.

During the summer months, Joseph Papp presents free **Shakespeare-in-the-**

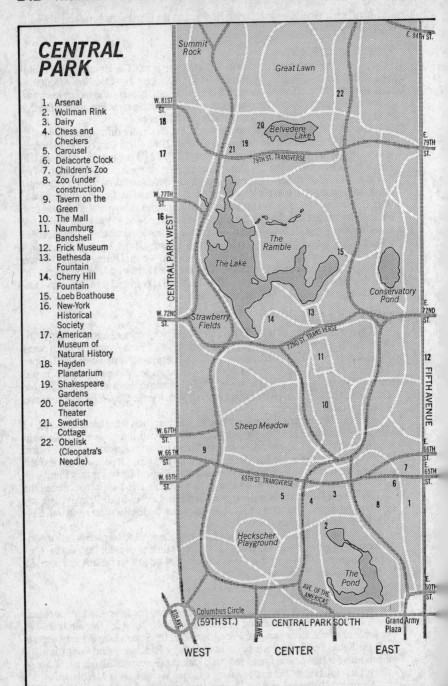

CENTRAL PARK

1. Arsenal
2. Wollman Rink
3. Dairy
4. Chess and Checkers
5. Carousel
6. Delacorte Clock
7. Children's Zoo
8. Zoo (under construction)
9. Tavern on the Green
10. The Mall
11. Naumburg Bandshell
12. Frick Museum
13. Bethesda Fountain
14. Cherry Hill Fountain
15. Loeb Boathouse
16. New-York Historical Society
17. American Museum of Natural History
18. Hayden Planetarium
19. Shakespeare Gardens
20. Delacorte Theater
21. Swedish Cottage
22. Obelisk (Cleopatra's Needle)

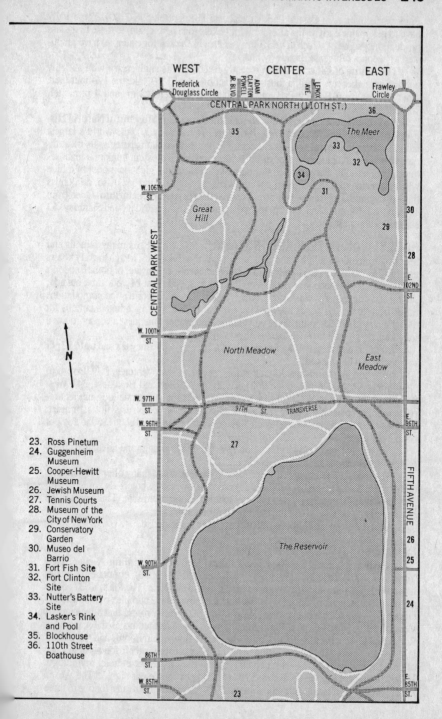

23. Ross Pinetum
24. Guggenheim Museum
25. Cooper-Hewitt Museum
26. Jewish Museum
27. Tennis Courts
28. Museum of the City of New York
29. Conservatory Garden
30. Museo del Barrio
31. Fort Fish Site
32. Fort Clinton Site
33. Nutter's Battery Site
34. Lasker's Rink and Pool
35. Blockhouse
36. 110th Street Boathouse

Park performances in Central Park's Delacorte Theater (tel. 598-7100). You usually have to get on line early in the afternoon for tickets (one per person) to these first-class productions, some of which (*The Mystery of Edwin Drood*, for example) have graduated to become full-scale Broadway hits.

The **Statue of Liberty,** which recently celebrated its anniversary with a highly publicized makeover, is still a must-see attraction. For $1.50, take the 1½-hour tour, which leaves from Battery Park every half hour between 9 a.m. and 4 p.m. (tel. 269-5755).

You could spend days rambling about in the **American Museum of Natural History** on Central Park West at West 79th Street (tel. 769-5100), the world's largest natural-history museum, with its collection of some 35 million artifacts. Its most famous attractions include the Star of India star sapphire, a crosscut hunk of a giant sequoia tree, various reconstructed dinosaur skeletons, and a gigantic model of a blue whale hovering over the museum's Wednesday-evening cocktail bar. Also, don't miss the **Naturemax Theater's** giant film screen or the **Hayden Planetarium.** Open from 10 a.m. to 5:45 p.m., and 10 a.m. to 9 p.m. on Wednesday, Friday, and Saturday. $3 suggested contribution.

HONEYMOON HOTELS AND HIDEAWAYS: New York has many famous and beautiful romantic hotels, but lodgings aren't exactly a bargain. Though the city boasts nearly 175,000 hotel rooms, they tend to be either small, expensive, or both. But don't let room sizes dissuade you, since you'll want to spend most of your time outside, seeing and doing things you won't find anywhere else in the world. Accommodations range from luxurious suites overlooking Central Park to rooms in hotels famous for their literary clientele. Whichever you choose, remember to request a corner room; a long look down a midtown avenue is always inspirational.

In addition to the city's 8.25% sales tax, a 5% city occupancy tax and up to $2 per room will also be charged.

New York **bed-and-breakfast** services, such as Urban Ventures, P.O. Box 426, New York, NY 10024 (tel. 594-5650) or City Lights Bed and Breakfast, 344 West 84th St., New York, NY 10024 (tel. 877-3235) offer such romantic lodgings as fireplace rooms in beautiful Upper East and West Side brownstones, artsy lofts, or quiet, private little apartments in Greenwich Village. Rates range from about $50 to $85 per couple per night.

The hotels listed below offer color TVs, air conditioning, and telephones in all rooms. Reservations are highly recommended.

Weekends are relatively slow for New York hotels, and many offer bargain rates at that time. Some of the best of these are noted below. Some hotels also offer theater packages, with the price of two tickets included in the room rate. This tends to be seasonal, and you should call the hotel for information.

All rates given are European Plan, i.e. meals not included.

Expensive

Newly remodeled, the 80-year-old **Plaza,** 59th Street and Fifth Avenue, New York, NY 10019 (tel. 212/759-3000 or toll free 800/228-3000), continues to attract newlyweds who equate honeymoons with old-world elegance. The Plaza's 837 rooms decorated in French provincial style rise above a labyrinthine complex of lobbies, restaurants, shops, and banquet rooms. Request one of the many rooms that offer a unique view of the length of Central Park. Such famous Plaza restaurants as the warm Oak Room, the Oyster Bar, the Palm Court, the stately Edwardian Room, and the kitschy Polynesian Trader Vic's are worth a visit, not necessarily for their food—better can often be found elsewhere—as much as for what they represent in hotel mythology. Honeymoon package: None. Rates: $200 to $750 per couple per night. ''The Westin Plaza Weekend'' offers accommodations at 50% off regular room rates for one to three nights, Friday through Sunday. "The Westin Plaza Champagne Weekend"—with a medium room and a bottle of champagne—is available for one to three nights, Friday through Sunday, at $190 per couple per night.

The Waldorf-Astoria, 100 East 50th St., New York, NY 10022 (tel. 212/355-3000). Everything in this Hilton Hotel–chain flagship seems larger than life—even the plush, marble-pillared main lobby is introduced by a smaller lobby that welcomes the visitor with ethereal harp music. Actually, the Waldorf-Astoria is two hotels: From the 20th floor up, it becomes the more expensive Waldorf Towers, with prices beginning at $260 per couple per night. The Waldorf-Astoria's elegant rooms are nice and big themselves—with comfortable mauve European decor, enormous marbled bathrooms, and wonderful views of Park Avenue—and the entire place recently underwent a $110-million restoration. The Waldorf's famous restaurants are an international potpourri of moods, and include a glamorous art deco Cocktail Terrace and the Persian atmosphere of Shah Abbas, one of the city's few Iranian restaurants. Honeymoon package: Two days / one night (arrival Friday, through Sunday), $190 per couple, including deluxe accommodations, champagne, breakfast in bed, and gratuities. Standard rates: $175 and way up. The three-day / two-night "Weekend at the Waldorf" package (Friday or Saturday arrival), $270 per couple, includes deluxe accommodations and welcoming cocktails in Peacock Alley.

Moderate

New York's chicest new hotel, **Morgans,** 237 Madison Ave., New York, NY 10016 (tel. 212/686-0300 or toll free 800/334-3408; reservations: tel. toll free 800/334-3408), is a study in tasteful simplicity. From the smartly tailored clerks and bellhops to the clean, well-lighted rooms, everything about the Morgan is *just so*. Decorated in pastels and grays, the small, quiet midtown hotel has gone all out to assure that its rooms look nothing like any other commercial hotels. For example, you'll find a black toothbrush in your black-and-white bathroom with a clear Plexiglas shower door; instead of bedspreads, beds are covered with comforters made from Brooks Brothers cotton shirting material; and all rooms have window seats. Although the hotel offers no special honeymoon packages, it is small enough that the staff will treat newlyweds to a complimentary bottle of champagne and special care. All rooms come with fresh flowers, complimentary continental breakfast, the *New York Times* delivered to your door, complimentary admission to the Palladium (one of New York's popular clubs), audio and video cassette recorders (and use of the hotel's extensive video library), a refrigerator, and full turndown service. Daily rates are $150 to $350 per couple, and a weekend rate of $115 per couple per night is available.

A very romantic and beautiful hotel, the **Golden Tulip Barbizon,** 140 East 63rd St., New York, NY 10021 (tel. 212/838-5700 or toll free 800/223-1020), is designed to compliment the building that houses it, a Manhattan landmark built in 1927. Decorated in various shades of pink and ochre, the Barbizon's rooms are intimate yet relaxing, and reflect the soothing charms of the early-20th-century Barbizon school of Impressionist painting. Surrounding the marbled lobby is a small shopping pavilion, the Barbizon Restaurant, and Cafe Barbizon, all designed to combine European elegance with American activity (Bloomingdale's, for instance, is just a few blocks away). Honeymoon package: None. Standard rates: $160 to $375 per night. The "Golden Tulip Weekend" package consists of three days / two nights (Friday arrival) for $99 per couple per night with champagne, continental breakfast in bed, and the *New York Times*.

New York's Murray Hill neighborhood still contains many fine 19th-century brownstones. The 248-room **Shelburne Murray Hill,** 303 Lexington Ave., New York, NY 10019 (tel. 212/246-1300 or toll free 800/637-8483), evokes the Victorian era from the moment you walk in the door and take in the lobby's Persian rugs, antique furnishings, and crystal chandeliers. The rooms themselves are quite large by New

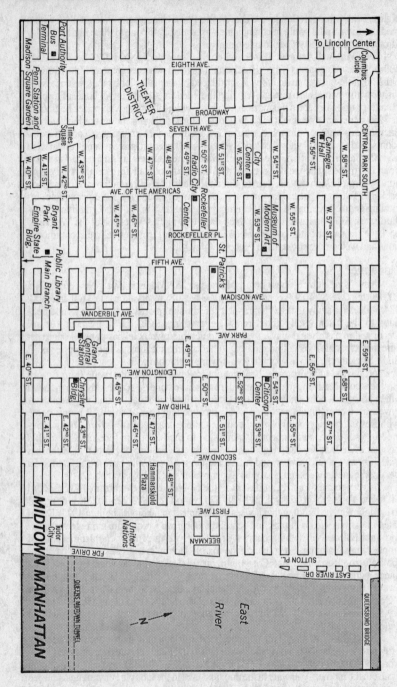

MIDTOWN MANHATTAN

York standards, and are furnished in extremely comfortable grandmotherly elegance. All the rooms and suites contain surprisingly large walk-in kitchens, and many also have balconies you can walk out on. The hotel is also close to Grand Central Station and the Madison and Fifth Avenue shopping districts. Honeymoon package: None. Standard rates: $140 to $190 per couple per night. "The Suite Weekend" package offers one to three nights at the Shelburne (Friday or Saturday arrival) for $75 to $97 per couple per night.

Lyden Gardens, 215 East 64th St., New York, NY 10021 (tel. 212/355-1230 or toll free 800/637-8483). Located on a quiet, dignified Upper East Side street, this little-known hotel is apparently protected from public acclaim by its regular guests, who probably wish to keep it to themselves. Walking into any of the rooms, you'll be a-mazed at their size and comfort, with large sofas and dining room tables that seem more appropriate in a home than in a hotel room. The decor is tasteful and relaxed, and the afternoon light filters pleasantly into most rooms. All Lyden Gardens rooms contain kitchens so fully equipped that you'll be tempted to eat all your meals in the hotel; it seems a perfect place to be alone together in. Honeymoon package: None. Standard rates: $125 to $175 per couple per night. "The Suite Weekend" package offers one to three nights (Friday or Saturday arrival) for $80 to $97 per suite per night.

Glittery, glossy, and *big,* the **Milford Plaza,** 270 West 45th St., New York, NY 10036 (tel. 212/869-3600 or toll free 800/221-2690), is notable for two aspects honeymooners may find irresistible: First, it's located smack dab in the middle of the theater district, close to Sardi's, Times Square, and the TKTS booth. Second, most of the Milford's 1,310 clean and modern rooms offer great views of the Hudson River. The hotel also contains three pretty good restaurants: Kippy's Pier 44, Celebrity Deli, and The Stage Door Canteen. Honeymoon package: None. Standard rates: $100 to $300 per couple. The "Lullabuy" package offers one to five nights for $85 to $92 per night per couple, including a daily continental breakfast, cocktail, and a table d'hôte dinner at Kippy's Pier 44 (not a bad deal).

Inexpensive

Located across the street from Lincoln Center, New York's cultural mecca, the no-frills **Hotel Empire,** Broadway at West 63rd Street, New York, NY 10023 (tel. 212/265-7400), is a perfect low-budget hotel for honeymooners who love operas, concerts, theater, and enjoy being on the doorstep of the trendy West Side scene. The Hotel Empire itself contains clean, old-fashioned, modestly furnished rooms decorated in pink and green, and you will be well taken care of by its attentive staff. The surrounding neighborhood contains many fine restaurants (such as Fiorello's, noted for its delicious pizzas, and The Saloon, with its gigantic menu and roller-skating waiters), and is within walking distance of Carnegie Hall, the Broadway theater district, and Fifth Avenue shopping. Honeymoon package: None. Rates: $90 to $125 per night.

We're in budget-basement territory here, but the **Palace International,** 429 Park Avenue South, New York, NY 10016 (tel. 212/532-4860), is still to be recommended for clean, albeit small rooms decorated in very contemporary designer grays. For the price, it's rather a nice deal, and the hotel aims to please with a helpful staff and by offering visitors a complimentary drink in the nearby Bombay Palace Indian restaurant. Located on the edge of Manhattan's midtown shopping district, the Palace is within easy access of the main transportation routes. Honeymoon package: None. Standard rates: $80 to $99 per night. The "European Weekend" package features one night (Friday or Saturday arrival) for $64, with continental breakfast and a 2½-hour bus tour of New York City. The "Summer / Winter Surprise Weekend Package" features two nights (Friday arrival) for $155 per couple, with breakfast, a bus tour of New York, and dinner for two at the Bombay Palace (Indian cuisine) or Zona Rosa (Mexican cuisine).

ROMANTIC RESTAURANTS: When they're not eating to live—you can grab a decent hot dog on any corner, or a tasty slice in one of the city's more than 1,000 pizza parlors—New Yorkers live to eat. From quaint bistros to unusual ethnic discoveries to luxurious four-star cuisine, New York has a restaurant for you. In this chapter, we have not included any of New York's well-known gourmet palaces with the stratospheric prices; instead, we've put together a tasty assortment of restaurants that offer excellent food and romantic atmosphere—all at moderate prices (about $45 to $80 per couple for dinner, plus drinks).

Moderate

One of the more intimate dining rooms, this candlelit jewel, **Le Café de la Gare,** 143 Perry St. (tel. 242-3553), is a special Greenwich Village secret. Entrées include simply prepared yet hearty fish and meat dishes—such as trout stuffed with cod and vegetables or rabbit with cabbage, bacon, and white wine sauce—from a menu that changes every other week. One of Le Café's staple dishes, however, is its highly recommendable garlicky cassoulet. A fixed-price menu ($17.50) includes soup, the special of the day, and dessert. In addition to Le Café's reasonable prices (dinner for two runs about $45), the restaurant doesn't serve its own liquor, so feel free to bring in your own bottle of wine. No credit cards accepted, however.

Union Square Cafe, 21 East 16th St., between Broadway and Fifth Avenue (tel. 243-4020). One of the highlights of the newly spruced-up Union Square area, this handsome café—with its split-level architecture, warm lighting, fresh flowers, Country French antiques, and attentive service—has quickly become one of New York's most highly regarded midrange restaurants. The restaurant takes fresh ingredients, many of which are purchased at the neighboring farmers' market, and turns them into creatively eclectic delights. While perusing the menu, nibble the lusty Sicilian olives and crunchy homemade croutons. Begin with a rich spaghettini alla puttanesca or a trusty, crusty duck confit, then move onto such toothsome entrées as grilled lamb steak, venison medallions, or a filet mignon of tuna. An unusual selection of dessert wines can accompany an apple tart or an Italian pear torte. A superb hamburger is available at lunchtime. Appetizers from $3.75 to $6.95, lunch entrées from $5.95 to $14.50, dinner entrées from $12.95 to $20.

Omen, 113 Thompson St., between Prince and Spring, SoHo (tel. 925-8923). At this fine Japanese restaurant, the food is so subtle and good, and the rural oriental ambience—lots of wood, bamboo, and brick—is so out of whack with the area, that one feels both physically and spiritually replenished after a meal. And what meals! Since the menu makes no distinction between entrées and appetizers, you are encouraged to mix and match. Here are some recommended options: avocado and shrimp with miso sauce, seafood and chicken stew, spinach and shiitake mushrooms with sesame, scallops with lemon juice, or marinated chicken with white radish and carrot. Omen soup is a warming winter favorite, and the restaurant also serves very good sashimi. Wash it all down with sake or Japanese beer. Prix-fixe meals are available for $16 to $21 per person, à la carte items range from $2 to $12.

The charming Parisian-style **Quatorze,** 240 West 14th St., Greenwich Village (tel. 206-7006), on funky 14th Street serves delicious bistro cuisine in sophisticated and romantic surroundings—handsome tile floors, warm red banquettes, brass railings, and white-jacketed waiters. You might begin with local oysters on the half shell or the house salad, a traditional bistro concoction of chicory with bacon and hot vinaigrette. Recommended entrées include the half-chicken grilled with herbs or the consistently well-prepared fish dishes. For dessert, don't miss the house specialty, Chocolate Regal. Appetizers from $4.75 to $6, entrées from $14 to $21.

The Black Sheep, 342 West 11th St., West Greenwich Village (tel. 242-1010). Located about as far west as you can get in the Village, in a storefront on the corner of Washington Street, this casually elegant bistro recalls the time when New York was still a small town, and horse-drawn carriages clattered along the cobblestoned streets. Classical guitar music strums in the background, while bright modern art accents the brick walls. The five-course, prix-fixe dinner offers extremely good value, serving well-prepared country French food—and plenty of it. For openers, the crudité platter, including a garden harvest of broccoli, artichokes, and carrots, could be a meal in itself. Your second course might be a country pâté or green lasagna. Entrées take advantage of fresh seasonal offerings, and might include a perfectly roasted free-range chicken, sautéed yellowtail, or a pink rack of lamb, piquant with mustard and pepper. A green salad clears your palate for the dessert specials—perhaps a white chocolate mousse, chocolate truffle, or strawberry biscuit. Five-course, prix-fixe dinner, from $23 to $34 per person.

Pesca, 23 E. 22nd St., Gramercy Park area (tel. 533-2293), aptly calls itself a seafood café. The warm beige and peach walls, bentwood chairs, massive floral arrangements, and pressed tin ceilings recall favorite restaurants on the grand boulevards of Paris, while the creative and tempting all-fish and seafood menu makes it hard for devotees to make up their minds. Long-time chefs Skip Dillon and Ralph Steiber have designed an innovative menu that covers all the favorites—broiled catch of the day or seafood cannelloni—as well as innovative specials that really come off. Many house dishes reflect Mexican or oriental touches. Sea scallops come deep fried in a tempura batter with shiitake mushrooms; tuna chili is sautéed with tomatoes, pepper, and spices, and served with fried sweet plaintains. Appetizers from $4.50 to $11.50 per person; entrées from $13.75 to $28.

The Gotham Bar and Grill, 12 East 12th St., between Fifth Avenue and University Place (tel. 620-4020) serves expensive but delicious and perfectly presented sausages, chops, and salads in a large, comfortably postmodern room that manages to simultaneously evoke activity and intimacy. The favorite restaurant of many food writers. Entrées from $18.50 to $26.

Oysters—raw and pan-roasted—are the specialty of the **Grand Central Oyster Bar and Restaurant** in the lower level of Grand Central Station (tel. 752-3334), a spacious room and adjacent masculine bar that remains the epitome of New York dignity and sophistication. Lunches and dinners begin at about $40 per couple and mount rapidly to the $80 to $100 range.

Inexpensive

Would you believe a 1¼-pound lobster for $10.95? How about a bluefish filet for $7.25? And you also get all the salad you can eat, fresh garlic bread, fresh veggies, and spuds. **Cockeyed Clams,** 1678 Third Ave. at East 94th Street, Upper East Side (tel. 831-4121), keeps its prices low by operating its own fishing boats. (For landlubbers, they also raise their own cattle on a farm upstate, allowing the restaurant to offer a 16-ounce sirloin steak with all the trimmings for $9.75.) The decor is a funky nautical mixture of lobster traps, fish netting, operating room lights on ships, and who knows what else.

The same management also operates **Hobeau's Restaurant,** 988 Second Ave. at East 52nd Street (tel. 421-2888) and **Squid Roe Restaurant,** 1468 Second Ave. at East 77th Street (tel. 249-4666), which all have similar decor and prices. No reservations accepted, so be prepared for a wait. Open for both lunch and dinner.

Gigantic portions of Brazilian favorites are served in large tureens at **Cabana Carioca,** 123 W. 45th St., midtown (tel. 581-8088), an intimate wood-paneled upstairs room filled with lovers, families, and local workers enjoying a late meal at the bar. Try the *feijoda completa,* Brazil's native dish, which combines delicious Portuguese sausage and black beans. Before dinner, sample a *caiparinja,* a powerful and tasty concoction of crushed limes and cane liquor. Entrees $8.50 to $13.50.

Known in the neighborhood as "the place with the line in front," the **Cucina Stagionale,** 275 Bleecker St., Greenwich Village (tel. 924-2707), modestly serves

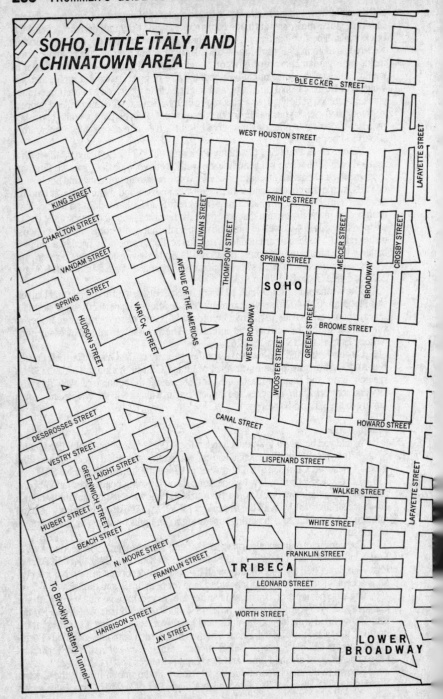

SOHO, LITTLE ITALY, AND CHINATOWN AREA

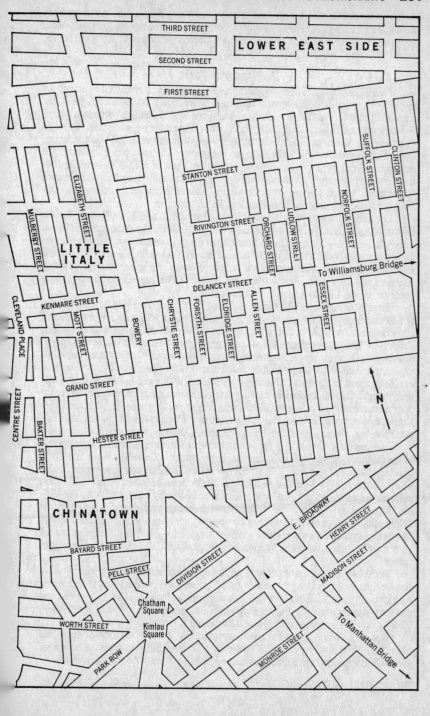

large portions of healthy Italian food at surprisingly low prices. The restaurant itself feels like an Italian grandmother's dining room, and as with most grandmothers, you'll have to bring your own wine since no liquor is served. Appetizers from $2 to $5.95, entrées $5.95 to $10.95.

2. Niagara Falls

This is the big one: The honeymoon center of the universe, as well as one of our fair planet's most incredible natural wonders. Ever since 1804, when Joseph Bonaparte (Napoleon's brother) and his American-born wife, Elizabeth Patterson, visited in celebration of their marriage, Niagara Falls has attracted newlyweds from the world over. Perhaps some subliminal vibration emanating from the 212,000 cubic feet of water that topple over the Falls each second inspires this ritualistic pilgrimage, or maybe honeymooners are drawn to the astounding sight of a 2,000-foot-wide, 184-foot-high cataract sending a cloud of mist billowing into the air. Its name, which means "thundering waters," comes from the Neutre Indians. Whatever the reason, Niagara Falls attracts approximately 15 million tourists per year.

Located halfway between Lake Erie (to the south) and Lake Ontario (to the north), Niagara actually consists of three separate cataracts. The American and Bridal Veil Falls lie in New York, on the eastern side of the river. Horseshoe Falls, the largest and most stupendous cataract, is on the western side, in Ontario, Canada. Goat Island —containing a park, a restaurant, and access to caves behind the rushing waters— separates the three falls. Below them, the Niagara River has gouged a stupendous gorge on its way to Lake Ontario, 13 miles north.

The city of Niagara Falls, New York (pop. 71,000), charms with its natural beauty and traditional upstate appeal. Along the shores of the Niagara River a number of attractive parks provide free access to the Falls. Naturally enough, much of Niagara Falls, New York, devotes itself to the voluminous tourist trade, with numerous hotels, restaurants, souvenir stands, and miscellaneous attractions. The annual Festival of Lights, for example, a 44-day holiday celebration that begins in late November, is an event-crammed hodgepodge of intriguingly lit festivity located in the downtown section of both Niagaras. Likewise, the Niagara Falls Summer Experience offers free outdoor ethnic festivals, concerts, dance, and theater performances outside the city's Convention & Civic Center during July and August. Despite its status as a tourist magnet, however, Niagara Falls, New York, remains a low-key, working-class town.

Niagara Falls, Ontario, on the other hand, seems to have gone all out in response to the fabulous view of the Falls one can enjoy from the Canadian shore lined with beautiful parks and gardens. Such attractions as the Elvis Presley Museum, the House of Frankenstein Wax Museum, and the Guinness Book of World Records Museum compete with the natural splendor provided at no charge by Mother Nature. The Clifton Hills section, adjacent to the Niagara River, becomes a whirlwind of activity at the height of the tourist season (April 1 to October 31), viewing towers punctuate the skyline, and people line the shores during the winter months—both during the day and the early evening hours, when the illuminated falls glow amid a rainbow of splendiferous colors.

For honeymooners whose tastes run more toward natural beauty, simply drive outside the city limits along the banks of the Niagara River, where you will find serene parks, country roads, and off-the-beaten-track historical towns. Hikers, campers, and curiosity seekers alike will find local color aplenty in the historic towns of Lewiston, New York, and Queenston and Niagara-on-the-Lake, Ontario.

Not only does Niagara Falls embody tradition, it's also the kind of place that offers something for every taste. If you wish your honeymoon to combine an active, event-filled vacation with a little undisturbed solitude, it could be just the place.

PRACTICAL FACTS: All that U.S. citizens need to come and go from Canada is some form of identification, such as a valid passport, birth certificate, or driver's license. To enter the United States, Canadians will need proof of citizenship, such as a passport or birth certificate.

Getting There

Reaching Niagara Falls is easy from most places in the United States or Canada.

By Air: Niagara Falls visitors usually fly into the Greater Buffalo International Airport, about 30 miles south. **USAIR, American, Brockway, Comair, Eastern, Empire, Mall, Piedmont, Republic,** and **United** are among the carriers that serve Buffalo's airport. There is also the Niagara Falls airport; it handles military and charter planes primarily.

By Train: The **Amtrak** station in Niagara Falls, New York, is at Hyde Park Boulevard and Lockport Road. For schedule information and rates, call the toll-free Amtrak number, 800/877-7245.

By Bus: The **Greyhound** and **Trailways** bus companies operate out of the Niagara Falls Transportation Center, 4th and Niagara Streets, in Niagara Falls, New York.

By Car: Buffalo, New York, is on Interstate 90 (I-90), the Governor Thomas E. Dewey Thruway. From Buffalo, take I-190 to Niagara Falls. From Toronto to Niagara Falls, Canada (or vice versa), take the Queen Elizabeth Highway.

Getting Around

By Bus: Niagara Scenic Bus Lines (tel. 716/648-1500) offers a regular shuttle service between the Buffalo Airport and Niagara Falls, New York, between 8:30 a.m. and 8:30 p.m. The hour-long ride costs $8 per person each way and will deliver you to your hotel.

By Car: A valid United States driver's license is sufficient to drive in Canada. Before leaving the United States, it's a good idea to pick up a sticker from your insurance company signifying proof of financial responsibility; otherwise, should you have an accident while in Canada, you may be detained for a few days while your insurance coverage is verified.

By Taxi: Taxi rates in Niagara Falls, New York, depending on the company, are about $1 for the first ⅑ of a mile and 10¢ for each ⅑ of a mile thereafter. Taxi fare between Buffalo and Niagara Falls is about $27.50.

Rental Cars: If you didn't arrive in the area via your own automobile, a rental car is strongly suggested so you can appreciate the beautiful scenery of Niagara's outlying areas. Many companies offer inexpensive weekly or weekend rates—beginning at about $60 per weekend or $175 per week—and cars may be rented at the Buffalo airport. A valid United States driver's license is sufficient to drive into Canada.

Language and Money

Although Canada is officially a bilingual country with both English and French spoken, one rarely hears French in Niagara Falls unless the speaker is a French tourist. In fact, one is much more likely to hear the native language of the area's significant Italian population.

The Canadian dollar is the official currency in Canada. At the time of this writing, one Canadian dollar equals about 65 U.S. cents. Unless otherwise noted, all prices in this chapter are given in U.S. dollars.

Most hotels and restaurants accept major credit cards, but check in advance to avoid difficulty.

Weather

The Niagara Falls area is pleasant during the late-spring through early-fall months, and turns rather cold during the winter. The average January temperature is an often windy 24°, while the average July temperature is 70°. March averages about 32°, and October about 50°. Evening hours will be relatively cooler. Expect snow toward the end of the year, when the area becomes a veritable winter wonderland. But thanks to the practiced snowplows of both the New York and Ontario governments, driving isn't much of a problem if common sense is used.

Clothing

Casual—lighter or heavier depending on the season. Bring hiking boots or a sturdy pair of walking shoes, the better to take in the scenery. During the winter, snow boots or galoshes will come in handy.

Time

Niagara Falls, Canada, and Niagara Falls, New York, both remain on Eastern Standard Time, except when Daylight Savings Time is in effect.

Telephones

The area code for Niagara Falls, New York, is 716. In Niagara Falls, Ontario, which you can dial direct from the United States, the area code is 416.

Shopping

As you might expect, you can choose from an enormous range of Falls-related souvenir and gift items in Niagara, from the many souvenir stores located close to the Falls—everything from snow scenes to *Maid of the Mist* pens (watch the boat sail from one end to the other).

The Niagara Falls area is also one of the continent's major factory-outlet centers. The **Factory Outlet Mall,** 1900 Military Rd. in New York, contains some 75 manufacturer outlets, with—according to *Consumer's Digest*—"bargains unequaled in the annals of consumer marketing." For example: the Pfaltzgraff Country Store (tel. 297-5706) offers second-quality stoneware at 50% of its regular prices; Candie's (tel. 297-9642) sells Nike, Reebok, and Bass shoes at discounts of up to 80%; and the Van Heusen Factory Store (tel. 297-8416) sells its regular line at a savings of 30% to 60%.

The **Rainbow Centre Shopping Mall** in downtown Niagara, New York, one block from the Falls, offers more than 60 shops and restaurants. For serious antiquing, browse **Lewiston Landings** (tel. 754-2144) in Lewiston, where four dealers share a single roof, or **Weezie's Antiques** (tel. 284-8173) in Niagara Falls, New York. Niagara Falls, Ontario, boasts several extremely drinkable—and reasonably priced—local wines, not to mention Canada's famous whiskey.

Each U.S. visitor can bring back, duty free, $400 worth of goods purchased in Canada for personal use if he or she is in Canada for at least 48 hours and has not claimed this exemption within 30 days. If the 48-hour or 30-day requirement isn't met, each person may only bring in up to $25 worth of items for personal or household use.

How to Get Married in Niagara Falls

In New York you can get married 24 hours after obtaining a marriage license ($10) at City Hall, 745 Main St., Niagara Falls, NY 14302 (tel. 716/278-8208). No blood test or physical is necessary. If you are 18 to 23 years of age, you'll need original proof of age and identification (for example, passport, driver's license, etc.). To be married by the mayor, phone a week or so ahead of time to make an appointment (a gratuity is expected).

In Canada, you must be 18 years of age or older, have identification, and pay approximately $25 for a marriage license, which can be obtained from Niagara Falls City Hall, 4310 Queen St. (tel. 416/356-7521; information: Niagara Falls City Hall, P.O. Box 1023, Niagara Falls, Ontario L2E 6X5). No blood test or physical is necessary. After the license is issued, you must wait three full days before getting married at the court house or by one of the justices of the peace whose names are provided through city hall. If you are in a hurry, the Toronto Registrar's Office may waive the waiting period. If you've been married previously, you'll need a decree absolute with the original seal and must see an Ontario lawyer who will obtain permission from the registrar general's office in Toronto, so don't expect to get married in a single day.

For Further Information

Contact the **Niagara Falls Convention & Visitors Bureau,** Carborundum Center, Suite 101, 345 Third St., Niagara Falls, NY 14303 (tel. 716/285-2400). **Niagara Falls, Canada Visitor and Convention Bureau,** 4610 Ontario Ave., Niagara Falls, ON, L2E 3P9 (tel. 416/356-6061).

ROMANTIC INTERLUDES: Honeymooners will have no problem finding ways to amuse themselves in Niagara Falls, both in the city and outside of town.

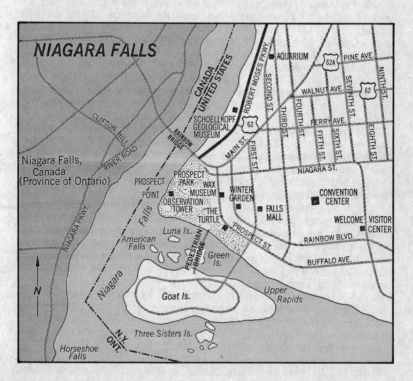

Most locals agree that the *Maid of the Mist* **boat ride** is the best way to really see the Falls. Slip on the traditional black rain gear provided free to all passengers and prepare yourself for a wet and wild close-up look as you are carried right to the base of the American Falls. The water roars and surges, testing the *Maid*'s powerful diesel engines. The boats depart at 15-minute intervals from both the base of the Observation Tower at Prospect Point (U.S.) and from the incline railway at the foot of Clifton Hill (Canada). The trip lasts half an hour and costs $4.75. Open mid-May through mid-October (tel. 284-8897 or 358-5781).

Spanish Aero Cars, a quaint tram (with a perfect safety record), carries 40 exhilarated passengers over Whirlpool Rapids, about three miles north of Niagara, from one Canadian point to another. The rapids are a 60-square-acre expanse of swirling green water enclosed in an awesome natural stone bowl. Massive tree trunks gyrate and splinter in the maelstrom, which snaps them like matchsticks. The $3 ride can be taken from mid-April through mid-October, depending on the weather (tel. 416/354-5711).

According to Indian legend, the earth was created upon the back of a giant turtle. **The Turtle,** a museum in Niagara, New York, houses **The Native American Center for the Living Arts.** Architecturally true to its name, the Turtle contains an exciting and diverse collection of Indian art and artifacts. Paintings, sculpture, and crafts by contemporary Native American artists share space with the carefully preserved handiwork of the Iroquois people. Browse through the Turtle's fascinating and diverse craft shop or take in the daily Iroquois dance performances (summer only). $3 admission (tel. 284-2427).

For yet another unique perspective on the Falls and surrounding area—bridges, parks, floral gardens, power stations—take one of the **helicopter rides** offered by Niagara Helicopters Ltd. The ten-minute jaunts ($38 per person) carry you from the company's Ontario landing pad south of the Falls over the Canadian side of the Niagara River, then back over the U.S. side. If you forget to bring your camera, the company will gladly lend you one; you just pay for the film (tel. 357-5672).

Ten miles north of the Falls, visit **Lewiston,** New York (pop. 16,000), a pleasant residential and agricultural community surrounded by shady trees, fertile farmlands, historic buildings, and a stunning natural escarpment overlooking the Niagara River and Lake Ontario.

Artpark, New York's sole park devoted to the arts, lies on Lewiston's southern perimeter. Containing a 2,400-seat theater for musicals, opera, dance, and concerts, Artpark hosts events from mid-June through September 1. Pack a picnic lunch and dine al fresco, then take in some jazz, classical music, opera, or dance in the theater (tel. 754-9001 during the season, and off-season 745-3377). Admission to the park is free; special events cost $5 and up.

Drive 12 miles north of Niagara Falls, Ontario, and savor the simple charms of historical Niagara-on-the-Lake, which was settled by British Loyalists more than two centuries ago. Handsome parks, museums, and houses carefully and handsomely renovated in traditional 19th-century styles sweep visitors into the past. Visit churches, forts, the 1847 Court House, an apothecary museum, and the site of a military camp dating back to the War of 1812. The area has many pleasant hiking and biking possibilities as well; bikes may be rented at the Pillar and Post Inn, at John and King Streets (tel. 468-2123), even if you're not staying there. Theater buffs won't want to miss the famous annual festival honoring playwright George Bernard Shaw, held from late April until mid-October at the Royal George Theater (tel. 468-2172). For more information, write the Niagara-on-the-Lake Chamber of Commerce, P.O. Box 1043, Niagara-on-the-Lake, Ontario L0S 1J0 (tel. 468-2326).

HONEYMOON HOTELS AND HIDEAWAYS: Plenty of hotel chains and smaller, lower-priced motels and hotels offer accommodations in Niagara. Many of these cater to newlyweds, usually through economical packages that include such honeymoon accessories as heart-shaped whirlpool tubs, champagne, stereo tape decks, waterbeds, and—ahem—mirrored rooms. Many attractive honeymoon packages are available.

High season runs from approximately April 1 to October 31, and low-season rates are a third to a half less. The price ranges quoted for hotels in this section reflect the low- and high-season rates, where applicable.

The full American plan (AP)—including breakfast, lunch, and dinner—is offered by several establishments, though usually not by the major chains.

In addition to a 7% state sales tax in New York, you'll also pay a 3% hotel tax. A 7% sales tax is levied in Canada.

Visitors wishing to truly integrate themselves into the area will want to check out **Rainbow Hospitality,** 9348 Hennepin Ave., Niagara Falls, NY 14304 (tel. 716/754-8877 or 716/283-1400), the only bed-and-breakfast service in western New York. Rainbow lists some 15 homes and small inns that range in price from $30 to $55. These include a 150-year-old antique-filled country home overlooking the Niagara River; an early 18th-century Greek-revival home with private baths, a veranda, and fireplaces; and a private, unhosted guest house.

A stately, curved, downtown landmark, this 220-unit **Hotel Niagara,** 201 Rainbow Blvd., Niagara Falls, NY 14303 (tel. 716/285-9321), offers a splendid view of the nearby Falls and surrounding area. Dark wood interiors provide the perfect antidote to cold winter days, while the cozy Indian Room cocktail lounge and dining room nostalgically remind one of the resort hotels viewed in such movies as—what else?—*Niagara* (which starred Marilyn Monroe). Most of the warm, simply furnished rooms overlook the Falls; some contain refrigerators. Honeymoon package: Three days / two nights: $115 per couple. Includes deluxe accommodations, a New York strip steak dinner, breakfasts, and champagne.

Located adjacent to scenic Goat Island and the parks lining the Falls, the **Holiday Inn Downtown at the Falls,** 114 Buffalo St., Niagara Falls, NY 14303 (tel. 716/285-2521), is loaded with features. In the Holidome you'll find a miniature golf course, exercise room, videogames, pool, sauna, whirlpool, restaurant, and a comfortable lounge that magically transforms itself into a jumping night spot. While not strictly romantic, the 194 rooms are modern, clean, and comfortable. The big bonus is that most of the accommodations offer splendid views of the Canadian shore. Honeymoon package: Three days / two nights: $189 to $277 per couple. Includes king-size bed, Châteaubriand dinner, and breakfast. Five nights / four days: $363 to $539 per couple. Includes Châteaubriand dinner, an additional dinner off the menu, breakfasts, champagne, souvenir glasses, souvenir photographs, and a honeymoon certificate.

Since **Oakes Inn,** 6546 Buchanan Ave., Niagara Falls, Ontario L2G 3W2 (tel. 416/258-5926), is one of the hotels closest to the Canadian falls, all the honeymoon suites lend themselves to happy gawking at the roaring waters below. Management has recently added an 18-hole miniature golf course and driving range, and plans to complete an additional tower with accommodations in 1988. Minutes away from both the Minolta and Skylon towers, the Oakes also offers two lounges (the subdued Redford Lounge and the rowdier Sports Bar), a sauna, an exercise room, and indoor and outdoor swimming pools. In addition to honeymoon suites containing such indulgences as waterbeds, stereos, and heart-shaped whirlpool baths in mirrored chambers, you might also look into the Oakes's unique Starlight Suite, which features a laser-disc-projected planetarium show right over your bed. Suites and rooms are tidy, comfortable, and modern. Honeymoon packages: Three days / two nights: $271 to $431 per couple. Includes champagne, one dinner, and breakfasts. Four nights / three days: $519 to $819 per couple. Includes the above plus a tour of Niagara Falls, cocktails, and a Niagara honeymoon certificate. Honeymoon suites, with a heart-shaped bath and waterbed, cost $115 to $215 per night.

Maple Leaf Motel, 6163 Buchanan Ave., Niagara Falls, Ontario L2G 3V7 (tel.

416/354-0841). This tidy little money saver boasts clean, spacious rooms at inexpensive prices. Located a mere 320 yards from the Falls, this very small hotel looks out on the Skylon and Minolta towers. Rooms are clean and comfortable in a no-frills roadhouse kind of way. Enjoy a picnic in the well-treed courtyard. Honeymoon package: None. Standard rates: About $19 to $39 per couple per day.

Located a few miles away from the Falls, the **Bel-Aire Motel,** 9470 Niagara Falls Blvd., Niagara Falls, NY 14304 (tel. 716/297-2250), is a small (22-room), one-story, and inexpensive alternative to the downtown area's hustle and bustle. Located in a commercial district populated by similar accommodations, the Bel-Aire is slightly nicer than the others, with a standard hotel decor a cut above the rest. All rooms include cable TV, and air conditioning. A heated pool and an adjacent café are pluses as well. Honeymoon package: None. Standard rates: $25 to $40 per couple per day.

ROMANTIC RESTAURANTS: In Niagara Falls, fine dining is available both on the ground and high in the sky. The area boasts a bevy of restaurants ranging from fast-food establishments to tony meccas of continental cuisine. At least once, you should sample two tasty and highly recommended upstate New York specialties: spicy Buffalo chicken wings appetizers (served with blue cheese dressing and celery), and a delicious sandwich dubbed the "beef on weck," which consists of roast beef on a salty kimmelweck roll. Delish.

Ask anyone on the Canadian side of the Falls where to get a good meal in a romantic atmosphere, and the **Casa d'Oro,** 5875 Victoria Ave., Niagara Falls, Ontario (tel. 356-5646), will inevitably be their first choice. A big, warm, baroque-style restaurant, the Casa's dining room is surrounded by plush red velvet and wall hangings guaranteed to put you in the mood for the fine traditional Italian haute cuisine. Start with regal clams casino, classic mushroom Daumont, or split a generous antipasto alla Casalinga, and don't forget to order at least one portion of the Casa's delicious garlic bread. Recommended entrées: poitrine de poulet Clunysoise (chicken with champagne sauce) and fettuccine Natacha (served with fresh poached British Columbia salmon in a tasty cream sauce). The local Inniskillin winery bottles a highly drinkable Riserva Privata for the restaurant. Select dessert from a large wagon of sweets, or split a delicious banana flambé. About $40 per couple plus drinks.

The Skylon Tower, 5200 Robinson St., Niagara Falls, Ontario (tel. 356-2651). While the food is good enough in the larger of the two tower observatories (Minolta Tower is the other) on the Canadian side of the Niagara River, you will probably be distracted by the panoramic view while the dining room revolves 775 feet above the splendor of Niagara Falls. During the winter, the restaurant offers a special four-course Châteaubriand dinner for two in honor of the Festival of Lights, with baked Alaska for dessert ($32). From 4:30 to 6:30 p.m., the Early Bird Dinner Special features either prime rib or chicken Cordon Bleu dinners for about $9. The restaurant's regular menu includes a wide selection of continental standbys and plenty of surf-and-turf dishes. Appetizers range from $4 to $5, entrées from $10 to $16. Downstairs, the Skylon Summit Suite Dining Room offers lavish buffets for lunch and dinner. A special Sunday brunch ($16 per couple) is served from 10:30 a.m. to 3:30 p.m.

Enjoy a leisurely and romantic Sunday drive north of Niagara Falls toward Lake Ontario for a hearty meal at **The Pillar and Post,** King and John Street, Niagara-on-the-Lake, Ontario (tel. 468-2123), a refurbished canning factory. The Post's special Sunday brunch (about $15 per couple plus drinks) includes an all-you-can-eat assortment of sausages, roast beef, soups, salads, hot cakes, French toast, and on and on. Sip a Bloody Mary, peruse the Sunday paper, then stroll down to the beach and gaze at the outline of Toronto hovering mysteriously on the lake's far shore.

The Cataract House Restaurant, off Third Street, Niagara Falls, New York (tel. 282-5635). Drop by this clean, unpretentious, and reasonably priced restaurant a little later in the evening, once the families have gone home, when it turns into one of the town's more happening spots. The Cataract, entertainingly decorated with historic photographs of the Falls, has a romantic charm all its own. Enjoy a Greek specialty such as creamy saganaki (flaming cheese), hearty moussaka, tasty pastitsio (seasoned ground beef and macaroni baked with bechamel sauce), or a simple yet delicious village Greek salad (Greek potato salad with regular Greek salad). Steaks, kebabs, ribs, and a variety of fish dishes are also available. For a snack, nibble on some spicy Buffalo chicken wings. Lunches from $3 to $5; dinner appetizers from $1 to $5, entrées from $7 to $13.

Relax in **The Wintergarden Restaurant,** Rainbow Boulevard, in downtown Niagara Falls, New York (tel. 282-1215), a tranquil oasis of enclosed greenery. Thousands of plants surround you as you enjoy the mesquite-grilled specialties. Dinner for two: About $40 plus drinks. **Carmelo's,** 425 Center St., in Lewiston (tel. 754-2311) serves fine Italian cuisine—primarily meats and seafoods—in warm, antique-filled surroundings. Top off your meal with Carmelo's Special, a unique and delicious coffee drink. About $40 for two, plus drinks. **The Red Coach Inn,** Z Buffalo Ave., in Niagara Falls, New York (tel. 282-1459), prides itself on its "Olde English" atmosphere, and justifiably so. The Red Coach specializes in prime rib of beef, but such hearty dishes as Australian lobster tail, Boston scrod with seafood sausage mornay, chicken alouette, and steaks are also available. Lunch for two, about $25; dinner, about $45 plus drinks. **The Top of the Rainbow,** 6732 Oakes Dr., in Niagara Falls, Ontario's Minolta Tower (tel. 356-1501) serves a variety of continental dishes—from loin of lamb diable to roast young duckling with a lingonberry sauce—in high-in-the-sky ambience. Lunch for two costs about $12 a couple; dinner, about $25 plus drinks. **Scalzo's,** 1602 Pine Ave., just outside downtown Niagara Falls, New York (tel. 282-5122), claims to be Niagara's oldest (not to mention finest) restaurant. In casual surroundings decorated with old theater and cinema posters, you can enjoy a large selection of Italian and American favorites. Daily dinner specials include a nine-ounce strip steak (plus the salad bar and an after-dinner cordial) for $7.50; a large lobster tail plus the salad bar and cordial is $12.50. Pasta dishes start at $5.50 per person.

Chapter XI

PENNSYLVANIA: THE POCONOS

1. Practical Facts
2. Romantic Interludes
3. Honeymoon Hotels and Hideaways

WELCOME to the only area in the world where resorts devote themselves primarily to newlyweds and honeymoons—the Poconos.

Maybe it's the mountains, their pinnacles softened by towering oaks and hemlocks. Maybe the reason is the sparkling lakes, ranging from little ponds by the willows where ducks paddle, to wide, blue expanses that invite vacationers to waterski and sail. Whatever the cause, the fact remains—the Poconos reign as "Honeymoon Capital of the World," attracting some 275,000 honeymoon couples annually from around the world.

What people commonly refer to as "the Poconos" is actually a collection of several mountains, part of the Appalachian chain, tucked in over 2,400 square miles in northeastern Pennsylvania. The region is bounded by the New York border to the north, Delaware River to the east, and the Lehigh River on the southwest. The whole scenic area lies eminently close to major East Coast cities—about 75 miles from New York and 85 miles from Philadelphia. As you might expect, the name "Pocono" comes from an Indian word meaning "a stream between the mountains"—a very accurate description of the landscapes you'll encounter.

In a sense, the modern honeymoon was "invented" in the Poconos. Until the 1940s, only the very rich and famous could afford them. Then Rudolf Van Hoevenberg started promoting stays at his farm on the hill to newlyweds—and the whole loving tradition began. Nature provided the mountains and streams, but the Pocono resorts created the glamour and excitement. Each Pocono resort provides a self-contained world for honeymooners, with everything—from sports to nightclubs—right on the property. The Pocono properties not only invented the honeymoon, they created the concept of the "all-inclusive resort." The price you pay for your room covers everything: meals (some do not include lunch), social activities, nighttime entertainment, and all the sports facilities, equipment, and action a body can pack in. Since the packages are all inclusive, planning a honeymoon budget is easy. You'll know how much your honeymoon will cost before you even leave home. Once you arrive at your honeymoon hotel, you can relax and enjoy the resort facilities completely, without worrying about how much it costs for a tennis game or Sunfish sail.

The sports options are especially extensive. In summer, lakes beckon for

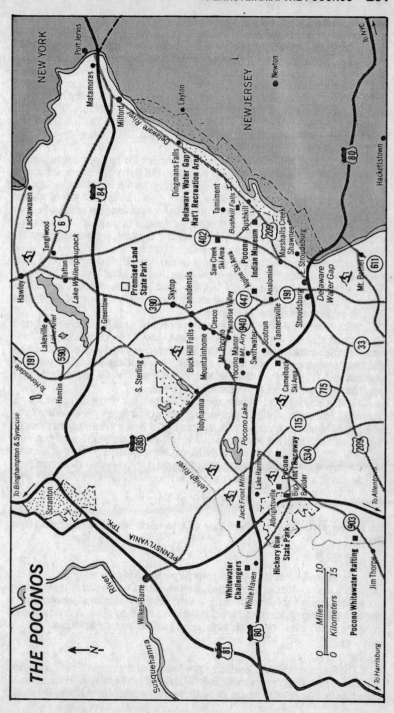

THE POCONOS

N

NEW YORK

Port Jervis

Matamoras

Milford

Delaware River

Layton

NEW JERSEY

Newton

To NYC

Hackettstown

80

Lackawaxen

84

6

Tanglwood

Clifton

Hawley

Lake Wallenpaupack

Dingmans Falls

Delaware Water Gap
Nat'l Recreation Area

Tamiment

Bushkill Falls

Bushkill

209

Marshalls Creek

Shawnee

E. Stroudsburg

611

Mt. Bethel

Lakeville

Lake Ariel

Greentown

Promised Land
State Park

Skytop

390

Canadensis

Saw Creek
Ski Area

Alpine Ski Area

402

Pocono
Indian Museum

Analomink

191

Delaware
Water Gap

To Honesdale

191

590

Buck Hill Falls

Mountainhome

Cresco

Paradise Valley

447

940

Tannersville

Stroudsburg

33

Hamlin

S. Sterling

Mt. Pocono

Pocono Manor

Mt. Airy

Swiftwater

Scotrun

380

Tobyhanna

Pocono Lake

Camelback
Ski Area

715

To Binghampton & Syracuse

Lehigh River

115

Pocono
Raceway

534

209

Scranton

Lake Harmony

Pocono
Int'l Raceway

Boulder

To Allentown

Jack Frost Mtn.

Albrightsville

903

PENNSYLVANIA TPK.

Hickory Run
State Park

Jim Thorpe

Wilkes-Barre

Susquehanna River

Whitewater
Challengers

White Haven

Miles   10

Kilometers   15

0

0

Pocono Whitewater Rafting

81

80

To Harrisburg

waterskiing, sailing, canoeing, and swimming. You can also swim and splash in large outdoor pools, many of which carry out the romantic motif by being shaped like wedding rings, bells, or hearts. Go bicycle riding along country roads, or play a round of golf—most resorts either have their own courses or can arrange for guests to play nearby. In winter, try snowmobiling, ice skating, or some of the best skiing in the East—both downhill and cross-country. Consider learning a new sport. Since the honeymoon package includes all equipment and instruction, it's a particularly good time to start. All year round, you can enjoy swimming, tennis, basketball, volleyball, and badminton, thanks to the modern indoor and outdoor facilities. You'll also find pool tables, video-game arcades, and health spas complete with state-of-the-art fitness equipment, whirlpools, saunas, and more.

Okay, enough about sports. What really makes the Poconos famous are the rooms, which are glittery, plush, and available with every amenity imaginable—saunas, sun lamps, and in-room swimming pools (too small for swimming laps, but ample for a splashing good time). And, of course, those famous heart-shaped tubs and whirlpools, with plenty of room for two people to luxuriate amid the bubbles. Beds are generally king-size, round or heart-shaped, surrounded by canopies, columns, and mirrors. Most rooms have a color TV, log-burning fireplace, and a mini-refrigerator where you can chill a bottle of champagne for a nightcap.

Razzle-dazzle nightlife adds more sophistication to a Poconos honeymoon. Each evening, there's a different show, from magicians and belly dancers to live bands, Las Vegas–style revues, maybe even a big-time headliner such as Tom Jones, Susan Anton, or Soupy Sales. At the disco, the band or theme varies each night—from New Wave to a down-home country hoedown.

Since most of the other resort guests are honeymooners also, the atmosphere is friendly and sociable. You'll find it easy to get to know other couples, since a social director makes introductions and arranges activities. Every day, the resorts schedule a full agenda: water polo, men's beauty contests, skeet-shooting instruction, plus competitions such as Trivial Pursuit or The Newlywed Game. Couples can join in the fun if they like, but there's never any pressure to participate.

Finally, a word about "Poconos people"—the folks who work at the resorts. Throughout the region, there's a long-term tradition of caring for guests with personal attention. The honeymoon hotels are still run by the families that founded them: the Wilkins at the Caesars Resorts, the Fardas at the Summit, the Poalillos at Penn Hills, and Emil Wagner and Carl Martens at the Mount Airy properties. Many staff members have worked at the same hotels for years. Both the resort owners and the employees will do everything possible to assure your honeymoon happiness.

1. Practical Facts

GETTING THERE: The Poconos are easy to reach from throughout the United States.

By Air
Newark and Allentown are the main airports serving the region. Newark is a major hub, and airlines such as **United, Eastern,** and **Continental** offer convenient nonstop and direct flights from the entire country. From the airport, all the honeymoon resorts can arrange ground transportation—even stretch limousines. Ask the resort for complete details when you or your travel agent make the room reservations.

By Car
The Pocono resorts are less than a two-hour drive from many East Coast cities. The main interstate highways are **Routes 80 and 84** from New York. From Philadelphia, take the Northeast Extension of the Pennsylvania Turnpike to **Route 209 east.**

By Bus
   Greyhound and **Martz Trailways** serve the area.

GETTING AROUND: Because the resorts are self-contained, you'll find practically everything you want right on the property. But to truly appreciate the scenic mountain region and explore the back country roads, you'll need a car. If you arrive by air, you can rent cars at both Allentown and Newark airports; rates run about $165 for six days, with the first 700 miles free.

WEATHER: The climate resembles that of nearby New York and Philadelphia, but will be about 10° cooler because of the elevation.

CLOTHING: By day, choose casual activewear and sportswear. Jeans are best for rugged sports such as horseback riding or skiing, while sneakers see you through everything from tennis to hiking. For evening, dress ranges from calico shirts for country evenings to sequins for gala champagne dinners. Many resorts also plan special "theme nights" during the week—Hawaiian night, toga parties, etc. Ask about the schedule before you go; you might want to bring along something appropriate.

TIME: The Poconos are in the Eastern Time zone, and observe Daylight Savings Time in the summer.

TELEPHONES: The area code for the Poconos is 717.

TIPPING: To cover tips, a 15% service charge will generally be added to your hotel bill. If so, you will not have to tip hotel employees individually.

SHOPPING: First stop should probably be the gift boutique at your resort, which stocks items from all over the world: antiques, pewter candlesticks, wicker baskets, and cut crystal.
   The region is also known for its antiques shops. Our number one favorite is the **Theo. B. Price Country Store** in Cresco owned by Maryann and Micky Miller (tel. 595-2501). Out on the front porch, you'll be greeted by life-size soft sculptures and various tempting knickknacks. You could spend hours browsing through the quilted pillows ($22 to $40), baskets (some priced under $10), and magnificent carved swan and duck decoys (from $120).
   Candles make popular honeymoon mementos; you can buy them for about 50% off regular prices at the **Pocono Candle Shop** (East Stroudsburg) and **American Candle** (Bartonsville) factory outlets. At the **Holley Ross Pottery** on Route 191 in LaAnna, you can watch free pottery-making demonstrations Monday through Friday at 11 a.m. and 3:30 p.m., then browse through their selection of soup crocks, quiche dishes, ceramic cannisters, and other gifts. Open daily May through mid-December (tel. 676-3248).
   Homemade candy is another treat. At **Callie's Candy Kitchen** on Route 390 in Mountainhome (tel. 595-2280), the sweet smell of chocolate wafts into your nostrils the moment you walk in. It's a child's fantasy, with giant lollipops, gummy bears, peanut-butter ribbon candy, and more. Chocoholics should head straight for the Pocono Mountain Bark—dark, milk, or light chocolate laced with raisins, walnut, coconut, or peanuts. The **Ella C. Ehrhardt General Store** in Newfoundland (no phone) sells old-fashioned penny candies—you'll have fun picking out an assortment.

Another good place to shop for gifts and souvenirs is **Memorytown, U.S.A.** just off Route 940 in Mt. Pocono. At the **Country Store,** you'll find homemade preserves, bags of spices, penny candy, pottery—even an antique spinning wheel. The **Red Corner Cupboard** carries dolls, brass items, carved wooden ducks ($15 to $25), cookie and muffin molds shaped like fruit and animals ($9 to $11), and some captivating mechanical banks. Also stop by **Pocono Mineral and Gem** in Colony Village, south of Canadensis on Route 447. Here, the jewelry displays create the effect of underground caves, with fine pieces made from semiprecious stones such as amber, turquoise, amethyst, and malachite sparkling in the depths. Prices start around $14 and climb well over $100.

Also check out the nearby city of Stroudsburg, which is one of the factory-outlet capitals of the world. Savings run from 20% to 60%. For the widest selection, head over to the **Pocono Outlet Complex** at 9th and Ann Streets. Best bets include the **Stroud Handbag Outlet** for handbags, wallets, attaché cases, and leather goods, and **The Potting Shed** for silk and dried flowers, as well as houseplants. The **Workout ROM** features women's activewear, including a large selection of leotards and tights from Danskin. Whatever your sport, you'll find a shoe that fits at **Sneak Preview,** which carries sneakers by Pony, Converse, and Nike. In addition to ribbons, the **American Ribbon Factory Outlet** has a wide selection of baskets.

DINING OUT: Some of the Pocono resort honeymoon packages are Full American Plan (Full AP), including breakfast, lunch, and dinner daily. Other resorts offer the Modified American Plan (MAP), including breakfast and dinner daily. Soda, wine, and cocktails are not included. See the individual resort listings for details.

Practically all the resorts offer free breakfast in bed daily, including specials such as Bloody Mary or champagne breakfasts. The three-course dinners are usually table d'hôte, giving you a choice among various selections for your appetizer, main course, and dessert. There are also theme dinners, such as Italian night with wine, international buffets, champagne dinners, Wild West barbecues, weiner roasts, and Hawaiian night, complete with leis and hula skirts. Most seating is at tables of from four to five honeymoon couples; you can also generally get a table for two if you prefer.

Since the Pocono honeymoon packages include meals, you will probably not be dining away from your resort. If you do go out, you'll find several absolutely top-notch restaurants in the area. **Fanucci's** on Route 611 in Swiftwater (tel. 839-7097) does terrific pasta, seafood, and veal dishes. Entrées for dinner priced from $9 to $16.50. Another favorite for Italian food is **Peppe's** in the Eagle Valley Mall near Stroudsburg (tel. 421-4460). Try the cannelloni bolognese or the striped bass marechiare, a house specialty. Entrées from $8.50 to $17. **The Inn at Tannersville** on Route 611 (tel. 629-9893) is the place for thick, juicy, char-broiled steaks; prices range from $2.75 for a hamburger to $8.50 for an eight-ounce steak. For lobster, try the **Beaver House** at 1001 N. 9th St. in Stroudsburg (tel. 424-1020); you can choose your lobster from a tank out front, and they often have four-pounders. A complete dinner with a 1½-pound lobster runs $21. At harvest time, stop at one of the many roadside stands for just-picked fruits and vegetables. They'll stay crisp and crunchy in the refrigerator in your room—or take some home as an edible souvenir of your honeymoon.

SPECIAL EVENTS: The Poconos pack in four full seasons of activity, and there are several annual events you should know about. Late May to early June is mountain laurel time, when the delicate, pale-pink blossoms cover the hillsides and valleys. Many Pocono towns plan **Laurel Blossom Festivals** with fairs and crafts shows timed to coincide with the peak displays of the flowers. Late September through early November, the Poconos blaze into full fall foliage, with hues of crimson, orange, and gold. One of the most peaceful ways to view the spectacle is on a float trip along one of the region's rivers: the Delaware, Lehigh, or Lackawaxen. (See details under "Romantic Interludes," which follows.) The autumn is also harvest season, and many of the ski areas stage **Oktoberfests,** complete with German-style oompah bands, folk dancers, and Bavarian foods. From the last week in February through the first week in March, the **Pocono Winter Carnival** celebrates with ski races, skating parties, ice-skating exhibitions, torchlight ski parades, snow-sculpture contests, and more. Contact the **Pocono Mountains Vacation Bureau** (see address below) for a complete calendar of events.

HOW TO GET MARRIED IN THE POCONOS: If you want to combine your honeymoon with a Poconos wedding, here's how to do it. Both parties must be over the age of 18. You both must appear at the Prothonotary Office at the Monroe County Courthouse at the same time. Bring with you the signed results of your blood tests (which can be performed in your home state), as well as a certified copy of the final divorce decree, if either of you was previously married. There is a three-day waiting period before the license can be issued. Contact the **Monroe County Courthouse,** Stroudsburg, PA 18360 (tel. 717/424-5100).

FOR FURTHER INFORMATION: Contact the **Poconos Mountain Vacation Bureau,** Box PR, 1004 Main St., Stroudsburg, PA 18360 (tel. 717/421-5791).

2. Romantic Interludes

Here are some special pastimes for lovers at and around the various Pocono resorts.

Most of the resorts have **photographers** who can snap candid pictures for your honeymoon scrapbook. Favorite poses include embracing in the woods, or toasting with champagne at a candlelight dinner. Most fun of all—don bathing suits, pour in some bubble bath, start running the water, and call the photographer—he or she will photograph you up to your necks in bubbles in your heart-shaped tub. Five-by-seven color photos cost about $7 each.

The **resort gift boutique** makes a great place to purchase your honeymoon souvenirs. Best bets: his 'n' hers sweatshirts imprinted with the resort name, or a stuffed animal for a bedroom mascot.

What better way to savor the beautiful Pocono scenery than on a **picnic lunch?** Head for **Bushkill Falls,** called "the Niagara of Pennsylvania," where sparkling waters tumble down a 100-foot cliff and then race through a boulder-strewn gorge. It's on Route 209 in Bushkill. Open daily from April through November, from 9 a.m. until dusk (tel. 588-6682). Closed in winter. Or visit the **Delaware Water Gap.** Perhaps the best-known landmark in the Poconos, it is a spectacular 1,200-foot gorge cut by the Delaware River through the Kittatinny Mountains. Explore the various hiking trails and take photos from the scenic overlooks. You'll find parking and a Visitor Center just east of Stroudsburg on Route 80.

The **Lehigh** and the **Delaware,** two of the mightiest rivers in the East, course through the Poconos. The Lehigh is more challenging, with several roiling Class III rapids for thrilling white-water rafting; the Delaware generally offers more tranquil runs perfect for canoeists. White-water rafting trips, including rafts, paddles, and experienced guide, run about $50 to $75 per couple. Contact **Jim Thorpe River Adventures** in Jim Thorpe (tel. 325-2570), or **Whitewater Challengers** in White Haven (tel. 443-9532). Both also offer peaceful float trips—excellent for viewing fall foliage. For canoe rentals as well as raft trips, contact **Kittatinny Canoes** in Dingman's Ferry (tel. 828-2700 or 828-2338), owned and operated by the Jones family for over 32 years.

From about mid-April through November, theatergoers flock to the Poconos for

summer-stock productions of long-run Broadway hits such as *West Side Story*, *Evita*, and *My Fair Lady*. Check out the performance schedules at **Shawnee Playhouse** in Shawnee-on-Delaware (tel. 421-1500), **Pocono Playhouse** in Mountainhome (tel. 595-7456), and **Playhouse by the River** in Mt. Bethel (tel. 897-6744). Ticket prices run about $10 to $14 per person.

Each season, **Pocono Raceway** in Long Pond stages a calendar of major events for NASCAR stock cars, motorcycles, Indy cars—even big-rig truck races. Races are usually held on Sundays, admission $30 to $50 per person, depending on the event. For a season schedule, contact Pocono Raceway, Box 500, Long Pond, PA 18334 (tel. 717/646-2300; toll free 800/RACEWAY) for ticket information.

If you want to try your own hand at the wheel, head over to **Pocono Action Park** in Tannersville (tel. 629-4411). Strap on your seat belt in the $12,000 Lola T-506s, wait until the light tree flashes green, and then zoom off, testing your skills and reflexes on a half-mile course of hairpin turns and straightaways ($2.25 per lap). Pocono Action Park also features bumper boats, baseball batting cages, and a new "Water World" with twister flumes and water slides. Open daily in season Monday through Saturday, 11 a.m. to 10 p.m.; Sunday, noon to 10 p.m. Admission is free; you just pay for the rides.

With 16 major **ski areas** and over 120 different trails, the Poconos is one of the East's major centers for downhill skiing. All have extensive snow-making facilities. **Camelback** is the largest area, with 25 trails and 11 lifts. Other choices include **Big Boulder, Elk Mountain, Jack Frost,** and **Shawnee,** all open for night skiing as well. **Alpine Mountain** in Analomink (tel. 595-2150), with a 500-foot vertical drop, has four lifts, including a quad chair, with 14 trails and slopes for all levels, from novices to experts.

Horseback ride along pine-fringed mountain trails—it's a leisurely way to appreciate the scenery. Some of the resorts have stables on the premises; at others, the hotel social director can arrange trail rides. Most resort honeymoon packages do not include horseback riding, which costs about $11 per person for 45 minutes in the saddle. Among the riding stables you can contact: **El-J Riding Stable** near Mt. Pocono (tel. 839-8725), **Shawnee Stables** in Shawnee-on-Delaware (tel. 421-9763), and **R.J.D. Stables** in Lake Ariel near Hamlin (tel. 698-6996).

3. Honeymoon Hotels and Hideaways

Choosing where to stay is probably the most important decision you can make when planning a Pocono honeymoon. Look for a place that features your favorite sports—and fulfills your heartfelt romantic fantasies.

The Pocono honeymoon packages are all-inclusive: The price of the room you choose determines the total cost of the honeymoon package. The basic honeymoon package runs six days/five nights, arriving on Sunday and departing on Friday. Other packages are usually available; check with the specific resort for details. Make reservations early: The most popular rooms are the most luxurious ones, and these often book up a year in advance. Most resorts require a deposit of $75 to $100 with your reservation. During the winter, some resorts offer special reduced rates; ask your travel agent.

Rates quoted do not include the 6% Pennsylvania state tax, which will be added to your bill. A 15% service charge to cover gratuities will also generally be added.

Some of the resorts are owned and operated by the same company. Since accommodations and honeymoon packages are often similar at all hotels under the same ownership, we have grouped them together.

Caesars Resorts

These four resorts have all the glitter and glamour of their sister hotels in Las Vegas and Atlantic City. Over the past three years, the company spent some $25 million refurbishing the properties and adding new facilities. As the star attraction, all four resorts feature the ultradeluxe "Champagne Towers." These multilevel suites have perhaps the ultimate fantasy—a whirlpool bath shaped like a champagne glass, with plenty of room for both of you and oodles of bubbles. The suite also has a heart-shaped swimming pool, sauna and massage table, combination shower/steam bath for two, round king-size bed, fireplace, and sunken living room with cushy furnishings done up in shades of burgundy, mauve, and pink.

Key A Round Club: No matter which Caesars Pocono resort you stay at, you are welcome to use the facilities at all four, giving you a chance to experience their different atmospheres. Just show your room key to identify yourselves as Caesars guests. To get around, guests at Pocono Palace, Paradise Stream, and Brookdale can hop the "Caesars Chariot" shuttle that runs among these three resorts.

Honeymoon package: At all four resorts, if you stay for four nights or more, you'll receive a bottle of champagne, decanter of bubble bath, honeymoon photo album, and a fire log. At certain times of the year, the package also includes a free day-trip to Caesars Atlantic City. And every morning, you can have breakfast in bed—free.

Cove Haven, Lakeville, PA 18438 (reservations: tel. 717/226-2101 or toll free 800/233-4141). "We give you three big A's—for atmosphere, accommodations, and activities," one honeymoon couple wrote in the guest book at Cove Haven, the flag-ship of Caesars resorts in the Poconos. Their comments accurately describe the unique features of this sophisticated resort in a countryside setting. The atmosphere is very secluded, about a 40-minute drive north of the other three Caesars properties. Thanks to its location on the shores of Lake Wallenpaupack, Pennsylvania's largest lake, Cove Haven is a perfect choice for couples who love water sports: waterskiing, speed-boat rides, paddleboats, and sailing are all on the agenda. In fact, whatever your favorite sports activity you can probably find it somewhere on the 110-acre property. On land, you can tee off on the driving range, play tennis, or go bicycle riding. In winter, you can enjoy downhill skiing, snowmobiling, tobogganing, as well as ice skating in the indoors Ice Palace. Even when it snows, you can enjoy the semitropical paradise of the indoor Harbourside Health Club with a heated pool; whirlpools surrounded by grot-toes, plants, and waterfalls; exercise equipment; saunas; steam baths; tanning tents; and a game room. In the brand new, year-round Sports Palace, you'll find three tennis courts, four racquetball courts, electronic games, and bocce ball—remember, all equipment (even the balls) are included.

If you love nightlife as well as the sporting life, the new, million-dollar Champagne Palace Nightclub features spectacular light shows, multilevel stages, a large dance floor, and live entertainment seven nights a week.

Cove Haven is the largest of the Caesars Pocono resorts, but it retains a close-knit, personable feeling. This is the kind of place where the staff—everyone from the bar waitress to the power-boat captain—will soon greet you by name. But your best friend will probably be "Honest Phil," the long-time social director. Phil has the knack of making people feel welcome, and he helps the different honeymoon couples get to know each other. And honeymoon history buffs will be intrigued to learn that the heart-shaped tub was "invented" at Cove Haven in 1963 by Morris Wilkins.

Accommodations: Cove Haven offers a wide range of rooms priced to appeal to all pocketbooks. Although the rooms do not have lake views, the sumptuous furnish-ings establish them as cozy love nests. All accommodations have color cable TV and air conditioning. The rates quoted are Modified American Plan (MAP) including breakfast and dinner daily. The Champagne Towers: Needless to say, the duplex champagne glass you see the instant you walk in the door gets all the attention, but the plush upholstery and thick carpeting will make you feel pampered, even when you're not up to your neck in bubbles. Six days/five nights: $1,254.75 per couple. The Garden of Eden–Apple: You get a triangular private pool surrounded by mirrors and wall mu-rals, as well as your own sauna. In the sunken bedroom, you'll find a round, king-size bed with mirrored headboard, and a fireplace to complete the romantic mood. Six days/five nights: $960.75 per couple. The Ultra-Modern: These split-level accommodations are absolutely huge, featuring a sunken living room with log-burning fireplace, king-size round bed surrounded by mirrors, and a sunken, Roman-style whirlpool bath. Six days/five nights: $824.25 per couple. Many different rooms and lengths of stay are available.

The **Paradise Stream Resort,** Mt. Pocono, PA 18344 (reservations: tel. 717/226-2101 or toll free 800/233-4141), provides elegance in a woodland setting. Throughout the resort, a Garden of Eden theme predominates. You can get snacks at the Poison Apple Deli, and every night, there's top-caliber entertainment in the Red Apple Lounge and Nightclub.

The resort offers a full range of sports. Go swimming in the outdoor, Olympic-size pool, play tennis, or get back to nature with a canoeing, fishing, or paddleboating excursion on Lake Eden. During the winter, you can zoom off on a snowmobile, ice skate on the pond out front, or head for the nearby ski slopes (you each get a free lift ticket). All year round, you can stay in shape at the new Fireside Health Club and Spa, with Universal fitness equipment, freeform whirlpool, rowing machines, stationary bikes, as well as European tanning tents to add that healthy glow. Also new for sports enthusiasts—a racquetball center.

Accommodations: Paradise Stream's low-rise units are nicely spread out over the property. You have many different rooms to choose from, including the Champagne Towers. All have color cable TV and air conditioning. Rates quoted are MAP, including breakfast and dinner daily. Champagne Towers: Glass walls and mirrors maximize the views in this four-level townhouse design with the champagne-glass-shaped whirlpool. Six days/five nights: $1,254.75 per couple. Garden of Eden–Apple: All private for you—a swimming pool heated to a cozy 90°, living room, and sunken bedroom with a king-size round bed surrounded by a mirrored headboard. Six days/five nights: $960.75 per couple. Lakeside Villa: Your own private cottage on the edge of the Lake Eden. Outside, your private balcony overlooks the shimmering waters; inside, there's a king-size round bed, cathedral ceiling . . . and a heart-shaped tub for two. Six days/five nights: $892.50 per couple. Many other rooms and packages are also available.

Pocono Palace, Marshalls Creek, PA 18335 (reservations: tel. 717/226-2101 or toll free 800/233-4141). The long driveway winds past pine trees to this intimate resort, nestled in a country club–like setting on 350 green, rolling acres. Here the outlook is definitely sporting. There's a regulation nine-hole golf course right on the property. And you never pay any greens fees, no matter how many times you play. You can also hone your skills on the driving range or putting green—and there's an excellent pro shop. Tennis players will want to round up another couple for a game of mixed doubles. Water sports are right on your doorstep, since the resort surrounds 25-acre Echo Lake—a perfect choice for waterskiing, speed-boat rides, paddleboat cruises, or sailing. If you want to relax, settle into one of the chaise longues on the private sandy beach. In addition to the lake, you can swim in the new outdoor heated pool, or soak your cares away in the warm, bubbling whirlpool. And if your honeymoon fantasies include horseback riding through the woods, Pocono Palace has its own stable of well-schooled mounts. In winter, the undulating golf course turns into a snowmobiler's dream, and there are new cross-country trails. Downhill racers each receive a free lift ticket for the nearby slopes.

Carrying out the Roman theme, the resort has the Noshorium for snacks, and the Gladiator Lounge and Nightclub for dazzling evening entertainment. When you want to work out, head for the Nattaorium, with an indoor heated pool, state-of-the-art gym with Universal exercise equipment, and tanning machines.

Accommodations: In this woodsy setting, you'll find many different room choices, all with air conditioning and color TV. Rates quoted are MAP, including breakfast and dinner daily. Champagne Towers: After a full day in the great outdoors, you'll love your great indoors, with the champagne-glass-shaped whirlpool for complete relaxation. Six days/five nights: $1,254.75 per couple. Fantasy Apple: Your own spacious triplex apartment, with a glass skylight illuminating your own private pool. A circular stairway leads to the round, king-size bed, and you have a private balcony overlooking the woods and Echo Lake. Six days/five nights: $1,102.50 per couple. Capri Suite: Just for you: a king-size round bed, log-burning fireplace, and a heart-shaped whirlpool bath surrounded by eye-catching, floor-to-ceiling mirrors. Six days/five nights: $824.25 per couple. Many other rooms and packages are also available.

Brookdale on the Lake, Scotrun, PA 18355 (reservations: tel. 717/233-4141 or toll free 800/233-4141). When you honeymoon at Brookdale, you'll feel as though you're staying at a private country estate. The resort encompasses over 250 acres of woodlands and meadows, all centered around storybook Brookdale Lake, a tranquil spot where swans glide among the willows. You can sail, canoe, set off in paddleboats, or stroll hand in hand along the shore and across a covered bridge. For a relaxing time, borrow some fishing rods—the lake is well stocked with trout. Then sun yourselves on the large outdoor patio deck around the heated pool that looks out over the marina and lake. And tennis players would have trouble imagining a more attractive setting than the two lakeside courts. In winter, explore the woods aboard snowmobiles or head over to Brookdale's own Frosty Mountain—perfect for tobogganing. Several major downhill ski areas are nearby, and each of you gets a free lift ticket. After a day on the slopes, jump into the heated pool at the indoor spa with floor-to-ceiling windows facing the lake, or warm yourselves through with a sauna. Over the next year, Brookdale is adding a new, indoor ice-skating rink, expanding the dining room and gift shop, and creating a new, million-dollar nightclub. The atmosphere at Brookdale is very friendly —after you've been here a day or so, the staff will greet you by name. Saxy Sal, the social director for over seven years and leader of the house band, really knows how to get people to mingle, and you'll soon be teaming up with other couples for volleyball or softball. Accommodations: Whether you crave elegant sophistication or country charm, you'll find accommodations to please at Brookdale. Rates are MAP, including breakfast and dinner daily. Champagne Towers: What's your fantasy? Curling in front of a blazing fire . . . splashing in your own heart-shaped pool . . . or sipping champagne while lolling in a whirlpool shaped like a champagne glass? You can do it all here. Six days/five nights: $1,254.75 per couple. Lakeview Villa: This huge sumptuous apartment (almost like a four-room suite) is done up in muted tones of burgundy and champagne, with brass accents adding an art deco touch. Your private balcony overlooks the lake, and there's a whirlpool bath for two surrounded by mirrors galore. Six days/five nights: $960.75 per couple. Brooklodge Suite: Newly redesigned, these accommodations have very sophisticated, modern furnishings, decorated in warm beige and taupe tones. The rooms feature a round bed with mirrored headboard and a whirlpool bath, and are conveniently located in the main lodge building. Six days/five nights: $824.25 per couple. Many other rooms and packages are also available.

Mount Airy/Strickland's/Pocono Gardens

These three resorts, all under the same ownership, all offer a different ambience and accommodations. Guests at any one have access to the restaurants and extensive facilities at the others. If you love lavish shows and entertainment, take note that hotel guests pay no cover charge to attend the nightclub shows starring famous headliners at Mount Airy Lodge.

Honeymoon package: If you stay at least four nights, you get free skiing, equipment, and instruction; free golf, cart, and equipment rental, and free horseback riding, depending on weather conditions.

Mount Airy Lodge, Mount Pocono, PA 18344 (reservations: tel. 717/839-8811 or toll free 800/441-4410). Julio Iglesias, Sergio Franchi, Jack Jones, Corbett Monica, Bobby Rydell—these are just a few of the big-name stars that regularly appear at

Mount Airy Lodge, a sumptuous 1,500-acre sports and entertainment complex in the heart of the Poconos. The sports facilities are absolutely first rate, starting with the challenging 18-hole golf course. There are two Olympic-size pools: one outdoors on the sundeck, the other indoors in the sports palace, which also has a health club, ice rink, and massage rooms. You can also get wet in the sparkling lake, the setting for waterskiing, sailing, paddleboating, plus sheer relaxation on a white sand beach. Try out your serve on 21 tennis courts, indoors and out (they're open 24 hours a day). Or hit the trails—the lush country paths surrounding Mount Airy—on horseback or bicycle. Still want more? Add in volleyball, basketball, archery, billiards, Ping-Pong, or skeet shooting—you'll have trouble fitting it all in. Come winter, there are seven ski slopes right on the property, with two double-chair lifts, and complete snowmaking. You can also cross-country ski, snowmobile, or ice skate.

At night, curtain's up—and Mount Airy turns on its full glamour. After a full-course dinner, check out the talent lineup in the Crystal Room, then move to the disco beat in the Club Suzanne. Then, perhaps a nightcap in the intimate Royal Lounge, before heading back to your suite.

Accommodations: Mount Airy gives you one of the widest choices of any Pocono resort, and several other rooms and packages are also available. Rates quoted are Full AP, including breakfast, lunch, and dinner daily. The Palace Suite: This suite features one of the largest in-room pools in the Poconos, with a totally private garden patio just outside the sliding-glass doors. There's also a valentine-red whirlpool tub lavishly backdropped by mirrors, Swedish sauna, drapery-framed king-size round bed, fireplace, and soft blue colors to create a seductive mood. Six days/five nights: $1,102.50 per couple. The Monarch: Recently redone in pale slate-blues and dusty pinks, the Monarch charms honeymooners with its king-size circular bed, heart-shaped whirlpool tub, oak-mantel fireplace, and very contemporary glass-and-chrome-accented living room. Six days/five nights: $997.50 per couple. Golden Suites: Very regal indeed, with a gold crown supporting the canopy over the king-size platform bed, sunken heart-shape tub, crystal chandelier, French-style furnishings, and gold wall coverings. Six days/five nights: $918.75 per couple.

Strickland's Mountain Inn and Cottages, Mount Pocono, PA 18344 (reservations: tel. 717/839-7155 or toll free 800/441-4410). It's a woodland setting, 400 acres dense with evergreens and rhododendrons. Many of the accommodations are built of wood and glass, and snuggle into the slopes like ski chalets; decks and skylights take advantage of the sunshine and views. In addition, Strickland's roster of sports activities will tempt you into the Great Outdoors. You have a choice of three outdoor heated pools, or there's a tranquil private lake just right for paddleboats. Go bike riding or horseback riding, play a few sets of tennis, or challenge each other to archery, handball, or bocce. Try to improve your handicap on the nine-hole golf course—or aim for a hole-in-one at miniature golf. In winter, let it snow, because Strickland's offers sledding, snowmobiling, and cross-country skiing. For downhill skiing, you have full use of Mount Airy's extensive lifts and slopes. Strickland's also has a large indoor sports pavilion for tennis, racquetball, ice skating, and roller skating, as well as a comfortably heated indoor pool. Pinball wizards can try their skills on a slew of video games. With all this activity, you'll really appreciate the meals served in Strickland's dining room, where huge hearths and stained-glass windows add to the hearty mountain atmosphere. After dinner, though, you'll feel like you're in the Big City, with entertainment by live bands or a New York–style revue.

Accommodations: Many of the most attractive accommodations harmonize with the mountain setting, using natural materials such as fieldstone, cedar, and redwood to create a mood of alpine elegance. Rates quoted are Full AP, including breakfast, lunch, and dinner daily. Several other rooms and packages are also available. The Timberline: For your honeymoon—your own cozy trilevel chalet nestled in the woods. Downstairs sofas flank the fieldstone fireplace and plank walls contribute a cozy, rustic feel. Upstairs you have a loft bedroom with mirrored ceiling, king-size bed, and a second fieldstone fireplace. There's also a Swedish sauna, sunken black whirlpool bath, and an oh-so-private deck for nude sunbathing, if you wish. Six days/five nights: $1,102.50 per couple. The Skytop: A private wood-and-glass mountain villa with a floor-to-ceiling stone fireplace in the living room and bedroom, outdoor balcony, and king-size bed illuminated by skylights. You'll also be pampered with a heart-shaped tub for two and private sauna. Six days/five nights: $1,050 per couple. Forest Chateau: Settle into your own cozy cottage for total privacy. The natural-stone fireplace casts its warm glow over the Mediterranean-style furnishings in the living room, there's a king-size round bed in your bedroom, sunken black tub for two in the bath, and a redwood terrace for sunning. Six days/five nights: $861 per couple.

Pocono Gardens, Mount Pocono, PA 18344 (reservations: tel. 717/595-7431 or toll free 800/441-4410). The feeling is very much that of an Italian villa: white ballustrades edge the terraces of the main building, columns frame arching windows, and marble statues stand in little nooks in the greenery. It's all very grand and glamourous. And very sporting, we should add, since Pocono Gardens not only has its own extensive facilities, but also shares those of Mount Airy Lodge, just minutes away. Right at Pocono Gardens, you can swim in the outdoor, Olympic-size heated pool, play tennis, croquet, volleyball, and softball. Pocono Gardens has its own private, clear-blue lake where you can cruise aboard a sailfish, canoe, or paddleboat, or stretch out your towels on a small, white sand beach. Nearby, there's waterskiing, 18 holes of golf, and horseback riding. In winter, the Poconos turn into a true wonderland, and you can enjoy favorite winter pastimes such as skiing (both downhill and cross-country), snowmobiling, and ice skating, both indoors and outside on the large lake. You'll want to spend lots of time around the indoor pool—shaped like an engagement ring and surrounded by statues and wraparound windows that let in the views of the snow-covered pine trees. At night, Pocono Gardens' dining room always has a festive air, with its marble columns and mirrors. Afterwards, there's star-studded entertainment every evening, and live music for dancing.

Accommodations: Each of Pocono Gardens' varied accommodations comes with air conditioning and a color TV. Several other rooms and packages are also available. Rates quoted are Full AP, including breakfast, lunch, and dinner daily. The Amorata: This room is similar to the Palace Suite at Mount Airy. Your private pool is large, and just outside the sliding glass doors you have a secluded garden terrace. Other features include a sauna, round bed framed by a gilt-and-blue-velvet headboard, and a heart-shaped whirlpool bath, artfully set off with mirrors. Six days/five nights: $1,102.50 per couple. The Sorrento-Capri II: Decorated in shades of blue, white, and gold, and accented by Provincial-style furnishings, this suite has a distinct Italianate ambience—enhanced by the mirrored Roman whirlpool bath. Six days/five nights: $997.50 per couple. Roman Forum Suites: Definitely for lovers of the dramatic, this room stars a king-size round bed set on a platform, backed by draperies, and highlighted by mirrors overhead. In the bath, there's a heart-shaped whirlpool bath, with mirrors and a crystal chandelier to add elegant finesse. Six days/five nights: $861 per couple.

Summit Resort

Owned by the Farda family, who have been part of the hospitality industry in the Poconos since 1952, the **Summit Resort,** Tannersville, PA 18372 (reservations: tel. 717/629-0203 or toll free 800/233-8250), offers practically every activity you can think of right on the property. Although all facilities are ultramodern, the Summit has the friendliness you can only find at a family-run resort.

The setting: a lush, green hillside above a large lake. The options: just about endless, what with tennis, bicycling, and boating, as well as horseback riding, archery, and water sports. That describes the Summit, a couples resort that believes in helping you live out your honeymoon dreams. Much of the action focuses on the main Summit Resort Center, a sleek wood-and-glass hilltop chalet. Here, all under one roof, you'll find the dining room, Moorish-motif Scheherezade Nightclub, and complete indoor sports facilities, including tennis courts, golf-driving range, basketball, ice skating, roller skating, complete fitness center, and large heated pool. Outdoors, you'll probably spend lots of time around the completely remodeled pool area with a waterfall, sundeck, sliding pond, and large whirlpool. During the winter, the Summit turns into a snowy wonderland, so grab your mittens and go tobogganing or snowmobiling. And the Summit is located near all the Pocono ski mountains—Camelback is just up the road.

You'll soon get to know the other honeymoon couples, thanks to Bob Beil, the longtime social director, who runs the Monday morning orientation tour of the property, and hosts Summit's own version of *The Newlywed Game*. Bob also performs a magic act, and his sleight-of-hand will soon have you wondering, "How did he do that?" Every day, the activity board lists a full swirl of events—picnic lunches, basketball games, trivia contests, skeet-shooting matches, or bowling derbies. Meal time is something to look forward to, especially since the Summit menu includes entrées such as sirloin steak, roast prime rib of beef, and chicken cacciatore. If you have an attack of the munchies between meals, head over to the new snack bar with café-style tables. The resort plans new additions for the coming year. The tropical atrium lobby (complete with waterfall, 20-foot rubber plant, bright blue parrot, and carp pond) is being expanded, two new racquetball courts are being added.

Honeymoon package: If you stay for four nights or longer, you'll receive a bottle of champagne, a bottle of bubble bath, a fire log, a honeymoon photo album, a Summit "Love Potion" cocktail (you also get to keep the glasses), and a horseback ride along scenic trails.

Accommodations: You have a varied choice of honeymoon headquarters, all with air conditioning and color TV. Rates quoted are Full AP, including three meals a day. Other rooms and packages are also available. Fantasia II: Soft earth tones set the seductive mood in this lavish suite. There's a private, glass-enclosed pool with mirrored walls and a woodland mural, fireplace, king-size round bed with mirrored canopy, a heart-shaped whirlpool tub backed with mirrors, plus a private steam bath and sauna. Six days/five nights: $834.75 per couple. Montserrat Villa: Here, you not only get a heart-shaped whirlpool, but a heart-shaped bed as well, in most units. Each suite is located in its own spacious villa, featuring a very secluded outdoor sun deck. Six days/five nights: $803.25 per couple. Shasta Penthouse: Decorated in shades of blue and rust, these accommodations feature a king-size bed, private balcony facing the Summit grounds, and a Roman-style sunken tub in bathroom. Six days/five nights: $619.50.

Penn Hills

In the mid-1940s Charles A. Poalillo, Sr. and his wife, Frances, came to the Pocono Mountains to retire. Instead, they discovered a small inn set by a lovely waterfall. They bought the property—and began developing **Penn Hills Resort,** Analomink, PA 18320 (reservations: tel. 717/421-6464 or toll free 800/233-8240). Today, honeymooners still love strolling through the woodlands to gaze at Rainbow Falls, and the Poalillo family maintains its tradition of friendly hospitality.

At Penn Hills Resort, honeymoon couples constantly find that they're able to enjoy the best of all worlds. The resort occupies over 500 acres, so there are plenty of woods and forests for hiking—and yet the accommodations are very chic and sophisticated. Penn Hills is located close to all the shops and factory outlets of Stroudsburg—and also right on a nine-hole golf course, Evergreen Park, and near its own ski mountain, Alpine.

Sports lovers will appreciate the enormous variety of Penn Hills' facilities: tennis courts, par course fitness cluster, softball, bocce ball—even a large outdoor swimming pool shaped like a wedding bell. There are two private lakes; Lake Pocahontas has small Paradise Island, an idyllic setting for paddleboats, canoeing, rowing, fishing, and other aquatic endeavors. You can enjoy many of your favorite sports all year, thanks to the large indoor sports arena, with volleyball, badminton, basketball, mini-golf, and a tennis court. You can even ice skate year round at the indoor Ice-A-Rama. When it snows, Penn Hills looks just like a Christmas card, and couples can take advantage of a wide range of winter sports. The resort is an excellent choice for skiers, since it owns Alpine Mountain, just three miles from the resort. Alpine has a 500-foot vertical drop, 14 trails and slopes, four lifts, 100% snowmaking capability, and is slated to add nighttime skiing in 1988. (Ask about the special ski packages.) Cross-country skiers can snap into bindings on the latest equipment and whoosh off along the stream and through the pine forests. Or you can turn into a kid again at the snow area complete with toboggan, sleds, and skibobs. Then head for something tropical—the indoor pool, sauna, or whirlpool. New for this year, Penn Hills is adding racquetball courts, Universal exercise equipment, and a steam room. It's always easy to round up a team for softball, or opponents at tennis, because social director Ernie Camlet introduces everybody around.

Whatever season you visit, you'll enjoy dining in the Garden Terrace, a greenhouse-like dining room overlooking the woods and lakes of the golf course. Penn Hills has always been known for its good food, especially Italian dishes, including some Poalillo family recipes. At night, everyone heads over to the Reflections nightclub and disco, with live entertainment nightly, and dance music ranging from Golden Oldies to New Wave.

Honeymoon package: If you stay for at least four nights, you receive a bottle of champagne, a bottle of bubble bath, a fire log, a honeymoon photo album, plus—free skiing daily at Alpine Mountain in winter, or free golf at the nine-hole regulation course in spring, summer, and fall.

Accommodations: This is just a small sampling of the rooms and package plans available at Penn Hills. All rates are Modified American Plan (MAP), including breakfast and dinner daily; all rooms have air conditioning and color cable TV. Penthouse Towers: This triplex townhouse is nestled into the mountainside, overlooking the swimming pool and gardens. In addition to the heart-shaped bath, there's an enticing round bed encircled with Roman pillars, a log-burning fireplace, all accented with a passionate red. Six days/five nights: $871.50 per couple. Mountain Terrace Villa: Your own individual mountainside chalet, decorated in nature's tones of beige, brown, and russet. The spacious suite has five separate living areas, a round platform bed with circular mirror above, fireplace, and a totally private terrace facing the woods. Six days/five nights: $871.50 per couple. Riviera Towers: These roomy accommodations have recently been redone in soft browns and beiges, with colorful modern art on the walls. There's a playground-size king-size bed, and either a heart-shaped tub or combo steambath/whirlpool in the private bathroom. All have a balcony overlooking the wedding-bell pool. Six days/five nights: $682.50.

Chapter XII

SOUTH CAROLINA

1. Practical Facts
2. Myrtle Beach
3. Pawleys Island to Georgetown
4. Charleston
5. The Island Resorts

HAS THE ROMANTIC in you ever yearned for the graciousness and quietude of the Old South? Does your mind conjure up landscapes of ancient oaks draped with Spanish moss swaying indolently in the breeze? Does your heart quicken at the heavy sweet scent of magnolias sent out in tendrils to tickle your nose? Have you pictured yourself in a wide-brimmed sunbonnet sipping a cool drink on the piazza as the sun sets over the harbor? If so, you can plunge into these antebellum scenes and sensations along the coast of South Carolina.

You will find yourself in a place where the natives are sincerely and unabashedly devoted to enjoying life—have been for centuries. And nothing pleases them more than sharing their largesse of ease and grace with a couple of newlyweds.

The heritage of the South Carolina coast is long and intricate. Some of young America's largest fortunes were amassed on the indigo and rice plantations around Myrtle Beach, and on the cotton plantations on the Sea Islands. Sea Island cotton once was rivaled only by Egyptian cotton as the finest in the world.

Ultramodern, ultraluxurious resorts now occupy land where mansions and slave quarters once stood; resorts that offer a host of active sporting opportunities or the opportunity to sit on an empty beach and watch the waves.

The South Carolina coast lies directly on the north-south flyways of many migratory birds. Spring and autumn, the air above and the marshes below are filled with exquisite creatures such as the snowy egret and the blue heron. When golfing, you might find yourself forced to abandon a slice hit too close to a lagoon whose resident alligator has taken a liking to your golf ball. On an afternoon's horseback ride through the woods you might come upon a glade where white-tailed deer feed. The natural beauties of the locale cannot help but further seduce you into a state of blissful escape.

From the bumper cars at Myrtle Beach to the piazzas of Charleston to the marinas on Hilton Head, a sorcerous blend of history, luxury, and simplicity will weave its spell about the two of you, and you too will appreciate some of the Old South's secrets for living the good life. After all, Captain Rhett Butler—a man who certainly knew plenty about how to enjoy himself—was a born and bred Charleston boy.

1. Practical Facts

GETTING THERE: South Carolina is accessible from any of the continental United States.

By Air

Airports at Myrtle Beach and Charleston, South Carolina, and Savannah, Georgia (serving Hilton Head Island), have incoming and outgoing flights daily. **Piedmont, Delta,** and **Eastern Airlines** serve these airports, usually with connecting flights from Columbia, S.C., or Washington, D.C.

By Car

From the north or south, the fastest route is to drive on **Interstate 95.** From the west the area is served by **Interstates 20** and **26. Rte. 17** runs north-south along the coast and will be your primary means of getting around.

GETTING AROUND: Public transportation in the area is rare to nonexistent. If you are flying in, all airports have **rental car** facilities. If you're in a sporty mood, reserve a convertible. Rental rates for a midsize, standard car are approximately $175 weekly.

Roads are generally well marked and well maintained. Rtes. 95 and 17 are major north-south highways, so many drivers tend to be in a hurry to get from here to there.

WEATHER: South Carolina's weather is close to perfect for about 9 months out of the 12. Spring arrives early in March, and Indian summer can linger well into November. During the height of the season, June through August, temperatures can climb into the 90s and beyond. March through May and September through November are by far the most pleasant months with warm days (75°) and cool evenings (60°).

CLOTHING: Pretty much anything goes around these parts. Some of the fancier restaurants in Charleston request a jacket and tie for gentlemen, so if you're planning to step out in style, you might want to check when you make your reservations. Otherwise dress is casual and cool. Most of the resorts and hotels require that you wear shoes and a cover-up for your bathing suit when not in the pool or beach areas. Proper golf and tennis attire are required on the fairway or the court.

TIME: The state is in the Eastern Time zone, and observes Daylight Savings Time.

TELEPHONES: The area code for all of South Carolina is 803. Most of the lodgings have toll free 800 numbers for reservations and/or information.

SHOPPING: The area around Myrtle Beach is chock-full of outlet stores for things like Hathaway shirts and Dansk pottery. These stores are concentrated around the **Waccamaw Pottery Outlet Park,** west of town on Rte. 501.

At the other end of the scale are the **antiques stores** and **art galleries** of Charleston. Some of the finest American and English furnishings from the 18th century on can be found in Charleston shops, such as **Elizabeth Austin and Company** at 165 King Street and **Century House** at 77 Church Street. Prices tend to be very steep, but quality is commensurate.

One of the most welcome additions to any home, new or otherwise, is a Pawley's Island hammock. When *GQ* magazine named the most luxurious things to do in the world, lounging in a Pawley's Island hammock ranked near the top of the list. Indeed, these marvels of the hand-knotters' craft have cradled julep-swilling South Carolinians ever since Captain Josh Ward gave up his riverboat and kept weaving the things until he found a pattern he liked. The hammocks are still handwoven, made of wool or 100%

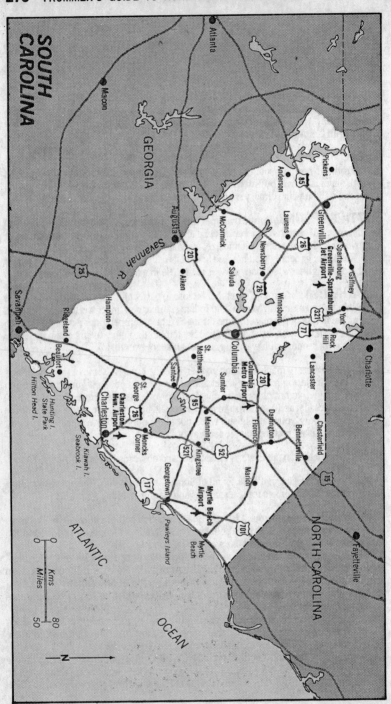

cotton rope. Prices start at $95. You can find them, among other places, at the **Pawley's Island Hammock Shop** on the east side of Hwy. 17 at Pawley Island (tel. 237-9122).

ABOUT ACCOMMODATIONS: Any taste and any budget can be accommodated here. Along the coast you can stay in 150-year-old cottages that once housed rice planters—some of whose paint might be original by the looks of it; or in a state-of-the-art villa equipped with microwave, washer/dryer, Jacuzzi.

It is impossible to pinpoint exactly when high season begins and ends. Some resorts recognize two seasons, some recognize three and four or more. Prices between lowest and highest seasons can vary as much as 50%, so be sure to contact each hostelry to find the exact rate for the particular month you'll be arriving. Prices quoted reflect the spread from the lowest low-season rate to the highest high-season rate, when applicable.

DINING OUT: Since the atmosphere around these parts tends to be quite relaxed, reservations are often unnecessary; however, the fancier Charleston restaurants and some of the small inns request that you call in advance.

Naturally the coastal waters supply the local eateries with mouth-wateringly fresh catches daily. The cuisine here is known as low-country, featuring such Southern standards as she-crab soup (a rich bisque), deviled crab (a spicy presentation of crabmeat in the shell), and oysters about a dozen different ways. Biscuits and hush puppies (deep-fried nuggets of cornmeal) are ubiquitous and irresistible.

HOW TO GET MARRIED IN SOUTH CAROLINA: No blood test is necessary. You must be 18 years old or older if you get married without parental consent. Whether applying by mail or in person, you must wait a full 24 hours after submitting application before license can be issued. Contact the county courthouse in the locale where you will be marrying for complete details.

FOR FURTHER INFORMATION: Contact: **South Carolina Department of Parks, Recreation & Tourism,** 1205 Pendleton St., Columbia, SC 29201 (tel. 803/734-0135); **Myrtle Beach Area Chamber of Commerce,** 1301 N. Kings Hwy., Myrtle Beach, SC 29578 (tel. 803/626-7444); **Georgetown County Chamber of Commerce,** 600 Front St., Georgetown, SC 29440 (tel. 803/546-8436); **Charleston Trident Chamber of Commerce,** Rice Mill Bldg., 17 Lockwood Blvd., Charleston, SC 29402 (tel. 803/723-7641); **Hilton Head Chamber of Commerce,** P.O. Box 5647, Hilton Head Island, SC 29938 (tel. 803/785-3673).

2. Myrtle Beach

Myrtle Beach is what you get when you mix la crème de la mer with a liberal dose of kitsch: a town that's fast and fun and doesn't take itself too stuffily. The great thing about Myrtle Beach is the way it easily assimilates the old and the new. High-tech high-rise condos peer down on mom-and-pop-operated motels. You can play golf on some of the world's toughest courses or pitch-'n'-putt past a plastic brontosaurus.

Myrtle Beach is the first resort you hit in South Carolina, just beyond the state's northern border. It has historically been the first beach destination for the southbound spring-beach crowd, and still has a giddy, good-time collegiate feel about it. There is a midway complete with rollicking roller coasters, pinball, cotton candy—just as you remember it.

This is not to say Myrtle Beach is only an old-time seaside town. On the contrary, Myrtle Beach has seen the future and is retooling from a vacationland of the 1940s and 1950s to a world-class resort for the 1980s and beyond. Assisting in this upscale uplift are the area's 30-odd championship golf courses, the slew of new-sprung restaurants, and a climate boasting more sunny, clear days than Florida. So if you're seeking sun, sport, and nonstop fun, Myrtle Beach provides the punch.

ROMANTIC INTERLUDES: Myrtle Beach appeals to active lovers; her attractions are outdoor and energetic.

When you've wearied of pinball and bumper cars down in town, around sunset, you might like to take a stroll or a jog up **Ocean Boulevard** north of 31st Street, an avenue bordered by big, beautiful beach houses—some Mediterranean, some Georgian, some indescribably idiosyncratic—which attest to Myrtle Beach's history as a resort of choice for the trust-fund set as well as for the fancy-free. Cactus, holly, and the ubiquitous palmetto (South Carolina's symbol) thrive in the sandy soil and salt air.

If your idea of togetherness is tees for two, the Myrtle Beach area's close to 40 **golf courses** should delight you. The varying character of the courses exceeds even your wildest dreams and ensures that golfers—from hackers to pros—can find 1, 2, or 20 just to their liking. Although most courses are open to the public, the local hotels and resorts tend to reserve the prime tee times. Your best bet is to arrange for a golf package when you make your hotel reservations. Options include:

Pine Lakes International Country Club, P.O. Box 2096, Myrtle Beach, SC 29578 (tel. 449-5134), Myrtle Beach's first, designed in 1926 by PGA chairman Robert White.

Carolina Shores Golf and Country Club, P.O. Box 66, North Myrtle Beach, SC 29597 (tel. 448-2657), the most heavily trapped course in the area; Tom Jackson, architect.

Bay Tree Golf Plantation, Rte. 2, Hwy. 9, North Myrtle Beach, SC 29582 (tel. 249-2026), three 18-hole courses with undulating greens designed by George Fazio and Russell Breeden.

"Romantic" is not quite the right word to describe **Waccamaw Pottery and Linen,** a cavern full of pottery, lamps, linens, gourmet food—perhaps "exhilaratingly enervating" comes closer to the experience, so grab a shopping cart, hold onto your hat (and your spouse), and go *nuts!* Here you'll find copper, brass, Christmas supplies, place mats, sheets, quilts, handcraft supplies, appliances, and acres of stemware, glassware, flatware, and china—in case you didn't get enough settings from Tiffany.

Prices are real low, 20% to 70% below retail, so just dive right in. At the **Outlet Mall,** Rte. 501, Myrtle Beach (tel. 236-4606).

HONEYMOON HOTELS AND HIDEAWAYS: Myrtle Beach's host of new resorts offers luxurious accommodations at reasonable rates. All those mentioned are right on the beach. Rates quoted reflect the spread between low- and high-season prices.

Smack dab on the beach, **Beach Colony Resort,** 5308 N. Ocean Blvd., Myrtle Beach, SC 29577 (tel. 803/449-4010; reservations: toll free 800/222-2141), is located a bit north of Myrtle Beach center, so during the height of season when the Strand can be crowded, their beach tends to have fewer bodies strewn about. The rooms are decorated in soft shades of mauve, green, and teal blue. They come equipped with a kitchenette in the sitting room and porches overlooking the beach.

On the ground level there is an indoor pool, whirlpool, exercise room, and saunas. Outside several other pools and whirlpools are attractively arranged on the boardwalk deck. Honeymoon package: None. Daily suite rates range from $45 to $100 per couple.

The Yachtsman, 1400 North Ocean Blvd., Myrtle Beach, SC 29577 (tel. 803/448-1441; reservations: toll free 800/331-8076). Opened in July 1986, this impressive sheath of sky-blue glass reflects sun, sky, and a new twist in local architecture. All the rooms feature floor-to-ceiling windows and views of the rippling Atlantic. Sitting rooms decorated in floral and bird prints in warm shades open onto oceanside decks equipped with comfy chairs perfect for sipping cocktails you've fixed at the wet bar in your kitchenette. The bath is equipped with a telephone and Jacuzzi—we suggest you take the former off the hook when employing the latter. On the premises you'll find an indoor and an outdoor pool, whirlpool with bar beside, saunas, and weight rooms. Honeymoon package: None. Daily rates for a one-bedroom suite with ocean view range from $50 to $120 per couple.

Kingston Plantation, 9770 Kings Rd., Myrtle Beach, SC 29577 (tel. 803/449-4177; reservations: toll free 800/421-5432), encompasses 145 acres, including a half-mile of oceanfront. There are a variety of accommodations on the property, including a Radisson all-suite hotel. Located on the beach, the Radisson is replete with all the amenities you'd expect: several restaurants, all overlooking the Atlantic; and an inviting lounge decorated with huge salt-water aquariums. Radisson honeymoon package (BP): $125 per couple per night. Includes a two-room suite, champagne on arrival, and breakfast.

Villas surround a wooded lake, which provides a home for ducks, crane, blue heron. Choose one of the upstairs one-bedroom suites, which have cathedral ceilings. All villa accommodations are decorated in corals and sea blues, and you can sit in front of your fireplace and enjoy a quiet evening together. In addition, all the villas have a kitchen, washer/dryer, and an outdoor deck. Honeymoon package: None. Rates for a one-bedroom villa run $39 to $69 per couple per night.

To attend to your athletic needs, there's a $3-million sports complex open to guests at either the hotel or the villas. Facilities include hard-surface and clay tennis courts, racquetball, squash, whirlpool, saunas, Nautilus equipment, and a swimming pool.

ROMANTIC RESTAURANTS: Myrtle Beach offers everything from candlelight and champagne to brews and burgers, so you can sup differently every night. Many of the area's best are located on Restaurant Row at the north end of town on Rte. 17.

Moderate

Among the prettiest and most romantic dining spots on Restaurant Row is **Gullyfield,** Rte. 17 (tel. 449-3111). Ask for a table in the garden room at the rear. Thanks to the white latticework, hanging ferns, and soft lights reflecting on the pines and magnolias outside the huge picture windows, you'll feel you're in a low-country gazebo. The food echoes the antebellum decor—fresh seafood, spicy-sweet fried chicken, embarrassingly ample desserts. Dinner for two with wine will run about $50. Also open for lunch.

Pier 14 (tel. 448-4314) doesn't have a particular address, but you can't miss it pushing its spindly way right out into the surf at the center of the Strand. Set some 35 feet over the water, this seafood restaurant comes equipped with frothy daiquiris, a dance floor, and a 360° view. You can eat indoors or take-out on the deck until midnight or beyond. There is live music Tuesday through Saturday, no cover charge. Pier 14 also serves breakfast and is the perfect place to fortify yourself after a long morning's walk on the beach. Dinner for two will run $25 to $45 depending on accompanying liquor(s).

Inexpensive

Buddy's Grill, 16th Avenue North, west of Rte. 17 (tel. 626-4792). Welcome to the best local joint around. You'll feel right at home when you walk in. Myrtle Beach High football memorabilia adorns the walls; a big grin adorns the face of your host, who named the place for his son, Buddy. It's basically a spot for burgers and such.

They make their own buns for the burgers, cut their own onions, and sliver their own potatoes for frying. Dinner for two, $10 tops.

3. Pawleys Island to Georgetown

Whereas Myrtle Beach is decidedly 1980s, the area south to Georgetown retains much more of an 18th century flavor.

Georgetown County once boasted the richest farmland, and the wealthiest farmers, in the Americas. First indigo and then rice provided the wealth. At one point the area supplied 80% of the world's rice. To grow rice you need plenty of marsh land which makes for very humid summers. To escape, the planters fled to such favorite haunts as Pawleys Island.

The Pawleys Island motto, "arrogantly shabby" sums up nicely the area's unconcern with things newfangled and fancy. Tradition, history, and legend take over here. One such legend involves the Gray Man who supposedly appears before a dangerous storm to at least one local resident, who then warns the other islanders to evacuate. Whoever sights the ghost is assured that his home will not be destroyed. The woman who saw the Gray Man before the hurricane of 1959 even returned home to find her laundry still hanging on the line where she left it.

One last word: Rumor has it that once you've dug your toes into Pawleys Island sand, you won't ever want to leave—you have been warned!

ROMANTIC INTERLUDES: Activities in this area tend toward the quiet and contemplative. Here are a few "just for the two of you" suggestions.

One of the most romantic settings in South Carolina, is **Brookgreen Gardens,** founded by Archer Milton and Anna Hyatt Huntington as the repository for their collection of American statuary. Although the statues tend to be overly sentimental, the gardens are magnificent. Here you can stroll beneath some monumental *Quercus verginiana fagaccae,* or live oak, so-called because, although a member of the oak family, this tree is an evergreen, thus appearing "alive" year round. If you're a serious naturalist, there are guided tours explaining the flora and fauna; or a self-guided, taped tour describing the artwork. Admission: $3 per person.

Should you so desire, you can have your wedding and reception at Brookgreen. It's hard to imagine a more perfect setting in April and May when the dogwood and azaleas are in full regalia. Brookgreen is located on Rte. 17 just halfway between Myrtle Beach and Georgetown (tel. 237-4218). Open everyday except Christmas, 9:30 a.m. to 4:45 p.m.

Take a **riverboat ride** around the creeks and through the swamp grass daily from 9 a.m. until dark. The **Wacca Wache Marina** in Murrells Inlet gives tours of varying length. It is a thrill to motor around the marshes past the old plantation sites along the Tee Dee River, scuttling ducks and alligators in your wake. Call for reservations, tel. 651-2994 or 651-7171. River tours and dinner tours are enjoyed aboard the *Island Queen II.* A three-hour tour costs $10 per person. Wacca Wache is located on the water in Murrells Inlet, 2 miles west of the Highway 17 Bypass.

Savor twilight's tranquility at **South Beach** on Pawleys Island. If you have the good fortune to be lodging on the island, just walk south until the island ends; otherwise, you can drive down to the beach, park, and enjoy the miles-from-nowhere sensation.

Time your visit to coincide with sunset—the beach sharpens to a point, so the sun sinks on the western side and the Atlantic pounds the east. Bring along a bottle of something crisp and dry and some of Yum Young's unbeatable barbecue (see "Romantic Restaurants"), and plenty of napkins—or if you're feeling très amoureux, you can just lick your fingers.

HONEYMOON HOTELS AND HIDEAWAYS: Georgetown County offers accommodations ranging from the quaint antique cottages of Pawleys Island to the anything but shabby cottages of Wachesaw Plantation. In addition, some of the cottages once used by plantation owners are available for rental by the week or longer, including the Summer Academy, which was a popular hot-weather hangout back in 1812. House rentals can be arranged through **Pawleys Island Realty,** P.O. Box 306, Pawleys Island, SC 29585 (tel. 803/237-4257). Weekly rates for an oceanfront duplex range from $500 in low season to $700 in high season.

Rates quoted reflect the spread between low- and high-season rates, when applicable.

Expensive

Wachesaw Plantation, P.O. Box 570, Murells Inlet, SC 29576 (tel. 803/651-0115). Spread out on close to 1,800 acres on the site of the Wachesaw and Richmond Hill plantations, Wachesaw fairly exudes aristocratic taste and meticulous planning. Wachesaw is essentially a private community—only 20% of the properties are available for rental—keeping the atmosphere small-town and uncommercial. Although the cottages are new, the architecture recreates the 18th-century ambience combining it with 20th-century amenities. Golf, a private marina, horseback riding, and the like, complete the facilities.

The cottages are decorated mostly with reproduction antiques, and the atmosphere is casually comfortable. A fully equipped kitchen, porches overlooking greens or courts or woods, and full housekeeping and catering services add a touch of luxury. You can also stop in for a brew or two at Kimbell's Cabin, a cozy, gentlemanly, converted hunting lodge overlooking the Wachesaw River and the 18th green. Honeymoon package: None. Rates for a villa are $150 per couple per night. Golf and tennis packages are available.

Moderate

1790 House, 630 Highmarket St., Georgetown, SC 29440 (tel. 803/546-4821). This lovely 18th-century home has been transformed into a bed-and-breakfast in the historic district of Georgetown. The downstairs has 11-foot ceilings to keep the rooms cool. Upstairs, the Rice Planter's Suite features a planter's bed with rice sheaves carved in the shafts, the scent of fresh flowers, and mellow sherry filtering through the air. Innkeeper Gay Forstbauer jealously protects her guests' peace and tranquility: "There is no TV, and we put telephones in the room only by request. We want to keep everything quiet, secluded, so our guests can be in and still be out." Honeymoon package: None. Accommodations for two includes breakfast indoors or on the veranda, and starts at $50 per night.

The **Tip Top Inn,** P.O. Box 1278, Pawleys Island, SC 29585 (tel. 803/237-2325), is a marvelous getaway from the modern world. Rooms are wood-paneled and simply furnished. The public room is decorated with expansive armchairs and antique lamps with yellowed shades. The paint's peeling, there are gaps in the floor boards, but somehow all of this adds to the charm of the place. You can set a spell on the front porch, steps away from the surf, and shoot the breeze with innkeeper Sis Kelly—a great source of local lore and information. Meals are "low-country food and lots of it," according to Sis—barefeet are encouraged. Honeymoon package: None. Standard rates include breakfast and dinner at noon; from $40 to $55 per couple per night; $265 to $360 per couple weekly.

ROMANTIC RESTAURANTS: Whether you prefer the fanciest of tables or the funkiest of fare, Georgetown cooks are known to spare no pains to ensure your dining is fine.

Moderate

Pawleys Island Inn at the Hammock Shops, Hwy. 17, Pawleys Island (tel. 237-8491). Set in a gaggle of clapboard shops on the east side of the highway, this restaurant is an uncanny reconstruction of an old inn: brick floors, rustic wooden tables, 250-year-old beams, walk-in fireplaces. The place is bustling almost anytime because of its cooked to perfection local catch such as grouper or scallops. You might like to try something from the mesquite grill—Black Angus steaks, swordfish, even buffalo. The wine list is one of the most extensive in the area. Dinner for two, about $60 with wine. Reservations are suggested.

Inexpensive

Murrells Inlet is a town with 18 restaurants at last count, and not much else. Most follow much the same pattern: casual atmosphere, paper place mats, beer, and an all-you-can-eat seafood buffet, stocked with fried shrimp, succulent oyster, deviled crab. It's tough to recommend one place over another, so just mosey on into town and stop at whichever strikes your fancy. All are extremely good for this sort of food, and all are reasonably priced. Dinner for two with beers should be a modest $20.

Yum Young's, west side of Rte. 17 north of Georgetown (no phone). This chicken-and-rib joint is one of the area's best-kept culinary secrets. It's a secret that practically keeps itself: The establishment is a most unprepossessing cinderblock shack beside the highway. Hours are irregular, but Thursdays around 5:30 are a good bet. Of course, if the hunting's good, George Young may be otherwise engaged. George has been grilling beef and pork ribs and barbecued chicken over a charcoal-and-oak fire for years. Inside you can pick up your order (business is take out): about $4 per pound. They also sell hog-head cheese and potato pie. While you're waiting, relax in the armchairs by the fireplace, and admire the cook-off trophies George has won displayed on the mantel.

4. Charleston

It is said that Charlestonians are very much like the Chinese: They eat a lot of rice; they worship their ancestors; and they speak a different language. Merely being born in the city does not qualify you as a native; one is not considered a Charlestonian until after at least three generations.

Today Charleston is prosperous, set on a harbor at the confluence of the Ashley and Cooper rivers. Much of its 18th-century graciousness still remains intact. In 1986, Charleston was voted the most livable city in America, and indeed it would be difficult to imagine a more perfect place to spend a week or a lifetime. Exquisite inns filled with antiques perpetuate Charleston's tradition of hospitality, fine restaurants serving low-country and haute cuisine abound, antique stores and art galleries will assist you in finding some local treasure for your home, and pretty pastel-painted houses with lacy verandas line the streets.

Special mention must be made of the **Spoleto Festival,** held in late May through June, when the city gives itself over to the loveliest of arts: dance, drama, music. When Gian Carlo Menotti was looking for a new world site to complement his festival in Umbria, Italy, the maestro landed in Charleston and searched no further. The event is nothing short of ecstatic. Needless to say, hotel and restaurant reservations and program tickets are snatched up fast, so if you plan to be in town for Spoleto, be sure to call well in advance. For information contact: **Spoleto Festival U.S.A.,** P.O. Box 704, Charleston, SC 29402 (tel. 803/722-2764).

To get started on your Charleston explorations, take a tour in one of the mule-drawn carriages, or a more comprehensive walking tour with a guide. **Palmetto Tours** (tel. 723-8145) and **Old South Carriage Company** (tel. 723-9712) run 50-minute carriage tours from the market area through the historic district; cost is $16 per couple.

Charleston Strolls (tel. 766-2080) will perambulate you about for two hours at $6 per person. Be sure to tell the guide you're honeymooning, and she'll be sure to include many of Charleston's romantic tales in her repertoire. You might also want to take in a showing of *Dear Charleston,* an independently made, 45-minute film shown at the **Preservation Society Visitors Center,** 147 King St. Admission $3 per person.

ROMANTIC INTERLUDES: It's hard to avoid romance in a place as rife with history and charm as Charleston. Here are a few extraordinary options.

Middleton Inn (also see "Honeymoon Hotels and Hideaways" section) will equip you for a delicious picnic with a difference. For $120 you can hire an **antique surrey.** A perfectly matched pair of horses, a coachman and a footman both in full regalia will whisk you off through the forest surrounding Middleton Plantation to your destination in a sequestered glen. There they will unpack and set a sumptuous picnic for you, complete with wine, then remove to a discreet distance while you disport yourselves as you will. They return to pack up your hamper and drive you home. Call 556-0500 for details.

If you're of a seafaring nature, you might like to take a spin around **Charleston Harbor** or go exploring the outer islands. Take a sunset or moonlight or overnight cruise on the *Evening Star,* a 56-foot wood-hulled schooner. Captain John will include hors d'oeuvres, cocktails, dinner, whatever you care to order, and sail you wherever you want to go. You make up the itinerary and the menu. You can sail the ship if you like or sit back and relax while Captain John mans the helm. Rates start at about $30 per person but vary widely. For information or reservations, call 723-8518.

Ask any Charlestonian what they would recommend to honeymooners, and they'll send you out to **Sullivan's Island** to watch the sun set. Porpoises swim and cavort close to shore as the sun wends its fiery way westward behind the spires of Charleston. Pack a picnic of champagne, or save your appetite for a meal at Guild's (pronounced guile's) Inn (see "Romantic Restaurants").

HONEYMOON HOTELS AND HIDEAWAYS: Charleston's dizzying array of accommodations allows you to fulfill your every fantasy.

Opened late in 1986, the **Omni Hotel** at Charleston Place, 130 Market St., Charleston, SC 29401 (tel. 803/722-4900), gives its ground floor over to a shopping gallery of marble, brass, and soft pastels occupied by Godiva, Polo, Gucci, Brookstone, and other tempting boutiques. Upstairs the rooms are comfortable, complete with a wet bar and low-country reproduction furniture. Try to get one of the suites with a private courtyard where you can have your breakfast served. Keep yourself in shape at the hotel's fitness center, indoor pool, sauna, steam room, and Jacuzzi. Honeymoon package: None. Superior rooms from $90 per couple per night, suites from $145 per couple per night.

The Indigo Inn, One Maiden Lane, Charleston, SC 29401 (tel. 803/577-5900; reservations: toll free 800/845-7639). You'll feel the low-country elegance the moment you step into the lobby, paneled in mellowed woods, liberally deployed with fine antiques. The rooms have the fluffiest comforters and pillows and your hosts will further assure your warmth and good spirits with a cordial and chocolates with evening turndown. In the morning, fortify yourself with the Indigo's famous hunt breakfast. Honeymoon package: $75 to $95 per couple per night. Includes breakfast and parking and bottle of wine upon arrival.

The honeymoon suite at **The Guild's Inn,** 101 Pitt St., Mt. Pleasant, SC 29464 (tel. 803/881-0510), can accommodate you with its all-encompassing four-poster, dormer windows, and Jacuzzi under a skylight. The atmosphere at the inn is friendly, informal—like staying with a family. Honeymoon Suite: $100 per couple nightly, including wine, breakfast, turndown.

Bed-and-Breakfasts

The most intimate and indigenous lodgings in Charleston are provided by the town's bed-and-breakfast inns. Though tough to select a favorite, here are some top choices:

Expensive: The **Maison Du Pré**, 317 East Bay St., Charleston, SC 29401 (tel. 803/723-5905), is the brainchild of Lucille Mulholland, who took up a radio station's offer to relocate some old houses that were in disrepair. Lucille placed them around a Charleston garden, which forms a most charming courtyard. All the rooms are decorated with antiques that Lucille has culled from all over the South and with some of her own watercolors. Breakfast and low-country tea are served in the parlor overlooking East Bay Street. The honeymoon suite, done up in soft pinks and ivory, has an antique sleigh bed and a claw-foot tub in the bathroom. Honeymoon package: $170 per couple per night. Includes champagne; continental breakfast; afternoon tea, wine, and cheese; carriage tour; nightly turndown service.

Moderate: The **Sword Gate Inn**, 111 Tradd St., Charleston, SC 29401 (tel. 803/723-8515), manages to outshine the formidable competition. Set back from the road on a quiet street, the Sword Gate (circa 1800) houses the last unadulterated ballroom in Charleston; the 14-foot ceiling,has gilding by Tiffany. Each afternoon there is wine and cheese and a chance to visit with Walter Barton, a most congenial host, who will tell you of the inn's resident ghost (who has a thing for shoes), and will share with you his exhaustive list of what to see and do in the area. Joel Fischer, honeymooning from Charlotte, NC, remarked, "So many inns these days confuse haughtiness with elegance. Here the service is very personalized." Honeymoon suites: $110 per couple per night.

Belvedere, 40 Rutledge Ave., Charleston, SC 29401 (tel. 803/722-0973). Host Jim Spell is an architect himself and has seen to it that this late-19th-century mansion has been perfectly restored, including the addition of woodwork and mantels from the Belvedere Plantation on the Cooper River. Only three rooms are available to guests, all with canopy bed, luxurious draperies, and private terrace overlooking Colonial Lake. Honeymoon package: None. Standard rate of $75 per couple per night. Includes continental breakfast, afternoon sherry, use of bicycles, and a most sincere welcome.

Middleton Inn, Ashley River Road, Charleston, SC 29407 (tel. 803/556-0500). Although it has a Charleston address, Middleton Inn is set deep in the woods west of the city proper beside the Ashley River. Among the laurels and pines is nestled a clean, crisp, ultramodern cluster of buildings, all picture windows and masonry, designed by Charlestonian W. G. Clark.

Clark's inn is truly magnificent, yet warm and comfortable. Your room looks through the trees out onto the river and is furnished with a marble bath, hand-turned ash furniture, and a fireplace all set to go. Honeymoon package: Four days/three nights: $375 per couple. Includes champagne, continental breakfast daily, and best of all, unlimited admission to the restored house and 65 acres of colonial gardens at next-door Middleton Plantation, permitting the two of you to wander alone among the camellias after the crowds depart at closing time.

ROMANTIC RESTAURANTS: Charleston cooking mmm-mmm-makes your mouth water just thinking about it. Must-haves: creamy she-crab soup, deep-fried hush puppies, and oysters *any* way.

Expensive

Phillippe Million, 2 Unity Alley (tel. 577-7472). Below a skylight you can sip selections from the wine bar while you wait for your table. The cuisine is nouvelle française, perfectly prepared and presented on delicate Limoges china. There are three prix-fixe menus with from five to eight courses, or you may order à la carte. Specialties include delicately prepared seafood, veal, and game in season. The eight-course menu degustation, $45 per person. Reservations are necessary.

Moderate

The **Supper at Seven Restaurant** at Guild's Inn, 101 Pitt St., Mt. Pleasant, SC 29464 (tel. 803/881-0510), seats only 34 for dinner in front of the fire in this 1888 building. The chairs and tables are waxed to a warm brilliance, the food is authentic low-country, and the welcome is real. You may just decide not to leave. Dinner for two: $50.

82 Queen Restaurant, 82 Queen St. (tel. 723-7591). There is a perfect table for two here in the garret upstairs overlooking the courtyard. The restaurant encompasses two 18th-century townhouses and a carriage house in which you'll find formal dining rooms with chinoiserie wallpapers and hunting prints. There is a raw bar stacked with plump oysters and such, frequented by the locals after work. Also a wine bar and pub in front with free popcorn, the game on TV, and a less formal atmosphere. The chefs work magic with oysters, shrimp, beef, and fowl. Do choose a bottle from their wine list of over 90 selections to accompany your meal. Dinner for two with wine about $75.

Ferrante's Restaurant, 32 Market St. (tel. 723-3614). This oh-so-romantic eatery owes much of its charm to its location in the Old Seaman's Chapel. The dining room features a heart-of-pine vaulted ceiling, a most secular mural of a postrevelric Bacchus and his handmaidens, and background piano music. Cuisine tends toward the Italian—veal, fresh pasta, and a bravura selection of gelati, Italian ices, and pastries from Ferrante's bakery. Dinner for two with all the trimmings will cost about $65.

Middleton Place Restaurant, Ashley River Road (tel. 556-6020), is set right in the center of Middleton Plantation (see also "Hotels" section), and is presided over by Edna Lewis, a soft-spoken woman who began cooking on a wood-burning stove in Freeton, Virginia. She has since gone on to international fame, hailed as one of America's greatest chefs. After extensive research she has designed a menu incorporating some of the foods which the Middletons would have served honored guests 250 years ago—pan-fried flounder, tenderloin of beef with chervil and tarragon, panned quail with country ham. Dinner for two will add up to about $65.

5. The Island Resorts

The coast of South Carolina is fringed with a string of barrier islands which once produced the finest Sea Island cotton. Recently these lands have been taken over by developers who have created fabulous, self-contained resorts, each one covering several thousand acres, including miles of sable-sanded South Carolina beach.

The island resorts—Wild Dunes, Kiawah, Seabrook and Hilton Head—are a veritable fantasyland for adults offering every kind of outdoor activity you can think of, from biking to beachcombing, tennis to tanning. The basic blueprint of all these resorts creates a community of golf, tennis, swimming pools, beaches, and fine dining. In addition, there are jogging and biking trails through the maritime forests and ancient moss-shaggy live oak and palmetto that are native to the Sea Islands.

Since the islands are so closely identified with the resorts that inhabit them, see "Honeymoon Hotels and Hideaways" for specifics on each. There are, however, a few facts that apply to all. When you check in, you are given a temporary membership card that serves as ID and as a credit card for the dining and diversions that you may pursue at the resort. Your accommodations will most likely be in a privately owned condo the resort or individual realtors rent for the owners. To be part of the rental program, the villas must meet certain minimum standards of decorating and upkeep and must include a standard list of appliances, such as dishwashers and air conditioners.

While Wild Dunes, Kiawah, Seabrook, and Hilton Head have many similarities, each one has its own distinctive flavor and appeals to a particular clientele. They all rank high on the most amusement for your money chart, you can have a spacious villa, complete with tennis, golf, biking, and beachcombing for about the same price you'd pay for a broom-closet-size room in a major city.

ROMANTIC INTERLUDES: Even if both of you are exquisitely satisfied with all the diversions available at the resorts, a change of scenery is a great change of pace from the nonstop tennis, golf, swimming, biking, boating, fishing . . .

The recommendations to visit **Beaufort** (pronounced "Byoofurt") are so persistent up and down the coast that your curiosity will certainly be piqued. The town is small, sleepy, and secluded. Porch swings and hammocks straddle verandas and wrought-iron fences enclose pretty gardens. If you like, **Historic Tours** (tel. 838-2129) provides escorted walks daily for $15 per person, or you can just wander about by yourselves. You might want to charter a boat and arrive from one of the island resorts by water.

Hunting Beach State Park, Rte. 1, Box 668, Frogmore, SC 29920 (tel. 838-2011). Located just a 20-minute drive from Beaufort on Hwy. 21, the park covers 5,000 acres, including a fine-sand, white beach. There are also several cabins available for rental (however, they're often booked over a year in advance), and a 200-site campground. In the park, you'll find hiking trails, lagoons, 125 species of birds, white-tailed deer, trout, bass. And complete and utter serenity. Admission: $2 per adult.

If you prefer more action, how about a **polo match** at **Rose Hill Plantation** (tel. 842-2828), located on U.S. 278, a short drive from Hilton Head. Admission is $4 per person, so pack up an ample tailgate picnic and go for a display of equestrian skills and thrills. The matches are held most Sundays beginning at 2 p.m., April through May, and October through December.

HONEYMOON HOTELS AND HIDEAWAYS: The sea island resorts will enchant you with their roster of sports and their acres of secluded beaches. Rate spreads reflect the difference between low- and high-season rates, when applicable.

Wild Dunes

When Ray Finch was developing **Wild Dunes,** P.O. Box 1410, Charleston, SC 19402 (tel. 803/886-6000; reservations: toll free 800/845-8880), he wanted golf-course designer Tom Fazio, and he wanted Fazio bad. He sent Fazio a letter saying, "I have a $1,000 bill here, you come take a look at the place, and if you're disappointed, the thousand is yours." Fazio came, saw, and was conquered: He whipped out *his* checkbook and wrote a check to Finch with a memo, "This is the finest strip of land I've ever seen."

So Wild Dunes got two spectacular Fazio golf courses and Ray Finch got a grand. And when you get an eyeful of Wild Dunes' spectacular facilities, you'll be a believer too. It *is* a mighty fine strip of land, massive dunes bordering verdant fairways, villas of wind-weathered wood peering out from among the trees, beach, pools, and tennis galore.

Accommodations at Wild Dunes are villas that are either beachfront, beachview, or near beach locations. Prices for a one-bedroom villa of course vary with location and season. Honeymoon package: Four days/three nights: $222 to $303 per couple. Includes a bottle of champagne and $50 in club cash on your ID card.

Kiawah

When asked why they chose **Kiawah,** P.O. Box 12910, Charleston, SC 29412 (tel. 803/768-2121; reservations: toll free 800/6KIAWAH), villa owners Gail and Don Moore from Richmond, Virginia, responded emphatically, "The beach. We looked at

other places in the area, but there is simply nothing like it on any of the other islands."
It's easy to be bowled over by Kiawah's ten-mile stretch of soft, buff-colored sand.

Of the three island resorts close to Charleston, Kiawah covers the most area. Each
of the two sections has its own golf course: East Beach has a Gary Player course, the
West has a Jack Nicklaus course; plus, there's a brand-new Tom Fazio course in the
middle. Each beach also has its own tennis courts, pools, and shopping.

Special activities abound on Kiawah. Besides the usual complement of sports,
dancing, and dining Kiawah offers island shopping at the open-air Straw Market, Jeep
safaris through the marshes, as well as fishing, crabbing, and terrific shelling.

Perhaps the most special activity is Kiawah's loggerhead-turtle program. Turtle
Patrol runs May through August, and you can help local naturalists go about their various tasks of studying the turtles and assisting in conservation. You can have fun at the
beach, learn a thing or two, and do something nice for the planet while you're at it.

Kiawah has 350 one-, two-, and three-bedroom villas in addition to a 150-room
inn. The inn rooms are a bit disappointing—small, dark, and the windows don't open
—so if you can, spring for a one-bedroom villa. Honeymoon package: Four days/three
nights for a one-bedroom villa in a wooded, lagoon or tennis setting: $495. Beachfront
villas slightly higher. Includes wine and a fruit and cheese basket upon arrival.

Seabrook Island

Seabrook Island, P.O. Box 32099, Charleston, SC 29417 (tel. 803/768-1000;
reservations: toll free 800/845-5531), is smaller, more private, and more exclusive
than its next-door neighbor, Kiawah.

In summer there are oyster roasts and dancing on the beach as the sun sets. Year-
round you can rent Windsurfers, Hobie cats, fishing, and crabbing equipment, with or
without instruction. You can grab a Frisbee or volleyball from the clubhouse and spend
an active day at the beach. Or sip margaritas by the pool overlooking the ocean. Meanwhile, tennis players can get a furious workout on any of Seabrook's 20 Har-Tru
courts, many lighted so you can make your sets last well into the evening, or on the pair
of golf courses: Robert Trent Jones's "Crooked Oaks" or William Byrd's "Ocean
Winds."

Seabrook offers a few things the other resorts don't, such as horseback riding,
English or Western, with instruction or on a trail ride through the marsh, forest, or
surf.

Four hundred of the choicest villas are in the rental program, giving a range of
options between tennis, golf, and beach locations. Honeymoon package (minimum
two-night stay): $174 to $253 per couple per night. Includes villa accommodations,
welcome fruit basket, choice of sports activities such as horseback riding, golf, bicycle
riding, and others. Daily rates per couple from April to October are $120 to $200; from
November to March, $100 to $175.

Hilton Head Island

Hilton Head is the progenitor of all these resorts. It has been around by far the
longest, and is not one resort, but rather a conglomeration of eight separate resorts.

The island is divided up into plantations, each an aggregation of villas, hotels,
homes, and facilities forming a complete resort, discrete unto itself. For the most part,
facilities at any given plantation are restricted for the use of its residents and guests.
Among the eight plantations, four are open to the public.

Expensive: Sea Pines Plantation, Hilton Head, SC 29928 (tel. 803/785-3333;
reservations: toll free 800/845-6131), is the original plantation and by far the largest
located on the southern tip of the island. Honeymoon packages: Four days/three nights
(EP): $375 to $525 per couple. Includes one dinner, champagne upon arrival, bicycles
for three days, and free tennis.

Hyatt Regency at Palmetto Dunes, P.O. Box 6167, Hilton Head, SC 29938 (tel. 803/785-1234; reservations: toll free 800/228-9000). The Hyatt's oceanfront rooms are stocked with luxurious soaps, fluffy towels, and an honor fridge jammed with goodies. Bedrooms are decorated in aquatic shades and maritime prints; outside, the terraces are perfect for overseeing activities on the pool deck and the beach just below. The entire hotel is loaded with possibilities. A terrific spa with weight machines, sauna, classes; Olympic-size swimming pools and Jacuzzis, indoors and out overlooking the beach. Also check out the head-spinning menus at the Cafe, Possum Point, and Hemingways. Then you can cap off your night with a turn around the dance floor to the band's hot licks at the Club Indigo. Honeymoon package: Three days/two nights (EP): $154 to $294 per couple. Includes deluxe oceanview accommodations, steak and eggs with champagne one morning, $25 food and beverage credits.

The **Hotel Inter-Continental Hilton Head,** Port Royal Resort, P.O. Box 4000, Hilton Head, SC 29938 (tel. 803/681-4000; reservations: toll free 800/327-0200), is the island's newest, reflecting a European-style polish and flair. The hotel's 416 rooms are decorated with elegant reproduction antiques, chintz draperies, and each has a balcony overlooking the sea. The sunny, soft-pink Brasserie features a Friday buffet dinner and a Sunday brunch buffet. The health club offers the latest equipment, saunas, massage. Evenings The Barony serves up fine continental fare, and the Battery Lounge features a top-40 band nightly. Honeymoon package (minimum two nights): $145 to $205 per couple per night. Includes upgraded accommodations with oceanview balcony, champagne with complimentary glasses, his-and-her complimentary terry robes, breakfast in bed daily, fresh flowers, turndown service, bike rental, discounts on golf and tennis.

Moderate: Shipyard Plantation and Port Royal Plantation, Hilton Head Management Company, P.O. Box 7000, Hilton Head, SC 29938 (tel. 803/785-4256; reservations: toll free 800/845-6135), are run by the same management company and offer 350 villas, 63 holes of golf, and 36 tennis courts. They are located along the eastern shore of the island. Nightly rates for a one-bedroom villa begin at $50.

Palmetto Dunes Resort, P.O. Box 5606, Hilton Head, SC 29938 (tel. 803/785-1161; reservations: toll free 800/845-6130). There are 3 golf courses here, 25 tennis courts, a system of lagoons and marina. Base price for a one-bedroom villa is $70.

Beaufort

This charming town has two bed-and-breakfasts of note:

Rhett House Inn, 1009 Craven St., Beaufort, SC 29901 (tel. 803/524-9000). This 1840s home has been restored by Steve and Marianne Harrison, authentically furnished, and filled with quilts and fresh flowers. Breakfast is served on the porch in your room or in the garden out back. Honeymoon package: None. Rooms are $65 and up, including breakfast and sherry or wine on arrival.

Bay Street Inn, 601 Bay St., Beaufort, SC 29901 (tel. 803/524-7720). Up the marble steps on the porch of this 1852 house looking out over the river you'll see a rope hammock dangling. The beautiful old wood floors support period Victorian antiques and canopy beds. Honeymoon package: None. Prices start at $50 including breakfast, afternoon sherry, and use of bicycles.

ROMANTIC RESTAURANTS: Wild Dunes, Kiawah, and Seabrook all realize when it comes to dining theirs is somewhat a captive audience, so they do their best to provide a variety of dining options. All villas have kitchens and catering can be provided, or you can cook your own—it's great fun to sauté up those fish or boil up a pot of those blue crabs you may have landed. If you feel like getting off-island here are some choices:

Oriental rugs, deep oak paneling, hand-painted ceilings, and a warm welcome by proprietors Debbie and Joe Belvedere are the hallmarks of **Anchorage House,** 1103 Bay St., Beaufort (tel. 524-9392). Specialties include Black Angus beef, fresh scallops and oysters, and a wine list featuring American varietals. Open for lunch and dinner, reservations recommended. Dinner for two with wine, about $70.

Just across the bridge from Beaufort, take your first sharp right to reach **Wilkops White Hall Inn,** Lady Island (tel. 524-0382), overlooking the Beaufort River. The dining room is spacious, focused on the large picture windows through which you can watch the boats making their lazy way upstream. The selection includes charcoal-grilled meats and the restaurant specializes in homemade soups, gumbos, chowders, and bisques. Open Tuesday through Saturday for lunch and dinner. Dinner for two: $60.

L'Etoile Verte, Plantation Shopping Center, Hilton Head (tel. 785-5277). This tiny restaurant seats only 40, and Chef Charlie likes to keep things low-key. The fish is from Hilton Head and Beaufort waters. The hand-written wine list emphasizes French wines and is extremely reasonable. Reservations for lunch are suggested, for dinner are necessary. Dinner for two with wine, $60.

Skull Creek, Hilton Head Plantation, Hilton Head (tel. 681-6700), seems an ominous monicker for a restaurant, but the place is most pleasant. Windows on all sides overlook the marina at Hilton Head Plantation (a private resort, but visitors are admitted to dine at Skull Creek). Try cocktails at sunset on the deck for starters. There is a good, if pricey selection of wine by the glass and a raw bar. Check out the chef's daily specials—always strong choices. Reservations requested. Prices for dinner for two from $50 to $80.

Chapter XIII

TEXAS: SAN ANTONIO

1. Practical Facts
2. Romantic Interludes
3. Honeymoon Hotels and Hideaways
4. Romantic Restaurants
5. Nightlife

LATE AFTERNOON. You relax over margaritas at an outdoor café, chatting and people-watching as the river that gives San Antonio its name glides by, not far from your feet. People laugh as they stroll along the walkways at the river's edge, speaking English, Spanish, or a melodious mixture of both. As a boat full of tourists being serenaded rounds the bend, the lilting voices of guitar-strumming mariachis fill the air with sweet-sad Latin love songs. Caught up in the enchantment of San Antonio's River Walk, you feel like you're in another country—a mixture of Europe and Mexico in a lushly landscaped, subtropical setting. Time itself seems to flow as lazily as the river.

Not that the city 20 feet above the river level isn't a bustling, modern metropolis of nearly a million inhabitants. Located in the heart of Texas, where the rolling limestone hills meet the flat, bushy ranching country that sweeps on to the Gulf of Mexico, San Antonio has always been a busy crossroads, a place of contrasts where Indian and European cultures, civilization and wilderness, genteel manners and Wild West ways all collided. Since its founding by the Spanish in the 18th century (making it one of the oldest cities west of the Mississippi), it has been a mission and military outpost, the battlefield that galvanized Texas' drive for independence, a rowdy frontier town where cowboys brawled and cattle barons lavishly spent their newfound wealth, and an oasis of civilization between New Orleans and San Francisco. By the 1920s it was Texas' largest city, sprouting jazzy skyscrapers in the latest art deco and neo-Gothic styles.

What makes San Antonio so romantic? First, it's your sense that the past comes alive at every turn. Here, says a tiled placard on the wall, was the shallow place where the Spaniards first forded the river. Or here, around a small mission church called the Alamo, Davy Crockett and 187 men were slain fighting for Texas' freedom. And here, just a stone's throw from that "cradle of Texas' liberty," Teddy Roosevelt is said to have recruited his Rough Riders in the bar of the Menger Hotel. Heroes and legends just seemed to gravitate to the Alamo City.

The pervasive Spanish and Mexican culture, however, is what most sets San Antonio apart from other cities today and gives it an exotic, seductive charm. It is apparent not only in the city's love of festivity and its lovely Spanish colonial architecture, but in its slower, more relaxed pace. It is apparent in the streets, where you hear Spanish spoken by half the population, and it is deliciously obvious in the wide array of Mexican restaurants, dishing up some of the best Mexican food this side of the Rio Grande. A picturesque place to enjoy this food is at an outdoor restaurant in Market Square, where you can also shop in a Mexican-style indoor market for everything from panchos to piñatas.

Although today San Antonio is no longer the biggest city in Texas, people still agree it's the prettiest. Deep down, it remains the romantic heart of Texas, a place where the past comes alive in beautiful settings.

1. Practical Facts

GETTING THERE: It's easy to reach San Antonio from most places in the United States. More than a dozen airlines serve San Antonio International Airport. By rail, limited passenger service is also provided by **Amtrak** (tel. toll free 800/872-8245). By car, San Antonio is an hour's drive from Austin, four hours from Houston, and five hours from Dallas.

GETTING AROUND: On arriving at the airport, you have several transportation choices. The **Airport Limousine,** which stops at all the major downtown hotels, leaves the airport every half hour from 6 a.m. to 9 p.m. Cost is $5 per person one way.

Taxis

Taxi fares in San Antonio are moderate. To go from the airport to downtown costs between $11 and $13; to go from Alamo Plaza on the east side of downtown to Market Square on the west costs $3 to $4.

Rental Cars

Rates for rental cars in San Antonio run from $20 per day (on weekends) to $40 per day (weekdays) per day for a compact car. Several major car-rental agencies have offices at the airport.

Public Transportation

VIA Streetcars, at 10¢ per ride, are the most economical way of getting around the downtown area, or from there to Fiesta Plaza, St. Paul Square, or the King William historic district. Most hotels can provide you with route maps listing hours and details.

WEATHER: With its mild winters and 300 days of sunshine a year, San Antonio has long been known for its pleasant climate. Though the winter months are not without occasional cold snaps (nights in the 30s), they have plenty of sunny, spring-like days with temperatures in the 60s. Spring and fall are the best times to visit, when it's warm (in the 70s and 80s) but not hot. Summers are generally hot and humid, though cooled somewhat by southeasterly breezes from the Gulf of Mexico.

CLOTHING: Dress tends to be casual during the day—along the River Walk you'll see plenty of jeans and shorts. In the fancier restaurants and in the evening, people dress up more (dresses and slacks), though few establishments require gentlemen to don coats and ties. During three-quarters of the year, comfortable cotton clothing plus a sweater or light jacket is recommended; in winter, take medium-weight cottons and wools plus a coat for cool days.

TIME: San Antonio is on Central Standard Time, the same as Chicago.

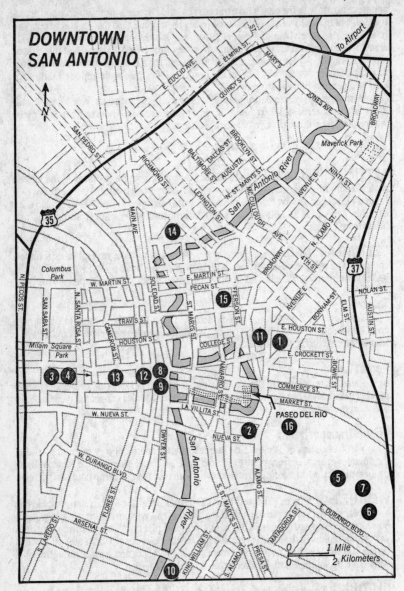

KEY TO NUMBERED SIGHTS

1. The Alamo
2. La Villita
3. Market Square
4. Fiesta Plaza
5. Tower of the Americas
6. The Institute of Texan Cultures
7. San Antonio Museum of Transportation
8. Main Plaza
9. Military Plaza
10. King William Historical Area
11. The Heart of Texas
12. San Fernando Cathedral
13. Spanish Governor's Palace
14. Southwest Craft Center
15. Travis Park
16. Convention and Visitors Bureau

TELEPHONES: The area code for San Antonio is 512.

SHOPPING: Almost like a branch of Mexico and Latin America, San Antonio makes a great place to buy ethnic clothing, silver jewelry, folk art, and other arts and crafts from south of the border. Western wear and cowboy boots can be good buys too, as well as crafts by local and regional artists.

For the widest selection of Mexican wares at the lowest prices, begin at **Market Square.** In the enclosed Mexican-style *mercado*, shops sell everything from embroidered dresses and *huaraches* (woven leather shoes) to onyx chess sets and bright piñatas. Mexican food aficionados can stock up here on tortilla presses, lime squeezers, and *molcajetes* (a mortar and pestle of lava rock, often used for making and serving guacamole). If you're buying several things from one vendor, you might try bargaining for a lower price. Among the shops out on the square, the **Tequila Tree** has high-quality regional crafts from Mexico; **DagenBela Galeria** offers silver and ceramics by regional artisan. In the barn-like **Farmer's Market** section, buy chains of braided garlic, strings of dried red peppers, and Mexican food ingredients. And when you're tired of shopping, grab a table at one of the outdoor restaurants and watch the crowd, and listen to the live music if there's a festival going on.

In and around River Walk **Mayan Tejidos de Guatemala** has South American fabric, weavings, Nativity scenes, silk-screened skirts, and wonderful folk-art necklaces bristling with birds, animals, jalapeño peppers, and even angels. Cowboys and cowgirls can lasso a bunch of bandanas in rainbow colors, silver buckles, concho belts, and other western wear at **Cross Western** store. Don't leave without stopping in **Santa's Christmas Shoppe,** even if it's July, for souvenir Texas icons—ceramic armadillos, Alamos, cowboy boots—to decorate your tree, along with a grand array of hand-painted wooden ornaments.

For crafts by local and regional artists, wander through **La Villita**, the historic village of cottages-turned-shops. Its **Lone Star Loomworks** features pretty hand-woven apparel, while animal lovers will like the fanciful birds and beasts of fabric, lacquer, clay, and papier-mâché that inhabit **Casa Manos Alegres.** Seek out spices and fixings for Mexican food at Old San Antonio Casa Gourmet. Gift shops in the **San Antonio Museum of Art,** the **Witte Museum,** and the **Southwest Craft Center** also carry unique handmade items, including ceramic jewelry.

Fans of folk art will find a feast for their eyes at these galleries: **Flight of Fancy,** 5938 Broadway (tel. 822-7467); **Milagros,** 324 West Sunset (tel. 821-5861); and **Papularis,** 4026 McCullough (tel. 824-0706).

And for unique "wearable art," try **Artwear,** 4833 McCullough (tel. 821-6465). The selection includes ceramic jewelry, hand-painted sweatshirts, handwoven clothing, and other one-of-a-kind items. Or do the San Antonio stroll in custom-made cowboy boots from one of the many bootmakers listed in the Yellow Pages of the telephone directory.

Last, you can afford to pour your favorite scent into your bath after a trip to the **House of International Fragrances,** 4711 Blanco at General Krueger Boulevard (tel. 341-2283), which sells reproductions of name-brand perfumes for as much as 80% off the retail price of the real thing.

HOW TO GET MARRIED IN SAN ANTONIO: Once you find the **Bexar County Courthouse** on Main Plaza, getting married in San Antonio is easy. At the courthouse get your marriage license for $25 from the County Clerk's office (tel. 220-2216). No blood test, witnesses, or waiting period is required, but you must have a valid driver's license, birth certificate, or military ID. After obtaining the license, you can be married by a justice of the peace (look up judges listed under Justice, Courts of Bexar County in the blue pages of the telephone book) or the officiant of your choice; the fee is usually around $25. A nondenominational minister, Reverend Fausto, has an office near the courthouse (tel. 222-9914). If you would like to be married in the picturesque little church of La Villita, call well in advance to make the arrangements (tel. 512/226-3593).

SPECIAL EVENTS: Nearly every month there's a public celebration or special event going on. Perhaps the best-known is December's **Fiesta de las Luminarias,** River Walk (tel. 227-4262). See the River Walk at night transformed into a fairyland of twinkling lights in the trees and *luminarias*—paper bags with candles inside—outlining the curving banks and arched bridges. Also take in **Las Posadas** on the River Walk (tel. 224-6163), a Hispanic folk tradition in which a singing, candle-bearing procession wends its way along the River Walk as it reenacts the Holy Family's search for an inn.

Note: From January 2 to about the middle of the month, the river in the **River Walk** is drained for cleaning and maintenance (tel. 229-7844). This is the only time the River Walk is not romantic, though a "mud festival" to celebrate the event is threatening to become a new annual tradition.

FOR FURTHER INFORMATION: Contact **Visitor Information Center,** 317 Alamo Plaza, San Antonio, TX 78205 (tel. 512/299-8155); or the **Convention and Visitors Bureau,** P.O. Box 2277, San Antonio, TX 78298 (tel. 512/270-8700).

2. Romantic Interludes

See San Antonio the old-fashioned way—in a **horse-drawn carriage.** Catch one around Alamo Plaza and tour the downtown and/or the King William area, the latter full of vintage Victorian mansions. Most of the buggies charge around $20 for a half hour, $40 for an hour (for two people). Call **Alamo Carriage Service** (tel. 534-1051) for more information.

Or see the city on the **San Antonio Trolley** (tel. 533-3992), which departs from the Alamo in good weather about every half hour during the daytime for a 40-minute tour of downtown and the King William district. $4 per person.

Take a leisurely ramble through history and some of San Antonio's most beautiful places. **La Mansion del Rio Hotel** on the River Walk has free pamphlets outlining two **walking tours** of the city. Don't miss the following attractions in or near the downtown:

The Alamo, the first Spanish mission established (1718) here, where the Mexican army massacred its defenders in 1836.

One of the original Spanish *acequias* (their irrigation and drinking water system) cuts through the peaceful, beautifully landscaped Alamo grounds.

La Villita above the River Walk, a quaint village of old adobe houses and pretty plazas now converted to crafts shops and restaurants.

The Spanish Governor's Palace, completed by the Spanish in 1749 as quarters for their military commander. The austere simplicity of its thick white walls contrasts with its dark wood rafters and more elaborate Spanish colonial furnishings.

San Fernando Cathedral, on Main Plaza, incorporates some of the walls of the original church started by the Canary Island settlers in 1738, making it the oldest parish church in the country that has continued to hold services.

Southern Pacific Railroad Depot and **St. Paul Square,** on Commerce east of downtown. Take the VIA Streetcar marked St. Paul Square/Fiesta Plaza to see these architectural gems, the square a collection of renovated 19th-century brick commercial buildings, the railroad station a fine example of the Spanish colonial-revival style. Be sure to go inside the station to see its beautiful woodwork, ornate coffered ceiling, and stained-glass window.

The **King William** historic district, south of downtown, where prosperous Germans built stately mansions and lacy gingerbread cottages in the latter half of the 19th century. Here **Steves Homestead,** a Victorian Mansion, restored and furnished in period style, is open to the public ($2 admission).

In the San Antonio area, you'll find many choice spots for laying out an al fresco spread.

Follow in the footsteps of 18th-century Spaniards by exploring the four Spanish missions south of downtown: **San Jose, Concepción, San Francisco de la Espada, and San Juan Capistrano.** Ample grounds surround each one, so you'll feel like you're in the country. The grandest and most romantic is Mission San Jose, with its elaborately carved limestone facade and the famous Rose Window that, according to legend, was sculpted by Pedro Huizar out of love for a woman left behind in Spain. Include a stop at the Espada Dam and Espada Aqueduct, the latter the only Spanish aqueduct in the United States. All four missions still serve as parish churches. For maps and directions, drop in at the **Visitor Information Center** on Alamo Plaza (tel. 299-8155).

Rent horses and wind through Brackenridge Park's lovely woods and thickets along the river. Contact **Brackenridge Stables,** 840 East Mulberry (tel. 732-8881). Or ride the miniature train, which can drop you off and later pick you up at four different stops along the way—including one near the Witte Museum. You can also rent paddleboats on the San Antonio River there, or catch the cable car for a lofty view of the downtown skyline and a trip to the Japanese Tea Gardens, a series of landscaped oriental pavilions and ponds. Then there's the San Antonio zoo, also built from the old quarry walls to create natural-looking habitats. Main entrance at 3800 Broadway, north of downtown.

On a hot day, cool off amid the spectacular scenery of the **Guadalupe River,** about 45 minutes north of the city. Take your picnic in an inexpensive styrofoam cooler (available at convenience and grocery stores) and rent three innertubes there (the extra for your cooler). You'll spend a relaxing day floating beneath tall, rocky bluffs and majestic cypresses hung with Spanish moss. For directions and information on water conditions and tube rentals ($3 to $5 a day), call **Rio Raft Co.** (tel. 1-964-3613) or **Whitewater Sports** (tel. 1-964-3800).

As the sun sets, sip champagne aloft in a **four-seater plane,** and watch the lights come on in the city below. You can bring whatever you want to eat and drink during the flight, which costs $35 per couple for 30 minutes. Call **Million Air** (tel. 828-9005). Or perhaps you fancy a romantic morning or afternoon ride over hills and fields in a balloon? The whole excursion takes about three hours, with an hour spent in the air, and the cost is from $225 to $300 for a couple. Take along some champagne and a picnic to enjoy the countryside when you land. Call **Alamo Balloon Port** (tel. 624-2041) or **The Balloon Group** (tel. 496-1818).

Glide down the San Antonio River on an **open boat** at twilight as you sip margaritas. Or after dark, enjoy a dinner cruise, or champagne by moonlight (weather permitting). Cruises at 5:30 p.m. (margaritas), 7:00 p.m. (dinner), and 8:30 p.m. (champagne), from $14.50 to $24.50 per person. For reservations call **Guido Kelley's River Cruises** (tel. 227-2787).

Feast on hot dogs and cold beer under the stars in an old-fashioned wooden stadium while the San Antonio Dodgers (the farm team for the Los Angeles Dodgers) play ball. For an extra treat, buy a ticket for the "Dodgers' Patio," where you can sit comfortably in lawn chairs—it's like watching live baseball in your own backyard—and be waited on. April through August, tickets $3 to $6 each (tel. 434-9311).

That's not all, folks—San Antonio has plenty more to captivate honeymooners of all interests and inclinations.

San Antonio Museum of Art, 200 West Jones (tel. 226-5544). Within this converted 19th-century brewery, see art ranging from pre-Columbian to contemporary American, including one of the best collections of Mexican folk art in the country.

Marion Koogler McNay Art Institute, 6000 North New Braunfels (tel. 824-

5368). Besides its fine Impressionist and post-Impressionist collection, this mansion-turned-museum is worth visiting for its interior courtyard alone, where hand-painted tile, carved stone columns, lush plantings, and fountains capture the romantic Spanish-Mediterranean style of the 1920s.

The **Southwest Craft Center,** 300 Augusta (tel. 224-1848), holds crafts exhibitions and classes in a beautiful stone convent built by French Ursuline nuns in the 19th century. The restaurant there is open for lunch.

Witte Memorial Museum, 3901 Broadway (tel. 226-5544). From prehistoric relics and gaudy tropical butterflies to the jewel-encrusted gowns of last year's Fiesta Royal Court, the Witte contains a delightfully eclectic assortment of historic, natural, and social flora and fauna.

The **Institute of Texan Cultures,** in HemisFair Plaza (tel. 226-7651), celebrates Texas' diverse heritage with displays covering 26 ethnic groups.

Buckhorn Saloon, Lone Star and Mission Road (tel. 226-8301). Order a brew at this historic saloon, which once accepted rattlesnake rattles as payment. The bar and its collection of horned game trophies were moved lock, stock, and beer barrel to their present location at the Buckhorn Hall of Horns on the grounds of the Lone Star Brewery.

San Antonio Botanical Center, 555 Funston Place (tel. 821-5115). Check out the new section, which contains a striking series of triangular and conical greenhouses set partially underground.

Sea World, scheduled to open in 1988 (tel. 523-3450). This will be the largest marine life park in the world, containing whales, dolphins, sea lions, and other specimens.

3. Honeymoon Hotels and Hideaways

From Victorian bed-and-breakfast inns to luxurious, sleek hotels, the Alamo city has accommodations to please most budgets, though most are in the moderate to upscale range. Every place listed is either in the downtown area or reasonably close to it, since this core, with its River Walk and historical buildings and plazas, is the romantic heart of San Antonio.

If you want to stay in a bed-and-breakfast, the **King William Bed & Breakfast Registry** (tel. 512/227-1190) lists several homes in the historic King William area, as well as contemporary accommodations on the River Walk. Rates per couple in the King William range from $44 to $121 per night; condominiums (all with kitchen), $82 to $140 per night.

Room rates, unless otherwise noted, do not include meals or the 11% hotel tax that will be added to the lodging bill. Most of the honeymoon packages, however, do include champagne on arrival and breakfast the first morning. All rooms are air-conditioned, a must during San Antonio's summer.

EXPENSIVE: In 1985 the three-story brick **Fairmount Hotel,** 401 S. Alamo St., San Antonio, TX 78205 (tel. 512/224-8800; reservations: tel. toll free 800/642-3399 in Texas or 800/642-3363 nationwide), attracted national attention—and enshrinement in the Guiness *Book of World Records*—when it was moved six blocks to its present site next to La Villita to save it from demolition. Now carefully restored and enlarged, this compact hotel attracts guests who like its rather private, residential atmosphere. New arrivals will notice the fresh flowers in the lobby and adjacent parlor, where tall windows reveal a fountain in a garden courtyard. Here guests can breakfast or lunch in fine weather. None of the hotel's 37 rooms and suites are alike, though all mix ivory and muted pastels with tiny prints and textured fabrics, classic furniture, and plants. Most rooms open onto a balcony or veranda and include a VCR with the TV (a videotape library is available to guests). All have queen-size beds, valet stand, marble bathroom with brass fixtures, lighted makeup mirror, additional telephone in the bath, and for an extra bit of pampering, full-length, hooded, terrycloth robes for you to use during your stay. Two rooms even come with stereos and canopy beds. The hotel restaurant, Polo's, serves innovative American cuisine, and its bar usually has live music nightly. Honeymoon package: $264 per couple for a room one night, $374 for two nights; $336 per couple for a suite one night, $517 for two nights. It includes a bottle of Perrier & Jouet champagne and two glasses on arrival, finger sandwiches, breakfast or brunch the first morning, and airport pickup and dropoff. Standard rate for a double ranges from $138 to $187.

MODERATE Presiding like a queen in lacy finery over the north end of Alamo Plaza, the **Emily Morgan Hotel,** 705 East Houston St., San Antonio, TX 78205 (tel. 512/225-8486; reservations: tel. toll free 800/356-LOVE in Texas or 800/824-6674 nationwide), takes its name from romantic Texas lore. Called "the Yellow Rose of Texas," the mulatto slave Emily Morgan so distracted the Mexican general Santa Ana with her beauty, the legend goes, that Sam Houston's early morning attack surprised him and clinched Texas' independence. Sleekly contemporary, yet as romantic as the legend, the 177 rooms of this 12-story Gothic-revival skyscraper are decorated in soft pinks and grays with sliding Japanese-like panels that open to reveal the large bath area. All guest rooms have telephone, cable television with movies, clock radios, hair dryers, and oversize towels; in addition, the Signature and Plaza rooms come with Jacuzzi tub, refrigerator, remote-control television, and king-size bed (Plaza rooms have a double-size Jacuzzi with a discreetly placed window overlooking Alamo Plaza). Guests can dine at the hotel's gourmet restaurant, Sarducci's, and hear a singer in the lobby bar most evenings. The premises also include an outdoor pool, fitness room with exercise equipment, and saunas. Honeymoon package: $132 to $176 per couple the first night, plus $94 each additional night. It includes a Signature or Plaza room, a bottle of champagne on arrival, continental breakfast the first morning, and a river barge ride. Rate for a standard double is $94 per couple per night.

One of the first hotels on the River Walk, the 22-story **Hilton Palacio del Rio,** 200 S. Alamo St., San Antonio, TX 78205-3229 (tel. 512/222-1400; reservations: tel. toll free 800/HILTONS), rose in record time using a new modular construction technique. But though contemporary in design, its decor evokes the Spanish colonial past with wrought-iron fixtures and balconies, stucco walls, and beamed ceilings. All 484 guest rooms have private balconies overlooking the River Walk or the Convention Center, and are furnished in basic contemporary style and dusky colors. Honeymoon package rooms are equipped with king-size bed, cable television with movies, telephone, coffee-maker, and sometimes a hairdryer and bath scale. Guests can choose from several hotel bars and restaurants, including a lobby piano bar, a riverside Irish pub, and the new Stetson Steakhouse. An outdoor pool and heated Jacuzzi are on the fifth floor. Honeymoon package: $132 per couple the first night, plus $96 for additional nights. It includes a bottle of champagne on arrival, mariachi champagne brunch on Saturday or Sunday or a full American breakfast the first morning, a special gift, and a 50% room discount on the next visit. Standard rates for a double range from $122 to $160 per couple per night.

At the head of a lushly landscaped section of the River Walk and across the street from the Convention Center, the 500-room **Marriott River Walk,** 711 East River Walk, San Antonio, TX 78205 (tel. 512/224-4555; reservations: tel. toll free 800/228-9290), bustles with life. In fine weather guests sip drinks on its patio beside the river, or admire the view of it from their balcony (half the rooms overlook the river). Even on cool days people swim in the heated pool, part of which is enclosed in a soaring glass shell like a high-tech terrarium. Comfortable, modern rooms are decorated with graphics and furnishings with a touch of the orient. Amenities for honeymooners include king-size bed, balcony with river view, cable TV with movie channel, telephone, and AM/FM radio. The upscale lounge beside the river, Gambits, features complimentary hors d'ouevres during happy hour and dancing later. Honeymoon package: $110 per couple the first night and $93 for additional nights. It includes a bottle of champagne on arrival and full breakfast in bed the first morning. Standard rate for a double: $138 to $149 per couple per night.

Centered around a 16-story atrium looking out on the river, the 632-room **Hyatt Regency San Antonio,** on the River Walk, 123 Losoya St., San Antonio, TX 78205 (tel. 512/222-1234; reservations: tel. toll free 800/228-9000), dazzles with sights and sounds. Lighted elevators float up and down the interior wall like space capsules, while a stream cascades and splashes through the atrium's river level. Here visitors stroll among boutiques or tarry at The Landing's riverside tables to hear Jim Cullum's jazz band. Yet along with this liveliness the hotel retains a laidback charm that's echoed in its guest rooms. Tawny earth tones and the natural textures of leather, rattan, unglazed ceramics, and Indian weavings give the rooms a comfortable, casual southwestern style. Remote-control TV, telephone, clock radio, and king-size bed are standard amenities. A rooftop sun deck has a swimming pool and heated Jacuzzi. Several good restaurants and lounges are also on the premises. Honeymoon package: $142 per couple for a king deluxe room the first night, plus $120 for additional nights; $219 per couple for a one-bedroom suite and $193 for extra nights. It includes a room with balcony overlooking the atrium, bottle of champagne, a steak-and-egg breakfast the first morning, and all taxes and gratuities on package items. Standard rate for a deluxe double is $127 per couple per night.

Tucked away behind the lovely gardens of the Alamo, the small **Crockett Hotel,** 320 Bonham, San Antonio, TX 78205 (tel. 512/225-6500; reservations: tel. toll free 800/292-1050 in Texas or 800/531-5537 nationwide), makes a nice retreat for honeymooners who like a quiet, leisurely ambience. Its lobby and public areas echo turn-of-the-century San Antonio with their tall potted palms, etched-glass windows, and ornate Victorian fixtures. Guests can breakfast in the airy, seven-story atrium, or dine regally at Lela B's while being regaled with Broadway tunes by its musical staff. Guest rooms likewise sing cheerfully with crisp cotton prints, fresh pastels, and tall, old-fashioned windows. With a Fountain room or suite, the couple receives a key to the rooftop garden terrace with heated Jacuzzi. All rooms feature king- or queen-size beds, telephone, radio, and remote-control TV; Fountain rooms and suites also come with a wet bar and icemaker. Honeymoon package: $153 per couple the first night for a deluxe room with sitting area, plus $76 for extra nights; $175 per couple for a Fountain room (a large corner room), plus $96 for extra nights; $252 per couple for a one-bedroom suite, plus $165 for extra nights. It includes a bottle of champagne and chocolate-dipped fruit on arrival, full American breakfast in bed, free parking, and tax and gratuities on package items. Standard rate for a double ranges from $94 to $121 per couple per night.

If basking beside a pool in a garden courtyard where fountains play is your idea of bliss, the **Four Seasons Hotel,** 555 S. Alamo at Durango, San Antonio, TX 78205 (tel. 512/229-1000; reservations: tel. toll free 800/268-6282), has created just such an oasis. Pheasants stroll the ample landscaped grounds, which boast the largest anaqua tree in North America. Here guests enjoy not only the large heated pool and Jacuzzi, but working out in the health club (which includes dry saunas), playing tennis on the lighted courts or croquet on a manicured lawn, and pedaling off to see the sights on a bicycle built for two (all available free to guests). The hotel, designed by San Antonio's most celebrated architect, the late O'Neil Ford, has the informal elegance and openness to the outdoors that he was known for, as well as exquisitely handcrafted details throughout. Most of the generous-size guest rooms have balconies overlooking the courtyard or the city, and are decorated with dramatic floral fabrics and classic furniture with a touch of oriental opulence. Amenities include king-size bed, telephone, bathrobes, hairdryer, cable TV with movies, complimentary shoe shines and morning paper, and fresh flowers in the bathroom. Guests can dine in the Anaqua Room, a highly regarded Continental/French restaurant, or take high tea or cocktails in the Palm Terrace. Honeymoon package: $151 per couple per night for a superior room; $215 per couple per first night for a junior suite, plus $275 per night thereafter. It includes a bottle of champagne, full breakfast the first morning, personalized matches, and free valet parking. Rate for a standard double is $129 per night.

With its tiers of white arches and wrought-iron balconies rising gracefully above the River Walk, **La Mansion del Rio Hotel,** 112 College St., on the River Walk, San Antonio, TX 78205 (tel. 512/225-2581; reservations: tel. toll free 800/292-7300 in Texas or 800/531-7208 nationwide), recalls the city's romantic Spanish past. Terra-cotta tile, dark beams against stucco, and stone fountains and courtyards could have come straight out of Spain. The rooms, clad in dusky rose and earth tones, with brick walls, beamed ceilings, and French doors, have private balconies with a riverside or courtyard view. For honeymooners they come with a king-size bed, remote-control cable TV with movies, telephone, radio clocks, dry bar, refrigerator, and bathrobes, while the extra-large Ambassador rooms include a couch and dining table with chairs. Guests can sip margaritas by the pool, where strolling mariachis sometimes play, or be serenaded at night by a classical Spanish guitarist in Las Canarias, a fine restaurant known for its paella, America Southwest cuisine, and Sunday brunches. Honeymoon package: "Romancing the River," $132 to $176 per couple per night. It includes a bottle of champagne and a box of chocolates, full American breakfast in bed the first morning, and a riverboat ride. Standard rate for a double: $127 to $176 per couple per night.

St. Anthony Inter-Continental Hotel, 300 East Travis, San Antonio, TX 78205, or P.O. Box 2411, San Antonio, TX 78298 (tel. 512/227-4392; reservations: tel. toll free 800/327-0200). Once host to cowboys and cattle barons, the lavishly re-stored St. Anthony on Travis Park recaptures the glittering grandeur it enjoyed when it opened in 1909. And opulent enough for a baroness is its Peacock Alley (just off the lobby), studded with stately columns and sparkling with gilt and crystal chandeliers. Seventeenth-century furniture, completes the splendid scene. Afternoon tea and cock-tails here are often served to the accompaniment of a pianist. Or guests can dine and dance the night away to a live orchestra at the St. Anthony Club restaurant. Travelers also enjoy the outdoor pool and hot tub on the tenth floor. The well-proportioned de-luxe king rooms come furnished with old-fashioned, Georgian charm, with wingback chairs, four-poster beds, and antiques in many of them. Of course they also have all the modern amenities—king-size bed, telephone, remote-control TV, clock radio, hairdryers, and even doorbells. Suites add scales and bathrobes. Honeymoon pack-ages: The hotel has a range of plans that include a bottle of champagne and continental breakfast in bed the first morning. "Sweetheart Package": $105 per couple for the first night plus $77 per night thereafter for a deluxe king room. "Precious Package": $160 the first night plus $105 per night thereafter for a junior or executive suite. "Truelove Package": $253 per couple the first night plus $88 each additional night; it consists of champagne, full American breakfast in bed, fresh flowers in the room, a framed 5-inch-×-7-inch professional portrait, a carriage ride, and a gift certificate for a night in a deluxe king room on the couple's first anniversary. Standard rate for a double from $87 to $142 per night.

Radisson Gunter Hotel, 205 East Houston, San Antonio, TX 78205 (tel. 512/227-3241; reservations: tel. toll free 800/228-9822). The footsteps of Will Rogers, Mae West, and Harry Truman have echoed across the marble floor of the Gunter's turn-of-the-century lobby. Arranged with classical symmetry, the lobby's dark walnut paneling contrasts with ivory columns and a coffered ceiling, carved intricately with friezes and medallions. Overhead hang the same chandeliers that lighted its 1909 opening. In this completely restored hotel, guests again relax on the second-floor ter-race over food or drinks, while watching the busy sidewalk scene below. The furnish-ings of the rooms share in the lobby's old-fashioned ambience, with wingback chairs, an armoire to hide the TV, and paisley or floral fabrics in soft blue, green, and peach. They also have a desk and table, lighted vanity mirror, telephone, cable TV with movies, telephone, and king-size bed. Besides a pub-type bar-restaurant and the European Cafe Suisse, the hotel has a Swiss bakery serving croissants and tempting pastries. The premises also include an outdoor pool. Honeymoon package: $109 per couple the first night plus $94 per night thereafter for a deluxe room. It includes champagne, full breakfast in bed the first morning, morning paper, riverboat ride, free parking, and tax and gratuities on package items (available Friday, Saturday, and Sunday only). Standard rate for a double is $94 per night.

INEXPENSIVE: **Menger Hotel and Motor Inn,** 204 Alamo Plaza, San Antonio, TX 78205 (tel. 512/223-4361; reservations: tel. toll free 800/241-3848). Opened in 1859, the matriarch of San Antonio hotels still stands regally on Alamo Plaza. Her original neoclassical lobby, where tiered columns reach three stories towards a skylight of gold-and-emerald glass, graciously testifies to the time when the Menger was a cultural landmark between New Orleans and San Francisco. It was here that the former president of the republic of Texas signed the register "Sam Houston and horse." And here, in the hotel bar that's a replica of the one in the House of Lords, Teddy Roosevelt recruited his Rough Riders. The famous Menger Garden Patio, where mint juleps were served and countless frontier tales exchanged, still blooms with tropical foliage. And although the dining room no longer numbers buffalo hump and deer loin among its entrées, it still serves its famous mango ice cream. Staying in the rooms in the oldest part of this hotel is a little like stepping into the past. Antiques (or antique reproductions) decorate most of them. Chenille bedspreads and old-fashioned bathrooms with tiny white tile add to the quaint charm. Rooms in the newer section are larger, with standard modern furnishings and balconies overlooking the swimming pool. Both types have double beds, telephone, and cable TV with movies. But if you really want to indulge in Texas-size Western fantasies, spring for the King Ranch suite, where the underside of the antique bed's tall, carved canopy is covered with shirred red fabric. The honeymoon package is called "River City Fling": $66 per couple per night (two-night minimum) for a room in either section; $105 per couple per night plus $94 for additional nights (no minimum) for the King Ranch suite or other suites. Package includes a bottle of champagne on arrival, continental breakfast each morning, and free parking (plus a carriage ride with a suite). Standard rate for a double is $79 per couple per night.

La Quinta Motor Inn, 1001 East Commerce, San Antonio, TX 78205-3303 (tel. 512/222-9181; reservations: tel. toll free 800/531-5900). In downtown San Antonio not far from the Convention Center, La Quinta offers clean, modern accommodations—in fact, its the nicest budget-price hotel in town. Simply decorated in browns and beige with geometric print spreads and contemporary furnishings, the rooms, though neither large nor luxurious, are comfortable. Many on the first floor have French doors that open onto the swimming pool courtyard. All come with king-size bed or two doubles, cable TV with movie channel, telephone with free local calls, AM/FM radio, and free parking. Complimentary coffee is available each morning in the lobby, while a 24-hour restaurant is just across the street. Honeymoon package: Standard rates of $66 to $72 per couple per night plus a complimentary bottle of champagne and turndown service with a fresh red rose.

Built of stone in 1894 by Edwin Terrell, a lawyer and statesman who served as U.S. ambassador to Belgium, **Terrell Castle Bed & Breakfast,** 950 East Grayson, San Antonio, TX 78208 (reservations: tel. 512/271-9145 or 512/824-8036)—with its turret, arches, and billowing balconies—reflects its original owner's love of the castles and châteaus of Europe. Inside, its new owners have carefully restored its elaborate Victorian woodwork, patterned parquet floors, and fireplaces. Several of its nine available rooms and suites have gas fireplaces, and all furnished with lovely antiques set off by floral prints and lace curtains. Guests are welcome to cook their own steaks on the gas grill in the park-like enclosed yard. Just up the street, guests can visit the historic Quandrangle of Fort Sam Houston, where Geronimo and his braves were held captive in 1886. Honeymoon package: Standard rates range from $79 (room with double bed and shared bath) per couple per night, to $87 (king-bed suite with private bath) per couple per night, and include a full American breakfast each morning and all taxes; honeymooners also get complimentary basket of candy and fruit on arrival. Some rooms have TV and telephone.

If the idea of eating breakfast beside a crackling fire in your room warms your heart, **Bullis House Inn,** P.O. Box 8059 or 621 Pierce, San Antonio, TX 78208 (reservations: tel. 512/223-9426), located just northeast of downtown, may please your pocketbook as well. Its rates of $31 to $50 per couple per night (including daily continental breakfast) make it one of the best bargains in town. The white-columned neoclassical mansion was built by cavalry general John Bullis, famous for his efforts to tame the Texas frontier in the late 1800s. Though most of the seven large, high-ceiling rooms share baths (including one with an old-fashioned claw-foot tub) and are not luxurious, they have comfortable, mix-and-match furniture and lots of character. Some of the rooms on the second floor have French doors with a view of the parade grounds of Fort Sam Houston across the street. Most come with TV's and clock radios; three have wood-burning fireplaces. Guests also enjoy the working fireplaces in the dining and living rooms, both with beautiful woodwork and period furnishings. A pay telephone on the ground floor is available to guests, as well as the kitchen in the youth hostel next door. Honeymoon package: Standard rates of $31 to $50 per couple per night plus complimentary bottle of champagne.

Staying at the **The Victorian Belle,** 147 Crofton, San Antonio, TX 78204 (reservations: tel. 512/227-1592 or 512/227-1190; King William Bed & Breakfast Registry), in the King William historic district is a little like visiting the ideal grandmother's house, full of gleaming carved woodwork and antiques, oriental rugs, patterned chintz in rich colors, and a solarium hung with well-tended plants. It's easy to slip into a turn-of-the-century mood there while stoking the fire or playing the old English piano in the parlor. The two guest units (one is a suite) on the second floor have tall windows that open onto the veranda, where honeymooners can enjoy their continental breakfast and a view of the residential neighborhood. Each is beautifully furnished with antiques and rich fabrics in blue, aqua, and peach, as well as a private bath, telephone, and TV. Honeymoon package: Standard rates of $55 to $64 per couple per night (which includes daily continental breakfast) plus complimentary bottle of champagne.

4. Romantic Restaurants

Whether you're in the mood for an exquisite French feast by candlelight, or some spicy tacos and enchiladas while mariachis serenade you, or you just suddenly have a yen for sushi, San Antonio offers a smorgasbord of excellent restaurants. Of course no one should leave town without trying its Mexican fare—some of the best in the country. Area specialties include *gorditas,* a kind of corncake filled with meat, cheese, and other goodies; *chiles rellenos,* peppers stuffed with cheese; and *fajitas,* flank steak marinated in spices, charcoal broiled, then sliced thin and wrapped in a flour tortilla. As for dress, most restaurants are casual (jackets are not required), although at the more expensive establishments people tend to dress up a little anyway. Nor are reservations needed at most restaurants, though it's best to call and check at the more expensive ones.

EXPENSIVE: Chez Ardid, San Pedro at Woodlawn, north of downtown (tel. 732-3203). Indulge in a shameless splurge at this elegant mansion turned premier French restaurant. After such starters as mussels steamed in wine and seafood sausage, followed by rack of lamb, and salmon with sorrel sauce, you'll feel as ethereal as the floating island dessert. Coat and tie, and reservations, required. Lunch for $6.50 to $14.50 per person plus drinks; dinner from about $45 to $100 per couple plus drinks.

MODERATE: Lela B's, 320 Bonham, in the Crockett Hotel behind the Alamo (tel. 225-6500). If the idea of being serenaded by your waiters with old Broadway favorites makes your heart sing, then prepare yourself for some enchanted evening. Don't be shy—you can join right in as you dine by candlelight on some of the most inventive American regional cuisine around. Among its biggest hits are the smoked pheasant sausages, and tenderloin of beef with jalapeño sauce. The tab for two: about $40 to $60 plus drinks. ·

P.J.'s, One River Walk Place, on the river north of the River Walk (tel. 225-8400). To get to this elegant, glass-enclosed enclave, just hop the "North Channel" river taxi from the River Walk. You'll dine royally on such contemporary French specialties as plateau de fruits de mer—fresh mussels, oysters, clams, shrimp, and lump crabmeat served with three sauces. Or if you just want cocktails, land there during happy hour (4 to 8 p.m. weekdays) and sample the complimentary hors d'oeuvres and live piano music (cool jazz on Friday and Saturday night) in the bar—also with a view of the river. Appetizers $3.50 to $9, entrées $13.50 to $18.50.

San Angel Room, in La Mansion del Norte Hotel at Loop 410 and McCullough (tel. 341-3535). Feast to your heart's content at one of the best Sunday brunches in town. Amid Spanish colonial surroundings you'll test your decision-making powers on a grand array of salads, seafood appetizers (such as smoked trout, fresh oysters, boiled shrimp), pâtés, marinated vegetables, cheese blintzes, and entrées that include mesquite-smoked roast beef—plus a special sauce for nearly everything. The sinful smorgasbord of desserts—buttery cakes, English trifle, brownies, even Belgian waffles—will finish you off. $16.95 per person with champagne (poured liberally after noon), from 10:30 a.m. to 2:30 p.m. The rest of the time the San Angel Room serves excellent paella and "New Southwestern" cuisine. Lunch will run about $25 per couple plus drinks; dinner, $40 to $50 plus drinks.

Grey Moss Inn, 19010 Scenic Loop Rd. about 45 minutes north of San Antonio (tel. 695-8301). Get a taste of the countryside, early Texas, and some of the best mesquite-grilled steaks around in this 1840s stone stagecoach stop. Sit outside on the patio under lofty oaks hung with Spanish moss, or inside under rafters as a fire crackles in the hearth. Save room for the homemade pies or praline parfait. A complete dinner for two: about $50 plus drinks.

Shogun on the Riverwalk, 412 East Commerce (tel. 222-2212). Sliding *shoji* screens and soft colors will show you just how romantic a Japanese tatami room can be. Whether you have a yen for sushi or feel tempted by tempura, you'll want to linger here before saying sayonara. If you want to keep your shoes on, you can sit at the sushi bar or tarry on the outdoor patio overlooking the River Walk. For a splurge, try the Love Boat—a little of nearly everything. Lunch specials run $3.75 to $8 each, dinner for two, about $25 to $50.

Ernesto's, 2559 Jackson Keller, northwest of downtown (tel. 344-1248). In a quiet, linen-and-candlelight setting, Ernesto serves what one local food critic aptly terms "Gour-Mex"—a happy marriage of French and Mexican cuisine with a decided seafood emphasis. Ernesto is often present, chatting with his guests and happy to explain his creations to gringos and nongringos alike. Appetizers, from $3.50 to $6; entrées, $9 to $19.95.

Cafe Rio, 4051 Broadway, just north of the Witte Museum (tel. 822-4233). After exploring the Witte or Brackenridge Park, head for Cafe Rio, perched above the San Antonio River. Choose a table next to the floor-to-ceiling glass panels that swivel open to let in the breeze. Veal dishes, pasta, and snapper florentine are all favorites. About $28 to $50 per couple plus drinks.

L'Etoile, 6106 Broadway, north of downtown (tel. 826-4551). Dishes like shrimp Toulouse Lautrec, Agnelotti à la creme (pasta stuffed with spinach, cheese, and ham, topped with cream sauce), and a sublime terrine of dark and white chocolate topped with raspberry sauce have made this restaurant a relatively new star in the firmament of French restaurants here. A sheltered outdoor patio framed with white lattice and hanging plants makes a romantic place to dine. Dinner for two from $26 to $45 plus drinks.

Taj Majal, 5305 McCullough in The Yard shopping center (tel. 824-1393). The dim lighting, rustling bead curtains, and soft twang of Indian music will make you feel like a maharaja and maharani as you partake of this ancient, richly spiced cuisine. A generous luncheon buffet offers a fine way of sampling it. Lunch buffet (all you can eat) $5.95 per person; dinner for two about $16 to $25 plus drinks.

Boudreaux's, at Commerce Street on the River Walk (tel. 224-8484). A quiet eddy beside a lively stream, this small, elegant restaurant charms like old New Orleans with its rough stone walls, kerosene lamps, and Chippendale-inspired chairs. And after the eye-opening Cajun margaritas (made with rum and rimmed with salt and cayenne), oysters Bienville, spicy gumbo, blackened prime rib, and bread pudding with whiskey sauce, you'll feel as happy as two crawdads in a Louisiana bayou. It has outdoor tables, too. About $20 to $40 per couple plus drinks.

Liberty Bar, 328 East Josephine St. (tel. 227-1187). A local favorite of those who know, this sedate but casual restaurant in a restored 1880s wood building serves down-home American cooking with an uptown flair. Crusty homemade bread slathered with locally churned butter compliments such seasonal specialties as hearty stew, scallop ceviche, steak tartare, and mesquite-grilled fish and chicken. And some swear the chocolate cake is the best in town. From about $10 to $35 per couple plus drinks.

At **Villa Italia,** 6322 San Pedro, north of downtown (tel. 340-0296), the freshly made pasta and its saucy permutations are as exuberant and generous as the decor—grapevines twine and wine bottles hang profusely above and around you. Add live violin and guitar music on Monday nights and you might be celebrating in the old country. Try the Roman Holiday for Two ($26.50)—godfather-size portions of antipasto, salad, manicotti, cannelloni, and lasagne with bread, coffee, and dessert. From $10 (for pizza) to $45 (for complete dinner) per person plus drinks.

A short drive through the country will lead you to **Stallion on the Roof,** Boerne Stage Road and Scenic Loop (tel. 698-2386), a small, intimate restaurant with French and American specialties. Dinner for two: $20 to $60 plus drinks.

INEXPENSIVE: Paesano's, 1715 McCullough, north of downtown (tel. 226-9541). This bustling Italian restaurant has been a San Antonio favorite for years—particularly because of its inimitable shrimp paesano: light, lemony shrimp swimming in a seductively simple sauce. From $10 (for pizza) to $28 (for complete dinner) per couple plus drinks.

Settlement Inn, north of San Antonio on Interstate 10 and Boerne Stage Road (tel. 698-2580). Settle in for some down-home barbecue in Texas-size portions, especially if you order the "Platter"—all the ribs, sausage, beef, barbecue sauce, green salad, beans, potato salad, green onions, hot biscuits, and honey you can eat. Sit at the picnic table under the stars, where a folk singer sometimes serenades diners, or inside by the fire in the rough-and-ready stone building, another stop on the old stagecoach line. About $16 to $24 per couple plus drinks.

On a balmy, breezy night, the sheltered courtyards of **La Fogata,** 2427 Vance Jackson, northwest of downtown (tel. 341-9930), are hard to beat for a romantic, outdoor place to eat fine Mexican food. Sip giant margaritas or piña coladas while fountains splash in the background. Be prepared to wait for a table. Best to go an hour before you're hungry. Lunch or dinner for two from about $10 to $23 plus drinks.

Rosario's, 1014 South Alamo, close to the King William neighborhood south of downtown (tel. 223-0453). In a funky hybrid of American-café art deco meets Mexico

City taqueria, Rosario turns out some of the most Mexican Mexican food around. Order thick corn gorditas with the black bean or tortilla soup, plus a side order of charbroiled onion, and you have a meal made in heaven—and mild enough for gringos. Live music on weekend evenings. Lunch or dinner for two from $5 to $15 plus drinks.

El Mirador, 722 South St. Mary's, south of downtown (tel. 225-9444). Every Saturday San Antonians line up to lunch on the famous Mirador soups: caldo xochitl (xochitl is Aztec for flower), a floating garden of chicken, avocado, tomato, scallions, rice, and mild herbs; and caldo azteca, a more pungent, peppery brew generously laced with tortilla strips, cheese, spinach, and other vegetables in a chicken base. The rest of the menu is simple but good Mexican fare (the special soups can only be had on Saturday). Be prepared to stand in line at this small, crowded eatery. Lunch for two: $5 to $10 plus drinks.

Lunch and browse in a sylvan setting beside Salado Creek at **Los Patios,** north of N.E. Loop 410 (tel. 655-6171), three restaurants and some boutiques nestled among trees. Try the **Gazebo** for salads, or the **Brazier** for grilled meats, fish, and a view of the creek. Lunch for two: $14 to $20 plus drinks. Should a craving for Mexican food—especially breakfast—strike at an odd hour, strike out for **Mi Tierra Cafe & Bakery** in Market Square (tel. 225-1262) or **Mario's,** 325 South Pecos just west of downtown near Fiesta Plaza (tel. 223-9602), both of them open 24 hours a day and frequented by singing mariachis around $10 to $20 per couple plus drinks. Also open 24 hours is **Taco Cabana,** 3310 South Pedro and other locations throughout the city (tel. 733-9332), a serve yourself taquería with good food for the right price: tacos from 69¢ to $1.50 each. Use the drive-through window to pick some up for a picnic or late-night snack. Lunch lightly on the fresh salads, inventive sandwiches, or zesty ceviche in the homey **Calico Cat Tea Room,** on Presa above the River Walk (tel. 226-4925). About $7 to $10 for two. Savor San Antonio's German heritage with a bowl of split-pea soup, a plate of wurst, and some cold German brew at **Schilo's,** on Commerce Street near the River Walk (tel. 223-6692), a picturesque deli lined with old wooden booths. Lunch for two from $3.50 to $7 plus drinks. Tacos, black bean soup, chiles rellenos (chiles stuffed with cheese), and grilled pork ribs will please your palate and pocketbook at **Cocula,** a cheerful, tiled Mexican eatery just across the street from the Alamo (tel. 223-2281). From about $5 to $20 per couple. Try **Thai Kitchen,** 445 McCarty, off San Pedro north of Loop 410 (tel. 344-8366), for hot and spicy Thai dishes in a simple setting. $15 to $18 per couple. Zesty Chinese food in a softly lighted, contemporary setting can be had at **Hunan Garden** (tel. 349-5427), 8069 Callaghan off Interstate 10. Weekend champagne brunch, $6 per person (includes champagne); dinner for two about $14 to $30 plus drinks. **Viet Nam Restaurant,** 3244 Broadway, north of downtown (tel. 822-7641) specializes in crab dishes. Lunch from $8 to $10 per couple plus drinks; dinner about $12 to $25 per couple plus drinks.

Picnic fare and snacks: For gourmet picnic fare try **Classic Dining at H.E.B.,** the huge supermarket at 4821 Broadway (tel. 820-3866) or **Ciao Seasonal European Kitchen,** 6539 San Pedro (tel. 340-1119). If a loaf of French bread, a fine wine, and some special cheese is your heart's desire (try the Saga with mushrooms!), the **Cuisinery** at 4233 McCullough (tel. 828-4672) can fix you up. For croissants, coffee, and pastries seek out the **Patisserie Suisse** at the Gunter Hotel, 225 East Houston St. downtown (tel. 227-3241). Pack up a parcel of hot tamales fresh from **Goa's Tamale Factory,** 1611 Culebra (tel. 732-8344), a bargain at $2 a dozen. Or cool off with an Italian ice or ice cream from **Justin's Ice Cream Co.** on the River Walk (tel. 222-2707).

5. Nightlife

Stop in at **The Landing,** on the River Walk in the Hyatt Regency Hotel (tel. 223-7266), to hear Jim Cullum's Happy Jazz Band. For disco, try **Royal Street**

Crossing on the River Walk (tel. 226-6256). Sip drinks at sunset 750 feet above San Antonio at **The Cloud Room in the Tower** at the Americas at HemisFair Plaza (tel. 223-3101). Take in dinner and the show at **Cabaret S.A.,** 315 East Commerce St. downtown (tel. 227-3676), where the tuxedo-clad waiters and waitresses stage a spirited cabaret in an elegantly restored building of the gaslight era. Four-course dinner and show, 7 to 10:30 p.m. (show starts at 9 p.m.), about $29 (including tax and tip) per person plus drinks. Jacket recommended and reservations required. Listen to the pianist at **Polo's,** a quiet, sophisticated place with turn-of-the-century ambience, in the restored Fairmount Hotel, 401 South Alamo St. downtown (tel. 224-8800). Or catch El Curro, a classical Spanish guitarist who frequently plays at **Las Canarias** in La Mansion del Rio Hotel, on the River Walk (tel. 225-2581). A change of pace from the River Walk is the North St. Mary's Street "strip," a growing collection of converted commercial buildings, now the scene of colorful restaurants and bars, some with live entertainment. Most of the places are within walking distance of each other. The crowd ranges from college kids (many from Trinity University) to elderly yuppies. Some favorites: **Nona's Homemade Pasta** (tel. 736-9896), for the belly dancer on Friday and Saturday after 9 p.m.; the Casablanca-theme **Cafe Americain** (tel. 737-2355), also with live music; the casual beach-shack atmosphere of **Playa Santa Maria** (tel. 737-1005), with appropriate flotsam-and-jetsam decor; and the outdoor patio at **Dos Guys** (tel. 225-2121), where local bands often play on weekends.

Part Two

CANADA

Chapter XIV

INTRODUCING CANADA

1. Practical Facts

STRETCHING FROM THE ATLANTIC to the Pacific, Canada is BIG. Although it is the second largest country in the world in area, its population is only about 25.5 million. And, since about 60% of that population lives in a relatively narrow band stretching roughly from Quebec City, Quebec, to Windsor, Ontario, you'll find plenty of elbow room outside of the cities.

Canada is divided into ten provinces that function much like the American states: Newfoundland (including Labrador), Nova Scotia, Prince Edward Island, New Brunswick, Quebec, Ontario, Manitoba, Saskatchewan, Alberta, and British Columbia. There are also two territories, the Northwest Territories and the Yukon Territory, which, although they account for 38% of Canada's landmass, have only a minuscule population. The nation is part of the British Commonwealth, and the queen of Great Britain is also queen of Canada. Despite the popular image, it is not all snow and ice, red-coated Mounties and grizzled fur trappers, and a populace saying "eh?" at the end of every sentence. The Mounties, in fact, are very rarely seen, usually just at state occasions and at events where the celebrated musical ride is performed. Telephones, electric appliances, railway tracks, and even TV programs are comparable to those south of the border in the United States—a border which is the longest undefended frontier in the world.

Although Canada and the United States are very similar, they share just enough differences to make travel to the north intriguing. In Quebec, sidewalk cafés, the aroma of fresh-baked baguettes, and the rapid-fire French recalls Paris. Bagpipes and kilts find themselves perfectly at home in Nova Scotia, where Gaelic is still spoken. Afternoon tea remains a tradition throughout the country. Add the influence of more recent immigrants—best reflected in the bounty of ethnic restaurants, from Chinese dim sum parlors to Greek tavernas selling retsina—and you find that Canada is a nation different enough to be foreign, yet not foreign enough to be unfriendly. Indeed, it is a world of difference, right next door.

1. Practical Facts

The following information will be useful wherever you travel in Canada.

ENTERING AND LEAVING: No passport or visa is required of U.S. citizens, but you will need proof of citizenship, such as an original birth certificate or voter's registration card.

LANGUAGE: Canada is officially a bilingual country, with both English and French being spoken. However, English strongly dominates in Ontario and Nova Scotia, while French is widely heard throughout Quebec. Sometimes, too, the English spoken uses a different accent from American speech, or words might be spelled differently: "harbour," in the British style, rather than "harbor." The French language also varies from what you would hear in Paris, resembling Old French a bit (the language has evolved from settlers who arrived in the 17th century).

MONEY: The official currency is the Canadian dollar ($Cdn), which is divided into 100 cents, just like the U.S. dollar. As we went to press, $1 Cdn was worth about 70¢ US. Unless otherwise noted, all prices in the following chapters are in U.S. dollars. Although American currency is sometimes accepted in Canada, it is always strongly recommended that you change your money into Canadian currency at a bank, which generally offers the most favorable exchange rate. If you will be arriving in Canada at night or during the weekend, it's a good idea to change some money into Canadian currency before you go, so you'll have funds on hand if necessary. As elsewhere in the world, traveler's checks are far preferable to carrying cash. Most major American credit cards are accepted in Canada, but always ask in advance to make sure.

ABOUT DRIVING: Speed limits are posted in kilometers—NOT miles—per hour. The most common posted speed limits are 100 km / h (62 mph) on super highways; 80 km / h (50 mph) on regular highways; and 50 km / h (30 mph) on city streets. Driving is on the right, as in the United States. If you will be driving your own car to Canada, it is recommended that you obtain a "Non-Resident Interprovince Motor Liability Card" from your insurance agent back in the United States. If you should be involved in a car accident while in Canada, Canadian police will accept this card as proof that you are, in fact, insured.

WEATHER: Canada is on the metric system, so temperatures are quoted in degrees Celsius. To convert a temperature in Celsius to Fahrenheit, multiply by 2 and add 30.

FOR FURTHER INFORMATION: For details about travel anywhere in Canada, contact: **Tourism Canada,** 235 Queen St., 4–6, Ottawa, ON K1A 0H6, Canada (tel. 613/954-3852).

Chapter XV

TORONTO

1. Practical Facts
2. Romantic Interludes
3. Honeymoon Hotels and Hideaways
4. Romantic Restaurants

TORONTO, capital of the province of Ontario, hugs the north side of Lake Ontario's shoreline. A metropolis of 3½ million, it contains almost 15% of Canada's population, and is the financial and commercial hub of the country. Hailed as "the world's greatest new city," Toronto pulsates with energy. Sidewalk cafés and wine bars overflow with talkers and revelers, jazz music wails from the clubs, and one of the world's liveliest theater districts—second only to London and New York—entertains both residents and visitors alike.

When the city was incorporated in 1834, its population was a scant 9,000, but its lakeshore position encouraged trade, travel, and manufacturing. Today, Toronto is one of North America's fastest growing cities, and is constantly undergoing renovation and rejuvenation. Downtown, day or night, the city bustles with activity. Old houses have not all fallen to the wrecker's ball, but instead, have been sandblasted and spiffed up with white paint, ornamental ironwork, and modern glazing. Present-day Toronto offers first-run plays, world-class ice hockey, ballet, baseball, opera, cricket, fine orchestras, rugby, and cinemas aplenty. You can browse through art galleries galore, both big and small, and explore many a cozy bookshop. There is a world-class zoo, with 4,000 inhabitants, a super astronomy observatory, and the Ontario Science Centre to stimulate your curiosity and intellect.

Get a bird's-eye view of it all from 1,815-foot CN Tower, the tallest freestanding structure in the world. It has three different observation decks, a revolving restaurant, and a popular disco with all the latest in sound and video. Check out Toronto's Harbourfront, 92 waterfront acres that have been turned into a recreational and cultural complex. Exercise your bodies by jogging, walking, or riding a bicycle, then drop by the Antiques Market, arts and crafts demonstrations, or galleries.

Until the 1950s, Toronto was a very stodgy British city, but an influx of wartime refugees from Europe produced a lively admixture of cultures—the city now has vigorous Italian, Greek, Ukrainian, Hungarian, German, Portuguese, Chinese, and Indian and West Indian communities. Toronto has consequently become a great dining city, with tempting ethnic restaurants of every sort. Every year, the city celebrates its international roots in June with Caravan, showcasing the culture of over 50 national groups at special pavilions. On the first weekend in August also, the West Indian community gets together for Caribana, a Carnival-type event complete with elaborate costumes.

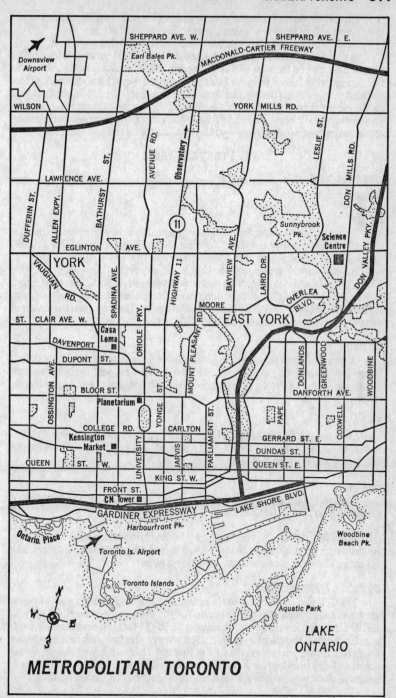

METROPOLITAN TORONTO

The end of August brings the greatest to-do of them all—the Canadian National Exhibition, with its air shows, entertainment, fireworks, and pizzazz.

The city is big, and scattered, but downtown, day or night, people, . . . well, . . . they walk! They walk above ground, and they walk below ground, in the world's biggest underground complex of stores, cinemas, offices, and restaurants, where the odd tree grows to 20 feet or more. Finally, the biggest surprise for visitors from less civilized metropolises is the fact that Toronto works as a city. It is clean, civilized, and the people are almost unfailingly polite. Everything functions smoothly—from telephones to taxis. Whichever aspect of Toronto you choose to explore—its parks or museums, waterfront or café society—you both should have a real good time.

1. Practical Facts

GETTING THERE: Toronto is a major transportation hub with excellent connections from all over the world.

By Air

Toronto's Pearson International Airport is served by almost all major international carriers. There are two terminals: Terminal Two is for **Air Canada, Air France, Swissair, Air Jamaica,** and **Aero Mexico;** Terminal One services other airlines.

To get to the city proper from the airport, the **airport bus** costs $5.55 (tel. 979-3511). It will take you to or from the downtown hotels; Royal York, Sheraton Centre, Hilton Harbour Castle, Chelsea Inn, Bond Place, Carlton Inn, Holiday Inn downtown, L'Hotel, Westbury, Park Plaza, Plaza II, and Ramada. **Taxi** fare from the airport to downtown will be approximately $17 to $18.50 per couple.

By Rail

Connections are made from the United States through service by **Amtrak** (toll free 800/872-7245) or **Via Rail** (tel. 416/366-1302). Rail passengers arrive right downtown, at the classically proportioned Union Station, making an impressive arrival.

By Bus

Lines serving Toronto from the United States are **Greyhound** (toll free 800/528-0447) and **Graycoach** (tel. 416/974-3511). Arrivals and departures are from the bus terminal, 610 Bay St., at Dundas.

By Car

The most popular U.S. entry points connect to **Hwy. 2, 401,** or the **Queen Elizabeth Way,** leading right to Toronto.

GETTING AROUND: Toronto, like New York and London, is a great walking city. Be sure to bring comfortable shoes for hoofing it. If you're going longer distances, take advantage of the city's excellent transportation system.

By Public Transportation

The **T.T.C.** (Toronto Transit Commission) has an 818-mile network of buses, subways, and trolleys. Adult cash fare is 74¢ ($1 Cnd). A two-fare ticket is $1.40 ($1.90 Cdn), and six tickets or tokens cost $3.70 ($5 Cdn). Interchangeable paper transfers are free, and must be obtained when you pay your fare. Ask for one, whether you need it or not; you may need it later in your trip. Drivers carry no change, so that tickets, tokens, or exact fare is necessary before boarding. Tickets or tokens can be bought at all subway stations and at stores displaying the T.T.C. ticket agent sign.

The comprehensive T.T.C. "Ride Guide" map is available at all subway stations, but if you are stuck, call 393-INFO, between 7 a.m. and 11:30 p.m. daily for more information.

Timetables are available by calling 484-4544.

Study the system. With your increased mobility, you'll be able to enjoy the experience of seeing the city even more, without the hassle of parking in the downtown core, where parking is about $6 for the day.

By Taxi

Taxis are metered and cost a basic 96¢, plus 15¢ for each third of a mile traveled. Service is very reliable, and you can hail cabs on the street. The usual tip is 10%.

Sightseeing Tours

Gray Line Sightseeing Tours operate from the bus terminal, at 610 Bay St. (tel. 979-3511) and have a variety of excursions from 1½ to 4 hours in length. This is a good way to get the lay of the land. Check your hotel to determine if it is a pickup point.

A 1½ hour tour in a 1920s **trolley car** rattles through Chinatown, the business district, and passes the old and new city halls, $9.60 per person. There are various central departure points. Contact Toronto Tours (tel. 869-1372).

Gray Line Toronto Harbour and Islands Boat Tours leave from the foot of Yonge Street (364-2412) in glass-topped boats.

WEATHER: Summer temperatures average 71°F, with lots of sunshine. July and August are the hottest months, with June and September being the most comfortable. May and October are somewhat cooler, at about 52°F, but are the prettiest times to visit for blossoms in springtime or colorful foliage in the autumn.

From November to April anything can happen, including snow storms, and heavier clothing should be in your suitcase.

CLOTHING: Torontonians are fairly conservative and reserved by U.S. standards. Proper dress always commands respect, and your wardrobe should include a jacket and tie for men and dress or suit for women for dining out in Toronto's fine restaurants. Otherwise dress for comfort.

TIME: Toronto is in the Eastern Standard time zone and observes Daylight Saving Time. However, dates from going onto, or off of, Daylight Saving Time may vary from U.S. practice, and you should check your railway or airlines to be on the safe side before traveling.

TELEPHONES: Local calls from a public call box are 19¢ (25¢ Cdn). In an emergency dial 911 for fire, police, or an ambulance. You can call Toronto direct from the United States; the area code is 416.

SHOPPING: Generally, store hours are 9 a.m. to 5:30 p.m. with late-night shopping till 9 p.m. on Wednesday, Thursday, and Friday. Many large supermarkets stay open for 24 hours daily, and small variety stores usually are open until 11 p.m.

Toronto is a shopper's paradise. If you don't know where to start, begin with the big department stores, such as **Eaton's, Simpson's,** or **The Bay.** For convenience and comfort in hot or cold weather, the glass-enclosed **Eaton Centre Galleria,** at 220 Yonge St., should be seen for its four floors of grace and space. It is replete with 300 shops, snack bars, and services. Don't miss it.

The Bloor-Yorkville area contains probably the widest selection of elegant shops and specialty boutiques, all rather upscale in price.

Creed's (45 Bloor St. West) and **Holt, Renfrew** (50 Bloor St. West) are both considered to be the ultimate in women's specialty store shopping, with designer fashions, furs, accessories, lingerie, shoes, cosmetics, and a selection of crafts. **Eddie Bauer** (50 Bloor St. West) has a wide selection of outdoor clothing for men and women. **Stollery's** (1 Bloor St. West) has the largest selection of high-class British men's and women's apparel in Canada. For crafts, head over to **The Guild Shop** nearby (140 Cumberland), which is Toronto's oldest crafts shop. Here you can find handmade objects and Inuit carvings.

College Park, at Yonge and College Streets, is one stop north of the Eaton Centre, and contains over 100 shops and restaurants in the heart of downtown.

Queen's Quay Terminal, at 207 Queen's Quay West, is an award-winning complex on the waterfront. It has about 85 shops.

For a completely different experience, take a streetcar along Queen Street West for the faded but genteel elegance of its secondhand stores, containing books and weird clothing. This is also a good area to find cheap grub. Going east you will pass streets with names like Hammersmith, Kenilworth, and Waverly, and end up in the Beaches neighborhood, which is the newest trendy residential quarter. While you are here, stop off for a stroll along the boardwalk adjacent to the lakeside.

The strength of the U.S. dollar against Canadian currency makes shopping a bargain for Americans in Canada. In addition, you can save even more money by getting a refund on the 7% provincial sales tax levied on goods and services, purchased, consumed, or used in Ontario. Generally speaking, visitors may apply for a tax refund on receipts totaling over $100 Cdn for nondisposable goods to be used outside Ontario. For application forms on this, and information on the 5% accommodation sales tax refund, write or call: **The Retail Sales Tax District Office,** 2300 Yonge St., 10th Floor, Toronto, ON, M4P 1H6 (tel. 416/487-1361), or **Ontario Travel,** Queen's Park, Toronto, ON, M7A 2R9 (tel. 416/965-4008).

HOW TO GET MARRIED IN TORONTO: You'll find it fairly easy to arrange a wedding in Toronto. You need a marriage license, which can be obtained from city hall, Bay and Queen streets (tel. 416/392-7341). The license costs $35 Cdn ($26.25 US). No blood test is required; for people aged between 18 and 21, a birth certificate is necessary. Three days after the application, you will need to declare the date, place, and officiant of your choice to perform the ceremony. If either of you is divorced, complications of arise. For complete details, contact: **The Office of the Registrar General,** McDonald Block Parliament Buildings, Toronto, ON, M7A 1Y5 (tel. 416/965-2026).

FOR FURTHER INFORMATION: Contact: **Metropolitan Toronto Convention and Visitors Association,** Toronto Eaton Centre, 220 Yonge St., Suite 110, Box 510, Toronto, ON, M5B 2H1 (tel. 416/979-3143 or toll free 800/387-2999 from NY, OH, MI, and PA).

2. Romantic Interludes

It might be cheering the **Blue Jays,** or the **Maple Leafs,** or perhaps a memorable evening of drama at the **Royal Alexandra Theatre.** Seeing the **National Ballet of Canada** is always a great idea, and so, too, is attending the **Toronto Symphony Orchestra** at spiffy Roy Thomson Hall. Other choices include a day at **Ontario Place,** with its bag full of attractions, or even at old **Fort York,** a restored garrison from the War of 1812, complete with soldiers carrying muskets who re-enact old battles. Here are a few more suggestions:

Located just off Toronto in Lake Ontario, the **Toronto Islands** are only a stone's throw away from the city—but remain a tranquil world apart ideal for a picnic.

Fenton's Food Shop, 2 Gloucester St. (tel. 961-8485), has elegant wicker picnic baskets, complete with linen, cutlery, and dishwasher safe, plastic champagne flute glasses for $81.40 (there are also some less expensive ones to choose from). Also at the store you can load up with such goodies as strawberry tarts, black Russian rye bread, marinated herring, smoked trout with mustard mayonnaise, tortellini with hazelnuts, chocolate bourbon pecan pie, and so on. **Movenpick**, at 165 York St. (tel. 366-5234) will also prepare a suitably tempting picnic lunch on 24 hours notice. You can also pick up bagels and fillings from a wide variety of delis to keep your costs down.

Arrange to rent **bikes** from **U-Pedal-It** at 180 Queen's Quay West (tel. 862-7684), then head for the nearby ferry dock at the foot of Bay Street, and prepare for a glorious day exploring Toronto's islands. Take a sweater, in case it is cool beside the lake.

The **ferry ride** takes only about 15 minutes (bikes are not carried on weekends). It costs 74¢ ($1 Cdn). For information and schedules, call 392-8194. The ferry stops at Centre Island, Ward's Island, and Hanlan's Point, all of which are interconnected by bridges. You can then pedal off through leafy lanes, alongside yacht-dotted marinas, or loiter by the lagoons or the boardwalk. Visit Centreville, with its make-believe turn-of-the-century village, or go on to see the farmyard beasties at "Far Enough Farm."

For starry-eyed lovers, what's more appropriate than the sky show at the **McLaughlin Planetarium**, 100 Queen's Park (tel. 586-5736)? Call for show times; admission is $2.25 per person. (Located next door to the Royal Ontario Museum—Museum subway stop.)

From Dixieland jazz to a World War II destroyer—that's what you'll find at **Ontario Place** (tel. 965-7711), a combination cultural center, playground, and plush green park. You can visit H.M.C.S. *Haida*, a Tribal-Class destroyer that saw action in the Second World War, cruise around peacefully aboard paddleboats—or raucously on bumper boats—or thrill to a wet-and-wild ride down the giant waterslide. Then head over to the Showboat, where musicians play some of the best jazz this side of New Orleans. Attractions also include musical shows and revues, orchestral performances, films at the Cinesphere, pubs, picnic areas, and the Canadian Baseball Hall of Fame. When you get hungry, you can dine in the fancy Trillium Restaurant, or other more casual places that serve German or Irish food. Open daily from 10 a.m. to 1 a.m. (until 11 p.m. on Sunday); admission is $3.75 per person.

Built in the style of a medieval castle, the 98-room **Casa Loma** mansion provides tangible evidence of the enormous wealth—and equally gigantic eccentricity—of Sir Henry Pellat, who was one of Toronto's most successful financiers in the early 20th century. The sprawling manse has towers, turrets, a Great Hall with a 60-foot ceiling, and hand-carved oak paneling. Located on Spadina Road, south of St. Clair Avenue. Open daily from 10 a.m. to 4 p.m.; admission is $3 per person.

Take your camera and sashay off to **Kensington market,** in the College and Dundas streets vicinity. In this colorful quarter, where Haitian, Portuguese, Jewish, and Caribbean immigrants have settled, you can buy stereos or salted fish, hear chickens cluck away, and buy fresh bagels or new sandals. Some of the nearby houses have been brightly painted Portuguese-style in a riot of color. Full of charm and character.

3. Honeymoon Hotels and Hideaways

As you would expect of the largest city in Canada, Toronto has a wide selection of hotel accommodations designed to suit all predilections and pocketbooks. All of the following have air conditioning, color TV, and private bathrooms. There is a 5% tax on rooms, which is not included in the hotel rates quoted here unless noted.

EXPENSIVE: The **Sutton Place Hotel,** 955 Bay St., Toronto, ON M5S 2A2 (tel. 416/924-9221; reservations: toll free 800/828-7881 nationwide; 800/462-1088 in NY), in midtown is subdued, with French Provincial–style furniture, and bright with floral fabrics. The clientele is genteel and well-to-do. The hotel is a haunt of Peter Ustinov, Donald Sutherland, Dick Van Dyke, and other personalities. The graceful chandeliers are bright but not overwhelming, and the designer-coordinated decoration and marble entrance tell you what to expect before you reach your room—pure excellence. You'll also feel quite grand when you dine in the stately, pillared, and tapestried Sansouci dining room. Honeymoon package (CP): $154.67 per couple for one night. Includes a deluxe room, a bottle of Henkell Trocken, continental breakfast for two, and all taxes and gratuities. An extra night is $105.82 per couple (room only).

For a romantic hideaway, consider the **Windsor Arms Hotel,** 22 St. Thomas St., Toronto, ON M5S 2B9 (tel. 416/979-2341), which offers a secluded, unobtrusive, central location, close to Bloor Street's high fashion and trendy Yorkville. It resembles a small English manor house in turreted style, with leaded-glass windows, polished brass accents, and dark woods paneling. Afternoon tea is served in a room plushly carpeted with oriental rugs and set off by coromandel screens for privacy. A discreet classic, it attracts many celebrities, among them the late John Lennon and the late Richard Burton. The 81 rooms are furnished highly individualistically as one would expect of an establishment worthy of inclusion in European Relais and Chateaux Guide.

The premises also contain four outstanding restaurants (see "Romantic Restaurants" section). Honeymoon package (BP): $144 per couple for one night. Includes a premium deluxe room, fruit basket, bottle of sparkling wine, and room service breakfast for two. Each extra night is $109.52 per couple (room only).

MODERATE: Located on the waterfront, the **Hotel Admiral,** 249 Queen's Quay West, Toronto, ON M5J 2N5 (tel. 416/364-5444; reservations: toll free in the eastern U.S. 800/387-1626), is new, romantic, and quietly grand. It sparkles with brass, glass, thick-carpeted hallways, and rich, dark mahogany woods, in the subdued elegance favored by its primarily business executive clientele.

Since it is situated on the waterfront, overlooking Toronto's islands and harbor, the hotel is a bit out of the way from the downtown shops and facilities. However, a shuttle bus runs every half hour, and can drop you at several downtown locations. Meanwhile, the lakeside locale offers serenity and comfort. In addition, it's adjacent to the long Harbourfront walks and bicycle paths and close to the boutiques of Queen's Quay West, Antique Market, and Harbourfront, with its book readings, art exhibits, and other happenings.

Honeymoon package (CP): $129.50 per couple for one night. Includes king-size bed, chilled bottle of champagne, deluxe fruit basket, and continental breakfast for two next morning.

A traditional Toronto hotel, familiar to generations, **The Park Plaza Hotel,** 4 Avenue Rd., Toronto, ON M5R 2E8 (tel. 416/924-5471; reservations: toll free 800/268-4927) is convenient to elegant Bloor Street, museums, the planetarium, and cinemas. The quiet understated decor is in subdued pastel tones. Fine dining is available in one of the city's best restaurants, The Prince Arthur Room, where a meal runs from $15.75 to $24.75 per person. The hotel is also noted for family-style dining in its very popular and more modestly priced Murray's Restaurant. Honeymoon package (BP): $123.75 per couple for one night. Includes luxurious suite accommodations, champagne, full breakfast, all taxes and gratuities. Additional nights are $85.84 per couple.

INEXPENSIVE: The **Venture Inn,** 89 Avenue Rd., Toronto, ON M5R 2G3 (tel. 416/964-1220; reservations: toll free 800/387-3933) is close to Yorkville, the Royal Ontario Museum, the planetarium, and Bloor Street's stylish shops. The style here is of a simple country inn, plainly furnished in honey-colored Canadian pine and homey print fabrics. It is spare, frill-free, and sparkling clean. Popular with no-nonsense travelers who favor function over extravagance without sacrificing comfort. Some rooms have water beds. Excellent value. Honeymoon package: None. Rates (CP): $68.40 per couple per night.

Built in 1929 **The Royal York,** at 100 Front St. West, Toronto, ON M5J 1E3 (tel. 416/368-2511; reservations: toll free 800/828-7447) helps keep the tradition of the great Canadian Railway Hotels alive and well. Not only is it Toronto's biggest hotel—it's the biggest in the British Commonwealth. Its château-style roof is a Toronto landmark. Conveniently located across from Union Station, its 1,600 rooms are popular with conventioneers, as well as with business people who favor its proximity to downtown. There are 14 places to wine and dine here, from 24-hour delis, to the splendor of the Imperial Room, where headliners such as Peggy Lee, Tony Bennett, and Tina Turner entertain. This is the hotel of choice for Royal and state occasions, and it has hosted dinners for the queen. Although the Royal York is considered the Grand Old Dame of Toronto hotels, the property is up to date in every respect without yielding its traditional and well-proven style.

Honeymoon package (EP): $63.64 per couple for one night. Includes deluxe (albeit a bit small) accommodation with a queen-size bed, a special gift, late checkout, and preregistration. Provincial tax is extra.

4. Romantic Restaurants

Toronto takes second place to none in its rich diversity of international food choice, style, ambience, service, or size and quality of its wine cellars. There are truly hundreds of fine places to eat and dine.

The Windsor Arms Hotel, 22 Thomas St. (tel. 979-2212). Unique for such a small hotel, The Windsor Arms contains four highly regarded restaurants, supervised by Chef Michael Bonacini, who trained at London's Dorchester Hotel. You can make reservations for all four at the number listed above.

The elegant, bright, and airy Courtyard Cafe with modern decor and sky-revealing canopy, is a Toronto favorite for seeing and being seen. The film, media, and theatrical luminaries congregate here to sign contracts or nod hellos at acquaintances. Colorful bright fabric streamers add a feeling of lightness and romance. The food is excellent, and the desserts are particularly scrumptious. This was the first Canadian restaurant to introduce cuisine naturelle. Lunch appetizers priced from $2.80 to $5.50; entrées from $6.70 to $11. At dinner, appetizers run from $2.80 to $5.50; entrées from $8 to $15.

The Grill is more country and gleams with burnished copper cookware. The emphasis here is most on food and less on style. Lunch, about $30 a couple; dinner, $30 to $40 a couple plus drinks.

The Wine Cellar is intimate and tiny, and your surroundings there are brick, masses of wine bottles, and interesting modernistic photographs. Dinner, about $30 to $40 a couple, plus drinks.

Modern decor, tapestries, and carpets in subdued tones are featured in The Restaurant. Emphasis here again is on food in the French manner. They offer a prix-fixe dinner for $29 per person, as well as a gourmet "tasting" menu for $135 per couple. À la carte dishes are also available.

Ed's Warehouse Restaurants, 270 King St. West (tel. 593-6676). This complex of five restaurants has become a Toronto institution, located just a few doors away from the showplace Royal Alexandra Theater.

All the eateries share the same flamboyant Ed Mirvish style, forests of Tiffany lamps, stained glass, paintings, marbles, enormous vases big enough to conceal Ali Baba, wood carvings, ancient clocks, etchings, bronzes, and hoary arcade novelty machines. All are riotously overdone and immensely popular, with a total seating capacity of 2,400.

Go to Ed's Warehouse for basic roast beef and steaks. Dinner for two, about $10 to $30, plus drinks. No jeans permitted, jacket (no tie) required for men.

Ed's Seafood serves favorites from the ocean such as lobster, sole, and crab. Dinner appetizers are priced from 60¢ to $4.50; entrées $4.50 to $16.50. No jeans permitted; jacket (no tie) required for men.

For favorites such as steak, roast beef, and lasagna try Old Ed's Restaurant. Complete dinners go from $12 to $20 per couple, plus drinks. No dress code.

Ed's Italian Room features hearty specialties such as veal, spaghetti, and chicken. Dinner, from $20 to $30 per couple, plus drinks. No dress code.

Ed's Chinese Restaurant serves an extensive Chinese menu. Dinner for two, about $10 to $25, not including drinks.

There are two restaurants at **Fenton's,** 2 Gloucester St. (tel. 961-8485), one at street level, one downstairs.

Fenton's upstairs is perfect for a great romantic occasion. The airy garden courtyard lit by scallop-shell lamps, and arrayed with flowers conveys an impression of eternal summer. The menu is studded with such delights as terrine of wild mushrooms, cream of leek soup with Stilton, and meringue poached in milk, caramelized, and served on English custard. Lunch from $25 to $40 per couple; dinner from $35 to $60 per couple.

Fenton's downstairs is eminently comfortable and cozy with brick walls, posters, and softly lit by crystal candle holders on each table. Cuisine is as superb as it is upstairs. The temptations include poached fresh Atlantic salmon and supreme of chicken with presto mousse filling. Desserts are a dieter's despair, featuring such delicacies as fresh fruit tart with whipped cream and brandied praline ice cream. Finish off with darjeeling tea, or a house specialty, apricot Ceylon tea. Dinners, about $30 per couple plus drinks. No cigar or pipe smoking until after 10 p.m.

Movenpick, 165 York Street (tel. 366-5234), pleases everybody with its Alpine ambience of red-checked tablecloths and bright, potted plants, Swiss canton banners, and gaily-colored cloth lamps. Among the steaming hot Swiss specialties are fondue, raclette, and walliser Filetspitzen (beef tenderloin strips in a red wine sauce, with Rösti). There is roasted rack of lamb and fettuccine primavera to round out an international menu.

Movenpick has four food stops in this one location. They include:

The Belle Terrasse; which is excellent for people watching. Dinner for two, about $20 to $40 per couple.

The Rossli (Little Horse) has fine dining amid Alpine decor, featuring typical Swiss dishes. From $20 to $40 per couple.

Let yourself go at the Veranda indulging in pastries and chocolate truffle prepared with Swiss chocolate, fresh heavy cream, and laced with Grand Marnier, champagne, or almonds. About $10 per couple.

The Grape and Cheese is secluded but companionable, and a relaxing spot for a drink or a snack. A gourmet buffet is featured on Wednesday and Thursday evenings for $14.85 per person. The Sunday brunch ($13.25 per person) is also a Toronto favorite, serving quiche lorraine, salmon coulibiac, omelets, sausage, and Bünderfleisch (air-dried beef) to satisfy hearty appetites. Picnic lunches are available on 24 hours' notice. Parking is free after 6 p.m.

For something different, try **The Groaning Board,** 131 Jarvis St. (tel. 363-0265) which proffers a lavish salad bar with over 70 different items for $10 per person, as well as various meat dishes. But the establishment is less known for its hearty fare than for its film show: award-winning commercial shorts from the Cannes Film Festival.

While in Toronto, take advantage of its international array of cuisines. Feel like dining Danish? Head for the **Copenhagen Room,** 101 Bloor St. West (tel. 920-3287). Buffet and entertainment on Tuesdays run about $32 per couple. For French food, sample **La Chaumiere,** 77 Charles St. East (tel. 922-0500), where dinner for two runs about $22.50 and up. Want something more exotic? You could eat with the Egyptians at **Stone Cottage Inn,** 3750 Kingston Rd. (tel. 266-6200), where there's usually belly dancing on Friday and Saturday nights. Entrées include Egyptian specialties such as falafel; dinner for two will run about $15 to $20 per couple. Craving a kiwi? Dine with the New Zealanders at **"For My Friends,"** 1051 Bloor St. West (tel. 536-9360). Their prix-fixe menu includes a salad; choice of lamb, chicken, veal, or fish, all accompanied by fresh vegetables; and a Pavlova—the New Zealand national dessert, made with kiwi fruit. Lunch, $11.25 per person; dinner, $12.75 per person. If your tastes run to good, plain roast beef and Yorkshire pudding, **Murray's Restaurant,** 172 Bloor St. West (tel. 922-3564) is very hard to beat for great food at moderate prices. Hamburgers run about $3, the roast beef, about $12 per person.

For good jazz, try the upscale **Café des Copains,** 48 Wellington St. East (tel. 869-0148), or **George's Spaghetti House,** 290 Dundas St. East (tel. 923-9887). But, best of all, is at **Ontario Place** (tel. 965-7711). Your admission charge lets you hear the striped-jacketed, straw-hatted Dixieland Band joyously play away, while floating along the waterways under sunny skies.

Chapter XVI

MONTREAL

1. Practical Facts
2. Romantic Interludes
3. Honeymoon Hotels and Hideaways
4. Romantic Restaurants

SHOULD YOU TWO—interested mainly in being alone together—honeymoon in a crowded metropolis? Yes, if it's Montreal. Here, if a couple kiss on a street corner while waiting for the light, the only looks they get are of approval.

There's more than that Latin spirit in Montreal to delight visitors. Americans love its French flair; Europeans wonder at its New World tempo. And in the small *quartiers* you'll find a relaxed mood, spiced by a joie de vivre that fosters romance in the midst of this three-million-strong bustling hive.

Surrounded by a majestic river and crowned by a forested peak, the city's ancestor, an Indian village, enjoyed a spectacular setting. Its beauty wasn't lost on the first tourist. Sailing up the St. Lawrence in 1535, the French explorer Jacques Cartier stopped at the island and climbed the mountain. *"Quel mont réal* (what a royal mountain)," he enthused and so the city got its name, a century before being born. The first settlers arrived in 1642. The colony soon grew into an important trading post and a base for the exploration of North America. Montreal briefly became the capital of New France, only to serve as the site of capitulation when the British took it in 1760. The French nobles left, Scottish merchants arrived, and the city settled down to get rich. There was a brief distraction in 1775 when the American army marched in. With them came Benjamin Franklin, who urged the citizenry to join the revolution. But by then Montrealers had had enough of changing masters; the Americans gave up and went home the following summer.

The next invasion came at the end of the last century with the hosts of immigrants. By then Montreal had become Canada's gateway: produce, machinery, and money streamed through here, as well as people on their way to the West. Of the people, many stayed. Montreal must have always had something especially attractive. After the 1760 conquest many British soldiers chose to settle; their descendants, named Jean-Louis O'Hara or Gérard Burns, help to make the "Paris of North America" the second largest French-speaking city in the world. But you hear Italian, too, spoken by 160,000 residents. You think New York is Jewish? The first synagogue of the New World was built here. At last count 80 ethnic groups have added their culture —and cuisines!—to this exciting mosaic.

Much of the original 17th-century city still stands, in the quarter known as Vieux Montréal. The entire 95 acres is officially designated as an historic site. In addition to the old quarters, you'll also want to explore Montreal's sophisticated, futuristic side—

especially the "underground city" where you can shop, dine, or go to a movie—all along nine miles of covered streets. So get ready to enjoy!

1. Practical Facts

GETTING THERE: You have many convenient ways to reach Montreal.

By Air

Flights from the United States and elsewhere in Canada land at Dorval Airport, 25 minutes from downtown. From here, it's $4.50 by **bus** (Aerocar, tel. 397-9999), $9 by **minibus** (Aero-Exec, tel. 866-AERO), $15 by **taxi**, $17 by **limo** (Murray Hill, tel. 937-5311) to reach the city proper.

Flights from outside North America land at Mirabel Airport, 45 minutes from downtown. Transportation to Montreal costs $7 by **bus** (Aerocar, tel. 397-3999), $34 by **taxi**, $38 by **limo** (Murray Hill, tel. 937-5311).

By Rail

There's one day and one night train from New York. From Toronto, six day trains and one overnight; all arrive at **Central Station.** For information in the U.S., call **Amtrak** (toll free 800/872-7245). In Montreal, call **VIA Rail** (tel. 871-1331).

By Bus

Buses arrive at **Terminus Voyageur** (tel. 842-2281).

By Car

The main approaches are from Toronto (**Hwy. 401** in Ontario, **Rte. 20** in Quebec) and New York (**Interstate 87** in the U.S., **Rte. 15** in Canada). For road conditions, call 514/873-4121.

GETTING AROUND: Once you arrive in Montreal, you'll find it easy to get around.

By Public Transit

The fastest way to get around is by **metro** (subway), which runs from 5:30 a.m. to 1:30 a.m. **Buses** are frequent, many run all night. Single tickets cost 75¢ ($1 Cdn); six tickets are $3.75; tickets are valid on both bus and metro (get transfers). Buses require exact change. Change and free maps are available at metro stations. For information, call Montreal's public transit system, which is known as **STCUM** (tel. 288-6287).

By Taxi

Flag them down or call 273-6331, 273-6351, or 277-2552.

By Car

Driving here gets a bit frenetic, seemingly more suitable for bullfighters than for distracted honeymooners. If you must drive, note that speed limits are posted in kilometers (45 km/h equals 28 mph, 100 km/h equals 62 mph), and no right turns are allowed on red lights. U.S. permits and insurance are valid.

If you want to rent a car, most of the major U.S. companies are represented in

Montreal. The weekend rate for a compact car is about $30 per day, with 200 km (124 miles) free.

LANGUAGE: The official language in Montreal is French. Most Montrealers are bilingual, but it creates goodwill if you start off in French ("Bon jour. Parlez-vous anglais?").

WEATHER: The climate is northern temperate, like the midwestern United States. May and September are usually the most comfortable. Summer has temperatures in the 70s. September and October are pleasant and often sunny (50° to 60° F). November is rainy. Winter, December to March, brings snow and temperatures between 14° and 20° F, dipping to 20° F below zero. Anything can happen in April.

CLOTHING: Montrealers dress. The better restaurants require jackets for men. Bring lightweight cottons for the summer, sweaters for the fall, and everything you've got, including snowboots, for the winter.

TIME: Montreal is in the Eastern Time zone. During the summer, Daylight Saving Time is observed, but the changeover dates do not always match those in the United States. If you want to know when the changeover date will occur, call an airline.

TELEPHONES: The phone system works similarly to that of the United States. You can dial Montreal directly from the United States; the area code is 514. Pay phones take Canadian coins. In emergencies, dial 911 (no money required).

SIGHTSEEING: To help you get oriented, you can join an organized sightseeing tour.

By Bus

Gray Line (tel. 280-5327) runs six tours, from 2½ hours to all day ($9 to $15), including an exploration of underground Montreal ($6). Departures from Square Dominion.

By Boat

All boats depart from Victoria Pier, at rue Berri. Cruises cost $5.25 or $10 for 1½ or 3 hours with **Montreal Harbour Cruises** (tel. 842-3871). Jet-boat trips through the rapids cost $23 for 1½ hours, wet gear provided, with **Lachine Rapids Tours** (tel. 284-5607).

By Horse-drawn Carriage

Calèche stands are on Nôtre-Dame (near Gosford), Place d'Armes, rue de la Commune (at Place Jacques-Cartier), Square Dominion, and on Mount Royal. They are $23 per hour.

SHOPPING: Stores are generally open from 9 a.m. until 6 p.m. from Monday through Wednesday, until 9 p.m. on Thursday and Friday, and on Saturdays until 5 p.m. **Small groceries** *(depanneurs)* sell food, wine, beer, and necessities until midnight. Ask your hotel clerk for the nearest 24-hour **pharmacy.**

What you buy here is limited only by your imagination and budget. The city prides itself on being an international trendsetter in fashion. Many **boutiques** on Sherbrooke and Crescent do not post prices—as the old joke goes, if you have to know, you probably can't afford it. The shops and **department stores** on Ste-Catherine cater to all tastes and budgets. For **antiques,** browse in the shops on Sherbrooke West, St-Denis, and Nôtre-Dame West. You'll find **art galleries** in Old Montreal and on Sherbrooke West. And buy a memento of your visit at the **Canadian Guild of Crafts** (2055, rue Peel) from a selection of Quebec, Indian, and Eskimo handcrafts, prints, and carvings.

HOW TO GET MARRIED IN MONTREAL: It will take considerable advance planning, because the law requires that your intentions be posted for 20 days. A civil marriage can take two months to arrange, but you can contact a clergyman 21 days ahead for posting and fly in for the ceremony. For details, contact the Canadian consulate in your home city.

FOR FURTHER INFORMATION: Contact the **Greater Montreal Convention and Tourism Bureau,** Box 889, Place Bonaventure, Montreal, PQ, H5A 1E6 (tel. 514/871-1595). In Montreal, you can stop in their offices at 174 est, rue Nôtre-Dame; 2, place Ville-Marie; airport information desks; or at Square Dominion (summer only).

2. Romantic Interludes

Its residents consider Montreal one big romantic interlude. When pressed for specific recommendations, they first want to know if you are staying for one week or three, then agree on these highlights.

Time shrinks in the historic quarter, **Vieux Montréal.** The narrow cobblestoned streets, laid out under the French colonial regime, run between 18th-century mansions. Warehouses line the waterfront where a hundred years ago a forest of ships' masts swayed. Hire a calèche, a horse-drawn carriage (about $23 per hour) to take you around.

But old is not staid in Montreal. The ancient streets are very much alive. After your ride you'll find the sidewalk cafés of Place Jacques-Cartier nearly full. It's time for an apéritif while listening to *chansons* (songs). Then dinner in a room of stone walls and oak beams.

If you prefer to visit on foot, begin at the tourist office (174 est, rue Nôtre Dame) to pick up a brochure and map for a walking tour.

Forests and meadows adorn **Mount Royal,** a place for all seasons and all people. Couples stroll, hikers—or skiers—puff on the slopes, bird-watchers stalk the woods, serious men steer model boats on the lake that's taken over by skaters in the winter. From Beaver Lake, a train-on-road or a calèche takes you up to the **chalet** and its terrace for the great panorama of the city embraced by the wide bend of the river.

The fresh air will make you hungry. Snacks are sold here, but for a good picnic you should pick up provisions before. Boulevard St-Laurent is the source of culinary nostalgia for Montrealers from the four corners of the world. Follow your nose north of Prince Arthur to Italian cheeses, Hungarian sausages, crusty French rolls or Jewish rye, Portuguese grilled chickens, Greek pastries.

Where to picnic in the 500 acres of greenery of the mountain? There are tables on the flats, but you'll be better off on the steeper slopes, fortunately unsuitable for Frisbee and soccer, but fine for the view and a pleasant afternoon just for two.

The opposite view, from the **river,** sets the city's skyline against the mountain. But there are many other attractions on the wooded islands. Visit Île Ste-Hélène for screams and laughs in La Ronde, the amusement park ($11.25 for all rides and entertainment). In the Vieux Fort the reincarnated forces of French marines and Fraser Highlanders parade and shoot it out three times a day. On the adjacent Île Nôtre-Dame, the site of Expo '67 opens in the summer for the "Man and His World" exhibition and the magnificent floral park, the Floralies.

Back on shore, the most pleasant part of the Old Port is where the docks have given way to spreading lawns and a fairground. The sightseeing boats dock at Victoria Pier. If you miss the Sunday breakfast sailing at 10 a.m., take a Love Boat Cruise at

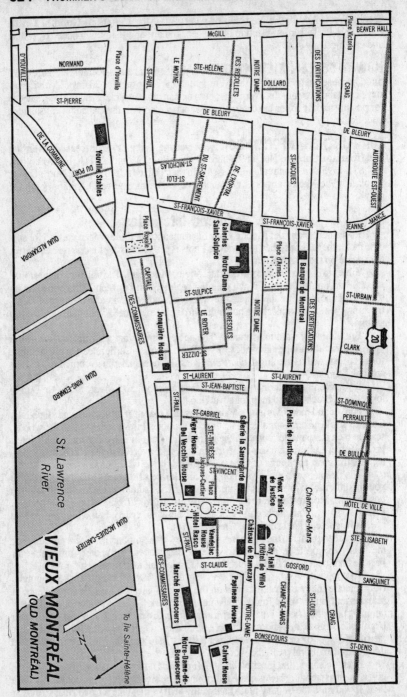

9 p.m. (3 hours, Thursday through Saturday, dancing and bar, $10.50 per person. For reservations, call 842-3871).

The theme of the opera played in Montreal's **Latin Quarter** is music and laughter, punctuated with the clinking of glasses and espresso cups, counterpointed by the arguments of students bent on changing the world. Passing eccentrics add more action. Your part in this performance is to be there, sit, and watch.

The stage is the countless bistros and bars of Rue St-Denis. Most popular are Le Faubourg St-Denis (no. 1662) for looking and talking and Le Grand Café (no. 1720) for mingling and listening to jazz and blues.

When you get hungry, grab a *croque-monsieur* (a Gallic grilled-cheese sandwich), croissants stuffed with anything from ham to chocolate, or find a place dedicated to food (see "Romantic Restaurants").

At the end of June there is music and dancing in the street during the festival international de jazz, when 400,000 fans invade concert halls and open-air venues to hear everything with a beat, from cerebral jazz to big-band swing and rock.

Near the Latin Quarter, on the Prince Arthur pedestrian mall, the quieter entertainment consists mostly of sitting in the sun with a drink and watching people. If you linger here into the evening, drop in for jazz and blues till after dawn at **Lola's Paradise** (3604, boul. St-Laurent), a loft filled with plants, Sally Ann armchairs, and the liveliest crowd in Montreal.

Sculptures grace the sidewalk outside the **galleries** on Rue Sherbrooke. The Museum of Fine Arts (1379 ouest, rue Sherbrooke; tel. 285-1600) displays collections of European, Canadian, Amerindian, and Oriental art, plus a major exhibit every summer (Tuesday to Sunday, 11 a.m. to 5 p.m., admission $1.50 per person). The Musée d'art contemporain (Cité du Havre, tel. 873-2878) has a permanent post-1940 collection and exhibits of contemporary artists (Tuesday to Sunday, 10 a.m. to 6 p.m., admission is free). The Palais de la Civilisation (Île Nôtre-Dame, tel. 872-4560) puts on "first-ever-in-America" expositions of seldom seen art treasures from other continents every summer.

Musical life centers on the Place des Arts (175 ouest, rue Ste-Catherine, tel. 285-4200) where concerts, opera, ballet, and popular shows are given in three halls. Théâtre St-Denis (1595 rue St-Denis, tel. 849-4211) features touring singers and groups, and is the main venue during the Jazz Festival.

The 1976 Olympic Games is now legend and, while the debate over the cost continues, the great **stadium** has become Montreal's pride. Impervious to weather under the retractable roof, it's the home of the Montreal Expos baseball team from April to September, and the Alouettes football team from July to November. Take in a game or join a guided tour of the complex ($3.40 per person; tel. 252-4737).

While in the area, visit the Jardin botanique (4101 ouest, rue Sherbrooke), the third largest botanical garden in the world ($1.50 admission to the greenhouses).

Ste-Catherine and its sidestreets downtown are in constant motion all day and most of the night. Shopping, dining, entertainment are packed into this square mile. And not even heat waves or blizzards can spoil your vacation in the air-conditioned comfort of Montreal's famous underground city. Over a thousand shops, a hundred restaurants, dozens of cinemas, eight hotels, train stations, and bus terminals are linked by nine miles of covered streets. A journalist once spent all of January here; he took the escalator from his hotel to shop, got his typewriter fixed, meet friends for dinner, see movies, and occasionally hopped on the metro to go to a concert; all that without parka and snow boots.

The liveliest streets, Crescent and its competing neighbors, are still aboveground, although the thousands of dancing feet may have weakened the foundations. In the crowded pubs, clubs, and discos everybody seems to know everybody else, and within minutes you, too, will be part of the scene.

3. Honeymoon Hotels and Hideaways

All the following rooms are air-conditioned, with private bathroom, telephone, color TV.

EXPENSIVE: Bonaventure Hilton International, 1, place Bonaventure, Montreal H5A 1E4 (tel. 514/878-2332; reservations: toll free 800/445-8667 in the U.S.; 800/268-9275 in Canada), is unique. Where else could you escape the crowded streets in minutes to a wooded retreat? It's just an elevator ride to the 17th-floor roof garden where outside your window pheasants peck under pine trees and ducks bob in the stream. Nothing else is rural about your quiet hideaway. The main dining room, decorated in lavish 17th-century French style, serves award-winning gourmet fare. A nightclub offers live shows and dancing. The heated outdoor pool is accessible in the winter: slip into the water indoors and swim out to where the stream rises over the snowbanks.

Honeymoon package: $184 per couple per night for a room; $270 per couple for a suite. Includes roses, a fruit basket, and sparkling wine; breakfast and free entrance to the nightclub are included. The "Magic of Montreal" package, without the extras, costs $174 per couple for two nights.

At the **Ritz-Carlton,** 1228 ouest, rue Sherbrooke, Montreal H3G 1H6 (tel. 514/842-4212; reservations: toll free 800/327-0200 in the U.S.; 800/268-3708 in Canada), you enter a world of elegance, polished brass, marble, wood-paneled walls, and hushed service in the classic tradition, preserved for 75 years. Breakfast comes on a wooden tray, the paintings on the walls are original, and the fireplace in your suite works. To Old World elegance the Ritz adds modern convenience, and routinely treats all guests like VIPs.

The dining room and garden have been the haunts of Montreal's crème-de-la-crème for generations. Their visitors from out of town wouldn't dream of staying anywhere else. They want to be part of the Ritz legend. So did Elizabeth Taylor and Richard Burton, who spent one of their honeymoons here. Honeymoon package: $160 per couple per night for a deluxe room; $280 per couple per night for a suite. Includes champagne, chocolates, and flowers.

Queen Elizabeth, 900 ouest, blvd. Dorchester, Montreal H3B 4A5 (tel. 514/861-3511; reservations: toll free 800/268-9143). The "Queen E" is Montreal's gateway: Airport buses stop at the side, trains arrive below, and escalators descend to the "underground city" and the metro.

Honeymooners find seclusion on the 19th floor, in "Entrée Gold." A private elevator whisks you to this small hotel within a big one. In the lounge a lavish continental breakfast is laid out in the morning, canapés in the afternoon; the honor bar is always open. The view is glorious and the crackling log in the fireplace entertains those who pass up the VCR (one in each room) and the choice of a 100 movies. Honeymoon package: $142 per couple per night. Includes a luxury suite, champagne, and a sightseeing tour.

MODERATE: Within strolling distance of the boutique and bistro streets, the **Château Versailles,** 1659 ouest, rue Sherbrooke, Montreal H3H 1E3 (tel. 514/933-3611; reservations: toll free 800/361-3664 in the U.S.; 800/361-7199 in Canada), is a small, elegant European-style hotel, housed in restored turn-of-the-century mansions. The rooms are furnished in style, some have a fireplace. Honeymoon package: $70 to $80 per couple per night. Includes a bottle of champagne.

Hostellerie Les Trois Tilleuls, 290, rue Richelieu, St-Marc, PQ, J0L 2E0 (tel. 514/584-2231), gives seclusion, scenery, and superb food away from the city (see directions under "Romantic Restaurants"). Your balcony overlooks a river and wooded islands. Explore them on an afternoon boat cruise; apéritifs are served on board. Dinner is a gastronomical delight for which jaded Montrealers take the 30-minute drive.

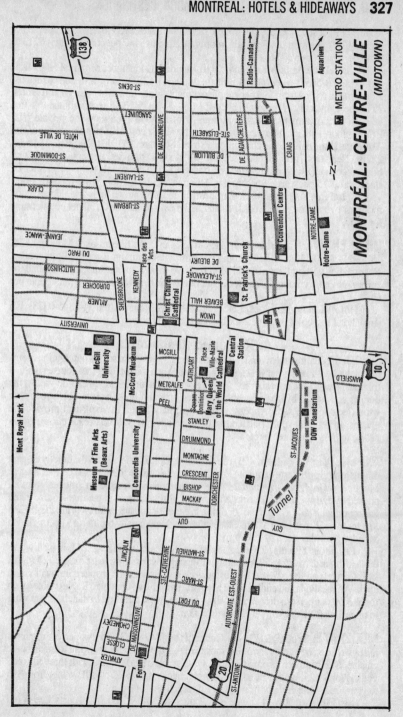

MONTRÉAL: CENTRE-VILLE *(MIDTOWN)*

Rooms (EP) cost $57 to $69 per couple per night; suites $135 to $162 per couple per night. With three memorable meals, rooms are $135 to $147 per couple; suites $213 to $240 per couple per night.

L'hôtel rue de la Montagne, 1430, rue de la Montagne, Montreal H3G 1Z5, (tel. 514/288-5656; reservations: toll free 800/361-6262). European and luxurious. Honeymoon rooms from $94 per couple per night; suites from $147. **Le Grand Hôtel,** 777, rue University, Montreal H3C 3Z7 (tel. 514/879-1370; reservations: toll free 800/361-8155). American and luxurious. Honeymoon rooms on the private "Le Privé" floor, with champagne, cognac, and breakfast cost $128 per couple per night. **Auberge Handfield,** 555, chemin du Prince, St-Marc, PQ, J01 2E0 (tel. 514/584-2226). Near Les Trois Tilleuls (see above). Rooms from $30 per couple per night; honeymoon suite with champagne and breakfast, $90 per couple per night. **Hôtel Le Baccarat,** 475 ouest, rue Sherbrooke, Montreal H3A 2L9 (tel. 514/842-3961; reservations: toll free 800/228-5150). European air in a downtown high-rise. Honeymoon room for two nights, with breakfasts and $22 meal voucher for $150 per couple; suite for $158.

INEXPENSIVE: Château De L'Argoat, 524 est, rue Sherbrooke, Montreal H2L 1K1 (tel. 514/842-2046). Charming, comfortable rooms in a restored townhouse. Near the bus terminal, metro, Old Montreal. No meals, but restaurants are around the corner. No honeymoon package, but the rate is the best value for $34 per couple per night.

Hôtel Manoir des Alpes, 1245, rue St-André, Montreal (tel. 514/845-0373), is a small hotel in a quiet street near Old Montreal. $30 per couple per night.

4. Romantic Restaurants

For the quality and diversity of its restaurants, Montreal stands out. Dining rooms of unabashed luxury serve *menus gastronomique,* eight or nine courses with a midmeal pause for a cool sherbet, or *trou normand,* a bracing sip of eau-de-vie. At the budget end, small bistros offer modest selections and invite you to bring your own wine (look for the sign, *Apportez vôtre vin*); they'll pull the cork and provide the glasses. In between you'll find a range of prices and styles, from French *cuisine bourgeoise* to fiery Szechuan fare.

EXPENSIVE: Le Fadeau, 423, rue St-Claude (tel. 878-3959). In the quietly elegant dining room you'll taste exquisite French nouvelle cuisine that has earned four stars in Montreal's *Guide gastronomique.* The restaurant makes its own smoked salmon, praised by Europeans who've tasted them all. Put your trust in the nine-course menu gastronomique ($45 per person) or dine à la carte for about $70 for two; lunches $12 to $18 for two. Wines from $20 to Château Lafite. Dinner daily 6 p.m. to 11 p.m.; lunch Monday to Friday noon to 2:30 p.m.

Les Trois Tilleuls, 290, rue Richelieu, St-Marc (tel. 584-2231), is well worth the half-hour drive from Montreal to a romantic river setting (east on Rte. 20 to exit 112, then left on Rte. 223). The cuisine is classic French with inspired innovations on duck. All meals should end with the luscious marquise au chocolat. Table d'hôte lunch for $13.50 per person; dinner $37.50 per person, wine selection to match. If you want to linger, read "Honeymoon Hotels" section.

MODERATE: Troïka, 2171, rue Crescent (tel. 849-9333). In this perfect romantic hideaway in a cozy cellar, strolling musicians set the mood for savoring Russian haute cuisine. Sample three caviars (Beluga, Ossetra, Sevruga) for $33 with three flavored vodkas for $8.25, before the main course (entrées priced $12 to $19). Wines from $15 to your limit. Dinner daily from 6 to 11 p.m.; closing at 3 a.m.

Les Filles du Roy, 415, rue Bonsecours (tel. 849-3535). The hearty fare of old

Quebec is served in an 18th-century mansion, where the surroundings bring back the days of la Nouvelle-France. Bring a pioneer appetite. Dinner for two with wine for about $45. Open daily from 11 a.m. to midnight.

Witloof, 3619, rue St-Denis (tel. 281-0100). In the middle of the Latin Quarter you find a corner of Brussels (rhymes with mussels, a specialty). Try the *waterzooi* of three kinds of fish, and sample the impressive selection of 15 Belgian beers. Dinner for two for about $40, beers from $3 to $10. Opens Monday to Friday at noon, Saturday and Sunday at 5 p.m., closes at 1 a.m.

Montreal has so many good restaurants, it's hard choosing among them. Here are some more choices.

La Marée (tel. 861-8126) and **Le St-Amable** (tel. 866-3471) are in a 18th-century house on Place Jacques-Cartier. Both are well respected by local gourmets. Lunch for two with wine for $40, Monday to Friday, noon to 3 p.m., dinner for two with wine for $70, daily 6 to 11:30 p.m. **Chez La Mère Michel,** 1209, rue Guy (tel. 934-0473) also has its followers, especially for the mousseline of lobster and pike. Lunch for two with wine for $35, Tuesday to Friday, 11:30 a.m. to 2 p.m., dinner for two with wine for $55, Monday to Saturday, 6 to 10:30 p.m. Closed Sundays.

La Raclette St-Denis, 1657, rue St-Denis (tel. 849-6576) specializes in raclette ($3.70) and fondues ($8 to $15). Remember that if you lose your bread in the melted cheese, you must buy your partner a drink (eau-de-vie for $4.50). Opens Monday to Friday at 11:30 a.m., Saturday and Sunday at 2:30 p.m., closes between 11 p.m. and 2 a.m. **La brioche Lyonnaise,** 1593, rue St-Denis, (tel. 842-7017) has sinful pastries, fine snacks and salads to eat there or take out; the upstairs room offers lunch and dinner, about $25 to $35 for two. Bring your own wine. Open daily from 8:30 a.m. to midnight; the kitchen works from 11:30 a.m. to 10 p.m.

Have a Sunday brunch (noon to 4 p.m.) in the sunny courtyard of **Au Cépage,** 482, rue St-Francois-Xavier in Old Montreal (tel. 845-5436). Omelets with bagel and croissant for $4.25 per person and bubbly by the glass.

Prince Arthur is not one restaurant but two rows of them, lining the pedestrian mall. Most let you bring your own wine. Lunch or dine in Greek, Vietnamese, or Italian style from $6 to $20 for two.

A must is the **Montreal Hebrew Delicatessen** (a / k / a Schwartz's), 3895, boul. St-Laurent (tel. 842-4813). No reservations, often a lineup for the famous smoked meat that's air-shipped to connoisseurs in New York and L.A. Sandwiches for $2.25, plates $4.50. Daily 8 a.m. to 1 a.m.

Chapter XVII

NOVA SCOTIA

1. Practical Facts
2. Halifax / Dartmouth
3. Nova Scotia's Trails
4. More Suggestions in Nova Scotia

CIAD MILE FAILTE—one hundred thousand welcomes—the traditional Gaelic greeting embraces the open, friendly hospitality of a place that hasn't quite caught up with the 20th century, a world where they still speak old-world French and the wail of bagpipes can be heard through the early morning mists.

Nova Scotia, the smallest of Canada's maritime provinces, lies in the Atlantic Ocean just east of the coast of Maine. Less than a million hearty people make their homes here, depending heavily on the bounty of the sea for both their livelihood and sustenance. What most of us don't realize is that Nova Scotia comes in two parts: a lobster-claw-shaped peninsula connected to the mainland by a very narrow isthmus; and Cape Breton Island, which is really a tight cluster of islands surrounding an inland sea, located at the northern tip. The untainted, natural beauty of Nova Scotia's rugged coastline and lush interior forest offer some of the most romantic and spectacular untamed settings to be found anywhere in the world. Over 100 lighthouses stand as lone sentries perched atop barren piles of granite boulders mercilessly pounded by a relentless sea, guarding calm, deep water harbors and secluded coves. Tiny fishing villages dot the 4,265 miles of shore in settings so stunningly beautiful you will feel certain you have stepped into a richly detailed painting. A land of exaggerated contrasts, Nova Scotia offers a variety of experiences all colored by a stubborn unwillingness to give up the romantic notions of the Golden Age of Sail. The sea is everywhere. It dominates life here and, in fact, no matter where you go in Nova Scotia you are never more than 35 miles from the water.

It is very possible the Vikings may have discovered Nova Scotia as early as A.D. 1000. We do know for certain that John Cabot, the great navigator and explorer, first sighted Cape Breton on June 24, 1497, where he planted the English flag and claimed the continent for England. It was not until 1605, however, that a permanent settlement was established—but by the French at Port Royal on the Bay of Fundy.

The British and French skirmished for control until 1713, when the Treaty of Utrecht transferred Nova Scotia to British rule. The French continued to contest England's claim until 1755, when disaster befell the Acadian community. Unwilling to declare an oath of allegiance to the British crown, fearing it might require they take up arms against their countrymen, the Acadians were forcefully expelled from the province. The tragedy of this evacuation was immortalized by Henry

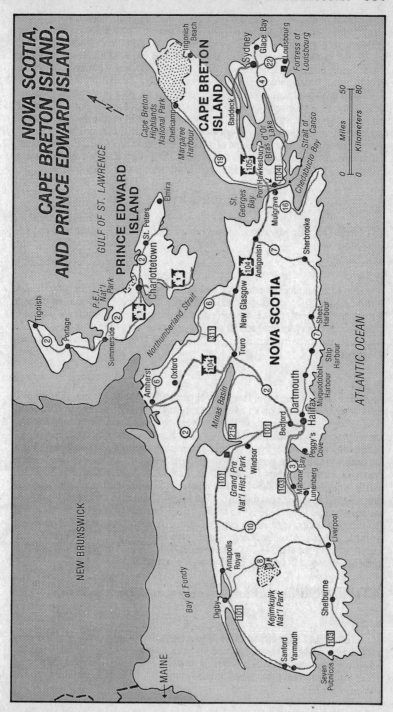

NOVA SCOTIA, CAPE BRETON ISLAND, AND PRINCE EDWARD ISLAND

Wadsworth Longfellow in his epic poem *Evangeline*. The scattering sent some Acadians to Quebec, Prince Edward Island, and Cape Breton Island, and some went as far as Louisiana, where they became known as Cajuns, a corruption of Acadian. In 1763, Britain was granted permanent possession under the terms of the Treaty of Paris. France finally relinquished her claims, but she held onto the tiny islands of St. Pierre and Miquelon, which remain French departments today.

From this tumultuous history, Nova Scotia has forged a peaceful, harmonious blend of the varied elements of its culture: an amalgam of French, British, Scottish, and native Indian heritages. As you travel around the province, take the time to get to know the Nova Scotians. They seem a bit reserved at first, but soon will warm to genuine friendliness. This is the kind of place where people take time for other people. If someone sees you stopped in your car perusing a map, they'll come over to offer you directions. In particular, they extend a very hearty welcome to honeymooners.

1. Practical Facts

GETTING THERE: Nova Scotia is easy to reach, thanks to excellent land and sea connections.

By Air
During the summer months **Air Canada** has regular daily direct flights to Halifax from New York, Boston, Toronto, and Montreal. **CP Air** makes connections through Toronto and Montreal. Off-season (generally November through April) you will have to connect through Montreal and Boston. Flying time to Halifax from New York is three hours and forty-five minutes; from Chicago, 4½ hours; from Boston or Montreal, 1½ hours.

By Sea
There are two wonderful **ferry trip** opportunities. The M / S *Scotia Prince* provides honeymoon suites on its overnight trip from Portland, Maine, to Yarmouth, Nova Scotia. The trip takes about 10½ hours and operates from May through October. The ship can accommodate about 250 cars and has full cruise facilities on board, including dining, dancing, live entertainment, casinos and duty-free shopping. Fares run from $40 to $58 per person, $85 to $115 per person for a deluxe cabin. Contact: **Prince of Fundy Cruises Limited,** P.O. Box 4216, Station A, Portland, Maine 04101 or call toll free, 800/341-7540 nationwide; 800/482-0955 in Maine. The **Marine Atlantis** *Bluenose* sails daily from Bar Harbor, Maine, to Yarmouth, Nova Scotia, and operates from mid-May to mid-October. The trip takes about six hours and there are sun decks, restaurants, bars, casinos, a snack bar, and duty-free shopping available. The *Bluenose* also accommodates cars. Fares run $23.25 to $31 per person. Telephone toll free: 800/341-7881 nationwide; 800/432-7344 in Maine, or write Terminal Supervisor, CN Marine, Bar Harbor, Maine 04609.

GETTING AROUND: You have a choice of ways to explore Nova Scotia.

By Car
The best and most efficient way to tour Nova Scotia is by car. If you arrive by ferry you can bring your own. Nova Scotia has a seat-belt law in effect, so buckle up! Anticipate your fuel needs, when driving as stations are often closed at night or on weekends. Speed limits are posted in kilometers—*do not confuse the figures posted with miles per hour.*

If you want to rent a car, you can do so at Nova Scotia's airports as well as in Halifax. Most of the major U.S. companies are represented. Sample rates for a one-week rental of a subcompact car run about $150 per week, with the first 840 miles free. Be sure to book your rental car in advance through your travel agent, the Check In Service, or direct to: **Avis** (tel. 902/742-3323); **Budget** (tel. 902/454-8501); **Hertz** (tel. 902/454-7431 or toll free 800/268-1311); **Auto Host** (tel. 902/425-3774); or, **Rent-A-Wreck** (tel. 902/454-6401).

By Air

There are connecting flights between Halifax and Sydney serviced by **Air Canada** (in Halifax, tel. 429-7111; in Sydney, tel. 539-6600) and **CP Air** (in Halifax, tel. 465-2111; in Sydney, tel. 564-4545).

By Bus

If you are not driving yourself, the most interesting way to get around is by bus. **Acadian Lines Ltd.** (tel. 902/454-9321) goes just about everywhere, as do **MacKenzie Bus Lines Ltd.** (tel. 902/543-2491), and **Zinck's Bus Company, Ltd.** (tel. 902/454-9321). If you are interested in more than just getting from one place to another, try **Nova Tours and Charters, Ltd.** (tel. 429-3702 or 463-0212); **Atlanta Tours** (tel. 423-6242); **Cabana Tours** (tel. 423-6066 or 423-8945); **Evangeline Tours** (tel. 542-9109); or **Bridge Tours** (tel. 422-8462).

Public Transportation

In Halifax the best way to get around downtown is on **foot,** especially during business hours when parking is a serious problem. However, there is a good **Metropolitan Transit System** that pretty well covers the entire metro area. The basic fare is about 45¢, and you will need exact change. For route information, call 426-6600.

By Taxi

Taxis are available but it is best to go to a cab stand and call for a pickup, as hailing cabs on the street can be difficult. The meter starts at $1.40 and the fare is based on both mileage and time. Depending on traffic, an average fare across town should cost around $5.50. Tipping is usually between 10% and 15% depending on how satisfied you were with the trip.

LANGUAGE: English is spoken everywhere, often with a lilting Scottish burr, a rolled French "r," or a clipped Brits accent.

TAXES: There is a 10% Health Services Tax levied on goods and services such as accommodations (hotel, motels, lodges, and inns); restaurant bills over $4 each; local telephone calls over 20¢, and most soft drinks and alcoholic beverages. Unless indicated otherwise, all prices quoted in this chapter do *not* include this tax.

WEATHER: Summer temperatures average 75°F during the day and 50°F to 65°F at night. In the fall it averages 55°F to 65°F during the day and 40°F at night. Spring is 48°F during the day, dropping to 35°F at night; and winter is 35°F during the day and 20°F at night.

The prime time of year to travel in Nova Scotia is from May through October. Evenings the temperature always drops by a few degrees and it is sometimes cool even in the summer. Along the coastline it can get very foggy and damp. Because the sea surrounds Nova Scotia, the weather is very changeable.

CLOTHING: Generally, from May to October you will want medium to lightweight, spring to early-summer-style clothing. It is most sensible to plan your wardrobe in layers so you can take off and add on as the temperature changes—and it does. From November to April you will need medium- to winter-weight clothing. Again, plan a layering system. You should pack some rain gear.

TIME: While in Nova Scotia you are in the Atlantic Time Zone, which means you are one hour ahead of Eastern Time. If it is noon in New York, it will be 1 p.m. in Halifax. Nova Scotia observes Daylight Savings Time in the summer.

TELEPHONES: You can dial Nova Scotia direct from the United States; the area code is 902.

SHOPPING: Native crafts and maritime arts should dominate your shopping list even though you will be able to make some good purchases of imported British wares. At various crafts shops in Halifax, you should keep a look out for those wonderful, expressive apple dolls, which have faces sculpted from apples. South of Halifax in Purcells Cove you will find impressive leaded-glass ware, and in Waverly, also near Halifax, you will find excellent silversmiths plying their craft. Along the Evangeline Trail in Middletown, shops sell special handcrafted wooden toys and in Wolfville you can pick up some pewter ware. On the Lighthouse Rte., a visit to the blacksmiths in East Dover is a worthwhile stop off and the native pottery found in Arichat off the Fleur de Lis Trail on Cape Breton Island has found its way into many homeward-bound collections.

As you meander around Nova Scotia you should make it a point to always stop in the local general stores. These are the center of all the action in some of these villages, some of which have populations as small as 30 people. If you are patient and willing enough to poke around, you are sure to find treasures for your collection of memories. See individual area sections for shopping recommendations for each area.

Before you leave on your trip you should write for the *Handcraft Directory,* Nova Scotia Department of Culture, P.O. Box 864, Halifax, Nova Scotia B3J 2V2 (tel. 902/424-4061). This is an excellent guide to the crafts of Nova Scotia and to the people who produce them.

ABOUT ACCOMMODATIONS: Accommodations in Nova Scotia range from world-class deluxe to local, rustic, and quaint, the last sometimes being euphemisms for a room in a clean, old bed-and-breakfast where more often than not you will be sharing a bathroom. Seasoned travelers will tell you that staying at these small inns is frequently one of the best ways to spend an intimate, memorable visit.

Unless otherwise indicated, rates are European plan. Travel in Nova Scotia is seasonal, so watch for reduced off-season rates. Not all hotels are open all year; we have listed the operating season, if applicable. Many Nova Scotia honeymoon packages are short—only one or two nights. If you want to stay longer, ask the hotel what the regular rate would be.

DINING OUT: Nova Scotia must chuckle a bit when they hear of all the fuss about "nouvelle cuisine," which features the freshest local ingredients, perfectly prepared and seasoned—because that's exactly how they've been cooking in this province for years. Lobster, of course, is king here, either simply boiled and served with drawn butter, or elegantly prepared with sauce Newburg or Thermidor. The region is also known for its superb scallops, halibut, haddock, and salmon. The low prices are amazing. On Cape Breton Island, for example, entrées rarely top $10. Please note, however, that prices and availability of fresh fish and seafood will vary with the seasons.

You'll probably want to sample some flavorful Nova Scotian dishes with their intriguing names. Solomon gundy appears as an appetizer on many menus; it's a marinated raw herring, generally served with onions. You'll also encounter rappie pie (an Acadian dish made with meat and potatoes), finnan haddie (smoked haddock), marakins (spiced sausage), Digby chicken (locally smoked herring), fat archies (cookies), and mharagh (a type of sausage; the squeamish should not inquire as to exact components). For dessert, take advantage of the fresh berries in season: a fine summer harvest of strawberries, blackberries, blueberries, rhubarb, cranberry, and apples.

For romance, nothing beats a picnic lunch of fresh-baked bread, lobster, and fruit, a repast best enjoyed while looking out over a bit of spectacular Nova Scotia coastline. Throughout the province, you'll find designated picnic areas and day-use parks, all marked with signs and equipped with complete facilities. Hint: You might want to invest in a pair of nutcrackers and some of those premoistened towlettes if you're planning on some lobster feasts—and who isn't?

In Nova Scotia the legal age is 19. There are still "dry" areas and bottled alcoholic beverages are sold only in Nova Scotia Liquor Commission (NSLC) retail stores. Hours may vary but generally they are open from 10 a.m. to 5 p.m. on weekdays, and Saturdays (until 9 p.m. on Fridays) and closed on Sundays.

In "licensed" restaurants you must order food with your alcoholic beverages and "licensed" lounges must have entertainment. Taverns and beverage rooms serve only beer by the bottle or on tap and frequently offer surprisingly tasty light meals.

HOW TO GET MARRIED IN NOVA SCOTIA: There is a five-day waiting period from the day you first apply for a license at the Registry of Marriage in the Halifax Town Hall. When you go to make your application bring along two witnesses (they must both be over 16 years of age); $20 Cdn; your birth certificate, and proof of your marital status. You must be 19 or have written parental consent. No blood or medical test is required. Your marriage ceremony will have to be performed by a clergyperson registered in Nova Scotia or by a judge of either the Family Court or County Court. To make specific arrangements and for additional information contact Mrs. Fogerty at 902/424-4373/4374. Either she or some one in her office will be very happy to help you sort out all the details. They are a delightfully cheerful group, eager to accommodate.

FOR FURTHER INFORMATION: Contact: **Tourism Nova Scotia,** 129 Commercial St., Portland, Maine 04101 (toll free 800/341-6096 nationwide; 800/492-0643 in Maine).

Also ask the tourism office to send you a captain's log book. If you don't get one before you arrive, be certain to pick one up at one of the local tourist bureaus in Nova Scotia. At each historic site you visit they will stamp your log book with a distinctive marker commemorating that specific site. It's a fun way to create a special collection of memories of your trip.

The **Nova Scotia Check In Service** is just possibly one of the very best and most efficient reservation and information services in the world. They can book all your reservations and confirm them for you. The telephone operators are very well informed, friendly, and more than eager to help. They are fully computerized, and from them you can get information on the weather, festivals, bus, train, and air schedules, ferry departure times, car rentals, hotels, motels, lodges, inns, campgrounds, or where to find that special quiet part of Nova Scotia to call all your own. Call toll free 800/341-6096 nationwide; 800/492-0643 in Maine; or write Check In, 1535 Dresden Row, Halifax, Nova Scotia B3J 2K3 Canada.

2. Halifax / Dartmouth

Haligonians, the 120,000 natives of Halifax, are blessed with a city of open spaces and beautiful parkland. Surrounded on three sides by saltwater and named the

"City of Trees," Halifax is the capital of the province and one of the oldest cities in Canada. Halifax Harbour is among the world's finest ice-free, deep-water natural harbors. It extends ten miles inland into the wide bowl of Bedford Basin and services over 3,500 vessels each year.

Founded in 1749 by Lord Edward Cornwallis and a band of 2,500 hearty Brits, Halifax was built to establish a British presence in the North Atlantic and to counterbalance the French Fort at Louisbourg, on Cape Breton Island. Subsequently, it served as a British naval base during both the American Revolution and the War of 1812. Today, Halifax is a charming sightseeing city, filled with special treats. On the front lawn of the library, around lunch time, you will encounter live entertainment, sometimes planned, sometimes spontaneous. Buy some snacks from the street vendors, spread out on the inviting lawn, and enjoy an impromptu picnic. If it gets too crowded, walk over to the Grande Parade on Barrington Street, where you can also enjoy a variety of free entertainments and delicious munchies from the pushcarts.

While you are at the Grande Parade you will see St. Paul's Church on the south side. It was built in 1749 and is the oldest structure in Halifax. Ask a native to help you locate the mysterious silhouette cast by a chink in the stained glass. On the opposite side of the Grande Parade is the city hall, built in 1890. It is a gem of Victorian architecture. A visit to Province House, oldest existing legislative building in Canada, on Hollis Street north of Prince Street, is also worthwhile. It is open year round and you can take a free guided tour during the week between 9 a.m. and 5 p.m. (no phone).

SHOPPING: There are three major shopping areas of interest in Halifax, each servicing different needs. The older, more established area is located along **Spring Garden Road.** Here the stores feature traditional wares, specializing in British imports. At **Historic Properties** and the **Barrington Inn Complex** you will find fine quality local crafts, pewter, top-of-the-line international manufactured goods, and **The Eskimo Gallery,** featuring artifacts, sculpture, and art works. The **Scotia Square Complex,** which is Halifax's main downtown shopping mall, features stores selling goods for your day-to-day needs.

ROMANTIC INTERLUDES: Several interesting sites are clustered in the downtown area, which extends from Lower Water Street to the Citadel and is bound by Cogswell to the north and Spring Garden Street to the south. The very best way to get around downtown is on foot, so park your car and get out your walking shoes.

The result of an extensive restoration program, **The Historic Properties** comprise 12 different buildings, some of which date to the early 1800s. Pick up a walking tour map at the tourist office located in the Old Red Store, which was once used for shipping operations. It will guide you to **Privateers Wharf** on Lower Water Street, where real pirates brought their booty for trade and storage and where the 143-foot schooner, the *Bluenose II,* docks just as ships tied up there over 200 years ago. Book passage on the *Bluenose II* for a two-hour cruise through Halifax Harbour and experience the thrill of traveling under full sail on an authentic tall ship. Enjoy the panoramic view of Halifax Harbour. About $10 per person (tel. 422-2678 or 424-5000). When you return, stop at the Clipper Cay Restaurant along side the wharf for a platter of fresh mussels or a steamed lobster before setting off to poke around the myriad of nautical craft shops, boutiques, galleries, and pubs.

Perhaps let one of Halifax's rickshaw drivers (they line up near Privateer Wharf and The Historic Properties) pull you through the cobbled streets. Head south to the Brewery Market (an actual brewery dating from 1820) where the **Maritime Museum of the Atlantic** is located in a restored 19th-century, well-stocked chandlery and dockside warehouse (1675 Lower Water St.; tel. 429-8210). Open all year, hours are 9:30 a.m. to 5:30 p.m. during the summer; until 8 p.m. on Tuesdays. Admission is free.

The full glory of the Golden Age of Sail is on display here, featuring scale models of vessels that plied the waters of Halifax Harbour. You can get a sense of their enormous size by standing near the actual figureheads, that were once proudly mounted on the prows of these elegant ships. Moored alongside the museum is the *Acadia*, a 900-ton hydrographic ship that charted the Labrador and Arctic coasts in the early part of this century. You can visit her during the summer months and get a taste of what life on board must have been like. Museum is open all year, but hours vary seasonally, so call for information (tel. 429-8210). Admission is free.

The star-shaped **Citadel** is a fortress located high on a hill overlooking the heart of the city and the harbor. Begun in 1749, the third and final version of the fortress was completed in the mid-1800s. Originally designed to house, feed, and arm an entire garrison, the fort was never attacked but nonetheless symbolized British imperial control in North America. There is an excellent **Army Museum** (tel. 422-5979 for the hours) offering a history of colonial warfare together with a collection of armor, firearms, uniforms, and other military memorabilia. You can visit garrison cells, restored ramparts, powder magazines, and a musketry gallery. Open all year; small admission fee in season.

In the very best British military tradition they still fire the noon-day gun from the top of the Citadel every day promptly at high noon. There is also a 50-minute sight and sound show, *The Tides of History*, that relates the city's story (a small admission is charged).

In addition to seeing the Citadel and surrounding grounds and historic buildings during the day, you should return at night for a romantic candlelight tour. Try to partake of one of the special cavalier dinner programs. Remember, you will need to book in advance. During the day visit, stop at the Tea Shop located at the fort and ask any of the Friends of the Citadel for details and reservations (tel. 902/425-3923).

Nestled just south of the Citadel, between Sackville Street and Spring Garden Road, are the **Public Gardens,** 18 acres of Victorian gardens originally designed in 1753. The gingerbread bandstand with its domed red roof, surrounded by velvet lawns and a riot of colorful flowerbeds, is a peaceful retreat.

Located at the entrance to Halifax Harbour, **McNabs Island,** an irregular chunk of land three miles long and ¾-mile wide, sits between the eastern passage and the main shipping passage into Halifax Harbour. Twice daily, **Harbour Island Tours** (tel. 422-9523) sets sail from the Maritime Museum of the Atlantic on a cruise of the harbor and a two-hour walking tour of McNabs Island, including a visit to Fort McNab (established between 1888 and 1892).

On the southernmost tip of the Halifax peninsula, surrounded on three sides by saltwater, is **Point Pleasant Park,** 186 acres of lush parkland open to pedestrians only. Bring along a picnic lunch and head for Black Rock Beach, where you can watch the passing ships, some only a few hundred yards away. On your stroll back through the park, look for the beautiful Scottish heather that grows wild here, the only place in North America that it does. Legend has it the seeds were shaken out of mattresses used by sailors newly arrived at the province. The park is open all year. Should you wish, you can drive to Black Rock Beach, where there is plenty of parking. However, you will still have to walk through the park, since cars are forbidden.

Two toll suspension bridges span The Narrows between Halifax Harbour and Bedford Basin, connecting Halifax to its sister city, **Dartmouth** (population 63,667). A delightful and inexpensive (25¢) way to get to Dartmouth is on the ferry that leaves from the George Street Terminal in Halifax (tel. 466-2215 for the schedule). As an added benefit you get a beautiful view of the harbor and a ride on the oldest continuing saltwater ferry system in North America; the first ferry made the crossing in 1752.

Founded in 1750, Dartmouth was once a whaling community. To see how these early settlers lived visit the Quaker Whaler's House at 57–59 Ochterloney Street, which was built in 1785 and is the oldest remaining house in town. Equally charming and from the Victorian era is the Evergreen House (26 Newcastle St.). There is a delightful main street shopping area near the ferry terminal and the gigantic MicMac Mall (tel. 466-2056), the largest shopping mall east of Montreal, offers over 150 stores in which to browse.

There are 23 lakes within Dartmouth's city limits and the two largest, Lake Mic-Mac and Lake Banook, are world-class quality for canoeing and Windsurfing. You can also water ski on Lake MicMac.

HONEYMOON HOTELS AND HIDEAWAYS: Halifax offers a wide range of honeymoon nests, from large hotels to intimate bed-and-breakfast inns.

Expensive

The **Delta Barrington,** 1875 Barrington St., Halifax, Nova Scotia B3J 3L6 (tel. 902/429-7410; reservations: toll free 800/268-1133), is open all year. Upon your arrival at this restored granite hostelry near Privateers Wharf you will be served a perfectly chilled glass of champagne. In your room you will find personalized matches, chocolates, and fluffy, luxurious bathrobes to be used during your stay (sorry, you can't take them with you). There are 200 rooms; an indoor heated pool; saunas; and a whirlpool. The dining room is licensed; there is also a cocktail lounge with a piano bar. Honeymoon package (BP): Two days/one night: $123.75 per couple.

The **Lord Nelson Hotel,** 1515 South Park St., Halifax, Nova Scotia B3J 2T3 (tel. 902/423-6331) is open all year. A local landmark, it is located opposite the beautiful Public Gardens. Your special honeymoon package puts you in a deluxe two-room suite with a king-size bed. Upon arrival you will discover a chilled bottle of sparkling wine with a single perfect rose. On your first morning you will be served a special honeymoon breakfast. Your suite will be stocked with magazines, a city map, and homemade chocolates. As part of the special package you will receive a discount at Avis and free parking. There is a licensed dining room open from 6:30 to 10 p.m. and a very popular lounge for a relaxing apéritif in the corner and live entertainment. Honeymoon package: Two days/one night: $120 per couple. Includes all taxes and gratuities.

The **Prince George Hotel,** 1725 Market St., Halifax, Nova Scotia B3J 3N9 (tel. 902/425-1986; reservations: toll free 800/565-1567). Open all year. This new and luxurious facility has 217 rooms and features the works: heated indoor pool, sauna, whirlpool, exercise rooms, sun deck, color cable television, air conditioning, two phones, and a mini-bar in your room. The management will roll out the VIP carpet for honeymooners. Rooms are contemporary, with floral-print fabrics done in soft tones of pink and blue; accommodations on the upper stories have views of the Citadel or harbor. Honeymoon accommodations will be upgraded to a one-bedroom suite if it is available. There is a fine licensed restaurant and café, plus pub serving light meals and a cocktail lounge with live entertainment. Honeymoon package: Two days/one night (BP): $112.50 per couple. Includes a champagne breakfast.

Moderate

Chateau Halifax, Scotia Square, Halifax, Nova Scotia B3J 1P2 (tel. 902/425-6700; reservations: toll free 800/268-9411). Open all year. Attached to Scotia Square and the indoor shopping complex, there are over 300 rooms in this hotel. Despite its size, they love to pamper honeymooners, so check on special honeymoon packages, as they vary with the time of year. You will have a heated indoor swimming pool and sauna at your disposal. The Crown Cafe is open from 6:30 a.m. to 11 p.m. and offers better than standard hotel dining, and the entertainment in Sam Slick's Lounge is always good and fun. Honeymoon package: Varies. Ask what they are offering for a special honeymoon package when you book. Standard rate (EP): $66 to $70 per couple per night.

Halifax Sheraton, 1919 Upper Water St., Halifax, Nova Scotia B3J 3J5 (tel.

902/421-1700; reservations: toll free 800/325-3535). Open all year. Not a typical big chain hotel by any means. This is an elegant harborfront deluxe hotel overlooking Historic Properties that guarantees you all the amenities. Your special honeymoon package room will have a dazzling harbor view and, at your request, a king-size bed. There is an indoor pool, sauna, whirlpool, exercise room, licensed sun deck, and indoor parking facility. And, if you arrive by private yacht, there is docking space. The Cafe Maritime serves a fine selection of local seafood. There is a harborfront lounge and terrace and a quiet bar in the lobby. Honeymoon package: Two days/one night (EP): $93.75 per couple. Includes a harborview room and a VIP amenity package, with nightly turndown service, chocolate truffles, and champagne.

The Apple Basket, 1756 Robie St., Halifax, Nova Scotia B3H 3E9 (tel. 902/429-3019). Open all year. A charming bed-and-breakfast in a beautiful Victorian home located in the heart of the city. Mrs. Michael Crowe loves to fuss over newlyweds. A lovely champagne breakfast served on a silver tray in your comfortable pineapple four-poster bed is included in your special honeymoon package. There are only three rooms available, and you will have to share a bath, but the special atmosphere and romantic coziness will compensate for that minor inconvenience. Honeymoon package: Two days/one night (EP): $37.50 per couple. This is a nonsmoking accommodation.

The Nova Scotian Hotel, 1181 Hollis St., Halifax, Nova Scotia B3H 2P6 (tel. 902/423-7231). Open all year. Located right in the middle of all the city's hustle and bustle, the Nova Scotian has a Grand Hotel feel. There are two wings. Rooms in the original wing are larger and have nice big windows that open wide to allow breezes to circulate. They are not air-conditioned, although rooms in the newer section are. All have been refurbished recently. Views overlook the harbor or city, and they offer free guest parking. A special treat here is the restaurant, L'Evangeline, which glows with romantic ambience and is well worth its moderate to expensive price ticket. There are 314 rooms, each equipped with free color cable TV. Honeymoon package: None. Rates (EP): $54.75 to $59.25 per couple per night for a room; $93.75 for a harborview suite (ask for a suite on a higher floor).

ROMANTIC RESTAURANTS AND NIGHT SPOTS: There is a staggering variety of eateries in Halifax. Most places ask that you dress appropriately for dinner, and it is wise to inquire if a jacket or jacket and tie are required when you book reservations (reservations recommended).

Set in an 1880s Victorian red-brick townhouse, **Fat Frank's,** 5411 Spring Garden Rd. (tel. 423-6618), is the most elegant, sumptuous restaurant in Halifax. Antiques and grace the high ceilinged rooms, and some original Gainsborough paintings hang on the walls. Fine Spode china and crystal set the mood for the haute cuisine that follows. The restaurant's owner, Fat Frank began his restaurant career under the tutelage of Henri Soulé at the renowned Le Pavillon in New York, and he adopted as his motto: "Do what you do best—and the best way you can." The cuisine lives up to these high standards. Although the menu changes every two weeks to take advantage of fresh seasonal delicacies, specialties generally include sweetbreads, guinea fowl, fresh salmon, and poultry dishes, as well as lamb, beef, or veal. They also do superb, homemade pastas. Appetizer prices, $3.50 to $6.50; entrées from $12.75 to $18.50. For dessert, try a chocoholic's dream come true—"Death by Chocolate," a rich chocolate pavé in a sauce anglaise. Desserts run $3 to $5.25. The restaurant is very small (only seating 32 people) and intimate, and the service is very discreet: prime ministers, princes, and the rock star Sting have enjoyed quiet dinners here. Well worth it. Open Monday through Friday for lunch and dinner; dinner only on Saturday; closed Sunday.

Through the floor-to-ceiling windows of **Clipper Cay,** Historic Properties and Privateers Wharf (tel. 423-6818) located right on the wharf, you'll have four-star views of the courtyards or Halifax Harbour. The ambience is softly romantic, with pink velvet wingback chairs, soft lights, and classic white china edged with gold. Fish and seafood are the specialties here. Start your meal with a shrimp cocktail, solomon gundy (raw herring marinated in spiced vinegar), the house pâté, or oysters (priced $3 to $6.50). As your entrée, you'll have a hard time deciding among the fresh catch of the day, which might include a fillet of salmon, scallops simmered in herb butter with white wine, or jumbo shrimp (all priced around $14.25). This is also the place for lobster, which will be in the $20 range, depending on market prices. Open for lunch and dinner, Monday through Friday; dinner only, Saturday and Sunday. They also have a downstairs lounge and terrace, serving light lunches as well as Sunday brunch.

Located in the city's oldest school building, where Anna Leonowens (of Anna and the King of Siam) founded her school, **Five Fishermen,** 1740 Argyle St. (tel. 422-4421) has a mellow, stained-glass-and-brass-rail ambience. Appetizers include a richly satisfying chowder, smoked salmon, and fresh oysters on the half shell, all around $3. Entrées spotlight fresh fish such as halibut and salmon ($10 to $15), as well as lobster (about $18 to $20). Another favorite is the steak-and-seafood combination platter, which pairs a prime cut with shrimp, lobster, or scallops ($17.50). Treat yourselves to their award-winning toasted almond cheesecake for dessert ($3). Open for dinner only.

The nautical decor, complete with varnished wood floors and lobster tanks, perfectly complements the downtown waterfront locale of **McKelvies,** corner of Bedford Row and Prince Streets (tel. 421-6161). Gigantic arched windows look out over some of Halifax's fine restored buildings. Jumpin' fresh seafood is the specialty here. Favorite appetizers include the chowder, seafood antipasto, or the two-fish pâté, priced $3.50 to $5.25. Fish entrées include the salmon Wellington, Cajun halibut (with lots of spices), or a classic seafood vol-au-vent (served in a puffed pastry), all in the $11 range. And, of course, there are succulent fresh lobsters, priced around $12. One of the nicest things about this friendly restaurant is the fact that they'll cook up your fish any way you like it—sautéed, broiled, or in a sauce. All the luscious desserts are made on the premises under the supervision of their Belgian pastry chef, including a rich cheesecake. Memorable parfaits as well ($2.25). Open for lunch and dinner. For one of the best deals in town, come by for an early dinner between 4:30 and 6:30 p.m. in the evenings—you can get two entrées for the price of one.

The sophisticated surroundings of **O'Carroll's,** 1860 Upper Water St., across from the Historic Properties (tel. 423-4405), feature lots of hanging plants, stained glass, some brick walls, plus other antiques, wood-paneled walls that come from the old Neptune Theatre. Especially at dinner time, when candles cast soft light on the tables, you'll enjoy the water view. Start off your dinner with some succulent Belon oysters, Atlantic salmon, the house pâté, or solomon gundy ($3.75 to $5.25). For dinner, choose a fresh lobster, served either Thermidor style or boiled ($16.50). Entrées also include shrimp scampi, poached filet of halibut, or steak in a peppercorn sauce, all priced around $13. All the desserts earn rave reviews, especially the chocolate amaretto cheesecake or hazelnut cheesecake ($3), gingerbread with hard sauce, and apple pie. O'Carroll's also has an oyster bar, featuring a piano player from 5 to 10 p.m., and live Irish folk music from 10 p.m. on.

When you want to go out at night, Halifax has surprising variety. **The Palace,** 1720 Brunswick (tel. 423-7154), across from the Citadel, features live jazz and rock music. Very popular with the enthusiastic crowds from the local university. **The Misty Moon,** 2219 Gottinger (tel. 422-5871) is open seven days a week until 3 a.m.; features live rock music. Admission charge varies according to who the featured performers are that evening. At **Gingers,** on Hollis Street near the Train Station (tel. 423-5660) you can drop by to hear live folk, blues, and bluegrass music, as well as some traditional maritime tunes. Every Tuesday is amateur night. **Brandy's,** 1712 Market St. (tel. 425-8357), is a good choice if you want to dance the night away. **The Cave,** 5244 Blower St. (tel. 429-3551). After you've closed down just about every place in town, head on over to this charming bistro. It serves up sensational desserts and is especially well known for its cheesecake.

3. Nova Scotia's Trails

Touring the scenic province is easy, thanks to a system of eight well-marked sightseeing "trails" for cars that wend their way along Nova Scotia's most spectacular sea coast and byways. For our purposes we have tried to arrange trips that could be accomplished easily within five to seven days. We are assuming that Halifax will be your starting point.

Tour #1: Go south along the Lighthouse Route to Yarmouth (where the ferries from Maine land, so if you come by ferry this would be your starting point), then north, along the Evangeline Trail back to Bedford and Halifax. Tour #2: Leaves Halifax through Dartmouth and heads north to Cape Breton Island, spending most of your time on the Coast Trail. If you do not tour by car, you can spend time in Halifax and fly to Sydney on Cape Breton Island to see the Cabot Trail, which is the most popular spot for visitors. A short, time-saving trip would cover Halifax and Peggy's Cove, then go across to the Glosscap Trail.

THE LIGHTHOUSE ROUTE: Leaving Halifax and following the south shore on the Atlantic Ocean, the Lighthouse Route courses along a wild, almost desolate coastline piled high with huge boulders; past long stretches of sand dunes and beaches; and, through fishing villages whose very existence depends on the sea.

There are 13 lighthouses guarding this 227-mile route between Halifax and Yarmouth. The south shore has a rich, proud maritime history along with a better-than-fair share of pirates, privateers, and smugglers.

Romantic Interludes

Peggy's Cove is a picture-perfect fishing village that has less than 100 residents, most of whom really are fishermen. The barren landscape is punctuated by gigantic rocks and the magnificent lighthouse, which is no longer in operation but serves as the post office. Because of its location (only 27 miles south of Halifax), this early-19th-century cove has become one of the province's showpieces. The piers piled high with lobster pots; the white steepled church and old pastel houses; the fishermen's shacks built on stilts in the harbor, all make this an artist's and photographer's mecca.

With over 350 islands scattered around, it's easy to understand why **Mahone Bay** was a haven for pirates and rum-runners with all its secret coves and tiny clumps of land. In Chester, there is a ferry that makes a run out to Big and Little Tancook Islands. Ask in town for the schedule, which changes daily. The five-mile trip is fascinating, and poking around Big Tancook Island takes you back in time to when the likes of Captain Kidd ruled the waves.

Off the western Shore of Mahone Bay is Oak Island. It is said that Captain Kidd buried most of his treasure here. Another legend has it that in June 1813, an American privateer, *Young Teazer,* was chased into the bay by a British man-of-war. There was a young British deserter aboard. Seeing no escape route, and knowing he would be hanged if he was captured, he threw a torch into the powder magazine and blew the works sky high. Locals claim that every year on the anniversary of the explosion, an apparition known as *The Fireship* can be seen drifting in the bay.

We told you this was pirate country and you will find that **Lunenberg,** founded in 1753, was also home to those legendary rascals. Situated on a hilly peninsula, Lunenberg has "front" and "back" harbors. The original *Bluenose* was built here in 1921; the replica, which you can sail upon in Halifax Harbour, was built here in 1963. The Fisheries Museum of the Atlantic (tel. 634-4794) has an aquarium featuring local sea life and there are two fishing boats open for your inspection. Here you will see the *Theresa E. Connor,* which was the last Lunenburg schooner to fish the Grand Banks with dories. You'll also see *The Cape Sable*, a dragger, and one of the original rum-runners. Should you be inclined to capture the real feeling of days of yore, give Dave Wilkie a call (tel. 543-9317) and ask him to arrange a schooner tour.

Located not too far south of Lunenberg, **The Ovens** (tel. 766-4621 off-season; 766-4230 in season), are a series of large caverns carved out of the rocky cliffs by the wave action of the ocean. On June 13, 1861, gold was discovered here and many of the old pits and tunnels remain open for exploration.

Continuing on, stop for a spot of high tea at the Tea Cup in **Shelbourne**. They serve a traditional repast, including Devon cream, fresh biscuits, and homemade jams. After your rest, take a walking tour of this small town, originally founded in 1783 by Loyalists fleeing the American Revolution. A visit to Ross Thompson House is a journey back in time to a fully stocked Loyalist store, the only survivor of its kind. At the John Williams Dory Shop you can still see the old wooden dories made in the traditional way.

The Seven Pubnicos was first settled by the Acadians in 1653, making it one of the oldest Acadian communities in the province. Today some of the settlements speak English; others still speak French. A special point of interest in Pubnico Harbour: This is a deep-channel harbor. About 30 feet down is Habitat-Subsea City, a precast concrete underwater habitat for scuba divers. It weighs 22.5 tons and is a seven-by-seven-foot dwelling anchored 30 feet under the surface of the harbor. If you are interested and you qualify, contact Doug Wilson (tel. 762-2059) for a visit.

Located in Arcadia, **The House of Four People,** was built on the original site of an ancient MicMac Indian camping grounds. It began as a French structure, then was added onto by the English and Dutch owners (consecutively). It was in this amalgam that Paul Revere took his mark degree in freemasonry.

Just before entering Yarmouth, stop at **Cheboque Point** lookout, famous for a brilliant display of lupine flowers during the summer months, and a spectacular view of the ocean and Tusket Island all year round. From May through August, the vain and showy shorebird called a whitewing (or Willet) prances about in great numbers, happy for all your attention.

Honeymoon Hotels and Hideaways

Whether you're looking for charm or convenience, you'll find many places to overnight along the Route.

Moderate: Best Western Oak Island Inn and Marina, Western Shore (between Mahone Bay and Chester), Lunenberg County, Nova Scotia B0J 3M0 (tel. 902/627-2600; reservations: toll free 800/528-1234). Open all year; off-season rates apply October 16 to June 15. This is a 70-unit romantic hideaway by the sea that offers breathtaking sunsets and quiet moonlight strolls along a private beach. The modern accommodations are located in a three-story building. An unhurried resort, it offers, if you want to participate, a full range of organized and not-so-organized activities. You have full use of all the facilities: a heated indoor pool; sauna; and tennis courts. Sailboat rentals or deep-sea fishing charters can be arranged. The licensed dining room, of course, specializes in seafood. Honeymoon packages: Two days / one night (BP): $71.25 per couple. Includes a deluxe waterfront room overlooking Oak Island (you are not actually staying on the island), breakfast, and a bottle of local vintage wine.

Best Western Bridgewater Motor Inn, 35 High St., Bridgewater, Nova Scotia B4V 1V8 (tel. 902/543-8171; reservations: toll free 800/528-1234). Open all year; off-season rates apply from October 16 through June 15. There are 47 rooms in these two-story buildings, and the main attraction is the genuine down-home Nova Scotian hospitality. The inn is located near the Wile Cording Mill on Victoria Road, a mill that dates from 1869 and still has the original machinery. All rooms have contemporary furnishings and a color TV. There are two excellent dining rooms, which are licensed.

There is also a lounge with entertainment; a heated indoor pool; sauna; and hot tub. Honeymoon package: Two days / one night: $63.75 per couple. Includes a bottle of wine and breakfast.

White Point Beach Lodge, White Point Beach at Hunts Point near Liverpool, P.O. Box 9000, Queens County, Nova Scotia B0T 1K0 (tel. 902/354-3177; reservations: toll free 800/565-5068). Open all year. The 300-acre grounds include an ocean beach, freshwater lake (perfect for canoeing), a heated pool, golf course, tennis courts, and boating facilities. Along the ¾-mile beach there is some of the best shell and driftwood hunting in Nova Scotia. There are 47 rooms, which all have patios that open out onto decks with wonderful views; and there are also 43 cottages that have living rooms with working fireplaces and one to three bedrooms. Host Doug Fawthrop organizes beach parties, with lobster boils and the works. Honeymoon package: Four days / three nights (EP): $202.50 to $221.25 per couple. Includes your choice of a cottage or a room, champagne, fresh-cut flowers; welcoming fruit basket; lobster dinner and glass of wine; choice of complimentary horseback riding or bike package; plus use of all the facilities except the golf course, which is extra.

Inexpensive: The Mahone Bay Inn, 680 Main St., Mahone Bay, P.O. Box 550, Nova Scotia B0J 2E0 (tel. 902/624-8078). Open all year. A charming bed-and-breakfast, meticulously restored by Esther and Gordon Bryant, this Victorian house was originally owned and built by a sea captain. There are five rooms (only one has a private bath) and the ones in front look out to sea. They serve a wonderful hearty breakfast of sausages, eggs, and freshly baked muffins. Bicycles, cross-country skis available for rental. There is also a sauna. Rates (BP): $30 per couple per night.

Romantic Restaurants

Because some of the accommodations are secluded, you'll probably take some meals at your hotel. The following places are also well worth a detour.

Moderate: Constructed in 1805, **Zwicker's Inn,** Mahone Bay (tel. 624-8045); occupies a charming "four-square"-style Georgian building, so named because it has four rooms on its main level. Mussel dishes are their specialty—the tender mollusks come practically from just outside their front door. Try them in the savory mussel soup, rich with cream (about $3). At lunchtime, they serve tasty light fare, such as a soup and sandwich, or soup and salad, for $4 each. They also have fish and seafood entrées priced from $5.25 to $6.75. At dinner, start off with one of the fine chowders, oysters, smoked salmon, or soused shrimp, served in a sweet-and-sour mayonnaise ($1.75 to $3.20). Entrées include a seafood casserole, poached halibut, oven-roasted lamb shank, steak, or their own "Heavenly Chicken," chicken breast simmered with white wine, mushrooms, shallots, and sour cream ($7 to $9). Zwicker's Inn is also known for their homemade German-style noodles. For dessert, top choices are the homemade ice cream, chocolate ambrosia (chocolate ice cream slathered in orange whipped-cream mousse), fresh tarts, and the Martha Washington raisin-and-honey cakes. Open all year.

Overlooking the water, **Dublin Bay House,** Hwy. 331 at Dublin Shore, near Lunenberg (tel. 688-2751) has a contemporary feel, with oak beams and big tables. The restaurant is owned by "Bell" and Mary Elizabeth Voegelin, who care passionately about serving their guests the freshest food, expertly prepared. For starters, sample one of the hot appetizers that change daily—hali-bits (halibut tidbits), shark bites (your chance to avenge yourself against *Jaws*), or swordfish snacks, all served with tartar sauce. They also do an excellent solomon gundy, artfully arranged on lettuce with onions and tart apples. A choice of soups comes with the entrées and depending on what's in season, selections might include cream of leek, green split-pea, or sorrel-pinto bean soup. Fresh bread baked on the premises accompanies the meal—dark rye, sour rye—even homemade croutons. The roster of entrées spotlights the bounty of the sea: broiled halibut topped with crab mousse, scallops (served sautéed, Newburgh, or au gratin), or a sublime lobster Newburgh that only uses lobster tail and claw meat. Priced about $9.75 to $11.50. Steak lovers will opt for the aged 1⅛-inch-thick sirloin steak, served either broiled or prepared tableside as steak Diane (priced $12.50 to $15). All entrées are garnished with more garden-fresh vegetables. The excellent wine list deserves special praise for its reasonable prices. For dessert, try one of the frankly decadent homemade ice creams and sherbets, or chocolate mousse, with home-baked ladyfingers topped with shaved chocolate. Open for dinner only; closed Mondays.

Inexpensive: The **Dutch Oven,** in Chester (tel. 275-5241) serves fresh natural food and plenty of it. Many of the breads are homemade, including the cinnamon buns, bran muffins, and the whole-wheat bread used for many of the sandwiches, such as a Halvarti cheese and alfalfa-sprout sandwich, or a smoked ham sandwich, priced around $3. But the real reason for coming here are the home-baked desserts, such as black-forest cake or a mocha torte ($2). Open from 8:30 a.m. to 5:30 p.m.

Don't expect anything fancy—**The Blarney Stone,** Hwy. 103 in Hebbs Cross, near Bridgewater (tel. 543-6229), is a real, family-style restaurant. But local residents highly recommend it for its terrific seafood at very moderate prices. Try a satisfying seafood chowder brimming with scallops, haddock, and lobster; or plates of halibut or scallops, served as you like 'em ($4.50 to $5). Desserts are simple, but simply delicious—a big slice of apple or rhubarb pie, for only $1. Open for breakfast, lunch, and dinner all year.

THE EVANGELINE TRAIL: The legendary romance and stirring history of the Evangeline Trail is captured in Longfellow's epic poem, *Evangeline,* recalling a girl's frantic and futile search for her lost lover, Gabriel, and immortalizing the tragic expulsion of the Acadians from their land in 1755.

The trail meanders north from Yarmouth to Halifax, taking you back in time to old Acadia. From the rocky shoreline cliffs and pebble beaches of the chilly Bay of Fundy, into the rich coastal forests and on to the fertile red earth of the lush Annapolis Valley, the trail travels through a land of picturebook settings.

Yarmouth (population 10,000), a harbor town, was first settled in 1761 and remains today the center of Nova Scotia's French-speaking community along this section of coast. The province's largest seaport west of Halifax, it has been dubbed the "gateway to Nova Scotia."

Before leaving Yarmouth you will want to poke around the center of town, where you can see the Runic Stone on Main Street, at the door to the Isaac Walton Memorial. It is believed that the cryptic writing on the stone was carved by Vikings who landed here several thousand years ago. Make a stop at the Firemen's Museum, also on Main Street, where you can see a collection of beautiful, early-20th-century fire engines (there is a 35¢ admission fee). And if you happen to be in town on a Saturday morning during April through December, you should experience the traditional farmers market displaying local produce and crafts.

Romantic Interludes

Begin your journey with a stop at the historic **Yarmouth Lighthouse** located at the very tip of Cape Fourchu (named by Champlain in 1640). The lighthouse, built in 1840, is accessible by car. A network of paths leads to the Lief Ericson Picnic Park, which overlooks an expanse of sea-washed rocks.

Continuing on the trail to Hebron you enter the **Lupine Trail** where, beginning in June, wild lupines blossom in a dazzling display of white, pinks, and blues.

The quaint drawbridge in the picture perfect fishing village of **Sanford** is said to be the smallest one in the maritime provinces. The scenery here has inspired many artists and photographers. When you pass through **Clare** you begin a drive on the longest Main Street in the world. Twenty-seven picturesque villages and towns are clustered around this section of Rte. 1 and 14 of them actually straddle the road.

At **Church Point** the horizon is dominated by the spire of St. Mary's Church, the tallest and largest wooden church in North America. The spire is a dizzying 185 feet tall and visibly sways in the buffeting winds sweeping off St. Mary's Bay.

The **Digby** harbor bristles with the sparkling white-and-blue boats of the world's largest scallop-fishing fleet. Besides the delicious and world-renown Digby scallops, you should try tasting some famous "Digby chicken," which is locally smoked herring. A side trip to Gilbert Cove Lighthouse, 12 miles east of Digby, is a prime seacoast setting for a lazy picnic.

The Annapolis Royal was the site of the original 1605 French settlement. At Fort Anne National Historic Park, located in the center of town, you can stroll the grassy earthworks of the original 18th-century fort, the most fought-over scrap of land in Canada. An exact replica of Champlain's original 1605 habitation has been built at the Port Royal Habitat National Historic Park.

Lower St. George Street is being restored to resemble the Victorian enclave it was in 1878. There is a pleasant boardwalk here along the Annapolis Basin, where the Grand Union flag still flies, proudly combining the English Cross of St. George and the Scottish Cross of St. Andrew.

The tides of the **Bay of Fundy** are the highest (and the lowest) recorded anywhere in the world, often reaching a difference of over 50 feet. At the Annapolis Tidal Power Project, where they are trying to harness the power of these waters, the tides rush in with such astounding force they actually reverse the course of the river. The causeway over the dam offers an excellent view of this phenomenon.

Grand Pré National Historic Park is located at the east end of the Annapolis Valley, north of Wolfville; this great meadow was the rich farmland reclaimed from the sea by a series of dikes built by the Acadians. A rough-cut stone church, built in the French style, houses Acadian cultural and historical displays. The steeply pitched roof crowned by a delicate steeple is a splendid background for the beautiful and poignant statue of Evangeline, sculpted by Philippe Hébert, which stands outside the church.

Honeymoon Hotels and Hideaways

Along your route, you can overnight at everything from grand old resorts to casual country inns.

Expensive: The Pines Resort Hotel, Shore Road, P.O. Box 70, Digby, Nova Scotia B0V 1A0 (tel. 902/245-2511). Open June to mid-October. A stone-and-cement castle built in a French Norman design, the Pines occupies a 300-acre parkland of landscaped lawns, flower gardens, and woodland. Owned and operated by the province of Nova Scotia, this luxurious resort in the grand style offers a wide variety of activities, from a dip in the outdoor heated pool to a walk on the pebbled shoreline where you can watch the fishermen at their work. Twice daily you can also witness the incredible Bay of Fundy tides, which average about 30 feet, and sometimes reach as high as 50 feet. There is a championship 18-hole golf course nearby and the inn can assist you in arranging activities ranging from a spectacular airplane excursion over the Annapolis Valley to a sailing charter to an adventure scalloping. Morning coffee and afternoon tea are served on the veranda overlooking the village and Annapolis Basin. There are 89 rooms in the main building and 30 cottages with one to three bedrooms. The elegant dining room has fine service, is licensed, and specializes in Digby scallops complimented by local wine. There is live entertainment, dancing, and you are asked to observe dress regulations. Honeymoon package: Two days / one night (Modified AP): $172 per couple. Includes two lobster dinners, green fees, tennis, swimming, fresh fruit, flowers, chocolate truffles, a personal gift, taxes, and gratuities.

Mountain Gap Inn, P.O. Box 40, Smiths Cove, Nova Scotia B0S 1S0 (tel. 902/245-2277). Open June 1 to October 15. A 45-acre seaside resort with a 1,000-foot tidal beach. Even though this is a large motel with 100 rooms and 13 cottages, your hostess, Anne Goddard, makes it seem cozy with her personal touches such as the fresh-cut flowers and chilled wine waiting in your room. The dining room is licensed and specializes in (guess what!) local seafood. There is a pool and tennis court and magnificent views of the Annapolis Basin. Honeymoon package: Two days / one night: $116.25 per couple. Includes dinner.

Moderate: The Harbour View Inn, P.O. Box 35, Smiths Cove, Nova Scotia B05 1S0 (tel. 902/245-5686 in summer; 416/445-1042 in winter). Open June 15 to September 15. A small, charming inn with nine rooms and one two-room suite known as the "Honeymoon Suite" overlooking the Annapolis Basin. There is swimming, tennis, and an excellent beach for clam digging. The dining room is licensed and specializes in Digby scallops, lobster, local garden-fresh vegetables and homemade bread. They have a good selection of local estate wine and either Mona or Philip Webb, the owners, will be happy to help you make the perfect choice to compliment your dinner. Honeymoon package: Two days / one night (MAP): $75 per couple.

The Olde (1890) Village Inn, Sandy Cove on Digby Neck, Nova Scotia B0V 1E0 (tel. 902/834-2202). Open May to October 15. Whether you're interested in some whale watching or bird watching, Dixie and Bob Van, your hosts, can pack a picnic for you and give you directions to the best sites. There are eight cozy rooms in the inn, some with Franklin stoves, and six rooms in the annex. You will have to share baths. Canoeing and sailing expeditions can be arranged as well as fishing trips. Honeymoon package: Three days / two nights (MAP): $180 per couple. Includes complimentary champagne on arrival and a picnic basket for a luncheon.

The Garrison House Inn, 350 St. George St., Annapolis Royal, Nova Scotia B0S 1A0 (tel. 902/532-5750). Open May through December. Anna and Patrick Redgrave have lovingly restored their inn, which was originally opened in 1854 as the Temperance Hotel. Located across from Fort Anne, it sits right in the center of an area rich in Canadian history. There are quiet little nooks and cozy corners everywhere. The fresh-cut flowers, native-patterned quilts on the beds, and hand-hooked rugs on the wide-planked floors blend to create a warm, intimate atmosphere. There is a lovely, licensed dining room that specializes in candlelight gourmet meals. Anna bakes the muffins for breakfast and the scones for high tea. There are five rooms with private baths and two rooms that share a bath. You might want to rent bicycles from the Redgraves, since this is an excellent way to explore the area. Honeymoon package: Two days / one night (MAP): $81.75 per couple. Includes dinner with wine, room with private bath, and breakfast in bed.

Milford House, South Milford, R.R. 4., Annapolis Royal, Nova Scotia B0S 1A0 (tel. 902/532-2617). Open mid-June to mid-September; two cottages are available year-round. Situated in a 600-acre preserve of lakes, streams, and woodland, this is a special haven that has people coming back year after year. As early as the 1860s travelers began stopping here to enjoy the peace and tranquility, the superb trout fishing, good moose hunting, and the simple pleasures of canoeing on a mirror-still lake or sitting in front of a crackling fireplace. In 1969, a band of devoted patrons organized a company dedicated to preserving this untouched property. Activity centers on the main lodge, a large white building furnished with lots of country antiques and the occasional moosehead. There is a large dining room that serves up enormous farm-kitchen breakfasts and generous-portioned dinners. Your muffins come hot from the oven, your fish is fresh from the stream, and your vegetables have been just pulled from the garden outside. You will be staying in one of the 27 cottages located within walking distance of the lodge along a tree-lined shore. The cottages are spaced far enough away from each other to ensure privacy; have old stone fireplaces in the living room, which are stocked with wood; a bathroom; a minimum of two bedrooms; maid service; and, bare-essential cooking facilities (enough to make your morning coffee or afternoon tea). This is a very special place to be; a wilderness setting of incomparable beauty. Honeymoon package: None. Rates (MAP): $78.40 per couple per night.

Sea Haven Guest House, Clementsport, R.R. 2., Annapolis Royal, Nova Scotia B0S 1A0 (tel. 902/638-8881; toll free 800/561-7105). Open mid-June through mid-October. Originally part of a 1750 land grant from the King of England, this New England–style colonial house is perched on a rise overlooking Annapolis Basin and is surrounded by 24 acres of flower, vegetable, and herb gardens. There are three sunny, comfortable rooms with private tiled baths. The house is furnished with an eclectic blend of traditional pieces, family heirlooms, and objects collected during innkeepers Patricia and Tom Edwards' travels through the Far East. Candlelight dinners are served in an elegant dining room set with crisp linens and antique china and silver. A full breakfast is available. The private beach is a perfect setting for a clambake, a refreshing swim, or a lazy nap in the afternoon sun. Honeymoon package: Three days / two nights (MAP): $138.75 per couple. Includes one champagne breakfast in your room, two dinners with wine, and a real old-fashioned English-style picnic lunch, served in a wicker basket and with silver goblets.

Inexpensive: The Manor Inn and Lakeside Motel, Hwy. 1, P.O. Box 56, Hebron, Yarmouth County, Nova Scotia B0W 1X0 (tel. 902/742-2487). Open May through December. Located four miles north of Yarmouth, the Manor Inn was built in the early part of this century. Surrounded by nine acres of flower beds and lawns, the grounds feature a beautiful rose garden. The white clapboard, colonial-style mansion is noted for its interior woodwork and splendid staircase built of South American mahogany. The two dining rooms have fireplaces decorated with Wedgwood-carved mantelpieces and feature local lobster, fresh seafood, and home-baked pies. In the concealed cocktail lounge, the original owner used to store his whiskey and serve friends during Prohibition.

There is nightly entertainment and dancing in the public lounge. The property has 29 rooms—six of which are located in the original building. There is good swimming at nearby beaches; excellent opportunities for boating and deep-sea fishing, and the area abounds with fields of wild flowers and berries. Honeymoon package: None. Rates (EP): in the Inn; $55.50 to $68.25 per couple per night; in the motel; $49.50 per couple per night.

Bread and Roses Country Inn, 82 Victoria St., P.O. Box 177, Annapolis Royal, Nova Scotia B0S 1A0 (tel. 902/532-5727). Open all year. A restored Victorian mansion built in 1885, this small inn is "dedicated to the concept that people require not only the basic essentials in life, but beauty and inspirations as well." There are nine spacious rooms decorated with antiques and each with a private bath. The original owner loved the richness of natural wood, and the fine paneling in the entrance hall and the splendid central staircase glows with the mellow tones of black cherry, black walnut, mahogany, oak, ash, and tiger maple, lovingly preserved by innkeeper Ron Philips. There are cozy tiled fireplaces and large bay windows in the parlor and dining room, where dinner is served during the winter months. A hearty country-style breakfast or a simple continental eye-opener is served in the morning and complimentary herb tea is served at 9 p.m. Smoking is permitted on the porch only. Honeymoon package: None. Standard rates (EP): $33 per couple per night.

The Hillsdale House, 519 St. George St., P.O. Box 177, Annapolis Royal, Nova Scotia B0S 1A0 (tel. 902/532-5727). Open all year. Ron Phillips, the proprietor of Bread and Roses Country Inn and the Blomidon Inn, has here restored an 1849 stately Victorian country inn, which he has lavishly furnished with authentic period antiques. Surrounded by a 15-acre estate, there is a tennis court, sauna, and exercise room. Ron can also rent you bicycles. The dining room offers fine country-style food nicely served. A full country-style breakfast is also available and high tea is served in lieu of lunch. There are 15 rooms and each has a private bath. Honeymoon package: None. Rates (EP): $37.50 per couple per night.

The White Elephant Inn, 94 Upper St. George St., P.O. Box 34, Annapolis Royal, Nova Scotia B0S 1A0 (tel. 902/532-7850 in summer; 514/932-5930 in winter; or write 446 Grosvenor Avenue, Westmount, Quebec H34 2S4). Open mid-May to mid-October. Najma and Charles Barton are understandably very proud of their 23-room mansion located in the center of town. Built in 1869 as a wedding present (it actually looks vaguely like the wedding cake), it is now a registered historic property. Carefully decorated with antiques, the house retains many of its original details. There are 12 guest rooms, 8 of which have private baths. Honeymoon package: None. Rates (EP): $27 to $33 per night.

Blomidon Inn, 127 Main St., P.O. Box 839, Wolfville, Nova Scotia B0P 1X0 (tel. 902/542-9326). Open all year (with special off-season rates). This is another inn owned by Ron Phillips, proprietor of Bread and Roses and the Hillsdale House. A three-story, late-1800s mansion, it has a classic mansard roof, bristling with chimneys for its seven fireplaces. Guest rooms are furnished with four-poster beds, plush sofas, and wing chairs, and lovely old oriental carpets. There are two licensed dining rooms, each with a welcoming fireplace, serving such specialties as apple-curry soup, stuffed haddock, prime rib, local lamb and veal, and sour cream blueberry pie. There are tennis courts for use by the guests and you can rent bicycles. Seventeen of the 21 rooms have private baths. Honeymoon package: None. Rates (BP): $22.50 to $33.75 per couple.

Romantic Restaurants

Many area inns and hotels have extremely fine dining rooms. Both they and the area restaurants specialize in Nova Scotia's fine fish and seafood.

At **Blomidon Inn**, 127 Main St., Wolfville (tel. 542-9326) dine elegantly in a restored 1877 Victorian mansion built by a sea captain. Antiques and gas lamps enhance the period ambience. They serve an excellent, three-course prix-fixe dinner for $16.50 per person, which includes soup or salad, the entrée, and dessert. Recommended entrées include the ample portion of roast prime rib and the chicken Elizabeth —chicken breast stuffed with crab, shrimp, and cheese. Finish off with the cheesecake or chocolate mousse. Open for lunch and dinner all year.

Old Orchard Inn, between Wolfville and Kentville (tel. 542-5751). Well-polished antique furniture, fireplaces, and candles on the table encourage the spirit of romance at this elegant inn with view of Minas Basin. As an appetizer, order some of the local seafood, such as the steamed mussels or the oysters ($1.65 to $6). If you can't decide what you want for your main course, they have a surf 'n' turf combination with a tenderloin and a fresh Nova Scotia lobster for $17.75. Finish your meal with a sweet bite—perhaps some black forest cake or cherries jubilee. Open for lunch and dinner all year.

Webster's, central Kentville (tel. 678-9390) is pretty much a local secret—and a local favorite because of its hearty portions and low prices. It occupies a restored old building, right in town, painted brown with red trim. Webster's is especially well known for its Friday night buffet—all you can eat for $7.50 per person. Other nights, you might want a heaping portion of their fish 'n' chips ($3.75) or steak-and-shrimp combination platter ($9.75). For your finale, dig into the chocolate-marble cheesecake or luscious strawberry shortcake in season.

If you have a hankering for fresh seafood, **The Cove**, The Harbour View Inn, Smith's Cove (tel. 245-5686), is bound to please. You can dine on an enclosed porch overlooking either the water or gardens. Start off with the house specialty, a mackerel pâté, or other Nova Scotia favorites, such as solomon gundy, mussels, or chowder (all priced around $1.15). Among the entrées, the seafood platter for two really stands out—a seaworthy combination brimming with lobster, clams, scallops, and two different types of fish. Entrées priced from $6 to $11.25, which includes digging-in privileges at the plentiful salad bar. For dessert, take aim on the fresh berries in season or the chocolate mud pie. Open for breakfast and dinner, summers only.

CAPE BRETON ISLAND: Cape Breton Island is really a cluster of islands that barely kiss the peninsula at its northernmost tip. It is the most popular area of Nova Scotia for visitors. One hundred and ten miles long and 87 miles wide, it offers some of the most breathtakingly beautiful scenery in North America, ranging from majestic bluffs that seem to rise right out of the raging sea to lush highlands that gently cradle lazy Scottish villages. The scenery unfolds in vistas that are alternately stark and pastoral. Gigantic waves pound the imperturbable cliffs; the water can get so rough, it churns up foam that flecks the shoreline. Tiny fishing villages huddle around snug harbors; white-and-red lighthouses stand in lone vigils on rocky promontories. Meanwhile, the softly rolling meadows of Margaree Valley where sheep graze recall the gentle countryside of Ireland.

As a souvenir of your visit, you might want to buy some of the hand-knit goods made from wool from some of those sheep you see cavorting on the hillsides. You can pick up some very attractive sweaters, socks, and mittens.

Romantic Interludes

There are three self-guided auto "trails" on the island—the Ceilidh Trail, the Fleur-de-Lis Trail, and the Cabot Trail. All three highlight the scenic beauty of Nova Scotia.

Sixty-seven miles long, the **Ceilidh** (pronounced kay-lee) **Trail** begins in Port Hastings and takes you through the heart of Gaelic country and joins the Cabot Trail in Margaree Harbour. This trail is suitable for biking, should you be so inclined, as it traverses easy, undulating countryside. It ends in Baddeck, an old resort town in a picture-perfect setting. You'll want to spend some time in Baddeck, where the Alexander Graham Bell Museum is located (tel. 295-2069). Here, you will experience the wonder of seeing how this inventor worked, with exhibits of Bell's experiments and research on the deaf, medicine, and marine life.

Beginning in Port Hastings and winding its way south to Port Hawkesbury on the Strait of Canso, the **Fleur-de-Lis Trail** takes you through Acadian country. At the old fortress at Louisbourg, you will step into the summer of 1744 and be greeted by costumed guides who actually play out the identity of a former inhabitant. Then stop and have an authentic lunch. Plan on spending a full day here, and, no matter what the weather looks like when you set out in the morning, take along a raincoat and a sweater. Guided tours are offered daily from June to September, 10 a.m. to 6 p.m. Admission is about $2 per person (tel. 733-2280).

Named for explorer John Cabot, who landed in Nova Scotia on the tip of Cape Breton Island in 1497, the 181-mile-long **Cabot Trail** is considered by those who have traveled it to be one of the most scenic drives in North America. This is a roller-coaster ride, so be prepared to see some of the most dramatic vistas you can imagine—vast plateaus of dense forests sweep out to spectacular cliffs, which plunge with heart-stopping abruptness into a raging sea. The road hugs the seacoast, rising and falling with the steep terrain. You'll get the best views if you follow the route in a counterclockwise direction, which puts you on the outer edge (ocean side) of the roadway. However, if you are not accustomed to driving narrow, winding, mountain roads, you'll probably feel more comfortable going in a clockwise direction, which allows you to stay on the land side of the road.

From Baddeck, head to the **Bras d'Or Lakes,** considered one of the most magnificent inland seas in the world. Here, 450 square miles of smooth, fog-free saltwater lies sheltered in the warm embrace of the surrounding hills. This is a sailor's paradise.

Should you want to try out your sea legs on your own or with the able assistance of either a charter or a tour guide, call any of the following. To rent or charter sails, contact: **Baddeck Marine and Sports** (tel. 295-2434); or **Bras d'Or Charter** (tel. 295-2713). To rent paddleboats or canoes or sign on for a tour, call **Anchors Aweigh** (tel. 295-2713). To sail on a 32-foot diesel schooner, the *Balaema*, call 235-2943.

Hike along secluded trails in the last remaining natural wilderness in Nova Scotia. **The Cape Breton Highlands National Park** is literally where the mountains meet the sea; where you will see cliffs soar over 1,200 feet out of the water. As you meander along the marked trails you will discover an abandoned gold mine, a charming replica of a Scottish sheep-crofter's hut sheltered by 300-year-old sugar maples, and may glimpse moose, deer, or some of the 185 different species of birds (including the bald eagle) who call this beautiful area home. Bring along a knapsack lunch and a sweater and wear your hiking shoes.

A stop at the small French fishing village of **Chéticamp** on the Gulf of St. Lawrence will give you a chance to do some whale watching and see ancient Arcadian crafts demonstrated at the Acadian Museum (tel. 224-2170) on Main Street (admission is free). This is the center of the island's Acadian community, where you can buy beautiful, traditional, hooked rugs and watch them being made at **Flora's Shop** (tel. 224-3139).

Located off the tip of Cape Dauphin at the mouth of St. Ann's Bay, Hertford and Ciboux (the outermost island) are known as the **Bird Islands.** Twice a day, boats run out to the islands, where you can watch seabirds in astounding numbers. Get in touch with **Boularderie Cruises** in Big Bras d'Or to arrange for your cruise out to these islands (tel. 674-2384).

Honeymoon Hotels and Hideaways

Because of the incredible natural beauty of Cape Breton Island, you'll probably want to linger for at least two nights. The Baddeck, Ingonish, and Chéticamp areas all make a good base for your explorations.

Inverary Inn Resort, Shore Road, P.O. Box 190, Baddeck, N.S. B0E 1B0 (tel. 902/295-2674). Open May through October. Over 150 years ago, this charming inn began life as a farm on the shores of Bras d'Or Lake. Now, when you visit you can stroll tree-shaded paths and fields blanketed with colorful wildflowers. You will have no doubt that you are smack in the middle of the New World's Scottish Highlands. The stone fireplace beckons with traditional warmth; the windows are shaded with colorful tartans. Scott MacAulay and his family will expend every effort to make sure that your stay is perfect. The popular breakfasts are a treat with fresh spiced-apple sauce, Scottish oatcakes, oatmeal topped with thick fresh cream, bannock (griddlecakes), and mharagh (a kind of sausage). There is a private beach, swimming pool, boat rentals, and three tennis courts. Specify if you want a room in one of the cottages or in the lodge. Honeymoon package: Two days / one night (EP): $70 per couple. Includes champagne on arrival.

The Keltic Lodge, P.O. Box 70, Ingonish Beach, Cape Breton Island, Nova Scotia B0C 1L0 (tel. 902/285-2880). Open all year. This is another resort operated by the provincial government and is one of the province's most elaborate properties—a classic and elegant resort. That does not mean that it is big—there are only 32 rooms in the main lodge, 40 motel-type rooms, and 24 cottages. Located along the Cabot Trail on the eastern shore of Cape Breton, surrounded by lavish gardens, the red-roofed lodge sits perched on a promontory thrust out into the Atlantic Ocean. Your vistas encompass ocean, mountain, fresh water, forest, and sandy ribbons of beach. This is also an outdoor activity wonderland. In addition to hiking along the trails in Cape Breton Highlands National Park (the lodge is right near the east gate entrance), there is golf, swimming, tennis, and boating available. During the winter, there is also fine skiing on Cape Smokey. The lodge dining room is open to the public as well as guests and has huge picture windows offering excellent seascapes. Rates (MAP): $95 to $110 per couple per night.

Normaway Inn, Margaree Valley, P.O. Box 10, Nova Scotia B0E 2C0 (tel. 902/248-2987). Open June 1 through October 31. On a secluded 250-acre property in the Margaree River Valley and located along the Cabot Trail, the setting here is classic, the food is sumptuous, and the service, supervised by host David MacDonald, is unaffected. The inn is centrally located and near Baddeck, Chéticamp, Cape Breton Highlands National Park, and Inverness western shores, where you find many uncrowded beaches that boast some of the warmest and best swimming waters in the province. The welcoming living room has a working fireplace and attached reading room. There are nine rooms in the inn and four two-bedroom cabins with fireplaces. There are tennis courts; nightly films on the area; walking trails on the grounds; rental bikes available; and salmon-fishing outfitting. Honeymoon package: Four days / three nights (some meals): $315 to $345 per couple. Includes sparkling wine on arrival, two candlelight dinners, daily breakfast, bikes for half a day; canoeing; choice of a boat tour to Bird Islands, horseback riding, windsurfing, or a whale-watching cruise (when available).

Romantic Restaurants

Cape Breton boasts some of Nova Scotia's richest lobster fishing grounds, so you'll find plenty of shellfish on local menus. As you're driving along, keep your eyes open for signs announcing different "lobster suppers," run by community groups to raise money for special projects. It's an excellent opportunity not only to sample claw-clattering-fresh lobster, but also participate a bit in local life.

Moderate: The Keltic Lodge, Ingonish Beach (tel. 285-2880). Since this grand old resort is located on a very slim peninsula, you'll dine with seaward views of either North Bay Ingonish or South Bay Ingonish. The dining room itself is formal, in a Scotian sort of way, with rich wood paneling and wooden columns. Their five-course, prix-fixe dinner at $22.50 per person is a very good deal indeed, highlighting the fresh fish and seafood of the province, such as salmon, halibut, and haddock, with a menu that changes nightly. For dessert, they're known for luscious pastries. Open June through mid-October, January through March; serving breakfast, lunch, and dinner daily.

Inverary Inn, Shore Road, Baddeck (tel. 295-2674). You'll relish the gracious atmosphere of this 150-year-old inn. In the main dining room, the menu includes the fresh Nova Scotia catch, such as haddock, lobster, or salmon; they also offer steak, roast prime rib, and an unusual and savory cranberry chicken dish (priced $7.50 to $10). For dessert, treat yourselves to a Canadian sundae (maple walnut ice cream topped with maple syrup), or one of the baked on the premises selections, such as the carrot cake. The Inverary is also in the process of adding a new gourmet restaurant; call and ask for complete details.

Laurie's Motel, Chéticamp (tel. 224-2400). Through the dining room windows, you can watch the boats come and go in the harbor. Much of the fresh catch with which the fishing boats return—lobster, crab, scallops, and halibut—star on the menu of this fine restaurant. Entrées are priced from $7.50 to $13.50; all are served with fresh vegetables, such as broccoli, cauliflower, or fiddleheads, and also come with a salad. Desserts—all made in Laurie's own kitchen—include an absolutely out-of-this-world mincemeat pie, as well as a berry-delicious strawberry shortcake ($1.50).

Inexpensive: The Chowder House, Rte. 19, north of Inverness (tel. 258-2545). Nothing but a small lunch restaurant, but ahh . . . the overstuffed lobster and crab rolls, and thick chowder that's practically a meal in itself. This is definitely a worthwhile lunch stop when you are driving along the Cabot Trail.

4. More Suggestions in Nova Scotia

We have only touched on the beauty and romance of Nova Scotia. In addition to the places we have guided you there is much more to see and exciting things to do, if you have the time.

THE MARINE DRIVE: This trail corkscrews its way along the rugged coastline from Halifax / Dartmouth to the Canso Causeway, entrance to Cape Breton Island, featuring one long, endless view of the ocean—a sportsman's paradise and a photographer's dream come true. En route, you will pass through tiny, sparsely settled fishing villages far off the usual tourist track. Along this remote, oft untraveled route there are two romantic, honeymoon hideaways worthy of mention.

Camelot Inn, Rte. 7, Musquodoboit Harbour, P.O. Box 31, Musquodoboit Harbour, Nova Scotia, B0J 2L0 (tel. 902/889-2198). Open all year. Ms. P. M. "Charlie" Holgate, the owner, personally welcomes you to her home. The 128-year-old inn looks out over a horseshoe bend in the river. There are four acres of surrounding woodland, river rapids, and excellent bird watching to keep you busy. The five rooms share two baths and a powder room. Expect to find some fine old antiques in the rooms, as well as cozy touches such as hooked rugs. Your day will begin with what Charlie calls her "no-lunch breakfast." She serves up generous portions of "Red River" cereal, a concoction that consists of stone-ground wheat and rye with whole flax, cooked together with plump raisins. Breakfast can also include fresh-squeezed juice, bacon, ham, sausage, and free-range chicken eggs together with a mouth-watering assortment of home-baked breads made from stone-ground flours. Breakfasts priced about $3 to $5. Dinner is served only to Charlie's guests and arranged pretty much to suit your schedule. The meal might consist of cream of spinach soup; fresh garden salad with Charlie's special garlic dressing; salmon in egg sauce, accompanied by fresh broccoli and parsleyed new potatoes, and chocolate cheesecake for dessert—prix-fixe at $18 per person. Rates (EP): a large room is $45 to $60 per couple per night; a small room is $40 to $50 per couple per night.

Liscombe Lodge, Liscombe Mills on Hwy. 7, Guysbourgh County, Nova Scotia B0J 2A0 (tel. 902/779-2307); off-season: Liscombe Lodge, P.O. Box 456, Halifax, Nova Scotia B3J 2R5 (tel. 902/424-3258). Open from late May to late October. If you have any interest in salmon or trout fishing, this is a place you should look into. Located on the Liscombe River just below the mill falls, there are several small chalets and cottages dotted along the river bank near the lodge. Honeymoon package: Two days / one night (MAP): $120 per couple. Includes use of small boats and fishing gear, tennis facilities, entry tickets to nearby Sherbrooke Village (an historic restoration), and champagne on arrival.

THE SUNRISE TRAIL: This takes you to the Northumberland Shore, where you will find yourself in the heart of lobster land. The scenery and weather recall the Scottish Highlands. There are over 35 secluded beaches, gently washed by the warmest waters in the North Atlantic. An average summer water temperature is 70°. In Pugwash you can watch the "gathering of the clans," a traditional Scottish-flavored event that will take you back to the days of yore.

THE GLOSSCAP TRAIL: This follows the Fundy shore. In the Minas Basin, the highest (and the lowest) recorded tides in the world occur. At low tide in Parrsboro, for example, you can see the dramatic effect—huge freighters and fishing boats stand stranded high and dry. This is also a region wealthy in prehistory. View ancient animal footprints near Parrsboro and see fossilized trees and plants in the 150-foot sandstone cliffs near Joggins. The rule is, if you find a fossil here that you can easily carry away by hand, it's yours!

In Truro you can see the phenomenal tidal bore on the Salmon River. A tidal bore is literally a wall of water, sometimes reaching as high as several feet, relentlessly pushed upstream by the power of the incoming tide. Tides at this part of the Bay of Fundy have measured up to 54 feet—the highest in the world. If you are interested, there is a thrilling white-water rafting tour that rides the tidal bore. Call Bill MacKay to reserve your raft position (tel. 755-5560 or 752-0899). You don't need any previous experience, just a sense of adventure. The trip takes about three to four hours and lunch is provided. The cost is $30 per person.

Chapter XVIII

INTRODUCING MEXICO

1. Practical Facts

A TROPICAL BREEZE wafts across the tiled terrace as a pitcher of margaritas is laid out and the sun starts its steady decline. The soft strains of a singer caressing Spanish words—*"mi amor, mi vida"*—drifts from the cantina below. The lapping waves carry in the tiny boat of the last fisherman with his catch.

The scene may seem familiar because you have been dreaming about spending your honeymoon in a place like Mexico, where the pace is unhurried, the people warm and hospitable, the food delicious and fresh, the music both soft and spirited, and the beaches long stretches of pure sand bordered by the sapphire blue of the Pacific or the crystal-clear turquoise of the Caribbean.

Mexico, the United States' southern neighbor, is a vast and rugged country encompassing mountain ranges, plateaus, jungles, deserts, colonial towns, and futuristic skyscraper-crowded cities. Nevertheless, it is its 6,212 miles of coastline—fronting the Gulf of Mexico and the Caribbean on the east, and the Pacific Ocean on the south and west—that draws most of the four million visitors from the United States each year. A large percentage are honeymooners who delight in Mexico's abundance of sun and sand.

The history of Mexico goes back hundreds of years, to about 1,500 BC, when the Olmec Mesoamerican culture was first established in the Gulf Coast area. Thousands of ruins of ancient cities still dot the countryside, mute witnesses to the rise and fall of the sophisticated civilizations built by the Olmecs and their successors, the Mayans and the Aztecs. Today, the story of their achievements and downfall are still being unraveled by archeologists.

In 1519, the arrival of the Spanish conqueror Hernán Cortés dramatically changed Mexico's course of history. Over a period of 30 years, Cortés and his Spanish troops took over the Aztec nation and all that is today Mexico, infusing Old World culture into the New World.

The early 19th century saw the drive for independence from Spain, led by Father Hidalgo and Captain Ignacio Allende. In 1821, this goal was finally achieved. The early years of the Mexican republic were turbulent. Government corruption and the need for land reform sparked the Mexican Revolution of 1911 to 1920, directed by leaders such as Pancho Villa and Emiliano Zapata. Reforms and the new constitution generated by this movement helped create the modern Mexico, a politically stable and democratic republic.

This history, the mixture of charming Latin culture, the ancient wonders of the Mayas and Aztecs, and plush, new hotels and modern conveniences, combine to make Mexico romantic. For starters, there's the pace of life. Mexicans say that Americans live to work, while Mexicans work to live. You'll see this zestful approach to life in the Mexicans' relaxed attitude toward time and their passionate embrace of good food, love songs, and laughter. Then there are the historical remnants, seen in the Spanish-style buildings with their wrought-iron grillwork, ceramic pots and tiles, archways and bouganvillea-draped terraces, and the vestiges from the more ancient period of the Mayas and the Aztecs with the great temples and pyramids that have endured for generations. All this and 20th-century hotels and restaurants, too.

Mexico is also for honeymooners who love the outdoors. The ocean affords opportunities for waterskiing, scuba diving, snorkeling, sailing, and parasailing. On land, you can try tennis courts, golf courses, horseback riding into the jungle or along the beach, or exploring highways and byways of the land by four-wheel-drive vehicles.

Mexico's resorts have managed to maintain their individualism without becoming sterile chrome-and-glass cities on beaches. Whichever destination you choose, you'll be sure to find romance—in this case defined as warm, sunny weather; long, clean beaches; friendly people; a relaxed pace; lively music and delicious food, all available alongside the luxuries of the modern age.

1. Practical Facts

ENTERING AND LEAVING: Americans need proof of U.S. citizenship, such as a valid passport. An authorized birth certificate or a voter registration card is also acceptable. You need to obtain a tourist card (available at travel agencies, Mexican consulates, and airlines serving Mexico) before you arrive. The cards are free and valid for 90 days. Make sure to keep the tourist card with you during your trip, as it's required by law; and you must present both it and your proof of U.S. citizenship upon leaving the country. Canadians must have a passport. Mexico has a departure tax of $10 per person, payable in either dollars or pesos at airport check-in counters.

GETTING THERE: As each year passes, more opportunities open up for traveling to Mexico from the United States.

By Air

There are nonstop flights from several U.S. cities to Mexico on **Pan Am, Western, American, TWA, Continental,** and the two Mexican airlines, **Mexicana** and **Aeromexico.** They fly from major U.S. cities directly to all the resorts mentioned in this book, or are sometimes routed through Mexico City, the hub of the country's air traffic. (For example, if you're flying from New York to Ixtapa, you'll probably need to connect to another flight in Mexico City; if you're flying from Los Angeles to Cancún, you'll probably also connect in Mexico City.) In recent years, numerous U.S. tour companies have contracted with airlines for charter flights to Mexican resorts. These generally cost less than regularly scheduled flights, but you won't have a lot of schedule flexibility. Check with your travel agent.

By Sea

Many luxury cruise ships sail to Mexico. Some stop at Mexican ports on their way around the world or through the Panama Canal; others sail year-round from Los Angeles or other west coast ports. Check with your travel agent for itineraries.

GETTING AROUND: With inexpensive taxis and a variety of other transportation, getting around in Mexico is easy.

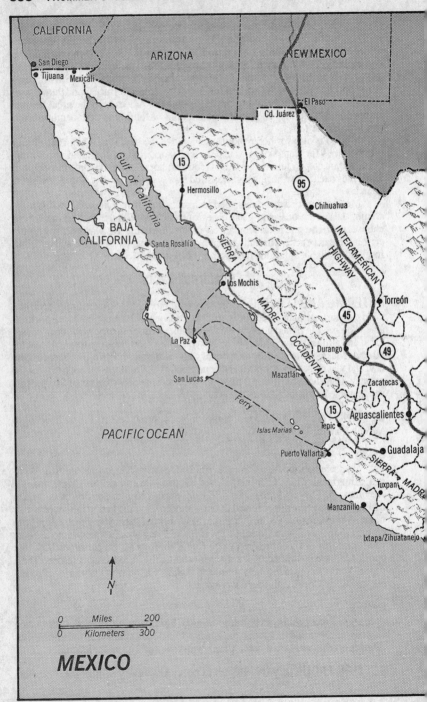

MEXICO

By Taxi

Taxis are so inexpensive and abundant in Mexico that they may be cheaper and easier than renting a car. There are no set rates for taxis and few have meters, so your best bet is to establish the price before you get into the car. (Your hotel doorman can help negotiate.) In some cities, you find that there are usual "going rates" between popular destinations; these are often posted at the front desk of your hotel.

Rental Cars

Major U.S. car-rental companies, such as **Avis, Hertz,** and **National** have offices in major resort cities, both at the airports and in town. Renting a car in Mexico is often more expensive than doing so in the United States (one of the few things in Mexico that costs more than back home). Sample car rates from Hertz are $25 a day for a standard transmission Volkswagen sedan (plus 17¢ per mile); $173 for a week's rental (the first 1,250 miles are free). You can often find deals at airport car rental desks where local companies have Volkswagen bugs with standard transmissions. But the high cost of car rentals makes hiring a taxi a cost-saving option: In many cases, it can be cheaper to hire a taxi for an all-day excursion. In order to rent a car in Mexico, you'll need a valid U.S. driver's license, a credit card, and your tourist card. Car insurance is extra and mandatory since your U.S. policy is not recognized. The advantage of booking through U.S. companies is that you can reserve the car in advance and a 24-hour emergency service may be available.

Renting and driving four-wheel-drive vehicles is a lot of fun in Mexico, allowing you to explore off-road areas which are inaccessible to regular cars. Mexican highways and roads between major destinations are generally in good condition, but it is not recommended you drive outside of cities at night—even the Mexicans avoid it if they don't have to—because of animals and other hazards that often block roads.

LANGUAGE: Spanish is the official language, but you'll be able to get along fine in the resort areas even if you don't know a word. Still, you might want to invest in a Spanish phrase book since it adds to the fun to learn a word or two, such as "*gracias*" (thank you) or "*cuanto*" (how much). Mexicans are usually thrilled when other North Americans make an attempt to communicate in their language, and will help you improve your vocabulary rapidly.

MONEY: As of this writing, the Mexican currency—the peso—is continuing a controlled devaluation in relation to the U.S. dollar; good news for U.S. travelers, who will continue to find low prices in restaurants and shops. The exchange rate "floats" on the international money market, and will fluctuate almost daily. You'll find the current exchange rate posted at banks, hotels, airports, and money exchange houses; banks usually offer the most favorable rates. Pesos come in various denominations, both notes and coins. Each peso is composed of 100 centavos and there are 5, 10, 20, and 50 centavo coins, which buy very little.

Traveler's checks are your best bet, change them a little at a time as you need the money. (Make sure you have proof of identity with you.) Although traveler's checks are readily cashed in the major resort areas listed in this book, they are not widely accepted in small towns well off the beaten tourist track. Most hotels and restaurants accept major credit cards; they usually do not take personal checks. Since the peso is indicated by the dollar sign ($), the same as for U.S. and Canadian currency, pay particular attention to prices quoted in stores.

Mexico has instituted a value added tax—called the IVA—which places a 15% surcharge on all goods and services except surface transportation. Think of it as a 15% sales tax.

Tipping in Mexico is almost the same as in the United States. Give waiters/

waitresses 10% to 20%, porters the equivalent of 25¢ per bag. Chambermaids who clean your room are generally tipped 25¢ to 50¢ a day. Tips to cab drivers are optional.

WEATHER: In general, Mexico has a dry season (November through April) and a rainy season (May through October), but travel in both periods is encouraged—it can always rain in the dry season too, and you'll find the rain in the "rainy" season usually consists of afternoon showers, which cause little inconvenience. The beach resorts are tropical almost all year round, with humidity and temperature rising in the summer months and becoming cooler in the winter.

CLOTHING: Casual and fun are the key words throughout Mexico, but some resorts have definite differences. Acapulco, for example, is dressy compared to Cozumel, where informal is the byword. Few restaurants at the resorts require men to wear a tie and jacket, but there are elegant establishments at which gentlemen feel more comfortable in an open-necked shirt and jacket. Women should bring along some fun evening wear—nothing too fancy—for the nicer restaurants and discotheques. For the day, bring cotton clothing, comfortable walking shoes, and several bathing suits. Although shorts are fine at the beach, do not wear them on shopping expeditions to town or in more conservative inland areas.

TIME: Mexico does not change to Daylight Savings Time. Most of the country is on Central Time, including all the resorts in this chapter. During the summer when Daylight Savings Time is in effect in the United States, Mexico is one hour later than Los Angeles and two hours earlier than New York: When it is noon in Mexico, it is 11 a.m. in Los Angeles and 2 p.m. in New York. During the winter months, the Mexican resorts are two hours ahead of Los Angeles and one hour behind New York.

TELEPHONES: To call Mexico from the United States, dial 011-52, and the local area code and number. For long-distance telephone calls within Mexico, dial 91 plus the area code and the number. Area codes for the major resorts are: Acapulco, 748; Puerto Vallarta, 322; Manzanillo, 333; Ixtapa/Zihuatanejo, 743; Cancún, 988; and Cozumel, 987. Use pay phones for local calls—they accept one-peso coins.

Placing long-distance telephone calls from your hotel may be the most convenient method to call home, but it is expensive, since the telephone company charges a 50% tax on international calls plus a surcharge. For dialing direct to the United States, dial 95, area code, and number. An alternative is going to the local Larga Distancia office in each city where operators place the calls for you. You can also make collect calls from your hotel (dial 96 plus the area code and number) and you'll avoid the tax.

The Mexican phone system functions quite well, but due to a shortage of lines it will sometimes take some time to place a call to the U.S. from your hotel.

SHOPPING: The variety and quality of merchandise found in Mexico can be overwhelming. Visitors may expect to find lovely handcrafts—the sarapes, embroidered blouses, ceramic vases, silver jewelry, and copper products—but they're often also pleasantly surprised to come across low prices on designer items by the likes of Ralph Lauren and Gucci. The resorts are home to so many modern shopping malls, tiny boutiques and open-air markets that vacationers often find themselves divving up their days between sunning and shopping.

In general, stores are open from 10 a.m. to 2 p.m., then closed for "siesta" break to reopen at 4 or 5 p.m. Evening is a good time to stroll and shop, because stores close at 7 or 8 p.m., just before dinner. The strength of the American dollar makes shopping a favorite activity and you'll be amazed at the prices you can obtain with some patient bargaining, a practice which is expected in markets and stalls, but frowned upon in stores. As a rule of thumb, start off by offering about 50% of the asking price; although the vendor won't agree, this launches the bargaining give-and-take. Usually, the final price will be about 65% of the original price.

Markets, bazaars, and vendors hawking wares on beaches yield some of the best buys, and also provide the chance to meet the locals, often the people who created the crafts with their own hands.

Mexico is rich in **handcrafts** that have been developed by people who blended Indian skills and European designs and techniques. Every state in the country specializes in a unique kind of jewelry, ceramics, artwork, embroidery, weavings, and such, so you'll find some resorts will have a profusion of certain goods. Yet most have large crafts markets that feature merchandise from all around the country. These include hand-blown glass from the village of Tlaquepaque outside of Guadalajara, the carved furniture of Patzcuaro, the onyx and pottery of Puebla, and the famous silver jewelry of Taxco. Pottery, for example, reflects the different styles of each state. Those from Oaxaca and Chiapas display pre-Hispanic influences, while those from Guanajuato and Puebla have a distinct Spanish flavor. Imaginary figures made from papier-mâché are found all over. Piñatas, important for Mexican fiestas and ceremonies, are made from clay pots covered with colored tissue paper. Cute, whimsical, nativity scenes—available all year—come in various sizes and bright colors. As far as traditional clothing, you'll see leather and woven belts, sarapes, sombreros, embroidered blouses and rebozos (Mexican shawls), and native dresses such as the Mexican wedding dress, all in white with colorful embroidery.

Puerto Vallarta is one of the best places in Mexico for shopping. Many of the finest shops and boutiques face the seaside promenade or parallel Morelos and Juarez streets. The **Mercado Municipal,** on the north side of the Rio Cuale, contains dozens of souvenir stalls. **Galeria Uno** at Morelos 561 sells an outstanding selection of Latin American art for collectors. You can choose from a selection of huaraches, the traditional Mexican leather sandal, at **Huaracheria Lety** (Juarez 472). If you don't see what you want, describe it, and the shoemaker will create it. **Joyeria Arodi** (with five locations, including in the Fiesta Americana and Sheraton hotels) specializes in custom jewelry made with fine gemstones.

Ixtapa and Zihuatanejo offer better and better shopping each year. **La Puerta** shopping center across from hotel row houses a number of good boutiques, including Florence, with an excellent collection of jewelry and embroidery; and Creaciones Alberto's, with gold and silver jewelry made to your specifications using semiprecious stones. The **Camino Real** has an outstanding mall with top-of-the-line stores such as Tane, which sells fine silver, and La Esperanza with high-quality crafts. **Zihuatanejo** has a high concentration of boutiques. The **State Handcrafts Store** near the zocalo is stocked with items from throughout Mexico. El Embarcadero contains embroidered clothing and weavings from Oaxaca and Chiapas. Next door, La Zapoteca, has sarapes from Oaxaca and hammocks from the Yucatan (both are on J. Alvarez near the zocalo).

Manzanillo has more limited choices, so shopping is less of an attraction. The downtown has a few boutiques, such as Boutique Grivel (Pasaje Oscarana), specializing in crafts and resort wear. At Barra de Navidad's neighboring Melaque (a ten-minute drive), Curiosidades del Mar sells all kinds of items made from seashells (on the corner of G. Farias and L. Mateos).

Acapulco, as you would expect, has a staggering selection. Your best finds will be resortwear—from skimpy bikinis for the beach to tinsely minidresses for the discos. Most of the finest shops line the Costera, especially from the point across the avenue from the Americana Condesa del Mar hotel west to El Morro beach. Here's where you'll find **Izod** (men's polo shirts priced from $10 to $15) and **Ellesse** (tennis tops or shorts about $20 each). For casual duds, check out **Aca Joe, Fiorucci,** and **Ruben Torres.** Women looking to enhance their bikini wardrobe should check out **Cocaine,** also on this stretch of the Costera.

For the most elegant resortwear, the no. 1 choice is the **La Vista** shopping mall near Las Brisas. The pink stucco buildings house an upscale selection of shops, including **Tane** for silver, **Girasol** for embroidered cotton dresses, and **Gucci** for leather goods. Acapulco is not known for local crafts, but you can browse through a selection of such wares from throughout the country at **Artesanias Finas Acapulco,** on Horacio Nelson around the corner from the Baby 'O disco. Quality is mixed, but with some care, you can winnow out the real finds: mother-of-pearl inlaid boxes from $4 to $40, silver bauble necklaces for $80 to $100, and leather attaché cases priced from $50 to $150. The store's currency exchange bureau also offers one of the most favorable rates for U.S. dollars in the city.

Cancún has modern plazas and malls stocking handmade goods from all over Mexico. At **Plaza Mexico** (corner of Tulum and Agua Avenues), stores offer some of the best from Mexico's various states. Ki-Huic, downtown off Avenue Tulum, is another big marketplace for handcrafts; stalls sell curios, sarapes, and blouses, and bargaining is the order of the day. Among the larger shopping malls is **Plaza Caracol,** which was Cancún's first (located at the convention center). Restaurants, fountains, refreshment stands, and bars offer respite along the walkways connecting the stores. Don't dismiss some of the stores at the hotels: The ones at the Camino Real and Sheraton are known for their excellent selections. Cozumel attracts hundreds of happy cruisers (from ships) who hit the beaches, as well as the numerous shops of the main town, San Miguel. In the same area near the main square, check out Galeria Oaxaca, which emphasizes the art of that state (Ave. 5 Norte). El Mercado de Artesanías, one block east of the square on Calle 1 Sur, is the place to pick up inexpensive souvenirs such as onyx chess sets, ceramic figurines and woven belts, while La Concha (Ave. 5 Sur) has some more rare items made in Mexico.

Benetton, Acapulco Joe, Ruben Torres, Gucci, Ralph Lauren. All names you would find in New York, Los Angeles. How about Puerto Vallarta and Cancún? Right alongside the artisan's markets in Mexico are some of the best-known names in clothing, jewelry, and leather goods in the world, at prices considerably lower than in the United States. In Puerto Vallarta, just a couple blocks north of the malecon (Diaz Ordaz 588) is **Aca Joe.** In the same area, you'll also find **Ocean Pacific** (Morelos 660), **Ruben Torres** (Diaz Ordaz 590), **Fiorucci** (Aldama 112), and **Gucci** (Juarez 402). One of the highlights of shopping in P.V. is a visit to the collection of **Sergio Bustamante** (Morelos 527), a world-reknowned artist who produces magnificent birds and other animals sculpted in metal and papier-mâché. In Acapulco, there is even a larger array, with **Polo Ralph Lauren** near the Diana Circle on the Costera. Across from the El Presidente Hotel you'll find the three casual clothes havens—**Fiorucci, Aca Joe's,** and **Ruben Torres**—and **Gucci. Cartier** is across from the Hyatt Continental. At **La Vista Shopping Center,** across from Las Brisas on a hillside overlooking the ocean, you'll find high-quality items from Mexico, Gucci, and Givenchy. This mall is across from Las Brisas, on a hillside overlooking the ocean. In Cancún, Benetton, the hottest brand name in Italian sportswear, is at **Plaza Caracol** in the hotel zone. Aca Joe is found at Ave. Tulum at the corner of Tulipanes. Aca Joe at Calle 2 Norte in Cozumel is another installation of the popular clothing chain. For more designer clothes check out **Los Cinco Soles** on Cozumel's Ave. **Melgar** stocks women's clothing as well as crafts. **Tucan,** also on Melgar, sells silk-screened fabric and clothes.

ABOUT ACCOMMODATIONS: The growth of tourism to Mexico in the last ten years has given birth to numerous new hotels in all price ranges. The results are a boon to honeymooners: In each resort you'll find a host of modern hotels that provide all the services and comforts you'll need.

Like the Caribbean, high season in Mexico runs from December 15 through April 15; low season rates are about 30% to 50% lower. Rates quoted in this section reflect the range between low-season and high-season prices. The federal tax of 15% is not included unless noted.

Ask your travel agent about honeymoon packages. At many resorts they give you a substantial savings—as well as perks such as chilled champagne and fresh flowers in your room.

Beachfront hotel rooms can be extra romantic, with balconies or terraces facing the ocean. Make sure your travel agent finds out if your room has a view (sometimes they cost $10 to $20 more per night). They can be booked at special request.

As in other popular resort areas around the world, Mexican hotels may have problems with overbookings in high season. For this reason, make sure you get the receipt for your room deposit from your travel agent. Take it along on the trip to present at the hotel desk if any problems arise.

Christmas and Easter weeks are the most crowded in Mexico and the resorts burst at the seams. You'll need to make reservations six months in advance for other high season dates.

DINING OUT: You may know it as the home of enchiladas, but you'll be pleasantly surprised by the range of delicious food in Mexico. Like the cuisines of France and Italy, Mexican cuisine consists of regional specialties. The Pacific resorts boast sumptuous fish and seafood: haddock, clams, oysters, lobster with palm hearts, stuffed snapper, shrimp in beer batter, *ceviche* (fish and seafood marinated in lime juice), and seafood grilled over mesquite or charcoal. There are also good, simple favorites such as steaks, spareribs, and kid grilled over coals, and beef and lamb skewered together and served over a bed of rice. The Yucatan is a mecca for Mexican gourmets. *Papadzul* is a classic of the area: a tortilla dipped in pumpkin seed sauce and filled with crumbled hard-boiled egg. Other specialties are lobster and shellfish, pompano, fish filet pit-roasted in banana leaves and *panuchos*—small fried tortillas filled with black beans, onions, hard-boiled eggs, and shredded roast suckling pig. For dessert, there's coconut dishes and almond cake and, as everywhere in Mexico, the delicious flan, or egg custard.

You will be pleasantly surprised by the quality of Mexican wines, especially the whites from Baja California. And, Mexican beer needs little introduction, having won international awards for their flavor and quality. Neither does tequila, one of the oldest drinks in the country, its origins dating to pre-Hispanic times. Traditionally, it is drunk straight with a lick of salt and a bite of lime. More to most Americans' tastes are margaritas—tequila mixed with lime juice and orange liqueur in a glass rimmed with salt.

Restaurants are some of the liveliest and romantic aspects of a Mexican honeymoon. You'll come across old haciendas turned into elegant dining rooms, thatched-roof beachfront eateries serving fresh shrimp swathed in butter and garlic, and American-style coffeeshops where ham, eggs, and orange juice dominate the breakfast menu. Dinner is eaten late by American standards—most Mexicans head out to restaurants around 9 p.m. and vacationers seem to follow suit. Reservations are rarely required, except in the most elegant and popular of spots. Check with hotel desks for information.

The food, beer, and tequila are quite tempting, but be careful not to overdo it. That's the best advice to prevent the mild traveler's diarrhea that hits some visitors to Mexico on their first trip. It's best to eat and imbibe lightly the first few days while your system adapts to a new climate and food. Drink only purified water. Most major hotels have water purification plants, so it's safe to drink the water and brush your teeth with it; other hotels provide bottled purified water in the rooms. Whenever in doubt in restaurants, ask for mineral water (agua mineral), or stick with beer, wine, and name-brand bottled soft drinks. Avoid ice cubes not made from purified water as well as fruits and vegetables you cannot peel. Don't be tempted by the food sold at street stands—that's where most Americans get their cases of Montezuma's Revenge. If it happens to befall you, take an ounce of liquid Pepto-Bismol or the equivalent in tablets every half hour for four hours. Lomotil and Kaopectate are other helpful agents; before you go, ask your doctor's opinion of these treatments. Don't let health concerns stand in your way of having a good time. Eating and drinking are an integral part of the Mexican vacation experience.

HOW TO GET MARRIED IN MEXICO: Mexican government officials in the United States advise not trying to tie the knot in Mexico unless you have patience and are planning to spend at least a week in the country. It may take that long to make an appointment with a civil judge and have the blood tests, the two basic steps needed to get married. After the ceremony, you'll need to register your marriage at a U.S. consulate or embassy in Mexico (check before you leave to make sure there's one at your destination). Then, when you return home, you'll need to file the certified copy of the marriage certificate at your county courthouse. Brides and grooms who have been divorced in the United States need to clear an added hurdle: They'll need to bring a certified copy of their divorce decree—translated into Spanish—to Mexico to present to the civil judge. To save time and energy in making these arrangements, check with the hotel you'll be staying at in Mexico before you leave. Some, such as romance-oriented Las Hadas and Las Brisas, can make all the arrangements necessary for a wedding ceremony as well as a champagne reception.

FOR FURTHER INFORMATION: Contact the **Mexican Government Tourism Offices** at the following addresses: In New York: 405 Park Ave., Suite 1002, New York, NY 10022 (tel. 212/755-7261). In Los Angeles: 10100 Santa Monica Blvd., Suite 224, Los Angeles, CA 90067 (tel. 213/203-8151). In Chicago: Two Illinois Center, 233 North Michigan Ave., Suite 1413, Chicago, IL 60601 (tel. 312/565-2785). In Houston: 2707 North Loop West, Suite 450, Houston, TX 77008 (tel. 713/880-5153).

Chapter XIX

ACAPULCO

1. Romantic Interludes
2. Honeymoon Hotels and Hideaways
3. Romantic Restaurants

ACAPULCO IS one of the rare resort destinations that lives up to its reputation. You'll feel as if you've been plunked down into a glossy color postcard. The Bahía de Acapulco (Acapulco Bay) flaunts one of the most famous stretches of beachfront hotels in the world. Like Waikiki, Ipanema, or Cannes, photographs of its hotel skyline are instantaneously identifiable even by people who have never been there. The splendid setting borders on the awesome: golden sands surround the sapphire-blue bay, all cupped by the green, jungly Sierra Madre Mountains that tumble seaward on three sides.

Acapulco is located on Mexico's Pacific coast, about 150 miles south of Mexico City. It is the southernmost of Mexico's developed resorts. Acapulco life centers on the Costera Miguel Alemáin, better known as the "strip," the broad avenue that threads its way along the coast. Many of the finest hotels front the Costera on one side, the beach on the other. Other honeymoon haciendas perch in the cliffs above the city, or to the east or west of town.

The city was founded in 1530 by the Spanish conquistadors. The beautiful harbor first served as a major port for Spanish trading ships carrying rare goods from the Orient—fine silks, porcelain, and ivory. During the 1950s, the first resort hotels were built toward the city's west end near Caleta and Catetilla beaches, and the influx of celebrities earned the city its nickname as "The Riviera of the West."

More so than other Mexican resorts, Acapulco has distinct tourist seasons. High season runs December through Easter; it's when most of the bejeweled jet-setters drop by their cliffside villas, and when parties, nightclubs, and restaurants throb most fervently. (It's also when you'll have the toughest time making reservations and squeezing yourselves into the discos.) But even Acapulco's off-season packs in more than enough action to satisfy the most energetic honeymooners, with plenty of sunshine, nightlife—and the pleasant addition of some elbow room.

There are really two, almost completely different, cities—Acapulco by day and Acapulco by night. When the sun shines (which averages about 149 days out of 151 during the winter season), Acapulco dedicates itself with full-blown hedonism to the delights of sand and sea. After dark, Acapulco transforms itself into party central, a town that greets each evening as if it were Mardi Gras. Couples sip cocktails on terraces before heading to some hilltop restaurant to dine—late—with the lights of the city spread out below their feet. And after dinner, they make a fashionably late arrival at the disco—several discos, actually, because club hopping characterizes the nighttime scene. "When," you may ask, "do we get time to sleep?"

Most Acapulco revelers we know would never hit the beach before 1 p.m.—just in time for their afternoon siesta. If you want rest and relaxation, go elsewhere. If you want to dance and party to the max, Acapulco is the perfect choice.

1. Romantic Interludes

Night or day, lovers will find plenty of ways to amuse themselves in Acapulco. Most of the major hotels have concessions for parasailing, waterskiing, Windsurfing, and sailing. Here are more options that really showcase the city's magic.

BEACH HOPPING: Acapulco's renown originally grew from that glorious crescent of **beach** that curves its way around the bay practically nonstop. Each section is known by its own name—about 23 different beaches in all. The search for the perfect beach by day makes as popular a pastime as club hopping at night. All beaches are public in Mexico, so the hotels have no control over them. As of this writing, the most fashionable stretch of Acapulco Bay for the see-and-be-seen set is **La Condesa,** which runs from the Hyatt Continental to the El Presidente hotels. Thatch-roof *palapas* (sun shelters) offer respite from the heat, and casual seaside cafés such as Paradise and Beto's (see "Restaurants" section) make for lively lunch spots. The surf is a bit rough here, however. **Icacos beach** lies towards the eastern curve of the bay near the Hyatt Regency and La Palapa hotels. Waters are calmer here, and the scene a bit less frenetic. **Revolcadero beach,** to the south of town near the Princess and Pierre Marques hotels, is another broad, tawny favorite. Be careful of the big breakers. Perhaps the most romantic option here is renting horses to ride along the shoreline. For sunset watching, head for **Pie de la Cuesta** about seven miles to the northwest of the city. Although you won't want to swim here (the surf is downright treacherous), you can stake out a hammock at water's edge, wrap your fingers around a cool tropical drink, and watch el sol dip slowly beneath the horizon. On the other side of the beach is peaceful **Laguna de Coyuca,** a freshwater lagoon that attracts birds such as herons, cormorants, and egrets. You can rent canoes or rowboats to skim the glassy surface of the lagoon, perhaps taking out some time for swimming or fishing. The cab fare from Acapulco proper is about $14 round-trip; ask the driver to wait for you. Remember that throughout Mexico, the sun is strong—use protective sun lotions.

DISCOS: According to a recent count, you could hit a different **disco** in Acapulco every night for three months. Acapulco clubs run the complete gamut, from cozy little boîtes to lavish dance palaces.

The current in-spot is **Fantasy,** where duplex floor-to-ceiling windows have a drop-dead view of Acapulco at night, lights sparkling like a contessa's necklace. Overhead, a galaxy of mirrored balls glitters; and the special effects roster includes soap bubbles, confetti, balloons, and giant video screens that replay the scene on the floor. Most spectacular of all—the fireworks that send down a shower of sparks that seems to merge with the city lights below. Be sure to ask for one of the special drinks, such as 7-Up with tequila (it foams up, and you chug-a-lug it down). Brandy is another showstopper, warmed, flamed, and then poured as a flaming blue waterfall in your glass. Located in the La Vista shopping mall near Las Brisas (tel. 4-67-27).

Baby 'O has ranked at the top for several seasons, with its distinctive "melted cave" facade. The music mix really keeps you moving, and the partying continues to dawn. On the Costera in town (tel. 4-74-74). **Boccaccio,** also in town, tends to attract an older, more sophisticated crowd, with its plush banquettes and mirrors (tel. 4-19-00). Other favorites include **Jackie 'O, Magic,** and **U.B.Q.**

Most of the discos open around 10 p.m., but the dance fever doesn't warm up in earnest until after midnight. Dancing until dawn is not a cliché here—often, the last reveler will not depart before sunup. The admission fee generally runs about $10 to $20 per couple, so be sure to allow plenty of room in your budget for boogeying.

THE CLIFF DIVERS AT LA QUEBRADA: *Las clavadistas* as they are called in Spanish, plunge 150 feet into a wave-tossed gorge surrounded by jagged rocks at La Quebrada, to the west of town. Yes, it's very touristy—but it's a don't-miss Acapulco attraction, demanding split-second timing on the part of the divers. One of the best perches for watching the spectacle is the terrace at the El Mirador hotel (admission fee is $3.50 per person plus drinks; arrive early to get the best seats). There's an afternoon show at 1 p.m., and several evening shows, usually at 7:15, 8:15, 9:15 and 10:30 p.m. The evening shows are by far the most dramatic, illuminated by torchlight and bonfires. For the exact schedule, check at your hotel.

LAS CALANDRIAS: And who more than honeymooners would more enjoy cuddling up in these charming **horse-drawn buggies** festooned with colorful balloons, and clopping down the Costera, completely oblivious to the hurly-burly of the city that surrounds them? Nicest time of all is at twilight, cooled by sea breezes and accented by the diamond-bright lights of the city. You can find *calandrias* for hire all along the Costera, especially in front of the major hotels.

BULLFIGHTS: If you want to experience this dazzling Mexican spectacle, *las corridas* (the bullfights) are held most Sundays during the winter season at **Cajetilla Stadium** and at other times during the year. Be advised that because of the bloodshed, this spectacle is not suitable for everybody, and animal lovers might prefer spending the afternoon at the **dolphin shows** at the **CICI aquarium** or the **zoo** in **Parque Papagayo.** You can make arrangements for bullfight tickets at your hotel front desk.

2. Honeymoon Hotels and Hideaways

Whatever season you visit, Acapulco's popularity makes it imperative that you make hotel reservations several months in advance. The off-season (approximately April through the beginning of December) represents a real travel bargain, with rates about 15% to 50% lower than in winter. Please note that winter rates are often MAP (including both breakfast and dinner); while EP (no meals) is available in summer. Price spreads reflect the difference between low- and high-season rates. Because the meal plans may vary between winter and summer, the difference in room rates can appear greater than is customary for Mexican hotels.

EXPENSIVE: **Las Brisas,** Carretera Escenica Clemente Mejia Avila No. 5255, Acapulco, Guerrero, 39868 Mexico (tel. 748-4-16-50; U.S. reservations: tel. toll free 800/228-3000), is romance—the most seductive resort in Mexico, and quite possibly the world. Certainly no setting could surpass this balmy perch on the hillsides above Santa Lucia Bay, Acapulco dramatically laid out beneath you. Accommodations are in white *casitas,* the Spanish word for small houses, carefully snuggled into the cliffs so as to maximize both views and privacy. Don't let the diminutive "ita" word-ending fool you, however. Rooms in the minivillas are graciously ample, with cool marble floors and sliding louvred doors opening onto the balcony and private pool. Perhaps it's the pools that lovingly establish Las Brisas' fairy-tale appeal. Lined with turquoise tiles, they are true oases, perfect for cooling refreshment, large enough so you can swim a couple of strokes. Every morning, your maid arrives with a basketful of tulipan (hibiscus) blossoms, which she gently positions on the surface. Although the rooms are air-conditioned, the cooling breezes that give Las Brisas its name usually keep temperatures comfortable.

When you finally budge from your room, you'll discover that the 110-acre Las Brisas is a complete, self-contained resort. All the pleasures of Acapulco lie a mere ten minutes' away, and right on the property, Las Brisas offers boutiques, five tennis courts, and its own discotheque. One of the nicest spots for sun-bronzing is its private La Concha Beach Club, centered around a seawater pool carved into the rocky hillside. The pool forms a natural aquarium, and colorful tropical fish are real amigos, loving to swim right up to you, and inquisitively nudge your toes. Las Brisas has three excellent restaurants on property: The Deli for casual dining, El Mexicano for creative regional cuisine, and Bella Vista, known for its white-glove service and dazzling views of Acapulco Bay (all three are open to guests and club members only). And there's room service 24 hours a day. Honeymoon package: Seven days / six nights (CP): $1,174.80 per couple. Includes casita with a private pool, welcome cocktails, basket of seasonal fruit, continental breakfast, and use of a Las Brisas pink-and-white jeep. Honeymoon package available April to December only; but other, different, packages are available. The guest relations staff at Las Brisas is also very experienced at handling all arrangements for couple who want to get married in Mexico; contact them for complete details.

MODERATE: Villa Vera Hotel and Racquet Club, Lomas del Mar #35, Acapulco, Guerrero, Mexico (tel. 748-4-03-33; U.S. reservations: toll free 800/233-4895 or 800/241-0767). At the swim-up bar, the sound of clinking glasses mingles with the beat of a Bruce Springsteen record. A huge inflatable dragon floats across the pool. As you stretch out on a blue-and-white striped towel on a lounge chair, you can see, through your toes, the Acapulco skyline and blue bay. Welcome to La Dolce Vita, Mexican style—Villa Vera.

Poised on a steep hillside above the city, Villa Vera provides an enclave of classy escape, ten acres of tropical gardens just minutes' drive from downtown. The hotel evolved from a private home; the villas originally accommodated the owner's friends. Thanks to a one-to-one staff / guest ratio, personalized service is still very much maintained, and since there are only 79 accommodations, the atmosphere remains distinctly club-like. Rooms, suites, and villas are tucked here and there in white buildings around the gardens. Furnishings are tasteful, comfortable rather than opulent. Superior rooms have two queen-size beds, cool marble floors, and green and white spreads. Each suite layout is different: Some have king-size beds, others feature huge balconies overlooking the bay or a private pool. Every room features a minirefrigerator, air conditioning, and a TV. The "racquet club" portion of the hotel name comes from the three clay courts (lit for night play), as well as resident pro and pro shop. But the main attraction of staying at Villa Vera is plugging into Acapulco's high-voltage social swirl. As one bronzed, gold-bechained playboy sighed, "Villa Vera is Acapulco." Honeymoon package: none. Superior room: $77 per couple per night summer season (EP); $125 per couple per night winter (BP). Villa with private pool: $159 per couple per night summer season (EP); $297 per couple per night winter season (BP).

At first glance, **Acapulco Princess,** P.O. Box 1351, Acapulco, Guerrero, Mexico (tel. 748-4-31-00; U.S. reservations: tel. toll free 800/223-1818 nationwide; 800/442-8418 in NYS; 212/582-1800 in NYC), is overwhelming and rather magical at the same time, built to resemble a massive Mayan pyramid set on the broad plain east of Acapulco. Cascades of bougainvillea tumble over the terrace railings, palm trees and ponds grace the atrium lobby, a rope bridge crosses the jungled lagoon, and flamingoes strut in the glades. The Acapulco Princess is a true self-contained resort, occupying 380 acres of gardens alongside Revolcadero Beach, about 25 minutes from Acapulco. It's a complete world, with 8 international restaurants, 4 bars, 2 18-hole golf courses, a disco, 11 tennis courts (9 lighted), elegant shopping arcade, and one of the world's great swimming pools, with inlets, lagoons, a waterfall, and a swim-up bar. Rooms either face the golf course or the ocean; oceanview rooms are more expensive but definitely worth it. They are absolutely huge, with beige marble floors, queen-

or king-size beds with colorful parrot-design bedspreads, rattan headboards, and a never-ending view of the blue Pacific. Honeymoon package: Eight days / seven nights: Summer: standard room: $783 per couple summer season (EP); $1,535 per couple winter season (MAP). Deluxe oceanview: $919 per couple summer season (EP); $1,982 per couple winter season (MAP). Includes welcome cocktails, bottle of domestic champagne, souvenir photo and honeymoon gift, his-and-hers T-shirts, use of chaise longue at pool, and all applicable taxes. Three-night packages, extra nights, and upgrades to suites are all available.

Acapulco Plaza Holiday Inn, Costera Miguel Aleman 123, Acapulco, Guerrero, Mexico (tel. 748-5-80-50. U.S. reservations: tel. toll free 800/HOLIDAY), one of the newest hotels on the strip, this is a three-towered hotel that is also one of the largest, with 1,000-plus rooms. Occupying a prime stretch of El Morro beach, just west of La Condesa, it features six restaurants, two freshwater pools, four tennis courts, a health club, arcades and arcades of boutiques, a disco, and live entertainment—making it a perfect in-town setting for action-loving honeymooners. Down at the beach, you can indulge in parasailing, scuba diving, Windsurfing, or waterskiing. The lobby itself is a tropical fantasy, with rushing waterfalls as well as parrots and peacocks adding to the sound effects. Half of the guest rooms are suites, and they come highly recommended, with a balcony overlooking Acapulco Bay, marble bathroom, and louvred separation between bedroom and living room. Decor is light and tropical, with rattan chairs and mauve and pink floral upholstery. All rooms offer air conditioning, color TV, a balcony, and a mini-bar, and room service runs 24 hours a day. Part of the Holiday Inn chain. Honeymoon package: Eight days / seven nights (BP): $849 to $1,147 per couple. Includes deluxe room with king-size bed, welcome drinks, full breakfast including one breakfast-in-bed with champagne, one dinner. Suite rates are from $158 per couple per night.

Hyatt Regency Exelaris Acapulco, Costera Miguel Aleman 1, Acapulco, Guerrero, Mexico (tel. 748-4-28-88; U.S. reservations: tel. toll free 800/228-9000), located along the far eastern edge of Acapulco Bay on relatively tranquil Icacos beach, this luxury, 23-story property offers understated elegance. The circular marble lobby is a knockout, with columns and huge potted plants. You'll find all the amusements you could want right on the property, with six restaurants and bars, sauna and massage room, three tennis courts, and a sprawling free-form pool with a swim-up bar and little footbridges. Any sport you want—from parasailing to waterskiing—is available down at the beach. The spacious rooms either face the water or the Costera; all feature air conditioning, a mini-bar, private balcony, and color TV. The color scheme is bright, with yellows, reds, and greens; rugs adapt an Indian-type design. For the most pampering, opt for a room on the Regency Club level, where you'll enjoy amenities such as an oceanview room, complimentary continental breakfast, an open wine bar in the afternoons, and complimentary hors d'oeuvres. Honeymoon package: Eight days / seven nights (BP): From $650 per couple low season. (Call for high-season rates.) Includes daily breakfast, welcome drinks, free tennis, and 50% discount on use of water-sports facilities. Regency Club rooms: From $110 to $170 per couple per night.

Playa del Secreto, Acapulco Sheraton Resort, Costera Guitarron 110, Fracc. Playas Guitarron, Apartado D160, 39359 Acapulco, Guerrero, Mexico (tel. 748-4-37-41; U.S. reservations: toll free 800/325-3535). The name reflects a lot of the charm: a hidden cove on the far side of Acapulco Bay, facing the mountain-framed skyline. This brand-new resort is set in a posh residential area to the east of the city, near Las Brisas resort. Four-story white stucco villas with traditional red-tile roofs occupy the steep hillsides; each room has a terrace or balcony fronting the bay. In addition to the small but charming beach, which lends its name to the resort, there's a large free-form pool, with arcing footbridges leading to a thatch-roof bar in the center. The accommodations are all condominium-style apartments, each with air conditioning, color TV, and completely outfitted with dishes and cooking utensils. You have a wide choice of apartments. The studios suit honeymooners perfectly, with spacious layouts, marble floors, blond furniture, and appealing details such as a shell-motif headboard or decorative Mexican pottery on the shelves. There's a restaurant right on the property, and the resort provides shuttle transportation into Acapulco. Honeymoon package: none. Studios range from $59 to $154 per couple per night (EP).

INEXPENSIVE: Maralisa Hotel, Enrique el Esclavo S/N, P.O. Box 721, Acapulco, Guerrero, Mexico (tel. 748-5-66-77 or 748-5-67-30; U.S. reservations: toll free 800/421-0767 nationwide; 800/252-0327 in California), is *it*—the real "find" in Acapulco, a true gem-like property that will have you whistling mariachi tunes as you lounge around the pool. The four-story white hotel is built surrounding a courtyard, Spanish style; small, balustraded balconies face the palm tree-lined terrace, gazebo / bar, and small pool. Wonder of wonders, the Maralisa is set on one of the prettiest stretches of El Morro beach, just off the Costera on a quiet side street. Another big bonus: Since the Maralisa is the sister hotel of that darling of the jet set, the Villa Vera, you share tennis and pool privileges. The rooms are simple but scrupulously clean, all with TV and air conditioning. And don't tell anyone, but the curtains and bedspreads are the same as you'll find at Villa Vera. All at about half the price, and beachfront to boot. Honeymoon package: none. Double room (EP): From $38 to $59 per couple per night.

3. Romantic Restaurants

Acapulco has the restaurant to suit your moods—from funky eateries on the beach to elegant continental showplaces that pull out all the stops.

MODERATE: El Campanario, Paraiso s/n Fracc. Condesa (tel. 4-88-30). Set in a ritzy residential neighborhood in the hillsides above La Condesa beach, this restaurant resembles a fairy-tale castle, with turrets and the tall tower that gives it its name (which means bell tower). The magic begins the moment you arrive and wend your way up the stone stairway, past a rushing waterfall and flaming torches. Piano music tinkles in the background, a perfect counterpoint to the panoramic views of Acapulco. You'll dine seated in heavy oak chairs that make you feel like a returning conquistador. The menu highlights both continental and Mexican specialties; We went Latin, and enjoyed superb ceviche, Aztec soup, red snapper (huachinango), and chicken serrano (served with mildly spiced pepper), plus an excellent flan for dessert. Dinner for two, about $45 per couple.

Madeiras, Scenic Highway near Las Brisas (tel. 4-43-78). Make your reservations several days in advance for this elegant continental dining spot on a cliff overlooking the city. (To take maximum advantage of the views, have cocktails on the terrace first.) Your four-course dinner will be served by candlelight, to the sound of live music. Chocoholics should be aware that there is a luscious chocolate torte for dessert. Four-course, prix-fixe dinner, about $17.50 per person.

Carlos 'n' Charlie's Bar & Grill, Costera Miguel Aleman (tel. 4-12-85). As the long lines will attest, this is probably the most popular spot on the strip. The atmosphere is simultaneously casual and outrageous—you never know when your waiter is going to pop up next to you on the dance floor, wearing a gorilla mask and waving a two-foot long unmentionable rubber object he has fastened somewhat below his mid-section. The menu features good food and plenty of it: seafood, steaks, salads, and ribs. Dinner for two: About $30 per couple. No reservations; open from 6 p.m. until 1 a.m.

INEXPENSIVE: Paradise, Costera Miguel Aleman at La Condesa beach (no phone). This thatch-roof restaurant located on one of the most popular sections of La

Condesa beach provides the perfect afternoon hangout. Once you wander in for lunch, you'll probably end up spending the whole afternoon, dancing to the live music and making new friends as you down frosty cervezas. Seafood is the specialty here—platterfuls of red snapper or garlicky shrimp. A complete lunch will run about $5 to $10 per person. Other similar beach-bars on the strip are **Beto's** and **Langosta Loca**, both nearby.

Chapter XX

PUERTO VALLARTA

1. Romantic Interludes
2. Honeymoon Hotels and Hideaways
3. Romantic Restaurants and Night Spots

ONCE A REMOTE FISHING VILLAGE, Puerto Vallarta has blossomed into one of Mexico's most popular resorts by virtue of its small-town charm and scenic beauty. Whitewashed stone houses with red-tile roofs and archways line the cobblestoned streets. The foothills of the Sierra Madres almost reach the ocean, and bougainvillea and other lush vegetation seem to meander across every balcony. Although today, Puerto Vallarta is more of a city than a village, the sight of a farmer with his burro plodding along a busy downtown street won't let you forget its small-town origins.

Heading from the airport to Puerto Vallarta, you'll take Paseo Diaz Ordaz, the beachfront drive that passes most of the modern, deluxe hotels that line the road about a mile or two north of downtown. When you see the cobblestone streets, the spire of the cathedral and the oceanside promenade, you'll know you've arrived in Puerto Vallarta proper. The city center is bisected by the Rio Cuale. In the middle of the river itself, you'll find five-acre Cuale River island, linked to the town by two arched bridges. The island is packed with restaurants and dozens of chic shops such as Ralph Lauren and Gucci, as well as numerous little curio outlets—contributing to Puerto Vallarta's reputation for having the best shopping of any Mexican resort. At the mouth of the river, the waterfront promenade—the *malecon*—forms the hub of Puerto Vallarta's social life. From early afternoon to the wee hours of the morning, lively bars and restaurants throng with gringos toasting their newly acquired tans with margarita after margarita.

If you're seeking beaches, then you're sure to find one that will please you in Puerto Vallarta or a bit farther south. The action-packed main beach in town, Playa del Sol, bustles with sun-worshipping North Americans, snacks stands, and even musical combos. You can try all the water sports here, including parasailing, Windsurfing, and waterskiing, or rent horses for a ride on the beach. If you're both seeking quiet and seclusion, follow the cliff-hugging highway south along isolated stretches of ocean to remote caves which await exploration. Renting a car, or, even more exhilarating, a four-wheel-drive Jeep, for a day trip is the best way to take it all in. Driving south you'll come across some spectacular hillside villas before catching a glimpse of Playa las Estacas, a small inlet with beautiful white sand at the Camino Real hotel. Along the way you'll see the huge, craggy Los Arcos rock formations which jut out from the sea. At Mismaloya, seven miles south, you can rent boats that will take you to Los Arcos for some of the best snorkeling in the area. Locals sell grilled fish in small stands on the Mismaloya beach. And on the hillside above, you can still see part of the set for the movie *Night of the Iguana*, which put Puerto Vallarta on the tourist map when Elizabeth Taylor dallied with Richard Burton during the filming.

Set aside a day to visit Yelapa, a village surrounded by jungle and ocean, and accessible only by boat. Hotel desks can arrange the trips, which leave each day for the 1 ½ hour cruise down the coast on the *Serape* and *Vagabundo* boats. When you get to Yelapa you'll find no roads and no electricity, only several small restaurants serving fresh seafood on the beach, a quaint Indian village, and a 150-foot waterfall, which you can explore by foot or by horseback. Cruises to Yelapa are about $12 per couple.

1. Romantic Interludes

Puerto Vallarta's settings make a variety of options available.

Each morning at 9:30 the *Bora Bora* trimaran **sails** to deserted Las Animas for a day of snorkeling and sunning at the kind of tropical beach you've probably fantasized about. You can also check at the Garza Blanca resort, where you can hire fishermen to take you to Las Animas in their private boats. For a three-hour cruise around Banderas Bay and to Los Arcos, natural arches formed in rock, sign on with El Vagabundo and Yelapa Yachts. Price is about $20 per couple, including lunch. At 5:30 p.m. each evening, the motor yacht *Serape* offers sunset cruises of the bay, with a buffet, live music for dancing, and two bars (about $14 per couple). Another day cruise is on the *Cielito Lindo* trimaran along the north shore, passing fishing villages, to isolated and beautiful Piedra Blanca (White Rock) beach. Price is about $20 per couple, including lunch. If you catch a fish, there is a cook on board who will prepare it for you. Hotel desks can arrange any of these and other sailing trips.

Stroll the **malecon.** Buy an ear of corn on a stick, or stop by for the best ice cream on the Mexican coast at **Helados Bing** (Ave. Juarez 280), before taking a moonlight stroll along the **promenade,** where you can watch the waves break on the beach beyond the swaying palms. Then poke your heads into one of the many shops and galleries downtown before crossing the bridges to Cuale Island. Saunter along pebbled paths winding through tropical gardens, then relax on one of the benches. At the foot of the steps of the southbound bridge, stop at the Franzi Café, which serves coffees, pastries, and exotic drinks, while a jazz band performs until midnight. Perhaps later, hop over to Le Bistro Café where tiny lights twinkle in the trees along the banks of the river, and recorded jazz is played all evening long.

Not all the action centers on the city or on the beaches in Puerto Vallarta. The **jungle** inland is surprisingly accessible. It can be explored by horseback, by car or Jeep, and by organized tour. Day-long Jeep safaris ride across the back-country plantations of mangroves and through lush green forests (Jeep rental is $60 per day). A horseback tour at **Rancho Victoria**—a real working ranch—is accompanied by a "ranchero," a Mexican cowboy, who leads groups past small villages and along a river where you can take an invigorating swim. Cost is about $20 per couple. Check with hotel desks for arrangements for tours or Jeep rentals. One fun way to experience the Tarzan-like ambience is by lunching at one of the two big jungle restaurants south of town—Chico's Paradise and Chino's Paradise (see "Romantic Restaurants" section). At either one you can splash around in pools and waterfalls before, during or after lunch, and sunbathe amid trees and squealing birds and monkeys (most of them in cages).

2. Honeymoon Hotels and Hideways

Puerto Vallarta's hotels have kept pace with the phenomenal popularity of the resort. Almost all of the big, modern hotels lie along the north shore, just outside of downtown. Becoming a big factor in Puerto Vallarta's accommodations scene are villas and condominiums, which offer all the amenities of a hotel, plus full kitchens. Unless otherwise indicated, difference in room rates reflects the spread between low- and high-season rates.

EXPENSIVE: Garza Blanca, Apdo. 58, Puerto Vallarta, Jalisco (tel. 322-2-10-23; U.S. reservations: tel. 918/665-2900 or 213/388-1151; toll free 800/331-0908, 800/421-0000, 800/252-0211). Puerto Vallarta's most exclusive—and expensive—hideaway is situated on a secluded stretch of Banderas Bay about ten minutes from downtown. Garza Blanca cannot be simply defined as a hotel. Yes, there are rooms, but none are "standard." The beachfront suites occupy two-story thatched-roof huts, with living rooms overlooking the beach. Bedrooms contain king-size beds. Chalet suites sit higher up, on a hillside affording panoramic views of Las Arcos. Each contains a living room, a large bedroom, and a private pool shaded by bougainvillea and jungle-like trees. For the ultimate in romantic dining, reserve one of the three or four secluded and candlelit tables set out each night on the beach in front of the hotel's restaurant. Honeymoon package: Seven days/six nights (EP): $900 per couple (chalet suite in low season); the seventh night is free. Includes welcome drink, tropical flowers and fruit in room, bottle of champagne, and boat excursion. High-season rates for chalet suites: $180 per couple per night.

MODERATE: Camino Real, Playa del las Estacas, Apdo. 95, Puerto Vallarta, Jalisco 48300 (tel. 322-2-00-02; U.S. reservations: toll free 800/228-3000), among the most luxurious of Puerto Vallarta's hotels, stands majestically on its own cove on Banderas Bay. The white-sand beach with its calm water is among the best in the area for swimming and water sports. Beautifully landscaped grounds greet guests even before they glimpse the bougainvillea-draped hotel from the highway. Each of its 250 rooms has views of the ocean. One of the two pools is a large, free-form swimming pool lined in Mexican tile and crossed by wooden bridges. Standard rooms are spacious and have bright Mexican decor, while the icing on the cake here are the two-story penthouse suites considered by some to be the most elegant accommodations in Puerto Vallarta (Elizabeth Taylor used to forsake her house in town for one of these suites). Each has a private pool with glorious ocean views and a circular stairway leading to a mammoth bedroom with king-size bed and private terrace. Honeymoon package: Eight days/seven nights: $600 to $850 per couple. Includes deluxe room, daily full breakfast, one dinner, bottle of champagne, flowers in room, souvenirs, and free admission to the discothèque.

You need never to leave the Krystal Vallarta, Ave. de Las Garzas, Puerto Vallarta, Jalisco 48300 (tel. 322-2-14-59; U.S. reservations: 713/784-2682 in Houston; toll free 800/392-4671 in Texas; toll free 800/231-9860 nationwide), to experience almost everything Puerto Vallarta has to offer. From Mexican fiestas on Saturday nights to bullfights in which guests can participate, the Krystal has it. Arched passageways, iron grillwork, red tile, and gushing fountains set a romantic mood. There is a host of daily activities from which to choose, including tennis classes with professionals, scuba lessons, basketball, soccer, and even donkey polo (participants whack a ball with a broom while astride a donkey). Six restaurants cater to a variety of moods and tastes, including a Japanese dining room and an Argentinian steak house. There is also a range in accommodations—a cluster of 38 villas with private swimming pools, master condominiums with kitchens, junior suites with king-size beds and living rooms, deluxe rooms with king-size beds and small sitting areas, and standard rooms. All have terraces or balconies overlooking gardens or the ocean, servi-bars, and TVs with reception of two U.S. channels. Baths in the suites and villas have large Roman-style bathtubs. Honeymoon package: none. Standard room rates: $60 to $155 per night. One-bedroom suites: $85 to $230 per night.

Fiesta Americana, Apdo. 270, Puerto Vallarta, Jalisco 48300 (tel. 322-2-20-10; U.S. reservations: toll free 800/223-2332). The dramatic lobby here—with its large, cone-shaped, thatched roof and waterfall—sets a delightful tropical atmosphere at this hotel located just five minutes from downtown Puerto Vallarta. Brightly colored rooms have color TVs and servi-bars. Balconies with pretty potted flowers add splashes of color to the pale orange facade of the hotel. For more luxury, book a room in the Grand Fiesta, an 81-room adults-only section of the hotel whose rooms have amenities such as complimentary evening cordials and turndown service, terry cloth robes, private lounge for continental breakfast, and afternoon hors d'oeuvres. The hotel has all you could ask for from a deluxe resort, including a variety of restaurants. Honeymoon package: Eight days/seven nights: $925 to $1150 per couple. Includes full American breakfast (one in bed with bottle of champagne), flowers in room, king-sized bed, and room tax.

Los Tules Condominiums, Apdo. 169B, Puerto Vallarta, Jalisco 48300 (tel. 229-90-2-46-60; U.S. reservations: 213/474-4041 or toll free 800/824-7102). Next door to the Fiesta Americana is Los Tules, a luxurious condominium village set amid banana trees and winding cobblestone streets. Units are attractively decorated and are ideal for honeymooners who would appreciate the at-home conveniences of kitchens and the other pluses of renting what are essentially fully-equipped and fully furnished apartments. Master studios contain king-size beds and terraces or patios. There are five tennis courts and nine swimming pools, located right off the beach. Honeymoon package: none. Standard rates: $45 to $110 per couple per night for studios; $86 to $175 for one-bedroom units.

Bugambilias Sheraton, Apdo. 333, Puerto Vallarta, Jalisco 48300 (tel. 322-2-30-00; U.S. reservations: toll free 800/392-3500 in Missouri; toll free 800/325-3535 nationwide). All the services you would expect from the Sheraton name are found at this sleek, modern hotel, whose six high-rise towers dominate the stretch of beach north of town. The largest hotel in Puerto Vallarta, the Sheraton is for couples who love being in the center of activity. There are four restaurants, five bars, Mexican Fiestas each night, in addition to a daily roster of activities, most around the huge pool area. Five tennis courts are available. All rooms have ocean views and modern decor. Honeymoon package: none. Oceanview room rates: $68 to $110 per couple per night.

Holiday Inn, Apdo. 555, Ave. De Las Garzas, Puerto Vallarta, Jalisco 48300 (tel. 322-2-17-00; U.S. reservations: 212/683-0060 in New York or toll free 800/ HOLIDAY). Two adjoining beachfront highrises set the stage here for a modern, first-class hotel. One tower contains 230 rooms and suites while the second is more ideally suited for honeymooners with 236 more lavish suites with private terraces. All rooms have a balcony, ocean view, cable TV and servi-bar. A lovely pool area, three restaurants, two bars, a discothèque, and tennis are other pluses. There are plenty of activites: volleyball games, parasailing, and other water-based sports among them. Honeymoon package: Eight days/seven nights: $780 per couple (low season only). Includes welcome cocktail, American breakfast each day (one breakfast in bed with bottle of champagne), one Mexican dinner, flowers in room, and an eighth night free.

INEXPENSIVE: Puerto Vallarta's famed cobblestoned streets begin just outside the **Buenaventura,** Ave. Mexico 1301, Puerto Vallarta, Jalisco 48300 (tel. 322-2-37-37; U.S. reservations: toll free 800/522-5568 in New York; toll free 800/223-6764 nationwide), which manages to create a feeling of seclusion even though it's just steps away from the bustle of downtown. With all the services of a more luxurious hotel and such a prime location, this modern hotel offers a really good buy. An attractive five-story atrium lobby is the centerpiece of the hotel. Rooms are clean, comfortable and nicely furnished. There are fashion shows and a Mexican Night once a week. Honeymoon package: none. Rates: $35 to $60 per couple per night.

Molino de Aqua, P.O. Box 54, Puerto Vallarta, Jalisco 48300 (tel. 322-2-19-07; U.S. reservations: toll free 800/423-5512 in California; toll free 800/826-9408 nationwide), set among gardens accented by fountains, stone walkways, and cages with parrots squawking inside, this hotel lies hidden away beside the Rio Cuale downtown. Older cabins are simple and clean with double beds and a terrace. There are also suites with ocean views in a new two-story addition on the beach. A casual, friendly atmosphere centers around and animates the two swimming pools. No frenzied activities or glitter of the high-rise resort hotels here. Honeymoon package: none. $38 to $48 per couple per night for cabins; $58 to $76 for suites. Tax and breakfast are included.

3. Romantic Restaurants and Night Spots

Puerto Vallarta's restaurants can be blissfully quiet or fun and crazy, so there's a definite range from which to choose, both downtown and in the hotel zone.

MODERATE: El Set, on the Mismaloya highway about two miles south of town (tel. 2-03-02). The hills of Puerto Vallarta afford many breathtaking views, but the setting of the El Set bar/restaurant, with its terraced seating and lush plants under a thatched roof, may afford the best of all. Famous for its "another lousy sunset in paradise" motto, El Set attracts Hollywood types and couples who enjoy watching the crashing ocean and twinkling of city lights, while sipping cool margaritas. Go for lunch and you can swim in the pool on the terrace. Seafood and steaks are specialties. Lunch for two from about $10; dinner about $25.

Chico's Paradise, off Mismaloya beach about 15 minutes south of town (no telephone, no electricity). Open daily from noon to 6 p.m., this is a place to spend the entire afternoon tucked away in the mountainous jungle. Wild, vibrant flowers, gushing waterfalls, and pools for swimming set the scene (make sure to bring swimsuits for a dip). Grilled steaks, spareribs, and Mexican food highlight the culinary offerings. Sample some of the delicious tequila and rum fruit-punch cocktails. Lunch for two with beer and wine is about $18 to $20. **Chino's Paradise,** also about 15 minutes inland from Mismaloya beach, has similar ambience, food, and prices to Chico's, although the two are not related.

La Hacienda, Aquacate 274 (tel. 2-05-90). Secluded from the hustle and bustle of town behind the walls of a former grand home, you've got the choice of a rustic, wood-beamed dining room or lush gardens for your dinner setting. Soft music and candlelight accompany such dishes as crêpes, French onion soup, Mexican platters, and grilled meats. Dinner starts at about $25 for two, with wine.

Daiquiri Dick's (tel. 2-05-66), Olas Altas 246, makes the perfect midday getaway spot after a morning on the beach. You can eat on the beach patio or in the indoor dining room decorated in nautical motif while indulging on an extensive menu, including crêpes Suzette for dessert. Lunch for two (hamburgers, sandwiches) runs about $8; dinner with drinks about $22 to $25. **Carlos O'Brian's** (tel. 2-14-44), Ave. Díaz Ordaz 786, is probably the wildest and most popular place in town, with live music and a party atmosphere. Lines to get in are not uncommon. Try the baked oysters, $3.50, or barbecued spareribs $4. **La Cebolla Roja** (tel. 2-10-87) has some of the best food on the malecon, with imaginative vegetable dishes and Mexican specialties. Lunch for two will run about $8 to $10; dinner about $20 to $30 with drinks. **Moby Dick** (tel. 2-06-55), just off the malecon on Cuale North has a kitchen open to view that serves, arguably, the best seafood in town. Excellent fresh lobster ($14.50) and whole red snapper ($4.50) are the delights. When you enter **El Morocco** (tel. 2-20-10) at the Hotel Fiesta Americana, you'll feel like you've stepped onto a movie set, thanks to the lavish, Casbah-like decor plucked straight from the Arabian Nights. Red snapper with orange sauce is delectable. Dinner about $30 for two. For dancing, head to **Capricco** (tel. 2-15-93) perched on a cliff and reached by funicular. A wild music-and-dance show erupts in the early morning hours (about 1:30 a.m.). It's on the highway to Mismaloya, about five minutes from downtown. You'll find live music for dancing or just listening at major hotels. Downtown, the notable—and raucous—dancing spots are **Sundance** (tel. 2-22-96) and **City Dump** (tel. 2-07-19).

Chapter XXI

MORE MEXICAN BEACH RESORTS

1. Manzanillo
2. Ixtapa / Zihuatanejo
3. Cancún
4. Cozumel

PLANTATIONS OF MANGOES and bananas, long beaches, craggy coves, and turquoise water—that's the stretch of coastline between Puerto Vallarta and Ixtapa often referred to as the Costa de Oro (Gold Coast).

1. Manzanillo

Manzanillo, an important commercial port for Mexico, has developed into a glittering, yet slow-paced resort in just a few years. Those looking for a lot of diversity (shopping, sightseeing, restaurants) or sizzling nightlife may be disappointed; those seeking quiet, luxurious seclusion will find this area ideal.

ROMANTIC INTERLUDES: Because of its remoteness, many of the attractions here are a bit distant from each other, but the drive in between is rewarding—through verdant, tropical landscape.

Rent a car and drive 35 miles north of Manzanillo along a modern highway bordered by tropical plantations to the quaint fishing village of **Barra de Navidad.** Along its long, curving beach, you'll find an authentic Mexican resort, with cantinas lining the beach and serving up the freshest seafood you'll find anywhere. Just spend the day dallying about here, soaking up the sun and the atmosphere of the laid-back town. Little boats on the lagoon at the east end of town will take you on private cruises for about $10 an hour.

Still by rented car, head inland on highway 110 about two hours to the quiet town of **Colima.** Along the way you'll see a spectacular active volcano and the Nevado de Colima mountains which are sometimes snow-capped. Founded in 1523 on an Indian site, Colima is an attractive town of simple colonial buildings and gardens. At the **Museum of Western Mexico Indian Cultures** you'll see some pre-Columbian statues—for which this area is famous. You can buy reproductions in small shops in town. The museum is open Monday through Saturday, 10 a.m. through 1:30 p.m.; admission is free. There's another museum here of quite a different sort—the **antique automobile collection** of Francisco Zaragoza Basquez, with 50 perfectly restored cars dating from 1886 to 1941. Automobile buffs will be thrilled. Check with the tourist office at Hidalgo 75 (tel. 333-2-43-60) to arrange an appointment to see the collection.

HONEYMOON HIDEAWAYS AND HOTELS: Hotels in this region stand out because their uniqueness as romantic spots. Rates quoted reflect the spread between low- and high-season rates.

Las Hadas, Apdo. Postal 442, Manzanillo, Colima (tel. 333-3-01-41; U.S. reservations: toll free 800/228-3000), is a fantasy come true for those who dream of a place where white spires rise out of green hillsides, where no cars are allowed, where fountains and statues greet you at every turn, and privacy is prized above all. The 203-room hotel is built in a style called by some Moorish, by some Mediterranean, and by others Disneyland. It was the dream of a Bolivian tycoon, Don Antenor Patino, who chose Manzanillo to build his "fairyland" retreat. Today, it's best known as the setting for Dudley Moore–Bo Derek movie *10*. Rooms are in white and muted colors to match the exteriors, with private balconies, marble floors, and servi-bars. A true "self-contained" resort, Las Hadas has its own 70-vessel marina, golf course, and ten tennis courts. There is a lagoon-size swimming pool surrounded by islands and waterfalls, a private cove with white, Arabian-style tents for shade, and a range of water sports available. Honeymoon package: Eight days/seven nights: $820 to $1,100 per couple. Includes junior suite with ocean view, sunset cruise, a dinner, bottle of champagne, flowers in room, and unlimited golf and tennis daily.

Hotel La Posada, Apdo. 135, Manzanillo, Colima (tel. 333-2-24-04; U.S. reservations: toll free 800/252-0211). If Mexicans had invented bed-and-breakfast inns they would resemble this hotel. Small—24 rooms—it exudes charm and relaxation, Mexican style. Surprise—it's actually owned and operated by an American, Bart Varelmann. Low-key and unpretentious, the only aspect of the hotel that is even slightly outrageous is its exterior—painted in what the hotel calls "passionate pink." From the fan-cooled rooms, a tiled patio leads to the beach a few yards away, a small pool, and plenty of trees. The large lobby contains comfortable sofas and game tables with chess and backgammon boards and a bar where guests serve themselves on the honor system. The owner's three cats may even wander over for a nap on your laps. Honeymoon package: none. Rates: $48 per couple per night (year-round), with breakfast.

Near Manzanillo

Hotel Plaza Careyes, Barra de Navidad-Puerto Vallarta Highway Km. 52, Jalisco (tel. 333-7-00-10; U.S. reservations: tel. 714/494-8129; toll free 800/227-0212 in California; toll free 800/458-6888 nationwide). About an hour north of Manzanillo and two hours south of Puerto Vallarta, you'll find utter serenity. Plaza Careyes is the result of the dream of an Italian banker, Giafranco Brignone, who sighted this spectacular coastline from an airplane almost 20 years ago and was inspired to build a hotel that combines the best of Europe and Mexico. The coast here, with its white-sand beaches, rocky cliffs, and turquoise waters, may be the most beautiful spot on Mexico's Pacific. The hotel does its best to show it off: Its horseshoe shape opens onto the beach and there are balconies or large patios from each room overlooking the ocean. There is a range of rooms, from standards with Arabian-looking canopied beds with mosquito netting, to "casitas"—actually apartments individually decorated in bright Mexican colors with original artwork. They contain living rooms, huge bedrooms with king-size beds, kitchenettes, and large terraces for private sunbathing; some have private swimming pools. Guests can occupy themselves by snorkeling, scuba diving, horseback riding, deep-sea fishing and tennis, but it's recommended that guests rent Jeeps when they arrive at Manzanillo (the nearest airport) for use during their stay, as there is no other way of getting around here. There are three restaurants and a disco at the hotel, but Gianfranco warns that those seeking the hustle and bustle of Puerto Vallarta will be disappointed: This resort deals in isolation and tranquility. Honeymoon package: Eight days/seven nights: $899 per couple (year-round), including a deluxe suite with king-size bed and living room, one candlelight dinner on the beach, breakfast each day, a two-hour horseback ride, and transfers from Manzanillo airport.

ROMANTIC RESTAURANTS: How can a restaurant help but be romantic along a stretch of coastline that is so beautiful and isolated?

L'Recif, Olas Altas, Manzanillo (tel. 3-06-24), actually hangs on the cliff next to the Vida del Mar Hotel. With one of the best ocean views of any restaurant in the area. L'Recif serves a cuisine that best can be described as French/continental. The bouillabaisse and seafood are outstanding (try the seafood combo plate). There is a large menu and good choice of wines. Dinners cost about $36 per couple, but you may want to come for lunch and take a dip in the pool on the terrace.

Pancho, on López de Legazpi in Barra de Navidad (tel. 7-01-76). This simple, rustic restaurant on the beachfront provides serious seafood eating. It specializes in a dish invented in this small town—camarones a la diabla (shrimp cooked in butter and hot sauce)—as well as oysters and ceviche. Lunch ranges from about $5 to $7 per couple.

2. Ixtapa / Zihuatanejo

Fifteen years ago this region consisted of nothing but Zihuatanejo (See-WHA-tah-nay-hoe), the quintessential Mexican "sleepy fishing village" with its picturesque boats and small harbor. Today, although its streets are all paved, and restaurants and boutiques flourish, you can still watch fishermen haul in the daily catch of oysters and marlin and see the local women shopping at open-air markets.

Ten minutes north is Zihuatanejo's glittery neighbor, Ixtapa, a resort as modern as Zihuatanejo is rustic. It stretches along six-mile-long Palmar Beach, covered with white sand and dotted with coconut palm trees. Here, the modern, high-rise hotels line up in a row, each offering deluxe accommodations, American-style service, and amenities (you can drink the water here), but each retaining a unique ambience. Most hotels have tennis courts, and you can partake of various water sports—parasailing, waterskiing, Windsurfing—on the beach. Because of the rough surf at Palmar, the hotels all boast huge, fantastic swimming pools, with whimsical additions such as bridges, waterfalls, water slides, and swim-up bars.

Across from the hotel strip, the Palma Real Golf and Tennis Club features a Robert Trent Jones-designed 18-hole golf course winding along the base of the mountains and finishing at the edge of the ocean. Also across from the strip lies La Puerta, the area's largest shopping area, containing restaurants and a plethora of stores selling handcrafts from all over Mexico and designer resort wear.

Although a rental car can give you the freedom you may want, it's not a real necessity here. The hotels, restaurants, and discos are all an inexpensive cab ride away from each other. A cab ride from Ixtapa to Zihuatanejo is about US $2.

Sometime during your honeymoon here you'll want to venture to one of Zihuatanejo's three beaches—La Madera, La Ropa, or Las Gatas—which have calm waters ideal for snorkeling. (Snorkeling equipment is available for rent at each beach.) La Madera is a small cove, about a 15-minute walk from Zihuatajeno's center. La Ropa, with possibly the best water for swimming, has some restaurants and a Windsurfing school. To get to remote Las Gatas, take a launch from the pier in Zihuatanejo (about $1).

ROMANTIC INTERLUDES: No honeymoon in Ixtapa is complete without a visit to primitive **Ixtapa Island,** a national park which shelters tropical birds and animals. There are some thatched-roof restaurants serving fresh seafood just steps away from white-sand or pebble beaches. The gentle surf and underwater conditions offer ideal conditions for snorkeling or diving. Hotel desks can arrange excursions (about $11 per person) or you can take a little boat to the island from Playa Quieta, a short taxi ride from Ixtapa hotels.

Stroll through **Zihuatanejo,** after dinner at one of the many seafood restaurants in town, saunter along the beachfront to the main square, as the townsfolk do. Sometimes cruise ships dock in the harbor, providing a pretty sight with their clear lights streaming from their stacks. You can soak up the rustic beauty of the town by rambling up Calle Alvarez and other streets, visiting the small shops and sharing a drink at one of the local cantinas.

HONEYMOON HOTELS, INNS, AND HIDEAWAYS: Just as Zihuatanejo and Ixtapa are different in character, so are their accommodations. Modern, luxurious hotels line the hotel strip of Ixtapa, while Zihuatanejo's inns are more rustic and family-oriented. As in the rest of Mexico's beach resorts, rates from April through November (low season) are cut by as much as half. Prices quoted reflect the spread between low-and high-season rates.

Camino Real, Playa Vista Hermosa, Ixtapa, Guerrero 40880 (tel. 743-4-33-00; U.S. reservations: toll free 800/228-3000). Another of the Westin chain's strikingly beautiful hotels, this one stands out for its angular design which blends into the jungle hilltop and affords spectacular views of secluded Vista Hermosa Beach. Each of the hotel's 441 rooms has a view of the ocean from a large lanai that comes with chaise longue and hammock for private sunbathing, and a marble-topped table in the shade for dining or watching the sunset. The 13 suites also have their own swimming pools. Recreation focuses on the beach (you get to it by walking down the steep staircase cut in a cliff or by a private elevator) and a complex of four swimming pools connected by waterfalls and fountains. There are four lighted tennis courts. Forty-five Jeeps are available to rent for those who want to explore the grounds and surrounding area. Honeymoon package: Four days/three nights (some meals): $299 per couple. Includes full breakfast daily, oceanview room with private balcony, flowers upon arrival, bottle of champagne, dinner for two including wine at La Esfera restaurant, one hour of tennis, welcoming cocktails. Available low season only. Standard rates: $80 to $115 per couple per night.

Hotel Villa del Sol, Playa La Ropa, Apdo. 84, Zihuatanejo, Guerrero 40880 (tel. 743-4-22-39). It's difficult to beat the isolation and private atmosphere of this unusual hotel, conceived by Helmut Leins, a German engineer who discovered this area on vacation years ago and never left. The hotel consists of just 17 bungalow-type rooms laid out amid gardens and streams. Rooms have ceiling fans and canopied beds; bathrooms are lined in hand-painted Mexican tiles and there is a split-level living room area. Breakfast and dinner at the hotel restaurant—considered by many to be the finest in Ixtapa/Zihuatanejo—are included in the price. You can be guaranteed privacy and quiet here: Children under 14 are not allowed. The hotel is on one of Zihuatanejo's calm coves and best beaches. Warning: Because of its uniqueness and size, reservations are required a year ahead in high season. Honeymoon package: none. Rates (MAP): $85 to $160 per couple per night.

Krystal, Boulevard Ixtapa, Apdo. 68, Ixtapa, Guerrero 40880 (tel. 743-4-26-18; U.S. reservations: toll free 800/231-9860 nationwide, in Texas: toll free 800/392-4671). This high-rise hotel—which resembles the bow of a ship thrusting toward the Pacific Ocean—is among the most sophisticated in Ixtapa. Chandeliers and polished Mexican granite accent the luxurious lobby. There are four tennis courts, a gigantic free-form pool with waterfall and toboggan slide, racquetball, and water sports. Honeymoon package: none. Standard room rates: $55 to $95 per couple per night.

Holiday Inn, Boulevard Ixtapa, Apdo. 55, Ixtapa, Guerrero 40880 (tel. 743-4-23-96; U.S. reservations: toll free 800-HOLIDAY), is an activity-oriented hotel with events planned all day around the huge tropical pool area. There is a tennis court and a lively disco. Honeymoon package: Eight days/seven nights: $650 to $750 per couple. Includes American breakfast each day (one breakfast in bed with champagne), one dinner, eighth night free.

Sheraton, Boulevard Ixtapa, Ixtapa, Guerrero 40880 (tel. 743-4-31-84; U.S. reservations: toll free 800/325-3535). You'll get a terrific view of the Sheraton's towering atrium lobby—the centerpiece of this 358-room hotel—from the glass elevators leading to your room. There are four lighted tennis courts. Honeymoon package: none. Standard room rates (with ocean views): $55 to $106 per couple per night.

El Presidente, Boulevard Ixtapa, Apdo. 95, Ixtapa, Guerrero 40880 (tel. 743-4-20-13; U.S. reservations: toll free 800/472-2427). This large hotel complex containing 440 rooms is both modern and traditional: Rooms in a newer, large tower building all face the ocean, while three hacienda-style buildings are set among tropical gardens and have a colonial flavor. There is a large swimming pool and two tennis courts. Honeymoon package: Eight days/seven nights, $725 to $775 per couple. Includes room with king-size bed, American breakfast each day, welcome cocktail, one candlelight dinner, bottle of wine in room, fresh fruit basket each day, and discount on rental car.

ROMANTIC RESTAURANTS AND NIGHT SPOTS: From thatched-roof, local hangouts in Zihuatanejo to sleekly elegant hotel restaurants in Ixtapa, this area will have the dining spot to fit your mood.

Villa del la Selva, Paseo del la Roca, near the Camino Real (tel. 4-20-96), advertises "private" sunsets, and as you sit at a small candlelit table on a terrace overlooking the sea, you might believe the sunset is, indeed all yours. The setting is sublime, amid lush vegetation and the crashing surf far below. Seafood and meat dishes are the specialties (red snapper with hollandaise is one favorite), all served by candlelight. It's also one of the most expensive restaurants in Ixtapa. Dinner for two with wine will run $25 to $35.

Gitanos, Bravo and 5 del Mayo, La Ropa Beach, Zihuatanejo (tel. 4-33-93). There are a few shaded tables on the beach in this popular seafood restaurant featuring the fresh catch of the day—so fresh, it comes straight from the boats docking at the pier a few yards away. Meat dishes are also available. You may want to eschew your hotel and head here for inexpensive breakfasts—less than $5 for two. Expect to pay $10 for lunch.

Da Baffone at La Puerta shopping center in Ixtapa (tel. 4-23-15) offers indoor and outdoor dining areas and fine dishes of pasta, veal, and other Italian specialties. Expect to pay from about $25 to $30 per couple for dinner with wine. **Villa del Sol,** at the Zihuatanejo hotel of the same name (see "Hotel" section), has a Swiss chef who prepares luscious European dishes. The menu changes each night, but always gives a choice of two entrées of meat or fish. The restaurant's candlelit tables overlook the ocean and, to make the atmosphere even more sumptuous, classical music accompanies the meal. Dinners run about $20 per couple with wine. **Coconuts** (tel. 4-25-18) in Zihuatanejo offers a romantic setting of candlelit tables arranged in a garden under twinkling lights. Entrées such as red snapper cost $6 to $7.50. Save room for delicious dessert specialties such as apple pie and coconut ice cream. **La Mesa del Capitan** (tel. 4-20-87), run by an Englishman, Oliver Jones, and his wife, ranks as one of Zihuatanejo's most popular restaurants. Steak and lobster are the specialties, with dinner entrées running from $5 to $7. **Christine's** at the Krystal Hotel is a disco with electrifying special effects straight out of Star Wars. In Zihuatanejo try one of the thatched-roof discos on the beach—**Ibiza** is one of the most popular.

3. Cancún

This idyllic resort just off the tip of the Yucatan peninsula consists of mainland Cancún city and a narrow island of sand, almost 15 miles long, surrounded by lagoons and the sparkling waters of the Caribbean. The area receives little rain and maintains a steady 80° average temperature year-round.

Cancún provides a haven for water lovers. The lagoons of Nichupte and Bojorquez to the west furnish secluded waters for waterskiing, Windsurfing, and jet skiing, while the Caribbean side has the water sports as well as white, porous sand ideal for sunbathing. Abundant marine life makes for terrific snorkeling and scuba diving everywhere on this coast. When you've had enough of the water, put on a pair of comfortable walking shoes, rent a car or join a day tour, and explore Mayan ruins. Chichen-Itza, the phenomenal and largest Mayan site in the Yucatan with its massive pyramids, makes a popular day trip (check hotel desks for tours, which run about $38 per person). If you can't find the time, don't despair: There are dozens of other Mayan sites, large and small, such as Coba, a jungle-covered city, and Tulum, 50 miles away (see "Romantic Interludes"). At night in Cancún, you can get a feel for traditional Mexico at the Ballet Folklorico (tel. 3-01-99), which entertains with music and dancing from all over the country. They perform every night except Sunday at the Convention Center; dinner and the show cost about $22 per person.

ROMANTIC INTERLUDES: Water sports and the ancient ruins nearby nicely fill out any honeymoon agenda.

The islands of **Cozumel** and **Isla Mujeres** are within a couple of hours' sailing time from Cancún. Hydrofoil service on the trimaran m/v *Mexico* is available at Playa Linda, next to the Calinda Hotel each morning for the 1½-hour trip to Cozumel (tel. 4-64-33 and 4-69-35). The boat drops you in the middle of San Miguel, the main town; you can shop and spend the day there, or explore the many beaches (see "Cozumel" section). Various boat trips to tiny **Isla Mujeres** are offered by travel agencies. These usually take a total of five hours and include lunch, drinks, and on-board live music for dancing for $10 to $32 per person. At Isla Mujeres the boats dock at El Garrafon beach, which has a terrific coral reef for snorkeling. The *Tropical* leaves each day at 9:30 a.m. from the **Playa Langosta Tropical Dock** (tel. 3-14-88); the *Manta Trimaran* (tel. 3-03-48 or 3-16-76) sails daily from the **Club Lagoon Caribe Cancún Hotel;** the *Fiesta Maya* motor yacht—with a glass bottom—visits Isla Mujeres each day from the **El Presidente** (tel. 3-18-04); the *Aqua-quin* trimaran leaves each day from the **Camino Real** (tel. 3-01-00, ext. 605); and *Don Diego* sails from the **Playa Blanca Marina**—you can even hang onto the spinnaker while under sail (tel. 3-06-06). The *Fiesta Pirata Tropical* cruiser also departs from **Playa Langosta** to Isla Mujeres (tel. 3-14-88). Check hotel desks for more information.

Tulum is one of Mexico's most stunning Mayan cities. Perched atop a cliff and overlooking the turquoise of the Caribbean, it invites you to wander around its fascinating temples and ruins. If you take an organized tour, you'll be allowed plenty of time to explore, followed by lunch at the beachside Akumal Hotel, then let loose for snorkeling at **Xel-Ha** (pronounced shell-HA), a national park with seaside coves filled with brilliant tropical fish (you can rent snorkeling equipment, change clothes, and take showers here). An organized bus trip can be booked through hotel desks for about $20 per person. You can also rent a car and visit both on your own. Tulum lies about two hours' down the coast from Cancún along a modern highway; Xel-ha is practically next door to the ruins.

Rent a car and set out on the highway south of Cancún City to find the dozens of **hidden beaches** along Mexico's Caribbean coast. You'll pass through relatively developed areas of Puerto Morelos, Punta Bete, and Playa del Carmen. Five miles from Playa del Carmen is **Xcaret** (Shka-ret), a cove fed by underground springs. The grottoes here have water so clear, you can see the rocks beneath. A little farther south is **Akumal,** a tranquil bay and underwater paradise with a marvelous beach protected from rough surf by a breakwater. Don't stop too long because you're also going to want to make it to **Chemuyil,** a small horseshoe-shaped cove. Its talcum-soft white sand is dotted with coconut palms and swaying hammocks.

HONEYMOON HOTELS AND HIDEWAYS: Hotel building in Cancún hasn't caught up with its phenomenal popularity: Hotels are often full in the high season. You must make your reservations early and pay in advance. Cancún's hotels also are among the most expensive in all of Mexico, but honeymoon packages cut down on costs.

During the off-season prices drop by about a third. Rates quoted reflect the spread between low- and high-season prices.

Moderate

Camino Real, Kukulkan Blvd., Cancún, Quintana Roo, 77500 (tel. 988-3-0100; U.S. reservations: toll free 800/228-3000). Like the other hotels in the Camino Real chain, this one stands out for its bold architecture and setting. Shaped like a pyramid, the hotel sits on the tip of Punta Cancún so that it's bordered on three sides by the blue of the Caribbean. All 281 rooms and 10 suites have private terraces from which to enjoy the sea views. A homey touch are the fresh flowers that are brought in each day. The suites contain living rooms and winding staircases leading to the bedrooms. Honeymoon package: none. Rates: $115 to $160 per couple per night.

Miramar Mission, Kukulkan Blvd., Cancún, Quintana Roo 77500 (tel. 988-3-1755; U.S. reservations: toll free 800/854-2026 nationwide; toll free 800/542-6028 in California), is a bit less expensive than Cancún's other deluxe hotels, yet it has all the activities and services most honeymooners would want. Attractive rooms and suites all overlook the beach or the lagoon and contain servi-bars and color TV with satellite reception from the United States. The hotel has a small health spa and minature golf. One of its two pools is the longest in Cancún and has lounge chairs built right into the shallow end for unusually cool sunbathing. Honeymoon package: none. Rates: $105 to $120 per couple per night.

Exelaris Hyatt Regency, Kukulkan Blvd., Cancún, Quintana Roo 77500 (tel. 988-3-00-04; U.S. reservations: toll free 800/228-9000), is an elegant hotel, with an architecturally striking circular lobby where classical music is played in the evenings. For royal treatment, stay at the Regency Club on the top floors where the personal service truly pampers. A new fitness club has its own pool, gymnasium, steam room, and Jacuzzi; in addition, there are two swimming pools and a large lagoon in which to swim. Honeymoon package: none. Rates: $110 to $150 per couple per night; $180 per couple for Regency Club.

Hyatt Cancún Caribe, Kukulkan Blvd., Cancún, Quintana Roo 77500 (tel. 988-3-00-44; U.S. reservations: toll free 800/228-9000). One of the first modern hotels in Cancún, this remains a favorite due to friendly atmosphere and a terrific location on a wide, secluded beach. Glass elevators provide a panoramic view. Honeymoon package: none. High-season rates: $110 to $150 per couple per night; $180 for Regency Club.

Fiesta Americana, Cancún Blvd., Cancún, Quintana Roo 77500 (tel. 988-3-14-00; U.S. reservations: toll free 800/223-2332). Built to resemble a Mediterranean village, this hotel's quaint atmosphere makes it unique among Cancún's hostelries. The buildings, painted in pastel colors and topped with red-tile roofs, surround a striking pool area with tropical landscaping. Honeymoon package: Eight days/seven nights, $1,200 to $1,450 per couple. Includes full breakfast each day (one in bed with a bottle of champagne), fresh flowers in the room, king-size bed and room tax.

Sheraton, Kukulkan Blvd., Cancún, Quintana Roo 77500 (tel. 988-3-19-88; U.S. reservations: toll free 800/325-3535). Two aspects of this resort set it apart from others on hotel row in Cancún: its location farther out and on a private beach, and the presence of a Mayan temple right on the grounds. Activities are central to the hotel's attraction, with a full roster of organized events each day. Suites have Jacuzzis. Honeymoon package: Four days/three nights; $500 to $625 per couple. Includes suite with Jacuzzi, bottle of champagne, breakfast each day, and one cocktail per person each day.

Inexpensive

La Posada del Capitain Lafitte, write Apdo. 1463, Merida, Yucatan 97000 (no telephone; U.S. reservations: tel. 303/674-9615; or toll free 800/538-6802 nationwide;

in Colorado, 303/674-9615). Just 37 miles south of Cancún City you can play Robinson Crusoe to your heart's content at this collection of bungalows. A five-mile stretch of secluded beach called Punta Bete provides the setting for 32 cabins tucked among a coconut grove laced with hammocks. Each cabin has a terrace, ceiling fan, private bath, double bed, and simple furnishings. A swimming pool, a rustic restaurant, and a bar, serving delicious seafood (broiled lobster tails) complete the setup of this hotel, where casual is the password. Honeymoon package: none. Rates: $34 to $42 per couple per night, including breakfast and lunch or dinner.

ROMANTIC RESTAURANTS AND NIGHTSPOTS: Chinese, German, Tex-Mex—these are some examples of the varied dining in Cancún. However, more than any other kind of cuisine, you'll find seafood, steak, and dishes of the Yucatan topping most menus.

Moderate

Mauna Loa, across from the convention center (tel. 3-06-93), is a kind of Mexican-style Trader Vic's with entertainment to boot. Twice each night, Hawaiian shows perk up the dinner atmosphere, turning this lagoon-side restaurant into a Polynesian paradise. Cuisine is Chinese, South Seas, and international. At 11:30 p.m. the Mauna Loa is transformed into a rocking discotheque called Krakatoa. Reservations for dinner/show are required; your hotel desk can make all the arrangements. Price is about $40 per couple.

Chac-Mool, next to the Hotel Aristos (tel. 3-11-07). Candlelit tables and background music by Vivaldi and Beethoven make the ambience here as delectable as the pasta, beef, and seafood specialties, among them lobster in cognac. You can choose a table on the outdoor terrace overlooking the floodlit beach or indoors where a statue of the Mayan god, Chac-Mool, oversees diners. Lunch for two is about $10; dinner with wine about $30 to $40.

Maxime (tel. 3-04-38) in the hotel zone is the most elegant restaurant in town (men must wear jackets) and reservations are suggested. Delicate French cuisine is the fare, with such entrées as boneless duck with olive sauce and, for dessert, orange soufflé. Dinner runs $40 to $50 for two with wine.

Blackbeard's (tel. 4-16-59) nearby on Ave. Tulum is a nice, rustic spot with Mexican ambience and delicious grilled shrimp, lobster, and steaks. A complete dinner for two runs about $25 with drinks.

Inexpensive

Los Almendros, downtown on Ave. Bonampark (tel. 4-08-07). When in Cancún, you may want to try dishes of the Yucatan, which are not fiery hot (no chilis are used). The cheerful dining room at Los Almendros sets the stage for such succulent fare as lime soup with chicken and turkey in a white sauce of capers, olives, and almonds. Try the more famous Yucatecan specialties, such as *cochinta pibil,* which is beef marinated for 24 hours in a sauce with a variety of spices and then wrapped in banana leaves; or *poc-chuc,* slices of pork grilled with spices, orange juice, tomatoes, and onions. Or, better yet, order the combination plate. Lunch or dinner will run less than $12 per couple.

Chocko's and Tere's (tel. 4-13-94), downtown at the intersection of Claveles and Tulum, is always hoppin', with a lot of laughter and often live music—from a guitarist or maybe a mariachi band—emanating from the bright dining rooms. Expect to pay about $18 per couple for a full dinner of seafood and wine. **Pizza Rolandi** on Ave. Coba 12 in Cancún City (tel. 2-01-62) is one of the most popular and inexpensive Italian restaurants in Cancún, with homemade pastas (fettuccine, ravioli, lasagne) and, of course, pizza as selections (pizzas for one hungry person are $3 to $5; pasta about the same). **Cafeteria Pop** (tel. 4-19-91) on Ave. Tulum near the Hotel Parador is the place for an unpretentious breakfast (eggs, bacon) or lunch (hamburgers). Your bill for two for either meal probably won't top $5. For a Mexican floor show, followed by disco dancing through the night, try the lively **Mine Company** at the Club Verano Beat near downtown. Or, if you're homesick for some country music, head over to the **Lone Star Bar** at the Hotel María de Lourdes.

4. Cozumel

Cozumel lies like a jewel off the coast of the Yucatan. Mexico's largest island in the Caribbean, it is framed in white sand and pristine water that sparkle in the year-round sunshine. Physically, just 44 miles south of the sophisticated planned resort of Cancún, but, in spirit, it's a world away. While Cancún is modern and luxurious, Cozumel is simple and relaxed—a haven for those just wanting to get away from it all.

Most of Cozumel is sparsely populated or uninhabited. All activity takes place on the west coast where the major hotels dot the beaches south of the island's only town, San Miguel. Charming and still untouched by mass tourism, San Miguel provides plenty of people watching in cafés and bars along the waterfront Avenida Rafael Melgar. There are dozens of small shops selling souvenirs, such as jewelry made from the black coral from the Palancar Reef, and designer resortwear.

ROMANTIC INTERLUDES: There is much to explore and do on this island, 28 miles long and 11 miles across. Cozumel is perfectly located for excellent snorkeling and other **water sports.** At **Parque Chankanaab,** nine kilometers (5½ miles) south of town, you'll find a natural underwater park and botanical garden where you can spend a day exploring caves and the colorful life of the lagoon (there is a small admission fee). Off the shore of the south of the island is **Palancar Reef,** one of the longest coral reefs in the world, and thus a magnet for scuba divers from all around the world. Cozumel is the closest Mexican resort to the Mayan ruins of **Tulum** and the lagoon of **Xel-Ha,** which are just across the water on the mainland (see the Cancún section). On Cozumel itself, you can explore small, yet interesting, Mayan relics and ruins, such as **El Caracol,** a temple; and **El Cedral,** a tiny shrine. You can explore these by renting cars, Jeeps, or mopeds at hotels or in town.

So-called **Robinson Crusoe cruises**—all day sailing and picnic lunch excursions —delight vacationers here. The most romantic of all journeys to **Isla de la Pasion** (with a name like Island of Passion, it's got to be good) for a barbecue and day of seclusion on an islet just north of Cozumel. En route, the crew dives and fishes for your lunch, which is an orgy of red snapper, conch, and shellfish grilled on the beach. All-day adventures are about $25 per person, including lunch. Your hotel desk can sign you up for this and other boat excursions, including several to the breathtakingly vibrant coral reef, **Playa Palancar** (particularly fun are the glass-bottom boat tours, both day and night, which run about $7 per person).

HONEYMOON HOTELS AND HIDEAWAYS: Cozumel does not have the luxury atmosphere of Cancún, but you'll still find hotels from deluxe to tourist class, and at lower prices. Like other resorts in Mexico the most modern, better hotels are located outside of town, while the less expensive and simpler properties are in the center of things.

Moderate

Sol Caribe, Playa Paraiso, Apdo. 259, Cozumel, Quintana Roo 77600 (tel. 987-2-07-00; U.S. reservations: toll free 800/223-2332). Dramatic Mayan architecture and an enormous free-form tropical pool mark this 220-room high rise, operated by the highly regarded Mexican hotel chain, Fiesta Americana. Lush plants and trees spread over the grounds, giving a feeling of a newly discovered Mayan city. All units have servi-bars and spectacular views of the Caribbean. There is a nice cove for swimming and all the services of a deluxe hotel. Honeymoon package: Eight days/seven nights: $875 to $1100 per couple. Includes room with king-size bed, full breakfast each day (one in bed with bottle of champagne), one dinner with wine, fresh flowers in room, and room tax.

El Presidente, Playa San Francisco, Cozumel, Quintana Roo 77600 (tel. 987-2-03-22; U.S. reservations: toll free 800/472-2427), also is run by another prestigious Mexican chain, El Presidente. The island's first deluxe resort, it has 189 rooms divided between a beachfront tower and a one-story wing. All rooms have colorful decor, ocean view, balcony, servi-bar and cable TV. The beach here is stunning. Honeymoon package: Eight days/seven nights: $1,100 to $1,200 per couple. Includes deluxe room, breakfast each day, candlelight dinner, fresh fruit in the room each day, one free hour of tennis, and a discount on an Avis rental car.

Inexpensive

Cabañas del Caribe, Pilar Street 9, Cozumel, Quintana Roo 77600 (tel. 987-2-01-61). For sheer coziness, you won't find anything else quite like this on Cozumel. This casual inn about three miles north of town consists of 50 small bungalows on the beach—some older cabañas while others in the coconut grove are new units. Some have the added luxury of private terraces, and all are clean and comfortable with private baths and air conditioning. There is a small swimming pool, two restaurants, and a bar. Rates: $60 to $80 per couple per night.

Hotel Villablanca, Apdo. 230, Cozumel, Quintana Roo 77600 (tel. 987-2-07-30), a quaint, 26-room hotel about two miles south of town, occupies the former grounds of a private home and still retains a feeling of intimacy. Lovely tropical gardens surround the units, which are set back across the road from the beach in a quiet location. Some of the rooms have sunken bathtubs and whirlpools; all are attractively decorated. There is a tennis court, small pool, a restaurant, and private dock. Honeymoon package: none. Rates: $45 to $68 per couple per night.

ROMANTIC RESTAURANTS AND NIGHT SPOTS: Lunch in Cozumel will probably be at a small restaurant at the beach or at your hotel, while you'll probably want to walk along the waterfront in town for dinner and nightlife. A specialty in restaurants is conch—or, in Spanish, *caracol*—found only in this area.

Moderate

Casa Denis, downtown San Miguel (tel. 2-00-67; hotel desks can make reservations), actually is a small wooden house owned by natives of the Yucatan, Jorge and Fatima Gutierrez. The restaurant was started by Fatima's father, Denis. The atmosphere is very homey—in a mi casa es su casa way. You'll walk through their living room, filled with wedding photographs, into a garden courtyard where dining tables are under a huge mango tree. Reservations are necessary because lunch and dinner is limited to 12 people (find another couple to share a table, as foursomes are required). Yucatecan and Cuban cuisine are the specialties of the limited menu, which changes each day. Dinner for two with wine are about $25.

La Ceiba (tel. 2-08-16 and 2-08-44). In the hotel of the same name, this restaurant features romantic dining in a garden near the beach. An international menu emphasizes local lobster and a seafood bisque. Serenades by strolling guitarists add to the atmosphere. Dinner for two will be in the $30 range, not including wine or tax.

Morgan's (tel. 2-05-84) is the restaurant to choose for the special night out. One of the most elegant places to eat in Cozumel, seafood and prime rib are the specialties. A dinner for two will be about $20.

Inexpensive

Las Palmeras, on San Miguel's waterfront (tel. 2-05-32). This bistro-like restaurant is popular all day long as a people-watching hang-out, probably because of its breezy location across from the ferry pier. You can get a reasonably priced breakfast or lunch, everything from hamburgers to Yucatecan specialties and there's often live music. Breakfasts of bacon and eggs will be about $1.75 while lunch and dinner entrees of seafood will run from $2.50 to $4.

Pepe's Grill (tel. 2-02-13) entices with soft lights and tables open to the Caribbean breezes. Meat and fish specialties run $5 to $6 per entrée for dinner. As in other Mexican resorts, most evenings you'll find a Fiesta Mexicana at one of the hotels, with mariachi bands and dancing along with a buffet. The El Presidente has one on Fridays, and the Sol Caribe's is on Wednesday.

Part Four

THE CARIBBEAN,
THE BAHAMAS, AND BERMUDA

Chapter XXII

ARUBA

1. Practical Facts
2. Romantic Interludes
3. Honeymoon Hotels and Hideaways
4. Romantic Restaurants and Nightlife

MILES OF SUGARY WHITE sand beaches. World-class resort facilities. Intimate restaurants. Las Vegas–type nightclubs. Whether your honeymoon plans include soft starry nights or bright disco lights—Aruba has it all.

The island is a tiny one, about 20 miles long and just 6 miles across at its widest point. Before it became a separate entity within the kingdom of the Netherlands in 1986, Aruba was part of the Dutch territories known as the Netherlands Antilles. Along with Bonaire and Curaçao, it had been included in the Leeward group of the Netherlands Antilles off the northern coast of South America—often referred to as the "ABC" islands. Aruba lies just 15 miles north of Venezuela and about 42 miles west of Curaçao. The country's new political status is a form of "commonwealth" with Holland, along with Bonaire, Curaçao, and the three windward islands of the Netherlands Antilles—St. Eustatius, Sint Maarten, and Saba, all located in the Caribbean more than 500 miles to the north of Aruba. Although Aruba has its own currency now, there haven't been any other changes that would affect couples who want to travel between Aruba and the other islands of the Netherlands Antilles.

Oranjestad, the capital city on the southwest coast, provides a number of clues to Aruba's early history. Fort Zoutman, built in 1796, and the Willem III Tower, built in 1868, are landmarks, and two of the earliest buildings in Aruba. The jumble of pastel-colored stucco walls topped with terra-cotta roofs and cupolas along Willhelminastraat aren't quite as old, but are fine examples of colonial shops and residences.

The island's first inhabitants were probably members of the Arawak Indian tribe that settled throughout the Caribbean. In 1499, Alonso de Ojeda, a Spaniard, was the first European to see the island. Subsequently, Aruba was visited by many pirates and buccaneers while its ownership was juggled between Spain, Holland, France, and England; the Dutch gained permanent possession in 1816.

Today Aruba has a population of 65,000, made up of people of over 40 different nationalities. Despite their ethnic diversity, Arubans share a spirit of warmth and graciousness. "Bon Bini" means "welcome" in the native language, and Arubans will go out of their way to make you feel at home wherever you travel on the island.

They throw a weekly Bon Bini Festival, which introduces visitors to the Aruban people and their culture by showcasing the local arts, crafts, foods, and music. The festivities take place every Tuesday from 6:30 to 8:30 p.m. in the court-

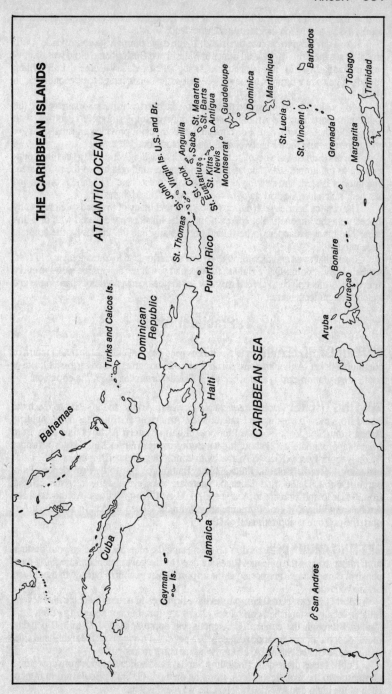

THE CARIBBEAN ISLANDS

ATLANTIC OCEAN

CARIBBEAN SEA

St. Thomas
St. John
Virgin Is. U.S. and Br.
Anguilla
St. Croix
St. Maarten
Saba
St. Barts
St. Eustatius
St. Kitts
Antigua
Nevis
Montserrat
Guadeloupe
Dominica
Martinique
Barbados
St. Lucia
St. Vincent
Grenada
Tobago
Trinidad
Margarita
Puerto Rico
Dominican Republic
Haiti
Turks and Caicos Is.
Bahamas
Cuba
Jamaica
Cayman Is.
San Andres
Bonaire
Curaçao
Aruba

yard of the Aruba Historical Museum in Fort Zoutman. Tickets are available at all hotels; the $1 admission includes a folkloric dance show.

Take a day or so to explore the island. If you drive through the countryside you'll probably see the ruins of the gold mines at Balashi and Bushiribana. Gold was discovered in Aruba in 1824; mining became Aruba's first industry. More than 3 million pounds of gold were brought to the surface before the mines ceased to be economical in 1916.

Most visitors to Aruba spend their time on the beaches in the resort area along the southwest coast. But the Aruban *cunucu* (countryside) is strangely beautiful, with many different areas to visit. For honeymoon couples, it provides unusual spots for private picnics and for leisurely or energetic exploration.

The north coast has a desolate beauty, and its crashing waves are a startling counterpoint to the limpid seas that lap the palm-fringed sand beaches of the resort area. The interior is stark and striking as well. No rain forests here. The land is brown and parched, much like the arid states of the southwest United States.

The cunucu bristles with clumps of cactus, and many of the roads are practically fenced with the impenetrable, spikey plants. The hillsides are covered with divi-divi trees: The branches appear to be folded horizontally into 90° angles by the constant trade winds.

Roads that twist and turn through Aruba's interior lead to Yamanota, at 617 feet, Aruba's highest point. Drive right to the top, and you'll see panoramic views in every direction. A great place to greet a new day, or to pop open a bottle of champagne and watch a magnificent sunset.

1. Practical Facts

ENTERING AND LEAVING: U.S. citizens need proof of citizenship, and a return or continuing ticket. Although a passport is preferred, an authenticated birth certificate or a voter registration card is also acceptable. The departure tax is $9.75 per person.

GETTING THERE: There's frequent air service to Aruba, and it's easy to reach the island from most places in the United States. **American Airlines** has daily flights to Aruba from New York (about a four-hour flight). **Eastern Airlines** flies daily from Miami (approximately a 2½ hour flight). Both American Airlines and Eastern Airlines fly daily from Puerto Rico to Aruba, with connecting flights from major U.S. cities including Newark, Boston, Philadelphia, Baltimore, Hartford, Providence, Pittsburgh, Detroit, Dallas, and Chicago. There are also several daily interisland flights from Curaçao and Bonaire to Aruba via **ALM Antillean Airlines.** All the hotels on Aruba are within a 15- to 30-minute drive from the Queen Beatrix International Airport; the taxi fare is approximately $10.

GETTING AROUND: Taxis don't have meters; the rates are based on your destination, rather than on the mileage. Rates are fixed by the government and are fairly inexpensive. Sample fares are posted at the airport; always confirm fares with the drivers before you ride.

Most U.S. **car-rental companies** have licensees in Aruba; there are also several reliable locally established companies. Jeeps are fun, but not necessary, even for a "safari" through the cunucu. Car rentals run approximately $30 to $40 per day; motor-scooter rentals are approximately $25 per day. Driving is on the right-hand side, as it is in the United States. Aruba uses international road signs.

Public **buses** make daily (including Sundays and holidays) loops from downtown Oranjestad to the main resort area, stopping on the L.G. Smith Boulevard in front of each of the high- and low-rise hotels. One-way fare is 90¢.

LANGUAGE: Aruba's native tongue is Papiamento, a language which evolved from Spanish, Dutch, Portuguese, and combines a sprinkling of African and French, as well as Caribbean Indian dialects. You won't experience a language problem though. Most Arubans are multilingual and speak several languages, including Dutch, Spanish, and English.

MONEY: The official currency of Aruba, introduced when the country gained equal status as a member within the Dutch Kingdom in 1986, is the Aruba florin (AFl), which fluctuates on the world market. At this writing, there are 1.77 florins to the U.S. dollar.

If you also travel to the nearby islands of Bonaire and Curaçao, make sure you don't confuse Aruba's square coin with the square coin of the Netherlands Antilles! In Aruba it's a 50-cent piece; in Bonaire and Curaçao it's a nickel.

U.S. dollars are accepted everywhere on the island. Although the hotels and the shops in the downtown shopping district accept major credit cards, many local restaurants require cash payment.

WEATHER: The climate in Aruba is dry and sunny, and it's always summer there! The trade winds are constant, and blow at a steady 15 miles per hour. So hold on to your hats—and forget about your hairdo!

The temperature in Aruba is almost always a warm 82°. There's only a slight change of temperature from day to night, and the temperature difference between summer and winter is only 2° or 3°. The average rainfall is 20 inches per year, which mainly occurs in brief showers during the months of October, November, and December. This isn't truly a rainy season, though, and if you do seek shelter, you'll be able to get right back onto the beach. The island lies completely outside the hurricane belt.

CLOTHING: Cool, casual, and informal summer clothes are the rule in Aruba, for both men and women. Dress-up clothes are fun, but not entirely necessary, for a night out in one of the elegant high-rise restaurants, nightclubs or casinos. Dress-up for men usually means a jacket, although some require ties; but it's not unusual to see jackets over polo-type shirts.

You should wear a cover-up over bathing suits once you leave the beach; bathing suits aren't permitted in the shopping or business areas.

TIME: Aruba keeps Atlantic Standard Time all year long. That means that during the winter, it's one hour later in Aruba than it is in U.S. east coast cities; during the summer, when eastern U.S. cities observe Daylight Savings Time, the time is the same.

TELEPHONES: You can dial Aruba direct from the mainland United States. The international dialing code is 011; the area code is 297-8; then dial the five-digit local number. When making calls in Aruba, just dial the five-digit local number. You can make local and international telephone calls through hotel operators. The average price for a three-minute call to the mainland U.S. is approximately $10.

SHOPPING: U.S. Customs regulations allow U.S. citizens a $400 duty-free quota.

Aruba is considered a free port, since the country imposes little or no tax on imported items. This means that you can get good buys on specific items, but it's important to shop carefully before you leave home, so that you can compare prices. Well-priced luxury items include perfume, table linens, china, crystal, and flatware; some jewelry and designer fashions are also attractively priced.

In Oranjestad, most shops are located along **Nassaustraat** and in the **Boulevard Shopping Center** opposite the harbor. Many stores in Oranjestad have branches in the **San Nicolas Shopping Center** at the eastern end of the island. The **Alhambra Ba-**

zaar, across from the Divi Divi and Tamarijn Beach hotels, has many international boutiques with items from all over the world. There are also shops in each of the hotels.

The **Aruba Trading Company** on Nassaustraat is something of a tradition in Aruba. It offers the widest assortment of merchandise on the island, and some of the world's finest brand names. **Spritzer & Fuhrmann** has three shops at the corner where Hendrikstraat meets Nassaustraat. You'll find over 300 patterns of china, crystal, and flatware with names like Lalique, Waterford, Baccarat, and Wedgwood. Spritzer & Fuhrmann also has shops in the Holiday Inn, the Concorde, and the Divi Divi Beach hotels.

Aruba's shops are also well stocked with merchandise imported from South America; best bets for local handcrafts include pottery, ceramics, and hand-printed or silk-screened T-shirts and dresses.

Arubans follow the siesta tradition: shop hours are from 8 a.m. to noon and 2 to 6 p.m. Although shops are closed by law on Sundays, if a cruise ship is in the harbor, special permits allow them to open. Aruba has no sales tax. For more information on shopping, check out *A Shopper's Guide to the Caribbean* (Prentice Hall Press, New York).

SIGHTSEEING: It's easy to hire a taxi for sightseeing; the driver guide will provide running commentary for $10 per hour. **De Palm Tours** (tel. 24400 or 24545) and **Pelican Tours** (tel. 23888) offer tours of Oranjestad, combined with either full-day (approximately $22 for six hours) or half-day (approximately $14 for 2½ hours) tours of the island.

HOW TO GET MARRIED IN ARUBA: Although Aruba extends a warm and cordial welcome to just-married couples, you won't be able to say "I do," while visiting. Marriages are permitted only if one of the partners has been a resident of Aruba for at least one year.

FOR FURTHER INFORMATION: Contact: **Aruba Tourism Authority,** Schuttestraat 2A, Oranjestad, Aruba (tel. 011/297-8/23777); **Aruba Tourism Authority,** Suite 2212, 1270 Avenue of the Americas, New York, NY 10020 (tel. 212/246-3030).

2. Romantic Interludes

Aruba has sophisticated resorts with all the amenities and plenty of opportunity for adventure, too.

For **day sails,** the *Mi Dushi* ("my sweet one" in Papiamento), a 76-foot Danish ketch built in 1928 and restored to its original splendor, leaves from the Tamarijn Beach Hotel. You can purchase tickets in advance at the De Palm tour desk in all the hotels (tel. 24400 or 24545). The multihulled *Blue Melody* and the *Octopus* set sail from the **Pelican Watersports Center** at the Holiday Inn (tel. 23600, ext. 329).

Sail into the sunset with your sweetheart! Most water-sports operators in Aruba offer **sunset cruises** complete with rum punch and snacks for approximately $40 per couple. The boats depart from hotel piers and cruise the calm waters of the southwest coast. Voyages usually last 2½ to 3 hours. The glass-bottomed *Dreamboat* cruises at sundown from the Aruba Palm Beach Hotel pier to the Surfside Beach close to the Talk of the Town Resort, where there's an open rum punch bar, an all-you-can-eat barbecue, a romantic bonfire, and dancing to the tropical sounds of a steelband (tel. 24400 or 24545). Tickets cost approximately $80 per couple. **Royal Sunset Cruises** runs a similar sail for about $30 per couple (tel. 23334 or 23888).

The beaches are beautiful, but the **cunucu** (countryside) has much to recommend it too! Rent a car, jeep, or motor scooter, pack a lunch, and don't miss the Natural Bridge, the highest and longest in the Caribbean; the massive boulder formations at

Ayo and Casibari; and the caves with Indian inscriptions at Guadirikiri and Fontein. Ride through Frenchman's Pass, where Arawak Indians defended Aruba against the invaders in 1700; you'll have panoramic views of the countryside and abandoned aloe fields. The roads in the country are rough, and poorly marked, but it's literally impossible to become lost; the divi-divi trees point to the southwest, in the direction of the major hotels.

Whether you gamble, or just watch the action, a visit to Aruba wouldn't be complete without a visit to one of the island's six **casinos.** Don't feel intimidated, even if you've never gambled before. The casinos are fun places, and in Aruba, the beach parties continue right into the gaming rooms. You don't have to dress up to gamble, but you won't look out of place if you do.

The **Alhambra Casino** (tel. 35000) is the only casino that's not attached to a hotel; it's in the Alhambra Bazaar, across from the Divi Divi and Tamarijn Beach hotels. The five hotel casinos include: the **Americana Hotel & Casino,** the **Aruba Concorde Hotel & Casino,** the **Aruba Holiday Inn & Casino,** the **Aruba Palm Beach Hotel & Casino,** and the completely refurbished casino at the **Golden Tulip Aruba Caribbean Hotel & Casino.**

In addition to 5¢, 25¢, and $1 slot machines, the casinos usually offer games of chance, including blackjack, roulette, craps, wheel of fortune, and baccarat. Video poker is becoming increasingly popular.

The **Seroe Colorado,** the residential area of the Exxon Corporation's Lago refinery is in a beautiful location, well maintained, and open to the public. Since the refinery closed, the executive homes and facilities are deserted. And so are the two sand beaches with their lush vegetation. **Baby Beach** and **Rodgers Beach** provide privacy and some of the best snorkeling on the island, with crystal-clear waters.

On the way back from **Seroe Colorado,** stop in at Charlie's Bar in San Nicolas (tel. 45086). You can get a light lunch, and take a look at the eclectic assortment of memorabilia that's been accumulating since 1941.

Try **island hopping.** Enjoy a touch of Holland on a one-day trip to Curaçao. Or bask for the day on a beach in Bonaire. **De Palm Tours** (tel. 24400 or 24545) and **Pelican Tours** (tel. 26003) run day-long tours to both Netherlands Antilles islands for approximately $150 per person. The one-day tours include airline tickets, airport transportation, sightseeing, lunch, and time to shop.

You can also make arrangements to spend a few days (or longer) on either Bonaire or Curaçao. Interisland schedules change frequently, so plan to confirm your flight at least two days in advance. We flew in a 20-seat Twin Otter, with very limited luggage capacity. It's a good idea to pack light, check in early, and tote essentials in a small carry-on bag, just in case your luggage travels on a separate plane.

3. Honeymoon Hotels and Hideaways

There is a 5% government room tax and an 11% service charge on all room rates. The service charge on food and beverage is 10% to 15% in lieu of gratuities at the hotels. Some properties also charge a $3 energy surcharge per day.

All of the hotels in Aruba have package rates that are very attractive. Some packages include meal plans that represent good value, but you should decide in advance whether you'd rather experience a variety of restaurants and types of food. High season runs from mid-December to mid-April; low-season rates are about 20% to 50% lower. Prices quoted in this section reflect the range between low- and high-season rates.

Aruba has 14 first-class hotels in its south-west coast resort area; casually elegant low-rise hotels are located on Druif and Manchebo beaches; stylish and sophisticated high-rise hotels on Palm Beach.

EXPENSIVE: Divi Divi Beach Hotel, L.G. Smith Blvd. 93, Aruba (tel. 011/297-

8/23300; U.S. reservations: tel. 607/277-3484 or toll free 800/367-3484 nationwide). A sense of privacy prevails at this self-contained resort with outdoor pool and Jacuzzi, where the atmosphere reflects barefoot elegance. All of the luxury "Lanai" and "Casita" rooms have oceanfront balconies or patios, just a few steps from the private beach. Deluxe accommodations are set back in trilevel, bougainvillea-draped buildings made of white stucco with dark wood trim that surround a free-form pool with a small island and a tea house accessible by a wooden foot bridge. Inside your room, you'll find fresh flowers everywhere. Floral prints in deep tropical greens complement the room's dark-wood furnishings, providing a soft, cool, oasis-like retreat. Honeymoon package: Eight days/seven nights (EP): $910 to $1,260 per couple. Includes: a bottle of champagne, a personalized gift, and a "just married" sign, a two-hour sailing cruise.

Golden Tulip Aruba Caribbean Hotel & Casino, L.G. Smith Blvd. 81, Aruba (tel. 011/297-8/33555; U.S. reservations: tel. 212/832-2277 or toll free 800/344-1212). The "Grand Dame" of the Caribbean is the only five-star deluxe hotel on the island. The hotel is stately, and English tea is served every afternoon in the Lobby Lounge. But lavish use of turquoise accents throughout the building and grounds promotes an ambience of tropical informality that will have couples feeling right at home. Situated on 1,500 feet of white sand beach, the resort has a water-sports center, a freshwater swimming pool with a sun deck, four floodlit tennis courts, a rooftop health and fitness center, a driving range, and a putting green. There are also four restaurants, a nightclub, and the most modern casino on the island. Honeymoon package: Eight days/seven nights (CP): $1,010 per couple year round. Includes: a bottle of champagne, keepsake honeymoon photograph, use of designer bathrobes, sunset cruise, a candlelight gourmet dinner, and more. Four-day package also available.

Aruba Palm Beach, L.G. Smith Blvd. 79, Aruba (tel. 011/297-8/23900; U.S. reservations: tel. toll free 800/345-2782 nationwide; 800/322-2782 in FL). Couples who want to experience a casual atmosphere while they enjoy high-rise conveniences will be more than happy in this 200-room hotel. The rooms are large and airy, with comfortable, modern furnishings, and in-room TV; each has an ocean view and a private balcony. For daytime activity, there's a spacious beach with complete water-sports facilities, a freshwater swimming pool, and tennis. In the evening, the Club Galactica features international entertainers; there's also a disco and a casino. Honeymoon package: Eight days/seven nights (EP): $970 to $1,035 per couple. Includes a bottle of champagne, island sightseeing tour, glass-bottom boat trip, sailing trip, round-trip airport transfers.

MODERATE: Aruba Concorde Hotel & Casino, L.G. Smith Blvd. 77, Aruba (tel. 011/297-8/24466; U.S. reservations: tel. 212/697-7405 or toll free 800/223-7944 or 800/442-8436). At 18 stories, this high-rise towers over everything else in Aruba. Soft rainbow hues decorate its southern wall, and with the little thatched sun umbrellas that line its beach, give the illusion of a tropical oasis with cosmopolitan conveniences. It's a lavish resort, and all 500 rooms have terraces with ocean views, closed-circuit television, movies, radio with private channel music, and an individual refrigerator. There are five restaurants and three cocktail lounges, a nightclub, and the Caribbean's largest casino. Outside, there's an open-air beachfront bar, an Olympic-size pool, facilities for water sports, and tennis courts. Honeymoon package: Eight days/seven nights (EP): $598 to $979 per couple. Includes: a bottle of champagne, private island cruise, phone call home to mom and dad.

The **Holiday Inn Aruba Beach Resort & Casino,** L.G. Smith Blvd. 230, Aruba (tel. 011/297-8/23600; U.S. reservations: tel. 800/HOLIDAY), on Palm Beach is like a miniature modern city. The lobby bustles with activity at all hours of the day and night, and there are more amenities than one couple could possibly make use of in a week. There's a beach, a pool, water sports facilities, four tennis courts, a health center with sauna, four restaurants and a deli, and the Palm Beach Room, famous for nightclub entertainment with international stars. The 400 rooms are furnished in a sleek, modern, no-nonsense style that is the trademark of the chain. Each has a private balcony and in-room TV. Honeymoon package: Eight days/seven nights (EP): $675 to $1,060 per couple. Includes bottle of champagne, lunch at Bali Restaurant, trimaran cruise.

The **Bushiri Beach Hotel,** L.G. Smith Blvd. 35, Aruba (tel. 011/297-8/25471; U.S. reservations: tel. toll free 800/622-7836), a 50-room hotel, is the smallest on the island, but there are plans to add almost 100 additional accommodations. The rooms and furnishings in the single-level building are simple; the Flamboyant Restaurant and Cocktail Lounge similarly low-key. There's a freshwater pool and a very pebbly beach. Honeymoon package: Eight days/seven nights (EP): $589 to $690 per couple. Package includes a bottle of champagne, two admissions to Bon Bini Festival, round-trip airport transfers.

4. Romantic Restaurants and Night Spots

Whether you're out for a ride in the country or a night on the town you won't go hungry in Aruba.

The island has a wide variety of restaurants, ranging from the indoor and outdoor coffee shops, main dining rooms, and specialty restaurants at the hotels, to moderate- and high-priced international and Aruban restaurants.

Restaurant prices are usually listed in both florins and U.S. dollars. A 10% to 15% service charge is almost always added to your bill.

EXPENSIVE: The **Red Parrot,** in the Divi Divi Beach Hotel (tel. 23300), is a casu-ally elegant dining spot that comes complete with piano music every night except Tues-day. The menu is sophisticated, and the food is simply superb. Although the service tends to be rather formal, it's softened by a warm and friendly manner. A mural made of light-colored stained glass and large windows framed with greenery give the fully enclosed air-conditioned restaurant a breezy, open-air feeling. Hot and cold appetizers have international origins and are priced in the $6 range; the German potato salad and sausage was particularly good. Entrées are priced between $19 and $25; we enjoyed the veal Oscar and the flaming duck. The dessert cart has confections that are inde-scribably delicious. You won't be able to make up your mind—but you can have a taste of a few things for under $4.

La Serre, in the Aruba Concorde Hotel (tel. 24466), sparkles and shimmers with bright glass and chrome against a deep-red and maroon decor. It overlooks the pool, where the reflections of hundreds of lights flicker in the water. As an appetizer, the escargot wrapped in flaky pastry is out of this world ($6). La Serre specializes in steaks and chops done to perfection, priced at $25. Dom Perignon tops the wine list, but don't let the $165 price throw you; the list is extensive, and there's an excellent selection at $16 to $20 per bottle.

Papagayo, upstairs at Boulevard Center, Oranjestad (tel. 24140) serves Italian specialties amid a profusion of lush plants. Entrées priced from $15 to $20.

MODERATE TO INEXPENSIVE: **Papiamento,** on Wilhelminastraat in Oranje-stad (tel. 24544). The setting for this intimate dining experience is one of Aruba's finest old mansions, where you'll have the undivided attention of your own personal chef. He'll prepare beef, chicken, or seafood specialties cooked to your individual taste on a sizzling marble tile, at your table. It's wonderful to watch, and delicious, too. Or try chicken cooked just for the two of you in a pottery "egg" that's cracked open at your table. Dinner for two: about $40 plus drinks.

The Bali, Oranjested Harbor (tel. 22131). How about dining in a floating restau-rant set in a typical Indonesian houseboat docked along the Oranjestad harbor? Seven

Indonesian specialties are priced at $10 each, or you can try the rijsttafel, an Indonesian smorgasbord, for $17. If you don't want a full meal, chicken, beef, and pork satay (shish kebab) are served with drinks at the bar that overlooks the harbor and a fleet of deep-sea fishing boats.

The New York Deli in the Alhambra Casino & Bazaar complex (tel. 25434) is open 24 hours a day. You can't beat the $2 breakfast special, served from 1 to 7 a.m. The overstuffed sandwiches really are; try to leave room for the cheese blintzes. **Charlie's Bar** in San Nicolas (tel. 45086) is famous for its grilled shrimp ($10), but also serves light meals, sandwiches, and hamburgers priced at under $5. Closed Sundays and holidays. **Brisas del Mar** on the waterfront in Savaneta (tel. 47718) specializes in Aruban-style creole seafood dishes. Entrées priced from $8 to $14, although lobster runs higher. The restaurant is open daily from noon to 3 p.m. and 6:30 to 10:30 p.m.

Don't miss Aruba's exciting nightlife. It starts late, and goes on till the early morning hours! Discos open after 10 p.m., including the **Roseland Ballroom** in the Alhambra Bazaar (tel. 35000), the **Scaramouche Disco** in the Boulevard Shopping Center (tel. 24954), and the **Visage Disco** on L.G. Smith Blvd. (tel. 22397) in Oranjestad.

During the high season, many nightclubs have an early show that starts close to midnight, and another in the early morning. Try the **Fandango Nightclub** in the Golden Tulip Aruba Caribbean Hotel & Casino (tel. 33555), the **Arubesque** in the Aruba Concorde Hotel & Casino (tel. 24466), and **L'Esprit Nightclub** in the Holiday Inn Aruba Beach Resort & Casino (tel. 23600).

Chapter XXIII

THE BAHAMAS

**1. Practical Facts
2. Nassau / Cable Beach / Paradise Island
3. Freeport / Lucaya
4. The Family Islands: The Abacos,
Eleuthera, The Exumas
5. More Suggestions in The Bahamas**

IF VARIETY IS THE SPICE of life, then The Bahamas couldn't be more highly seasoned. Starting only 50 miles off the coast of Florida, this chain of 700 islands (some not much larger than rocks) stretches into the Atlantic, almost reaching the Caribbean. The country's 200,000 people live on only a handful of these islands, leaving the rest uninhabited. The shapes and sizes of the islands and their offshore cays (pronounced "keys") are as varied as the lifestyles of their residents.

Which Bahamas are you looking for? The one that gives you something to do during every waking hour? Extensive shopping? Golf, tennis, and all kinds of water sports? Historical sights? Or the one that invites you to do nothing at all—except, of course, have beach after beach all to yourselves? The one that allows you to go barefoot or the one that tempts you to dress up every night? The one that lets you indulge in gourmet delights or the one that keeps you coming back for more homestyle local cooking? The best thing about honeymooning in The Bahamas is that you can have it all.

You may have heard it said that there are two sides to every story. Well, The Bahamas story has at least three: Nassau / Cable Beach / Paradise Island, Freeport / Lucaya, and the Family Islands. Each of these destinations is strikingly distinct. On the northern coast of the island of New Providence, Cable Beach, adjoining Paradise Island, and Nassau, the historic capital, offer more action than all the other Bahamian islands combined. While Grand Bahama's youthful Freeport / Lucaya can give Nassau a run for its money in the nightlife department, the pace here is generally more relaxed. Far removed from either New Providence or Grand Bahama are the rest of the Bahamian islands, collectively known as the Family Islands. Here life revolves around the blessings of nature, from the quiet empty beaches to the spectacular offshore reefs.

Columbus first brought The Bahamas to the attention of Europe when he arrived in 1492 to find Arawak Indians living peacefully on these predominantly flat, beach-rimmed islands. The exact place where he first landed in the New World is under dispute, but it is generally thought to be the southerly Bahamian island of San Salvador. Spanish explorers soon lost interest in The Bahamas and the British began reshaping the islands. The first wave of Europeans came from Bermuda in 1648, settling on Eleuthera after fleeing religious persecution at home. For decades, ruthless pirates ruled the shores, hiding out in the quiet inlets and among the tiny cays. During the 17th and 18th centuries, Nassau was the home base of pirates who preyed on Spanish galleons transporting gold and silver from the New World to Europe. Then in 1718, Captain Woodes Rogers put an end to the plundering and became the first royal governor of The Bahamas.

Although The Bahamas gained its independence from Britain in 1973, there is still a marked British flavor to the country: you'll drive on the left, you can watch the changing of the guard at Government House in Nassau, and you can enjoy steak-and-kidney pie or fish-and-chips washed down with ale at many of the pubs. However, because of the proximity to the United States, Americans will also find much that is familiar. The Bahamian dollar, for instance, is on par with the U.S. dollar, so that the two currencies can be used interchangeably.

Now this is not to say that The Bahamas does not have a distinctly Bahamian character. The colorful lilt in the English spoken, the easygoing pace of life (even in bustling Nassau), and the homegrown Junkanoo and Goombay music—which give rise to the festive Junkanoo parades at Christmastime and New Year's—are only a few examples of what the word "Bahamian" means.

Honeymooners who want to get an inside look at The Bahamas, from the point of view of its residents, should consider participating in the People-to-People Program. This free program introduces Bahamian couples to visitors with similar interests for picnics, shared meals, personalized sightseeing tours, or any other activities you'd like to arrange (contact a Bahamas tourist office).

No matter which island you choose—and to appreciate the variety of The Bahamas, you may decide to sample more than one—The Bahamas has a gentle way of helping romance thrive.

1. Practical Facts

ENTERING AND LEAVING: American citizens are required to have passports as well as round-trip or onward-bound tickets. Canadians can use a passport or a birth certificate as proof of citizenship. When flying home, you'll each pay a $5 departure tax.

GETTING THERE: Many airlines and cruise ships serve the Bahamas.

By Air

Flight time from Miami to Nassau is just over a half hour, and from New York to Nassau, about 2½ hours. **Bahamasair** flies from Newark, Atlanta, and several Florida cities to Nassau and Freeport. **Delta** will take you to Nassau from Atlanta, Boston, New York, Detroit, Dallas, or Fort Lauderdale. **Eastern** has flights from ten U.S. cities to Nassau and Freeport. **Pan Am** jets into Nassau and Freeport from New York, and **United** flies there from Chicago. In addition, several small airlines fly from various Florida cities.

For interisland travel, **Bahamasair** has flights to almost all the Family Islands. **Chalk's International** will take you from Florida to Nassau, Bimini, and Walker's Cay.

By Sea

If you want to ease into The Bahamas, a cruise provides a leisurely, fun-filled means of getting there. The kind of voyage you choose will depend on the size of the ship you want, the facilities (some of which are so extensive that you'll think you're in

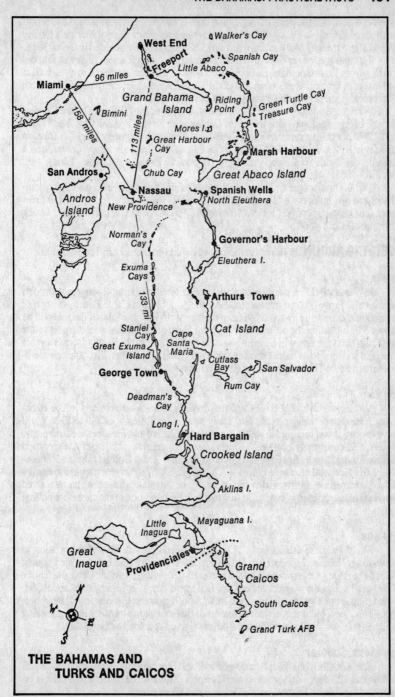

Walker's Cay

West End

Freeport

Spanish Cay

Little Abaco

Miami

96 miles

Grand Bahama Island

Riding Point

Green Turtle Cay
Treasure Cay

Bimini

158 miles

113 miles

Mores I.

Great Harbour Cay

Marsh Harbour

San Andros

Chub Cay

Nassau

Great Abaco Island

Andros Island

New Providence

Spanish Wells
North Eleuthera

Norman's Cay

Governor's Harbour

Exuma Cays

Eleuthera I.

133 mi

Arthurs Town

Staniel Cay

Cat Island

Great Exuma Island

Cape Santa Maria

Cutlass Bay

San Salvador

George Town

Rum Cay

Deadman's Cay

Long I.

Hard Bargain

Crooked Island

Aklins I.

Little Inagua

Mayaguana I.

Great Inagua

Providenciales

Grand Caicos

South Caicos

N W E S

Grand Turk AFB

**THE BAHAMAS AND
TURKS AND CAICOS**

a resort hotel), and the ports of call. Some lines combine stops at Nassau and Freeport with visits to various Family Islands; others even give you a taste of Florida's Disney World along the way. Airfare from certain U.S. cities is often included in the package.

The 800-passenger *Costa Riviera,* for instance, spends seven nights at sea, departing from Ft. Lauderdale, calling at St. Thomas, St. John, and St. Croix, as well as at Nassau. The cost ranges from $2,025 to $3,390 per couple, including air fare from 100 cities. (Contact **Costa Cruises,** tel. 305/763-3980.)

With three outdoor whirlpools, a casino, and room for 1,100 guests, the *Starship Royale* cruises for four nights from Port Canaveral to Nassau and Salt Cay. The $1,040 to $2,090 per couple rate includes a three-night hotel stay at Disney World, admission to Magic Kingdom and EPCOT Center, a tour of the Kennedy Space Center, *and* a rented car with unlimited mileage. (Contact **Premier Cruise Lines,** tel. 305/783-5061.)

The 950-passenger *Carnival,* with a casino and five swimming pools (four outdoors and one indoors), sails weekly for four nights from Miami to Nassau and Freeport. The cost, per couple, is from $890 to $1,795. (Contact **Carnival Cruise Lines,** toll free 800/232-4666.)

GETTING AROUND: Transportation is varied and convenient in The Bahamas.

By Taxi

In Nassau and Freeport: Taxis, which are metered, wait for passengers at airports and hotels. From Nassau International Airport to a hotel in Cable Beach, the two of you should expect to pay about $9; from the airport to Paradise Island, the ride will be about $18 including the $2 bridge toll. From Freeport's International Airport to the hotel districts, the fare will be from about $5 to $8. Taxis in the Family Islands are not metered and tend to be more expensive than in Nassau or Freeport. Taxi tours are available throughout The Bahamas for about $16 an hour.

By Car

Visitors with valid U.S. or Canadian driver's licenses can rent cars in The Bahamas. *Note that driving is on the left.* Daily rates range from about $45 to $72. You'll save money if you rent by the week. Agencies in Nassau and Freeport are at airports, hotels, and downtown locations. In high season, you may want to make a reservation before leaving home. In addition to local companies, **Avis, Budget, Dollar Rent-A-Car,** and **National** also have offices in The Bahamas. You can rent cars in the Family Islands (sometimes from taxi drivers), but many of the models have been battle scarred by years of use on bumpy roads. Be sure to check the condition of the car before pulling off.

By Bus

Many Paradise Island and Cable Beach hotels provide free transportation to downtown Nassau. Freeport hotels that are not located on the beach offer frequent shuttle service to the shore. If you'd prefer to get around Nassau, Cable Beach, or Freeport/Lucaya the way Bahamians do, hop into a jitney, or minibus, for about 75¢. With reggae or calypso pulsing on the radio, you'll pass through residential neighborhoods and see a picturesque side of the islands that many tourists miss. For sightseeing tours in large or small air-conditioned buses, sign up at a hotel activity desk.

By Motor Scooter

Some hotels in Nassau, Paradise Island, and Freeport rent mopeds for about $25 a day plus $20 deposit. Be sure to wear helmets. Motor scooters are also available on some of the Family Islands, such as Exuma and Eleuthera.

By Bicycle

Especially on some Family Islands, bikes are a good way to get from one place to another. Some resorts rent bikes for about $10 a day; others make them available to guests at no cost.

LANGUAGE: English is the national language. If you listen carefully, you'll hear Irish and Scottish influences along with the West Indian lilt. Also, Bahamians frequently interchange v's with w's, so don't be surprised if people say "You're velcome" when you thank them. This pronunciation is thought to date back to 18th-century English.

MONEY: Although The Bahamas has its own currency, U.S. dollars are also accepted throughout the islands. However, once you see the Technicolor Bahamian bills, you may want to forgo your monotonous American green. Since the U.S. dollar and the Bahamian dollar are equal in value, you'll often receive change consisting of both currencies.

The service charge is often included in restaurant checks. If not, tip about 15%. This percentage also goes for taxi drivers and tour guides. Porters are tipped about $1.

WEATHER: Temperatures average in the 70s during the winter season (December through April) and the 80s during the summer. Evenings tend to be slightly cooler. The summer months get a bit more rain, but showers are usually too brief to interfere with outdoor life.

CLOTHING: During the winter season, men will need jackets and ties at the more expensive restaurants at night. However, for the most part, even in high season, dress tends to be casual. Air conditioning and mild evenings can necessitate a shawl or jacket for women. Bahamians prefer that visitors confine beachwear and short-shorts to the shore or the pool only.

TIME: Eastern Standard Time is in effect in The Bahamas, and Daylight Saving Time is observed in the summer. Therefore, when it is 8 a.m. in New York, it is 8 a.m. in The Bahamas, year-round.

TELEPHONES: To call The Bahamas direct, dial (809) and the seven-digit local number.

SHOPPING: Although The Bahamas is not a duty-free territory, bargain hunters may have trouble parting company with Nassau, Paradise Island, and Freeport. Prices can be 25% to 45% lower than in the U.S. for some imports such as crystal, china, woolens, linens, French perfumes, watches, cameras, and liquor. You don't even have to leave the larger hotels to start dipping into your pocketbook—many have arcades with lots of tempting shops. But most visitors agree that it is more fun to venture out.

In Nassau, stores line Bay Street, the main thoroughfare, all vying for your attention. For Seiko and Rolex watches, jewelry, English bone china, Limoges porcelain, and much more, stop in at **John Bull** on Bay Street between East Street and Elizabeth Avenue. The **Brass & Leather Shop,** on Charlotte Street off Bay, sells wallets, belts, Bottega Veneta luggage, and the like.

Many shops, boutiques, and restaurants in Freeport, are clustered in the International Bazaar. **Midnight Sun** here is where you'll find a wide selection of Scandinavian bargains, and the **Discount Bazaar** is also worth checking out. The new multi-million-dollar **Port Lucaya,** a dining, shopping, and entertainment complex, is across from the Holiday Inn and the Lucaya Beach Resort and Casino.

Handmade straw goods are sold on most Bahamian islands, but the variety is greatest in Nassau and Freeport. Pick up straw hats to keep the sun off, or buy straw bags to carry suitcase overflow on the way home. Don't be shy about bargaining—no one expects you to pay the first price you're quoted.

CASINOS: Visitors over age 21 are welcome to gamble in the casinos, which are located in Nassau, Paradise Island, and Freeport/Lucaya.

ABOUT ACCOMMODATIONS: New Providence, Paradise Island, and Grand Bahama offer every kind of hotel from big and brassy to quiet and unassuming.

Hotels add a 6% room tax to rates. Many also add a 15% service charge. High season runs from about December through April. During the summer (or "Goombay") season, rates are about 20% to 50% lower. The price ranges given for hotels in this chapter reflect the spread between low- and high-season.

DINING OUT: Throughout the islands, restaurants serve continental food along with local favorites. It is best to make reservations at most restaurants. Conch—the meat of that large shell you put to your ear to hear the roar of the ocean—is king on Bahamian menus. Pronounced "conk," it is served in a variety of forms: cracked (pounded tender and fried), raw as salad, in bite-size fritters, and in chowder. Other specialties are baked crab, local lobster, and okra soup. Grouper heads the list of fish—it's on breakfast, lunch, *and* dinner menus. Side dishes include mildly sweet johnny cake, peas and rice, and fried plantain. Try one of the country's prized rum cocktails: a goombay smash, a yellow bird, or a Bahama Mama. For dessert, sample guava duff, made from slices of the fruit rolled in dough and boiled.

HOW TO GET MARRIED IN THE BAHAMAS: If you've always dreamed of an island wedding, why not make it happen? Before applying for a marriage license, which costs $20, one of you must have spent at least 15 days in The Bahamas. Pick up the application in New Providence at the Registrar General's Office, East Hill Street, P.O. Box N-532. While no blood test is required, you'll need to show proof of identity, such as a passport, and proof of divorce (if applicable).

FOR FURTHER INFORMATION: Contact **The Bahamas Ministry of Tourism,** P.O. Box N-3701, Nassau, The Bahamas (tel. 809/322-7500); **The Bahamas Tourist Office,** 150 East 52nd St., New York, NY 10022 (tel. 212/758-2777); or one of the tourist offices in eleven other cities throughout the United States; or the **Family Islands Promotion Board,** 255 Alhambra Circle, suite 420, Coral Gables, FL 33134 (tel. 305/446-4111).

2. Nassau / Cable Beach / Paradise Island

Home of Nassau, the historic capital, New Providence Island is The Bahamas' most popular destination. Seven miles across at its widest point and 20 miles long, it is only an hour by air from Miami, Florida. Dreamy beaches, great snorkeling, scuba diving, and other water sports, old forts, pastel-colored colonial homes, nonstop nightlife, casinos—it's all here.

The island has three main resort areas, all close to each other: Nassau, Cable Beach, and Paradise Island.

Nassau, the capital, is made for strolling. In particular, you'll want to check out Bay Street, the broad main thoroughfare, which is bordered by shops, boutiques, restaurants, banks, and the famed straw market. In addition to all kinds of straw goods, you'll see T-shirts and jewelry made from shells. Hone your bargaining skills with the friendly craftswomen—no one expects you to pay the first price you're quoted.

Near the straw market is flower-filled Rawson Square, across from the pink-and-white government buildings. In the courtyard formed by these buildings is a statue of a youthful Queen Victoria. Christopher Columbus has the honor of standing before nearby Government House, the colonial mansion that is the official residence of the British-appointed governor general. You may not be in London, but the changing of the guard does take place here every other Saturday at 10 a.m. Climb the 65 steps of the queen's staircase, hewn from solid limestone. At the top you'll find the crumbling remains of Fort Fincastle and you'll have a sweeping view. Still guarding the entrance to Nassau Harbour, Fort Charlotte, dating back to 1788, is one of the city's well-preserved forts.

The bridge that connects Paradise Island to New Providence arches majestically (the toll is $2 by car, 50¢ by moped, and 25¢ on foot, round-trip). For a spectacular vision, stand on the bridge at sunset. Not too long ago, Paradise Island was nothing but farmland and was known as Hog Island. Now its sparkling beaches are backed by high-rise hotels and its casino and Las Vegas–style nightlife draw travelers from all over. Secluded Cabbage Beach is a romantic cove that seems to have been carved into the eastern shore just for honeymooners. Ferries run between Nassau and Paradise Island (about $1.50 per person each way).

ROMANTIC INTERLUDES: For a romantic tour of historic downtown Nassau, sit back and relax in one of the surreys that leave from Rawson Square. Your driver will certainly entertain you with intriguing tales about the way things were.

You'll find a medieval cloister standing in **Versailles Gardens** on modern Paradise Island. These peaceful grounds with a dramatic view of the harbor invite hand-in-hand strolls. Near Fort Charlotte in Nassau, the **Botanical Gardens** (tel. 323-9575) attract nature lovers. Open daily from 9 a.m. to 4 p.m.; admission is $1 per person. At **Ardastra Gardens** (tel. 323-5806) nearby, you can not only enjoy the flowers—trained flamingoes (the national bird of The Bahamas) put on a great show at 11 a.m., 2 p.m., and 4 p.m. Open daily from 9 a.m. to 4:30 p.m.; admission is $5 per person. When you need a break from shopping, board the 97-foot *Nautilus* ($30 per couple) for a two-hour, day-time cruise to the underwater **Sea Gardens.**

Try **parasailing,** which is available at several hotels on Cable Beach or Paradise Island Beach. You'll be strapped to a parachute tied to a boat. As the boat takes off, you'll rise slowly into the air and the folks on the beach will grow as tiny as pebbles in the sand. What a view! Coming back to earth is no problem. You'll descend as gently as you rise. About $25 a ride.

Moray eels, bright parrot fish, sea turtles, spiny lobster, and sea cucumbers are just a few of the creatures you'll see on the multicolored coral reefs at **Coral World's Underwater Observatory** (tel. 328-1036). Get nose to nose with "man-eating" sharks—you'll peer at each other through the glass. Not far from the heart of downtown Nassau, Coral World is on a cay connected to the mainland by an arching bridge. Allow a couple of hours to visit the many exhibits and to stop for a bite at the oceanfront restaurant. Open daily from 8:30 a.m. to 6 p.m.; admission: $10 per person.

Most hotels can arrange **snorkeling and diving** excursions for the novice as well as for the experienced. Qualified scuba divers can visit "James Bond Reef," which was featured in the movies *Never Say Never Again* and *For Your Eyes Only.*

One-tank dives run about $29; three-tank dives about $66. If you've never dived before, but think you would like to try, sign up for an introductory resort course, which runs approximately $59 per person.

HONEYMOON HOTELS AND HIDEAWAYS: Whether your pleasure be a 200-year-old mansion or a modern high-rise, you'll find something to suit in Nassau, Paradise Island, and Cable Beach.

Expensive

The Royal Bahamian, 5775 N.W. 11th St., Miami, FL 33126 (tel. 305/262-1397 or 809/327-6400; U.S. reservations: toll free 800/822-4200). Quieter and more dignified than most Cable Beach hotels, this posh resort was born in 1946 as a private club. Peacocks grace the imaginatively landscaped grounds and afternoon tea is served. The lobby, with its marble floor and Georgian furnishings, opens onto a courtyard with a fountain in the center. The 170 individual rooms and villas, done in smoky pinks and bright blues, come equipped with terry-cloth robes, and the modern baths are stocked with all kinds of toiletries. Relax by the pool, with its breezy café, or take advantage of the variety of water sports offered at the beach. If you prefer to be alone together when you take a dip, book one of the two villas with private pools. Pamper yourselves with mud baths or massages in the health spa. Honeymoon package: Eight days/seven nights (EP): $812 to $1,510 per couple. Includes a welcome gift, a bottle of champagne, and a half-day cruise. Four days/three nights package also available.

Cable Beach Hotel & Casino, Box N-4914, Nassau, New Providence, The Bahamas (tel. 809/327-6000; U.S. reservations: toll free 800/822-4200). All 700 balconied rooms in the two wings of this pleasure center face the long, wide beach. These beige concrete buildings offer facilities galore, including restaurants, shops, tour operators, and nightly entertainment. Musical extravaganzas in the casino's 1,000-seat theater are the highlights of many an evening. The bright glass-enclosed lobby is spacious and overlooks the pool. In addition to all the water sports available on the beach, you'll find tennis, squash, and racquetball courts in the Sports Centre across the street, and the championship 18-hole Cable Beach golf course is nearby. Rooms are very modern, with rattan furnishings to add an islandy touch. Honeymoon package: Eight days/seven nights (EP): $1,043 to $1,505 per couple. Includes a bottle of champagne, a full-day lagoon cruise, and admission to the casino show. Four days/three nights package also available.

Ocean Club, Box N-4777, Nassau, New Providence, The Bahamas (tel. 809/326-2501; U.S. reservations: toll free 800/321-3000). Before its transformation into a Resorts International hotel, this colonial-style mansion built in the 1960s was owned by millionaire Huntington Hartford and run as a private club. Each of the 71 guest rooms, including those in suites and villas, has two double beds. Rooms come complete with thick terry-cloth bathrobes, sitting and dining areas, telephones in the bedrooms and baths, and both air conditioning and ceiling fans. Try a villa if you'd like an enclosed patio with a Jacuzzi. The broad, stark-white beach stretches for two miles. Slabs of flagstone create walkways through the flowering grounds and around the pool, which overlooks Versailles Gardens. This medieval cloister was imported from France and reconstructed here stone by stone. The garden's gazebo overlooking the harbor is a favorite spot for wedding ceremonies. Afternoon tea is served near the nine Har-Tru tennis courts, four of which are lit for evening games. Golfers have trouble staying away from the 18-hole championship golf course. Honeymoon package: Eight days/seven nights (EP): $1,100 to $2,308 per couple. Includes a champagne breakfast in bed the first morning, a reception for honeymooners, admission to the show at Le Cabaret Theatre, a free round of golf, and Ocean Club tote bags. Four days/three nights package also available.

Paradise Island Resort & Casino, Box N-4777, Nassau, New Providence, The Bahamas (tel. 809/326-3000; U.S. reservations: toll free 800/321-3000). Once two separate hotels, this extensive resort on stunning Paradise Island beach now has more than 1,100 rooms. Located in several buildings, the stylish rooms all have refrigerators and color satellite televisions. King-size beds are available upon request. In the afternoon, the beachside pool reverberates with activity. Bingo and other games follow entertainment by a live band. There is no need to leave the hotel to go shopping, since you'll have a good selection of stores. Many consider the revue at Le Cabaret Theatre the hottest casino show in The Bahamas. Inquire about the Club Paradise program, an all-inclusive hotel package featuring a gourmet dining plan, all water sports, golf green fees, weekly Bahamamian night, beach barbecues, and daily cocktail parties. Note that hotel rates are cheaper during the week than on weekends. Honeymoon package: Eight days/seven nights (Full AP): From $2,123 per couple. Includes all meals, a bottle of champagne, admission to the show at Le Cabaret Theatre, a reception for honeymooners, a free round of golf, and his-and-her nightshirts. Four days/ three nights package also available.

Moderate

Sheraton Grand, Box SS-6307, Paradise Island, The Bahamas (tel. 809/326-2011; U.S. reservations: toll free 800/325-3535). This beachfront high rise is a stone's throw from the Paradise Island casino. The sunny lobby is decked out with a reflecting pool surrounded by plants, and high-backed wicker chairs stand next to the floor-to-ceiling windows. Delicious meals are served in several restaurants, including the bar and grill on the patio next to the swimming pool. The 360 colorful guest rooms have sitting areas, refrigerators, and balconies. Practically every water sport is available right on the property (there are tennis courts lighted for day or night play), and the hotel staff is always on hand to help with arrangements for any other activities. Honeymoon package: Eight days/seven nights (EP): $880 to $1,113 per couple. Includes an ocean-view room with private balcony, a bottle of champagne, honeymooners' reception, complimentary tennis, surprise gift, and tote bag. Four days/three nights package also available.

Paradise Paradise Beach Resort, P.O. Box SS-6259, Paradise Island, The Bahamas (tel. 809/326-2541; U.S. reservations: toll free 800/321-3000). Water sports are the main events at this casual, relaxed hotel in a quiet area. Some guests are convinced that the protected waters and the wide sandy expanse make this beach the best on Paradise Island. Even when the hotel is completely full, the beach and bean-shaped pool are far from crowded. All water sports and other activities (such as daily bike tours of the island) are included in room rates. The 100 rooms, handsomely decorated in blue and white, are equipped with mini-bars, color televisions, and king-size or double beds. Honeymoon package: Eight days/seven nights (EP) $702 to $1,330 per couple. Includes a bottle of champagne, admission to the show at Le Cabaret Theatre, and complimentary land and water sports. Four days/three nights package also available.

Sheraton British Colonial, Box N-7148, No. 1, Bay Street, Nassau, New Providence, The Bahamas (tel. 809/322-3301; U.S. reservations: toll free 800/334-8484). This 325-room resort dating back to the 1920s is the dowager queen of Nassau, appealing to visitors who don't want to choose between sandy shores and city living. This is the largest downtown hotel and is the only one with a beach. Set in eight acres of gardens, it is right on Bay Street, the heart of Nassau's shopping district. An Olympic-size pool, three lighted tennis courts, and a nine-hole golf course are only a few of the many facilities. Rooms have been recently redone with contemporary furnishings in bright greens and blues, and are very spacious. Honeymoon package: Eight days/seven nights (EP): Up to $966 per couple. Includes one bottle of champagne each day, a honeymoon photo, and T-shirts. Four days/three nights package also available.

Graycliffe, Box N-10246, West Hill Street, Nassau, New Providence, The Bahamas (tel. 809/322-2796 or 809/322-2797). This 12-room hotel across the street from Government House has the distinction of being the only member of the prestigious "Relais et Châteaux" chain in The Bahamas. Set in a colonial mansion more than two centuries old, it has retained the feeling of an elegant private home. The large rooms, with colorful names such as Yellowbird and Hibiscus, are individually decorated with antiques and tile floors. Some have walk-in closets and dressing rooms. Spacious bathrooms gleam with glass-enclosed stall showers and old-fashioned tubs that invite bubble baths. Thriving gardens and a stone walkway surround the swimming pool. The excellent food, served in a variety of settings, draws a constant stream of diners. Honeymoon package: None. Rates (EP): $155 to $168 per couple per night.

With 411 plush rooms, the **Nassau Beach,** Box N-7756, Nassau, New Providence, The Bahamas (tel. 809/327-7711; U.S. reservations: tel. 212/541-4400 or toll free 800/223-5672), accommodates its guests in high style. The lobby sparkles with marble and tile floors. Decorated in eggshell, tangerine, and reds, the guest rooms pamper visitors with white rattan upholstered furniture, marble baths, and dressing areas. The fare at the variety of restaurants ranges from all-American steak to Polynesian surprises. Accompanied by music and other entertainment, the weekly Junkanoo buffet eases visitors into the island spirit and allows them to sample Bahamian culinary specialties. At night the popular Out Island Bar is filled with couples shaking a leg or two. A tennis pro is on hand at the six-court tennis complex and water sports are available on the hotel's strip of Cable Beach. Honeymoon package: Eight days/seven nights (EP): Up to $1,200 per couple (high season). Includes an oceanview room, a bottle of champagne, a fruit basket, breakfast the first morning, one dinner, and the show at the Cable Beach casino. Four days/three nights package also available.

ROMANTIC RESTAURANTS AND NIGHTSPOTS: Honeymooners have plenty of choices in Nassau, Paradise Island, and Cable Beach.

Expensive

Graycliffe, Nassau (tel. 322-2796 or 322-2797). This grandiose old mansion is one of the best places to dine in style. Begin lunch or dinner with cocktails in a drawing room furnished with antiques. Then get ready for the elegant gourmet fare served at tables sparkling with Royal Copenhagen china and silver imported from Britain. From the hot and cold hors d'oeuvres to the Italian pastries, each item on the elaborate menu is more tempting than the last. Bahamian crawfish in puff pastry with cream and saffron, pâté of Abaco wild boar with walnuts, filet mignon with mushrooms and tomatoes, roast duck with tropical fruit and calvados brandy—they all compete for your attention. Be sure to make reservations. Dinner for two will easily cost $100 or more. Jackets are required for men.

Buena Vista, Nassau (tel. 322-2811 or 322-4039). In the main dining room, of this early 19th century manor house plants hang in archways and the pink walls, trimmed in white, are decorated with paintings. Lush foliage surrounds the enclosed patio, with its terra-cotta tile floor. As candles flicker in hurricane lamps and ceiling fans gently stir the air, the pianist sings everything from "Waltzing Matilda" to songs from *Fiddler on the Roof.* Smoked dolphin with whipped horseradish sauce, avocado stuffed with lobster, or cream of garlic soup are good ways to begin. Memorable entrées follow such as shrimp scampi, rack of lamb, duck in Grand Marnier sauce, and quail with wild mushrooms. Finish off with baked Alaska for dessert. Jackets—and reservations—are required. Dinner for two will cost about $80.

At **The Courtyard Terrace,** Paradise Island (tel. 326-2501) in the luxurious Ocean Club resort the sky makes a starry ceiling, tall palms rustle in the breeze, and a long rectangular pool with a fountain serves as a centerpiece. Candles flicker shadows over tables topped with Irish linen, and Wedgwood china. Try goose liver pâté with truffles, Bahamian conch chowder, or cream of asparagus soup, and hearts of palm salad. House specialties include filet of beef stuffed with crabmeat, and well-seasoned pan-blackened red snapper. Pear belle Hélène (vanilla ice cream, pears, and chocolate sauce) or coconut cake are hard to resist. Live music floats down from the balcony above. Plan to spend $90 or more on dinner for the two of you.

Round House, Cable Beach (tel. 327-7921 or 327-7922). This intimate restaurant is housed in what was once a guard house for the surrounding homes. Nettie Symonette, your friendly host, ensures that patrons never forget her international treats. Various versions of shrimp, lobster, and conch are on the menu along with steak. Expect to pay about $95 for dinner for two, unless you arrive before 7 p.m., when the special, a complete dinner, will cost about $40 per couple.

Moderate

Café Martinique, Paradise Island (tel. 326-3000). When you're in the mood for a taste of France, reserve a table at Café Martinique. Wall-to-wall windows look out to the lagoon. Fans hang from a white latticework ceiling, and white wicker chairs surround the tables. Entrées include grilled Coho salmon or *fruits de mer,* a selection of seafood. Boneless veal sautéed with mushrooms, apples, and French apple brandy is also an excellent choice. Since the sinful desserts are so time consuming to prepare, the dessert menu will be offered before the entrées. Consider chocolate soufflé or soufflé au Grand Marnier. Although the candlelit dinners are superb, Sunday brunch is just as popular. You can dine outdoors on the terrace. Expect to pay about $60 and up for dinner for two. Men are required to wear jackets.

Local and imported seafood, from conch chowder to lobster, is on the menu at **Gulfstream,** Paradise Island (tel. 326-3000). Begin with fresh cherrystone clams or oysters. Plan to spend about $60 per couple for dinner. Closed Mondays. Only dinner is served at **Julie's,** Paradise Island (tel. 326-2011), where gourmet selections include Bahamian bouillabaisse. A meal for two will cost about $80.

Inexpensive

Marietta's, Nassau (tel. 323-2395) is an all-time favorite near the Paradise Island bridge. Many diners come to this casual restaurant for the crab soup. Dinner for two should cost about $25. When you're shopping in Nassau, a good place to stop for a plentiful Bahamian buffet lunch is **Hotel Corona,** Nassau (tel. 326-6815). About $20 per couple. Ask a Bahamian to point you in the direction of the best "boil" fish" in town, and chances are you'll end up at the **Shoal,** Nassau (tel. 323-4400). Dinner for two should run $30.

Nassau, Cable Beach, and Paradise Island days stretch into the wee hours of the morning. Few leave New Providence without trying their luck at its two casinos. The **Cable Beach Casino** (tel. 327-6000) is flashy and modern, with lots of neon. The theater here, whose 1,000 seats are often packed, hosts wildly entertaining musical extravaganzas (about $36 per couple). You may think you've stumbled into Las Vegas at **Le Cabaret Theatre in the Paradise Island Casino** (tel. 326-3000). The revues here are full of feathers, sequins, and bare skin (dinner and the show will cost about $80 per couple; the show and two drinks will be about $50 for the two of you).

Most of the large hotels have nightspots. Some of the most popular among Bahamians as well as vacationers include **Trade Winds Lounge** and **Club Pastiche,** both in the Paradise Island Resort & Casino; and, in Nassau, **Peanuts Taylor's Drumbeat Club** (tel. 322-4233) on West Bay Street (where limbo dancing and a fire ritual are done to Afro-Bahamian music); the **Pink Pussycat** at Delancy and Augusta streets; and the **Palace** on Elizabeth Avenue.

3. Freeport / Lucaya

Dazzlingly modern, Freeport is barely three decades old. Together with adjoining Lucaya, it is known as The Bahamas' second city. Freeport/Lucaya sits on Grand Bahama, north of Nassau and only 80 miles (a half-hour flight) from Florida.

Freeport/Lucaya blends natural beauty with casinos, large-scale resorts, extensive shopping, scores of restaurants, nightspots, cruise ship ports, and golf courses. The twin cities were certainly planned to be eye-pleasers: broad landscaped highways, glistening marinas, tall apartment buildings and condominiums, gardens, and parks. Many of its quiet beaches are free from the shadows of high-rise hotels and the grounds surrounding the pretty private homes burst with flowering shrubs.

Almost everyone who lives here is from somewhere else—Nassau, the Family Islands, Canada, the United States, Europe. Celebrating the island's multicultural flavor, the International Bazaar in Freeport is one of the places few visitors miss. A Japanese *torii* gate stands at the entrance. Along narrow, winding alleyways lined with boutiques and restaurants, you'll travel around the world from Mexico to Morocco, China to Sweden, Ghana to France, and then some. Be sure to check out the markets selling Bahamian straw goods and arts and crafts. Shady plazas with fountains and cafés make pleasant rest stops. Not to be outdone, Lucaya now has a shopping and entertainment complex called Lucayan Village, across from the Holiday Inn and the Lucayan Beach Resort.

ROMANTIC INTERLUDES: Many of your most special moments will center on the superb beaches.

Said to be world's largest glass-bottom boat, the *Mermaid Kitty* leaves from the dock near the Lucayan Beach Resort & Casino several times a day. You'll be treated to a diving show and visit sites including a shipwreck teeming with brilliantly colored marine life. Make reservations at your hotel's activities desk or just show up at the dock. Cost is about $11 per person.

The **Underwater Explorer's Society,** commonly known as UNEXSO (tel. 373-1244), has its headquarters across from the Lucayan Beach Resort & Casino. Scuba-dive beginners will appreciate the thorough instruction and the opportunity to learn the basics in a tank that is 18 feet deep—far more helpful than the usual swimming pool lessons. The three-hour resort course is $59. Experienced divers will be thrilled by the excursions to a variety of dive sites, including wrecks, caves, and a one-mile drop off. One tank dives cost $29; three-tank dives are $66.

Pack a picnic and rent a car for a drive to the **Lucayan National Park,** at the eastern end of the island. These 40 secluded acres thrive with wild tamarind, cedar, and ming trees. The wonderfully wide beach is the star attraction. Off West End Road, at the **Rand Memorial Nature Centre** you can take a guided tour and learn about some of the 200 species of birds and the varieties of plants. You probably won't be able to resist photographing each other by the pool filled with pink flamingos. But Grand Bahamas' love affair with nature doesn't end here. The **Garden of the Groves,** also on West End Road, bursts with waterfalls and hanging gardens. At the entrance, be sure to stop at the **Grand Bahama Museum** ($2 per person), where fascinating artifacts of the Lucayan Indians are displayed.

Rent mopeds or a car, take a taxi (arrange with the driver to come back for you)—no matter how you do it, don't miss the unpeopled, palm-fringed **beaches** off Midshipman Road. There is something about a deserted shore marked only by two sets of footprints—yours! The undulating turquoise and jade waters never looked so good, and it's difficult to remember sands that felt this soft.

As far as romantic fantasies go, it's hard to top riding **horses** along a quiet white sand beach lined with palms, wispy pines, and glossy-leafed sea-grape trees. Bring this vision to life and try other equestrian adventures at **Pinetree Stables** (tel. 373-3600); about $25 an hour per person).

HONEYMOON HOTELS AND HIDEAWAYS: Modern is the key word here— after all, the resort is only 30 years old.

Bahamas Princess Resort & Casino, P.O. Box F-207, Freeport, Grand Bahama, The Bahamas (tel. 809/352-6721; U.S. reservations: tel. 212/582-8100 or toll free 800/223-1818 or 800/442-8418). More than 900 rooms in two buildings make up this hotel near Freeport's famed International Bazaar. Although there is no beach at the hotel itself, complimentary shuttle buses whisk guests to the shore from both the low-rise Country Club and the high-rise Tower, across the street from each other. The Tower, next to the Princess Casino and the International Bazaar, is topped with striking Moorish minarets and this North African motif is echoed by the intricate tilework of the dramatic circular lobby. In addition to a ten-kilometer jogging trail, the Tower sports a pool, six tennis courts, and several good restaurants. The free-form pool at the Country Club, which also has six tennis courts and some fine eating spots, is known for its hot tub and free-form pool with a waterfall. Honeymoon package: Four days/three nights (EP): $320 to $440 per couple ($92 to $138 per couple for each additional night). Includes welcome rum swizzles, a bottle of champagne, a souvenir photo, and a princess discount booklet.

Xanadu Beach & Marina Resort, 7814 Carousel Lane, Richmond, VA 23229 (tel. 804/270-4313 or 809/352-6782; U.S. reservations: toll free 800/222-3788). This 185-room resort was once the hideaway of Howard Hughes. With dark wood paneling, backgammon tables, and a wrought-iron gate where you'd expect to find the door, his cozy private library is much the way he left it. When the reclusive millionaire dined in the hotel's gourmet Escoffier Room, no other guests were allowed. The nearby Persian Room, with muted lighting and hand-painted silk wall hangings, offers French selections. Guest rooms are comfortably modern and gaily decorated. You can indulge in a variety of water sports at the beach near the marina, or simply float in the pool. A taxi ride away from other hotels and the International Bazaar, Xanadu offers evening entertainment. Honeymoon package: Eight days/seven nights (EP): Up to $818 (or $1,203 for a one-bedroom suite) per couple. Includes a bottle of champagne, one breakfast in bed, a honeymoon photo, and a paddleboat ride.

The **Lucayan Beach Resort & Casino,** P.O. Box F-336, Lucaya, Grand Bahama, The Bahamas (tel. 809/373-7777; U.S. reservations: tel. 305/463-7760), a 248-room resort, is built around a lighthouse. Climb to the top for a sweeping view of the area. A lamplit walkway bordered by stone columns leads to the hotel and casino. The huge lobby is airy and elegant, with plush sofas and armchairs in various sitting areas. You'll cross a bridge over a wishing well to get to the circular main dining room. Each of the large rooms, with balconies or terraces and walk-in closets, has two double beds. Lush plantings dot the grounds. Sip cocktails at the poolside bar, play volleyball on the beach, or try some tennis or Ping-Pong. Also, be sure to check out the hotel's shops. Honeymoon package: Eight days/seven nights (EP): from $610 per couple. Includes a bottle of champagne, admission to the casino show, and a honeymoon photo.

Holiday Inn Lucaya Beach Resort, P.O. Box F-2496, Freeport, Grand Bahama, The Bahamas (tel. 809/373-1333; U.S. reservations: toll free 800/HOLIDAY). A 505-room hotel, the Holiday Inn buzzes with activity day and night. Boutiques, restaurants, a liquor store, beauty parlors, water sports, and poolside bingo, volleyball, shuffleboard, hat and balloon dances, or nightly entertainment—you name it, they've got it. The mini–straw market by the pool allows for open-air shopping. The good-size rooms are attractively decorated. Honeymoon package: Eight days/seven nights (EP): $860 to $1,200 per couple. Includes a breakfast for two, honeymooners' weekly party, a champagne dinner for two at Neptune's Table restaurant, and discount booklets. Four days/three nights packages also available.

ROMANTIC RESTAURANTS AND NIGHTSPOTS: Moonlight on the water,
Vegas-style shows, and the casinos . . . who can ask for anything more?

Pier One, Freeport Harbour (tel. 352-6674). Perched on stilts, this seafood restaurant is almost completely surrounded by water. At night, lights twinkle on the water. Sip cocktails on the balcony off the bar while watching the sun set. The ceiling beams are hung with plants and fish nets. Starfish, pots, and pans decorate the wood-paneled walls. Ask to be seated by the "Lovers' Lane" street sign. Dinner for two will be about $60 and up.

The Stoned Crab, Lucaya (tel. 373-1442). Be sure to make reservations and to bring hefty appetites when you visit this crowd-pleaser on quiet Taino Beach. While you dine, you'll hear the waves lapping the shore as the moonlight dances on the water. The menu boasts all kinds of crab dishes, from crab and avocado salad to snow crab claws, plus fish and freshly baked raisin bread. Only dinner is served. A meal for the two of you could cost $70 or more.

Stop at **Café Valencia,** Freeport (tel. 352-8717), for lunch when you're ready for a break from shopping in the International Bazaar. You'll enter the restaurant through a tiled patio that leads to a bar/lounge with beige-tile floors and rattan furniture. Buffalo chicken wings, Caesar salad, pasta, and minced lobster (a Bahamian specialty) along with—you guessed it—paella. A complete lunch for two will start at about $20. Dinner will be about $50 for two.

Work up an appetite in the Princess Casino, then spend your winnings on a gourmet meal in the **Crown Room,** Freeport (tel. 352-6721). Dinner for two will cost about $60. Many consider **Marcella's,** Freeport (tel. 352-5085) the best Italian restaurant on the island. Dinner for two: $30 and up. **Scorpio's,** Freeport (tel. 352-6969) offers cracked conch, minced lobster, and other island favorites. Expect to pay about $25 per couple for dinner. After lunch at **Black Beard's,** Lucaya (tel. 373-2960), which overlooks Fortune Beach, take a dip in the Atlantic. Lunch, featuring hearty local fare, runs about $20 and up for two. When touring the west coast of Freeport/Lucaya, **Freddie's,** Hunters (tel. 352-3250) makes a good lunch spot. Although the emphasis is on shrimp, lobster tails, and other seafood, you'll also find pork chops and steak on the menu. Lunch for two will be about $25. At the **Buccaneer Club,** Holmes Rock (tel. 348-3794), dramatic sunsets accompany the Swiss and Bahamian dishes on the menu. Call for complimentary transportation from your hotel. Plan to spend about $50 per couple.

The Princess Casino, at the Lucayan Beach Hotel (tel. 373-7777), is the island's newest gambling spot. Freeport sports another **Princess Casino,** in the Princess Tower (tel. 352-6721). **Electric City Disco, Restaurant, and Bar,** Freeport (tel. 352-6681) is open until 4 a.m. It serves good Bahamian food and has poolside dancing. For live jazz, try the **Skipper's Lounge** at the Princess Country Club (open every night except Thursday). You'll move to disco, calypso, and reggae at **Sultan's Tent** in the Princess Tower. Other lively after-hours spots are **Panache** at the Holiday Inn; **Studio 69** on Midshipman Road; **Yellow Bird** at Castaways Resort; and the **Palace II** on East Sunrise Highway.

4. The Family Islands: The Abacos, Eleuthera, The Exumas

The friendly Family Islands, full of natural splendor, are for those who like empty beaches, exceptional diving and snorkeling, and life at an easy, slow pace. They're for newlyweds who can make their own nightlife, who don't mind waiting until the weekend for most parties and musical entertainment, and who won't miss casinos. On some islands, one of the most popular and festive activities is helping to unload the weekly mail boat, which brings supplies—and livestock—from Nassau.

These islands are so friendly that many resorts don't even use keys for guest rooms (you can lock up your valuables in safety deposit boxes, if you like). Although most dining out will happen in your hotel, there are also some excellent local restaurants specializing in fresh, homestyle Bahamian fare. Most of the accommodations that follow are air-conditioned. Those that are not are cooled by trade winds and ceiling fans.

THE ABACOS: The northernmost part of the Bahamas, the Abacos are one of the most developed parts of the Family Islands. This 130-mile-long archipelago, shaped like an arm bent at the elbow, is about 75 miles north of Nassau and about 200 miles east of Miami, Florida. The Abacos have long been the shipbuilding center of The

Bahamas and paradise for sailors. Your hotel staff will be pleased to make arrangements for you to charter a boat for sailing, fishing, or just plain exploring.

Many visitors are surprised by the New England flavor of three of the prettiest islands, Green Turtle Cay, Elbow Cay, and Man-O-War Cay. But once you learn the history of these islands, it all makes sense. The Abacos were settled by Loyalists, who, choosing to remain under the British Crown, fled New England and the Carolinas during and after the American Revolution. Today the fishing villages of New Plymouth on Green Turtle, Hope Town on Elbow Cay, and Man-O-War Cay are favorite sightseeing stops. Ferries will take you from Marsh Harbour to Elbow and Man-O-War cays (about $8 per person round-trip if you're returning the same day or $6 per person each way if you're staying overnight); and from Treasure Cay to Green Turtle Cay (about $6 per person each way).

New Plymouth sports several beautifully restored historic homes, one of which houses a museum. Stop at a local restaurant to sample one of the Abacos specialties—wild boar or turtle steak.

South of Green Turtle, Hope Town is known for its red-and-white-striped lighthouse, which can be seen from almost any point in town, and for its long wide beaches with high grassy bluffs. Climb the 120 feet to the top of the lighthouse for a nonstop view of the area. Cars are banned from the center of town.

Romantic Interludes

For newlyweds with an adventurous spirit, the Abacos offer a variety of cays to explore.

While it's easy to stumble onto amazing **beaches** in The Bahamas, the Abacos have some of the country's most outstanding sandy shores. Treasure Cay, with its self-contained resort, sports a strip stretching almost four miles. Hilly Green Turtle Cay is surrounded by quiet bays and empty expanses where you can swim and relax undisturbed. The candy-striped Hope Town Lighthouse stands guard above Elbow Cay beaches; even those that border the picture-perfect town are never crowded.

Don't be fooled by the size of the **Albert Lowe Museum** in New Plymouth on Green Turtle Cay. This tiny museum is packed with intriguing memorabilia. The history of the Abacos is told through old photographs, model ships, paintings, antique furniture, and the architecture of the restored Loyalist home that houses the museum. Founded by Alton Lowe, one of the country's best-loved painters, the museum was named for his boat-building father. (Open from about 9:30 to 11:30 a.m., then from 1 to 3 p.m. Admission: $3 per person.)

You'll come across another slice of history in Elbow Cay's Hope Town. Named for the South Carolinian woman who founded the town in 1783, the **Wyannie Malone Museum** has exhibits detailing the colorful history of the island. (Open 10 a.m. to noon. Admission: $1 per person).

If you're curious about **boat building,** take the ferry from Marsh Harbour to Man-O-War Cay (about $8 per person round-trip). Craftsmen line the waterfront, where the marina is chock-full of bobbing boats. Nowadays most boats are made of fiberglass. But if you strike up a conversation with one of the men at work, he'll probably tell you a bit about the old days, when boats were painstakingly made of wood. Even if you're not in the market for new sails, stop by **Uncle Norman Albury's Sail Loft.** The canvas sold here is no longer used to catch the wind. Instead it is dyed bright colors and sewn, by hand, into tote bags.

Honeymoon Hotels and Hideaways

You'll be surprised by the wide range of accommodations the Abacos offer.

Abaco Inn, Hope Town, Elbow Cay, Abaco, The Bahamas (tel. 809/367-2666). There are only ten rooms in this peaceful, casually elegant hotel on a narrow strip of land a short drive from Hope Town. The ocean crashes on one side of the property and the calm bay bathes the other. You'll have a choice of three beaches. The main building, which houses the bar/lounge and dining room, is paneled in Abaco pine and has tiled floors and ceiling fans. Served on two waterfront terraces, the five-course gourmet dinners are delicious. Guest rooms, in cottages, are simple, each with its own hammock and private patio, and they come with books left by previous guests. Host Ruth Maury is always happy to arrange water sports, including scuba diving, snorkeling, sailing, windsurfing. Honeymoon package: Eight days/seven nights (EP): $550 to $605 per couple. Includes a bottle of champagne, use of Sunfish and windsurfer for a day, and a boat trip to a deserted island for an intimate picnic with wine.

Hope Town Harbour Lodge, Hope Town, Elbow Cay, Abaco, The Bahamas (tel. 809/367-2277; U.S. reservations: toll free 800/626-5690). Not only is this lodge right in picture-perfect Hope Town, but it is also on a gorgeous beach. And you won't have to walk far to find a sandy stretch just for the two of you. The gray clapboard buildings, trimmed in pink, are perched on a rise above the main road. From the front, the view is of the boat-filled harbor, and the back overlooks the pool and the ocean. Be sure to request a double bed when you make reservations. In addition to the 21 cheery guest rooms in the main house, a private cottage called Butterfly House is also available for rent. The food—prepared by Norris Smith, a young Bahamian chef who has trained in France, Switzerland, and Germany—is unforgettable. Honeymoon package: none. Rates (EP): $66 to $73 per couple per night.

Treasure Cay Beach Hotel and Villas, P.O. Box 4183, Treasure Cay, Abaco, The Bahamas (tel. 809/367-2847; U.S. reservations: toll free 800/327-1584, nationwide; or 800/432-8257 in Florida). On the east coast of Abaco, this 205-room resort is a village in itself. When you check in you'll receive a map showing you how to find the tennis courts, four pools, the marina packed with yachts and other sea craft, and the shopping center, which boasts a bank, post office, pharmacy, and boutique. You can stay in an individual room, a suite, or a red-roofed villa. The snow-white beach is nearly four miles long and never crowded. Guests have complimentary use of snorkeling gear, and sailing and green fees are also included in room rates. Dick Wilson designed the 18-hole golf course. Evening entertainment includes poolside buffets. Honeymoon package: Seven days/six nights (EP): From $807 per couple. Includes a bottle of champagne, an island excursion, and a honeymoon gift.

Green Turtle Club and Marina, P.O. Box 270, Green Turtle Cay, Abaco, The Bahamas (tel. 809/367-2572; U.S. reservations: tel. 305/833-9580 or toll free 800/327-0787). The ferry to Green Turtle Cay will let you off at a white clubhouse with a green awning at the edge of a marina. You'll be welcomed with Tipsy Turtles, the club's special brand of cocktail. Yachting club flags decorate the ceiling beams, and dollar bills, put there and signed by visitors, paper the walls. Guests stay in 30 individual rooms, suites, and waterfront villas. The roomy units have modern baths and sliding glass doors. A swimming pool is on the grounds and two beaches are short walks away. The snorkeling and diving in this area is excellent. Take one of the daily complimentary boat trips into the town of New Plymouth or stroll in for exercise. Honeymoon package: Eight days/seven nights (EP): From $616 per couple. Includes a bottle of champagne and a deserted island picnic for two. Four days/three nights package also available.

Bluff House Club and Marina, Green Turtle Cay, Abaco, The Bahamas (tel. 305/564-2621; U.S. reservations: tel. 305/564-2621; or toll free 800/327-0787). Built on a hill high above a tantalizing beach, Bluff House offers individual rooms, suites, villas, and even "treehouse" accommodations. In the 32 units, the decor includes weathered wood paneling, wicker upholstered chairs, and ginger-jar lamps. Sliding glass doors in the main house lead to the oceanview pool deck. Inside, the lounge is split-level, with a driftwood coffee table and colorful framed posters. Staff will arrange tennis, fishing, snorkeling, and diving excursions. Ferry rides to the town of New Plymouth are complimentary to guests. Plan to diet after you leave! Honeymoon package: Eight days/seven nights (EP): From $555 per couple. Includes a bottle of champagne and a half day's use of a power boat or Sunfish sailboat. Four days/three nights package also available.

ELEUTHERA: The pencil-thin arc called Eleuthera takes you back to the very beginning. Barely five miles across at its widest point, this island was where the first settlers, the Eleutherian Adventurers, set up camp in 1648. Since they had come to escape religious persecution in Bermuda, they used the Greek word for "freedom" when they named their new home. They were followed by other Bermudians and English settlers, many of whom brought their slaves and later by British loyalists and freed slaves from America.

Just 70 miles east of Nassau, Eleuthera is 100 miles long. After New Providence and Grand Bahama, it is the most developed island in The Bahamas. Throughout Eleuthera you'll find blue holes, inland bodies of water teeming with fish, and caves awaiting adventurous souls. During the late 19th century, Eleuthera was a prime source of pineapples. A visit to the plantation in Gregory Town will allow you to sample pineapple rum. You may have heard about pink sand, but you've got to see Eleuthera's beaches to believe it. Many of the palm-shaded deserted beaches have a rosy hue from bits of coral and shells.

Harbour Island, off the northern coast, is famous for its pink sand beaches and for charming Dunmore Town, the first capital of The Bahamas. Affectionately referred to as "Briland" by residents, this petite oasis is truly captivating. You'll think of Cape Cod when you see the small wooden houses, but the palm trees and the turquoise water will remind you that you are in The Bahamas.

Spanish Wells off the northern coast of Eleuthera received its name when Spanish galleons sent sailors ashore for fresh water. Today it is reminiscent of the suburban United States with brightly painted houses, colorful gardens, and neat lawns. Like Man-O-War Cay in the Abacos, the many blond-haired blue-eyed residents may surprise you. Fishing is the island's main industry and you can buy some of the freshest lobster around.

Romantic Interludes

The action in Eleuthera revolves around water sports, but the land also holds some intriguing sights.

Ships were not the only victims of the Devil's Backbone, a magnificent spine of reefs off Eleuthera's northern coast. A **Civil War train** met its end here as well. This Union locomotive plunged into the depths from a barge on its way to Cuba in 1865. In a kaleidoscopic blast of color, fish and other sea creatures swim in and out of the rusted wreckage. This is one of the dive sites offered by the **Romora Bay Club** (tel. toll free 800/327-8286) and **Valentine's Dive Center** (tel. 333-2142), both on Harbour Island.

The narrowest point on the island has come to be known as the **Glass Window.** Here the crashing surf has whittled the land down to a sliver, so that the dark blue of the ocean on one side is only a few feet from the turquoise of the shallower sound on the other side. A human-made bridge now crosses the gap where a natural rock arc once was.

For a real adventure, go spelunking in one of the many caves that dot the island. The entrance to one of the largest is marked by a sprawling fig tree said to have been planted as camouflage by pirates who had hidden treasure inside. Your hotel will put you in touch with a local guide, who will lead you through labyrinths of passageways, past stalagmites and stalactites in various configurations, and below bats (of the harmless variety) clinging to the ceilings.

Honeymoon Hotels and Hideaways

Eleuthera has some of the country's best accommodations, from the small and casual to luxurious resorts that receive royal patronage.

Expensive: Windermere Island Club, P.O. Box 25, Rock Sound, Eleuthera, The Bahamas (tel. 809/332-2538; U.S. reservations: tel. 212/839-0222). If you want to follow in the footsteps of Prince Charles, Princess Diana, and Prince Andrew, Windermere Island is just the place for royal treatment. Notables and ordinary folk all come for seclusion, privacy, and pampering. Connected to the mainland by a bridge, this opulent resort is on its own private island. The beautifully decorated suites, villas, and private homes for rent are so distant from each other that you won't have any trouble finding a spot to be alone together. Begin breakfast with fresh pineapple or pawpaw served on your private balcony while you gaze at the deserted white beach. The day's end brings candlelit gourmet feasts. Perfect your tennis game or try an array of water sports. Honeymoon package: none. Rates (FAP): $231 to $475 per couple per night.

Moderate: Cotton Bay Resort Club, P.O. Box 28, Rock Sound, Eleuthera, The Bahamas (tel. 809/334-2101; U.S. reservations: toll free 800/843-2297, 800/225-4255, or 800/327-0787). Known for its spectacular Robert Trent Jones–designed golf course, Cotton Bay was once a private club catering to millionaires. The decor epitomizes the best of the tropics, with rattan, wicker, and *Casablanca*-style fans. Combining rustic charm with luxurious comfort, most of the 77 rooms look out to the Atlantic. You'll easily find a place to call your own on the long powdery beach. Scuba diving, tennis, and boating are among the sports available. A local guitarist entertains guests gathered in the octagonal lounge for drinks before dinner. Dining under the stars on the pool terrace couldn't be more romantic. Honeymoon package: Eight days/seven nights (MAP): $770 to $1,130 per couple. Includes a bottle of champagne and free airport transfers.

Inexpensive: Runaway Hill, P.O. Box 31, Harbour Island, Eleuthera, The Bahamas (tel. 809/333-2150; U.S. reservations: toll free 800/327-0787). Staying at this small inn that was once a private home is like visiting old friends. The lounge is decorated with wicker furniture on a glossy black-and-white tile floor. Well-thumbed books have been left by previous travelers in the guest rooms, each of which is individually decorated. The fresh, delicious meals, which draw many visitors from other hotels, are served on the veranda above the swimming pool and pink sand beach. Carol Becht, who runs this eight-room inn with her husband, Roger, writes the menu by hand every day. Honeymoon package: Eight days/seven nights (EP): From $500 per couple. Includes a bottle of champagne.

Romora Bay Club, P.O. Box 146, Harbour Island, Eleuthera, The Bahamas (tel. 809/333-2324; U.S. reservations: toll free 800/327-8286). Overflowing with tropical flowers, bushes, and trees, Romora Bay borders both the beach and the harbor sides of the island. A popular activity, especially for honeymooners, is being marooned all day for an "X-rated" picnic on a deserted island. The 30 comfortable rooms have private patios or balconies, and there is an excellent dive program offered. Honeymoon package: Seven days/six nights (EP): From $528 per couple. Includes an "X-rated" picnic trip to a deserted island.

Pink Sands, P.O. Box 87, Harbour Island, Eleuthera, The Bahamas (tel. 809/333-2030 or 809/333-2060). How about waking up to the sweet aroma of breakfast? At Pink Sands, a cook will prepare your morning meals in the kitchen adjoining your bedroom. All you have to do is roll out of bed and sit down to eat. Your enormous cottage, cooled by a ceiling fan, will feature a dining and sitting area and a dressing room. Narrow paths wind past the 49 units, through the lush beachfront property. Tennis courts and water sports are available for the asking. Dinner, a casually elegant affair, is served in the open-air dining room, where tables surround a fireplace. At the Pink Sands Harbour Lodge in town, you can treat yourselves to dramatic sunsets while sipping cocktails. Honeymoon package: none. Rates (EP): From $55 per couple per night.

THE EXUMAS: Although the Exumas are said to have a cay for each day of the year, the population of this chain is concentrated on Great Exuma, the largest of the islands. Stretching for 100 miles between New Providence and Long Island, these islands are heaven for sailors and water-sports enthusiasts. When you fly in you'll see tiny islands strewn through swirls of turquoise in more shades than you thought existed. It's as if Mother Nature had pulled her fingers through the water, leaving a whimsical design.

In the center of George Town, the pink-and-white administration building resembles a dignified Government House in Nassau. The pastel-and-white color scheme of this and other buildings in town makes taking photos hard to resist. Women selling a multitude of straw goods set up shop in the shade of the huge fig trees that border the main road. A few scuba diving operations, boutiques, and other stores are clustered here.

Rent a car or hire a taxi for a drive up north, and you'll pass tiny farming settlements and a few good home-style restaurants. Palm, banana, tamarind, and citrus trees grow along the road. Stop for a swim at deserted Three Sisters beach, where three huge dark rocks rise out of the aquamarine water side by side.

If your honeymoon happens to fall at the end of April, you'll be swept up in the excitement of the annual Family Island Regatta. The partying surrounding these three days of sailing races is stretched out for at least a week.

Romantic Interludes

Both on land and at sea, nature has given newlyweds plenty to discover in the Exuma cays.

Long, narrow Stocking Island lies across Elizabeth Harbour from George Town. Edged with some of the world's most powdery sand, this island lures romantics with countless **secluded coves** and inlets. Pack a picnic, or get hot dogs at the beach bar. The calm waters of the harborside are speckled with sailboats. You can walk out on a sandbar stretching at least 40 yards into the bay. Red and black starfish wash gently ashore. If you're into bonefishing, all you have to do is cast your lines off the dock. On the other side of the island, the shelling is excellent. Peace and Plenty Hotel provides daily complimentary ferry service to the island for its guests.

Lying on and around some of Exuma's most dramatic cays, the **Exuma Land and Sea Park** has been declared a national park. It encompasses more than 20 miles of striking coral reefs, brilliant fish, and other marine life, as well as nesting areas for flocks of birds. Since some of the colorful underwater spectacles are only three to ten feet down, snorkeling is extremely exciting here. To tour this region north of Great Exuma, make arrangements through your hotel to charter a boat.

Honeymoon Hotels and Hideaways

Once a sponge market and then a private home, **Peace and Plenty,** P.O. Box 55, George Town, Exuma, The Bahamas (tel. 809/336-2551; U.S. reservations: toll free 800/327-0787), has settled comfortably into its latest incarnation as a hotel. The hospitality here is truly Bahamian. Many residents socialize with visitors at the bar, which is decorated with anchors, nets, and other nautical touches. At breakfast, the grits and boiled fish—a Bahamian specialty—are favorites. Weekend parties often take place on the pool patio and it seems as if the whole island turns out to wiggle their hips under the stars. Many of the 32 large rooms have sweeping views of Elizabeth Harbour, which attracts more than a few boaters. Some rooms are air-conditioned and others have ceiling fans. A complimentary ferry ride takes guests to the quiet beaches of Stocking Island, just across the water. Honeymoon package: Eight days/seven nights (EP): From $492 per couple. Includes use of Sunfish sailboat for a day.

5. More Suggestions in The Bahamas

Some Bahama-philes are convinced that you've never really seen the Bahamas until you've taken a good look below its shimmering waters. At least two islands should not be missed by serious—or even semi-serious—divers or snorkelers. Right off the beach-fringed eastern coast of Andros is an extraordinary 120-mile-long barrier reef while on Long Island, divers can learn that sharks need not be frightening after all.

Small Hope Bay Lodge, P.O. Box N-1131, Nassau, New Providence, The Bahamas (tel. 809/368-2014; U.S. reservations: tel. 305/463-9130 or toll free 800/223-6961). Since scuba diving is the house specialty, nondivers are invited to take lessons free of charge at Small Hope Bay, one of the few accommodations on massive, undeveloped Andros. Guests are also encouraged to learn to snorkel here. At a rustic lodge, where jackets, ties, and shoes are virtually unheard of, soaking in a hot tub or having a massage might seem to be unlikely activities. However, not only is a hot tub right on the beach, but you can arrange for expert hands to relax your muscles after a hard day of diving, snorkeling, biking, or simply cooling out in a hammock. The palm-shaded beach begins just outside each cabin door. The 20 pine and coral units are decorated with distinctive batik wall-hangings and pillows. This colorful cloth is dyed at the local Androsia workshop, which makes resortwear sold throughout The Bahamas. Meals, hearty and plentiful, are served at tables where various members of the Birch family dine with guests. Honeymoon package: Eight days/seven nights (FAP): From $1,100 per couple. Includes a bottle of champagne and breakfast in bed.

Stella Maris Inn, P.O. Box SM-105, Stella Maris, Long Island, The Bahamas (tel. 809/336-2106; U.S. reservations: tel. 305/467-0466 or toll free 800/327-0787). The waters off the coast of Stella Maris on Long Island provide a wealth of thrilling dive sites. For the adventurous, learning to dive (safely) with sharks is one of the special attractions of this 50-room German-owned inn. Sailing, Windsurfing, waterskiing, deep-sea fishing, and snorkeling around the brilliant offshore reefs are also favorite pastimes. Cottages, apartments, and individual rooms dot the sprawling hilly grounds that border the ocean. You'll have a choice of three swimming pools and two tennis courts. On weekends, the Stella Maris is where the action is: local musicians play up a "rake and scrape" storm. Honeymoon package: Eight days/seven nights (EP): From $508 per couple. Includes a bottle of champagne and one day's use of a rental car or Jeep.

Chapter XXIV

BARBADOS

1. Practical Facts
2. Romantic Interludes
3. Honeymoon Hotels and Hideaways
4. Romantic Restaurants

BARBADOS IS a little farther from U.S. shores than some other Caribbean locations—perhaps 45 or so extra minutes on a plane. But if you choose this extraordinary island for your honeymoon, you'll be well rewarded, since it combines the most delightful features of all the islands in one. It has more than its share of natural beauty —azure water, pristine beaches, graceful palm trees, warm, flower-scented breezes. But even more beguiling is the Barbadians' deeply personal approach to visitors. Although the hotels are sophisticated and know how to provide every amenity, you'll never be "processed" or shoved around in an impersonal way. Hotel managers greet you, check on you, coddle you until you feel like a guest in a private home. But much as visitors are cherished, Barbadians haven't sold out to big-time tourism; they mightily resist turning their island into an artificial, plasticized world designed to capture tourist dollars. They're proud of their native culture, which is vibrant, unspoiled, and, for the most part, devoid of grinding poverty and racial resentments. Even the simplest dwellings have a spruced-up dignity, and the humblest Bajan has the same sense of self-respect. They address you with an attitude that says "I'm a pretty terrific person. What about you?"

Barbados is one of the Windward Islands of the Lesser Antilles, an island chain that swings east from Puerto Rico, then south and back west again as it skims the coast of South America. The island is shaped rather like a pear that leans to the west—21 miles long (north to south), and 14 miles wide at the widest point (total area: 166 square miles).

Because it's the most easterly of all the Caribbean islands, it has three quite different sea coasts. The east coast, the northern end of which is aptly named the Scotland district, is a wild, forlorn area—hilly, picturesque, and populated mostly by farm animals that graze along the mountainsides. The rough, blue-gray Atlantic breakers start their shoreward roll from miles out, and as they crash, fill all the rocky bays with an eerie sea mist. In sharp contrast, the west coast, bathed by the much more gentle Caribbean Sea, has been sculpted and polished for the international visitor. One after another, elegant, low-rise hotels and vacation homes (one of them belonging to Claudette Colbert) cozy up to the beach, the waves almost lapping their terraces. Guests wander across green lawns landscaped with hibiscus and bougainvillea, bathe in brilliant blue swimming pools, or sit in the sand under a palm tree and watch a glowing sunset. At the southwestern elbow of the island, you'll find Bridgetown, Barbados' capital, with its fine duty-free shops centered along Broad Street. Barbados' curving south coast (the bottom of the pear) is also peppered with pretty hotels, generally more moderate in price. The beaches are wider, breezier and wavier than on the west coast. In the afternoons, colorful flotillas of windsurfers try to keep their boards balanced and sails high.

As early as 1511, Barbados was spotted by Spanish and Portuguese sailors, who named it "Isla de los Barbados" (Island of the Bearded Ones), perhaps referring to the native ficus tree whose aboveground roots grow down from its branches in a beard-like fashion. But it was a British trading party that took possession of the island in 1625, and England governed the island for the next 350 years. In 1627 the first settlers arrived to grow tobacco and cotton, but sugar proved to be a better economic bet. The island was deforested, sugar was planted everywhere, and plantation owners prospered. But since growing, harvesting, and refining sugar required a large workforce, Africans were imported, and the institution of slavery was established on the island.

In 1834, slavery was abolished on Barbados. Over the years, sugar became less lucrative, and Barbadians turned to tourism and light industry to balance their economy. Sugar is still grown on the island, especially in the interior, and its by-products, molasses and rum, are among the island's major exports. Barbados became independent from Britain in 1966, but it still retains membership in the British Commonwealth. The Barbadians (also called "Bajans") maintain cultural links with England, as well—they like cricket, polo, afternoon tea, and low-key good manners. Their parliamentary government is stable, and there is little crime. Bajans from all walks of life seem to get along with a minimum of racial and class tensions, probably because all people are free to advance in commerce and the professions as they wish. (Interracial marriages are not unusual.) As a tourist, you'll feel the goodwill and gentle interest of almost all Barbadians. Once when we asked directions in Bridgetown, an elderly woman walked us to our destination, delighted to point out the shortcut we surely would have missed. Her attitude is not unusual.

Barbados is not the place for hustle and bustle, glitz and glitter. No gambling here. The island's attractions are subtle and tasteful in the British tradition. This is paradise for honeymooners who enjoy natural beauty, water sports, history, and nightlife that's upbeat and elegant but not gaudy.

1. Practical Facts

ENTERING AND LEAVING: American and Canadian visitors will need proof of citizenship, plus a ticket for onward or return departure. Passports are always best (they allow you to use shorter, quicker lines), but you can get by with a birth certificate, along with a photo ID such as a driver's license. There is a departure tax of $8 U.S., payable when you check in for your return flight.

GETTING THERE: Barbados is a little over 4 hours from New York, 5 hours from Toronto, and 3 hours and 15 minutes from Miami. The island is easy to reach without stopping and changing planes, especially from the major east coast United States cities. The following major air carriers serve Barbados nonstop (or one stop only) from the United States and Canada. From New York and Boston: **American Airlines, Eastern Airlines, Pan American, B.W.I.A.** From Miami: **Eastern Airlines, B.W.I.A., Pan American.** From Toronto and Montreal: **Air Canada.** You can connect from Midwest and west coast cities via Miami or San Juan. From Barbados, it's also fun to island-hop to Martinique, Grenada, St. Lucia, and other nearby islands via **Tropic Air, Air Martinique,** or **B.W.I.A.**

GETTING AROUND: Barbados offers buses, taxis, rental cars, "mokes," and even motorbikes and bicycles for your convenience. To get the best transportation for your

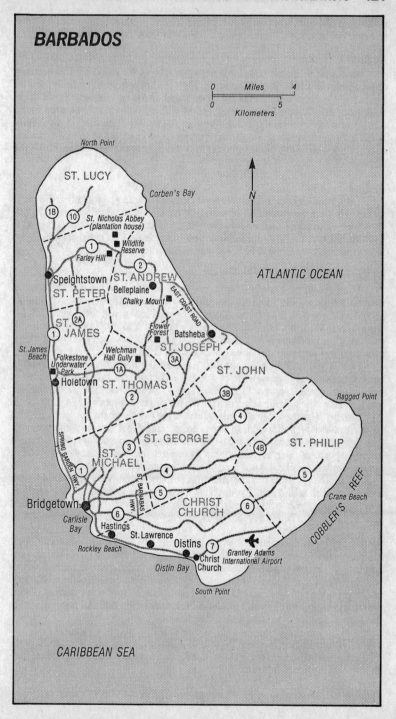

BARBADOS

0 —————— Miles —————— 4
0 —————————— 5
Kilometers

North Point

ST. LUCY

Corben's Bay

N

(1B) (10)   St. Nicholas Abbey
              (plantation house)

(1)   Wildlife
Farley Hill   Reserve

              (2)

Speightstown ST. ANDREW   ATLANTIC OCEAN

ST. PETER   Belleplaine
             Chalky Mount

ST. (2A)   Flower   EAST COAST ROAD
(1) JAMES   Forest   Batsheba

St. James   ST. JOSEPH
Beach   Welchman
Folkestone Hall Gully
Underwater
Park   (1A)   ST. JOHN
Holetown   ST. THOMAS
                              (3A)
              (2)
                        (3B)   Ragged Point

                              (4)

SPRING GARDEN HWY. ST. GEORGE   (4B)   ST. PHILIP

ST.   (3)
MICHAEL   (5)
(1)
                    (4)
ST. BARNABAS HWY.

              (5)
Bridgetown   CHRIST   (6)
Carlisle   (6)   CHURCH
Bay   Hastings
                                        COBBLER'S REEF
Rockley Beach St. Lawrence Oistins (7)   Crane Beach
                    Christ   Grantley Adams
Oistin Bay   Church   International Airport

              South Point

CARIBBEAN SEA

dollar, first find out where your hotel is located relative to other sights you'd like to see, restaurants where you'd like to dine, etc., then plan your vacation time accordingly.

By Bus

Buses give you most miles for your money all over the island (fare between any two points is 75¢ Bds. in exact change). They're comfortable and reliable, and the routes include many areas of interest. State-owned buses are blue with a gold stripe; those from the privately owned line are yellow with blue stripes. All buses run from 5 a.m. to 11 p.m. Routes and schedules are available from the Board of Tourism. Some hotels have courtesy van service to and from the airport and shuttle service to Bridgetown; check when you make your hotel reservations, or ask at the front desk once you arrive.

By Taxi

Taxis are always there when you need them, and the drivers friendly and eager to please. They are expensive, however. There are no meters; fixed rates are charged between various points on the island. Sample rates: Airport to west coast hotels; $7 to $10 US. Ask your taxi driver or the desk clerk at your hotel for a rate sheet. It's always wise to ask what the fare will be before you take a ride.

By Car

These are easy to come by from several local companies. Popular in Barbados are mini-mokes, dune-buggy-like vehicles with canvas roofs and open sides. They rent for about $5 U.S. to $7 U.S. a day less than cars. A mini-moke runs about $150 U.S. per week; a car, $175 to $200 U.S. (Add on 5% tax and a $25 collision waiver to this estimate.) Use credit cards for car rental if you can: otherwise you must leave a large cash deposit. Car rental companies do not accept personal checks.

Even if you only drive for one day, you'll need a Barbados visitor's driving license (international licenses will not suffice). To obtain one, take your own state or international license, along with $10 Bds to the police station in the town nearest your hotel, and the officials will write out a license for you on the spot.

Driving is on the left in Barbados and steering wheels are on the right; careful at those roundabouts (traffic circles)! Roads are generally (not always) well paved, but tend to be narrow and curvy (those on the mountainous east coast are often steep and like roller coasters). Driving is European style with lots of dodging and passing. Main arteries are well marked, but it's easy to get lost on secondary roads, especially at night. A couple of driving hints: Avoid traffic jams by steering clear of the Bridgetown area during rush hours. And if you wish to have dinner in a restaurant far away from your hotel, better visit the area in daylight first, spring for a taxi, or wait until the end of your stay when you know the roads better.

MONEY: The Barbados dollar is worth just about 50¢ US, and stays constant since it is officially tied to the U.S. dollar. To figure how much Barbadian goods and services cost in U.S. dollars, just divide the amount of the Barbadian price tag in half. Shops will accept U.S. and Canadian cash, plus traveler's checks. Some hotels, restaurants, and larger stores will take major U.S. credit cards, but ask first; don't assume. Hotels, stores, and banks all offer pretty much the same rate of exchange. All prices quoted in this section are in U.S. dollars, unless otherwise indicated.

LANGUAGE: English has been the official—and only—language since 1627, when the British landed and laid claim to the island. Bajans speak it with a lovely West Indian lilt—which tends to be catching.

WEATHER: During the winter, temperatures range from 68° to 85°; summer temperatures from 76° to 87°, but the island is constantly refreshed and cooled by steady northeast trade winds. The island boasts more than 3,000 hours of sunshine per year, the rainiest months being September, October, and November. February and March tend to have the driest weather. Rain seldom lasts long; the trade winds blow storm clouds quickly by.

CLOTHING: Bajans aren't stuffy about clothing, but they have the British regard for neatness and decorum. Bathing suits are for beach and pool area only; when you adjourn to the terrace for lunch, don a shirt or cover-up. Tour the island in pants and a shirt, or an informal dress; no short shorts or halter tops, please. Many hotels and restaurants require men to wear jackets, some of the more elegant establishments also request ties during dinner; for special occasions during the winter season, some tony hotels require dinner jackets. Wardrobes are more casual in the summer. Check dress codes with hotels and restaurants in advance.

TIME: All year, Barbados is on Atlantic Standard Time, which is one hour ahead of Eastern Standard Time. In winter, when it's noon in New York, it's 1:00 p.m. in Barbados. However, when Daylight Savings Time is in effect, the time will be the same in both places.

TELEPHONE: You can reach Barbados direct from the United States by dialing area code 809 and the seven-digit number. The phone service on the island is good. Most hotels have phones in the rooms, and local calls are free. Minimum charge for a three-minute call to the United States is about $12.

SHOPPING: Do you want to fill out your English china or crystal pattern, or warm yourself in British woolens this winter? In Barbados you can buy these items at 20% to 50% less than in the United States! Excellent buys are also found on perfumes, Irish woolens and linens, Liberty silks and cottons, gold and silver jewelry, watches and liquor—especially Barbados rum. Hot spot for shopping: **Broad Street** in **Bridgetown,** where the finest department and specialty stores are located. These include C.F. Harrison, Cave Shepherd, DaCosta's, Y. DeLima, and India House, plus several fine jewelry stores. Shopping hours are 8 a.m. to 4 p.m. on weekdays (afternoons are less crowded), 8 a.m. to noon on Saturdays. Smaller branches of some of these stores are in the Barbados shopping malls: **Sunset Crest** on the west coast, **Skyway Shopping Plaza** in Hastings on the south coast. Many of the finest hotels have their own boutiques, as well.

Barbados has a special in-bond purchasing system to help U.S. and Canadian tourists realize greatest savings on imported goods. Here's how it works. In the duty-free section of stores carrying imports, you'll see all goods have two price tags—take-away, and in-bond. If you buy at the lower in-bond price, your purchased goods will be delivered to the Chamber of Commerce section in the Departure Hall at the airport. You pick up your packages there before you leave. To take advantage of in-bond savings, you must make your purchases at least 24 hours before your departure time. Inform the sales clerk of your departure date plus your airline and flight number, and save any invoices to give to the airport official so that you can claim your packages. It all works very smoothly.

Be sure to check out local Bajan handcrafts, as well. Some of the most tasteful items—children's toys and clothes, basketry and other woven items, place mats, and ceramics—are to be found at the Best of Barbados shops (six different locations throughout the island). The owner and guiding spirit of Best of Barbados is designer Jill Walker, who is known throughout the island for her bright watercolors and hand-printed fabrics. Local straw work, batik, pottery of Arawak Indian design, and African-style jewelry made from shells can be seen at **Pelican Village,** Harbour Road,

Bridgetown, with its individual thatch-roofed stalls. Also in Bridgetown, check out the **Handicraft Emporium,** Princess Alice Highway; and **West Indies Handcrafts and Articrafts,** Norman Center, Broad Street.

Don't forget that you can bring $400 worth of goods back to the United States duty free; a 10% duty will be collected on purchases over that amount. A hint when purchasing liquor: Although you can bring in only one quart of liquor duty free, you might consider buying several bottles of Barbados rum anyway. Even after you've paid the duty, you'll probably be spending less than you would in your local liquor store.

HOW TO GET MARRIED IN BARBADOS: Tying the knot in Barbados is easy but takes a bit of planning. Here's what to do. You must be on the island at least six days before the marriage can take place, and you must make arrangements for the ceremony with clergy or magistrate before you apply for your license. You also need a blood test. Although you can get them on the island, it's better to have it done at home, and bring the official results with you. Also beforehand, purchase the special $12.50 stamp needed to make the license legal at a Barbados post office. On the fourth day after your arrival, you may apply for your license at the Ministry of Legal Affairs, Marine House, Christ Church (tel. 427-5420). Have identification with you—either a valid U.S. passport or a birth certificate plus a photo ID with signature, such as a driver's license. Also bring original or certified copies of divorce papers, if applicable. If one of you is widowed, bring proof of former marriage, plus death certificate of spouse. You will also need to show your airline tickets and the immigration cards you filled out on the aircraft. Your license will cost $50 and will be issued on the spot. There is a three-day waiting period before the marriage can take place.

FOR FURTHER INFORMATION: Contact: **Barbados Board of Tourism.** Barbados: P.O. Box 242, Bridgetown, Barbados (tel. 809/427-2623,2624). New York: 800 Second Ave., New York, NY 10017 (tel. 212/986-6516). Los Angeles: 3440 Wilshire Blvd., Suite 1215, Los Angeles, CA (tel. 213/380-2198/9). Or call toll free in the United States, 800/221-9831.

2. Romantic Interludes

Barbados waters are beautiful, clear, and warm—and there are so many ways you can enjoy them. Many hotels offer free **water sports** to their guests; this means that you can use their small sailboats, windsurfers, snorkel gear, and maybe even go waterskiing, without charge. For divers, there are a number of fine dive shops on the island.

Arguably, the best reefs for snorkeling on the island can be found at Folkestone Underwater Park, next to the Coral Reef Club on the west coast. This sanctuary for underwater life is also devoted to marine research. Snorkelers can follow an underwater trail, while scuba divers will find excellent reefs for steep, drop-off diving. If you think you'd like scuba, but you're not quite sure, call **Les Wotton's Dive School** next to Folkestone Park (tel. 422-3215; evenings 432-0833). Les, who is a wonderful character in his 70s, personally takes beginning divers down to the reefs each afternoon, after thorough (and reassuring) shallow-water instruction. He conducts expeditions for intermediate and experienced divers as well. He keeps his groups small and safe, so call several days ahead to reserve your place; his dives cost $30.

Vistas of land and sea are spectacular on this island, and since Barbadians want visitors to see them to advantage, they have established a number of **gardens and walking paths** that you should not miss. The brick paths at **Flower Forest** (tel. 433-8152) meander up and down a mountainside covered with tropical trees and exotic flowers. Beyond the vegetation, lush green mountains loom. There's a lovely, romantic gazebo and benches where you can sit and soak it all up. Entrance fee, $3. Animal lovers must visit the **Barbados Wildlife Reserve** (tel. 422-8826). You stroll along a yellow brick path quietly observing the free-roaming animals—otters, raccoons, alligators, deer, tortoises, and a new family of wallabies—while the lovely Barbados "green" monkeys soar overhead. Not smelly or confining, the reserve is beautifully kept by people who cherish animals. Entrance fee, $2.50. Be sure to visit the ruins of Farley Hill, an elegant old plantation house destroyed by fire in 1965 after it served as the site for the filming of *Island in the Sun,* starring Harry Belafonte. Behind the burnt-out mansion, you can walk up the hill under towering mahogany trees to the lookout, from where you can see the whole Scotland district, the Atlantic Ocean, and "Sleeping Napoleon," a strange cluster of huge rocks that simulate the profile face and belly of a reclining man. Take a picnic with you to Farley Hill; many hotels will prepare a box lunch if you ask them a day in advance.

Barbados has a **beach** for every taste. Top contenders start with St. James Beach along the west coast. Lunch at **Sandpiper Inn** (tel. 422-2251) or **Treasure Beach** (tel. 432-1346), then walk down the curving strand, wading in the warm, gentle water and surveying all those elegant hotels. Crane Beach, south coast: This magnificent strip of pink sand beneath towering limestone bluffs is one of the most marvelously unspoiled beaches in the West Indies. Have a wonderful seafood lunch atop the bluff at the Crane Hotel dining room and enjoy the view. Every fish on the menu is highly recommended. Bathsheba Beach, east coast: When the poet John Keats wrote about "perilous seas in fairylands forlorn" he must have had in mind a beach like Bathsheba—foggy, mysterious, pounded by turbulent surf. Native surfers love it; you can see them far out on their boards, waiting for a wave. Wade only; rough surf and underwater rocks makes swimming perilous. Plan for lunch at the **Bonito Bar** (tel. 433-9034), a tiny, unpretentious restaurant specializing in native cuisine. The owners will delight in showing you Brooke Shields' and Mick Jagger's signatures in their guestbook.

Learning about Barbados' sugar economy is far more interesting than you would at first expect. Start by visiting the excellent **Barbados Museum** (tel. 427-0201 or 427-1956), housed in the old military prison at Garrison, St. Michael. You'll be able to view flora and fauna of the island as well as archaeological items, antiques, and artifacts from the plantation days. Open Monday through Saturday, 9 a.m. to 6 p.m. And do not miss **St. Nicholas Abbey,** St. Peter (tel. 422-8725 or 422-2446), a sugar plantation still in operation but open to the public. The owner, Lieut. Col. Stephen Cave sometimes conducts tours himself and will give you the whole history of his family, closet skeletons and all. Sadly moving are the carefully written records of the plantation slaves, remembered only by their first names and estimated worth. A wonderfully detailed home movie, taken in 1935 by Cave's father, gives fascinating insights into the plantation culture and the techniques of harvesting and refining sugar. Open Monday through Friday, 10 a.m. to 3:30 p.m. Entrance fee; $2.50. Other privately owned "plantation great houses" are open to the public; of special interest are **Villa Nova** in St. John (tel. 433-1524) and **Sunbury Plantation House,** Highway 5, St. Philip (tel. 423-6270).

Half-day **sailing cruises** with lunch, drinks, and perhaps a stop for swimming and snorkeling will give you a wonderful lesson on how to be lazy in the tropics. Some hotels have their own boats (the Coral Reef Club owns the *Anna Kareena,* for example), and a cruise might be included as part of your honeymoon package. If not, you can call **Tiami Exclusive Sailing Cruises Ltd.** (tel. 428-8276) for a lunch or cocktail cruise on a graceful catamaran; $60 per couple. If you prefer lively parties and large boats, cruise on the pirate ship *Jolly Roger* (tel. 436-6424, or 436-6425) or the riverboat *Bajan Queen* (tel. 436-2149). Both offer moonlight cocktail cruises for $60 per couple, including drinks, meal, and round-trip transportation. A guide called "Inns and Outs of Barbados," which you'll probably find in your hotel room, gives dates for full moons for a year . . . so take note!

3. Honeymoon Hotels and Hideaways

Barbados boasts some of the most romantic accommodations in the islands, with plenty of choices to suit all moods and inclinations.

Bajan prices are upscale; even moderate prices are a bit on the high side. But the good news is you don't have to be afraid of more modest places: They may be basic and no-frills (even romantically seedy), but they'll seldom be junky, cheap, or dirty. Except on the breezy south coast, most hotels give you a choice of air conditioning or a much more picturesque "punkah" ceiling fan. Telephones in the room are almost universal, but televisions are rare.

When trying to find the right place for you, remember that although posh resorts are found throughout the island, most of them are concentrated on the Caribbean (west) coast. The main buildings of many of these properties were once elegant estates or vacation homes. When the hoteliers bought them from their original owners, they added guest space by building free-standing cottages (or, more recently, low-rise condo-style units) on the surrounding land, which has been landscaped into a veritable Eden.

Several of Barbados' most prestigious west coast resorts, including Cobblers Cove, Coral Reef Club, and other properties, have joined together to form "The Elegant Resorts of Barbados" collection. Among other features, guests staying at participating hotels can take their meals at any of the member resorts, and enjoy various social facilities. Special package rates are also available from May through mid-December. For details, contact "The Elegant Resorts of Barbados," toll free 800/235-3505.

On the south coast, the resorts around St. Lawrence Gap, a lively little harbor town of restaurants, night spots, and mall shops, are great for young, informal honeymooners who like action and the company of others. Some of the loveliest hotels are found farther east along the south coast, but they tend to be isolated from the rest of the island, best for honeymooners who want a leisurely pace, natural beauty, and privacy. Some of the least expensive hotels are found on the rugged east coast (where the Bajans themselves go on vacation), but this area is extremely secluded. If you go there, plan to do a lot of reading, hiking, or watching the waves roll in.

You'll get the best deals on hotel rates between mid-April and mid-December—from 30% to 50% lower than in the high season. Liveliest time during off-season is the Crop-Over Festival that celebrates the completion of the sugar cane harvest. It's held during the last two weeks in July and positively busts loose with fairs, parades, and cultural events.

Prices in this chapter reflect the spread between low- and high-season prices. Unless otherwise indicated, the rates are European Plan (EP), which means no meals included. You can purchase a meal package in most hotels, or pay as you go. When figuring costs, remember that 5% government tax and 10% service charge will be added to your bill.

In addition to the major resort hotels, there are a number of small hotels, apartment hotels, and guest houses. You can obtain a complete list by writing the Barbados Board of Tourism and requesting the brochure entitled "Hotel and Guest House Rates." Another way to go is to rent a luxury villa complete with housekeeper and/or cook. For information about villas, contact: West Coast: **Bajan Services,** Seascape Cottage, Gibbs, St. Peter, Barbados (tel. 809/422-2618); or **Alleyne, Aguilar & Altman,** "Rose Bank," Derricks, St. James, Barbados (tel. 809/432-0840). South Coast: **Ronald Stoute & Sons Ltd.,** Sam Lord's Castle, St. Philip, Barbados (tel. 809/432-6800).

WEST COAST: One of the most venerated hotels on the island, **Coral Reef Club,** St. James Beach, Barbados (tel. 809/422-2372; U.S. reservations: 212/535-2445 or toll free 800/223-1108), combines British grace with West Indian warmth. You'll be met on arrival by at least one member of the O'Hara family; Budge and Cynthia have managed the hotel since 1956, and now are joined by their three attractive and friendly children. You'll have your own secluded cottage/suite, one of 75 on 12 beachfront acres, landscaped with palms and a multitude of flowering plants. The rooms have high ceilings, white walls, and are decorated with splashy, cool-color native prints. Patio chairs and loungers are comfortable. You can play tennis on the property, or snorkel next door at Folkestone Park. The restaurant is just fine, with a wide variety of choices from continental cuisine to native fruits, vegetables, and fish. (The cooks regularly get creative with homegrown products, and the results are scrumptious.) Best of all, you get a meal plan that offers exchange dining with 13 other of the finest west-coast hotels, so you can sample different restaurants without fuss and bother. Internationally known, Coral Reef Club is a member of the French group Relais et Châteaux and the British Prestige hotels. Honeymoon package: From April to mid-December: eight days/seven nights (MAP): $1,025 per couple. Mid-December to April (MAP): $250 to $370 per couple per day, depending on size of room or suite, and whether it has an ocean view. Includes two bottles (!) of rum, a sailing cruise, round-trip hotel-to-airport transfers.

Staying at the impeccable **Cobblers Cove**, St. Peter, Barbados (tel. 809/422-2291; U.S. reservations: 212/832-2277 or toll free 800/223-6510), is like renting a private villa with an attentive staff and sharing it with some people who turn into friends. This spiffy little resort consists of a small but elegant main house (formerly a plantation owner's vacation home) and 38 dew-fresh suites set in a U-shape surrounding the terrace, pool, and bar. The living room of the suites opens onto outdoor sitting areas that are cleverly designed to give you a good view of beach and pool but without allowing others to see you. Manager Richard Williams, the world's nicest perfectionist, and his lovely wife, Jan, keep Cobblers spotless and efficient, but never in a way that makes guests uptight. Specially chosen European chefs make Cobblers' restaurant one of the best on the island. Take advantage of the free water sports or curl up in a beach chair or in the hotel's tastefully decorated sitting room for a good read. Beware: The delicious drinks from Cobblers' bar have actually won awards! Honeymoon package: eight days/seven nights (EP): $1,111 per couple. $300 more for meal plan and exchange dining. Includes full American breakfast, lobster dinner with champagne, flowers and fruit in room, sailing cruise, round-trip transfers to airport and to Bridgetown. Package is only available April through mid-December.

If you want nothing less than total opulence for your honeymoon, **Grand Barbados Beach Resort**, P.O. Box 639, Bridgetown, Barbados (tel. 809/426-0890, U.S. reservations: 212/840-6636 or toll free 800/223-9815), is for you. This gorgeous seven-story pink edifice right on the water has recently been upgraded to offer guests everything their hearts desire, from valet parking to satellite TV and a hairdryer in every room. Are you hungry? There are three restaurants at Grand Barbados from the Golden Shell (plush carpets, brocaded chairs) to The Boardwalk, offering Bajan-style lunches and snacks. Most striking are the pier lounge chairs where you can enjoy view and sun; at the end is the Schooner Restaurant and, yes, the famous pier suites—all you can see from your windows is the blue of sea and sky. But the suites are available as part of a honeymoon package only during low season. Honeymoon package: eight days/seven nights (EP): High season, $1,570 per couple; Low season, $995 per couple for deluxe ocean view room; $1,975 for pier suite. For about $80 per couple per day, you can purchase a meal plan that includes dining options at Da Luciano's and Kokos Restaurants, a Bajan Queen or Jolly Roger dinner cruise, and a dinner theater evening at the Museum.

Coconut Creek Club Hotel, St. James Beach, Barbados (tel. 809/422-2741, U.S. reservations: 212/696-1323 or toll free 800/372-1323). This small hotel is pretty, friendly, and gives you a lot for your money. It's built on a low bluff overlooking the Caribbean, so views from the rooms are marvelous; guests walk to their beautiful beach down a short flight of limestone steps. Rooms have smooth tile floors and rattan furniture accented with floral print draperies and bedspreads. The management tries to arrange for honeymooners to have oceanfront rooms, whatever price package they book, and gives couples who return for their anniversaries free bottles of champagne. Water sports are complimentary; exchange dining on the MAP enables you to eat at some of the west coast's finest hotel restaurants. Honeymoon package: eight days/ seven nights (MAP): $840 to $1,330 per couple.

SOUTH COAST: Marriott's Sam Lord's Castle, St. Philip, Barbados (tel. 809/ 423-7350; U.S. reservations: 212/603-8200 or toll free 800/223-6388). According to legend, the pirate Sam Lord used false beacons to lure ships onto the reefs. After the vessels foundered, he added their plunder to his treasure chest.

At any rate, Sam's marble and mahogany mansion with its Regency antiques is now the focal point of a 72-acre resort hotel, one of the plushest on the island. You might want to stay in one of the ten bedrooms in the castle itself and perhaps get a canopied four-poster bed covered with a brocade bedspread. Or you might choose a gaily decorated cottage room (or suite) with a king-size bed and a sliding glass door opening onto your own sunny terrace. It may take you your entire honeymoon to sample from the four restaurants, walk the beach, play on the night-lighted tennis courts, swim in the three swimming pools, and just explore the property. Every night there's an extravaganza of some sort—seven-course feasts, folkloric shows, beach barbecues, rum punch parties. And the hotel's activities desk can arrange just about any other activity on the island you want to try. Honeymoon package: eight days/seven nights (EP): $791 to $1,296 per couple for a moderate room; $1,001 to $1,576 per couple for the castle; and $1,596 to $2,486 per couple for a suite. Includes beachside picnic for two, mini-moke for two days, free movies and tennis, transfers to and from the airport and Bridgetown.

If you like informality and a casual good time, you'll like **Sand Acres Hotel,** Maxwell Coast Road, Christ Church; Barbados (tel. 809/428-7141; U.S. reservations: tel. 212/535-9530 or toll free 800/223-5581), a simple well-managed group of condos on a beautiful, breezy beach. Suites, which include living room, bedroom, and kitchen are neatly furnished with touches of wicker and bright bedspreads. Sliding glass doors lead to your own small terrace with views of pool and beach. Sand Acres is not a full-service hotel, so unit rates are low, but it has a sparkling pool (the hotel's focal point), tennis, shuffleboard, and a fun, beach-bar–style restaurant, called Ron's. You're just a step from the beach, so you'll go to sleep lulled by the surf and the trade winds singing in the trees. If you want super restaurants and lively night spots, they're only a short walk away at St. Lawrence Gap. Honeymoon package: None. Standard rates per unit: Low season, $45 to $59 per day; high season, $91 to $115 per day, depending on size.

Ginger Bay Beach Club, St. Philip, Barbados (tel. 809/423-5810; U.S. reservations: 212/535-9530 or toll free 800/223-5581), is a little gem of a hotel where peace and quiet reigns. Each suite (and there are suites only—no rooms), has wall-to-wall carpets, mahogany furniture, and a balcony facing the awesome sweep of Crane Beach. The entire hotel is decorated with exquisite taste; the exterior is painted pink with island flowers delicately stenciled in white here and there. You reach the beach by walking down into the hotel's own limestone grotto. There is a freshwater pool, tennis, and a fine restaurant, Ginger's, which specializes in smoked meats and fish. Honeymoon package: None. Suites: $99 to $210 per couple per day.

Crane Beach Hotel, St. Philip, Barbados (tel. 809/423-6220; U.S. reservations: 212/832-2277 or toll free 800/223-6510). Have you ever dreamed of honeymooning in a high-ceilinged room with a four-poster bed and a door opening onto one of the world's most beautiful beaches? Crane Beach Hotel, high atop a bluff overlooking the famous beach, can match your fantasy. Your first view of this white limestone hotel with its sapphire pool surrounded by Greek columns and a balustraded terrace will remind you more of an ancient temple than a full-service hotel. But it has two bars, four tennis courts, boutiques on the property, and a restaurant known for its excellent seafood. Honeymoon package: eight days/seven nights (EP): $1,350 per couple, year round. Includes a Superior Room plus a bottle of champagne, a Jolly Roger cruise, a free mini-moke for two days.

Pink and white, airy and light, **Southern Palms Beach Club,** St. Lawrence Gap, Christ Church, Barbados (tel. 809/428-7171; U.S. reservations: 212/832-2277 or toll free 800/223-6510), has the easy yet orderly atmosphere that typifies Barbados. Rooms are bright and white-walled, with tables and headboards of blonde bamboo, accented with flower-splashed fabrics. Their beach is long and beautiful; jog down the waterline or try sailing or Windsurfing (water sports are free). Eat in the arcaded restaurant or walk a few steps to St. Lawrence Gap and enjoy the many eating spots there. The hotel's activities desk will arrange tours, trips, golf. Honeymoon package: None. Double bedroom per couple per day (EP) Low season: $82 to $125; high season: $145 to $185, depending on room size.

EAST COAST: A tiny eight-room hotel, truly far from the madding crowd, **Kingsley Club,** Box 297, Cattlewash, St. Joseph, Barbados (tel. 809/433-9422) has the relaxed atmosphere of a British colonial outpost. Its low room rates are attributable to its isolation on the wild coast of the Scotland district, never to its lack of charm, and its restaurant always gets good reviews. You'll love the breezy turn-of-the-century porch, with its wicker tables and chairs, rather like a veranda on a summer hotel in Maine. Seven rooms only. Honeymoon package: None. Rooms are $34 to $45 per couple per day.

4. Romantic Restaurants

Food in Barbados is good—and getting even better. Hoteliers are ceasing to import the "right kind of fish," frozen, from Europe, and are taking advantage of the local catch, which is excellent. When you eat chubb, grouper, snapper, and dolphin, you can be sure it was swimming just a few hours before. Caribbean spiny lobsters are larger than their New England cousins and their meat is sweet and delicious. On the exotic side, try turtle or a local delicacy called "sea egg," which is actually the meat of a sea urchin. The Barbados equivalent of the American burger is the flying fish sandwich, typically served fried with french fries and cole slaw. Eat it with tartar sauce, to which you've added a tiny bit of spicy mustard sauce. Outstanding! Most restaurants offer Bajan specialties on their menu in addition to American or continental cuisine, so you'll have a good opportunity to try the local vegetable specialties: cou-cou (corn meal and okra), eddoes (a potato-like vegetable), yams, cassava, and breadfruit. There will be a full array of tropical fruit as well, and a variety of marvelous drinks made with Barbadian rum, one of the smoothest in the world.

When you book a hotel, check whether it has exchange dining. If so, you can buy the meal package (either breakfast and dinner or all three meals) and eat dinner at other hotels and restaurants which participate in the plan.

This roundup will give you an idea of the great variety of restaurants Barbados has to offer.

EXPENSIVE: Built in 1645, **Bagatelle Great House,** Highway 2A, St. Thomas (tel. 425-0666), was the home of Barbados's earliest governors. Its entranceway, a picturesque double stairway with wrought-iron railing, makes it a favorite place for wedding receptions. The cuisine is an elegant mix of Bajan and continental. For appetizers you can have West Indian fish cakes with pepper dip or escargot bourguignon, homemade pumpkin soup or vichysoisse. Entrées feature braised pheasant, beef Wellington, shrimp creole, or local fish. Complete dinners run about $80 per couple (tax, service charge, and liquor not included).

Josef's, St. Lawrence (tel. 428-3379). Dress up for Josef's. This small, exclusive hideaway is low-key, elegant, expensive—and reputedly has the best continental cuisine on the island. Especially well-regarded is Josef's way with meat; try filet mignon with sauce béarnaise ($19), rack of lamb ($16.50), veal Cordon Bleu ($13). Local fish (dolphin, kingfish, barracuda) are fixed continental style. Tempting appetizers (terrine of shrimp and salmon with green sauce, for example) are $6 and under.

MODERATE: **Pisces,** St. Lawrence Gap, Christ Church (tel. 428-6558). As you sit at your candlelit table on Pisces' open terrace and watch the Gap's harbor lights twinkle, you'll know you're at Barbados' most romantic restaurant. Pisces features the freshest seafood, imaginatively prepared, Bajan style. For appetizers, try kingfish ceviche (pickled in a lime marinade) for $2.50 or fillets of flying fish stuffed with caviar and chopped egg for $3. For an entrée, try blackened dolphin, coated with Cajun spices and pan fried ($12) or a Pisces platter with a variety of local fish for $15. There are also several lobster dishes for $20 to $23 each.

Dinner Theater (tel. 435-6900). Have dinner, learn a little about Barbados history, and take in a show all at the same time by reserving a spot at a dinner theater performance, all run by the same outfit. Tuesdays, see *Barbados, Barbados,* a musical comedy based on the life of Barbados' most infamous madam, held at Boiling House, Balls Estate, Christ Church. Thursdays and Sundays, see *1627 and All That,* a folkdance performed by members of the Barbados Dance Center, held in the courtyard of the Barbados Museum of Garrison, St. Michael (tour of museum included). One price of $30 per person includes transportation to and from your hotel, hors d'oeuvres, buffet dinner, the show, and all drinks!

Atlantis, Bathsheba Beach, St. Joseph (tel. 433-9445). Do not miss manager Enid Maxwell's extraordinary island buffet served after church on Sundays. Tourists and islanders line up near the buffet tables to see the food brought in, and each dish is labeled so you know what you're getting. This is Bajan food untouched by European hands—pepperpot, pumpkin fritters, salt-fish stew, yam pie, fried chicken, roast pork and more—all with creole spices. Fill up your plate and eat at your oilcloth-covered table over looking Bathsheba's small fishing fleet and the pounding Atlantic surf. All you can eat: $18 per person. Drinks extra.

INEXPENSIVE: **Bamboo Beach Bar,** Paynes Bay, St. James (tel. 432-0910). Sun worshippers can stay at this barefoot bar through lunch and dinner and never leave the beach. Good, basic food is served here at reasonable prices, such as a toasted cheese, ham, and pineapple sandwich for $3. Luncheons in a basket—burgers, or shrimp with chips and salad—vary from $4.25 to $10. Dinner prices a bit more expensive, but the food is just as healthful and basic. Try creole shrimp for $12.50 and a chicken casserole flavored with rum for $9.

Barbados has a lot of great places when you just want to hang out. Sit at your harborside table and watch the boats go in and out of Bridgetown at the **Waterfront Cafe** (tel. 427-0093). Open for lunch and dinner (dinners from $7.50); live entertainment. Need a TV fix? **T.G.I. Boomers,** St. Lawrence Gap (tel. 428-8439) is a garden restaurant with a satellite television, and good American/Bajan meals reasonably priced. Off season, get a bacon-and-egg breakfast for under $4. Lunches run about $5; dinner $5 to $12. A great pub-style bar and restaurant is **The Ship Inn,** St. Lawrence (tel. 428-9605). Meet island people, listen to impromptu performers, and sing along. Great bar snacks at $5 to $6. All you can eat buffet, $18 per person. **The Barbados Windsurfing Club,** Oistin's Bay (tel. 428-7277) offers good, inexpensive food in a friendly atmosphere right on the beach. It's famous for its rotis—chicken, beef, or shrimp curry wrapped in a light pastry. Lunches $10 to $20 per couple.

Chapter XXV

BERMUDA

1. Practical Facts
2. Romantic Interludes
3. Honeymoon Hotels and Hideaways
4. Romantic Restaurants in Hamilton
5. Nightlife in Hamilton
6. Romantic Restaurants Elsewhere in Bermuda
7. Nightlife Elsewhere in Bermuda

THEY TELL THE STORY about the famous watercolor artist who arrived in Bermuda and intended to remain two weeks. He ended up staying over 40 years. "I want to get the color of the water right," he explained. Certainly, capturing the proper nuance of Bermudian ocean blue is difficult, because at any given time, the sea reflects hundreds of shades—pale aqua, peacock turquoise, a most royal blue, and every gradation in between.

The colors are what you tend to remember most about Bermuda. Flowers bloom and burgeon everywhere: magenta bougainvillea tumbling over railings, pale pink oleander hedges lining roadways, fragrant purple passion flowers climbing up limestone walls. Both prim little cottages and large mansions are painted pastel shades of pink, lavender, mint, and yellow, and topped with white step roofs that positively sparkle in the sunshine. Bright green casuarinas bob in the breeze. And, of course, there are the blush-pink, coral sand beaches, gently bathed by the surf.

The word "fairyland" might be overused, but it perfectly describes the ambience and landscapes of Bermuda. Contrary to what most people believe, Bermuda is not a Caribbean island, but rather lies in the Atlantic Ocean about 600 miles due east of North Carolina's Cape Hatteras. Although palm trees flourish, the climate is actually subtropical. Bermuda is not just one island, but rather is composed of approximately 150 different ones, many linked by bridges and causeways. When seen from the air, the island group resembles a fish hook, and the chain is about 22 miles long and 2½ miles wide at its broadest part. Built on the pinnacle of an extinct volcano, the islands are fairly flat, formed from lava, coral, and sandy limestone.

Ever since its earliest history, Bermuda has seemed tinged by magic. The islands were discovered in 1503 by a Spaniard, Juan de Bermúdez, who named the islands, but did not settle them. Because of the treacherous reefs, early seafarers feared that the islands were inhabited by spirits. A shipwreck actually led to the settlement of Bermuda. In 1609, Admiral Sir George Somers was on his way to the new British colony in Jamestown, Virginia. Instead, he ran aground on Bermudian reefs in a hurricane, totally destroying his ship, the *Sea Venture*. Miraculously, everybody on board—some

150 people—were unharmed. Also to their wonder, the islands were richly stocked with food supplies—fish, birds, turtles, prickly pear, and even wild pigs (left by the Spanish). It took passengers and crew nearly a year to build two new, small pinnaces, constructed from the remains of the *Sea Venture* and native Bermudian cedar. These two ships, named the *Deliverance* and the *Patience,* sailed for Virginia in 1610. Tales of their adventures soon reached England, and William Shakespeare used these legends of "the still-vex'd Bermoothes" as the source for his play, *The Tempest.*

The first formal settlement of Bermuda was established in 1612 at St. George's, at the eastern end of the island, and the first parliament sat in 1620 (making Bermuda's parliament the third oldest in the world, after Britain and Iceland). Slaves were brought to the islands in 1616, mainly to work as household servants and carpenters. Slavery was finally abolished in 1834.

Bermuda's population today numbers just over 54,000. It is Britain's oldest self-governing colony, administered by a governor who is the official representative of the queen, and a two-house parliament. The island is divided into nine parishes, all with names recalling the old country: St. George's, Hamilton, Smith's, Devonshire, Pembroke, Paget, Warwick, Southampton, and Sandy's. Hamilton, Bermuda's capital, is located roughly in the middle of Bermuda, in Pembroke Parish. As you travel around the countryside, you'll observe the many links with British traditions: the white-uniformed cricket players, automobiles driving on the left, and the ritual of afternoon tea. Another local custom you'll notice is the gracious hospitality with which visitors are treated. Bermudians (known as "Onions") make everyone feel like honored guests, not mere tourists, and honeymooners receive especially warm welcomes.

Because Bermuda is so compact, you'll find it easy to explore from top to tip. Start your sightseeing in Hamilton, the capital, the center for shopping, dining, and nightlife. Take a photo of the Birdcage, where a Bermuda-shorts–clad bobby (policeman) directs traffic. Intersperse your shopping forays along Front Street with a bit of history. You'll want to see city hall, the Bermuda Cathedral, and Sessions House, where Parliament meets (you can attend sittings). Then stroll over to pretty Par-La-Ville Gardens on Queen Street. Here, the Bermuda Library has a collection of Bermuda newspapers dating back to 1787 and other memorabilia, such as a sea chest that belonged to Sir George Somers, considered Bermuda's founder. Stop by the Perot Post Office, named for William Bennett Perot, Bermuda's first postmaster. Mr. Perot, who designed Bermuda's first stamp, was a bit eccentric—he used to carry letters in the crown of his top hat while delivering mail.

Continue your explorations west to Somerset, east to St. George's, or down to the south shore beaches (see details under "Romantic Interludes,"). As you whiz along on your scooters or in the pink-and-blue buses, you'll get the feel for the postcard-pretty scenery that Honeymooners will be intrigued by Bermuda's moongates, round arches of coral stone shaped like a full moon. According to Chinese legend, moongates symbolize happiness and unity, and lovers who walk through them are assured good luck and happiness. The tradition was brought to Bermuda by a sea captain. You'll find moongates throughout Bermuda, and you'll surely want to walk through several different ones on your honeymoon.

Much of the charm of Bermuda comes from its love of traditions. Change is never undertaken lightly. After all, this is a place that did not permit private automobiles until 1946. Page one of the daily newspapers still announces "lighting up time"—the hour when carriage lanterns must be lit. Neon signs are expressly forbidden. Fifty years from now, if you return to Bermuda for your golden wedding anniversary, you'll probably find the gentle island very much like it is today.

Maybe those early mariners were right, and Bermuda is enchanted. Not by sea spirits, however—but because of the beautiful surroundings and the hospitable Bermudians themselves. Mark Twain, who often wintered here in the early 1900s, wrote,

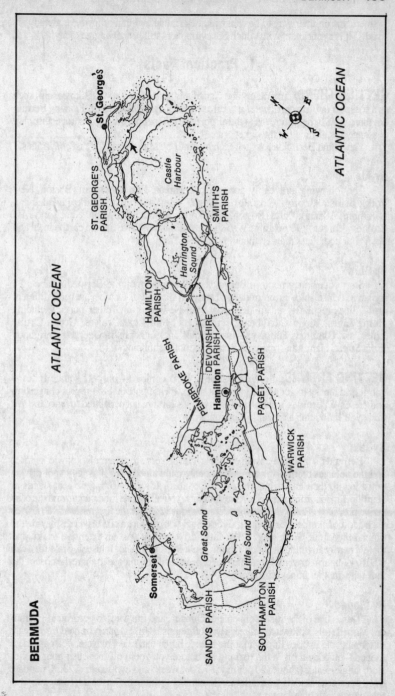

BERMUDA

ATLANTIC OCEAN

ATLANTIC OCEAN

St. George's

ST. GEORGE'S
PARISH

Castle
Harbour

SMITH'S
PARISH

Harrington
Sound

HAMILTON
PARISH

PEMBROKE PARISH

DEVONSHIRE
PARISH

Hamilton

PAGET PARISH

WARWICK
PARISH

Great Sound

Little Sound

Somerset

SANDYS PARISH

SOUTHAMPTON
PARISH

"Americans on their way to heaven call at Bermuda and think they have already arrived." It is a sentiment with which honeymooners still heartily agree today.

1. Practical Facts

GETTING THERE: Americans and Canadians must show proof of citizenship, such as a passport or birth certificate, as well as a return or ongoing ticket. Leaving Bermuda, there is a $10 departure tax at the airport; the $30 per person port tax for cruise ship passengers is included in the ticket price.

You'll find Bermuda easy to reach by air or by sea from major east coast cities.

By Air

The following airlines fly nonstop to Bermuda: **Pan American** (Boston, New York); **British Airways** (Orlando); **Eastern** (New York/JFK, Newark, Philadelphia, Baltimore, Atlanta); **Delta** (Boston, New York), **American** (Boston, New York), **Air Canada** (Toronto). Flying time is so short, you'll barely have time to eat the meal and open your book: less than 1½ hours from New York.

By Ship

Start your honeymoon in Bermuda with a honeymoon to Bermuda—aboard a romantic cruise ship. From mid-April through the end of October, several different cruise lines regularly sail to Bermuda from New York and other ports, including **Home Lines, Royal Caribbean Cruise Line, Sun Line Cruises, Ocean Cruise Lines,** and **Chandris Fantasy Cruises.** Ships dock either in St. George's or right on Front Street, Hamilton—extremely convenient for shopping.

GETTING AROUND: Because Bermuda is so compact—only 21 square miles— you'll find it easy to get where you want to go. Please note that to prevent congestion and preserve Bermuda's unhurried lifestyle, visitors are not permitted to rent cars. We think you'll find this a veritable blessing.

By Taxi

Bermuda's taxis are absolutely tops: The drivers are extremely knowledgeable, and the vehicles themselves are meticulously maintained (you'll usually spot drivers polishing up their cars while they wait for fares). It's easy to find taxis at stands in Hamilton and in front of hotels. At restaurants, you telephone for a pickup and the cabs arrive promptly. Rates are fairly moderate: about $2.40 for the first mile, and $1.20 for each additional mile. For in-depth sightseeing, you can hire a taxi driver displaying the official blue Tour Guide flag. To qualify, drivers must pass an extensive exam, and there's hardly anything they don't know about Bermuda. The sightseeing rate for a cab is $16 per hour—extremely reasonable, especially if you choose to share the cost of the tour with another honeymoon couple.

By Moped

This is one of the most convenient, chipper, and fun ways to get around Bermuda. Mopeds (also known as scooters or motor-assisted bikes) can be rented from many different cycle liveries throughout the island. If you can ride a bicycle, you can ride a moped—practice a bit in the parking lot before you zoom off into rush-hour traffic. Both single-seater (about $20 per day; $72 per week) and two-seater ($28.50 per day; $110 per week) models are available. Remember—driving is on the left (use caution in the roundabouts), and wear your helmets.

By Bicycle

Bermuda is fairly flat, so bicycle riding makes for peaceful touring. Rates run about $10 per day for the first day; $5 for each additional day.

By Ferry

You'll definitely fall in love with Bermuda's jaunty ferries, which ply many different routes between the various islands, including Hamilton to Somerset or Hamilton to Ireland Island at Bermuda's northernmost tip. It's more like taking a sightseeing cruise than mere transportation. Fares are very inexpensive: from $1 to $2, depending on how far you are going. If you like, you can take your bikes or scooters on board, and then cycle back (a very popular excursion goes from Somerset back along the South Shore beaches).

By Bus

Bermuda's blue-and-pink buses provide another inexpensive, efficient way to get around the island. Bus rides run $1 to $2, based on distance. You must have exact fare in coins—paper money is not acceptable. You can also use tokens. You can get both tokens and fare information at your hotel.

LANGUAGE AND MONEY: Very proper English is spoken—you might even come home with a bit of an English accent. Although the U.S. dollar is accepted everywhere, the legal tender is the Bermuda Dollar (BD$), which is officially pegged to the American currency: 1 Bd$ = 1 US$. Also like the U.S. dollar, the Bermudian currency is divided into 100 cents. Traveler's checks and credit cards are accepted in most—but not all—restaurants, shops, and hotels. Be sure to ask in advance.

WEATHER: Bermuda is subtropical and has two real seasons: spring and summer. Summer temperatures prevail from late May until mid-November, the warmest months being July, August, and the beginning of September, with temperatures in the mid-80s (10° cooler in the evening). From November through April, temperatures range in the 60s and 70s. Rainfall is fairly evenly divided throughout the year and usually comes in the form of passing showers; all-day storms are very infrequent.

CLOTHING: During the warmer months, dress for summer—bring bathing suits and nice cotton sportswear. Also take along light sweaters or wraps for evenings. From December through March, bring spring and fall-weight clothing: light wools, plus a raincoat or windbreaker. Part of the fun of a Bermuda honeymoon is dressing up a bit—most restaurants require that men don a jacket and tie in the evenings, and women will have plenty of opportunities to wear trousseau finery. Dress is conservative—a legacy of Bermuda's British heritage. Bathing suits and bare feet are acceptable only at the beach and pool, not in town, public areas of hotels, nor aboard mopeds. Tennis whites are required on most courts.

TIME: Bermuda is on Atlantic Standard Time during the winter and observes Daylight Saving Time in the summer, so it is always one hour ahead of U.S. east coast cities. When it is noon in New York, it is 1 p.m. in Bermuda.

TELEPHONES: You can call Bermuda direct from the United States. First dial "809" (the area code) and then the seven-digit phone number.

SHOPPING: The wide selection of stores and fine quality of merchandise makes shopping a highlight of many Bermuda stays. Stores painted cheery shades of yellow, orange, pink, and green line Hamilton's Front Street, and you'll enjoy strolling from one to the other under the covered promenades. Many of Bermuda's best-known stores such as Cooper's, Smith's, and Trimingham's also have branches in St. George's and many hotels.

Although Bermuda is not a duty-free port, taxes are quite low, and you will find that prices are substantially lower than at home on many items, especially British imports. In addition, Bermuda has no sales tax. Recently, duties have been substantially lowered on watches, cameras, ceramic figurines, and jewelry, so this merchandise generally represents an especially good value. Best shopping bets include:

China and crystal: Consider using some of your wedding checks to fill out your patterns—all at substantial savings. Compared with U.S. prices, you can generally save from 40% to 50% on fine bone china from Wedgwood, Royal Doulton, Aynsley, Royal Worcester, Spode, Minton, and other lines. On crystal, prices run about 30% to 40% lower on Waterford, Orrefors, Lalique, Baccarat, Galway, and others. You'll also find similar savings on decorative figurines from Lladró, Boehm, and Royal Copenhagen. The stores are all very experienced at packing purchases for you to carry to the United States. Also, they can arrange to ship items home for you. Although costs will be higher than if you carried items with you, you will still realize substantial savings over stateside prices.

Clothing and accessories: You'll find a large selection of classic sportswear, such as Shetland sweaters and Harris tweed jackets, which run about 30% to 50% less than the United States. Ditto for cashmeres by Jaeger and Pringle, and raincoats from Burberry. Other good buys include cotton rugby shirts, woolly Icelandic sweaters, and authentic kilts and blazers.

Imported cosmetics and perfumes: Save from 20% to 30% on makeup from European companies, such as Orlane, Christian Dior, Chanel, Lancôme, and Yves Saint Laurent. Savings are similar on fragrances such as Chanel No. 5, Opium, L'Air du temps, Joy, and other famous scents.

Watches and jewelry: Currently a very good deal in Bermuda, thanks to the recent 20% reduction on local customs duty. A Concorde watch priced at $1,175 on Madison Avenue in New York was selling for $735 in Bermuda. You'll find similar savings on more inexpensive, "fun" time pieces, such as Swatch watches.

Art and antiques: Bermuda has several well-known watercolor artists, and a painting of a one of your favorite landscapes will always bring back fond memories of your honeymoon. You can also browse through old prints, nautical curios, and fine English and Bermudian antiques. Remember that you can bring back antiques over 100 years old and original art duty-free: Just make sure to get proper certificates when you make your purchases.

Wines, liquor, and liqueurs: You'll get the best savings (up to 40%) on English gin and Scotch, as well as local Bermudian potions such as rum for swizzles. Please note that if you want to take liquor home, it is sold "in-bond"—you must purchase it at least 24 hours before your departure, and the store will deliver it to your airplane or cruise ship before you leave.

Linens and fabrics: To show off your new china and crystal, set your table with Irish linens, Brussels lace, or Portuguese hand-embroideries. If you sew, you can save on fabric by the yard: English tweeds, Scottish tartans, Italian and French provincial-style cotton prints.

Only in Bermuda: Look for unique items either made in Bermuda or specially designed for the country. One of the most popular choices include gold or silver charms or jewelry, shaped like the Bermuda longtail bird, surreys, or seashells. Many stores feature items made from local Bermuda cedar, including bookends, candlesticks, and classic Bermuda handbags, with a wooden handle and fabric cover that can be unbuttoned and changed with the season. For a fragrant souvenir of your honeymoon, consider perfumes made from Bermuda's own blossoms: lilies, passion flower, oleander, jasmine, and roses. You can buy them at Bermuda Perfumeries in Bailey's Bay, as well as many stores in town. To make an authentic Bermuda fish chowder or spike your Bloody Mary's back home, pick up some spicy Outerbridge's Sherry Peppers. And when you want to brew up rum swizzles, you'll need Bermuda black rum, such as Black Seal. Also consider Bermuda Gold liqueur, made from loquats.

All of the following stores are located on Front Street, unless otherwise noted. Many also have several branches in hotels.

A.S. Cooper & Sons, Ltd.: The oldest china and glassware store in Bermuda, Cooper's carries Wedgwood, Minton, Royal Doulton, Belleek, Aynsley, Royal Copenhagen, Villeroy & Boch, and other fine china; Waterford, Orrefors, and Atlantis crystal; and Georg Jensen silver. They also have a fine men's shop, and their ladies' shop carries Jaeger sportswear.

H.A. & E. Smith Ltd.: Serving Bermudians for nearly 100 years, Smith's has the exclusive for Burberry raincoats and accessories, and has one of the widest selection of Shetland sweaters for both men and women, in up-to-date, fashion-right colors and designs. You'll also find bone china by Royal Doulton and Minton, Lladró figurines, and Waterford crystal. They also sell wool tartans and Liberty prints by the yard, cosmetics, and fragrances.

Trimingham's: You'll find one of the largest selections in Bermuda: sweaters, woolens, and other fashions, French perfumes, as well as china by Royal Worcester, Meissen, and Aynsley, Irish crystal by Waterford and Galway, Hermès and Liberty silk scarves, Italian leather accessories, as well as original-design gold jewelry.

Astwood Dickinson: Your stop for jewelry and watches, including timepieces from Patek Philippe, Omega, Movado, and Concord; plus a wide selection of Bermuda charms.

Bluck's: Carries Lalique, Baccarat, Waterford, Spode, Royal Doulton, Royal Worcester, Minton, and others.

Crisson's: Look through their selection of fine jewelry and gemstones, as well as watches from Rolex, Piaget, Mercier, Cartier, Ebel, Raymond Weil, and others.

Benetton: A new addition to Bermuda, this line found around the world features colorful casual clothes—knits and cottons, skirts and sweaters, you name it! All very well made, very fashionable—and priced about 30% less than back home.

Pegasus Prints and Maps (Pitts Bay Road across from the Hamilton Princess): Collectors of antique maps and prints will delight in browsing through their displays of maps and prints, including fine botanicals, caricatures, engravings of horses, fox-hunting, birds, and shells. Also a wonderful selection of inexpensive Bermuda map reproductions.

Irish Linen Shop: Fine linens from Ireland, to be sure, but also hand-embroideries from Madeira, Brussels lace, and an exclusive selection of the famous Souleiado line of French provincial cottons and accessories.

Bananas: Want something that says "Bermuda"? You can probably find it here —T-shirts, umbrellas, beach bags, and towels.

Bermuda Book Store (Baxters) Ltd.: Both a bibliophile's and a Bermudaphile's paradise, with an extensive selection of books about Bermuda (from ghosts to antiques), as well as European periodicals, plus thrillers and romances for beach reading.

And for liquor: **Gosling Bros., Bermuda Wines & Spirits,** and **Frith's** all have extensive selections of the most popular brands, and can make complete arrangements for in-bond delivery.

Each U.S. citizen can bring back $400 worth of goods duty free, including one liter of liquor and one carton of cigarettes. If you bring back more, you'll have to pay Customs duty. On the first $1,000 worth of goods over your $400 duty-free allowance, you will be taxed at a flat rate of 10% of the retail value of the goods. For a complete explanation of U.S. Customs regulations, see the introduction to this book.

SPORTS: If you're interested in the sporting life, you'll have plenty of opportunities to enjoy your favorite pastimes in Bermuda.

Golf: Bermuda is especially well known for its eight challenging golf courses. Many of the holes at the tough **Castle Harbour Golf Club** (tel. 293-8161) feature breathtaking views of the Atlantic. Robert Trent Jones designed the courses at **Port Royal Golf Course** (tel. 234-0974) and **St. George's Golf Club** (tel. 297-8067). Other public courses include the Belmont Hotel, **Golf & Beach Club** (tel. 236-1301); **Ocean View Golf & Country Club** (tel. 292-6758); and **Princess Golf Club** (tel. 238-0446). The **Riddells Bay Golf & Country Club** (tel. 238-1060) and **Mid Ocean Club** (tel. 293-0330) are private; introduction by a member is required. Daily greens fees run from about $15 to $55; if a hotel has a golf course, greens fees sometimes are reduced for guests.

Tennis: Tennis has been a Bermudian passion for over 100 years. In fact, it was a Bermudian, Mary Gray Outerbridge, who introduced the game to the United States. There are over 100 courts on the island, many lighted for night play. In the hotel listings that follow, we mention which properties have tennis courts; and many hotels permit both guests and visitors to play. Court time might be free or very inexpensive (about $4 per hour) for hotel guests; up to $10 per hour for visitors. Please note that tennis whites are preferred on all courts, and are mandatory on several.

Snorkeling and scuba diving: Bermuda has the clearest water in the western Atlantic, and you'll be dazzled by the variety of fish and coral you can observe. Snorkelers might want to take one of the half-day boat trips offered by **Grotto Diving** at the Grotto Bay Beach Hotel (tel. 239-2915), **Nautilus Diving** at the Princess Hotel (tel. 238-2332), **Skin Diving Adventures & Blue Water Divers** at Somerset Bridge (tel. 234-1034), and **South Side Scuba** at the Sonesta Beach Hotel (tel. 238-1833). Half-day trips run about $20 and generally include snacks and rum swizzles. The reefs that surround Bermuda have claimed the lives of many a vessel, and scuba divers will want to explore famous shipwrecks such as the *Mari Celeste*, an 1863 paddle steamer; and the *Minnie Breslauer*, an English ship that ran aground in 1783. All the above operators also run scuba diving programs; a one-tank dive costs about $45. They also offer an introductory "learn to dive" program that will first teach you the basics, then take you out for a supervised shallow-water dive, about $60. Bermuda also has several unique "helmet-diving" operations, in which you wear a Jules Verne–style helmet and walk along the sea bottom (you do not have to know how to swim). It costs about $22.50 per person; contact **Hartley Helmet Diving Cruise** (tel. 292-4434) or **Hartley's Under Sea Adventure** (tel. 234-2861) for details.

Other water sports: Bermuda has world-class conditions for other activities, such as sailing, deep-sea fishing, Windsurfing, and waterskiing. Many Bermuda hotels have their own water-sports facilities, or can make outside arrangements for you. For complete information about all sports in Bermuda, get a copy of the free "Bermuda Sportsman's Guide," issued by the Bermuda Department of Tourism.

SPECIAL EVENTS: No matter what time of year you honeymoon, there's sure to be fun going on.

Bermuda Rendezvous Season: Every year from mid-November until early March, Bermuda welcomes vacationers with a series of special events: crafts demonstrations, fashion shows, golf tournaments, a performing arts festival. Every day, there are different free programs: a guided walking tour of Hamilton; a skirling ceremony with kilted pipers, drummers, and dancers at Fort Hamilton; tours through the Botanical Gardens or Camden, the official residence of the premier. Get complete details from the Bermuda Department of Tourism.

January through mid-February—Bermuda Festival. Spotlighting classical music, dance, jazz, drama, and entertainment.

January—Bermuda International Marathon. Attracts top runners; also a 10K race.

Late March to mid-May—Open Houses and Garden Tours. Every Wednesday, many residences are open to the public.

Good Friday. Traditional kite-flying day.

Late April—Invitational International Race Week. Yachtsmen from all over the world compete.

May 24—Bermuda Day. With dinghy races and the annual half-marathon.

Mid-June—The Queen's Birthday. Celebrated with a military parade in Hamilton.

Mid-June—Yacht Races. In even-numbered years, it's the Newport-to-Bermuda race; in odd years, the Annapolis-to-Bermuda contest.

Late July—Cricket Festival. Two days of matches.

October/November—Convening of Parliament. The governor opens Parliament amid traditional military ceremonies.

December 26—Boxing Day. Appearances of the Bermuda Gombey Dancers and various sporting events.

HOW TO GET MARRIED IN BERMUDA: It's hard to imagine a more romantic setting for a wedding than Bermuda, with its pink sands, aqua waters, and pretty gardens everywhere. If you want a church wedding, a favorite is the Bermuda Cathedral in Hamilton. Most nonchurch weddings can be performed in the registry (by appointment); other locales can be arranged with the consent of clergy. You might want to incorporate Bermudian traditions into your wedding, such as arriving at the ceremony in a horse-drawn carriage. It's also a custom for the bride and groom to have separate wedding cakes (which can be small): the groom's wrapped in gold paper, the bride's in silver. And you'll certainly want to walk through a moongate together for good luck. Here's how to make arrangements.

1. No blood tests or health certificates are required.

2. Obtain a "Notice of Intended Marriage" form, available from the Bermuda Department of Tourism offices in New York, Boston, Chicago, Atlanta, and Toronto.

3. Send the completed form, along with $86 (must be a bank draft made payable to the Accountant General, Hamilton, Bermuda—personal checks not accepted) to: The Registrar General, Government Administration Building, Parliament Street, Hamilton HM 12, Bermuda.

4. The notice will be published by the registrar in Bermuda newspapers. Fourteen days later, the license will be issued. You do not have to be present in Bermuda during the waiting period. The license will be mailed to your home address, unless you request it to be held in Bermuda for your arrival. The license remains valid for three months.

5. The fee for a marriage in the registry is $89; the marriage certificate costs an additional $12 to $18.

Many hotels can help you make wedding arrangements; you can also contact the Bermuda Department of Tourism at one of the addresses below if you have specific questions.

FOR FURTHER INFORMATION: Contact the **Bermuda Department of Tourism.** Bermuda: Global House, 43 Church St., Hamilton 5–24, Bermuda (tel. 809/292-0023). New York: Suite 201, 310 Madison Ave., New York, NY 10017 (tel. 212/818-9800 or toll free 800/223-6106 nationwide; 800/223-6107 in NYS). Atlanta: Suite 2008, 235 Peachtree St., NE, Atlanta, GA 30303 (tel. 404/524-1541). Boston: Suite 1010, 44 School St., Boston, MA 02108 (tel. 617/742-0405). Chicago: Suite 1070, Randolph-Wacker Building, 150 North Wacker Dr., Chicago, IL 60606 (tel. 312/782-

5486). Toronto: Suite 1004, 1200 Bay St., Toronto, ON, Canada M5R 2A5 (tel. 416/923-9600).

2. Romantic Interludes

Bermuda may only be 21 square miles in size, but every inch seems packed with romantic possibilities.

Yes, the **sands** really are pink—tinged a rosy hue by tiny specks of pink coral mingled in with the sand. Complete the pretty picture with crystal-clear waters the color of molten turquoise and stark limestone formations that jut out of the water like some strange, prehistoric sea dragons—and you know why Bermuda's beaches rank among the best in the world. Many of the beaches are public, and you'll have fun trying out the different strands. You'll soon note an unusual phenomenon—the beaches never seem to get crowded, mainly because there are over 20 fine ones to choose from.

Bermuda's most celebrated sands lie along the South Shore. Horseshoe Bay is a favorite—one of the longest sandy stretches on the island, it has a water-sports concession, snack bar, and toilet facilities. Warwick, just nearby, is another top choice. Honeymooners will want to get to Jobson's Cove early to set up their beach towels in one of the small caves that line the shore. Reef-enclosed Church Bay offers excellent snorkeling. Long Bay is shallow—perfect for sunbathers and nonswimmers. John Smith's Bay has some of the pinkest sands on the island.

What goes together as well as love and marriage? Certainly, a leisurely ride in a **horse-drawn Bermuda surrey,** which will slowly wend its way down Front Street, then softly clop along roads just outside of town (one popular route takes in the elegant residential area called Fairylands). As you mosey along, the driver will regale you with a delightful blend of Bermuda fact and fiction. A single horse-drawn carriage runs about $10 for a half hour for two; you can find carriages for hire along Front Street in Hamilton.

Perhaps you'd rather explore Bermuda from **horseback.** You'll trot along country lanes bordered by hibiscus and oleander, and wooded bridle paths. The calibre of the horses is generally excellent. **Spicelands Riding Center** on Middle Road in Warwick (tel. 238-8212 or 238-8246) offers a wide range of programs for both experienced and novice riders. We highly recommend the morning breakfast ride, which follows back roads to the beach for a long canter along the surf. Afterwards, back to the stable for a hearty ranch-style breakfast. It costs $33 per person. Spicelands also runs guided rides along the historic Railway Trail, $16.50 per person for the one-hour excursion. All rides are accompanied by qualified instructors; long pants and shoes with hard heels are recommended.

One-and-a-half-million years of nature's handiwork has gone into sculpting **Crystal and Leamington Caves,** high vaulted grottoes eroded in the porous limestone rock from which Bermuda is formed. Crystal Caves were discovered in 1907 by two schoolboys looking for a lost cricket ball. What they found was a cavern filled with stalactites and stalagmites, and crystal-clear Cahow Lake. Located near Bailey's Bay, Crystal Caves are open daily except some Saturdays; admission is $2.75 per person (tel. 293-0640). Leamington Caves covers nearly two areas of crystal formations as well as several underground pools and a large grotto. Located near the Plantation Restaurant near Bailey's Bay, Leamington Caves are open Monday through Saturday, 9:30 a.m. to 4:30 p.m.; admission is $2.75 per person (tel. 293-0226).

Spend the day exploring the western part of Bermuda, **Sandys Parish.** From Hamilton, you (and your mopeds or bicycles) can hop aboard the ferry to Ireland Island ($2 per person). If you're fascinated by legends of sunken galleons and pieces of eight, head for the **Maritime Museum** at the Royal Navy Dockyard (open daily from 9 a.m. to 5 p.m.; admission $4 per person). Here, you can view the treasure recovered from a ship that foundered on the reefs off Bermuda in 1595. Then start wending your way back toward Hamilton. Perhaps stop to picnic near Ely's Harbour, or swim at

Mangrove Bay (rumored to have been a smugglers' harbor). Visit Fort Scaur—once known as the Gibraltar of the west, Bermuda has had 22 forts built on its 21 square miles. From the ramparts, you'll enjoy sweeping views of the entire west end of the island. In Somerset, you'll want to pass by Somerset Bridge, the world's smallest drawbridge. For more great views, climb 117 feet up to the top of Gibbs Hill Lighthouse (admission 75¢ per person). Built in 1846 of cast iron, this lighthouse affords some of the most panoramic vistas of Bermuda. Continue meandering back along South Road, stopping for refreshing swims at the beaches.

In 1620, the Pilgrims landed at Plymouth Rock. By that time, **St. George's** had already been settled for eight years, and the industrious residents had already built themselves a fort, a church, and the State House—which still stands today. Today, St. George's has been extensively restored, and visitors will delight in stepping back in time as they saunter along its narrow streets and alleyways, many with historic (or amusing) names, such as Blockade Alley, The King's Parade, and Old Maids' Lane. Start at Town Hall, where *Bermuda Journey*, a new multimedia, audiovisual presentation, traces the history, culture, and heritage of Britain's oldest colony (admission $3.75 per person). Then go to Duke of York Street and climb the broad flight of brick stairs to white-painted St. Peter's Church, the oldest Anglican church in the western hemisphere. View the silver communion service, a gift from King William III in 1698. You'll enjoy poking through the Tucker House Museum on Water Street, filled with wonderful antiques, such as a Waterford chandelier, a splendid Bermudian highboy, and a clock dating back to 1660 (it still keeps good time). Open Monday through Saturday, 10 a.m. to 5 p.m.; admission $2. The Carriage Museum on Water Street displays a wonderful collection of old conveyences—buggies, surreys, and shays. Open Monday through Saturday, 10 a.m. to 5 p.m.; admission $1 per person. In Kings Square, you'll want to have your photos taken in the stocks and pillory, used by early settlers to punish miscreants. Then cross the small bridge over to Ordnance Island, where you can view the life-size replica of the *Deliverance,* the vessel that carried the shipwrecked settlers from Bermuda to Jamestown. Open daily from 10 a.m. until 4 p.m.; admission is $1.50 per person. Nearby, check out the ducking stool—a replica of the instrument used to subdue suspected witches and nagging wives. Just a bit outside of town, stop by Fort St. Catherine, a 19th-century fortification. You'll probably feel a chill as you walk through the underground galleries and magazines and view the heavy muzzle-loading defense guns. There's also a fun display of replicas of the British Crown Jewels. Admission $1 per person.

St. George's also has a fine selection of shops and boutiques. Frangipani carries very fashionable cotton sportswear for women. There are also outlets of Crisson's, Smith's, Trimingham's, Cooper's, Bluck's, and other top stores.

3. Honeymoon Hotels and Hideaways

Bermuda has some of the most unabashedly romantic hotels in the world. In addition to large, sophisticated self-contained resorts, you'll also find several uniquely Bermudian accommodations, such as elegant cottage colonies. Because of the wide selection, it is extremely important for you to decide exactly what kind of lodgings you want for yourselves—large or small, located in town or at the beach. Here's a brief overview of the kinds of accommodations available in Bermuda; they are grouped according to these categories in the hotel write-ups which follow.

Large resort hotels: These are usually complete worlds, with everything you need for honeymoon happiness right on the property: several restaurants, nightclubs, entertainment, boutiques, moped rentals, concierge service, tennis courts, often even golf courses. Most have their own beach or beach club, and many plan special daily activities for honeymooners. You usually have a choice of meal plans.

Small hotels: Although the services and facilities at the small hotels will be less extensive than at the major resort properties, they usually have a restaurant, bar, swimming pool, and water-sports equipment rental for snorkel gear and small sailboats. Some small hotels lodge their guests within one main building; others have separate cottages surrounding the main house. Various meal plans are usually available.

Cottage colonies: A unique Bermudian institution, these feature separate cottages or cottage units scattered throughout landscaped grounds, affording maximum privacy. At the same time, the cottage colonies have all the facilities of a resort hotel, including a main "clubhouse" with dining room, bar, informal entertainment, beach and/or pool. Many of the cottages have small kitchens where you can prepare a light meal; at some, a maid comes in the morning to prepare your breakfast to order. Meal plans are generally BP or MAP.

"The Bermuda Collection": Seven of Bermuda's finest and most luxurious small hotels and cottage colonies have joined together to form "The Bermuda Collection": Cambridge Beaches, Glencoe, Lantana Colony Club, Newstead, Pompano Beach Club, The Reefs, and Stonington Beach Hotel. Each of these hotels is a true "gem," as you'll read in the write-ups which follow. By banding together, they have been able to plan joint social activities for their guests, and share services and facilities. In particular, guests at these hotels on the MAP (Modified American Plan) for meals can participate in "Carousel Dining," a dine-around program permitting them to take their meals at any of the seven different resorts—all of which are known for their superb restaurants. Contact the individual hotel or cottage colony for complete details.

Housekeeping cottages: These are similar to the cottage colonies in that lodgings are in separate cottages or wings, but there is no clubhouse. Some are apartment-type units with full kitchens. Rates usually are EP, without meals.

Guest houses: Most of these occupy old Bermuda mansions, which have been refurbished and modernized to accommodate guests. Bedrooms might be in the main house, or in separate units. Often, there is a dining room where some meals are served. The atmosphere tends towards the casual and informal; the meal plan will generally be CP.

When you compare Bermuda hotel prices with those in other destinations, remember that most Bermuda rates are MAP, including lunch and dinner daily. (Resorts in other parts of the world usually do not include any meals in their room rates.)

Although mid-November through March is considered the low season for Bermuda, not all hotels reduce their rates. On occasion, some facilities close temporarily for renovation during the winter, so be sure to check the hotel for details if you will be honeymooning at that time. Important—not all Bermuda hotels accept credit cards. Be sure to confirm your method of payment in advance. Also note that a 5% Bermuda government tax and a service charge to cover tipping (usually 10% or $8.50 per day for MAP guests) will be added to your final bill. Several hotels and guest houses also add an energy surcharge. Ask for travel agent for complete details.

LARGE RESORT HOTELS: Marriott's Castle Harbour Resort, P.O. Box HM 841, Hamilton 5, Bermuda (tel. 809/293-2040; U.S. reservations: tel. 212/603-8200 or toll free 800/831-1000.) The drive in is impressive: The long road passes through the manicured fairways of the golf club, and winds through tunnels formed by overarching palm trees, cedars, and casuarinas. When the car pulls up in front, a doorman wearing a white uniform with polished brass buttons and a feathered topee rushes to open the door for you. Yes, Marriott's Castle Harbour is definitely back, after a $60-million renovation that has restored it to the top rank of Bermudian resorts. The 395-room property occupies a 250-acre estate in the exclusive Tuckers Town area, with spectacular views of Castle Harbour and Harrington Sound. The main building has been returned to its original, old world splendor. A cedar entranceway lined with gilt mirrors leads to a magnificent circular lobby, with marble floors and exposed cedar beams.

Castle Harbour boasts extensive sports facilities—most notably, the 18-hole, 71 par, 6,435-yard championship golf course designed by Robert Trent Jones. The first hole, where you tee off over the roadway towards the ocean, is considered among the most spectacular in the world. For your sporting pleasure, the resort also has three heated swimming pools, a complete assemblage of water-sports facilities (including Windsurfing, waterskiing, snorkeling, Hobie cat, and Sunfish rentals), and a new beach club located just minutes' away on one of Bermuda's finest beaches, next to Natural Arches. (A convenient beach shuttle runs constantly.) Stay in shape at their new health spa, which boasts a Jacuzzi, saunas, and Universal exercise equipment. One of the nicest places to sun yourself in winter is the Olympic-size Harbour pool, framed by the Romanesque limestone archways. Glass jalousies front the oceanside, acting as a wind break to keep you toasty warm.

You'll have a tough time deciding whether you prefer the accommodations in the original building or in the brand-new wing. The latter, shaped like a futuristic white pyramid, cascades down the steep cliffside to the very edge of the water, and each room has a spacious balcony. In the original buildings, proportions are larger, and you'll find wonderful old-fashioned touches such as the huge walk-in closets. However, most of the older rooms do not have balconies. All the accommodations are decorated in a classic contemporary style, with English-style furnishings, floral bedspreads in soothing shades of muted rose and slate blue, and walls tinged with the subtlest shade of pink. All rooms are air-conditioned and have color TVs. The property has three bars and six restaurants, including Mikado's—the only Japanese restaurant in Bermuda (see write-up which follows).

Honeymoon package: Seven days/six nights: $955.80 (winter—BP) to $1,765.80 (summer—MAP) per couple. Includes champagne and fresh flowers upon arrival, one day's use of moped or one 18-hole round of golf for two, free tennis, a traditional afternoon tea, manager's reception, and souvenir gift.

Beach lovers, take note—the **Elbow Beach Hotel**, P.O. Box HM455, Hamilton 5, Bermuda (tel. 809/236-3535; U.S. reservations: toll free 800/223-7434), is located on the longest, broadest, most exquisite strands in Bermuda, two miles of pale-pink sands and clear, cobalt waters. Overlooking the south shore in Paget Parish, the Elbow Beach provides perfect honeymoon headquarters for couples who want absolutely everything right on the property—from dancing under the stars to tennis to moped rentals. Shoppers will delight in prowling through the arcade that houses outposts of some of Bermuda's finest stores, including Trimingham's, Crisson's, and Cooper's. And, when you feel like wandering off, the property is conveniently located, just ten minutes from Hamilton.

Practically all of the 300 rooms are located in the four-story white hotel that crowns the hillside; there are also some lanai units and suites located in the gardens that line the paths down to the beach. The resort encompasses 35 lushly landscaped acres. At the water-sports concession at the beach, you can make arrangements for sailing, waterskiing, diving, or fishing charters. In addition, Bennie Hall at the hotel's tour desk is something of an island institution—she can set you up with anything from horseback riding to glass-bottom boat tours. If you prefer a swimming pool, you'll have plenty of room to swim laps in the large, free-form pool.

Most honeymooners choose either a junior suite or a superior room, both with king-size bed and an oceanview terrace. The two accommodations are virtually identical: The suite has a wall separating the living and bedroom areas. Elbow Beach is currently going through renovations, and rooms are being redone in soft tones of beige and off-white, with subtle accents of pale mauve, pink, and green.

You can dine in three different restaurants: The Surf Club down at the beach is especially nice for lunch, with its jaunty blue-and-white striped umbrellas placed out on the terrace. There's entertainment every night, such as calypso music or a steel band, and every Saturday and Monday night in season, you can dance under the stars to live music at the Beach Terrace. Honeymoon package: Seven days/six nights (MAP): $1,765.80 to $1,929.96 per couple for a superior room. Includes bottle of German sparkling wine, Elbow Beach cook book, welcoming drinks, invitation to weekly honeymooners' champagne party, invitation to weekly rum swizzle party, free admission to nightclub for one evening, souvenir honeymoon photograph album, and more.

Located on a peninsula thrust out into the ocean, the **Sonesta Beach Hotel,** P.O. Box HM1070, Hamilton 5, Bermuda (tel. 809/238-8122; U.S. reservations: toll free 800/343-7170), has not just one beach waiting for you, but three, all set on sheltered coves just off the Atlantic. The architecture is rather dramatic: the broad three-story, U-shaped building seems to embrace the sea from its rocky promontory. Lovers will want to stroll out to Honeymoon Point, a rocky spit that overlooks the ocean. On your way back, pass through the very pretty moongate, to assure yourselves good luck. Although the Sonesta has 400 rooms and spreads out over 25 acres, the feel remains intimate and personalized. By day, much of the activity centers around the three beaches, where you can rent equipment for Windsurfing, snorkeling, helmet, or scuba diving, or sign up for a glass-bottom boat ride. Day or night, tennis is complimentary for guests on the six courts, and golf on a Robert Trent Jones–designed course lies just minutes away at the Port Royal Golf Course. Pamper yourselves at The Spa, which offers individually tailored health and fitness programs. Sign up for a facial or massage or work out in an aerobics class or on the exercise equipment.

One of the advantages of the Sonesta is that you are right on the beach—and, since there are three sandy coves to choose from, they never seem crowded. You can also swim in a huge, heated outdoor pool—or a large indoor one, located under a glass dome. All of the rooms have a private balcony and all have recently been redone in very contemporary shades of mauve and aqua, with king-size beds available on request. Consider one of the split-level minisuites, with a sunken living room. There are three different restaurants: the Port Royal dining room, the Greenhouse restaurant, or in Lillian's, a new, Art Deco–style supper club serving grilled specialties. (On the MAP plan, you will have to pay extra to dine at the Greenhouse or Lillian's.) Every night, there's entertainment and music for dancing.

Honeymoon package: Seven days/six nights (MAP): $1,563.84 per couple for a minimum room to $2,406.24 for a deluxe room. Includes: airport transfers, one room-service breakfast, a half-carafe of wine at dinner daily, manager's rum swizzle party, souvenir photograph, one dinner in the Greenhouse Restaurant (the others are in the Port Royal), one scuba lesson or tennis lesson, use of mopeds for one day, honeymoon champagne party.

Grotto Bay Beach Hotel and Tennis Club, P.O. Box HM1291, Hamilton 5, Bermuda (tel. 809/293-8333; U.S. reservations: toll free 800/225-2230 nationwide; 800/982-4770 in MA). If you're looking for a casual, laid-back place, where outdoor good times provide the prevailing modus operandi, then Grotto Bay is your perfect honeymoon choice. This place is really fun. You'll feel right at home, thanks to the friendly, relaxed atmosphere. Grotto Bay offers all the amenities of the larger hotels, combined with the intimacy of a small (only 171 rooms) resort. There's always something going on—tennis clinics, a make-your-own-hat competition, photography lectures, or nature walks. Much of the enthusiasm and energy percolates from E. Michael Jones, the recreation and social director, who can always come up with new ways for couples to have fun. In addition to the usual water sports (aquatrikes, snorkeling, waterskiing, and sailing), you can rent a Boston whaler (about $70 for half a day), and take off for one of the dozens of nearby uninhabited islands for a picnic. Back at Grotto Bay, you'll want to do your sunbathing at aptly named Honeymoon Beach, reached by passing through a moongate. And for honeymooners who really want something different, there's Cathedral Cave, with its very own underground lake. If you like, E. Michael will lock you in there for an hour, all by yourselves. At night, you can dance in one of the world's oldest discos—Prospero's Cave, set in another real, honest-to-goodness cavern complete with stalactites and stalagmites. No wonder Grotto Bay seems to have the happiest bunch of guests on the island.

Part of the outdoorsy, informal atmosphere comes because of the layout. Accommodations, located in nine separate lodges, are spread out over the 20 acres of gardens and beaches. Each room has a balcony with a water view. All are decorated fairly similarly, with blue wall-to-wall carpeting, blue-and-white floral bedspreads, and a white, rattan-edged dresser. If you want to splurge, opt for the "ELE" ("Every Little Extra") rooms that come with nightly turndown service, color TV, and in-house video hook-ups.

Honeymoon package: Seven days/six nights (MAP): $1,238.76 to $1,738.80 per couple for a superior room. Includes a tote bag, use of mopeds for a day, champagne in room upon arrival, boat cruise, scuba lesson, two rum swizzles, one half-day of snorkeling, honeymooners' wine and cheese party, walking tour of Baily Bay including admission to the Dolphin Show.

On the island of Bermuda, the **Southampton Princess Hotel, Golf, Beach, & Tennis Club,** P.O. Box HM1379, Hamilton 5, Bermuda (tel. 809/238-8000; U.S. reservations: tel. 212/582-8100 in New York City, or toll free 800/223-1818 nationwide; 800/442-8418 in NY), is an island of luxury—and absolutely impeccable after a $20-million renovation. You'll find just about every creature comfort you could desire on the 100-acre estate that crowns a hillside on Bermuda's south shore. All 600 rooms have terraces that overlook either the Atlantic Ocean or Great Sound. As the name implies, the resort features complete golf, tennis, and beach facilities. For golfers, there's an 18-hole, par 3 course, with 2,600 yards of manicured terrain that challenge both the experienced and the novice golfer. Tennis players can work on their strokes on 11 courts (7 lit for night play). The private beach, reachable by shuttle from the main hotel, is one of Bermuda's finest. At the water-sports concession, you can rent snorkel or scuba gear, or arrange fishing trips. There are also both outdoor and indoor swimming pools. For those whose favorite sport is shopping, the Southampton Princess' arcades contain 12 stores, including Smith's, Trimingham's, Calypso, and Cooper's.

All the rooms at the Southampton Princess have just been redone in scrumptious pastels, the better to focus attention on the startling blue ocean seen through the sliding glass doors leading to the balcony. Rooms are all fairly similar, with a small, tea-rose-tone couch and a writing desk with rattan chair; all have air conditioning and a color TV (hooked up to a satellite dish) discreetly tucked in the armoire.

If you like, you could dine at a different restaurant every day of the week, including two that are generally numbered amongst Bermuda's finest: the Newport Room with its nautical ambience, and the Waterlot, a 300-year-old inn. For entertainment, there's a spectacular dinner show and revue at the Empire Room, the island's largest nightclub; and dancing at the Neptune Lounge and Touch Club.

Honeymoon package: Five days/four nights for a superior room. Winter: $550.80 per couple (EP); summer: $1,578.96 per couple (MAP). Includes welcoming rum swizzles, admission to the "Follies" show plus two drinks, bottle of champagne upon arrival, honeymoon photo album, traditional Bermuda cedar marriage goblet, Princess totebag and cookbook, airport transfers.

The Princess Hotel, P.O. Box HM837, Hamilton 5, Bermuda (tel. 809/295-3000; U.S. reservations: tel. 212/582-8100 in New York City; toll free 800/223-1818 nationwide; 800/442-8418 in NYS). For over 100 years, the Princess in Hamilton has epitomized gracious service. The hotel was named in honor of Princess Louise, the daughter of Queen Victoria who became the first member of the Royal Family to visit Bermuda. Today, thanks to a $14-million renovation to celebrate her centennial, The Princess reigns more regally than ever over Hamilton Harbour.

The Princess is located on Pitts Bay Road, just a few minutes' walk from all the Front Street shops. The imposing pink palace is set right on the edge of the harbour, surrounding lush gardens, palm trees, goldfish ponds, and large outdoor swimming pools. As is characteristic of older hotels, each of the 452 rooms has a slightly different layout and view. All have air conditioning and color TV. Rooms, recently redecorated, have a substantial, British feel. Furnishings might include a moss-green velvet couch, captain's chest, or Bermuda prints on the walls; the modern bathrooms have a spring-like floral wallpaper. You definitely can enjoy the best of both worlds: proximity to Hamilton, plus complete use of all the beach, sports, and dining facilities at the Southampton Princess (a water shuttle runs between the two properties several times daily). The Princess in Hamilton itself has four excellent restaurants, and top-caliber shows in the Gazebo Lounge, which has a wraparound view of Hamilton's twinkling lights.

Honeymoon package: Five days/four nights, for a superior room (EP): $548.64 to $894.24 per couple. Includes welcoming rum swizzles, bottle of champagne upon arrival, honeymoon photo album, traditional Bermuda cedar marriage goblet, Princess cookbook and tote bag, his-and-hers T-shirts, daytime shuttle ferry to the Southampton Princess Beach Club, airport transfers.

Club Med, St. George's Cove Village, P.O. Box GE 59, St. George's 1, Bermuda (tel. 809/297-8222; reservations: toll free 800/CLUB MED). Vive l'amour! Take Gallic charm and a penchant for romance, add in Club Med's reputation for nonstop activities and sports, and set it all in beautiful Bermuda—and voilà . . . you have a captivating retreat for a *lune de miel* (honeymoon). This resort is a bit different from the 106 other Club Meds around the world. First of all, it looks like a hotel (which it was during its past incarnations under management by Holiday Inns and Loews Hotels); the ten-story property surmounts a hillside overlooking the town of St. George's and the Atlantic Ocean. Guests, known as G.M.'s (Gentils Membres) are encouraged to leave the compound (in fact, one excursion takes guests to Hamilton by boat for sightseeing and shopping). You'll also have five restaurants on site to choose from, free of charge. You can work out with Chinese chopsticks one evening, twirl pasta at the Italian restaurant the next, sample Moroccan delicacies such as pastilla or tajine, down a pint in a pub set in an old fort, or dig in to Club Med's justly renowned buffets. Finally, this isn't a singles resort: couples, including many honeymooners, predominate. What Club Med/Bermuda shares with its compatriot properties is the carefree bounty of sports and activities available—all free to guests. Facilities include tennis (nine all-weather courts), archery (giving you the proper yeoman feeling, it's located in the moat of Fort Victoria), volleyball, basketball, aerobics, and a fully equipped fitness center. Down by the true-blue, ultraclear waters of the Atlantic, you can take up sailing, Windsurfing, snorkeling, or kayaking, climb aboard for a catamaran ride or improve your tan on the wooden sun deck or pink-sand beach. Golfers can tee off at reduced rates on the St. George Golf Course, just down the hill from the hotel-village —18 challenging holes designed by Robert Trent Jones. Every week, special events are planned—perhaps a carnival night, or a Mexican-style fiesta. Everything is very informal and spontaneous, and men do not have to wear jackets or ties in the restaurants. And, if you want something different for your nightlife, head for the nightclub located in Fort St. Victoria, located in an honest-to-goodness fortress, built to defend St. George's. True to the Club Med concept, this resort is all-inclusive: all you have to pay extra for are the "bar beads," used to buy additional drinks (you get free wine and beer with meals). Honeymoon package: Eight days/seven nights (all-inclusive land rate): $810 to $1,188 per couple, depending on week selected. Includes champagne upon arrival, guaranteed oceanfront room, two packets of beads, Club Med honeymoon T-shirts, a VIP "goodies" basket, plus a weekly champagne party for newlyweds hosted by the "Chef de Village." Combined air and land packages are available; contact Club Med for details. Property is closed January through March.

Overlooking Hamilton Harbour and Great Sound, the **Belmont Hotel, Golf & Beach Club,** P.O. Box WK251, Warwick 7, Bermuda (tel. 809/236-1301; reservations: tel. 212/541-4400 in New York City, or toll free 800/223-5672 nationwide), occupies a distinctly country-club–like setting, 110 acres of lush green verdure that undulate to the water's edge. All 150 rooms are located in the main building. If you love golf and tennis, this is your place. The hotel adjoins the fairways of its own 18-

hole, par 70 championship course designed by Robert Trent Jones, with a complete pro shop on the property. Play tennis on three all-weather courts—the hotel also regularly schedules tournaments for guests. The very large, sea-water pool that overlooks the harbor is not only fun to swim in, but also to watch—there are underwater portholes, so you can peek at the aquatic antics down under. For those who prefer to feel the pink sand squish under their toes, there's a private beach club just five minutes' away by free shuttle. One of the biggest bonuses of the Belmont is its location—just a three-mile drive from Hamilton. Better yet—hop the ferry right at their private dock. After a scenic ten-minute cruise, you'll arrive right on Front Street.

Following its multi-million-dollar refurbishment, the Belmont radiates tip-top form. The lobby has the warmth of an English club, accented by Bermuda cedar paneling and brass chandeliers. Rooms, also all recently redone, face either the gardens, the golf course, or Hamilton Harbour. Furnishings evince distinguished elegance: a Queen Anne–style headboard and highboy, rattan armchairs, plush wall-to-wall carpeting, and a color cable TV. The Belmont is a Trusthouse Forte property. Honeymoon package: Four days / three nights (EP): $332.64 to $502.20 per couple. Includes breakfast during the summer season, afternoon tea, rum swizzle party, bottle of champagne, Sea Garden cruise, unlimited tennis.

Bermudiana Hotel, P.O. Box HM842, Hamilton 5, Bermuda (tel. 809/295-1211; reservations: tel. 212/541-4400 in New York City; toll free 800/223-5672 nationwide). A country club setting in the midst of Hamilton—that's what you'll enjoy at the Bermudiana Hotel, which faces out over Hamilton Harbour and the Royal Bermuda Yacht Club. The 230-room property has recently refurbished its lobby area, pool area, and rooms, so everything looks freshly inviting. Rooms have an English decor, with Queen Anne–reproduction headboards and nightstands, as well as island accents, such as a rattan seating group and Bermuda prints on the walls. When you feel cosmopolitan, Hamilton's finest Front Street shops and restaurants are just a short stroll away. If you feel sporty, the Bermudiana has a large salt-water pool, two lighted, all-weather tennis courts, and an indoor freshwater pool. Since the Bermudiana is a Trusthouse Forte hotel, guests enjoy full exchange facilities with the Belmont Hotel, including special privileges on the 18-hole golf course and use of the private beach club at Discovery Bay. Honeymoon package: Four days / three nights (BP): $502.20 per couple. Includes room with a king-size bed and color cable TV (upgrade to suite if available), afternoon tea daily, bottle of champagne upon arrival, manager's rum swizzle party, harbour cruise, unlimited tennis.

SMALL HOTELS: For couples seeking an island of romance on the island of Bermuda, **Harmony Club,** P.O. Box PG299, Paget 6, Bermuda (tel. 809/236-3500), provides the perfect getaway. Not only is Harmony Club Bermuda's first all-inclusive resort catering to couples only—it also weaves an ambience that is first-class all the way. Ensconced in a park-like enclave just two miles from Hamilton, the seven-acre luxury property has only 71 rooms. The property exudes Bermudian charm, with its columned entrance, pink-painted main building and cottages topped by white peak roofs, and showplace gardens—the head gardener has been with the property (formerly called Harmony Hall) for 45 years, and he manages to coax snapdragons to grow to eye-level. Personal, elegant touches abound. The main building is constructed around a 200-year-old residence, and you'll find fine architectural details impossible to replicate today—parquet floors, Bermuda cedar-paneled walls. All meals are served sit-down style, and you'll sup off fine crystal, silver, and china. Adding to the romantic glow, dinner is by candlelight every evening. With awareness of the kinds of privileges fun-loving honeymooners would appreciate, Harmony Club includes free use of a motor scooter throughout your stay. Among the places you might like to go are Oasis and The Club, two of Bermuda's hottest clubs, where Harmony Hall guests are admitted without a cover charge. For sports lovers, there's tennis on two courts or 1,000-feet of blush-pink sands at the private beach at Discovery Bay. Right at Harmony Club, the swimming pool has been refurbished, with the addition of a California-style wooden sun deck, saunas, miniwaterfall, and a moongate that you can walk through for good luck. Since Harmony Club is a Trusthouse Forte hotel, guests enjoy special golf privileges at the Belmont Golf and Country Club.

The property lends itself particularly well to privacy, since most rooms are located in small cottages scattered around the gardens, lawns, and courtyard. (There are also some equally nice accommodations in the main house.) Rooms are big and airy; sunlight streams in the windows framed by tie-back drapes. Most rooms have private terraces or balconies; be sure to request a king-size bed if you prefer one, since some rooms have two doubles. Much of the magic at Harmony Club comes from general manager Jean Pierre Auriol and his wife, Martine, who have the deft savoir faire to create an ambience in which romance blossoms. Honeymoon package (all-inclusive): Eight days / seven nights: $1,865.16 to $2,167.56 per couple. Among the features the package covers: airport transfers; champagne upon arrival; traditional English afternoon tea daily; evening cocktail party with hors d'oeuvres; all meals, unlimited wines, spirits, and liquors; use of hotel club room. Please note that the rate also includes all taxes, gratuities, and service charges.

The Reefs, 56 South Rd., Southampton 8–08, Bermuda (tel. 809/238-0222; reservations: toll free 800/223-1363). Casual elegance—that's what you'll find at this picturesque resort located on Bermuda's beach-studded south shore. The 65 rooms are set in two-story pink buildings that sashay down the coral bluffs towards the reef-sheltered sea. What makes The Reefs extra special is its private beach—a good-size stretch of pink sands, with that clear, aquamarine water beckoning you to jump on in. When you add in the personal attention given to guests by owners Bonnie and David Dodwell, you'll understand why The Reefs is usually booked solid all year, and 60% of its guests are returnees.

Recently refurbished, the clubhouse (built around a 200-year-old farmhouse) has a cozy piano bar, as well as that expansive outdoor terrace just made for sipping rum swizzles at sunset. All the rooms capture a warm, island ambience, with wicker and rattan furnishings, terra-cotta floors with area throw rugs, framed Bermuda maps and prints on the walls, and a color scheme incorporating nature's palette: sea-foam greens, peaches, lilac, rose, and slate blue. Most rooms (except the Clubhouse and Poolside accommodations) face westward to the ocean, giving you on-the-brink views of the sunset from your balcony and terrace. In summer evenings, you can dine at the new restaurant poised on a beachside terrace. More music comes with the live entertainment nightly—singers, a combo, or a calypso band. A member of the Bermuda Collection. Rates: Winter (MAP): $138.24 per couple per night (poolside lanai), to $181.44 (surfside lanai). Summer (MAP): $213.84 per couple per night (poolside lanai) to $276.48 per couple per night (surfside lanai). Honeymoon package: $36 additional. Includes champagne upon arrival, half-day Sea Garden cruise, souvenir photograph, swizzle party, and a gift for the bride.

Even in an island of beautiful locales, the **Pompano Beach Club,** 32 Pompano Beach Rd., Southampton 8–01, Bermuda (tel. 809/234-0222; reservations: tel. 617/358-7737 in Massachusetts, or toll free 800/343-4155 nationwide), setting leaves you gasping at nature's handiwork. Poised at the edge of limestone cliffs, the pink buildings overlook a panoramic view of shoreline where reefs and sandbars color the water two startlingly different shades of blue. At low tide, the water often gets so shallow, you can walk over 250 yards out into the Atlantic—and still have your head well above water. Much of the warmth and hospitality of Pompano comes from David and Aimee Southworth (the family has owned and operated Pompano for over 30 years). They're young and enthusiastic, and know just the places and activities to recommend for newlyweds. Pompano itself offers seclusion and privacy on Bermuda's southwest coast in Southampton parish, about a half-hour's drive from Hamilton. The 54 rooms are located in seven separate units, all named for different sport fish. Each room offers that dramatic sea view, although layouts differ slightly: some have kitchenettes, others are studios, some have a separate bedroom or sitting area. The honeymoon package features a studio room with double bed, sitting area, private bath, and outdoor porch.

Thanks to the sandbar and protective reefs, Pompano offers excellent swimming, snorkeling, and Windsurfing. The sand beach is rather small, so for sunbathing, you'll probably prefer the stunning white pool deck, thrust out toward the Atlantic. Park your lounge chair under a yellow umbrella, or swim in the heated freshwater pool. There's also tennis on a clay court and golf at Port Royal Golf Course right next door (Pompano is only 500 yards from the first tee). The oceanview Cedar Room is an atmospheric place to dine, with its solid cedar furnishings, coral stone pillars, and excellent food. A member of The Bermuda Collection. Honeymoon package (MAP): Seven days / six nights: $1,008.72 to $1,267.92 per couple, depending on time of year. Includes studio accommodations, bottle of champagne, a gift for the bride, airport transfers, tickets to the Maritime Museum, round-trip ferry tickets to Hamilton. Package not available December and January, when rates for a studio are $82:.08 per person per night (EP).

Waterloo House, P.O. Box HM333, Hamilton 5, Bermuda (tel. 809/295-4480; reservations: toll free 800/468-4100), occupies one of the most delightful settings you could possibly imagine. Two-story buildings painted a pale persimmon color and accented by trim white shutters surround a garden courtyard leading out to Hamilton Harbour. Although the inn is less than a three-minute walk from Hamilton's Front Street, you'll definitely feel more like you're a guest in an elegant English country house (the property was originally built as a private residence). There's a cozy, at-home ambience: You can sit down at the upright piano in the lounge, or challenge each other to a very British game of skittles (somewhat like billards). Each of the 35 rooms is different—some have balconies and water views, others face the garden. All are very bright, cheerful, spacious, and well laid out, decorated with English-style furnishings, captains' chests, and overstuffed armchairs. When you wake up in the morning, the sun comes streaming in through the windows, and the colorful harbor throbs with activity. And because the rooms face onto the courtyard rather than busy Pitts Bay Road, the only sound you'll hear in the morning is the chirp of the bananaquits and the quack of the ducks. There's no beach, but you can take a dunk in the small pool in the courtyard. Guests also enjoy beach privileges at the very exclusive Coral Beach Club, for a small fee. Since Waterloo House is associated with Horizons & Cottages and Newstead resorts, guests enjoy exchange dining and other activities. Waterloo's own restaurant is excellent and, in summer, you can dine on the large terrace overlooking Hamilton Harbour. Honeymoon package: Seven days / six nights (MAP): $997.92 (summer) to $1,056.24 (winter) for a standard room. Includes bottle of champagne upon arrival, a picnic lunch for two, one day free tennis or golf, one day free admission and transfers to the private Coral Beach and Tennis Club.

Rosedon, P.O. Box HM290, Hamilton 5, Bermuda (tel. 809/295-1640; reservations: toll free 800/225-5567). This white house with the aqua shutters set on a low hillside just minutes away from Hamilton's Front Street envelops you in turn-of-the-century graciousness. Built as a private residence in 1906, it is one of Bermuda's most captivating small hotels. A grand circular driveway edged with bright blooming flowers sweeps up to the front door, flanked by leaded-glass windows. When the mansion was built, no expense was spared. Fine woods such as oak, cherry, mahogany, and California redwood were imported for the paneling. This wealth of charm and detail is still appreciated by guests today. Pathways wind through lush gardens to the modern, two-story wings where most of the 43 guest rooms are located. Accommodations are simple—not fancy, but rather are comfortable and clean, with bright quilted bedspreads, jalousie windows, floral-print drapes, and beige carpeting. All rooms have air conditioning and a minifridge. The wings surround a large garden courtyard that has a large, heated pool at its center; all around, brick walkways meander past the palms, oleanders, and hibiscus that add color and fragrance to the grounds. For ocean swimming, Rosedon guests enjoy beach privileges at Elbow Beach Surf Club, with the hotel providing free transportation. Honeymoon package: Seven days / six nights (EP): From $684.72 to $1,032.48 per couple, depending on room and time of year. Includes bottle of champagne upon arrival, gift for the bride, daily afternoon tea or a drink by the pool, a picnic lunch, rum swizzle party, a half-day Sea Garden cruise.

Stonington Beach Hotel, P.O. Box HM523, Hamilton 5, Bermuda (tel. 809/236-5416; reservations: tel. 212/661-4540 in New York; toll free 800/223-1588 nationwide). A modern luxury hotel, Stonington Beach occupies a prime location on one of Bermuda's finest south shore beaches. It's the same two-mile strand shared with the Elbow Beach Hotel right next door, but much more tranquil, since Stonington is set at the far eastern end. Although the hotel attracts many honeymoon couples, the ambience is low-key: no group parties or games, but a lot of quiet enjoyment.

Because the property is small (only 64 rooms), it retains an intimate feel. The accommodations, all with panoramic ocean views, are situated in beige buildings with traditional Bermudian white step-style roofs, tucked amid the rolling lawns of the green hillside. Every room has attractive modern decor, an oceanfront balcony, and a ceiling fan as well as air conditioning. The public areas are especially inviting, including a Regency-style library where you can pick up copies of the *London Times* or the *Economist*, and settle in for a good read in front of the fireplace. The English-style Norwood Dining Room serves excellent cuisine. Outdoors, there's a large freshwater pool and two tennis courts screened behind bougainvillea. Both service and upkeep are superior, thanks to General Manager William Mulder, who was educated at the renowned Swiss Hotel School in Lausanne. You'll get doubly good attention, since the front-desk staff includes some students from Bermuda College's Department of Hotel Technology, all supervised in their duties by professional managers. A member of The Bermuda Collection. Honeymoon package: Seven days / six nights (BP): $1,097.28 to $1,343.52 per couple for a superior room. Includes a chilled bottle of champagne and fruit basket in your room upon arrival, unframed watercolor print by a local artist, English afternoon tea daily, Monday evening wine-tasting party, free daytime tennis, airport transfers. MAP is also available.

Get a feel for the real Bermuda at **Glencoe**, P.O. Box PG297, Paget 6, Bermuda (tel. 809/236-5274; reservations: toll free 800/468-1500), an intimate resort located in a quiet, residential area on the edge of Salt Kettle Bay. For the past 30 years, the property has been owned and managed by Reggie Cooper, who has nurtured its growth from a small guest house accommodating 22 people to its present 80-guest capacity. Although the property has grown, it hasn't really changed: It retains an informal but elegant atmosphere—a Bermuda-style country inn, centered around an historic 18th-century house that is now the main building. The rooms occupy graceful, two-story pink buildings, with balconies and terraces trimmed with white latticework and wooden railings. No two rooms are alike, although most offer water views. Furnishings carry out the light tropical motif—many have open-beam cathedral ceilings, rattan chairs and dressers, and bright floral print fabrics. Calla lilies and oleander line the garden paths that lead to the two swimming pools and patios. If you prefer an ocean beach, Glencoe guests enjoy privileges at Elbow Beach. During the day, you can watch the yachts and Bermuda-fitted dinghies come and go from their moorings in the bay, or take off yourself aboard a Sunfish or Windsurfer. Deep-sea fishing, scuba diving, tennis, and golf can all be arranged easily. At night, there's excellent dining both indoors and out, with sweeping views of sunset over Little Sound. Glencoe definitely offers the best of both worlds. Although it enjoys a secluded location, it is just five minutes away from Front Street, Hamilton, via the ferry that leaves from the nearby dock. A member of The Bermuda Collection. Honeymoon package: None. Rates (MAP): $151.20 to $194.40 per couple per night. BP also available.

Newstead, P.O. Box PG196, Paget 6, Bermuda (tel. 809/236-6060; reservations: toll free 800/468-4111). Imagine an English country manor with assorted guest houses transplanted to the edge of Hamilton Harbour, and you very much have the picture of Newstead, a pretty collection of moss-green-painted cottages just across the sparkling blue waters from Hamilton. The main building, dating back to the 19th century, contains a very grand ballroom-size living room, with exposed cedar beams, floral chintz couches, and exceptionally fine English antiques and original 19th-century oil paintings. Every afternoon, guests gather here for a traditional tea. Afterwards, form a foursome for bridge in the card room, or take up skittles, an English game that resembles billiards. Hamilton is just a short drive or five-minute ferry ride away.

Rooms are located in different cottages that ramble down the hillside facing the harbor and Hamilton. (There are also 16 rooms in the main house.) There's a total of 55 rooms, each a unique gem: The most deluxe accommodations have private terraces right on the harbor. The furnishings seem to come from an English country manse: overstuffed wingchairs, Queen Anne headboards, and old-fashioned floral fabrics. Everything feels comfy and lived-in, not formal. And what would be a good country house without sports? Newstead has just added two new tennis courts; and there's sailing and deep-water swimming from the private docks, as well as a large heated pool. For surf-bathing, Newstead guests enjoy privileges at the very posh Coral Beach Club for a small fee. Since Newstead is also a companion resort of Waterloo House and Horizons & Cottages, there's also a dine-around program with those properties. At Newstead's own dining room, you'll dine by candlelight beneath crystal chandeliers and open-beam ceilings. Newstead is also part of The Bermuda Collection. Honeymoon package: Seven days / six nights (MAP): $1,135.20 to $1,293.60 per couple. Includes a bottle of champagne and free tennis.

Mermaid Beach Club, P.O. Box WK250, Warwick 7, Bermuda (tel. 809/236-5031; reservations: toll free 800/441-7087 nationwide; 800/292-9695 in PA). A millionaire's beach at a bargain price—that's what you get at this south shore hotel long known as a one of Bermuda's best values. The 86 rooms are located in two-story beige buildings that cozy up to a long stretch of soft pink sands, just a pebble's throw from other fine south shore beaches, such as Warwick Long Bay and Jobson Cove. Most rooms have ocean views, as well as verandas or patios. Although the decor is simple, rooms are cheerful and tropical with rattan chairs and tables, plump white couch, and green, fern-leaf motif draperies. All are air-conditioned. Some rooms have a small kitchenette; there's a convenience store on the property where you can buy groceries, as well as a small restaurant. Tennis, golf, and all water sports can be arranged. Honeymoon package: Seven days / six nights (MAP): $957 to $1,421.20 per couple. Includes flowers for the bride, a two-hour Sea Garden cruise, a bottle of champagne, a free cocktail daily, and complimentary snorkel equipment.

COTTAGE COLONIES: **Horizons and Cottages,** P.O. Box PG198, Paget 6, Bermuda (tel. 809/236-0048; reservations: toll free 800/468-0022). Fresh as a summer's day, gracious as the "welcoming arms" stairway built of Bermuda sandstone, scenic as a longtail's view from on high—that describes Horizons, part of the crème de la crème of Bermuda cottage colony society. The property crowns a hillock and offers you nearly 360° of horizons, including a postcard-perfect view of the very elegant Coral Beach Club. Because the resort encompasses nearly 30 acres, you'll feel completely secluded—yet Hamilton is less than three miles away. The clubhouse is built around a 17th-century farmhouse that once belonged to the Middleton family. Oriental carpets and valanced windows help complete the feeling of old Bermuda. Manager Wilhelm Sack runs a crack ship—one of the reasons that Horizons is the only Bermudian hotel that is part of the prestigious Relais et Châteaux group. Rooms in the main house have just been redone using colors that come straight from a floral bouquet—soft peach and pistachio, with daffodil-yellow towels in the bathroom. The rooms that will really win your hearts are in the ten delightful cottages, which have names such as "Morning Glory," "Sea Cloud," and "Wind Song." Each is unique: Some have fireplaces, others sunken living rooms with Mexican tile floors, all with islandy furnishings made of rattan, ceiling fans, and an Impressionist's palette of pastels: pinks, aqua, yellow, and coral. All fabrics and accoutrements are crisp and new. Views overlook the water or gardens. Especially in the morning, you'll have time to savor your surroundings: A maid will prepare your breakfast to order in the separate kitchen, which you can then enjoy on your balcony. This, indeed, is the good life. And when you also want good sports, you'll find that Horizons has a heated swimming pool, three all-weather tennis courts, nine-hole mashie golf, and an 18-hole putting green. Full golf and all water sports can be easily arranged. Horizons is especially well known for its excellent cuisine, and many of the herbs and vegetables come from their own gardens. In summer, candlelit dinners are served outside on the terrace. Afterwards, settle into a cozy, English-style pub with a dart board and skittles for some friendly competition. Three nights a week there's entertainment, and every Sunday evening, you can dance underneath the stars. Guests at Horizons also can enjoy the facilities of its companion resorts, Newstead and Waterloo House. Honeymoon package: Seven days / six nights (MAP): $1,283.04 to $1,684.80 per couple. Includes bottle of champagne, afternoon tea daily, complimentary golf and tennis on the property, and an introduction to a private beach.

Lantana Colony Club, SB 90, Sandys 9, Bermuda (tel. 809/234-0141; reservations: toll free 800/468-3733). Set on 20 acres of lushly gardened, lovingly tended grounds at Bermuda's west end, Lantana embraces guests with a feeling of elegant repose. Since there are only 55 rooms, the ambience is distinctly uncrowded. Very private pink cottages with the traditional white-step roofs sit discreetly tucked under palm trees, behind hibiscus hedges, along impeccably manicured lawns. The large pool area near the beach is exquisite: edged with tile and backed by a trim pink cabana. At the pink, coral-sand beach, you can rent Sunfish and other small boats, Windsurfers, and snorkel gear for exploring the clear-as-glass waters of Great Sound. It's easy to reach Hamilton without disrupting the relaxed pace—just hop the nearby ferry for a peaceful, 40-minute cruise in. But you'll find plenty of pleasures right at Lantana: tennis on two all-weather courts, a putting green, and a superb croquet lawn (both John H. Young II and his wife, the owners, are international tournament-level players). Perhaps your favorite moments will come as you just stroll around the property, which has often been called a "museum without walls" because of the bronze sculptures by renowned artists such as Desmond Fountain and John Robinson that grace the lawns and glens. You'll also be captivated by some of the fanciful topiary creations. Accommodations—suites, one-, and two-bedroom units—are all differently delightful—you might find terra-cotta floors, rattan rugs, a ceiling fan, and fragrant cedar-wood armoires. Many have terraces, and some have water views. The resort just completed $900,000-worth of improvements and refurbishments.

For lunch, you'll enjoy the La Plage waterfront restaurant, shaded by the seagrape trees. Dinners are served in the formal dining room, with guests rotated night by night toward—and finally into—the Solarium, which has to be the most lavishly romantic dining spot in Bermuda. Chandeliers with their crystals formed like dangling bunches of grapes, spotlit hanging plants, white wrought-iron furniture, and glimmering hurricane lanterns on the table weave a spell that is complemented by the exquisite cuisine. Part of The Bermuda Collection. Honeymoon package: None. Rates (MAP) run from $162 to $243 per couple per night (winter); $216 to $297 per couple per night summers, depending on proportions and views.

Cambridge Beaches, 30 King's Point, Sandys 9-08, Bermuda (tel. 809/234-0331; reservations: toll free 800/468-7300), is the type of place that can proclaim on its brochures, "Cambridge Beaches *is* Bermuda"—and nary a voice would beg to differ. The property is, in fact, Bermuda's original cottage colony, and it continues to reign as one of Bermuda's premier facilities for ambience and service. Owned by the Trott family (whose ancestors came over on the *Sea Venture*), the 25-acre estate is almost completely surrounded by water on a slender peninsula that curves out into Great Sound. The "Beaches" of the property's name actually number about six. Personalized service is the by-word here—guests are always greeted by name. No wonder about 60% of the guests are repeat visitors. You'll have fun browsing through the plaques in the clubhouse that honor the returnees—some of whom have come for 60 years. The whole place has a substantial, old-guard Bermudian feel, from the cedar reception desk to the old beam ceilings and the crewel-work fabrics on the furniture.

Cambridge Beaches is that marvelous anachronism—a resort run exclusively for the pleasure of its guests. The 75 guest rooms are spacious, located in pink-painted, white-roofed cottages scattered hither and yon amongst the gardens, lawns, and shoreline. No two rooms are the same. Most have honest-to-goodness antiques: genuine cedar chests and secretary desks that are worth in the thousands. The decor recalls an English country house, with the comfortable feel of furnishings that have been passed down through generations. You'll find wing chairs poised by the fireplace, bright floral fabrics (unfortunately, some chairs are covered with vinyl), and white chenille bedspreads. Some rooms have working fireplaces, and many have water views. Eighteen rooms boast newly renovated bathrooms with Jacuzzis.

Sporting options include a large swimming pool stationed just at water's edge, all those fine beaches, three tennis courts, and all water sports are available right on the property. Meals are served either in the open-beam, cathedral-ceiling dining room, or out on the terrace fronting Mangrove Bay, where white wrought-iron chairs surround a 300-year-old tamarind tree. Part of The Bermuda Collection. Honeymoon package: Six days / five nights (MAP): From $1,000 per couple. Includes a bottle of champagne.

Pink Beach Club & Cottages, P.O. Box HM1017, Hamilton 5, Bermuda (tel. 809/293-1666; reservations: tel. 212/696-1323 in NY; toll free 800/372-1323 nationwide). The name is appropriate, because this cottage colony fronts a ⅓-mile of the rosiest coral sands in Bermuda. The entire property radiates discrete elegance: Just a small brass plaque next to the cedar door announces "Pink Beach."

Pink cottages with green shutters and steep white roofs spread out over the expansive, 18-acre property filled with well-tended gardens. Whether you choose a cottage or studio, the rooms are big, all with private patio or terrace, and most with a fine water view. Furnishings are a bit mix 'n' match—some orange carpets cheerfully coexist with green bedspreads—but Pink Beach regulars (about 60% of the guests are repeaters) prefer the homey, lived-in look. The most spectacular accommodations are plunked right at the very edge of the sea, their coral-stone terraces merging gradually, perfectly with the jagged rocks.

Start off your day with an ample English breakfast (kippers, anyone?), cooked to order by your maid in the kitchen adjoining your cottage. Then head off for a game of tennis on the two all-weather courts, or golf at Marriott's Castle Harbour or the exclusive Mid Ocean Club (Pink Beach can arrange an introduction). Lunch is served under the graceful colonnade by the large, salt-water pool. Dinner is a formal affair, with jackets and ties required for gentlemen every evening. Picture windows face out over the ocean, with guests gradually rotated to the windowside tables during the course of their stay. There's entertainment six evenings a week, and the beach is softly lighted at night; hand-in-hand strolls definitely encouraged. Honeymoon package: None. Rates (MAP): $232.20 (studio) to $297 (executive suite) per couple per night during the high season; 25% less during the off-season.

Fourways Inn, P.O. Box PG 294, Paget, Bermuda (tel. 809/236-6517; reservations: tel. 212/535-9530 in NY; toll free 800/223-5581 nationwide). Bermuda's brandnew cottage colony continues the tradition of elegance and excellence established by its neighboring Fourways Restaurant (see "Romantic Restaurants"). The two-story pink cottages sit atop a hillside on Middle Road, and each room has a sweeping view of Hamilton Harbour and Great Sound. Because of the central location, golf, tennis, the beach, and the ferry to Hamilton are conveniently nearby. Adding to the feeling of elegant intimacy, there are only ten guest rooms, and their classic, yet contemporary decor ranks them among Bermuda's finest. Floors are of cool pressed marble. Rattan sofas and traditional Bermudian open-beam cathedral ceilings mingle easily with English Chippendale-style chairs. The bathrooms win the award for best in Bermuda, hands down—they're huge, thoughtfully outfitted with niceties such as a scale and hairdryer. Movie stars and arbitragers, please note: These are the only hotel bathrooms in Bermuda equipped with phones. The downstairs rooms are one-bedroom suites, upstairs, you have deluxe studios; each has a kitchenette and a well-stocked private bar. To make your honeymoon home even more enjoyable, you get a continental breakfast of flaky rolls and croissants from the Inn's pastry shop, the morning local paper, and fresh flowers. In your minifridge, you'll find fresh milk and orange juice daily. All this—plus Bermuda's finest restaurant next door. Honeymoon package: Seven days / six nights (CP): $1,263.60 to $1,587.60 per couple (high season). Includes bottle of champagne, cocktails in the bar each evening, admission to Oasis nightclub, glass-bottom boat cruise, and a honeymoon cake. Call for low-season rates.

HOUSEKEEPING COTTAGES AND GUEST HOUSES: If you want seclusion —and you want it right on the beach, **Marley Beach Cottages**, P.O. PG278, Paget 6, Bermuda (tel. 809/236-1143 or 236-8910; reservations: tel. 516/482-6272 in NY; toll free 800/247-2447), could be just the ticket. The small (11-unit) group of cottages cluster around a lovely pool and Jacuzzi, all perched on a bluff overlooking the south shore and Marley Beach. (Because of the breathtaking location scenes from *Chapter Two* and *The Deep* were filmed here.) Marley Beach itself appears in many travel photos: It is a deep pocket of pink sand, sheltered by jagged boulders and casuarinas. The property is about five miles from Hamilton, two miles from the Southampton Princess. Every one of the pink cottages, offers a spectacular view of the sea, rocks, and covelets. Owned and operated by June and Giff Stanton, the resort (formerly known as the Cottages at Marley Beach) is personable, informal, and relaxed. All of the rooms have been rebuilt over the past year, and each has slightly different layout and furnishings. All come with fully equipped kitchens—right down to the toaster and butter knives. Top choice for honeymooners would be the spacious Sandcastle Studio, with its beige tile floors, bright chintz upholstery, rattan furnishings, and jaunty awning that unfurls over the terrace facing the ocean. Or how about "Heaven"—a privately owned cottage that's often for rent. It has a fireplace and fantastic water views. Honeymoon package: Eight days / seven nights (EP): $604.80 to $864 per couple for the Sandcastle Studio. Includes a bottle of wine. "Heaven" apartment: $122.47 to $174.96 per couple per night. Many other charming accommodations are available.

    Clear View Cottages, 10 Sandys Lane, Hamilton Parish 2–10, Bermuda (tel. 809/293-0484; reservations: toll free 800/468-9600), are romantic—and a good deal too! Located on Bermuda's north shore near Bailey's Bay and Flatts Village, and just five miles from St. George's, the pink-painted cottages face seaward from a rolling green hillside. Each of the 11 units is different—some are studios, others one-bedrooms, all have either a full kitchen or kitchenette, as well as a veranda or patio (some even have fireplaces). Each is air-conditioned and comes with a TV. Rooms have an airy, Bermudian feel, with exposed-beam cathedral ceilings, peacock-style wicker chairs, and decorative wicker elephants that double as tables. Everything is fresh, clean, and inviting. Since no meals are included, you can cook your meals in the kitchen or the barbecue grills on the terraces, arrange to dine in Clear View's restaurant, or try any of the other fine dining spots on the island. Clear View has two large pools, there's good snorkeling and swimming in the waters just off shore as well as at nearby Shelly Bay Beach, and a scenic route for jogging along the old railroad path down at the water's edge. Honeymoon package: Eight days / seven nights (EP): $801.36 to $876.96 per couple. Includes wine and fresh flowers.

Astwood Cove, 49 South Rd., Warwick 7–06, Bermuda (tel. 809/236-0984; reservations: tel. 617/879-8102 or toll free 800/225-2230 nationwide; 800/982-4770 in Massachusetts). Built around an 18th-century dairy farm (some of the original structures have been incorporated into the property), Astwood Cove is a cluster of 18 pristine white apartments that surround a free-form pool. Set on a low hill on Bermuda's south shore, the property overlooks woods and the sea. Astwood Cove is owned and operated by Gaby and Nicky Lewin, who make their guests feel welcomed and comfortable. The accommodations include studios and suites, all with air conditioning, ceiling fans, and private terraces or patios. Fully equipped, the kitchens come with fine English bone china, wine glasses—even salt and pepper shakers. Standard rooms are at pool level; superior rooms occupy the second story and have high cathedral ceilings. Lush green gardens set off the crisp white paint of the buildings: You'll find not only brilliant flowers, but also herbs such as rosemary, thyme, and dill, while an orchard supplies fresh grapefruits, bananas, loquats, and peaches in season. Just across the road, you can swim at Astwood Cove beach, where you follow the footpaths through the casuarinas to pocket-size, private dollops of sand surrounded by limestone boulders. Honeymoon package: Eleven days / ten nights (EP): $496.80 to $648 per couple (winter); $820.80 to $972 per couple (summer). Includes fruit bowl, bottle of wine, flowers, and one free sauna.

Loughlands Guest House and Cottage, 79 South Rd., Paget 6–06, Bermuda (tel. 809/236-1253). This big white house with green shutters on the crest of a hill in Paget exudes charm and character. The foyer is crammed with magnificent antiques— a towering grandfather clock, Chinese rugs, and bibelots tucked on the sideboard. The main house has 18 guest rooms; there are also seven rooms in the cottage. Although rooms differ slightly, all have private bath. You'll find richly old-fashioned touches such as chenille bedspreads, lace tablecloths, chintz draperies, and quilted floral bedspreads. Bathrooms retain their original 1920s mosaic tiles. The feeling is one of homey contentment; not posh, but eminently comfortable. Rooms in the cottages offer more privacy, but less ambience. Since the property rambles over nine acres, you'll definitely think yourselves staying at a private Bermudian estate. There's a new tennis court and a large swimming pool; Elbow Beach is just minutes away. Honeymoon package: None. Rates (CP): $64.80 to $97.20 per couple per night.

4. Romantic Restaurants in Hamilton

Bermuda offers everything from cozy British pubs where you can bend your elbow with a pint of Watneys on tap to elegant dining palaces that are truly international in scope.

Be sure to try some Bermudian dishes during your stay. Most menus feature "Bermuda fish"—the fresh catch of the day, usually grouper, snapper, or rockfish generally served pan-fried or broiled. Another specialty is fish chowder, served with a flourishing addition of black rum and spicy sherry peppers. If you honeymoon between September and April, you'll want to savor the succulent Bermuda lobster, or "guinea chicks"—small lobsters that are very tender and sweet. More local favorites include mussel pie, conch stew, Hoppin' John (black-eyed peas and rice), and shark hash—it's quite savory, and served on toast. To wash it all down, order rum swizzles (potent blends of rum with fruit juices), or a Dark and Stormy (made with black rum and ginger beer). Because so much of the foodstuffs are imported, restaurant prices tend to be quite high: Figure that a lunchtime hamburger at the Bermudian equivalent of a coffee shop will run about $6.95 per person. Many restaurants require men to wear jackets and ties in the evenings; ask when you make reservations. Also note that some hotels offer dine-around programs with associated properties.

Most restaurants automatically add a service charge of 15% to your bill to cover gratuities. Ask the waiter if you are not sure. To whet your appetite, pick up a copy of *Dining Out in Bermuda,* sold in most local bookstores. It costs $2 and lists complete menus and prices for Bermuda's most popular restaurants.

For convenience, we've grouped all the Hamilton restaurants together, followed by other dining spots around Bermuda.

EXPENSIVE: Once Upon A Table, 49 Serpentine Rd., just off city hall (tel. 295-8585). Old Bermuda is alive and well at this charmer in Hamilton located in a former private residence. The Victorian surroundings seem made for romance: full-length lace portieres frame the windows, bentwood chairs surround tables set with pale pink linens, archways separate the different rooms, paintings of flowers counterpoint blossoms on your table. Although the menu highlights continental dishes, you also will find intriguing Bermudian specialties, such as shark hash or corn fritters. The chef has a delicate hand with fish, such as the perfectly poached grouper in fresh sorrel sauce, accompanied by broccoli, new potatoes, and carrots. Other favorites include duck à l'orange, rack of lamb, or chateaubriand for two. The restaurant pulls out all stops for dessert: chocolate mousse, served with a sauce anglais; a pear poached in sauterne, aswim in raspberry sauce. Dinner for two, from $80 to $100 with drinks.

Located up a tall brick staircase from Front Street, the **Penthouse,** Front Street (tel. 292-3414), is one of Bermuda's most elegant restaurants. The place practically has two identities. At noontime, it is the power center for Bermuda's elite. The prime minister and various members of parliament often lunch here. But in the evening, the Penthouse transforms itself into a seductive rendezvous for lovers. The blue Souleiado fabric creates a soft, warm decor, along with the fresh flowers on the table and mirrored ceilings. Try to get one on the cushy booths that line the walls. The menu has international flair, with a decided French accent. Start with the lobster bisque with cognac or shrimps on a bed of spinach, served in puff pastry (appetizers $5.25 to $12). As your entrée, consider the pan-fried sea scallops ($27) or rack of ramb ($51 for two people). A suitable finale will be the crêpes Suzette, flamed tableside. Their wine list is superb and, thanks to careful buying, extremely reasonably priced, including a fine St. Emilion 1983 for $14. Most notably, if you have a yen for a special dish, the Penthouse chef will prepare it for you, if the ingredients are in-house. Dinners will run $80 to $100 a couple, plus wine.

MODERATE: Loquats, 95 Front St. (tel. 292-4507). Light and breezy, this is one of the only restaurants in Bermuda that feels distinctly tropical. Here, you'll enjoy a really nice dinner that won't break your budget. Located on the second story of a Front Street building, Loquats takes advantage of its setting by placing a few tables out on the white-pillared terrace for al fresco dining with a glorious view of Hamilton Harbour. Inside, the main dining room is airy, with a high cathedral ceiling, light-wood floors, potted orchids, back-lit louvred Bermuda shutters, and stucco walls. The menu is witty: "Dunk and crunch" is raw veggies with a dip ($5), while "muscargot" translates as snails stuffed into mushroom caps ($8.50). They also serve a definitively hearty fish chowder and a tender, meaty marinated conch salad. Entrées emphasize specialties from the charcoal grill and rôtisserie: Cornish hen, baby back ribs, filet mignon, or scampi ($13.50 to $21.50). You can also have a simple burger for $8. Details count for a lot, and the guiding hand in the kitchen knows it. You can order good wines by the glass: a Pouilly Fumé for $4.75, or a Sutter blush zinfandel for $3.50. Desserts, known on the menu as sweet afterthoughts, are the sort of tummy-pleasing favorites you wish mom used to make: apple brown betty with whipped cream, a hot fudge brownie, or pecan pie ($3.50 each). And yes, they serve excellent brewed decaffeinated coffee. And no, men don't need jackets or ties.

New Harbourfront, Front Street opposite the Ferry Terminal (tel. 295-4207 or 295-4527). In nice weather, dine on the terrace overlooking Front Street, watching horse-drawn carriages clop along the road and ferries chug into the landing. Indoors, the ambience is more formal, with country French tables and a baby grand piano contributing background music during the evening hours. Lunches can be casual—a tuna fish sandwich ($8.50) or broiled Bermuda fish ($16). For dinner, start off with the giant stuffed mushrooms ($9.45), then move on to the scampi riviera, sautéed in brandy with fresh tomatoes, baby clams, and herbs ($24.50); or the grilled sirloin steak ($19).

The Hog Penny, Burnaby Hill (tel. 292-2534). Bermuda's oldest English-style pub, and certainly one of its most popular, complete with wood paneling, half-timbered trim, and antique copper and brass dangling over the bar, all producing the proper dark, clubby feeling. If you fancy a pint, they have Watney Red, Webster's Yorkshire Bitter, and John Courage Lager on tap. At lunchtime, choose a Hog Penny burger ($8.50), shepherd's pie ($12.50), or one of their excellent curry dishes (from $13). Their early evening special, a three-course dinner for $17.25 per person, is an especially good deal. For dinner, try the roast prime rib ($16.75) or Bermuda fish ($15). There's lively entertainment each evening from about 9:15 p.m. until 1 a.m., and you can sing along with the guitarist or make requests.

The Lobster Pot, Bermudiana Rd. (tel. 292-6898). When you want really good seafood, head to this Hamilton restaurant with the hybrid England-by-the-South Seas decor. A bamboo screen worthy of Sadie Thompson stands at the entrance, there's a British timbered ceiling and huge hearth, while an old fishing dory and miscellaneous lobster traps loll here and there among the fishing nets. You'll find all your favorite fish dishes on the menu: from fish 'n' chips to cold lobster salad at lunch, Bermuda rockfish, tuna steak, and, of course, Bermuda lobster and guinea chicks in season. Lunch entrées priced from $5; dinner entrées from $16.25 to about $27 for the lobster or guinea chicks.

Fisherman's Reef, Burnaby Hill, opposite the Flagpole (tel. 292-1609). At this nautical motif restaurant, you'll feel as if you're dining 20,000 leagues under the sea, thanks to the portholes and illuminated slides of fish that form the backdrop. You can choose your own Maine lobster from the tank out front. The menu also lists all your favorite fish, plus steak and veal specialties. Fish entrées priced from $14.50; steaks from $18. Or order an aptly named "Bermuda Triangle," a combo plate with a filet mignon, broiled fresh fish, and grilled scampi.

Julie Fong's, Pitts Bay Road, across from the Princess Hotel (tel. 295-2167). The decor at this newly opened oriental restaurant is stunning. Black-and-gold lacquer panels hang on the walls, white Chinese lanterns illuminate the pagoda-like central area, and booths are set off behind bamboo partitions. The menu is mostly Chinese, but also features some dishes from Vietnam—where the owner was born. Start off with spare ribs or hot-and-sour soup ($3.75 to $5). Entrées ($13.50 to $16.75) include shredded beef with vegetables, beef satay, or hot and spicy shrimp with scallops.

INEXPENSIVE: Portofino, Bermudiana Road (tel. 292-2375 or 295-6090). Come for a touch of the old country. A portrait of Mona Lisa grins from the wall, wine bottles hang from the ceiling, and posters of pasta and the Piazza San Marco clue you in that the name of the game here is pizza. Order up a Marathon, with tomatoes, mozzarella cheese, ham, mushrooms, red and green peppers, and olives ($8) or a vegetarian pie with artichokes, green peppers, and mushrooms ($8). All are excellent. They also have reasonably priced pasta and veal dishes, priced $8 to $15.

5. Nightlife in Hamilton

Currently the hot spot in Bermuda is **Oasis,** with a disco nightclub. At 69 Front Street, tel. 292-3379 or 292-4978. **The Club** (tel. 295-6693) is also popular; it's on Bermudiana Road. At each, the cover charge is about $15 per couple; jackets required for men. At **The Princess** in Hamilton (tel. 295-3000), the Gazebo Lounge with its wraparound views of the city offers different shows nightly. At 9:30 p.m., it's curtain's up on local performers such as singer / comedian Gene Steede, singer George Smith, or the Bermuda Strollers, whose act combines calypso, reggae, R & B, and humor. At 10:30 p.m., there's a Broadway-style revue featuring singing and dancing. Cover charge is $27 per person, which includes two drinks.

6. Romantic Restaurants Elsewhere in Bermuda

EXPENSIVE: **Tom Moore's Tavern,** Harrington Sound Road, Walsingham's Bay (tel. 293-8020). It's hard to imagine a more poetically romantic locale than this Bermuda residence dating back to the 17th century. Here, under a giant calabash tree in the front yard, the Irish poet Thomas Moore is said to have written his farewell to the lady and the island he loved: "Farewell to Bermuda, and long may the bloom / Of the lemon and myrtle its vallies perfume . . ." The restaurant has been beautifully restored and refurbished, and everything reflects the utmost good taste. Seated in a tapestry-covered chair, you'll dine off the finest bone china from Luxembourg and crystal from Germany. The cuisine features superb renditions of classic French recipes, such as oysters poached in champagne and quail stuffed with pâté, truffles, and morels, and baked in a delicate puff pastry. Very expensive, but worth it. Count on spending at least $100 for two, with wine.

Built in 1727 of coral stone and cedar, **Fourways,** No. 1 Middle Rd., Paget (tel. 236-6517), was the private home of the Harvey family for two centuries. Today, meticulously restored, it retains its classic Bermudian charm and ranks as one of Bermuda's most celebrated restaurants. In the main dining room, polished brass chandeliers hang from the massive cedar beams, coral stone archways create intimate nooks, while candlelight, fresh flowers, and classical music complete the haute ambience. The food lives up to its reputation for finesse. The rich lobster bisque is flamed with cognac; ceviche gains a colorful new twist when made with white sea scallops, pearl-gray swordfish, and rosy salmon. Main dishes include a roast duckling with a poached pear, chateaubriand for two, or chicken breasts with a subtle chive, cream, and pink peppercorn sauce. For dessert, try pure ambrosia: the individually prepared souffles, including a favorite made with Bermuda's own black rum. Open for lunch and dinner; expect to pay $100 to $130 for two.

MODERATE: **Plantation Club,** Harrington Sound Road (tel. 293-1188). Under the ownership of Christopher and Carol West, this bright yellow 1930s home with the trim white shutters has become one of Bermuda's most captivating restaurants. Fresh, springtime colors create the sunny mood of an outdoor gazebo. Hanging baskets of philodendrons and ferns overhead, and little nosegays of daisies and freesias on the tables, complete the greenhouse picture. In nice weather, you can also dine outside under the bright yellow-and-white marquee surrounded by gardens (which are spotlit at night). The menu stars a string of delectable dishes at both lunch and dinner. Luncheons are light—an assortment of sandwiches, salads, and hamburgers (priced $5 to $9.50). Dinner choices reflect creativity and panache. Hot appetizers include a mousseline of Bermuda fish served with watercress sauce, and chicken and mushrooms served in a puff pastry ($6 to $9). For your entrée, choose among such items as charcoal-broiled yellowfin tuna ($17) or lamb "loquat," a mignon of lamb grilled and accompanied by a loquat chutney ($19.50). The restaurant closes annually from mid-December through February.

Mikado Steak House, Marriott's Castle Harbour (tel. 293-2040). Tradition-loving Bermuda doesn't easily embrace trends—so it's the ultimate compliment that this brand-new restaurant at Marriott's Castle Harbour has zoomed into prominence as Bermuda's "in" spot. Make reservations far in advance—it's *that* hard to get into.

Mikado is Bermuda's only Japanese restaurant, and it is drop-dead gorgeous. The decor delights in the dramatic: The entranceway is filled with cherry blossoms and shoji screens; you enter over a little bridge that crosses a pond. Mikado features teppan-grilled items, with chicken, beef, and seafood items prepared by your chef right in front of you. Your four-course, prix-fixe meal includes miso or clear soup, salad, a shrimp or scallop appetizer, as well as your main course. Complete dinner priced from $19 to $27 per person, depending on which entrée you choose. Whatever you do, don't miss the fried ice cream for dessert. It's rolled in a crunchy coating, quick fried, and topped with honey or chocolate sauce ($3.50).

Henry VIII Pub and Restaurant, South Shore Road, Southampton (tel. 238-0908 or 238-1977). For a fine evening, try this traditional inn located conveniently near the Southampton Princess and Sonesta Hotels. The British atmosphere comes through nicely thanks to the exposed beam ceilings hung with a miscellany of brass artifacts. At lunchtime, both the atmosphere and the menu are lighthearted. In addition to salad platters and sandwiches, you'll find good pub fare, such as fish-and-chips, steak-and-kidney pie, and an excellent rendition of Bermuda's own mussel pie. Lunch for two should run about $20 per couple plus drinks. In the evening, the setting is more formal. The royal menu specialties include the court jester (an array of broiled seafood); steak Anne Boleyn, flavored with Armagnac; and prime ribs with Yorkshire pudding. In season, Henry VIII features both Bermuda lobster and guinea chicks. Dinner for two: about $60 per couple plus drinks. Also check out what's happening at "The Oak Room," the English pub right next door. In particular, try to catch pianist Jimmy Keys, who plays requests and really knows how to get the audience involved.

Fisherman's Wharf, Somers Wharf, St. George's (tel. 297-1515). One of the nicest choices for seafood in Bermuda's east end. You'll know the catch is fresh—at the dock just outside, the fishing boats tie up, along with glamorous yachts from all over the world. In nice weather, you can dine outside overlooking the harbor; inside, the decor continues the nautical ambience with captain's chairs at the tables, and fish nets hanging from the ceiling. Start off with a Bermuda fish chowder, liberally laced with rum and sherry peppers, then savor some rockfish ($17), guinea chicks ($25), or a filet mignon and shrimp combo ($21). For a spectacular finale, order the banana fritters, flamed with Bermuda black rum.

INEXPENSIVE: Dennis's Hideaway, St. David's (no phone). This simple, family-run place is the place if you want to try real Bermudian food: from chowders and conch fritters, to shark hash, mussel pie, fresh Bermuda fish, turtle steaks, and conch stews. Outside, you'll dine at large, family-style tables. No liquor is sold. Dinner will be about $20 to $30 per couple.

7. Nightlife Elsewhere in Bermuda

When you want big-time entertainment and a lavish show, head over to the extravaganzas at the **Southampton Princess.** Greg Thompson's "Follies" is a glittering salute to the best of Broadway, with talented singers and dancers performing numbers from hit shows like *Grease, West Side Story,* and *Cabaret.* Showtime is 10:30 p.m.; admission is $29 per person, which includes two drinks. For reservations, tel. 238-2555. Also at the Southampton Princess, you can catch "Bermuda Is Another World," a dinner show celebrating the music and dance of the island. Doors open at 6:30; the four-course dinner is served at 7 p.m. Tickets cost $25 per person. For reservations, tel. 238-2555.

Chapter XXVI

BONAIRE

1. Practical Facts
2. Romantic Interludes
3. Honeymoon Hotels and Hideaways
4. Romantic Restaurants
5. Nightlife

IF YOU CRAVE an uncrowded and unspoiled island for your honeymoon—this is it! The flamingoes outnumber the people on Bonaire.

Located 50 miles off the coast of Venezuela, Bonaire is the second-largest island in the Netherlands Antilles. It ranks as one of the best diving destinations in the world, but not all of the arid coral reef's allure lies beneath the crystal-clear waters. Bonaire has couple-size coves, idyllic beaches, and dramatic vistas. Its greatest attraction, though, is a totally unhurried atmosphere.

The white-trimmed, ocher-colored buildings in the miniature capital of Kralendijk on the west coast provide a clue to the island's colonial heritage. Bonaire was discovered in 1499 by Amerigo Vespucci; Spain, Holland, France, and England vied for possession until 1816, when the Dutch took permanent possession.

Kralendijk is just a few blocks long, but it provides the center for all activity on the island. One of its two main streets runs along the waterfront, where the casual open-air restaurants are located. Stop in at Karel's Beachfront Bar, overlooking the protected harbor and the uninhabited islet of Klein Bonaire. It's just the place to ease into your vacation, and to watch for the green flash at sunset.

Diving dominates the activity (and the conversation) on Bonaire, where you'll be able to see coral formations and improbably colored fish along the beach right in front of your hotel. This is a protected environment; the Bonaire Marine Park encompasses all land and water from the high water tidemark to a depth of 200 feet. Many of the best dive sites lie immediately off-shore.

But there are things to see above the high-water mark, too, so rent a car or jeep and head for the hills. Bring a mask and snorkel, though. The island is only 24 miles long and less than 7 miles at its widest point; all roads eventually lead to the beach, and there will be plenty of opportunities to stop for a swim.

The northwest part of the island is mountainous, with desert-like terrain studded with giant cactus that soar as high as 30 feet. The road out of town winds along the curving coast, before it begins to climb through the hills. At Gotomeer, a salt-water lake, you can usually spot hundreds of flamingoes flaunting their pink plumage quite close to the road. You'll continue to climb, until the road crests along a ridge called "Para Mira," where there's an observation point with panoramic views in all directions. Down below, you'll see the orange roofs of Rincon, Bonaire's oldest village, which was settled in the early 1600s, and the road that leads from the town to the entrance of Washington/Slagbaai National park, a 15,000-acre wildlife preserve is clearly visible.

The park's northern coast is made up of volcanic rock cliffs and wildly desolate bays that are popular spots for hiking, picnicking, and sunbathing. It's impossible to swim off the rugged coral cliffs, but if you continue on to the secluded coves along the western edge of the park, you'll find a number of private, protected beaches.

The southern part of Bonaire is as flat as a pancake, except for the mounds of snow-white salt crystals of the Antilles International Salt Company. Within the salt-works property, there are protected breeding grounds for more than 10,000 flamingoes. Access is strictly prohibited, but from the road, you can often see hundreds of the birds taking off for Venezuela in the sunset.

At the southern tip of the island, the coral-hued sands of the Pink Beach attract beachcombers. Although this is the longest stretch of beach on Bonaire, it's not unusual to have it all to yourself. On the opposite coast, the shores of the almost completely landlocked Lac Bay are piled with conch shells, and its waters form a natural aquarium filled with exotic marine life.

There's not much nightlife on Bonaire, but that doesn't mean that everything stops when the sun goes down! The scuba divers are still out there, and if you walk along the beach, you'll be able to see the torches of the night divers flickering underwater.

In the evening, Kralendijk's two main streets throng with people, and the downtown area comes to life. Music spills from the al fresco bars and restaurants, and the town takes on a carnival air. It doesn't last long, though, and soon the only music you'll hear will be from E Wowo, Bonaire's only disco. If you're determined to stay up late, head for either the Bonaire Beach or Flamingo Beach Hotel. Each has a small casino that stays open until just before the sunup.

1. Practical Facts

GETTING THERE: U.S. citizens need proof of citizenship and a return or continuing ticket. Although a passport is preferred, an authenticated birth certificate or a voter registration card is also accepted. The departure tax is $5.75 per person for those returning to the United States; the tax is $2.75 for departures that include an overnight stay on Aruba.

American Airlines provides daily flights from New York to Aruba and Curaçao, with an **ALM Antillean Airline** connection to Bonaire. ALM offers flights from New York on Friday, by way of Haiti. **Eastern Airlines** provides daily flights from Miami to Aruba and Curaçao, with an ALM connection to Bonaire. ALM also has several daily interisland flights to Bonaire from Aruba And Curaçao. In season, you can also often find reasonably priced direct charters; ask your travel agent for details.

Only small planes could land at the Flamingo International Airport until a new refueling facility was opened in late 1986. The Bonaire Government Tourist Office is hopeful that the new facility will result in more direct flights from the United States in the near future.

Bonaire's hotels are just minutes from the Flamingo International Airport; the taxi fare is approximately $5.

GETTING AROUND: Taxis don't have meters; the rates are based on your destination, rather than the mileage. Rates are fixed by the government; sample fares are posted at the airport. You should always confirm fares with drivers before you ride.

A **rental car** is almost a necessity on Bonaire; there's no public transportation, and taxi rides to scattered points of interest are expensive. There are a number of rental

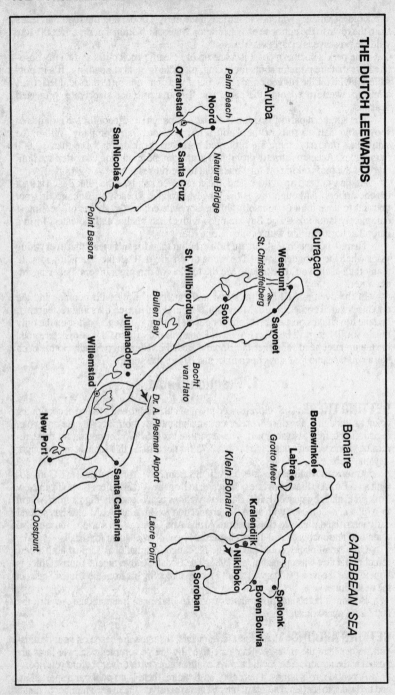

companies on Bonaire; car and jeep rentals run approximately $30 a day; scooters are approximately $25 a day. Driving is on the right-hand side, as it is in the United States. Bonaire uses international road signs.

LANGUAGE: Bonaire's native tongue is "Papiamento," a language which evolved from Spanish, Dutch, and Portuguese and combines a sprinkling of African and French, as well as Caribbean Indian dialects. You won't experience a language problem, though. Most Bonaireans are multilingual, speaking several languages including Dutch, Spanish, and English.

MONEY: The currency of the Netherlands Antilles is the guilder (NAF), which fluctuates on the world market. At this writing, there are 1.77 guilders to the dollar.

The guilder is divided into 100 cents, and there are coins of 1 cent, 2½ cents, 5 cents (square nickel), 10 cents, 25 cents, and the 1 and 2½ guilder coins. Bank notes are issued in denominations of 1, 2 ½, 5, 10, 25, 50, 100, 250, and 500 guilders.

If you also travel to Aruba, don't let the square coin confuse you! In Bonaire and Curaçao the square coin is a nickel; in Aruban currency it's a 50-cent piece.

U.S. dollars are accepted everywhere on the island. Although the hotels accept major credit cards, many restaurants and shops require cash payment.

WEATHER: The climate in Bonaire is dry and sunny, and it's always summer there. The temperature hovers at a warm 82°, cooled by pleasant trade winds. There's only a slight change of temperature from day to night, and the temperature difference between summer and winter is only 2° or 3°. The average rainfall is 22 inches per year, which occurs in brief showers during the months of October, November, and December. This isn't truly a rainy season, though, and if you do seek shelter, you'll be able to get right back onto the beach. The island lies completely outside the hurricane belt.

CLOTHING: Cool, casual, and informal clothes are the rule in Bonaire, for both men and women. You'll practically live in a bathing suit—so bring a couple with you. Although some women dress for dinner in sundresses, jackets for men are rarely seen.

TIME: Bonaire keeps Atlantic Standard Time all year long. That means that during the winter, it's one hour later than it is in U.S. east coast cities; during the summer, when U.S. cities observe Daylight Saving Time, the time is the same.

TELEPHONES: You can call Bonaire direct from the mainland United States. The international dialing code is 011; the area code is 599-7; then dial the four-digit local number. When making calls in Bonaire, just dial the four-digit local number.

You can make local and international telephone calls through hotel operators. The average price for a three-minute call to the mainland United States is approximately $10.

SHOPPING: U.S. Customs regulations allow U.S. citizens a $400 duty-free quota.

Most of Bonaire's shops are located along Kaya Grandi in Kralendijk. Although Spritzer & Fuhrmann and Littman Jewelers have small shops located there, for the most part, the shopping in Bonaire is for inexpensive items, especially printed T-shirts. Two of the best boutiques are located in the Flamingo Beach Hotel and the Bonaire Beach Hotel; the dive shops carry the latest in snorkel, scuba, and photography gear. Local arts and handcrafts include wood carvings and jewelry made from black coral, and silver and gold jewelry decorated with flamingo motifs. Shop hours are from 8 a.m. to noon and 2 to 6 p.m., daily except Sunday.

SIGHTSEEING: A number of sightseeing operations offer tours of the island and

Washington/Slagbaai National Park, including **Archie Tours & Transport** (tel. 8630), **Bonaire Sightseeing Tours** (tel. 8300), and **Flamingo Tours** (tel. 8310). Half-day island tours are priced at approximately $15; day-long excursions to the national park cost $35.

HOW TO GET MARRIED IN BONAIRE: Although Bonaire extends a warm and cordial welcome to just-married couples, you won't be able to say "I do" while visiting. Marriages are permitted only if one of the partners has been a resident of Bonaire for at least one year.

FOR FURTHER INFORMATION: Contact: **Bonaire Tourist Bureau,** Kaya Grandi, Kralendijk, Bonaire, N.A. (tel. 011/599-7/8322 or 011/599-7/8649). **Bonaire Tourist Bureau,** 275 Seventh Ave., New York, NY 10001 (tel. 212/242-7707).

2. Romantic Interludes

Bonaire is for couples who love the outdoors, above or below the high-water mark!

You'll probably get the urge to at least try **diving** while you're in Bonaire. Introductory dive programs and resort courses run about $80. You'll learn everything you need to know about equipment and technique in the morning, and you'll be diving in the afternoon. Contact the **Bonaire Scuba Center** at the Bonaire Beach Hotel & Casino (tel. 8448), **Dive Bonaire** at the Flamingo Beach Hotel & Casino (tel. 8285), or **Captain Don's Habitat** (tel. 8290).

All of the dive operations on Bonaire offer specially priced dive packages; snorkelers and nondivers can go out on the dive boats on a space-available basis for approximately $12 per person.

You can bring home one-hour videos of your underwater escapades shot by Jerry Schnabel at **Photo Bonaire** (tel. 8285) at the Flamingo Beach Hotel, or Andre Nahr at **Sand Dollar Dive and Photo** (tel. 8738) at the Sand Dollar Beach Club.

Rent a jeep (a car will do), and "safari" through the 15,000-acre **Washington/Slagbaai National Park,** located at the northern tip of the island. You'll discover an ever-changing landscape, waves crashing against coral cliffs on the northern coast, and idyllic beaches with mysterious caverns and caves to the west. The roads are rugged and dusty, but safe and well marked.

Flamingos usually congregate near the beach at Playa Funchi (also one of the best picnicking, swimming, and snorkeling spots on the island) and in the brackish waters of Gotomeer. Whether you're a serious "birder" or not, you can't help but be awed by the unusually large numbers of birds (including brightly colored parakeets) that appear in the early morning and late afternoon at Put Bronswinkel, Posi Mangel, and Salinja Slagbaai.

The park is open seven days a week from 8 a.m. to 5 p.m., except for major holidays. Admission is $2 per person.

You can rent a **sailboard** or **sunfish** for $10 per hour, or make arrangements for single or double **waterskiing** for $35 per hour through the **Poseidon Nemrod Club** (tel. 8761). For $10 per person, with a four-person minimum, they'll water-taxi you over for a picnic or barbecue on the uninhabited island of Klein Bonaire. If you do go out to this 1,500-acre desert island, wear running shoes (not sandals) and a hat. There's a rough coral beach, and the cactus doesn't provide shade from the sun. Poseidon can also arrange full- or half-day sailing charters and sunset cruises. **Karel's Watersports** (tel. 8434) opposite the Zeezicht Restaurant, and run by its owners, rents couple-size motorboats for approximately $10 per hour, and everything you need for waterskiing for $35 per hour.

Pack a basket with Dutch cheese, breads, some wine, or a bottle of champagne, and head for a picnic on your own **private beach.** There are so many spots on Bonaire that you can have all to yourselves, that it may be hard for you to choose. It could be at Boca Cocolishi, in the national park, with its protected swimming basin and black-sand beach. Perhaps you'd prefer Lac Bay or the Pink Beach at the southern end of the island.

The boulder-strewn, white-sand beach at out-of-the-way Nukove, on the western coast, may be the most romantic spot on Bonaire. Waves lap the sands that seem to sparkle, and a cooling breeze rustles through the greenery shading the fringes. Off a little-used road, just before Playa Funchi, Nukove is well known to the scuba divers who begin shore dives there. It has to be the diving community's best-kept secret.

3. Honeymoon Hotels and Hideaways

Bonaire offers a wide range of accommodations, from resort facilities to small waterfront bungalows, apartments, and condominiums. You won't find any high-rises; most accommodations don't have telephones or TV in the rooms; many aren't air-conditioned. There is a 5% government room tax and a 10% service charge on all room rates. The service charge on food and beverages is 10% to 15% in lieu of gratuities at the hotels.

All accommodations listed are within a mile of Krajendijk, the capital. High season runs from about December 15 to April 15; low-season rates are about 20% to 30% lower. Prices quoted reflect the spread between low- and high-season rates.

Relaxed and casual, the **Flamingo Beach Hotel & Casino**, Kralendijk, Bonaire, N.A. (tel. 011/599-7/8285; U.S. reservations, tel. 607/277-3484 or toll free 800/367-3484), perfectly captures the mood and feeling that pervades Bonaire. The architecture is Spanish style, with red-tile roofs, white stucco walls, and dark-wood trim; the decor is tropical, with cool cotton fabrics in floral prints. All 150 rooms are air-conditioned, with sheltered patios or balconies. There's an intimate feel to this beachfront resort, which includes a freshwater swimming pool and secluded outdoor Jacuzzi. Its "barefoot casino" is housed in a beautifully restored manor house, a historic Bonairean landmark.

The dining facilites are outstanding. In particular, breakfast at the Calabas Terrace is a real treat: fresh muffins and pastries, and mounds of sliced tropical fruits are just the beginning. Dive Bonaire operates from a pier on the grounds. Honeymoon package: Eight days/seven nights (EP): $579 to $895 per couple. Includes deluxe accommodations, a bottle of champagne, two-hour cruise, round-trip airport transfers.

Bonaire Beach Hotel & Casino, P.O. Box 34, Bonaire, N.A. (tel. 011/599-7/8448; U.S. reservations: tel. 212/840-6636 or toll free 800/223-9815). This self-contained resort is located on Playa Leche, a 600-foot, sugar-white sand beach. The 145 air-conditioned rooms and suites occupy 11 attractive low-rise buildings that sprawl across 12 landscaped acres. The open-air Beach Bar is really two bars in one; one side faces the beach, the other the sun-shaded patio. The rooms are simply furnished and decorated with nautical artwork and motifs. The Bonaire Scuba Center operates from a pier on the grounds. Honeymoon package: Eight days/seven nights (EP): "The Snorkel Honeymoon" costs $830 to $980 per couple, including three guided snorkel trips. "Learn to Dive Honeymoon" runs $1,336 to $1,488 per couple, including a complete certification course. Rates also include complimentary in-room flowers and wine.

Cap'n Don's Habitat / Hamlet, P.O. Box 88, Bonaire, N.A. (tel. 011/599-7/8290; U.S. reservations: tel. 802/496-5067 or toll free 800/345-0322). "Habitat is a concept—an attitude—not a hotel," philosophizes Captain Don, who runs this unique diving- and nature-oriented retreat. Lush vegetation and landscaped palms, flowering plants, and bougainvillea ensure a sense of privacy for fewer than 50 guests. Loll in a hammock, or enjoy the companionship of kindred spirits at the open-air restaurant and bar. Habitat offers comfort in a natural environment; there are economy accommodations with private baths, nine two-bedroom Mediterranean-style cottages, and eight air-conditioned luxury oceanfront villas. The dive operation is staffed by expert dive masters and certified instructors and is considered one of the best in the Caribbean. Honeymoon package: none. Standard eight day/seven night rate (CP): $513 to $733 per person includes breakfast, six days of boat dives, and airport transfers. Nondivers can use the à la carte plan with room rates from $373 to $502 per person per week. Full AP is available for an additional $28 per person per day.

4. Romantic Restaurants

There are a number of fine restaurants featuring a wide variety of international cuisine in Kralendijk and along the waterfront. The fish and seafood here is fresh, fresh, fresh! This is the place to try turtle steak—we've never had any prepared better.

Restaurant prices are usually listed in both guilders and U.S. dollars; a 10% to 15% service charge is frequently added to your bill. Unless otherwise noted, all restaurants are in Kralendijk.

Chibi Chibi, at the Flamingo Beach Hotel & Casino (tel. 8285/8485). Don't miss this trilevel open-air restaurant cantilevered over Calabas Reef—it's just spectacular! The reef is lighted from underwater, and you can toss bread to the best-fed fish in the Caribbean! We were hard-pressed to choose our favorite appetizer: The escargot in mushrooms ($6) in a light garlic butter sauce was superb, the gazpacho ($2.50) with crispy, crunchy, garden fresh vegetables, was perfectly chilled. Seafood and steaks priced at $15 to $20. Open from 6:30 to 10 p.m. nightly. Reservations recommended.

Den Laman Aquarium Restaurant & Bar, next to the Bonaire Beach Hotel & Casino (tel. 8955). Here's a unique dining experience: A 9,000-gallon aquarium filled with sharks, moray eels, turtles, and exotic reef fish forms two walls of this restaurant. The denizens are to look at, not to eat, but you can choose a lobster from the tank on the open-air patio. Entrées range from $10 to $21. The Coral Reef combo ($15) is out of this world, and the turtle steak ($14) may be the best in the Caribbean. Open from 6 till 11 p.m. nightly, except Tuesdays. Reservations recommended.

Zeezicht Restaurant & Bar, overlooking the harbor and Klein Bonaire (tel. 8434). This popular hangout exudes lots of character; it's been operated by the same family since 1929. Because of the fine views, prime tables are on the veranda; inside, the decor is crisp, white, and nautical, with lamps made of foot-long conch shells hanging over the bar. Seafood is the specialty here. If you can't make up your mind, try the Special no. 2 ($15)—a smorgasbord of lobster, conch, oysters, shrimp, and octopus. Breakfast ranges from $2 to $4; lunch from $5 to $10; complete dinners from $10 to $20. The menu is varied with the emphasis on seafood. Open daily from 8 a.m. to 11 p.m. No reservations taken.

Lisboa Terrace, in the Hotel Rochaline (tel. 8286). The whitewashed walls with classic arches frame travel poster-like views of the fish market, the harbor, and Klein Bonaire. It's a casual place, featuring local seafood dishes and special pizzas. Go for the Rochaline Special Appetizer ($6), half of a melon-size avocado literally stuffed with shrimp, and the special broiled lobster ($21.50), indescribably delicious. Other appetizers priced under $4. Entrées priced from $7 to $12. Open daily from 8 a.m. to 11 p.m. Reservations recommended.

Egretta Bar & Restaurant, located in the Lac Bay area of Sorobon and well worth the 15-minute drive it takes from Kralendijk to get there. The decor is an eclectic mix of cactus, European antiques, and noisy macaws, and it works beautifully. The luncheon menu features homemade soups and Dutch-style sandwiches priced at less that $4. Dinner entrées priced at under $15. There's no phone, but the restaurant is open daily except Monday from 8 a.m. to 11 p.m.

Bistro des Amis on Kaya L.D. Gerharts (tel. 8003 or 8770). Elegant, and excellent. Save room for the homemade ice cream. Dinner for two: $40 plus drinks. Seatings at 7 and 9 p.m.; reservations absolutely necessary. **Rendez Vouz,** on Kaya L.D. Gerharts (tel. 8454 or 8539). Vegetarian dinners priced under $8, seafood specialties under $13. Dinner from 6 to 11 p.m.; espresso and cappuccino served all evening at the bar.

5. Nightlife

Despite the focus on outdoor activities, the fun on Bonaire doesn't stop when the sun goes down. Bonaire's only disco, **E Wowow** (tel. 8998) is located on Kaya Grandi, and opens for business every night. On weekends, you can dance to live pop and soft rock at the **Pirate House,** on the second level of the Zeezicht Restaurant (tel. 8434). There's also blackjack, roulette, and slot-machine action at the **Flamingo Beach Casino** (tel. 8285 or 8485) and the **Bonaire Beach Casino** (tel. 8448) from 6 p.m. till the early morning hours.

Chapter XXVII

BRITISH VIRGIN ISLANDS

1. Practical Facts
2. Tortola
3. Virgin Gorda
4. Jost Van Dyke
5. Peter Island
6. More Suggestions in the B.V.I.

SUNSET. The three-masted barquentine cruises across the horizon, her square-rigged sails silhouetted against the crimson sun. Overhead, a black and red frigate bird gyres slowly, its seven-foot wingspan catching the rising thermal. Along the shore, fishermen haul in huge seining nets, heavy with yellowtail and grouper.

It's a scene that could have happened 300 years ago—or one that you could witness today, honeymooning in the British Virgin Islands.

Located in the Caribbean Sea about 60 miles east of Puerto Rico and right next to the United States Virgin Islands, the B.V.I. encompasses about 50 different islands. These range in size from 12-mile-long Tortola, site of Road Town, the capital, to teeny lava rock outcrops like the Indians where only the seabirds roost. Only 16 of the islands are inhabited; just 7 even offer tourist accommodations.

What makes the B.V.I. so romantic? First of all, it's the sheer number of emerald-green, palm-thatched, bougainvillea-draped islands that surround you. All of the B.V.I. (with the exception of Anegada) surround the 22-mile-long Sir Francis Drake Channel—creating a veritable pleasure bowl for vacationers, especially sailors. Stand on the deck of a boat or atop a mountain and gaze around you—your glance can take in over 20 islands at a time. Then look again. On the fringes of many of these jungled, green islands, dazzling white, coral sand beaches catch your attention.

If your honeymoon agenda includes the search for the perfect beach, you'll find many candidates here. Strands like Cane Garden Bay on Tortola, White Bay on Jost Van Dyke, the Baths on Virgin Gorda, and Deadman's Bay on Peter Island easily belong on any "Best in the World" list. Meanwhile, the warm, transparent Caribbean Sea convinces all beholders that the color blue can exist in infinite gradations.

The division of the island chain into the United States and the British Virgin Islands owes more to the whims of history than the imperatives of geography—the two groups lie less than a 45-minute ferry ride from each other. The islands were discovered by Christopher Columbus in 1493. "Very mountainous," he recorded in his diary. "And very green down to the sea. A delight to see." He was so struck by their beauty and purity, he named them after the legendary followers of St. Ursula.

For the next hundred years, the islands snoozed peacefully, ignored by the major European powers until 1595, when Sir Francis Drake led a fleet through the channel that now bears his name. The English, Dutch, and Spanish disputed possession until 1672, when England annexed Tortola.

However, the major power in these islands was an international gaggle of pirates, cutthroats, and brigands who plundered treasure ships heading from Mexico and South America to Europe. Buccaneer legends still pervade the region. Robert Louis Stevenson reportedly based Treasure Island on tales about Norman Island. The island Jost Van Dyke is named for a Dutch pirate; on Dead Chest Island, the notorious Blackbeard is said to have marooned some of his men, giving rise to the "Yo, ho, ho, and a bottle of rum" ditty.

Towards the end of the 17th century, the islands regained middle-class stability when many English planters arrived to farm the land. Today, the B.V.I. has a population of about 11,000 and is a British territory, administered by a governor appointed by the queen. Although the official language is the queen's English, warmed by West Indian accents, and pub menus highlight traditional English favorites such as fish 'n' chips and Pimm's Cup, the official currency is the U.S. dollar.

The British Virgin Islands is perfect for couples who really want to get away. Very few hotel rooms have televisions; "air conditioning" usually comes via the trade winds or Casablanca-style ceiling fans; and you won't need to ride an elevator to get to the beach. This low-key lifestyle has attracted some high-powered vacationers. Paul McCartney, Steven Spielberg, and Neil Young have all cruised the B.V.I. aboard yachts, and a crowned monarch and his queen were recently spotted on a buffet line at Peter Island.

Honeymooners who love sports and the outdoors will find plenty to do in the B.V.I. Such as sailing. What Aspen is to skiers or Mt. Everest is to climbers, the B.V.I. represents for sailors—namely, the best in the world. Even if you're not sailors yourselves, you can hop aboard one of the many day sails that embark for uninhabited cays, or charter a yacht with a skipper.

Scuba divers and snorkelers will also find top-class conditions, with visibilities of 60 to 150 feet, and varied sites to explore—from underwater caves to coral forests and shipwrecks. On land, you can play tennis, saddle up for horseback riding, or take a hike.

Wherever you go, you'll discover another natural resource of the B.V.I.—its friendly people. Some friends recently rented a car on Tortola, and told the rental agent that they wanted to return the vehicle later in the evening, when the office would be closed. Was that a problem? "No problem," the agent smiled. "Just leave the keys in the car—and don't lock the door."

Now, we're not recommending that people leave keys in unlocked cars. But the story illustrates the openness and the warmth of B.V.I. residents. As you motor along, other drivers will toot their horns in greeting; children wave as they ride home on donkeys. You'll feel very welcome here—almost as though you've come home yourself.

1. Practical Facts

GETTING THERE: Americans need proof of U.S. citizenship. A valid passport is preferred; however, an authenticated birth certificate or voter registration card is also

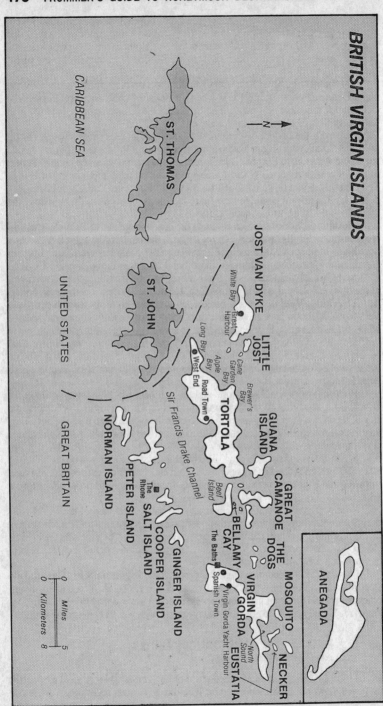

BRITISH VIRGIN ISLANDS

CARIBBEAN SEA

ST. THOMAS

N

ST. JOHN

UNITED STATES

GREAT BRITAIN

JOST VAN DYKE

White Bay
Great
Harbour

LITTLE JOST

Long Bay
Cane
Garden
Bay
Apple
Bay

West End

Brewer's
Bay

Road Town

TORTOLA

GUANA ISLAND

GREAT CAMANOE

THE DOGS

Beef
Island

BELLAMY CAY

The Baths

Virgin Gorda Yacht Harbour

Spanish Town

VIRGIN GORDA

North
Sound

EUSTATIA

NECKER

MOSQUITO

Sir Francis Drake Channel

NORMAN ISLAND

PETER ISLAND

The
Rhone

SALT ISLAND

COOPER ISLAND

GINGER ISLAND

Miles
0   5
Kilometers
0   8

ANEGADA

acceptable. There is a departure tax of $5 per person if you leave by air, $3 per person if you depart by boat.

It's easy to reach the B.V.I. from most places in the United States.

By Air

Although there are currently no direct flights from the continental United States, you can take advantage of several convenient connecting flights daily from San Juan, Puerto Rico, and St. Thomas, in the U.S. Virgin Islands.

To Tortola: The airport is located on Beef Island, at the far eastern end of Tortola. From San Juan, you can fly into the Beef Island Airport on **American Airlines, Air BVI,** and **Crownair.** From St. Thomas, you can take Air BVI or Crownair into the Beef Island Airport; the **V.I. Seaplane Shuttle** lands at West End. Consequently, the sea plane is more convenient if your hotel is on the western side of the island.

To Virgin Gorda: Both Air BVI and Crownair fly daily from San Juan and St. Thomas; American Airlines and **Eastern Metro** fly from San Juan only.

To Anegada: Air BVI flies from Beef Island, Tortola.

Since the airplanes that fly into the B.V.I. are quite small, they have limited luggage capacity. To help assure that your luggage gets on the same flight that you do, check in early and pack light. To play it safe, take a bathing suit and personal essentials with you in a small carry-on bag.

By Sea

Frequent, convenient, and inexpensive ferries—Bomba Charger, Native Sun, and Speedy's Fantasy—connect the B.V.I. with both St. Thomas and St. John in the U.S.V.I. The ferry ride takes about one hour from St. Thomas to Tortola (Road Town), about 20 minutes from St. John to Tortola (West End). The ferries are your best bet if you have a lot of luggage.

GETTING AROUND: Once you arrive in the B.V.I., you have a wide choice of transportation.

By Taxi

Taxis are available only on Tortola and Virgin Gorda. Rates between destinations are fixed by law and are charged per person, and vary according to the number of people in the cab. Rates are moderate. For example, Road Town, Tortola to the airport costs approximately $15 per couple. Although fares are reasonable, expenditures can add up if you will be taking a lot of taxis.

Rental Cars

Once again, these are only available on Tortola and Virgin Gorda. Rentals run about $30 to $45 per day. Driving is on the left. You will need a temporary B.V.I. driver's license; it costs $5 and is available from rental car agencies. To obtain one, you will need to show a valid U.S. driver's license.

Jeeps are the most fun. Rental car companies do not permit their conventional two-wheel-drive cars on some of the island back roads, which can be steep, bumpy, and curving—but which also lead to the most beautiful scenery and vistas. Jeeps allow you to explore everywhere on the islands.

LANGUAGE AND MONEY: The queen's English is spoken, often with a West Indian lilt. The U.S. dollar is the official currency. Most hotels and restaurants accept major credit cards, but ask in advance just to be sure. Travelers checks are widely accepted; personal checks are not.

WEATHER: The B.V.I. offers practically perfect year-round weather, with little variation between the seasons. Temperatures range from 77° to 85° in winter, 80° to 90° in summer. Evening temperatures run about 10° cooler. Constant trade winds provide breezy refreshment. Tropical storms might occur from late August through October. These usually pass through quickly and you can go right back to the beach.

CLOTHING: Dress tends to be very casual. Bring lightweight, comfortable clothing, including several bathing suits—you'll be living in them all day. Off the beach, local custom requires that you wear cover-ups over bathing suits. For men, jackets (no ties) are required for dinner at Little Dix Bay, Peter Island, and some other elegant restaurants, but these resorts are the exception in the B.V.I., not the rule.

TIME: The islands remain on Atlantic Standard Time all year. In winter, this means that when it is noon in New York, it is 1 p.m. in the B.V.I. In summer, when Daylight Saving Time is in effect, the time is the same in the B.V.I. as in U.S. east coast cities.

TELEPHONES: You can call the B.V.I. direct from the mainland United States. First dial 809 (the area code), then the seven-digit phone number. All B.V.I. phone numbers begin with 49. When making local calls in the B.V.I., omit the 49 and just dial the last five digits.

SHOPPING: Like everything else in the B.V.I., shopping is a relaxed experience. You'll find some fine souvenir and gift items, but nothing like the enormous range of duty-free merchandise sold by stores in the U.S. Virgin Islands. If you're interested in some real "power shopping," plan on spending your last day in St. Thomas before flying home.

Best bets in the B.V.I. include unique island items—B.V.I. Sea Salt, dapper T-shirts emblazoned with the Union Jack, and Pusser's Rum, distilled according to the original recipe used by the Royal Navy. Also, since there is no duty levied on British imports, you can find bargains on English china, fabrics, and food (such as Fortnum and Mason teas). Liquor prices on Scotch whisky are quite good, but you can only bring home one liter per person duty-free.

You'll find the best selection of merchandise in Road Town, Tortola; Spanish Town, Virgin Gorda; or in boutiques in the resorts (the one at Little Dix Bay is particularly nice).

In Road Town, many of the plantation-period buildings clustered around Main Street now house interesting boutiques. Browse through—you'll find a wide choice of items that might strike your fancy, from genuine pieces of eight at the Collectors Corner to English antiques and books at Past and Presents. Carousel and the Cockle Shop stock china by Wedgwood and other English items.

Go bonkers—to **Bonkers Gallery,** this is, for high-style casual clothing imported from France, Italy, and around the world. **Carib Handprints** carries silk-screened prints handmade by local craftspeople. **The Shipwreck Shop,** located in one of the oldest buildings in Tortola, sells baskets, hammocks, and other tropical handcrafts from around the world. **Sunny Caribbee,** a spice and herb shop, offers such invaluable elixirs as "West Indian Hangover Cure" and "Arawak Love Potion." **Zenaida** specializes in fabrics, artifacts, and jewelry from the exotic corners of Africa, Asia, and the South Pacific.

Each person can bring home $400 worth of goods to the United States duty-free. However, if you also stay in the U.S. Virgin Islands (where the duty-free allowance is $800 per person), you can buy $400 worth of merchandise in the B.V.I., plus $400 in goods in the U.S.V.I.

ABOUT ACCOMMODATIONS: That old expression about "running the gamut" applies to the assortment of accommodations available in the B.V.I.

High season runs approximately December 15 through April 15; low-season rates are about 20% to 50% lower. The price ranges quoted for hotels in this section reflect the low- and high-season rates.

At many hotels and resorts, especially in more secluded island areas, room rates are Full American Plan (AP), including breakfast, lunch, and dinner. Consider this when reviewing room rates, so you can compare the value you are getting for your money.

A 7% accommodation tax, plus a 10% to 12% service charge, will be added to hotel bills. Even at the finest resorts, rooms seldom have air conditioning, and instead are designed to rely on the cooling trade winds and ceiling fans. If air conditioning is important to you, check in advance.

One of the most romantic B.V.I. honeymoons isn't on land, but aboard a luxury yacht. More than 300 charter boats are available, either crewed or bare boat, and rates compare to those at a luxury resort. For information about yacht charter in the B.V.I., contact: **The Moorings, Ltd.,** 1305 U.S. 19 South, Suite 402, Clearwater, FL 33546, tel. 813/535-1446 (in Florida), or toll free 800/535-7289; **Caribbean Sailing Yachts, Ltd.,** Box 157, Road Town, Tortola, B.V.I., tel. 809/494-2741; **Virgin Islands Charteryacht League,** Homeport, St. Thomas, U.S.V.I. 00802, toll free 800/524-2061.

DINING OUT: Practically every restaurant worth its salt shaker requires advance reservations. In high season, these should be made several days ahead. Some restaurants —especially those that cater to boaters—ask you to place your meal orders in advance by telephone or ship-to-shore radio. Many restaurants monitor VHF Channel 16.

If you like fish, the fresh local catch is always a best bet. Finny favorites include yellowtail snapper, "old wife," grouper, and dolphin (the fish, not the mammal). And thanks to the islands' British heritage, you'll find authentic renditions of fish 'n' chips, bangers 'n' mash, and roast beef with Yorkshire pudding.

HOW TO GET MARRIED IN THE B.V.I.: The territory warmly welcomes couples who want to say "I do," and planning a B.V.I. wedding is easy.

You must be in the territory three days before you can be married. You can get an application form then at the attorney general's chambers on Main Street, Road Town. Bring along proof of identity, such as passports, birth certificates, and certified proof of marital status. Blood tests are not necessary. You must have two witnesses with you to verify receipt of the license.

After obtaining the license, you go to the registrar's office in Road Town. You can be married either by the registrar (fee is $10), or by the officiant of your choice. For details, contact: **Registrar's Office,** P.O. Box 418, Road Town, Tortola, B.V.I. (tel. 809/494-3701 or 494-3492, ext. 303/304).

FOR FURTHER INFORMATION: Contact the **B.V.I. Tourist Board.** Tortola: P.O. Box 134, Road Town, Tortola, B.V.I. (tel. 809/494-3134). New York: 370 Lexington Ave., Suite 412, New York, NY 10017 (tel. 212/696-0400). San Francisco: 1686 Union St., San Francisco, CA 94123 (tel. 415/775-0344).

2. Tortola

Although Tortola is the center of commerce and the largest of the British Virgin Islands, the site of the capital, and reigns as one of the premier yacht charter centers in the Caribbean, it remains far off the beaten path for tourists. Life's pace moves no faster than the shiny, plump brown cows that saunter home slowly for the afternoon milking. You'll find it a wonderful hideaway for relaxation—interrupted, perhaps, by some poke-around sightseeing.

What activity there is centers on Road Town, located about midway on Tortola's south coast. Road Town has been the capital of the B.V.I. since 1774; 80% of the country's population resides here. The town cheerfully and haphazardly blends the old and the new. On Main Street, where most of the shops are clustered, the many original buildings reflect traditional plantation architecture. Meanwhile, along the waterfront, state-of-the-art marina developments such as the Village Cay Marina and the Moorings boast everything for the visiting yachtsman—from haul-out and dry-dock facilities to gourmet provisioning (ripe brie, anyone?) and designer boutiques.

Tortola is easy to explore by car or Jeep. The island is small—about 12 miles long and 3 miles wide—and you could drive around it in about two hours if you didn't stop to sightsee or swim. Since Tortola is hilly inland, and flat along the coast, it's practically impossible to get lost. When in doubt, drive downhill, and you'll hit one of the main roads that circle the island.

Moving along Tortola's south coast from Road Town, the island tends to be more desert-like, bristling with loblolly pines, wild tamarind, and 12-foot-tall agave cactus that rise like sentinels across the hillsides. On the northern side, vegetation flourishes in lush profusion—mangroves along the shore, then, further inland, groves of banana trees and golden mangoes, accented by colorful outbursts of hibiscus, flamboyant, and bougainvillea. Here, small settlements like Apple Bay and Carrot Bay reflect a West Indian lifestyle.

Along Tortola's north shore, you'll also find the kind of beaches you fantasize about—broad, diamond-white, powder-soft swaths of fine, coral sands, rimmed with glossy green coconut palms that provide shade. Check out Long Bay, a sweeping strand toward Tortola's west end that's never crowded. If the surf's up, watch bronzed surfers at Little Apple Bay. Follow the steep, winding road past the ruins of an old sugar mill to Brewers Bay. The wide beach is perfect for Frisbee, while the protected harbor makes for a quiet swim.

ROMANTIC INTERLUDES: For honeymooners, Tortola is ripe with romantic promise—on land and at sea.

At 1,780 feet, **Sage Mountain** is the highest point in the Virgin Islands. You'll need a four-wheel-drive vehicle to handle the steep terrain. Take along a bottle of champagne, then follow the trails through the rain forest. If you think you've gotten to the end of the road—you haven't. Keep going until you reach the clearing about a mile below the summit. As night falls, the tiny coqui frogs start their plaintive chirp, the lights of Road Town sparkle like diamonds below, and the wraparound view takes in St. Thomas, St. John, and most of the B.V.I.

The **White Squall,** an 80-foot schooner, takes you to either the Baths (sea grottoes) on Virgin Gorda, or caves on Norman Island (tel. 4-2564). The **Shadowfax,** an elegant 60-foot catamaran and one of the fastest boats in the islands, also calls on the Baths (tel. 4-2175). Both day-cruises include lunch, libations, and time for snorkeling. It costs about $110 per couple.

Thanks to introductory **dive** programs, you can learn about scuba equipment and techniques in the morning, and be swimming with the fishes in the afternoon, on supervised, open-water dives. Cost for the introductory resort course runs about $60. On Tortola, contact **Underwater Safaris,** P.O. Box 139, Road Town (tel. 4-3235, or toll free 800/535-7289), or **Aquatic Centres,** P.O. Box 108, Road Town (tel. 4-2858/9, or toll free 800/345-6296). Full certification courses and trips for certified divers are also available.

A loaf of bread (French-style baguette), a jug of wine (some cabernet sauvignon, perhaps), and your own true love—what better way to spend a sun-kissed afternoon? Get all the gourmet fixin's at two shops that specialize in yacht provisioning: The **Ample Hamper** at the Village Cay Marina and near The Moorings (tel. 4-2784); and **The Gourmet Galley** at The Moorings (tel. 4-2332).

What a beach—a mile and a half of sparkling white sands, surrounding one of the truest, bluest harbors imaginable. It's popular, lively fun—yet very unspoiled. **Cane Garden Bay** bottom is sandy all the way out, making it perfect for water sports. Go waterskiing, or rent a Hobie cat or Windsurfer, and skitter across the bay. Then join the genial crowd that congregates under the shade of the palm trees at Rhymer's Beach Bar or Stanley's Welcome Restaurant.

Rhymer's usually features live entertainment, and you can rent Windsurfers or arrange a glass-bottom boat ride. Stanley's has a rope swing out front and Stanley himself presiding inside. The decor is memorable—a colorful assemblage of T-shirts hangs overhead, and bumper stickers plaster the walls—gifts from visitors from around the world.

HONEYMOON HOTELS AND HIDEAWAYS: Tortola offers about the widest range of accommodations in the B.V.I.—everything from full-scale resorts (with so many facilities, you might never want to leave the property), to campgrounds. In addition, room rates tend to be the most moderate in the B.V.I.

Rates quoted reflect the spread between low- and high-season prices.

Moderate

Sugar Mill Hotel, Box 425, Tortola, B.V.I. (tel. 809/495-4355; U.S. reservations: tel. 212/840-6636 or toll free 800/223-9815). Built on a hillside overlooking Apple Bay on Tortola's beach-fringed north shore, this intimate hideaway (only 20 rooms) surrounds the restored ruins of a 360-year-old rum distillery. You'll feel right at home thanks to the warmth of the American owners, Jinx and Jeff Morgan, who are also noted food and travel writers.

Contemporary, cheery, and comfortable, all rooms have balconies, kitchen facilities, and views of the sea or gardens. Decor reflects cool island casualness, with tile floors, rattan furnishings, and cotton spreads on the bed. You can borrow books from the little library, and the honor bar stays open 24 hours a day. The circular freshwater pool occupies the site of the old treadmill, and there's good snorkeling off the small but delightful beach. After a full day of activity (or serious sunbathing), the superb restaurant is a great place to come home to. "The people who are happiest here," says Jinx, "Are those who appreciate natural beauty and remain open to new experiences and people." Honeymoon package: Eight days/seven nights (EP): $698 to $1,050 per couple. Includes a bottle of champagne, a dinner for two at the restaurant, a full-day sail on a charter yacht, and more. Five-day package also available. Closed August 1 to September 30.

Set in a 50-acre estate along aptly named Long Bay Beach near Tortola's West End, **Long Bay Hotel,** P.O. Box 433, Tortola, B.V.I. (tel. 809/495-4252; U.S. reservations: tel. 212/725-5880 or toll free 800/223-5695 outside NY), offers easygoing escape, seclusion, and a low-key lifestyle. There are only 37 rooms, located in small villas and cottages sheltered here and there among the palms and hibiscus. If you want air conditioning, choose the hillside studios, which have a kitchenette, dressing area, and large balcony overlooking the sea and neighboring islands. For the best views, request a room high up on the hill. Beach buffs should opt for the cabanas, built on stilts and located just 30 feet from the water. The cabanas have an amply proportioned deck and patio, as well as a kitchenette. Both types of rooms are priced similarly, and are decorated simply, with rattan furniture and cool cotton fabrics. In addition to the mile-long beach, there's a saltwater pool, a tennis court, and two good restaurants (the one at the beach occupies a former rum distillery). Honeymoon package: Eight days/seven nights (includes some meals): $714 per couple. Includes a bottle of champagne; all breakfasts; four dinners by candlelight; unlimited free tennis and use of snorkel gear; and either an island tour or use of a self-drive Jeep for the day. Package not available from December 15 to April 15.

Treasure Isle Hotel, P.O. Box 68, Road Town, Tortola, B.V.I. (tel. 809/494-2501; U.S. reservations: tel. 212/355-6605 (call collect) or toll free 800/221-4588). Nestled into the cliffside, this self-contained resort overlooks the harbor and Sir Francis Drake Channel. It's a perfect choice for honeymooners who want to check in and find a full bevy of activities right on their doorstep—without having to bestir themselves to Road Town, just a mile away. Lush, tropical gardens surround the low-slung, contemporary-style buildings. All rooms are air-conditioned and have a private balcony with view of the harbor. Every room is painted a different color—including pinks, blues, greens, and purple,—so ask in advance if you have strong preferences. Treasure Isle appeals to many water-sports enthusiasts, since the Offshore Sailing School and an Aquatic Centres Dive Shop are located right on the premises. The facilities also include a mooring dock, squash and tennis courts, and freshwater pool (complete with a porthole, so you can peer out from under water). Although there's no beach, the resort runs trips twice a week to nearby Cooper Island, reachable by ferry for $12 per couple. Fine restaurant. Honeymoon package: None. Standard eight days/seven nights rate (EP): From $678 to $909 per couple. Includes a full-day sail on a charter yacht, free bottle of Pusser's Rum, use of rental car one day or a day trip to Virgin Gorda.

Prospect Reef Resort, P.O. Box 104, Road Town, Tortola, B.V.I. (tel. 809/494-3311; U.S. reservations: tel. 212/841-1111 (in NYC) or toll free 800/223-0888 nationwide). This stylish, contemporary resort complex is the largest in the B.V.I. (131 rooms), yet it retains an open, spacious feeling thanks to its 40 acres of beautifully landscaped grounds. You can play tennis day or night on six floodlit courts, and take lessons from the resident pro. The fully equipped health spa features Universal gym equipment, aerobics classes, plus a licensed massage therapist. For divers, an Aquatic Centres dive shop is located right on the premises. The resort also has marina facilities, a nine-hole pitch and putt course, two freshwater pools, a small but perfectly loungable sand beach—all just a few minutes from Road Town on Tortola's south coast.

The low-rise, white-painted buildings offer a range of accommodations, all tastefully decorated with rattan furniture, tile floors, and natural fabrics in cool blue and white tones. The garden rooms, facing the lagoon, are air-conditioned; the reef rooms command spectacular views across the channel. Louvred windows and sliding doors leading to terraces allow you to bring the outdoors in, complete with the rustle of palm leaves and the fragrance of oleander. Honeymoon package: Eight days/seven nights (EP): $715 to $1,055 per couple (garden rooms); $769 to $1,198 (reef studios). Includes welcome rum punch, bottle of champagne and a fruit basket, and a full-day sail to nearby islands including lunch.

Very Inexpensive

Brewers Bay Campground, Box 185, Tortola, B.V.I. (tel. 809/494-3463). If you crave the stars overhead and soft sands under your sleeping bag, then this is the place for you—located right on one of Tortola's most beautiful north shore beaches. They have all the amenities—charcoal grills, a commissary, even a bar and restaurant. Honeymoon package: None. Bare sites cost $5.35 per night, prepared sites with tents are $17.12.

ROMANTIC RESTAURANTS: Tortola's fine selection of restaurants makes dining out well worthwhile.

The Sugar Mill, Apple Bay (tel. 5-4355). The setting—an old sugar mill—would be romantic enough. But add flickering candles on the tables, original—and extremely high caliber—Haitian art on the coral stone walls, and innovative cuisine, and the Sugar Mill earns its reputation as one of the best restaurants in the islands. Caribbean—but with a California flair best describes the menu created by owners Jinx and Jeff Morgan, who have authored several cookbooks and write regularly for *Bon Apetit* magazine. Specialties include roast honey-lime duck with fried plaintains, seafood creole, and one of the tastiest conch stews around. Many of the ingredients—from fresh herbs to coconuts—are harvested right on the property. Prix-fixe, three-course dinner for two with wine: About $45.

Sky World, Meyers (tel. 4-3567). See how many islands you can count from your perch at this hilltop restaurant. On clear days, the views sweep all the way to Anegada, Virgin Gorda, and Puerto Rico. Located on Ridge Road, just ten minutes from Road Town, Sky World is open from 10 a.m. until 9 p.m. We like it best for lunch, when the menu includes light entrées such as hearty fish chowder ($4.75), conch fritters ($6.75), or pasta of the day. Or come by for cocktails, when the setting sun blazes over the Caribbean, then linger for a six-course dinner feast starring different fish and lobster entrées every day, prix fixe at $28 per person.

The Last Resort, Bellamy Cay (tel. 5-2520). This unique pub-cum-music hall is a real B.V.I. institution, so popular with yachting folk, it's hard to find room for your dinghy at the dock. (The island is also reachable by ferry from Tortola.) It's known for it's wildlife—of all varieties. Chocolate the Donkey pokes his head in through the back door to guzzle beer, cats snooze in armchairs, and a monster dwells in a corner of the ladies' room (you'll see what we mean). At 9:30 p.m., British entertainer Tony Snell puts on a wickedly funny show spoofing everything from charterboat captains to matadors and the Bermuda Triangle. The dinner menu includes homemade soups, roast beef with Yorkshire pudding, and a help yourself hot buffet. Dinner is about $40 for two; you can also just have drinks and watch the entertainment (there's a $2.50 per person cover charge.)

Fort Burt Hotel, Road Town (tel. 4-2587), built around a 300-year-old fort, specializes in Old English favorites like steak-and-oyster pie as well as fresh lobster done up four different ways, including lobster Chaucer—fit for a king in a cream sauce with caviar ($28). There is also a three-course, prix-fixe dinner priced from $16.50. In the British Navy, the "pusser" was the purser, who handed out the daily ration of grog. **The Pusser's Landing,** right on the harbor in West End (tel. 5-4554), carries out this nautical theme. The menu hits the spot with burgers, barbecue chicken, and other casual fare. Try the famous rum drinks such as "The Pusser's Pain Killer" or "Nelson's Blood"—sure to inspire feats of derring-do. Entrées priced from $6.50 to $12. For local dishes such as papaya soup, coconut chicken, and soursop sherbet, head to **Mrs. Scatliffe's** in Carrot Bay (tel. 5-4556) or **The Apple** in Little Apple Bay (tel. 5-4437). A complete dinner for two runs approximately $30 to $45 per couple plus drinks. **Brandywine Bay Restaurant,** just outside Road Town (tel. 5-2301), is set on a former private estate overlooking Drake's Channel. Great views, and the sophisticated menu highlights specialties from around the world—caviar crêpes, beef yakitori, pepperpot seafood gumbo, and some excellent pastas. Entrées priced from $15 to $20. **De Place,** Road Town (tel. 4-3885), has the best disco on the island; you can also watch satellite TV in the lounge).

3. Virgin Gorda

There are beaches, to be sure, about 20 of them. And an extraordinary seaside grotto formed from massive boulders that look like they tumbled from the hands of a giant. But what makes Virgin Gorda so special to visitors who return again and again is the sheer number of things you can do, all here on this little island most people never heard of.

Located at the eastern end of Sir Francis Drake Channel, Virgin Gorda is the second largest of the B.V.I. The island covers about 8.3 square miles and has a population of about 1,000. What makes this particular Virgin "gorda" ("fat" in Spanish) is Virgin Gorda Peak, the highest point on the island.

Most of Virgin Gorda's residents live on the southwest coast near Spanish Town, which was capital of the B.V.I. in the 18th century. But for vacationers, most of the action centers on the yacht harbors.

North Sound (officially named Gorda Sound) throbs with activity. Windsurfers and Sunfish zip across the sapphire blue waters; power boats head out for deep-sea fishing or waterskiing. Along the shore, happy hour tipplers gather in convivial waterfront bistros for some serious sunset watching.

Virgin Gorda Yacht Harbour, on the island's southwest coast, lies just a short drive from Spanish Town. The waterfront shopping center caters to boaters, with good markets, wine stores, a dive shop, and several boutiques selling resortwear and island handcrafts. Just inland in "The Valley," you'll find most of the island's services (the airport, taxi rentals), and hotels and restaurants.

ROMANTIC INTERLUDES. Great watersports and a genial, gregarious life ashore make Virgin Gorda a favorite of both sailors and landlubbers.

The famous **Baths** on Virgin Gorda's southwest coast are sea caves and grottoes formed from huge granite boulders—some as large as houses. The entrance to the caves is deceptively simple, set in a little circular palm grove that looks like a desert oasis from the tales of Ali Baba. Inside the caves, voices echo against eons of rock, and shafts of sunlight penetrate the shadows. From one cave, you can swim out to the bright turquoise sea, where more fallen stones create a surreal backdrop for snorkelers. Bring deck shoes or sneakers for rock climbing, a picnic lunch if you want to spend the day (no snack bars).

You'll find superb **snorkel** sites all around the North Sound area. Long Beach reef has huge stands of elkhorn coral. The diving is so good, Jean Michel Cousteau takes groups here. Rocky Beach (at the northeastern end of Moskito Island) offers some wonderfully spooky underwater caves. Off Eustatia Island, you can spot an ancient anchor and three cannons. Half-day snorkel trips run about $25; introductory scuba lessons cost from $60 to $85 per person. For certified scuba divers, one-tank divers are $45 to $50. Contact **Kilbrides Underwater Tours** at North Sound (tel. 4-2746) or **Dive B.V.I. Ltd.** at Virgin Gorda Yacht Harbor (tel. 5-5513).

For something different, board *Flipper*, a semisubmersible craft, for a one-hour underwater tour of Eustatia Reef (tel. 4-2746). The sea fans and gorgonians look so close, you feel that you could reach out and touch them.

Rent a Jeep—it's the best way to get to know Virgin Gorda. Head for Virgin Gorda Peak, a 1,370-foot summit. The peak area is National Park and has good hiking trails. At the southeastern end of the island, you can visit Copper Mine Point, where the Spaniards who first settled the island mined the ore. To cool off, seek out some of the secluded beaches that dot the island. Favorites include Savannah Bay, Pond Bay, and Valley Trunk Bay, a long white strand dotted with coconut palms. Jeep rentals are available through Speedy's Car Rental for $35 per day (tel. 5-5235).

HONEYMOON HOTELS AND HIDEAWAYS: The key words to describe Virgin Gorda resorts are "understated elegance." Accommodations are casual—but in the ultimate best taste.

Rates quoted reflect the spread between low- and high-season prices. Also note that most hotels on Virgin Gorda offer Full American Plan (AP).

Expensive

To our way of thinking, **The Bitter End Yacht Club**, Box 46, Virgin Gorda, B.V.I. (tel. 809/494-2746; U.S. reservations: tel. 312/944-5855), is the quintessential B.V.I. resort—exuberant, young, gregarious, with a seafaring, outdoors-loving outlook. It seems to be the Virgin Gorda good times center—dinghies chug, cocktail glasses clink, and Windsurfers whoosh through the waves. It's the perfect place for people who want a yachting atmosphere while living ashore. (If you do want to live aboard, they also have Cal 2-27 yachts complete with maid service.) Set on a hillside above North Sound, each villa has a private thatch-roofed deck overlooking the harbor; stone stairs and gravel paths crisscross gardens where hummingbirds hover near bougainvillea, frangipani, and oleander blossoms. The rooms themselves are delightful, done up with teakwood louvres, natural stone walls, rattan furniture, colorful cotton bedspreads, and batik wall hangings. You'll feel like you are living in a posh tree house. The beachfront villas, just a few steps from the sea, are bigger, but the hillside villas are real nice too, nestled in the gardens and offering wonderful harbor views.

Best of all, take advantage of the water-sports facilities. Guests enjoy unlimited day sailing, with a choice of more than 80 boats—Lasers, Rhodes 19s, even rowing sculls—all with free instruction. The week-long package also includes sailing regattas, daily snorkel trips, and all-day powerboat trips. Small but lively beach and an "in" restaurant. Honeymoon package: None. Standard eight days/seven nights package (Full AP): From $1,386 to $2,310 per couple (hillside villas); $1,771 to $2,695 (beachfront villas).

Biras Creek Hotel, P.O. Box 54, Virgin Gorda, B.V.I. (tel. 809/494-3555/6; U.S. reservations: tel. 212/696-1323 or toll free 800/372-1323). Very private, very elegant—that captures the ambience of this lush, 130-acre estate at the southeastern corner of North Sound. Perched atop a narrow promontory of land separating the tranquil harbor from the pounding sea, the resort's main stone building seems almost like a medieval fortress. Down below, walkways and marked nature trails wind through lush tropical gardens to the 32 secluded, yellow stucco guest accommodations (all are L-shaped, two-room suites), screened by almond trees, palms, and sea-grape trees for privacy. The decor of the modern, ultracomfortable rooms creates a tropical feeling. Swim at secluded Deep Bay Beach or in the hexagonal freshwater pool overlooking the sea—a real knockout. Guests enjoy complimentary use of bicycles, snorkeling equipment, Windsurfers (plus instruction), and 12- to 14-foot sailboats, plus day trips to other beaches nearby. There's also free tennis and courtesy rackets; The courts are lighted for night play. Gourmet restaurant. Honeymoon package: Eight days/seven nights (Full AP): $1,853 to $2,115, depending on view. Includes round-trip transfers between Virgin Gorda airport and the resort, a bottle of champagne, sunset cruise. Package not available in the high season; the resort is closed September and October.

Relaxed and casual, **The Tradewinds,** P.O. Box 64, Virgin Gorda, B.V.I. (tel. 809/494-3151/2; U.S. reservations: tel. 212/696-1323 or toll free 800/372-1323), is located near to all the North Sound action, but in a tranquil location at the quiet end of the harbor. It just recently merged with the Bitter End Yacht Club. Wooden stairways climb past palm trees and bright magenta bougainvillea to the 19 peak-roofed cedarwood cottages cradled by the hillside. Each of the accommodations gives off a wonderfully airy feeling, with a private balcony overlooking the harbor, two queen-size beds, tile floors, rattan furniture, sitting area—and a huge shower surrounded by plants that could practically accommodate your entire wedding party. Guests enjoy free use of water-sports equipment such as Windsurfers, snorkel gear, and day-sailers, plus tennis at nearby Biras Creek, its sister resort. The Tradewinds' own good-size beach offers peace and quiet; there are also free day-trips to nearby secluded beaches. When you get thirsty, try the beach bar, located in a genuine 1924 Scottish cutter; there's also a fine restaurant. Honeymoon package: Eight days/seven nights (Full AP): $1,590 to $2,195 per couple. Includes round-trip transfers between Virgin Gorda airport and the resort, a bottle of champagne and a fruit basket upon arrival, a sunset cruise, T-shirts, and more. Package currently not available high season, but this may change.

Little Dix Bay, P.O. Box 70, Virgin Gorda, B.V.I. (tel. 809/495-5555; U.S.

reservations: tel. 212/586-4459 or toll free 800/223-7637 nationwide; 800/442-8198 in NY). This intimate retreat (a Rockresort property) is elegant—without being stuffy. Here is a place where you can relax completely, knowing that you will be cared for, cosseted, and catered to. Impeccably landscaped grounds sprawl over 500 acres, and even by Virgin Islands standards, the waters lapping the half-mile-long, crescent-shape beach are an ultraclear, turquoise marvel. The 84 accommodations, tucked here and there along the beach under sea-grape trees and palms, offer privacy. Built of native stone and fine hardwoods such as purple heart, locust, and ash, they harmonize with the beautiful setting. Some rooms have hexagonal layouts, others rectangular, all have a private balcony or terrace, and plenty of louvres to let in the trade winds.

At the resort, the emphasis leans toward water sports and tennis. Guests enjoy free use of seven tennis courts, small sailboats, snorkel gear, bicycles, and waterskiing; horseback riding is available for a small fee. There are also free day-trips by Boston whaler to various secluded beaches and coves on Virgin Gorda; you can arrange to take along a picnic lunch. Both restaurants, the elegant Main Pavilion and the more informal Sugar Mill, are excellent. With all these amenities, you may never want to leave the property—but if you do, the shops and restaurants of the Virgin Gorda Yacht Harbor lie just over the hillside. Honeymoon package: Eight days/seven nights (Full AP): $1,942 to $2,173. Package not available December 20 through March 31.

Drake's Anchorage, P.O. Box 2510, Virgin Gorda, B.V.I. (tel. 809/494-2254; U.S. reservations: toll free 800/624-6651). How about honeymooning on your own private island? Drake's Anchorage occupies a 125-acre isle at the entrance to North Sound, well known for its beaches and snorkeling. The neat and cozy cottages sit right on the beach; each has a white-railed balcony overlooking the harbor. The tropical furnishings are simple, but comfortable, and convey a classy, castaway feel—tile floors, wicker headboards, natural fabrics, stone walls, floor-to-ceiling louvres, and Haitian wallhangings. You'll feel like you have the whole island to yourselves because there are only ten rooms (two of these are suites), plus two luxury villas. (Reserve the villas way in advance, since they book up fast.) Guests have free use of all water-sports equipment, including snorkel gear, day-sailers, and boat trips to nearby deserted islands. Terrific restaurant. Honeymoon package: Eight days/seven nights (Full AP): $1,319 per couple (cottage accommodations).

Moderate

Guavaberry Spring Bay, P.O. Box 20, Virgin Gorda, B.V.I. (tel. 809/495-5227). Where do people who live in the Virgin Islands go for a vacation? Often, to this unique retreat owned by Betty Row. The location is excellent, nestled amid massive boulders near the famous Baths, and just a few minutes from the golden sands of Spring Beach. Each of the 16 individual, hexagonally shaped units (they are built on stilts) has complete living, kitchenette, and dining facilities—complete with daily maid service. Furnishings are modern, made of teakwood. Meanwhile, the wraparound balconies let you take advantage of the panoramic views. There's a small commissary on the property where you can buy most everything except fresh veggies, and town is quite close by. Honeymoon package: None. Standard rates: $68.20 to $108.90 per couple per day for a one-bedroom villa.

ROMANTIC RESTAURANTS: Ask charter-boat captains to name the best restaurant in the B.V.I.; **Drake's Anchorage** Moskito Island (tel. 4-2254) will be the hands-down winner. It's located at water's edge, on a private island at the entrance to North Sound. This stone-walled restaurant with stunning Caribbean views serves up—an elegant amalgam of West Indian and French cuisine. You'll have trouble deciding what to order. Should it be the rich tomato soup or a tender conch salad? Each entrée arrives cooked to perfection: coquilles St-Jacques in a light cream sauce; fresh Caribbean lobster served with drawn butter; filet of beef au poivre, flamed in cognac and cream, and served rare as requested. For your finale, save room for a member of the dessert Hall of Fame: the chocolate mousse. Five-course, prix-fixe dinner from $55 to $72 per couple; lunch, about $25 per couple; good selection of reasonably priced French and Italian wines. Rum punch party and pig roast every Thursday in season.

Biras Creek, North Sound (tel. 4-3555). Great views and gourmet cuisine—that describes your dinner at this luxury resort. First sip cocktails on the circular terrace with a 360° panorama of North Sound, the Atlantic Ocean, and the Caribbean Sea— then head inside to the batik-cushioned rattan armchairs and flickering hurricane lamps in the dining room. Specials for the six-course, table d'hote gourmet dinner might include a scallop consommé, pâté maison, veal Cordon Bleu, lobster meunière, or shrimp scampi. Another favorite is the curry lunch, held every Sunday. Excellent, extensive wine list. Three-course lunch, $27 per couple; prix-fixe dinner, $72 per couple plus drinks. No formal dress is required for dinner, but men are required to wear long pants after 6 p.m.

The Bitter End, North Sound (tel. 4-2746). Whether you come for champagne breakfast, rum grog lunch, or full-course dinner, you'll enjoy the excellent food and animated crowd at this popular gathering spot overlooking North Sound. The dining room, under its thatched roof, is open to the trade winds, and every table offers ringside views of the magnificent yachts coming and going in the harbor. Colorful burgees (ship's flags) flutter in the breezes, gifts of visiting yachtsmen who wanted to leave a little of themselves behind at their favorite island watering hole. At lunchtime, the serving table positively groans under the weight of the hot and cold buffet, including chicken, ribs, roast meats, and seafood fritters. At night, first help yourself from the appetizer buffet, soup cauldron, and salad bar, then enjoy some fresh fish, grilled steak, or island specialty such as chicken coconut or lobster supreme, made from juicy lobsters, fresh from the restaurant's fish pens. Three-course prix-fixe lunch, about $27 per couple plus drinks; five-course prix-fixe dinner, $53 per couple plus drinks.

Little Dix Bay Hotel, near Virgin Gorda Yacht Harbour (tel. 5-5555, ext. 20-22). Taste the lifestyle of this chic resort at lunch or dinner. The main Pavilion Dining Room is a masterpiece of contemporary island architecture, with a shingle roof supported by Goliath-size purple heart timbers—some weighing more than 3,000 pounds. The Pavilion is completely open-sided to take advantages of the trade winds and a postcard-perfect view of shimmering Little Dix Bay. The luncheon smorgasbord serves up a luscious harvest of tropical fruits, chunky chicken salad, enough cold cuts (roast beef, ham, and turkey) to do a New York City deli proud, plus hot specials such as shrimp and pasta. For dessert, delights include a kiwi-banana cream pie, a molasses-rich pecan pie, and some very toothsome chocolate chip cookies. At dinner, the menu highlights both continental and Caribbean specialties (jackets required for men most evenings). For more informal dining, try the stone Sugar Mill, which serves broiled lobster and other dishes. Start your meal with a potent Pelican Smash cocktail. Lunch, $33 per couple; dinner, $75 per couple plus drinks.

Dishes such as curried shrimps with green peppers and roast rack of lamb with rosemary butter have made **Chez Michelle,** near Virgin Gorda Yacht Harbour (tel. 5-5510) an island favorite. Lunch entrées from $4 per person; dinner entrées from $13.50. **The Tradewinds,** on North Sound (tel. 4-3151) has an open-air restaurant that offers tasty fare and great views—especially nice for lunch. Lunch entrées from $6; complete dinner with either soup or salad and coffee, from $45 per couple.

4. Jost Van Dyke

No cars, no roads, no airport, and only about 130 permanent residents—yes, this is the island for honeymooners who crave escape. According to legend, the island is named after a Dutch pirate, a contemporary of Sir Francis Drake. What the island lacks in amenities, it compensates for with its scenery. White Bay is one of the prettiest beaches you can encounter, with long white sands edged by coconut palms, and two reefs to protect the waters and provide good snorkeling. Just around the bend, you'll find Great Harbour, a favorite yacht anchorage.

HONEYMOON HOTELS AND HIDEAWAYS: Because of its fine beaches and lively beach bars, Jost Van Dyke is a "must" for cruising charter boats. Although accommodations on land are limited, they are comfortable and offer the opportunity to get away from it all. Completely.

Rates quoted reflect the spread between low- and high-season prices.

White Bay Sandcastle, P.O. Box 9997, St. Thomas, U.S.V.I. 00801 (tel. 809/494-2462). There are only four cottages in this secluded resort situated snugly on beautiful White Bay. You'll almost expect to see Robinson Crusoe snoozing beneath a palm tree. Although there's no electricity, passive solar power runs the stereos and heats up the water for showers; you have gas lamps to read by. Each of the octagonally shaped wooden cottages is cozy, tidy, and private, plunked right on the edge of the beach. Furnishings are simple—but the view through the big glass windows is worth a million dollars. Help yourself from the honor bar; borrow books or cassettes from the library. Guests also enjoy complimentary use of Windsurfers, snorkel gear, and Sunfish. Excellent restaurant; the beachside Soggy Dollar bar makes a great afternoon hangout. Honeymoon package: None. Room rate (Full AP): $192 to $209 per couple per day.

ROMANTIC RESTAURANTS: If your idea of romantic dining encompasses cocktails fueled by a fiery sunset, followed by a dinner under the stars, then you're in luck.

When Billy and Lisa Hawkins say that all pies, cakes, and breads are homemade at their **White Bay Sandcastle** resort (tel. 4-2462), they aren't kidding. Even the coconuts for the fried shrimp and limes for the Key lime pie come from their backyard. Every night under the rustling palms at the beach's edge, they serve a four-course, set dinner costing about $60 per couple, including a glass of wine.

In Great Harbour, check out the string of casual, folksy beach restaurants that line the waterfront. Jost Van Dyke habitués speak of **Rudy's Mariners Rendezvous** with the same reverence that Scarlett O'Hara regarded Tara. It's a good place to down lobster, barbecue chicken, and a frosty beer; every Tuesday and Saturday night, there's a complete beachside pig roast ($16 to $30 per couple). **Foxy's,** another Jost Van Dyke tradition, has a lobster dinner priced from $8.50 per person. Or try **Happy Laury's,** with Laury himself behind the bar. The menu features lobster (starring a three-pound monster, for $22), barbecued chicken and ribs (about $10 to $13.50 per person), and you can shoot a game of pool between courses. None of these places has a telephone—just drop in.

5. Peter Island

Picture a perfect, half-moon-shaped sweep of fine, white coral sands that roll on for a mile. The bay is calm, clear, the color of molten turquoise; palm trees curve gently, sculpted by the constant trade winds. This is Deadman's Bay, perhaps first among equals of exquisite, B.V.I. beaches. Deadman's Bay is the crown jewel of Peter Island—and of the very exclusive Peter Island Resort.

Peter Island Hotel and Yacht Harbor, P.O. Box 211, Peter Island, B.V.I. (tel. 809/494-2561; U.S. reservations: toll free 800/346-4451; or 800/562-0268 in Michigan). Peter Island ranks—justly—among the world's most exclusive island retreats, a preferred port of call of yachtsmen, celebrities, and the jet set. The island is completely private. The resort owns most (1,800 acres) of the 1,956-acre island; there are also some private estates. A bevy of sports awaits right on your doorstep—tennis, horseback riding, snorkeling, Windsurfing, and sailing—all complimentary for guests. Four secluded beaches around the island account for five miles of coastline.

For the most spectacular accommodations, choose the one of the 20 cedar-and-stone beach house rooms in the two-story villas fronting Deadman's Bay. The spacious rooms are the most luxurious in the B.V.I., furnished with Mexican tile floors, peacock-style wicker armchairs, and pastel-colored fabrics. But the biggest star (next to the views from the huge balcony or terrace overlooking the bay) is the bathroom and adjoining plant-filled garden atrium.

The 32 Harbour House rooms, situated between Sprat Bay and the Sir Francis Drake Channel, all have a veranda or patio, and are air-conditioned. The A-frame buildings have a modern, Scandinavian design, warmed by cheery, tropical decor. As you would expect, special touches pamper guests—accommodations have his and hers sinks in the bathroom, a mini-refrigerator, and you'll find a hibiscus on your pillow every night. Or, if you really want to splurge, there are six private villas, including the free-form, white, Eagle's Nest villa—surrounded by a moat leading to a large swimming pool. Honeymoon package: Seven days/six nights (Full AP): $1,380 per couple (Harbour House rooms); $1,859 (Beach House rooms). Package not available December to April. Private villas: $630 per day to $3,500 per day for the Eagle's Nest.

Peter Island has two restaurants open to both guests and visitors. Advance reservations are very necessary (tel. 4-2561). In the Main Dining Room, candlelight flickers on the tables, accenting the rough-textured stone walls and colorful tropical motif paintings. The menu features continental favorites such as filet mignon with béarnaise sauce, as well as fresh fish (grouper, snapper) caught by the resort's "own" fishermen. Lunch, $26.50 per couple; dinner, $77 per couple plus drinks. Jackets required for men. For casual lunches and dinners (highlighting barbecued chicken or steak, and a salad bar), try the open-air Beach Bar. The view of Deadman's Bay can't be beat. Lunch $28.50 per couple; dinner $55 per couple plus drinks.

6. More Suggestions in the B.V.I.

Since the various isles and cays that make up the British Virgin Islands lie so close to each other, much of the fun comes from exploring different places. Join one of the day sails from the main islands, or charter a yacht yourselves. Here's a roundup of the most popular anchorages.

Norman Island reportedly provided Robert Louis Stevenson with the model for his *Treasure Island*. A French pirate supposedly hid his booty in one of the four huge sea caves on the island's northwest coast, so you can live out all your childhood fantasies of searching for buried treasure. Then head outside for what may be the best snorkeling of your lives. The water is absolutely transparent, with easily 100 feet of visibility, and hundreds of yellow-and-black sergeant majors and big yellowtail snappers greet you when you dive in. You can reach the island only by boat, with Norman Bight a favorite anchorage. At the bight, dinghy over to the *William Thornton,* an old (1915) Scandinavian freighter that's now a floating bar and restaurant (tel. 4-2564).

Salt Island is best known for the wreck of the R.M.S. *Rhone,* a royal mail vessel that sunk on the rocks during a violent hurricane on October 29, 1867. The wreck is probably the most popular dive site in the entire Caribbean, and underwater scenes for *The Deep* were filmed here. Because of the superb visibility (generally over 100 feet), snorkelers as well as scuba divers can view the ship's shattered remains, which lie only 20 to 80 feet down.

Since the wreck is a national park, and it is illegal to take catch here, you'll encounter lots of big, happy fish who nudge up against divers for handouts (they like potato chips).

Anegada sits apart from the main B.V.I. group, about 20 miles northeast of Tortola. Its Horseshoe Reef offers superb dives, especially shipwrecks. Over 100 vessels have foundered in the treacherous shallows, including the British frigate H.M.S. *Astra,* and the *Paramatta,* which sank over 100 years ago—both popular dive sites. The island lies so low in the water (its highest point is only 28 feet above sea level), Spanish sailors named it "the drowned island." In addition to its diving, Anegada offers fine beaches on its north and west coasts. For total escape, book one of the 12 rooms at the **Reefs Hotel,** or drop by for a barbecued lobster, chicken, or steak (tel. 4-3425). Dinners run from $35 to $50 per couple.

Also consider **Great Dog,** which has wonderful coral forests for snorkelers to explore; and **Cooper Island,** with sparkling Manchioneel Bay and a good restaurant. Along the rocky shores of Guana Island, you can often catch your own lobster dinner. There's also fine snorkeling off of **Necker Island, Green Cay,** and the **Indians.** For more buccaneer tales, stop by **Dead Chest Island.** According to legend, Blackbeard buried his treasure here—along with the 15 men who carried it ashore.

Chapter XXVIII

THE CAYMAN ISLANDS

1. **Practical Facts**
2. **Grand Cayman**
3. **Cayman Brac**
4. **Little Cayman**

TUCKED IN THE BRITISH WEST INDIES 480 miles south of Miami and 180 miles north-northwest of Jamaica, the Cayman Islands are a world unto themselves: properly British, yet seeming more like Florida than a foreign land. They are friendly, safe, comfortable—and above all, fun. Romantic? Oh yes. Do you want secluded beaches of talcum-fine, pure white sand? Hammocks swaying beneath the palms? Dinner by candlelight in an old Victorian home? Or do you prefer a little more action— limbo on the beach, party boats at sunset, feeding fish by hand?

You'll find it all on the three Cayman Islands—Grand Cayman, Cayman Brac, and Little Cayman. The islands hunker down close to the blue Caribbean—both Grand and Little Cayman are flat, and the ridge that runs along the spine of Cayman Brac rises only 140 feet above sea level. But don't let the low-slung profile fool you. These islands are actually the tops of a submerged mountain range cut by valleys that plummet 6,000 feet deep. The upper "slopes" are lined with some of the finest scuba reefs in the world: underwater forests of antler coral, canyons lined with blood-red sponges, tunnels filled with lobster, drop-offs so sheer you can't see bottom, and fish so friendly they nibble cheese from your fingers. All this in water clear enough to eye a clump of coral 200 feet away.

Back on land, the Caymans give you your choice of pace—slow, medium, or fast. Grand Cayman offers life in the fast lane—at least speedy by Cayman Islands standards. (After all, these are islands that have chosen the turtle as their official mascot.) On Grand Cayman, you'll have enough to keep you busy—yacht cruises, innumerable dive shops, nightclubs, and duty-free shopping—along with plenty of peace and quiet when you prefer. Cayman Brac provides even more of a chance to catch your breath—paired with fantastic diving and hiking. There are caves and quaint towns to explore, plus hotels where all-in-one packages do, indeed, take care of everything. And Little Cayman is the true escape, with simple cottages on the beach, tarpon ponds among the mangroves, and mile upon mile of sands.

Change has come so quickly here in the past two decades, it's hard to remember the Caymans were once just sleepy fishing villages; even harder to picture a time when bloodthirsty pirates roamed the islands. Christopher Columbus started it all in May 1503, stumbling across these three long, flat clumps of coral covered with iridescent-backed turtles and surrounded by translucent, cobalt water. He promptly dubbed them Las Tortugas and sailed away. Twenty years later, Spanish sailors, mistaking the local iguanas for crocodiles, renamed the islands Caimanas, which turned to Caymans when the islands were ceded to Great Britain in 1670.

By the 17th century these waters had become a highway for Spanish galleons laden with Inca gold—and a hideout for pirates. The vessels provided easy pickings for pirates the likes of Captain Henry Morgan and Blackbeard, whose treasure is rumored to lie in crevices of Cayman caves to this day. Despite their notoriety, the pirates' reign lasted barely 30 years, leaving a legacy of skull-and-crossbones beach names (Pirate's Point, Bloody Bay), an annual pirate festival (last week of October), and the official island symbol: a peg-leg turtle dressed in pirate's clothing.

By 1788, the piracy was long gone. In fact, when ten Jamaican ships foundered on a Grand Cayman reef, islanders slogged through treacherous seas to rescue the seamen. In gratitude, England's King George III granted the islands a tax-exempt status—which remains to this day. Today, the total lack of taxes has brought the Caymans more riches than any pirate could have dreamed of, the gold of business profits from banking and tourism.

The Caymans are a British crown colony, with a legislative assembly and a governor. And while the islanders' English comes with a decided Jamaican lilt, you'll find Whitbread's Ale, steak-and-kidney pie, and dart boards in the pubs.

For couples on a visit, the biggest problem is finding time for it all . . . time to nose about the pastel pink towns and roam the beaches of Grand Cayman, to climb through the caves and hike the orchid trails of Cayman Brac, to bicycle the unpaved back paths and fish the tarpon ponds of Little Cayman.

Above all, share some time with the Cayman Islanders—friendly people who are never too busy for a chat or to help strangers find their way. Stop in a native restaurant and you'll probably leave with the family recipe for conch stew. Hire a cab and you'll like as not get a mini-tour of the island, complete with tips on the hottest night spots and restaurants of the moment. That friendliness and comfort, that feeling you're a member of the family come home for a visit, is what's most precious about a Cayman stay.

1. Practical Facts

GETTING THERE: Americans and Canadians can use various proofs of citizenship (passport, birth certificate, voter's registration, or certificate of naturalization). However, a valid passport will speed things along. An onward or return ticket is also required. Departure tax is $7.50.

Cayman Airways offers regularly scheduled jet service from Miami and Houston to Grand Cayman and Cayman Brac, as well as 15-passenger "Trislander" interisland service to all three islands. Cayman Airways also arranges regular charter service from several major U.S. cities. Some of these charter flights operate only during the winter season, others year-round. For further information, telephone toll free 800/422-9626.

Northwest Airlines has regular jet service from Miami to Grand Cayman. Telephone toll free 800/447-4747.

Several cruise lines also call at Grand Cayman. Check with your travel agent for details.

GETTING AROUND: There are lots of transportation options on Grand Cayman, fewer on Cayman Brac, almost none on Little Cayman.

Taxis

Taxis are available on Grand Cayman and Cayman Brac. Taxi rates on Grand Cayman are controlled by the government and based on four people per taxi. Sample rate: from airport to Seven Mile Beach, $10. (tel. 9-2275 or 9-2811 for taxi dispatch.)

Rental Cars

Auto, moped, and bicycle rentals are available on Grand Cayman and Cayman Brac. (On Little Cayman, you can arrange with the one island hotel to take you around.) By law, rental cars cannot be picked up at the Grand Cayman airport (they can, however, be dropped off there). To get your rental car, you will have to take a taxi or walk to the car rental office (a few are located across from the airport).

Cars come big and small, standard shift and automatic, with air conditioning and without. In addition, you can rent vans and jeeps. Rentals run from about $16 to $43 per day, $110 to $225 per week. You'll need your U.S. driver's license to obtain a temporary Cayman license (available at the car rental counter for a $3 fee).

Mopeds and scooters range from $30 to $44 for a three-day rental. Warning: Don't ride mopeds or scooters on Lighthouse Road on Cayman Brac. Some riders have been seriously injured on this undulating sand and rock road, which is no way to end a honeymoon.

On Grand Cayman, bicycles rent for about $7 a day ($10 for a tandem). Some hotels, especially on the smaller islands, make bikes available for guests free of charge.

A tip: Get the Esso road map, generally available at their gas stations. It's small and extremely detailed, including every paved road on Grand Cayman. Best of all, the plainly marked Esso gas stations make great landmarks when you're trying to figure where to make that critical left turn. Finally, whatever you are riding, remember: *Drive on the left.*

Public Transportation

On Grand Cayman, **buses** serve the Seven Mile beach area (where most hotels and condos are located), running hourly between West Bay on the north end and downtown George Town to the south. Buses are also available to eastern destinations (e.g.; Bodden Town). The fare is $1.25.

LANGUAGE AND MONEY: English is the official tongue, spoken here with traces of Scottish and Welsh and flavored with a Caribbean lilt. The Cayman dollar (abbreviated CI$) is fixed at U.S. $1.25, making the U.S. dollar worth 80¢ Cayman. Prices in island shops and restaurants might be given in either Cayman or U.S. dollars, so be sure to ask. Unless otherwise noted, all prices given in this book are in U.S. dollars. American and Canadian currency is accepted virtually everywhere, as are major credit cards and traveler's checks. Personal checks are usually not accepted, unless drawn on a local or (sometimes) Miami bank.

WEATHER: The climate is delightfully balmy year-round. Winters average 75°, summers 80°. Most rainfall occurs in the summer months, but that's when you'll get the calmest conditions for scuba diving. In fact, one dive operator on Grand Cayman is so confident of his ability to find good diving in summer, he promises a refund if you're blown out of the water between April and December. Winter brings an occasional "nor'wester" that shakes the palms and roughens the seas somewhat. But even when that happens, dive operators just trundle over to the lee side of the island.

CLOTHING: Casual dress is accepted virtually everywhere, meaning men can leave the coat and tie home. Even the fanciest restaurants will settle for a "casual but elegant" look. Skimpy beachwear is frowned on away from the beach, although the

Caymanians are too polite to say anything. Occasional cool and breezy winter evenings make taking a light wrap or sweater a good idea.

TIME: The Cayman Islands remain on Eastern Standard Time year-round. In the summer, this means that honeymooners arriving from New York or Washington, D.C. should set their watches back one hour.

TELEPHONES: You can call the Caymans direct from the United States and Canada. First dial area code 809, then the seven-digit phone number. All Cayman phone numbers begin with "94," so when in the islands, you can omit the "94" and just dial the last five digits.

SCUBA DIVING: Some of the best diving and snorkeling in the world awaits you in the Caymans. Here all the elements come together: beautiful corals and sponges, colorful tropical fish, sheer walls with tunnels and caverns to explore, and, most important, knowledgeable and dependable dive operators.

On Grand Cayman, there are 17 dive operators, ranging from the huge fleet and many locations of **Bob Soto's Diving** (whose founder virtually invented Caribbean dive vacations), to smaller, more personalized operations such as **Quabbin Dives.** Most are clustered around the Seven Mile Beach area, and many will pick you up on the beach behind your hotel or condo. But if you're staying in another area, "not to worry," as they say here. Most resorts located away from the mainstream have their own, or nearby, dive operators.

On Cayman Brac and Little Cayman, you'll be diving with the operator attached to your hotel. There's always a good choice of diving destinations, and the diving off Little Cayman is the best in the islands.

Most dive trips consist of two dives: the first on a wall to about 100 feet, and the second (after a suitable surface interval) on a shallower reef at 30 feet or so. Remember to bring something to feed the very friendly fish—Cheeze Whiz, hot dogs, or an ear of corn are good choices.

SHOPPING: Grand Cayman is no St. Thomas but you'd be surprised at the little treasures you can find here as well as on Cayman Brac.

Each of you can bring back $400 worth of merchandise from the Cayman Islands. The tax-free status means bargains, especially on European imported goods such as watches, gold chains, fine porcelain, exotic perfumes and, most notably, china and crystal, whose prices are 30% to 50% off those in the United States.

Save your liquor shopping for the airport on Grand Cayman, since that's the only place spirits are sold duty free. If you can, avoid shopping in George Town on Thursdays, when the place is packed with cruise-ship passengers.

Grand Cayman has the serious shopping centered on George Town, the downtown area. The main shopping area is concentrated in a few blocks near the dock. The various Kirk Freeport stores (there are several) and the multitude of shops in the nearby Anchorage Centre seem to carry just about everything.

In this cornucopia, several shops stand out. **Treasure Cove** near the Kirk complex for china, porcelain, and crystal; **Colombia Emeralds International** in the Anchorage Centre for watches and gold chains; **Kirk Freeport Plaza** for Chinese cloisonné and Japanese pearls; **Heritage Island Crafts** for all kinds of Caribbean craftwork from Caymanian palm baskets to Jamaican carvings.

And then, there's black coral, a dense, bushy growth taken from deep water. It polishes up to such a high luster, it looks like a gemstone. Craftspeople on most Caribbean islands dabble in black coral, but here, it is a true art.

There must be 30 places on Grand Cayman that sell black coral, a dozen of them along Fort Street (downtown), alone. Also on Fort Street, you'll find a place called **Black Coral And . . .** , where artist Bernard K. Passman has woven polished black coral and gold into exquisite forms. There's a tiny sports car, a saxophone with each key done in gold, a cancan dancer with gold stars in her skirt. It's museum-quality stuff, with prices to match. But go in for a look, even if you can't afford to buy.

Mitzi, another black coral artist, also has a shop downtown. But if you want real bargains and a tour of Mitzi's studio to boot, drive back to the Turtle Farm area and just follow the signs that say **Coral Art Collections.** Delicate pendants sell for as little as $20, hearts inlaid with gold for $60.

On your drive around the island, keep an eye out when you reach the town of Pedro for **Ralph Terry's** house. There's a sign out front and a porch filled with mugs, walking sticks, napkin holders, vases, even foot massagers carved of everything from mahogany and cherry wood to poison ivy.

Cayman Brac has a half-dozen tiny shops with local craftware scattered along the north shore road. The two that stand out are **Idalee's Black Coral And Jewelry** and **N.I.M. Things.** You can't miss Idalee's. It's the home of Eddie Scott, the woodshop teacher in the local high school. Eddie built half the house himself, carving the ginger-bread trim and hand-making the two frontyard lighthouses in his workshop.

Ask Eddie to show you the scuba diver he carved in black coral with a knife (before electricity came to the island). It's so detailed, you can see the buckle on the diver's belt. Then indulge yourself in a piece of his black coral jewelry, which he sells for a fraction of the cost of comparable pieces on Grand Cayman.

N.I.M. (Native Island Made) Things in Spot Bay specializes in caymanite. It's a layered stone that polishes up to a rainbow splash of pinks, oranges, blacks, and browns and makes great jewelry and paperweights.

ABOUT ACCOMMODATIONS:
Except for a few knockout exceptions that are fairly new arrivals on these islands, Cayman accommodations tend to be the "white bread" of the Caribbean. Rooms are clean, attractive, and modern—but lacking in personality and character. You'll find no real surprises, but then, people choose the Caymans because of the water sports, beaches, and sightseeing—not the bedrooms. Really cheap accommodations in the way of campsites and cabins simply do not exist. Nor do those very exclusive, very expensive hideaways frequented by folks who don't mind spending $500 a day for their digs.

There are a handful of hotels, but mostly what you find are condos. And in truth, a condo is a good way to go. For virtually the same price as a single room, you get your own fully furnished apartment with a kitchenette, plenty of space, and daily maid service. By rustling up some of your own breakfasts and lunches, you can save enough for guilt-free dinner splurges at some of the islands' finer restaurants.

As a rule—but with plenty of exceptions—Cayman hotels offer honeymoon packages; condos do not. (When you make your condo reservations, however, let them know that you are honeymooners—often you'll get a complimentary bottle of champagne.) If you are scuba divers, consider taking the dive package rather than the honeymoon package; it will probably offer you better value.

The hot spot of Grand Cayman is Seven Mile Beach, with its many hotels and condos, water-sports shops, barbecues, and door-to-door scuba pickup service. Those seeking a bit more quiet head for Spanish Cove (the northern nub of land above Seven Mile Beach) or, better yet, the north side of the island towards Rum Point.

High season is December 15 through May 15, with low season rates running 20% to 35% lower. Most hotels and condos on Grand Cayman are European Plan (EP), meaning they don't provide meals. Hotels on Cayman Brac and Little Cayman, where restaurants are scarce, all offer Full American Plan (AP). A 6% accommodation charge and 10% to 15% service charge is added to hotel bills.

Twenty years ago on Grand Cayman, air conditioning and freshwater showers were a luxury, but no longer. A couple of the posher places even have fresh water in the swimming pools (a real luxury on an island where every drop of fresh water is manufactured). Cayman Brac hotels also now have freshwater showers and air conditioning. But don't expect such coddling on Little Cayman, where the beachfront cottages come equipped with ceiling fans and special spigots for drinking water, period.

DINING OUT: Casual is the byword here. Even the ritziest restaurants don't require a coat and tie. Reservations, however, are another story, especially during high season.

Restaurants run the gamut from gourmet French to Burger King with a marvelous conglomeration of native spots in between. Unfortunately, nothing is cheap. The top restaurants tend to be very good and very expensive—count on spending at least $100 per couple. The next down are good but still very expensive. Your best bet, especially if you like fish, is those native places that serve up a potpourri of conch stews, fritters, and fried fish.

HOW TO GET MARRIED IN THE CAYMANS: A Cayman marriage is the perfect start to a Cayman honeymoon. A special nonresident marriage license may be issued upon application to the governor and payment of a $200 fee.

At least one of you must apply in person and have been in the Caymans three days. Blood tests aren't necessary. You can use a minister or a lay marriage officer registered with the chief secretary's office.

For details, write to administrative secretary, Government Administration Building, George Town, Grand Cayman, B.W.I.

If you want to add a spice that your friends back home are guaranteed not to have, arrange for all this to be done underwater, either in scuba gear or on a submarine. Both are becoming popular (see "Romantic Interludes").

FOR FURTHER INFORMATION: Contact: **Cayman Islands Department of Tourism.** Grand Cayman: P.O. Box 67, George Town, Grand Cayman, B.W.I. (tel. 809/949-7999). Atlanta: P.O. Box 900024, Atlanta, GA 30329 (tel. 404/934-3959). Chicago: 333 N. Michigan Ave., Suite 905, Chicago, IL 60601 (tel. 312/782-5832). Dallas: 9794 Forest Lane, Suite 569, Dallas, TX 75243 (tel. 214/931-2224). Houston: 9999 Richmond Ave., Suite 131, Houston, TX 77042 (tel. 713/977-0604). Los Angeles: 3440 Wilshire Blvd., Suite 1202, Los Angeles, CA 90010 (tel. 213/738-1968). Miami: 250 Catalonia Ave., Suite 2312, Coral Gables, FL 33134 (tel. 305/444-6551). New York: 420 Lexington Ave., Suite 2312, New York, NY 10170 (tel. 212/682-5582). Tampa: P.O. Box 824, Tarpon Springs, FL 34286 (tel. 813/934-9078). Toronto: Earl B. Smith Travel Marketing Consultants, 234 Eglington Ave. E., Suite 306, Toronto, ON M4P-1K5 (tel. 416/485-1550).

2. Grand Cayman

Here's where you'll find fun in the sun with a touch of sophistication—but not so much you can't just hole up and relax.

Actually, Grand Cayman is more than just a beachfront playground. Thanks to the total lack of taxes and complete privacy for business transactions, this clump of coral is home to 480 banks, 456 insurance companies, and 18,000 other assorted corporations.

This business atmosphere brings a crack efficiency to this otherwise relaxed Caribbean isle. There's no looseness in, say, the scuba operations. Trips leave when they should. Equipment operates. Divemasters know the reefs. And it's the same with other island activities, from fishing to sightseeing tours.

Despite its weighty name, Grand Cayman is rather small—22 miles long and 8 miles wide—and flat. Its highest point reaches only 60 feet above sea level. The island looks like a reversed letter "L" on its back. The leg that sticks up along the western end embraces the powder-fine sands of Seven Mile Beach, the main resort area. This, and the crook of the "L" where George Town (the Cayman Island capital) sits, form the center of island life. You'll find most of the island's 2,000 condo and hotel rooms here, many of them conveniently located on the beach for that starlit, midnight swim.

What's to do? Just about everything. Along the beach there's waterskiing, jet-skiing, Windsurfing, sailing, paddleboating, or exciting parasail flights. Check with **Aqua Delights** at the Holiday Inn (tel. 7-4444) and **Surfside Watersports** at Le Club Cayman (tel. 7-4224).

Then, of course, there's diving and snorkeling (some of the best in the world). Most dive operators will pick you up on the beach. Many have representatives in the hotels, or stop in at their shops along West Bay Road. Further out, there's fishing: snapper, grouper, and barracuda year-round; dolphin, wahoo, and tuna in spring; and marlin in midsummer.

On land, there's tennis (free for guests, a small fee for nonguests) at the Holiday Inn, Cayman Kai, Caribbean Club, and other hotels. And there's golf at the Britannia. Jack Nicklaus designed a special "Cayman ball" that weighs a third of a regular ball and travels only half as far, so you can play 18 holes in the space that would generally accommodate 9.

If you can tear yourself away from all this, there's the rest of the island. Tight on time? Do a guided tour (two to six hours) via **Tropicana Tours Ltd., Gray Line, Rudi's Traveler's Transport, Elite Limousine Service,** and **Greenlight Tours.** (Make arrangements at your hotel front desk.)

Better yet, do it on your own. Start with a stroll through George Town, an incongruous mix of whitewashed colonial stone buildings and modern glass structures. (You'll be surprised how many of them house banks.) Then head over to the shopping district, which centers on a few blocks near the docks.

Leaving George Town, continue past Seven Mile Beach to that eerie expanse of jagged, blackened coral called Hell. (Many couples mail their postcards here—the postmark, of course, will read "Hell.") Nearby, hit the Turtle Farm, literally crawling with turtles (27,000 of them). The littlest critters are barely bird-size, and love to be tickled under the neck.

Now go back down Seven Mile Beach, past George Town, and head out around the island. It's hard to get lost, since there's only one road that circles the island plus a single crossisland route. The island is flat and sandy, covered with thick sea-grape scrub interlaced with coconut palms, the peeling, red-barked gumbo limbo, bread-fruit, and flaming poinciana.

You drive through tiny towns of low, pastel houses and offshore, the Caribbean sparkles with a half dozen shades of coral-studded blue.

On your tour of the island, you'll pass the Pirate Cave, with its antique lanterns and other leftover tools of early life; the Blow Holes, where waves spew 30 feet through coral cracks; the endless deserted beaches of the north shore; and, finally, Rum Point. Take the crossisland road to save time on the way back.

ROMANTIC INTERLUDES: Fast lane or slow, on land or at sea, it's all here on Grand Cayman.

You'll find plenty of **beaches** where you'll be totally by yourselves. Barkers lies north of Seven Mile Beach, past Spanish Cove along the top of the northernmost point. Turnoffs lead to its three miles of pure, white sand shaded by sea-grape trees. To reach Smith's Cove, go south of George Town past the Grand Old House restaurant to find the crescent of sand surrounded by ruggedly beautiful ironshore (coral weathered a dark gray). East End is appropriately on the far east end of Grand Cayman, past the village of Gun Bay. Beyond the Tortuga Club, paths lead off to a string of deserted coves. Along North Side untouched beaches stretch all the way from Old Man Bay to Rum Point. Storms and sea currents bring driftwood and shells here, so picnic and then go beachcombing for treasures.

The *Atlantis* (tel. 9-7700), a 28-passenger vessel built especially for **underwater touring,** takes you along the top of the Cayman "wall" at 65 feet, past gardens of coral and tropical fish. Day trips $45 per person, night dives (which go a little deeper) $55 per person. Located next to Government Dock, downtown George Town. For something truly out of the world, ride the **Research Submersibles Ltd.** (RSL) (tel. 9-3870) sub to 800 feet down. You'll glide along the Cayman wall past rare black coral and perhaps pay a visit 790 feet down to the *Kirk Pride,* an island freighter that sank some ten years ago. It's still laden with cargo. These are genuine research subs: not for the claustrophobic. Two hundred dollars per person and worth it. Office located next to the Burger King on the waterfront north of George Town.

Various **boats,** both power and sail, make North Sound snorkeling trips. While you stop to swim through the reefs, the crew fishes for your lunch, which is served on a secluded spit of sand around a bonfire. Or take a sunset dinner cruise aboard a sailboat, making your way down Seven Mile Beach while the sun sinks slowly in the west. Some cruises feature cocktails and dinner. Contact **Ron Ebanks Charter Boat Headquarters,** (tel. 7-4340) for these and more.

The incomparable reefs, served by two dozen **dive** operators, draw most people to Grand Cayman. The famous Cayman Wall starts a scant 300 yards off shore. Closer in is Devil's Grotto, a twisting maze of coral-encrusted tunnels that *Skin Diver* magazine rates as one of the ten best shallow dives in the world. At the Aquarium, yellowtail and grouper are so tame, you can feed them by hand (Cheese Whiz in a can is best).

Boats give door-to-door service along Seven Mile Beach, picking up divers as they wait on the beach in front of their hotel. For certified divers, most hotels have special dive packages that include their trips to the reefs. If you want to learn, there's a one-day resort course ($75) or a full NAUI/PADI (National Association of Underwater Instructors; Professional Association of Diving Instructors) open water certification that takes five days ($300).

One highly recommended dive shop is **Bob Soto's Diving, Ltd.** (tel. 9-2022). Not only is this the largest operator in the Caymans, Soto is one of the pioneers of Caribbean diving, having established his shop way back in 1957. Another excellent outfit is **Quabbin Dives** (tel. 9-5597), known for its individualized services.

For a **wedding** you'll really remember, tie the knot at 40 feet . . . or even 800. For scuba divers, the wedding party plus divemaster goes down and runs through the ceremony using underwater slates to say their "I do's." Then you come back up to the boat and repeat the ceremony verbally before the clergy or justice of the peace (there are no scuba-certified marriage officers). You can even have the whole thing videotaped. Total package for ten people, including videotaping, costs about $600. Contact **Surfside Watersports,** (tel. 7-4224) or in the United States toll free 800/468-1708.

For nondivers, there are the submarines. The RSL subs are a bit cozy, but you can squeeze in the pilot, minister, and couple in one sub and a small wedding party in another sub. You'd have the ceremony, then come up for the reception on a party boat. Figure the whole thing—subs, party raft, video—at about $2,500. Contact RSL (tel. 9-3870). The *Atlantis* sub holds 28 people and you could have it, complete with champagne and decorations, for 90 minutes for $900. Contact **Atlantis** (tel. 9-7700).

HONEYMOON HOTELS AND HIDEAWAYS: Whether it's a condo or a hotel room, the center of parties and excitement or some private hideaway, Grand Cayman has it.

Prices quoted reflect the spread between low- and high-season rates. Package rates usually include tax and service while single day rates do not.

Expensive

Hyatt Regency Grand Cayman, Box 1698, Grand Cayman, B.W.I. (tel. 809/949-1234; U.S. reservations: tel. 212/972-7000 or toll free 800/228-9000). By far the most luxurious thing to hit the Caymans, this brand new, 235-room hotel has everything: free-form pool with swim-up bar, waterfall in the courtyard, concierge on duty to help you with everything from renting a car to getting your clothes ironed and, out back, the Britannia golf course. The resort is located just two miles from George Town. With their blue-and-white facades, the colonial-style buildings look like Wedgwood villas. All rooms and suites have their own verandas, with views of water, foliage, or the golf course. Decor blends elegance with an easygoing island style. Look for natural furnishings of bleached ash, rattan, teak, and mahogany. And on an island where space is so tight even the golf balls are engineered to fall short, this place (hotel, golf course, beachfront complex with dive shop, hotel, and pools), sprawls across 88 acres.

Honeymoon package: Four days/three nights: $700 to $869 per couple. Includes daily breakfast, champagne and flowers on arrival, candlelit dinner, afternoon snorkeling trip, and use of two mopeds for a day.

Moderate

Holiday Inn Grand Cayman, Box 904, Grand Cayman, B.W.I. (tel. 809/947-4444; U.S. reservations: tel. 901/767-8050 or toll free 800/421-9999), is party central, right on Seven Mile Beach, the magnet for all hot action on the island. Until recently, it was the largest hotel (213 rooms), the only full-service hotel, and one of the few places around with a telephone in each unit. The rooms are standard Holiday Inn issue (though those at oceanfront have king-size beds instead of two doubles). It's what's outside that makes the difference: a huge beach studded with coconut palms and a thatch-roof bar (the island spot for sunsets), a free-form swimming pool with stools in the water so you can sip your rum punch in ultimate weightless comfort, tennis courts, reservation booths for the Bob Soto dive operation, and Aqua Delights, a water-sports concession. Inside, George Novak, the Barefoot Man, does Cayman folk music nightly in the lounge and outside, twice a week, there's a beachside barbecue.

Honeymoon package: Eight days/seven nights (EP): $1,040 to $1,732 per couple. Includes champagne, a dinner for two at the gourmet restaurant, an evening cruise, and gift pack. Three- and five-day packages also available.

Villas of the Galleon, Box 1797, Grand Cayman, B.W.I. (tel. 809/947-4433; U.S. reservations: toll free except Florida, 800/232-1034), is how you get close to the Seven Mile Beach action without drowning in it. You've got the Holiday Inn with its parties and beach bar on one side, and Surfside Watersports on the other, while enjoying the quiet and convenience of a condo. The beige stucco-and-wood buildings look like something from a Florida resort community, with individual porches, modern furniture, and all the conveniences, including a kitchen and a comfy queen-size bed. It's hardly 50 steps to the ocean and there are handy "dunk" tanks to rinse scuba gear. Best of all, this is a regular stop for the scuba boats: door-to-door service. There's no honeymoon package, but if you let someone know in advance you've just been married, you'll find a bottle of cold champagne in your room. Rates (EP): $145 to $175 per couple per day for one-bedroom villa.

Villas Pappagallo, Box 952, Grand Cayman, B.W.I. (tel. 809/949-3568; U.S. reservations: toll free except Florida, 800/232-1034). You don't HAVE to go to the other side of the island for seclusion. You can have it right here in West Bay, on the peninsula north of Seven Mile Beach. There's nothing on either side of this condo resort except empty beach. With its beige stucco set off with black wrought-iron work and red-tile roofs, there's a Mediterranean feel. Loads of lush greenery—hibiscus, palms, sea grape—carpet the grounds. Inside, the units are a cut above the usual island condo, with dishwashers, ice makers in the refrigerator, and a rock coral wall that looks like a reef, with individual chunks of brain, star, even lettuce coral. For a touch of real luxury, you can have a cook come in for $30 to $35 a day to do your meals. As for activity, forget it. "No barbecues, no parties, no sailboat tours, none of that," says assistant manager Joan Dell, adding, "but we do have quiet. . . . REAL quiet."

Honeymoon package: None. Rates (EP): $135 to $165 per couple per day for one-bedroom villa.

Retreat At Rum Point, Box 46, North Side, Grand Cayman, B.W.I. (tel. 809/947-9535; U.S. reservations: toll free 800/423-2422). Rum Point, located on the northside of the island, is where you come on Grand Cayman if you really want to get away from it all. The three-story beige stucco buildings are surrounded by a rainbow of tropical flowers: yellow oleanders, flame hibiscus, purple bougainvillea. Inside, it's king-size beds, cane furniture, and a modern kitchen all overlooking a beach with talcum-fine sand and an offshore reef. There's tennis, racquetball, a sauna and fitness center, the resort's own dive shop, and a freshwater pool. Plus you can arrange for that ultimate bit of pampering, your own personal cook, for another $40 a day.

Honeymoon package: None. Rates (EP): $130 to $160 per night per room for one-bedroom villa.

Villa Caribe, Box 1410, Grand Cayman, B.W.I., (tel. 809/947-9636; U.S. reservations: toll free 800/367-0041). This isn't your biggest, ritziest, or most action-packed resort on Grand Cayman—but it's one of the friendliest and among the least expensive. The small (14 rooms) hotel overlooks a protected bay fringed with coral reef on the quiet, north side of Grand Cayman. The rooms are spare, but they do have king-size beds. Owner James Terry, retired police chief of the island, literally built the place with his own hands. These days, he lounges around in shorts and bare feet, chumming with the guests. The result is a guest book filled with sweet comments. The beaches on either side are empty and there's hardly a sign of civilization. It's the kind of place where dressing for dinner means putting sandals on your feet.

Honeymoon package: Nine days/eight nights (MAP): $1,214 to $1,324 per couple. Includes airport transfers, bottle of wine on arrival, sunset cruise.

ROMANTIC RESTAURANTS: This is where Grand Cayman shines, with a wide choice of restaurants—from fancy to footloose.

Expensive

Le Diplomat, Grand Pavilion Hotel, Seven Mile Beach (7-4666). With its crystal chandelier, etched-glass wall, flickering candlelight and gourmet French food served on Wedgwood china, this place is easily the most elegant restaurant in the Caymans. French with a Caribbean touch is how you might best describe the food. Among their truly special dishes are the scallop mousse, lobster Caribe (lobster slices sautéed in whisky sauce), and absolutely not to be missed: the bananas flambé (bananas flamed in liqueurs, brown sugar, butter and citrus fruits, then poured—still burning—over ice cream). Dinner for two with wine: about $100.

Elegant with a native touch, **Ristorante Pappagallo,** West Bay (9-1119), nestles beneath a huge palm-thatched roof (100,000 leaves) on a spit of land in the middle of a bird sanctuary. Inside, the walls are ringed with bay windows housing tropical birds. The food here is northern Italian: pastas of all kinds, an array of seafoods, and absolutely the best veal on the island. For something really special, try the linguine in salsa di aragosta, a sinfully creamy lobster sauce, and finish with Caribbean Coffee: coffee, coconut rum, and Tia Maria, all set afire with a flourish. Dinner for two with wine: about $80.

Grand Old House, just south of George Town on South Church Street (9-2020). There's a genteel feel to this century-old Caymanian plantation-house-turned-restaurant. The white frame house with its veranda, ceiling fans, Tiffany lamps, wicker chairs, and the huge stuffed marlin over the door is truly one of a kind. In keeping with its decor, the menu is Caribbean gourmet: turtle steak, mesquite-grilled local fish, lobster, and conch, plus an array of continental dishes. Don't miss the turtle-and-rum chowder, chock-full of tender chunks of meat, or the white chocolate mousse, laced with huge chunks of white chocolate and raspberry sauce. Chef Tell, the well-known TV personality, recently took over the place. Alas, some old favorites from the menu are gone. But service has improved immensely. Dinner for two with wine can easily hit $100.

Moderate to Inexpensive

Crow's Nest Eatery, just past Grand Old House (tel. 9-6216) has its own beach and, better, its own offshore island where you can snorkel after munching one of their fabulous turtle steaks ($13.75) or fresh fish ($11). **The Lone Star Bar & Grill,** Seven Mile Beach (tel. 9-5575) is Tex-Mex with a touch of fish and has one of the island's few big-screen TVs plus a lively happy hour. Tacos and enchiladas run about $8. **Wrecks' View Craft Shop,** past Gun Bay on East End (tel. 7-7438), opens as a restaurant only on Sundays, noon to 3:30 p.m. This funky little spot on the sand serves down-home native chow: whelk, conch and turtle stew, ribs, chicken plus "heavy cake," a dense, sweet concoction not to be missed. You can get out of here for about $5 per person. In George Town, head to **Lord Nelson Pub,** Trafalgar Square (tel. 7-4595) and **Cayman Arms,** downtown (tel. 9-2661) for the likes of steak-and-kidney pie, good British ale, and a jolly game of darts (about $9 to $12 per person). **Lighthouse Club in Breakers** on South Sound Road (tel. 7-2047), draped outside with huge chains and anchor, decorated inside with tables of split tree trunks and assorted wreck paraphernalia, is located right on the ocean. It serves up conch in every imaginable form, elegant dishes such as lobster Thermidor ($23), plus some German specialties, such as sauerbraten ($16.25).

3. Cayman Brac

Everyone talks about the good old days on Grand Cayman, when the beaches were empty, the hotels small, the pace of life turtle slow. But the Grand Cayman of 30 years ago still exists. To find it you need only head 86 miles northeast to the Brac.

Cayman Brac, 12 miles long and 1 ½ miles wide, has secluded beaches, but also enough creature comforts (meaning air conditioning, freshwater showers, restaurants, and some nightlife) to keep people happy. The island's 1,500 residents live in a scattering of small towns on the north coast, leaving the south side empty except for a couple of interesting caves and fine beaches.

Fishing is fantastic, whether you borrow a rig from your hotel and cast for bonefish from the beach or go out with a guide (some of the Caymans' best fish guides live here) for tuna, wahoo, or marlin.

Underwater, you'll find more of that fabulous Cayman diving, only here, it's practically untouched. Southside diving features great tunnels and caves, sandy chutes leading to sheer walls coated with coral and sponges, shallow forests of huge coral that looks like antlers. The north side has seven-foot-tall basket sponges in only 50 feet of water and the soft corals and tiny critters that macrophotographers love.

Between dives and fishing, tour the island. The hotels offer guided trips, or you can rent a car or scooters. There's the **Brac Museum** in Stake Bay, an old house filled with lanterns, old dental tools, and other marvelous tidbits from turn-of-the-century Brac life, and there's Spot Bay on the northeast side, a town of little pastel houses ringed by breadfruit, bananas, and flaming poinciana.

ROMANTIC INTERLUDES: Great diving, great exploring, and great people make this island everyone's favorite.

Take Bluff Road, turn off on Lighthouse Road, and you'll wind six miles down a roller-coasting rock path to the far eastern tip of the island. There you'll find the **Brac** (bluff in Gaelic), a coral spine that runs up the middle of the island, ending in a sheer,

140-foot-high cliff that plummets straight to the sea. There, surrounded by cactus and palms that seem to glow in the setting sun, you can pick your way across rugged, blackened coral or, better yet, just sit on the bluff's edge and watch the birds.

Caves honeycomb the limestone spine of the Brac. The Bat Cave (two miles east of the west-end crossisland road) is an abstract painting of muted colors: black, white, gray, coral, and green. A hole in the ceiling drips with vines and leaves, and somewhere in the farthest recesses are, indeed, bats. But the best of the caves is called, simply, Great Cave (at road's end on the southeast side of the island). Inside is a delicate lace of stalactites, fluted, crystallized walls, and the most profound silence on this earth. For the most comfort, wear sneakers and old, washable clothes, and bring a flashlight.

At the far east tip of the island, beyond the entrance to Great Cave, lies a very special **beach** that has no name. There's little sand. Instead, you walk on a carpet of marble-size pieces of perfectly preserved coral braided with vines and purple flowers. Off in the distance, the bluff hangs there, striped with the black, rust, and white of mineral drippings, its harsh edges softened by the mist of crashing waves.

HONEYMOON HOTELS AND HIDEAWAYS: There are only three tourist hotels on this island and they're all quite similar, with simple, modern decor, and niceties such as air conditioning. Prices quoted reflect the spread between low- and high-season rates. Note some prices here include airfare from Miami, all meals, and liquor.

Brac Reef Beach Resort, Box 235, Cayman Brac, B.W.I. (tel. 809/948-7323; U.S. reservations: 813/229-5359 or toll free 800/327-3835, outside FL; and 800/233-8880, FL), is the quieter of the two southside hotels. There's no daily schedule of activities beyond diving and beachside barbecues. Instead, what this place has is a wide beach studded with coconut palms, flowering oleander, and cool forests of sea grape hung with hammocks. The rooms are plain but comfortable, and outside, there's not only a freshwater pool but a Jacuzzi. Since the hotel next door had a bar over the water, the Brac Reef went one better, making their bar a double-decker with swinging loveseats.

Guests have unlimited use of paddleboats, Windsurfer, and metal detectors for beachcombing (real doubloons have been found). Honeymoon package: Eight days/seven nights (Full AP): $1,749 per couple. Includes airfare from Miami, all meals and liquor, rental car or scooter, picnic boat trip to Little Cayman, bottle of champagne each night, and two days' use of snorkel equipment. Other packages range from three to eight nights. Available only April 15 through December 15 (approximate).

Think of the **Tiara Beach Hotel,** Stake Bay, Cayman Brac, B.W.I. (tel. 809/948-7313; U.S. reservations: 607/277-3484 or toll free 800/367-3484) as a low-key Club Med. Daily scheduled fun runs the gamut from crab races and sandcastle-building contests to snorkel tours. Newly renovated, the Tiara has a South Seas look, with palm thatch, bamboo wallpaper, and fresh-cut hibiscus everywhere. Like the Brac Reef, the older rooms here tend to be plain. But the hotel has undergone extensive renovation, and the newest rooms are something special, with open air bathrooms that have their own Jacuzzis.

Guests have unlimited use of bicycles, Windsurfer, and paddleboat. Honeymoon package: Eight days/seven nights (Full AP): $1,320 to $1,654 per couple. Includes upgraded room, all meals and liquor, bottle of champagne on arrival, and a free night when you return on your anniversary.

Buccaneer's Inn, Box 68, Cayman Brac, B.W.I. (tel. 809/948-7257; U.S. reservations: 504/292-7772 or toll free 800/535-9968). Until ten years ago, this was the Brac's only hotel, catering mainly to divers. It's still a real diving hotel—and the place to go if you're on a tight budget. Like Topsy, the hotel's restaurant and 34 rooms just sort of grew here and there across the property, which sits on a gentle rise of ironshore beach overlooking the Brac's north shore. Rooms are clean but spartan. Folks are friendly here and shore diving is unlimited, plus there are the expected dive, snorkel, and beach party trips around the Brac and over to Little Cayman.

Unlike the other two hotels, this place is more à la carte, with meals, diving, tax, and service not included. Even so, you save about a third over the other two hotels. Honeymoon package: $92 per couple per night. Includes airport transfers, welcome drink, champagne, breakfast.

ROMANTIC RESTAURANTS: If you're expecting gourmet French tidbits by candlelight, this is not your place. Native food and local atmosphere, however, are plentiful.

Lagoon Bar, a mile up from the southside hotels (8-7213). Strictly native, down to its plentiful helpings of fried fish (Cayman style, with onions and green peppers), turtle steaks, and the occasional stewed cow foot. Like most native spots on the Brac, it's all plywood—the walls, the floor, even the tables. An island band does a mean mix of reggae, calypso, and country-and-western on weekends. Lunch or dinner for two about $15.

La Esperanza, north side (8-8531), looks like a wood shack on the sand with a scattering of picnic tables about. Inside, the ubiquitous plywood tables are set with ketchup, hot sauce, and dominoes—a giveaway that this is the main northside watering spot for locals. More Cayman fried fish, conch stew, turtle steak. Barefoot island atmosphere is what you really get here. Lunch for two about $10.

4. Little Cayman

This island is the kind of place newlyweds dream about—ten miles of palms and orchids lined by talcum-fine, absolutely uninhabited sand.

Aside from 27 locals (including hotel staff), Little Cayman is deserted. There's one hotel, no outside restaurants, no bars, no telephones, no TV. Nothing but legendary fishing: bonefish practically at your front door, tarpon in a landlocked mangrove lake that boils with their frenzy.

Diving here is among the best in the world: walls of encrusted coral starting at barely 20 feet and plunging to infinity, stands of fragile staghorn fingers and sponge cups by the hundred, forests of rare black coral and visibilities approaching 200 feet. The diving is so good, folks motor over from Cayman Brac five miles away.

For a break, swing in your hammock beneath the palms, island drink in hand. Or hike the crossisland nature trail, an ancient footpath used by early settlers, lined with orchids, cactus, and delicate bromeliads.

ROMANTIC INTERLUDES: Relax and enjoy, that's the key here.

All for you, a stretch of powder-fine pink sand, rimmed with coconut palms, and protected by a ring of offshore coral. The lagoon is mirror calm, the water crystal clear. And there's nobody here at **Point O' Sand** on the far east tip of Little Cayman but the two of you.

Owen's Island, 11 acres of beach, trails, and mangrove forest, sits so close to the Southern Cross Club, you can actually walk to it (the water's only chest deep). Most folks, however, get a lift from the hotel, then spend their hours snorkeling, picnicking, and exploring the forest.

Have a day of **fishing** in the southside lagoon, where the bonefish sometime run so thick, their fins carpet the top of the water. Or go out in a small boat for snapper, jack, and grouper. Your guide ($70 a half-day per couple) knows the best spots and has all the fishing gear. Then sit back while he cooks your fresh catch over a fire.

HONEYMOON HOTELS AND HIDEAWAYS: This is the ultimate getaway. Prices reflect the spread between low- and high-season rates and include all meals, but no fishing or diving.

Other hotels have come and gone on this island but only the **Southern Cross Club,** Little Cayman, Cayman Islands, B.W.I. (tel. 809/948-3255; U.S. reservations: 317/636-9501), seems to endure. This very private collection of cabins on the beach is a glorified fish camp. There's no air conditioning, and even the bath water is salt. But the beds are clean and comfortable, the plumbing works, and the louvered windows let the breezes waft through—simplicity as you like it. The cabins are scattered about the sand, surrounded by palm trees strung with hammocks so you can lie back and watch the setting sun. What a place to be together!

Honeymoon package: None. Standard rate (Full AP): $180 to $220 per couple per night. Includes airport transfers, snorkeling, and bicycling.

Chapter XXIX

CURAÇAO

1. Practical Facts
2. Romantic Interludes
3. Honeymoon Hotels and Hideaways
4. Romantic Restaurants and Night Spots

IF CITY SIGHTS and balmy tropical nights rank high on your honeymoon agenda, "the little Europe" of the Caribbean is the place to go.

Located just 35 miles off the coast of Venezuela, Curaçao is the largest island in the Netherlands Antilles. Most of the 175,000 inhabitants live in and around the capital city of Willemstad. There, reconstructed colonial fortresses mix with modern highways and bridges, and with the futuristic superstructures of one of the largest crude oil refineries in the world.

Although Curaçao was discovered by the Spaniard Alonso de Ojeda in 1499, Spain, Holland, France, and England contended for its possession until 1815, when the Dutch established their dominance. One hundred years later, an oil refinery spurred Curaçao's prosperity. Today, the refinery is one of the largest, and Curaçao's harbor one of the busiest, in the world. A constant flow of traffic bustles in and out of Schottegat Bay, which also has one of the largest dry docks in the region.

The best way to see Willemstad is on foot; and one of the best places to start is at the Queen Emma Floating Bridge, which spans the entrance to Schottegat Bay. From the west, or Otrobanda side of the bay, you'll have a perfect view of Curaçao's Handelskaade, or ferry landing, surely one of the most easily indentifiable waterfronts in the world. The pastel buildings on the Punda side of the bridge look like a multicolored Amsterdam. Each reflects the Dutch architectural heritage, but the white-trimmed facades, and the tiled, peaked roofs also display an unmistakable tropical influence. The pontoon bridge opens 20 to 30 times a day to allow ships to enter and leave Schottegat Bay, but you won't be stranded if it opens while you're admiring the Handelskaade. Free ferries shuttle pedestrians across the harbor entrance whenever the bridge is open.

When you cross over to the Punda side of Curaçao, you'll be in the midst of the downtown and shopping districts, and not far from the historical renovations at Fort Amsterdam, the current seat of government. A short walk brings you to the floating market, where small sailboats that have crossed the ocean from Venezuela tie up. There's a fish market there, too, where South American and local fishermen sell fresh snapper, grouper, yellowtail, and conch.

The floating market is proof positive that you're in the tropics. But where are the palm trees and the stretches of white sand beach? The best beaches in Curaçao aren't in front of the hotels, so you'll have to venture away from Willemstad's urban sprawl.

You won't find long stretches of sand, but there are 38 small coves and inlets along Curaçao's southern coast that are perfect for a day in the sun.

There are a number of public beaches on the southern coast to the west of Willemstad; only Santa Cruz has rest-room and changing facilities. Don't miss Knip Bay (local people refer to it as "love city"), where there are actually two separate coves. Both are lovely, but if you follow the trail that curves to the left, you'll end up at the more secluded one. To the east of Willemstad, there's a public beach with facilities at the Curaçao Sequarium complex. The private beaches at Jan Thiel Bay and Santa Barbara have rest-rooms and changing facilities. Admission to each is under $5.

Back in the city, Curaçao has the kinds of attractions one would expect in a cosmopolitan center. There's the Curaçao Museum, the Botanical Gardens, and a zoo. The Center for Performing Arts serves up a full season of entertainment, and the Curaçao Stadium has regularly scheduled soccer and baseball games. Unique to Curaçao, though, is the Chobolobo Distillery, where the famous Curaçao of Curaçao Liqueur is prepared. Made from a recipe traced to the 18th century, the liqueur is distilled in antique copper vats that bristle with valves and levers. Bottling in the traditional blue delft containers is still done by hand. After touring the facility and sampling the orange-flavored liquid you'll know that you have found the perfect gift to bring home to family and friends.

1. Practical Facts

GETTING THERE: U.S. citizens need proof of citizenship and a return or continuing ticket. Although a passport is preferred, an authenticated birth certificate or a voter registration card is also acceptable. The departure tax is $5.75 per person.

There's frequent air service to Curaçao, and it's easy to reach the island from most places in the United States. **American Airlines** and **ALM Antillean Airlines** have daily flights from New York. ALM and **Eastern Airlines** fly daily from Miami. There are also several daily interisland flights from Aruba and Bonaire via ALM. The hotels in the Willemstad area are about 20 minutes from the International Airport; the taxi fair is approximately $10.

GETTING AROUND: All points of tourist interest are easily accessible by paved roads, so you have various transportation options to choose from.

By Taxi

Taxis don't have meters; the rates are based on your destination, rather than on the mileage. Rates are fixed by the government and are fairly inexpensive. Sample fares are posted at the airport; ask your driver to confirm the rate before getting in the car.

By Car

Many American car-rental companies have licenses in Curaçao; there are also several reliable local companies. Car rentals run approximately $30 to $40 per day. Driving is on the right-hand side, as it is in the United States. Curaçao uses international road signs.

By Public Transportation

The hotels on the outer edge of Willemstad run free shuttle-bus transportation to and from the downtown area during the day. And there's a fleet of yellow buses that operate from Wilhelminaplein to most parts of Curaçao.

LANGUAGE: Curaçao's native tongue is "Papiamento," a language which evolved from Spanish, Dutch, and Portuguese and combines a sprinkling of African and French words, as well as Caribbean Indian dialects. You won't experience a language problem, though. Most Curaçaoans are multilingual, speaking several languages, including Dutch, Spanish, and English.

MONEY: The currency of the Netherlands Antilles is the guilder (NAf), which fluctuates on the world market. At this writing, there are 1.77 guilders to the U.S. dollar.

The guilder is divided into 100 cents, and there are coins of 1 cent, 2 ½ cents, 5 cents (square nickel), 10 cents, 25 cents, and the 1 and 2 ½ guilder coins. Bank notes are issued in denominations of 1, 2 1/2, 5, 10, 25, 50, 100, 250, and 500 guilders.

If you also travel to Aruba, don't let the square coin confuse you! In the N.A. currency used in Curaçao and Bonaire the square coin is a nickel; in the Aruban currency it's a 50¢ piece.

U.S. dollars are accepted everywhere on the island. Although the hotels and shops in the downtown shopping district accept major credit cards, many local restaurants and shops require cash payment.

WEATHER: The climate in Curaçao is dry and sunny, and it's always summer there! The temperature stays a warm 80°, cooled by pleasant trade winds. There is only a slight change of temperature from day to night, and the difference between summer and winter is only 2° or 3°. The average rainfall is 20 inches per year, and it occurs in showers of short duration during the months of October, November, and December. This isn't truly a rainy season, though, and if you do seek shelter, you'll be able to get right back on the beach. The island lies completely outside the hurricane belt.

CLOTHING: Cool, casual, and informal summer clothes are the rule in Curaçao, for both men and women. Dress-up clothes are fun, but not entirely necessary, for a night out in the city or in the elegant hotel restaurants, nightclubs, or casinos. Dress-up for men usually means a jacket but no tie.

You should wear a coverup over bathing suits once you leave the beaches and pools of the resort hotels; bathing suits or revealing outfits aren't permitted in the shopping or business areas.

TIME: Curaçao keeps Atlantic Standard Time all year long. That means that during the winter, it's one hour later in Curaçao than it is in U.S. east-coast cities; during the summer, when U.S. cities observe Daylight Savings Time, the time is the same.

TELEPHONES: You can call Curaçao direct from the mainland United States. The international dialing code is 011; the area code is 599-5; then dial the five- or six-digit local number. When making calls in Curaçao, just dial the five- or six-digit local number.

You can make local and international telephone calls through hotel operators. The average price for a three-minute call to the mainland United States is approximately $10.

SHOPPING: U.S. Customs regulations allow U.S. citizens a $400 duty-free quota.

Although Curaçao no longer offers the kinds of bargains that made it a famous duty-free shopping destination, you can still get good buys on certain items: fragrances, jewelry and watches, designer clothing, china, crystal, flatware, and linens. Shop carefully before you leave home, so that you can compare prices; don't forget that sales taxes on high-ticket items in the United States can raise prices considerably.

Start your shopping on **Breedestraat,** lined with elegant stores that are institutions in the city. At the foot of the street, in a landmark 1709 building, is **Penha & Sons,** the exclusive distributor for many famous perfumes, including Lanvin, Chanel, Patou, and Yves Saint Laurent. There are also two floors of designer clothing for men and women at excellent prices.

You'll find four **Spritzer & Fuhrmann** stores on Breedestraat: One showcase china tableware, crystal stemware, and china and porcelain figurines; another focuses on optical goods including chic frames, opera glasses, binoculars, and barometers. Their "house of watches" branch features an extensive selection of Swiss timepieces; the main store, with its revolving figurines and carillon chimes that sound every quarter hour, specializes in diamond and gold jewelry, prestige watches, and exquisite clocks.

As you continue up Breedestraat, you'll come to **Gandelman Jewelers,** the only manufacturing jeweler in the Netherlands Antilles. This is the place to purchase a genuine "made in Curaçao" memento of your honeymoon. Gandelman's creates contemporary designs and settings, but the intricate gold filigree pieces are uniquely Curaçaoan. The **New Amsterdam Store** is next, with fabulous discounts on hand-embroidered linens. At **Kan,** housed in a beautifully renovated 18th-century gabled building, you'll find a splendid collection of Swiss watches, exquisite jewelry, and a fine selection of gift items. The ocher and white building with the balcony is the **Yellow House,** famous since 1887 for its selection of fragrances.

The centrally located **Gomezplein,** a popular plaza with sidewalk cafés, runs perpendicular to Breedestraat. Along with many adjacent narrow side-streets in Willemstad's shopping district, the Gomezplein has been closed to vehicular traffic and turned into a pedestrian shopping mall, where you'll find small boutiques with casual clothing and accessories, and gift shops carrying local items, including dolls dressed in traditional Curaçaoan costumes, and paintings by local artists. The famous Curaçao Liqueur in the traditional blue delft containers is also a good buy. This is something uniquely Curaçaoan; only a limited number of bottles is exported each year. Recently, many shops carrying electronic equipment have also moved into the Gomezplein area.

Stores are open Monday through Saturday from 8 a.m. to noon, and from 2 p.m. to 6 p.m.

SIGHTSEEING: A number of sightseeing operations, including **Casper Tours** (tel. 53010), **Daltino Tours** (tel. 61400), and **Taber Tours** (tel. 76637 or 76713) offer sightseeing excursions. Willemstad city tours cost approximately $30 per couple; half-day tours of the island cost approximately $30 per couple; full-day tours run $60 per couple.

HOW TO GET MARRIED IN CURAÇAO: Although Curaçao extends a warm and cordial welcome to just-married couples, you won't be able to say "I do" while visiting. Marriages are permitted only if one of the partners has been a resident of Curaçao for at least one year.

FOR FURTHER INFORMATION: Contact: **Curaçao Tourist Board,** Plaza Piar, Willemstad, Curaçao, N.A. (tel. 011/599-9/613397 or 011/599-9/611967). **Curaçao Tourist Board,** 400 Madison Ave., New York, NY 10017 (tel. 212/751-8266).

2. Romantic Interludes

Curaçao offers honeymoon couples all the attractions of a cosmopolitan city center, just minutes from exciting new recreational facilities.

Curaçao Underwater Park and Seaquarium, a 12.5-mile stretch of coral reef along Curaçao's southeast coast, is a paradise for scuba divers. Permanent mooring buoys protect the fragile reef from being damaged by the anchor of dive boats at 16 sites, including a wreck dive and several wall dives.

The underwater park stretches from Koral Specht to East Point, with many points accessible by car. The park's headquarters, though, are located just east of the Princess Beach Hotel, where a brand-new recreational complex has been developed. There's a sandy beach with lifeguards, changing facilities, lockers, and showers, two three-story wet-and-wild water slides, and a shop which rents Windsurfers, Sunfish, and other water-sports equipment.

Underwater Curaçao, a fully equipped dive shop in the recreation complex, can provide underwater equipment rentals and scuba diving instruction. Nondivers can follow the snorkel trail. You can also float over the reef in a glass-bottom boat.

The unique Curaçao Seaquarium displays the world's largest collection of tropical fish and coral in their natural habitat. Admission is $5 for adults and $2.50 for children.

The underwater park is a good place to unwind after a day in the city. There's often entertainment in the evening, and boats are available for sunset or moonlight excursions. The park has a first-class restaurant adjacent to the Seaquarium, and an open-air bar.

Rent a jeep (although a car will do) and drive 30 minutes from Willemstad to **Mt. Christoffel National Park** (tel. 640363), a 4,000-acre wildlife preserve. There a 35-mile network of well-marked roads winds through the hilly park leading to several breathtaking lookouts. Keep your arms inside your vehicle if your windows are open— much of the roadway is overgrown with spiny cactus and other scratchy vegetation. You can drive the shortest of four color-coded circuits in about an hour; the longest in under three hours. If you'd like to do some hiking, three of the routes provide access to footpaths that wind 1,239 feet up to the top of Christoffel—and the top of Curaçao— providing 360° panoramas. Although the path isn't difficult, it's best to go in the early morning, before it gets hot. Bring your own refreshments, since there are no services within the park. Open seven days a week from 8 a.m. to 3 p.m. Admission is $1.50.

3. Honeymoon Hotels and Hideaways

Curaçao's first-class hotels include a recently refurbished high-rise in the downtown area and a number of modern resort facilities on the outer edge of Willemstad. There is a 5% government room tax and a 10% service charge added to all room rates. The service charge on food and beverage is 10% to 15% in lieu of gratuities at the hotels.

The **Princess Beach Hotel & Casino,** Dr. Martin Luther King Blvd., Willemstad, Curaçao, N.A. (tel. 011/599-9/614944; U.S. reservations: tel. 212/840-2039 or toll free 800/221-4588), on the western edge of the Curaçao Underwater Park, is great for couples who like the outdoors, but don't want to give up any comforts! The accommodations are motel-style simple, but rooms under construction will be more luxurious. Most rooms have sitting areas, and those that face the ocean have sliding glass doors and patios. The Dive Curaçao & Watersports facility is part of the resort, so you can rent equipment or take diving instructions just a few steps from your room. When it's time for relaxing, there are two private white-sand beaches lined with thatch-roof umbrellas, snack tables and chairs, and an Olympic-size saltwater swimming pool surrounded by full-length lounge chairs covered with brightly colored, overstuffed pillows. The casino is the most modern on the island, and there's live entertainment every evening at the Patio Bar. Honeymoon package: Five days/four nights (EP): $325 per couple. Modified American Plan is available for an additional $30 per person per day. Includes welcome cocktails, casino coupons worth $10, Curaçao T-shirts or hats, a glass-bottom boat trip for two.

Holiday Beach Hotel & Casino, P.O. Box 2178, Willemstad, Curaçao, N.A. (tel. 011-599-9/625400; U.S. reservations: tel. 212/840-6636). Each of the rooms in this four-level, self-contained resort has a sliding glass door opening onto its own balcony and spectacular views of the ocean. It's located on Rif Beach, to the west of Willemstad. The rooms are comfortable and colorful; the white rattan furniture is accented by drapes and spreads in tropical shades of orange, yellow, and green. You can loll on the private beach or around the pool, or enjoy unlimited water sports and tennis. The Holiday Beach also has dancing, entertainment, and gambling at the Casino

Royale. Honeymoon package: Eight days/seven nights (EP): $475 to $666 per couple. Includes a bottle of champagne, casino coupons worth $20, scuba diving lessons in the pool for two.

Las Palmas Hotel & Vacation Village, Piscardera Baai, Willemstad, Curaçao, N.A. (tel. 011/599-9/625200; U.S. reservations: tel. 203/849-1470 or toll free 800/622-7836). This white stucco, orange-roofed village is made up of a 100-room low-rise hotel and close to a hundred one- and two-bedroom villas with kitchenettes, sliding glass doors, and terraces scattered across the property. The accommodations have a light and breezy feeling; most of the furnishings are built-in European style, and have orange lacquer accents. It's a casual, low-key resort on Piscadera Bay, on the outskirts of Willemstad, with a swimming pool and lighted tennis courts on the grounds. A short walk away lies the private beach with complete water-sports facilities. Honeymoon package: None. Standard eight days/seven nights rate (EP): $546 to $686 per couple for a standard room; villas are $135 per couple per day.

In the heart of the Punda section of downtown Willemstad, the **Curaçao Plaza Hotel,** P.O. Box 229, Willemstad, Curaçao, N.A. (tel. 011/599-9/612500; U.S. reservations: tel. 212/661-4540 or toll free 800/223-1588), is built on the foundation of one of the forts that guarded the entrance to Santa Anna Bay. Its architecture blends beautifully with Willemstad's colonial gable-roofed houses, but the hotel has a thoroughly modern and sophisticated atmosphere. It was recently remodeled and refurbished, and you'll enjoy the state-of-the-art disco and casino. Although the location rules out beach facilities, a free shuttle bus will transport you to nearby hotels, where you'll enjoy complete beach privileges. Honeymoon package: None. Standard eight days/seven nights rate (EP): $490 to $630 per couple.

4. Romantic Restaurants and Night Spots

For a special dinner in a unique setting, search out a restaurant located in one of Willemstad's landmark buildings. Local fare has a strong Dutch influence, with many dishes using Dutch cheeses and Indonesian spices.

Restaurant prices are usually listed in both guilders and U.S. dollars; a 10% to 15% service charge is almost always added to your bill.

MODERATE

Fort Nassau, Fort Nassau, Willemstad (tel. 613086 or 613450). This unique restaurant perched high above the Schottegat Harbor provides a charming setting and spectacular views of the dollhouse-size buildings of the Punda. It's in the ruins of a 200-year-old fortress, and winding, low-ceilinged passageways lead to the many-windowed dining room. Cold and warm appetizers are priced under $7. Entrées are truly international, and priced at $12 to $15. We enjoyed scampi a l'Indienne, mildly seasoned with curry, and Hawaiian chicken breast, served with pineapple and melted cheese. Desserts include a number of ice cream confections at $4. The wine list is extensive, with most selections in the $20 to $30 range. Open for lunch (noon to 2 p.m.) Monday through Friday. Dinner daily (6:30 to 11 p.m.). Reservations recommended.

Bistro Le Clochard, Rif Fort, Willemstad (tel. 625666 or 625667). Set in the vaults of the 18th-century Rif Fort, the bistro's rustic interior is dark wood and white stucco; a picture window provides a sentry's view of the harbor and the Queen Emma Bridge. Gourmet Swiss and French cuisine include creamy fondues, wonderful bouillabaisse from fresh local fish, and French onion soup. The desserts are out of this world; try the vanilla ice cream flavored with Cheri-Suisse liqueur or the crêpes with strawberries and Grand Marnier. Appetizers are priced under $10. Entrées priced between $15 and $25. Wines range from $20 to $25. Open for lunch from noon to 3 p.m. and dinner from 6 p.m. on weekdays; dinner only, from 6 p.m.; on Saturday; closed Sunday.

Bellevue Restaurant, in Parera, overlooking the Dutch naval base (tel. 54291 or 54294). This family-owned-and-operated restaurant is a hangout for local bigwigs and government officials, and you'll see lots of meeting and greeting, hand shaking and back slapping. At $12, the special Funchi Table is a bargain. It combines *funchi* (a white type of cornbread) with five local delicacies: Keshi Yena (gouda cheeseball stuffed with chicken and spices and baked), a stewed fishball, stewed goat meat, stewed codfish, and a vegetable stew of the day. Open daily except Sundays for lunch from noon to 2 p.m. and for dinner from 7 till 10 p.m.

Inexpensive

Jaanchie's, in West Point at the far end of Curaçao (tel. 640126). If you go to the national park, this is a "must stop" place for lunch. Jantje Christiaan runs a large, open-air, family-style restaurant that his father started in 1939. Ask to see some of the guestbooks that date back to 1962, and don't forget to add your name to the current one. Although Jaanchie's provides standard steak, chicken, and pork-chop fare, this is the place for fish. Don't even ask for a menu—just order the daily special (wahoo is Jantje's favorite, but the catch of the day could be barracuda, red snapper, or grouper) with funchi and fried bananas. A generous portion is $6, an extra large serving is $8. Open 7 days from 10 a.m. to 6 p.m.

For nightclub shows or disco dancing try **Infinity** (tel. 613450), located downstairs from the restaurant in Willemstad's Fort Nassau. Infinity has an intimate atmosphere in the midst of glittering lights. It's open every night till 2 a.m. **Naick's Place** (tel. 614640) in Salinja stays open till 4 a.m., and has a disk jockey spinning the latest European and U.S. hits. **The Studio Club** (tel. 612272), also in Salinja, has live entertainment; reservations essential on weekends.

More casual places include **De Tempel** (tel. 613410) in Wilhelminaplein, where art exhibits and jazz sessions are held in a former synagogue. You can play cards or darts, or listen to music at **The Pub** on Schottegatweg Oost (tel. 612190). **The T Cafe,** in Salinja (tel. 615940) and **Tap Maar In** on Santa Rosaweg (tel. 77344) are best known for their happy hours in the early evening.

Chapter XXX

GUADELOUPE

1. Practical Facts
2. Romantic Interludes
3. Honeymoon Hotels and Hideaways
4. Romantic Restaurants and Night Spots

A FAR-FLUNG PIECE OF FRANCE, Guadeloupe attracts honeymooners seeking understated adventures. It is actually a butterfly-shaped pair of islands divided by a stream. Basse-Terre, the green, mountainous western wing covers 312 square miles. Flatter, drier Grande-Terre, to the east, spreads over 218 miles. Along with Martinique and the rest of the French Caribbean, this Leeward Island in the Lesser Antilles is an overseas region of France. This means that its 330,000 residents are citizens of France and enjoy all the same rights as their European compatriots.

Most of Guadeloupe's larger hotels are clustered in Grande-Terre's centrally located Gosier. This beachfront village boasts a casino and several lively discos. The stores in nearby Pointe-à-Pitre, the main town, draw shoppers and browsers. Fish, fruit, and vegetables are piled high at the open-air market and ferries leave from the dock for offshore islands, such as peaceful Terre-de-Haut.

Along Grande-Terre's southern coast are old sugar mill towers, cane fields, and the stunning beaches of Sainte Anne. Saint François is a fishing village with another spectacular beach. An 18-hole golf course is near the Meridien, the only large hotel in the area, and Guadeloupe's second casino is at the marina.

More than half of fertile Basse-Terre, with its banana plantations, waterfalls, volcano, and cloud-topped mountains, consists of the Parc Naturel. Go hiking or take a drive through this scenic area where fluffy pines stand next to palms and towering bamboo stalks.

Columbus came upon Guadeloupe in 1493. The resident Carib Indians valiantly fought off Spain's attempts to claim it. The island fell into French hands in .1635 and the French and British squabbled over control until 1763, when the island was restored to France. After the abolition of slavery in 1848, East Indians were brought in to work in the fields.

Since tourism was almost nonexistent in Guadeloupe before the 1970s, the calm lifestyle of the island is still very much as it has always been: French, accented with African and East Indian influences. People greet each other with kisses on both cheeks and French wine flows with lunch and dinner. Topless bathing is the norm on most beaches. The local beguine music has a rousing African beat and the creole spoken by almost everyone combines French with West African words.

A honeymoon in Guadeloupe means indescribably delicious food, water sports galore, quiet beaches, and a chance to get next to nature in the French version of the tropics.

1. Practical Facts

GETTING THERE: In addition to a return or onward-bound ticket, Americans need proof of U.S. citizenship. While a valid passport (or one that has expired within the last five years) is best, an authenticated birth certificate or a voter's registration card is also acceptable. For Canadians, a valid passport is required. A departure tax will be included in your air fare.

You'll have no problem reaching Guadeloupe, no matter how you travel.

By Air

Flying time is about three hours from Miami and just over four from New York. **American Airlines** jets in from New York, Newark, and other U.S. cities by way of San Juan. **Eastern** offers direct flights from Miami and flies from New York, Newark, and other U.S. cities via San Juan. **Air France** will take you from Miami and San Juan, and **LIAT,** the airline of the Caribbean, flies from many other islands. Local airlines with flights to Les Saintes, St. Barts, and other islands include **Air Guadeloupe** and **Caraibes Air Tourisme.**

By Ship

Cruise ships dock downtown in Pointe-à-Pitre, near the shopping district. Immigration and customs officials board right away and passengers are cleared within a few minutes. The larger ships—more like aquatic resorts—have extensive facilities, such as swimming pools, health spas, and water-sports platforms. Some cruise lines include air fare to the point of embarkation in their rates.

The 750-passenger *Cunard Countess,* for example, boasts an outdoor pool and a casino. The year-round, 14-night cruises leave from San Juan for Tortola, St. Martin, St. Thomas, and other islands in addition to Guadeloupe. Rates range from $3,565 to $6,100 per couple. (Contact Cunard Line, tel. 212/661-7505.) One of the most romantic cruises is on a 126-passenger yacht, the *Fantôme,* which was launched in 1927. Aristotle Onassis once purchased it as a wedding gift for Princess Grace and Prince Rainier. The year-round, five-night cruises go from Antigua to Guadeloupe and other islands. Rates are $1,300 per couple. (Contact Windjammer Barefoot Cruises, tel. 212/686-4868.)

GETTING AROUND: There are several convenient ways to get to know Guadeloupe.

By Taxi

You'll be able to find taxis at Raizet International Airport, in both Pointe-à-Pitre and Basse Terre, and at major hotels. Since cabs do not have meters, check the rates, which are posted at taxi stands and the Office of Tourism, before getting into a cab. Many drivers don't speak much English, so if you don't speak French, take along a dictionary or phrase book. From 9 p.m. to 7 a.m., a taxi ride will cost 40% more than during the day.

By Bus

If you want to save money and you're at least semicomfortable with a bit of French, climb into the vans that crisscross Guadeloupe. In downtown Pointe-à-Pitre, the jitneys at Gare Routière de Mortenol will take you to Grande-Terre hotels and other locales. The vans at Gare Routière de Bergevin are headed for places in Basse-Terre. From Pointe-à-Pitre all the way to southern Basse-Terre, the ride is only about $3 per person.

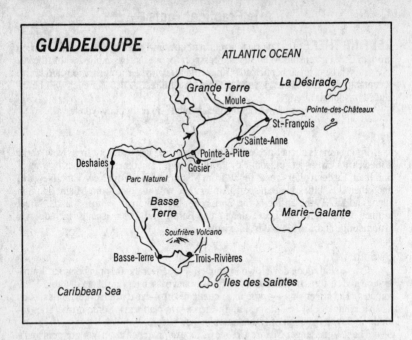

By Rental Car

The excellent road system makes driving a pleasure in Guadeloupe. Be forewarned, however, that local drivers always seem to be in a hurry. You're required to have a valid license or a temporary permit in order to rent a car. You'll save money by renting by the week. Using a credit card will allow you to avoid the $250 to $400 cash deposit. Especially if you're traveling during the winter season, you may want to make a reservation before you leave home. **Avis** (tel. 82-33-47), **Budget** (tel. 82-95-58), **Hertz** (tel. 82-00-14), and others have offices at Guadeloupe's international airport. Some also have branches in Pointe-à-Pitre, Basse-Terre, and many hotels. Local companies include **Guadeloupe Cars** (tel. 82-10-94) and **Agence Azur** (tel. 82-90-43).

By Ferry

You can fly to Terre de Haut, an offshore island in the group known as Les Saintes. But when the water is calm, the trip is wonderful by sea. Ferries depart from Pointe-à-Pitre on Grande-Terre (a 1¼-hour ride) and from Trois-Rivières on Basse-Terre (a 30-minute ride).

LANGUAGE: If you speak French but don't understand conversations you overhear, you're probably listening to creole, Guadeloupe's second language. This patois combines French, Spanish, English, and words from West African languages. Unless you speak French, be sure to take along a phrase book and a dictionary. The larger hotels have English-speaking staff, but you'll need to know some French if you plan to venture beyond the tourist areas.

MONEY AND TIPPING: As in France, the franc is Guadeloupe's official currency. You'll get the best exchange rates at banks, which open Monday through Friday at 7:30 a.m., close from 12:30 to 2:30 p.m., then reopen until 5 p.m. U.S. dollars are accepted at some shops, restaurants, and hotels. Some stores give an additional 20% discount when you pay with traveler's checks.

Restaurant checks often include the tip, so ask if you're not sure. Hotel rates also frequently include the service charge for your room maid and other staff. Otherwise, a tip of 10% to 15% is fine. It is not necessary to tip porters, but if you are so inclined, you can give one franc per bag. Most taxi drivers, many of whom own their cabs, don't expect tips.

WEATHER: During the day, temperatures average in the high 70s and low 80s. Although the weather is warmest in the summer, there is very little variation in temperature throughout the year. Trade winds blow constantly, keeping the weather pleasant year-round. Rainfall is usually brief, followed by sunshine.

CLOTHING: Like life in general in Guadeloupe, dress is also a relaxed affair. Men hardly ever wear jackets at dinner and ties are almost nonexistent. However, evening attire tends to be somewhat dressier during the winter season than during the summer. Women should pack a shawl or light sweater for cool evenings or air-conditioned restaurants and clubs. Also, women won't need their bikini tops at hotel beaches, but can certainly wear them if they prefer. Beachwear should only be worn at the poolside or the ocean.

ELECTRICAL CURRENT: Electricity is 220 volts ÀC, 50 cycles, so you'll need converters and adapter plugs for your hairdryer or other appliances. Some hotels keep converters and adapters on hand, but it's best to bring your own.

TIME: Guadeloupe is on Atlantic Standard Time, which is an hour later than Eastern Standard Time. When it is 10 a.m. in New York during the winter, it is 11 a.m. in Guadeloupe. However, when Eastern Daylight Saving Time is in effect, the time is the same in Guadeloupe and U.S. east coast cities. Time is told in the French way here; for example, 1 p.m. is called 13 hours.

TELEPHONES: To make direct calls to Guadeloupe, dial 011-590, then the six-digit local number.

SHOPPING: French imports such as cosmetics and perfumes are excellent buys, along with crystal and china. Mostly found in Pointe-à-Pitre, stores are open Monday through Friday and Saturday mornings. During the week, they close for lunch from noon to 2:30 p.m. Try **Vendôme** (rue Frébault, Pointe-à-Pitre) for watches, jewelry, and imported fashions for men and women. With several locations in Pointe-à-Pitre and Basse-Terre, Rose'bleu has a large selection of crystal and French cosmetics. If you'd like clothes made of the vibrantly colorful madras cloth used for head ties by some local women, visit **Le Bambou** (rue de la Liberté) in St. François. You are each allowed to take home $400 worth of purchases duty-free. For a change of scenery and an appealing selection of shops, plan an excursion to St. Bart's, one of Guadeloupe's dependencies.

CASINOS: In the mood for roulette wheels and blackjack? Place your bets at the centrally located Gosier-les-Bains, the casino next door to the Arawak hotel, or at Casino la Marina, near the Meridien and Hamak hotels in St. François. Guadeloupe's gambling crowd tends to dress up somewhat. Admission to the casinos is about $10 and you'll need to show your passport or driver's license with a photo.

HOW TO GET MARRIED IN GUADELOUPE: If you are considering beginning your honeymoon in Guadeloupe with a wedding, you should know that one partner must have lived in the French West Indies for at least 30 days before filing the marriage license application. Applications are available at the local *mairie* (town hall). You'll need to have a birth certificate, proof of citizenship, proof of divorce (if applicable), and a medical certificate—all accompanied by French translations. (For the medical certificate, a list of qualified English-speaking doctors is available by contacting the American Consulate in Martinique, Immeuble Place Pere Labat, 14 rue Blenac, 97206 Fort-de-France; tel. 596/63-13-03, or your local French Consulate.) Allow at least ten days after filing the application for the publication and posting of the marriage banns (the official announcement of your intention to marry). You may be asked to take a blood test and witnesses will be necessary. A religious wedding may only be performed *after* the civil service. The minister, priest, or rabbi must be given a certificate of civil marriage (certificat de célébration civile) before performing the religious ceremony.

FOR FURTHER INFORMATION: Contact the **French West Indies Tourist Board,** 610 Fifth Ave., New York, NY 10020, 212/757-1125 or **Office Departemental du Tourisme de la Guadeloupe,** B.P. 1099, Angle des Rues Schoelcher et Delgrès, 97110 Pointe-à-Pitre, Guadeloupe, French West Indies, 590/82-09-30.

2. Romantic Interludes

According to Jacques Cousteau, **Pigeon Island,** off the western coast of Basse-Terre, is "one of the world's ten best" places for scuba diving. You'll swim side by side with spotted, striped, and iridescent fish darting in and out of coral configurations and waving ferns. To see the deep, make arrangements at the **Nautilus Club** (tel. 86-70-34) on Malendure beach, **Les Heures Saines** (tel. 82-77-58) at Bas-du-Fort Marina, or dive operations at hotels in Gosier. The uninitiated can take lessons through places including **Aqua-Fari** (tel. 84-15-00) at **La Crèole Beach or Karukera** (tel. 84-12-93) at the PLM Callinago.

Snorkeling is particularly exciting along the western and southern coasts of Basse-Terre; at the St. François reef, near Grande-Terre's southern coast; and around Ilet de Gosier, just offshore from Gosier hotels, most of which provide equipment.

Much of the land in lush, mountainous Basse-Terre is part of the **Parc Naturel,** or Natural Park. Pack a picnic and go exploring. Near the entrance to the park in the north, follow a rocky path to La Cascade aux Écrevisses (Crayfish Falls)—be sure to wear good walking shoes. The path is dappled with sunlight peeking through the thick, overhanging trees. The falls are great for a refreshing dip. There is a zoo and botanical garden in this area, where you'll find plants and animals native to Guadeloupe, from iguanas and land crabs to friendly raccoons.

Route de La Traversée highway cuts across the island from east to west, through tropical forests, past lakes and valleys, and between the pair of mountains aptly called Les Deux Mamelles (the Two Breasts). Going north along the west coast, you'll come to Deshaies. Here you'll find one of Guadeloupe's most prized beaches, in a bay enclosed by hills and mountains.

Head south on Basse-Terre toward the quiet, picturesque capital of Guadeloupe, also called Basse-Terre. Tiny villages, a flower nursery, and the Hindu temple of Changy dot the countryside. The most accessible part of the three-tiered Carbet Falls is reached on foot (about a 20-minute walk). The source of the river that feeds the falls is in the famed 4,813-foot **Soufrière volcano.** Steam and sulfurous fumes often burst from it. You can drive to the foot of the crater. Park at Savane-à-Mulet and touch the ground. You'll feel the intense heat of the subterranean lava. If you're ready for an adventure, climb to the edge of the volcano to peek into the boiling crater.

In Grande-Terre at Pointe-des-Châteaux, the narrowest part of Guadeloupe, the calm Caribbean meets the turbulent Atlantic. Here a dramatic series of rocks rises from the water looking like huge **abstract sculptures.** When you come to view this stunning example of nature's handiwork, be sure to bring your cameras and your appetites. Good casual seafood restaurants dot the road to Pointe-des-Châteaux. The coves off the road are good for secluded swimming and the beach at Pointe Tarare is reserved for nude bathing.

Deshaies, on the western coast of Basse-Terre, is a good place to charter a **sailboat.** Here a bay enclosed by hills is rimmed by Grande Anse, one of Guadeloupe's most inviting beaches. Try a romantic moonlight sail on the catamaran *Papyrus* (tel. 82-87-26). At the Marina de St. François, **Evasion Marine** (tel. 84-47-28) offers one-week and two-week sailing courses. Companies specializing in boat and yacht charters include **Locaraibes** (tel. 91-07-80) at the Bas du Fort Port de Plaisance, and **Basse-Terre Yachting** (tel. 81-11-45) at the Marina de Rivière-Sens. Check hotel desks for more information about bareboat or crewed sailboats.

For a change of pace, take a day trip to a **nearby island.** Beach-fringed Terre-de-Haut, in the group of tiny islands called Les Saintes, is anchored off the southern coast of Basse-Terre. You can fly here, but the breezy ferry ride is more romantic. At the dock where you arrive, children sell tourments d'amour, freshly baked coconut or banana tarts that are not to be missed. When you leave the colorful town square, you'll see far more pedestrians, goats, cows, and iguanas than cars along the narrow, roller-coaster roads. On the way to the beach, either on foot or in a minibus taxi, you'll pass small cottages with bright flowers spilling over their front fences. The unending view from Fort Napoleon and the gardens there are worth the steep trip. Fishing boats tie up in the bay in front of Le Foyal Restaurant, which serves unusual dishes like seafood pizza.

Fly over to St. Barthélemy. Those who have come to know this small island 140 miles north of Guadeloupe affectionately refer to it as St. Barts. The name of the capital, Gustavia, recalls the island's Swedish heritage. Especially during the annual August Festival of St. Barthélemy, boats fill the rectangular harbor. La Langouste Restaurant is the place to try fresh local lobster. Then visit some of the duty-free shops. Rent a mini-moke (an open-air jeep)—the island is so hilly that if you're not going up, it's only because you're going down. Even in high season, you'll have no trouble finding an empty beach. In some areas, old women wearing the starched white bonnets of their ancestors from Normandy sell tempting straw goods outside their homes.

3. Honeymoon Hotels and Hideaways

Most hotels are in seaside Gosier and nearby Bas du Fort. If you don't need to be near other hotels, try quieter areas like St. François on Grande-Terre and Deshaies on Basse-Terre. Sprinkled throughout the island, the smaller hotels, many of which are charming family-run inns, are collectively known as Relais Créoles.

High season runs from about mid-December through mid-April; low season rates dip about 20% to 50%. The price ranges given for hotels in this chapter reflect the low- and high-season rates. A 10% or 15% tax and service charge is generally included in room rates. In some resort areas, you'll also pay an additional government tax of approximately $1 per person per day.

EXPENSIVE: Auberge de la Vieille Tour, 97190 Gosier, Guadeloupe, F.W.I. (tel. 590/84-23-23; U.S. reservations: tel. 212/757-6500 or toll free 800/223-9862). The reception area of this comfortable hotel is in the tower of a sugar mill dating back to 1835. Equipped with balconies, mini-bars, and direct-dial telephones, the 80 modern rooms have been built onto this old structure. Book a deluxe room if you want television and closed-circuit videos. Wander through the gardens surrounding the tower, float on your back in the fresh-water pool, stretch out on the private beach, or join a volleyball game. Nude bathers are whisked over to the Ilet de Gosier, just offshore. Most nights during the high season, guests flock to the gourmet dining room, relax at the piano bar, or dance to the infectious music of a steel band at the beachside Ajoupa restaurant. Tennis courts are lit for night games. The small town of Gosier is a brief walk away. Honeymoon package: Eight days / seven nights (full breakfast, served in your room the first morning): from $1,130 per couple. Includes a bottle of local rum, a fruit basket, one candlelit champagne dinner, and admission to a disco.

Known as the Frantel Guadeloupe in its previous life, the **PLM Azur Marissol**, Bas du Fort, 97190 Gosier, Guadeloupe, F.W.I. (tel. 590/90-84-44; U.S. reservations: tel. 212/757-6500 or toll free 800/223-9862), has 200 rooms, including 50 bungalows. About a ten-minute drive from Pointe-à-Pitre, it is within walking distance of a handful of restaurants, cafés, and other hotels. Glossy leaves of banana trees and other greenery decorate the grounds. The beach is human-made, but it's hard to tell, and the pool lets you take a break from the sand. Guests also amuse themselves with Sunfish sailboats, pedal-boats, volleyball, tennis, and shopping in the boutiques. The tiled rooms have mini-bars, and baths are French style, with separate toilets. You'll find televisions in deluxe rooms. If you have a taste for pizza, the poolside snack bar is the place to go. Gourmet meals are served up at Le Grand Baie. After dark, Le Foufou reverberates with disco and island sounds. Honeymoon package: Eight days / seven nights (full breakfast, served in your room the first morning): from $1,080 per couple. Includes a bottle of local rum, a fruit basket, one candlelit champagne dinner, and admission to a disco.

Fleur d'Épeé-Novotel, Bas du Fort, 97190 Gosier, Guadeloupe, F.W.I. (tel. 590/90-81-49; U.S. reservations: tel. 212/354-3722 or toll free 800/221-4542). There always seems to be a flurry of fun-filled activity at this hotel. Located in three wings of a three-story building, most of the 180 attractive rooms have balconies. The Fleur d'Épée shares a beach with the PLM Azur Marissol, and like its neighbor, it attracts a casual, young crowd. A large swimming pool, pedal-boats, all kinds of water sports, Ping-Pong, and volleyball keep guests moving. Shops in the lobby draw many browsers. Gosier hotels and Pointe-à-Pitre are each about a ten-minute drive from here. Honeymoon package: Eight days / seven nights (BP): from $1,000 per couple. Includes a bottle of champagne, a lobster dinner, and a shopping tour of Poite-à-Pitre.

Hamak, 97118 Saint François, Guadeloupe, F.W.I. (tel. 590/88-59-99; U.S. reservations: tel. 212/477-1600 or toll free 800/223-1510). In a quiet part of the island 25 miles from the airport, Hamak is conveniently located across from an 18-hole Robert Trent Jones–designed golf course and near the marina. Pamper yourselves in a luxurious beachfront bungalow. Reclining in your personal hammock on your front patio, you'll be lulled by the surf at the small beach. Out back is another patio and an outdoor shower (lush foliage ensures privacy). Furnishings include twin or double beds, sitting areas with a couch and a desk, and modern kitchenettes. Villas and duplexes are available. Jimmy Carter, Giscard d'Estaing, and other leaders knew what they were doing when they held the 1979 international summit at Hamak. Rainbow-colored Sunfish speckle the water, which sparkles an amazing shade of pale turquoise in this area. Many guests play tennis when they are not taking advantage of water sports. The Méridien Hotel and a casino are right nearby. Honeymoon package: none. Rates (CP): $165 to $336 per couple per night.

MODERATE: **Arawak**, 97190 Gosier, Guadeloupe, F.W.I. (tel. 590/84-24-24; U.S. reservations: tel. 212/832-2277 or toll free 800/223-9862). At ten stories, the 160-room Arawak rises high on a nice stretch of private beach. A broad, breezy lobby welcomes visitors to the hotel, which has one of Guadeloupe's two casinos right on the premises. Water-sports facilities are available, and a pool and tennis courts also keep guests busy. At night, live entertainment sizzles at the West Indies Bar. Cheerfully furnished, the spacious rooms have mini-bars. Both superior and deluxe rooms come with televisions and closed-circuit video. Honeymoon package: none. Rates (CP): $63 to $145 per couple per night.

La Créole Beach Hotel, Pointe de la Verdure, 97190 Gosier, Guadeloupe,

F.W.I. (tel. 590/84-26-26; U.S. reservations: toll free 800/465-4329). At the end of the Gosier hotel strip, the 156-room Créole Beach has not one but two beaches, one of which has long attracted those who prefer to bathe in the buff. No matter what kind of water sport you want to get into, chances are you'll find it here—if not at the beach shared with the other hotels. Tennis courts can be used by day or night. Bursts of bougainvillea, hibiscus, and other colorful blossoms are sprinkled throughout the nicely landscaped grounds. All of the large guest rooms have televisions, telephones, and open onto balconies or terraces. Many have two double beds. Honeymoon package: none. Rates (FAP): $112 to $185 per couple per night.

Sernida's Hotel & Restaurant, Dampierre, 97190 Gosier, Guadeloupe, F.W.I. (tel. 590/84-29-29; U.S. reservations: tel. 212/840-6636 or toll free 800/223-9815). In this intimate seven-room hotel, guests are treated like relatives. All rooms are air-conditioned and the eye-catching wooden furniture is locally made. In addition to personal attention, a truly breathtaking view of the ocean and offshore islands comes as part of the package. Surrounded by flowers, a miniature windmill sits in a pleasant garden near the restaurant. At the tables, artfully rolled white napkins are bent U-shaped in the glasses. The delicious creole cooking keeps most of the tall-backed chairs occupied at meal times. Honeymoon package: none. Rates (CP): $50 to $73 per couple per night.

Cap Sud Caraïbes Hotel, Chemin de la Plage, Petit Havre, 97190 Gosier, Guadeloupe, F.W.I. (tel. 590/88-96-02; U.S. reservations: tel. 212/840-6636 or toll free 800/223-9815). In a tranquil residential neighborhood near Sainte Anne, this 12-room hotel sits high above the water. A tiled staircase with a dark wooden bannister snakes around the outside of the pink building. While dining in the cozy breakfast room near the pool, you'll have a stunning view of the ocean far below. On a clear day—and there are many in Guadeloupe—you can see the islands of Les Saintes, Dominica, and Marie-Galante. The beach is not far from the hotel. Rooms are all decorated with color-splashed paintings. Some have terraces and sunken tiled bathrooms. Honeymoon Package: none. Rates (CP): $94 to $100 per couple per night.

With 271 rooms, the **Hotel Méridien,** 97118 Saint François, Guadeloupe, F.W.I. (tel. 88-51-00; U.S. reservations: tel. 212/265-4494 or toll free 800/223-9918), is the largest hotel in drowsy Saint François. This is a good choice for couples who want the bustle of a resort in low-key surroundings. A gorgeous beach and the Méridien's proximity to the 18-hole golf course, the marina, and the casino add to its appeal. Tennis courts, extensive water sports, and a swimming pool are available to guests. Rooms are comfortably stylish, with tropical touches. You'll choose among several restaurants, from casual to gourmet, and nightlife on the premises can be quite lively. Honeymoon package: none. Rates: (EP) $94 to $210 per couple per night.

4. Romantic Restaurants and Night Spots

Guadeloupe's renowned creole cuisine combines the best of delicate French food with the spice of Caribbean cooking. Characterized by light sauces, dishes are flavored with lime, basil, thyme, and mint. Seafood steals the show on many menus, with favorites such as sunfish, red snapper, soudons (tiny clams), lambi (conch), langouste (clawless local lobster), and steamed baby shark. You can also sample roast duckling and fricassee of goat. For a sweet surrender, try coconut custard, mango sherbert, or a lemon soufflé.

If you're in Guadeloupe in August, don't miss the legendary Fête des Cuisinières (Festival of Women Cooks). Come hungry—food is free. Festivities include music, dancing, and a procession of the cooks, all decked out in traditional madras dresses. If you taste something you just can't get enough of, don't worry. Many of the cooks run local restaurants.

EXPENSIVE: Auberge de la Vieille Tour, Gosier (tel. 84-12-04). The old sugar-mill tower out front lets you know you've arrived at this gourmet hotel restaurant. Chandeliers hang from beamed ceilings in the main dining room. Waitresses wear colorful creole madras dresses. Table d'hôte and à la carte selections include seafood crêpes, roast lamb with saffron, and clams in escargot butter. The wine list is long and good. About $70 for dinner for two.

La Canne à Sucre, Pointe-à-Pitre (tel. 83-58-48). Few people who like to eat leave Guadeloupe without spending at least one evening with Gérard and Marie Virginius. They have converted this old home into a gourmet restaurant with an international reputation. The dining area is a study in pink and white—pink ceiling beams, pink borders around the shuttered windows, white lace curtains. Paintings and elaborately framed mirrors decorate the walls, and ceiling fans stir the air. Flower bouquets sit beside lamps with fringed shades. The menu tempts diners with rich pumpkin soup, coquilles St-Jacques, pig's feet, red snapper cooked in coconut milk, chicken stuffed with conch, and grilled lamb chops. Side dishes include purée of bananas and purée of yams. Chocoholics won't be able to resist the chocolate mousse with amandine white sauce. Expect to spend about $70 per couple.

Hidden in an undistinguished shopping center, elegant **La Plantation,** Bas du Fort (tel. 90-84-83), is open for dinner only. The chef continually changes his highly creative nouvelle cuisine dishes—try the duck breast with pears. Reservations are essential. Closed Sunday nights. The cost: about $70 per couple including wine. Hammocks are strung across the dining room ceiling at **Hamak,** Saint-François (tel. 88-59-99). Fish brochette with Indian rice is a delicious choice, and a favorite for dessert is vanilla ice cream topped with toasted almonds, pineapple, and caramel sauce. Plan to spend $60 and up per couple.

MODERATE: Fruit de la Passion, Bas du Fort, Gosier (tel. 91-21-91). There are not even ten tables in this roadside restaurant located on a front porch. The young chef / owner is always on hand to ensure that the creole food is as attractively presented as it is delicious. Diners feast on dishes such as freshly caught fish and beef brochette, accompanied by red rice and vegetable garnishes—and served on square wooden plates. Meals begin with light, puffed accras (cod fritters) or lobster bisque with a dash of sherry. Coconut or passion fruit ice cream are on the menu for dessert. Cooking is done on an outdoor grill. Hung with paintings and starfish, low bamboo and wood-paneled walls leave the dining area open to the sun or stars. Dinner for two: $25 to $45.

Le Karacoli, Deshaies (tel. 28-41-17). When you're touring northern Basse-Terre, plan to have lunch here. The breezy patio, set back from stunning Grand Anse beach, is shaded by tall palms pierced by shafts of sunlight. Tables are covered with red-and-white plaid or checkered tablecloths. Owner Lucienne Salcede has made sure that all meals here are memorable. Begin as Guadeloupeans do, with potent punch made with rum and pieces of tropical fruit. Conch or crab in a cream sauce comes in a clam shell. Try blood sausage, lobster salad, grilled kingfish, or curried lamb—all served with rice and peas. For a delicious finale, order a flambéed banana flanked by scoops of ice cream. Then stretch out on the beach. The cost is about $20 or $30 per couple.

At **Balata,** Gosier (tel. 91-50-41), the owners from Lyon combine the spice of creole with French regional cuisine. Save room for something from the dessert trolley. Dinner for two: $40 and up plus drinks. Closed Sunday nights and all day Monday. Specialties at **L'Accras,** Sainte Anne (tel. 88-22-40), include conch in a creamy white sauce, steak, and local vegetables. A meal for two will cost about $20 to $35.

INEXPENSIVE: Chez Lucile, Le Moule (tel. 84-51-63). This no-frills restaurant may *look* plain, but there is nothing plain about the creole food. A recent visitor remarked that eating here was "like having your own mother cook for you"—providing, of course, that your mother can cook up a storm. Try spiny lobster, broiled "catch of the day," blood pudding, and that bite-size staple, accras. Bring your bathing suits: Chez Lucile is in a small fishing village with an irresistible curve of beach. A meal for two can be well under $20.

La Nouvelle Table Créole, Saint-Félix, Gosier (tel. 84-28-28). Before moving to these large, oceanview quarters with ten vacation bungalows on the grounds, Jeanne Carmelita (known as Madame Jeanne) spent three decades running a small restaurant nearby. Try the red snapper grilled with ginger, blaff (a spicy fish stew), beef brochette, or lobster fricassée. Some evenings a steel band plays during dinner. The cost for two will be about $15 to $25.

NIGHTLIFE: Nightlife is most active in the Gosier area. Some clubs charge an admission fee of about $10. At **Mandingo** (Gosier) live bands will show you what beguine is all about. Spend a romantic evening listening to jazz or calypso at **West Indies** (Arawak Hotel, Gosier). If you want to combine dinner with discoing, check out Elysées Matignon (Bas du Fort), which plays a lot of European popular music.

Chapter XXXI

JAMAICA

1. **Practical Facts**
2. **Montego Bay**
3. **Negril**
4. **Mandeville**
5. **Ocho Rios**
6. **Port Antonio**

IRIE. It's a word you'll see emblazoned on T-shirts, headlined on posters announcing festivals, and hear threaded through the sensuous, syncopated rhythms of the reggae music. Irie . . . it means a joyous welcome—and it neatly summarizes the happy mood of a honeymoon in Jamaica.

The name Jamaica comes from the Arawak Indian word *Xaymaca*, meaning "land of wood and water." Indeed it is. The country packs amazing geographic wallop into its 4,411 square miles. For vacationers, the chief attractions are the powdery coral sand beaches that curve gracefully along the island's north coast—shores that have become the centerpieces for some of the most celebrated resorts in the Caribbean: Montego Bay, Ocho Rios, Port Antonio, and Negril. But in addition to its beaches, Jamaica has waterfalls, plateaus, plains, rivers, mineral springs, caves, coves, and the forest-clad Blue Mountains, which run through the island's interior. Soaring up to 7,402 feet tall, the peaks rise higher than any mountains in the United States east of the Mississippi.

Located in the northern Caribbean about 700 miles from Miami, 550 miles due north of the Panama Canal, Jamaica is one of the three islands that form the Greater Antilles. It is the third largest Caribbean island, measuring some 146 miles from east to west and 51 miles from north to south at its widest point. It has a population of about 2.5 million, making it the largest English-speaking island in the Caribbean.

Nature has treated Jamaica well. The countryside is lush, rich, bounteous. If ripe mangoes or bananas don't plop right into your hands, they—or other sweet tropical treats such as genip, papaya, and naseberry—never seem more than an arm's length away. When you drive along country roads Technicolor vistas succeed each other like scenes from a movie. You'll pass velvety green polo fields, undulating acres of sugarcane, old sugar mill ruins, quiet coves, and rocky cliffs pounded by the sea.

Jamaica was originally settled by the peaceful Arawak Indians, who probably came to the island from the South American mainland some 1,300 years ago. Christopher Columbus was the first European to see it, sailing along the north coast in May 1494. He called it "the fairest isle that eyes have beheld, mountainous, and the land seems to touch the sky." In 1510, the Spanish cemented their claim to Jamaica by founding a permanent settlement at New Seville. The capital was moved to Villa de la

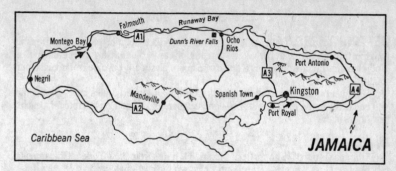

Vega (now Spanish Town) in 1534. In 1655, a British expeditionary force of 6,000 soldiers trounced 500 Spaniards at Kingston Harbour, snatching the rich island prize for England.

Because of Jamaica's central location, the British used the island as a base for plundering Spanish treasure ships. This form of legalized piracy was known as privateering. The practice was so widely condoned that the notorious buccaneer Henry Morgan was named lieutenant governor of Jamaica—and even received a knighthood for his efforts. Jamaica's Port Royal (just south of Kingston) established itself as the pirate headquarters. Its swashbuckling reign as "the wickedest city on earth" came to an abrupt end on June 7, 1692, at 11:43 a.m., when a tremendous earthquake hurled one-third of the city into the sea.

The pirate era was over. In its place, the English turned to agriculture, growing indigo, tobacco, and cotton, before settling on sugar as the chief cash crop. During the 1700s, over 700 plantations flourished on the island, making Jamaica the richest British colony. Of course, there was a dark side to this prosperity. Sugar meant slavery, and thousands of Africans were brought to toil in the fields. Some slaves were freed, others escaped. They became known as the Maroons (from the Spanish word *cimarron*, meaning "untamed"), and inhabited the thickly wooded reaches of Jamaica's backcountry. Slavery was finally abolished throughout the colony in 1838.

From 1866 until 1944, Jamaica was a British Crown Colony. In 1962, Jamaica became a fully independent nation within the British Commonwealth. The nation is a parliamentary democracy, with a well-established two-party system.

Jamaica's motto is "Out of Many, One People," which recognizes that the country is a true ethnic melting pot. Most of its citizens come from African or Afro-European descent, but there are also many British, Chinese, Indians, Portuguese, Germans, and other West Indians. Nowhere is this international hodgepodge more evident than in Jamaican cuisine. Saltfish—which along with ackee is the national dish—was a staple of Portuguese sailors. Goat curry, a frequent lunch special, uses Indian spices. And afternoon tea, a legacy of the British, is still an island tradition.

Because of Jamaica's variety, honeymooners can plan a trip that perfectly matches their interests. Since the island has over 200 miles of beaches, it is a prime area for water sports—swimming, Windsurfing, waterskiing, deep-sea fishing, snorkeling, scuba diving, and sailing. But couples can also hike along mountain trails, explore deep beneath the earth on a spelunking (caving) expedition, play golf or tennis at a luxury resort—or improve their polo game at a week-long clinic. At the same time, Jamaica's rich historic and cultural heritage makes sightseeing well worthwhile. You can visit old plantation great houses (maybe you'll meet one of the resident ghosts), browse through art galleries and crafts markets, climb to the top of a 600-foot waterfall, or spend a lazy afternoon drifting down a languid river aboard a bamboo raft.

1. Practical Facts

GETTING THERE: Both Americans and Canadians require proof of citizenship (passport, birth certificate, or voter's registration card), plus a return or ongoing ticket. Upon leaving Jamaica, there is a departure tax of about $4, payable in Jamaican currency.

Frequent nonstop and direct flights from major United States cities means that you can leave home in a snowstorm—and be sunning yourself on a Jamaican beach a few hours later.

By Air

Jamaica is only 1½ hours from Miami, 3¾ hours from New York or Chicago, and 6 hours from Los Angeles. The country has two international airports: Manley International, about 20 minutes from downtown Kingston; and Sir Donald Sangster International, ten minutes east of Montego Bay. Most airlines fly to both airports. Sangster Airport serves Montego Bay, Ocho Rios, and Negril; Manley Airport is your best bet for hotels located in Kingston, Mandeville, and Port Antonio.

Air Jamaica, the island's national carrier, flies from New York, Philadelphia, Baltimore / Washington, Atlanta, Miami, Tampa, Los Angeles, and Toronto. **American Airlines** flies from New York. **Eastern** flies from New York (to Kingston and Montego Bay) and Atlanta (to Montego Bay only). All international flights must be confirmed 72 hours before departure.

The big news is Air Jamaica's weekly supersonic service aboard the Concorde. From mid-December through mid-March, flights depart Saturdays from New York to Montego Bay and return. Flying time is only 1¾ hours. Round-trip Concorde flights are approximately $1,299 per person; one-way Concorde flight and one-way subsonic economy class is approximately $979. Fares are higher during holiday periods.

By Sea

Jamaica has become increasingly popular as a port of call for cruise ships sailing from New York and Port Everglades, Miami. The liners usually put in at Montego Bay or Ocho Rios; some stop at Port Antonio. The M/V *Regent Star* (registered in The Bahamas) is currently the only major vessel based year-round in Jamaica. It also calls at Costa Rica, the Panama Canal, and Aruba.

GETTING AROUND: Since Jamaica's major resort areas are all located fairly near each other on the north coast, it's easy to get to know several of them during your honeymoon. You have several transportation choices.

Airport Transfers

How you get from the airport to your hotel depends on whether the transfer is included in your vacation package. If your package includes the hotel transfer, you will have a voucher to give to the company representative at the airport. Even if your package does not include the transfer, your travel agent can set up the transportation in advance. This is highly recommended, since otherwise you might be stranded or have to pay a high individual taxi fare. Sample taxi fares are from $5.50 to $14 per person from Sangster International Airport to Montego Bay hotels; $71 to Ocho Rios, and $56 to Negril.

Intra-island Air

Trans-Jamaican Airlines, Ltd., links the island's major resort areas. Sample one-way airfares are $24 from Manley Airport (Kingston) to Port Antonio; $33 from Manley Airport to Negril. For reservations, call 809/923-8680, 809/923-6664, or 809/923-8680.

Taxis

Taxis provide excellent, reasonably priced transportation for short trips (for example, from your hotel to a crafts market). You'll usually find several cabs available at hotels and resorts. If you're going to a remote location (like a great house or a rafting trip), arrange for the driver to return at a designated time to pick you up. Many well-known island restaurants in the resort areas also provide a free shuttle service from major hotels for their patrons. JUDA (Jamaica Union Drivers Association) is the main taxi service on the island; they have offices throughout the island, including Montego Bay (tel. 952-0813) and Ocho Rios (tel. 974-2292).

Although there are some metered cabs, most Jamaican taxis are "Contract Carriages" that charge fixed rates between points. Verify what the fare will be before you take the taxi; at your hotel, you can ask the doorman to double-check the rate. Away from hotels, you can summon a taxi either by telephone, or by flagging them down in the street. Contract carriages can be recognized by the bright red PPV (Public Passenger Vehicle) plates.

Many Jamaican cab drivers also make knowledgeable tour guides. Ask your hotel front desk to make arrangements with someone qualified. Rates are quite inexpensive if you share the ride with another couple.

Jamaica also has a system of public minibuses that ply various popular routes. Although they have no fixed schedules, they run frequently and are quite inexpensive. However, they tend to get crowded, and most visitors either call a cab or rent a car.

Rental Cars

These are a very popular option, since Jamaica has an excellent system of paved roads linking the entire country. Major car-rental agencies have branches at airports and the resort areas. It's a good idea to reserve your car in advance, since popular models (especially air-conditioned vehicles) tend to be in short supply. To rent a car, you must be at least 21 years of age and have a valid driver's license.

Sample rates for a subcompact car with automatic transmission from **Avis Rent-A-Car** range from about $65 per day (for a one- or two-day rental), to about $180 for three-day rentals, or $280 for a one-week rental, all with unlimited mileage. In all cases, you pay for gas, which is quite expensive: about $2.50 per imperial gallon (an imperial gallon is about ⅕ bigger than a U.S. gallon). Gas stations are usually open from 7:30 a.m. until 7 p.m. Mondays through Saturday. Many are closed on Sunday.

Driving is on the left; most rental cars have steering wheels on the right. You should adjust to this quickly. What takes a little more getting used to is the Jamaican driving style. Many Jamaican drivers seem to relish overtaking slower moving cars on blind curves, and avoid using directional signals with a relentless passion. In the country, cows and goats consider that they have equal rights to the asphalt. None of this is a major hazard nor should prevent you from enjoying your drive. Just maintain a sense of humor, practice good defensive driving techniques, and honk on blind curves.

Sightseeing Tours

Many different ground operators offer organized tours to Jamaica's most popular tourist attractions—Dunn's River Falls, Martha Brae or Rio Grande river rafting, Rose Hall great house, plus day trips to Negril. Ask at your hotel's front desk for details and costs.

LANGUAGE: English is the official language. You also might hear Jamaicans speaking a local patois, which mixes English with Caribbean words and cadences—quite difficult to understand. This dialect reflects the different nations that have influenced Jamaican culture. Shoes are called *shampatas,* adapted from the Spanish *zapatos.* The words *duppy* (ghost) and *bankra* (basket) come from Africa.

Jamaicans are also extremely polite. Whether you're in a shop or asking driving directions, always begin your conversation with "good morning," "good afternoon," or the like.

MONEY: The official currency is the Jamaican dollar, which is written: J$. As we go to press, the official exchange rate is $1 US equals about J$5.50. Check the Jamaica Tourist Board or your bank for the current exchange rate. Unless otherwise noted, all prices in the book are in U.S. dollars. When traveling in Jamaica, always double-check which dollar-rate stores, taxi drivers, and others are quoting.

Jamaican currency laws are quite strict. Tourists must pay all bills in Jamaican dollars, and it is illegal to take Jamaican currency out of the country. Since you cannot exchange Jamaican dollars in the United States, make sure that when you return home, you allow sufficient time at the Jamaican airport for changing your money. Airport exchange bureaus are open to service all incoming and outgoing international flights. Save your currency exchange receipts—you must present them when exchanging extra Jamaican dollars at the end of your honeymoon.

The Jamaican currency system uses bills of various denominations: J$1, J$2, J$5, J$10, etc. Coins are 1¢, 10¢, 20¢, 25¢, and 50¢. Banks are open from 9 a.m. until 2 p.m. from Monday through Thursday; from 9 a.m. until noon and again from 2:30 p.m. until 5 p.m. on Friday. They are closed on Saturday, Sunday, and holidays. In addition, most island hotels, cruise ships, and duty-free shops can change your money; ask in advance. The exchange rate is about the same as you will get at the airport or the bank. Many hotels, restaurants, and shops accept major credit cards, but ask in advance. Your bill will be written up in Jamaican dollars, then charged to your account in U.S. dollars. Traveler's checks will usually be accepted, but you will get your change in Jamaican dollars.

Most Jamaican hotels and restaurants add a service charge of 10% to your bill. If this has not been done, tip waiters 10% to 15% of the bill; leave chambermaids $2 per couple per day. Give porters and bellboys $1 per bag. Taxi drivers get 15% of the fare.

WEATHER: From December through March, the coolest months, daytime temperatures range from the high 70s to the mid-80s. Summer temperatures run about 80° to 90°, somewhat warmer inland. Phrases like "black velvet" come to mind when describing the balmy evenings, which are about 5° to 10° cooler. Constant breezes moderate the climate; these blow from the water during the day, from the land at night. Remember that Jamaica is a mountainous country and temperatures are lower in the hills. The average daily temperature is 86° at sea level, 63° in the mountains.

From May through early June, and again from October until early November is generally the rainy season, although this pattern has wobbled a bit in recent years. Rains usually come in the form of passing showers.

CLOTHING: Dress casually by day in shorts, swimsuits, and lightweight sports cloths. Wear bathing suits and short shorts only at the beach—they are not appropriate garb for city streets. If you are going to the mountains, bring a light sweater or jacket.

At night, dress standards vary at the different resorts. In Negril, dressing up usually means putting on a clean T-shirt, while some of the posh grand resorts in Montego Bay, Ocho Rios, and Port Antonio require men to wear a jacket and tie to dinner—perhaps even black tie certain nights. Throughout the island, wardrobe codes tend to be more permissive in summer, when a jacket (no tie) admits men to most fine places. Ask your travel agent to check in advance.

Many hotels and beaches (especially those in Negril) have areas that are designated as "swimsuits optional." Nude beaches?! Perhaps the best feedback we've gotten about this au naturel phenomenon comes from the woman who said, "For the first ten minutes, I felt embarrassed because no one was wearing any clothes. For the next ten minutes, I felt embarrassed because I was the only one wearing clothes. Then I took my clothes off—and wondered what all the fuss was about anyway.''

In any event, confine your nude sunbathing to the designated places—it's illegal elsewhere on the island.

TIME: Jamaica stays on Eastern Standard Time all year. In winter, Jamaican time is the same as New York's. In summer, when it is noon in New York, it is 11 a.m. in Jamaica.

TELEPHONES: You can call Jamaica direct from the United States; dial 809 (the area code), and then the number. When placing calls from Jamaica, be aware that a government tax of 50% will be added to hotel charges on all overseas calls. When making long-distance calls, it is a good idea to use a credit card or to call collect.

ELECTRICAL CURRENT: Although most hotels use 110 volts (just as in the United States), some have 220 volts, 50 volts (as in Europe). Many hotels have converters available, but ask your travel agent to check this out.

SHOPPING: Jamaica offers tempting buys on both items produced on the island and fine European imported goods. In general, store hours are from 8:30 a.m. until 5 p.m. on weekdays, from 8:30 a.m. until 6 p.m. on Saturdays. For specific store recommendations, see the appropriate resort area information.

Imported Goods

Jamaica's in-bond prices mean that you can save from 20% to 50% on imported merchandise. Best buys include Swiss watches, French perfume, and English china, porcelain, and crystal. Most stores are clustered together in the main tourist areas; prices tend to be the same in the different resorts. Stores often have exclusivity, carrying different brand names and patterns, so shop around.

"In-bond" means that goods technically never enter the country, so no duty is charged on them. In some countries, you cannot take purchases with you from the store; instead, they will be delivered to your departing flight or cruise ship. However in Jamaica, American tourists with proof of identity who pay in U.S. dollars, traveler's checks, or with credit cards, can take all their purchases with them except for consumables, such as liquor and cigars. These must be picked up upon departure at the cruise-ship pier or airport. Large in-bond shops such as Chulani's, which sells perfumes, cameras, crystal, and more, have outlets in most of the major resort areas.

Locally Made Items

Jamaica has a flourishing folk crafts tradition, rich with African, Indian, and European influences. Goods include straw work, baskets, and paintings. Wood carvings made from lignum vitae, a native hardwood, are popular, formed into statues, book-ends, and salad bowls. Also look for colorful resort fashions, made from fabrics silk-screened on the island, and jewelry made from local agate, black coral, and semiprecious stones.

For the widest selection, check out the crafts market in Montego Bay; there are also crafts markets in Negril, Ocho Rios, and Port Antonio. Entrepreneurs also set up "shop"—or at least their wares—near major tourist attractions such as Dunn's River Falls and patrol the public beaches at the major hotels. Designs and prices tend to be similar at the different outlets, so browse around until you find something you like. Many of the merchants also can execute designs to order. At all outdoor markets, haggling is accepted. As a rule of thumb, start by offering the vendor (called a higgler) one-third to one-half of the asking price; the final price will be somewhere in the middle. Sometimes vendors will be overly persistent about hawking their merchandise; just politely but firmly say no.

Consider taking home a taste of Jamaica, such as Tía María, a coffee-flavored liqueur, other exotic liqueurs made from pimento (allspice) or ginger, or one of the mellow island rums. Although you can't bring Jamaica's succulent fresh fruits back to the United States, you can return with them preserved in tangy chutneys. Best of all, buy a couple of bags of rich Blue Mountain Coffee—Jamaica's volcanic soil produces some of the finest beans in the world. (Make sure you buy the 100% brew.) Or perfume yourselves with Jamaica's own tropical scents: Royall Lyme or Royall Bay Rhum for the groom, White Witch perfume or Khus Khus toilet water for the bride. Also fun for women—getting their hair braided like Bo Derek in *10*. It can be done at little shacks along many Jamaican beaches; the braids stay in for a couple of days, if you take care of them. Depending on the elaborateness of the do, prices range between $10 and $30.

For fine art, the island center is Kingston. You can also view and buy works by well-known artists such as Edna Manley and Mallica "Kapo" Reynolds at Harmony Hall in Ocho Rios.

ABOUT KINGSTON: Kingston, Jamaica's capital, is a bustling metropolis with a population of about 700,000, making it the largest English-speaking city in the western hemisphere south of Miami. Although most vacationers bypass it in favor of the beach resorts, Kingston is well worth exploring, because it represents the heart and soul of the nation. Many of the north coast resorts offer day trips to the capital, or you can stop by on your way back to the states, returning via Kingston's Manley Airport. Places to visit include:

The National Gallery of Art, 12 Ocean Blvd. (tel. 922-1563), down on the waterfront, with a superb collection of paintings and sculpture by contemporary Jamaican artists. It also exhibits portraits, engravings, and maps dating back to the 17th century. Open Monday through Saturday, 10 a.m. to 5 p.m.; admission $1 per person.

Devon House, 26 Hope Rd., was the 19th-century home of George Stiebel, one of the Caribbean's first black millionaires, who made a fortune mining in South America. It has been beautifully restored by the Jamaica National Trust, with elegant period furnishings and paintings. Small crafts shops located in what once were the stables sell some of the best crafts on the island. Open Monday through Saturday, 10 a.m. until 5 p.m.

Port Royal, favorite lair of marauding buccaneers such as Henry Morgan and Blackbeard, was largely destroyed by earthquake and tidal wave in 1692. Today, a walk through what remains provides a fascinating glimpse back to the time when the *Jolly Roger* ruled the Caribbean. Stop by St. Peter's Church, which contains a silver plate rumored to be a gift from Morgan. Fort Charles, built in 1656, now houses the Maritime Museum. The Old Naval Hospital is now a museum displaying Port Royal artifacts recovered by divers and archeologists, including Spanish armor, guns, swords, and a watch that stopped at the exact moment of the cataclysmic earthquake. All are open daily from 9 a.m. until 5 p.m.; there are small admission fees. You can reach Port Royal by ferry from Kingston, or by driving west past the airport along the narrow Palisadoes peninsula.

SPECIAL EVENTS: Throughout the year, Jamaica serves up festivals, sports events, and happenings that delight both locals and visitors.

Negril Reggae Festival (January / February) is a series of concerts headlining major performers.

Chukka Cove Cup (late January) is a polo tournament near Ocho Rios with four competing teams, each with a high handicap player.

Manchester Golf Week (March), held at the Manchester Club in Mandeville, is Jamaica's oldest golf tournament, and attracts leading local and international players.

Miami to Montego Bay Yacht Race (mid-March). Ocean-going yachts compete in this annual race.

Jamaica Sailing Week and Easter Regatta (late March/early April). Yacht crews compete in the week's races, while landlubbers will enjoy the beach parties and pig feasts.

Jamaica International Marlin Tournament (late May) is a marlin fishing tournament in Ocho Rios.

Trelawny Carnival (late May). Held at Falmouth (about midway between Montego Bay and Ocho Rios), the three-day festival features steel bands, drum corps parades, historical tours, Jamaican crafts and food markets, and three nights of concerts at Burwood Beach headlining top calypso, soca, and reggae performers.

Independence Day (first Monday in August) Parades, native dance, music, arts, and crafts animate the streets of Kingston and the parish capitals.

Reggae Sunsplash (late August). This is it—Jamaica's biggest musical event. Held in Montego Bay, it's part concert, part carnival, and part beach party. The festival turns on five nights of sizzling reggae and rock. Advance hotel reservations are very necessary.

Junkanoo (Christmas). Brightly costumed dancers take to the streets throughout the country, whirling and twirling to the rhythms of Caribbean drums and bamboo fifes.

MEET-THE-PEOPLE PROGRAM:
If you want to delve past the tourist level and join in Jamaican life, this superb program run by the Jamaica Tourist Board makes it possible. You'll be introduced to Jamaicans who share similar jobs, hobbies, or interests with your own—maybe even other newlyweds. You might join a couple for afternoon tea or dinner, play a game of tennis or golf, go horseback riding or birdwatching. Nearly 700 Jamaican families participate. The program is absolutely free, but you might want to bring your hostess a small gift (such as a bouquet), or pick up the restaurant bill or sightseeing admission fees. Contact the local Jamaica Tourist Board at one of the addresses that follow, giving your name, length of stay, main interests, and when you will be available.

ABOUT ACCOMMODATIONS:
Jamaica boasts an extraordinary number of accommodations that are best in class—luxury resorts that revel in the graciousness of the plantation era, posh villas staffed by a retinue of servants, and all-inclusive resorts where you never need to spend a Jamaican dollar. But what makes Jamaica so remarkable is the wide choice of excellent accommodations available to suit all tastes and pocketbooks—including inexpensively priced, family-run hotels, and simple cottages right by the side of the sea.

The high season runs from mid-December through mid-April. Winter rates often include two or three meals a day (Modified American Plan or American Plan). During the low season (mid-April through mid-December), rates are about 25% to 50% lower, and hotels often offer the European Plan (no meals). A 10% service charge is usually added to the bill. Jamaica also levies a room tax of about $10 to $15 a day (winter), $5 to $10 a day (summer), depending on the hotel category.

The Elegant Resorts

Several of Jamaica's most exclusive properties have joined together to offer vacationers the opportunity to sample several different resorts. Guests can dine at the different resorts and even stay overnight, subject to availability. Participating properties include Half Moon Club, Round Hill, and Tryall Golf and Country Club in Montego Bay; Plantation Inn and Sans Souci in Ocho Rios; and Trident Hotel and Villas in Port Antonio. For details, call the "Elegant Resorts" hotline toll free, 800/237-3237.

All-Inclusive Resorts

Jamaica is known for its all-inclusive properties, where everything—accommodations, meals, drinks, sports, entertainment—often even cigarettes—is covered by a single package price. The cost depends on the category of room you choose. The only additional expenses you will incur will be for souvenirs and perhaps some sightseeing excursions. Here are some points to consider when selecting an all-inclusive resort for your honeymoon.

- What exactly is included? Price variations between resorts are usually explained by exactly what features are covered. How many meals a day are offered? Are menu choices limited or can you order à la carte? What sports are included—do you have to pay extra for diving or horseback riding? Are any sightseeing excursions included?
- Couples resorts versus "everyone" resorts. Some resorts cater to couples only; others allow all comers—couples, singles, and families. Each setup creates a different ambience.

The Inns of Jamaica

Some of Jamaica's finest small, personalized properties located throughout the country—from the Blue Mountains to the north-shore beaches—have put together this program. These inns are all intimate and service-oriented, averaging only 26 rooms each. Prices run as low as $27 a night—even during the high season. Various packages include airport transfers and use of a rental car, all reasonably priced. You can get complete details from the Jamaica Tourist Board.

Villa Rentals

This is another popular option in Jamaica. Here, a villa is really any rental property, from cottage to mansion, going for anywhere between $800 and $4,500 a week. Many have a private swimming pool; most come complete with staff (maid, cook, gardener). The cooks are generally true treasures, equally adept at whipping up Jamaican pepperpot soup, soufflés, or hamburgers. Some villa owners have agreements with nearby hotels permitting house guests to use the resort facilities. To get a list of villa representatives in Jamaica, contact the Tourist Board or the **Jamaica Association of Villas and Apartments** (JAVA), 200 Park Ave., New York, NY 10166 (tel. 212/986-4317). They represent over 300 rental properties.

One particular rental villa that might tickle your fancy is Goldeneye, the beachfront house near Ocho Rios where Ian Fleming created Agent 007—James Bond—and wrote all 13 original Bond novels. It rents for $2,800 per week in the winter; about $1,800 per week in the summer. Contact **Travel Resources**, P.O. Box 1043, Coconut Grove, FL 33133 (tel. 305/444-8583 in Florida; toll free 800/327-5039 nationwide). Travel Resources also has a wide variety of other luxury villas for rent.

DINING OUT: Good food is one of the great pleasures of Jamaica. The island's ample dimensions and agricultural bounty means that most of the fruits, vegetables, meats, and fish that appear on menus are ultrafresh, often coming from the restaurant's own backyard. Visitors can find an international array of cuisines—from elegantly sauced French classics to perfectly British afternoon teas, fiery Indian curries, stir-fry Chinese—and delicious Jamaican specialties that combine the best of all worlds.

In recent years, more and more Jamaican hotels have instituted the European

Plan, allowing guests to try the island's fine restaurants. Most restaurants include a 10% service charge in the bill; if not, tip waiters 10% to 15% of the total.

Both at your hotel and in restaurants, you'll often find Jamaican favorites appearing on the menu side-by-side with continental choices. One local delicacy is Caribbean rock lobster, served either simply grilled, or dressed up with sauce Thermidor or sauce Américaine. For an appetizer, you might want to try the hearty soups—pepperpot, with spinach, okra, and meat; or callaloo, made with a leafy vegetable resembling spinach. Jamaica's national breakfast dish is saltfish and ackee—a savory concoction of cod cooked with a local vegetable that tastes like scrambled eggs, seasoned up with onions, garlic, and pepper. Goat curry reflects the Indian influence on Jamaica cuisine, *escaveche* (marinated fish) the Spanish. Popular side dishes include squash, yams, sweet potatoes, pumpkin (boiled or mashed with butter), green bananas or plantains (boiled or fried), plus rice and peas (rice simmered with red beans, onions, spices, and salt pork).

For a Jamaican-style lunch, try jerk chicken or pork, a dish that originated with the Maroons. The meats are seasoned with spices, then barbecued slowly over a pimento-wood fire. It's served at many hotel beach bars and food stands that line the north coast road. If you want a snack, get patties, pastries filled with highly seasoned meat and bread crumbs.

To quench your thirst, Jamaica has developed smooth, cooling beverages. First and foremost is Red Stripe beer, well rounded and "hoppy." If you want something nonalcoholic, try a fruit punch, blended from the island's harvest, or "bellywash"— the local name for lemonade. Finish your meal with Blue Mountain coffee, Tía María, or rum.

Then we get to jelly coconuts, the consumption of which combines refreshment with ritual. These young green coconuts are sold by roadside vendors whose salesmanship rivals that of P. T. Barnum. With a subtle flourish of their machetes, they first hack off the coconut top, leaving a small hole through which you drink the sweet liquid inside. For an encore, the coconut is cut in half so you can scoop out the delicate jelly in the center, using a thin piece of the shell.

HOW TO GET MARRIED IN JAMAICA: More and more couples are choosing to say their "I do's" in Jamaica. Favorite sites include beautiful gardens or beaches on your hotel grounds, and various island attractions, such as Dunn's River Falls and Shaw Park Gardens in Ocho Rios, or Athenry Gardens in Port Antonio. Most Jamaican hotels offer all-inclusive wedding packages that cover the services of the officient, processing the license, witnesses, champagne, flowers, and the wedding cake. They can also arrange for a photographer.

No blood tests or physical exams are required. You must bring birth certificates and be on the island for 24 hours before filing for a license. There is a J$12.50 stamp duty fee. People who have been married before should bring certified copies of their divorce decrees. Once the license has been issued, it is valid for three months, and the couple can be married immediately. The Jamaica Tourist Board can assist you in meeting and making arrangements with a marriage officer. For approximately US $100 to $150, the marriage officer will obtain the license for you and perform the ceremony.

Most couples incorporate Jamaican traditions into their ceremony. You might be married under an arch made from braided coconut leaves festooned with hibiscus and other flowers. Brides can put a leaf of sweet basil or a leaf from the noo-noo bush in their shoes or stockings for good luck. Or arrange for a "show bread"—an elaborately braided loaf with a bird on top to symbolize peace or two birds to signify love.

FOR FURTHER INFORMATION: Contact the **Jamaica Tourist Board** at the following addresses: 21 Dominica Dr., New Kingston, Jamaica (tel. 809/929-8690); 3440 Wilshire Blvd., Los Angeles, CA 90010 (tel. 213/384-1123); 1320 South Dixie Hwy, Coral Gables, FL 33146 (tel. 305/665-0557); 36 South Wabash Ave., Chicago, IL 60603 (tel. 312/346-1546); 866 Second Ave., New York, NY 10017 (tel. 212/688-7650 or toll free 800/223-5225).

The Jamaica Tourist Board also maintains centrally located offices in the island's main tourist areas: Cornwall Beach, Montego Bay (tel. 952-4425); Visitors Service Bureau, Negril (tel. 957-4243); Ocean Village Shopping Centre, Ocho Rios (tel. 974-2570); City Centre Plaza, Port Antonio (tel. 993-3051); or Rafter's Rest, Port Antonio (tel. 993-2778).

2. Montego Bay

Montego Bay was Jamaica's original tourist destination. As early as 1908, the local citizens' association ran advertisements in American newspapers inviting tourists to "Come South—to Montego Bay, the most beautiful spot in Jamaica." From being Jamaica's first vacation resort, Montego Bay has become Jamaica's premier vacation resort, a magnet for royalty, rock stars, and honeymooners from around the world. The moment you set eyes on the broad, crescent-shaped harbor, you'll know why Montego Bay reigns as Jamaica's number one tourist destination. Partly, it's the splendid natural setting—clear, aquamarine waters surrounded by lush green hills. Mainly, it's the spirit—the knowledge that this place subscribes to the pleasure principle. Lazing on a soft white beach feels right here. So does dancing until dawn, bantering with the old fruit lady in the market, prowling for backstairs ghosts in 200-year-old great houses, or shopping 'til you drop. Whatever kind of honeymoon you crave, Montego Bay embraces and encourages your desires.

Located on the northwestern coast of Jamaica, the town is better known to both Jamaicans and just-arrived tourists as MoBay. The second largest city in the country, it is sometimes referred to as The Republic—a tribute to the independently minded local landowners who threatened to secede from the central government in Kingston during the 19th century.

It is significant that most of the town has developed around the beaches rather than the harbor, because life here revolves around the sea and sand. Some of the finest beaches in the Caribbean scallop the shoreline from Tryall east to Rose Hall. There's no one main resort area per se; the major tourist hotels have been built around the various strands.

Because of its excellent beaches and clear waters, the area lends itself to all water sports. Most of the major hotels offer snorkeling, scuba diving, Windsurfing, and sailing right on the property; there are also Windsurf rental shops at Doctor's Cave Beach. You can charter boats for deep-sea fishing from **Seaworld** (near Rose Hall, tel. 953-2180). On land, golfers can tee off on four 18-hole championship courses: Tryall, Ironshore Golf Club, Half Moon Golf Club, and the Wyndham Rose Hall Beach Hotel's Golf Club. Most hotels have tennis courts, several lighted for night play. Horseback riding can be arranged through the hotels or direct with various stables: **Seawind** (tel. 952-4070), **White Witch** (no phone), and **Good Hope Plantation** near Falmouth (tel. 954-3289).

Good roads link Montego Bay with other resort areas, permitting easy day-trips. The seven-mile beach at Negril is about a two-hours' drive (47 miles); spectacular Dunn's River Falls and the other Ocho Rios attractions also take about two hours to reach (67 miles, but it is a straighter road). But whether you use your resort as a base for exploring the rest of Jamaica, or never wander further than the beach bar, Montego Bay will reward you with sun, fun, and honeymoon bliss.

SHOPPING: Since Montego Bay is the commercial and shopping hub of this northwest part of the island, it offers the widest selection of stores, boutiques, and crafts vendors. The **Crafts Market** located near Harbour Street is perfect for picking up souvenirs—jipajapa hats, straw bags, wooden carvings, and more. For in-bond shopping for luxury items, try the shops at your hotel or the major shopping areas: **City Centre** and the **Casa Montego Arcade** in Montego Bay, and **Holiday Village** across from the Holiday Inn Hotel. At Casa Montego, for example, you can find major duty-free outlets such as **Swiss Stores** (watches from Rolex, Patek Philippe, Rado, and Swatch); and **Bijoux** (imported liquor and liqueurs, English bone china, including Wedgwood, Royal Doulton, and Aynsley; plus Lalique and Waterford crystal). City Centre features **La Belle Creole** (cameras and electronics, imported embroidered linens, and watches by Cartier, Corum, Seiko, and Swatch); and **Chulani** (cameras by Nikon, Minolta, and Canon; crystal by Lalique and Baccarat; china; electronics; perfumes and cosmetics; and watches by Ebel, Girard-Perregaux, and Seiko); and others. Holiday Village offers **Casa de Oro** (cameras by Canon and Minolta; electronics; linens; and watches by Cartier); **China Craft** (china by Wedgwood, Minton, and Royal Worcester; crystal by Waterford, Lalique, and Baccarat; figurines by Lladró, Hummel, and Royal Doulton; embroidered linens); and **Tropicana** (jewelry and watches by Piaget, Concorde, Movado, and Seiko). The Holiday Inn, Half Moon, and Trelawny Beach Hotels all have especially fine shopping arcades.

Check out some shops that sell some uniquely Jamaican items. At **Blue Mountain Gems,** Mike O'Hara creates one-of-a-kind jewelry pieces made from exotic gemstones, such as agates, found in the riverbeds of the Blue Mountains. The shop also sells black-coral necklaces, batiks, and large wooden salad bowls (located at Holiday Village). On the north coast road just east of Falmouth, stop by **Caribatik,** where American Muriel Chandler designs and handcrafts clothing and wallhangings. Prices start at about $100 and climb into the thousands; the store is open Tuesday through Saturday, 10 a.m. until 3 p.m.

ROMANTIC INTERLUDES: In Montego Bay, your "problem" won't be deciding what to do, but rather finding the time to pack it all in.

If tales of ghosts and witchcraft tickle your fancy, don't miss **Rose Hall Great House.** The house's notoriety derives from Annie Palmer—a woman best known as "The White Witch of Rose Hall."

Fact and legend intermingle in the history of Annie. Born Annie Mae Patterson in England, she moved to Haiti with her parents. Orphaned at a young age, she became the protégé of a Haitien voodoo priestess. She moved to Jamaica, where she married John Rose Palmer—whom she allegedly poisoned soon afterward. Annie married several more times and took on several lovers—all of whom she murdered when they grew tiresome. Finally, she was strangled by her own slave/lover when she was 29.

Thanks to American millionaire John Rollins, Rose Hall has been beautifully and accurately restored. The house is part of the Jamaica National Trust. Knowledgeable guides lead you through the corridors and rooms, gleefully relating the most lurid details of Annie's life. It's all a tremendous amount of fun. Downstairs, there's a souvenir shop where you can buy books and postcards—there's even an Annie Palmer Frisbee.

Rose Hall (tel. 953-2341) is located just nine miles east of Montego Bay and is open daily from 9:30 a.m. until 6 p.m. Admission is $5.50.

If ghost stories provide the literary motif for Rose Hall, poetry is the medium at **Greenwood Great House,** which was built by the family of Elizabeth Barrett Browning (she wrote "How Do I Love Thee," among other works). The Georgian-style house was built in 1780 by Sir Richard Barrett, a cousin of Elizabeth's father.

The house has been opened to the public by owners Bob and Anne Betton. At Greenwood, they have assembled one of the finest collection of period furnishings in the Caribbean. In addition, there's an appealingly quirky collection of antiques: a 16th-century court jester's chair, a chamber pot manufactured by Royal Crown Derby, and old musical instruments in perfect working order—including a player piano that tin-kles out "Daisy, Daisy."

Greenwood (no phone) is open daily from 9 a.m. until 6 p.m.; admission is $4.50. This great house is 14 miles east of Montego Bay.

Maybe this is the ultimate Jamaican fantasy—drifting slowly down a sparkling river shaded by almond trees, picnicking on mangoes in leafy glades, swimming in freshwater pools so clear, you can see every pebble on the bottom. The raft trip on the **Martha Brae River** is one of the most soothing interludes you can have during your honeymoon. A skilled raftsman poles your two-seater craft down broad channels and gentle rapids. Be sure you wear bathing suits under coverups so you can swim.

The raft trips depart from Martha Brae Rafter's Village, about three miles south of Falmouth. The rafts operate daily until about 4:30 p.m. and cost $28 per couple.

Make some fine feathered friends at the **Rocklands Feeding Station** bird sanctu-ary run by Lisa Salmon, one of Jamaica's best-known naturalists. Birds will eat right out of your hand, including doves, finches, and Jamaica's famous "doctor bird"—a type of hummingbird. If you want to learn more about Jamaica's birds, pick up a copy of the definitive *Field Guide to the Birds of the West Indies*, written by James Bond. (Ian Fleming, part-time Jamaica resident and creator of superspy 007, named his hero after the ornithologist.) Rocklands (tel. 952-2009) is located a mile from Anchovy, east of Montego Bay. It is open daily from 3:30 p.m. until sundown; admission is $4 per person.

For Jamaica's newest adventure, sign up for one of the **rail tours,** which depart from Montego Bay Rail Station.

Governor's Coach Tour. All aboard a replica of the train once used for official travel by the governor of Jamaica. Complete with a calypso band and a professional guide, the train chugs 40 miles into the heartland of Jamaica. Stops include Catadupa, where seamstresses hang out rows of bright fabrics along the railroad tracks. Choose your favorite pattern for a shirt, sundress, or skirt—and the made-to-order garment will be ready for you on the afternoon return trip three hours later. You'll also explore Ipswich Caves, filled with stalactites and stalagmites; and tour Appleton Sugar Facto-ry, where you'll learn how rum is made and then sample rums and liqueurs. The trip costs $33 per person, including snacks, rum punch, and round-trip transfers from Montego Bay Hotel. For schedules and reservations, call 952-2887 or 952-1398.

Mandeville Rail Tour. Explore the cool mountain countryside of Mandeville, lo-cated 2,000 feet above sea level in the Manchester Mountains. En route, the train stops at Balacava, where you can have dresses and shirts made to order at the market. You can pick up your new wardrobe later that afternoon. Then, you continue to Williamsfield, where you'll board a bus for Mandeville, considered the most English town in Jamaica. After a visit to a private home garden filled with exotic orchids, you'll have a buffet lunch at the family-run Hotel Astra, where the specialties include Jamai-can dishes. The train tour costs $44 per person; for departures and reservations, call 953-2859.

More formally known as the **Hilton High Day Tour,** this program gives you the chance to discover the interior regions of Jamaica—and get a bird's-eye view of it all from a hot-air balloon. You'll journey by motorcoach to St. Leonards, where you'll be greeted by Norma Hilton-Stanley at the 350-acre banana plantation that has been in her family for seven generations. Here, you can ascend over 300 feet into the air aboard a tethered hot-air balloon. After a real Jamaican breakfast, you can go horseback riding through the countryside or stroll to the German-style town of Seaford. At lunchtime, help yourself to the buffet spread that includes roast suckling pig, roasted breadfruit, rum punch, and other Jamaican specialties. The excursion costs $53 per person; for information, call 952-3343.

HONEYMOON HOTELS AND HIDEAWAYS: Since Montego Bay is the largest resort area in Jamaica, it also offers the widest range of accommodations—couples-only resorts, ultraelegant hotel compounds, high rises, and guest houses. Rates quoted reflect the spread between low- and high-season prices.

Ultraluxurious

The Half Moon Club, P.O. Box 80, Montego Bay, Jamaica, W.I. (tel. 809/953-2211; U.S. reservations: tel. toll free 800/237-3237). Certain resorts feel right the instant you walk in. The Half Moon Club is one of them. From the moment you drive through the wrought-iron gate, you know this 400-acre resort is a class act. The reception area is located beneath a loggia surrounding an open-air courtyard, where two absolutely humongous palms tower overhead, and the patter of water from an hexagonal fountain soothes the senses. Service is impeccable, gracious yet friendly, thanks to the careful direction of longtime Managing Director Heinz Simonitsch. Simonitsch is one of the legendary hoteliers of the Caribbean, having served as president of both the Caribbean Hotel Association and the Jamaica Hotel Association, and the personal attention he lavishes on the resort really shows. Fresh hibiscus flowers brighten rooms daily, room service orders arrive promptly and piping hot, and a lady never has to glide out her own chair in the restaurant. No wonder the hotel has been named one of the 300 best in the world.

The resort takes its name from the perfect crescent-shaped beach it surrounds—a one-mile stretch of fine white coral sands and a tranquil bay, sheltered by a protective reef. At water's edge, a fleet of Windsurfers, Sunfish, and Hobie cats awaits your pleasure.

Honeymooners usually opt for the deluxe oceanview rooms in the two-story wing fronting the beach on one side, lush gardens on the other. The downstairs rooms convey an English feeling, with Queen Anne–style furnishings and glossy parquet floors. Bathrooms are large, and there's a minifridge. The upstairs rooms reflect a more tropical motif, with tile floors and a huge eat-in terrace—perfect for breakfasts overlooking the sea. All rooms have air conditioning. If you want to splurge, reserve one of the generously proportioned private "cottages" that come with swimming pool big enough to swim laps in.

Name your favorite sport, and you can probably indulge in it right on the property. Half Moon Club has 2 main pools, 13 tennis courts (4 lighted), 4 lighted squash courts, an aerobics room, sauna, massage room, Nautilus-equipped gym, and an 18-hole championship golf course just across the road. Introductory snorkeling and scuba lessons are provided free. You'll welcome the opportunity to work out, because the Seagrape Terrace restaurant is excellent. And if you want to mellow out completely, try one of the bartender's prizewinning concoctions, such as a Gold Label Float or a Top Hat. Honeymoon package: There's none per se; most couples take the Half Moon Plan, which includes an oceanfront room, airport transfers, fruit basket, flowers, a shell necklace, golf-green fees, tennis, squash, a glass-bottom boat trip, and more. Four days / three nights (EP): $462 to $715 per couple; extra nights $132 to $209.

All-Inclusive Resorts

If all the world loves lovers, then **Sandals,** P.O. Box 100, Montego Bay, Jamaica, W.I. (tel. 809/952-5510; U.S. reservations: tel. 305/271-0045 or toll free 800/327-1991), must rank as the most popular address in the universe. It definitely is to the couples who check into this luxurious all-inclusive resort for twosomes only. And not just any hand-holding pairs—at any given time, about 50% of the guests are honeymooners. The resort occupies a stellar location along the largest private beach in Jamaica.

Gordon "Butch" Stewart, the owner of Sandals, has designed a seemingly unstoppable roster of activities. Absolutely everything is included in your room price—meals, snacks, drinks, entertainment, transfers, tips, and every sport you can name (plus some you probably couldn't, such as crab racing). Only cigarettes, massages, and day trips aboard the 45-foot catamaran cost extra. The list of things to do covers two sides of an elongated piece of paper: glass-bottom boat rides, waterskiing, volley-ball games, tennis, free scuba lessons and dives, and—literally—hundreds more. An enthusiastic and energetic young staff known as "Playmakers" make sure the fun keeps happening, whether it's the weekly Olympics or theme nights (centered on pi-rates, masquerades, or togas) that enliven evenings. At night, you dine by candlelight on the open-air, oceanfront terrace, then can head over to the Skydome nightclub, which headlines a different show every night, from reggae to magic. If you've overin-dulged at the ample buffet spreads, the gym stays open 24 hours a day.

Sandals has six categories of rooms—all of which combine a breezy tropical feel-ing (high ceilings, white furniture, cotton spreads, jalousie windows, floral-patterned drapes) with the finer creature comforts (king-size beds, air conditioning, paddle fans, and in-room hairdryers). All rooms (except for 12 standard units) have balconies. As you'd expect, the most expensive accommodations sit right on the sea. Whichever kind you choose you'll have plenty of elbow room, since the three-story units are spread out, and the resort occupies 19 acres of grounds. The complex is located just behind the Montego Bay airport, and it has become a Sandals tradition to wave at the departing planes.

Sandals not only specializes in honeymoons—it's also a popular place for wed-dings. They can make all the arrangements—and it's all free for resort guests.

Sandals offers a wide variety of all-inclusive packages, ranging from four to eight nights. For an eight-day, seven-night package, sample rates are: Superior oceanview room: $1,904 to $2,282.50 per couple. Deluxe beachfront: $1,986.60 to $2,387 per couple.

Sandals Royal Caribbean, P.O. Box 167, Montego Bay, Jamaica, W.I. (tel. 809/953-2231; U.S. reservations: tel. 305/271-0045 or toll free 800/327-1991). An entrance portico framed by graceful columns. Afternoon tea served daily. Buildings named after British royal homes. And the all-inclusive package includes . . . croquet? That gives you some idea of the upscale, Euro-style romantic atmosphere that pervades Sandals Royal Caribbean, the newest member of the Sandals resort group.

Like its sister property, Sandals Royal Caribbean is an all-inclusive resort for couples only. The party atmosphere begins the moment you arrive, when a calypso band breaks into song in the lobby. New arrivals receive a welcome basket brimming with goodies—scarfs, suntan oil, Tia Maria, and Blue Mountain coffee. Much of the activity centers on the pearly-white beach that stretches the length of the property. Water sports run the aquatic gamut—sailing, Windsurfing, waterskiing, pedaling an aquatrike, snorkeling (excellent near the offshore reef), and scuba diving (the intro lesson and one dive a day are included). Beach buffs can tan all over at the swimsuit-optional private island reachable by boat (yes, you wear clothes on the boat). On land, there's tennis day or night on the lighted courts, volleyball, golf, and a health club with a weight room. Now's a good time to learn a new sport, because instruction and equip-ment are free. Even in the middle of a game, most guests stop to observe another San-dals tradition—waving at the planes taking off from nearby Montego Bay airport.

Sandals Royal Caribbean prides itself on its fine cuisine. Breakfast and lunch are served buffet style, but dinner is an elegant, sit-down, à la carte bash every night. Other gracious features here: You can order breakfast in bed, and you can have before-dinner drinks served on your porch or patio. At night, sing along at the piano bar, or head for the disco, where there's live entertainment every night.

The pink-painted guest units are spread out over the property, tucked in palm groves or sidling up to the sea. Rooms are large and cheery, air-conditioned, and king-size beds are available on request. Room layouts are fairly consistent throughout the resort; the top-of-the-line rooms are located on the oceanfront, away from the activity surrounding the main building.

If you'd like to combine your wedding with your honeymoon, Sandals Royal Caribbean will gladly oblige. They can set up the complete ceremony—and it's all free for guests.

Sandals Royal Caribbean has all-inclusive packages ranging from four to eight days in length. For an eight days / seven nights package, sample rates are: lanai room: $1,793 to $2,068 per couple; deluxe beachfront: $1,980 to $2,332 per couple.

Carlyle on the Bay, P.O. Box 412, Montego Bay, Jamaica, W.I. (tel. 809/952-4141; U.S. reservations: tel. toll free 800/327-1991 nationwide; 800/231-1645 in Florida; 305/271-0045 in Miami). Words like "gem-like" and "intimate" come to mind when describing this pristine resort located in Montego Bay, within walking distance of Doctor's Cave and the area's fine shopping. Situated on a tiny cul-de-sac just off the main road, the white, colonial-style facade positively sparkles in the sunshine. The hotel's walkways and arcades surround a white tiled courtyard, with a large pool and Jacuzzi at its center. The resort is owned by Gordon "Butch" Stewart, the moving spirit behind Sandals and Sandals Royal Caribbean, and the Carlyle on the Bay has just adopted an all-inclusive format, admitting couples, singles, and families who appreciate the sophisticated atmosphere.

Although the hotel was built less than 20 years ago, it conveys a gracious, Old Jamaica feeling. Original Jamaican art brightens the walls of the rooms, which have all been newly refurbished. Each of the 50 rooms has a slightly different layout, but all feature air conditioning, telephone, and a hairdryer in the bathroom. Not all rooms have balconies; the deluxe rooms have better views of the pool, ocean, or beach just beyond the coconut palms and the bougainvillea blossoms. Just across the street, you can swim on a small public beach. There's tennis available right on the property, a new health spa, as well as water sports such as snorkeling, scuba diving, sailing, and glass-bottom boat rides. The Plantation Restaurant serves both native and continental cuisine, with live entertainment every night. Indicative of the charm and grace of this resort, you can opt for room service at no extra charge.

Because Carlyle on the Bay is just a block away from the heart of Montego Bay, guests can easily get involved with the local culture. Jamaican culture, in fact, is very much part of this resort. The "fruit lady" comes around selling paw-paw, soursop, or other fruits in season; local craftspeople visit several times a week to demonstrate wood-carving or straw-weaving techniques. It all adds up to an experience that is warm, intimate, and uniquely Jamaican. Honeymoon package: None. Standard eight days / seven nights package: From $1,456.40 per couple, low season. Call for high-season rates. Includes three full meals daily, snacks, unlimited drinks, and room service.

Jack Tar Village, Montego Beach Hotel, P.O. Box 144, Montego Bay, Jamaica, W.I. (tel. 809/952-4340; U.S. reservations: tel. 214/670-9888 or toll free 800/527-9299). So you want an all-inclusive resort, you want to be in the center of Montego Bay and all its shopping and clubs, and you want a white-sand beach and waters so transparent you can play tag with a parrot fish 30 yards away? Then consider Jack Tar Village, Montego Beach, part of the famous, all-inclusive chain with properties throughout the Caribbean. This four-story resort is located on the main Montego Bay thoroughfare, and right near Doctor's Cave Beach, probably the clearest stretch of waters in Jamaica. Given such a sublime aquatic positioning, much of the day's activities centers on the water: Windsurfers, pedal boats, waterskis, snorkel gear, and Sunfish await your pleasure. (You can also retreat beneath the thatch-roof sun shades that dot the sands.) Every day, there's a full roster of special events—from reggae lessons to toga parties and cooking classes. You can work on your serve on three tennis courts (free instruction included), then unwind with a massage or sauna (also included). Since there are only 130 rooms, you'll never feel crowded. The rooms here are really big; we prefer the accommodations in the Sunset Lodge, which have been recently refurbished and are even larger and nicer than the rest. All rooms have ceiling fans, air conditioning, a balcony, and full front oceanview; if you get a ground-floor room, you're literally on the beach. Honeymoon package: None. Standard rate: $253 per couple per night. Includes all meals, limited wine during lunch and dinner, unlimited drinks, most water sports (except deep-sea fishing, scuba lessons, and glass-bottom boat rides), nightly entertainment, airport transfers, all applicable taxes, tips, and service charges. The resort admits a fun-loving mixture of couples, singles, and families.

Trelawny Beach Hotel, P.O. Box 54, Falmouth, Jamaica, W.I. (tel. 809/954-2470; U.S. reservations: tel. 212/397-0700 in NY; or toll free 800/223-0888 nationwide), offers the best of both worlds—seclusion, plus plenty of activity when you want it. The 6-story, 350-room resort is located in Falmouth, just 23 miles from Montego Bay and 44 miles from Ocho Rios, permitting easy access to island "musts" such as Dunn's River Falls and rafting on the Martha Brae River. But in between sightseeing excursions, couples can relax on the fine beach, or indulge themselves to the hilt in the sports and activities programs at this all-inclusive resort. Complimentary activities for guests include snorkeling cruises, Sunfish sailing, Windsurfing, waterskiing, and glass-bottom boat rides. There's also tennis on four lighted Laykold courts and tennis instruction, aerobics and exercise classes, Jamaican dialect and reggae dance lessons, nightly entertainment, and daily shuttle service to Montego Bay for sightseeing and shopping. And, if you've ever wanted to try scuba diving, you can—for free. Trelawny's rates include both the introductory resort course and a one-tank dive daily, all under the supervision of certified dive masters. The resort bills itself as an "inclusive resort for everyone," and predominantly attracts a mix of families and couples, especially honeymooners. "Islanders," the name for the guest relations staff, make sure that the array of amusements continues nonstop. But one of the nicest aspects of Trelawny is that you'll never feel any pressure to participate and can opt for a snooze under the beachside palms if you prefer. Most meals are served buffet style; there are also theme dinners, such as a poolside Jamaican barbecue.

Thanks to the H-shaped layout, views are maximized, and the honeymoon package includes an oceanview room with king-size bed. All rooms are air-conditioned and have private balconies, radio, and telephone. Whenever possible, furnishings utilize wicker and floral-print Jamaican fabrics for island ambience, and the grounds are impeccably landscaped with palm trees, hibiscus, and bougainvillea. Honeymoon package: Eight days / seven nights (MAP): $1,181.40 to $1,496 per couple. Includes a horseback ride along the beach, "honeymoon dinner" with wine and wedding cake, champagne and a fruit basket with Jamaican liqueur in the room, his-and-hers T-shirts, $100 gift coupon for use on a return visit. Taxes, gratuities, liquor, and transfers from the Montego Bay airport are not included. Different length packages and Full AP are also available. If you want to tie the knot in Jamaica, Trelawny features a $125 wedding package, which includes the services of a justice of the peace, marriage license, witnesses, domestic champagne, native flowers, and wedding cake. Call 212/397-0700 for details and requirements.

First-Class Hotels

Definitely the first choice if you want to be at the center of the action, the **Holiday Inn Montego Bay,** P.O. Box 480, Montego Bay, Jamaica, W.I. (tel. 809/953-2485; U.S. reservations: toll free 800/HOLIDAY), is the largest hotel in Jamaica, with 516 rooms. Somehow, the hotel seems much smaller—almost folksy—because it is low rise (only four stories) and is nicely sprawled along a fine stretch of golden sands just a few miles east of Montego Bay proper. There's always something happening—a poolside crab race; horseback riding down at the beach, snorkeling on the reef just offshore, volleyball, rum-swizzle parties, or a backgammon tournament. Tennis anyone? You can play day or night on four lighted courts. Need to buy some souvenirs? Just across the road, Holiday Village offers a wide variety of crafts shops as well as in-bond stores.

When you get hungry, you can dine at your choice of four restaurants. There are three different bars, one set on an island in the center of the large free-form pool. And after dark, the Witch's Hideaway nightclub and the Thriller disco offer the most exciting nightlife in Montego Bay (even the locals come here).

The rooms have all the deluxe, stateside amenities you expect from the Holiday Inn chain: radio, telephone, and air conditioning. Top-of-the-line choices for honeymooners are the King Leisure oceanfront rooms, with king-size beds and a balcony thrust out over the ocean. Honeymoon package: Eight days / seven nights (EP): $787.60 to $1,072.50 per couple. Includes King Leisure oceanfront room, fruit basket, flowers in room, bottle of Tía María, a dinner for two, sightseeing excursions, T-shirts.

Moderately Priced

Richmond Hill, P.O. Box 362, Montego Bay, Jamaica, W.I. (tel. 809/952-3859). This 18th-century great house positively exudes Old World charm, with its pillars and awnings, timbered ceilings, oriental-design rugs, and Queen Anne–style antiques. It sits 500 feet above Montego Bay, an airy perch overlooking both town and harbor. During the 1700s, it belonged to the Dewars, members of the Scottish clan of whiskey fame. Today, although a bit of the grandeur has faded, the charm still remains. The rooms are of moderate size, most furnished with English-style furniture, wall-to-wall carpeting, and velvet drapes—atmospheric albeit a bit heavy for the tropics. Each room is different; some have air conditioning, but all open onto verandas. There's no beach, but the hotel compensates very nicely by running a shuttle to Doctor's Cave in town. Best of all, there's a large, sublimely photogenic pool on the outdoor terrace. Superb restaurant (see "Romantic Restaurants"). Honeymoon package: Seven days / six nights (BP): $767.80 per couple year-round. Includes deluxe accommodations, airport transfers, sightseeing tour of Montego Bay, welcome drink, bouquet of flowers, breakfast daily, two dinners for two.

ROMANTIC RESTAURANTS: As Jamaica's most popular resort, Montego Bay

offers the most dining choices, with everything from elegant hilltop restaurants to roadside stands selling jerk pork. Many of the restaurants listed below provide free shuttle transportation for patrons from their hotels; call them for details.

Seagrape Terrace, Half Moon Club (tel. 953-2211). A perfect red hibiscus floats in a glass bowl. Flames flicker in the hurricane lamps. In the background, a trio plays numbers such as "Satin Doll," "Strangers in the Night," and "Yellow Bird," that fit this sophisticated atmosphere as much as the black velvet night and the lapping waves. This is part of the Jamaican good life at the Seagrape Terrace at the Half Moon Club. You'll dine at an elegantly set table on the outdoor gallery or terrace, which face the calm bay. At terrace center, gay Japanese lanterns bob in the branches of the giant sea-grape tree, for which the restaurant is named. As much as possible, the menu spotlights fresh Jamaican ingredients. Conch might substitute for veal in a traditional schnitzel; chicken is poached in coconut milk; a fresh snapper is filleted, then stuffed with lobster, callaloo, and cream sauce. Be sure to save room for the desserts, which might include mango or coconut mousse, or banana crêpes flamed with Jamaican rum and brown sugar. Six-course, prix-fixe dinner for two: about $60 per couple plus drinks.

An Evening on the Great River, just west of Montego Bay (tel. 952-5047 or 952-5097). As the fishing boat moves up the torchlit river, you start to hear the calypso rhythms. Once you arrive, you're handed a rum punch, and you settle in for the good times. "The Evening on the Great River" includes a buffet-style Jamaican dinner, open bar, dessert, and coffee. There's also entertainment by local dancers and musicians, plus a chance for you two to show off some fancy steps while you dance under the stars to the live band. Definitely a fun evening. Held Sundays, Tuesdays, and Thursdays, $56 per couple, including transportation to and from your hotel.

The Diplomat, 9 Queen's Dr. (tel. 952-3353). The setting has all the glamour of a 1930s movie set—Italian marble floors, oversize sofas in the drawing room, and big French doors opening onto the veranda. Fred Astaire and Ginger Rogers would not look misplaced hoofing it to the Gershwin, Porter, and Berlin tunes played on the grand piano. If the Diplomat has the feel of a private villa, that's because it is—only the downstairs terrace area is open for dinner in the evening. You'll dine on the columned terrace overlooking the classic motif swimming pool, which in turn overlooks all of Montego Bay, sparkling lights and moonlit harbor included. The well-prepared continental cuisine lives up to the setting. Start off with the lobster cocktail or the pepperpot soup (about $3.50). Entrées include fresh fish meunière, lobster, or steak (entrées about $18 to $25). Definitely worth the splurge.

Calabash, Queen's Highway (tel. 952-3891). Another favorite perch for lunching or dining above Montego Bay, this one some 500 feet above the harbor. You'll be seated on a breezy terrace with flower pots and white ballustrades, which form a dazzling contrast to the turquoise Caribbean. For lunch, you'll find first-rate Jamaican favorites such as ackee and saltfish or curried goat, as well as classic dishes like chicken simmered in sherry (complete lunch from $20 per couple). At dinnertime, the menu gets more elaborate and more expensive, with highlights such as Jamaican lobster ($18.50), Caribbean fish ($13.50), veal with peppers and sherry ($16), or filet mignon ($16.50), served with rice and peas or a potato casserole.

Cascade Room at the Pelican, Gloucester Avenue, Montego Bay (tel. 952-3171). Spotlit grottoes and waterfalls weave the magic at this rendezvous that is very popular with lovers, located within walking distance of most of the downtown hotels. In addition to the seductive atmosphere, the Cascade Room is also one of the best seafood restaurants in Montego Bay. The specialty here is every conceivable manifestation of lobster: Newburg, curry, or creole, served stuffed back in its own shell with a Thermidor sauce, simply broiled, or arranged on a skewer for shish kebab (about $18). Landlubbers can opt for one of the steaks broiled to order (about $17), and you both might like to share a slice of their delectable coconut cream pie ($3). Open for dinner only; When making reservations, be sure to specify the Cascade Room—the Pelican Restaurant out front is a casual diner.

Richmond Hill, Union Street (tel. 952-3859). The attractions here are twofold—the once-upon-a-time charm of a plantation great house dating back to the 18th century, and the postcard-perfect views of Montego Bay, as seen from 500 feet up. Lunch and dinner are served on the broad, white-balustered terrace that surrounds the pool, where a sculpted swan and cherubs provide just the right classic touch. Lunches are casual and not too expensive: The light fare of sandwiches or salads should run you about $20 per couple. If you're planning to come for dinner, time your arrival for sunset—Richmond Inn offers prime views. The special four-course dinner including soup, salad, lobster or fish, and dessert is a steal at $25 per person. Otherwise, entrées such as a sirloin steak are $21.

A good place for your first taste of jerk chicken, pork, or fish is the **Cotton Tree Jerk House and Bar** on Queens Drive near Malvern Gardens or the **Pork Pit** on Gloucester Avenue in town (neither place has a phone). Portions run about $4 a person. If you want to dine under the stars and beside the water, check out **Marguerite's by the Sea** on Gloucester Avenue in Montego Bay (tel. 952-4777). Seated on a high-backed rattan chair, you can look out over the transparent blue waters near Doctor's Cave Beach. Choose from the fresh catch of the day, lobster, beef, or chicken dishes. Lunch, about $25 per couple; dinner, from $40 per couple.

NIGHTLIFE: When you want to go out dancing, you'll have several hot spots to choose from. **Disco Inferno** at the Holiday Village (no phone) draws the most action, with its huge bar, large dance floor, and live acts (often three different bands a night). You can also try the **Witch's Hideaway** across the street at the Holiday Inn (tel. 953-2485). **Evita's** attracts a lot of couples. It's located west of town, and has inspiring views: indoors, there's an eight-foot TV screen; outdoors, you look over the Great River and lights of Montego Bay (tel. 952-2301).

3. Negril

The slightly hedonistic aura that pervades Negril is neatly summarized by the anonymous entry in a hotel guest book: "Come to Negril and live, mon!" Negril, located at the western tip of Jamaica, is less a place than a state of mind—a mental condition characterized by sensuality and indolence. This is a place that bewitches vacationers, transforming them into folk for whom the most energetic event of the day is watching the sunset.

Negril is located about 47 miles west of Montego Bay, about two hours' drive. The area's supreme natural attraction is its seven miles of beach, coral sands as soft as talc that unfurl along the shores of two well-protected bays: Negril Harbour (formerly known as "Bloody Bay") and Long Bay. At West End on the island's very tip, the sands give way to dramatic ironshore (weathered coral) cliffs, explaining the spot's nickname as "The Rock."

What people commonly refer to as Negril stretches from the edge of Negril Harbour to the Lighthouse, at the very western tip of the island. "Town" is actually a modern minimall located on a roundabout; here you can buy picnic supplies at the supermarket or oil your hips at the very happening Com"pulse"on disco. If you follow Lighthouse Road west from the roundabout, you'll pass small, wooden-front restaurants such as Chicken Lavish and Sweet Bite, and tiny, fancifully named cottage accommodations called Moon Glow, Home Sweet Home, Mirage, and Catch A Falling Star. The road ends at the Negril Lighthouse, located some 100 feet above sea level. At Lighthouse Park, steps lead down the cliff face to the sea.

The vibes in Negril are truly friendly. This is a "people place," a legacy of the time when hospitable rural families took in long-haired, flower-bedecked hippies who had discovered the fine beach. Since the area is also a popular vacation spot for islanders, you'll be able to get to know Jamaicans, not just other tourists. A love of reggae forms the common bond here—sensuous bursts of music waft suddenly from passing cars and beachside restaurants; video screens feature Tosh and Marley rather than Springsteen and Genesis. There's little shopping to speak of—you might be able to round up a couple of commemorative T-shirts at the shopping plaza in the village. But you will bring home memories of snorkeling together through a cave, sharing a Red Stripe beer and a fish fry under a palm tree, or rewarding a particularly boffo sunset with a standing ovation. If you want to truly relax and get away from it all, this is the place.

ROMANTIC INTERLUDES: Negril itself is the romantic interlude. In a place so completely committed to pleasurable lethargy, recommending any activity seems to be a contradiction. But here, nevertheless, are a few suggestions:

Named for the owner, with a tip of the fedora to *Casablanca* and Bogie, **Rick's Café** (tel. 957-4335) is the heart and soul of Negril. Vacationers don't just visit Rick's, they make a pilgrimage. Late afternoon every day, sun-bronzed bodies rouse themselves from along the seven-mile stretch of sand and slouch off to this watering hole out on the coral cliffs toward the West End of town. The main event, of course, is the setting sun, which earns a standing ovation when it puts on a particularly flashy crimson show. For a supporting cast, there are also amateur cliff divers, who hurl themselves off the rocks with either perfect swan dives, or ridiculous belly flops.

The same superb views of shore and sea that make Rick's numero uno for sunset watching also make it a scenic choice for your meals. Light lunch entrées such as a lobster and veggie omelet, sandwiches, and burgers fall in the $5 to $7 range. At dinnertime, the menu gets more elaborate, with entrées such as red snapper baked in white wine ($10), steak kebab ($13), or a steak and lobster "surf 'n' turf" combo topping off the list at $18.

So you'll look like an experienced Negrilian when you arrive at Rick's, please note that you have to exchange your cash for bar beads at the desk out front—the bartender does not accept money. Credit cards are not accepted.

Because of its long isolation from the rest of Jamaica, Negril has no "must-see" historic sights. Its most interesting attractions are on, near, or under the **water.** **Snorkelers** will want to explore the caves along the ironshore at West End. **Scuba divers** can make arrangements through the **Negril Scuba Centre** at the Negril Beach Club Hotel (tel. 957-4220). For a bird's-eye view, sign up for **parasailing** at **Ray's Parasailing** (no phone) on the beach at the Sundowner, or at the **Negril Tree House Club** (tel. 957-4287). Various entrepreneurs along the beach can take you **waterskiing.** Horseback riding isn't generally considered a water sport—but it is when you can canter along the surf's edge as you can in Negril. You can rent horses from **Horseman Riding Stables,** tel. 957-4216.

The many restaurants along Negril's beaches are not just places to eat—they form the central focus of an entire day's nonactivity. In addition to having lunch or dinner, you can stake out a palm tree or a chaise longue, and practice your suntanning. For a lowdown on favorite hangouts, see the restaurant write-ups that follow.

HONEYMOON HOTELS AND HIDEAWAYS: Charela Inn, P.O. Box 33, Negril, Jamaica, W.I. (tel. 809/957-4277), with its red-tile roof, arched walkways, wrought-iron grillwork, and garden courtyard, has a Spanish ambience. Owners Daniel Grizzle and his French-born wife Sylvie have created an inn with charm and personality right in the center of Negril's Long Bay beach. There are only 36 rooms, all with air conditioning, ceiling fans, wall-to-wall carpeting, and a queen-size four-poster bed on request. Every room has either a terrace or a balcony; we prefer the upstairs accommodations because of the high ceilings, which add an airy feel. Honeymoon package: None. Deluxe room (EP): $88 to $121 per couple per night. In winter, MAP (including full breakfast and a five-course dinner at the excellent restaurant) is also available; it costs $176 per couple per night.

Foote Prints on the Sands Hotel, Negril P.O., Jamaica, W.I. (tel. 809/957-4300). The name is doubly fitting. Not only is this tiny hotel (only 12 rooms) right in the middle of Negril's seven-mile-long beach, it's also run by the Foote family (Dane, Audrey, and Ingrid), who delight in spending time with guests and recommending places and activities of interest. The hotel's architecture is highly unusual—it vaguely resembles an Egyptian pyramid with portholes. Inside, accommodations are furnished simply but cheerfully. Everything is spic-and-span; each room has a terrace. And, since the hotel is right on the beach, you'll soon be making your own footprints along the shore. Honeymoon package: None. Standard rate (EP): $56 to $78 per couple per night.

Rockhouse, West End, Negril, Jamaica, W.I. For reservations, contact: Leisure Travel, P.O. Box 78, Park Ridge, IL 60068 (tel. 312/699-1726 or 312/296-1894). You may never have seen anything quite like it—and least, not east of Tahiti nor west of Africa. Rockhouse is really a collection of Rockhouses—seven thatch-roof, round villas planted at the very brink of the limestone cliffs. Catwalks and bridges traverse inlets where the sea has bitten deep into the rock. Some of the cottages even overhang the water, so you can hear the sea surging right under your feet. Very magical. Best news of all for escapists who like their creature comforts as well: accommodations come complete with all the amenities: a queen-size bed, rattan rugs, tables, chairs, and a real bathroom with an open-air shower, well screened by lush greenery for privacy. Kerosene lanterns illuminate the property at night; there is also some limited electricity (yes, you can use your hairdryer). For lodgings, we recommend the villas, which are larger than the studios. Floor-to-ceiling glass windows take advantage of the views of cliffs and shimmering turquoise sea. When you want to swim, there's no sand beach—ladders descend from the rocks into the crystal-clear water, and skinny-dipping and all-over tans are encouraged. Snorkelers will want to poke around the underwater caves nearby. In the dining room, where dinner costs about $10 per person. Many local cafés also lie within easy walking distance, including Rick's. But since Rockhouse is near the very end of West End's Lighthouse Road, you'll probably want to rent a car, bike, or moped so you can get around. Honeymoon package: None. Villas (EP): $99 to $121 per couple per night.

Situated on one of the best stretches of Negril's seven-mile-long Bay beach, **T-Water Beach Hotel,** Box 11, Negril, Jamaica, W.I. (tel. 809/957-4270; U.S. reservations: tel. 212/519-0634 or toll free 800/243-9420), is run by the Segre family, who started up the hotel in the late 1960s. The low-rise hotel sits under the palms and sea-grape trees at water's edge. Each of the 70 rooms is air-conditioned, and has ceiling fans and private baths. Decor is a bit basic, with a double bed, wall-to-wall carpeting, and white furniture, but everything is neat and scrupulously clean. Rooms face either the ocean or garden. Honeymoon package: None. Superior room with garden view (BP): $71.50 to $82.50 per couple. Beachview suite (BP): $110 to $165 per couple. MAP available for an additional $13.20 per person per day.

Sundowner Hotel, P.O. Box 5, Negril, Jamaica, W.I. (tel. 809/957-4225), was one of Negril's first resort hotels, started by Rita Hojan. Today, it's still a small (25-room), convivial, family-style place, the kind of hotel where guests chat with each other under the huge breadfruit tree at the center of the dining terrace, or snorkel over to the coral reef just a few strokes offshore. All of the rooms have sea views and are air-conditioned, with mini-refrigerators, ceiling fans, and a patio or terrace. Make sure you request a king-size bed—some rooms have two doubles. The accommodations are bright, basic, and very clean. Honeymoon package: None. Superior room (MAP): $126.50 to $143 per couple per night.

ROMANTIC RESTAURANTS: Negril Tree House Club, Long Bay (tel. 957-4287), is a place where you'll be tempted to plunk your beach towel for the entire day. The Tree House Club is situated on one of the finest stretches of Negril beach, with shallow, turquoise waters and that powdery white sand. (Designated nude beaches lie to the left and right.) For lunch, start off with a creamy banana daquiri—diligent research has determined it's the best in Negril. Then move on to the lobster sandwich, succulently crammed with shellfish. The lunch tab should run about $16 per couple; lobster dinners about $30 per couple.

Xtabi, West End (957-4336). Located at the far west of Negril, Xtabi has no beach; instead, you sunbathe on the flat rocks along the cliff. A circular stairway hewn from the rock wends its way down to the sea. There's excellent snorkeling, including some sea caves. When you get hungry, try one of their tender conch steaks (about $8).

Kaiser's Café, West End (no phone). After sunset, the party crowd clears out of Rick's, and heads over to Kaiser's just a wee bit down the road. What Rick's is to sunsets, Kaiser's represents for nocturnal drinking and dancing. The bartender whips up a potent medley of tropical drinks, and there's a live band nearly every night. This is also the only club in Negril with videos, which feature reggae stars such as the late Peter Tosh and the late Bob Marley. Sit out on the plateaus of lava rock thrust out over the sea and enjoy.

Mariner's Inn, West End (tel. 957-4348). If you've been yearning for a lobster that hangs over the side of your plate, head for Mariner's Inn, located out on the cliffs between Xtabi and Rick's. While you dine outdoors by candlelight, you can watch blowholes in the coral along the shore shoot columns of mist two to three feet up into the air. In addition to lobster, the menu features fresh fish, including an excellent pan-fried snapper. A complete dinner will cost you about $40 per couple.

Le Vendome, Charela Inn (tel. 957-4277). Out front, water splashes in the fountain adorned with a sailfish. On the terrace, high-backed white wrought-iron chairs nestle beneath the plump coconut palms. In front of you, nothing impedes the view of Long Bay beach and the blue Caribbean. When you take into account the excellent food, a table for two at Le Vendome makes a delightful place for honeymooners to hold hands. At both lunch and dinner, Le Vendome specializes in Jamaican and Caribbean favorites. For lunch, try the steamed fish with ackee, curry goat, or roast chicken (about $4 to $10 for entrées). At dinner, choose from dishes such as lobster served grilled or creole style or a roast leg of lamb (entrées from $11 to $18). In addition, there's a different, five-course dinner special nightly, a very good deal at $20 per person. Le Vendome also has a fine, reasonably priced wine list.

Start off your day with breakfast at the **Silver Star** on Lighthouse Road in West End, just west of the roundabout (no phone). Seated on a covered patio, you'll enjoy a hearty American-style meal, complete with eggs or pancakes, whole-wheat toast, jam, peanut butter, and great coffee. About $10 per couple. For jerk chicken and other Jamaican dishes, check out **Chicken Lavish** (tel. 957-4410) over toward West End. Portions run about $5 per person. Satisfy your sweet tooth at the **Sweet Bite Café** in West End, just east of Kaiser's. Ask for two forks to share the enormous slices of chocolate or Grand Marnier cake (about $2.50 each).

4. Mandeville

Situated practically in the center of Jamaica, on a plateau some 2,000 feet above sea level, Mandeville gives you a look at a different aspect of Jamaica from the beach resorts. Here, in the Manchester Mountains, you'll find wild orchids and some of the country's most prestigious schools, 19th-century buildings and a bustling street market. When you visit an old great house, you'll most probably be shown around by the owner himself. (It all adds up to that elusive quality so sought by discerning travelers—the "real Jamaica.")

The fact that Mandeville is located in a parish named Manchester seems appropriate, since Mandeville has often been called the most British town in Jamaica. Certainly, the landscape with its lush, green, rolling hills looks like the English countryside, and the town itself is named for a former British governor. Mandeville is built around a typical English green, and many fine Georgian buildings dating to the early 1800s remain intact, including St. Mark's Church and the Courthouse. Because of the high elevation, temperatures here remain much cooler than at the coastal resorts, averaging in the 70s in summer, the 60s in winter. This moderate climate helped establish Mandeville as one of Jamaica's first tourist areas, a popular "hill station" with the early British settlers, who would summer here.

With its central location and excellent network of highways, Mandeville makes a convenient base for exploring the rest of the island. Honeymooners in particular will want to explore the little-known south coast beaches, such as Great Pedro Bay and Treasure Beach. On the way, stop for a glimpse of Lover's leap, a 1,500-foot sheer cliff that plunges to the Caribbean.

ROMANTIC INTERLUDES: If you share special interests, such as history, birdwatching, or horticulture, you can pursue them in the Mandeville area. **Marshall's Pen,** an 18th-century great house on a 300-acre cattle ranch, once belonged to the Earl of Balcarres, governor of Jamaica from 1795 to 1801. Its current owner, Arthur Sutton, will give you a personally guided tour, and explain the history of the antiques and paintings you'll see. The property also has hiking trails and a bird sanctuary. Contact Robert Sutton at 809/962-2260. **Goodwin Stables,** owned by Mrs. Pamela Goodwin, a champion show jumper, is the center of **equestrian activities.** After your ride or jumping lesson, Mrs. Goodwin's husband, the colonel, will offer you some of his celebrated homemade orange or grapefruit wine. **Mrs. Stephenson's Gardens** are known for their exquisite varieties of orchids and are the site of an annual flower show at the end of May. Mrs. Stephenson herself will show you around. To arrange visits for any of the above, contact Diana MacIntyre-Pike at the Hotel Astra, tel. 809/962-3265.

HONEYMOON HOTELS AND HIDEAWAYS: If you want to get beyond the usual
tourist destinations and be treated like a friend—not a guest—this is the place.

The story of the **Hotel Astra,** 62 Ward Ave., Mandeville, Manchester, Jamaica, W.I. (tel. 809/962-3265 or 962-3377), is inseparable from that of its co-owner and manager, Diana MacIntyre-Pike, a one-woman dynamo and the area's unofficial tourist information center. Her family has been in the hospitality business in Jamaica for over 38 years, and ran some of the first guest cottages in Negril.

Diana's experience, warmth, and enthusiasm have created a friendly, homey hotel—personalized, but run with crackerjack efficiency. The Astra has 20 rooms, and participates in the "Inns of Jamaica" program. Each room is modern and comfortable, with its own telephone and private bathroom. The hotel has a large pool and sauna; there are also some special health and fitness programs (aerobics, yoga, stress reduction, and massages) that can be arranged by appointment. Hotel service is especially impressive: A phone call to Europe came through in about one minute flat, and the Astra's guest information booklet (personally signed by Diana) tells you not only everything that you need to know about the hotel, but the Mandeville area as well.

Diana's personalized service goes as far as plopping you in her car and driving you off for an orientation tour—what has been called "Di's Whirl Around Mandeville." It's a perfect introduction to the area, and will help you decide which attractions you want to pursue in depth. Since Diana seems to know not only everyone in Mandeville, but also everyone in Jamaica, she'll gladly help you arrange special sightseeing and visits. Honeymoon package (EP): $40 to $90 per couple per night. Includes complimentary bottle of wine and a fruit basket.

ROMANTIC RESTAURANTS: The choices here aren't so much romantic as at-
mospheric, and you'll have many opportunities to try real Jamaican dishes.

Hotel Astra (tel. 962-3265). Whether you come for lunch or dinner, you're sure to find many Jamaican specialties on the menu. Meals are served in the Zodiac Dining Room, a pleasant, friendly spot with tapestry-design wall coverings and draperies. For starters, there might be pumpkin soup or a beef soup laden with vegetables. Your main course will center around beef, chicken, or fish, accompanied by different local dishes, such as rice and peas, or stamp and go (made with codfish), or akkra (vegetables). Everything is very, very good, and the friendly waiters will be glad to identify any unidentified objects on your plate. Complete lunch, from $40 per couple; dinner, $55 per couple. After dinner, you might want to sip some rum or brandy in the "Revival Room," a Jamaican-style pub built from old oaken run casks.

Located some 600 feet above Mandeville, the veranda of **Bill Laurie's Steak House,** Bloomfield Gardens (tel. 962-3116), offers one of the best vantage points for viewing the town and the softly rolling countryside. Every inch of the place is crammed with automotive memorabilia—license plates from around the world, old car photos, and various old cars. Inside the restaurant proper, a friendly, pub-like atmosphere prevails: The bar stools are old rum casks and pewter tankards belonging to the regulars hang on the walls. The steaks and chops here are excellent, and should run you about $50 per couple, including salad, vegetable, and "chips" (French fries). Open for dinner only.

5. Ocho Rios
If you know a little Spanish, you'll be surprised to learn that this town was not

originally called "eight rivers." The Spanish first referred to this area as *choreras*, meaning waterfalls, for the cascades which tumble down the verdant hillsides. With time, the English settlers altered the spelling and the pronunciation, to the name we know today.

Like its name, Ocho Rios is not quite what it seems at first glance. Although high-rise luxury hotels line the harborfront, and multi-million-dollar villas dot the hillsides, the place still retains the friendly atmosphere of the fishing village and banana-shipping port it was just 20 years ago. Ochee, as Jamaicans affectionately call it, is just a small town at heart.

Ocho Rios is located on Jamaica's north coast, about midway between Montego Bay and Port Antonio, each about a two hours' drive (70 miles) away. True to its fishing village roots, Ocho Rios life still centers around the broad, curving harbour—only now, sleek cruise ships drop anchors, instead of tiny skiffs. The harbor also provides the focus fmr water sports, such as waterskiing, Windsurfing, and sailing. Ocho Rios is one of Jamaica's most historic areas, dating back to Christopher Columbus, who is said to have landed at Discovery Bay, west of town. During the 20th century, Ocho Rios has been closely associated with movie stars and writers such as Noel Coward and Ian Fleming, both of whom owned houses in the vicinity. They were lured by the same secluded beaches, dense fern forests, and rushing waterfalls that captivate honeymooners today.

SHOPPING: Since Ocho Rios is so compact, you can walk to town from many of the most popular hotels and villas. Shoppers will want to check out three major centers. **Pineapple Place,** on Main Street, has Three Stars and Roshan for arts and crafts and other souvenirs; Jamaica Fashion for perfume, liquor, and T-shirts; and Attraction Discount Houses for liquors, batiks, and coral jewelry. For in-bond shopping for cameras, electronics, perfumes, and crystal by Baccarat, Lalique, and Swarovski, go to the Chulani's. Casa de Oro offers duty-free savings on watches by Piaget, Concorde, Cartier, and Movado; perfumes such as Giorgio and Obsession; plus jewelry, table linens, and cameras.

Coconut Grove Shopping Centre, opposite Plantation Inn, specializes in local crafts items. In particular, check out Selection for hand embroidery and black-coral jewelry. Coconut Grove also has duty-free shops such as Somi's for linens and gold jewelry.

At **Ocean Village Shopping Centre,** on Ocho Rios Bay, you'll find The Swiss Store for duty-free watches, including Omega, Tissot, Patek Philippe, and Rolex. Mohan's carries cameras by Nikon, Canon, Minolta, and Pentax. Americana Shops specializes in crystal by Lalique, Waterford, and Baccarat, plus china by Royal Doulton, Wedgwood, Royal Worcester, and Aynsley. Hemisphere, at the Americana and the Sheraton Hotels, carries Waterford, Wedgwood, and Sevres. For woven-straw items and wood carvings, check out the colorful stalls of the adjacent **Ocho Rios Crafts Market.** Nancy's China and Crystal Palace, opposite the crafts market, offers savings on a wide variety of in-bond goods: Lladro figurines, Waterford crystal, Royal Doulton china, and jewelry. You'll also find an excellent selection of popular crafts, especially wood carvings, hawked by vendors just inside the entrance to Dunn's River Falls. For the finest quality selection of local crafts and gift items, head over to **Harmony Hall** (see details under "Romantic Interludes"). Most hotels also have shopping arcades.

ROMANTIC INTERLUDES: Near Ocho Rios, you'll find some of the most romantic places in all of Jamaica.

Dunn's River Falls, a sparkling cascade, is perhaps the island's best-known sightseeing attraction, a beautiful spot where waters tumble and splash over wedding-cake tiers of smoothed rocks before ending at a white sand beach and the Caribbean.

So grab your spouse's hand, and start climbing! An experienced guide will lead you up the natural stone staircase to the top of the 600-foot falls. Along the way, you'll stop to swim in crystal-clear pools and relax in natural whirlpools. Be sure to bring a bathing suit (there's a changing room available at the base of the falls), and wear old sneakers to protect your feet. Admission to the falls area is about 75¢ per person; the guided climb costs an additional 50¢ a person.

A Victorian house dating from 1886, **Harmony Hall** has been lovingly restored, right down to the very last curlicue in the gingerbread fretwork. Today, it serves as a gallery of arts and crafts, showcasing the work of some of Jamaica's best artists and craftspeople. The roster of painters and sculptors who have exhibited work here includes Edna Manley, Mallica "Kapo" Reynolds, and George Rodney. Styles of the works range from intuitive to highly sophisticated. You can also browse through beautiful batiks, shell jewelry, and antiques. Original oil paintings start at about $100, ceramic sculptures of Jamaican cottages are $5, or you can bring home a "taste of Jamaica" in the form of Blue Mountain coffee or island spices such as sage or nutmeg starting for about $3. Open daily from 10 a.m. to 6 p.m.; admission is free (tel. 974-4222).

Located to the southwest of town, the **Fern Gully** rain forest is an officially protected reserve, running three miles along an old river bed. Over 550 varieties of native ferns flourish here, everything from the 30-foot-tall tree fern to the tiny film fern, with translucent leaves that are only one cell thick. The reserve is perfect for a short hike or picnic in the shade.

Two different legends exist about the origins of **Runaway Bay.** According to one account, it was the place from which escaped slaves launched their dugout canoes and headed for freedom in Cuba, just 90 miles away. The alternate theory maintains that the Spanish governor of Jamaica hid here after the British took over the island in 1658. Whichever explanation you prefer, the spot is fascinating because of the nearby **Green Grotto Caves,** which you can visit. On the 45-minute tour, you'll go about 120 feet underground, passing natural rock formations that look like sculptures. There's also the underground lake which gives the caves their name. The caves are open daily from 9 a.m. to 5 p.m.; admission is $2.50 per person.

Firefly was the home of Noel Coward, the playwright, composer, and dramatist whose elegance and savoir vivre seem so in tune with Jamaica. During his lifetime, Coward often entertained his celebrated friends here, including Winston Churchill, Laurence Olivier and Vivien Leigh, Katharine Hepburn, and the Queen Mother.

Located 20 miles east of Ocho Rios in the hills above Oracabessa, the house is now part of the Jamaica National Trust. All the belongings remain exactly as they were on the day Coward died in 1973—right down to his silk shirts and bathrobe in the cupboard, and the sheet music ("Three Little Words") on the piano in the living room. The ruined lookout is said to date from his time. Open daily from 10 a.m. to 4 p.m.; admission $2 per person.

Chukka Cove is the largest full-scale equestrian center in the Caribbean, and whether you're looking for an enjoyable **trail ride**—or a serious three-day event clinic —you'll find top-notch horses and facilities. Choose from a complete range of activities. On the one-hour trail ride, you'll head through a working coconut and banana plantation Papillon Cove, where scenes from that movie were filmed ($12.50 per person). More experienced riders will enjoy the six-hour day trip up to a 2,000-foot-high mountain ridge, passing wild orchids and a coffee plantation en route ($55 per person). Other programs combine a stay at a luxury resort with a polo clinic, eventing clinic (Captain Mark Phillips, a former member of the British Olympic Team, has taught here), or trekking. Polo matches are held here every Thursday during the winter. For complete details and schedules, contact **Chukka Cove Farm Ltd.,** Richmond, Llandovery, P.O. Box 160, Ocho Rios, Jamaica, W.I. (tel. 972-2506).

HONEYMOON HOTELS AND HIDEAWAYS: Even in a country known for luxury resorts, Ocho Rio dazzles vacationers with elegant choices—grand and gracious Old Jamaica inns, sleeky modern high-rise hotels, all-inclusive couples resorts, personable small hotels and cottages, and private villas.

Ultraluxurious

Jamaica Inn, Ocho Rios, Jamaica, W.I. (tel. 809/974-2514; U.S. reservations: tel. 203/438-3793 in CT; 212/697-2340 in NY; or toll free 800/243-9420). A clean, fluffy towel awaits you, even after your umpteenth return from the beach. The bed is freshly made, even after an afternoon nap. It's details like these that move Jamaica Inn beyond the realm of merely beautiful hotels, into the ranks of the truly great ones. Everything remain classically just so—white archways and columns lead to the reception area, white balustrades line the dining terrace overlooking the sea (a view that has often graced the Jamaica posters). At any given time, there are never more than 90 guests on the property, and since the two-story, U-shape inn spreads out over more than 6 acres, including 700 feet of beachfront, you'll enjoy plenty of elbow room around your chaise longue. Ambience is assured, rather than showoffy—this is the kind of place where the only sport on the property is croquet. (Ah, yes, there's a lovely oval-shape freshwater pool, good snorkeling, and tennis, golf, and horseback riding can all be arranged.)

As you would expect, rooms are spacious and classic, with chenille bedspreads, floral chintz draperies, and magohany headboards. But what really wins over guests lies just outside—the huge, private terraces or balconies that are really outdoor living rooms, taking advantage of Jamaica's balmy climate. Ask for a downstairs room—the patios are larger, and you can pop right over the railing onto the sand from many of them. All rooms are air-conditioned, most have views of both the mountains and ocean, and the hotel is situated so that you'll generally have a four-star view of the sunset. Superb restaurant. Honeymoon package: None. Oceanfront double room (MAP): $181 to $275 per couple per day. April through December, there's a seven days/six nights "Paradise Package" (MAP) for $1,315.60 per couple, which includes lots of extras such as sightseeing trips and the "Evening on the White River." And, if we wanted to splurge, we can't think of any place more romantic than the White Suite —absolutely gigantic, completely surrounded by terraces, and very secluded on the brink of a promontory (Winston Churchill slept here). From $275 to $440 per couple per night.

Pretty and pink, **Sans Souci Hotel and Club,** P.O. Box 103, Ocho Rios, Jamaica, W.I. (tel. 809/974-2353; U.S. reservations: tel. toll free 800/237-3237 nationwide; 305/666-3566 in Florida), meanders down the cliffside above a tranquil, reef-protected cove on the Caribbean. The buildings combine West Indian and Italian architectural elements, with archways, white lattice-framed balconies, and a distinctive campanile-type structure that houses the elevator to the pool. The whole property positively sparkles after a $4-million renovation. There are only 80 rooms and suites, each different in size and layout. Pink and yellow predominate—in the soft floral print upholstery, oomphy cushions on the sofa, and original prints of native Jamaican flowers. Proportions are ample, and the rooms are so comfortable, you'll want to move right in.

A lot of care is lavished on guests, so that your stay will be truly *sans souci*— without care. Equally appealing are the fanciful touches at the resort. Rolly the Parrot (a/k/a Sir Walter Raleigh) holds court amid the white wicker, chintz, and hanging plants of the reception area, there's a human-scale chessboard down by the pool, and the new health club facilities have been named "Charlie's Spa" to honor the resident turtle mascot. Water lovers can avail themselves of the two swimming pools (one spectacularly thrust over the rocks), as well as the powdery white beach that's the focus for sailing, scuba diving, snorkeling, and other sports. Tennis is complimentary on the two courts. And there's low-key entertainment nightly: Delroy Stephens tinkling the ivories in the Balloon Bar, or perhaps Ches and the Calypso Ticklers syncopating to the rhythm of the surf. The Casanova Restaurant is excellent. A member of the "Elegant Resorts of Jamaica." Honeymoon package: Eight days/seven nights (some meals): $1,091 to $1,507 per couple. Includes airport transfers, welcome cocktails and fruit basket, a bottle of champagne, one full breakfast on your balcony, one dinner at Casanova Restaurant, sightseeing tours, and more.

Plantation Inn, P.O. Box 2, Ocho Rios, Jamaica, W.I. (tel. 809/974-2501; U.S. reservations: tel. toll free 800/237-3237 nationwide; 305/666-3566 in Florida). "Plantation Inn? I'd go back there in a minute," replied one dreamy-eyed woman, some four years after her honeymoon. Maybe it's the open-air corridors, thickly overhung with climbing vines. Maybe it's the proper English afternoon tea, served from a silver teapot, or the white columned entrance portico where Scarlett O'Hara would feel right at home. Probably, it's the sum total of all these exquisite details that establish Plantation Inn as one of Jamaica's great resorts.

Imagine an antebellum southern mansion transplanted to a low hillside above two fine north coast Jamaican beaches, and you've pretty much gotten the picture. At the far side of the lobby, latticework archways open onto a broad terrace. Here, seated in a graceful white wrought-iron chair, you can take high tea or dine overlooking the pool and beaches.

Each of the 65 rooms and 14 suites is air-conditioned, and each has a private balcony with a wrought-iron railing overlooking the sea. Ask for rooms in the new section. Recently refurbished, they are breezy and tropical with white bamboo furniture and rattan rugs. Junior suites come with large terrace living areas complete with couches and a dining table.

Plantation Inn doesn't just have a private beach, it has a private bay, edged by two crescent-shape beaches. Just 100 yards offshore, you can snorkel over a coral reef. Learn to windsurf, or sail a light dinghy. Back on land, there's tennis on two courts (one lighted for night play), and horseback riding and golf can be arranged. Superb restaurant. A member of "The Elegant Resorts of Jamaica." Honeymoon package: Eight days/seven nights (MAP): $1,399.10 to $2,332 per couple. Includes deluxe room with private balcony, airport transfers, free use of watersports equipment, sightseeing tour of Prospect Plantation, a bottle of champagne.

All-Inclusive Resorts

Couples, P.O. Box 330, Ocho Rios, Jamaica, W.I. (tel. 809/974-4271; U.S. reservations: tel. 516/868-6924 in NY; toll free 800/858-8009). As the name implies, this all-inclusive resort located just east of Ocho Rios admits twosomes only. No singles. No families. No children.

Couples has been called a place created by romantics for romantics, and it lives up to its reputation. The mood is blissful, but lighthearted—part Garden of Eden, part summer camp, thanks to the amazing roster of sports available. Everything is included: sailing, Windsurfing, snorkeling, and scuba diving down at the beach; squash, racquetball, and a state-of-the-art gym with Nautilus equipment and free weights. Want to participate, but don't know how? Take advantage of the free lessons.

The romance comes not only from the clientele, but also because of the tranquil setting on an 800-foot, half-moon-shape beach. Just offshore, there's a tiny, vintage Robinson Crusoe island you can swim to (or take the launch): Tower Island, reserved for nude sunbathing. The white, red-roofed main hotel was constructed way back when—"when" being a time when people knew how to build things right. Accommodations are big, and even have walk-in closets. Rooms have been refurbished with lovers in mind: with king-size beds, air conditioning, and private balconies, each with a mountain or a sea view. Request a room on the fourth floor of the main building: although a tad smaller than the rest, they have lots of character, with a sunken living area and triangular bathroom.

Breakfast and lunch are served buffet style on the veranda, with choices of both American and Jamaican dishes. Dinner is a sit-down affair at convivial tables of four or five couples, with a four-course, table d'hôte menu that often include steak or lobster (or both, if you prefer). With lunch and dinner, you get unlimited free wine. In fact, you could eat, drink, and be merry nearly 24 hours a day, if you like, what with afternoon hors d'oeuvres, free cocktails, midnight snacks, and a piano bar that doesn't close down until the last guest departs. And, if you want to tie the knot in Jamaica, Couples can handle all wedding arrangements. Honeymoon package: None. Ocean-view room: Eight days/seven nights: $1,947 to $2,178 per couple. Mountainview rooms are $70 per couple per week less.

Eden II, P.O. Box 51, Ocho Rios, Jamaica, W.I. (tel. 809/972-2300; U.S. reservations: tel. 212/661-4540 in NY; toll free 800/223-1588). What components do you seek in your portion of honeymoon paradise? A private, secluded beach? Unlimited sports such as tennis, waterskiing, and scuba diving? The carefree spirit engendered by never having to ask how much something costs, never having to pay a tip or fee? That's what you'll find at Eden II, an all-inclusive, couples-only resort situated on 22 garden acres fronting Mammee Bay, west of Ocho Rios.

Eden II packs in an energetic repertoire of sports and instruction. On the water, there's Windsurfing, scuba diving, and snorkeling, along with lessons, if you need to hone your skills. Back on terra firma, you can opt for tennis day or night, horseback riding, or the Nautilus fitness center. Even greens fees and transfers to a nearby golf course are included. What makes Eden II different, however, are some ingratiating personalized touches. Room service will deliver a continental breakfast to your room. Waiters at the pool and beach will fetch you drinks (included, of course). Dining is à la carte four nights a week. And, when the time comes to go to bed, the nightly turndown service tucks you in nicely.

Palm trees, golden jasmine, and scarlet poinciana add vibrance and lushness, recalling the resort's garden namesake (there is also a Temptations bar, Garden of Eden dining room, and Paradise disco). The hotel itself is a substantial, seven-story structure (it served as a Hilton in a past incarnation), painted soft pink and sea-foam green to lend a tropical air. Most of the 263 rooms have king- or queen-size beds, but be sure to reserve them in advance. All have comfortable modern furnishings, air conditioning, and views of the sea or gardens (the oceanview rooms cost more). The main buildings surround a large, zigzaggy pool, perfect for swimming laps or staging some vigorous volleyball competitions.

During the day, an action-packed schedule can keep you on the move from sunup to well after moonrise: beach volleyball, aerobics classes, a couples massage class, hair-weaving demonstrations—even jaunts to Dunn's River Falls or to Ocho Rios for shopping. Every night, there's a different theme, such as Oldies' Night, or a Toga Party. If you want to get married in Jamaica, the folks at Eden II can arrange all the details of a dandy wedding party for approximately $175. Honeymoon package: None. Eight days/seven nights: Gardenview: $1,790.80 to $2,035 per couple; Ocean-view: $2,065.80 to $2,343 per couple.

Jamaica, Jamaica, P.O. Box 58, Runaway Bay, Jamaica, W.I. (tel. 809/973-2436; U.S. reservations: tel. 516/868-6924 in NY; toll free 800/858-8009 nationwide). Sip wine on a hansom-cab ride through lanes close-hemmed by bougainvillea and oleander. Move to the beat of both reggae and rock 'n' roll in the disco. These are just some of the warm, colorful, and romantic aspects of the island you'll encounter at Jamaica, Jamaica, an all-inclusive resort located at Runaway Bay, about a half-hour's drive (18 miles) west of Ocho Rios.

One could not ask for a more attractive natural setting, poised at the edge of one of the longest beaches on Jamaica's north coast. The architecture of the buildings is especially pleasing: none looms taller than the sheltering coconut palms, and the wings are angled to maximize views and privacy. Upstairs rooms have balconies, the downstairs ones have terraces; all are air-conditioned and have fresh, modern furnishings decked out with batik-like fabrics. The resort's lobby fulfills all your tropical fantasies, with waterfalls, squawking parrots, a jungle of plants, and hanging basket chairs.

Since Jamaica, Jamaica admits all adults over the age of 16, an upbeat, energetic atmosphere permeates the resort. For the sports-minded, there are three swimming pools: a gigantic free-form, a lap pool, and a volleyball pool. Down at that gorgeous beach, you can set sail on a Sunfish or Windsurfer, go snorkeling, or cruise aboard a 40-foot catamaran. Improve your tennis or golf game, or pump some iron in the Nautilus-equipped gym. Perhaps learn two of Jamaica's favorite national pastimes: soccer and cricket. In addition, you can sign up for the weekly tanning contests, fashion shows, beach Olympics, and goat racing. There's a daily shopping shuttle to Ocho Rios and excursions to Dunn's River Falls. If you prefer peace and quiet, Jamaica, Jamaica encompasses over 27 acres, so you can always get away to a hammock under a palm tree.

One of your favorite aspects of Jamaica, Jamaica is sure to be the food prepared by the resort's award-winning chefs, who prepare recipes from around the world. Breakfast and dinner are buffets, while dinner is generally sit-down, offering you a choice of continental, Jamaican, or low-calorie dishes. And, for the unstoppable, there are also afternoon hors d'oeuvres and midnight snacks. Jamaica, Jamaica attracts many honeymooners, and the resort offers them his-and-hers T-shirts and invitations to a special all-newlyweds cocktail party. Here, everyone will want to sample the drink called "Matrimony," said to guarantee a long marriage and passionate nights. Honeymoon package: None. Standard eight days/seven nights package: $1,705 to $2,178 per couple.

Jack Tar Village, Runaway Bay, P.O. Box 112, Runaway Bay, Jamaica, W.I. (tel. 809/973-3503; U.S. reservations: tel. 214/670-9888 or toll free 800/527-9299), is the kind of place where the guests write virtual love notes in the big register in the lobby: "Wonderful Jamaican hospitality!" "Thanks for all the smiles." "Fabulous!" If you're looking for an intimate scale all-inclusive resort with plenty of warm Jamaican friendliness, Jack Tar Village at Runaway Bay could be just your ticket to paradise. Part of the charm is the setting itself: The main building of the resort is a plantation great house dating to 1655. But what really makes the resort is General Manager Ned Wong, who positively delights in spoiling his guests—especially honeymooners.

Although the resort is small (only 52 rooms), you can choose from a wide range of accommodations. Couples who prefer something old-fashioned should request accommodations in the original great house, where some rooms have king-size, four-poster beds. (Be sure you reserve these in advance.) More modern types will enjoy the villas, which each have three contemporary apartments with huge balconies overlooking the sea. Although the sports facilities aren't as elaborately all-encompassing as at the larger resorts, you'll pretty much find anything a body could aspire to in the tropics. There's a fine private beach, and the reefs just offshore teem with colorful fish. You can make friends with them while snorkeling or cruising aboard Sunfish, rafts, or a glass-bottom boat. Practice your serve on the full-size tennis court (not lighted), play some tennis or chess, or unwind with a massage. At mealtime, you'll sit either on the outdoor terrace or in the formal dining room, decorated with Jamaican Victorian furniture. Most of the socializing centers around one of the two pools, especially the one near the shingle-roof gazebo bar at water's edge. Honeymoon package: None. Standard rate: $198 to $290 per couple per night.

First-Class Hotels

Sleek, modern, and elegant, the 325-room **Americana Hotel,** P.O. Box 100, Ocho Rios, Jamaica, W.I. (tel. 809/974-2151; U.S. reservations: tel. toll free 800/223-1588), has all the facilities and panache of the well-known chain. The high-rise hotel is set on a completely private beach on Mallards Bay, just a short walk from the heart of Ocho Rios and the crafts market, and right across from the Mallards Beach Hotel. The property has just completed a million-dollar refurbishment, and everything looks spanking new. The pool area has been enlarged, and the water-sports facilities have been expanded, and now feature waterskiing, jet-skiing, snorkeling, scuba diving, fishing trips, and cruises. Most importantly, all the rooms have been redone and now have a breezy island feel, the white furniture accented by pretty pastel tones of pink, lavender, and blue. Framed paintings of local landscapes adorn the walls. All the rooms are basically the same, with oceanview balconies, air conditioning, a telephone, and radio; they will try to honor requests for king-size beds. Room prices vary according to elevation: accommodations on the higher floors are considered more deluxe. The Americana has two restaurants, a snack bar, a cocktail lounge, two lighted tennis courts, freshwater swimming pool, and a shopping arcade. Honeymoon package: None. Superior room: $82.50 to $119.90 per couple per night. Deluxe room: $93.50 to $137.50 per couple per night. Various meal plans are also available.

Mallards Beach Hotel, P.O. Box 245, Ocho Rios, Jamaica, W.I. (tel. 809/974-2200). The Americana's neighbor on Mallards Bay, this 370-room hotel (formerly the Sheraton) is similar in modernist, high-rise outlook. It too is practically a self-contained resort, with four restaurants, three bars, entertainment, and a shopping arcade. Thanks to the prime Mallards Bay location, a bevy of water sports awaits right on your doorstep: deep-sea fishing, snorkeling, scuba diving, sailing, waterskiing, and glass-bottom boat rides. You can team up for doubles on the two lighted tennis courts, or line up some players for volleyball. All rooms are air-conditioned and have been recently redecorated, and now sport cool, tropical fabrics. Here, the various room categories do boast different amenities. The superior and deluxe rooms have a balcony; the standard rooms do not. Honeymoon package: Eight days/seven nights (some meals included): $1,190.20 to $1,492.70 per couple. Includes ocean- or mountainview room with balcony, airport transfers, welcome cocktails, fruit basket, full American breakfast daily, two dinners, half-day sightseeing tour. Three-night package also available.

Moderately Priced

Nestled on the shores of Cutlass Bay, **Shaw Park Beach Hotel**, P.O. Box 17, Ocho Rios, Jamaica, W.I. (tel. 809/974-2552; U.S. reservations: tel. 203/438-3793 or toll free 800/243-9420), is located right near the classiest stretch of Ocho Rios, just down the road from the Jamaica Inn and Plantation Inn. The mouth of the White River lies just to the east; almond trees, palms, and other lush foliage shade the walkways. It is a small hotel with friendly appeal. The lobby looks like an English drawing room transplanted to the tropics. All the rooms face the ocean and all are air-conditioned; most also have a balcony or terrace. Rooms are clean, simple, and comfortable, with wall-to-wall carpeting and bright floral spreads on the bed. Standard rooms, which are mostly located in the east wing, have showers only, no bath tubs.

Thanks to its location on a 1,500-foot-long beach, Shaw Park offers a good collection of water sports: sailing, snorkeling, scuba diving, waterskiing, Windsurfing, and glass-bottom boat rides are all available at a nominal charge. Tennis is free on two flood-lit courts. The outdoor terrace right over the water makes a nice spot for a casual drink. There's entertainment six nights a week from the resident band, as well as special native cabaret shows, calypso singers, and some informal wagering on crab races. Honeymoon package: Eight days/seven nights (BP): $861 per couple (available low season only). Includes deluxe double room, airport transfers, welcoming drink, flowers, bottle of wine, one dinner, free daytime tennis, and free snorkeling, sailing, and Windsurfing. Winter rate for a deluxe double (BP): $170.50 per couple per night.

Hibiscus Lodge Hotel, P.O. Box 52, Ocho Rios, Jamaica, W.I. (tel. 809/974-2676). Intimacy and oodles of charm—that's what you'll find at this small, personable inn steeped in the traditions of Old Jamaica. Although the property is conveniently near the center of town, you feel secluded from the hustle and bustle, since it is surrounded by three acres of lush gardens. Purple cattleya orchids snuggle in the crooks of trees, grapefruit and avocado trees flourish—a veritable Eden. Rooms are modern and simple to basic in decor, with private baths. Most have ceiling fans—no air conditioning. All the rooms face the Caribbean, but very somewhat in layout: Some are closer to the water, others have larger balconies. Not fancy or posh, but completely endearing. Hibiscus does not have a sand beach, but there's a stone sun deck dramatically thrust out over the water, and you can swim in the crystal clear, reef-protected waters right from there. Honeymoon package: None. Double-room rates (EP): $41.80 to $56.10 per couple per night.

ROMANTIC RESTAURANTS:

Jamaica's black velvet nights seem particularly seductive in Ocho Rios, where most of the best restaurants also come with beautiful views.

The Ruins, on the Turtle River, Ocho Rios (tel. 974-2442 or 974-2789). Built around the ruins of an old sugar mill (it even has the requisite resident ghost), The Ruins has a setting that seems to be made for lovers, set in a glade shaded by palm trees by the edge of a waterfall. You can dine on an open terrace by the side of the waterfall and river, or beneath a thatch-roof gazebo. The menu features an intriguing combination of Chinese, Jamaican, and continental specialties: everything from fish creole to a T-bone steak to Lotus Lily lobster, stir-fried with ginger and oyster sauce (entrées from $10 to $17). Either before or after your meal, you can wander up the paths and bridges that climb past the ferns and moss-covered boulders to the top of the falls, or browse through the gift shop that carries some pretty hand-painted *pareus* (sarongs). Given the fairy-tale setting. The Ruins is a perfect spot for a wedding, and Cleveland Hoo, the general manager, will be glad to help you with all the arrangements. Open daily for dinner, and for lunch Monday through Saturday. Reservations recommended.

Almond Tree, Hibiscus Lodge (tel. 974-2813). For al fresco dining with a Caribbean view, head for the Almond Tree, set cliffside some 30 feet above the sea. The white wrought-iron railings and chairs on the terrace contrast with the bright blue of the sea, which laps against the rocky shoreline. The lunch menu features crisp, crunchy salads, priced from $6 (chicken) to $10 (lobster). For starters, you might want to sample one of Jamaica's classic soups, such as pumpkin or pepperpot (about $2.50). At dinnertime, the chef has a deft hand with both continental and Caribbean dishes such as veal scaloppine ($10), breaded butterfly shrimp ($13), or broiled red snapper ($9). Reservations required.

The Little Pub Restaurant & Cocktail Bar, Little Pub Complex, Ocho Rios (tel. 974-2324). The Little Pub calls itself the "Home of Lobsters and Fun," and it delivers nicely on both counts. The restaurant is set in the courtyard of this small shopping center, surrounding the oldest standing building in Ocho Rios (1871). You'll sit on white wrought-iron chairs under the palm trees. The lobsters come prepared in a variety of styles—Thermidor, creole, or curried—but we prefer ours simply grilled and dipped in lots of butter (about $12). At lunch, you can get juicy burgers for about $5. Other than lobster, the dinner menu features a variety of grilled items: king fish, sirloin steak, shish kebab, or chicken, priced from $12 to $16. For dessert, you can set your night afire with some bananas flambé ($5). The fun really gets going thanks to the evening entertainment: the Stone Fire Band nightly, plus special performances and shows by entertainers such as The Mighty Digger. Reservations recommended.

Nights on the Rivers. In Ocho Rios, you'll find two special evening events that take advantage of the area's natural attractions. **Dunn's River Feast** (check your hotel desk or call 974-2619) is an evening of Jamaicana centered around the famous falls, which are illuminated by torchlight. There's an open bar and Jamaican buffet feast served beachside, with the emphasis on local dishes. Then get ready to enjoy the live music and John Canoe (a kind of calypso) dancers, or join in yourself for the limbo contest or goat races. Held every Wednesday at 7 p.m., price $28 per person.

A Night On The White River (tel. 974-2619) takes you by canoe up the torchlit river, frogs and crickets chirping in the jungly vegetation. You'll disembark for a buffet dinner—barbecue chicken and ribs, washed down with plenty of rum punches from the open bar. For entertainment, you'll enjoy limbo dancers, fire swallowers, and live music for dancing. Held Monday and Tuesday evenings at 7 p.m., price $28 per person.

Even if you're not staying at Jamaica Inn, Sans Souci, or Plantation Inn, you can drop over for lunch, afternoon tea, or dinner. At any one of the three, you'll enjoy excellent food, panoramic sea views, and experience the gracious service that is a Jamaican hallmark. **Jamaica Inn** (tel. 974-2514) offers a ballustered dining terrace under the rustling palm trees. The five-course, prix-fixe dinner ($27.50 per person) spotlights both Jamaican and continental dishes. **Plantation Inn** (tel. 974-2501) serves an especially atmospheric high tea every afternoon on the open terrace from 4 p.m. to 5:30 p.m. Choices include sweet cakes and tiny tea sandwiches served from a mahogany and silver cart. About $4 per person complete with tea or coffee. The Plantation Inn also serves an elegant five-course, prix-fixe dinner for $33 per person. **Casanova at the Sans Souci** (tel. 974-2353) offers both outdoor dining on the poolside terrace, and indoors in the main room (although the wide-open windows make you feel as if you're outdoors anyway). Dinner will cost about $30 to $35 per person. Reservations required for all.

6. Port Antonio

The drive east from Ocho Rios along Jamaica's north coast plays hide-and-seek with the sea. Alternately, the road opens onto awesome vistas of mountain and sea coast, then plunges deep into bamboo forests and dense sugarcane fields, so close to the road that foliage swishes against the car windows as you pass. The route takes you through the towns of Oracabessa and Port Maria (with their busy markets on Fridays), and runs along the base of mountains that plummet straight to the sea. Some 2 hours and 67 miles after you leave Ocho Rios, you'll arrive in perhaps the lushest and most tropical part of Jamaica, what poet Ella Wheeler Wilcox called "the most exquisite port on earth"—Port Antonio.

Today, Port Antonio still retains a quiet, old-world charm, heavily tinged with movie-star and jet-set connotations. There are two ports actually—east and west harbors—both surrounded by steep, jungly hillsides. The town is an historic one, originally settled by the Spanish. It staked its initial claim to fame as the center for the banana trade in the 19th century. Because of the rich profits the bananas yielded, they soon became known as "green gold." According to legend, the banana planters grew so wealthy that one "Banana Day" (any day a ship was loading), they would light their cigars with $5 bills. Prosperity ended abruptly with the outbreak of Panama disease, which destroyed nearly the entire crop. The industry never recovered.

Into this sleepy ex-banana-port sailed the yacht *Zacca*, owned by Errol Flynn. The swashbuckling actor acquired substantial real estate holdings here, including Navy Island, which he supposedly won in settlement of a gambling debt. Flynn's widow, Patrice Wymore Flynn, still lives in the area. Another interesting footnote: Flynn receives credit for making river rafting a popular attraction for vacationers. The rafts were originally used to bring bananas to market, and Flynn, true to form, started racing them down the river and wagering on the results.

Another fascinating story concerns the Folly, a mansion built in 1906 by millionaire Alfred Mitchell for his wife Annie Tiffany (daughter of the founder of the Fifth Avenue store). By 1938, the entire structure collapsed: Sea water had been used in mixing the concrete, and the supporting iron rods rusted through. Today, only a jumbled pile of ruined columns remains, and the site makes a hauntingly beautiful spot for a stroll or a picnic.

Despite its reputation as an oasis for the rich and famous, Port Antonio remains refreshingly innocent, and is still largely unspoiled by tourism. For a uniquely Jamaican experience, stop by the market held Thursdays through Saturday, and sample some savory jerk pork served with hard-dough bread. Perhaps pick up some Irish moss, which can be brewed into a tea said to be an aphrodisiac. No high-rise buildings mar the profile of the main town, which is dominated by the Georgian Courthouse and the brick parish church, Christ Church, which dates from 1840. Queen Street has some more good examples of Georgia architecture. The town is looking pretty spiffy these days, ironically thanks to Hollywood connections once again: It was used as the setting for the Robin Williams' movie, *Club Paradise*. It is precisely this interplay between show business and local Jamaican culture, glamour and down-home roots, that makes Port Antonio so intriguing to honeymooners.

SHOPPING: Your options are quite limited here. In town, there's **Sang-Hing's Freeport Giftland,** with a small selection of duty-free figurines and perfumes. For local crafts, try the **weekly market** or the **pier** on those days when cruise ships come to town. If you're really looking to buy, plan to spend time in Montego Bay, Ocho Rios, or Kingston.

ROMANTIC INTERLUDES: The choicest options center around Port Antonio's lush surroundings.

According to legend, The **Blue Lagoon** is bottomless; more scientific types have determined that it's about 180 feet deep. In any event, it's beautiful—crystal clear, sapphire-blue waters fed by freshwater springs said to have amazing rejuvenating powers. Located a short drive west of Port Antonio, the lagoon is framed by white beaches and green cliffs. For a small charge, you can waterski or take a glass-bottom boat ride to view the reef and colorful fish; better yet, bring your bathing suit and go for a swim (absolutely free). It's also a fine spot for a picnic.

The only sounds are the chirps of the June bugs in the surrounding jungle and the wind rustling through the stands of bamboo. For a true oasis of peacefulness and bliss, head over for the rafting trip down the **Rio Grande,** which has its headwaters in the Blue Mountains, and runs all the way to the Caribbean. This particular journey runs about eight miles, and takes about two to three hours. Seated on a bench just big enough for two, you'll float down the river on the 33-foot-long raft, propelled by an experienced skipper with a stout pole. Along the way, you can stop for a swim in the crystal waters (remember your bathing suits), or for a drink at a little riverside stand. To reach the embarkation point, you can either take an organized tour from your hotel, or drive your rental car. If you drive, you can hire a licensed, insured driver to bring your car to the journey's end (this costs about $8). The raft trip itself costs $30 per couple.

Located just east of Port Antonio a bit past the Blue Lagoon, the **Nonsuch Cave and Gardens of Athenry** are located on a 185-acre working coconut and banana plantation. The journey is worth it just for the drive: The road to the plantation winds up through the hills and offers splendid vistas of the mist-covered Blue Mountains. At Nonsuch Cave, you can catch up on the past 1½ million years of history. The caves were discovered in the 1950s by someone looking for a lost goat. During the guided tour of the caves, you'll pass stalactites, stalagmites, fossilized marine animals, and artifacts left by the Arawak Indians, the original inhabitants of Jamaica. Then, if you've ever wondered where many of your favorite kitchen spices came from, join the guided tour of the gardens. You'll view coconuts, thyme, pimiento (allspice), bay leaf, ackee, nutmeg trees, vanilla vines with their fragrant seed pods, and other plants and flowers typical of Jamaica. There's also a charming restaurant, where you can lunch al fresco and admire the views. The property is open 9 a.m. to 5 p.m., and $4.25 per person admits you to both the caves and gardens.

Waterfalls, rivulets, and deep rock pools make **Somerset Falls** a cool change of pace from the beach. Go swim and splash in the tumbling waters. The forests are lush and jungly, thick with croton, banana plants, bamboo, and huge red ginger lilies. Bring a picnic lunch; there's also a small restaurant. Located ten miles west of Port Antonio, just past Hope Bay.

HONEYMOON HOTELS AND HIDEAWAYS: Port Antonio offers a small, but select, collection of places to stay.

Ultraluxurious

Trident Villas and Hotel, P.O. Box 119, Port Antonio, Jamaica, W.I. (tel. 809/ 993-2602; U.S. reservations: tel. 212/689-3048 in NYS or toll free 800/235-3505), is the kind of place that makes you wish that your honeymoon could, in fact, go on forever. The 14-acre setting is a marvel, right on the brink of rocky bluffs at the edge of the Caribbean. And where the rocks end, the lovingly tended verdure of Trident's manicured lawns begin, dotted with palm trees, gazebos, and flowers. The one- and two-story white cottages and villas are scattered along the edge of the cliffs, providing maximum privacy and panoramic impact. Each of the 27 accommodations is different and delightful, and all come furnished with antiques and have large balconies or verandas. But the pièce de résistance will surely be the view of the pounding surf, just beyond your terrace. Each room has a large paddle fan, to enhance the cooling trade winds that usually comfort this coast.

The ambience is a gracious blend of Jamaican plantation hospitality and English country house tradition. Waiters in crisp uniforms walk along the paths, ferrying breakfasts to the guests. High tea becomes high art when served on white linen tableclothes on the brick terrace. Adding the final regal touch, white and blue peacocks and peahens strut regally across the ample lawn. No wonder the hotel attracts a regular clientele among the rich and famous, including Peter O'Toole, Jimmy Cliff, and Twiggy.

Trident has a small, private beach with a protected sand cove for swimming. If you get hungry or thirsty, the beach boy will whisk lunch and cocktails right to your chaise longue. In addition, there's a stunning free-form pool by the main house (it's been photographed for several magazines). The little gazebo at the end makes a cozy nook for two lovers to gaze out over the blue, blue Caribbean. Honeymoon package: Eight days/seven nights (MAP): $1,771 per couple. Includes deluxe oceanview suite with living room, bedroom, and balcony, airport transfers, welcome cocktail, afternoon tea daily, and daily tennis. Available April 15 through December 15 only. Winter rate for a junior suite (MAP): $325 per couple per day.

All-Inclusive

Fern Hill Club, P.O. Box 28, Port Antonio, Jamaica, W.I. (tel. 809/993-3222; U.S. reservations: tel. toll free 800/423-4095). "You've got to see this place," said the honeymoon couple we met while rafting on the Rio Grande. "We love it and are coming back for our first anniversary next year." We took their advice—and discovered Fern Hill Club, which must be one of the best-kept secrets in the Caribbean. A secret, at least, to most Americans—the property is Canadian-owned, and is extremely popular with vacationers from Canada, especially honeymooners. Fern Hill Club is an all-inclusive resort, with accommodations both in deluxe and standard rooms, as well as extremely spacious, well-appointed, and modern villas. The villas are nestled in the foothills of the Blue Mountains, and offer travel-poster-caliber views of Port Antonio, just a ten-minute drive away. Villa accommodations each have different, but assuredly impeccable, furnishings, and fully equipped kitchens. Not that you'll have to cook—meals are served down at the main building on one of the three patios. Floor-to-ceiling louvres all around guarantee a breezy island ambience. (There's also air conditioning.)

Fern Hill's hillside location precludes a beach on the property, but they run a free shuttle to the beach at San San and Frenchman's Cove. There's complimentary snorkeling and Windsurfing, as well as tennis. Every day, you can participate in special activities—sightseeing tours through Maroon country, trips to the Rio Grande for rafting, beach parties, and sunset cruises, as well as live entertainment nightly. And, [our honeymooning friends ask us to add, "The staff really make the place. They'll help you with anything you need. Just great people!" Honeymoon package: None. Villas: $1,276 to $1,735.80 per couple per week. Standard rooms: $1,045 to $1,535.60 per week. Covers airport transfers; welcome rum punch; breakfast, lunch, and dinner daily; beer, local liquors, and wine with dinner; shuttle bus to beaches.

Moderately Priced

Bonnie View Hotel, Port Antonio, Jamaica, W.I. (tel. 809/993-2752). As the sign out front will tell you, this is one of the oldest continuously operating hotels in Jamaica. The view, in fact, does live up to its name: Set some 600 feet above Port Antonio, the panorama encompasses the east and west harbors to the north, the Blue Mountains to the southwest. The rooms themselves are quite simple but very tidy, with plain tile floors, private bathroom with shower, and jalousie windows, which take advantage of the cool, upcountry breezes (no air conditioning, because it's usually 10° cooler here than in town). Each room has a private balcony facing the mountains or sea. There's a large freshwater pool, and the dining terrace makes a very attractive perch for a light lunch. In the evenings, you can dance to calypso music at the bar pavilion. Honeymoon package: None. Double room: $55 per couple per night year-round.

ROMANTIC RESTAURANTS: From elegant restaurants with white-glove service to casual stands by the sea, Port Antonio offers something to please.

Expensive

Trident Hotel Restaurant (tel. 993-2602). A silver candelabra flames on the table set with English bone china and fine cutlery. Antique tapestries and crystal chandeliers adorn the white stone walls. Another world . . . almost another century . . . that's the feeling captured when you dine at the Trident Restaurant. Dinner is served promptly at eight, a five-course, fixed-menu gourmet treat that gracefully balances both Jamaican and continental dishes, exquisitely prepared. The waiter, wearing a red vest, starched white shirt, black bow tie, and—yes—white gloves, murmurs the name of each dish as he serves it. "Blinis, sir, served with Russian caviar." "How would you like your roast beef, madam?" (said as he wheels a silver trolley to your table). "Jamaica fruits flambéed." "Viennese pastries." After dinner, there's a musical combo at the bar, or an occasional spur-of-the-moment sing-along around the grand piano in the oriental-carpeted lounge. The fixed dinner costs $45 per person. Jacket and tie required for men in the winter season; jackets only, May to December; cocktail attire for ladies. Reservations required.

Inexpensive

Boston Bay Beach (no phones). The beachside stands at Boston Beach are generally conceded to have the best jerk pork and jerk chicken on the island. After all, the dish originated here, a staple of the Maroons who inhabited the nearby hinterlands. Portions are sold by weight—a half-pound to three-quarters of a pound should do you nicely, and cost about $5. Just dig in with your fingers. Afterwards, take a siesta, then cool off with a swim. Boston Beach, located east of Port Antonio and the Blue Lagoon, is a public beach, donated to the government during the 1950s by Robin Moore, author of *The Green Berets*.

The terrace at **Bonnie View Hotel** (tel. 993-2752) serves light sandwiches and salads for lunch, with a side order of the best views of Port Antonio and Navy Island. About $10 per person. Built by an old sea captain in typical New England style, **DeMontevin Lodge** (tel. 993-2604) is the place to head for soul-satisfying Jamaican food—pepperpot soup, breadfruit, home-style chicken with vegetables, and desserts such as banana cream pie. Dinners about $20 per person.

Chapter XXXII

MARTINIQUE

1. Practical Facts
2. Romantic Interludes
3. Honeymoon Hotels and Hideaways
4. Romantic Restaurants and Night Spots

NIBBLING FRESHLY BAKED croissants, a newly married couple breakfasts at a seaside café. They think of the gourmet meal they had the night before prepared by an award-winning French chef. Snatches of French conversations float by as they gaze into the harbor filled with masted boats. That afternoon, they are planning to drive through the hilly countryside sprinkled with red-roof houses. No, they are not in the French Riviera. It's true that they are honeymooning on French soil, but they are not in France. The sun glistens on the Caribbean, not the Mediterranean. The ancestors of most of the people they see came from Africa, not Europe. And in addition to French, they've heard the musical patois called Creole. They are in Martinique, in the West Indies.

Separated by Dominica from Guadeloupe, its sister island, 425-square-mile Martinique is in the eastern Caribbean. About 350,000 people call it home. Residents are quick to remind visitors that their mountainous island is as much a part of France as Hawaii is of the United States. While the serene Caribbean Sea soothes one side, the tumultuous Atlantic throws itself against the other.

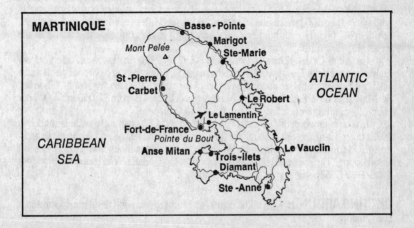

Start getting acquainted with the island in Fort-de-France, the capital. Backed by mist-covered mountains, this city faces a busy harbor. Wander along the narrow, winding streets, past women selling fruits and vegetables by buildings with fretwork balconies. Ferries cruise across the bay to Pointe du Bout and Anse Mitan, the two main beach resorts. Some of the island's best restaurants are here, along with stunning beaches where snorkeling is particularly colorful, and there are hotels in all shapes and sizes. You'll find one of the island's two casinos in Pointe du Bout (the other is just outside Fort-de-France in Schoelcher).

A drive north of Pointe du Bout along the Caribbean coast will take you past sugarcane fields, banana plantations, and undulating hills. Small fishing villages dot the shore. Diamant, a small village in the south, is known for the massive rock that juts 600 feet out of the ocean just offshore. Some of the island's most attractive beaches are in this area.

As palm trees sway in the breeze and the clear water ripples turquoise, then navy, Martinique will give honeymooners more than a taste of France.

1. Practical Facts

GETTING THERE: Americans must have a valid passport, a passport that has expired within five years, a voter's registration card, or an authenticated birth certificate. For Canadians, a passport is necessary. You'll also need to show a return or ongoing ticket. The departure tax will be included in your air fare.

Whether you fly or sail, traveling to Martinique is hassle-free.

By Air

Martinique is about three hours from Miami and just over four from New York. All international flights land at Lamentin Airport, about five miles from the capital of Fort-de-France. **American Airlines** offers flights from New York, Newark, and other U.S. cities via San Juan. **Eastern** has direct flights from Miami and Atlanta; it also flies from New York, Newark, and other U.S. cities via San Juan. **Air France** will fly you in from Miami or San Juan, and **Air Canada** from Montreal and Toronto. Both **Air Martinique** and **LIAT**, the Caribbean's local airline, connect Martinique with other Caribbean islands.

By Sea

If you decide to sail to Martinique you'll have a wide choice of boats, from yachts with fewer than 100 passengers to enormous vessels with over a thousand. The pools, health spas, nightly entertainment, and seemingly endless meals make some of the larger ships seem like floating hotels.

Carnival Cruise Lines (tel. toll free 800/232-4666), for instance, offers seven-night cruises on the *Festivale*. Among the many facilities are three outdoor pools and a casino. Leaving from San Juan on Sundays, year-round, the ship stops at St. Thomas, St. Martin, and Barbados as well as Martinique. The cost is from $2,050 to $4,000 per couple, including air fare to San Juan from 140 U.S. cities.

If you prefer something smaller, the *Mandalay*, a 72-passenger yacht launched in 1923, takes 12-night sails throughout the year between Grenada and Antigua. In addition to Martinique, ports include Mustique in the Grenadines and Les Saintes off Guadeloupe. The cost is $2,730 and up per couple. (Contact **Windjammer Barefoot Cruises,** 212/686-4868.)

GETTING AROUND: With taxis, buses, and cars for rent, on-island transportation is convenient.

By Taxi

You'll find taxi stands at the airport, downtown Fort-de-France, and the larger hotels, Cabs are not metered, so be sure to check at your hotel to find out how much your ride should be. The fare from the airport to Pointe du Bout hotels runs about $19 for two people with luggage. Note that between 9 p.m. and 6 a.m., fares increase by 40%. If you speak some French and you want to save money, look for collective taxis (TCs). These eight-seat limousines and vans congregate at Pointe Simon on the waterfront on Fort-de-France and run from early morning to about 6 p.m.

Taxi tours are most economical when you join forces with another couple. A half-day sightseeing tour will run from about $28 to $40 for two to four passengers. Many drivers speak some English.

By Bus

The no. 3 bus leaves about every half hour from the airport for the harbor in Fort-de-France. The fare is about 50¢ per person.

For a half day or full day of sightseeing by bus, try **Roger Albert Voyages** (tel. 71-44-44) in Fort-de-France or **Carib Tours** (tel. 76-32-56) in Pointe du Bout. Tours include historic sites, dramatic scenery, beaches, and often, stops at restaurants for creole specialties.

By Ferry

Ferries go between Fort-de-France harbor and the resort areas of Pointe du Bout, Anse Mitan, and Anse à l'Ane. The fare is about $1 each way or $1.50 round-trip. While the boats go to and from Pointe du Bout from early morning until about midnight, boats to the other two areas stop running in the late afternoon.

By Rental Car

You'll need a valid driver's license to rent a car. Most roads are well marked and well paved, but many of the most scenic are narrow and winding, so drive carefully. Especially during the winter season, it is best to make advance reservations for a rental car. In Martinique, you'll find rental agencies at the airport, in Fort-de-France, and at some hotels. As in France, car rentals and other businesses close for lunch from about noon to 2:30 p.m.

The following companies are among those that have offices in both the United States and Martinique: **Avis** (airport: tel. 79-26-86; Fort-de-France: tel. 70-11-60), **Budget** (airport: tel. 79-22-88; Fort-de-France: tel. 71-69-68), and **Hertz** (airport: tel. 79-28-22; Fort-de-France: tel. 60-64-64). You'll save a few dollars at local companies, such as **Carib Rent-a-Car** (tel. 70-12-34) at the airport; **Resort** (tel. 71-68-74) and **L.A.M.** (tel. 71-47-37), both in Fort-de-France; and **Safari Car** (tel. 66-06-26) and **Pinville et Fils** (tel. 66-03-06), both in Anse Mitan. Rates run from about $12 a day plus about 12¢ a mile to about $32 a day plus about 25¢ a mile. Credit cards are accepted at most rental agencies; if you don't have plastic, be prepared to put down a cash deposit of between $180 and $300.

LANGUAGE: French is the official language. Creole, a patois incorporating words from French, Spanish, English, and West African languages, is also widely spoken. Staff members of many restaurants and the larger hotels speak some English, but you'll need to know at least a little French if you plan to do much exploring. So, if you don't speak French, be sure to take along a phrase book and a dictionary.

MONEY AND TIPPING: The French franc is the official currency of Martinique, and its value in relation to the dollar changes daily. Local banks give better exchange rates than hotels. Banks are open Monday through Friday, from 8 a.m. to 4:30 p.m., and are closed for lunch from noon to 2:30 p.m. U.S. dollars are accepted at some shops, restaurants, and hotels. In addition, several stores give an additional 20% discount when you make purchases using certain credit cards or traveler's checks in dollar denominations. Most large hotels accept credit cards.

The tip (or service charge) is often included in restaurant checks and hotel rates, in which case it is not necessary to leave a tip for your room maid. Ask if you're not sure. Tip 10% to 15% when the service charge is not included. Porters don't usually expect tips, but if you'd like, you can give one franc per bag. Most cab drivers don't expect to be tipped either.

WEATHER: Daytime temperatures average in the high 70s and low 80s year-round, with the weather somewhat warmer during the summer months. Evening temperatures can be 5° to 10° cooler. Refreshing trade winds blow continually and rainfall is usually too brief to disrupt the beach scene for long.

CLOTHING: The attire in Martinique is generally casually chic. Women tend to wear dressier evening outfits during the winter season than during the summer. Pack a shawl or light sweater for cool nights or air-conditioned restaurants and clubs. Men rarely wear jackets at dinner, and ties are seldom seen. Bikini tops are scarce on most hotel beaches. Beachwear should be restricted to poolside and seaside.

ELECTRICAL CURRENT: Unlike the United States, electricity is 220 volts AC, 50 cycles, so you'll need converters and adapter plugs for your iron, razor, hairdryer, or any other electrical appliances you might bring. Some of the larger hotels will lend converters and adapters to guests, but it's best to bring your own.

TIME: Martinique is on Atlantic Standard Time, which is one hour later than Eastern Standard Time. During the winter this means that when it is 9 a.m. in New York, it is 10 a.m. in Martinique. However, when Daylight Saving Time is in effect, the time is the same in Martinique and U.S. east coast cities. You'll notice that time is told in the French way here, so that for example, 1 p.m. is called 13 hours.

TELEPHONES: To call Martinique from the United States directly, dial 011-596, then the six-digit local number.

SHOPPING: Martinique offers bargains on an array of honeymoon mementos. Although the island is not duty free, the 20% tax reduction discount on luxury items purchased with traveler's checks or credit cards makes for some excellent bargains. Together the two of you can take home up to $800 worth of goods duty free. The best buys by far are in French imports, including designer fashions, perfume, and fine wines. Local rum is also a popular purchase. The majority of the island's shops line the narrow side streets of Fort-de-France. Most stores close from about noon until 2:30 p.m. during the week. Unless you like crowds, avoid shopping when cruise ships are in, and on Saturdays, when stores are only open in the morning.

For a wide selection of crystal, china, cosmetics, jewelry, watches, and leather goods, head for **Roger Albert** (on rue Victor Hugo). The treasure trove at **Cadet Daniel** (on rue Antoine Siger) includes gold and silver jewelry, Lalique crystal, and Limoges china. Roger Albert and Cadet Daniel are two of the stores that give additional discounts on items bought with some credit cards and travelers' checks. Near the cathedral, **Au Printemps** (on rue Schoelcher) is a branch of the famous Parisian department store. It carries a good selection of French fashions, fancy kitchen gadgets, gourmet foods, and other imports. You'll also find small boutiques in the capital selling French resortwear for both women and men, such as skimpy high-fashion bikinis and Cardin bathing trunks.

In addition to imports, Martinique has some tempting home-grown goods. **La**

Case à Rhum (avenue de la Liberté) sells local rums and other alcohol. The **Caribbean Art Center,** across from the Office of Tourism near the Fort-de-France harbor, specializes in colorful appliquéd wall-hangings, pottery, and straw bags, among other handmade finds. Take a stroll through **La Savane,** an attractively landscaped park where more crafts are sold. You'll see handmade creole dolls clad in bright madras dresses and the island's trademark bakoua hat (pointed and wide-brimmed). Then recover from all your shopping by relaxing by the lily pond in the parc **Floral et Cultural.**

While you're touring the Atlantic coast, stop in at **Ella,** a gourmet boutique specializing in local spices, homemade preserves, jams, and liqueurs. Just north of Trinité, this pleasant shop is in the village of Bézaudin, near Sainte Marie.

CASINOS: Feeling lucky? The Méridien hotel, in Pointe du Bout, is the home of one casino, while the other resides in La Batelière hotel, just outside Fort-de-France. Men don't need jackets and ties, but dress tends to be elegantly casual. You may be asked to show some form of identification with a photograph.

HOW TO GET MARRIED IN MARTINIQUE: In order to tie the knot on this tropical island, one partner must have resided in the French West Indies for at least 30 days prior to filing the marriage license application. Applications are available at the local mairie (town hall) upon presentation of a birth certificate, proof of citizenship, proof of divorce (if applicable), and a medical certificate—all accompanied by French translations. For the medical certificate, a list of qualified English-speaking doctors is available from the American Consulate in Martinique (Immeuble Place Père Labat, 14 rue Blenac, 97206 Fort-de-France, Martinique, F.W.I.; tel. 596-63-13-03) or your local French Consulate.

After filing the application, allow at least ten days for the publication and posting of the marriage banns (the official announcement of your intention to marry). You may be asked to take a blood test, and witnesses will be necessary. A religious wedding may only be performed *after* the civil service. The minister, priest, or rabbi must be given a certificate of civil marriage (certificat de célébration civile) before performing the religious ceremony.

FOR FURTHER INFORMATION: Contact the **French West Indies Tourist Board,** 610 Fifth Ave., New York, NY 10020, tel. 212/757-1125; **Office Departemental du Tourisme de la Martinique,** B.P. 520, 97206 Fort-de-France, Martinique, French West Indies, (001)596/63-79-60.

2. Romantic Interludes

The legacy of famous lovers, secluded natural wonders, and activities best done in pairs make Martinique perfect for newlyweds.

Le Jardin de Balata (tel. 72-58-82) is a tropical botanical garden deep in a thick rain forest. To get here from Fort-de-France, you'll drive up a steep, winding road through the picturesque suburb of Didier and you'll look down on the busy capital. In the garden, paths are bordered by ferns as large as trees, fragrant multicolored flowers, and gurgling brooks. Their peaks caught in the clouds, mountains stand in the distance. The reception area, in the gracious 60-year-old vacation home of the owner's grandmother, is attractively decorated with antiques and old photographs of island residents. Dolls, colorfully decked out in madras outfits, are on display along with bright creole hats once worn by local women. Le Jardin de Balata is open every day from 9 a.m. to 5 p.m. and admission is about $5. Nearby **Sacre Coeur de Balata,** a lovely church, bears a startling resemblance to its Parisian namesake.

Following La Trace road to the Atlantic side of the island, you'll cross one of the most spectacular parts of the rain forest. Towering bamboo and high walls of vegetation in endless variations of green create a tunnel-like passageway.

Pack a **picnic lunch**—maybe some freshly baked croissants, cheese, a bottle of wine, a few ripe mangoes—and drive to Caravelle, a scenic peninsula that pokes out into the Atlantic near Trinité. There are campsites in this idyllic nature preserve, as well as the impressive ruins of Dubuc Castle. Once the home of a wealthy 18-century family, the castle now lies in ruins. The only remains are the crumbling walls of the slave cells, a dam, a mill, and sheep pens. The view from these ruins is truly breathtaking.

Martinique has several intriguing museums—all small enough to squeeze in between trips to the beach. Begin at the **Musée de la Pagerie** near the village of Trois Ilets, a brief ferry ride from Fort-de-France. The museum sits on the grounds of the plantation where Napoleon's empress Josephine was born in 1763. Along with portraits of the Empress, her bed, and invitations to balls in Paris, you'll find a steamy love letter she received from Napoleon (with an English translation). The museum is about $1 per person.

North of here, **Carbet** is the place where Columbus is said to have landed. This village is also known for its unusual dark sand beaches. Here the **Gauguin Museum** commemorates the work completed by the legendary French painter during his four-month stay on the island in 1887.

Further north, you'll come to **Saint Pierre.** Once a sophisticated city called "the Paris of the West Indies," it was two centuries old in 1902 when the now dormant Mont Pelée volcano erupted violently. Three minutes was all it took to destroy the entire city, killing the 30,000 inhabitants. At the **Musée Volcanologique,** remains of the disaster are on display—petrified spaghetti, a half-full bottle of perfume fused shut, a huge melted church bell, disfigured clocks all stopped at the same time.

The golden expanse in southern Martinique known as **Les Salines** is easily one of the most stunning beaches in the Caribbean. At one end of the crescent, you'll see the silhouette of Le Diamant in the distance. You may find it difficult to tear yourselves away from these calm, turquoise waters. But keep in mind that there are some excellent creole restaurants nearby that are great for lunch.

Trot on horseback through sugarcane fields, past banana plantations, and along scenic mountainsides and seashores. **Ranch de Galochat** (tel. 76-43-97) in Anse à l'Ane, will even have riders picked up in and returned to Pointe du Bout, about 15 minutes from the stables. The cost is about $25 per person for the 1½-hour ride.

For bareboat or skippered **yacht charters,** try **Voile et Vent Antilles** (tel. 66-00-72) at the Pointe du Bout Marina or **Ship-Shop** (tel. 71-43-70) in Fort-de-France. Yacht charters range about $400 a weekend for a yacht with two double cabins to about $3,000 a week for one that sleeps eight.

After a few days of romping around Martinique, board the *Wind Star* for a seven-day cruise through the Grenadines. This chain of islands is surrounded by some of the clearest water you'll ever see, water that shimmers turquoise, teal, and navy. At 440 feet, the four-masted *Wind Star* is among the world's longest sailing ships. As the billowy sails catch the wind, you'll swim in a salt water pool, go snorkeling, waterskiing, or Windsurfing off the boat, and dine on the freshly caught lobster. Stops at islands along the way give the 150 passengers ample opportunity to play tennis, golf, and go deep-sea fishing. The *Wind Star* sails weekly from Martinique and back. A seven-night cruise will cost $4,330 to $5,790 per couple. Contact **Windstar Sail Cruises,** 7415 N.W. 19th St., Miami, FL 33126 (tel. toll free 800/258-SAIL in the U.S.; 800/341-SAIL in FL; and 800/525-SAIL in Canada).

3. Honeymoon Hotels and Hideaways

The hotel you choose will depend on whether you want to be in the thick of things, a stone's throw from the action, or as far away from it as possible. In addition to modern beachfront high rises and medium-size hotels, there are cozy inns, collectively known as the Relais Créoles. Some are in historic homes; many are renowned for their excellent creole cuisine; all are friendly, casual, and best for visitors who speak at least a little French.

Most of Martinique's tourist hotels speckle the waterfront in the Pointe du Bout/ Anse Mitan area, a brief ferry ride from the capital. This is where the nightlife is the liveliest—beginning with some of the island's most popular restaurants, a casino, and musical entertainment. If you're looking for seclusion, consider Leyritz Plantation, up north in Basse Pointe, or Manoir de Beauregard, down south in Sainte Anne near the island's most breathtaking beaches.

High season runs from about mid-December through mid-April; low-season rates dip about 20% to 50%. The price ranges given for hotels in this chapter reflect the difference between low- and high-season rates. A 10% or 15% tax and service charge is generally included in room rates. In some resort areas, you'll also pay an additional government tax of approximately $1 per person per day.

Leyritz Plantation, 97218 Basse Pointe, Martinique, F.W.I. (tel. 596/75-53-08; U.S. reservations: tel. 212/477-1600; or toll free 800/223-1510). Tucked away at the northern end of the island, the 50-room Leyritz Plantation blends modern comforts with living history. The old rum distiller has been turned into a health spa where you can pamper yourselves in the solarium, Jacuzzi, or massage rooms. Dormitories for plantation workers have been transformed into guest rooms, and the main house is furnished with antiques including oriental rugs and day beds. Stone walkways wind past lush vegetation and old buildings with red-tile roofs. From the hotel, you can appreciate the sweeping vistas of banana groves and distant mountains. Hosts Charles and Yveline de Lucy de Fossarieu give people the personalized attention that brings guests back year after year. The restaurant draws people from all over the island for lunch. When you want a break from the swimming pool, transportation is provided to a nearby beach. Almost a two-hour drive from the capital or the airport, Leyritz Plantation is for people who want total relaxation. Honeymoon package: None. Rates (CP): $44 to $137 per couple per night. Health spa packages available.

Conveniently located just outside the capital, **La Batelière Hotel-Casino,** Schoelcher, 97200 Fort-de-France, Martinique, F.W.I. (tel. 596/71-90-41; U.S. reservations: tel. toll-free 800/223-9862), sprawls over 18 acres of flowering grounds. Wicker furniture with bright floral cushions decorates the spacious lobby. A long, canopied bar overlooks the round pool and one of the three restaurants faces the small beach. In addition to Windsurfing, waterskiing, and other water sports, the hotel has scuba facilities with licensed instructors. The glass-bottom *Aquarium* takes groups on snorkeling excursions. Playing on the six tennis courts is free during the day; there is a small charge at night. In each of the 218 comfortable guest rooms, a wall of sliding glass doors leads to a seaview or gardenview terrace. At night, guests flock to Club 21, the hotel's popular disco, and the casino, which sports three American-style roulette tables and five blackjack tables. Honeymoon package: Eight days/seven nights (EP): $800 to $1,390 per couple. Includes a bottle of champagne, a half-day glass-bottom boat cruise, admission to Club 21 disco, and discounts on sightseeing, shopping, and car rental.

Bakoua Beach Hotel, 97229 Pointe du Bout, Martinique, F.W.I. (tel. 596/66-02-02; U.S. reservations: tel. 212/696-1323). The name of this hotel comes from the pointed, broad-brimmed straw hats worn by fishermen. Swaying palms, frangipani, and other bright flowers surround the hillside and oceanfront buildings. Some of the 100 rooms have balconies that face the water while the patios of others are right on the beach. Many members of the friendly, accommodating staff have worked here for years, and the resort is a favorite of visiting celebrities (Jean-Paul Belmondo and Paul McCartney stayed here). Bakoua Beach offers a variety of water sports, tennis courts, and a pool perched high above the ocean. During the afternoons and evenings, the circular bar is a popular hangout. In the adjoining Châteaubriand, the large, open-air beachfront dining room, a thatched roof covers the dance area. Dinner is accompanied by live music. The chef blends the best of French cooking with creole specialties. Once a week, an elaborate buffet is followed by a performance of Les Grands Ballets de la Martinique, which shows off the island's African roots. Honeymoon package: Eight days/seven nights (BP): $825 to $955 per couple. Includes a bottle of champagne, a fruit basket, round-trip ferry tickets to Fort-de-France, and the buffet dinner/folkloric dance performance.

PLM Azur Carayou, Pointe du Bout, 97229 Trois Ilets, Martinique, F.W.I. (tel. 596/66-04-04; U.S. reservations: tel. toll free 800/223-9862). Formerly the Frantel Martinique, this 200-room hotel sits at the edge of the bay facing Fort-de-France. The grounds, which resemble a botanical garden, are interlaced with footpaths. Balconied rooms in bungalows look out to the bay, the marina, or the flower-filled gardens. Guests can swim or sunbathe at the beach or float in the circular swimming pool and gaze at the bay. Sports include sailing and tennis. If you want TV and closed-circuit video, book a deluxe room. Boutiques on the premises make shopping convenient and Le Vesou discotheque is one of the island's hottest spots. Honeymoon package: Eight days/seven nights (BP): from $980 per couple. Includes a bottle of local rum, a fruit basket, and one candlelit champagne dinner.

Méridien-Trois Ilets, 97229 Pointe du Bout, Martinique, F.W.I. (tel. 596/66-00-00; U.S. reservations: tel. 212/265-4494; or toll free 800/223-9918). If you like being near other hotels and you don't want to go far to gamble, the Méridien, with a casino on the premises, is a good place to stay. Not only are there many other hotels within walking distance, but the Méridien is right near the dock for the ferry to Fort-de-France, just across the bay. The breezy lobby is open to the palm-shaded pool. At the small beach, Windsurfers and other water sports equipment are free to guests. Take the full-day picnic sail on the *Old Nick* with Captain Cap at the helm, or board the glass-bottom *Aquarius* for a snorkeling trip. Room service is available 24 hours a day in the 303 guest rooms, some of which have king-size beds. The Anthurium restaurant is known for its delicious gourmet food and Von Von disco is the place to shake a leg or two. Honeymoon package: None. Rate (EP): $93 to $210 per couple per night.

Le Calalou Hotel, 97229 Anse-à-l'Ane, Martinique, F.W.I. (tel. 596/76-31-67; U.S. reservations: tel. 212/840-6636; or toll free 800/223-9815). On a beautiful beach a short drive from other hotels, Le Calalou attracts many guests from France and Canada. Visitors enter the open-air reception area after walking along a palm-lined path, under an awning, and through a wrought-iron gate. Her limbs elongated, the abstract statue of a woman holding a broken chain above her head stands in tribute to the abolition of slavery. Upholstered rattan decorates the beachfront bar/sitting area, while white garden furniture fills the breezy dining room. Tall palms and flowering bushes grow in abundance on the property. The 36 air-conditioned rooms in bungalows, some of which are right on the water, are cheerfully done in wicker and bright colors. Some rooms have double beds and terra-cotta tile patios. There is a barbecue every Friday night in season. Fort-de-France is a ferry ride away. Calalou is closed in October. Honeymoon package: None. Rates (MAP): $133 to $155 per couple per night.

Diamant-Novotel, Pointe de la Chéry, 97223 Diamant, Martinique, F.W.I. (tel. 596/76-42-42; U.S. reservations: tel. 212/354-3722; or toll free 800/221-4542). This self-contained resort buzzes with activity. Staying here, you may not feel the urge to wander far. To get to the round dining room from the open lobby, you'll walk over a bridge stretching across the large pool. The 180 individual rooms and suites are spacious, some with balconies and dramatic views of Diamond Rock. Scuba facilities and licensed instructors are available at the hotel's beach, and other beaches are nearby. For many, evenings bring visits to the nightclub. When you make reservations, simply let the hotel know you're honeymooners and you'll receive V.I.P. treatment. Your room will be upgraded to a seaview accommodation and, along with a fruit basket, you'll find a bottle of chilled champagne in your room upon arrival. Honeymoon package: None. Rates (Full AP): $88 to $187 per couple per night.

The first in the area, the **Auberge de l'Anse Mitan,** 97229 Anse Mitan, Martinique, F.W.I. (tel. 596/66-01-12; U.S. reservations: tel. 212/840-6636; or toll free 800/223-9815), has long been popular with vacationing Martiniquais. The small white building sits at the edge of the bay and guests dine on the shaded veranda facing the water. The cozy dark-paneled lobby is shared with the bar and sitting room, whose walls are hung with maps. Tiled floors give this inn a European flavor. All of the 20 guest rooms are air-conditioned. Five are huge, and some have two double beds. Old photos and drawings decorate the walls, making the rooms truly home-like. Honeymoon package: None. Rates (CP): $54 to $60 per couple per night.

Manoir de Beauregard, 97227 Sainte Anne, Martinique, F.W.I. (tel. 596/76-73-40; U.S. reservations: tel. 212/832-2277; or toll free 800/223-6510). An ornate wrought-iron gate thrown wide invites you into this 18th-century manor house. The stark white building with thick stone walls is set off by a weathered orange-tile roof. Wicker rockers, a wicker couch, a heavy dark wood desk, and gray-and-white-checkered tiles made of marble decorate the reception area. The 27 air-conditioned rooms are furnished with high four-posted beds, tall armoires, and other antiques. All rooms have modern baths. Manoir de Beauregard has a swimming pool and the hotel is a short drive from Les Salines, considered by many to be the island's best beaches. It is also within walking distance of the town of Sainte Anne. Honeymoon package: None. Rates (CP): $50 to $88 per couple per night.

St. Aubin Hotel, B.P. 52, 97220 Trinité, Martinique, F.W.I. (tel. 596/69-34-77; U.S. reservations: tel. 212/840-6636; or toll free 800/223-9815). Perched on a hill overlooking the Atlantic, a carpet of sugarcane fields, and colorful gardens, St. Aubin was once a private home. It was built around the turn of the century and has been painstakingly restored by Guy Foret, a former restaurant owner originally from Normandy. This small hotel is an excellent place to perfect the art of enjoying undisturbed peace and quiet. Wide, airy verandas, with gingerbread fretwork railings, surround both the ground floor and the second story. Just inside the salmon-colored building, high archways lead to a tiled sitting area furnished in blond wicker. Across the entranceway, the sunny dining room opens onto the front veranda. The hotel's 15 rooms, with double beds or twins, all have private baths. Take a dip in the pool or head for the beach in Trinité, a five-minute drive away. Honeymoon package: None. Rates (CP): $66 to $72 per couple per night.

4. Romantic Restaurants and Night Spots

For visitors and Martiniquais alike, eating out is a cherished activity. Whether you have a taste for elegant French cuisine, highly seasoned creole dishes, or a marriage of the two, you'll find a surprisingly wide selection of excellent restaurants. Most are in the Fort-de-France/Pointe du Bout/Anse Mitan area, connected by ferries. If you stay in another part of the island, dining out and evening entertainment will center around your hotel.

You'll need reservations for dinner at the most popular restaurants—and it's difficult to find a restaurant in Martinique that isn't popular. Escargots and soufflés will tempt you on some menus. On others you'll find Creole specialties such as accras (bite-size cod or shrimp fritters), blaff (fish stew spiced with garlic, lime, and bay rum berries), crabes farcis (stuffed crabs), and langouste (clawless native lobster). Landlubbers can begin with blood sausage or paté en pot (a thick mutton soup), then try tender beef or chicken dishes. Meals are accompanied by French wine and potent rum punch made with fruits such as coconut, guava, and pineapple.

La Grand' Voile, Pointe Simon, Fort-de-France (tel. 70-29-29). The high point of many a vacation in Martinique is a meal at this restaurant overlooking the bay. Near the Yacht Club, it is decorated with nautical touches, such as buoys suspended from the ceiling by the bar. Owners Muriel Palandri and Dominique Laval have imported the very best of the cuisine from their native Toulouse, known for its gourmet food. If you would like a sweeping view of the water to accompany your meal, try to be seated near the window. French and creole selections include scallops Grand Voile, stuffed crab, and mouth-watering beef dishes. About $60 and up per couple for dinner. Closed Sundays.

Typic Bellevue, Blvd. de la Marne, Fort-de-France (tel. 71-68-87). Try "créole pastry flambé," curried chicken, frogs' legs, or turtle steak by candlelight on a breezy terrace. Just outside the center of Fort-de-France, this restaurant is reminiscent of a roadside inn. Dinner will be about $30 to $40 for two. Closed Saturday afternoons and Sundays.

La Biguine, route de la Folie, Fort-de-Folie, Fort-de-France (tel. 71-40-07), a small duplex restaurant, is in an old home in the capital. Downstairs, the informal grill serves light meals such as beef and chicken brochette. Upstairs, the more upscale menu offers delights like escargots, crayfish in a creamy red sauce, lobster salad, and duck laced with pineapple sauce. For dessert, try fresh fruit sherbet. Presided over by Gérard Padra, formerly of the Bakoua Beach Hotel, La Biguine continues to grow in popularity. Reservations are a must. Dinner upstairs will be about $40 and up per person, including drinks and tip. Closed Sundays.

La Belle Époque, Didier (tel. 70-36-22). A handsome old home is the setting for this pleasant restaurant in a suburb of Fort-de-France. The emphasis is on French cuisine, with a smattering of creole thrown in. Entrées range from veal kidneys in mustard sauce to shrimp with passionfruit juice. Expect to pay about $60 for a complete dinner for two. Closed on Sundays and Mondays.

L'Amphore-Anse Mitan (tel. 66-03-09). A short walk from the Bakoua Beach Hotel, this restaurant faces the water. At night, the music of crickets accompanies the mellow tunes of a guitarist who welcomes requests from diners. High-backed wooden chairs surround the small tables, and brick archways separate sitting areas. Choose your lobster fresh from the tank, or try tenderloin with green-pepper sauce, duck l'orange, or coquilles St-Jacques. Appetizers include creole blood sausage, accras (cod fritters), and sea urchins. But whatever you do, be sure to save room for dessert: passionfruit and lemon mousse, bananas cooked in a cream sauce, sinfully rich chocolate cake with vanilla ice cream and hot fudge—you may have to dine here more than once. A complete dinner, including drinks and dessert, will be about $40 per couple. Closed Mondays.

If popularity with residents is a measure of a restaurant's worth, then **Le Matador,** in Anse Mitan (tel. 66-05-36), is undoubtedly a winner. Surrounded by bright vegetation, this creole dining spot is owned by a former hotel chef. Home-style specialties include crabes farcis (stuffed crabs), red snapper, and for the adventurous, octopus and curried mutton. Dinner should be about $30 or $40 for two. Closed Tuesdays. The view from the waterfront veranda, of purple bougainvillea, masted boats, and the misty mountains of Fort-de-France is almost as good as the food at **Auberge de l'Anse Mitan,** in Anse Mitan (tel. 66-01-12). Spicy creole fish and crab are specialties. Dinner for two: about $30. Two other Anse Mitan Creole restaurants are well worth visits: **La Bonne Auberge** (tel. 66-01-55) has bright madras fabric draped artfully across white tablecloths. About $40 per couple for dinner. Closed Wednesdays. And **La Villa Créole** (tel. 66-05-53) is run by a brother and sister: She cooks and he strums the guitar. About $40 and up per couple for dinner. Closed on Sundays. When in the Les Salines area, take a break from the beautiful beaches with lunch at **Manoir de Beauregard,** in Sainte Anne (tel. 76-73-40). A large fishing boat sits in the dining room, which serves puffed accras de crevette (shrimp fritters), avocado stuffed with crab, veal cutlets, broiled sirloin, and herbed lamb. Dinner for two should be about $40 and up. The stone building that now houses the restaurant at **Leyritz Plantation,** in Basse-Pointe (tel. 73-53-08 or 75-53-92), were once a chapel and storage room. Lunchtime tour groups make this restaurant busy at midday, but the food is worth a stop. The savory seafood, beef, and chicken dishes are accompanied by local vegetables such as taro root, bread fruit, and red beans. A complete lunch for two will be about $35.

Martinique has many night spots where you can let your hip bones slip. They are located in and outside of hotels, and you'll hear American and European popular music, as well as beguine (the local sound), reggae, and salsa: **Number One** (in Trinité, near the St. Aubin Hotel); **Club 21** (at the Batelière Hotel, Schoelcher); **Von Von** (in the Hotel Méridien, Pointe du Bout); **Vesou** (at the PLM Azur Carayou, Pointe du Bout); and **L'oeil** (in Ducos), one of the newest additions. Most are closed Sunday and/or Monday nights. Try to catch the spirited **Les Grands Ballets de la Martinique,** a dance troupe that rotates among various hotels after dark.

Chapter XXXIII

PUERTO RICO

1. Practical Facts
2. Romantic Interludes
3. Honeymoon Hotels and Hideaways
4. Romantic Restaurants
5. Nightlife

HOW DO YOU LIKE your romance? With a "salsa" beat and the seductive tug of a blackjack table? How about a deserted beach and the whisper of trade winds in the palms? Or perhaps accompanied by a coffee or a cognac in a moonlit 17th-century Spanish courtyard?

Nestled between the Dominican Republic and the U.S. Virgin Islands, a combination of history, size, and location has blessed Puerto Rico with variety—variety of everything—that is rarely found on a Caribbean island. Add to that its accessibility from the U.S. mainland—less than 3½ hours from New York—and you may find that Puerto Rico offers just the honeymoon you are looking for.

One thousand miles southeast of Florida on the northern rim of the Caribbean island chain, Puerto Rico is 100 miles long and 35 miles wide, with the Atlantic Ocean to the north and the Caribbean Sea on the south. But there really are two Puerto Ricos: San Juan, the island's lively capital, center of its tourism industry, and home to most of the hotels and resorts, and "out on the island," a local term referring to everything else. But within the two there is remarkable, even startling, variety. Old San Juan, for example, beautifully restored and dating back to the 16th century, lies gracefully only minutes away from the most dazzling, throbbing resorts and casinos in the Caribbean. Lovely coffee plantations-turned-paradors perch on dark, rich hillsides of the Central Cordillera, in contrast to the open, cactus-covered hills of the southwest rolling onto the miles of deserted beaches of Cabo Rojo. The choice is yours—which Puerto Rico appeals the most?

Puerto Rico's history, rather unique in the Caribbean, has contributed enormously to its present character. The island was discovered by Christopher Columbus in 1493. Unlike many other Caribbean islands, whose nationalities changed every time the powers of Europe fought a war, Puerto Rico was held by the Spanish for nearly 400 years. The Spaniards conquered the local Taino Indians as early as 1508, and Juan Ponce de Leon (who would later go on to seek the Fountain of Youth) became its first governor. Despite several attempts by Britain and Holland to change the course of history, the island remained Spanish until 1898 when the Spanish-American War gave Puerto Rico to the United States. Today, Puerto Rico is a U.S. Commonwealth, and its people are U.S. citizens.

This uninterrupted history of Spanish influence has left a lasting impact on Puerto Rico. It certainly is the most European of the Caribbean islands; in fact, much of it, particularly Old San Juan and some of the smaller historic towns such as Ponce and San German, are strongly reminiscent of Spain. And it is not just in the landmarks that reflect the island's heritage. While influenced, of course, by Caribbean tastes and customs and later by American lifestyles, Puerto Rico's cultural life, its religious life, even the local cuisine, today remain strongly Spanish in character. Virtually no day in Puerto Rico goes by, for instance, without the celebration in some small town of its patron saint. In the luxuriant traditions of Europe, Christmas on the island is celebrated for weeks, rather than just one public holiday.

This is not to say that Puerto Rico has ignored its other influences. Its Indian ancestry is recognized in the preservation of several ceremonial and religious centers out on the island, including the Gaguana Indian Ceremonial Park, located on the central mountains near Utudo, and the Tibes Indian Ceremonial Center, on the south coast, just outside Ponce. The island's African heritage is particularly vibrant in the town of Loiza, dating back to the 16th century and still populated with residents descended from African slaves who were brought over to work in the sugar plantations. Using coconut *vejigante* masks, dances, and feasts, the town honors that heritage in a festival held once a year.

Puerto Rico's American heritage has produced the modern lifestyle of the island. Fast-food chains, for example, abound in new San Juan and the larger cities out on the island. English is spoken across the island. And American political ties—although Puerto Rico is internally self-governing—have resulted in many practical benefits. Roads are good, telephone communications plentiful, U.S. investments have contributed to the island's economy. But don't come here looking for Miami Beach; despite its American affiliation, which makes travel here virtually hassle-free, Puerto Rico is delightfully and decidedly foreign.

Puerto Rico's size and location also combine to create a variety of natural environments and attractions. Its Atlantic beaches have been described as the "Hawaii of the Caribbean," because of their excellent surf. The Caribbean National Forest—also known as El Yunque—is one of only two tropical rain forests in the United States. Portions of the tiny islands of Vieques and Culebra off Puerto Rico's east coast are preserved as wildlife sanctuaries. The Caribbean coastline is noted for its expansive and uncrowded beaches. In the northwest a recently opened Camuy Caves Park offers a glimpse of one of the world's largest and most beautiful underground cave systems.

Puerto Rico's variety is not limited to natural wonders and the contrasts of old and new. The range of activities, for example, is extensive. From casinos to history, art galleries to baseball, rum tasting to sunbathing there is a remarkable choice of things to do. Water sports include sailing, snorkeling, scuba, deep-sea fishing (some 40 world record catches were made offshore here), and the traditional resort activities such as Windsurfing. Other sports include golf at some of the Caribbean's best-known courses, tennis on more than 100 courts, many of which are lighted for night play, horseback riding, hiking, and cycling. Spectator sports include Puerto Rico's famous winter baseball league action (where many of the mainland's stars spend their offseason), horse racing, the San Blas Marathon, sailing regattas, and fishing tournaments.

A trip to Puerto Rico has only two absolutes: the weather, regardless of the month, is honeymoon weather, and the hospitality is warm and genuine. After that, you're on your own. Don't come looking for ski lodges but just about anything else is possible. In Puerto Rico you can plan the honeymoon.

1. Practical Facts

GETTING THERE: Because Puerto Rico is a U.S. Commonwealth, no passports or visas are required for U.S. citizens. However, it is always wise to travel with a valid form of personal identification. U.S. Customs regulations also apply to Puerto Rico

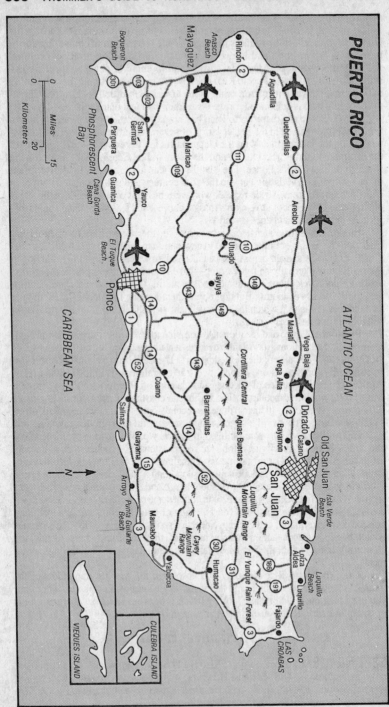

and there are no duties on items purchased there and brought to the mainland. There is, however, inspection by the U.S. Department of Agriculture.

Nonstop and direct air service to Puerto Rico is available from a number of U.S. cities, including New York, Boston, Newark, Miami, Dallas/Ft. Worth, Chicago, Baltimore, and Philadelphia. **American Airlines** and **Eastern Airlines** have recently made San Juan their hub for all Caribbean operations and other carriers that fly there include **TWA, Delta,** and **American Trans Air.** Most flights are to San Juan, the island's capital, but there is also service available to Aguadilla on the northwest coast.

Puerto Rico is also a major port of embarkation for a dozen international cruise lines and other ships call there on a regular basis throughout the year. Ask your travel agent for details.

GETTING AROUND: Public transportation in Puerto Rico is plentiful and varied, and rental car companies are well represented, particularly in San Juan.

Taxis

All taxis authorized by the Public Service Commission use meters except for long-distance chartered trips. While more expensive than other means of public transportation, taxis are the most efficient way of getting around San Juan. Rates are roughly equivalent to those in major U.S. cities and there is a nominal extra charge for suitcases, home calls, and for waiting. Cab companies are listed in the telephone directory and taxi stands are plentiful at hotels and locations in the city. Taxis can also be hailed from the street. The approximate cost of a taxi from San Juan's international airport to the Condado area is $5 to $10, depending on your hotel.

Rental Cars

Most of the major car-rental companies are represented in Puerto Rico, including: **Avis** (toll free 800/331-1212), **Budget** (toll free 800/527-0700), **Hertz** (toll free 800/654-3131), **National** (toll free 800/227-7368), and **Thrifty** (toll free 800/367-2277), all of which can be booked in advance from the U.S. mainland with rates comparable to U.S. cities.

Carros Públicos

Automobiles with license plates ending in P or PD are public cars and operate as inexpensive taxis, often between towns on the island. They do not use meters, but the Public Service Commission requires that they be insured and fixes routes as well as reasonable rates.

Buses

The San Juan metropolitan area is amply, though often erratically, served by a bus system that is inexpensive (25¢) and an excellent way to get a feel for the city. The most popular route for visitors runs from Rio Piedras to San Juan (use no. 1 or 2) and includes the hotel section of Condado, the university, and many of the historical attractions, including the Old City.

LANGUAGE AND MONEY: The language of Puerto Rico is Spanish. However, only in the smallest of towns is there any difficulty communicating in English, and even then goodwill usually makes all things known. Currency is the good old U.S. dollar and major credit cards are accepted almost everywhere in San Juan and in most of the areas out on the island that are visited by tourists.

Service charges are generally not automatically added to hotel or restaurant bills and 15% is standard tipping policy.

WEATHER: Decidedly tropical, the climate of Puerto Rico is favored by trade winds that make for pleasant weather year around with average temperatures in the high 70s and low 80s. The central mountain region is cooler and more humid, while the southwest part of the island is quite dry, much like the American southwest. Evening temperatures drop about 10° to 15°. Temperatures during the winter months may reach into the low 70s.

CLOTHING: What you wear largely depends on where you stay. The large resorts in San Juan can be quite formal in the evenings—jackets and ties for the men, dresses and skirts for women—and short shorts are discouraged except for beach and recreational use. Out on the island, dress is quite casual. Throughout the year, light, summer clothing will suffice, but you might want to bring light coverups for restaurants and casinos, which are *very* well air-conditioned.

TIME: Puerto Rico operates all year on Atlantic Standard Time, which is one hour ahead of Eastern Standard Time. When it is noon in New York, it is 1 p.m. in Puerto Rico. When Daylight Savings Time is in effect, the times are the same.

TELEPHONE: The area code for Puerto Rico is 809, and you can dial direct from the United States. There are public pay telephones in San Juan and most of the towns and cities of the island.

SHOPPING: While Puerto Rico is not a duty-free port and therefore superdiscounts are rare, imported goods, including jewelry, clothing, perfumes, porcelain, and china are available in shops and boutiques in Old San Juan and in most of the larger resorts. Old San Juan, in particular, is a pleasant shopping area, with stores often staying open late in the evening. Among the locally produced items of note are the *santos,* small wooden religious carvings; handmade lace called *mundillo;* and *quatros,* a guitar-like instrument that comes in several sizes. Puerto Rico also is the world's leading rum producer. Cigars are also a favorite gift to take home.

Special shops include: **Jewels of the World,** 150 Fortaleza in Old San Juan, for jewelry, particularly gold; **The Butterfly People,** 152 Fortaleza, for unique glass-enclosed tropical butterflies and other gifts; **La Plazoleta,** at pier 3 in Old San Juan, for crafts; the **Hathaway Factory Outlet,** 203 Cristo St., for shirts at sizable discounts; and the **Dexter Shoe Factory Outlet,** 1126 Ashford Ave., for discounted shoes made here and in Maine.

HOW TO GET MARRIED IN PUERTO RICO: Puerto Rico requires a blood test and a marriage license, both obtained in San Juan. You can get the blood test through a private physician (your hotel can recommend one) and the marriage license from city hall, Plaza de Armas. Allow two or three days for each. While most of the island's citizens are Catholic there are also Protestant and Jewish places of worship where marriages can be performed.

FOR FURTHER INFORMATION: Contact: **Puerto Rico Tourism Company,** 1290 Avenue of the Americas, New York, NY 10104, (tel. 212/541-6630) or toll free 800/223-6530.

2. Romantic Interludes

In addition to such activities as golf, tennis, water sports, gambling, and fine dining, Puerto Rico offers some special opportunities to make a honeymoon all the more memorable.

The tiny **Old City of San Juan** (barely ten square blocks on the western tip of the metropolitan area) has been called "an architectural masterpiece in the Caribbean." Quite simply, there is nothing like it. Other islands have their museums and restored fortresses and buildings, Puerto Rico has an entire living, breathing city that is a step back several centuries in time. It has museums but it is not a museum itself; on the contrary, much of Puerto Rico's most exciting life takes place here, but in an atmosphere that is far more European than tropical.

Wander the narrow streets that are paved with stones originally used as ballast by the Spanish fleets. Climb the hill to **San Juan Cathedral** (no phone) in the center of the old city, first built in 1540 but continually restored, and containing the body of Ponce de Leon. Further on, at the tip of the old city, is **El Morro Castle** (tel. 724-1974), which has protected the city's busy harbor for 400 years. This enormous, six-level fortress is open daily from 8 a.m. until 6:25 p.m., and guided tours are available. Follow the massive city walls along the cliffs overlooking the sea and stop in at the **Cristo Chapel,** built to commemorate a miracle. Hundreds of years ago, horse races were conducted through the narrow streets of Old San Juan. When a young jockey and his mount plunged over the city wall, a spectator vowed to build a chapel on the spot if his life was spared. According to the legend, he was, and the graceful chapel overlooks the harbor, usually filled with cruise ships.

Visit **La Fortaleza,** the oldest governor's mansion still in use in America. Built in 1540 and remodeled in 1848, the building is open Monday through Friday, 9 a.m. to 4 p.m. (tel. 721-7000). Or stop in at the many museums, including **Casa del Libro** (tel. 723-0354), with one of the Caribbean's finest collections of rare books, the **San Juan Museum of Art and History** (tel. 724-1875), or the **Casals Museum** (tel, 723-9185), commemorating Pablo Casals, the noted cellist and conductor. Or shop at the many stores and boutiques. Night or day, Old San Juan is a perfect interlude. But do it on foot; much of the old city is closed to all but pedestrian traffic.

Be big spenders and take the nighttime **ferry** from Old San Juan across the bay to Catano. In the evening there is no reason to get off in Catano, and each way will cost only a dime. There is no other view of San Juan's lights, castles, and churches by night quite like it.

Puerto Rico produces 14 different kinds of rum. Just across the bay from San Juan is the **Baccardi factory.** You can reach the free samples by public transportation, ferry, or by car. The plant can put out 100,000 gallons a day, so don't worry about it running out. Forty-five minute free tours are offered Monday through Saturday between 9:30 a.m. and 3:30 p.m. (tel. 795-1560).

You might consider giving the casinos a rest and visit the nearby **U.S. Virgin Islands.** By hydrofoil (tel. 721-5177) it's only two hours and $65 per person to St. Thomas, and St. John and St. Croix are no more than a stone's throw farther. If you prefer to fly, a number of local as well as international carriers can get you there and back in time for dinner.

Cabo Rojo and **Phosphorescent Bay** on Puerto Rico's southwest corner are some of the island's most romantic settings. Don't try them on a day trip from San Juan, but if you're out on the island for a few days, it is a must. Towering cliffs plunge into the sea from the edge of open country that resembles the American southwest. Miles and miles of unnamed beaches make you wonder how something so perfect can have so few visitors. In the tiny village of Parguera, is Phosphorscent Bay which, on moonless nights, sparkles with an intensity most casino and disco operators can only wish for, as millions of microscopic animals light up the water. There are several paradors nearby for comfortable accommodations, including Villa Paraguera, on the bay itself.

You might consider a change of pace from the glamour and bustle of San Juan's 20th-century lifestyle and remove yourselves to a **country inn** where time seems to stand still. There's one with therapeutic baths, another on a tiny island, and several only seconds from the beach. See details under "Honeymoon Hotels and Hideaways."

These are two islands off Puerto Rico's east coast, reachable by air from San Juan or by ferry from Fajardo. **Vieques** in the last few years has developed a reputation as an "in place" for romantic escapes, with a picturesque Parador Esperanza and lazy, secluded beaches. **Culebra** is, for the most part, a wildlife preserve and particularly interesting for day trips. Both provide a wonderful contrast to the sophistication of San Juan.

3. Honeymoon Hotels and Hideaways

The best honeymoon hotels in Puerto Rico come in two varieties: large, glamorous resorts with extensive facilities, private beaches, nightlife, and entertainment; and small, secluded country inns. With few exceptions, the hotels of San Juan are in the former category: high-rise structures along the beaches of Condado or Isla Verde where the accent is on glittering activity often 24 hours a day. Enormous casinos, swimming pools and beaches, tennis and nearby golf facilities, a choice of several restaurants, supper clubs and lounges are all standard features of these hotels, which differ only in style and decor. Rooms are fully air-conditioned and equipped with all the conveniences of home, including color TVs and VCRs at many of them. Such amenities as room service and special honeymoon packages are also standard. An additional benefit to a honeymoon hotel in San Juan is proximity to other resorts: Most of the larger hotels are within walking distance of several others so that restaurants and entertainment need not be limited to only your resort.

Out on the island the large resorts, too, have a wealth of facilities and services to offer the honeymooner, often including sailing marinas, deep-sea fishing, snorkeling and scuba diving, horseback riding, tennis and golf. In contrast, the handful of gracious paradors scattered throughout Puerto Rico provide an escape from everything. Modest in accommodations as well as price but lacking nothing by way of appeal or service and local hospitality, these country inns are for the couple who needs only each other, a good meal or two and beautiful scenery to start off married life.

SAN JUAN: There are a number of perfect honeymoon hotels in San Juan and Old San Juan for you to choose from.

Expensive

Condado Plaza Hotel & Casino, 999 Ashford Ave., Puerto Rico 00902 (tel. 809/721-1000; reservations: toll free 800/468-8588). With an airy, tropical feel to it (accomplished by the use of pale wood paneling and wicker furniture), the glamorous Condado Plaza is one of the hotels on Puerto Rico's Condado strip that fronts both the Atlantic Ocean and the Condado Lagoon. Continental, Italian, and French restaurants provide a cosmopolitan flair and, for lighter snacks, there is a poolside cafe. Six lounges keep the entertainment going around the clock, sports facilities are abundant, including two lighted tennis courts and a water-sports concession. There is also a casino.

Honeymoon package: Eight days/seven nights (EP): from $1,053.80 per couple for a standard room; to $1,185.80 per couple for an oceanview room. Includes accommodations with a king-size bed and balcony, welcoming cocktails, T-shirts, admission to disco, San Juan Bay cruise, discount coupons. The Condado Plaza also offers a unique seven-night package that includes a stay in the tiny Esperanza Beach Club on the island of Vieques. Ideal for honeymooners, the package ranges from $1,206 to $2,214 per couple.

Caribe Hilton International, P.O. Box 1872, San Juan, Puerto Rico 00903 (tel. 809/721-0303; reservations: toll free 800/223-1146), is the granddaddy of the Condado resorts, in some ways the one that sets the standards. Muted pastel colors, tropical plants, and open spaces (about 17 gardened acres) give the hotel a soothing quality, and its location, perched on the beach across from the historic Fort Jeronimo, is breathtaking. Juliana's, the hotel's disco and supper club, is considered "the" place to be seen in San Juan. Honeymoon packages (EP) of three or seven nights range in price from $538 to $1,254 per couple.

The **El San Juan Hotel & Casino**, P.O. Box 2872, Isla Verde, San Juan, Puerto Rico 00902 (tel. 809/791-1000; reservations: toll free 800/468-2818), has become, if anything, even more glamorous since its recent $40-million renovation. Spectacular chandeliers, brass, and polished wood help create an atmosphere of European sophistication in the tropics. The hotel features Puerto Rico's only wine bar and a Palm Court provides an air of almost sinful luxury. Some of the suites have their own private Roman baths and private balconies add a touch of intimacy. Five restaurants, three clubs, and a selection of lounges offer the opportunity to make variety the theme of the honeymoon. Honeymoon package: Eight days/seven nights (EP): From $1,500 per couple. Includes airport transfers; accommodations with color cable TV, VCR, and mini-bar; breakfast in bed one morning; one dinner for two at La Veranda restaurant; flowers and fruit basket upon arrival; city tour of Old San Juan.

Moderate

Condado Beach Hotel, Ashford Avenue, Condado, Puerto Rico 00905 (tel. 809/721-6090; reservations: toll free 800/223-9869). Does the Roaring '20s appeal to you? The Condado Beach was built by no less than the Vanderbilts in 1919 and, handsomely restored, still maintains that devil-may-care atmosphere. It is also smack dab in the heart of Condado's late-night casino action. Entertainment and decor focuses on the 1920s. Honeymoon package: Eight days/seven nights: $816 per couple. Includes oceanfront room if available, full American breakfast daily, two welcoming drinks, a bottle of champagne, T-shirts, a souvenir photograph, one dinner at the hotel restaurant, and various coupons and discounts.

Gran Hotel El Convento, 100 Cristo St., San Juan, Puerto Rico 00902 (tel. 809/723-9020; reservations: toll free 800/468-2779), is a hotel like no other in Puerto Rico. Set in what was a 17th-century convent across a cobblestone street from the San Juan Cathedral in the Old City, El Convento is a complete change from all other San Juan hotels. Built around a courtyard that contains a gracious, al fresco restaurant, this is the place for friendly, European elegance, comfortable rooms, and a location unrivaled by other hotels. Within walking distance of all the historic attractions of the old cities, the museums, restaurants, and bars that make Old San Juan unique in the Caribbean, a stay at the El Convento is more like being in Spain than being in the tropics. Honeymoon package: None. Rates (EP) are $88 to $121 per couple per night.

OUT ON THE ISLAND: Dorado is 25 miles west (a 40-minute drive) of San Juan. Here Hyatt Hotels has recently spent some $50 million to renovate and improve two self-contained resorts. A mile apart and connected by a free shuttle bus system, the hotels' guests can make use of both properties' extensive facilities and amenities, including restaurants.

Hyatt Dorado Beach Hotel, Dorado, Puerto Rico 00646 (tel. 809/796-1600; reservations: toll free 800/228-9000), the smaller and slightly more exclusive of the two, sits in tropical splendor on the ocean's edge, seemingly centuries away from the pace of life back home. The focus here is on the resort's natural beauty, which is unmatched on the island. Two Robert Trent Jones–designed golf courses and seven all-weather tennis courts have made Dorado a favorite among athletically inclined honeymooners. Dorado, along with its sister resort, are favorite vacation retreats for the celebrities of Hollywood and New York. Honeymoon packages: Eight days/seven nights (MAP): from $1,806 to $2,294 for a standard room. Includes airport transfers, air-conditioned room with private balcony, welcoming drink, champagne and fresh flowers upon arrival, one hour of tennis or greens fees for one round of golf daily, admission one night each to El Coqui Disco and Casa de Oro nightclub, use of bicycles, all applicable taxes and gratuities. Honeymoon package not available mid-December through mid-April.

Hyatt Cerromar Beach Hotel, Dorado, Puerto Rico 00646 (tel. 809/796-1010; reservations: toll free 800/228-9000), may be the splashiest resort in the Caribbean, with the recent installation of the world's longest swimming pool (1,776 feet), which winds through the hotel's splendid grounds. Almost twice the size as Dorado (506 rooms), Cerromar also provides the best in sporting facilities in a breathtaking natural surrounding. Two golf courses, 14 tennis courts, a private casino, a supper club, as well as a disco, plus a health club ensure that honeymooners may become exhausted but never bored. Honeymoon package: Eight days/seven nights (MAP): $1,106 to $1,564 for a deluxe room, depending on when you go. Includes airport transfers, air-conditioned room with an oceanview, welcoming drinks, bottle of champagne and fruit basket upon arrival, breakfast in bed your first morning, one hour of tennis daily or greens fees for one round of golf, admission one night to El Coqui disco and Casa de Oro nightclub, all applicable taxes and gratuities. Package not available mid-December through mid-April.

Palmas del Mar, P.O. Box 2020, Humacao, Puerto Rico 00661 (tel. 809/852-6000; reservations: toll free 800/221-4874). "At Palmas a high rise is a seaside cliff, not a condominium tower. And no building can be taller than the tallest tree," is the way the architect of this lovely 2,700-acre resort puts it, and quite accurately. There may be no resort in the Caribbean that is more beautifully suited to its natural environment. And that's what people come here for—to enjoy Puerto Rico's beauty and its bountiful sports activities. In addition to one of the island's most comprehensive sailing and fishing marinas, Palmas has a golf course, tennis courts, riding stables, a casino, five freshwater pools, a fitness center, and three miles of perfect beaches. Honeymoon package: Four days/three nights (EP): from $402 per couple at the resort's Candelero Hotel to $498 per couple for a one-bedroom villa, complete with living room, dining area, and fully equipped kitchen. Includes free golf, tennis, a sunset trail ride on horseback, and use of bicycles.

Paradores puertorriquenos, Puerto Rico Tourism Company, 1290 Avenue of the Americas, New York, NY 10104 (tel. 212/541-6630 or toll free 800/223-6530; reservations: tel. toll free 800/443-0266). Modeled after Spain's successful system, the paradors of Puerto Rico are a collection of government-sanctioned and monitored country inns. Each must be situated in a historic building or a site of exceptional beauty and all are noted for their fine kitchens. These are not luxury resorts; service is simple and gracious, there are no large-scale facilities, although a number do have tennis courts, swimming pools and access to some of the island's most spectacular beaches. What they afford the honeymoon couple is an unforgettable opportunity to see the island of Puerto Rico, meet its people, sample its cooking—all in great comfort, with the assurance of being well cared for. Rates vary from roughly $30 to $70 per night per couple, with meals as little as $15 for two.

The great charm of the paradors is their contrast to the bustle and glamour of San Juan and their individual characters. Some are perched on cliffs overlooking the ocean, others are in small fishing villages. The paradors are generally quite small and have become extremely popular with American as well as European visitors, so book well in advance. Contact the Puerto Rico Tourism Company for a complete list and description of these hotels. Meanwhile, here are some of our favorites:

Parador Vistamar, Route 113, Quebradillas. High atop a cliff overlooking the sandy beaches of the Atlantic Ocean on Puerto Rico's northwest coast, Vistamar has 35 air-conditioned rooms, a restaurant, two swimming pools, and a tennis court as well as beach access. There is even live entertainment on weekends. $35 to $40 per couple per night.

Parador Hacienda Juanita, Route 105, Maricao. A restored coffee plantation high in the Central Mountains of Puerto Rico. The 21-room inn was originally built in 1830 and, while renovated, the historic atmosphere remains intact. A swimming pool and tennis court blend in nicely with the surrounding lush forests, towering palms, waterfalls, and flowers. From $30 per couple per night.

Villa Parguera, Route 304, Lajas, is in the fishing village of Parguera on the southwest coast. This is the site of Phosphorescent Bay, which sparkles like millions of stars on moonless nights, and the hotel itself, with 50 air-conditioned rooms and a swimming pool, offers the opportunity to sample rural life in Puerto Rico at its best. The restaurant specializes in seafood. From $32 to $55, per couple per night.

Parador Baños de Coamo, Route 546, Coamo, is built on the oldest thermal springs in America, which were once visited by Franklin D. Roosevelt in the 1920s. The Indian cultures of Puerto Rico discovered the medicinal waters more than 300 years ago. The hotel has 48 rooms, a swimming pool, and a tennis court in addition to the baths. Coamo is on the south coast. $40 per couple per night.

4. Romantic Restaurants

You may think that all you need is love on a honeymoon, but a bite of food now and then is not a bad idea. Here too, Puerto Rico means choices. The larger hotels and resorts all have an assortment of restaurants, ranging from inexpensive coffeeshops to elegant supper clubs complete with floor shows. In San Juan, the choice of restaurants is unlimited: Italian, French, Chinese, continental, nouvelle cuisines, and, of course, Caribbean dishes and Puerto Rico's own *cocina criolla* (creole-style cooking).

Out on the island the dining rooms of the paradors are noted for their excellent quality, particularly the local dishes, and a dinner can cost as little as $15 for two. Along the coast, especially in the southeast, southwest, and northwest, don't hesitate to try the tiny seaside cafés where seafood may be only minutes from the water and two can dine for practically nothing.

San Juan

Ali-Oli, at the Excelsior Hotel in Miramar (tel. 725-7700), is a real favorite among local food afficionados and one of the city's trendier eating places, Ali-Oli features nouvelle cuisine dishes and Puerto Rican cuisine in an atmosphere that is appealing, simple, and appropriate for a Caribbean setting. About $40 for two, without wine or drinks.

Cafe del Puerto, overlooking San Juan's Harbor at Pier 3 in Old San Juan (tel. 725-1500); is a charming open-air café above the Puerto Rican Crafts Plaza just across the street from the cruise-ship docks. Wonderful for a drink to celebrate the sunset or for an informal lunch of burgers, salads, or seafood. Lunch is $15 to $30 for two, plus drinks. (Note: at dinner, this is a private club.)

La Mallorquina, 207 San Justo (tel. 722-3261). Patios and ceiling fans enhance the tropical mood in what is reputed to be the oldest restaurant in San Juan. La Mallorquina specializes in local favorites, the cocina criolla dishes served with sophistication. About $20 to $40 for two, plus drinks.

La Zaragozana, 356 San Francisco (tel. 723-5103), may be the place for the extraspecial romantic meal with full flourishes. Tableside guitars or strolling violins are just the beginning at this elegant hacienda complete with a splash of fountains in a courtyard. Traditional Spanish and Cuban dishes, as well as typical Puerto Rican favorites, including many "flambées". Dinner runs $45 and up for two, plus drinks.

Los Galanes, 65 San Francisco (tel. 722-4008). Take a step or two back in time and dine in this restored townhouse nestled in the heart of the old city. Continental cuisines as well as Puerto Rican favorites are served with a Spanish colonial flair, including antique-looking tableware. Dinner will be $40 and up for two, plus drinks.

Scotch & Sirloin, 102 Ashford (tel. 722-3640), is best for a complete change of pace, when the yearning is for steak and seafood. This restaurant in the La Rada Hotel in Condado has a small menu, but what it does it does very well. About $20 to $40 for two, plus drinks.

On the Island

The **Puerto Rico Tourism Company** has just launched a new restaurant program called "Foods of Puerto Rico," modeled after the successful parador system, which gives a seal of approval to eating places out on the island. Selected for their authenticity, these restaurants specialize in traditional Puerto Rican cooking, featuring such favorites as *asopao,* a chicken and rice soup, and *lechon asado,* roast suckling pig.

El Buen Cafe, Barrio Carrizales, is the first selection for inclusion in the program. The restaurant, on the northern coast road from San Juan and only a half hour from the Camuy Caves, features such dishes as goat and veal fricassee, Puerto Rican steak and onions, and fresh fish and seafood. It is open for lunch and dinner, about $20 to $30 per couple.

Anchor's Inn, Route 987, Fajardo (tel. 863-7200). In keeping with its seaside location, this restaurant has a salty appearance and features steaks and seafood. Lunch and dinner, about $15 to $30 for two, plus drinks.

Mayagüez Hilton, Route 104, Mayagüez (tel. 832-7575). For those traveling on the west coast this hotel features a good restaurant offering international dishes. Lunch and dinner, $15 to $30 for two, plus drinks.

Villa Parguera Hotel, Route 304, Parguera (tel. 899-3975), is one of the better seafood specialty restaurants on Puerto Rico's south coast. For those visiting the Phosphorescent Bay, lunch and dinner here are real treats, expect to pay $15 to $30 for two, plus drinks.

5. Nightlife

The island's gambling casinos must, by law, be part of a hotel. Conveniently, most of the major resorts in San Juan are contained in the Condado and Isla Verde sections of the city, and it is not only possible but common for visitors to stroll along in the moonlight from one to another until the money runs out. Puerto Rico's casinos vary only in minor degrees: color themes in the decor, location in the hotel, for example. Otherwise, they are all large, noisy, glittering, and glamorous. Try them all. Most of the larger hotels have casinos, as do the two Hyatts in nearby Dorado and the self-contained Palmas del Mar resort in Humacao.

Supper clubs and discos, too, are found in the larger hotels of San Juan for the most part, although a few are located in other parts of the city. Many of the supper clubs feature big-name entertainment as well as folkloric shows. Consult your hotel concierge or the weekly guides to entertainment available in hotels for up-to-date information on who's appearing where. Among the more popular are **Club Caribe** in the Caribe Hilton, **Club Tropico** at the El San Juan, and the Condado Plaza's **Latin Fever** show.

Chapter XXXIV

ST. MAARTEN/ ST. MARTIN

1. Practical Facts
2. Romantic Interludes
3. Honeymoon Hotels and Hideaways
4. Romantic Restaurants

LISTEN CAREFULLY and you'll hear the sugar birds as you wend your way along the beach past the blossoming oleander and bougainvillea to the two narrow main streets of the island's largest city—Philipsburg. Even here, where cars still pass in slow single file, the noises evoke a land that echoes its history: the gentle lapping of waves; the fluid mix of English, French, and Dutch; and the calling of men from the boats that ply the harbor combine to form a picture that overlaps century-old traditions with modern vitality.

France and the Netherlands share this small, 37-square-mile island, the smallest land mass in the world to be governed by two separate countries. When honeymooning here you have choices you won't find anywhere else, for this island is unique. Here you can opt to spend time exploring the quiet, green pasturelands and fields of the French side for half the day, then join the bustle and excitement of the developing towns and their casinos on the Dutch side.

Situated in a string of three islets called the Dutch Windwards, St. Maarten/ St. Martin lies 144 miles east and just barely south of Puerto Rico. To the immediate northeast are Saba and Sint Eustatius (also known as Statia), sister islands ruled by the Dutch. South and west lies St. Barthélemy, fondly referred to as St. Barts, kin to the French side of St. Martin.

Before the island claimed its dual nationality, Columbus supposedly anchored off its shores on November 11, 1493, the feast day of St. Martin of Tours (some historians claim he landed offshore of Nevis). Until the French corsairs arrived in the 1500s, the island was virtually left alone; only the Amerindians lived on its flatlands and rolling hills. The pirates liked the many bays and coves of St. Martin; the irregularities of its near-heart shape hid their ships when they retreated after plundering Spanish galleons bearing golden treasures from Mexico.

An early Dutch exploratory team landed in the 1600s but didn't stay long; nor did the French who took refuge on the island in 1629 after they were shipwrecked by a hurricane.

Later that year, however, the French returned, having been driven off of St. Kitts by the Spaniards. The Dutch came again too, two years later, and initiated the unique plan of cohabitation that exists in slightly altered form to this day. These early settlers picked the salt from the Grand Case salt pond, following in the historical footsteps of the Amerindians, who called the island *Salouiga*, "the land of salt."

The somewhat peaceful coexistence became marred by a Spanish takeover a few years later that produced one of the United States' earliest figureheads. Dutchman Peter Stuyvesant, who governed New York City when it was known as Nieuw Amsterdam, lost his leg in a battle to capture St. Maarten for his native country.

The year 1648 marks the true colonization of the island. On a day in late March the two countries signed a Partition Treaty at Mont des Accords (Mount Concordia), a site you can still hike to. One hundred and twenty-four years later a boundary—a stone wall—was established. Today there is only a small stone monument and back-to-back signs that say "Welcome to Sint Maarten" and "Bienvenue en Partie Française." Actually, legend tells that two men, one French and one Dutch and both drunk, paced off the island. The Frenchman had the greater stride apparently, but the Dutchman got the more valuable property.

Through sugar boom, slavery, and growing cotton, the island has survived with a certain spunk and a generous amount of friendly sophistication. Foreigners have always played a large part in the island's growth. Even in 1775 plantation owners and other inhabitants were speaking English as a common language. The population of outsiders now outnumbers the indigenous population.

Philipsburg, the capital of Dutch St. Maarten, stands on a slender strip of land outlined on one side by the Great Bay of the Caribbean and on the other side by the large Salt Pond. Its alleyways, called *steegjes,* join Front Street to Back Street, the only two main thoroughfares in town. It's a busy city compared to the calmer maze of streets that comprise Marigot, the capital of the French side. The harborside ambience permeates this very French town, even on the more built-up streets, where the international boutiques are. Women pass by with baguettes under their arms, and a small cart with a red-and-white checked umbrella, an *île aux glaces*, sells ice cream at the edge of

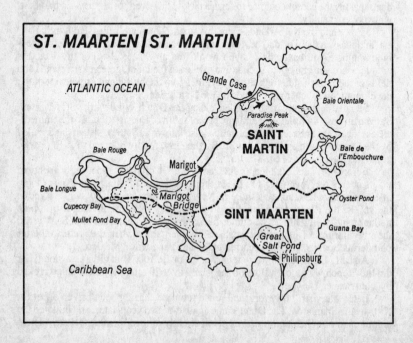

the water. Grand Case, the only other developed village on the island, is a few minutes past Marigot. It's a one-street main town known for its many restaurants.

Outside of the cities the land is a bit scrubby, a little like parts of the Italian countryside, with a smattering of cactus mixed in. When you head inland toward Colombier or Paradise Peak, however, you see a part of the island many tourists miss. This is where the land turns lush and tropical. Although bougainvillea, hibiscus, and frangipani grow by the sea, the growth in the interior surrounds you with a cool, almost tactile presence. This diversity appeals to many sports-minded vacationers. The inviting crystal-clear beaches draw scuba and snorkel aficionados, while the peaks here and on Saba and Statia lure hikers.

1. Practical Facts

GETTING THERE: For St. Maarten, Americans need to show proof of citizenship. A valid passport is preferable, but you can also use one that is expired, provided that it's not more than five years out of date. An original birth certificate with a raised seal, or a photocopy with a notary seal, or a voter's registration card will also suffice. St. Martin requires one piece of identification with a photo, but there are no customs stops between the two sides of the island, so it is highly unlikely that you would be required to show your picture ID. You also must have a confirmed room reservation and a return ticket.

There is a departure tax of $5 per person, which you do not have to pay if you are going from St. Maarten to Saba or Statia.

The island is one of the most popular in the Caribbean, so you can reach it easily by plane, usually with only one change or by a direct flight.

By Air

All flights to and from the United States use Juliana Airport on the Dutch side of the island. **American Airlines** now offers some nonstop flights from New York and San Juan and one-stop flights from Boston and Dallas. **Pan Am** and **Antillean Airlines** (ALM) also have nonstop service from New York. Passengers coming from Miami or Philadelphia can take advantage of **Eastern's** direct flights to St. Maarten. For travelers coming from other cities, connecting flights are available in New York, Miami, and San Juan.

The other Dutch islands—Aruba, Bonaire, and Curacao—connect with St. Maarten via ALM, and **Winward Islands Airways** (WINAIR) has daily service from half a dozen other Caribbean islands. In addition, **Prinair** flies in and out daily from Puerto Rico.

The island has another, much smaller airfield outside of Grand Case. Esperance Airport serves **Air Guadeloupe** for its daily flights to and from St. Barthélemy.

Take note if you're flying from Puerto Rico that baggage has been known to get delayed sometimes. The bags usually show up the next day by mid-afternoon. Plan accordingly if it's at all possible.

To Saba and Sint Eustatius: Regularly scheduled flights leave Juliana International Airport via Windward Islands Airways International (tel. 599/5-44230 or 599/5-44237).

By Sea

Ferries and sightseeing boats ply the waters between St. Maarten and St. Barts, Anguilla, and Saba. Most of the boats to St. Barts and the *Style,* which takes you to Saba, are day sails primarily for tourists. More specific information is available at your hotel activities desk or at the tourism offices in Philipsburg and Marigot.

The ferry to Anguilla leaves from and returns to Marigot six days a week (not on

Monday), catering as much to islanders as to tourists. Inquire in Marigot at the tourist office for schedules.

GETTING AROUND: You can explore the French or the Dutch side by taxi or by rental car. Following are the details.

By Taxi

Taxi fares are set, rather than metered, and are based on two-person occupancy. If you're coming from the airport, you should know that additional passengers raise the fare only $1 more per person. The daytime fares are reasonable, ranging from $4 to $16 from the airport to most major hotels and guest houses. Past 9 p.m. the rates go up 25% until midnight, when the fares become 50% more than daytime rates. There are two main taxi centers, one in Philipsburg by the harbor and the other in the center of Marigot. Either can arrange for a 2½-hour island tour ($30) or you can hire a taxi for $10 an hour, plus $2.50 for each additional 15 minutes.

By Rental Car

A valid driver's license is all that's needed. Although you can make a reservation for a car from the United States, once you get to the airport in St. Maarten, you must check in at the rental car counter. Even then you won't be able to drive away immediately. Regulations require that the car be delivered to your hotel.

Japanese and Korean cars are common, although Peugots do show up. Make sure the car you rent is fitted with seatbelts, and check tires, lights, etc., before you take the car out. And don't be shy if you'd like to exchange the car for another; that is, if one is available.

Driving can be hazardous, as there are embankments and gutters along the sides of some of the roads. Drivers are more casual here than in the United States, and it's not uncommon for cars to pass, barely missing oncoming traffic. Also, be aware that most insurance companies do not cover accidents on dirt roads, which is a problem because many of the major hotels lie at the end of some unpaved pathway.

Don't be surprised either at the goats and cows wandering by the side of the road. After wondering whether they ever get hit, I saw a small goat buckle under a van. Miraculously, he fit directly under the wheels and bounced back up with only a forlorn bleat. Still, they do stray into cars' paths, and you might not be as lucky as the driver of that van.

By Bus

The bus system runs infrequently but regularly. Opt for a rental car or taxi for island exploration; you'll be able to go farther, into more interesting places, and you can set your own pace.

LANGUAGE AND MONEY: Although Dutch is the official tongue and Papiamiento is the local dialect in St. Maarten, English is the prevailing language. You should have no problems communicating with people. On the French side, however, you may run into a few people who don't speak English, but they'll be the rarities. However, if you're unfamiliar with French food, you may find it handy to bring along a menu translation guide.

The money situation is also very simple. Although the Netherlands Antilles florin (NAF) and the French franc are the official currencies for the Dutch and French sides, respectively, the dollar is accepted throughout the island. In fact, the dollar is used more widely than the florin. Even some vending machines accept American coins.

WEATHER: Temperatures remain at a pleasant 80° or 85° year-round, with the added comfort of breezy trade winds.

CLOTHING: Dress is casual, even in the casinos, although a few people do don evening apparel for special nights out. Bring at least two bathing suits for the beach, and a coverup for hotel common areas. A sweater or light wrap for women and a lightweight jacket for men will be sufficient for the occasional cool night.

TIME: The island is on Atlantic Standard Time, which means that in winter there is a one-hour time difference between St. Maarten/St. Martin and the east coast of the United States; when it is noon in New York it is 1 p.m. in Philipsburg and Marigot. When Daylight Savings Time goes into effect on the East Coast, the island then keeps the same time as New York.

TELEPHONES: To call Dutch St. Maarten from the United States, use the international calling code 011, then dial 599-5, then the local five-digit number. For French St. Martin, it's 011-590 plus the local six-digit number you want. Calling long-distance from the island to home is not always easy, so plan ahead if you can, with enough time to try again. If you're staying on the Dutch side and you want to call Marigot or Grand Case, dial 06, then your local number. Calls originating from the French side must begin with 3.

SPORTS: St. Maarten is a sports lover's paradise on land and at sea. If you're interested in exploring the waters around the island, ask **Ocean Explorers** (tel. 45252) for their free diving guide. It's not only a good beginner's booklet, but a great introduction to the offshore treasures of the island, describing underwater caves as well as the sunken ship the H.M.S. *Proselyte*, a British frigate that went down in 1801.

Sailors make use of the numerous marinas, at the same time that Windsurfers, waterskiers, and parasail adventurers are frolicking on the calm waters of Simpson Bay Lagoon. On the shores of the lagoon within the Mullet Bay Resort is the island's only golf course, an 18-hole layout designed by Joseph Lee. For tennis, visitors can play on one of the almost 50 courts on the island. Serious athletes may appreciate the new sports center outside of L'Habitation; **Le Privilege** (tel. 873737) offers tennis, squash, archery, bodybuilding, aerobics, yoga, and more. It's a complete sports village with restaurant, studio lodging, and nightclub.

If it's nightlife you want, you'll find plenty of it at the island's eight casinos in and around Philipsburg. Hotels often sponsor nights of dinner dancing and some even have discos. **Night Fever,** a disco in Colombier, is an interesting adventure into island life.

And that's what your honeymoon on St. Maarten/St. Martin should be: an adventure. The people are friendly, the island is easy, and your only thoughts should be of relaxation and love.

SHOPPING: Because of its duty-free status, St. Maarten offers some of the best shopping buys in the Caribbean, especially on high-priced items such as jewelry, watches, fine crystal, porcelain, and silver—from all over the world and at prices usually between 20% and 60% off what you'd find in the United States. More than 500 shops on the Dutch-held side of the island alone are duty-free. Most accept travelers check and credit cards, and almost all price their goods in dollars. Hours are generally from 8 a.m. to 12 noon and 2 to 6 p.m., although the shops by the casinos tend to keep later hours.

Philipsburg is a shopper's paradise. It's as if Front Street exists only for tourists with money to spend. Mirrored and chromed emporiums vie with small gingerbread-trimmed cottages to get travelers' attention.

If you're planning to buy a watch, dinnerware, camera, or appliance, do a little research before you get on the plane. Write down model numbers and names of specific items, with the price (including tax). Although the savings can be big, they can also be disappointing, especially on cameras and appliances where savings can be better in New York discount houses.

Two of the biggest and most-recognized names on the island offer jewelry and watches at huge discounts, and both have offices in New York that can service the timepieces when necessary. **H. Stern Jewellers** on Front Street offers savings of 25% to 40%. Open half-circle earrings in 14k gold with 10 rubies for each ear sell for $255; a ¼-inch thick solid 14k gold bracelet, for $820. Sapphires, diamonds, coral, onyx, pearls, lapis—the jewelry within these doors is both bold and staid; you can take your choice. The name watches are all here: Rolex, Piaget, Concorde, Corum, Baume & Mercier, and more. **Spritzer & Fuhrman** tempts shoppers at three locations (Mullet Bay by the casino, Marigot, and the airport). Watches, with as full a range as H. Stern, are usually 25% to 40% off U.S. prices; jewelry, 20% to 35% off; and Limoges, Lalique, Lladró, and other fine crystal and china, from 40% to 60% off.

Oro de Sol Jewelers in Marigot and Philipsburg offers a similar line of watches, jewelry, and porcelain in addition to perfume and a good selection of china. You can get a full dinner service at 35% below their normally low prices if you take advantage of their occasional sales. The price range is enormous; for example, one place setting of Villeroy & Boch "Geranium," $190; George Jensen beaded silverware five-piece place setting for $556; Puiforcat "Cannes" five-piece place setting, $4,969.

Little Switzerland (in Philipsburg and Marigot) also has china, crystal, and watches. An 18k Rolex Lady Presidential that sells for $6,950 stateside was selling for $5,500 in St. Maarten. The perfumes here and on the island in general can be as much as half off what you'd pay in the United States. Chanel No. 5 practically jumps off the shelves for $63 for ½ ounce, compared to the $100 price quoted in New York. Opium at ¼ ounce brings in $62.50 at home but only $50 on the island. There are many perfume and figurine shops on Front Street. Most of the prices are similar, varying perhaps by a few dollars. It's probably not worth your time comparison shopping. Other stores offering scents and cosmetics include **Printemps,** the **Yellow House,** and **Penha.**

International boutiques include **La Romana** (on Front St. and in Mullet Bay), where you can indulge in designer fashions—Fendi, Krizia, Gianni Versace, Giorgio Armani, and Bottega Veneta among them—often at savings of 25% to 30%. **Leda of Venice** draws you in with Missoni ties for $40, Missoni sweaters for approximately $295 to $350, and cotton Polo shirts for $27. For leather goods, try **Maximoflorence** in Philipsburg, which offers briefcases and handbags primarily, with a smaller selection of shoes and belts.

Marigot's boutiques worth checking out, besides those already mentioned, include **Sonia Rykiel, Lancel,** the ubiquitous **Benetton,** and **Chez Anael,** which has Christian Dior clothes and much more.

Stéphane Kélian, whose shoes from Paris include designs by Claude Montana, has a shop in Mullet Bay. Prices in New York ranged from $98 to $290, while those at the resort varied from $48 to $120. Next door, **Optiques Caraibes** had Vuarnet glasses at $60, and neighboring **NAF-NAF** of France sold cotton jumpsuits that looked eminently comfortable for approximately $40 to $50.

What you really want is a souvenir of the island; head for **Impressions** in Philipsburg. Batik pareus sell for $28, and you can walk away with striking hand-painted Haitian pegboards for $24 to $38. The store specializes in handcrafts and can package items for shipping and mailing. Only a few paces away, **Batik Caribe** has smaller souvenir items such as sea urchin spines for 10¢ and shells from 10¢ to $1 and up. Shell chimes make a nice gift at $26 and up, as do the batik dresses for $48. In Marigot, **Samson & Co.** has beautiful wooden trays for $20, batik kimonos for $30, and bright festive tropical earrings at a range of prices. Numerous other shops in both shopping towns have T-shirts, lacy linens from Asia, and cheaper coral or glass jewelry.

One last note for those of you going on to Saba. In the 1870s, one of the Saban women who had gone to study in a convent in Caracas, Venezuela, came back with the skills to make "Spanish work," or what has now become known as "Saba lace." After a brief period when the islanders almost lost their knowledge of how to make this delicate lacework, Saba again produces it for tourists. The prices vary greatly.

ABOUT ACCOMMODATIONS: If you know what you want, you can probably get it here. The island's dual identity encourages differences. You'll find an assortment of accommodations to suit a variety of tastes and budgets.

For those who have never visited the island, the general rule has been that St. Maarten had the big, casino-oriented resorts while St. Martin was known for quiet, small hotels. There's a grain of truth in that, but only a grain. The Dutch side of the island has two of the most attentive and most beautiful hotels on the island—the Caravanserai and the Oyster Pond Yacht Club—not to mention the smaller guest houses in and around Philipsburg. At the same time, St. Martin has been developing larger resorts such as L'Habitation and condominium complexes not mentioned here. Still, the French side of the island for the most part is quieter and more isolated.

The prices listed in this section reflect the range from low season to high season. Generally, high season runs from December 15 through April 15. Some hotels have instituted a shoulder season, with corresponding mid-range rates, so if you're traveling within a week or two of the beginning or end of high season, it might be worth your while to delay the trip until the hotel's official low season starts. The summer rates can be as much as 30% to 50% lower than winter rates for the same accommodations.

European Plan (EP) rates—with no meals included in the cost—seems to be the most widespread, although Modified American Plan (breakfasts and dinners included) rates are surfacing here and there.

All hotel bills include a 5% room tax in St. Maarten, and most also add a 10% to 15% service charge in lieu of tipping. St. Martin's hotels may—or may not—add a $1 per day per person room tax. A few hotels on the island add an energy surcharge, especially for air conditioning. Ceiling fans, however, are very effective; and some of the nicest accommodations are cooled only by the gentle whirr of their blades. Also, the current here matches that of the United States (although many of the French hotels provide double-duty outlets for appliances using European or American current), so there's no need to bring adapters. In addition, some of the bigger, newer resorts come equipped with individual built-in hairdryers, so if you plan to travel with one, you might ask and save yourself the extra few pounds.

DINING OUT: St. Martin is known as the culinary capital of the Caribbean. The quality, consistency, and variety of the restaurants is truly remarkable, especially considering that many of the ingredients are flown in from all over the world. No matter what season you're traveling, make dinner reservations as soon as possible, preferably when you're making the hotel reservation. During high season, reserve at least one week in advance if at all possible; in summer, it's still a good idea to make reservations beforehand because the hours and days of operation may change depending on the numbers of tourists and the whim of the owners.

In most cases, a 15% service charge will be added to the bill, so tip only if you feel that your service was above the norm. Skim the menu, however, to double-check that service is indeed included as part of the total cost of the meal.

Don't get confused. In some restaurants *entrée* means "appetizer" rather than "main course." The main course dishes are usually listed under the headings *poissons* (fish) and *viandes* (meat).

HOW TO GET MARRIED ON ST. MAARTEN/ST. MARTIN:
On the Dutch side, you'll have to establish residency one year prior to the wedding date. True to the romance of the French, you don't have to wait quite so long—only 30 days. Either you or your spouse will have to have lived on St. Martin for the 30-day period prior to your application for a license. Once that is established you need to present proof of American citizenship, such as a valid passport or birth certificate. Or you can present proof of divorce, if that is applicable.

FOR FURTHER INFORMATION:
Contact **Mallory Factor Inc.,** 275 Seventh Ave., New York, NY 10001 (tel. 212/989-0000). **St. Maarten Tourist Bureau,** De Ruyterplein, Philipsburg, St. Maarten (tel. 22337). The **French West Indies Tourist Board,** 610 Fifth Ave., New York, NY 10020 (tel. 212/757-1125). **French Government Tourist Office,** 9401 Wilshire Blvd., Beverly Hills, CA 90212 (tel. 213/272-2661). **St. Martin Tourist Information Bureau,** Waterfront, 97150 Marigot, St. Martin, F.W.I. (tel. 875326).

2. Romantic Interludes

With lively casinos, lush mountain peaks, and hidden coves, the island offers one of the most diverse arrays of romantic activities in the Caribbean.

It's wonderful and exceedingly tempting! All of the island's **beaches** are open to the public. Many of the famous—and not so famous—hotels front the beaches but anyone can wander onto their strands and revel in their distinctive characters. Some of the more spectacular include Cupecoy, nestled into the cliffs; horseshoe-shaped Guana, isolated and quiet, known for its good body-surfing waves; and more lively Baie Rouge, a long semicircle of sand with a wave-washed arched rock at one end. Also notable are the nude beach at Orient Bay and the fine-sanded, good swimming beach by the Caravanserai; the latter, which lies at the end of the airport runway, provides unusual entertainment—you can watch the planes come in right overhead, with their landing gear already out and ready to touch down.

The presence of **casinos** in St. Maarten makes one of the biggest differences between the two sides of the island. At night, when only a few restaurants and a dance place or two remain open in St. Martin, the Dutch side sparks with activity at its eight casinos and the nearby discos. You'll probably want to look in on the excitement even if you're not planning to gamble. Mullet Bay Resort's **Grand Casino** (tel. 593-8600), the largest on the island, seduces its visitors to play standard, progressive, and electronic slot machines; blackjack; roulette; craps; and more—even poker at the bar! Although times may vary slightly from winter season to summer season, the commotion usually begins at 1 p.m. and lasts until 3 a.m. Monday through Saturday. Sunday hours run from 8 p.m. to 3 a.m. An added inducement is a policy to accept credit cards for chips. The minimum varies and not all the casinos offer the service, so if it's important to you, call the casinos beforehand.

No beaches! Yet verdant Saba, an extinct volcanic peak that juts its nose up above water, draws a steady stream of curious travelers who want to spend an active day hiking the steps carved out of the rock mountain or scuba diving at one of the most well-known sites in the Caribbean. Only four Hansel-and-Gretel–like villages house a total population of 950. Day trips by boat, on the *Style* (tel. 22167), depart at 8:45 a.m. four days a week from the **Great Bay Marina** in Philipsburg. For $45 per person, you'll be back by 4:30 p.m. the same afternoon. For longer stays, contact **WINAIR** (tel. 44230 or 44237) about flights and fares.

Sister island to Saba and St. Maarten, **Sint Eustatius** (fondly known as Statia) lies 17 minutes away by **WINAIR** (tel. 44230 or 44237). While there, take in the historic sights of the second oldest synagogue in the western hemisphere, the **St. Eustatius Museum** in the 18th-century Doncker/De Graaff House, and the remains of warehouses once stacked with arms for the American colonists during the revolution. The other highlight not to be missed is the **Quill;** this extinct volcano is topped by a tropical rain forest dignified with majestic giant cedar trees and memorable iridescent hummingbirds.

Saddle up and ride into the waves. The Dutch side's **Crazy Acres Riding Center** offers an extravagant three-hour **horseback riding** excursion venturing through verdant countryside to a crystalline beach. The regularly scheduled trip ($40 per person), which leaves at 9 a.m., includes no more than eight people along with two experienced escorts. For a special treat, ask them to arrange a private beach picnic. Call Valerie (tel. 42503, ext. 201; or 44309, ext. 201) or check with your hotel's activities desk.

The 46-foot red-and-white ketch *Gabrielle* departs **Bobby's Marina** in Philipsburg Harbor every day at 9 a.m. for a refreshing sail to a secluded beach for swimming, snorkeling, and picnicking. They provide the snorkel equipment and underwater camera; you bring the 110 film. The $55 per person fee includes lunch, beer, and soda but not the port tax. For information and reservations, call 22366 or 23170 after 6 p.m., or contact your hotel activities desk.

If you'd rather **sail** without the company of strangers, try renting a Hobie catamaran for $30 per couple for an hour. The first time you rent, you'll go out with an instructor who'll teach you the ropes. After that, you're on your own. Ask for Maria Harris at **Red Ensign Watersports** located at the Oyster Pond Dock. If you must call, you'll have to go through the Oyster Pond Yacht Club receptionist (tel. 23206). For a splurge, ask about chartering a three-cabin monohull boat complete with skipper. The price for sailing *a deux:* $350 for the boat for the day. Call Anne-Marie Bruffaerts at **Happy Bay's Vacances Yachting** at 873333 or 873232, ext. 1422.

Right off the beach, within walking distance, the shallow reefs of **Dawn Beach** begin. This is a good spot for beginning snorkelers, who haven't become accustomed to submerging themselves yet—when the surf is calm. You may want to call the Dawn Beach Hotel (tel. 22929) and ask their water-sports center about surf conditions. Snorkeling equipment there costs $10 a day per person.

Tintamarre and **Pinel**—these two **islands** off the coast of St. Martin attract snorkelers in droves. The superb reefs are further supplemented by the sunken hull of an old tugboat. **Vacances Yachting,** which operates out of the harbor at L'Habitation (Anse Marcel) is one of the nicest points of departure. Choose from monohull and catamaran sailboat charters of six-person groups. With so few people you can keep the outing flexible and decide as a group how you want to schedule the time. Lunch, open bar, and gear are included in the $60 per person fee. Call Anne-Marie Bruffaerts at 873333 or 873232, ext. 1422.

You can clown next to the clownfish or try to tickle a sea cucumber and get it all down on **videotape.** For $50 for the two of you **Maho Watersports** will film you, edit the tape, and add music and initial subtitles. They're on the beach at Mullet Bay Resort (tel. 44387 or 42801, ext. 379).

It's late in the day and the horizon is clear: take note that you may be witness to an exceptional **sunset.** The bright orange disc renders the turquoise water translucent for the most extraordinary effect. Head for the **Caravanserai** hotel near the airport in St. Maarten (tel. 42510) for a civilized drink in their newly renovated oceanfront gazebo or climb into the ruins of Fort Marigot, high on a hill just north of town.

Between Marigot and Grand Case you'll see a sign for **Paradise Peak,** the highest point on St. Martin. The 1,500-foot summit lies at the end of a narrow, curving road that passes through some of the lushest landscapes on the island. The vista once you get there is quite spectacular too, with clear views of Anguilla, Marigot, and Philipsburg. Plan the journey for the early morning—you won't want to hike the last few steps in the heat of the noon sun.

3. Honeymoon Hotels and Hideaways

You'll find a wide choice of accommodations on the island—from resort villages with casinos, shopping centers, and discos to quiet hideaways known for their tranquillity and exclusivity.

The rates quoted below reflect the spread between low- and high-season prices.

THE FRENCH SIDE: Here are the choices for St. Martin.

Very Expensive

La Samanna, B.P. 159, 97150 St. Martin, F.W.I. (tel. 590/875122; U.S. reservations: tel. 212/696-1323). Tucked into the greenery of Baie Longue, this intimate, Mediterranean-inspired resort welcomes an exclusive but ever-so-casual crowd. The white stucco buildings and thatch-roof terraces create an atmosphere that is known to soothe even the most savage business executive. Power brokers the world over have supped quietly in anonymous glory here. Nothing offensive meets the eye. Each of the 85 rooms—whether the air-conditioned main-house chambers or the spacious beachfront "apartments" cooled by ceiling fans—is fitted with a fully equipped kitchen, tasteful natural wicker and rattan appointments, chaise longues on the terraces, fresh flowers, and lovely tiled sinks. As of 1987, the resort has switched over to the Modified American Plan (breakfasts and dinners are mandatory), but the price includes all water sports (except for lessons), use of the three tennis courts, and easy access to the 1½-mile stretch of isolated beach. Fine restaurant. Honeymoon package: none. Rates (MAP): $480 to $1,820 per couple per day. Closed August 31 to November 1.

Expensive

Happy Bay, B.P. 170, 97150 St. Martin, F.W.I. (tel. 590/875520; U.S. reservations: tel. 212/840-6636 or toll free 800/223-9815 outside NYS). Dramatically situated with the rolling hills of La Savanne on one side and the ocean on the other, Happy Bay is slowly establishing itself as a gracious, European-style resort. Forthright elegance is the key here, with cherry-hued wooden furniture, king-size beds, room telephone, and a bathroom outfitted with marble bath, separate shower, and double sinks. As lovers' retreats, the suites especially radiate warmth; soft peach and green bargello fabric covers the canopy bed's headboard, plump loveseat, and chair—and the pond appears heart-shaped from the terraces. Butterflies flirt with jacaranda and hibiscus blossoms, while the outer fields attract an occasional egret. All can be seen from the stunning dining room, open to breezes and exceptionally well put together, with a modern chandelier hanging as counterpoint to the white balloon-cloth-draped ceiling. Extras include use of a rental car, smooth Porthault bed linens, and on arrival, a bottle of Dom Perignon, a smaller bottle of French perfume, and a Davidoff 500 cigar. Jean Payot, the assistant manager, lends a friendly hand when planning activities and water sports off their isolated beach. Honeymoon package: none. Rates (EP): $180 to $680 per couple per night.

La Belle Creole, B.P. 118, Marigot 97150, St. Martin, F.W.I. (tel. 590/875866; U.S. reservations: 800/HILTONS). This extravagant resort complex was once the dream of Claude Philippe (former vice president and general manager of the Waldorf-Astoria), who envisioned it as an elegant retreat. He planned for it to resemble a French Mediterranean village with a central square and cobblestoned streets. His dream was never fulfilled and the property lay abandoned until a few years ago. Conrad International (of Hilton fame) rehired Robert Cabrera, the original architect, to complete the 27 buildings on 25 acres of land. Now due to open February 1, 1988, the hotel will offer five categories of rooms, twice-daily maid service, and full concierge desk. Breakfast is on the house each morning—French continental–style, with croissants and brioche—and a complimentary welcome surprise such as a bottle of champagne or fruit basket should greet you on arrival. A lovely tropical expanse with a three-acre lagoon marks it as a place to watch. This may indeed be a newfound paradise. Honeymoon package: none at this time. Rates: $225 to $490 per couple per night in winter; summer rates have not yet been set.

Moderate

L'Habitation de Lonvilliers, P.O. Box 230, 97150 St. Martin, F.W.I. (tel. 590/ 973333; U.S. reservations: 212/757-0225 or toll free 800/847-4249 outside NYS). The magnificent approach to L'Habitation winds its way up to a spectacular vista then curves down again to sea level at Marcel Cove. Standing on the flat of the land is an imposing mix of architecture with Disneyesque color and eclecticism: rustic lodge, balconied buildings à la New Orleans, and an elaborate Georgian plantation–style main house. To complete the fantasy, the planners installed a gazebo surrounded by flower-lined blue pebble walks. In the main house, a broad double staircase of marble leads down to the reception area and lounges. The 253 good-size rooms, inspired by the same imagination, flaunt fanciful headboards, geometric bedspreads, and pink marble sinks. All the rooms have either an efficiency or full kitchen, private balcony, and air conditioning. For privacy away from the central areas, request the quiet one-bedroom apartments by the marina causeway, where birdsong from the nearby 150-acre nature reserve replaces the murmur of more active guests. At your disposal is a freshwater pool, a children's playground, shuffleboard, volleyball on the 1,600-foot beach, and for a fee, tennis, squash, fitness equipment, and water sports. There are also international boutiques and two restaurants. Honeymoon package: Eight days / seven nights (EP): $1,351 to 1,526 per couple. Includes a bottle of champagne on arrival, a dinner for two and wine at their restaurant, La Belle France, a honeymoon dinner served in the room. Five-day package also available. Closed August 31 to October 2.

Grand Case Beach Club, Grand Case 97150, St. Martin, F.W.I. (tel. 590/ 875187; U.S. reservations: tel. 212/661-4540 or toll free 800/223-1588 outside NYS). New Yorker Daniel Acciani and his family bring an upbeat atmosphere to this lively 76-room beachfront hotel just outside of Grand Case. Choose between studio and one-bedroom accommodations; the latter offer king-size beds with bamboo headboards, sitting area partitioned by a folding door, and balconies off the living room and bedroom. If you opt for a studio, request double beds (some are twin-bedded). Both types of rooms come with air conditioning, equipped kitchenette, and dining area. Beach buffs will prefer the oceanview, where you can hear the surf as a gentle lullaby through the night. A nice touch much appreciated by the guests are the inviting two-person hammocks strung along a strip of planted land just above the beach. Good restaurant. Water-sports center on the property. Honeymoon package: Eight days / seven nights (EP): $635 to $2,016 per couple. Includes a bottle of champagne at dinner, flowers, breakfast daily, use of artificial grass Omnicourt tennis court day and night. Four-day package also available.

Le Galion, Baie de l'Embouchure, 97150 St. Martin, F.W.I. (tel. 590/875177; U.S. reservations: tel. 212/840-6636 or toll free 800/223-9815 outside NYS). Tucked into a corner of the island near the nude beach at Orient Bay, Le Galion attracts a laidback, young set, who don't mind a little sand on the floor. One honeymooning couple remarked, "We're treated like family guests rather than clients. They've been gracious, warm, hospitable—and Germaine makes a stiff drink!" Manager Michel Bernard has been known to open a bottle of champagne spontaneously to welcome newlyweds, but it's an action of the moment. Here you're likely to see the guests Windsurfing and sailing in the quiet bay, playing cards in front of the restaurant, or playing tennis. The newly renovated, capacious one-bedroom cottages make a nice splurge for romantics. Air conditioning, kitchenettes or refrigerators, televisions, and patios bring high-tech comfort to an otherwise low-key and understated resort of only 63 units. Honeymoon package: None. Rates (EP): $130 to $385 per couple per day.

Inexpensive

Bertine's Guest House, Savana Grand Case, 97150 St. Martin, F.W.I. (tel. 590/875839). Open all year, but call to confirm. Friendly and charmingly modest, Bertine's appeals to the casual bed-and-breakfast crowd. The four petite rooms have a half-size refrigerator, ceiling fan, and folding aluminum chairs made cozy with patterned fabric cushions. Owners Bernard and Christine Poticha, originally from Chicago, and their small staff add a personal air that makes up for what the place lacks. The restaurant, which overlooks the untouched beauty of the hills above Grand Case and offers a sweeping view of the bay from afar, welcomes the public. Breakfast isn't included in the rates, but coffee's available to early risers. Honeymoon package: None. Rates: $35 to $55 per couple per day.

THE DUTCH SIDE: Here are the selections for St. Maarten.

Expensive

Mullet Bay Resort, SunResorts Ltd., N.V., St. Maarten, Netherlands Antilles (tel. 42801; U.S. reservations: 212/593-8600 or toll free 800/468-5538). A megaresort with over 600 rooms and suites, casino, disco, eight restaurants, and eight bars, Mullet Bay feels more like an expatriate village on the island than a hotel. A country-club atmosphere predominates, primarily because of the resort's 18-hole Joseph Lee golf course—the only course on the island—which sprawls throughout the property, giving an open, landscaped effect to the 172 acres. Whether you're sports minded or not, the emphasis here is on leisure. Besides the golf pro and staff, the facility offers 14 all-weather tennis courts and pro shop, two salt-water pools, jogging path with exercise stations, and for the more sedentary crowd, two major tax-free shopping centers with international boutiques, food stores, and gift shops. The water-sports activities take advantage of the ¾-mile stretch of beach in addition to the lagoon and Mullet Pond, the two bodies of water that define the inner horseshoe shape of the resort. To ease guests' explorations, a courtesy bus calls at designated stops every 15 or 20 minutes. All accommodations have air conditioning, terrace, wall-to-wall carpeting, and king-size bed. The roomier suites feature separate parlor / living room and full kitchen. Medical clinic on grounds. Honeymoon package: Eight days / seven nights (EP): From $1,463 per couple during the summer; inquire for winter rates. Includes champagne and cheese tray on arrival, honeymoon dinner with wedding cake, rental car for four days, unlimited golf and tennis, breakfast daily, three additional dinners. Four-day package also available.

Moderate

Reserved and romantic, **Oyster Pond Yacht Club,** P.O. Box 239, St. Maarten, Netherlands Antilles (tel. 599-5/22206 or 23206; U.S. reservations: tel. 212/696-1323 or toll free 800/372-1323 outside NYS), is a newlywed's dream. Just a few minutes from the French border on the eastern coast of the island, the yacht club sits on a spit of land with Oyster Pond on one side and the Caribbean on the other. You're more isolated here than at most of the other accommodations on the island, and tranquility is supreme. Children under 12 are not welcome, a policy that reflects the attitude and lifestyle of this sophisticated, 20-room resort. Fashioned after a villa with a central courtyard and tower (with a lovely suite in it), the stone and stucco buildings were constructed in the 1960s; then in the early 1980s everything but the main structures underwent extensive renovation. The result: an impeccable vacation hideaway embellished with pastel-cushioned, white wicker, and rattan appointments, arched patios, and blooms and greenery everywhere. Take note of the door plaques, another example of the evident attention to detail. Each carries the name of a beloved or famous boat—*Fandango, Harlequin, Passage* (for *Windward Passage*, one of the greatest racing boats of its time)—and was carved in Newport in 1983 during the Americas Cup race. Good restaurant. Tennis. Adjacent watersports center. Honeymoon package: none. Rates (EP): $170 to $310 per couple per day.

The Caravanserai, P.O. Box 113, Philipsburg, St. Maarten, Netherlands Antilles (tel. 599-5/42510; U.S. reservations: tel. 212/840-6636 or toll free 800/223-9815 outside NYS). Yes, it's right next to the airport, but it's situated so perfectly that you can take delight in watching the planes come in to land—usually between 9 a.m. and 9 p.m. One of the treasures of this tasteful but stylish 85-unit hotel is room number 19, whose unique terrace dramatically juts out into an outcrop of highly textured rock carved out by the crashing ocean. Then there are the *caravanserai*, ten rooms built around a courtyard, reminders of the sleeping quarters in the 1600s for Eastern caravans. Other views overlook the ocean or the garden. At 4:30 you'll want to relax in a wicker couch by the arched colonnades of the beautiful Palm Court, where tea is laid out. The service is friendly and indulgent; what you can't find here—water sports, casino, golf course, disco—you'll find at sister establishment Mullet Bay, just minutes away. The Oasis restaurant is a well-known spot for watching the sunset, especially now with its new wrought-iron gazebo bar. Honeymoon package: Eight days/seven nights (EP): From $778 to $979 per couple during the low season; inquire for high-season rates. Includes champagne, honeymoon dinner with wedding cake, rental car for four days, unlimited golf and tennis at Mullet Bay, breakfast daily, three additional dinners. Four-day package also available.

Inexpensive

Mary's Boon, P.O. Box 278, St. Maarten, Netherlands Antilles (tel. 599-5/44235; U.S. reservations: tel. 212/986-4373). At the gate, two painted sentries keep guard in front of black-and-white painted gatehouses. The garden path leads up to a cozy guest house that would fit as easily in Provincetown, Massachusetts, as it does here. The breezy front room attracts bibliophiles with eclectic tastes. Books are everywhere, backgammon tables stand ready in the bar room, and local art fills the wall space, occasionally broken by the delicate frame of a wicker bird cage. The 12 rooms on the ocean and by the airport (you *can* hear the planes) sport simple, urbane, and unadorned furnishings. You'll find twin beds pushed together, twin burners, and a one-sink efficiency kitchenette. This has the feel of a New England bed-and-breakfast turned tropical. Request the balconied upper-floor rooms that overlook the beach. Although children will be absent from the scene, you'll probably meet one of Rush Little's six dogs. Honeymoon package: none. Rates (EP): $60 to $110 per couple per day. Closed September and October.

The Pasanggrahan, P.O. Box 151, Philipsburg, Netherlands Antilles (tel. 23588), features the comforts of a relaxed but well-run guest house right on Front Street. The veranda invites people watching, while the interior induces guests to share stories and sit back. This is a place that will please diehard city dwellers who crave being able to step out of their hotel into a bustling world of tourists and islanders. Personal attention, air conditioning, and beachside lounging out beyond the tropical backyard are the pluses here. Rates range from $54 for the standard beachfront room to $110 for the more romantic Queen's Room.

SABA AND STATIA: Captain's Quarters, Windwardside, Saba, Netherlands Antilles (tel. from St. Maarten 04-2201; U.S. reservations: tel. 212/840-6636 or toll free 800/223-9815). A quaint ten-room inn that was a sea captain's house in the 19th century, Captain's Quarters hides its guests away in either wood-frame guest cottages or in the main house where the honeymoon suite is located. Antiques and four-poster

beds make the secluded stay a joy, as does the remarkable pool, the only one on the island. Honeymoon package: none. Rates (EP): $65 to $95 per couple per day. For MAP rates, add $25.

The Old Gin House, P.O. Box 172, Lower Town, St. Eustatius, Netherlands Antilles (tel. from St. Maarten 03-2319; U.S. reservations: tel. 212/535-9530 or toll free 800/223-5581). If you like black-sand beaches, *quiet* nights, and the feel of being truly away from it all, you'll love Statia. The 20 rooms of this made-for-romance hideaway give you two choices; six face the beach, the others, across the street, front the pool. The charming inn stands on the site of a building that once housed a cotton gin. Although the building is a modern reconstruction, it captures the feel of the past without neglecting the amenities of the present. Run by a former art director of a major advertising company and his wife, who taught art, the many-beamed inn flourishes under their care. Each room is individually decorated with comfortable and interesting antiques. The restaurant serves up notable gourmet fare on beautiful Spode china. Honeymoon package: none. Rates (EP): $100 to $130 per night for two.

4. Romantic Restaurants

The island's restaurants deserve their world-class reputations. As much as you like one restaurant, be adventurous and go someplace new the next time. From Chinese and Indonesian to the finest French and Italian, the restaurants alone will lure you back to St. Martin / St. Maarten.

EXPENSIVE: Le Poisson D'or, Marigot (tel. 875033). Water laps gently at the base of the dining terrace, capturing the best of a romantic moonlit night. Inside, stone walls with arched entrances provide a backdrop for exquisite oil paintings. But it's the cuisine here that draws crowds from every corner of the world. From the simple to the sublime, the food is in a word—wonderful. Lobster and vegetables in a light vanilla cream sauce. Breast of duck with a lime and cinnamon sauce. And an exquisitely prepared pasta with flawless scallops. The inspired combinations work with a sensitivity rarely found outside the best restaurants of New York City and France. As beautiful to the eye as to the palate, the creations at Poisson D'Or merit the expense. Dinner for two with appetizers, dessert, and wine runs from about $125 per couple and up.

Messalina, Marigot (on the Boulevard de France). A classic beauty that oozes romance, this impeccable restaurant overlooking the square and harbor in Marigot enfolds its diners in a skyscape of blue with white clouds. The fresco-like painting is set off by gold moldings that are in turn accentuated by delicate peach and sand wall colors. The ambience and food match the decor. Classical music plays softly in the background, while crystal chandeliers add a soft light to the scene. Choose from a diversity of Italian specialties, from lobster minestrone to fresh pappardelle in pesto sauce to osso buco. Selections for lunch are more limited but no less delicious. You'll have to drop in to make a reservation; they don't have a phone yet. When you do, ask for a balcony table. Lunch for two with soft drinks and antipasti, about $60; dinner, appetizers from $6 to $12, pasta appetizers from $9 to $14 (add 50% for pasta as a main course), entrées from $17 to $24.

Casual and chummy, both the tourists and the staff at **Sebastiano's,** Grand Case (tel. 875348), seem to have a good, high-spirited time. Here you'll find down-home northern Italian cooking. The chef, Sergio, hails from Milano and makes a mean matriciana sauce and a superb scaloppine alla pizzaiola. The fresh pasta dishes are priced from $9 to $12 (add $4 if served as a main course or shared); the appetizers run from $5 to $12; entrées, from $15 to $20. Dessert will add another $5 or so to the bill. Wine selections range from $13 to $27. MasterCard and Visa accepted, but not American Express.

Le Tastevin, Grand Case (tel. 875545). Chef Daniel Passeri brought treats from Burgundy to Grand Case at L'Auberge Gourmande; now, across the street and on the water, at Le Tastevin he and chef Frederic Blain are offering delicious, well-prepared nouvelle cuisine to tempt even the most diehard traditional *saucier*. The beachfront terrace drips with bougainvillea and is especially nice for lunch, when you can choose from such excellent appetizers as a smooth pâté of tuna in a sweet pepper ring or home-made rough-grained chicken liver pâté, both garnished beautifully with a tomato rose. The poached langouste Tastevin and the charred chicken present simple but elegant fare executed by a knowing hand—and it is this simple elegance that makes Tastevin the gem that it is. Lunch for two with appetizers, beverage, and a shared dessert: $58; dinner, from $64. Wine list starts at $14. Closed Wednesday and in June and July. MasterCard and Visa accepted, but not American Express.

La Rhumerie, Colombier (tel. 875698). The best of French creole cooking awaits you in this charming house set in the lush interior of the island. Madame Le Moine, who brought fame to Marigot's Cas' Anny restaurant (then called Chez Lolotte), has outdone herself here; with an herb and vegetable garden out back, she uses the freshest of ingredients for such delectable items as conch creole style and courtbouillon of crayfish. For an authentic taste of the French West Indies, try the ac-cras (fish fritters) and the house's special homemade—and potent—fruit-imbued rums. Take a stroll down the pastoral road before you head in to eat; the scents and sights outside are a perfect complement to cuisine indoors. Lunch per person, appetiz-ers from $5 to $8.50, entrées from $12 to $17; dinner for two with appetizers, dessert, and two rum drinks, from $80. No credit cards accepted; traveler's checks and person-al checks with passport or picture license are welcomed.

La Samanna, Baie Longue (tel. 875122). This most exclusive and picture per-fect of resorts on the island opens its doors to the public for breakfast, lunch, dinner, and drinks. The atmosphere bespeaks relaxed gentility, taste, tranquillity. The back-drop: aquamarine water and perennial blossoms. Straw chairs with blue-fringed cush-ions, ceiling fans, white stucco walls—each element helps to evoke a lifestyle of leisure and pleasure. Even the table setting, a blue-and-white Rosenthal wave pattern, adds to the effect. Feast on sautéed foie gras with truffle sauce, osetra caviar, rack of lamb, roasted free-range chicken and the like; dieters will appreciate the dinner menu, which notes low-calorie dishes. If you just want a peek at the place, go for the conti-nental breakfast ($13 per person) from 8 a.m. to 10 a.m. Figure on at least $50 for two for lunch and $100 for dinner, not including drinks or wine. American Express ac-cepted, but not MasterCard or Visa. Closed August 31 to November 1.

Bilboquet, Pointe Blanche. You can't call for reservations here. The island is small enough and the directions to Bilboquet complicated enough that American hosts Bob Donn and Bill Ahlstrom ask that you drive up to the house at least a day in advance to leave your name and hotel room. The five-table restaurant-cum-house sits high above the village port of Pointe Blanche. One wrong turn and you'll end up where the cruise boats and freighters dock. Artifacts from Latin and South America hang about the walls and punctuate the bookcases, providing an eyeful while the dinner is being prepared. In keeping with the size of the house, the menu is limited to two entrées and diners must arrive between 7:30 and 8 to be seated. To further establish a cozy and tranquil atmosphere, the hosts allow no more than four to a table. The prix-fixe dinner is $45 per person not including wine. No credit cards are accepted, only travelers checks. Follow signs for Pointe Blanche, turn left at the Pot Rum factory; take another left at Vinomar, then another left up Pigeon Road.

MODERATE: West Indian Tavern, Philipsburg (tel. 22965). It's a little touristy but loads of fun late at night. The West Indian Tavern has a funky, somewhat offbeat air, with brightly colored parrot planters, lots of greenery, vivid red, green, and white gingerbread trim and trellises, and parasol-covered ceiling lights. On Sunday, Tues-day, and Thursday nights, strolling guitar players wander from the terraced tables to the backgammon barroom and tropical verandah. Creole dinners are served until midnight; the bar and veranda stay open an hour later. Appetizers from $5.95; main dishes from $14.95. Happy hour drinks are 99¢ from 4 to 6 p.m.

Bamboo Garden, at the Mullet Bay Resort (tel. 2801, **ext.** 367). Undoubtedly the best gourmet Chinese food on the island. Manager Leo Lee moved from a thriving restaurant on Long Island, New York, to work his wonders here. Most of the ingredients are flown in fresh every week from New York's renowned Chinatown. The Peking duck and crisp beef with orange rind are standouts. Ask for directions at the front desk of the resort. The restaurant, in the hillside building, sports a fantasy-like Polynesian decor that's at once festive and genial. Appetizers from $1.75; main dishes from $10.25. The chef also offers two special dinners, one for $40 for two, the other for $60.

For Indonesian fare, try the **Wajang Doll's** (tel. 2687) rijsttafel. A 14-dish spread costs $14.90 per person; the 19-dish version is $21.

INEXPENSIVE: **Waves** at the Grand Case Beach Club outside of Grand Case offers a lunch of sandwiches, ribs, fried shrimp, and the like for $4.50 to $8.50 at their polygonal restaurant that juts out into the sea (tel. 875390). **Sam's Restaurant and Pub** on Philipsburg's famous Front Street (tel. 2989) is the hot spot for music and carousing after the lights are out Tuesday through Saturday. Burgers are $3.95 and up; grills and poultry from $8.95; fish and shellfish, $11.50 and up. Lunch is very reasonable, from $2.95; and you can even pop in for a breakfast of bagel and cream cheese ($1.75).

Most likely, you'll be sitting next to locals at **Callaloo** (no phone), off Front Street next to Batik Carib and Impressions. Grab a slice of pizza at this Philipsburg institution for an inexpensive lunch. **Zemi by the Sea** on Front Street in Philipsburg (no phone) also offers low-priced, ultracasual lunches overlooking the harbor. Featuring health foods, delicious fresh fruit drinks, and a pleasant wood deck, the price can't be beat: breakfasts from $2.75 up, lunches from $2.50. If you're strolling in Marigot, stop in at one of the few omelet places, such as the **Pink Tea Room** by the Hotel Palm Plaza (no phone); prices from $3.50. **Etna per dolce vita** in Marigot on Kennedy Avenue serves up homemade ice cream and cookies in the afternoons and early evenings. Flavors run from the expected chocolate and coffee to unusual soursop, passion fruit, and rose. Cones and cups for $1.25, hot fudge sundae for $2.75.

Chapter XXXV

UNITED STATES VIRGIN ISLANDS

1. Practical Facts
2. St. Thomas
3. St. Croix
4. St. John

"ISLE 95 WEATHER. . . . Mostly sunny today, high about 82°. Mostly clear tonight, temperatures around 75°. Winds from the east at about 12 knots per hours. Sunny tomorrow." That's the weather report you'll hear on the radio practically every day of the year in the United States Virgin Islands.

Blessed with about 300 sunny days a year, crystal-clear waters the color of molten turquoise (and sapphire, and aquamarine), plus pure white, powder-fine beaches, the U.S. VI has become known as America's Paradise. The island group is composed of St. Thomas, St. John, and St. Croix, plus about 50 tiny islets and cays, most of them uninhabited. St. Thomas turns on the glamour full force, tempting visitors with a cosmopolitan array of duty-free shopping bargains and fast-lane nightlife. Life centers on its red-roof capital, Charlotte Amalie, which arcs around a harbor as famous as that of Rio de Janeiro or Monte Carlo—and equally pleasure loving. Nature reigns on St. John, the lushest of the isles, where two-thirds of the land is national park, and a string of unspoiled beaches with evocative names such as Hawksnest and Cinnamon Bay are strung like pearls along the northern coastline. Life's pace moves mighty slow here— the whole island seems to have hung up a "Do Not Disturb" sign. St. Croix combines a rich history with modern pleasures. Christiansted, its capital, looks very much as it did 300 years ago, with its yellow-painted fort and arcaded promenades lining the waterfront. But it is also thoroughly up-to-date: Many of those old buildings now house duty-free shops and gourmet restaurants, and you'll enjoy coming home to your luxury hotel after a full day of explorations. St. Croix also packs in the most geographical diversity of the islands, with everything from cactus-strewn desert on its far eastern end to dense rain forest on the west. And exotic as the vistas are, you'll feel right at home, because the U.S. VI are an American territory. English is spoken, the currency is the dollar, you don't need a passport, and satellite dishes pick up all the big televised games from the United States.

Located about 18° north of the equator, the island group spreads out over 14,000 square miles of sparkling blue waters. Puerto Rico lies 40 miles to the east, the British Virgin Islands immediately to the west. St. Thomas and St. John are neighbors, less than three miles apart from each other across Pillsbury Sound; St. Croix is 35 miles to the south. While both St. Thomas and St. John have their north shores bathed by the

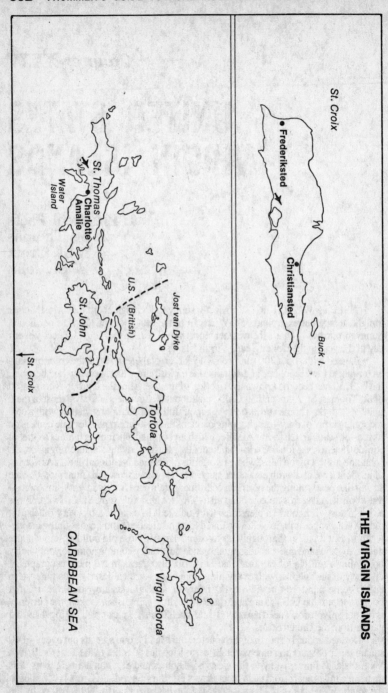

THE VIRGIN ISLANDS

St. Croix

● **Frederiksted**

● **Christiansted**

Buck I.

St. Thomas

Water
Island

● **Charlotte
Amalie**

St. John

U.S. (British)

Jost van Dyke

Tortola

Virgin Gorda

CARIBBEAN SEA

St. Croix

Atlantic, and south coasts lapped by the Caribbean Sea, St. Croix is completely sur-rounded by the Caribbean. It's easy to travel between the islands: St. Thomas and St. John are linked by a 20-minute ferry ride; while St. Croix is joined to its sister islands by both seaplane and regular air service.

Whether you approach the region by sea or air, you'll be amazed by the sheer number of mountainous, green islands you'll see looming out of the water—about 100 in all, between the U.S. and British Virgin Islands. The islands look exactly as you imagine Caribbean isles should, with glossy coconut palms, sugar-white beaches, and colorful flowers everywhere: white and pink oleander, orange flamboyant, scarlet poinsettias, and bougainvillea blossoms in magenta, crimson, and orange.

Although jungly vegetation covers most of the hillsides, you can still discern the jagged contours, testimony to the islands' fiery volcanic past. You'll wonder how they looked to Christopher Columbus, when he sailed through the channel after so many days at sea. "Very mountainous," he recorded in his 1493 diary, "And very green down to the sea. A delight to see." In appreciation of the islands' beauty and number, he named them Las Virgines, after the legendary followers of St. Ursula. Columbus didn't stay long—the resident Carib Indians gave him a fierce welcome—but he did christen St. Croix, St. Thomas, and St. John. For the next 400 years, possession of the islands seesawed between the great European powers—Spain, the Knights of Malta, France, England, Holland, and Denmark. Because of the lack of any strong govern-ment, piracy flourished during the late 16th and early 17th century. The islands' many bays and secret coves became hiding places for the likes of Captain Kidd and Edward Teach, better known as Blackbeard. (Blackbeard clearly was one of the first to realize the importance of public image. To terrify his victims, he braided his chest-length beard with colored ribbons and stuck lighted matches in his hair so that he would look truly fiend-like.) Finally the Danes established domination and a modicum of control, taking over St. Thomas (1672) and St. John (1683), and finally buying St. Croix from the French in 1733. The diligent Danes set about organizing the islands for profit. To encourage trade, St. Thomas became a free port in 1724, while St. John and St. Croix devoted themselves to sugarcane cultivation. For nearly 100 years, sugarcane ruled as king in what was called the Danish West Indies. But cane cultivation was only profit-able when dependent on the cruelties and horrors of slavery. After the abolition of slavery in 1848, the sugar industry dwindled. In 1917, the Danes sold the islands to the United States for the then-exorbitant sum of $25 million, and the stars and stripes began flying over Government House and other public buildings. Today, the United States Virgin Islands are an American territory, presided over by an elected governor and legislature, and residents are U.S. citizens (although they cannot vote in federal elections).

The best thing about a honeymoon in the U.S. VI is the wide range of possibilities open to you. If you enjoy sports, you'll want to take advantage of the world-class con-ditions for scuba diving, snorkeling, and fishing. In particular, consistent trade winds and deep cruising waters make the U.S. VI and neighboring B.V.I. a spectacular pleasure for sailors. You can also play tennis, golf on championship courses, saddle up for a ride through the rain forest or along the shore, or perhaps take up Windsurfing or waterskiing. Meanwhile, lazy bodies can bronze themselves on a bevy of beaches, many of which—such as Magens Bay on St. Thomas, Trunk Bay on St. John, and Buck Island near St. Croix—show up on various "Most Beautiful in the World" lists. In fact, relaxation is so much a way of life hereabouts, Virgin Islanders have a special expression to describe it—"just limin'," they say. Count on doing plenty of "limin' " on your honeymoon.

1. Practical Facts

GETTING THERE: No passports are required for U.S. or Canadian citizens. However, you will need proof of citizenship, such as an original birth certificate or notarized copy, or a voter's registration card, for re-entry into the U.S. mainland.

Frequent flights from throughout the United States make it easy to reach paradise. In addition, the islands are one of the most popular Caribbean ports of call for cruise ships.

By Air

To St. Thomas: **American, Pan Am, Eastern,** and **Midway** fly nonstop from New York. **Delta, TWA,** American Airlines, Pan American, and Eastern connect to St. Thomas via San Juan. Midway flies from Chicago.

To St. Croix: American, Pan Am, Eastern Airlines, and Midway all serve the island, first stopping in St. Thomas.

To St. John: You must fly to St. Thomas, then take the **Virgin Islands Seaplane Shuttle** or the **Red Hook ferry** (see details which follow) to St. John. Some of the St. John hotels run private ferry shuttles for their guests.

By Ship

Charlotte Amalie in St. Thomas is the number one port in the U.S. VI. Over 700,000 cruise passengers a year visit this sparkling blue harbor surrounded by steep green hillsides, and they rate it as their favorite port of call. Among the lines calling at St. Thomas are **Carnival, Commodore, Costa, Chandris, Cunard, Holland America, Home Lines, Norwegian Caribbean, Ocean, Princess, Regency, Royal, Royal Caribbean, Royal Viking, Sitmar,** and **Sun Lines.** St. Croix has become increasingly popular, with ships putting in either at Christansted or Frederiksted. No large ships call at St. John, only the ultrayachts, such as the *Sea Goddess*.

INTERISLAND TRAVEL: Because each of the three U.S. Virgins has such a different personality, it's fun to island hop during your honeymoon. Convenient seaplane and ferry service makes it convenient, too.

By Seaplane

The **Virgin Islands Seaplane Shuttle** (affectionately known to area residents as "The Goose"), links St. Thomas, St. Croix, St. John, Tortola (British Virgin Islands), and San Juan (Puerto Rico). The flight is really nifty, and you get great views of the islands from the air. It costs $32 one way and $64 round trip. For reservations and information, see your travel agent or call 809/773-1776 or toll free 800/524-2050.

By Ferry

The Virgin Islands ferries provide another scenic, convenient way to do island sightseeing. The St. Thomas–St. John ferry runs between Red Hook, St. Thomas, and Cruz Bay, St. John every hour between 7 a.m. and 10 p.m.; fare is $2 per person each way for the 20-minute ride. There is also ferry service between the U.S. and British Virgin Islands: from St. Thomas to Tortola, Virgin Gorda, and Jost Van Dyke; and from St. John to Tortola. For information about fares and schedules, call the **Native Son** (tel. 809/774-8685) or **Bomba Charger** ferries (tel. 774-7920). Note: Proof of citizenship is required to enter the B.V.I.

GETTING AROUND: Good taxi service and widely available rental cars make it easy to get around all three islands.

By Taxi

Taxis are available on all three islands. Rates are fixed by law and charged per person, based on the number of people in the cab. Rates are quite reasonable: From the St. Thomas airport to Charlotte Amalie will be $4 per person; from the airport to the

Red Hook ferry to St. John, about $9.50 per person. The most expensive taxi ride from the airport to a hotel on St. Thomas will be about $12 per couple. There will be an extra charge of 75¢ for each suitcase. Drivers are required to carry copies of the designated taxi rates, so ask to see it if you have any questions. Tipping is not required, though you might want to give something extra if you have received special service. Although tariffs are inexpensive, taxi fares really start to add up if you will be taking several a day. If you plan on bopping around a lot, rent a car. On St. John, taxi service gets a bit spotty after 9 p.m. If you are arriving on the island from the mainland later than that, make sure you make arrangements with your hotel for a pickup from the ferry dock.

By Rental Car

The major car-rental agencies are represented on St. Thomas and St. Croix, with desks right at the airport. For a subcompact car, for example, **Avis Rent-A-Car** charges $46 per day and $210 per week (unlimited mileage; two-days advance reservation required). Avis also rents Jeeps, as do several local companies, including **Caribbean,** in St. Thomas (tel. 774-6811, 776-7811, or toll free 800/524-2041), and **Caribbean Jeep & Car Rental** in St. Croix (tel. 773-4399). On St. John, Jeeps are definitely the way to go on the steep, winding roads. Contact **St. John Car Rental** (tel. 776-6103). On all three islands, Jeep rentals run about $55 per day. In order to rent a car or Jeep, you *must* have your driver's license.

Remember—*driving is on the left,* a holdover from the Danish colonial days. Steering wheels will also be on the left, the same as on the Mainland.

LANGUAGE AND MONEY: The U.S. dollar is the official currency, and English is the language, sometimes warmed and flavored with a West Indian lilt. You might hear a bit of "talkin' broad"—using Creole dialect, which mixes in Portuguese, French, Dutch, English, and African words, reflecting the varied heritages that have influenced these islands.

GETTING ALONG: The Virgin Islanders are extremely polite, reserved people. A simple "good day" is a must when dealing with them, rather than starting right in with a question. In return you will be treated with courtesy.

WEATHER: With such a blessedly perfect climate, you almost wonder why they bother with a daily weather report. The U.S. VI has sunny, warm weather year-round. Summer temperatures average about 82°, winters, around 77°—just a 5° difference. Thanks to the cooling trade winds, the islands remain comfortable during the summer. May and September to December tend to get the most rain, but even then, most precipitation tends to fall in passing showers. Days without any sunshine are rare.

CLOTHING: No matter which island you visit, casual is the byword. Pretty much anything goes, except for bathing suits in town or in shops. Some fancy restaurants require jackets and ties for gentlemen in the winter season (usually jackets only in summer), but such guidelines are rare. You will be most comfortable in lightweight cotton clothing. Because of the balmy climate, you probably won't even need a cotton sweater or sweatshirt, even at night.

TIME: The U.S. VI remains on Atlantic Standard Time all year. In winter, when it is noon in New York, it is 1 p.m. in the U.S. VI. In summer, when the mainland observes Daylight Savings Time, the hour is the same in east coast cities as it is in the U.S. VI.

TELEPHONES: You can dial the U.S. VI direct from the mainland; the area code is

809. Once in the islands, the phone system functions pretty much as it does back on the mainland. Coin-operated pay phones are everywhere; local calls cost 25¢ for the first five minutes.

POSTAGE: Once again, you're in familiar territory. The islands are part of the U.S. postal system and use the same rates and stamps as the rest of the country.

SHOPPING: America's paradise is also a shopper's paradise. From the time of the Danes, the islands, and most notably St. Thomas, have been duty-free ports. Not only do the U.S. VI offer low prices and a wide selection, Americans also get double the U.S. Customs exemption permitted from other Caribbean islands—$1,600 per couple. For details, see the section on U.S. Customs, which follows.

Charlotte Amalie on St. Thomas has the widest selection and the most shops, which line Main Street and the quaint alleyways leading to the harbor, as well as at **Havensight Mall,** at the West Indian cruise ship dock. Many of the best-known stores, such as Little Switzerland and Colombian Emeralds, have branches both in St. Thomas and St. Croix. Meanwhile, St. John is known for island-made fashions, handcrafts, and gifts. When shopping, look for stores that belong to the V.I. Retailer's Association: Members display the logo, which depicts a gift-wrapped box. Member stores agree to offer the highest quality goods at the lowest possible price, and stand behind their merchandise. In the islands, most stores are open 9 a.m. to 5 p.m., Monday through Saturday. Hotel boutiques often close later. In St. Thomas, the Havensight Mall stores stay open until 9 p.m. on Fridays.

Here's a general introduction to the shopping bargains you can find in the U.S. VI. For details about where to shop, see the write-ups on each of the islands.

China, porcelain, and crystal. Fill out your china and crystal patterns, at prices about 40% to 60% lower than back home. You'll find all the most prestigious lines, including Wedgwood, Royal Worcester, and Villeroy & Boch china; as well as crystal from Waterford, Lalique, Baccarat, and Orreförs. Porcelain figurines by Lladró, Goebel-Hummel, and Royal Copenhagen are also good value. Note: Even if a store carries a certain line, it may not stock your particular pattern. To find out who carries what, contact: In St. Thomas / St. John: **Virgin Islands Retailers Association,** P.O. Box 1295, St. Thomas, USVI 00801 (tel. 809/774-7305). In St. Croix: **St. Croix Visitors Bureau,** P.O. Box 4538, Christiansted, USVI 00820 (tel. 809/773-0495). You might also want to check out a copy of *A Shopper's Guide to the Caribbean* (Prentice Hall Press, New York).

Table linens. Set your table with fine linens. Take your choice—stores carry everything from delicate laces and hand-embroideries to easy-care drip-dries.

Jewelry and watches. Savings can run up to 50% on classic timepieces from Rolex, Movado, Patek Philippe, Piaget, Concord, and other famous lines; also gold chains, jewelry, and unset gemstones.

Leather goods. Gucci, Fendi, Bottega Veneta, and Louis Vuitton all have outlets in St. Thomas, with savings of about 30%.

Perfume and cosmetics. Save from 20% to 30% on your favorite brands, such as Yves Saint Laurent's Opium and Paris, Chanel No. 5, Oscar de la Renta, and Nina Ricci L'air du temps. Stock up on your favorite cosmetics too—prices are about 20% lower.

Liquor, wines, and liqueurs. These are the best value of all, often sold at up to 60% off the U.S. mainland prices. You'll get especially good values on Scotch whiskey and English gin, Russian vodkas, and imported liqueurs. In addition, the U.S. Customs allowance is particularly generous. Each of you can bring home, duty free, one gallon of liquor, plus a sixth bottle, provided that the latter is made in the U.S. VI, such as the justly celebrated Virgin Islands rums. So you don't have to lug the bottles around with you, the various retailers can deliver your purchases to your airplane or cruise ship, upon your departure. (Note: Check your home state about excise taxes.)

Clothing. From Courrèges and Guy La Roche to Benetton, you can update your wardrobe in style. You'll find very good selections of bathing suits and casual cotton clothing—an especially good bet if you had trouble finding these items back home before your honeymoon.

Cameras and accessories. All the big-name brands are here: Nikon, Vivitar, Canon, Minolta. Stores also stock binoculars, video cameras, stereo components, calculators, etc. On all these items, you should shop very carefully: Sometimes, prices are comparable to what you would pay at a discount outlet back home. Also make sure that your purchases are covered by a guarantee and that you can get them serviced on the mainland.

Art and antiques. Original art and antiques over 100 years old are exempt from Customs duty. Make sure you get a certificate of authenticity at the time of purchase.

Made in the U.S. VI. For a very special memento of your honeymoon, bring home items made in the islands. In addition, locally made merchandise is duty free (ask for a certificate of origin if your purchases exceed $25). Things you might want to bring home include leather sandals, silk-screened or batik fashions, shell jewelry, straw hats and bags, and wood carvings. Another pleasing souvenir—tropical scents for him and her made from local flowers and spices. To help you re-create some of your favorite island recipes, browse through the good selection of local cookbooks. You can also pick up island-made seasonings, spices, and teas.

ABOUT U.S. CUSTOMS: Because the Virgin Islands are part of the United States, returning citizens have certain privileges. As mentioned previously, each of you has a duty-free allowance of $800 worth of goods—which translates as $1,600 per couple (you can "pool" your allowance). If you buy more, you can each bring back an additional $1,000 worth of merchandise, and pay a flat 5% duty on its value. Over that amount, you will pay duty as assessed by U.S. Customs. If you want to send gifts to friends and family back home, you can mail presents (valued at $100 per recipient per day). This is over and above your duty-free allowance.

Another convenience: When returning home to most U.S. states, you clear Customs in the islands before boarding your plane.

ABOUT ACCOMMODATIONS: The U.S. VI has the largest lineup of hotels in the Caribbean, and whatever kind of accommodations you crave, you're sure to find something to suit: from luxury suites to a bare tent site with ocean view, with lots of choices in between, and at all price ranges. High season generally runs from December 15 to April 15; low-season rates will be about 20% to 50% lower. Rates do not include the 7½% government tax, which will be added to your bill.

If you want to do something different—and very romantic—on your honeymoon, how about chartering a yacht? The U.S. and neighboring British Virgin Islands offer some of the premier cruising waters in the world, and St. Thomas is the home port for one of the world's largest sailing fleets. You don't even have to know an anchor from a mizzenmast. You can charter a crewed yacht, with a captain and crew who do everything for you, from navigating through straits to giving snorkeling lessons or whipping up some poached grouper with tarragon sauce. Rates are comparable to those of a luxury resort. For information about chartering a yacht in the U.S. VI, contact: **Virgin Islands Charteryacht League,** Homeport, St. Thomas, U.S.VI. 08802 (tel. toll free 800/524-2061); **Le Boat, Inc.,** P.O. Box E, Maywood, NJ 07607 (tel. 201/342-1838 in NJ or toll free 800/922-0291 nationwide); **Charter Concepts,** 423 Shoreline Village Dr., Suite C, Long Beach, CA 90802, (tel. 213/491-1999; or toll free 800/521-1678 nationwide; 800/221-2793 in CA); **Lynn Jachney Charters,** P.O. Box 302, Marblehead, MA 01945 (tel. 617/639-0787 or toll free 800/223-2050); **The Moorings, Ltd.,** 1305 U.S. 19 South, Suite 402, Clearwater, FL 33546 (tel. 813/535-1446 or toll free 800/535-7289 outside of FL); **Nicholson Yacht Charters,** 9 Chauncy St., Cambridge, MA 02138 (tel. 617/661-8174 or toll free 800/662-6066); **Ocean Escapes,** P.O. Box 6097, Newburyport, MA 01950 (tel. 617/465-7116 or toll free 800/227-8633 outside of MA). **Virgin Islands Water Safaris,** Yacht Haven Marina, Long Bay Road, St. Thomas, USVI 00802 (tel. 809/776-5950 or toll free 800/524-7676); **Russell Yacht Charters,** 2750 Black Rock Turnpike, Suite 175, Fairfield, CT 06430 (tel. 203/372-6633).

DINING OUT: From French haute cuisine to mama mia's veal scaloppine or local lobster, you'll find most nationalities represented in the U.S. VI's fine restaurants. The fresh catch of the day is usually excellent, especially yellowtail snapper and dolphin (the fish, not the mammal). You'll probably soon become addicted to the delicious Caribbean lobster (sometimes called langoustine), and conch, served in fritters, salads, and chowders. Although it would seem logical that since you are on an island, the fish will always be fresh, that is not always the case. Ask before you order.

Also try some of the Virgin Islands' West Indian–style dishes, which are spicy, but not hot. Popular main courses are curries (especially goat or lamb) or garlic chicken. These might be accompanied by fungi (little dumplings made from cornmeal). You'll also want to try callaloo soup, a stick-to-your-ribs concoction with ham, crab, and greens. More West Indian treats are the patés (pronounced "patties"), spicy little meat pies. Wash it all down with mauby, brewed from tree bark (believe us, it tastes great), or soursop juice, a smooth, sweet-tart drink made from the delicious fruit.

Speaking of fruits, you'll want to sample whatever the islands have in season. In addition to the aforementioned soursop, try star apples, fig bananas, guava, and papayas. Perhaps the best reason on earth for June brides—and June honeymoons—are mangoes, which are in peak season then.

HOW TO GET MARRIED IN THE U.S. VI: If you've always fantasized about having your wedding in a tropical paradise, here's your chance. You can get married in a church or courthouse, or have an outdoor ceremony at the beach or in a beautiful garden. Many Virgin Islands hotels can help you make all the details, including arranging for flowers, a photographer, etc.

1. No blood tests or physical examinations are necessary.
2. Obtain an "Application for Marriage" form from the Territorial Court of the Virgin Islands. For St. Thomas and St. John: P.O. Box 70, Charlotte Amalie, St. Thomas, USVI 00801, Attention: Viola E. Smith, Clerk of the Court. For St. Croix: P.O. Box 9000, Kingshill, St. Croix, USVI 00850, Attention: Family Division.
3. Mail the $25 license fee, along with the completed form, which must be notarized (include a copy of the county clerk's certificate verifying that the commission of the notary public has not expired), back to the territorial court.
4. There is an eight-day waiting period before the marriage license can be issued; during this time, the application is posted for public inspection. (This waiting period can be waived; inquire in advance.)
5. If you want to be married by a judge of the territorial court, a date and time will be scheduled by the court office; fee is $50. If you prefer a religious ceremony, write directly to the officiant.

FOR FURTHER INFORMATION: Contact: **Virgin Islands Department of Commerce,** P.O. Box 6400, Charlotte Amalie, USVI 00801 (tel. 809/774-8784) or the

Virgin Islands Tourist Information Office. In Chicago: 343 S. Dearborn St., Suite 1008, Chicago, IL 60640 (tel. 312/461-0180). In Miami: 7270 N.W. (12th St., Suite 620, Miami, FL 33126 (tel. 305/591-2070). In New York: 1270 Avenue of the Americas, New York, NY 10020 (tel. 212/582-4520). In Los Angeles: 3450 Wilshire Blvd., Los Angeles, CA 90010 (tel. 213/739-0138). In Washington, D.C.: 1667 K St., N.W., Suite 270, Washington, DC 20006 (tel. 202/293-3707).

2. St. Thomas

Neat white houses with bright red roofs step-placed on the verdant hillsides. A broad blue harbor where million-dollar yachts bob at anchor, awaiting the whims of pleasure-seekers. A street where all that glitters in shop windows is real gold—bejeweled treasures gathered from the four corners of the globe. Tranquil turquoise bays, long white beaches, the flashing lights of a disco, insinuatingly sensuous steelband rhythms—these are the sights and sounds that come to mind when you mention, "St. Thomas."

St. Thomas is the most cosmopolitan of the Virgin Islands, as known for its nightlife and duty-free shopping as it is for its beautiful beaches. The second-largest island in the group, it measures 13 miles long and 3 miles wide. Most of the action centers on Charlotte Amalie, the capital of the U.S. VI, located practically in the middle of the island's south shore. Charlotte Amalie is, deservedly, one of the most photographed harbors in the world, a sapphire gem set in the midst of emerald-green hills. Just off the harbor, quaint alleyways are lined with elegant, duty-free boutiques selling luxury goods from all over the world. Many of these shops are located in thick-walled, 300-year-old warehouses, where merchants once stored rum and molasses for trade—and pirates hid their ill-gotten booty. Reflecting the town's Danish origins, many streets still have Danish names, such as Kongen's Gade and Dronningens Gade—better known as Main Street.

Intersperse your shopping forays with visits to Charlotte Amalie's historic sights. Founded in 1691 and named for a Danish queen, the town has many beautifully restored buildings that will whisk you back in time. Stop by Fort Christian, the oldest structure in St. Thomas, dating back to the late 17th century. The fort is now a museum of Virgin Islands' history. (Open Monday through Saturday, 8 a.m. to 5 p.m.; admission is free.) Visit Government House, a typical 19th-century West Indian structure. Today, it is the official residence of the governor, but the second-floor reception room is open Monday through Friday, 8 a.m. to noon, and 1 p.m. to 5 p.m.; admission is free (tel. 774-0001). Take each others photographs on the 99 Steps, which clamber up Government Hill to Lille Tarne Gade. Nearby, view Blackbeard's Tower, where the cut-throat pirate supposedly kept watch for treasure galleons to plunder (today it is part of a hotel and restaurant). If you are fascinated by the exploits of Sir Francis Drake, climb aboard the replica of his *Golden Hinde*, moored down at the waterfront. The ship serves as a nautical museum. Open Monday through Saturday, 9 a.m. to 5:30 p.m.; guided tours are $5.

Sightseeing around the rest of St. Thomas is covered under "Romantic Interludes." Now, let's turn our attentions to one of St. Thomas' most renowned attractions: the duty-free bargains.

SHOPPING: St. Thomas offers some of the biggest shopping values in the Caribbean. Many of the best-known stores have branches both in town (along Main Street, the alleyways, and the waterfront); as well as at the Havensight Mall complex at the West Indian dock. Charlotte Amalie stores are open 9 a.m. to 5 p.m., Monday through Saturday; the Havensight shops also stay open late and on Sundays if cruise ships are in town. To plan your shopping expeditions, pick up a free copy of *St. Thomas This*

Week, which has the most complete, up-to-date listing of stores and the merchandise they carry. Here's a rundown on some of the largest shops and their specialties. All stores are in town, unless otherwise indicated.

Animal Crackers Fun Factory: For the child in us all, delightful stuffed monkeys that jabber and roll up their tails, bright cotton parrots, teddy bears dressed up in three-piece suits, pinafores, doctors' uniforms, and other delights (Royal Dane Mall in town).

Benetton: All the latest fashion-right casual clothing from the popular Italian-based chain, and all at duty-free prices. Two different stores.

Bookchand's Linen Center: For embroidered sheets, pillowcases, and tableclothes.

Bookchand's: Cameras and accessories, including lines by Minolta, Canon, Nikon.

Cardow Jewelers: The treasure chests of Blackbeard or Captain Kidd could not have glittered more brightly than the display cases of this jewelry store, offering adornments to suit all budgets. There's a special, 100-foot-long chain bar, featuring 14k and 18k gold chains.

Caribbean Marketplace (Havensight Mall): Wonderful selection of "Made-in-the-U.S. VI" products that will help you bring the sunshine home: Caribbee Hot Sauce, guava jelly, papaya chutney, Virgin Islands cookbooks, and two mixes you might find handy: Arawak Love Potion and the West Indian Hangover Cure—purported to bring peace to mind and body.

Cartier (Les must de Cartier): A boutique carrying their most popular items: the watches, lighters, pens, wallets, and jewelry.

Colombian Emeralds: Both uncut and set emeralds and other gemstones. Note: unset emeralds enter the U.S. duty free.

Down Island Traders: For island-made items such as jellies, candies, seasonings, and teas.

The English Shop: Fine tableware from all over the world: Spode, Wedgwood, Limoges, Minton, and Noritake china; Swarovski, Gorham, and Stuart crystal; figurines by Lladró, Bing & Grøndahl, Belleek; and much more.

Gucci: In their own boutique on the waterfront near the entrance to Riise's Alley, this outlet carries one of the most comprehensive Gucci collections in the Caribbean.

The Leather Shop: Fine goods from the best manufacturers, including Fendi and Bottega Veneta. Selection covers handbags, wallets, attaché cases, and more.

Linen House: Specializing in decorative tablecloths, place mats, and hand-embroidered goods in all styles and colors.

Lion in the Sun: High-fashion clothes for men and women from Kenzo, Yamamoto, Saint Laurent Rive Gauche, Sonia Rykiel.

Little Switzerland: For jewelry, watches, and crystal, including watches by Rolex, Baume & Mercier, and Concord; Waterford, Lalique, and Baccarat crystal; china from Wedgwood, Aynsley, Royal Worcester, and Villeroy & Boch; and Lladró and Goebel-Hummel figurines. They have four shops, including one devoted to the Rosenthal Studio line. (For information, call toll free 800/524-2010.)

Purse Strings: Excellent selection of handbags, wallets, and other items, including eel-skin accessories.

Purse Strings Boutique: Specializes in one-of-a-kind accessories: belts, jewelry, shoes, and sweaters.

A.H. Riise: In their several different stores, they carry watches (Patek Philippe, Ebel, Concord, Heuer, and Swatch), original art, china and crystal (Royal Copenhagn, Herend, Wedgwood, Lalique, Baccarat, Orrefōrs, jewelry, flatware, perfumes, and cosmetics. Also an excellent liquor store.

Royal Caribbean: For cameras and accessories from Yashica, Vivitar, Canon, and others.

Scandinavian Center: Contemporary designs from Georg Jensen, Royal Copenhagen, Bing & Grøndahl, as well as sterling silver jewelry.

The Silver Vault: A wide selection of sterling silver jewelry, from designer pieces to West Indian bangles.

H. Stern: The internationally known jeweler has five outlets in St. Thomas, selling spectacular jewelry, and fine watches from Concord, Corum, and Movado.

Sweet Passion: Carries one-of-a-kind antique pieces (in Royal Dane Mall in town).

Mr. Tablecloth: Fine linens, lace dresser scarfs, and place mats.

Towel & Sun: Great selection of knock your socks off beach towels.

Tropicana Perfume Shoppes: Perfume and cosmetics—and nothing but—including Opium, Shalimar, Ralph Lauren, Anais Anais.

Louis Vuitton: This is the only Vuitton shop in the Caribbean, and they carry the entire line from France: handbags, luggage, and accessories.

ROMANTIC INTERLUDES: With its beautiful beaches and crystal-clear waters, St. Thomas is indeed a tropical paradise.

Red-roof Charlotte Amalie is only part of the St. Thomas experience. The sightseeing jaunt outlined below is based on renting a car and doing it yourselves; there are also several tour companies that can take you around (ask at your hotel; rates run about $16.50 per person).

How about starting off with a look at St. Thomas—underwater? You won't even get wet at **Coral World,** a unique underwater observation tower that descends 15 feet under the ocean surface. Through the huge glass windows, you can view the colorful coral reef and the abundant fish. Try to time your visit for the daily fish feeding (including sharks) at 11 a.m. Open daily from 9 a.m. to 6 p.m.; admission is $9 per person.

You'll definitely want to see—and swim at—Magens Bay, which usually appears on the "Most Beautiful in the World" list of beach connoisseurs. The broad, U-shaped harbor is edged by a mile of sugar-white sand. With its full facilities—food, beverages, and water-sports equipment rentals—Magens is highly popular, and gets a bit crowded. If you honeymooners want to escape from the world a bit, just stroll on down to the far ends. There's a small admission charge: 50¢ per car, plus 50¢ a person. (It's located off of Route 35 on the north shore.)

To get a bird's-eye view of where you've just been, take Rte. 40 to **Drake's Seat,** where Sir Francis himself is supposed to have kept watch for Spanish galleons. The view of Magens Bay, and the rugged outlines of about 100 U.S. and British Virgin Islands in the distance, is truly breathtaking.

If you want to linger over the splendid vistas, head over to Mountain Top, off Rte. 33. They are known for their high-octane banana daquiries, and also have a small gift boutique.

Your sense of wanderlust will undoubtedly get piqued by the views of all these lovely deserted islands that rise out of the blue Caribbean. How about getting a closer look—on a **day sail** that takes you out to a deserted island where you can swim and snorkel, then enjoy a picnic lunch? Many different charters are available. **Sea Adventures** at Frenchman's Reef Hotel (tel. 774-9652) offers a deluxe sail for $65 per person, which includes lunch, snacks, plus free snorkeling equipment and instruction. Snorkel sites include the wreck of the *Cartanser Sr.*, a 191-foot World War I freighter. Other day trips include the yacht *My Way*, which cruises to uninhabited Little Hans Lollick island. It costs $60 per person, which includes all snorkeling equipment and instruction, lunch and all-day bar, and free use of an underwater camera (tel. 776-9547).

What two newlyweds could resist a splendid stretch of white coral sands named **Honeymoon?** This excursion is a bit off the beaten path, but very simple to accomplish from Charlotte Amalie. Honeymoon Beach is located on the western side of Water

Island, in the middle of Charlotte Amalie Harbor. Water Island has some private residences and is linked to Charlotte Amalie by a ferry that departs from Sub Base, just west of Charlotte Amalie. The ferry runs every half hour; 7 a.m. to midnight from St. Thomas, 7:30 a.m. to 11:30 p.m. from Water Island. The fare is $3.85 per person. With its palm trees and beach bar, Honeymoon makes a great place to while away a day. Since the beach faces west, it provides ringside views of the sunset.

HONEYMOON HOTELS AND HIDEAWAYS: Although St. Thomas has one of
the widest selections of hotels in the Caribbean, you'll be pleasantly surprised to find that there is no one big "strip" of high-rise hotels. In fact, with only one exception, there are no high rises at all. Hotels are found all around the island, both in town (Charlotte Amalie), and along the north and east coasts. In St. Thomas, a beachfront hotel really is right on the beach—and usually, that beach is exclusive (at most, two hotels might share a stretch of sand). Many properties are located on quiet coves. Remember —no spot on St. Thomas is more than a half-hour's drive from Charlotte Amalie. Whichever hotel you choose, you'll be near to the fine shops and restaurants in town.

High season runs approximately December 15 to April 15; summer season rates can be up to 50% lower. Prices quoted here reflect the difference between low and high season rates.

Moderately Expensive
Even in an island known for magnificent vistas, you won't quite believe the views you'll see from your private balcony at **Point Pleasant Resort,** Estate Smith Bay, St. Thomas, USVI 00802 (tel. 809/775-7200; reservations: toll free 800/524-2300 or 800/645-5306): The almost blindingly blue waters of Pillsbury Sound, the Windward Passage, and Sir Francis Drake Channel, with emerald-green isles such as Thatch Cay, Tortola, Jost Van Dyke, St. John, and dozens of others dotting the sea all the way to the horizon. Set on a steep hillside on Water Bay, on St. Thomas' northeastern shore, Point Pleasant Resort is a very special place run by a very special woman, Ruth Pfanner. She and her late husband Gunther envisioned a resort that would do justice to the spectacular 15-acre locale. They succeeded brilliantly. Nature paths wind down the cliffside past serrated boulders that date back to the island's earliest formation, bright orange hibiscus blossoms where hummingbirds dart and hover, and tall agave cactus.

Accommodations are set in white buildings with cedar-shingled roofs, angled into the cliffs to take maximum advantage of the dazzling views. Rooms have quarry-tile floors, rattan furnishings, sisal area rugs, tropical flower-print fabrics, and all have kitchenettes and large private balconies with water views. The studios are slightly larger than the efficiency units, and have a separate bedroom area screened off by louvred doors. Although rooms have air conditioning, you'll probably prefer to rely on the trade winds and ceiling fans, with the soothing tempo of the waves to lull you to sleep. If you'd rather not walk down (or more probably, back up) the rather steep paths, a jitney shuttles guests around the property. Point Pleasant has three freshwater pools and a small sand beach tucked amid boulders; you can also stroll over to neighboring Pineapple Beach and Coki Point. Tennis, Sunfish, snorkeling equipment, Windsurfers, and an introductory scuba lesson are all complimentary for guests. Point Pleasant gives guests free use of a car for four hours daily—just sign up on the sheet, and you've got your wheels for exploring the island. There's plenty going on right at the resort, too, with excellent dining at the Agave Terrace restaurant, overlooking the water, and different events daily, from a manager's cocktail party or a calypso steel band. Honeymoon package: Eight days / seven nights (EP): $1,218 to $1,642 for an efficiency apartment. Includes airport transfers, champagne and fresh flowers in the room, full-day sail to a neighboring island including lunch. MAP available for $75 per couple per day.

Bolongo Bay Beach and Tennis Club, P.O. Box 7337, St. Thomas, USVI 00801 (tel. 809/775-1800; reservations: toll free 800/524-4746). A beautiful, secluded bay . . . the intimacy of a small resort . . . sports facilities galore. . . . That's what you'll find at Bolongo Bay, a very unique honeymoon retreat just a ten-minute drive from Charlotte Amalie. Dick and Joyce Doumeng, the owner / managers, are warm and caring hosts, and their enthusiasm and attentiveness pervade the entire operation. The whole resort positively radiates relaxation and good times, and even first-time guests feel like long-lost friends from the moment they check in. You'll soon feel right at home, waving at Debbie, the resident manager, or asking Mr. Green, the head bartender, to whip you up one of his mysterious tropical concoctions, such as a Blue Caribbean. The bay itself is lovely, sheltered by a coral reef that makes for excellent snorkeling (gear and instruction are free). Sports lovers will also want to take advantage of the free Sunfish sailboats and lessons, four tennis courts (two of which are lighted), plus a day sail aboard the club yacht. Best of all, if you've ever wanted to learn how to scuba dive, now's your chance—a free scuba lesson is included, and Bolongo Bay's St. Thomas Diving Club is recognized as one of the best scuba operations in the U.S. VI. Every day, you can participate in different guest activities. For dining, there's the delightful open-air Sea Shells Restaurant.

Your room is a perfect honeymoon haven. The two-story white buildings are right on the beach: All you have to do is scamper down the stairs (from upstairs), or hop off the balcony (downstairs), and you can go for that refreshing morning dip. All rooms have beachfront views, private balconies, 22-channel color TV, telephones, wet bars and kitchenettes, air conditioning and ceiling fans. The resort has recently added 45 new rooms, and the 32 previous rooms have all been completely refurbished, so all the accommodations have a spanking-new feel. All these "pluses" add up to the reasons why Bolongo is so popular with honeymooners. Honeymoon package: Eight days / seven nights (some meals): $1,248 to $1,524 for a superior efficiency room. Includes airport transfers, welcoming rum cocktail, flowers and champagne in your room, continental breakfast daily, and three dinners (including one with a bottle of wine).

"New Adventures Club," Bolongo Bay Beach and Tennis Club, P.O. Box 7337, St. Thomas, USVI 00801 (tel. 809/775-1800; reservations: toll free 800/524-4746). If you've been yearning for "something different" for your honeymoon, how about some romance on the high seas? Dick and Joyce Doumeng of Bolongo Bay resort have put together a unique package that combines a stateroom on a luxury yacht, with use of all the facilities of Bolongo Bay Beach and Tennis Club. The yacht is the *Mohawk II,* which sleeps just eight couples, each in private, air-conditioned staterooms. For five days, the *Mohawk* is based at Bolongo Bay, making day trips to attractions such as Buck Island and Magens Bay. On land, you're able to enjoy Bolongo's tennis courts and restaurants, and explore St. Thomas itself. Then the *Mohawk* cruises to the British Virgin Islands, with calls scheduled at Tortola and the famous Baths on Virgin Gorda. Honeymoon package: None. Rates: Eight days / seven nights (some meals): $935 to $1,166 per couple. Includes yacht accommodations, continental breakfast daily, three lunches, three cocktail parties, St. Thomas island tour, admission to Coral World, St. John island tour, Sunday brunch, one lobster dinner, barbecue dinner, West Indian buffet dinner, and a scuba resort course. Air fare and a $116 per couple charge for gratuities and B.V.I. port taxes are extra. Package runs Monday through Monday.

Frenchman's Reef Beach Resort, M.P.O. 7100, Charlotte Amalie, St. Thomas, USVI 00801 (tel. 809/776-8500; reservations: toll free 800/524-2000). Set spectacularly on a promontory that guards the entrance to Charlotte Amalie harbor, Frenchman's Reef is top choice for couples who want the luxury and amenities of a self-contained resort. Right on the property, you'll find 6 excellent restaurants, 24 shops in an air-conditioned mall, 4 lighted tennis courts overlooking the beach, 2

Olympic-size swimming pools, and the largest water-sports and scuba-diving center on St. Thomas. The property fronts Morning Star Beach, a long, slim strand lapped by the Caribbean. Charlotte Amalie is only five minutes away by car; ten minutes by shuttle ferry that drops you right downtown. Frenchman's is the closest St. Thomas comes to having a big hotel, with 424 rooms. The main building is eight stories tall and built into the cliff. There are also 96 cushy units in the new, luxury Morning Star Beach Club villas. All are air-conditioned and come with a color TV. Room rates vary according to view: hillside, harbor, or ocean. If you can, opt for the Morning Star accommodations, which are located in five, two-story buildings right on the beach. Rooms are really BIG, and you'll enjoy the pampering touches, such as a concierge for personalized service, telephones in the bathroom, use of plush bathrobes, plus a complimentary wine-and-cheese welcome basket. All the facilities of the main resort are right on your doorstep. And, if you'd like to get married in the Virgin Islands, the social activities staff can help you with all the arrangements. Honeymoon package: Eight days / seven nights (EP): Low season: $1,342 to $1,639 for a room; $1,745 to $1,976 for the Morning Star Beach Club. High season: $1,572 to $2,034 for a room; $2,203 to $2,550 for the Morning Star Beach Club. Includes welcoming cocktails, tennis court use (unlimited for Morning Star accommodations), a moonlight cruise, champagne, his-and-hers T-shirts, round-trip airport transfers. MAP available for $45 per person per day.

Located on one of St. Thomas' prettiest palm-fringed coves, **Limetree Beach Hotel,** P.O. Box 7307, St. Thomas, USVI 00801 (tel. 809/776-4770; reservations: tel. 212/355-6605 or toll free 800/221-4588), offers honeymooners a secluded retreat —all just ten-minutes' drive from downtown. You'll have plenty of room to spread out, because the property encompasses 23 acres, right on the crystal-clear waters of Frenchman's Bay Cove. Set on gently rolling hillsides covered by well-tended greenery, the three-story villas surround the freshwater swimming pool and gardens. Although the locale is beautiful, what really makes couples return to Limetree to celebrate their anniversaries is the friendly, experienced staff, headed by general manager Dale Shakespeare. Furnishings are modern and tropical; all rooms were recently renovated and have a color TV; all are air-conditioned. You can practice your tennis strokes and join a weekly clinic with the resident pro (there's free tennis during the day, with a small charge for night play), or take a free snorkeling or intro scuba lesson. At night, you'll enjoy the entertainment—perhaps a West Indian steel band, limbo show, or other fun activities. You'll also want to make friends with Limetree's mascots: the giant iguanas who bask by the pool. They are very tame, and rather handsome, in a prehistorically sauve way, and they'll munch tidbits right out of your hand (hibiscus blossoms are a preferred delicacy). Honeymoon package: Eight days / seven nights (CP): $1,104 to $1,569 per couple for a superior room. Includes airport transfers, beachfront accommodations with upgrade if available, tropical flowers in room, welcoming rum cocktail, bottle of champagne at dinner one evening, manager's cocktail party, day trip to town, twilight cocktail cruise. Plus: either use of a car for a day with unlimited mileage, or a full-day sail to St. John, including snorkeling equipment and instruction.

Bluebeard's Castle, P.O. Box 7480, St. Thomas, USVI 00801 (tel. 809/774-1600; reservations: toll free 800/524-6599). There might—or might not—have been a swashbuckling pirate named Bluebeard. But whether or not he really existed, the legends of his exploits have left a romantic tradition—one that is continued by this top-notch hotel that commands a sweeping view of Charlotte Amalie and its harbor. The white-painted, red-roof buildings and the stone watch tower are a St. Thomas landmark, perched on their hillock just above the town. After a $6-million program of construction and renovation, the 20-acre resort complex is in tip-top condition. Both the studios and the one-bedroom suites have been beautifully redone with beige tile floors, rattan furnishings, and fabrics done in soft beiges and jungly floral prints. From the large balconies, you can behold the postcard-perfect view of Charlotte Amalie from many rooms. All rooms have air conditioning, ceiling fans, and color cable TV; most also have wet bars and a minifridge. For something really unique, consider the honeymoon room located in "The Castle"—the 300-year-old stone watchtower. Although the room is small, it is perfect for couples with a penchant for history and romance ($160 to $210 per couple per night).

Bluebeard's has two hard-surface tennis courts, both lighted for night play. There is a beautiful saltwater pool overlooking the town and cruise ships docked at the harbor. Because its in-town location precludes having a beach, the hotel runs a shuttle to Magens Bay twice a day. Bluebeard's has two fine restaurants; in particular, the Terrace Restaurant offers stellar views of the harbor. Honeymoon package: Eight days / seven nights (EP); $1,115 to $1,425 per couple for a standard room. Includes round-trip airport transfers, welcome cocktail, bottle of champagne at dinner one evening, souvenir Royal Copenhagen plaquette, his-and-hers terry velour robes, introductory scuba lesson, cocktail reception, $25 gift certificate redeemable at Bolero shop, a full-day tour with lunch to St. John. MAP available for $92 per couple per day.

The **Stouffer Grand Beach Resort,** P.O. Box 8267, St. Thomas, USVI 00801 (tel. 809/775-1510; reservations: toll free 800/HOTELS 1), has to rate as one of the most stunning hotels on St. Thomas. It sprawls out over gardens, hillsides, and beachfront on Pineapple Bay, on St. Thomas' northeastern shore. The low-rise hotel has a decided island flavor using natural wood shingles and West Indian–style windows and archways. As its centerpiece, the resort surrounds one of the most glamorously spectacular pools on the island, with free-form angles and fountains to add pizzazz. Rooms are decorated with equal panache, done in dusky rose and forest green, with the light touch of rattan furnishings. Amenities will vary: Some will have balconies, wet bars, or Jacuzzis. If you prefer the cooling trade winds to air conditioning, be aware that not all rooms have windows that open, so make sure you check things out in advance. For sports enthusiasts, the resort has a fitness center, lighted tennis courts, Sunfish, Windsurfers, and snorkeling gear, all free to honeymoon guests. Although the quality of service at this hotel had been a bit inconsistent, the property has just changed ownership and come under the Stouffer flag; increased attention to detail is promised. Honeymoon package: Eight days / seven nights (EP): $1,257 to $1,334 per couple for a standard room. Includes airport transfers, bottle of champagne, sunset cruise, manager's cocktail party.

The **Mahogany Run,** Box 7517, St. Thomas, USVI 00801 (tel. 809/775-5650 or 809/775-5000; reservations: tel. 212/683-1907 or toll free 800/221-4588 or 800/524-2038), set on 325 acres of rolling hillsides (including the famous 18-hole championship golf course), this hotel is the largest resort on the island. It is back in business under a new management company, after financial problems caused the brief closing of the resort in the fall of 1986. You'll enjoy complete privacy and spaciousness here, because all the units are lavishly appointed condominium apartments. Nestled into the contours of the rolling hills, the low, white, stucco buildings with shingled roofs overlook the golf course, hillsides, or ocean. Since all the apartments are condominiums, they are individually decorated and have fully equipped kitchens. The bathrooms are very special, filled with plants and huge plate-glass windows overlooking the sea (nobody can see in—nobody's out there, except the fishes!). And you'll have complete mobility, because your room rate includes the free use of a rental car during your entire stay. Although there is no beach, Magens Bay is just a mile away, and there is a pool on the property. Honeymoon package: none. Rates: $150 to $222 per couple per night for one bedroom.

Moderate

Carib Beach Hotel, P.O. Box 340, Lindburg Bay, St. Thomas, USVI 00801 (tel. 809/774-2525; reservations: tel. 212/355-6605 in NY; toll free 800/221-4588 nationwide), is a casual resort with a warm island friendliness, and also offers the advantage of being right on a beach—yet only ten minutes away from Charlotte Amalie. All 100 accommodations are air-conditioned and carpeted, and have been recently redecorated. It is definitely worth springing for the superior rooms, which all have ocean views; the standard accommodations face the parking lot. Although the property is near the airport, the noise is not obtrusive, but you do hear the planes. Lindburg Beach is small, but sparkling, and you can rent Sunfish, snorkel gear, and Windsurfers from the water-sports concession. You can also sun yourselves on the large deck surrounding the freshwater pool. At least one evening, you'll want to dine at the new Tonga Reef restaurant, where the carved totems, wooden masks, and waterfall make you feel like you've been swept off to the South Pacific rather than the Caribbean. Menu choices include Polynesian, West Indian, and all-American dishes. Honeymoon package: Eight days / seven nights (EP): $805 to $1,037 per couple for a superior room. Includes airport transfers, welcome Coco-Loco drink, manager's cocktail party, fresh flowers in room, $10 gift certificate at Cardow's (jewelry), T-shirts, one-hour use of Sunfish, use of snorkel gear for one day, bottle of champagne at the restaurant, 25% discount on auto rental, full-day trip to St. John.

ROMANTIC RESTAURANTS: What's your choice—elegant French cuisine, piquant West Indian specialties, or casual fare with a seaside view? You'll find something to please in St. Thomas. Reservations are a must at all the better restaurants. Not all places accept credit cards, so ask in advance.

Expensive

Fiddle Leaf Restaurant, Watergate Villas (tel. 775-2810). Exquisite cuisine and stunning Art Deco surroundings establish Fiddle Leaf as one of the best restaurants in St. Thomas—and the whole Caribbean, for that matter. Owner Pat LaCorte uses only the freshest ingredients for imaginative recipes that combine the best of American and French regional cuisines. The restaurant itself is beautiful, done in black and white, with red-tile floors and trelliswork adding a dramatic accent. From appetizer to desserts, all dishes come with elegant touches that make a meal memorable, such as the ethereal seafood boudin (like a sausage), which arrived draped in a spinach leaf, and adorned by a "rose" carved from a tomato ($7.20). Entrées include filet mignon, stuffed with brie cheese and served with a red-wine sauce ($24), New Orleans blackened fish ($21.50), or a Santa Fe roast game hen, cooked with chiles and cilantro and served with black bean fritters and pumpkin flan ($21.50). For dessert, indulge in the velvety smooth délice au chocolate ($5.50) or a fresh fruit cobbler ($6). For both its cuisine and its ambience, Fiddle Leaf was a gold medal winner in the recent "Great Events" restaurant awards.

Hotel 1829, Kongens Gade (near Government Hill), Charlotte Amalie (tel. 776-1829) is one of St. Thomas' best and most historic restaurants. Originally constructed in 1829 for a French sea captain, the hotel is now owned by Baron Vernon and Eva Ball—the baron actually being a self-made American millionaire who bought the title some years ago. (Backgammon players, take note: The baron is also the former World Backgammon Champion. You can sometimes pick up a game with him.) Under head chef Gerhard Hofmann, who has been with the hotel for 20 years, the menu features continental specialties such as rack of lamb, flambéed peppersteak filet mignon, and fresh (and nothing but fresh) fish, such as a sautéed yellowtail with lime or succulent Caribbean lobster. For dessert, make sure to place your order for one of the sublime soufflés: chocolate, Grand Marnier, or raspberry spiked with whipped cream. Since entrées are priced from $24, count on spending about $80 per couple for dinner, plus drinks.

Jimmy'z, 41 Constant, above Charlotte Amalie (tel. 776-4655). This place is so popular, people wait on long lines to get into the disco. During the winter, a week in advance is not too far ahead to make your dinner reservations. Why all the fuss? Jimmy'z is, quite simply, the most drop-dead gorgeous restaurant on the island—with elegantly executed nouvelle cuisine that soars to the occasion. Carpeting, tablecloths, and the high-backed chairs are all covered in a leopard-print design—yet somehow, the effect is consummately classy, never glitzy. The dining pavilion opens to the outside, allowing oleander-scented breezes to waft through the air. Fine china, crystal stemware, and hurricane lamps cast a romantic spell over the tables. Jimmy'z staff is always helpful, considerate, and knowledgeable. The list of specialties will certainly whet your appetite. As an appetizer, try the lobster ravioli served with a red pepper timbale or scallops with braised fennel (priced $7.50 to $10). Perhaps share one of the homemade pastas ($12.50). Entrées combine tastes and textures: lobster, shrimp, and scallops in a champagne sauce; twin filet mignons, with black pepper and cognac; or marinated duck breast with green peppercorn sauce (priced $18.50 to $24). "Everything we had was delicious," one couple raved. "We were really impressed—and we go to lots of restaurants." Top off your meal with one of the pastries from the dessert cart, then boogie on out to the dance floor, which has an excellent stereo and light system. Couples who dine at the restaurant do not have to pay the disco cover charge of $10 per person.

Moderate

L'Escargot. Both locations are popular with locals in the know. In town—at the Royal Dane Mall (tel. 774-8880). Set in one of the old Danish warehouses, the restaurant has the traditional high ceilings and stone walls. Open only for lunch, the selections include quiches, eggs Benedict, and salad platters, priced about $8 to $15. Country restaurant, near the sub base, just west of Charlotte Amalie (tel. 774-6565). Located just a short drive out of town, the garden setting provides a tranquil oasis for relaxed lunches and dinners. The salad bar is a favorite ($4 as an appetizer, or $8 by itself). Entrées include roast prime rib, seafood, pasta, and grilled specialties. Dinner for two should run about $45 plus drinks. Excellent wine selection.

Harbourfront, on the harbor near the USO (tel. 776-0200). Definitely a top choice for lively atmosphere and some of the best seafood in town. Open windows and ceiling fans add a balmy touch, the 40-foot brass bar draws a fun-loving crowd of mariners, ancient and otherwise, while the huge saltwater aquariums display neon-bright tropical fish. Whether you opt for meat or seafood, be prepared for the huge portions—such as giant-of-the-deep Caribbean lobsters, or roast prime rib that drapes gently over the edge of your plate (smaller servings also available). Dinner for two, about $40 per couple plus drinks.

Piccola Marina Café, at the Red Hook ferry landing (tel. 775-6350). From your table on the outdoor deck of Piccola Marina, you'll look out at the million-dollar sailing yachts moored at the docks. It's owned by Pat LaCorte, who also owns the superbly elegant Fiddle Leaf. Here, the atmosphere is definitely casual, attracting a congenial group of folks waiting for the St. John ferry, yachtspeople, and locals coming by for good food and good times. Favorite dishes include homemade pastas and sauces, and mesquite-grilled specialties. Dinner will run about $40 per couple, plus drinks. Also open for lunch and Sunday brunch.

St. Thomas has so many good restaurants, this list can go on and on. Here are some more favorites, grouped according to atmosphere or location.

For lunch in Charlotte Amalie: William and Daniels, Main Street, above Scandinavian Center (tel. 776-8877). Located on the second floor overlooking the hustle and bustle of Main Street, William and Daniels is known for its impeccable attention to detail, excellent food, and moderate prices. There's a different quiche of the day each day and a fresh-fish special, as well as international dishes such as chicken français and steak tartar. Open for lunch only; about $30 to $40 per couple. Café Amici, Riise's

Alley (no phone). Located in the brick-walled open-air alleyway, shaded by palm trees, the place feels like an Italian sidewalk café transplanted to the tropics. Excellent light fare—veal, pasta, fresh fish, and salads, priced from about $8 to $15. **Green House Bar and Restaurant,** on the waterfront (tel. 774-7998). The tables overlooking the waterfront make a great spot for people watching and imbibing the general downtown hubbub—as well as rum drinks such as the Cruzan Confusion and Sly Mongoose. Salads and burger platters run about $8 to $10. Also live rock music Tuesday through Sunday evenings, 9:30 p.m. to 2 a.m. **The Crazy Cow,** Raadets Gade (tel. 774-8518). Make any and all efforts to sample the hamburgers and tropical milkshakes, in luscious flavors such as banana and mango. Lunch, about $15 per couple.

Dinners with a view: Agave Restaurant, Point Pleasant (tel. 775-4142). Perched on the cliffs overlooking Pillsbury Sound on St. Thomas' north shore, Agave specializes in local and nouvelle cuisine. Specialties include chicken Martinique and stuffed Caribbean lobster; entrées priced from $14.50 to $24. A gold medal winner in the recent "Great Restaurants Event." **Entre Nous,** Bluebeard's Castle (tel. 774-1600). You'll look out over the classic view of Charlotte Amalie—especially beautiful those evenings when the cruise ships are in port, lights glittering like Christmas trees. Dinner for two, about $80. **Blackbeard's Castle,** above town (tel. 776-1234). Another four-star view of St. Thomas harbor, along with excellent American nouvelle cuisine, and piano entertainment nightly. Dinner for two, about $80. **The Gazebo Restaurant,** Frenchman's Reef Hotel (tel. 776-8500). Through the floor-to-ceiling windows, you'll have spectacular views across the harbor to the sparkling lights of Charlotte Amalie. The dinner menu features lobster, grouper, shrimp, and king crab, as well as roast prime ribs and veal parmigiana. Entrées run about $15.50 to $28.50 (for a mixed shellfish platter). Every Friday night, there's a lavish West Indian buffet, featuring suckling pig, leg of lamb, pumpkin fritters, pâtés (spicy meat pies), and more. All you can eat for $33 per person.

In Frenchtown: This district just west of Charlotte Amalie gets its name from the French fishermen from St. Barts, who migrated here in the late 19th century. Today, the area retains a fishing village atmosphere; it also boasts several excellent restaurants. **Alexander's Café** (tel. 774-4349). An open-air restaurant on the water featuring Austrian food. Entrées from $9 to $13. **Café Normandie** (tel. 774-1622). Candlelight sets the romantic mood at this small, air-conditioned restaurant. The five-course, prix-fixe dinner (starting at $19 per person, depending on entrée) includes soup, salad, sorbet, and a choice of specialties such as beef Wellington, Caribbean lobster, veal, or game. For dessert, take the word of the wise, and order a slice of the memorable chocolate fudge pie. **The Quarter Deck** (tel. 776-9708). Casual, with an exuberant seafaring spirit, the Quarter Deck overlooks the small harbor where many yachts tie up. For lunch, start off with the fish soup ($2.50), then move on to salads, sandwiches, and hamburgers (about $8). The complete fish dinner, including garlic bread and salad, is a good deal at $12.50. **Famous** (tel. 774-8651). This funky, 30-seat hideaway owned by Bobby DeVingo specializes in fresh pastas (including a mean fettuccine Alfredo), yellowtail français (sautéed in batter and served with a lemon butter sauce), and an oriental stir-fry with chicken, shrimp, beef, or lobster. Entrées are all priced under $12.

Local food: Daddy's, near the Red Hook dock (tel. 775-6590), is known for its conch in lemon butter sauce, conch fritters, fish dishes (try the fresh catch fried or West Indian–style), or fresh lobster, served with fungi and rice. For dessert, sample the Key lime pie. Meals are served on the garden patio. Dinner only, about $40 per couple. **Eunice's Terrace,** 67 Smith Bay, just east of the Coral World turnoff (tel. 775-3975). Enjoy a feast of local specialties on the open-air veranda—conch fritters; broiled, boiled, or fried fish; lobster; and steak. All are served with local sweet potato, and a choice of peas and rice, or fungi; green banana or fried plaintains. On Saturday nights, try the specials, including souse and callaloo. Honeymooners might like to try "The Eunice Romance"—a rum potion rumored to have aphrodisiac powers. Lunch, about $30 to $40 per couple; dinner, about $40 to $50 per couple.

And—would you believe honest-to-goodness Texas barbecue? Austin native Bill Collins has two barbecue stands, one on the St. Thomas waterfront, the other in Red Hook. **The Texas Pit** pork ribs, beef ribs, brisket, and chicken cook slowly over a cool fire, for maximum flavor and juiciness. They're served with cole slaw and potato salad. The stands open up about 6:30 p.m., and close at about 11 p.m., when everything is sold out. About $8 for a heapin' portion.

3. St. Croix

Located roughly 35 miles south of St. Thomas and St. John, St. Croix is literally a place apart—and an island of contrasts. It has all the attributes you would expect of a tropical isle: sugar-white beaches, palm trees, and cascades of colorful flowers everywhere you look: bougainvillea, oleander, and the yellow ginger thomas, the territorial flower. But it also has vistas you would not anticipate: Rolling meadows where contented cows graze, arid plains where only cactus can grow amid the rocks, and a damp, shady, rain forest where ferns grow nearly as large as trees, and vines dangle from mahogany tree limbs. A strong feeling of history pervades the entire island. Ruins of sugar mills dot the landscapes. The town of Christiansted, with its waterfront arcades and massive yellow fort guarding the harbor, remains virtually unchanged from 200 years ago, when it reigned as capital of all the Danish West Indies. Main roads make frequent 90° turns, since their routes skirt what had been the boundaries of early estates. At the same time, St. Croix offers a sizable amount of very contemporary pleasures: Old waterfront buildings now house duty-free boutiques and gourmet restaurants, rock music reverberates down narrow alleyways, and luxury resorts cater to the body and soul.

About 6 miles wide and 23 miles long, St. Croix is the largest of the Virgin Islands. The original inhabitants were the cannibalistic Carib Indians, who called the land Ay Ay. The island's recorded history formally began on November 13, 1493, when Christopher Columbus landed at what is now Salt River on the north coast, his first stop in the Virgin Islands. If you look at old maps of the estates on St. Croix, some plantation names recall the nationalities who settled here: Frederikshaab, Campo Rico, Tipperary, Oxford, and Bonne Esperance. Other names reflect the hopes of the early settlers—and the sober realities they encountered: Wheel of Fortune, Prosperity, Barrenspot, Adventure, and Little Profit.

St. Croix's basically flat terrain proved admirably suited to sugarcane production, and by 1800, the island was one of the wealthiest in the Caribbean. However, the collapse of sugar prices and the abolition of slavery ended the prosperity of the plantation era, and, like Sleeping Beauty, St. Croix peacefully dozed for nearly 100 years. In many ways, this slumber was a blessing, because it helped preserve the rich architectural heritage of the island.

You'll have fun exploring St. Croix because of its variety. The two main towns, Christiansted, on the north coast, and Frederiksted, on the west, lie at opposite ends of the island, with most of the attractions and resorts spread out in between. Sightseeing features many changes of pace—from plantation Great Houses, to botanical gardens, to spectacular beaches such as Grape Tree and Davis Bay. Although you won't find the go-go lifestyle of St. Thomas, St. Croix offers one of the tastiest assortment of restaurants in the Caribbean, and evening entertainment that ranges from mellow jazz to rock and reggae, or perhaps a performance by the island's Quadrille dancers, who curtsy and follow French calls, much as Crucians did 100 years ago. And whether you're filling in your china pattern at a duty-free shop, or sunning yourself by the side of a sparkling blue bay, you'll have plenty of elbow room, so you can truly enjoy. This feeling of intimacy amid wide-open spaces is exactly what makes St. Croix so appealing to honeymooners.

SHOPPING: St. Croix's stores offer just the right blend of famous names and serendipitous finds. Like St. Thomas, St. Croix features duty-free prices on a wide range of items: china, crystal, jewelry, watches, perfume, and liquor ranking among the best buys. Prices tend to be the same on both islands, and some stores, such as Little Switzerland, have outlets on both. Because the St. Croix stores are less crowded, shopping tends to be a much more relaxed experience. You'll also be able to browse through an interesting selection of island-made crafts and designs. Although Frederiksted has a few small boutiques, practically all the noteworthy shopping is in Christiansted. Most of the shops are located on the waterfront, on King Street, or in the arcades off of Strand Street. Top Christiansted choices include:

Benetton: An especially good selection of trendy, well-made cotton sportswear —at about 30% less than you'd pay back on the Mainland. On King Street.

Colombian Emeralds: Both unset and mounted gemstones, as well as Omega watches.

Crucian Gold: Handmade, island-designed 14k and 18k gold jewelry. 57A Company St.

Happiness Is: For locally crafted items, such as silk-screened clothing, seashell wind chimes, wood carvings, and jewelry. Pan Am Pavilion.

Many Hands: Handmade arts and crafts, pottery, jewelry, plus original works by local artists on display. Pan Am Pavilion.

Lisa's Sandal Shop: Treat your feet to a pair of handmade sandals, made to measure and ready in two to four days. Commanche Walk.

Little Switzerland: The place to go for fine china (Aynsley, Rosenthal, Wedgwood), crystal (Lalique, Baccarat, Waterford), watches (Rolex, Baume & Mercier) and many other elegant lines. On King Street.

The New Continental: Everything from china and crystal to gourmet accessories. Caravelle Arcade.

Spanish Main: Hand-screened, island-designed fabric, both by the yard and in ready-to-wear fashions. Pan Am Pavilion.

Violette's: Carries the largest selection of perfume in St. Croix, as well as cosmetics (Orlane, Lancome, Clarins), Dupont and Dunhill lighters, gold and costume jewelry, Seiko watches, men's and ladies' fashions—all at duty-free prices. Caravelle Arcade.

ROMANTIC INTERLUDES: With its rich history and varied geography, St. Croix offers many pleasant dalliances for lovers.

Located off the northeastern coast of St. Croix, **Buck Island** is a national monument, administered by the National Park Service. It's reached by a 45-minute sail from Christiansted. Both neophyte and expert snorkelers will relish the opportunity to explore the underwater wonders of the coral reef. Off the east end of the island, there's a fascinating, marked, underwater trail that takes you over huge stands of elkhorn and staghorn coral, past bright purple sea fans, and through coral grottoes. You'll spot multicolored parrot fish and damselfish, schools of yellow-and-black-striped sergeant majors, and some very dignified French angelfish, who generally cruise by in pairs. Afterward, the boat sails over to the west side of Buck Island, where you can swim and sun on the pristine white, coral-sand beach and picnic under the shade of the sea-grape trees.

Many different cruises to Buck Island are available. In particular, honeymooners will enjoy the trips offered by Captain Mark Sperber of **Mile-Mark Charters,** headquartered at the King Christian Hotel (tel. 773-2285). He's young and fun, and will delight in sharing his knowledge of St. Croix with you. In addition to his sleek trimaran, Mark has a new, specially designed glass-bottom boat that will give you a sneak preview of the underwater world. During the full moon, he also runs evening sails out to the island. Other boats that go to Buck Island include the *Teroro II*, a 42-foot trimaran (tel. 773-3161 or 773-4041); and catamarans and trimarans from **Caribbean Sea Adventures** (tel. 773-5922 days; 773-2100 ext. 740 evenings). Half-day sails run about $22 per person; full-day sails are $27.50; all include snorkel equipment and instruction. The half-day sails go to the snorkel trails only, and do not stop at the beach. Lunch is usually not included; you can pick up sandwiches in Christiansted.

One of the best ways to appreciate the lush, primeval beauty of St. Croix's **rain forest** is from **horseback.** Get into the saddle with **Jill's Equestrian Stables,** (tel. 772-0305), run by Jill Hurd, whose family runs Sprat Hall Hotel. Both beginning and experienced riders will appreciate Jill's well-schooled mounts, which range from Crucian ponies to thoroughbreds. On your guided ride, you'll pass the remains of old sugar plantations, and pass beneath towering mahogany trees. Jill will explain the history of the area, and point out the tropical fruits in season, which you'll be able to sample en route. Bring your cameras—saddle bags are provided—and you'll want to take photos of the spectacular views, which take in the beach at Sandy Point, Frederiksted, and Mahogany Valley. The 1½-hour ride costs $33 per person. During the full moon, there are also romantic evening rides ($50 per person).

Step back in time on a walking tour through **Christiansted,** much of which has remained virtually unchanged for over 200 years. The wharf building, the fort, and several other buildings are a national historic site. Your first stop should be the Visitor's Bureau located in the Scalehouse, a 19th-century building where imports and exports were once weighed. Here, you can pick up walking tour maps of Christiansted and Frederiksted. Highlights include:

Fort Christiansvaern. Built of yellow brick brought from Denmark as ballast in sailing ships, the fort was completed in 1749. Here, you can pick up maps for a self-guided walking tour. You'll shudder when you view the cells, only four feet high, and the tiny dungeon, which held the worst offenders. Then come back to the daylight—and the splendid view of the harbor from the ramparts of the Water Battery—a great place to take photos of the cannon and the harbor. Open Monday through Saturday, 8 a.m. to 5 p.m.; admission is free.

Steeple Building. Completed in 1753, this was the first Lutheran Church on St. Croix. It is now a small museum tracing the history of St. Croix—from the Indians through the reign of the Danish West India and Guinea Company. Open Monday through Friday, 9 a.m. to 4:30 p.m.; Saturday, 9 a.m. to noon; admission is free.

Government House. If you have any susceptibility to atmosphere, you'll be enthralled by the 18th-century Government House, facing King Street. For over 100 years, this was the seat of the Danish colonial government in the West Indies. The most impressive room is the second-floor ballroom, lined with tall gilt mirrors and lighted by sconces—you'll almost imagine that you can see dancers sweeping across the floor. Also pause in front of the portrait of Peter von Scholten, who served as governor general from 1828 to 1848. Von Scholten's story is a rather poignant one. A far-sighted man and a humanitarian, he instituted many reforms, including requiring free, compulsory education for slave children. No doubt, von Scholten's views were influenced by Anna Heegaard, the former slave who became his mistress after his Danish wife deserted him. During an uprising in 1848, von Scholten issued a proclamation freeing all the slaves in the Danish West Indies. Although the Danish king had previously agreed to emancipation, von Scholten was recalled to Denmark and convicted of acting without authority. He never returned to St. Croix, nor saw the woman he loved. The portrait of von Scholten that hangs in the Assembly Room is a fine one, and it almost seems to communicate the full weight of this tale.

Site of the Crugar hardware store. Born on the nearby island of Nevis, Alexander Hamilton worked as a clerk at this store from about 1766 to 1773, before leaving for America. The store was located on King Street, across from Government House, where the Little Switzerland shop now stands.

Because of St. Croix's sprawling dimensions, it is best to divvy up your sightseeing. The island's **west end** offers an interesting blend of historic great houses and forts, natural beauty, and white-sand beaches. Driving from Christiansted, your stops could include:

The St. George Village Botanical Gardens. The gardens display the exotic flowers and trees of the island against the coral stone and brick walls of what was once a 19th-century African workers' village. Depending on what month you visit, you might view one of the spectacular annual displays, such as the quarter-acre bed of red and white poinsettia, which bloom every winter. Various parts of the original village are also being restored, and on Thursdays, volunteers demonstrate metal-forging techniques in the blacksmith shop. The gardens are also a popular spot for weddings. If you would like to get married here, contact the St. Croix Visitors Bureau to arrange permission. Located just off Centerline Road (Rte. 70), the gardens are open daily from 8 a.m. to 3:30 p.m.; admission is free.

Cruzan Rum Distillery. Learn how rum is made at this working distillery—and get to sample some of the product. You'll walk through the plant surrounded by wooden kegs, and get a whiff of the intoxicating fumes from the distillery. Finally, you'll be able to quaff some of the potent rum (they make a 151 proof), and try their drink of the day. The free guided tours run Monday through Friday, 8:30 to 11:15 a.m., and 1 to 4:15 p.m. Located on West Airport Road (tel. 772-0799).

Estate Whim Plantation Museum. Get a feel for the plantation era of the late 1700s, when St. Croix was one of the richest sugar-producing islands in the Caribbean. Built by Christopher Mac Evoy, Jr., in the late 18th century, the three-room great house is built of stone and coral, mortared together by molasses. It combines architectural features of the famous châteaux of Europe, modified to accommodate tropical living (for example, a dry moat surrounds the house, to reduce humidity). The great house has been beautifully restored with period furnishings. Then stop by the cookhouse for some piping hot johnnycakes (fried breads), before strolling around the rest of the property, which includes a stone windmill and a steam mill. Stop by the gift shop, where you'll find some charming souvenirs and gift items. The great house is a national historic site managed by the St. Croix Landmarks Society. Located on Centerline Road near Frederiksted; open daily from 10 a.m. to 5 p.m.; admission is $3 per person.

Frederiksted. While Christiansted retains a decidedly Danish colonial feel, the ambience at Frederiksted is very Victorian, with many buildings boasting elaborate fretwork and gingerbread trim. Although the town was founded in 1751, much of it was destroyed in a fire in the late 1800s, and houses were reconstructed in the curlicued style of the time. Today, the excellent harbor makes Frederiksted a popular cruise-ship port, but it still retains a sun-washed, almost sleepy, mood. Start your explorations with a visit to the visitors bureau, located in the old Customs House at the corner of Strand and Custom House Streets. Here, you can pick up maps for a self-guided tour. Stop in at historic Fort Frederik, where the first foreign salute to the new stars and stripes flag supposedly occurred in 1776. Here too, in 1848, Governor Peter von Scholten issued his proclamation emancipating the slaves: "All not free in the Danish West Indies are from today free." Many elegantly restored buildings line Strand Street, fronting the harbor, including the fine Victoria House (7–8 Strand St.). There are also several shops for browsing, and cafés for relaxing.

The rain forest. From the tropical sunshine, escape to the cool of St. Croix's rain forest. Take Creque Dam Road just north of Frederiksted. You'll pass beneath towering mahogany trees and yellow cedar. At St. Croix Leap in the rain forest, you'll come across a group of talented woodcarvers with their works for sale. Don't hesitate about buying a large sculpture or some chairs—they can arrange to ship items home for you.

From here, you can return towards Christiansted on the Scenic Road, which runs along the island's mountainous backbone.

HONEYMOON HOTELS AND HIDEAWAYS: St. Croix has a wide range of places to stay—from breezy, island-style inns to a brand-new, superluxurious resort. If you decide to stay in Christiansted, you'll have its bevy of fine restaurants and shops right on your doorstep. Although there's no beach in town, you can take advantage of lovely beach and excellent water-sports facilities at Protestant Cay, in the middle of the harbor; it's just two minutes away by ferry.

Rates quoted reflect the difference between low- and high-season prices.

Moderately Expensive

The Buccaneer, Box 218, Christiansted, St. Croix, USVI 00820 (tel. 809/773-2100; reservations: tel. 212/586-3070 or toll free 800/223-1108). This pink-painted colonnaded resort occupies one of the most historic sites on St. Croix, part of a 17th-century estate belonging to Charles Martel, a Knight of Malta. Today, owned by the Armstrong family, it is still St. Croix's premier luxury resort, located just a mere wink (about four miles) from Christiansted. The Buccaneer offers guests the best of both worlds: A rolling green hilltop location (great views) that undulates its way down to not one, but three of St. Croix's finest beaches. After its recent redecoration, the lobby has a great house feel, with its ceiling fans and new wicker furnishings. All rooms have just undergone a thorough refurbishment, and feature a minifridge, air conditioning, and a private terrace or balcony. Although smallish, the superior rooms have water views and are located on either the top floor of the main building or near the beach dock. Deluxe rooms are large, high-ceilinged, and set right on the waterfront, with a combined sitting area/bedroom, and private terrace. The Buccaneer is a complete, self-contained resort with eight tennis courts overlooking the Caribbean, an 18-hole golf course, and water-sports facilities for snorkeling and scuba diving. At the new health spa, you can indulge in various treatment programs such as massage and acupressure, as well as work out on the exercise equipment. At the Brass Parrot restaurant, many of the veggies served were harvested right from the Buccaneer's own gardens. Honeymoon package: Eight days/seven nights (some meals): $1,063 per couple (superior room); $1,206 per couple (deluxe room). Includes breakfast daily, bottle of champagne, Tuesday night buffet, one hour tennis court time daily, sunset cocktail cruise, a snorkel lesson, daytime shuttle transportation to Christiansted, 7½% government tax, 5% room service charge. Package is not available during the high season.

Carambola Beach Resort and Golf Club, P.O. Box 3031, Kingshill, St. Croix, USVI 00850 (tel. 809/778-3800; reservations: tel. 212/586-4459 in NYC; toll free 800/442-8198 in NYS; 800/223-7637 nationwide). Located on the north shore along one of St. Croix's prettiest beaches, the Carambola Beach is the just debuted, newest Rockresort, the prestigious group that also includes Caneel Bay on St. John, and Little Dix Bay on Virgin Gorda. The property occupies 28 secluded acres on Davis Bay. Like the other members of the Rockresort family, the striking thing about Carambola is not only its luxury, but also the concern for the environment (one could almost say reverence) with which it was developed. Built of stucco, wood, and stone, the resort incorporates both Danish and West Indian architectural motifs. The 156 guest accommodations occupy two-story, six-unit clusters, completely surrounded by palm trees, hibiscus, and bougainvillea. Every room has an ocean view, and a separate sitting and sleeping area. There's also a room-size screened-in porch with built-in banquettes where guests can read, relax, and enjoy the scenery and trade winds. Accommodations are air conditioned. In addition to the splendid beach, guests can cool off in the large, free-form swimming pool, play tennis on four courts, or tee off on the 18-hole, Robert Trent Jones–designed Carambola Golf Course (formerly known as Fountain Valley). Carambola has two excellent restaurants: Saman, the main dining room;

and the Mahogany Room, which showcases gourmet continental and Caribbean cuisines. Honeymoon package: Eight days/seven nights (Full AP): $1,964 to $2,233 per couple. Includes a bottle of champagne, trip to Buck Island, manager's cocktail party, and a special honeymoon gift. Package not available mid-December to April.

Moderate

For honeymooners who really want to escape, the **Grapetree Beach Hotel**, P.O. Box Z, Christiansted, USVI 00820 (tel. 809/773-0340; reservations: tel. 212/661-4540 in NY; toll free 800/223-1588 nationwide), offers a secluded locale at the far eastern end of St. Croix, a beautiful region characterized by broad, flat plains and a spectacular offshore reef that colors the sea two startlingly different shades of blue. All of the rooms and suites face the ocean; each is air-conditioned and has a terrace. Decor is bright and modern. Some rooms are set beachside, others perch up in the hills overlooking the Caribbean. Grapetree is an excellent choice for sports lovers, with two lighted tennis courts and a diving facility run by Caribbean Adventures right on the property. The hotel has two restaurants: a snack bar at the pool and a waterfront restaurant. At night, the resort often features special entertainment and activities, such as calypso bands, jazz trios, "pirates' night," or crab racing. Honeymoon package: Eight days/seven nights (EP): $721 to $1,105 per couple (superior room); $759 to $1,183 per couple (deluxe room). Includes airport transfers, complimentary bottle of rum, bottle of champagne at dinner, free daytime use of tennis courts, group snorkeling instruction and free use of snorkel gear for one day, transportation to Christiansted one day, and more. Also inquire about rates at its sister property, the Grapetree Bay Hotel.

King Christian Hotel, P.O. Box 3619, Christiansted, USVI 00820 (tel. 809/773-2285; reservations: toll free 800/524-2012). Friendly and hospitable, this landmark inn usually appears in the photos you see of Christiansted harbor. The three-story hotel is located right on the dock, and its yellow-painted facade, blue shutters, and shopping arcade fit right in with the historic structures which surround it. About the only thing old-fashioned at the King Christian itself, however, is the attention to detail and dedication to personal service. Owner Betty Sperber and her staff will help you plan excursions to suit your interests—from sails to Buck Island, to golf at the Carambola course. All rooms are air-conditioned and have private baths. The superior rooms have a modern decor and feature two double beds, color cable TV, minifridge, and a large dressing area. Best of all, each has a spacious balcony overlooking the waterfront, providing ringside seats for watching yachts come and go in the harbor and spectating at sunsets. Although the minimum rooms have neither a balcony nor a harbor view, the price is certainly right. Whichever accommodations you choose, you can swim and sun yourselves in the freshwater pool in the central courtyard shaded by towering palms. Thanks to the hotel's superb location, you're right at the center of Christiansted activity. Honeymoon package: Eight days/seven nights (EP): $682 per couple for a superior room. Includes airport transfers, sail to Buck Island, a dinner by candlelight, bottle of rum, and a $12 gift certificate. Package not available during the high season, when the rates are $82.50 per couple per night for a standard room; $115.50 per couple per night for a superior.

Club Comanche, 1 Strand St., Christiansted, USVI 00820 (tel. 809/773-0210), exudes plenty of character and charm. No two rooms are alike, but many have romantic mahogany four-poster beds; all have a color TV and most are air-conditioned. There are two sections: an original building (dating to the mid-1700s), which has been updated with contemporary amenities, but still has plenty of West Indian atmosphere ($75 to $105 per couple per night for a room with a king-size bed). Club Comanche also offers more modern additions, which are located by the pool and the harbor. If you favor one-of-a-kind accommodations, choose the honeymoon suite that occupies the landmark sugar-mill–design structure on the harborfront. Your sleeping quarters, complete with a king-size bed, have a little spiral stairway leading to the balcony on the roof, where you can sun yourselves or watch Christiansted harbor shimmer in the moonlight ($97 to $149 per couple per night).

Sprat Hall Plantation, Route 63 (P.O. Box 695), Frederiksted, St. Croix, USVI 00840 (tel. 809/772-0305). Step back in time to all the romance of the plantation era at Sprat Hall, the oldest great house in the Virgin Islands. Dating from about 1670, the house is indeed a beauty, with a gracious front porch surrounded by archways, and rooms decorated with fine mahogany antiques. All rooms in the great house have four-poster beds. In room no. 5, the four-poster is an especially fine specimen, with a carved pineapple design. Room no. 3 is the only air-conditioned part of the great house (the breezes alone usually keep everything cool). Only nonsmokers can stay in the great house—a rule that is strictly enforced. The place is run by Joyce Hurd, whose family is one of the oldest on St. Croix. She supervises the excellent kitchen (see "Romantic Restaurants" write-up that follows), and shares old-time hospitality and warmth with her guests. Sprat Hall is located at St. Croix's west end, just north of Frederiksted. Beachgoers will enjoy the fine stretch of sand at the Sprat Hall Beach Club, and horseback riders will appreciate the easy proximity to the stables, run by Joyce's daughter, Jill. Don't expect modern luxuries or conveniences per se: its charms are casual, rather than highly refined. But for couples who want to experience a long-ago way of life, Sprat Hall could be just the ticket. (If you prefer a little more modernity in your lives, there are also Sprat Hall's Arawak cottages, which are air-conditioned and decorated simply.) Honeymoon package: none. Rates (EP): great house rooms: $88 to $121 per couple per night. Cottages: $55 to $132 per couple per night.

Inexpensive

The Tamarind Reef Beach Club, P.O. Box 1112, Christiansted, St. Croix, USVI 00820 (tel. 809/773-0463; reservations: toll free 800/524-2036). Seclusion, personalized service, a great beach, and just five minutes' away from Christiansted—those are just a few of the good things going for this comfy retreat on St. Croix's north shore. You couldn't ask for a more idyllic tropical setting: the 16 bungalow-style units snuggle beneath rustling palms and shiny sea-grape trees, and are poised right at the edge of the sea, looking out towards Green Cay and Buck Island. Although the rooms are furnished simply, they have everything you need—rattan furnishings, bright floral-print fabrics, a ceiling fan, efficiency kitchen, and outdoor patio. Daily maid service keeps everything looking clean and spiffy. The studios are one large room; the superior rooms have a divided sitting/sleeping quarters. In addition to the crescent-shaped beach, there's a large swimming pool, and guests can use the Sunfish sailboat and snorkel gear for free; Windsurfer lessons and rentals can be arranged. You'll probably spend many indolent hours around the poolside bar, which concocts admirable piña coladas. Honeymoon package: Eight days/seven nights (CP): $316 to $563 per couple. Includes airport transfers, welcome cocktails, oceanfront accommodations, bottle of champagne and bottle of rum, sail to Buck Island, nightly shuttle transportation to Christiansted, and shuttle to tennis and golf facilities nearby.

ROMANTIC RESTAURANTS: St. Croix seems to specialize in open-air eateries with a lively, convivial atmosphere. Some of the most attractive restaurants are set in the second stories of the old buildings that line Christiansted's narrow streets. Unless otherwise noted, all restaurants are in Christiansted. Reservations are a necessity, and since not all places take credit cards, you should ask in advance.

Set right on King's Wharf overlooking the harbor, the **Chart House,** King Christian Hotel, Christiansted (tel. 773-7718), is a great favorite with locals and visitors alike. Try to get a table by the window, so you can watch the passing parade of old salts and assorted glitterati. The restaurant is part of the well-regarded U.S. chain, but it far and away surpasses the ordinary with its excellent food and nautical ambience. The first and biggest hit is its 40-item salad bar, the largest in the islands. For your entrée, seafaring types will want to try one of the teriyaki platters, with shrimp and/or lobster; landlubbers will happily dig into the juicy prime rib. For dessert, request two forks, and start excavating into the huge slab of chocolate mud pie. Dinner for two, about $60 plus drinks.

Tivoli Gardens, Pan Am Pavilion (tel. 773-6782), a second-story charmer upstairs on Strand Street, recalls its Copenhagen namesake with the trellises, hanging plants, and tiny white lights that create a fairy-tale—yet tropical—atmosphere. Owner Gary Thomson often strums old favorite songs on the guitar, and the sounds of classics from the 1930s, 1940s, and 1950s somehow seem right in the island atmosphere. The menu spotlights an international array of dishes, from lobster-stuffed mushroom caps to steak Diane, fresh fish, stir-fry chicken orientale, and even a warming rendition of Hungarian goulash. Dinner entrées include salad, bread, and fresh vegetables. For dessert, everybody's favorite is the chocolate velvet. Dinner for two, about $50 plus drinks.

Comanche, 1 Strand St. (tel. 773-0210), is actually two restaurants: one on the second story of the hotel; the other, directly across the street and facing the waterfront. Open for breakfast, lunch, and dinner, Comanche has been St. Croix's most popular restaurant for nearly 40 years. For breakfast, head over to the hotel side and try to snare a table on the outdoor balcony (these are a favorite with regulars, so it might take some persistence). From this perch, you can watch the comings and goings of citizens down below on Strand Street, and the acrobatics of the bananaquits (sugar birds), zooming in for a sweet treat from the bird feeders. Breakfast: about $10 to $15 per couple (very good eggs Benedict). At dinnertime, the waterfront side wins out for the atmosphere. Here, the most romantic seating comes in the peacock-backed wicker chairs. The menu offers a combination of down-island and continental specialties, from callaloo to duck à l'orange. They are especially well known for their curries. Dinner for two, about $60 plus drinks.

Time and time again, **Top Hat,** upstairs at 52 Company St. (tel. 773-2346), distinguishes itself as being one of the best restaurants in St. Croix. Set on the second story of a townhouse, Top Hat is owned by a Danish husband-and-wife team, Bent and Hanne Rasmussen. The restaurant serves Danish specialties—appetizers such as smoked salmon, home-brined herrings, and split-pea soup. For your entrée, try frikadeller (Denmark's beloved national meatball), wienerschnitzel, or one of the changing roster of specials. To maintain authenticity, chug-a-lug icy cold aquavit and beer with your meal. Dinner for two will run about $80 plus drinks, but you will not be disappointed. Open November to May only.

Donn's Anchor Inn, 58A King St. (tel. 773-0263). When it's dining with a water view that you're after, head straight for Donn's Anchor Inn with its second-floor, open-air deck overlooking Christiansted harbor. It's a pleasant stop for breakfast, lunch, or dinner. For a leisurely breakfast, make your selection from 14 different omelets or opt for the memorable French toast, topped with real whipped cream (about $7 to $8). The lunch menu is casual, with burgers and salads (about $10 per person). At dinnertime, the fresh fish is the way to go: conch fritters or conch salad for starters, followed by fresh Caribbean lobster. Finish off your meal with a slice of the homemade cheesecake. Dinner for two will run about $60 plus drinks.

Sprat Hall Plantation and **Sprat Hall Beach Club,** one mile north of Frederiksted (tel. 772-0305). If the thought of West Indian specialties such as conch chowder, chicken curry, or pork loin in orange sauce make your mouth water, this is the place for you. Joyce Hurd, whose family has lived on St. Croix for generations, dishes out authentic island cuisine. Lunch is served on the terrace at the Sprat Hall Beach Club, set on a very lovely white-sand beach on St. Croix's west coast. Lunch features conch soup, salads, the fresh catch of the day—and some ambrosial pumpkin fritters. After lunch, you're welcome to spread out your beach towels on the sand, and enjoy the crystal-clear waters here on St. Croix's lee shore. Lunch will run $20 to $30 per couple.

For a very special dinner that will whisk you 300 years back in time, make reservations for the dining room at Sprat Hall Great House, the oldest plantation great house in the Virgin Islands. Many of the fruits and vegetables come right from Sprat Hall's own gardens. Do not pass up the conch, steeped in butter and spiked with just a hint of sherry. The menu constantly changes to take advantage of what's fresh, but might include fish and lobster dishes, beef burgundy, or leg of lamb, all accompanied by rice or potatoes, and four or five different fresh vegetables. Cap off your meal with one of Mrs. Hurd's specialties, such as soursop ice cream or soursop pie. Reservations at the great house are absolutely essential, since you are, in effect, dining in a private home. A very special experience. Dinner for two, about $50.

4. St. John

If you ask a St. Johnian how far his island is from St. Thomas, the populous Virgin Islands capital, a slow grin may spread over his face. "About twenty minutes . . . and a hundred years," he'll reply, only half joking.

St. John is the most truly virgin of the U.S. islands, a smidgen of unspoiled paradise surrounded by sapphire-blue seas. Located about two miles east of St. Thomas across Pillsbury Sound, it measures only nine miles long and five miles wide, making it the smallest of the major islands. About two-thirds of St. John is national park, donated to the U.S. government in 1956 by Laurance Rockefeller to preserve its pristine beauty for generations to come. If your top honeymoon priority is beaches, you've come to the right place. A necklace of several line the island's north shore, all blessed with crystal-clear turquoise bays and white sands so soft, they're almost fluffy.

Long before Christopher Columbus came, St. John was inhabited by Indians—first, the gentle Arawaks, who were subsequently displaced (and/or devoured) by the ferocious Caribs. Many Indian artifacts have been found, and you can view mysterious petroglyphs (rock carvings) along trails through the island's interior (see details which follow). The Danes settled at the protected harbor of Coral Bay in 1718. Viewing St. John's rather siesta pace today, you'll find it hard to believe that the island was once of the most prosperous sugar-producers in the region. A violent slave rebellion in 1733, and the subsequent abolition of slavery in 1848, ended the plantation era. For nearly 100 years, the island remained virtually undisturbed, while old coral stone walls crumbled, and lianas entangled themselves in the vanes of sugar mills. In recent years, nature-loving vacationers have discovered St. John's serene beauty, and they have made it a haven for peaceful escape.

What action there is centers on Cruz Bay, the main town located on St. John's west coast, where the St. Thomas ferry puts in. Here, time seems to have politely decided to stand still. Roosters crow and scamper across the main square, dogs snooze under the benches, and the town's no. 1 car rental agency operates out of a hut. The whole place is about three blocks long and two blocks wide. Don't be misled by the funky side, however. St. John is a preferred port of call for the rich and famous, who anchor their yachts in secluded bays, or ensconce themselves in luxury resorts. St. John attracts a mixed-bag clientele—CEO's and craftspeople, campers and yachtsmen, movie stars and, of course, starry-eyed honeymooners. All come to immerse themselves in the sun, the seclusion, and the magnificent beaches. St. John is the kind of place you'll feel like you've "discovered"—and you'll sincerely hope it never fully joins the 20th century.

SHOPPING: The Cruz Bay shops are one of the better-kept secrets of the Virgin Islands. You won't find large, duty-free emporiums; instead, individualistic boutiques specialize in fine, one-of-a-kind crafts items.

Many of the best shops are clustered in Mongoose Junction, a minimall built of coral stone and ballast brick to resemble the ruins of the sugar plantations that dot the island. Here, **The Canvas Factory** carries canvas bags in all different sizes. **R & I Patton Goldsmithing** makes original-design gold and silver jewelry on the premises. Many pieces incorporate island motifs such as scallop shells, seahorses, or petroglyph symbols. **Wicker, Wood, and Shells** sells all that—as well as St. John basketwork, straw hats, and some charming bird feeders made from coconut shells. **The Fabric Mill** offers framed wall-hangings, Haitian cottons, and batiks imported from Indonesia and the Netherlands. **The Clothing Studio** displays hand-painted clothing. **The Donald Schnell Ceramic Studio** has a beautiful selection of handcrafted platters, mirrors, and wind chimes, as well as exquisite hand-blown Christmas ornaments.

Elsewhere, try **Coconuts Tropical Clothing Company** for women's clothing and accessories. They have two outlets, one on the North Shore Road heading out of town, the other around the corner from the Lutheran Church. If you're looking for very fashionable casual clothing—the kind of dresses that you can wear over a bathing suit or to the office in summer—this is the place. **Batik Caribe,** also on the back street, carries hand-painted T-shirts by local artists (the large ones make great beach coverups), and brilliantly colored batik *pareos* (sarongs) and wall-hangings from Barbados. For T-shirts, head for **Stitches** or the **Art Project.**

ROMANTIC INTERLUDES: To best appreciate St. John, rent a Jeep and follow the winding roads, taking in the scenic lookouts over the north shore beaches and heading for the top of Bordeaux Mountain, the island high point. As you travel along, keep your eyes open for the furry mongooses, which often scurry across your path. Here are some attractions you might like to take in.

Ask a knowledgeable **beach** connoisseur to name the ten best beaches in the world—and it's possible that five of them will be on St. John. Part of the pleasure of a St. John sojourn involves trying out the different strands that fringe the island's north shore. You'll want to check out:

Hawksnest: A big, beautiful bay where scenes from Alan Alda's *The Four Seasons* were filmed. Facilities include toilets, picnic tables, and barbecue pits.

Trunk Bay: Ringed by sea-grape trees, this broad, white beach and calm blue bay with a tiny islet in the middle must be one of the most-photographed sites on St. John. Part of the national park, the beach is also known for its marked underwater snorkeling trail. Snorkel gear rental, a snack bar, and showers are located right at the beach.

Cinnamon Bay: Characterized by its long sweep of sand with cast-up, sunbleached driftwood pieces, Cinnamon also has a teeny offshore island that's a favorite with snorkelers. Novice snorkelers will enjoy exploring the shallow reef at the bay's eastern end. Cinnamon is part of the national park campground and offers a snack bar, water-sports equipment rental, and guided snorkel tours several times a week. Call 776-6201 for details.

Big and Little Maho Bays: Ringed by manchineel trees, these tranquil, horseshoe-shaped harbors have no public facilities—just beautiful beaches.

Francis Bay: Because it's the most isolated of the beaches, it usually is the least crowded—a sparkling white crescent that seems to roll on forever. Toward the east end at Mary Point, you can often spot turtles.

If you want to take along a picnic lunch, you can get all the fixin's at the **St. John Pub,** right near the ferry dock in Cruz Bay, or at the **Mongoose Restaurant** in the Mongoose Junction center.

Next to the sheer beauty of the island, the next thing that will surprise you about St. John is the very visible and caring presence of the National Park Service, which administers about two-thirds of the island. In addition, park rangers run a wide variety of **hikes, historic tours,** and **snorkel tours** that enable visitors to get the most out of their stays on St. John. Program schedules vary; write or call for details: **Virgin Islands National Park,** P.O. Box 710, St. John, USVI 00830 (tel. 809/776-6201). Events include:

Historic bus tour: The three-hour tour retraces the island's story from the time of the Arawak Indians to the Danish colonists through the present. Along the route, the park ranger will fill you in on local lore, such as plants used in folk medicine, or the story of Easter Rock, a huge boulder said to march itself to the sea every Easter. You'll also learn about St. John's unofficial mascot, the mongoose. The tour is free, but the bus transportation costs $12.50 from Cruz Bay. No charge if you bring your own car or Jeep.

Guided hikes: A favorite is the guided walk down Reef Bay Trail. It's the best kind of hike—downhill all the way—and concludes with a cooling swim and a boat ride back to Cruz Bay. Along the way, hikers pass rain forest and mango groves, as well as ruins of an old sugar plantation and intriguing petroglyphs (rock carvings) attributed to the early Arawak settlers. The return boat ride costs $7.50 per person. The park service also publishes excellent hiking trail maps of the island; you can pick them up at the Cruz Bay Visitor Center.

Snorkel trips: Held at Cinnamon Beach, the program teaches you safe snorkeling techniques and provides an excellent introduction to the fish that live on the coral reef. (Bring snorkel gear, which you can rent at Cinnamon Bay.)

"The best part of our trip!" That's how two honeymooners described the **snorkel day trip** they had taken. Cruises head to the British Virgin Islands or some uninhabited cay. Popular day sails from St. John include **Water Lemon Cay,** a postage-stamp-size islet in Leinster Bay with superb snorkeling; and also **Sandy Cay, Great Thatch,** and **Tobago.** Crewed charters that take six to eight passengers are available out of the major resorts as well as **Cruz Bay Watersports** (tel. 776-6234) and **St. John Watersports** (tel. 776-6256), both in Cruz Bay. Costs run about $30 per person for the half-day sail (includes snacks); $55 for the full-day sail (includes lunch).

At the beautiful **Annaberg Sugar Mill** overlooking Leinster Bay and the British Virgin Islands, you can retrace the history of St. John's plantation era. You can pick up a self-guided-tour map at the entrance and walk through the ruins of the slave quarters, mill, and outbuildings. Several times a week, St. Johnians demonstrate island cookery or crafts, such as basketweaving.

HONEYMOON HOTELS AND HIDEAWAYS: Although St. John does not have a vast number of different hotels, it offers an extremely wide choice of accommodations: everything from ultraposh resorts to seaside sites where you can pitch your own tent. The amazing thing is—all are, in their own way, superb. Rates quoted reflect the difference between low- and high-season prices.

Expensive

Caneel Bay, Virgin Islands National Park, St. John, USVI 00830 (tel. 809/776-6111; reservations: tel. 212/586-4459 in NYC; toll free 800/442-8198 in NYS; toll free 800/223-7637 nationwide). St. John owes much of its luxury-hideaway cachet to this elegant Rockresort, which spreads out over not just one, but seven, diamond-white beaches on the island's north shore. The resort encompasses a broad, 170-acre peninsula that seems to reach out to embrace the sea. Located within the boundaries of the national park, Caneel Bay is designed to enhance the beautiful natural environment. Guest accommodations are inobtrusive, screened by palm trees (15 different varieties), and color-splashed gardens bright with hibiscus, oleander, bougainvillea, and ixora. Ruins of an 18th-century sugar mill have been incorporated into one of the restaurants. There are only 168 rooms, all in low-profile buildings situated around the property. The decor utilizes coral stone walls, dark bamboo furnishings, and ceiling fans. There is no in-room telephone, television, nor air conditioning. Thanks to this combination of luxury and seclusion, Caneel Bay has become a preferred hideaway for the famous. Mrs. Vincent Astor, Mel Brooks and Anne Bancroft, and Henry Kissinger all stayed here.

Honeymooners will appreciate the fact that the Caneel Bay experience is all-inclusive. The sports facilities are superb, with guests enjoying complimentary use of the seven tennis courts, a fleet of small sailboats, snorkeling equipment and instruction, and bicycles. With seven beaches to choose from, you're sure to be able to find one where yours will be practically the only sets of footprints in the sand. One beach you'll want to check out—the strand appropriately enough named Honeymoon. Day sails, deep-sea fishing, horseback riding, waterskiing, scuba diving, and Windsurfing are all available at an extra charge. In addition, all meals are included, with guests having their choice of Caneel's three excellent restaurants: the Beach Terrace, Turtle Bay Estate, or the Sugar Mill. Honeymoon package: Eight days/seven nights (Full AP): $1,881 to $2,112 per couple. Includes deluxe accommodations, transfers from St. Thomas, sunset cocktail cruise, a bottle of champagne with dinner one evening, manager's reception, and a memento from the gift shop. Also inquire about packages that combine stays at Caneel Bay with a holiday on Little Dix Bay, its sister Rockresort on Virgin Gorda; or with a crewed or bareboat charter of a luxury Hinckley yacht. Packages not available mid-December through April 1, when the rate for a deluxe room (Full AP) is $330 per couple per night. Rates do not include gratuities or the 7½% U.S. VI hotel tax.

The first new luxury hotel in St. John in 30 years, the **Virgin Grand Beach Hotel,** Great Cruz Bay, St. John, USVI 00830 (tel. 809/776-7171; reservations: tel. 212/661-4540 or toll free 800/223-1580), just opened its doors in December 1986. Built into the hillside, the 264-room resort overlooks its own 1,200-foot secluded beach on Great Cruz Bay (which is a mile outside of the town). Accommodations are clustered in several different complexes along the beach and hillsides. The resort aims to go first class all the way, offering guests special features such as use of an exclusive airport lounge in St. Thomas, private ferry transport to St. John, plus an array of room amenities: air conditioning, cable color TV, wet bars and refrigerators, and marble bathrooms with baskets filled not only with shampoo and soap, but also sunscreens. Sports facilities are extensive, including a huge free-form swimming pool (complete with its own islands and waterfall) and six lighted tennis courts. Down at the beach, guests can zip off on sailboats, Windsurfers, or a private yacht, and snorkel gear is available for rent. At mealtime, you have a choice of three restaurants. Honeymoon package: Eight days/seven nights (Full AP): from $2,825 per couple (standard room); from $2,979 per couple (deluxe room). Includes oceanview accommodations with balcony or terrace; split of champagne with fruit and cheese basket upon arrival; all meals and nonalcoholic beverages; welcome cocktails; fresh flowers in room; complimentary use of small sailboats, snorkel gear, beach floats, and tennis courts; choice of day sail, island tour, or scuba lessons.

Inexpensive

Maho Bay, P.O. Box 310, Cruz Bay, St. John, USVI 00830 (tel. 809/776-6240; reservations: tel. 212/472-9453 or toll free 800/392-9004). For couples who love an easygoing, natural lifestyle amid incredibly beautiful surroundings, Maho Bay offers the best honeymoon value in the entire Caribbean. The resort is a community of 100 ultracomfortable tent cottages located within a private preserve in the national park. It's camping—with real beds and plumbing. The cozy tents are set on wooden decks overlooking the sea, and have three rooms: living room, bedroom (some with a double bed draped behind mosquito netting), and a cooking area, plus an open porch for sunbathing. Centrally located bath houses are equipped with modern toilets, sinks, and showers. The guiding spirit behind Maho, Stanley Selengut, has created a resort that lives harmoniously with its surroundings. Frangipani and hibiscus splash scarlet against the jungle greenery, orchids nestle in the crooks of tree branches, and peacocks strut along the walkways. At mealtime, guests can cook on the propane stoves in their tents (you can pick up supplies at Maho's convenience market), or head over to the breezy pavilion-deck restaurant. Here, St. Johnians bring in food that they have prepared in their own homes; a rich, cheese-laden lasagna, perhaps, or poached mahimahi (fish), or spicy West Indian chicken. The Maho cottages are perched just above some of St. John's finest beaches, Little Maho and Francis Bay. The resort runs extensive water-sports programs, with Windsurfers, Sunfish, and day sails all available. Maho is also the cultural center of St. John, hosting an eclectic series of special events throughout the year, ranging from jazz festivals to health, photography, and astronomy workshops—all free to guests. It all adds up to a very unique experience—and isn't that what honeymoons are all about? Honeymoon package: $48 to $60 per couple per night, based on a seven-night stay. Includes a bottle of champagne. They'll also give you one of the more secluded cottages with a superb view and a double bed.

    Cinnamon Bay Campground, P.O. Box 120, Cruz Bay, St. John, USVI 00830 (tel. 809/776-6330; reservations: tel. 212/586-4459 in NYC; toll free 800/442-8198 in NYS; toll free 800/223-7637 nationwide). The soft lap of the waves, starlit nights, and sunny days on one of the most beautiful of St. John's beaches—the best things in life, if not free, are a very good deal at Cinnamon Bay Campground. The word "campground" is a bit misleading here, since the area has three different kinds of accommodations, all suitable to couples with different thresholds of "roughing it." Cottages are indeed real apartments, with two concrete walls and two screened walls. They come provided with electricity, real beds (twins, so you'll have to resort to some ingenuity), linens (changed weekly), a picnic table, barbecue grill, two-burner propane gas stove, ice chest, water container, cooking and eating utensils ($48 to $61 per couple per night). The tents are extremely commodious and comfortable, built on platforms and equipped with camp cots and pads, linens (changed weekly), and the other features of the cottages, except electricity ($40 to $51 per couple per night). Bare sites are just that: a cleared area with a picnic table and a built-in charcoal grill; you bring everything else ($11 per couple per night). The four bath houses with showers and flush toilets are kept clean and sparkling. If you don't feel like cooking yourselves, the Raintree Terrace cafeteria serves breakfast, lunch, and dinner.

ROMANTIC RESTAURANTS: Whether you're dining elegantly at a posh resort, or just limin' at a local hangout, you'll find that St. John's restaurants have plenty of personality and downright great food. Only the Sugar Mill at Caneel Bay is romantic in a soft candlelight/tropical flower sense; instead, the rest of these recommendations exude plenty of energy and fun—romanticism at its most spirited and adventure-loving best. Reservations are necessary all over, and not all places accept credit cards.

Expensive

    Sugar Mill, Caneel Bay (tel. 776-6111). Sample the elegant Caneel Bay lifestyle at this restaurant built around the ruins of an old sugar mill—the only restaurant on the property that is open to nonguests. At lunchtime, you'll be treated to the four-star views from the Sugar Mill terrace, with panoramic vistas of (or so it seems) all 100 of the U.S. and British Virgin Islands. Lunch selections include both cold platters, such as a papaya and lobster salad ($14), or Danish-style sandwiches with roast beef and baby shrimp ($11.50), as well as hot dishes, such as the grilled fish of the day ($11) or fried shrimp with guava-mustard sauce ($10.25). For dinner, the Sugar Mill sets out a lavish buffet, with music from a steel band to set the mood. Every night, the grill buffet features three different entrées: one shellfish, one fish, and one meat. The dishes might include lobster, steak, shrimp kebabs, barbecue ribs, chicken, or crab claws—and you can dig into just one, or sample all three. But remember—a whole table filled just with desserts also awaits. Prix-fixe at $43 per person; served from 7 p.m. to 8:30 p.m.

Moderate

Il Bucanière Restaurant and Cruz Quarters Bar, Cruz Bay (tel. 776-6908). Located right behind Cruz Bay Park and across from the ferry dock, this seems to be the favorite local hangout—probably because the broad terrace and comfortable cast-iron chairs make this a prime spot for people watching. The food's pretty good too. Lunch tends to be casual, with a selection of omelets and burger platters, which should run you about $30 per couple. At dinner, you get more substantial entrées, such as fresh fish and lobster, pastas, and specials such as shish kebab. Dinner for two, about $40 plus drinks.

The Backyard, Cruz Bay (tel. 776-6862), is another favorite local gathering spot, the kind of place where residents thumb through stateside magazines to catch up on the latest news (of about two weeks ago), dogs doze off in the corners, and the bartender asks you if you want a glass with your beer. If you're the type of person who doesn't need a glass, you'll fit right in with the crowd. Open for both lunch and dinner. Each evening, the menu features a different international cuisine—West Indian, Mexican, Oriental—even a "movie night" featuring a film on the big-screen TV, with a side order of hot dogs, French fries, and other munchies. It's a fun way to plug into the local lifestyle. Lunch, about $20 per couple; dinners, about $30.

Frank's, Cruz Bay (tel. 776-6352). Located just a stroll up the hill from the ferry dock, this restaurant features dishes prepared by the owner's son, Richard Erdos, who is a graduate of the Culinary Institute of America. Some of the best entrées apply haute cuisine touches to local ingredients, such as the "puffed" lobster tail or fresh fish, baked in a pastry shell and swathed in a bisque sauce. Another specialty is Frank's chicken, sautéed with prosciutto and mushrooms in a white wine sauce. Adding to the ambience, there's folk music on Fridays, jazz on Saturdays and Sundays. Dinner for two, about $40.

Inexpensive

Mongoose Restaurant, Café, and Bar, Mongoose Junction, Cruz Bay (tel. 776-7586). Decks clamber between the levels, residents trade gossip at the bar, and a stream adds its rushing rhythms to the general hubbub—that describes the animated atmosphere at this local favorite that is open for breakfast, lunch, and dinner. It's an especially convenient lunch spot if you're shopping in town. Choose from fresh salad platters, sandwiches, or burgers (priced $7 to $10).

The Lobster Hut, Cruz Bay (tel. 776-6533) specializes in everyone's favorite crustacean, which you can pick out from their tank—only $6.95 per pound (you gotta call in advance if you want one for dinner). The place is, literally, a hut, but an extremely nice one, with candles on the table at dinner. **Meada's,** Cruz Bay (tel. 776-7571) isn't always open, but when it is, it serves four-star West Indian delights, such as baked chicken with peas 'n' rice, sweet potato, and fungi. Dinner for two, about $20, so give them a ring. **Hercule Pâté Delight,** Cruz Bay (tel. 776-6352) is just a casual sidewalk stand, but its food is high art. They serve meat, chicken, and fish pâtés (deep-fried pies), only $1.75 each. As a beverage, try ginger beer (tart and tingly), mauby, or soursop juice. For dessert, stroll across the street to the **Nature's Nook** fruit stand, where you can get the pick of the harvest—papaya, mangoes, genip, whatever is in season.

SUGGESTED READING

NOW THAT YOU HAVE SELECTED your honeymoon destination, here's a list of other specialized touring guides you may wish to consult in planning your itinerary. They are all published by Prentice Hall Press in New York and are available in bookstores or directly from the publisher.

The United States

NEW ENGLAND

Frommer's Dollarwise Guide to New England, by Tom Brosnahan
Frommer's Guide to Boston, by Faye Hammel
Marilyn Wood's Wonderful Weekends, by Marilyn Wood

CALIFORNIA

Frommer's Dollarwise Guide to California, by Mary Rakauskas
Frommer's Guide to Los Angeles, by Mary Rakauskas
Frommer's Guide to San Francisco, by Mary Rakauskas
The Serious Shopper's Guide to Los Angeles, by Jennifer Merin

FLORIDA

Frommer's Dollarwise Guide to Florida, by Marylyn Springer and Donald A. Schultz
Frommer's Guide to Orlando, Disney World, and EPCOT, by Marylyn Springer

GEORGIA

Frommer's Dollarwise Guide to the Southeast, by Susan Poole

HAWAII

Frommer's Hawaii on $50 a Day, by Faye Hammel and Sylvan Levey
Frommer's Guide to Hawaii, by Faye Hammel
Frommer's Dollarwise Guide to Cruises, by Marylyn Springer and Donald Schultz

NEVADA

Frommer's Guide to Las Vegas, by Mary Rakauskas

NEW YORK

Dollarwise Guide to New York State, by John Foreman
Frommer's New York on $50 a Day, by Joan Hamburg and Norma Ketay
Frommer's Guide to New York, by Faye Hammel
Marilyn Wood's Wonderful Weekends, by Marilyn Wood

PENNSYLVANIA
Frommer's Dollarwise Guide to the Mid-Atlantic States, by Patricia Tunison Preston and John Preston
Frommer's Guide to Philadelphia, by Jay Golan
Marilyn Wood's Wonderful Weekends, by Marilyn Wood

SOUTH CAROLINA
Frommer's Dollarwise Guide to the Southeast, by Susan Poole

TEXAS
Frommer's Dollarwise Guide to Texas, by Rena Bulkin

Canada
Frommer's Dollarwise Guide to Canada, by Tom Brosnahan, John Godwin, and Marilyn Wood
Frommer's Guide to Montreal and Quebec City, by Tom Brosnahan
Frommer's Dolllarwise Guide to Cruises, by Marylyn Springer and Donald A. Schultz

Mexico
Frommer's Mexico on $20 A Day, by Tom Brosnahan
Frommer's Guide to Cancún, Cozumel, and the Yucatán, by Tom Brosnahan
Frommer's Guide to Mexico City and Acapulco, by Tom Brosnahan
Frommer's Dollarwise Guide to Cruises, by Marylyn Springer and Donald A Schultz

The Caribbean, The Bahamas, and Bermuda

Caribbean
Frommer's Dollarwise Guide to the Caribbean, by Darwin Porter
Frommer's Dollarwise Guide to Cruises, by Marylyn Springer and Donald A. Schultz
A Shopper's Guide to the Caribbean, by Jeanne and Harry Harman

THE BAHAMAS AND BERMUDA
Frommer's Dollarwise Guide to Bermuda and The Bahamas, by Darwin Porter
Frommer's Dollarwise Guide to Cruises, by Marylyn Springer and Donald A. Schultz

THE $35-A-DAY
TRAVEL CLUB

IN THIS BOOK we'll be loking at how to get your money's worth as well as enjoyment from your honeymoon, but there is a "device" for saving money and determining value on *all* your trips. It's the popular, international $35-A-Day Travel Club, now in its 25th successful year of operation. The Club was formed at the urging of numerous readers of the $$$-A-Day and Dollarwise Guides, who felt that such an organization could provide continuing travel information and a sense of community to value-minded travelers in all parts of the world. And so it does!

In keeping with the budget concept, the annual membership fee is low and is immediately exceeded by the value of your benefits. Upon receipt of $18 (U.S. residents), or $20 U.S. by check drawn on a U.S. bank or via international postal money order in U.S. funds (Canadian, Mexican, and other foreign residents) to cover one year's membership, we will send all new members the following items.

(1) *Any two* of the following books

Please designate in your letter which two you wish to receive:

Frommer's $-A-Day Guides
Europe on $30 a Day
Australia on $25 a Day
Eastern Europe on $25 a Day
England on $40 a Day
Greece including Istanbul and Turkey's Aegean Coast on $30 a Day
Hawaii on $50 a Day
India on $25 a Day
Ireland on $30 a Day
Israel on $30 & $35 a Day
Mexico on $20 a Day (plus Belize and Guatemala)
New York on $50 a Day
New Zealand on $40 a Day
Scandinavia on $50 a Day
Scotland and Wales on $40 a Day
South America on $30 a Day
Spain and Morocco (plus the Canary Is.) on $40 a Day
Turkey on $25 a Day
Washington, D.C., & Historic Virginia on $40 a Day

Frommer's Dollarwise Guides
Dollarwise Guide to Austria and Hungary
Dollarwise Guide to to Belgium, Holland, & Luxembourg
Dollarwise Guide to Bermuda and The Bahamas
Dollarwise Guide to Canada
Dollarwise Guide to the Caribbean
Dollarwise Guide to Egypt
Dollarwise Guide to England and Scotland
Dollarwise Guide to France
Dollarwise Guide to Germany
Dollarwise Guide to Italy
Dollarwise Guide to Japan and Hong Kong
Dollarwise Guide to Portugal, Madeira, and the Azores
Dollarwise Guide to the South Pacific
Dollarwise Guide to Switzerland and Liechtenstein
Dollarwise Guide to Alaska
Dollarwise Guide to California and Las Vegas
Dollarwise Guide to Florida
Dollarwise Guide to the Mid-Atlantic States
Dollarwise Guide to New England
Dollarwise Guide to New York State
Dollarwise Guide to the Northwest
Dollarwise Guide to Skiing USA—East
Dollarwise Guide to Skiing USA—West
Dollarwise Guide to the Southeast and New Orleans
Dollarwise Guide to the Southwest
Dollarwise Guide to Texas
(Dollarwise Guides discuss accommodations and facilities in all price ranges, with emphasis on the medium-priced.)

Frommer's Touring Guides
Egypt
Florence
London
Paris
Venice
(These new, color illustrated guides include walking tours, cultural and historic sites, and other vital travel information.)

Arthur Frommer's New World of Travel 1988
(From America's #1 travel expert, a sourcebook of vacations that cater to the mind, the spirit, and a sense of thrift. Guaranteed to change the way people travel and to save them hundreds of dollars.)

A Shopper's Guide to the Caribbean
(Two experienced Caribbean hands guide you through this shopper's paradise, offering witty insights and helpful tips on the wares and emporia of more than 25 islands.)

Beat the High Cost of Travel
(This practical guide details how to save money on absolutely all travel items— accommodations, transportation, dining, sightseeing, shopping, taxes, and more. Includes special budget information for seniors, students, singles, and families.)

Bed & Breakfast—North America
(This guide contains a directory of over 150 organizations that offer bed & breakfast referrals and reservations throughout North America. The scenic attractions and major schools and universities near the homes of each are also listed.)

Dollarwise Guide to Cruises
(This complete guide covers all the basics of cruising—ports of call, costs, fly-cruise package bargains, cabin selection booking, embarkation and debarkation and describes in detail over 60 or so ships cruising the waters of Alaska, the Caribbean, Mexico, Hawaii, Panama, Canada, and the United States.

Dollarwise Guide to Skiing Europe
(Describes top ski resorts in Austria, France, Italy, and Switzerland. Illustrated with maps of each resort area plus full-color trail maps.)

Guide to Honeymoon Destinations
(A special guide for that most romantic trip of your life, with full details on planning and choosing the destination that will be just right in the U.S. [California, New England, Hawaii, Florida, New York, South Carolina, etc.], Canada, Mexico, and the Caribbean.

Marilyn Wood's Wonderful Weekends
(This very selective guide covers the best mini-vacation destinations within a 175-mile radius of New York City. It describes special country inns and other accommodations, restaurants, picnic spots, sights, and activities—all the information needed for a two- or three-day stay.)

Motorist's Phrase Book
(A practical phrase book in French, German, and Spanish designed specifically for the English-speaking motorist touring abroad.)

Swap and Go—Home Exchanging Made Easy
(Two veteran home exchangers explain in detail all the money-saving benefits of a home exchange, and then describe precisely how to do it. Also includes information on home rentals and many tips on low-cost travel.)

The Candy Apple: New York for Kids
(A spirited guide to the wonders of the Big Apple by a savvy New York grandmother with a kid's-eye view to fun. Indispensable for visitors and residents alike.)

Travel Diary and Record Book
(A 96-page diary for personal travel notes plus a section for such vital data as passport and traveler's check numbers, itinerary, postcard list, special people and places to visit, and a reference section with temperature and conversion charts, and world maps with distance zones.)

Where to Stay USA
(By the Council on International Educational Exchange, this extraordinary guide is the first to list accommodations in all 50 states that cost anywhere from $3 to $30 per night.)

(2) A one-year subscription to *The Wonderful World of Budget Travel*
     This quarterly eight-page tabloid newspaper keeps you up to date on fast-breaking developments in low-cost travel in all parts of the world bringing you the

latest money-saving information—the kind of information you'd have to pay $25 a year to obtain elsewhere. This consumer-conscious publication also features columns of special interest to readers: Hospitality Exchange (members all over the world who are willing to provide hospitality to other members as they pass through their home cities); **Share-a-Trip** (offers and requests from members for travel companions who can share costs and help avoid the burdensome single supplement); and **Readers Ask . . . Readers Reply** (travel questions from members to which other members reply with authentic firsthand information).

A copy of *Arthur Frommer's Guide to New York*

This is a pocket-size guide to hotels, restaurants, nightspots, and sightseeing attractions in all price ranges throughout the New York area.

Your personal membership card

Membership entitles you to purchase through the Club all Arthur Frommer publications for a third to a half off their regular retail prices during the term of your membership.

So why not join this hardy band of international budgeteers and participate in its exchange of travel information and hospitality? Simply send your name and address, together with your annual membership fee of $18 (U.S. residents) or $20 U.S. (Canadian, Mexican, and other foreign residents), by check drawn on a U.S. bank or via international postal money order in U.S. funds to $35-A-Day Travel Club, Inc., Frommer Books, Gulf + Western Building, One Gulf + Western Plaza, New York, NY 10023. And please remember to specify which *two* of the books in section (1) above you wish to receive in your initial package of members' benefits. Or, if you prefer, use the last page of this book, simply checking off the two books you select and enclosing $18 or $20 in U.S. currency.

Once you are a member, there is no obligation to buy additional books. No books will be mailed to you without your specific order.

NOW, SAVE MONEY ON ALL YOUR TRAVELS!
Join Arthur Frommer's $35-A-Day Travel Club™

Saving money while traveling is never a simple matter, which is why, over 26 years ago, the **$35-A-Day Travel Club** was formed. Actually, the idea came from readers of the Arthur Frommer Publications who felt that such an organization could bring financial benefits, continuing travel information, and a sense of community to economy-minded travelers all over the world.

In keeping with the money-saving concept, the annual membership fee is low—$18 (U.S. residents) or $20 U.S. (Canadian, Mexican, and foreign residents)—and is immediately exceeded by the value of your benefits which include:

(1) The latest edition of any TWO of the books listed on the following pages.

(2) An annual subscription to an 8-page quarterly newspaper *The Wonderful World of Budget Travel* which keeps you up-to-date on fastbreaking developments in low-cost travel in all parts of the world—bringing you the kind of information you'd have to pay over $35 a year to obtain elsewhere. This consumer-conscious publication also includes the following columns:

Hospitality Exchange—members all over the world who are willing to provide hospitality to other members as they pass through their home cities.

Share-a-Trip—requests from members for travel companions who can share costs and help avoid the burdensome single supplement.

Readers Ask . . . Readers Reply—travel questions from members to which other members reply with authentic firsthand information.

(3) A copy of *Arthur Frommer's Guide to New York.*

(4) Your personal membership card which entitles you to purchase through the Club all Arthur Frommer Publications for a third to a half off their regular retail prices during the term of your membership.

So why not join this hardy band of international budgeteers NOW and participate in its exchange of information and hospitality? Simply send $18 (U.S. residents) or $20 U.S. (Canadian, Mexican, and other foreign residents) along with your name and address to: $35-A-Day Travel Club, Inc., Gulf + Western Building, One Gulf + Western Plaza, New York, NY 10023. Remember to specify which *two* of the books in section (1) above you wish to receive in your initial package of member's benefits. Or tear out the next page, check off any two of the books listed on either side, and send it to us with your membership fee.

Date_____

**FROMMER BOOKS
PRENTICE HALL PRESS
ONE GULF + WESTERN PLAZA
NEW YORK, NY 10023**

Friends:

Please send me the books checked below:

FROMMER'S $-A-DAY GUIDES™

(In-depth guides to sightseeing and low-cost tourist accommodations and facilities.)

☐ Europe on $30 a Day $13.95
☐ Australia on $25 a Day $10.95
☐ Eastern Europe on $25 a Day $10.95
☐ England on $40 a Day............... $11.95
☐ Greece on $30 a Day................ $11.95
☐ Hawaii on $50 a Day................ $11.95
☐ India on $25 a Day $10.95
☐ Ireland on $30 a Day................ $10.95
☐ Israel on $30 & $35 a Day $11.95
☐ Mexico on $20 a Day $10.95

☐ New Zealand on $40 a Day $10.95
☐ New York on $50 a Day............. $10.95
☐ Scandinavia on $50 a Day........... $10.95
☐ Scotland and Wales on $40 a Day..... $11.95
☐ South America on $30 a Day $10.95
☐ Spain and Morocco (plus the Canary Is.) on $40 a Day $10.95
☐ Turkey on $25 a Day $10.95
☐ Washington, D.C., & Historic Va. on $40 a Day $11.95

FROMMER'S DOLLARWISE GUIDES™

(Guides to sightseeing and tourist accommodations and facilities from budget to deluxe, with emphasis on the medium-priced.)

☐ Alaska........................... $12.95
☐ Austria & Hungary $11.95
☐ Belgium, Holland, Luxembourg $11.95
☐ Egypt............................ $11.95
☐ England & Scotland $11.95
☐ France........................... $11.95
☐ Germany......................... $12.95
☐ Italy............................. $11.95
☐ Japan & Hong Kong $12.95
☐ Portugal (incl. Madeira & the Azores) . $12.95
☐ South Pacific..................... $12.95
☐ Switzerland & Liechtenstein $12.95
☐ Bermuda & The Bahamas........... $11.95
☐ Canada $12.95
☐ Caribbean $13.95

☐ Cruises (incl. Alaska, Carib, Mex, Hawaii, Panama, Canada, & US) $12.95
☐ California & Las Vegas $11.95
☐ Florida........................... $11.95
☐ Mid-Atlantic States $12.95
☐ New England..................... $12.95
☐ New York State $12.95
☐ Northwest....................... $11.95
☐ Skiing in Europe $12.95
☐ Skiing USA—East $11.95
☐ Skiing USA—West $11.95
☐ Southeast & New Orleans........... $11.95
☐ Southwest....................... $11.95
☐ Texas........................... $11.95

TURN PAGE FOR ADDITIONAL BOOKS AND ORDER FORM.

It's 2 am.
It's far from home.
It's more than
a tummyache.

**American Express Cardmembers can get
emergency medical and legal referrals, worldwide.
Simply by calling Global Assist.**℠

What if it really is more than a tummyache?
What if your back goes out? What if you get into a
legal fix?

Call Global Assist – a new emergency referral
service for the exclusive use of American Express
Cardmembers. Just call. Toll-free. 24 hours a day.
Every day. Virtually anywhere in the world.

Your call helps find a doctor, lawyer, dentist,
optician, chiropractor, nurse, pharmacist, or an
interpreter.

All this costs nothing, except for the medical
and legal bills you would normally expect to pay.

Global Assist. One more reason to have the American Express®
Card. Or, to get one.

 For an application,
call 1-800-THE-CARD.

Don't leave home without it.®

If you lose cash on vacation, don't count on a Boy Scout finding it.

Honestly.

How many people can you trust to give back hundreds of dollars in cash? Not too many.

That's why it's so important to help protect your vacation with American Express® Travelers Cheques.

If they're lost, you can get them back from over 100,000 refund locations thro out the world. Or you can hope a Boy Sc finds it.

Protect your vacation.